Patterns of Government

Patterns of Government

The Major Political Systems of Europe

Third Edition

Samuel H. Beer
Harvard University
Adam B. Ulam
Harvard University
Suzanne Berger
Massachusetts Institute of Technology
Guido Goldman
Harvard University

Under the Editorship of
Samuel H. Beer and **Adam B. Ulam**

Random House, New York

Third Edition, Revised, Reset, and Printed from New Plates, 1973

987654321

Copyright © 1958, 1962, 1973, by Random House, Inc.

Library of Congress Cataloging in Publication Data

Beer, Samuel Hutchison, 1911–   ed.
Patterns of government.

Includes bibliographies.
1. Comparative government.   2. Europe—Politics—
1945–   I. Ulam, Adam Bruno, 1922–
joint ed.   II. Title.
JN12.B4   1972   320.3   72–681
ISBN 0–394–31387–9

Manufactured in the United States of America. Composed by The Haddon Craftsman, Inc., Scranton, Pa. Printed and bound by The Kingsport Press, Kingsport, Tenn.

Designed by James McGuire

Preface

It has been ten years since the last edition of *Patterns of Government* appeared. In that time a great deal has happened in the world of politics and in the discipline of political science. This edition reflects both sorts of change. In it the authors examine the deep-seated and urgent political problems that the past decade has brought into prominence in England, France, Germany, and Russia, and in other advanced societies. In their analyses, moreover, the authors take advantage of new and more sophisticated ways of studying political change, finding particularly valuable the idea of modernization.

A major strength of this book in previous editions was its use of both theory and history in the study of contemporary politics,[1] an approach that has been followed again. Its authors have held that present patterns of political behavior can be best explained if we have an understanding of how they originated and what characteristics they displayed in the past. In taking this general view, the authors have followed the example of some of the leading figures in modern political science, from Montesquieu to Weber, who used history to enlarge the body of empirical political theory and then used that theory to analyze and explain the historical process as it flows from the past through the present into the future.

Giving substance to its commitment to empirical theory, this book in previ-

---

[1] For a sophisticated discussion and illustrations of this approach, see Melvin Richter (ed.), *Essays in Theory and History: An Approach to the Study of Social Science* (Cambridge, Mass., 1970).

ous editions adopted a systems approach, with emphasis upon political culture as a leading variable. The present edition uses the same framework of analysis. It also integrates with this framework certain concepts, taken from modernization theory, that enhance the power of the analysis to explain change. In accord with this shift of emphasis from static to dynamic analysis, the Introduction is entitled "Modern Political Development."

Thus each country is studied as an example of a highly developed modern polity, an approach that emphasizes certain features the countries have in common. These common features, moreover, are shown to have resulted from a course of historical development moved by similar forces, passing through similar phases, and culminating in a complex of similar problems. These problems are not accidents of history, nor have they first shown themselves only in recent times; they have been produced by the long-run forces of modernization. I call them "the disorders of modernity."

This stress on the common traits of modernity and modernization does not mean that major differences do not divide the four systems dealt with in this book. On the contrary, from the viewpoint of both human values and system dynamics, the Russian dictatorship diverges—and this book argues, will continue to diverge—from the three democracies. To see what is common helps one see the differences more sharply. As an expert on the country he is writing about, each author is accordingly concerned not only with its common modernity, but also with the traits and tensions that are unique to it. This is not a book merely of generalities. While stressing interpretation, its pages carry a substantial load of fact. Its level of analysis is not so "scientific" that the reader will have difficulty connecting what is said in it with everyday happenings in political meetings, legislatures, or government offices. If he visits any of the countries treated here, the book will help him recognize and understand the political life he sees in the streets, reads about in the newspapers, and discusses with the people who live there.

Not the least value of the book, I would claim, is that it will help the American student understand his own country. There is some tendency today for Americans to turn their eyes away from foreign countries and to focus on the ills and excitements of our own land. But isolationism is no more the way to understand America than to help her. In this book, comparison with an America seen as typically modern is never far in the background of analysis. To see how deeply our problems resemble those of other modern polities should help restore perspective to our view of our own condition.

With regard to most of the volume, this edition is less a revision than a new work. Two of the authors are new: Suzanne Berger, who wrote the section on France, and Guido Goldman, who wrote the section on Germany. I have drastically altered and expanded the Introduction and have written a completely new section on Britain. Adam Ulam's section on Russia has been updated and revised. As a new feature, substantial statistical appendixes have been compiled by Glenn Robinson.

In addition to the political tables, which are unique, the appendixes include economic data, arranged comparatively so as to supplement the extensive discussion of economic problems and policies in the text. Roberta Wilson compiled the Index.

I conclude with a request. Over the years this book has benefited greatly from comment and criticism by teachers and students of political science at universities and colleges throughout the country. Many of these views are reflected in the body of this new edition and in the Instructor's Manual. I want to ask anyone who reads the book or uses it in a course to write the authors and let them have his or her thoughts on how it can be improved. We will, of course, acknowledge such help in the fourth edition.

Cambridge, Massachusetts   Samuel H. Beer
April, 1972

Contents

II   The British Political System
Samuel H. Beer

III The French Political System
Suzanne Berger

IV   The German Political System
Guido Goldman

V   The Russian Political System
Adam B. Ulam

Statistical Appendixes

Index

1
Modern Political Development

Samuel H. Beer

One
Modernity and
Its Disorders

This book is about the modern political system and its problems. Although we deal here with only four countries—Britain, France, Germany, and Russia—this distinctive political order flourishes in all advanced countries, bringing with it characteristic benefits and burdens. Moreover, most of the countries presently considered to be not advanced are also trying in their various ways to achieve a similar standing.

Thirty or forty years ago a book on this topic would have emphasized economic events and their consequences for government and politics. The interwar world brought to a climax the harsh problem of unemployment that had plagued industrial countries for generations. From this economic crisis new political fanaticisms arose that threatened to end not only the capitalist system of property relations, but also, in many countries, any hope for a democratic and liberal regime. As a result, political science in the thirties was obsessed with the prospect that a solution of the economic problem would bring to an end the old freedoms.

The concerns of government today still include the economy. Postwar governments have found inflation to be as intractable as prewar governments found deflation. These difficulties will be examined in some detail, since they tell a great deal about the modern political system. Yet the problems that seemed to the prewar generation not only crushing but also insoluble have yielded to human control. Governments have demonstrated that they know how to achieve full employment and yet maintain democracy and freedom. When they have tolerated unemployment, as they have sometimes done in trying to restrain inflation, the magnitudes have been so slight as to have passed as indexes of prosperity in the thirties. Today the kind of issue that shakes the economic planning boards is how

3

to increase the GNP by 5 rather than 2 percent per year. Viewed from the perspective of the Great Depression, this age of affluence would seem to have little to call a problem.

Yet if some of the problems today are less serious, others are more fundamental than those of the interwar years. They are more fundamental in the sense that they are rooted in the nature and structure of modernity itself. During the interwar period, it seemed to many students of politics that the advanced countries were confronted with a choice between a communist order in which the economic problem was solved but liberty was extinguished and a liberal order in which freedom was maintained but the economic problem could not be solved. The choice was sometimes put as "either liberty or groceries." Today it is readily seen that both sorts of regime, communist and liberal, are highly developed modern polities deeply disturbed by problems proceeding from their very modernity. These problems and disorders are visible in the Western democracies, including the United States. They also afflict Soviet Russia.

To identify the common problems of the modern polity is not to deny the major differences among the four systems being considered. On the contrary, from the viewpoint of human values as well as of system dynamics, the Russian dictatorship diverges from, and very probably will continue to diverge from, the three democracies. Seeing what they have in common only helps us see more sharply and understand more clearly their differences.

The Loss of Purpose

At the heart of the matter is the coincidence of loss of purpose with dominance of technique. Each has deep roots in the political culture of modernity and a long history of development in the modern period.

Loss of purpose here means not a loss of resolve or nerve, but rather a faltering or relaxation in people's sense of moral direction. This change is related to one of the great strengths of modernity, its liberating and democratic spirit. For modern government, the main legitimizing principle is democracy. Even modern dictatorships try to clothe coercion in the trappings of plebiscites and populistic propaganda. Yet democracy is a remarkably empty doctrine. It legitimizes what the people will, but it does nothing to give their will object and content.

The liberating thrust of modernity was a powerful weapon against the external coercions of monarchic and aristocratic rule and against the thought control of a monopolistic church, releasing vast energies and freeing more and more groups from the impositions of premodern regimes. Yet apart from such negations, the democratic doctrine holds up neither a vision for a people to pursue, nor an ideal by which an individual can mold his life. If the members of a nation—or a class or a group—do have a conception of common purpose, democracy will enable them to express it and to work for it. If they are trying to give themselves some such guide, democracy will provide them with the freedoms to seek it. But where positive goals are lacking, democracy itself will not supply them. People do ask for a purpose in life, seeking to find something greater than themselves with which to identify—a cause, a movement, a historical or moral reality. In this quest, the central legitimizing principle of modernity is at best neutral.

Without exaggeration, the criticism can be pushed harder. The modern spirit, it can be argued, is hostile not only to external but also to internal restraints. It is at war not only with the established authorities of earlier times, but also with the ethical systems inherited from them. It has been a major force in the attack on Puritanism, Victorianism, and traditional moralities generally.

We may well applaud these efforts as part of a necessary moral housecleaning in modern times and look forward to a "new" morality, better adapted to the needs of man and the age. This surely has been a recurrent mood in modern times. Yet by now experience must make us wonder whether any ideal of group or individual life can withstand the powerful negative thrusts of modernity. Any ethics, new or old, must impose restraints and direct behavior. In principle this immediately opens it up to attack as an illegitimate restraint upon deviant wishes. The repressions of the superego are no more to be tolerated than the oppressions of a ruling class. The liberating ethos of modern political culture is not merely neutral toward the problem of purpose but actively hostile to any solution.

These are, of course, only tendencies, not fully accomplished developments. Yet no one can fail to recognize the decline of purpose and the confusion and doubt over ideals that this decline entails in all advanced countries today. Its political consequences notoriously afflict the democracies and are central to the problem of legitimacy of government. But neither do dictatorship and authoritarian rule offer a ready and lasting solution. In Russia, Marxist-Leninist ideology did provide a firm moral basis for the Communist party and thus ultimately for the legitimacy and stability of the regime. But boredom and disgust with the spirit and tenets of that ideology grow constantly, confronting the rulers of party and state with their most critical challenge.

The Dominance of Technique

If the liberating spirit of democracy constitutes one of the moving forces of modernity, another and probably even more powerful force is science. At once an attitude, a method, and a body of specialized knowledge, science has increasingly influenced modernization. In recent years it has fathered a technological revolution that is transforming the world.

As an attitude the scientific approach—questioning, empirical, rationalist—has devastated the religious and philosophical conceptions on which the old political and personal moralities were founded. The long struggle between science and religion, in which religion has continually been forced back to an ever narrower range of influence in modern culture, is only one of the more familiar episodes. Nor has science, as attitude, method, or specialized body of knowledge, been able to supply the foundation for a new normative order. Quite properly not. The concern of scientific method, as of the various sciences, is with *how* something can be done, not with *why* it ought or ought not to be done. Being concerned with the means, science cannot answer questions relating to ends. In these ways, science has weakened the hold of old values without generating new ones. In relaxing a sense of moral direction, its effects have coincided with those of the democratic spirit.

When we think of the positive effects of science, we mean above all its techno-logical consequences. From the earliest days of modern society, the application of new scientific knowledge to practical problems has been a major source of eco-nomic development. Increasingly, it has given the modern world the mastery over nature that the early philosophers of modernity passionately willed. Industrializa-tion is the leading instance, a qualitative leap in the extension of human power over the environment that has no parallel in recorded history. Yet as the course of industrialism shows in its later as well as its earlier phases, this extension of human power has a tendency to create new problems as fast as it solves old ones. Thus the factory system raised human productivity to a new level, yet at the same time created the industrial city with its unprecedented and unanticipated social prob-lems. As pollution in its many forms today gives evidence, an environment remade by man can be as hostile as pristine nature. The seemingly uncontrollable effects of technology afflict planned as well as unplanned economies, communist as well as capitalist states. Surely the most sobering instance of this distinctively modern disorder, a technology that has gotten out of control, is the development of nuclear weapons. We have learned that problem solving is a principal source of our problems.

The irony is that the instruments invented to facilitate the achievement of human goals lead to consequences their inventors never intended. It is the old story of industrial civilization, of the machine taking control. Modern technology does achieve remarkable results. At the same time, its unanticipated consequences for man and environment embody goals no one intended or even foresaw. Means dictate ends. Technique is dominant.

Politics illustrates an even more important facet of the problem. Public policy gets more and more complex and technical. In part this is because the problems of a developing society become more and more complicated. Yet we can also distinguish the heightening of complexity caused by the growth of knowledge itself. Government policies to deal with inflation, for instance, are complex because such factors as wages and prices are intricately interrelated with one another and with other economic factors. But these policies are also complex because the econo-mists' knowledge is increasingly sophisticated. For both reasons modern govern-ment makes constantly greater demands on professional expertise, and the professional-bureaucratic complex grows in numbers, competence, and power.

But how can the policy output of this situation be understood by the public in a degree sufficient to enable it to exercise democratic control? In spite of a rapidly rising level of education among voters, the gap between their capacities and the realities of the world continuously widens. But insofar as public policy escapes from popular comprehension and control, the opportunity is opened up that this vast, growing power will be exploited by some body more competent, although a good deal smaller, than the democratic electorate. Such an elite may serve purposes that are selfish or benevolent, ideological or traditional. Inherent in the situation is the possibility that this elite may consist of the very professionals and bureaucrats called into existence by the various technologies.

In their bureaucratic role, their task is simply the exercise of their knowledge and skill; ends and goals presumably come from some other source. But as democratic control relaxes—or as authoritarian control relaxes—the bureaucrat is left to follow the momentum of his expertise, practicing his skill and extending its sway. Again and in a more serious sense, technique becomes dominant.

The Response of Modernity

Modernization theory helps the political scientist understand the political systems he confronts in the developed and developing countries of the contemporary world. It enables him to see common features in systems that are otherwise very different. It enables him to identify problems common to these regimes that might otherwise be neglected or blamed on passing and parochial causes. Since these problems are rooted in the nature of modernity, it follows that modernity must take the blame for them. Far-reaching as such criticism may be, however, it does not necessarily imply that modernity itself was a wrong turning and a mistake but only that the modern polity, like any other political order, has the vices of its virtues.

In developing a critique of political modernity, I am not going to rail against science, technology, and the rationalist spirit. I am too fond of their fruits, material and ideal, and too much the creature of that nourishment. Quite apart from my preferences, which are interesting only because they are widespread, the point is that these dynamic forces of modernity cannot be made to reverse themselves and somehow take us back to a premodern age. We may bitterly regret that science and technology have burdened the world with nuclear weapons. But even if all nuclear weapons were destroyed, the knowledge of how to make them would remain, thus leaving intact the fundamental menace. Some vast physical catastrophe, such as a nuclear war itself, could eliminate the menace of nuclear war by reducing mankind to a prescientific condition. Conceivably, a similar result could follow from the cultural catastrophe of the thoroughgoing Luddite revolution recommended by some of the romantic enemies of industrial civilization. Since not many of us can wish for eventualities such as these, we are left with less grandiose alternatives. We can become more sophisticated about the second-order consequences of specific branches of technology; we can try to plan the directions of growth of the sciences; and we can learn to be more sensitive to the needs of affectual life. This strategy is merely what a mature modern outlook itself advises. In this spirit I offer my critique of modernity as an organizing axis for an explanation of the disorders of the highly developed modern polity.

Before turning directly to the topic of modernity and modernization, I wish first to explore the nature of the polity. Chapter 2 will develop a model of the political system reduced to its essentials, concluding with a statement of the problem of order that inheres in the polity itself. Chapter 3 on political culture and Chapter 4 on political structure will elaborate this sketch of the basic model. After these considerations of what can be called political statics, I shall turn to problems of dynamics. The mechanisms, trends and stages of political modernization will be examined in Chapters 5, 6, and 7. The final chapter will return to the questions broadly posed in these introductory pages, showing in more detail how modernity gives rise to the distinctive disorders of the contemporary polity.

Two

A Model of the Political System

The field of political science, like politics itself, is a scene of controversy. Among scholars differences of opinion rooted in ideological conflict may be further exacerbated by professional pride, so that the contention among intellectuals often exceeds that among men who are actually competing for power. These disagreements extend to fundamental questions. They concern definitions, methodology, and results; how research should be carried on, what is meant by politics and government, and to what extent major hypotheses have been substantiated. In this respect political science shares the fortunes of the social sciences generally, which, in contrast with the natural sciences, are in greater or lesser degree marked by severe and widespread controversy.

These disagreements should not be concealed. Neither should they be exaggerated. Rational inquiry in the spirit of scientific method makes progress even with regard to the complex and volatile subject matter of political behavior. In the course of time, continuing inquiry discredits some views and strengthens support for others. While enjoying nothing that compares with the success of the natural sciences, political science does constitute a gradually accumulating body of knowledge.

The Use and Abuse of Political Models

These incontestable generalities about political science need to be kept in mind. They mean that there is no single definition or model of the political system that is generally accepted among political scientists. They mean that whatever approach we take to a piece of research will necessarily be a choice among various possible approaches. So far as writers can do so economically and relevantly, they should make clear the nature of this choice by indicating the premises, analytical and normative, from which they proceed. For they are bound to have in mind some sort of answers to basic questions such as: What is a political system? What are its principal elements or functions? What are the main forces that under appropriate conditions give rise to development or at least to change? If the writer will attempt an honest answer to these questions he will by no means guarantee himself immunity from criticism, but he should make it easier for the reader to know what he is driving at and may very well enhance his own understanding of his task.

The study of comparative politics raises these questions with special force. If we were trying to give an account of the political system of only a single country, we might well be content to employ the headings provided by conventional discourse. Superior studies of American national government have been made in terms of a conceptual framework no more sophisticated than a fourfold division of the main elements into "the party system," "the Congress," "the presidency," and "the civil service."

For comparing political systems, however, terms with a higher level of generality are needed. Thus several Western democracies could be compared with respect to "the electorate," "the party system," "the legislature," "the executive," and "the bureaucracy." While such a scheme might be suitable for countries in Western Europe, it could only distort the study of Soviet Russia. There is in Russia an organization that calls itself a party. But in contrast with the major role of parties in democratic countries, its function is to control public opinion rather than to reflect it. Similarly, the Supreme Soviet is called the legislature, but it would be a waste of time to give this body the kind of attention called for by the House of Commons or the French Assembly.

Difficulties of this kind force us to a still higher level of generality. Although many structures of the Russian political system are very different from those of Western democracies, certain basic functions of government are performed in all countries. In any political system, for instance, there must be some way in which the main goals of governmental action are determined. In a democratic country this policy-making function may be performed by means of an intricate interplay among electorate, party system, and legislature. In Russia, on the other hand, it centers in the upper organs of the Communist party. In this sense, similar functions are performed by radically different structures in Russia as compared with the democratic countries of the West.

In comparative politics, as in any kind of comparison, the identification of differences depends upon the presence of underlying similarities. Two things totally different in every respect could not be compared. Political systems can be compared because they have in common the characteristics that make them political systems.

A logical implication of these truisms would seem to be a search for the basic functions that characterize any political system. These would consist in functions performed by differing structures within the system as well as functions performed by the political system as a whole in relation to the society of which it was a part. The search for some such model of the political system has inspired the long history of political theory. It has produced a rich body of hypotheses, though hardly universal agreement.

The variety of models available to the aspiring student of politics can be illustrated by looking at three approaches offered by modern political theorists. It will be neither necessary nor convenient to develop fully their implications for political analysis. But I will stress their conceptions of the relation of the polity to the social and economic environment, a point of fundamental importance on which their authors differ radically.

Very early in modern times John Locke sketched the classical liberal model of the political system. A brief passage from his *Second Treatise of Government* (1690) will indicate its outlines:

> . . . there and there only is political society where every one of the members hath quitted this natural power [to preserve his property—that is, his life, liberty and estate], resigned it up into the hands of the community in all cases that exclude him not from appealing for protection to the law established by it.

In this model the members of a political system are not divided into antagonistic classes but constitute a fundamentally harmonious community united by the common purpose of protecting private property. Power is exercised by "men authorised by the community," and the purpose of its exercise will be the severely limited one of protecting each man's life, liberty, and estate.

The perspective on politics expressed in this model directs research toward a particular kind of problem, raising certain questions and suggesting in reply certain hypotheses. Although the community is fundamentally harmonious, the relations between government and community remain problematical. Government may breach its trust and deviate from an impartial protection of the rights of the citizens. Yet in the Lockean model, such deviations do not result from conflicts deeply rooted in human nature or class structure. They may therefore be controlled by adaptations in the machinery of government.

A preoccupation of the political scientist starting from Lockean premises, therefore, is to investigate the mechanisms—such as the division of power, checks and balances, rotation in office, and frequent elections—by which governments may be kept faithful to their trust. The product of such concerns has not been insignificant. Witness the long line of practical governmental reform in American history running from *The Federalist* to the present day.

During the era of industrialization, the Marxists developed their socialist model. A key passage in Friedrich Engels' *Origin of the Family, Private Property and the State* (1884) reads:

As the State arose out of the need to hold class antagonisms in check, but as it, at the same time, arose in the midst of the conflict of these classes, it is, as a rule, the State of the most powerful, economically dominant class, which by virtue thereof becomes also the dominant class politically and thus acquires a new means of holding down and exploiting the oppressed class.

The true believer will accept this statement as an article of faith. The political scientist uses it as an instrument to stimulate and facilitate research. Such research will have a distinctive direction. The relation of the economy to the polity becomes the crucial object of inquiry, with more particular questions focusing on the role of economic classes in policy making and the influence of economic development on political development. In the light of this model, political life itself will have little autonomy. Political change will be a "reflex" or "echo" of economic change, and the role of political and intellectual elites will reflect their economic class position in the mode of production.

In neither the Lockean nor the Marxist model is the political process itself an important source of change. In the Lockean view men are "naturally" rational and bring a real though limited morality to their dealings with one another, independently of any social or political conditioning. This value system, inherent in their humanity, constitutes an underlying consensus, making social harmony possible even though government performs severely limited functions. Those functions consist mainly in settling conflicts that have arisen outside the polity. Disequilibriums occur in the environment; government intervenes in an effort to reestablish balance. From the consequences of such "inputs" from the environment, governmental activity and political development result. The political process is essentially reactive, not autonomous. In the Marxist model, needless to say, the role of political life is even more restricted. The polity responds to conflict externally generated, that is, to the basic conflict of class that determines political development in the post-gentilic and precommunist stages of history. Its response, however, is already determined by the economic position of the owning class, which is also the ruling class. In this model the polity is not reactive, but merely reflexive.

A very different view of the relation of polity and society is set forth in the model of that other great modern, Jean Jacques Rousseau. Far from being merely reactive or reflexive, his polity is autonomous and creative. Its powerful role is indicated in these lines from the *Social Contract* (1762):

The passage from the state of nature to the civil state produces a truly remarkable change in the individual. It substitutes justice for instinct in his behavior, and gives to his actions a moral basis which formerly was lacking. Only when the voice of duty replaces physical impulse and the cravings of appetite does man, who, till then, was concerned solely with himself, realize that he is under compulsion to obey quite different principles, and that he must now consult his reason and not merely respond to the promptings of desire.

The drift of Rousseau's argument is clear and striking: The state is the source of human values. It does not simply reflect a value system inherent in human nature or produced by the economy. On the contrary, it is from the polity that men acquire their sense of "justice" and a "moral basis" for their actions. The significance of this broad hypothesis for political analysis is sharpened as Rousseau continues, spelling out the effect of ongoing political life upon the individual:

> By dint of being exercised, his faculties will develop, his ideas take on a wider scope, his sentiments become ennobled, and his whole soul be so elevated, that, but for the fact that misuse of the new conditions still, at times, degrades him to a point below that from which he has emerged, he would unceasingly bless the day which freed him for ever from his ancient state, and turned him from a limited and stupid animal into an intelligent being and a Man.

The virtue of the Rousseauist approach is that it may induce the student of politics to take seriously the hypothesis that the polity itself is a source of social and individual purpose. In this view the source of political "output" is not merely a political reaction to economic or social "input," but forces generated within political life itself. Moreover, what the political process creates is not trivial. These purposes, arising out of political conflict and maturing through political development, engage the motivations of members at deep levels of psychic commitment and identification.

In this view the polity is not merely a reactive mechanism to social and economic conflict. On the contrary, its vision of justice and value may well be the cause of conflict. It is not merely a device for solving problems thrust upon it by the environment; rather its conception of purpose creates problems by setting goals that challenge the environment. It is certainly not simply a decision-making process; on the contrary, its most important process is the course of political development from which emerge the values and standards by which decisions are made. Acting as members of the polity, men have not only a wide autonomy, but they also use that autonomy for crucial tasks of individual and collective self-development.

The Necessity to Choose

These three models of the polity are still very much in use and in dispute among political scientists. They do not exhaust, but only illustrate, the variety that the student of politics has available to him. It is impossible not to have in mind some such model—or confusion of models—when one starts on a piece of research. To make use of such a theoretical device, however, does not mean that one must inevitably confirm the hypotheses implied by it. Objective scholarship is possible, though by no means easy, and the results of research have been known to force the modification and even abandonment of long-cherished models. Yet the act of initiating inquiry represented by the adoption of a model is, in effect, a choice that directs research in a certain direction and toward certain answers and thus diverts it from other directions and other types of answers.

The adoption of a model is a choice in two senses. In the first place, a model identifies what is causally important. It singles out certain elements of the political system as those on whose effects attention will be focused. In the second place, the adoption of a model consists in a choice among ethical concerns. Analytical interest centers on causal sequences, but unavoidably the analyst gives attention to the sequences that have a bearing on human welfare. Politics and government are studied because people are interested in their relation to mankind or, more likely, some part of mankind.

In this sense, then, political inquiry will not be "value free." Any model of causal sequences will involve effects. These effects will occupy some place, high or low, in some scheme of evaluation. To investigate these sequences, therefore, is to investigate what happens to some human values. Even if the subjective concern of the student is pure intellectual curiosity, the objective concerns of his inquiry involve values. Moreover, the fact that no student of politics really does investigate effects that in his scheme of values are completely trivial confirms the common-sense conclusion that subjectively as well as objectively political inquiry will not be free of ethical concerns. Rational inquiry does make progress. Yet the controversies that have swirled around the nature of politics and government will not be settled by a few seminar meetings or journal articles.

The sources of bias will be examined in the discussion of ideology in Chapter 3. They are acknowledged here partly as a warning, but especially to alert the reader to a challenge of the following pages. In those pages a model of the political system will be developed. I believe this model to be well suited for understanding the modern polity. Yet it is a choice among analytic possibilities and, moreover, a choice that will conflict on a fundamental level with some of the classic perspectives on politics that have flourished in the past and still flourish today. Given the inevitably controversial nature of political science, I regard that as a virtue.

The Means-End-Consequence Continuum

The fact that we are dealing with human action suggests a general and quite simple scheme. Two elements of any human act are the *end* being pursued and the *means* used to reach it. A third element is the *consequence*—the outcome of the whole process. This scheme applies to instrumental action by an individual. It can also be applied to action by a collectivity, such as a political system. The analogy is not total; it does not mean that groups have personalities or that the state is a person. Yet a political system is like a personality system in that both are action systems. In both, goals are set, means are used to pursue them, and results flow from the process. Thus the means-ends-consequences scheme provides a starting point for constructing a model of the political system.

John Dewey spent a lifetime examining this basic category of human action from every conceivable viewpoint—logical, ethical, esthetic, and social—and founded on it a complex and imposing philosophy.[1] In developing the implications of the idea, we can do no better than follow some of the main lines of his account.

The relation of means and consequence can be compared to the relation of cause and effect. Like causes, the means are antecedent conditions that lead to some change in a situation. In politics they are instrumentalities of power by which policies are implemented; in economics, productive capacities from which goods and services flow. Means and causes are alike in another respect: Causes do not merely give rise to effects, but also enter into them and become them, as in processes of physical transformation. Similarly, while means and consequences are analytically distinguishable, in the process of action the consequences arise from and are constituted by the means. Dewey wrote:

> Paints and skill in manipulative arrangement are means of a picture as end, because the picture is *their* assemblage and organization. . . . Flour, water, yeast are means of bread because they are ingredients of bread; while bread is a factor *in* life, not just *to* it. A good political constitution, honest police-system, and competent judiciary, are means of the prosperous life of the community because they are integrated portions of that life. Science is an instrumentality of and for art because it is the intelligent factor *in* art. . . . The connection of means-consequences is never one of bare succession in time, such that the element that is means is past and gone when the end is instituted. An active process is strung out temporarily, but there is a deposit at each stage and point entering cumulatively and constitutively into the outcome. A genuine instrumentality *for* is always an organ *of* an end.[2]

Means become consequences, as causes become effects. Yet in human action this continuum depends on instrumentalities, physical and technical, that are guided at every stage by some end-in-view. Unlike causes in a purely natural setting, the means employed in human action include not only physical entities but also the technique that makes the objects productive of results. Indeed, such skill, knowledge, and technique convert these entities into instruments of action. Here is a primary difference from purely natural process—unless, of course, we can make the case for teleology and immanent ends in nature. In analyzing natural processes, we start from a paradigm with only two terms, cause and effect, but to analyze human action, in addition to means and consequence, we need a third term, the end or goal. Again, while the end-in-view is an analytically separable aspect of the means-end continuum, it is not physically or chronologically distinct. Dewey laid

---

[1]John Dewey (1859–1952) was a philosopher, exponent of pragmatism, and long-time professor at Columbia University. Among his principal works are *Experience and Nature* (1925, 1929), *Human Nature and Conduct* (1922), *The Public and Its Problems* (1927), and *Liberalism and Social Action* (1935).

[2]Dewey, *Experience and Nature,* 2d ed. (New York, 1929), pp. 367–368.

great stress on this fact: that "the difference between means and end is analytic, formal, not material and chronologic." He wrote:

> The end-in-view is a plan which is *contemporaneously* operative in selecting and arranging materials. The latter, brick, stone, wood and mortar, are means [of building a house] only as the end-in-view is actually incarnate in them, in forming them. Literally, they *are* the end in its present stage of realization. The end-in-view is present at each stage of the process; it is present as the *meaning* of the materials used and acts done; without its informing presence, the latter are in no sense "means"; they are merely extrinsic causal conditions.[3]

In Dewey's model of human action, means do not exist apart from ends. We can analytically isolate a pattern or set of means and consider its possibilities and capacities; but in the actual world of process, these means will be serving some ends. Thus in the world of politics, any system of power will be used for some end or purpose, and as in the paradigm of individual action, this purpose will give it meaning.

Conversely, the consequences of any sequence of action become elements in the starting point of new action. They modify the environment and so become part of the means that the actor may use in further action as, for instance, a program of redistribution may so modify the economic environment as to create a new set of political forces. Moreover, this environment, as the situational aspect of the continuum of action, affects any new end-in-view that emerges. Goals, ends, objectives are not something "mentalistic" that are conceived apart from the helps and hindrances to their achievement presented by the situation. The model has built into it an allowance for the effect of situational or structural factors on purposive behavior. One major example is the way consequences of one sequence help shape the purposes pursued in a new sequence of action. Continuing his homely figure of speech about house-building, Dewey wrote:

> The house itself, when building is complete, is "end" in no exclusive sense. It marks the conclusion of the organization of certain materials and events into effective means; but these materials and events still exist in causal interaction with other things. New consequences are foreseen; new purposes, ends-in-view, are entertained; they are embodied in the coördination of the thing built, now reduced to material, although significant material, along with other materials, and thus transmitted into means.[4]

Finally, the distinction between end and consequence directs attention to another fundamentally important difference between natural process and human action. In the former, causes always have their appropriate effects. But in action, the means adopted by actors do not always lead to the end the actors propose. There will

---

[3] *Ibid.*, pp. 373–374.
[4] *Ibid.*

be consequences, but they may not be those intended. What is more interesting, the results may include the intended consequences and yet also a complex of new conditions that were quite unanticipated and that work against the desired end. The contingency of human effort, whether individual or collective, (in contrast to the necessity of nature) cannot be neglected by the social scientist. But he must be particularly interested in that variety of failure which results when human action defeats itself. The irony of counterproductive effort is deeply rooted in the possibilities of human action.

> Man finds himself living in an aleatory world; his existence involves, to put it baldly, a gamble. The world is a scene of risk; it is uncertain, unstable, uncannily unstable. Its dangers are irregular, inconstant, not to be counted upon as to their times and seasons.
>
> . . . Everything that man achieves and possesses is got by actions that may involve him in other and obnoxious consequences in addition to those wanted and enjoyed. . . . While unknown consequences flowing from the past dog the present, the future is even more unknown and perilous; the present by that fact is ominous.[5]

The Problem of Political Order

The basic paradigm of action by an individual provides the starting point for constructing a model of the political system. For any polity will be an action system —a system of means directed to certain ends producing a flow of consequences. But the means-ends-consequence paradigm does not have a specifically political dimension. It emphasizes the action of an individual, while political relations must involve a number of people. Economists can use the life of Robinson Crusoe to illustrate the fundamentals of their science, but the political scientist lacks a focus for his special discipline until Friday appears. Yet simply to add a social dimension does not make the paradigm into a political model since other sets of human relationships also are social-action systems without being polities. The political involves a special kind of relationship among the members of the action system. One essential, as the example of Friday in the world of Robinson Crusoe suggests, is that someone is giving orders to someone else. The political involves command-obedience relations, or what some political scientists term "domination" or "imperative control."

So long as we are concerned with the action of only one individual, politics does not arise. But let means and ends, those two elements of any action system, be differentiated and thereby associated with different actors, and a command-obedience relationship—and problem—comes into existence. It is interesting to specu-

---

[5] *Ibid.*, pp. 41, 43.

late on what a polity would look like if there were no such differentiation of roles. Those who determined the ends of governmental action would be identical with those who carried them out; governors and governed would be the same—a perfect democracy à la Rousseau. In modern representative democracies, on the other hand, the eye is immediately struck by the distinction between a highly organized governmental machine that issues orders and the mass of the population that carries them out. This is by no means the last word on the distribution of power, and in due course we shall consider the complications. It need only be noted here that in all historical polities the differentiation between those who govern and those who are governed is marked and fundamental.

In order to clarify and elaborate the distinction, it will be useful to use terms developed by Max Weber in his classic analysis of the phenomenon of "domination" (in German, *Herrschaft*). In a political system we can identify, on the one hand, a "chief" or "supreme authority" (*Herr*) and, on the other, an "administrative staff" (*Verwaltungstab*), whose action is "primarily oriented to the execution of the supreme authority's general policy and specific commands."[6] A principal value of Weber's analysis is that it identifies the basic political relationship as being between the element that determines the ends for which the power of the polity will be used and the element that constitutes the power to carry out those ends. In this way it shows the identity of the two basic processes of the political system with the two basic processes of the action system. The decision making of the chief determines the ends; the decision executing of the staff constitutes the means. The essential function of the "chief" in the Weberian model is the determination of ends, while the essential function of the "administrative staff" is the implementation of these ends. Thus is framed the primordial political problem of maintaining cohesion between the two basic elements of the polity, those who give commands and those who carry them out.

To focus on the relationship between the chief and the administrative staff passes over the question of how these two elements may be able as an integrated whole to control a still larger body. This is convenient for analysis, since it sets aside for the moment the possibility that this latter kind of control might be based solely on nonlegitimate means, such as force or manipulation, and concentrates on the essential question of how—and how far—chief and staff are cohesive and on the role of conceptions of legitimacy in maintaining this cohesion. The basic hypothesis is that such a conception of legitimate authority shared by chief and staff is indispensable to their cohesion.

This model of the polity, it must be emphasized, is not an account of the origin of the state. Its validity does not depend upon there ever having been an historical

---

[6]Max Weber, *The Theory of Social and Economic Organization,* A. M. Henderson and Talcott Parsons (trs.) (New York, 1947), p. 324. Weber (1864–1920), a German sociologist and political economist, developed his analysis of the role of conceptions of legitimacy especially in a section entitled "Types of Authority and Imperative Coordination" in the volume translated by Henderson and Parsons.

polity composed of a man who was a "chief" and a group constituting his "administrative staff." At the same time, the imagery it suggests, bringing to mind the simpler polities of tribal or feudal society, gives substance to the distinction being drawn. We think, perhaps, of the Indian chief who with regard to the means of hunting buffalo or fighting enemies is helpless in comparison with the assembled might of his braves and warriors, yet who by his authority is able to wield their power. Similarly, in the modern democratic polity, the power—in the sense of "power to," that is, the instrumentalities of physical strength, money, technology, property, and so forth—rests largely with the people, the governed. But they use this power in obedience to the commands of government in a crucial degree because they hold these commands to be legitimate. Similarly, within the governmental machine itself, the bureaucrats, who are in possession of the essential skills and tools of governmental action, carry out the orders of law makers and chief executives because these orders are believed to be legitimate. We sometimes think of those who issue the orders as being those who have the power. But this conceals the *essential political problem, which is precisely and paradoxically why those with the means of power obey those who have only authority.*

The polity is an action system that enables a number of people to decide on ends and to pursue them. This statement has no necessary implication of democracy. It can equally well apply to a system in which one "chief" determines the ends. What the statement does mean is that however many take part in deciding on ends, all members basically accept the decisions. Thus what was otherwise a number of people incapable of acting purposively as a unit now acquires that capacity.

To acquire this capacity of unified purposive action is to acquire a political order. The political order is the system the members see and intend, the legitimate system of government. Yet in this political order, within various structures and between structures, those who govern and those who are governed will be differentiated. Governors and governed are potentially, though not inevitably, in conflict. Any political order contains within itself a major source of disorder.

Politics and Class

This analysis of political order and disorder can be contested. The principal source of conflict could be found outside the polity itself, as when it is argued that the economy produces a conflict of classes, which in turn is reflected in the polity. By contrast, I am arguing for the autonomy of the political. I would, for instance, question whether any economic class can act as a cohesive unit unless it has some kind of political system. Moreover, I would hypothesize that once such a system is established to govern the class, it may well be disrupted by the essentially political conflict of governors and governed—a hypothesis richly substantiated by the history of organizations based on economic class.

The model does tell us something about class and class conflict. But the classes it identifies, being based on the differentiation of governor and governed, are essentially political, not economic or social. To use Weber's terms, the "administrative staff" is the elementary form of the governing class. Between it and the other members of the system there exists a command-obedience relationship from which arises a problem of political order. This governing class may also acquire privileges in the form of private property, and considering its political power, it is almost certain to do so. Yet its basis and social function are political, and the flow of causation is from its activity as governing class to other functions. Thus, even if economic differentiations resulting from private property were removed, a governing class might very well persist. This model, in short, makes the persistence of a governing class in Soviet Russia, in the form of the Communist party, not a problem, but a natural occurrence readily assimilated to the basic concepts of our analysis.

At the same time, this approach with its stress on the political prevents us from taking for granted the capacity of any group for unified purposive action. It means we will doubt that economic class solidarity, however helpful, can remove the necessity for a political system. Moreover, its formulation of the basic political problem means that the governing class itself must be governed. Thus in Russia today, the problem of political order arises not only with regard to the authority of the Communist party in relation to the wider population, but even more acutely with regard to the relations of the party leaders and the rank and file. In a system in which terror and physical violence have played so large a role, especially under the dictatorship of Stalin, these relationships present with special vividness the vital importance of legitimacy in creating authority that can control power.

The model does not imply that conflict is inevitable in political systems. It does, however, point to the continuing possibility of conflict at whatever level there is differentiation between the two basic functions of any action system. Conceptions of legitimacy, supported by other forces, may effectively integrate the system. The political problem may be solved. The order may survive and flourish. Yet the model does not let us forget that quite apart from the projection into the polity of conflicts from nonpolitical sources—economic, religious, ethnic, and so on—the political order itself is problematical, containing within itself the possibility of disorder. Nor is disorder always bad, for conflict can be a principal motor of political development.

Politics and Vision

Theories of government often start from the premise that conflict among men arises from essentially nonpolitical causes—economic, psychological, ideological—and then go on to show how government is a response to this state of conflict, its function being perhaps to reconcile conflicts, suppress them, or exert force on behalf of one of the parties. In these models the extrapolitical situation determines the basic function of government.

But this merely responsive model of the polity underestimates the human imagination. Men use the polity for a far wider spectrum of purposes. Individual action shows a great variety of patterns to which men may commit themselves singly. The same is true of collective action by means of the polity. In our model we also begin from the fact that human behavior is purposive: hence the great stress on the means-ends-consequence continuum. This formula represents a fundamental category of human action that in its political form has given rise to an enormous variety of patterns of government. Like the individual, the polity is not responsive, but creative. The polity can as autonomously as the individual generate complex patterns of purposive activity. Using the word in a sense that is not utopian or sentimental, I will say that a polity, like an individual human being, will have its "vision." Political vision and political imagination are not mere incidents and ornaments of the political process, but fundamental and continuous forces in any political system.

At the same time that purposive action is undertaken by means of a polity, however, the possibility of conflict is brought into existence by the polity itself. The differentiation of ends and means in the form of governors and governed can hardly be avoided in any except perhaps the smallest and simplest societies. Yet this distinction creates the structural conditions for conflict. In this sense the political order itself is the source of one of its major disorders.

The Four Variables

The terms *means, ends, consequences,* and *legitimacy* suggest the principal elements of the model and their basic relationships. But we also need some terms that are closer to conventional usage in political analysis.

The term *pattern of interests* will be used to refer both to the process by which ends-in-view are determined and to those ends themselves. (1) As process, the pattern of interests consists of the fundamental business of policy making and goal setting in the polity. (2) We can also abstract from this process the ends-in-view or intentions entertained by the various groups and bodies taking part in it. "Interests" seems the best term to catch the general meaning, which, of course, is not confined to self-interest, material interest, or short-run interest, but includes all sorts of ends-in-view. In addition to the term pattern of interests, such terms as *pattern of policy making* and *pattern of basic decision making* will be used as synonymous, when the context makes them appropriate.

The term *pattern of power* also has a dual meaning. (1) Looked at statically, it means those instrumentalities, material and nonmaterial, that are available for carrying out the ends-in-view embodied in decisions on policy. These are the instrumentalities of power of the polity. The bureaucracy, military and civilian, is a leading element, but the pattern of power of the modern polity also includes organized groups in the private sector and even the ordinary citizen and his resources, insofar as they can be mobilized in the service of government decisions. (2) In its second meaning, the pattern of power refers to these facilities as they actually operate in the political and governmental process—for instance, the army fighting wars or the civil service implementing a program of conservation or welfare.

The *pattern of policy* is the output of the system. It is distinguished from the pattern of power as consequence is distinguished from means. The output of government consists of the specific powers of government in the process of being exercised. When we look at this process as policy and output, however, we are thinking of its relation to a further environment, such as the effect of a redistributive welfare program upon the society.

Finally, the *pattern of political culture* refers especially (but not only) to those orientations toward action which are called conceptions of legitimacy. Distinguishing this element of the political system is indispensable if we are to isolate and examine the crucial grounds of political order by which the pattern of power and the pattern of interests may be integrated.

Three

Political Culture

Analytically the problem of political order is to explain why some men give orders and others obey. This problem can be presented in a fairly simple stimulus-response model. The command is the stimulus and the response is the required action. We observe the chief giving a certain command to his braves and the action they sequentially and repeatedly take. In a sense we can observe the orders going out from the Internal Revenue Service and the response of millions of citizens as they pay their income taxes. These two sets of actions, stimuli and responses, are all that we can observe; it would be an immense relief if we could confine our attention to them and not have to concern ourselves with such unobservable entities as the "thoughts," "purposes," or "feelings" of the subjects being studied.

Such a confined investigation would indeed be the procedure of a strict behaviorism. That approach has been adequate to studying physical reflexes and to developing certain important laws of the association of input and output events in relation to human and other organisms. A strict behaviorism, however, has never made much headway in political science (or indeed in any other social science) because it cannot provide the complex framework necessary to explain most phenomena of peculiarly human significance.[1] In order to study these phenomena, we must suppose between stimulus and response a set of intervening variables of great complexity. The variables include that whole world of motivation, conscious and uncon-

---

[1] A psychologist, Charles E. Osgood, discusses this problem in his "Behavior Theory and the Social Sciences," in Roland Young (ed.), *Approaches to the Study of Politics* (Evanston, Ill., 1958).

scious, personal and cultural, which at an earlier date some philosophers of social science thought they had banished as "spooks" and "soul stuff."[2] Today political scientists are careful to call themselves not behaviorists, but behavioralists. And indeed the innovations in method and theory associated with the latter term give even greater emphasis to the subjective and psychological aspects of political action than did the traditional American approach to the study of politics. Broadly speaking, the function of the term "political culture" is to make sure that political analysis will give this aspect of political action the serious and systematic attention it warrants.

Origins of the Concept

In the long perspective of political inquiry, it is no innovation to stress such factors. The classic studies of political behavior—such as those of Montesquieu, Alexis de Tocqueville, Walter Bagehot, and James Bryce—have recognized the powerful role of ideas. One may cite Tocqueville's famous chapter in *Democracy in America* (1835–1840) on the "Principal causes which tend to maintain the democratic republic in the United States," in which he attributed the main influence to "manners," that is, "the moral and intellectual characteristics" of Americans. The question of method—the role of ideas and values and how they are to be studied—was sharply focused in the furious debates conducted mainly by German philosophers during the latter part of the nineteenth century. Taking this *Methodenstreit* as his point of departure, Max Weber, who by no means neglected the importance of structural forces, developed a sensible approach that, moreover, could actually be used in research, as he showed in his brilliant studies of the role of conceptions of legitimacy in political systems.

In American social science, the leading figure in importing and developing Weber's viewpoint has been Talcott Parsons.[3] His action frame of reference is based on the premise that human behavior cannot be explained unless the observer grasps its meaning to the persons interacting. Such meanings are shared among members of a system by means of a common culture. A culture is an "ordered system of symbols"—of which words are the most familiar, but by no means the only example—that enables members of a system to see and sense in quite similar ways the situation, physical and social, in which they find themselves. In a social system, he writes, the members' relation to their situation is "defined and mediated in terms of a system of culturally structured and shared symbols."[4] It was a natural next step for the concept of culture to be applied to the subculture

---

[2] The pejorative expressions are from Arthur F. Bentley's classic, *The Process of Government* (Chicago, 1908).

[3] Among the works of Talcott Parsons, a professor of sociology at Harvard, are *The Structure of Social Action* (1937), *Essays in Sociological Theory*, rev. ed. (1954), and *The Social System* (1951).

[4] Parsons, *The Social System* (Glencoe, Ill., 1951), p. 6.

of that particular subsystem called the polity.[5] Thus the concept of political culture has provided a way of systematically thinking about and analyzing the "ordered systems of symbols" that play a crucial role in giving substance to the actions and interactions of human beings.

The political culture of a people gives them an orientation toward their polity and its processes. To be oriented is to have a sense of direction—in the simplest meaning, to know where you are in relation to the points of the compass. To be politically oriented would mean, in general, knowing how your government operates—having a "cognitive map" of the polity—and also knowing how it ought to operate and what it ought and ought not do—having a "normative map." Insofar as a people share such a cognitive and normative map, they will usually be able to act together, understanding what each is doing and avoiding conflict and dissension. "Usually" is the most we should say in this respect, since a political culture can have the effect of creating distrust and promoting dissension. Even then, however, it is performing the function of orientation—to a malevolent and unreliable world—giving members a sense of what is happening and what they can and ought to do. Insofar as a political culture is shared by the individual—that is, internalized in his personality system—it constitutes that very complicated intervening variable between the stimuli of the political situation and the responses of the political actor.

Culture exists because of the capacity for symbolic behavior that is especially, if not exclusively, characteristic of human beings. Symbolic behavior makes it possible for people to communicate, and so to learn from one another and to accumulate and pass on what they have learned from one generation to another. Language is the leading example of symbolic behavior. Through it we are able to communicate meanings—the ideas, values, and emotions that give life significance. Indeed, a great deal of social interaction consists in little more than the communication of such meanings. As anyone who has ever been to a cocktail party knows, social interaction can go on at a furious pace, crushing egos, creating and dissolving liaisons, and leading to triumphs and failures of factional purpose without anyone's moving more than a few feet from the spot in which he was originally standing.

As this example may suggest, language, while the leading kind of symbolic behavior, may be the lesser part. Tones of voice, body movements, who walks up to whom, and who is walked up to can communicate far more than mere words. In a school room, for instance, as much teaching is accomplished by what the teacher does as by what he says. The class is an action system with the instrumental purpose of getting certain bits of knowledge into the heads of children. At the same time, and also consciously and intentionally, it is designed to inculcate certain norms of conduct by the example of how the class is conducted.

---

[5]See especially Gabriel Almond, "Comparative Political Systems," *Journal of Politics,* 18 (1956).

Political life itself is especially rich in such symbolic behavior. The purely ceremonial occasions and institutions are well-known: Bastille Day in France, the Fourth of July in the United States, May Day in Moscow, the opening of Parliament in London. But the mixtures of instrumental and symbolic behavior are even more important. The national convention of an American political party is, instrumentally, a means of selecting a presidential candidate and drawing up a platform. But its symbolic aspect—while not perfectly understood or entirely intended—gives it a major teaching function. Only in this light can we make sense of its practices, which are highly dysfunctional when measured against the instrumental purpose: For instance, the number of delegates and alternates is huge, unwieldy, and unnecessary, but symbolizes populistic values. Thus while serving to select candidates and write platforms, the political convention has also been for generations a school that propagates American political culture.

Belief Systems

A moment of introspection will assure any political scientist that the world of political culture, as an operative element of the personality system, tends to be disorderly, ambivalent, and confused. If the concept is to be used in analysis, however, we must try to identify its main elements and to establish schemes of classification, even though such efforts must inevitably exaggerate the formality of the subject matter. I will follow here a division suggested by Parsons' classification of cultural-pattern types into belief systems, systems of value orientation and systems of expressive symbols.[6]

A political belief system is the "cognitive map" of a political culture; its function is to "define the situation." On the one hand, there is an objective reality, which the individual cannot change merely by his thinking and feeling, which he will incorrectly perceive at his peril, and to which he must adapt at least to the extent of using the right tools to control it. This is the situational or structural aspect of social action. But perception of the social, as of the natural, environment does not begin from a tabula rasa. The individual brings to his perception of the political situation a more or less coherent body of existential propositions about politics and government. Such ideas may extend to general orientations toward the political capacities and tendencies of mankind—for instance, optimistic folklore that "you can trust the people" and pessimistic folklore that "you can't change human nature." At a less general level, a political belief system will state what a particular political system is and how it operates. Survey research in the Western democracies does not encourage us to think that for most people this knowledge extends to details of constitutional principles or governmental machinery. Yet we should

---

[6]Parsons, The Social System, p. 327.

not underestimate the definiteness—and in many cases, the sophistication—of the ideas of the ordinary voter.

A function of an individual's political belief system is to help him perceive and interpret political events in his environment. Political events, however, are not mere physical realities. What the individual perceives in a political situation is not only the physical behavior of other individuals and groups—leaders, parties, legislatures, and so on—but also and especially the *meaning* of their physical behavior —a large part of which physical behavior is itself purely symbolic, for example, talking. The sheer physical behavior of the principals in a portentous Cabinet crisis, for instance, may be far less complicated than that involved in a game of sandlot baseball. The facts that the memoirists will reveal are such things as the heightening emotional tension on the part of the Prime Minister and his faction, the bluffing by his opponent, the coolness of some, the panic of others, the moral failure of still others, and the clever tactics and stupid blunders that led to the final breakup. A political situation consists of such subjective and psychological factors and forces as well as the overt, physical behavior with which they are associated.

Political culture is at once the source of the meanings with which men invest their behavior and the instrument by which those sharing a common political culture perceive and understand those meanings. A slight movement and a few words are understood by the man originating them and by the man to whom they are directed as a sincere gesture of friendship because both have the same cultural background. We can say that political culture coordinates political action, provided it is remembered that this can mean ordering not only harmonious action but also severe conflict, as when only a common subculture made the refined insults of the *code duello* intelligible and effective. Communication is a necessary foundation of political conflict. As Henry VIII remarked of the king of France, "Francis and I understand one another very well. We both want Calais." In the absence of some elements of common culture, there is no communication and so no political, or indeed human, conflict, but only the blind clash of physical forces.

If a common political culture performs such a function for members of a political system, it is evident why the political scientist must gain access to the same cultural background if he is to understand and explain their behavior. Such understanding, it must be emphasized, is just as necessary for structural as for cultural analysis. A political situation may exercise powerful compulsions on the people in it, and analysis of the regularities that may be set up by such structural forces is one of the most important and exciting kinds of political analysis. Yet a political situation, as we have seen, is not to be understood apart from the meaningful action of its participants. The very compulsions that it exercises upon them depend in large part upon the meanings they find in the situation. If we are to understand these compulsions, we must understand the meaning given the situation by the common culture of the participants.

A stimulus-response model for political analysis is not useless. Even if the analyst has only a limited knowledge of a political culture, he may find situations that are similar in terms of those limited categories. He can isolate such situations, compare them, and conceivably find similar consequences flowing from them. Such a correlation is not to be disdained. Yet there is always the chance that it has overlooked crucial explanatory and causal factors. There may be important similarities that would have been revealed by a better understanding of the purposes, style, and operative ideals of the people being studied. If so, the situations will have been incorrectly identified and compared, and the correlation will have no predictive power.

Or again, actions that are superficially similar may be very different in terms of the different cultures involved. For instance, attending church by Protestants or Catholics has an entirely different significance from going to the mosque for Moslems. In such a case, what seems to be the discovery of a uniformity—the correlation of attending church or mosque with some sort of other behavior—may be false and misleading. The chance of such error, substantial enough when one is comparing systems within the same general cultural region, such as Europe, is even greater when countries in different cultural regions are being compared. The attempts by some social scientists to approximate the modernizing process in developing countries today with that in Europe in recent centuries abundantly illustrate the dangers.

Systems of Value Orientation

Values are standards of selection among alternatives of action.[7] Even the most tightly compelling situation leaves open some choice to the individual confronting it, although it may be only the choice between sink or swim. Some acts of choice may be purely reflexive or instinctual, and some may be totally determined by unconscious motivation. A basic hypothesis of the action frame of reference, however, is that standards defining what is desirable and worthwhile play an important role. The response of the individual to a situation will depend not only upon the "cognitive map," but also upon the "normative map" that he brings to the perception of the situation.

Values may be classified as cognitive, appreciative, and moral. Cognitive values include such standards as the rules of logic or scientific inquiry. These are norms setting out correct methods of thinking and conducting research. Appreciative values are conceptions of what is worthwhile for an individual to have or be. They include definitions of success or excellence, such as the classical standards of arete or Renaissance notions of virtu, and, as these references suggest, vary from one culture to another. They range from the high valuation of military prowess and monastic austerity in the medieval world through the reversal of values by modernity, which gives an equally high place to secular success in money making and bureaucratic problem solving.

Moral values, which constitute the third class, are standards of choice defining

---

[7] *Ibid.,* p. 12.

rights and duties between individuals and groups. Typically, they lay down rights and duties in such relationships as those between parent and child, husband and wife, old and young, and buyer and seller and regulate conduct in sexual, family, economic, and other social spheres. Political values are a subclass of moral values regulating command-obedience relationships and other questions of what is right and good for the collectivity. Among political values, it is important to distinguish between conceptions of authority and conceptions of purpose.

Any scheme of classification will exaggerate the sharpness and formality of such cultural elements as they actually function in personality and action systems. The distinction between belief systems and value systems itself may need at times to be severely qualified. Looked at from the viewpoint of modern philosophy, the difference between existential and normative propositions—between statements of what "is" and what "ought to be"—seems fundamental and indeed unbridgeable. Looking at the matter historically, however, we readily see that in some cultural systems the distinction between "is" and "ought" has not been drawn with such sharpness. In classical thought, for instance, with its stress on teleology and an objective moral order, the difference between what actually happens and what ethically ought to happen was not marked. In importing into my classification of cultural patterns a distinction between belief systems and value systems, I may be succumbing to a cultural outlook that is peculiarly and parochially modern. For, as we shall see, the modern stress on subjectivity in the realm of values logically leads to a rigid separation of this realm from the world of objective reality.

While typical modern philosophies insist on a sharp separation between fact and value, in actual practice modern political culture is less than faithful to this standard. As the great "isms" of the contemporary world demonstrate, modern political man—however illogically—does continually leap back and forth between fact and value in constructing and using the "maps" by which he tries to understand and control political situations. To such maps, which are at once cognitive and normative, it is useful to apply the term "ideology." In this sense Marxism-Leninism is an ideology. On the one hand, it purports to be an objective, indeed scientific, description and explanation of the development of world history. Specifically, it lays down as a matter of fact that Russian society will be led through the present stage of socialism by the Communist party, acting as the vanguard of the proletariat. Strictly understood this system of belief does not state what "ought" to happen or what anyone "ought" to do. Yet no reader can miss the tone of moral exhortation in which these descriptions and predictions are uttered. Nor would any political scientist fail to observe that Marxist-Leninist ideology embraces political values that endow the Communist party leaders with authority and their policies with the ethical sanction of common purpose.

The systems of thought that men follow in actual political behavior are prone to be ideological. In plain words this means that the propositions political actors offer as nothing but the unvarnished truth are in fact heavily laden with their value preferences. To demonstrate this we need not turn to some Germanic *Weltanschauung*. Ask anyone what he thinks are the causes of crime, poverty, political corruption, war, economic productivity, or any other such topic of current interest and you almost certainly will get an answer bringing with it a strong whiff of ideology. Nor can the political scientist or social scientist be snobbish about the matter. He is likely to catch the ideological scent in the writings of his colleagues as well as in the talk of the man in the street.

Sources of Bias

The sources of ideological bias may be psychological. One of the uses of the concept of political culture is that it makes it easier for political scientists to use the skill and knowledge of the depth psychologist. With his help they may detect the influence of family structure and early childhood experience in people's adult conceptions of what politics is and ought to be. Ideology can also have a sociological source, as when we detect the influence of economic class in the differing interpretations of the same situation by persons occupying different positions in the mode of production.

Position in the polity can also independently be a source of ideological bias. Governors and governed commonly look at the same situation differently. For instance, according to Karl Mannheim, there is a bureaucratic ideology that leads government officials to interpret a revolutionary situation as essentially a problem in administration.[8] The differences of outlook spring from different positions in the authority structure, and they proceed in part simply from different lines of experience. The politician and the bureaucrat, while acting in the same situation, will have different roles and functions and so will be alert to different facts and causal sequences. Both may be correct in seeing respectively the political and the administrative causes of governmental breakdown. They have different interpretations because they are ignorant of one another's experience.

Yet as in the case of economic class bias, there may be something more. Differing views may reflect an element of interest as well as ignorance. We say we can detect the effort of an individual or group to maintain his or its power position. Giving rise to interest are such factors as personal survival and professional pride. But also and perhaps most interesting is the role of moral and political values: the unwillingness of an individual—or group, or party, or political class, whether governors or governed—to admit some factual state of affairs because according to their value system it ought not to exist. In this sense the democrat is as reluctant to admit that the people may be corruptible as the aristocrat that his class may be decadent. Again, when a political scientist simply lays out some empirically substantiated proposition about political behavior on a sensitive subject, he may be violently attacked as wicked by people whose ideology includes the denial of this proposition.

Finally, in this brief suggestion of the many sources of ideological bias, we should mention the methodological source. By this is meant the possibility that in some

---

[8]See Karl Mannheim's discussion of bureaucratic conservatism in his *Ideology and Utopia: an Introduction to the Sociology of Knowledge* (New York, 1936), pp. 104–106.

degree a value commitment is inevitable in the process of conceptual thought itself. I say possibility because this is a complex and contested question among philosophers, which makes it feasible in this context only to sketch the problem. The problem centers around what is called the "inductive leap" in scientific inquiry. The main object of such inquiry is to arrive at general laws that make prediction possible with a high degree of statistical probability. The basis for generalization is the observed sequence of antecedent and consequent in numerous instances. How many such repetitions must occur before the observer has "enough" to justify his predicting that the sequence will recur with a certain probability?

In reply to this question the observer might say that he relies upon a general law derived from previous experience regarding the necessary empirical basis for successful prediction. Having found that in the past a certain number of repetitions has sufficed to provide a ground for prediction, he applies this rule to his present inquiry. Needless to say, this general law itself remains unvalidated, since it presupposes a convincing answer to the question of "how many is enough." Induction alone cannot validate induction.

For reasons such as these, "the theory of Induction" is, in Alfred North Whitehead's words, "the despair of philosophy."[9] Yet people do go ahead generalizing from past experience and, moreover, offering predictions and basing action on such predictions. In so doing they are making what is called an "inductive leap," that is, adding something to inquiry not itself strictly derivable from induction. The force impelling them to make this leap and guiding them while making it would seem to be some value preference. Ideally, perhaps, pure science can wait, holding belief in suspension indefinitely through all mutations of the data. Purposive men, however, must act for goals and according to standards. But since the data will always be in some degree inconclusive, they would remain suspended in inaction unless at some point they made an ethical commitment.

The practical effects of this methodological problem are only too easy to observe. Since we have no rule of "how many is enough," the way is open for ideological choice. When we do not like the generalization experience seems to indicate, we ask for more data and prolong the inquiry. When results conform to preferences, on the other hand, our inclination is not to waste time in further research. To the behavior of the men—or parties or nations—that we feel are on our side, we do not apply quite the same stringent reality tests as those by which we try our enemies and opponents.

Moreover, while the problem of the "inductive leap" applies to any type of scientific inquiry, it is more acute in some fields than others. In physical science the uniformities are massively dependable in comparison with the data with which the political scientist must work. Uniformities in political behavior can be detected. Their ratio of statistical probability, however, will be relatively low. Also, the generalizations of political science are not only in this sense "soft" in relation to

---

[9]Alfred North Whitehead, *Science and the Modern World* (New York, 1935), p. 35.

uniformities of behavior; they also depend heavily upon a changing historical context. This means that even such generalizations as political science achieves may well be invalidated as new uniformities emerge in the course of historical development. For one reason or another, in political analysis the gap between data and generalization is only too often a veritable abyss. If the political scientist is to bridge this gap and conclude his inquiry with success, the temptation is very great to rely upon some ethical or ideological commitment to buoy him up as he reaches from wobbly data toward firm conclusions. If political science is rarely "value-free," one reason is the intrinsic variability of political behavior.

Systems of Expressive Symbolism

In a book about politics, it is easy and natural to write about belief systems and value systems. They are rather bookish subjects, the kind of thing we can handle in a seminar, classifying, criticizing for internal consistency, and analyzing for logical implications. This is not to deny their great influence on political behavior, especially in the modern polity, which more than other regimes is built on general ideas and broad ideals. Yet without being at all anti-intellectual, we must recognize that in any political culture there is another whole order of symbolism that is particular rather than general, that bears a heavy load of affect, and that is geared even more intimately into human motivation. While most students of politics readily acknowledge the importance of this level of political culture and this aspect of political action, they find it much harder to talk clearly and systematically about it. Parsons' notion of expressive symbolism[10] is a helpful starting point, although not everything to be said in this section faithfully reflects his views.

What expressive symbols are and what functions they perform can be illustrated if we will reflect briefly on the sources of solidarity of certain small groups, such as the family or neighborhood. Such groups, often called primary or "face-to-face" communities, usually involve bonds of self-interest. In the family, for instance, there is a division of labor that up to a point is advantageous to all. Likewise, common values normally define what is worthwhile and what a person's rights and duties are. But obviously the intense solidarity of such a group (we are making the assumption of harmony for the sake of illustration) is based on something much more personal. The picture of the group that each member carries in his head is not of a general structure, nor of types, but of actual people with names and individual tastes and temperaments. The life of the group consists in the interaction of these distinctive individualities, and the basis of its solidarity is the attachment of each member to their particularities. Adequately to describe the life of the group, the observer could not stop at a report of its cognitive and normative conceptual

---

[10]Parsons, *The Social System, op. cit.,* Chap. IX, "Expressive Symbols and the Social System: the Communication of Affect."

framework. He would have to give in some detail an historical account of how concretely the group lived and worked together. The common culture of the group, in short, includes not only its conceptual symbols, but also an array of highly personalized representations that are, so to speak, condensations of the group's history. These expressive symbols constitute an important level of the group's culture and function to regulate its conduct and maintain its solidarity.

Nationality as Expressive Action

What is obvious in the case of primary communities also in an important way holds true of larger secondary communities, even those very large secondary communities called nations. The importance of the nation in relation to the modern political system can hardly be exaggerated. "The nation," writes Rupert Emerson, "is today the largest community which, when the chips are down, effectively commands men's loyalty . . ."[11] When political scientists analyze the basis of national solidarity, they stress the importance of a common culture, which involves common political ideals as well as a shared outlook as shown by a common language. But they also give great stress to historical experience. Concluding his authoritative definition, Emerson specifies that a nation will normally be "shaped to a common mold by many generations of shared historical experience." This emphasis on history goes back to the earliest students of nationality and nationalism. Nearly a hundred years ago Ernest Renan, in one of the earliest and still one of the most profound works on the subject, denied that the basis of nationality was race, geography, language, religion, or a mere community of interest and stressed the importance of a common historical experience. He concluded his account with the famous assertion: "The existence of a nation is a plebiscite of every day, as the existence of the individual is a perpetual affirmation of life."[12]

The language may be a bit florid for our taste, but it brings out not only the historical origin, but especially the concreteness of nationality as an objective of action. The "plebiscite of every day" is the people voting with their feet as they move through the intricate and particular patterns handed down to them from the past; by this behavior they affirm the national vision.

Not the great historic moment nor some abstract moral quality, but the daily round of interconnected activities constitutes the substance of nationality. These activities have value in themselves, as well as, no doubt, being instrumental to other values. After characterizing this kind of action theoretically, we shall turn to the principal question of its relationship to political culture.

Some acts are performed as means to an end, other acts are performed as ends in themselves. Action, either individual or social, that is taken for its own sake is

---

[11]Rupert Emerson, *From Empire to Nation: the Rise to Self-Assertion of Asian and African Peoples* (Cambridge, Mass., 1960), p. 95.

[12]Ernest Renan, *What Is a Nation?* (1882).

called *expressive action,* in contrast with *instrumental action.* In the case of purely instrumental action, the individual performs the act in order to reach a situation in which he satisfies some need. The action constituting the gratification of that need is expressive action. Such action need not be crudely hedonistic; it may express the need to care for others. The needs and dispositions that are so expressed are not merely instinctual, but have been conditioned by appreciative and moral values. In terms of the means-ends-consequences formula, the acts expressing these needs and dispositions are the realization of the ends-in-view that have guided the course of action. "The essential point," writes Parsons, "is the primacy of 'acting out' the need-disposition itself rather than subordinating gratification to a goal outside the immediate situation or to a restrictive norm."[13]

Needless to say, this distinction is often blurred by relativities. Much instrumental action is also expressive. Some people enjoy their work as well as the leisure to which it leads; politicians may enjoy running for, as well as holding, office. Likewise, patterns of action that are strongly expressive and valued highly for their own sakes are often instrumental to other ends. An educational system aims at raising the cultural level of the citizenry; but a higher cultural level also presumably means that as voters the citizens will show more sense in solving the problems of the polity. In spite of these relativities, it is obvious that men and groups and nations do act for some ends and value such action for its own sake. Nationality, as we have seen, consists in such patterns of expressive action.

Expressive Symbolism

Members of a political system not only act out the patterns of expressive action, but they also talk about them. Or to put the matter more broadly and accurately, they refer to these patterns of action by systems of symbols. The symbol systems include cognitive and normative maps. But people also refer to the patterns of expressive action by means of another level of political culture consisting of systems of expressive symbols.

A first characteristic of these symbols is their particularity, corresponding to the particularity of the expressive action to which they refer. They are typically the stories, legends, folklore, heroic examples, and popular histories by which a nation —or an ethnic community, or other solidary group—pictures itself to itself. Just as history as the sequence of concrete and unique events is the main source of patterns of expressive action, so history as historiography, the account of what supposedly happened, is a principal type of expressive symbol. Both the normative-cognitive symbol and the expressive symbol are regulative mechanisms of the political culture; both condition action in the political system. But they operate differently, one teaching by precept, the other by example. Nor can the latter be reduced to the former. On the contrary, generalities are notoriously ambiguous, depending upon illustration and example to clarify their meanings. Moreover,

---

[13]Parsons, *The Social System, op. cit.,* p. 384.

examples may influence behavior directly and without being reduced to a rule by the person acting. The person acting may be quite decisive, yet be unable to reduce the meaning of his act to a rule or to describe conceptually what he is doing.

A political culture, in short, will normally include an order of symbols that functions in this particularistic way, not only to describe but also to regulate action. Students of political culture should recognize—as some emphatically do—that there are severe limits to a survey of attitudes that asks only for general answers to general questions. Subjects of such an inquiry may seem uninformed, uninterested, and downright stupid simply because the inquirer has not reached for the right level of political symbolism.

The importance as well as the complexity of expressive symbols is heightened by the fact that they include complex patterns of action. Ceremonies are an obvious case. A May Day parade in Moscow, for instance, with its contingents from trade unions, ethnic groups, sports organizations, and the various armed services, is a representation or symbol of the national life (according to the orthodox view). It says by means of action what could also be said in words in a patriotic speech; but the parade says it much more effectively because of the heightened emotional impact of action, especially mass action, in contrast with mere words. Such ceremonies, common to all countries, teach by example, but by example acted out. As symbols they refer in various ways to the polity, presumably strengthening its authority structure and common purpose. Ceremonial occasions are themselves instances of expressive action, patterned social behavior performed for its own sake. By means of them commitment to a regime is acted out and so is revived and reinforced.

In most political systems, a great deal of behavior has such a symbolic aspect and function, even when not nominally ceremonial. When, for instance, a Member of Parliament rises in his place in the House of Commons and puts his question to a Minister at Question Time, he is seeking, say, to bring out some error of administration, to show the superiority of his party's position, or to demonstrate his own dialectical skill. This is the instrumental aspect of his action. At the same time, this act of participation expresses an attitude toward the House, an attitude of acceptance and identification. It is part of a play, a secular liturgy, put on for the benefit not only of members, but also the outside world—to show them in little how Britain is governed.

It is essential, of course, that the behavior conform to the House of Commons manner. Speakers should not be unintentionally rude; their tone of discourse should be conversational, and the general style of speech and behavior should conform not only to the rules of procedure of the House and its conventions, but also to a complex of examples and precedents that could never be reduced to a code. Unspoken though these criteria may be, they constitute a rigorous discipline and perform an important function. In political speech as in rhetoric generally, style must fit content if communication is to be effective. But how can someone call for a revolution and echo the cries of a distressed proletariat when standing in a back row without a desk to pound or a tribunal from which to orate and addressing a class enemy as "the Right Honorable Gentleman"? It is no wonder that, as Aneurin Bevan remarked, the House of Commons "softens the acerbities of class feeling."

As this discussion suggests, a principal function of expressive symbolism is to facilitate identification. The roots of identification are psychological—indeed, according to Sigmund Freud, they are basically sexual[14]—and add powerful undergirding to human communities. The object with which the individual identifies may be a nation, an ideological movement, a party, ethnic community, or other solidary group. To say that identification occurs with solidary groups is simply to take note of two aspects of the same process. Identification is essentially an emotional bond, a sense of belonging, which thereby creates a solidary relation with the group. A solidary relation stands in contrast with relations resulting from calculations of interest, as in the case of employer and employee, and with relations resulting from agreement on an ideal, as in the case of membership in a pressure group promoting some social cause.

While the concept of identification and the psychological analysis of its roots are contemporary, the vital role of emotion in politics has frequently had to be rediscovered, perhaps because of the inevitably rationalistic bias of most scholarly writers. Among the classic political philosophers few had as sensitive an understanding of the role of expressive symbolism as Edmund Burke. His critique of the notion that the polity can be founded solely upon a self-interested contract or ideological consensus is still sound political science. In his *Reflections on the Revolution in France* (1790) he summed up his outlook in this attack on the abstract rationalism of the French philosophes:

> On the scheme of this barbarous philosophy, . . . laws are to be supported only by their own terrors, and by the concern which each individual may find in them from his own private speculations, or can spare to them from his own private interests. In the groves of *their* academy, at the end of every vista, you see nothing but the gallows. Nothing is left which engages the affections of the commonwealth. On the principles of this mechanic philosophy our institutions can never be embodied, if I may use the expression, in persons; so as to create in us love, veneration, admiration, or attachment. But that sort of reason which banishes the affections is incapable of filling their place. These public affections, combined with manners, are required sometimes as supplements, sometimes as correctives, always as aids to law.

Conceptions of Legitimacy

The problem of political order arises when in systems of action that unite men in purposive action some men give orders to others. A basic hypothesis of the

---

[14]See especially Sigmund Freud, *Group Psychology and the Analysis of the Ego,* James Strachey (tr.) (London, 1922).

approach to politics taken in this book is that we cannot explain with regard to some particular system how this problem is solved—or fails to be solved—without an understanding of the political culture of the system. Structures of political domination owe their stability and continuity significantly to the support they receive from systems of belief, values, and expressive symbolism. Such supportive cultural patterns can be called conceptions of legitimacy. To an important extent these shared elements of political culture lead the governed to obey because they feel an obligation to obey and the governors to command because they feel a right and duty to do so. In this way political culture may legitimize, shape, and stabilize the command-obedience relations of a polity.

These assertions can be clarified and developed and their conflict with other major perspectives on politics brought out if we take up some of the objections. The first, which is perhaps also the most ancient, is that domination in a polity depends not upon shared values, but simply upon force. If the polity is not merely a holdup, it is an institutionalized holdup. "Without justice," asked St. Augustine, "what are kingdoms but great robber-bands?"

Two points need to be made in reply. First, it must be granted that any survey of polities in time or space will turn up more than a fair number of instances of one body of men holding another body of men in subjection primarily through force and violence. The Nazi occupation of various countries in Europe would start off the list with a substantial number of entries. Indeed, the territorial boundaries of any polity will contain some persons whose relation to the polity is essentially determined by force.

The fact that one body of men may hold another body in subjection, however, diverts attention from the real political problem, which reappears in the relations of command and obedience in the governing body itself. That body can exercise force against the other only because it is an action system within which domination is based on more than force. In this sense, as David Hume pointed out, force ultimately rests on opinion. Persons who are dominated solely by force are not related to the polity as members of it but as objects of it. Such a class of polities would be "tax-gathering states," such as the Mogul empire in India, which, resting on conquest, established a regularized system of tribute and otherwise left the subject peoples free to follow their own ways.

Another objection arises when human action is considered from an economic perspective. Where there is free exchange, command-obedience relations also arise. A buyer puts in an order at the store; the employer orders the employee to do some piece of work. In this economic model, however, the power to issue orders is based neither upon force nor upon legitimacy, but upon a material quid pro quo. Theoretically, the bargainers are equal, and one party has only the power to order the other to perform his part of the contract that comes from the threat that he will not perform his own; enlightened self-interest sustains the structure of domination. Students of politics from philosophers of the social contract and utilitarian schools to the "political economists" of today would argue that enlightened self-interest is a sufficient bond to account for the stability of polities.

It cannot be denied that self-interest, material and otherwise, is often a significant incentive in support of political structures. In the modern polity the stress on output and performance makes the satisfaction of citizen expectations especially important in explaining acceptance or rejection of the system. Yet, analytically, it seems impossible that a mere balance of interests could account for the continuance of a political order, and empirically and historically legitimacy has always been an important influence.

A third objection arises from a psychological approach to politics. The explanation of command-obedience relations is found at the level of unconscious motivation rather than rational calculation of self-interest or conscious compliance with norms. Early childhood experiences with parental authority have profound influence in laying the groundwork for adult attitudes toward government. Political identification with a nation, party, or ethnic group is rooted in psychological mechanisms developed in infancy. To admit the role of such forces and, indeed, to insist on their importance is not to say that they are by themselves sufficient wholly to determine action. The mechanisms of identification may derive ultimately from infant sexuality, but what the individual identifies with—whether tribe or nation, revolutionary leader or traditional monarch —will depend also upon what kind of polity and political culture he is born into. Psychology has not reached the point where it can explain away conscious motivation based on beliefs and values or the structural determinants arising out of the historical situation.

So much for three major lines of criticism of the model of a polity put forward in this book. By contrast they serve to bring out its significance. Also, as major hypotheses explanatory of the strength and weakness of domination, they point out forces that may be present alongside political values. Such forces may work with political values, or work against them. Loyalty to a political system is enhanced if it is seen by its members as an essential condition of their material well-being. On the other hand, economic incentives can undermine support for a polity, as when the growth of a market turns loyalties from local and regional governments to the jurisdiction responsible for the wider economy. Whatever the role of these other forces, however, the political relationship gains its special character from values conferring legitimacy.

In normal usage, the term legitimacy refers to the status of a child born in wedlock and therefore having full filial rights and obligations. By extension it is used to refer to the fact that something is in accord with established legal forms or requirements, or more broadly, with recognized rules and principles, as in the phrase "legitimate drama." Thus, under hereditary monarchy, the legitimacy of the heir was crucial to establishing his right to rule and the obligation of subjects to obey. Where primogeniture prevailed, the elder son could claim to be the legitimate heir against his juniors, as when the supporters of the elder against the younger branch of the Bourbon monarchy in nineteenth-century France called themselves Legitimists.

Authority and Purpose

The term legitimacy acquired an even broader and deeper meaning when the years succeeding the French Revolution in Europe raised the question of not merely who was the rightful heir to the monarchy, but whether monarchy itself was a legitimate form of rule. The questions can be grouped under two main headings, *conceptions of authority* and *conceptions of purpose*. The first question is who or what has authority. That is, when do orders, such as those embodied in a system of laws, carry with them the obligation of obedience on the part of the members of the polity? Does such authority flow from the will of the king? Or do governments derive "their just powers from the consent of the governed"? The constitution writing that has punctuated the history of so many countries since the late eighteenth century has attempted many answers to this question. The concern of these attempts was not with the content of the commands of government, the substance of the law, but rather with procedure: How were laws to be made and especially how were the persons who made the laws to be chosen? In monarchic Europe, parties seeking change advocated such reforms as the restriction of the royal veto, the creation of elected legislatures where they did not exist, the expansion of their powers where they did, the division of the legislative body into two houses, the extension of the suffrage, and the liberalizing of rights of free speech and political association. These proposals, broadly concerned with procedures, reflect the concern of modern constitutionalism with the problem of authority.

As the political controversies of the time show, the question of legitimacy also involves the purpose of the regime. Parties had differing ideas of the legitimate social order that the polity was to serve. The movement from the controlled economy of mercantilist days to the freer economy of laissez faire was a source of conflict, as well as the occasion for the liberalizing of the structure of authority. Indeed, the "liberals" of the early nineteenth century were at once champions of a rather more popular government and of a free economy and society, as the constitutions they drafted show by their protection of religious toleration, civil liberty, and private property. Modern constitutionalism has been concerned with substance as well as procedure.

Legitimacy is conferred by conformity with the fundamental purposes of the polity as well as by conformity with the accepted structure of authority. Conversely, legitimacy can be strained in either of two ways. A polity can show the most scrupulous regard for constitutional procedures and yet alienate its members by disregarding their fundamental rights. Similarly, it may, with perhaps the best will in the world, take action to promote human welfare, yet act in so arbitrary and irregular a way as to spread confusion and distrust among the people. Legitimacy can be strained by disregard of procedure or substance, the norms of authority or the goals of common purpose.

In a modern political order, conceptions of legitimacy relate mainly to the policy-making process—what I have called the pattern of interests. Norms of authority lay down how these decisions are to be made; definitions of common purpose set out broadly what they should and should not be. Written constitutions, while often a less than accurate guide to conceptions of legitimacy, show the same emphasis in their concerns. They usually set forth the extent and rights of the electorate and the organization and powers of the main branches of government —legislative, executive, and judicial. These systems of rules are at once positive and negative. They say who and what shall have certain functions and also, at least implicitly, that others shall not have them.

Normally, certain limits on what government may do will also be specified— typically, in the form of protections of civil liberties. But there will be a fairly clear indication of what the power of government is to be used for. For example, the long and detailed list of powers of the two levels of government, state and federal, in the Bonn constitution makes clear the broad scope and the general fields of governmental action. In recent years, moreover, constitutions often include state- ments of rights of citizens and duties of government that require extensive positive action, such as social security programs and control of the economy. Modern constitutionalism, in short, is concerned not only with establishing restraints on government, but also with giving guidance and a sense of direction to it.

In terms of the model of the polity used in this book, the interesting fact is that conceptions of legitimacy are much more concerned with the pattern of interests —the determination of ends and the ends themselves—than with the pattern of power—the means and the process by which such purposes are carried out. In a people's views of how their government ought to be conducted—as in the usual written constitution—there is a concentration of attention on the first of these broad functions. This makes good sense, at any rate from the viewpoint of the standards of political modernity. The pattern of power, precisely because it is instrumental, should be readily subject to reorganization and reshaping for the more efficient achievement of policy objectives.

Insofar as this is the case, bureaucracies, as leading instrumentalities of power, are more adaptable than party systems, legislatures, or cabinets. The discrepancy also poses a problem: Rapid social and economic development often make radical reform of the policy-making institutions as necessary as radical reform of the policy-implementing institutions. Yet the great encrustation of affect and values built up over the years may make any movement toward adaptation exceedingly difficult. In Britain, as Ivor Jennings has said with regard to Parliament, being ancient is important. It may also be a vast impediment to efficiency, responsive- ness, and control of the bureaucracy. The very conditions that heighten legitimacy may impede changes necessary for greater effectiveness. Moreover, the normal tension of a command-obedience relation that subordinates bureaucrats to politi- cians, is liable to be further exacerbated by the fact that the world of the politician clings to its archaic ways, while the bureaucracy is straining to modernize.

Political Culture and Political Order

When referring to any particular political system, it would be more accurate and helpful to speak of political cultures rather than political culture—as we have learned to speak of public opinions in the plural rather than the singular. The reason is to guard against the term's lulling us into the assumption that any polity must have a single, coherent, harmonious cultural base. Such an unwarranted assumption tends to make political culture the source of order and to contrast it with the forces of conflict, which supposedly come from other quarters, such as the economy. Nothing could be further from the truth or from the understanding of those who have developed the term. Culture is important in explaining action precisely because it causes conflict as well as concord. In most political cultures there will be pronounced differences depending upon level of education—the elite-mass distinction. In the European past this difference was much greater than today, as when in the nineteenth century Walter Bagehot was able to distinguish between the outlooks of the great mass of English people who felt that the Queen ruled and the educated 10,000 who knew that it was the Cabinet and Parliament.[15] In that case, Bagehot found the two political cultures complementary rather than conflicting, their function being to sustain the rule of an efficient elite. In the case of France, on the other hand, the persistence of the "revolutionary tradition" among large sections of the lower class (not to mention the intellectuals) has for long periods in modern French history been a major ground for a continuing condition of barely suppressed civil war. Political culture may contribute to the solution of the problem of political order. It may also be a major barrier to its solution.

By way of summary of this chapter, I wish to return to certain propositions set forth when discussing models of the polity in Chapter 2. There I used some ideas of Jean Jacques Rousseau to put forward a broad hypothesis about the function of the polity. The essential point was the autonomy and creativity of political life. It is certainly not my intention to try to lay down as a universal law that any polity will have these properties. I do mean, however, to warn against and, if possible, to shake the conventional but misleading assumption that the polity can play only a reactive or reflexive role in relation to its social and economic environment. The emphasis on the concept of political culture in this introduction and in this volume should help make the point. It ensures, I trust, that the political scientist will not lightly neglect the meanings that constitute an inseparable dimension of political behavior. It helps bring out the crucial function of political values and beliefs in solving—and sometimes in exacerbating—the problem of political order. Not least important, it directs inquiry toward a proper appreciation of the creative—and sometimes destructive—role of intellectuals in political development.

But what I wish especially to stress is that the concept of political culture opens the way toward understanding how and why politics sometimes reaches to such extraordinary depths of the moral life of individuals. Man is a social animal, and certainly for most people it is vitally important to live in a purposive human community. By taking part in such a community they realize major values of

---

[15]Walter Bagehot, *The English Constitution* (1867).

personal achievement and social obligation. Moreover, through the polity they often give shape to these values and seek to express them in action. In this role the polity is not a mere arbitrator of conflicts or auxiliary to economic ownership. On the contrary, as shown by the power of modern nationalism, members of the polity may find in it a central agency in developing and realizing values essential to their individual sense of identity and significance. Political culture is the system of ordered symbols in which such a people express this developing vision of a common life. In it, therefore, the political scientist finds a major ground for understanding and explaining the conflicts and commitments of political man.

Four

Political Structure

A fundamental hypothesis of the approach to political analysis developed in these pages is that conceptions of legitimacy critically affect political behavior and, more specifically, that solutions to the problem of political order cannot be achieved without the support of such ideal forces. To say this is to attribute an important causal role to political culture. In later chapters on modernity and modernization it will be argued that the cultural orientations of modernity have been crucial to the emergence and development of the structures of the modern state and that the intellectual classes, as creators and bearers of political culture, have been major agents of both stability and change.

At the same time, I cannot stress too strongly that this emphasis on the role of ideal forces does not by any means exclude a role for structural causation, in particular the consequences of political structures. A major dynamic of the development of the modern polity has been its structural (or situational) tendencies, and one of the most challenging tasks of the political scientist is to identify and explain the uniformities that result from these tendencies. The purpose of the present chapter is to elaborate the meaning of the three main elements of structure—the patterns of interest, power, and policy—and in so doing to emphasize the possibilities of structural, in contrast with cultural, analysis. Because of this dual stress, the model of the polity developed in these pages will be called the cultural-structural model of the political system.

The Pattern of Interests

The pattern of interests has a dual aspect: It can be looked at as the process by which the ends of the polity are determined or as that array of ends itself. We may ask why it is necessary to distinguish this pattern as a separate element or variable of the political system. Does not political culture take care of the matter? Conceptions of authority set forth how and by whom policies ought to be made, and conceptions of purpose set forth the basic outlines and limits of those policies. Will not the pattern of interests simply be a faithful reflection of these cultural guides? The answer is obvious. Important as conceptions of legitimacy may be in shaping the political process, a major task of analysis is to assess the other forces that enter into this process and the gap between its actual contours and the ideal maps of the system. In examining the pattern of interests, we try to study the actual process by which policy, in the broadest sense, is made as well as the purposes brought to that process and winning out in it. If nothing more, the function of specifying this variable is to warn the political scientist, like all academic people an inveterate theoretician, to remember reality.

The dual aspect of this pattern—that it includes both process and purpose—has been insisted on. A major use of this notion is to hinder a one-sided concern with power—the fairly common tendency of political scientists to study how a decision is reached without regard for what participants were after and what they achieved. But the very process by which ends are determined will be significantly shaped by the type of ends being pursued. E. E. Schattschneider has laid down a general rule, which is so important and well-substantiated that I like to think of it as "Schattschneider's law": "There has been a different theory of political organization for every major concept of public policy."[1] He derives this hypothesis from a "functional concept of politics"—a type of structural analysis—which develops the notion, strongly appealing to common sense, that the purposes people try to accomplish will crucially affect the way they go about trying to accomplish them. Taking an approach that shares the premise of this volume that politics is essentially purposive action, he quotes approvingly from John H. Hallowell:

> One of the inadequacies of the definition of politics as a struggle for power is that it obscures, if it does not obliterate, the *purposes* in terms of which power is sought and used and the conflict of purposes out of which politics emerges. For it is the conflict of purposes that characterizes politics—not the struggle for a 'power' divorced from all purposeful motivation.[2]

Not only does the concentration on power obscure something normatively important. As Schattschneider's law points out, it also neglects a crucial causal relation-

---

[1] E. E. Schattschneider, "United States: The Functional Approach to Party Government," in Sigmund Neumann (ed.), *Modern Political Parties: Approaches to Comparative Politics* (Chicago, 1956), p. 195.

[2] *Ibid.*

ship—that "new policies have inevitably produced new kinds of politics," and (I suggest) vice versa. This relationship needs to be kept in mind when the major periods of political modernization in Europe are being identified. For example, in Western European countries in the past one hundred years there has been a shift from an individualist to a collectivist politics. In political parties this has meant a change from the loose, "cadre" parties of the nineteenth century to the "mass" parties of the twentieth. One reason why party organization changed in this important manner is that during this period the welfare state and the managed economy were being developed. Social democratic parties, for instance, were pushing for programs that were based in considerable part upon explicit class interest and that often required sustained and disciplined political and parliamentary action for their successful enactment and operation. This politics of redistribution involves at once a distinctive type of purpose and a distinctive type of organized political base. Therefore, if the political scientist is to understand the "power struggle" itself, the process in which people and groups compete for authority and exercise it, he must consider what ends the various participants have in view.

Earlier discussion of a model of the polity supposed only a single-step differentiation by which the pattern of policy making was distinguished from the instrumentalities of execution. The spectrum of historical polities, ranging from the primitive tribe to the Greek polis, the Roman Empire, the medieval *regnum,* the modern nation-state, and the totalitarian dictatorship—to mention only a few examples from Western history—displays a great variety of further differentiation with regard to both functions. Structural analysis of these patterns has interested political scientists for a long time. The classic formulation in *The Federalist* papers of the doctrine of the separation of powers as a condition of liberty and the rule of law reflected this concern. Similar inquiries have dealt with such questions as the effects of the structure of representation—for instance, proportional representation; the structure of the party system—for instance, the two-party versus the multiparty system; the structure of legislative power—for instance, bicameralism versus unicameralism; the structure of legislative-executive relations—for instance, presidential versus parliamentary government; the structure of territorial authority —for instance, federalist versus unitary governments.

A major transition in the development of the modern polity has brought to the fore the structural analysis of certain features of the organization of parties and pressure groups. The shift from individualist to collectivist politics has greatly increased what may be called the degree of concentration among such political formations.[3] Large-scale organization among parties and producers groups, such as unions, trade associations, and professional groups, has been legitimized by new attitudes regarding the proper role of class in politics and the meaning of democracy. Such organizations have seemed necessary to represent the demands of class

---

[3] I am summarizing here from my *British Politics in the Collectivist Age,* rev. ed. (New York, 1969), especially the Epilogue.

and subclass groupings and, even more so, to give a solid base of support for the widening scope of governmental policy. These intended functions have on the whole been fairly well carried out. What structural analysis shows, however, is that a complex of unanticipated consequences—or latent dysfunctions—has tended to bring important changes in the pattern of interests of collectivist politics.

Any detailed discussion of these changes and the unintended uniformities of behavior to which they have led belongs in the main body of this volume, under the accounts regarding particular countries. Here I will only suggest some of the tendencies that have been realized in Western democracies, in greater or lesser degree depending upon the circumstances. One characteristic of the mass party that has long been observed is the tendency to produce a new kind of elitism. Because this tendency of political concentration has much in common with similar tendencies of economic concentration, it may be termed managerialism. Another closely related consequence of size and complexity in political formations is bureaucracy, or, to use a more general term, formalization. When we turn to the relations of the massive political units of collectivist politics, whether parties or pressure groups, we find important unintended patterns. The interactions of the great organized producers groups with contemporary governments, while legitimized as advice and consultation, in fact often constitute a kind of bargaining. In relation to the consumer groups constituting the mass electorate, on the other hand, the competition of closely matched political parties tends to become a kind of bidding. One result of these processes of bargaining and bidding is to bring the policies and proposals of the parties closer together. The effect of the structure of the situation confronted by the parties, both as governing entities and as competitors for power, is to produce a convergence of positions and a decline of ideological conflict. This new group politics of the collectivist stage of political development can also seriously impede decisive governmental action. The vast economic power of the producers groups gives them influence amounting almost to a veto over some governmental decisions. Likewise, the competition for the votes of consumption-oriented voters can prevent parties and governments from taking steps demanded by the long-run needs of economy and society. The new group politics, in short, can produce what has been called pluralistic stagnation.

Most or all of these tendencies—managerialism, bureaucracy, bargaining, bidding, convergence, and pluralistic stagnation—can be detected in the politics of any of the Western democracies. They are behavioral uniformities that flow from certain basic characteristics of the modern polity in its collectivist stage of development, in particular from political concentration and the wide scope of governmental policy. While consequences of collectivist politics, they are, however, unintended, second-order consequences. They do not flow directly from the political culture of the system concerned—indeed, they may be sharply in conflict with the expectations and intentions of the actors. Rather they are second-order consequences of the situations created by the structures that are directly sustained by the political culture. They are identified and explained by structural, rather than cultural, analysis.

The Pattern of Power

Power of some sort is involved in every phase of the political process. But the concern here is with the set of instrumentalities, material and nonmaterial, by which the political-action system works to achieve its ends. The power with which we are concerned is only the kind that may be called "the power of the state."

The descriptive task is to discern the pattern in these instrumentalities and their operation. In terms of the Weberian model, the task of describing and analyzing the pattern of power depends on the distinction between the "administrative staff" and the "supreme authority." In the highly developed modern polity multiple interrelations and overlapping between these two elements complicate the analysis. In spite of these complexities, the modern polity generally differentiates the structures performing the policy-making function from those that carry out policies. Bureaucracies, civil and military, are the obvious examples of the latter. Yet it is evident that the "power of the state" is not limited to them. Certainly in the contemporary democratic welfare state, with its wide and detailed intervention in economic and social life, many bodies nominally in the private sector are in fact indispensable to the effective execution of programs and policies. Chief are the organized producers groups, whose skills and cooperation must be won for the service of policy. The citizen has a role in the pattern of power as a member of these groups: for example, the trade unionist carrying out the terms of an incomes policy, the employer advising the planning council, and the doctor serving in the national health service. But the citizen also has a role in the pattern of power as an individual—for example, as draftee or taxpayer. Among the resources that make up the power of the state are the citizens, whether organized or unorganized, who are regularly mobilized by the polity in pursuit of its purposes. In the liberal democratic state this role of the mobilizable citizen is presumably limited, although, as in the case of the British defense effort during World War II, mobilization by a liberal democracy may in some circumstances be more total than mobilization by a totalitarian dictatorship. In any case, when polities are being compared, a crucial question is how far and under what conditions citizen activities and resources can be mobilized by government—that is, included in the pattern of power.

If we were concerned with the European states of a few generations ago, it might seem feasible to draw the boundary delimiting the polity where the civil and military bureaucracy impinged on the environment. But today large sectors of what used to be the economic environment have been directly incorporated into the pattern of power by such means as the nationalization of industry. Moreover, where there has not been outright nationalization, economic planning and control have created such close and intricate linkages between the huge bureaucratic sector of the polity and major organized units of the so-called private sector that private bureaucrats perform crucial roles in the implementation of policy. Indeed, in Soviet Russia the ordinary citizen is in effect an employee of the state, if employee is not too mild a word.

While the pattern of power must be conceived broadly, it may be useful for purposes of analysis to distinguish between inner and outer rings or sectors. We may wish to distinguish between the central coordinating and planning ministry and the departments constituting its bureaucratic environment. Similarly, we may wish to examine the input and output relations between the civilian bureaucracy as a whole and the structures linking it with the private sector. In the developed modern polity, however, the pattern of power has a broad reach, including all activities used by the polity in pursuit of its ends.

Among the devices for making feasible the further incorporation of citizens into the pattern of power, one of the most effective in the course of political modernization has been the democratization of the pattern of interests. In a modern representative democracy the voters, the ultimate burden creators, are, roughly speaking, the citizens, the ultimate burden bearers. In theory this means that since those giving orders are much the same as those carrying them out, there should be no clash. And in fact the tremendous increase in state power among the democracies tends to bear out the theory. On the other hand, the increasingly roundabout system of producing and implementing decisions in the developed modern polity means that often the ultimate burden bearers find the policies unrecognizable. As a result, the distinction between governors and governed is acutely felt. This raises sharp problems of legitimizing the massive mobilization of effort involved in the welfare state and the managed economy, which in large part have themselves been called forth by the extension of democratic authority.

While norms of authority emphasize the procedures of policy making in the modern polity, they also relate to the structure of policy implementation. Written constitutions sometimes enter this field. Under a separation-of-powers doctrine, a written constitution may prescribe the differentiation of the law-executing and law-adjudicating functions from the law-making function. On the whole, however, written constitutions leave the organization of the bureaucracy open; and this very openness, when understood in the context of modern attitudes, is intrinsic to a crucial normative orientation of political modernity. The high valuation put on the efficiency of government by the rationalism of modern political culture means that instrumentalities should be subject to constant adaptation for the sake of better performance. In government as elsewhere tools and technology can and must be continually improved. It follows that the fundamental law should not try to fix their structure or operation once and for all but should leave them open to the influences of advancing knowledge and technique.

It is important to see the positive dynamic of these modern attitudes in the field of public administration and bureaucracy. They are as influential as are the factors more usually stressed by modern constitutionalism, namely, the restraints under which bureaucratic power must be exercised. There are strong practical and normative reasons why restraints are commonly stressed. But we will completely miss the spirit and dynamic of modern bureaucracy if we do not also recognize the major place given in modern political culture to heightening state power, efficiency, and performance.

The Pattern of Policy

Like the pattern of interests, the pattern of power has a dual aspect. It can be looked at, statically, as the complex of instrumentalities of "state power" or, dynamically, as these instrumentalities being used to carry out policy decisions. The static view would be a kind of table of organization. It would include an enumeration and classification of persons and material things, along with the skills and technologies in which the men and tools are embedded. Such an approach to the military bureaucracy, for instance, would give a picture of the various missions for which the armed forces were prepared and the types of situations with which it was believed they could cope. In contrast to this static approach, a dynamic analysis would examine how policy was carried out, as, for instance, in an administrative case study.

The pattern of power in the latter dynamic sense is closely related to the pattern of policy. The difference is that when we analyze the pattern of policy we are looking at the relation of policy implementation to a further environment. For example, the policy decision to have a national health service is implemented by the establishment and operation of the service, which in turn has effects upon the environment in such respects as the health of the citizens, their productive efficiency, their modes of organizing for political action in the health field (not to mention on the plane of political culture), and their long-run attitudes toward government in the age of the welfare state. The term "output" catches the meaning of policy in this context. To continue with economic language, we can think of the pattern of power as productive capacity that has an output in the form of governmental programs. These programs themselves enter into further stages of social action, which as instrumental and expressive action are analogous to production and consumption in the economy.

The kinds of questions raised by the concept of the pattern of policy include the classification and comparison of patterns of policy; their development over time; the analysis of their structural tendencies; and the relations of mutual influence between the political system and its social and economic environment.

A striking trait of the modern polity in recent generations and throughout modern times has been a vast expansion in the scope of policy. The pattern of policy has grown in both variety and magnitude, more functional areas being differentiated and the total output itself increasing. In policy as in politics, to pick up a previous theme, there has been a shift from individualist to collectivist patterns. Greater governmental intervention for redistribution of wealth and control of the economy has produced the welfare state and managed economy in the three democracies studied in this book. With appropriate qualifications, a similar pattern of policy can be discerned in the Soviet Union.

In the democratic setting, one tendency of greater governmental intervention is to create leverage over their controllers for those being controlled. Some years ago E. P. Herring stated the point in a striking and widely valid generalization:

The greater the degree of detailed and technical control the government seeks to exert over industrial and commercial interests, the greater must be their degree of consent and active participation in the very process of regulation, if regulation is to be effective or successful.[4]

Ironically, a pluralizing and decentralizing of power is a likely result of the attempt to centralize it. As a result, in the managed economies of Western Europe, the great organized producers groups have become so closely linked with government as to create a new system of representation alongside the formal system of representation based on elections. The nationalization of industries, even to the point of state socialism, does not solve the problem. For higher authority must reckon with the skill, knowledge, and power of the people actually in charge of industry, whether they are called bureaucrats or capitalists. It is in this connection that a major function of the one-party system comes into play. So long as its own internal authority structure remains coherent, a body like the Communist party of the Soviet Union may be able to offset the polycentric tendencies of the planned economy. As the cycle of movement toward and away from centralization in Russia shows, however, there is no simple and stable solution.

The feedback of consequences from the pattern of policy on other aspects of the polity is crucially important. Indeed, this interaction of other patterns upon policy and of policy upon them is the major reason why we can refer to the polity as a "system": Each of the main variables is mutually interdependent with the others, and a change in one variable will have effects on the others. As the scope of policy grows these effects on other patterns become more pronounced. Sometimes the effects are quite deliberate, as when, as a matter of policy, it is decided to change the pattern of interests or pattern of power—for example, to extend the right to vote or to introduce the merit system into the bureaucracy. Constitution making is one of the more ambitious expressions of this typically modern effort to use state power to alter the way in which state power is directed, organized, and used.

More interesting to the political scientist are the unintended consequences of policy for the rest of the society and for the political system itself. As state power increases and the scope of policy expands, this topic becomes more important. There develops a whole spectrum of what one writer has called "hidden policies." These are not the products of willful deception by bureaucrats or selfish manipulation by special interests—although the groups slighted by them will probably think so—but of the fact that a constant raising of the level of complexity and technicality makes control of the consequences of public policy ever more difficult. To take an American example, consider the huge interstate and defense highway system started in the fifties. Designed to improve highway transportation between cities and states—which it did—this program also had unintended effects that spread like

---

[4]E. P. Herring, *Public Administration and the Public Interest* (New York, 1936), p. 192.

shock waves through the urban centers of the country. In the opinion of one very knowledgeable observer,

> [It was] a program which the twenty-first century will almost certainly judge to have had more influence on the shape and development of American cities, the distribution of population within metropolitan areas and across the nation as a whole, the location of industry and various kinds of employment opportunities (and, through all these, immense influence on race relations and the welfare of black Americans) than any initiative of the middle third of the twentieth century.[5]

Yet these effects were not considered when the program was conceived, had no part in the project descriptions, and for a long time went unrecognized by outside observers.

The practical lesson to be learned from such experiences is that "government must seek out its hidden policies, raising them to the level of consciousness and acceptance—or rejection—and acknowledge the extraordinary range of contradictions that are typically encountered."[6] The theoretical lesson is that the student of the modern polity must be alert to the massive dysfunctions that are inherent in so complex and technical a system of activity.

Mobilization of Interests and Power

If we think of policy as the output of the political system, it is inevitable that we should also ask if there are comparable inputs. As the various elements of the polity are interdependent, so also is the political system itself interdependent with the other systems constituting society as a whole. While the polity will affect this larger environment through its outputs, it will itself be affected by inputs from that environment.

If we follow our model of the polity, two of these lines of input from the environment will affect respectively the pattern of interests and the pattern of power. In the history of European modernization the classic instance is the impact of industrialization. It brought into existence new economic strata, the commercial and industrial capitalist classes, which in turn put forward a whole new spectrum of policy demands and supported a system of parties and pressure groups to push these demands.

The process by which the needs of these groups were converted into explicit demands upon and within the polity was not merely reflexive but included a crucial and complex phase, which can be called the *mobilization of interests.* The objective position of a class or group in the economy does not automatically and

---

[5]Daniel Patrick Moynihan, "Policy vs. Program in the '70's," *The Public Interest,* 20 (Summer 1970), p. 94.

[6] *Ibid.*

instantly make the group aware of what its interests are and endow it with an organized mode of pursuing them. A necessary intervening stage is the growth of class or group consciousness. Class needs will remain ineffective until they are made articulate and given some form of organized support. In the period of political development that accompanied industrialization, the mobilization of interests included such crucial transformations as the extension of the suffrage, the development of media of political communication, and the rise of political parties and pressure groups. How this took place—for instance, by parliamentary or revolutionary means—depended in great degree upon features of the existing political system.

Comparable to the mobilization of interests is the *mobilization of power*. Industrialization greatly increased the resources, material and nonmaterial, present in the various nations of Western Europe: the wealth of individuals, their skills, and their organizations. Again, this did not mean that these resources automatically would be incorporated into state power. But sooner or later in all European polities the personnel and skills of the rising classes were used to enhance the power of the state in reforms of the civil and military bureaucracy.

This common process of mobilization of power displayed differences depending upon national differences among the polities. And today differences remain, not only in the character of the respective bureaucracies, but also in the degree to which the polity can mobilize the resources of its citizens. Citizens may resist the state by evading such typical burdens as heavy income taxation, military conscription, and economic regulation. On the part of the bureaucracy, failures of support range from the endemic friction between bureaucrats and politicians to an acute crisis of authority resulting in a coup against the regime by military or civilian officials.

A mark of the modern polity is often said to be its ability to satisfy a greater "load" of political demand. The vast mobilization of interests that has continued through the modern period has been a main reason for the expansion of the scope of policy. The rise of democracy, the extension of participation, and the refinement of tastes and needs have been major background conditions for the mounting output and increasing centralization of the modern state. But our model will not let us forget the intervening variable: the mobilization of power. Whether such inputs of power will be adequate to the outputs sought by rising political demands is never wholly assured, but has been and remains a major problem of the modern state.

Economy and Environment

For the liberal democracies the environment also includes the economic system. In these systems, the interaction between polity and economy is of central importance to the political scientist. In the crucial processes of modernization, the mobilization of interests and the mobilization of power, we can trace the emergence in the economy of new classes whose skills and demands often provide the foundation for major steps in the development of the polity. At the heart of this concern of the political scientist with what went on in the unregulated economy is the fact that again and again economic developments have confronted the polity with entirely unanticipated conditions, massive compulsions to which it had to respond and in some degree yield, and which at times seemed to dominate the life and purposes of the polity. Liberty for the economy seemed to mean a loss of liberty for the polity. Freedom of choice in the economy seemed to mean a diminution of freedom of choice for the polity.

Needless to say, the economic freedom that led to the separation of polity and economy in the liberal era is by no means a permanent feature of human affairs. Normally, on the contrary, what people in the liberal order call the economy is part and parcel of the polity. For Aristotle economic activity was clearly subject to the needs and purposes of the polis. Likewise in the case of the medieval manor, the activity of people in fields, shops, and markets was essential to material subsistence. But this activity constituted an integral part of the instrumentalities of the feudal regime, which by law and custom minutely directed and regulated it. These life-supporting spheres of action were as fully incorporated into the medieval polity as their present-day equivalents in any modern socialist regime.

In such cases, the economy is part of the polity, specifically of that element I have called the pattern of power, and it is incorrect and misleading to speak of the economy as separate from the polity, or as interacting with or having effects upon the polity. The huge public sector of the present-day modern state does not interact with the polity; it is part of it. The nationalized industries of some contemporary polities, for instance, do not interact with the polity any more than the bureaucracy interacts with the polity; like the bureaucracy, they are part of the polity.

This is not to say, however, that to nationalize industry or to incorporate the economy into the instrumental complex of the polity necessarily eliminates the old problem of coercion on human choice by unanticipated consequences. The source of the problem is simply transferred from outside the polity to within it. A huge bureaucracy and public sector of the polity now become the scene of developments that continually strain at human control. Freedom of choice continues to be menaced, although now by the bureaucratic instruments set up to serve it. Means still threaten to determine ends, and the "machine" to master man and human purpose.

Five

The Dynamics
of Modernization

After a brief eclipse, history is making a strong comeback in political science, largely under such headings as "development" and "modernization." A period of neglect was healthy, since it obliged political scientists to think out what they really wanted to use history for. They certainly had to get rid of that dreary chapter, vaguely entitled "Historical Background," with which the textbook author used to preface his or her account of a country's government and politics and which constituted a kind of catch-all of turning points, fundamental declarations, great statesmen, national characteristics, and bare and meaningless chronology.

History as Development

The subject matter of political science is political behavior wherever and whenever it takes place. The narrower the empirical base of the study, the less dependable will be our generalizations. The wider the empirical base, the firmer will be the foundation for our generalizing efforts. Individuals must specialize; but for the study of politics as a whole, an aspiration to the status of a science is incompatible with parochialism in space or time. Responding to this need, comparative study has broadened its concerns to include all parts of the world. The same rationale compels political science to seek out and welcome evidence of political behavior in times past. This interest with history as past behavior is a concern that social scientists generally are coming to share. Concluding his magisterial study of the 1793 revolt of the French Vendée, a leading sociologist, Charles Tilly, admonishes his colleagues: "Sociologists have cut themselves off from a rich inheritance by forgetting the obvious: that all history is past social behavior, that all archives are brimming with news on how men used to act, and how they are acting still."[1]

Stated in these terms the case for the study of history is strong. Yet it is a case for the study of history in only one meaning of the term. To study history as past behavior will broaden the basis of fact on which to build the discipline. Like the extension of study to non-Western countries, it increases the varieties of political behavior coming under inquiry and so widens the scope of knowledge. To argue for history in this vein, however, implies that, though past behavior will often differ in many vital respects from present behavior, this difference does not consist in or come from the fact of its pastness. History is to be consulted and used for the sake of difference, but not for that special kind of difference that resides in its pastness. In short, this case for studying the past presumes that the time dimension is irrelevant. But when the political scientists who advocate the study of the past say that the discipline can benefit from the use of history, they also mean that the time dimension is of the essence.

The concept of development recognizes the importance of the time dimension. It treats the evidence of past behavior not as data cut off from their temporal context, but on the contrary as intimately connected with the flow of events in earlier and later time. In common speech, some entity—a structure or institution or system—is said to have "grown out of" or to have "developed" or "evolved" from its previous history. This means that a study of its past is an important way of understanding and explaining the entity. It means that something can be learned about the entity by the study of its past that cannot be learned in any other way.

There is no single meaning that must be adopted as the definition of the term development. The essential question is how useful any definition proves to be in organizing material and directing research. In common usage three notions are often associated with the idea. The principal one is the notion of directionality or trend in the historical process. Along with this go the notions that such directional change occurs in stages and that, with regard to causation, each stage is produced by the preceding stage. Several successive stages of an entity, each caused by the preceding stage, with the whole process showing a trend—this is the distinctive pattern of historical process to which the concept of development calls attention as a possibility to be looked for and tested by research and theorizing.

The concept of development briefly sketched in the preceding paragraphs will provide the organizing idea for the remaining chapters of this Introduction. The first part of the Introduction was concerned with setting forth the cultural-structural model of the political system that indicated the general functions and problems of the polity and identified its basic elements and their relationships. In contrast with this static view of the polity, the concept of development directs attention to change and its dynamics. Specifically, the concern here is with long-run change

---

[1]Charles Tilly, *The Vendée* (Cambridge, Mass., 1964), p. 342.

in the modern polity. The concept of development can be used when studying change in nonmodern polities. As I shall have occasion to mention, the medieval polity also developed in what may be called rather inelegantly a process of "medievalization." The subject here, however, is modern political development, or, to use a convenient synonym, political modernization.

The argument can be briefly stated. The first general proposition is that modern political culture constitutes an orientation toward action that gives the basic threefold structure of the polity a distinctive character, such that we can speak of "the modern polity" as a general type. Insofar as it is governed by this orientation, moreover, the modern polity tends to produce consequences, intended and unintended, which show directionality over time. Furthermore, the modern polity displays not only the quantitative change embodied in these trends, but also qualitative change as its structure moves through successive stages. With regard to both trends and stages, the four polities dealt with in this book have followed a course of development that is similar in important respects. Because of this common course of development, these political systems have not only common features, but also common problems—the disorders of modernity.

The task of the present chapter is to describe the orientation given to political action by the culture of modernity and to show how the structures supported by this orientation produce the trends distinctive of political modernization. Chapter 6 will turn to the specific form taken by the basic structures of the modern polity, relating them so far as possible to the political culture of modernity. Chapter 7 will show how these structures have changed from one period to another, their culmination being the distinctive patterns of the highly developed polity of the present day. Chapter 8 will be concerned with the problems that follow from this common structure and common development.

Cultural Modernization

Since the polity is a system of purposive human action, it aims at control, and its development will involve an increase in the capacity to control. A present-day student of politics may immediately think of the kind of instrumental problem solving that the modern polity practices: pragmatic, secular, empirical, technological. Yet it is of the utmost importance to recognize that purposive action can involve many other varieties of motive and conduct. It can be transcendental and ritualistic, as in the manipulation of the gods by ancient kings. It can be frozen in a "cake of custom"—to use Walter Bagehot's phrase—that validates the perpetual efficacy of certain instrumentalities and permits no adaptation or flexibility. It can be based on a sharp separation between man and nature that makes nature a clearly defined object of mastery, as in the West. Or it can posit a continuum including man and nature in a unity, as in the Orient.

Scientific Rationalism

Purposive action can be detected from the earliest ages of human existence. In a broad sense, the struggle for mastery over "nature" and "history" has characterized human behavior since men first made tools and weapons and established laws. This will appear to be an unexceptionable and even obvious generalization. Yet the point needs to be stressed, since some students try to identify modernity with man's effort to control his natural and social environment. In their view, modernization begins when men first attempt to control their environment, seek knowledge for this purpose, and acquire a sense of human competence. Moreover, this distinctive situation is held to have emerged only in recent centuries, before which men passively accepted their environment and regarded any effort to change it as futile and even sacrilegious. Such an attitude of acceptance is sometimes said to be essential to the traditionalist mind in contrast with the modern, rationalist mind.

This approach must be shunned if we are to get at the heart of modernity. It does make easy the task of defining what is meant by the modern by reducing it to the broad category of human effort to control the environment. But the facts of history and prehistory contradict this conception, making it clear that men have sought to control their environment—in some sense of that word—from the time that we can call them men. Tools, weapons, and laws are the obvious examples, but magic and religion have also been means of control. In this sense rationalism of *some* variety begins with man himself, *Homo sapiens.*

An essential distinguishing trait of modernity is a unique kind of rationalism from which it derives a powerful dynamic. This component of modern culture is scientific rationalism: the beliefs and values supporting both the pursuit of scientific knowledge and the use of this knowledge to control the natural and social environment—as defined and understood by science. A main current in modernization is the distinctive process of rationalization that is buoyed up and driven on by this cultural premise, a process consisting in the expansion of scientific knowledge and the consequent impact of this knowledge upon culture and social structure.

Rationalism has taken many forms. Ancient and medieval philosophers were rationalist through and through, and Plato and Thomas Aquinas have left us supreme examples of rationalist thought—general, systematic, and logically coherent. Much as it owes to this earlier rationalism, science is a distinctively different sort of rationalism with different conceptions of what is meant by "knowledge," "control," and "environment." It is a rationalism that is not only systematically ordered, but also empirically founded, experimentally tested, and oriented toward a wholly secular sphere of operation.

It is this last point that is most important. Medieval thought was teleological. Its search for the laws governing nature and society was hemmed in and directed by a pervasive belief that an objective moral order governed the human and natural environment. In this view all things had their proper role and purpose in a divinely ordered cosmos. All ranks and orders of men, like all kinds of physical objects, fitted into a cosmos that was at once natural and moral. The alchemists, one may recall, thought of the metals with which they worked as "noble" and "base," and when performing their experiments they were as careful to pray and stay morally pure as to weigh out quantities accurately. The rejection of such a realm of purpose, objective to and yet controlling all men and things, is crucial to scientific progress, giving it in effect (if not always in theory) a single-minded concern with the secular world.

Moreover, scientific rationalism is not only an outlook, but an attitude, a propensity to action. It gives high value to the pursuit of scientific truth and to its application in technology as the means of mastering nature and history. "Knowledge is power," said Francis Bacon, one of the most far-seeing and forceful of the philosophers of modernity. The search for power is intrinsic to any form of purposive activity. But the scientific attitude makes its objective a unique kind of power and offers a unique method of achieving it. Scientific rationalism has consequences. They constitute the multiple and complex processes of scientific and technological rationalization that are a main current of modernization. The leading example is industrialization, that immense transformation of economic life, which, in Max Weber's words, consists in "the extension of the productivity of labour, which has through the subordination of the process of production to scientific points of view, relieved it from its dependence upon the natural organic limitations of the human individual."[2]

Voluntarism

It would simplify the study of modernity if it could be focused solely on the cultural complex associated with the scientific attitude. Some writers do find the essential dynamic of modernization in "the unprecedented increase in man's knowledge . . . that accompanied the scientific revolution."[3] Yet there is undeniably another related but distinguishable element in the culture of modernity. In the opening pages of this book, while sketching the problems of the modern polity, I suggested that these problems could be traced not only to the scientific attitude, but also to what I called "the liberating spirit of modern democracy."

It is fairly common to join democracy and science as the twin engines of modernization. For more recent times this formulation is satisfactory. In political development the focus on democratization directs attention to major aspects of change ranging from the rise of universal suffrage in the last century to the establishment of the welfare state in recent generations. Underlying the democratic norm, however, is an even more general and more powerful idea. This other major premise of modernity is most accurately called voluntarism.

---

[2]Max Weber, *The Protestant Ethic and The Spirit of Capitalism,* Talcott Parsons (tr.) (New York, 1958), p. 75.

[3]Cyril E. Black, *The Dynamics of Modernization: A Study in Comparative History* (New York, 1966), p. 7.

The term immediately calls attention to its contrast with the intellectualism of premodern and medieval thought. Medieval teleology was intellectualist in that it found the fundamental source of the moral law not in will—not even in God's will —but in an objective and unchangeable order. Voluntarism reversed this view, making human wishes the basis of legitimacy in public policy and, indeed, generally in the whole sphere of purpose, individual and collective. Its imperative was the phrase that François Rabelais, a major prophet of modernity, inscribed over the entrance to his abbey of Thélème: *Fais ce que tu voudras*. The will of the sovereign, whether king or people, became the ultimate basis of morally binding commands. Human needs as expressed in human wishes became the basis of the "rights of man." In contrast, the medieval (and classical) view held that the commands of the regime derive their moral force from a teleological order external to the human will.

In political thought the old medieval limits on law making were now relaxed. As has often been remarked, the basic approach to conceptions of legitimacy was reversed. While in the medieval view authority was based on law, in the modern view law is based on authority. The Constitution of the United States, for instance, and the other laws depending upon it gain their binding force from the will of "we, the people." There was, of course, some law making in the Middle Ages. Yet in practice it was strongly restrained by custom, and in theory it was conceived as serving an ideal order that severely limited the options open to men. Characteristic of this attitude was the fact that although many kings were attacked and overthrown, the monarchic regime itself was virtually never challenged. Sharply in contrast stands the modern period when voluntarism opens the door wide to continual changes in regime. The idea of an unlimited authority to make law—the idea of sovereignty—is an essential of political modernity.

Such, briefly, are the major premises of modernity: scientific rationalism and voluntarism. Can either of the concepts be derived from the other, or from some further inclusive idea? I think not. Yet there are important relations between them. Both reject teleology; the denial of final causation in nature going along with the denial of an objective ethic for man. Also, they are related as definitions of means and of ends. Modern rationalism incites men to extend their power over nature and society through science and technology. But as we have observed in our opening critique, while science can create powerful instrumentalities, it cannot answer the question of what they are to be used for. Modernity assigns this question of purpose to voluntarism, rejecting the guidance of teleology, religion, or tradition and leaving the identification of purpose to human subjectivity.

This is the meaning of that quintessentially modern definition of the end of man as "the pursuit of happiness." It is as distinctive of our time and culture as was the pursuit of salvation for the Middle Ages. Happiness has no objectively defined content, but is simply a way of referring to the gratification of whatever men may want. On the one hand, scientific rationalism gives a definition of means that is increasingly precise and differentiated in specialized bodies of knowledge. On the other hand, voluntarism makes the ends for which this power is used as various and changing as human wishes.

Democratization

I have said that one of the expressions of voluntarism is democracy. On the face of it, voluntarism seems to leave open the question of whose wishes are to govern. An elitist answer could be conceived that would put so high a value on the wishes of the few that the many would be wholly excluded from power. When we first see voluntarism pushing aside the old medieval restraints, its first champions are not the mass of the people, but the rulers. Historically, voluntarism spread from the top down, and the seat of legitimacy shifted gradually over generations from the will of the king, or of the king-in-parliament, to the will of the people.

There is a certain logic to this trend. In contrast with classical and medieval notions, there is in voluntarism an openness that readily becomes a tendency toward democracy. Perhaps the reason is simply that although it is hard to deny that knowledge of the good, on which premodern conceptions based legitimacy, is unequally distributed throughout society, it is self-evident that every man has wants to satisfy. If we are faithful to human appetite as our standard of valuation, we are pretty sure to come out with an equalitarian view of the ultimate foundations of power.

Given the nature of the present study the relevance of voluntarism to political development has been stressed, but its dynamic has been much broader. A prime characteristic of the process of modernization has been the multiplication and sophistication of human wants. In economic development it is a commonplace that goods and services that are luxuries in one period become everyday necessities in the next. People who thought of themselves as comfortably middle class a hundred years ago would be regarded as far below the poverty line today. Each stage in the prodigious growth of productive power of the modernizing countries has been accompanied by an equally prodigious increase in the wants that people exert themselves to satisfy. We cannot take such an expansion of wants for granted. It has been not only legitimized but powerfully propelled forward by the voluntaristic norm. Voluntarism is a constant goad to the conception and assertion of new wants, for new wants are not merely legitimate, but desirable. After all, the more wants satisfied, the greater the sum of happiness achieved. The voluntaristic norm supports and incites the use of the imagination for the multiplication of human wants. This expansion of appetite has also been a part of the great democratic revolution of modern times, affecting both economic and political development.

The dependence of modern economic expansion upon a parallel and supporting evolution of tastes in quality is readily recognized. Advertising, for instance, elicits new wants and tastes, as when producers create the consumer demand they are preparing to satisfy with a new line of goods. Moreover, this process of demand creation has been indispensable to economic modernization. If people were to return to the standards of contentment of three hundred years ago, the modern economy would collapse. The same holds of politics. A return to the political expectations of that earlier age would shrink the functions of government to unrecognizably tiny proportions. Like the modern economy, the modern polity also depends upon a massive and continuous process of demand creation. Joseph A. Schumpeter elucidates this function of political competition. Referring to the group demands put forward in the political arena, he observes:

> Such volitions do not as a rule assert themselves directly. Even if strong and definite they remain latent, often for decades, until they are called to life by some political leader who turns them into political factors. This he does, or else his agents do it for him, by organizing these volitions, by working them up and by including eventually appropriate items in his competitive offering.[4]

In the polity as in the economy there is interdependence between the processes of rationalization and of democratization. As the power and productivity of the modern state and modern economy increase, a growing and appropriately differentiated demand is provided for the new activities and products being made available.

The Intellectuals and Demand-Creation

In both processes the work of the intellectual classes is crucial. This is obvious with regard to rationalization, which grows out of the inventive and innovative achievements of scientists, engineers, and specialists in the various branches of advancing technology. But the complementary process of maintaining and creating demands also depends upon a certain type of intellectual. It is the function of this class of intellectuals to shape the tastes, preferences, and ideals of each generation. Among them are the creative minds that have set their marks on successive stages of modernization. In the development of political culture these include such men as John Locke, Edmund Burke, Jean Jacques Rousseau, Karl Marx and Friedrich Nietzsche.

But the culture of modernity has been sustained and driven forward not only by political philosophers. Poets and preachers, economists and historians, have also developed its basic symbols as they bear on the meaning of individual and social life. Percy Bysshe Shelley's famous asseveration that "poets are the unacknowledged legislators of the world" has much sociological merit. At this level of concern, intellectuals deal with the more general principles that inform the norms and beliefs of everyday conduct. They may express this concern in conservative or in radical ways. They may reinforce the symbols of the established order, or they may devote themselves to the imaginative creation of new models of action.

The history of modern culture has been especially marked by the proliferation of new visions of social and political order. From the philosophes of the eighteenth

---

[4]Joseph A. Schumpeter, *Capitalism, Socialism and Democracy,* 2d ed. (New York and London, 1947), p. 270.

century to the socialist intelligentsia of the present day, radical intellectuals have shaped the political demands of a society that is increasingly mobilized by and for political action. In conceiving new styles of political and economic order these intellectual leaders have shown as much creativity as the great scientists have shown in conceiving new theories of nature. Such styles and formulas, whether old or new, are propagated throughout the society by a highly differentiated complex of roles—by teachers, journalists, advertising men, agitators—that are distinctive to modernity. The developing political consciousness of modern man owes as much to them as his developing power and productivity owe to the myriad of technicians and skilled workmen who preserve the old technologies and apply the new.

Economic Modernization

The previous discussion has sought to characterize the attitudes that distinguish modern Western society from the Western societies that preceded it. I have not argued that there was a complete break. Clearly, on the contrary, there were major continuities. Indeed, I would accept Arnold J. Toynbee's argument that one of the major "intelligible fields of historical study" for the social scientist is Western Christian civilization.[5] What this means is that the continuities in European history for the past 1500 years are so fundamental as greatly to transcend the differences between the medieval and modern periods. The new attitudes, however, which with increasing prominence spread throughout Europe from the seventeenth century onward, did involve matters of very great, if not ultimate, importance.

Moreover, these ideas had consequences. The chain of effects descending from them transformed behavior and social structure, bringing into existence the distinctive traits of modern society. I wish in particular to focus attention upon two distinguishable, but interrelated, processes—increasing *differentiation* and increasing *scale*. Operationally, these embody the two basic orientations of modernity and by their interaction create the ever larger networks of social, economic, and political interdependence that characterize modern society. The general image of this evolution is familiar. Communities were at first small, relatively self-subsistent and similar in economy, polity, and culture—as was still the case with the village and manorial society of late medieval times. Gradually these communities were drawn together by ties of political and governmental activity, trade and industry, education and communication. This increasing interdependence introduced outside influences into the original communities, disrupting their solidarities and at the same time reshaping the fragments and binding them into vast, impersonal, highly differentiated, highly interdependent social, economic, and political

---

[5] Arnold J. Toynbee, *A Study of History,* abr. ed. (New York and London, 1947), "Introduction."

wholes. Such, in brief and impressionistic terms, is the manner of creation of what Emile Durkheim called "the great society."[6]

The general formula exhibited in this process characterizes development in many different modes and different ages. Indeed, the Middle Ages displayed a process of development—we may call it "medievalization"—that also followed this general formula in the creation of its own special sort of highly developed society. My concern here is to elucidate the mechanisms of that special form of development that we call modernization—to say more precisely how the basic orientations of modernity were expressed in increasing differentiation and increasing scale and how these two processes interacted to create the large, complex networks of interdependence constituting the great society. The concepts of differentiation and scale can be used in the analysis of social, economic, or political processes. Their meaning and their manner of interaction, however, can be most readily illustrated from economic analysis, from which they originally derived. While my interest is primarily political, it will best serve the purposes of clarity to consider first the economic significance of the terms.

The Division of Labor

In economic analysis differentiation is more commonly referred to as the *division of labor*. The eighteenth-century economist Adam Smith, who invented the term, was also the first to explore systematically its influence on productivity. On the very first page of his great work *An Inquiry into the Nature and the Causes of the Wealth of Nations* he introduces the topic, going on to illustrate it with his famous description of the pin factory in which specialization—the division of the business of making a pin into about eighteen distinct operations—increases the productive powers of labor hundreds of times over what it would be if each man worked separately, making the whole pin by himself. Smith argues that the tendency to division of labor arises from exchange, holding that it is the prospect of getting a larger return from marketing what he produces that incites the individual to raise his productivity by specialization. From this relationship it follows that "the division of labour is limited by the extent of the market." As the market is widened—for instance, by improvements in transportation—a higher degree of specialization becomes feasible, since its greater production can now be absorbed. In short, as the scale of the economy increases, so also does the division of labor within it. And as scale and differentiation increase, productivity rises.

Writing in 1776 Smith reflected—and analyzed—the experience of the first phase of economic modernization in Britain. This was the era of the "commercial revolution" when, as his analysis suggests, extension of the market (that is, increase in the scale of the economy) within Britain and abroad greatly stimulated agriculture and industry. The discovery of America, he observed,

---

[6]Emile Durkheim, *The Division of Labor in Society,* George Simpson (tr.) (New York, 1933), p. 222. The original version in French was published in 1893.

by opening a new and inexhaustible market to all the commodities of Europe
. . . gave occasion to new divisions of labour and improvements of art, which,
in the narrow circle of the ancient commerce, could never have taken place for
want of a market to take off the greater part of their produce.

Smith was not unaware of the importance of machines and made their invention
one of the principal reasons for the increase in productivity resulting from specialization. Yet he wrote before the second great phase of economic modernization
in Britain, when the industrial revolution made new machinery the principal means
of a vast economic advance. Writing after a hundred years of industrialization in
Britain, Alfred Marshall in his *Principles of Economics* (1890) still made the division
of labor central to his analysis of economic development. Like Smith he was
acutely aware of the importance of scale, laying great stress on how "man's power
of productive work increases with the volume of work that he does." Naturally,
he was far more aware of the importance of the organization of the individual firm.
But although he wrote at a time when the modern corporation was coming to be
widely used and British managers were making their first large-scale experiments
with industrial combinations, he still assumed that the free market controlled the
firm, not vice versa.

After another long interval, which has seen "the organizational revolution" and
the rise of collectivism in economics as in politics, John Kenneth Galbraith takes
a very different view of the role of the market. In his *New Industrial State* (1967)
he argues that the classical relation has been reversed, the great oligopolistic firms
now tending to control the market rather than the market the firms. In spite of these
many differences, he still finds that the division of labor is central to economic
development. Writing when science has come even more prominently to the fore
as the principal motor of advance, he stresses the role of technology, "the systematic application of scientific or other organized knowledge to practical tasks." Still
the "most important consequence" of technology is "in forcing the division and
subdivision of any such task into its component parts." The division of labor is very
largely derived from specialized branches of scientific knowledge and is carried on
by machines. As in the Smithian example, however, it depends upon an expansion
in the scale of the economy. Only thus can its increases in productivity be used.
Economies of scale resulting from such specialization are a main reason for the
creation of huge business organizations and the effort to create larger trading areas
such as the Common Market.

One reason these three discussions of the mechanism of economic development
are interesting is that they correspond to three main periods in European economic
modernization, the commercial revolution, the industrial revolution, and the organizational revolution. The last section of this chapter will consider this scheme
and its relation to parallel stages of political development.

Interaction of Specialization and Scale

The two processes of the mechanism of economic development are *division of labor* (or specialization) and *increase in scale.* Smith stressed the division of labor itself as the source of improvement in "the productive powers of labour." The present analysis, which finds the dynamic of economic growth in the advance of science and technology, puts the emphasis upon some step forward in scientific knowledge that, in turn, when applied to economic processes, involves their division and subdivision. Such an improvement in productivity can take place prior to an expansion of the market, as we see in the present phase of scientific advance, when a leaping technology continually presents us with goods and services we never dreamed of, let alone demanded in the marketplace. Hence, the constant need to keep the market adjusted by the cultivation of appropriate new tastes among potential buyers.

Yet the factor of scale can also vary independently. As Smith saw it, a widening of the market stimulates further division of labor. Such an expansion of scale could be brought about by more efficient modes of transportation, as when canals and then railways opened up markets in eighteenth- and nineteenth-century Europe. It could also be brought about by political means, as when the French Revolution through an act of governmental centralization struck down local imposts and other burdens on free trade within the country. Similarly, a change in cultural standards, by producing new tastes for more consumption goods and services, could sharply stimulate economic activity.

The first proposition to derive from this analysis is that *the two processes, increase in differentiation and increase in scale, can vary independently.* Either type of process—for instance, a new stage of productivity resulting from greater specialization, or a new level of demand resulting from a widening of the market —can be the primary process of change. Neither theoretically nor empirically is there reason for saying that one is more important than the other. While science and technology have driven forward the productive power of the economy through new stages of specialization, so also has the growing scale of modern economies initiated new thrusts forward. The fact that each can be and has often been an independent variable should be kept in mind when we come to consider the political embodiment of these two types of social process.

The point is obvious in the case of economic development, which, depending on the situation, may be driven forward by initial changes in either specialization or scale. When these concepts are applied to other spheres, however, this dual possibility is sometimes lost sight of. In Durkheim's classic discussion, *The Division of Labor in Society,* from which I have borrowed a great deal, he makes specialization derivative. Defining "density" essentially as I have defined "scale"—that is, as the "number of social relations"—he insists that the division of labor follows from an increase in density, not vice versa. Similarly, Godfrey and Monica Wilson, in *The Analysis of Social Change* (1945), find that the crucial difference between a segmented and developed society is the difference in scale, upon which, as in

Durkheim's account, the extent of differentiation is said to depend. Citing the work of the Wilsons, Scott Greer in *The Emerging City: Myth and Reality* (1962) also makes the increase in scale the primary process of change in urbanization and the source of differentiation of social roles. In applying the concepts of scale and specialization to political development, it seems clear to me that we should return to the lesson of economic analysis and approach any concrete situation with an open mind, ready to find the initiation of change on either side.

The second proposition is that *the two processes interact, mutually reinforcing one another.* An increase in scale promotes economic specialization; an advance in specialization encourages the search for markets where the added product can be disposed of. From time to time, each has taken the lead in stimulating economic development, as when the voracious markets developed by the commercial revolution conditioned the great leaps forward in technology of the industrial revolution, and the rise in productivity in the later nineteenth century promoted the search for markets in the later stages of European imperialism. While each may vary independently, if an advance in one sphere is to be maintained, it must meet with an appropriate and concomitant response in the other. This "functional" relationship does not in itself constitute a causal connection. It is, however, readily translated into activities that do bring about effects with regard to technological advance or market expansion, as the case may be. Such a mechanism of interaction, it may also be observed, is properly called a mechanism. It is not an instance of the influence of ideas. On the contrary, it is a type of process in which "pressures," "opportunities," and "structures" are the basis for explaining the generation of change. The cultural orientations of modernity motivate distinctively new types of behavior. But once these floods of consequence have been sent forth into the world, they interact with profound effect on one another in ways that may be only dimly understood or barely perceived and not at all intended by contemporaries. The industrial revolution, the rise of the factory system, the creation of the great manufacturing city were only in part—in small part—the intentional creations of their time.

The third proposition concerns the overall result of development. *Together the increase in specialization and the increase in scale constitute a growth in interdependence.* As Alfred Marshall said, drawing an analogy between economic development and organic evolution, the development of the organism, whether social or physical, involves, on the one hand, an increasing subdivision of functions between its separate parts and, on the other hand, more intimate connections between the parts, each becoming less and less self-sufficient and so more and more dependent upon the others. Economic development involves such a growth in interdependent complexity as more and more complex networks of exchange join together the increasingly differentiated parts of the growing economy.

In the conventional image of such development, the expansion of the economy is seen as involving a spread of exchange from a limited to a wider area, bringing more and more people into the system of relationships. That did often happen, as, for instance, in the expansion of the European economy to include trade with America in the seventeenth century. Yet it is crucially important to understand that economic development—and development generally—can take place and often has taken place quite apart from any increase in the number of individual units included in the expanding system. An increase in scale consists in an increase in the number of exchange relations. This can occur within an economic system and does not require physical expansion to include more people or more territory. The same number of individual units can be arranged in a simple, segmented economy or in a complex, developed economy.

The terms used in this analysis of development can be explained graphically. Figures 5.1 and 5.2 contrast schematically a segmented and a developed economy.

Figure 5.1 A Segmented Economy

Figure 5.2 A Developed Economy
(Relations of Only *A* and *B* Shown)

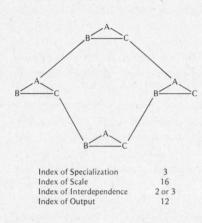

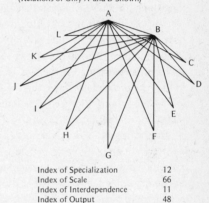

Index of Specialization	3	Index of Specialization	12
Index of Scale	16	Index of Scale	66
Index of Interdependence	2 or 3	Index of Interdependence	11
Index of Output	12	Index of Output	48

Figure 5.1 represents a segmented society with a very simple division of labor, consisting of three occupations (or members), *A, B,* and *C,* as indicated by the index of specialization. The society contains four local communities, identical in number of members and occupations and linked by simple ties of exchange. The lines show exchange relations. The scale of the economy is indicated by the total number of interrelations, 16. The interdependence of the members is slight, each having only 2 or at the most 3 connections with other members. Given the primitive level of specialization, productivity is low. Supposing the productivity of each member to be equal, it can be represented by 1, making the index of total output 12. Figure 5.2 presents the contrast of a developed economy. In this figure the division of labor has increased to the point of there being 12 occupations. The local communities have been dissolved into a single system. Supposing that each individual unit stands in an exchange relation with all other units, the index of scale will have risen to 66 and the index of interdependence to 11. Supposing also that productivity, like specialization, has increased fourfold, the index of output will be 48.

Political Modernization

The general ideas expressed in these familiar terms of economic analysis have an equally important, though less familiar, application to the study of political development. Increases in differentiation and scale have also characterized political modernization, the upshot being the great networks of interdependent complexity and centralized power that we call modern states.

In the course of political modernization, the dual orientation of modernity has been expressed in the pattern of interests and the pattern of power, respectively, of the modern polity. Scientific and technical advance has made its impact on the mobilization of power, while the thrust toward equality and democracy has been expressed in the mobilization of interests (see Chapter 4). Most studies of the modern state have shown an overwhelming concern with the latter topic. It has long been an interest of historians and political scientists to trace the course by which political demand has broadened and deepened, involved more and more people, and been made effective in the political arena. This is the story of the rise of constitutionalism and popular government; of how over time civil, political, and social rights were made effective. Even where major defeats have taken place, as in the modern dictatorships, there has been an immense growth in political scale in the sense that the spectrum of interests imposing demands and extracting satisfactions from the state has vastly increased. The populations of the various modern polities have grown, but even more important have been the unremitting increase and variegation of demands for new and more activities and services by the state. Like the modern economy, the modern state depends upon this vast and mounting demand to maintain its activity.

Along with the mobilization of interests has gone the mobilization of power, surely no less important, although much neglected by scholars. In part driven by the demands of the groups, classes, and leaders who have constituted the effective citizenry at various times, the modern state has continually developed its potential for acting on man and nature. This story has not been told in the detail it deserves. There are histories of the "output" of the modern state—from mercantilism, through laissez faire, to the welfare state and socialism. But the mobilization of power—like the growth of productivity in the economy—consists in the increase of the *capacity* to produce outputs. Its history is the history of the development of the "extractive" and "repressive" functions: not only the rise of bureaucracy, but also the expansion of the tax system, the police, and especially the armed forces. It has often been remarked that the huge productive capacity developed by the modern economy is totally unprecedented when seen in a long historical perspective. The power of the modern state is no less a historical wonder, reflecting a capacity for policy outputs as vast and unprecedented as the productivity of its remarkable economic system. The centerpiece in this mobilization of power has been the growing capacity of the civilian and military bureaucracy, fed by knowledge in law, economics, engineering, and the proliferating specialties of modern science and technology.

The Power-Interest Dynamic

In political modernization not only are the processes of increasing differentiation and increasing scale analogous to processes of economic modernization, but so also are certain mechanisms. A principal mechanism of economic development, as we have seen, is the mutual interaction of specialization with scale, of the technologically driven division of labor with growing markets, internal and external. In political development specialization and scale also interact, stimulating one another. An increase in the scale of political demand puts new requirements on the state, which often can be met only by an expansion of the state's bureaucratic capacities and possibly by further mobilization and control of the private sector. Thus, for instance, the demand for a national health service, made effective in a democratic polity by electoral victory, leads to the erection of a new ministry, to the establishment of a complex of relationships with the medical profession, and to a method of financing out of special charges and/or general taxation.

Influence also runs in the opposite direction, from the pattern of power to the pattern of interests. In this instance the advance of the instrumentalities of state power to a higher level of skill and capacity stimulates new demands upon their performance. An army, for instance, that has been mobilized and trained for a prolonged crisis may, although the crisis has passed, by its very existence give rise to proposals that it be used to defend some items of national interest that otherwise would have languished for attention. Or again, the reform of the civil service by the elimination of corruption and the institution of an effective merit system will tend to increase the efficacy of the state, and for that reason lead interested groups to see in it a means of achieving their ends. More specifically, the establishment of a special department to handle some field of policy often elicits demands for special programs adapted to the department's expertise. Whichever way the flow of influence, the politician is likely to play an important role. His more familiar role is to represent some interest in the policy-making structures of the polity. But he also often acts to communicate the new ideas and information about wider capacities to a latent public, rather like the salesman for a new product, who brings it to the attention of the consumer hitherto unaware of its availability and virtues.

A contemporary illustration of this typical mechanism of political modernization is the tendency to technocracy. As I observed in the introductory pages, modern government makes constantly greater demands on professional expertise, and the professional-bureaucratic complex grows in numbers, competence, and power. The advances of science and professional knowledge are often such that they can be applied directly to the formulation of governmental programs, as, for instance, new discoveries in medicine may be directly translated into action in the field of public health. Such advances continually open up new possibilities of policy. But they are produced by only a few specialists, who, moreover, are usually associated with the established bureaucracy in the relevant field. From these circles the initiative in policy making proceeds, the politician performing the essential functions of communicating the new possibilities in layman's language to the voting public and cultivating a potential demand for them. The process of demand creation elicits the support of the voters, but the initiative is taken by the technocrats and the primary choice is theirs.

Some of the new federal programs of the United States in recent years provide illustration. The poverty programs of the mid-sixties were striking examples of what has been called "the professionalization of reform." They did not originate from the demands of pressure groups of prospective beneficiaries; on the contrary, as Patrick Moynihan has observed, in the origins of the poverty programs the poor were not only invisible, but also silent.[7] With regard to such elements as the community-action program, the basic ideas and governmental initiative came, respectively, from social scientists and reforming bureaucrats. The beneficiary groups and local and state authorities were no more prepared to understand them than the general public. This created a crucial function for politicians, from the president to congressmen; they had to explain the new programs and win consent for them. One congressman has described this important aspect of the legislator's relationship with his constituents. Referring to the antipoverty programs and other new and complex federal programs, he reported the lack of understanding among the public reflected in the constant questioning by

> state and local authorities, officials of private organizations and individuals on how the programs work. It is more than a question of red tape and filling out applications. Many local leaders may not understand the legislation or see its relevance to their communities. The Congressman or Senator, by organizing community conferences, mailing materials and in other ways, can supply important information, interpretation, justification and leadership in his constituency . . . These activities of explaining, justifying, interpreting, interceding, all help, normally, *to build acceptance for government policy,* an essential process in democratic government [emphasis added].[8]

A general theme of political modernization, in short, has been this power-interest dynamic, that is, the mutual interaction and stimulation of state power and political demand. The mobilization of interests and the mobilization of power interact to promote the growth of one another. The significance of this mechanism is that it constitutes in the polity (analogously to similar mechanisms in the economy) a means by which the two main dynamic forces of modernization, so to speak, cross over and affect one another.

---

[7]Daniel Patrick Moynihan, "The Professionalization of Reform," *The Public Interest,* 1 (Fall 1965), p. 8.

[8]The Hon. John Brademas, "The Emerging Role of the American Congress" (Unpublished paper, 1966).

Nation Building by the State

Analogies between polity and economy are instructive only up to a point. For in spite of their similarities, they are two very different types of system for concerting human action. The heart of the difference is the contrast between *legitimate domination* and *mutual adjustment*.[9] The liberal economy consists of a number of entities, each pursuing its separate purpose and achieving the action it seeks from others by mutual adjustment, of which the most obvious example is payment in exchange for goods or services. The polity, on the other hand, secures action by imperative control, based on mutually shared conceptions of legitimacy. Hence, although both economic and political modernization produce ever larger systems of complex interdependence and although each has processes by which these systems are coordinated, the processes themselves are fundamentally different.

In the welfare state, for instance, the state uses its powers to subsidize programs that are made available to all, or to specified categories of persons. In this instance, the polity is a means of concerting action for welfare objectives, using its characteristic powers of imperative control to finance programs and lay down the regulations under which they will be administered. The program creates a new network of interdependence between those who pay for and administer it and those who benefit from it. In the course of political development, these networks of interdependence, maintained by imperative control, become larger and more complex as the scope of governmental policy is extended.

These structures of interdependence, moreover, have constituted a principal means of nation building by the modern state. It is well recognized that economic development promotes national integration by increasing the interdependence of the members of a polity. Political development similarly promotes national integration by creating networks of interdependence that utilize community resources to satisfy community needs. The more traditional regulatory functions of the state may perform this function, imposing burdens for the sake of benefits. Redistributive policies illustrate this nation-building effect of political modernization even more clearly. These may involve a sharing of resources between regions, as when an enlightened despot of the eighteenth century undertook military fortifications, civic building, and other public works in the less wealthy provinces of his domain. In more recent times, the thrust toward equality has brought significant redistribution between classes. Gunnar Myrdal has analyzed how these policies of the welfare state and a set of attitudes supporting them have heightened national integration in many countries during the past half century. He writes:

In internal politics, people can succeed in circumscribing the scope of partisanship; they have a basic level of personality where they think and feel in terms

<hr>

[9]The term is taken from Charles E. Lindblom, *The Intelligence of Democracy: Decision Making through Mutual Adjustment* (New York, 1965).

of "we." The national Welfare State has immensely enlarged the number of people who are capable of feeling this "belongingness" to the nation.[10]

This increase in integration, it should be noted, is not only a sentiment, a powerful emotion of identification (see Chapter 3). It is also a fact of objective political structure, consisting in new networks of interdependence created by growing centralization.

Because of its powers of legitimate domination, the polity can achieve objectives not available to the market. This is true of welfare programs that are provided at little or no cost to beneficiaries. There are also a vast number of objectives, such as national defense, education, and so on—often called "public goods"—which benefit most or all members of the community, but which would almost certainly not be sufficiently funded if their support were left to the market and the voluntary action of beneficiaries. At the same time, the fact that the polity's powers of imperative control depend upon generally shared conceptions of legitimacy severely limits the use of these powers. Perhaps the gravest limitation is their restriction within the territorial boundaries of the particular polity concerned. The great strides in social justice accomplished by the welfare state in recent decades have been confined by national boundaries. André Malraux has given the reason: "I subordinate social justice to the nation because I think that if one does not base oneself on the nation, one will not make social justice, one will make speeches."

Modern nation states have shown great capacity for extending their control over ever larger areas of the social and natural environment within their borders. But normally conceptions of legitimacy are shared only by members of a particular nationality. If the polity is to pursue objectives bearing upon the further environment, although it may use force, purchase, bargaining, and other means, it is deprived of one of the principal grounds for its efficacy within its own national boundaries, the attribution of legitimacy to its dictates by members of the polity. Thus, although the economic relations among men have developed to such an extent that we can speak of a world market and world economy, there is no world polity, or anything approaching it. This disproportion between political and economic development is strikingly exhibited in Europe. Economic development has created a vast, complex system of trade and industry. Yet the boundaries of the political systems of the area have barely pushed beyond their medieval origins. Only in recent years have the states of Western Europe made the first tentative steps to erect a larger political system.

---

[10]Gunnar Myrdal, *Beyond the Welfare State: Economic Planning and Its International Implications* (New Haven, Conn., 1960), p. 185.

Approaches to Measurement

An essential of the concept of development is the notion of directionality, or trend. Directionality, which refers to the quantitative dimension of development, means that each successive stage or period shows greater achievement or accomplishment according to some standard. Economic modernization consists in increases in specialization, scale, output, and interdependence. Analogous processes characterize and drive forward political modernization. In political as in economic modernization these processes are intrinsically capable of being measured, although it is not always easy to find indexes that are precisely accurate. (1) *Specialization* is the central process by which the power of the polity is advanced, just as it is the central process by means of which the productive capacity of the economy grows. The civilian and military bureaucracy is the principal field of activity to which this increase in state power can be most readily traced. The indicators would reflect the multiplication and differentiation of functions and agencies that have accompanied the mobilization of power. (2) *Scale* in the modern polity has been increased perhaps most notably by the growth of participation. Conventional indicators of this aspect of the mobilization of interests comprise data on such changes as the increasing numbers of persons enfranchised; the growing membership of political associations, such as pressure groups; the increase in members and supporters of political parties. (3) *Interdependence* in the polity results from government action imposing burdens and conferring benefits. Measurement of the redistributive effects of welfare state programs would be an indicator of interdependence.

(4) *Output* consists in the actual exercise of the state's power. On balance most modern states have shown not only a capacity to carry a growing "load"; they have actually assumed ever greater burdens and responsibilities. Their activities have sometimes shifted from one field to another, leaving free spheres that were previously subordinated to state authority. Disregarding these differences in fields of activity, however, we can discern a fairly steady expansion of output as a whole.

When this expansion of output is viewed as taking place within a single polity, it may be called *centralization*. What centralization means in this context is that from one point in time to another, a greater sum of the demands of the members of the polity and a greater sum of their resources have been mobilized and related to one another by the state. Output has expanded; that is, a greater demand is being met by a greater exertion of power. In comparison with what the polity did at the previous point in time, it has become more centralized.

To be sure, the structures by which these growing networks of interdependence are articulated may employ all sorts of decentralizing devices, ranging from federalism and functional representation to regional planning and administrative deconcentration. These devices are quite compatible with growing centralization on the part of the state as a whole. It will be useful therefore to distinguish between *primary centralization,* meaning this basic expansion of state activity, and *secondary centralization,* meaning the extent to which the activity of the state is controlled by one decision-making center. Thus, for example, a polity in which all industry was nationalized would have a high degree of primary centralization. At the same time, if it also had—let us say—a strongly federal structure, it would be characterized by a low degree of secondary centralization. The process of primary centralization does not necessarily imply that a greater *proportion* of needs and resources will be politicized—that is, there will not be an inherent trend in modernization toward socialism. Primary centralization means simply that at later stages, in contrast with earlier stages, greater magnitudes of needs and resources have been mobilized to produce a greater output.

Measuring primary centralization presents difficulties but is in some degree possible. It is a beginning to know, for example, how many people with a certain illness were treated by the health service, or how many missions were flown against an enemy by the air force. Then comparisons with previous levels of state activity can be made. Also, insofar as governmental activities can be accurately evaluated in money terms, they can be amalgamated to obtain an index of total state activity and so can provide the basis for measuring changes in primary centralization over time. Rough as such indicators must be, they do constitute significant data, and we shall have occasion to use them in this book.

If we wish to get some idea of the demonstrated power of the state, the problem is much more difficult. The questions now concern the curing, not merely the treating, of the sick and the defeat, not merely the bombardment, of the enemy. Output budgeting in its various forms attempts to answer this sort of question, giving to government an estimate of the actual effects of its programs on the natural and social environment in such a form that they can be measured against costs. Without attempting to be quantitative, historical accounts give impressions of how the demonstrated power of the modern state has grown over time, for example with regard to physical safety or public health.

The growing power of the modern state in its external relationships is even harder to measure. Yet when looked at from a broad historical perspective, the impression of rapid and overwhelming increase is marked from an early date. We can get some idea of the change from the contrast between the military competence of European and non-European regimes in medieval and modern times. The long conflict with the Moslem peoples, beginning with the earliest invasions of Europe in the eighth century and continuing through the Crusades to the defense against the Ottoman Turks in the sixteenth century, gave victory now to one side, now to the other and hardly showed the Europeans to be superior. Then in the seventeenth century the tide rapidly turned. In spite of the brief Ottoman revival in the latter part of the century, the Christian states showed growing ascendancy in military technology, discipline, and administration. Under the Hapsburgs the Austrian monarchy, then in the first stages of modernization, reconquered Hungary and ended the Turkish threat once and for all.

This shift in the balance of power against Islam after a long equilibrium is only one episode in the sudden upsurge of European armed power in the world. As the early generations of modernity passed and European imperialism got under way, the new regime—the modern state—showed growing military superiority over the non-European regimes—tribal, patrimonial, and imperial—that had flourished for centuries. The early pages of Western expansion are studded with stories of the overthrow of ancient polities by relatively small European forces, sometimes only a handful of adventurers. There were the exploits of the conquistadors in Mexico and Peru, the Portuguese along the African coast, and Clive in India; Napoleon's casual invasion of Ottoman Egypt; and the easy penetration of China in the nineteenth century. Modernization brings rising power in external, as well as in internal, affairs. But imperialism, like socialism, while a real possibility, is neither inherent in modernization nor inevitable in modern history.

Figure 5.3 Political Modernization : Processes and Trends

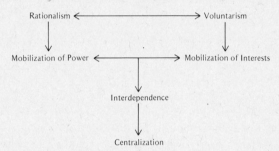

By way of summary, it may be helpful to conclude this discussion with a highly schematized view of the processes and relationships constituting political modernization. Figure 5.3 suggests the interaction of the main premises of modernity on the cultural plane in the development of European thought. It also shows how this dual orientation of modern political culture is expressed respectively in the two political processes, the mobilization of power and the mobilization of interests, which in turn mutually condition and stimulate one another in the power-interest dynamic. From the mobilization of power and interests flows a growing interdependence among the members of the polity as the expansion of policy shows a trend toward greater centralization.

Six

Elements of the Modern Polity

In two major areas of structure the cultural premises of modernity are directly expressed. Modern voluntarism has produced no more characteristic doctrine than the idea of the sovereignty of the state. Modern rationalism has led to that distinctive type of administrative staff called bureaucracy. The third element of any polity, the pattern of policy, is characterized in modern times by an intense secularism, which has taken more concrete form in the powerful thrust of national—and sometimes imperial—development. With regard to behavior and attitudes, each of these new structures contrasts sharply with the corresponding structure of the medieval polity.

Sovereignty and Bureaucracy

Sovereignty, the idea of an unlimited authority to make law, was abhorrent to the medieval conception of a fixed, detailed, and objective moral order binding on men and nations. In fully developed form, the doctrine gives to the authoritative policy-making organ a superiority to any subsystem within the borders of the polity and, likewise, complete independence with regard to any authority outside. In what is usually cited as the first explicit statement of the doctrine, Jean Bodin, the French jurist and political philosopher, in his *Six Books of the Commonwealth* (1576), defined sovereignty as "supreme power over citizens and subjects, unrestrained by law." He argued that the "well-ordered state," if it was not to be a prey to anarchy, must have within it somewhere—preferably in a monarch—this supreme and indivisible source of authority.

While Bodin granted that the sovereign was bound by divine law and the law of nature, Thomas Hobbes shed these premodern restraints, arguing in *Leviathan* (1651) that "Soveraigne Power" was absolute, indivisible, and indispensable to any viable commonwealth. Hobbes might seem to lean toward one man as the proper repository of such power, but the doctrine of sovereignty did not lack democratic versions. In Jean Jacques Rousseau's *Social Contract* (1762) the sovereignty of the general will is restrained neither by any other political or legal authority nor by any putative moral or natural law. The sovereign people makes law and morality for all its members.

The theory of sovereignty and the attitudes associated with it marked a major transition in political development. They broke from the old medieval notion of the hierarchic, corporate, organic Christian society as a permanent and unchangeable model. Now the regime itself began to be questioned. The issue of the legitimacy not merely of this or that claimant to the crown but of the political order itself and, indeed, of the social, economic, and religious orders became a common subject of political conflict. Likewise, the idea became accepted that the laws and the regime could legitimately be changed from time to time, whether by revolution or reform or by a popular or an autocratic will, depending upon the beliefs of the groups involved.

In England sovereignty in its theoretical and practical meanings—as both a theory of government and a wide-ranging exercise of law-making power—emerged in the seventeenth century. There is a lively and learned argument over whether or not political modernity came to England with the Tudors. The answer depends very much on how we define the term. The fact that decides the issue for the present analysis is that, in spite of the voluminous legislation by Tudor monarchs, the framework of purpose expressed in law and policy remained essentially medieval in its insistence upon a hierarchic and corporate community based on a religious consensus. We enter a world of modern legislation and policy making only with the civil wars of the early seventeenth century. Of this period Charles H. McIlwain concluded succinctly: "Practical parliamentary omnipotence begat a theory of parliamentary sovereignty."[1] But even before these events, the idea of sovereign power had affected English political thought. Early in the century the great chief justice and jurist Sir Edward Coke put the matter in words that became proverbial: "Of the power and jurisdiction of the Parliament for making of laws in proceeding by Bill," he wrote in his *Institutes of the Laws of England* (1628), "it is so transcendent and absolute, as it cannot be confined either for persons or causes within any bounds."

In France sovereignty also became clearly discernible in the seventeenth century. In contrast with English sovereignty, however, it was not parliamentary, but

---

[1]Charles H. McIlwain, *The High Court of Parliament and Its Supremacy* (New Haven, Conn., 1910), p. 93.

royal. While Louis XIV (1643–1715) did not actually utter the words *"L'État, c'est moi,"* the phrase nicely sums up the legal theory of the Bourbon monarchy. "As the king wills," it was said, "so the law wills." Franz Neumann writes of seventeenth-century ideas:

> To both [Richelieu and Bossuet] the monarchy was divine. But the divinity of that institution was no longer meant to imply, as it did to Bracton and almost all medievalists, limitations upon that power. There were none except those that the monarch's conscience imposed upon himself. Divine and natural law were in Bossuet's terms only a *puissance directive,* a counsel lacking *puissance coactive,* the coercive power. Bossuet's formula, *"Tout l'état est en la personne du prince,"* merely generalizes Louis XIV's alleged slogan, *"L'État c'est moi."* In theory the power of the monarch was as absolute as it was comprehensive.[2]

For Russia, Prussia, Spain, Austria, and the lesser principalities of continental Europe, it was France not England that provided the model in theory and practice for modernizing rulers in the seventeenth century. Indeed imitation was sometimes so slavish as to be nonfunctional. At the court of Frederick William the Great, Elector of Brandenburg, that prince, although a faithful husband and strict Calvinist, appointed a lady as "the king's mistress" for the sole reason that such a figure was known to grace the court of the Grand Monarch. In actual practice, of course, the rulers of the time were far from absolute and, in comparison with what states today can do, could mobilize and control only a tiny fraction of the lives and resources of their subjects. It was an age of aristocracy rather than autocracy, although then as later, Russia was an exception.

Bureaucracy

It is often said that bureaucracy is the core of the modern state. The implication of the present account is that the more political aspect of modernity—sovereignty—came first. Once will and *raison d'état* had driven out teleology and the restraints of custom, the pragmatic spirit could enter into the instrumentalities of administration. The new flexibility in ends required a new flexibility in means. If the sovereign, whether king, parliament, or people, was to innovate and reform at will, an instrumentality of state power would be needed that could be readily adapted to new needs, given new rules defining its objectives and procedures, and subjected at all times entirely to the will of the supreme power. These properties were lacking in the administrative staff of the medieval state, which derived from a feudal regime that had dispersed and decentralized political and economic power under the legitimation of baronial and corporate right.

Modern bureaucracy provides the flexibility and efficiency required by the new norms. Its members have no personal rights in the means of administration; they

---

[2]Baron de Montesquieu, *The Spirit of the Laws,* Thomas Nugent (tr.) (New York, 1949), Introduction by Franz Neumann, pp. xix–xx.

exercise authority only on the basis of office. They achieve their positions of authority according to law, which usually requires specialized training and demonstrated competence. Their relation to the sovereign authority is purely instrumental, advisory, and subordinate.[3] Since the human heart strongly resists being governed solely by standards of impersonal merit, no bureaucrats have ever fully lived up to this modernist ideal, not even the superb and austere civil servants of Prussia and their successors in imperial and republican Germany. Some bureaucracies have been slower to adapt to the modern spirit than others. All have shown distinct national differences.

In the early modern period on the continent of Europe the prevailing model was a royal sovereign, assisted by a council and various more or less specialized officials. They directed and managed an administrative staff, which was appointed by the central power and which operated directly in provincial and local as well as central affairs. The lead in establishing this model was given by France. There the principal task of the emerging bureaucracy was to overcome the "appropriation"—to use Weber's term—of public powers by feudal authorities and local and provincial bodies, which persisted in spite of the long history of centralization under the medieval monarchy. This change was largely accomplished between the last quarter of the sixteenth century and the middle of the seventeenth century, the structure of the absolutist regime being completed in the reign of Louis XIV. The principal means employed by the centralizing monarchs and their great counselors, such as Richelieu and Colbert, were the intendants (precursors of the present-day prefects), who carried the royal will into all parts of the realm. Upon this basis the structure of Bourbon power was founded. As Alexis de Tocqueville observed in *The Old Regime and the Revolution* (1856), his searing criticism of the old regime, "all real authority was vested in the intendants."

If France set the basic pattern for the new regime of bureaucratic monarchy, it was Germany, and above all Prussia, that developed its potentialities most rapidly and fully. Herman Finer has written,

Indeed it is plain that energies as mighty as those which England devoted to the creation of parliamentary institutions were in Prussia turned to the establishment of administrative institutions. While England was founding the constitutional state by the bloody struggles between the Stuarts and the Parliamentarians, Frederick William, the Great Elector of Brandenberg [1640–1688] in struggles as bloody, consolidated his state, uprooted the remnants of feudal administration, and created the administrative organization indispensable to efficient absolute monarchy.[4]

---

[3]Again Weber is the standard source for the model of the modern bureaucracy. Max Weber, *The Theory of Social and Economic Organization*, pp. 329–340.

[4]Herman Finer, *The Theory and Practice of Modern Government,* rev. ed. (New York, 1949), p. 724.

In Britain, as this passage suggests, the new administrative system serving the sovereign Parliament differed greatly from the Continental model. The uprising of 1640 had destroyed the beginnings of a royal bureaucracy that had been created by the Tudors and Stuarts. The monarchy did dispose of the services of some permanent officials—by the eighteenth century the Customs and Excise Service numbered 10,000—and was served by new and growing central instruments, such as the Treasury Board, which had already established its dominance over the spending departments. But the main burden of carrying out the laws and performing other duties of administration was borne by largely unpaid members of the aristocracy and gentry. They served as lords lieutenants, justices of the peace, and vestrymen in the counties and parishes of a still agrarian England. In comparison with the French or Prussian systems, the rising British bureaucracy was small, amateur and inefficient. Yet it would be questionable to say that the bureaucracy was decentralized, if by that is meant that it lacked coherence and common purpose. Once the struggles of the seventeenth century subsided, these members of the governing class displayed a strong sense of their own and their country's interests and, moreover, as members of Lords and Commons, had often made the laws in the first place.

Reformism and Secularism

In this book's model of the polity two of the leading elements of the modern political system are sovereignty in the pattern of interests and bureaucracy in the pattern of state power. As for the third element, the pattern of policy, the programs and activities of modern governments constitute efforts to control the natural and social environments. But this does not distinguish and characterize the modern pattern of policy, since all political systems aim at control of some kind and in some sense. The stress on flexibility and instrumentalism suggests a more precise meaning. Modern control in contrast with some patterns of control is continually renewed; reform, adaptation, and reconstruction go on constantly. Certainly this renewal is an empirical trait of modern policy making and of the meaning given to it by the communities involved. At the same time, modern political culture has a utopian strain that runs contrary to this conception. In these utopian views it is held that with regard to important features of the regime and, indeed, of the social and economic orders, change can and should stop at some point. This aspiration appears in the socialist vision of society and history. Yet early individualists, such as John Locke, made hardly any more allowance for the fact that in some circumstances change might become desirable and likely, even with regard to the fundamentals of their schemes. In the British tradition the first political philosopher fully to accept change as an object of state policy was Edmund Burke, whose conservatism intrinsically involved recognition of the continuing need for reform as a normal aspect of government.

Granting that modernity in policy means an effort of control that is continually changing in its specific methods and aims, we must ask whether such efforts of control have any distinctive general character that pervades their many variations. Comparison with the medieval polity immediately brings out the secularism of modernity. Negatively, the behavioral index of this great change to secularism consisted in the growing separation of state from church. As the modern state emerged, it detached itself from the church and from religion, more and more regarding itself neither as subject to a church nor as an aspect of a religious community, and setting its aims and weighing its achievements in terms of accomplishments in this world.

Some writers characterize the Reformation as the time when this act of withdrawal took place and hence as the origin of political modernity. But, again, as with sovereignty and bureaucracy, it is the seventeenth century that marks the clear emergency of secularism as the dominating theme of policy. Religious toleration in law and in practice is a primary indicator. In France, the Edict of Nantes (1598) granting toleration to Protestants constitutes a beginning, in spite of the later efforts to turn back, as in the revocation of 1685. In Britain, while the Toleration Act of 1689 applied only to Protestants not conforming to the Church of England, the spirit of the times also secured a considerable degree of freedom of religious worship for Roman Catholics. With regard to Germany, the termination of the Thirty Years War (1618–1648) by the formula of *cujus regio ejus religio* marked a fundamental break with the centuries-long commitment of the European peoples to the principle that a major, if not the major, task of organized society was to protect and propagate the correct religious faith and form of worship. Again Russia was an exception, seeming to maintain the medieval commitment in its toleration of only a single faith—unless the slavish subjection of the Orthodox church to the state by Peter the Great (1682–1725) is seen as a kind of secularization of religion for the sake of nation building.

Modernity, however, is not just the rejection of medievalism. It has its positive themes. One is the pursuit of happiness. But apart from its negation of the old transcendent aspirations, happiness is an empty guide to collective, as well as individual, behavior. Hedonism may be deeply modern, but as a proposed description of the rationale of modern policy, it does not much help the political scientist to identify the themes that have given coherence to the diverse activities of the modern state.

A more serious possibility is capitalism. It has often been argued that in Western Europe—and the farther west, the more this is true—the emergence of the modern state came about at the same time as the transition to a new individualist economy. This economy was based on individually owned property, which was used to pursue profit by means of a free market in goods and labor. Moreover, it is said, the function of the state was to protect and promote this mode of production and the interests of the owners.

This general hypothesis has added immensely to the understanding of early modern history. Its basic flaw is that it is too narrow to cope with the meaning and consequences of modernity. Modernity embraces both socialism and capitalism, collectivism and individualism. Soviet Russia, with a socialist economy, is a modern state, as are Germany, France, and Britain with their capitalist economies. To refer to all four as modern is not to deny vital differences. But the identities among these modern states, with regard to basic elements, course of development, and virtues and vices, make comparison fruitful—and this book possible.

The modern state has served and has been served by various types of economy. Its main traits of structure and development have not been a mere reflection of an autonomously developing economy, but, on the contrary, have displayed their own dynamic, often dictating the course of economic development itself. As Charles Tilly has pointed out, the rise of the capitalist economy did not consist merely in the release of a "natural" force, but represented, rather, a deliberate choice by the state and the groups controlling it to undermine peasant communities, to break up local networks of exchange, to nationalize the distribution of food, and in other ways to give a distinctive direction to economic development.[5] To put the point quite sharply: Capitalism did not just develop blindly but was "invented" and imposed upon a premodern economy by the political action of the early modern state.

Moreover, not only are individualism and collectivism both compatible with modernity, but in thought and practice they both came forward in the very early stages of modernization. In English political thought a current of economic collectivism has run strongly at least since the days of those early prophets of communism, Gerrard Winstanley and the Diggers of the era of the civil wars. As for actual patterns of policy, during the age of mercantilism, which stretched from the sixteenth century through the eighteenth, so great a degree of control was exercised by the state that one authority refers to what was the freest system in Europe during its early generations as England's "first planned economy."[6] Later, after liberal economic ideas and policies had reached their peak in the nineteenth century, the policies of Western nations again moved toward state intervention, with the result that it is more common to speak of them today as having "mixed" rather than "capitalist" economies. Individualism and collectivism are two warring twins of modernity, and their impact on development has been cyclical rather than successive.

Liberalism is a possible characterization of modern policy that touches a more fundamental level of values. Religious toleration, which arose with political modernization, meant that liberty with regard to ultimate concerns was now guaranteed to the individual. In Western Europe modernity also in due course brought other individual freedoms, cultural, political, and economic. In the case of many countries, the course of liberalization has so closely paralleled the course of modernization that it is easy to infer that they are identical.

---

[5]Charles Tilly, "Food Supply and Public Order in Modern Europe" in Tilly (ed.), *The Building of States in Western Europe* (forthcoming, Princeton University Press).

[6]E. Lipson, *The Growth of English Society: A Short Economic History* (New York, 1950), p. 142.

Yet modernism is not identical with liberalism. Little as we may like to admit it, a strong and highly developed modern state may be oppressively autocratic and despotically illiberal. Under a totalitarian regime, science and technology can flourish, while the democratic thrust of voluntarism is contained by systems of ineffectual participation.

Liberty is a continuing and perhaps unique concern of Western society. It has, however, given rise to different political doctrines as men changed their views of the nature of the individual, his capacities, and his destiny. It was a central issue of the conflicts and controversies of medieval polities. While highly prized, liberty then meant something very different from what it came to mean under the influence of modernity. To begin with, when referring to medieval thought and practice, we should speak of "liberties," since liberty had a different substance depending upon the rank and function of the individual and his group in the organic hierarchy of Christian society. The practical meaning of this assertion is shown in both title and content of *Magna Carta Libertatum* (1215)—the Great Charter of Liberties—which sought to guarantee for individuals and communities their differentiated and appropriate spheres of freedom. Moreover, these guarantees of medieval constitutionalism were not only differentiated; they were also inflexible. For the members of each rank and order of men there were proper patterns of conduct, made known by custom, law, and religious teaching. It was the purpose of the polity to protect and support each member in his station and its duties. For the individual, to be free meant being free to imitate these models of propriety and so to serve God.

Under the influence of modernity, liberalism has given almost the opposite meaning to liberty. It is now the right to innovate, to be different from anyone else, to develop individual creativity. Modern liberty means not imitation of what objectively is best, but creation of what subjectively pleases most. The modern conception of liberty brings us back to the pursuit of happiness, which apart from its negations is an empty category for philosopher or social scientist.

Nationalism and National Development

Hedonism, capitalism, and liberalism, while all thoroughly secular, are either too broad or too narrow to characterize the overriding theme of the pattern of policy of the modern state. We get much closer to a viable and meaningful generalization with nationalism or—if that term has acquired too pejorative a connotation—nation building and national development. The relation of nationality and modernity is a question of the first importance. It has two major aspects. On the one hand, nationality stands in relation to the modern state as something "given," something derived from a source outside of and, indeed, usually antecedent to modernity. On the other hand, modernization has affected nationality, the development of the nation having been the central object of policy in most modern states.

The modern state is commonly referred to as the modern nation-state, and few if any modern states have managed to survive without a basis in common nationality. Nationality demonstrates this powerful function perhaps most vividly in the limitations it sets on the effectiveness of the modern state. In many parts of the world, there are compelling economic, social, and strategic reasons for much larger political systems. Indeed, we can make a strong case for world government. In the absence of a common nationality, however, little progress is being made in the various efforts toward regional integration. Even the states of Western Europe, although intimately allied in culture and institutions, move at a snail's pace, if at all, toward a united Europe.

Crucial as nationality may be to the modern polity, however, its origins are very often premodern. The various nationalities of Europe descend from the Middle Ages. It was the rising national monarchies of the thirteenth century that finally brought about the defeat of the medieval papacy in its long struggle for dominion over the temporal power. This premodern heritage gave to the European modern state a vitally important unifying force, differing in kind from the bonds of self-interest, ideology, and common purpose that typically derive from modernity. The categories of modernity release energy, stimulate the intelligence, and encourage the creation of powerful instrumentalities and comprehensive organizations. Yet it seems that they cannot themselves create the strong solidary groupings and close-knit communities that we find in traditional societies. The typical social group of modern society, the bureaucratic organization, may be far more efficient, but it has far less solidarity than the typical group of traditionalist society, the tribe, clan, or other kinship group. The nationalities inherited from the medieval past had such a solidary character and gave to the emerging modern state an indispensable basis for unity and effectiveness.

The relation between modernity and nationality has been complex. In each of the four states examined in this book, a dominant nationality provided an initial basis of unity for the political system. Yet this force has not been without rivals within the borders of the state. In the earlier phases of modernization, the strength and unity of the British polity depended upon the solidarity of English nationality, but to this day its rivals in the form of Scottish, Welsh, and (emphatically) Irish nationality have never been wholly absorbed into the British nation. Similarly, in France, which also entered the modern period with a strongly based national monarchy, we still see the force of other territorial loyalties, as in the very powerful regional movement in Brittany. The German nationality also goes back to the Middle Ages. But in contrast with English and French experience, the splintering of the medieval German polity made the national question one of desperate urgency in the modern period. Today German federalism is a recognition of the continuing strength of regional and subnational loyalties. In Russia, the Great Russians of the medieval kingdom of Moscovy provided the national nucleus from which the centuries-long conquest of the vast empire of the present day was launched. But the welcome the Ukrainians gave to the invading Nazi armies during

World War II was an act of national liberation from Great Russian domination as well as of resistance to Stalinist dictatorship.

While a dominant nationality has been an indispensable basis of the polity in all four countries, it has never been able completely to absorb its rivals or permanently set at rest their claims for some kind of political expression. One of the most fascinating aspects of contemporary European politics is the revival of these lesser nationalities as political groups demanding a reversal of the long trend to centralization in the modern state and some degree of political autonomy for their members.

National Development

"States have made nations," William T. R. Fox has said, "far more often than nations have made states."[7] If we stretch the term "state" to include medieval polities, this generalization is strongly supported by European history. As Ernest Renan pointed out in *What Is a Nation?* (1882), the nations of Europe, which first appeared after the fall of the Carolingian empire, owed their character to the fusion of various peoples under the rule of medieval dynasties.

While the modern polity has rarely founded a nation, it has often developed one. Characteristically, modern states have promoted economic interdependence by such measures as the creation of a single national market governed by a single system of law. They have promoted cultural uniformity by such means as a national system of public education. As we have seen, primary centralization as a specifically political aspect of modernization has served to elaborate the networks of interdependence and the sentiments of identification that underlie national solidarity. Given a basis in common nationality, the modern state has on the whole and in most cases enormously increased the capacity of its members for concerted action. Although nationality has usually set stubborn limits to the boundaries within which the domination of a modern state will be accepted as legitimate, within those boundaries, the state has powerfully promoted integration. In comparison with previous polities, the immensely greater proportion of national resources that the modern state has mobilized internally for the welfare state or externally for national defense dramatizes the accomplishment. The income tax and military conscription show what the modern state has been able to make of nationality.

Even for a regime so self-consciously internationalist and ideological in its origins as Soviet Russia, nationality has been an indispensable support and a profoundly shaping influence. The two greatest challenges of the Stalinist period were industrialization and the war against Nazi Germany. In confronting these challenges, the Communist leaders increasingly turned to nationalist sentiments to summon up the energies of the people. "In a period of great reconstruction and of great purges," Ulam says of the mid-thirties,

---

[7] William T. R. Fox, in his Introduction to Amitai Etzioni, *Political Unification: A Comparative Study of Leaders and Forces* (New York, 1965).

the regime was also instinctively reaching for all the elements of stability it could find, and one of the most important ones was Russian partriotism. It seemed to be saying to the dominant nation of the Soviet Union: "The regime may be tyrannical, and it may be subjecting you to all kinds of sufferings and privations, but it is your government, and it is doing it for the greatness of your country."

Similarly, during World War II,

> Russian patriotism was . . . rediscovered by the Soviet regime to be its major asset, and the natural instinct of the people to fight for their government, no matter how oppressive, against a foreign foe, to be a surer basis of its power than even Marxism-Leninism.[8]

The premises of modernity return only a thin and flat reply to the old question of human purpose. Science can tell us how to pursue and increase power, but not what to use it for. The rejection of teleology frees modern men from old disciplines and restraints, but otherwise the pursuit of happiness is an empty answer to our question. On this vacant scene nationalism easily intruded. Amidst the abstractions of modernity it provided something concrete: a language; a set of tastes; ways of eating, drinking, working, courting, and raising a family—"a plebiscite of every day," in Renan's powerful phrase. To protect these valued specifics and to express them in promoting economic, social, and political development, nationalism gave body to the patterns of purpose and policy. Capitalism and education, armies and bureaucracies, although driven forward by identical forces of modernity, in each country received a special stamp from the unique character of its nationality. To make the nation more of a nation has been—for good and for ill—the overriding theme of the massive and growing activities of the modern state.

To identify this strong, continuing theme of national development is not to overlook other objects of policy. Modern polities have been peculiarly rent by class conflict. One reason was the radical shift in political culture from inequality to equality. When men accepted without question the need for hierarchy, finding its justification in a multitude of religious and philosophical reasons, the edge of relative deprivation in material, social, and political advantages could not fail to be dulled. The growing cult of equality in modern times, however, makes the many actual disparities among men and classes ever more painful to bear and harder to defend. Modernity did not create the class struggle, but it did immensely enhance it. Class and group struggle has been a principal motor of policy making in the modern state. These opposing interests, however, have been qualified and limited in appearance and in reality by some subjection to a national interest. During the industrialization of Soviet Russia, as we have just

---

[8]See Part 5 of this book, "The Russian Political System," Chapter 3.

seen in Ulam's comment, the harshness of rule by the Communist elite was softened by the appeal to "the greatness of your country." In general, where modern states have displayed stability in spite of the inevitable divisive forces generated by social, economic, and political structures, one reason has been the pervasive feelings and beliefs of a common nationality.

Seven

Stages of Political Modernization

In political culture and political structure, the modern polity is unique. Beginning in the sixteenth and seventeenth centuries, the sovereign, bureaucratic nation-state has come more and more to prevail in the West. It has not only prevailed, it has also developed, growing steadily in power, participation, centralization, and integration. In the developed modern polity of the present time the three basic elements of structure have acquired specific form as separate elements and as a system. This polity can be found in the four countries examined in this book, as well as in all other Western and some non-Western countries. The specific characteristics of the modern polity can be briefly summarized as follows:

1. Its policy-making structure is partisan and participatory.
2. Its power structure is corporatist and technocratic.
3. Its policy is collectivist in economic and social spheres.

Development by Stages

How did the modern polity acquire these traits? If we take the concept of development seriously, it implies that the modern polity has moved in a certain direction, measurable by various indexes, and that it has passed through identifiable stages in reaching its present structure. The notion of stages itself has certain implications. It directs attention especially to the possibility that history is not merely continuous flux, but is marked by alternating periods of stability and transition. Anyone who has read a great deal of history may be pardoned if he concludes that every historian finds in his period of special study a "time of transition," leaving it to preceding and succeeding times, about which he knows less, to provide the stability without which transition is meaningless. Yet in spite of its difficulties, the concept of stages is not useless. In political modernization, significant periods of relative stability occur when the basic structures of a polity remain much the same, in contrast with other periods when new features emerge and become dominant.

Indeed, in British political development each main period of stability is unmistakably marked by the occurrence at mid-passage of an exceptional lull in political controversy and party conflict. The most recent of these moments in British politics, as in Western politics generally, the 1950s, has been spoken of as marking "the end of ideology." More accurately, what characterized these years, like previous moments of lull, was not the end of ideology, but a consensus on ideology. Typically, a period of struggle between an old and a new political order, often embodied in party conflict, had given way to a time when the new order in some substantial part had been established and had won wide acceptance in the active political community. Between the earlier and later stages each of the three basic elements of the polity had changed significantly. In the case of Britain in the fifties the collectivist polity, over which sharp political battles had been fought for a generation or more, came to maturity and won general acceptance.

Another interesting hypothesis that may be attached to the notion of development by stages is the proposition that the transitions from one order to another have been mediated by "revolutions," meaning by this term at least substantial collective violence by one group to change the regime defended and controlled by another group. The suggestion directs attention to a fascinating subject and plausible hypothesis. Some revolutions have been moved by purposes and ideals strongly colored by modern values. Probably the leading case was the French Revolution with its thrust toward extending political power, strengthening the rule of law, encouraging the "career open to talents" in bureaucracy and economy, and centralizing law, government, and politics. The Puritan revolution in England, on the other hand, is a very ambiguous case. What the more ardent revolutionaries aimed at was deeply hostile to the modern, secular spirit, although the outcome of their failure was a great stride toward modernity. Rather similarly, the Russian Revolution promoted changes sharply opposed to some of its original ideals. Deeply egalitarian and utopian in conception, it was rapidly taken over by the overwhelming urge to modernize of the Stalinist regime. Even more ironic has been the upshot of the Nazi revolution, which, although inspired by romantic elitist fantasies, had the effect of sweeping away traditional social remnants in economy, bureaucracy, and army that had long impeded German modernization.

Apart from such ambiguities in purpose and intent, the role of revolution in modernization is even more seriously circumscribed by the leading part that established governing classes have commonly played in the transition to a more developed modernity. The principal case is Britain, where the governing classes, displaying great continuity throughout the modern period, have managed and in many respects have directed the great transitions of this time. In France the monarchy had not only taken the lead toward modernity in the seventeenth century, but also with the support of part of the privileged classes was striving to modernize policy and administration in the years just before the Revolution. In crucial respects the Revolution carried out what the *ancien régime* had attempted. In Germany also, as Guido Goldman shows, bureaucratic and aristocratic groups from the days of the Great Elector repeatedly took the lead in modernization, often anticipating the modernizing demands of excluded groups by absorbing both demands and groups into their own dynamic. In Russia the Revolution was in one sense an exception to the pattern of development from the top that had prevailed from the days of Peter the Great. Yet once the new group had won power, striking resemblances appeared, as the Communist leaders continued, although more ruthlessly and perhaps more rapidly, the modernizing effort of their predecessors.

In sum it must be emphasized that revolutions do not inevitably consist in the rising up of modernizers against traditionalists. On the contrary, revolution may occur when a modernizing regime falters in its effort of further development. To return once again to the French example, in the eighteenth century the Bourbon monarchy was modernizing, although at a slower pace than in its electric years under Louis XIV. Moreover, it had the support of a part of the privileged classes. A larger part, however, resisted, and the nobiliary reaction, an antimodern move, constituted one of the main precipitating causes of the Revolution. Overcoming the resistance of these groups that had blocked the modernizing efforts of the monarchy, the French Revolution carried forward the work that the Old Regime had instituted and failed to complete.

Such an interpretation, it should be added, greatly helps comparative study of modernization in France and England. If we start with the premise that revolutions are needed to accomplish the transition from premodern to modern regimes, it must follow that both the Puritan and French revolutions performed such similar functions. This is historically and empirically absurd for many reasons, not the least being the fact that France was the leader in political modernization. The solution is to give up the untenable premise and to recognize (1) that transitions can occur without revolutions—as in the case of early modernization in France—and (2) that they may be precipitated in the course of modernization by defects of regime and policy—as in the case of the French Revolution.

A third proposition that has sometimes been attached to the notion of development is the hypothesis of cumulation. The contention is that in each stage the modern polity has acquired certain features that have remained in succeeding stages. The developed modern polity of the present time, therefore, embodies accomplishments of previous eras as well as the present era of modernity. The idea does sometimes fit the facts. In a classic essay on the growth of English citizenship, T. H. Marshall has shown how the present conception was built up over a long history, in each of three stages a distinctive and notable advance being made.[1] The seventeenth and eighteenth centuries established civil rights in the legal sense of the rule of law and protection against arbitrary action, as, for instance, by establishing habeas corpus. In the nineteenth and twentieth centuries political rights were added, as the franchise was extended and the rights necessary to make the vote effective, such as freedom of speech and of the press, were secured. In recent generations social rights have come to be guaranteed by the growth of the welfare state.

The hypothesis of cumulation points to a kind of explanation of present structures by means of the examination of their origins. Vice versa, it constitutes an interpretation of development as the successive production of features retained in the end product. In this latter guise, it sounds a hopeful note and could be used to fill out the vision of progress. But applicable as it may be in some instances, it cannot obscure the vast discontinuities in even the most gradual and incremental development. Any historical change inevitably means the loss of things and qualities—the death of persons and the fading of their impression on contemporaries, the destruction of old institutions by the emergence of new ones, and the decay of a unique quality of life enjoyed or endured by a class or by society as a whole.

To hold that there are certain stages through which the process of political modernization must inevitably pass is a very dubious proposition. Human ingenuity, imagination, and plain historical accident have ways of playing havoc with rigid schemes. Looking back over the three hundred years or so of European modernization, we cannot fail to be impressed with how the peculiarities of a country's heritage, its individual leadership, and the odd conjunctures of events have served to impress unique and lasting marks on its polity.

Yet with all due qualification, we can still see significant similarities in the sequence of phases through which the four countries have passed. Broadly speaking, there are three stages: the aristocratic, the liberal, and the collectivist. Since some nations have modernized sooner and more rapidly than others, the dates for each stage are not the same for all countries. Very roughly, if the seventeenth century saw the beginning of modernization, the eighteenth was the age of aristocracy, the nineteenth was the age of liberal democracy, and the twentieth has been the age of collectivism. The general pattern is that in each nation in each stage there is a stable and distinctive complex of structures that in certain fundamental respects resembles those of other nations in the same stage.

The Aristocratic Stage

The term "aristocratic stage" becomes more appropriate as we pass from East to West. In England this was the age of the Whig aristocracy. Great landowners, descendants in many cases of families who had fought the Stuarts, they dominated

---

[1] T. H. Marshall, *Class, Citizenship and Social Development* (New York, 1965).

the coalition of governing classes and had allies among the gentry and mercantile strata. Under this leadership, these classes, a miniscule proportion of the total population, governed the country through Parliament and the dispersed amateur bureaucracy of the time. Although modernizing, it was by no means an egalitarian regime. Because of the decline in the number of small landowners, the electorate had probably diminished as compared with what it had been in the seventeenth century. The ghastly treatment of the poor and the lower classes, while it had begun to call forth a humanitarian protest, still prevailed generally. Yet Whig constitutionalism, in the name of the Revolution of 1688, established English liberty on so firm a foundation as to win the admiration of enlightened minds on the Continent, such as Montesquieu and Voltaire, initiating the attempts at imitation that have lasted into recent times.

It was not only constitutionalism and liberty that won this admiration, but also prosperity and especially power. The Whigs were nation builders and empire builders of genius and vision. Although economically based mainly in land, they perceived the British interest in an expanding commerce. Sharing the premises of mercantilism common throughout Europe in their day, they constructed an elaborate protective system and by diplomacy and war supported colonial and commercial aggrandizement. Although the system has been called "parliamentary Colbertism,"[2] it did not extend to the detailed regulation of the internal economy attempted in France. Yet in Britain, as elsewhere, the purpose of mercantilist policy was to foster home production, native shipping, and ultimately national power. Adam Smith may well have been right about the vices of the system, but it did at least coincide with that immense commercial revolution that prepared the markets for the industrialization of Britain.

Throughout Europe the principal accomplishment of the first stage of political modernization was to build up the instrumentalities of state power on an unprecedented scale. Britain may seem backward if we think only of civilian bureaucracy. But in these combative generations of the seventeenth and eighteenth centuries the armed forces were a crucial component of the pattern of power; and with respect to her navy, British achievement was great and highly functional to her expanding commerce. Generally, the mobilization of power included and presupposed the creation of a system of taxation. In a larger sense it usually also presupposed a significant degree of economic modernization. This does not mean industrialization. As the case of Britain, economically the most advanced country, shows, the material basis of this first stage of political modernization consisted in a great expansion of trade, which was so great as to be called a "commercial revolution" but which depended typically upon cottage industry and manpower. When it came, industrialism added overwhelmingly to the forces of modernity. But in eighteenth-century Britain the modern state had sent down strong roots and shown vigorous growth long before the Industrial Revolution.

---

[2]William Cunningham, *The Growth of English Industry and Commerce in Modern Times. The Mercantile System* (Cambridge, England, 1912), Part 3.

In the eighteenth century France, which, as Suzanne Berger contends, had been in basic respects the first regime to modernize, began to lose its place as the model for Europe. While the Bourbons had taken the essential first steps in creating a bureaucracy, the system, judged by later standards, was still imperfectly centralized, insufficiently impersonal, and inadequately trained and specialized. Central authority could not readily control the huge body of officials, whose upper levels enjoyed hereditary tenure and titles of nobility. The fact that most offices were purchasable—the "venality" of offices—depressed standards of competence. Only later in liberal and democratic periods did the French civil service acquire its thorough-going commitment to competence in the person of the specialized *fonctionnaire*. Having, so to speak, chosen absolutism as its mode of modernization, the Bourbon monarchy proved unable to complete the indispensable next step of creating a bureaucratic instrument that would do its will. Thus, when the monarchy attempted to put its finances in order, the resistance of the nobility, entrenched in the bureaucracy, the law courts, and the provincial assemblies, precipitated the Revolution.

Yet the accomplishments of the Bourbons had been massive, one of their most critical achievements having been the creation of a system of taxation. The importance of this feature to modernity is so great that Joseph A. Schumpeter has called the modern state the "tax state" *(Steuerstaat)*. The financial straits of their declining days should not be allowed to obscure the immense advances the Bourbons had made over medieval fiscal methods. In France as elsewhere that meant above all moving away from an extractive system based largely on payments in kind and services. Under the feudal method of mobilizing power vassals performed military service in return for their fiefs, public works were accomplished by forced labor, officials lived off fees, and indeed the royal court found food and shelter by prolonged visits with wealthy noblemen. The establishment of a system of taxation meant that there could be a full-time paid judiciary, bureaucracy, and military and that wars and public works could be based on supplies purchased and controlled directly and fully by the central authority—all essential ingredients of modern centralization. Such an extractive system presupposed an exchange economy that would provide the money and the appropriate points of extraction. At the same time, the vast and continually growing demands of modernizing authority also promoted the growth of such an economy, as in forcing landowners to find a market for their produce in order to have the means of paying their taxes.

The work of national integration had also been carried forward under the Bourbons. Georges Lefebvre wrote:

> Toward national unity there had been indeed great progress, without which the Revolution would have been impossible. A thousand ties had been woven among Frenchmen by the development of communications and commerce, by the education given in colleges, by the attraction of the court and Paris.[3]

---

[3]Georges Lefebvre, *The Coming of the French Revolution,* R. R. Palmer (tr.) (Princeton, N. J., 1947), p. 20.

But local and class particularism was still strong in spite of the efforts of the monarchy. In unifying the legal system, nationalizing the market, further centralizing government, and many other ways, the Revolution of 1789 and Napoleon I achieved what the Old Regime itself had attempted.

Like France, Germany also chose the road of absolutism to modernity. As Goldman notes, this was in great part a consequence of the political disintegration resulting from the Thirty Years War. Along with the geopolitical position of Germany in the midst of potentially hostile neighbors, this meant that the military strain would be powerful in the policies and instrumentalities of the modernizing principalities, especially Prussia. There the remnants of the medieval estates were crushed by the monarchy and the energies of the nobility absorbed into the powerful bureaucracy of the eighteenth century. This system showed its capacity when the challenge of revolution came in the Napoleonic period. As Goldman observes, the Prussian bureaucracy carried through a

revolution from above which largely forestalled the social and political revolution which never occurred in Germany. The result was a talented and efficient, if still privileged and oligarchic, civil service, the mandarin core of the much-heralded *Beamtenstaat* and the civilian compeer of its military establishment.

In eighteenth-century Russia, to an even greater extent than in Germany, an autocratic regime with a strong modernizing thrust was established that not only barred the way to constitutionalism and representative government but also subjected all elements of society—peasantry, nobility and clergy—to the state. Not only was serfdom maintained and even strengthened, but the position of the upper classes was also far weaker than in Western Europe. "Noblemen's privileges," as Ulam writes, "were made dependent on their direct service to the state, and the nobility, as a class, was amalgamated with a bureaucratic caste."

It is necessary to dwell on these long-ago scenes if we are to understand the modern state and its tendencies and possibilities today. Democracy and liberty are, and have been for some time, under severe challenge in the West. It would be reassuring if we could find some kind of inherent support for them in the basic forces of modernity, especially in the scientific rationalism that is so sharply defined and powerful a constituent in the modern state. It would be especially helpful to know whether the dictatorial forms of the modern state in our time are inherently stable, or whether their modernity will divert them toward convergence with the liberal democratic regimes. The developments in Prussia and Russia in the eighteenth century, however, are a warning that the modern state in its autocratic form can make great strides in building up its characteristic instruments of power without suffering intolerable strains for lack of liberty.

This empirical lesson of history can be put into the general terms of power-interest dynamics. It would appear that the mobilization of power, as in the expansion of the extractive functions of the state, will strongly stimulate and support the demands and purposes pursued by means of the state. The new purposes, however, need not represent a trend toward democratization. On the contrary, the active political community may remain relatively small in numbers while its visions of national development and imperial expansion increase and multiply. The equilibrium of power and interests will be maintained, but under conditions that will hardly please the liberal democrat. Crucial questions for analysis are whether the growing capacities of the state were used for egalitarian purposes and what the role of political structure was in the determination of the choices made. In this light, the lessons of the nineteenth and twentieth centuries, while still ambiguous, are rather less gloomy. The immense mobilization of power accomplished by all European states in this time seems to show that a wider degree of participation is almost inevitable.

The Liberal Democratic Stage

If the accomplishments of the first stage had been especially marked in the mobilization of power, the emphasis in the second was on the mobilization of interests. Moreover, this increase in political scale meant not only a new order of magnitude in the scope and complexity of political demands, but also a thrust toward wider political participation. At the same time, the mobilization of power went forward. The nineteenth century saw the perfecting of a system of civil service—specialized, impersonal, hierarchical—immortalized in Max Weber's famous model. It was also the time, especially in its later decades, when the income tax spread, a mechanism of extraction that can rightly be compared with conscription. These mounting drafts on the resources of society were often major reasons why participation was extended. Also, needless to say, democratization and the efforts of ruling groups to avert it by assuaging popular needs constituted a large stimulus to the mobilization of power.

In advances toward liberal democracy the era left its mark on political history. In Britain the structure of citizenship was further elaborated by the addition of political to civil equality, mainly through the gradual and, except for a brief flare-up over women's suffrage, less and less contentious extension of the franchise. One basic condition making possible the historic advance of 1832 when the franchise was extended to the middle class was the very weakness of bureaucracy that epitomized Britain's lack of modernity. "Whig liberty" meant that the governing class was free from the menace of a royal bureaucracy or a large standing army. But it also meant that the demands for power of a burgeoning middle class could not be resisted.

Yet this rise in participation did not signify a proportionate diminution in the influence of the governing class. In great degree the middle class in the early part of this period accepted the political leadership of the upper social strata, as did the working class in turn when it received the vote and was drawn into political activity. According to a long line of observers, both foreign and domestic, the stability and progress of the British polity owe much to the survival of such traditionalist structures and sentiments.

At least the nineteenth-century British example bars the generalization that aristocratic survivals are intrinsically destabilizing—as the case of Germany may seem to imply. Indeed it will be argued in the section on Great Britain that more recent British experience further suggests not only that certain traditionalist survivals may be functional but also that a thorough-going modernity has a large potential for instability and ineffectiveness.

Britain in this period does challenge the proposition put forward earlier that the overall trend in the modern state has been toward primary centralization. It will be remembered that primary centralization is a relative growth in activity or, more precisely, an increase in the sum of the needs and resources of the members of the polity that are mobilized and related to one another by the state. While we can no longer accept the older view that for much of the nineteenth century Britain practiced a policy of strict laissez faire, it is nevertheless true that there was a sharp shift away from the intervention of the mercantilist system, involving an immense dismantling of old laws and controls. In this sense, Britain experienced a swing from collectivism to individualism.

Even though the withdrawal of control was accompanied by new sorts of intervention—for example, the first attempt to regulate factory labor in 1802—the shift in policy patterns was marked. The three sets of figures in Table 7.1 give rough indications of what happened.

Table 7.1 Government Expenditure (1900 prices)

	Total Expenditure (in Millions of Pounds Sterling)	Per Capita Expenditure (in Millions of Pounds Sterling)	Total Expenditure (as percentage of G.N.P.)
1792	17	1.2	11
1822	49	2.3	19
1850	62	2.3	12
1900	268	6.5	15
1938	851	17.9	30.1
1955	1,309	25.7	37.3

DATA SOURCE: Alan T. Peacock and Jack Wiseman, *The Growth of Public Expenditure in the United Kingdom* (Princeton, N. J.: Princeton University Press, 1961), Tables 1 and 2.

The first column reflects the steady expansion of state activity from the late eighteenth to the mid-twentieth century. The sums are in constant prices and so show a relatively greater sum of resources being taken and used by the state from one point in time to the next. The second column, which measures per capita expenditure, brings out the impact of laissez faire. Conventionally, historians have said that there was a period of reduced governmental intervention in the second quarter of the nineteenth century. The table shows not a reduced, but at any rate a constant level of per capita expenditure. The third column, which sets forth total governmental expenditure in comparison with GNP, suggests a later major change in policy pattern. As industrialization moved forward after the Napoleonic Wars, governmental expenditure, even though rising, took an ever lower portion of the national product. This trend, however, was reversed toward the end of the century, the change coming between 1890 and 1900. During the interwar years the index mounted sharply. It is in these decades that the rise of the welfare state and what I have called the collectivist stage of modernization are usually placed.

Looked at in a broad perspective, the pattern of development in France was very much the same as that in Britain. This must be emphasized, because comparisons of the two countries are usually employed to display contrasts and dissimilarities. That is a useful way of bringing out their more subtle features, precisely because in the context of European, not to mention world, politics, Britain and France are and long have been very much alike. During the nineteenth century the French bureaucracy was perfected; patronage was finally eliminated and professional training built into the system to create the *fonctionnaire*. The franchise was extended to the point of universal male suffrage, although not with the majestic gradualism of the British experience. Industrial capitalism arose, although later than in Britain and leaving a larger agrarian sector of peasant owners. By 1914 France, like Britain, was a powerful, democratic, industrialized state that had achieved a level of national integration comparable to its power and prosperity. The proof came when it sustained the staggering losses of World War I—1.4 million military deaths—yet fought on for four years without serious internal dissent.

The differences between Britain and France at this time hinge mainly on certain peculiarities of the French Revolution, the event that inaugurated the French transition to the liberal democratic age. It was a highly self-conscious, modernizing revolution. Reason, science, democracy, secularism, and national progress were proclaimed and pursued by its leaders with fanatical commitment. In the language of the revolutionaries, France was only then breaking out of the Middle Ages. In fact, as we have seen, the French monarchy had long since accomplished that transition; the significance of the revolutionary period was that it moved France not into modernity but from the early to the middle period of modernization. In this sense, its function was similar to that of the great British reforms of the early nineteenth century. Accurate or not, the revolutionary claims were made with a grand style that gave an indelible character to a wide spectrum of French political behavior. From the calling of the Estates General to Waterloo, the drama of men and factions created a repertory of role models to which the French revert with what amounts to repetition compulsion—consider the events of May 1968, for example. The term may not be clinically exact, but it brings out the fact that in the development of the polity, as of the individual, the choices made and attempted at crucial moments of decision can determine a whole pattern of typical behavior for generations to come. As a result, whenever there is renewed crisis and confusion, men revert to these old designs of response, especially when the originals were executed with the superb aesthetic power of the great revolutionary and Napoleonic figures. In the nineteenth century, let the tocsin sound however faintly, and instantly countless French hearts acknowledged the nation's call for a new Robespierre, Saint-Just, Danton, and, not least, Napoleon.

The result of this peculiar past is that, as Suzanne Berger writes, French politics represents "the tradition of modernity." Since the revolutionary period, there has always been available in the past a detailed model for any modernizing regime. Curiously, therefore, French progressives, while trying to construct the future, have looked backward for guidance. This has imparted not only the atmosphere of traditionalism to their behavior, but also its rigidities. The central conflict over legitimacy in French political culture, for example, turns on the clash of presidential and parliamentary regimes, the strong executive versus the representative legislature. These two can be reconciled, as the British experience shows. But French reactions have long been fixed by the template of historical memory that opposes the *regime conventionnel* of the Revolution of 1789 to the Bourbon or Napoleonic executive. As any tourist knows, the political graffiti on Parisian walls cannot be appreciated without a knowledge of what Berger calls "political archaeology." These slogans still proclaim not only *"La commune vaincra"*—after all that was only one hundred years ago—but also *"Vive le roi."*

The German experience may not appear to fit under the title of liberal democratic stage that I have given to this second phase of modernization. In Germany liberal democracy did not rise and unfold increment by increment, as in Britain, nor by spasmodic advance and retreat, as in France. Although industrialism came with a mighty rush in the second half of the nineteenth century, these years only underline the lesson that capitalism does not necessarily or effortlessly bring liberalism and democracy. That this correlation can be found in British and French history does not make it any more natural than the correlation of capitalism with authoritarian government in Prussia—not to mention Russia. The essence of this stage of German political development, as Goldman brings out, is that a bureaucratic-aristocratic regime continued to be sufficiently adaptable to maintain the privileged position of its landowning and military elites and to assure their dominance in an alliance with the new industrial and commercial classes. Moreover, the regime had the power—if necessary the armed force—to crush any thrust for power by liberals or democrats, as in 1848. The contrast with Britain in this respect shows the importance there of "Whig liberty" for peaceful parliamentary reform and for the entrance of the middle class into the active political community. If in 1832 the Duke of Wellington had commanded a large standing army and a centralized bureaucracy on the Prussian model, it is hard not to believe that he would have suppressed the demand for the reform bill instead of winning the Lords' acquiescence to it.

The German bourgeoisie, as Goldman shows, were reconciled with an authoritarian state and a conservative social order. Indeed, they lent their support to the suppression and restraint of those very freedoms with which they were identified in Britain and France. From this alliance the capitalist classes reaped substantial material advantages; as German national unity was achieved under Prussian hegemony, they benefited from the usual opportunities for modernization that arise from a wide national market. The state also supported a massive system of external protection and internal subvention, including public construction and ownership of railroads. From such measures German capitalism acquired a special character contrasting with the capitalism of Britain.

These peculiarities were further developed by the advanced policy of social security carried out in the latter part of the nineteenth century. While the socialist and trade-union movement nonetheless continued to grow, it cannot be denied that the working class, like the middle class before it, was in significant measure reconciled to the established order. In Germany, as in France, the socialists in the legislature voted war credits in 1914. Indeed, considering how deeply the problem of national identity had perplexed Germany for most of the nineteenth century, the population as a whole during World War I showed a solidarity remarkably high and in no way inferior to that of Britain and France—in four years the military deaths were 1.8 million. Only toward the end, when confronted by defeat, did the system begin to crack.

As Goldman shows, the peculiarities of modernization in Germany's liberal democratic era prepared the way for the fatal weaknesses of Weimar. Yet it is crucial not to be preoccupied with the causes of that tragic episode of German political development. The imperial system between 1871 and 1914 was in many respects progressive and promising. While it was a *Beamtenstaat* (bureaucratic state), it was also a *Rechstsstaat* (rule–of–law state), in which a highly trained bureaucracy and judiciary gave the country an administration of the law that was impartial and incorruptible. Likewise, the regime moved toward a more popular government—after 1871 the lower house of the imperial legislature was elected by universal manhood suffrage, although to be sure the effect of this provision was more than overbalanced by the predominance of conservative Prussia in the whole scheme. Under the Weimar Republic a liberal democratic constitution was adopted. In spite of its failings, the politics of this regime were open and responsive —by no means doomed from the start to collapse in fascism.

Ulam remarks that in the nineteenth century "Russia stood as the fortress of militarism and national and social oppression, a seeming exception to all the rules of historical development as propounded by liberalism." In the previous century its modernizing monarchs, like other enlightened despots, had sought to improve education and raise bureaucratic efficiency. In the course of time, science took root and flourished; progress in such subjects as celestial mechanics, for instance, laid the groundwork for the later Soviet achievements in space. Although coming late to industrial development, once Russia entered the industrial race, its rate of growth compared favorably with that of advanced countries. During the last decade of the nineteenth century Russian increases in the production of iron and coal exceeded those of Britain, Germany, or the United States. Yet in spite of these undoubted advances in political, economic, and cultural modernization, the Russian polity showed only the faintest traces of movement toward liberalism and democracy.

Indeed, it is a question whether the economy itself could properly be called capitalist. Capitalism requires a free market in labor as in goods, but the great bulk of the Russian work force was held in serfdom until 1861. Even thereafter, as Ulam

shows, the powers of the *mir,* the village organization, were not only anti-industrial, but anticapitalist in spirit and effect. Generally, the extensive system of governmental intervention established in the days of Peter the Great survived strongly
in the nineteenth century, when the countries of Western Europe were throwing
off the collectivist restraints of mercantilism. While industrialism finally did take
hold and thrive, the mode of production was capitalistic in an even more qualified
sense than that of Prussia, because the government exercised a critical directing
role in industrialization. The Russian experience again reinforces the hypothesis
that modernization is compatible with a highly authoritarian regime.

Yet the Russian case also suggests that the power and efficiency that modernity
brings can only be partially realized by an old-fashioned autocracy. As measured
by at least three of the indexes of political modernity—power, participation, and
national integration—Russia on the eve of World War I lagged far behind the other
three polities. The war confirmed these indications, revealing incredible inefficiency in the bureaucracy and armed forces, as a series of terrible defeats, in which
military deaths ran to 1.7 million, undermined popular support for the regime and
precipitated revolution.

The tsars had learned only too well how to restrain and control political mobilization. During the nineteenth century, although the regime showed little movement toward liberal democracy, the pressures were there. The doctrines of the
French Revolution spread to Russia and, despite the fierce repressions of the tsarist
police-state, deeply affected small groups of the upper classes, especially the
intellectuals. These doctrines inspired a long series of efforts toward achieving
liberation. The regime did not respond either by granting a modicum of real power,
as happened in Britain and France, or by conceding material advantages, as in
Germany. Of course, it could not have conceived of the Soviet solution of participation without power. When the years before the revolution led to some movement toward constitutional monarchy, the steps were small and faltering. Although
economic modernization does not necessarily imply liberal democracy, it seems
clear that the mobilization of power in the modern state requires a commensurate
mobilization of interests of some sort. In this sense the inability of the regime to
modernize its instrumentalities of power derived from its failure to modernize its
politics.

The Collectivist Stage

With due allowance for profound national differences, the previous pages have
sketched the common course of modernization. The focus has been dual. One
theme has been the linear trends toward greater power, scale, interdependence,
and centralization that prevailed through all stages. Another theme has been the
qualitative changes in regime for each stage—the distinctive configurations of
policy, the new forms of bureaucracy, and the shifts in the constellation of governing classes and intellectual elites. Since the form and fortunes of the four polities

during the third stage of modernization is the subject matter of the principal sections of this book, it is not appropriate to continue this country-by-country sketch. A few general propositions will be offered, however, about how these regimes achieved their present common structure and what common problems are inherent in it.

When we ask how and why states changed from nineteenth-century liberalism to the age of the welfare state and planned economy, one plausible approach is to start with the development of the economy. When discussing economic modernization at an earlier point, I observed that in the British case the modern era in economic development can be divided into the periods of the commercial revolution, industrial revolution, and organizational revolution. By the last category I mean especially the rise of the modern corporation to a place of dominance in economy, but also the spread of large-scale organization in such forms as employers associations, trade unions, farmers and peasants groups, and professional associations. Under such influences, it is often argued, the market economy of the old classical economies declined and ceased to perform its function of efficiently allocating resources among various uses and rewards among various factors of production. Slumps and stagnation resulted within nations and in the world economy, forcing governments to intervene more and more drastically to supplement and supersede the automatic working of the market.

Such an interpretation is not implausible when applied to the British experience. If we take the longer and wider view imposed by modernization theory, however, the greater importance of political factors appears. Even in individualist thought the national purpose of economic development was well understood and highly valued. Adam Smith made his central concern the problem of how to heighten the annual increase in the wealth of nations. Also, as the practice of the continental countries shows, some governments intervened extensively even in the heyday of economic liberalism. To recur again to an observation of Charles Tilly, when capitalism arose, it did not come into existence as a "natural force" independent of state policy but, on the contrary, had to be encouraged, promoted, and often forcibly imposed by comprehensive state action. The liberal economic order, in short, was in great degree a creature of public policy—which might well be expected to change in fundamentals again in the course of political development.

Such a shift in fundamentals took place, especially with the rise of working-class politics, in the latter part of the nineteenth century. Most strikingly this new factor took form in the emergence of socialist parties, but it also had its impact on the liberal parties and, indeed, as the German and British cases show, upon conservative sectors. That powerful thrust of the modern spirit for equality that had been expressed in guarantees of legal rights and political rights now found expression in the demand for social rights. The formulation of these demands came overwhelmingly from reformist and radical intellectuals. The electoral—and physical—force to support them derived from the newly enfranchised and recently urbanized working class.

The beginnings of the welfare state go back to a time when the capitalist economy was at its prime and the standard of living of the working class was rising. Viewed from this perspective, the planned economy was an accidental offshoot of the welfare state. To put the matter very simply: As the state developed massive programs of expenditure, it was inevitable that its actions would profoundly affect the economy and only logical that it should attempt to calculate and control these effects.

Still another source of state intervention that springs from the deeper undercurrents of modernity is the development of problem-solving knowledge and skills. This development has gone on constantly during modern times. In the liberal democratic era, for instance, the policy of "sanitation," which constituted an obvious and major departure from laissez faire, was vastly stimulated and in many respects made possible by advances in scientific knowledge—particularly in the emergence of the science of bacteriology, with all that it implied for control of disease. Perhaps the major example of the transforming effect of knowledge on public policy was the impact of Keynesian economics. This new knowledge of economic process gave direction to the huge expenditures of the welfare state; it also did much to legitimize them.

The key processes in the transition to this third stage are to be found not so much in the interrelations of economy and polity as in the internal processes of the polity, especially in what I have called the power-interest dynamic. Generally in Western Europe, the rising tide of democratic demands worked with the growing scope of scientific possibility to create the massive structures of the collectivist pattern of policy. This interrelationship can be observed even in Russia. It does not apply to the Revolution, when in the name of equality a new and far more effective modernizing elite was put in power. Once the task of industrialization had been accomplished in the time-honored Russian manner, however, the pressures for higher material well-being and even for "liberalization" began to assert themselves. Although Russia has been at the autocratic extreme throughout the modern period, some observers profess to see in these pressures some signs of convergence with attitudes in the democratic welfare states of Western Europe.

The forces that led to these changes in the pattern of policy also transformed power structure and politics. Political parties have an intrinsic connection with modernization. They presuppose and grow out of large-scale law making, the legitimacy of opposition, and organized and continuous political combat. Parties can be found in all stages of modernity, but, like the bureaucracy, they take different forms, depending upon the values and structure of the prevailing regime. The collectivist age typically brings forth the programmatic mass party. Both adjectives are exaggerations, but they serve to mark radical changes in form and process from the parties based on small cadres and broad principles that prevailed before the arrival of universal suffrage. The new socialist parties are usually the innovators, but older parties have known how to adapt.

In this time of transition, class and class interests have become much more explicitly the center of political controversy. The philosophy and rhetoric of this new definition of the political situation derived from powerful intellectual elites, of which the various Marxist schools were the more influential. As a result, the political demands of substantial parts of the working-class electorates of different countries were shaped by socialist doctrine, and class membership became an important determinant of political behavior and party allegiance. As we shall see in the discussions of the various party systems, however, class never became more than one among several determinants: The correlation is closest in Britain, where other bases of party allegiance, such as religion and nationality, are weak. In Germany these other factors have cut across class divisions, as in religious groupings, such as the Zentrum party of Weimar, or in the persisting force of Bavarian regionalism.

In France class analysis breaks down completely as an explanation of party allegiance. In a striking tabulation Berger shows that occupation and economic status display almost no correlation with French party affiliation; parties of the Left have much the same class profile as parties of the Right. The main formative influence in France has been the conflict of Church and state. This conflict, which culminated in the late nineteenth century at the time that large-scale political parties were first being formed, has not only continued to serve as the principal axis of division between Left and Right, but also to color the whole of French politics with the high ideological fervor of a struggle over ultimate values. In Britain, on the other hand, where class division has been strongest, the issues, having been seen as essentially economic and quantitative, have been handled in a spirit of compromise and practical reform.

While there have been common trends in the patterns of participation, the national differences have remained strong. The French party system, with its multiplicity, indiscipline, and ideological overtones, contrasts with the British system, with its dualism, high cohesion, and sturdy pragmatism. With regard to the bureaucratic element of the collectivist state, however, the common traits are far more marked. The Weberian model is not a bad approximation of the common ideal. The emergence of the managed economy has added to this model a strong element of corporatism, as the powerful producers organizations of the contemporary economy have been drawn into close relationships with the formal agents of the state. Generally, also, the advance of science and the greater complexity of public policy have given the bureaucratic expert ever greater influence.

Such similarities in bureaucratic structures reflect the tendency of science to have a uniform impact. Moreover, the bureaucracy is in the realm of instrumentalities and is therefore more flexible and responsive to modernization. Parties, on the other hand, are more deeply involved in the world of expressive symbolism and consummatory values. Like the formal machinery of government in which they are embedded, they are strongly colored by national character and national history. For example, Berger finds that French parties can be best understood by a kind of political "archaeology," which reveals the historical roots of their parochialism and resistance to change. In general, national differences, whether deriving from a premodern heritage or from peculiarities of national development, have managed to survive strongly even in the present era of the highly developed modern polity.

Eight
Problems of the Developed Modern Polity

The previous pages have shown how a complex of common influences affects all countries, and not trivially but in sufficient degree to justify speaking of the modern state as a distinctive type of polity. Among other things this means that its common features produce similar patterns of consequences, which appear as problems to members of these states.

National differences affect these patterns of consequences. So, for instance, the ancient autocratic tradition of Russia greatly enhances the authoritarian tendencies of industrialism and bureaucracy. Yet these tendencies are inherent in the political and economic features of modernity and in some degree also appear in the other three modern societies. Similarly, certain peculiarities of German political culture and structure weakened the resistance of Weimar democracy to the demagogic mass politics of the Nazis. Yet the impact of modernization elsewhere has also created the political weaknesses that lead to fascist movements, even though these movements have been able to seize power in only a few cases. A principal virtue of carrying on comparative study with the aid of modernization theory is that its concepts help us see the sources of such tendencies and eventualities, which otherwise might be overlooked if national traits alone were considered responsible. The disorders of modernity afflict all advanced countries, but in different degrees.

The Problem of Effectiveness

The problems of the highly developed modern polity may conveniently be considered under two headings: the problem of effectiveness and the problem of authority. The first centers on the question of performance: To what extent does a state achieve the ends pursued through it? How well does it bear its "load" of problem solving? It may seem paradoxical that effectiveness is presented as a primary problem of the modern state, since it is in this sphere of performance and power that political modernity has scored its most distinctive successes. Yet the very order that is responsible for these successes also intrinsically gives rise to counterproductive tendencies. It has the vices of its virtues. Modernization has endowed the instrumentalities of the state with unprecedented power over man and nature. At the same time, because of their size and complexity, it is exceedingly hard to subject these instrumentalities to coherent, overall control. They continually threaten to break loose from the purposes of public policy and to drag along the whole polity on a chaotic and unintended course.

It is supremely ironic, not to say dangerous, that these powerful agencies, with their great potential for gratifying human wishes, should also be so prone to frustrate them. In the days of laissez faire in the nineteenth century, men rightly feared the unregulated economy as the source of coercive social forces. Today the polity, including the very instruments designed to modify and control the economic environment, has joined and in some countries superseded the economy as the machine that threatens to master man. Bureaucratization matches industrialization as a source of blind development. Every modern state is confronted with an unending struggle to subject to control its agencies of control. The first problem of a highly developed modern state is to master its own inordinate power.

When speaking of the state machine threatening to master man, I refer not to the problem of tyranny or other intentional abuse of authority but to the problem of control. This prospect threatens dictatorial regimes as well as liberal democracies. The menace of *accidental* nuclear war hangs over both sorts of polity. Less terrifying, but more typical of the problem, are the latent dysfunctions that burden, disrupt, and distort the huge bureaucratic machines of the modern state.

The public sector in Russia is virtually all-encompassing: Every factory and every store is owned and run by the state, and every acre of land is under its control. Adam B. Ulam describes and analyzes the difficulty of making the controls over this huge public sector respond to the will of the Communist elite. He traces, for instance, the cycle of centralization-decentralization-recentralization produced by the forces of Soviet bureaucracy. There are special qualities in this process deriving from the nature of the dictatorship. But the process also displays a dynamic that will be familiar to students of administration in the democratic countries. Overcentralization, needless to say, plagues the command economy of the Soviet regime as well as the democratic welfare state. In Russia as elsewhere, to make savings in personnel, to avoid wasteful duplication, and to give greater initiative to people on the spot are standard reasons for reforms of administrative decentralization. So also is recentralization a familiar consequence in modern regimes, democratic or dictatorial, when the decentralized structure works to put local interests ahead of what the central decision makers regard as the national interest.

Incoherence and Incompetence

To say that there is a problem in subjecting the vast complex of power mobilized by the modern state to coherent control implies that an effort is being made to assert such control and that there is some more or less unified will or scheme of priorities issuing from the politics of the system. This assumption is legitimate as a device for isolating and identifying tendencies inherent in the modern pattern of power. It brings out the fact that incoherence in the pattern of policy may proceed from such objective forces and need not be referred back to some conflict or disorientation in the directing will of the state. In practice, of course, the directing will of the state is itself often the source of chaos and ineffectiveness. The tendency of the pattern of interests to produce incoherent decision making is a major and common problem of the modern polity.

The terms coherence and incoherence do not have the connotation of deep seriousness. Yet, fragmentation in the polity and incoherence in the policy-making process have led to some of the more profound and characteristic failures of the highly developed modern state. The most tragic case was the fall of the Weimar Republic. Under this system, based on the best models of liberal, democratic constitutionalism, the public will splintered into a multitude of political parties, which were represented in the legislature with meticulous accuracy and fairness through a proportional system. In consequence, as Guido Goldman shows, no single party was ever strong enough to form a majority government, and Cabinets, being necessarily based on multiparty support, were short-lived and often paralyzed by internal disagreement. The resulting lack of governance, which the Germans strikingly referred to as "pluralistic stagnation" *(pluralistische Stockung),* greatly promoted the economic and political disorder that discredited self-government and strengthened the appeal of the authoritarian extremists.

Nor have the dire results of democratic pluralism been confined to Germany. The multiparty system of France had similar, although not such tragic, effects on the policy making of the Third and Fourth Republics. *Immobilisme* was a characteristic failing of governments under these constitutions. Charles de Gaulle made it a principal object of denunciation in his attack upon the "regime of parties." As Suzanne Berger points out, the new constitutional and political regime of 1958 represented an attempt of the French polity to shake off this typical weakness of multiparty democracy. Moreover, two-party democracy itself is by no means free of the basic flaw. A majority party may perform its conventional function of "aggregating interests," yet in the course of this process commit itself to compromises and respond to pressures to such an extent that its policies are as short-sighted and conflicting as those of a multiparty coalition. In Britain, the home of party dualism and strong Cabinet government, the power of pressure groups in recent years has been a major reason for the inflationary tendencies that have done much to frustrate a policy of sustained economic growth. The system of collectivist politics, which became stabilized in the fifties, was based not only on a consensus among the main political groups, but also upon a balance of pressures that severely limited the scope of decisive action.

Modernization promotes pluralism through its characteristic process of division of labor. The disruptive tendencies of that result are further enhanced by the egalitarian thrust of modernity. The basic doctrines of egalitarianism—that every man is the best judge of his own interest and that all men are the best judge of the common interest—brush aside the claims of traditional governing classes and of professionally trained elites. The resulting demands on the part of voters for plausible rhetoric and immediate gratifications can only further diminish the effectiveness of public policy.

In the face of these familiar vices of modern democracy, it is not absurd to suggest that an authoritarian system, as in Soviet Russia, is more functional to the needs of the modern polity, at any rate in its more advanced stages. Given the inevitable complexities of policy and the inevitable pluralism of social strata in these later stages, it would seem prudent to entrust the democratic electorate with only a restricted role in the governmental process. From a general view, it appears that a mature industrialism tends strongly toward a hierarchical form of organization. Trade unions do arise and acquire powers of collective bargaining in free countries. Yet the prerogatives of management are maintained and the typical firm or corporation is run from the top, not from the shop floor or by the shareholders. This being so, it would seem logical to believe that the hierarchical form would also be more suitable for the governance of the economy as a whole. Such a government would tend to reduce the distorting and frustrating pressures with which a free society obstructs the orderly and effective conduct of affairs. An authoritarian regime would presumably have a better chance of ensuring that a unified and professional outlook would prevail among the decision makers.

The experience of Russia, which was burdened by a rigidly autocratic tradition, a particularly dogmatic version of Marxism, and a large traditional sector in its economy, may not be a fair test of this hypothesis. But even after making allowance for these special national circumstances, the implications of the Russian experience are that the authoritarian version of the modern polity also has its own deep-seated dysfunctions. The question is not the liberty or humanity of such a regime. The case for this sort of regime is precisely that these values are sacrificed for the sake of a higher achievement according to that other criterion of modernity, effective performance—that is, in terms of this analysis, the power of the state over the social and natural environment.

Now if we pass over for the time being the question of whether the Soviet regime meets the two requisites of effectiveness already mentioned (coherence and professional competence), it is still clear from Ulam's account that it confronts serious problems in meeting two other requisites, the need for criticism and the need for active cooperation and consent among the governed. As Ulam observes, an authoritarian system of administration promotes efficiency, but "only up to a certain point." If any complex system of action is effectively to pursue its goals, there must be provision for a constant feedback of informed criticism into the decision-making process. In a liberal regime, a major function of its liberal institutions is to make possible a flow of reports, criticism, and counterproposals from within the bureaucracy and from the society at large. By many means, formal and informal, from the press, parties, pressure groups, legislative committees, and systems of administrative oversight, messages get through—admittedly confused by an immense amount of static—regarding the empirical relevance and technical appropriateness of governmental action. To governments these messages may be "thorns of criticism," to use Otto von Bismarck's words. Yet, as he himself recognized when he coined the phrase in his later years, they are indispensable in the long run to effective performance.

That further requisite, the need to mobilize consent among the governed, becomes ever more critical as the scope of policy grows. The process of primary centralization means that government touches more and more people in more and more ways. Among the democratic regimes, contemporary governments impose large and growing burdens upon their citizens, not only in the form of deprivations of money, time, effort, and so on—as in the payment of taxes or the performance of military service—but, even more important in these days of the welfare state and managed economy, in requiring intricate patterns of behavior—such as conformity to wage and price "guidelines." In Russia this immediate impact is multiplied by the far wider responsibilities of the regime. For either type of polity, as the scope of government action grows, sheer coercion is less and less adequate as a base of obedience. In countless ways, not mere conformity to orders but willing cooperation expressing intelligent understanding is necessary if the modern state is to achieve its goals.

Traditionally, one major means of mobilizing the consent needed by the modernizing state has been to extend the circle of participation. One function of the democratization of the polity in Western Europe has been to win consent, support, and cooperation for its growing activities. The extension of the franchise has paralleled the progress of primary centralization. Similarly, the rise of functional representation, which has brought organized producers groups from business, labor, and agriculture into close consultation with governmental departments, has been in great part impelled by the need of governments to have the advice and cooperation of the leaders and members of these groups.

Having foregone the means of performing these functions that are provided by liberal democracy, the Soviet regime has attempted to find substitutes suitable to its form of rule. For example, the congress of representatives of collective farms held in 1969 had as its purpose to boost the morale of the collective peasant and to emphasize the importance of that branch of the agrarian economy. Broadly speaking, the main instrument for performing both the function of watching over and checking the bureaucracy and the function of arousing and maintaining support among the populace for the regime has been the Communist party. Its presence and functioning justify referring to the Soviet regime as "partisan and participatory." In the liberal democracies also political parties provide criticism and help win support for the regime by giving the governed a sense of participation. The single party of the Soviet Union, however, performs these functions in a totally different manner, reflecting the will of the Communist elite rather than the purposes and interests of a democratic electorate.

It would seem that any modern authoritarian regime must find it necessary to have such a party apparatus to carry out functions indispensable to the effective performance of the polity. But the commitment to a one-party system itself entails further consequences that are severely dysfunctional. Such parties are usually highly ideological, and probably could not perform their task of mobilizing consent unless they were. Yet an ideological commitment hampers flexibility and adaptation and may embody conceptions of empirical reality that conflict with scientific advance. The grotesque and wasteful results of Lysenkism in Russia illustrate the dangers. Moreover, although the pluralism of the democratic electorate is repressed by "democratic centralism," conflicts within a small ruling elite can be even more intense and destructive. For this reason, in an authoritarian system there may be, even in a collegial regime (that is, a regime in which supreme authority is shared by a body of colleagues), a tendency toward one-man rule—a kind of Hobbesian logic leading to an absolute sovereign. Yet the irrationalities of autocracy, whether Stalin's paranoia or Khrushchev's "hare-brained schemes," are highly dysfunctional to the purposes of modernity. While liberty and democracy are less needed by modernity than was once supposed and while there is no reason to expect an inevitable liberalization of the Soviet regime, Soviet authoritarianism, as Ulam's account demonstrates, creates tensions and contradictions that could lead to major disruption.

The effectiveness of modern democracies is threatened by inherent tendencies toward incoherence of the public will and incompetence in the ruling powers. Yet the authoritarian alternative also suffers from severe deficiencies at both levels of the political process. The public will may be unified in a degree beyond the reach of pluralistic democracy, but the means by which this unity is achieved tend to create rigidities that are at least as counterproductive as the immobilism that may afflict popular government. Moreover, while unchecked authority nominally creates the opportunity to put the highest professional competence in command of the instruments of state power, the same structure impairs the adaptive and responsive capacities of the system at every level. Democratic incoherence and incompetence are matched by the rigidities and irrelevancy of authoritarian systems.

No doubt the most serious question of all is whether terror is inherent in modern authoritarianism. The destructiveness and dysfunctionality of terror are plain from the record of tragic and colossal blunders of Stalinism, ranging from collectivization to the "permanent purge." The notion of a single and incontestable truth that is embodied in the ideological one-party system makes the toleration of honest differences of opinion virtually impossible. Every critic and every dissident must appear to authority as a traitor and plotter. But given the complexity and fluidity of modern social change, differences of opinion are bound to arise. The effort to repress them and prevent them will therefore follow. In this sense, Stalinism was inherent in Leninism.

The Problem of Authority

The other major problem afflicting the developed modern state is the problem of authority. Any polity confronts the task of legitimizing the exercise of power by its rulers. But a special problem of authority afflicts political modernity, going back to its very beginnings. This problem arises from the fact that the basic attitudes of modernity, rationalism and voluntarism, mount a harsh and powerful attack upon the foundations of traditional authority, while themselves providing only vulnerable substitutes. The regimes produced by medieval political development had been sustained by doctrines grounded in a universal religious faith and by sentiments engendered by ancient communities founded on locality and lordship. The "acids of modernity" deeply eroded these foundations of legitimacy. The secularization of the state, whether or not there was outright separation of church and state or disestablishment of the church, deprived it of explicit ecclesiastical support. More seriously, the scientific and rationalistic attacks on religion weakened its old doctrines of civil order, which had justified as well as defined and limited the role of the polity. At the same time, the old bonds of communal attachment were worn away both by the new values celebrating contractual association and by the vast mobility of a modernizing society.

In place of these older grounds of political obligation, modern thought offers characteristic substitutes. In keeping with the nature of modernity, these can be neither transcendental nor traditional, but are contractual and ideological. In the first place, the state is sharply seen as an instrument of benefits to its members, in return for which they contribute support. Over time the content of the benefits has changed, from mere law and order and defense to the goods and services of the welfare state, as have the material embodiments of support, such as taxes, military service, and cooperation with the managed economy. Yet in practice, as in theory, the transaction remains essentially economic, a kind of mass purchase by citizens from the state of things they could not conveniently get through the market and individual action. As an economic transaction, moreover, the delivery of support depends upon the purchasers continuing to feel that they are getting full value for their contribution. Intrinsically, therefore, like customers in the market, they are free to withdraw support when their expectations are not fulfilled. Such attitudes put great emphasis upon the output efficiency of the modern state, a responsibility which, given the modern stress on high instrumental performance, the modern state has vigorously sought to meet. The economic and rationalist character of the relationship, however, has made the acceptance of modern authority precarious in contrast with the acceptance of forms and persons in traditional societies.

Ideologies constitute the second characteristic means by which modern states seek legitimacy. Three centuries of modernity have produced a dazzling variety of them in contrast to the massive uniformity of opinion that, apart from the conflict of *imperium* and *sacerdotium,* marked the previous thousand years. The conflict of "isms," which is typical of and indeed unique to modern times, has given rise to continual controversy over conceptions of authority and common purpose and to frequent efforts to change regimes. As systems of thought and ideals, ideologies have had and continue to have enormous influence. On the other hand, so long as they merely express intellectual belief and moral conviction, they fail to draw on the other strong grounds of motivation inhering in habit, emotion, and identification that supported traditional solidary groups. Like the bonds of contract, the bonds of ideology depend heavily upon conscious, rational processes, and so they suffer from a certain fragility.

These limitations of contract and ideology give rise to the classic problem of authority in the modern state. The course of modern political development provides abundant illustrations of this problem. The historical record, however, also shows that the authority and cohesion of the polity have been strongly supplemented by other supports. First is the fact of nationality. Deriving from premodern sources, nationality has provided a focus of identification, engaging deep-seated affectual energies and supporting a kind of solidarity similar to that in traditional communities. The modern states that have survived have been nation-states.

We need not dwell here on nationality, as its role has been given a good deal of attention in previous pages. A second source of support, which needs more attention, is economic class. Although usually thought of as a source of division and conflict, economic class must also be seen as a major instrument in maintaining the cohesion of the polity: In modern political development it functions as a source of stability as well as of movement. As a stabilizing factor, economic class has a twofold effect. In the first place, a sense of class is a powerful aggregating influence. Nowadays, the division of labor multiplies almost indefinitely the occupational groupings within the working force. In turn, these groupings form the basis for much of the organization of the pressure-group sector of the pattern of interests. Economic class, however, transcends these groupings, constituting a basis for concerted action among a wide portion of the electorate. In Britain, for instance, the strong dualism of class identity among voters has been one of the principal bases for the two-party system. The aggregating function of this factor can be seen by comparison with countries, such as the United States, where a weaker sense of class identity coincides with far less solidary party behavior.

Moreover, not only does class help suppress the pluralism of the modern mass electorate, but when attached to a political party, it also enhances the voters' sense of efficacy. In the huge electorates of present-day democracies, it is hard for the individual to see his participation as having influence on the polity. Indeed, where such large numbers are involved, the act of voting is so insignificant as to make little sense from the point of view of the lone individual. But while individuals cannot win elections, a class can. The voter who identifies with a class and its party can have feelings of victory, power, and self-government when this party wins elections or in other ways influences the state. In this way class can strengthen the familiar device of participation as a means of creating support for the modern polity.

Class can perform this function of aggregating economic interests because it is not itself solely an economic phenomenon. As the case of the United States shows, merely having a highly developed industrial economy is a necessary but not sufficient condition for a strong sense of class and a high level of class cohesion in political behavior. The latter types of behavior, as seen in European countries, depend also upon a political culture that still bears the marks of its origins in the hierarchical, corporate society of premodern times. As I argue in my discussion of class and politics in Britain, a "sense of degree" deriving from such a political culture prepares the perceptions of the British voter, making him more liable to find social stratification and to identify with a class.

The New Fragmentation

In general, the problem of authority is solved to the degree that the commands of government and the behavior of citizens coincide. Such coincidence will depend upon two variables: the burdens imposed upon citizens and their grounds for compliance. There is reason to believe that certain conditions created by the later stages of modernization make this equilibrium much harder to achieve than it was in earlier stages, and so raise the problem of authority to a new plane of intensity. With regard to burdens, it takes no prolonged argument to show that their weight is vastly increased in the era of collectivist policy. This is a period of growing intervention by the state, which progressively extends its regulatory and extractive activities. One rough indicator of the trend is the increase in taxation, not only absolutely but also as a percentage of the national income. There are complex questions of the changing incidence of these burdens. Yet it seems highly likely that, for comparable individuals or groups, the gross burden of state action has increased immensely in the course of the past two generations in the countries of Western Europe.

The further question of net burden and of the perception of that burden turn attention to the other side of the equation, the grounds of compliance. It is with regard to this variable that the most complex and subtle transformations have been taking place. On balance it would seem that both the rational and nonrational grounds for compliance have been weakening. Initially, at any rate, as Gunnar Myrdal has observed (see Chapter 5), the welfare state with its panoply of benefits surely heightened political integration. On the other hand, the connection between burdens and benefits has been obscured by the inherently complex and technical modes of action of the modern polity. Budgets for five years or so have become common; a government can hardly launch, let alone complete, a major program or change of program within the old annual cycle. Furthermore, the technical aspects of problems and programs—for example the economics of inflation—are so difficult as to defeat all but professionally trained minds. All this makes it hard for the individual to connect burden and benefit, to see the immediate sacrifice as a necessary cost of the ultimate outcome. Whether he values that outcome as a quid pro quo for himself or as a fulfillment of his ideals, the loss of rationale diminishes his willingness to tolerate the readily perceivable and relentlessly mounting costs.

The essential point is familiar to historians of democratic theory. The plausibility of that idea as the foundation of a viable polity depended not only upon an explicit belief in the rational competence of the voter but also upon an implicit assumption that the operations of government would remain comprehensible. We may think highly of the common man and yet conclude that modern government transcends his comprehension and patience.

Characteristic processes of modernization are also eroding the nonrational grounds. The most interesting change is what appears indubitably to be a decline of class as a factor shaping political behavior. In Britain, the country in which class has been outstandingly important, the behavioral indexes of this decline are striking. In Germany there are indications, such as the growing independence of voters, that suggest a similar trend. In France, as Berger shows, class is of little significance as a basis of party allegiance. The reasons for this decline inhere in modernization and can be found generally in advanced countries. Affluence, bureaucratization, and corporatist representation all play their familiar parts. Moreover, the rational, pragmatic, calculating spirit undermines not only sentiments of deference and noblesse oblige but also old solidarities of class identification. Sometimes the decline of class has been gradual, as in recent years; at other times it has been abrupt, as when the Nazi revolution, as Goldman shows, destroyed the powerful Junker class with its filiations in army and bureaucracy. In the long run, despite some powerful countercurrents, modernization in the past two or three centuries has deeply eroded the class distinctions inherited from the awesome inequalities of medievalism.

It may seem curious to speak of the decline of class in view of the role that class-based economic organizations have played in recent years in making difficult the attempts of Western governments to manage and control their economies. A principal problem has been the difficulty of coping with inflationary pressures. In particular, attempts at more programmatic planning, as by the Labour government of Harold Wilson, have foundered on the problem of controlling the wage-push elements of inflation. But even in *étatist* France governments have been unable to effectuate an incomes policy. As Berger observes, planning was forced by the wage-price problem to recede from its more ambitious efforts. Although Germany with its "social-market" economy has not attempted control on so wide a scale as France and Britain, the government of Willy Brandt has found its ambitious social program frustrated by the compulsions of an inflationary economy. Both social-democratic Sweden and free-enterprise America have been confronted by a wage-push inflation that has proved intractable.

It is not an adequate analysis to blame these trends on the "monopoly power" of labor organizations. We must note that the same basic problem afflicts countries with strong and with weak labor organizations. A more fundamental condition than

monopoly power is almost the very opposite—that is, the absence of strong authority in the trade-union sector. Effective control of the economy, whether we call it
planning or not, requires organization of the various sectors, on the side of both
management and labor, in such a form that firm and binding agreements can be
made between the planning government and the agents of production. This necessity has been a principal cause of the rise of corporatism in the present stage of
modernization.

Oligopoly in business facilitates such negotiations and agreements, but the organization of business is often incommensurate with the needs. On the labor side, the
problem is still more acute. Even where the top trade-union leadership is aware
of the necessities of economic control, as they often are, they have been losing
the capacity to bring along their rank and file. As a result the wildcat strike has
become typical, tending to displace the old-fashioned official, nationwide strike.
Governments cannot plan because labor itself has been losing its behavioral coherence. Entirely in contrast to the situation in the 1930s, it is not a polarization of
classes that constitutes the problem, but rather a fragmentation of classes.

Generally, a politics of fragmentation characterizes the new trends of the present
phase of modernity. This new politics rejects the corporatistic structures of economic planning and management. It emphasizes ad hoc voluntary associations, in
contrast to permanent, class-based parties. In its eyes, participation in decision
making becomes almost as important as the content and effect of the decisions
themselves. Partly for this reason, centralization is shunned and local and regional
forms preferred. One powerful current is represented by the revival of old nationalisms, as in Celtic Britain or Breton France. Sometimes it seems as if the energies
withdrawn from the old solidarities of class are being projected upon the even
older solidarities of regional nationality and that a communal politics might displace
the class politics that has reigned so long.

Some observers see precisely such a future for European politics as communal
loyalties flourish, nationality declines, and, they hope, European integration creates
a wider polity. There is good reason to connect the rise of communal loyalties with
the decline of nationality and to find a reason for the fragmentation of politics and
the weakening of national authority in the changing function of the nation-state
abroad. In this respect there are again parallels between the experiences of Russia
and the democratic countries. With regard to Russia, Ulam attaches great importance to this connection, which he examines in some detail. The rise of dissent in
recent years reflects some loss of authority as compared with the old days of
high-pressure industrialization and Stalinist terror. While such dissent is neither
organized, widespread, nor fundamental, Ulam does see some possibility that a
"drastic change" might arise from developments in the international situation,
specifically within international communism. The internal authority of the regime
and its Communist elite has depended heavily upon the leadership by the Soviet
Union of a unified, world-wide movement that promised to go on from strength
to strength. The failure of communism to progress and, more important, the divisions within the movement and the assertion of a rival leadership by Communist

China have weakened the hold of the authoritarian regime upon the loyalty and support of the Russian people. Ulam speculates that disillusionment with the regime and internal pressures for its liberalization could ultimately reach the point of undermining its ideological and organizational foundations.

Over the past generation the nations of Western Europe have suffered a not entirely dissimilar eclipse. Their role in the world has been reduced by the loss of empire, as in the case of Britain, France, Holland, and Belgium, and by the loss of influence in the face of the two superpowers, Russia and the United States. More recently and more importantly, the state apparatus of these nations has appeared to be less and less important not merely as an instrument of imperialism and influence but as an instrument of defense. The détente that developed between Russia and the United States in the sixties, dating especially from the nuclear test ban of 1963, has reduced the widespread fears of the Cold War period, as can readily be seen in the decline in defense budgets. In the West European countries, as in Russia, it is reasonable to suppose that a loss of external function has promoted a loss of internal authority. This decline in national authority gives the old communal loyalties the opportunity to assert their centrifugal claims.

Major problems of the advanced polities of the present day derive from fundamental traits of political modernity. To be sure, as other forces have shaped these political systems, so also problems can be found that derive from sources extraneous to modernity and modernization. The old and acute problem of liberty in Russia, for example, has such roots, and the tensions it creates cannot be explained merely by reference to the forces of modernization. Yet while modernization does not and should not pretend to explain everything about the polities we call modern, it does serve to bring out traits, trends, and problems of fundamental importance. At certain times in the past, such as the 1930s, the ideas of capitalism and capitalist development have similarly served to light up the nature of many contemporary problems. Today modernization theory performs this function of helping us understand the polities in which we live and which we may seek to preserve, change, or supersede.

Select Bibliography

General Theory

Almond, Gabriel, and G. Bingham Powell. *Comparative Politics: A Developmental Approach.* Boston: Little, Brown, 1966.

Deutsch, Karl. *The Nerves of Government: Models of Political Communication and Control.* Glencoe, Ill.: Free Press, 1963.

Easton, David. *A Systems Analysis of Political Life.* New York: Wiley, 1965.

Friedrich, Carl J. *Man and His Government: An Empirical Theory of Politics.* 2 vols. New York: McGraw-Hill, 1963.

Macridis, Roy O. *The Study of Comparative Government.* New York: Doubleday, 1955.

Merriam, Charles E. *Systematic Politics.* Chicago: University of Chicago Press, 1946.

Parsons, Talcott. *The Social System.* Glencoe, Ill.: Free Press, 1951.

Richter, Melvin (ed.). *Essays in Theory and History: An Approach to the Social Sciences.* Cambridge, Mass.: Harvard University Press, 1970.

Shils, Edward (ed.). *Toward a General Theory of Social Action.* Cambridge, Mass.: Harvard University Press, 1951.

Weber, Max. *Theory of Social and Economic Organization.* A. M. Henderson and Talcott Parsons (trs.). New York: Oxford University Press, 1947.

Modernization and Development

Apter, David. *The Politics of Modernization.* Chicago: University of Chicago Press, 1965.

Black, C. E. *The Dynamics of Modernization.* New York: Harper & Row, 1966.

Durkheim, Emile. *The Division of Labor in Society.* George Simpson (tr.). New York: Free Press, 1933.

Greer, Scott. *The Emerging City: Myth and Reality.* Glencoe, Ill: Free Press, 1962.

Huntington, Samuel P. *Political Order in Changing Societies.* New Haven, Conn. and London: Yale University Press, 1968.

Lerner, Daniel, *et al. The Passing of Traditional Society: Modernizing the Middle East.* Glencoe, Ill: Free Press, 1958.

Mannheim, Karl. *Man and Society in an Age of Reconstruction.* New York: Harcourt, Brace, 1940.

Moore, Barrington. *Social Origins of Dictatorship and Democracy.* Boston: Beacon Press, 1969.

Organski, F. K. *The Stages of Political Development.* New York: Knopf, 1965.

Rostow, W. W. *Politics and the Stages of Growth.* Cambridge, England: Cambridge University Press, 1971.

Rustow, Dankwart. *A World of Nations: The Problems of Political Modernization.* Washington, D.C.: Brookings Institution, 1967.

Tilly, Charles (ed.). *The Building of States in Western Europe.* Forthcoming.

Wilson, Godfrey, and Monica Wilson. *The Analysis of Social Change.* Cambridge, England: Cambridge University Press, 1945.

2

The British Political System

Samuel H. Beer

One

The Modernity of Tradition in Britain

Writing shortly before World War I, A. Lawrence Lowell of Harvard could introduce his classic work on British government and politics with this encomium:

> Measured by the standards of duration, absence of violent commotions, maintenance of law and order, general prosperity and contentment of the people, and by the extent of its influence on the institutions and political thought of other lands, the English government has been one of the most remarkable in the world.[1]

Nor were these merits lost on the governed. "The typical Englishman," he observed,

> believes that his government is incomparably the best in the world. It is the thing above all others that he is proud of. He does not, of course, always agree with the course of policy pursued . . . but he is certain that the general form of government is well-nigh perfect . . .[2]

Fifty years later an eminent French observer, although no less Anglophile than Professor Lowell, felt compelled to make a different report. Having observed how the French early in the eighteenth century came to admire "the governance of England" and to spread its praises throughout Europe, Bertrand de Jouvenel noted

---

[1] A. Lawrence Lowell, *The Government of England*. 2 vols. (New York, 1908), Preface.
[2] *Ibid.*, p. 507.

the sharp decline of this appeal in recent years. Although, in his view the British had formulated most of the new twentieth-century goals of government, during the past generation they had failed to display their usual leadership in showing how these goals could be best pursued. With understatement so British as to include the characteristic double negative, he concluded: "Surely Britain is not incompetently governed: that is not the point; the point is that its governance is not of such conspicuous excellence as to invite imitation."[3]

This gentle chiding by a courteous foreign friend is only a pale intimation of the storm of savage criticism that the British have directed against themselves during the past decade. Its crescendo was especially marked in 1963 by a special issue of *Encounter,* a decorous, highbrow journal with an international standing. The title of the special issue, "Suicide of a Nation?" did not exaggerate the harshness of its contents. Typically one contributor began:

> Each time I return to England from abroad the country seems a little more run down than when I went away; its streets a little shabbier, its railway carriages and restaurants a little dingier; the editorial pretensions of its newspapers a little emptier, and the vainglorious rhetoric of its politicians a little more fatuous . . .[4]

Through the intervening years this mood of national self-criticism has persisted. In the early seventies a perceptive journalist, reporting "the lacerating self-contempt of the past few years," could say that "Britain is living out a quiet agony."[5]

While the target of these attacks has not been confined to politics and government, they have provided a central focus of criticism. The performance of the polity is felt to be poor on many counts. As a ground of discontent, "loss of empire" has played a much smaller part than many foreigners imagine. Whatever the subconscious, psychological reactions may be, Britons explicitly show few regrets over the end of empire in Africa or the Indian subcontinent. Loss of status as a world power is considered a more serious matter. In 1945 toward the close of Britain's heroic performance in the war against Hitler, Churchill could still appear to meet with Stalin and Roosevelt on a plane of equality, but the situation is very different today. A failure to adjust to her reduced circumstances in a world of the two superpowers has troubled the sense of national purpose. The dissolving Commonwealth has not provided a substitute role, nor has the continuation of the wartime alliance with the United States. The third option, entering Europe, gave rise to the humiliations of de Gaulle's vetoes and then to the no less painful agonies that accompanied acceptance.

---

[3] *Government and Opposition,* 1 (October 1965), 135–136.

[4] Malcolm Muggeridge, "England, Whose England?" *Encounter,* 21 (July 1963), 14.

[5] Patrick O'Donovan, "Who Do We Think We Are?" *The Observer* (London), June 27, 1971.

Economic Failure

Dissatisfaction with the performance of the polity, however, has been more sharply focused on economic policy than on foreign or colonial policy. In the view of politicians, experts, and leaders of opinion, the British economic record since World War II has been deeply disappointing and well below what it could have been. In his budget speech of March 30, 1971, the Conservative Chancellor of the Exchequer reflected this judgment, placing the blame—it should be noted—on previous Conservative as well as Labour Governments:

> For many years, under one Government and another, the economic perfor-
> mance of our country has been poor. Over these years we have become accus-
> tomed to unfavorable comparisons with other industrial countries—slow
> growth, recurring balance of payments weakness, faster-than-average inflation,
> a low rate of investment, a falling share in world exports, and increasingly bad
> industrial relations . . .
>
> If we are realistic we should recognize that unless there is a change in the trend
> —a change not only compared with the last five or six years, but with the trend
> over the last two decades and more—the prospect is that by 1980 our standard
> of living in this country will have fallen considerably behind that of most of the
> countries of western Europe.[6]

The economic problem, which centers on the question of more rapid growth, may be a problem without a solution. Conceivably there could be objective conditions that ineluctably condemn the British economy to a performance inferior to that of other advanced countries. If this were true, it would be a mistake to regard the inability of public policy to improve economic performance as an indication of failure in the political system. Political leaders and other students of the question, amateur and professional, however, have largely rejected this argument. Party spokesmen and prospective Prime Ministers have persisted in perceiving the problem as one that could be solved in some sense by political and governmental means.

Certain broad comparative reasons support their belief. In the first place, the British economy turned in a superb record of performance during World War II. This was the Britain that invented radar and the jet engine, built the Mulberries—huge floating docks used during the Normandy invasion—and, although starting far behind Germany, reached a much higher level of mobilization. In those years Britain excelled in the very spheres of material production in which today she is compared so unfavorably with many other European countries. Her record was a story not of slow-moving traditionalism, but of a highly competent, adaptable, modernizing people who showed supreme ability in that most modern of activities, total war. "You defeated us," said Albert Speer, Hitler's Minister for Armaments,

---

[6]814 *H. C. Deb.* 1358–1359 (30 March 1971).

"because you made total war and we did not." The basis of this economic achievement was political, as British leaders attest by their frequent efforts to recapture "the spirit of Dunkirk."

In the second place, the economies with which the British economy compares unfavorably are in the same broad stage of development. We are not comparing Britain with countries in the early stages of industrial "takeoff," but with countries that have been industrializing for more than a hundred years and that have—this is the rub—reached and surpassed the British standard of living. In 1939 at the outbreak of World War II the real product per head in Britain was the highest in the world, except for the United States. Then after the war the other advanced countries moved forward rapidly. Appendix A gives comparative figures for selected countries of Western Europe. Whether the basis is the growth rate of gross national product or the growth rate of gross national product per capita, Britain ranks at the bottom of the list. By 1970 in product per person, Britain had fallen behind not only the United States, Canada, Australia and New Zealand, but also among Western European countries: Sweden, Germany, Switzerland, France, Denmark, Norway, the Netherlands, and Belgium, in that order. By the end of the next decade it seems likely that Britain will also have been surpassed by Finland, Japan, and perhaps even Italy and Austria.

Some critics ridicule the "international G.N.P. race," and, no doubt, a blind effort to increase production, without regard to what is produced, who gets the increment, and what the side effects are, can be self-defeating. On the other hand, without improvements in productivity there is little chance of advances in economic welfare. Where economic growth lags, hospitals and schools do not get built and real wages stagnate. When we recall that Britain was one of the pioneers in constructing the welfare state, it comes as a shock to see how poorly she compares with the other states of Western Europe in this respect. During the postwar period Britain has ranked below both Germany and France in percentage of national income spent on social welfare and, in recent years, below all members of the European community. To be sure, higher welfare expenditures are not identical with a higher standard of living, since they can be more than offset by low wages. In the comparison of Britain with the continental countries, however, this factor does not greatly change the picture. In hourly earnings of manual workers (both male and female) in manufacturing industry Britain does stand above Italy and France, but falls below the other four members of the Common Market—Luxembourg, Germany, the Netherlands, and Belgium, in that order. As we shall see in more detail when we look at the pattern of policy of contemporary Britain, there are urgent needs, public and private, that could utilize a greater output of material goods and services.

Britain's industrial supremacy in the long past, the prodigies of her war economy, and the lead in recent times by countries with variously structured economies support the presumption widely and strongly shared in Britain that if her people went about the matter in the right way, they too could have the high, continuing rate of economic growth required by their public and private needs. To say in what sense the roots of the problem are political and how the failure to take such action is a fault of the political system is best left to the more detailed discussion later. Yet the general direction in which analysis leads will be briefly indicated at this point.

It will not be denied that there are specifically economic causes that contribute to Britain's problem. No doubt her position as a massive importer and exporter puts her in an exposed position in the international economy, which is made still more delicate by the use of sterling as a reserve currency by many other countries. As a result, Britain must often take steps to depress her internal economy in order to protect her balance of payments. Also, looking at her problems in the context of comparative economic development brings out important differences between Britain and other countries. Because she was the first to industrialize, Britain does have, relative to most continental countries, a smaller sector of agriculture and self-employment whose resources can be drawn into more efficient employment in large-scale industry.

Yet we can readily conceive that these problems might have been dealt with satisfactorily if it had not been for other difficulties, which are in essence political. One set of major difficulties was related to the new group politics, which emerged powerfully after the war and to which later chapters will devote a good deal of attention. In the new politics the votes of groups of consumers were pursued by the two major parties in an intense and unrelenting competition in promises of prospective benefits. As a result, consumption, both public and private, was encouraged and the proportion of national product devoted to investment depressed, long-run economic growth being sacrificed for the sake of the immediate benefits of the welfare state and private consumption. The new group politics was also involved in the inability of Governments to control the cost-push element in Britain's chronic inflation, especially in very recent years, the pushing up of wage costs by trade union pressure. Unable to reach agreements that would provide the necessary restraint, Governments of both parties have been forced to resort to severely deflationary measures, with the result that for perhaps one-half of the years since the war the operation of the economy has been deliberately depressed by public policy. Under these conditions of "stop-and-go" economic policy, economic growth could hardly fail to lag.

The failures of economic policy are serious in their own right. They are also felt and perceived as a sign and an example of a general loss of governmental effectiveness. The values of modernity charge the polity with major tasks in controlling the environment external to the political system, of which the economy is only one major sector. Failures of economic policy therefore suggest a loss of capacity to control social change in general and a loss of grip on the nation's destiny. The problem of economic policy raises this larger question of a decline in the power of the polity to adapt, to change, to cope, to solve problems that was displayed by the long success story of Britain in modern times.

Bentham and Burke

As de Jouvenel's comments suggested, British excellence in the art of government is an old story. If, therefore, we are to understand the reasons for that excellence in the past and to perceive what basic changes may have taken place and whether these account for recent deficiencies, an explanation with an appropriate time dimension must be sought. In the vast literature about British government and politics, a familiar approach promises to have the explanatory power that is required. Broadly, this approach points to the integration of both modern and traditional elements in the British polity as the grounds for its achievement. The emphasis—to borrow the title of a superb study of modernization in India—is upon "the modernity of tradition."[7]

The line of analysis is twofold: The branch emphasizing the contribution of modernity may be called the Benthamite hypothesis; that emphasizing the contribution of tradition, the Burkean hypothesis. The former directs attention to precisely those elements which constitute the cultural premises of modernity, rationalism and voluntarism. It finds in the attitudes and structures deriving from these premises the factors explaining both the responsiveness and effectiveness of British government. It is the straightforward modernist view that the liberated intelligence is a sufficient basis for political order and progress. The free marketplace of ideas tends to winnow the sound from the unsound among proposals for public policy. Election of governments gives society the means for making sure sound proposals are registered at the seat of power. The trained intelligence of the bureaucrat in turn refines these proposals so as to solve the problems originally giving rise to criticism and reform. Indeed, intelligence, whether in or out of government, is the principal and sufficient motor of the whole process of adaptation and improvement. If modernity has faults, the remedy is more modernity.

To this British version of the political theory of the Enlightenment, the Burkean hypothesis represents a skeptical but constructive reaction. In contrast with intelligence, this view points to the role of sentiment in binding men into political communities and supporting the structures by which they concert public action. Tradition is necessary to stabilize men's sense of decency. Regardless of the extent of the suffrage, a viable polity requires strong and able leadership in the form of a governing class. Tradition, hierarchy, community—these are the elements stressed in the Burkean hypothesis. They create lasting behavioral solidarities, from the "little platoons" to the great "establishments," which at once satisfy the human heart and provide a basis for effective governance. Nor is their existence incompatible with reform. On the contrary, Burke was the first British political philosopher to state explicitly and systematically the argument for continuous adaptation of public policy, making the case

---

[7]Lloyd and Susanne Rudolph, *The Modernity of Tradition: Political Development in India* (Chicago, 1967).

for reform as a normal means of both conservation and improvement.

The use of this dual approach can be illustrated by two periods of major achievement in British political development. The first is the great age of·reform in the early part of the nineteenth century, when Britain fundamentally altered both her political system and her economic policy, setting for the world a pioneering example of peaceful, progressive reform. The second centers on the first half of the present century, when in response to the strains of industrialism and the rise of the working class, a period of social reform was inaugurated that ultimately led to the construction of a welfare state and managed economy—again by peaceful, parliamentary means.

The Great Age of Reform

As the record of Europe in the past and of developing countries today shows, the potential for large-scale collective violence within modernizing countries is very high. One of the particularly critical periods of transition is the onset of industrialization. Even now when the experience of many countries has made it a familiar phase of economic development, industrialization imposes severe strains on a society. All the greater and harder to control were the dangers faced by Britain when, first among nations she, so to speak, blundered into the Industrial Revolution. Again and again during the forty years after Waterloo observers foresaw the imminent outbreak of revolution. In 1817 a Swiss historian and economist visited England and was terrified by the spectacle. He predicted that unless economic development was drastically slowed down, society would pass through a series of crises ending in the destruction of civilization by a mob of angry workers.[8] Writing in 1844 of the horrors of working-class life in England's huge urban centers, the young Friedrich Engels declared that the transformation of England since 1760 had been as great as that between Bourbon France of 1789 and the France of his day. Declaring that "prophecy is nowhere so easy as in England," he foresaw a war of the poor against the rich that would be "the bloodiest ever waged."[9]

Tension centered on the great increase in numbers of two new classes created by economic modernization: the commercial and industrial capitalists and the wage-earning proletariat. While the industrial working class excited fear in conservatives and hope in socialists, it was hardly well enough organized or well enough led to be a serious revolutionary threat by itself. But the industrial working class as the potential followers of middle-class revolutionaries on the model of the French insurrectionists presented a far more formidable threat against the entrenched power of aristocracy.

---

[8]Charles de Sismondi, quoted in Elie Halévy, *England in 1815* (London, 1949), p. 382.

[9]Frederick Engels, *The Condition of the Working-Class in England in 1844* (London, 1950), p. 296.

The issues were political and economic and in both respects touched interests of fundamental importance. The political issue consisted in the fact that the aristocracy and gentry had a virtual monopoly on the formal instruments of authority in the state, the main seat and symbol of this oligarchic system being the unreformed House of Commons. The issue of economic policy arose from the restrictive burdens of the mercantile system, which in the eyes of traders and manufacturers increasingly meant the Corn Laws, the tariff protecting the production of grain and thereby the economic base of the landed classes. The essence of the story is that in the upheaval of 1832 the landed classes voluntarily agreed to share their authority with the commercial and industrial classes in a reformed Parliament, which, fulfilling the gloomy predictions of its opponents, proceeded in the next few years to whittle down and finally repeal the Corn Laws, establishing free trade as a pillar of public policy. In spite of great turmoil and some violence, the transition to a liberal polity suitable for an industrializing society and designed effectively to promote further economic modernization was accomplished.

Britain's free institutions—free, that is, in comparison with the typical regime of the day—could claim a large share of the credit. Overwhelmingly, the initiative for reform came from outside established government circles. A relatively high level of freedom of speech, press, and association was therefore indispensable to the spread of reform ideas throughout the society, while a powerful elected legislature, biased as it may have been, provided linkage to the seats of authority. One of the most striking changes in the politics of the early nineteenth century was the vast proliferation of voluntary associations formed for political purposes. Notable examples can be found in the late eighteenth century, such as the various bodies aiming at parliamentary reform. But these earlier associations were failures and during the wars with revolutionary France were brutally suppressed. From the 1820s, however, this new kind of pressure group became a power in British politics. Among them were the political unions agitating for reform before 1832, the London Workingmen's Association, the various Chartist groups, the Short Time Committees for the Ten Hours Bill in the 1840s, and that great Victorian exemplar of the reformist pressure group, the Anti-Corn Law League, which, founded in 1839, triumphed in 1846. While political parties already flourished in Parliament and in the active political community, it was less they than the new pressure groups that were the source of reform in policy.

In the case of free trade and repeal of the Corn Laws, the sequence of events is a classical illustration of how free institutions and the free marketplace of ideas are supposed to work. Properly the story begins with Adam Smith, who diagnosed the burdens of economic growth of the old protective system and bequeathed to later generations an inclusive but practical scheme of reform. Practical intellectuals like him, mainly economists, continued to urge the case in books and in the press and before committees of Parliament. In time they were joined by merchants and manufacturers—in 1820 there took place a famous meeting of London merchants at which they declared themselves in favor of free trade—and gradually some M.P.s and even Ministers began to relax their defense of the protective system. The organization of the Anti-Corn Law League was the last phase. It used all the devices that pressure politics has made familiar since that time: mass meetings, petitioning, intensive lobbying of Ministers and legislators, a huge publication effort, intervention in elections to support friends and defeat enemies. Finally, the parties and their leaders began to respond. As might be expected the first were the Liberals. But it was the Conservative Leader Sir Robert Peel, elected to serve "the sacred cause of protection," who, in a reversal of position that set one of the most fruitful precedents of modern politics, led the way to its abolition in 1846. "I will not withhold the homage which is due to the progress of reason and truth," he said, "by denying that my opinions on the subject of protection have undergone a change."[10]

Tocqueville on England

This modernist account, while true, is a little one-dimensional and needs a few Burkean qualifications. It will be helpful to look for guidance to an acute foreign observer. During the nineteenth century the success of Britain in avoiding revolution, enacting progressive reform, and achieving unprecedented prosperity and dominance as a world power was a source of painful, but often penetrating, reflection by thoughtful Frenchmen. Undoubtedly the weightiest of them was Alexis de Tocqueville, whose *Old Regime and the French Revolution* (1856), a study in which he frequently contrasts France and England, has shown the same enduring value as his *Democracy in America* (1835–1840).

If we turn to de Tocqueville's analysis, our attention is directed not only to Britain's free institutions, but also to the character of the men who held power under them. In explaining the tragedy of the French Revolution, his recurring theme is the contrast between the upper classes of France and England. In medieval times, he observes, both countries had similar institutions, including a Parliament of estates and a class of nobles. In both, the nobility performed important functions, especially as leaders and rulers in their localities and in the national Parliament. As the two nations moved into modern times, however, their paths diverged. In England the feudal aristocracy maintained its political function, developing into a modern governing class and continuing to exercise its leadership through Parliament and in the countryside. In France, on the other hand, this transformation was not accomplished, the aristocracy being loaded with privileges but deprived of effective authority in great matters of state. The medieval Parliament, in effect, ceased to exist; the last meeting of the Estates-General took place in 1614, while the function of governing under the Bourbon monarchy was vested in a bureaucracy ramifying from Paris. But a bureaucracy owing its authority only to its official status could not perform the essentially political function of a modern governing class. The English aristocracy and gentry, however, retained their contact with other classes, their

---

[10]83 *H. C. Deb.* 69, Third Series (22 January 1846).

rule in Parliament, and their political function, shaping the course of public affairs, guiding opinion, and lending authority to new ideas. In turn, they were not confronted with the rage for equality that afflicted France, but, on the contrary, maintained their ancient prestige in a highly deferential nation.

This traditionalist model of British politics lights up important aspects of the great age of reform. While the agitation for the act of 1832 was strongly urged by classes poorly represented in the old Parliament, there was also in Parliament a core of aristocratic advocates of reform that had a continuous history going back half a century. They had kept the cause alive and lent it their prestige through the long years of repression. A youthful member of this earlier aristocratic movement became the Earl Grey, who as Prime Minister carried the Reform Act of 1832. Moreover, his Cabinet was equally aristocratic and boasted a larger total acreage of land than any preceding body of Ministers. The foreboding aroused by this step toward popular government must not be underestimated. Even to the young Gladstone, as he later recalled, there was "something of the Anti-Christ in the Reform Act of 1832." Yet the measure was shaped and forwarded by a body of men who commanded the very peaks of power and prestige and whose political, economic, and social interests were deeply identified with the established order.

Lord Grey was confident that the reform would renew what he regarded as the "natural alliance" between the Whig party and "the people." While his hopes for a partisan monopoly were dashed, in a larger sense his expectations were overwhelmingly confirmed. The new electorate of middle-class and lower-middle-class voters—far from sending representatives of their own class and economic interests to dominate the new House of Commons—preferred men of landed wealth and members of the aristocracy and the gentry. In the Parliament that finally repealed the Corn Laws, only 17 percent of the members were businessmen. Among those who voted for repeal as well as those who opposed it, the landed classes greatly predominated.

Looking ahead, we may note that the deference that the middle class had shown to the aristocracy was similarly displayed by the working class toward the upper classes as the franchise was gradually broadened in later years. Recording his impressions of British politics in 1908, A. L. Lowell observed that "the upper classes in England rule today, not by means of the political privileges which they retain, but by the sufferance of the great mass of the people and as trustees for its benefit." Moreover, he continued,

> the sentiment of deference or snobbishness becomes, if anything, stronger as the social scale descends. The workingman, when not provoked by an acute grievance to vote for a trade union candidate, prefers a man with a title, and thus the latest extensions of the franchise have rather strengthened than weakened the hold of the governing class upon public life.[11]

---

[11]Lowell, *op. cit.*, II, p. 508.

Hardly second to its governing class, a further reason often cited for the stability and effectiveness of British government is its pragmatic style of politics, the contrast being drawn with the ideological style of French, German, and other continental polities. Tocqueville's comparative analysis also puts forward an explanation of this crucial characteristic. In his view perhaps the most fateful consequence of the political abdication of the French aristocracy was the resulting vacuum of leadership. In this situation, toward the middle of the eighteenth century, the radical intellectuals of the Enlightenment—the philosophes—took the lead in forming public opinion. Lacking any contact with practical politics as well as the guidance of a true political class, these men of letters believed and taught that a new social and political order could be constructed "by simple elementary rules deriving from the exercise of human reason and natural law."[12] The results were violence, disorder, and ultimately dictatorship.

This same reasoning explains why Britain in contrast with France produced not radical but practical intellectuals, such as the economists who demonstrated the vices of the mercantile system and the Benthamite reformers who conceived most of the great measures of reform that have given the period its fame. Not only did free institutions give them access to the seats of power, but the traditions of the governing class made it open to ideas for change. William Pitt himself, before the crisis of the war with revolutionary France made him into the stern enemy of reform, befriended Adam Smith and was receptive to his ideas.

The free institutions of modernity were indispensable to the British achievement of avoiding revolution, admitting new classes to power in the state, and adjusting public policy to the needs of an expanding economy. Yet these institutions were balanced by strong premodern and aristocratic elements. Or rather they were integrated with these vigorous survivals. The elected Parliament functioned in a social and economic context that assured the dominance of the traditional elites. But these elites themselves harbored modern attitudes that prepared them to accept and even champion ideas of reform.

Indeed it is wrong to contrast even in this dialectic way British free institutions and traditional survivals. For British liberty itself had a twofold character, making it at once modern and traditional. It included the brisk modern liberty of the free marketplace—in thought as in trade—where merit, sharply judged on utilitarian grounds, gained the day, and the contest was open to all. At the same time British liberty meant protection and support for standing in the old ways. Liberty to innovate and to rise in the world survived, because it was modulated by imitation of the past and disdain for excessive mobility.

---

[12]Alexis de Tocqueville, *The Old Regime and the French Revolution* (New York, 1955), p. 139.

Founding the Welfare State

The second episode relates to the rise of socialism and the early phases of the welfare state. Resulting from the dual thrust of modernization toward industrialization and participation, these events have been paralleled in all European countries. On one hand, economic development brings into existence the typical class structure of the capitalist economy, confronting managers and owners with a growing urban proletariat. On the other hand, the democratic ethic is propagated in a form that legitimates not only demands for political equality, but also economic equality.

The potential for self-destructive conflict is evident, and late-nineteenth- and twentieth-century history richly documents it. The conflict of classes makes effective government difficult at a time when the growing complexities of a mature economy require even more government intervention. If the conflict centers on the clash of two large class-based parties, it raises the danger that strong ideological positions may so sharply separate the contenders that they will not feel it safe to tolerate the peaceful alternation in power of the democratic method. Or if, as is more usual, the class conflict proliferates into a multiparty system, the task of constructing a stable and steady majority may be virtually impossible. Yet the need to plan and control the economy in its internal and domestic aspects mounts relentlessly, requiring strong government and coherent policy. The interwar history of most European countries, dominated by the rise of highly organized and militant extremes on Left and Right and the massive conflict of communism and fascism within nations and between nations, vividly illustrates the tragic possibilities.

In comparison with the other countries studied in this volume, Britain handled these problems with outstanding success. This is not to deny that there were ugly moments. The general strike of 1926 brought out more than two and a half million workers for nine days in what was taken to be an effort to coerce the government by direct action. Yet the conflict did not lead to violence and, as the British never fail to remind one, at Plymouth the strikers and policemen whiled away the hours by playing football together. Shortly afterward understandings were reached between employers and unions, which in effect made the strike obsolete as a means of industrial conflict—at any rate until the recent rise of the unofficial walkout.

The culminating success came after World War II. In 1945 the Labour party took power, backed by a huge parliamentary majority and committed to far-reaching social and economic reform. In the succeeding years the essential structures of the welfare state and managed economy were created. Viewed in historical perspective, the political success was impressive. A vast industrial proletariat mobilized by economic modernization had been effectively integrated into the polity, while the needs of this class, transformed into practical governmental programs, had given drive and direction to a comprehensive reconstruction of policy.

There is a simple Benthamite way of telling this story and explaining what happened. Its main explanatory variable is the practical good sense of the British workingman who uses politics to improve his conditions of work and life under advanced industrialism. In the first phase interest centers on the skilled workman whose unions developed rapidly after the middle of the nineteenth century. His purposes in politics were concrete and practical—they were called "the interests of labour"—and related to such things as the discriminatory master and servant law, which concerned the individual workman, or the burdens on trade union activity arising from legislation or judicial decision. The Trades Union Congress (T.U.C.), founded in 1868, and affiliating unions organized on a nationwide basis served as a lobby in relation to the central government. The two big parties, the Liberals and the Conservatives, competing for the votes of the skilled urban workmen enfranchised by the act of 1867, were modestly responsive to these pressures. The period provides a nice illustration of the Benthamite principle of "dislocability," that is, the way in which representative government enables the voter to control the representative by threatening to switch his support in order to defeat —or "dislocate"—him.

A second phase was entered with the rise of the "new unionism" of the 1880s. The unskilled workers that were members of these organizations had greater need for government intervention to protect their interests, and consequently we find the first serious efforts to form an independent party. Yet Lib-Lab collaboration dominated the years until World War I, producing such achievements as the vast political and social reform program of the Liberal government elected in 1906. Finally, however, as Liberal support for further reform faltered, especially in the straitened circumstances of postwar capitalism, the working class was obliged to turn to a more radical alternative. In 1918 the Labour party, founded mainly by trade unions at the turn of the century, officially adopted a socialist ideology and in the following years won increasing support among the working class.

This party was a very different sort of political formation from the small, loose parties, dominated by their parliamentary leaders, that had arisen in the great age of reform. Labour was a modern mass party enrolling millions of members, both directly through individual memberships and indirectly through trade union affiliation. It was strongly cohesive in its behavior out of Parliament as well as within. Above all, it was the source of the program that, item for item, was carried out by the Labour government of 1945–1951. If pressure groups had been the source of ideas in that earlier period, in this instance the source was party. Like the economy itself, the polity had moved from an individualist to a collectivist phase, party government representing the new instrument by which the democratic will was made effective. At the same time, the old disciplines of Cabinet government were strengthened and put in the service of coherent policy making, necessitated by the growing responsibilities for managing the economy.

Behind this success story does lie the practical, good sense of the British workingman. But how do we account for that? "Practical good sense" is not something we can take for granted, as the comparative study of socialism in various countries immediately reveals.

Schumpeter on England

How to account for British success was precisely the central problem for Joseph A. Schumpeter, an eminent Austrian economist of the last generation, when he summed up "almost forty years' thought, observation and reflection on the subject of socialism" in his classic, *Capitalism, Socialism and Democracy* (1942). He looked at the development of socialism broadly in the whole European context. But his special concern was with the contrast between Germany on the one hand and Britain on the other. The crucial difference was in the ideology and rhetoric of the two socialist movements. In Germany Marxism with its corrosive doctrine of capitalist exploitation and its prophecy of ultimate violent revolution supplied the beliefs, values, and expressive symbolism of the Social Democratic party, by 1914 the largest socialist party in the world. To be sure, many of the party's leaders were by then dedicated democrats who, even in imperial Germany, would have been ready to accept step-by-step reformism. But these facts were not admitted publicly in official utterance. On the contrary, the party clung to "a Marxist phraseology of unsurpassed virulence, pretending to fight ruthless exploitation and a state that was the slave of slave drivers."[13]

One result was to intensify the hostility toward the socialists of the other parties, already less than eager to share power with them. Hence, when social reform did come, it came from above, so to speak, as in Bismarck's social security legislation, and not from a political base that included the working class. Moreover, after World War I, when the Social Democrats did finally assume their place as a party of government, rather than revolution, the old patterns of intransigence and alienation were perpetuated by a massive Communist party. Thus the fateful polarization of politics under the Weimar Republic, which helped prepare the way for Nazism, had roots in the spirit and direction given to German socialism by Marxism many years before.

In contrast, Schumpeter emphasizes, British socialism was Fabian rather than Marxist, meaning that it took its character from the writings of the small group of intellectuals who founded the Fabian Society in 1884. While the Fabians generally accepted the central doctrine of socialism, namely, the common ownership of the means of production, they also laid great stress upon step-by-step measures of reform and, most important, upon the necessity and possibility of achieving their ends by peaceful, democratic means. That the new party of the working class adopted this style of politics was not because it had no other choice. In the later years of the nineteenth century in Britain, as in other countries, many varieties of socialism were being offered to the masses. The Social Democratic Federation, founded three years before the Fabians, was distinctively Marxist and for years struggled with litttle success to win over opinion and gain a following.

The influence of intellectuals is not to be underestimated. In a real sense, whether Fabian or Marxist, they were the teachers of the working class as it

---

[13]Joseph A. Schumpeter, *Capitalism, Socialism and Democracy* (New York, 1942), p. 342.

emerged into political consciousness and had the power, within limits, to make or mar their students. Yet if we are to understand why the British working class were more inclined to respond to their Fabian than their Marxist teachers, we cannot fail to take into account the long-established, pragmatic, and nonideological style of British political culture. Moreover, these attitudes, supporting the conviction that free institutions could be made to work, had been greatly reinforced by the achievement of the great age of reform itself. The power of these precedents is made clear by Bernard Shaw, one of the original Fabians, in a later comment on what the society set out to do:

> It was in 1885 that the Fabian Society, amid the jeers of the catastrophists, turned its back on the barricades and made up its mind to turn heroic defeat into prosaic success. We set ourselves two definite tasks: first, to provide a parliamentary program for a Prime Minister converted to Socialism as Peel was converted to Free Trade; and second, to make it as easy and matter-of-course for the ordinary respectable Englishman to be a Socialist as to be a Liberal or a Conservative.[14]

In a country exceptionally prone to follow tradition, the tradition of an effective modern polity was an important condition for the continued effectiveness of that polity. Moreover, structures that had shaped the experience producing this tradition continued to function. In what is almost an echo of Tocqueville, Schumpeter attributes primary importance to Britain's governing classes. Discussing what enables democracy to work, he cites as "the first condition . . . the human material of politics—the people who man the party machines, are elected to serve in parliament, rise to cabinet office." If this human material is to be of sufficiently high quality, "the only effective guarantee is in the existence of a social stratum itself a product of a severely selective process, that takes to politics as a matter of course."[15] This stratum should be "neither too exclusive nor too easily accessible for the outsider." It should draw on circles whose members have shown ability in fields of private endeavor but should also endow them with a specifically political tradition giving them a professional code and a common fund of views. What this elite contributes to government is emphatically not expertise or specialized knowledge, as with the bureaucrat, but, on the contrary, the prime political ability "to handle men." Nor is this an ability that comes as easily to the modern businessman as to the aristocrat.

England, according to Schumpeter, had such an elite, which "after having proved itself able to avoid an analogon to the French Revolution and to eliminate the dangers threatening from dear bread . . . continued to know how to manage social situations of increasing difficulty, and how to surrender with some grace."[16] Like France in Tocqueville's analysis, however, Germany failed to develop such a

---

[14]Bernard Shaw (ed.), *Fabian Essays.* Jubilee edn. (London, 1948), p. xxxiii.

[15]Schumpeter, *op. cit.,* pp. 290–291.

[16]*Ibid.,* p. 321.

political class. Under the empire the government, meaning by that the large and well-trained bureaucracy, took the initiative in matters of social policy. During the Weimar Republic (1919–1933), although politicians, members of Parliament, and Ministers were overwhelmingly honest, reasonable, and conscientious, most of them were otherwise "distinctly below par." In Germany it was still true that "ability and energy spurned the political career. And there was no class or group whose members looked upon politics as their predestined career."[17]

The important consequence of these contrasting conditions was not that in one country concessions were made to working-class demands while in the other they were refused. Indeed, in matters of social security imperial Germany was years ahead of Britain. The important point—paradoxically a tragic fact—is that these benefits came from above, being designed and introduced by the bureaucracy. Not that in Britain the initiative for reform came wholly or even largely from the working class and its organizations. Indeed, the Liberal Government that came to power in 1906 was on many points more innovative and progressive than the Labour party of the day.

The crucial fact was that again, as brought out in Tocqueville's analysis, the British political class maintained contact with the "other classes." While Bismarck did promote real and substantial social reforms, he also attempted to suppress the socialist movement in a twelve-year-long battle, which succeeded only in creating a chasm between the established leadership and a large part of the working class. This was from 1878 to 1890. At about the same time, Disraeli was forging that long-lasting alliance between an upper-class leadership and a lower-class following that was to make the Conservative party dominant in the age of democracy. His government (1874–1880) put through a program of social reform, modest by our standards, but remarkable for its time; and between 1886 and 1900 the Conservatives won a majority of the two-party vote in four successive general elections. This could not have been done without massive support from the working class. After Disraeli's death, the London *Times* remarked: "In the inarticulate mass of the English populace, he discerned the Conservative workingman as the sculptor perceives the angel prisoned in the block of marble."

During the interwar period and on to the present the Conservative party, the party *par excellence* of the governing class, continued the work of Disraeli and Lloyd George in developing social reform to meet the ills of industrialism. Moreover, as the Labour party took the place of the Liberals as the other of the two major parties, more and more young men who were marked by unmistakable signs of the English upper classes—with regard to speech, dress, manners, and education —appeared in Labour's ranks. Indeed, by 1950 Winchester, one of the more distinguished and exclusive "public" schools, had educated all three Ministers who presented the Labour Government's budget of that year, a coincidence of which the Ministers showed that they were mindful by presenting to the school library

---

[17] *Ibid.*, p. 291.

a specially bound volume of *Hansard* "as a memorial of an unique event never likely to be repeated."

In the political development of European countries two periods of special danger have been the transition from an aristocratic to a liberal polity and the transition from a liberal to a collectivist polity. Sometimes these transitions have brought tragic violence, and sometimes they have been aborted. The previous analysis of the success of Britain in accomplishing the transitions brings out in broad outline how the integration of modernist and traditionalist elements might account for the achievement of British government. We need to be cautious in trying to summarize the reasons. They are deeply embedded in history, and history, because it is concrete, has a way of being very complex. Keeping this caution in mind, we can say that the theme running through the previous analysis has been the union of hierarchy and liberty. Both the Burkean and the Benthamite hypothesis are necessary to the explanation. This does not mean that the separate accomplishments of each factor can be totalled together. The essence is that, contradictory as they may seem, hierarchy and liberty have been interdependent. Whig lords, whose arrogance was beyond compare, were yet the authors and defenders of Whig liberty. British trade unionists threw off the old subordination of their forefathers and fought doggedly for their rights against powerful interests. Yet they also knew how to accept the leadership and authority necessary for successful long-term organization. In British political development, modern and traditional forces have often been opposed. But the more durable truth has been their interdependence. As Benjamin Constant remarked almost 200 years ago: "England is the country where on the one hand the rights of the individual are most carefully safeguarded, and on the other, class distinctions are most respected."[18]

Cabinet Government and Party Government

The role of political elites, while properly given great attention by students of British government, is inseparable from the institutions within which these elites operate. The two principal institutions of the British polity are cabinet government and party government. If we ask how policy is made responsive to the wishes of the political community, the key structure is party government. Based upon the competition of two strongly cohesive, programmatic parties, party government is held to promote responsiveness in two ways. First, because of party unity the voter can hold responsible the candidates of the majority party for what government does when that party is in power. If the party he supports wins a majority, it will act together in the exercise of authority, presenting to the electorate a highly visible object of support or attack. The system makes government responsible by creating a linkage

---

[18]Quoted in *Encounter*, 21 (July 1963), p. 19.

between the casting of a vote and the acts of government such that voters can exercise ultimate control.

Second, party government also makes government responsive in terms of program. Each of the competing formations presents a statement of the politics it proposes to carry out if it wins the majority. This enables the electorate to control not only who will govern, but in broad outline what they will do. Moreover, since the parties are not the mere Tweedledum and Tweedledee of "ins" versus "outs," but represent significantly different approaches to the common purpose, the respective programs will have coherence. This is important for the implementation as well as the making of policy, since the coherence of a government's program means that the massive, far-flung, interdependent activities of the modern state will be directed toward compatible and mutually supporting goals. In contrast a government that, as in the United States, is based on a system of parties with loose cohesion and without unifying principles will tend to produce a series of "casual majorities," whose objectives may be inconsistent with one another and shaped by no deliberately thought-out view of policy as a whole.

Two-party competition, unity among partisans in the legislature and executive, programs based on distinctive political outlooks—these are the main ingredients of the doctrine of party government. Its consequences are not only to make government democratically responsive, but also to create the conditions of policy making and execution highly favorable to effective problem solving. The party program converted into a mandate by victory at the polls provides a coherent basis for policy making, while the steady support of partisans ensures government leaders of the legislative power necessary to carry out their mandate and—perhaps even more important—assures them of the continuous and prolonged support indispensable if policy is to be reflectively matured and adapted to the environment over a period of time. Finally, all along the line from the formation of policy through its implementation, a steady partisan majority guided by a coherent program gives leaders the base from which to resist the distorting demands of pressure groups.

So stated, party government could conceivably be adapted to various constitutional structures, whether presidential or parliamentary. Its main principles have seemed sufficiently transferable to generate a long and lively controversy among American political scientists as to whether party government should (and could) be brought to these shores. But party government obviously fits best with the constitutional structures of its country of origin. From the constitutional viewpoint, the key element in the British solution to reconciling democracy and effectiveness is cabinet government.

In contrast with presidential government, cabinet government means that the heads of the executive departments and the chief figure among them, the Prime Minister, sit in the legislature and are responsible to it in the sense that they must not only account for their actions to the legislature, but also resign from office if the legislature insists. This norm of the parliamentary responsibility of Ministers has, however, characterized British government at times in the past when, in comparison with recent generations, the Cabinet and Prime Minister had far less influence over Parliament and could depend upon it with far less confidence for support in legislation and expressions of confidence. The development of the cohesive, strongly led political party in the collectivist era has probably had as much effect upon this aspect of the British constitution as the constitution has had upon the shape and structure of party.

Nevertheless, cabinet government obviously adds to the efficacy of party government. It avoids the temptations of conflict and the opportunities of deadlock present when the chief executive and the legislature are elected separately, as under the American system. The leader whose party wins a majority becomes Prime Minister and in turn chooses from among his principal lieutenants in the parliamentary party the members of his Cabinet. This body is the chief executive, and although it is plural rather than unitary, the primacy of the Prime Minister and the norm of collective responsibility as well as the common acceptance of party program and principles provide the solidarity necessary for coherent government. Moreover, including in the deliberations of this chief executive persons who are also in charge of the various departments of state means that the knowledge and experience of the administrator are directly worked into policy making.

Such is the conventional model of party and cabinet government that is commonly used to explain the success of the British polity in combining responsive and effective government. It is an impressive case supported by long experience. If recent years have seriously disrupted the record of performance, we must inquire whether this familiar analysis of how the system works is still correct or whether changes, both internal and external to the political system, have finally rendered it out of date. The questions deriving from these premises will constitute a framework for the later chapters concerned with particular sectors of the British system. The discussion of parties, Parliament, the Cabinet, Civil Service, and policy will focus on the working of party government and cabinet government today.

The Bipolar Conception of Authority

The institutions of party government and cabinet government, like the interrelationships of followers and elites, also illustrate the modernity of tradition. Cabinet government, with its norms defining the authority of the Prime Minister and the responsibility of Ministers, is an institution that has grown up in fairly recent times to meet the needs of democratic Britain in the age of the welfare state and the managed economy. Yet in crucial respects this highly modern structure depends upon attitudes deriving from a medieval past. In a brilliant essay L. S. Amery, a Conservative politician and thinker of the past generation, has expounded the dual nature of the British conception of authority.[19] This conception he distinguishes from the Continental view of representative government, which derives from the

---

[19] L. S. Amery, *Thoughts on the Constitution* (London, 1947).

French Revolution and which makes political power a delegation from the individual citizen through the legislature to an executive dependent on the legislature. In contrast, the British constitution, today as in the distant past, has two basic elements: an initiating, directing, energizing element—nowadays the Cabinet—and a checking, criticizing element—nowadays the House of Commons and especially the Opposition. Given this notion of authority, it follows that "Parliament is not, and never has been, a legislature, in the sense of a body specially and primarily empowered to make laws." The function of legislation is mainly exercised by Ministers, while the principal task of Parliament is to secure full discussion and ventilation of all matters as a condition of giving its assent to what the Government does. "Our system," he concludes, "is one of democracy, but of democracy by consent and not by delegation, of government of the people, for the people, with, but not by, the people."[20]

The bipolar structure that Amery traces back to the Middle Ages and makes the central feature of the British constitution does not mean that Britain is not democratic. It means rather that British democracy has grown up within a certain framework of authority to which it has been obliged—perhaps at the sacrifice of some consistency—to accommodate itself. The idea of the mandate expresses the belief that Governments are responsible to the people for their major acts and policies. As the suffrage has been broadened and particularly since the Reform Act of 1867, this idea has been taken more and more seriously. In 1903, for example, Joseph Chamberlain raised the tariff question so that at the next general election the public might give a "mandate" on it. In 1923 Stanley Baldwin, the Conservative Prime Minister, dissolved Parliament, not because of an adverse vote of confidence or a defeat on policy, but solely, he alleged, because he felt he could not undertake tariff reform (then a very important issue) without obtaining an expression of popular will on the matter. The principle of the mandate is certainly a part of British political culture, and, what is more, is frequently acted upon.

But mandate theory has never fully replaced the idea of independent authority. Even in the heyday of mandate theory some very important policy decisions were made without mandate, and without in the least outraging anyone's constitutional feelings. Thus Baldwin, who felt he could not reform the tariff without a specific mandate, gave women equal suffrage without the slightest suspicion of one. Much more important, it seems to be generally recognized that the Government ought sometimes to ignore its lack of a mandate or even to act counter to a mandate, if doing so would be definitely in the national interest—a loose principle, which may cover a multitude of independent actions. The case most frequently cited to make this point is the famous "Baldwin Confession" about Britain's failure to rearm against the Nazi threat before 1935. Baldwin argued that until 1935 every government had been given a mandate for disarmament and collective security under the League of Nations and that the country's mind on the issue had been revealed

---

[20] *Ibid.*, pp. 11–12, 20.

emphatically at general elections and by-elections. Hence he felt that rearmament could not legitimately have been undertaken until 1935, when some sort of mandate for it was given. The position taken against this argument by Baldwin's opponents was that the Government—having had, as it claimed, a clear apprehension of the military danger and the futility of the League of Nations—should have acted in the best interests of the nation anyway; that in fact it was its *duty,* as the Government of the country and His Majesty's Ministers, to do so, regardless of any electoral consequences. It may be true that one or the other conception of the authority of government is invoked only when it is politically convenient to invoke it, but the great point is that both conceptions can be used for political convenience. Both conceptions have solid roots in British political culture.

Speaking always with an acute sense of relativity—that is, with regard to what is humanly possible and with regard to what other countries have accomplished—we may say that the story of British government in modern times is a story of high achievement. With all due qualifications, the record of effectiveness and responsiveness has been remarkably good. It is precisely this long record of achievement that makes the disappointments and failures of recent years disturbing to the British and intellectually challenging to the political scientist.

Has the balance between tradition and modernity been thrown off in some undesirable way? Has modernity run to excess, introducing deficiencies that in the past were more likely to trouble the unstable countries of the continent? Or is it the other way around? Has Britain lost her old ability to adapt traditional elements to developing modernity? Or, finally, have the old formulas at last become obsolete, whether we think of the complementary elements of party government and cabinet government or of the older, persisting structures that underlie these contemporary mechanisms? That is to say, has a phase of political development been reached that makes out of date the modernity of tradition? These spacious doubts and broad perspectives will inform the more particular problems and hypotheses that will be considered in the following chapters.

Two

Cabinet and Prime Minister

As increase in scale entails greater specialization, the expansion of policy of a modern polity normally leads to a growth in the number of departments and other agencies of state power. This raises the classic problem of how to achieve coherence in policy. Coherence means at least avoiding overlapping and conflict. This is no mean feat when one considers the capacity of government programs unintentionally to produce problems for one another—their "hidden policies." But coherence means more than just absence of conflict. It also means there is some positive drive uniting these numerous and far-flung activities—not necessarily some simple goal, such as "victory" in wartime, but rather a system of priorities that marshals energy and purpose to some fronts and withdraws them from others. Moreover, this unity has a temporal dimension. Programs change, of course; however, they do not simply zigzag in response to arbitrary thrusts on the rudder, but show continuity, as perseverance in tackling a problem is maintained and innovation builds on previous achievement.

Coherence, a bland and abstract word, may not seem to deserve being put forward as a major criterion of public policy. Yet the loss of coherence describes some of the more tragic and characteristic failures of the highly developed modern state. Fragmentation in the polity and in the processes of policy making leads to a loss of control over the nation's destiny and the dominance of the blind forces of technique. If politics is to be a process of social choice, the first requisite is that the instruments of governance should themselves be subject to control.

According to the conventional model, cabinet government has virtues that are highly relevant to this complex of problems. Because the Cabinet includes the men in charge of the principal branches of the executive, the system is said to produce positive and coherent action. By their common membership in the Cabinet, Ministers are enabled and obliged to make the action of their respective departments compatible and mutually supportive. Thanks to their party majority in the legislature, they are freed of the inconsistencies that the casual majorities of a leaderless legislature will impose on public policy.

The source of these virtues is, in the first place, the fusion of powers. In contrast to the separation of legislative and executive powers found in the American system, the Cabinet joins these powers in one body. This fusion does not consist merely in the fact that the executive actions of the individual departments and of the government as a whole are directed by a body of men who are also members of the legislature. The important point is that these men, while exercising the whole panoply of executive powers, also in effect command the legislative power, including that crucial power of any polity, the power to tax and spend. The men exercising these powers can be deprived of them, but this does not lead to the recapture of these powers by the legislature; the same massive authority is simply given to a new set of men. Cabinets come and go, but the Cabinet continues.

Not only does the Cabinet exercise a fusion of executive and legislative powers, but it also gains from the dual nature of the British conception of authority. The decisions of the Cabinet enjoy legitimacy—that is, they are accepted and obeyed —in large part because they are regarded as expressing the wishes of the voters through the mechanisms of party government. But there is no denying that the Cabinet is also conceived as having a wide sphere of independent authority. This further support of its powers derives from Britain's monarchic past. Any Cabinet acts within a complex of constraints and supports, serving to mark out the sphere within which it can in fact freely make decisions. One crucial support for a wider sphere of decision making is the ancient expectation among members of Parliament and Britons generally that "the Queen's Government must be carried on."

In the eighteenth century "the executive authority of the King was put in commission and it was arranged that the commissioners should be members of the legislative body to whom they are responsible."[1] But this was not just an event of the eighteenth century. The conception of cabinet authority that originated in this way continues to be a living force in British government and politics. Not least, it impresses the members of the Cabinet themselves. An ex-member recently described how Ministers, while gathering at Number 10 Downing Street for a Cabinet, laugh and joke and call one another by their first names, as one would expect of political colleagues. But once they enter the Cabinet room and the meeting starts, "the whole atmosphere changes." Members now address their remarks only to the Prime Minister, and even the oldest of friends refer to one another in the third person and by their ministerial titles. For "here is no longer a set of individual men,

---

[1] Sir Courtenay Ilbert, quoted in Patrick Gordon Walker, *The Cabinet* (London, 1970), p. 14.

but the collective sovereign power of the state."[2] The Cabinet is "not just a meeting of persons but a continuing body, that has for centuries been the seat of ultimate authority."[3]

From a decision-making structure so admirably fashioned it should not be strange if the output in policy and administration were coherent, decisive, and relevant. Yet a closer look at cabinet government today suggests that it is not working as the conventional accounts say it does but, on the contrary, suffers from such fragmentation in structure, incoherence in action, and immobility in responding to problems as to remind one of the less happy moments of those political systems burdened with a separation of powers or a multiparty system. A Minister in the Wilson Government contends that "the major problem of government today" is "how to make informed collective decisions at the cabinet level on economic and financial strategy." He concludes that the failure to solve this problem has relegated the Cabinet to "the margin of politics."[4] A common complaint among civil servants and outside observers is that British government is greatly overcentralized. As a result of the overload on central government generally and on the Cabinet in particular, many important decisions, they claim, are made quickly and badly, or properly, but with vast delay; while, as many observers have remarked, pressure groups have gained far wider opportunities than in the past. Hence, because of internal pressures forcing decisions away from the center and external pressures drawing them toward the periphery, what looks like a tightly centralized and neatly coordinated system is tending to become polycentric, pluralistic, and unintentionally dispersed.

What may seem an opposite view is also heard. This is that cabinet government has developed into prime ministerial government. A leading member of the Wilson Government has compared the present position of the Prime Minister with that of the American President and concluded that a Prime Minister may well exert "greater power than a President."[5] A professorial authority writes: "Now the country is governed by the prime minister."[6] There is no such simple answer to the question of who governs Britain. But, like the talk about prime ministerial government, the second statement does at least suggest that the Prime Minister has been gaining in authority in relation to the Cabinet. This is quite compatible, however, with a general fragmentation of cabinet authority. If the collective function of the Cabinet were to decline, it would be natural for the Prime Minister to loom as a relatively greater figure, but this would not necessarily halt the general trend toward less coordination of decision and more dispersion of authority.

---

[2]Patrick Gordon Walker, *Encounter,* 6 (April 1956), 19.

[3]Walker, *The Cabinet, op. cit.,* p. 106.

[4]Harold Lever (former Financial Secretary to the Treasury), in *The New Statesman,* 80 (30 October 1970), 552.

[5]R. H. S. Crossman (former Secretary of State for Social Services), *The Myths of Cabinet Government* (Cambridge, Mass., 1972), p. 6.

[6]John P. Mackintosh, *The British Cabinet,* 2nd ed. (London, 1968), p. 529.

Bearing in mind the conventional model of cabinet government sketched in the previous pages, as well as current criticisms of this model, we may now take a more detailed look at how a Cabinet is constituted and how it works.

Making a Cabinet

The first step in constituting a Cabinet is the appointment of a Prime Minister. This act is performed by the Sovereign, but is so hedged by conventions of the Constitution and by political circumstance as to leave her virtually no freedom of choice. The basic convention is that the Sovereign must appoint whatever leader is capable of commanding the support of a majority in the House of Commons. The occasion to act may occur when a general election has reversed the positions of the two main parties in the House. In such a case the Queen's function is simply to ask the known leader of the successful party to form a Government. If this leader were to die or become incapacitated, each party would undoubtedly avail itself of its established procedure for the election of a leader—which the Conservatives have had only since 1965—making obvious and inevitable the Queen's choice.

It must be mentioned that a Cabinet could also be brought down by a defeat in the House of Commons. Such defeats are unknown in this day of two-party dominance and tight party unity. But the basic rule of parliamentary government still obtains; namely, the Cabinet must retain the support of a majority of the House, and the rise of a third party or a decline in party cohesion could again, as in the past, subject a Government to defeat in the House of Commons. In case of such a defeat, under the conventions of British government a Government would have two courses open to it. The Prime Minister might dissolve Parliament and appeal to the electorate by means of a new election, or he might decide to resign. If he chose to resign in the midst of party confusion, conceivably the Queen could be confronted with a choice among several leaders of Opposition parties, each of whom had a chance of forming a Government. Presumably, the convention that the Sovereign must not get involved in politics would lead her to seek and follow the advice of the outgoing Prime Minister and other party leaders.

The first task of the Prime Minister is to choose his Cabinet and Government. The Cabinet formed by Edward Heath after the Conservatives won the election of June 18, 1970, consisted of seventeen members. It included the heads of the old and important departments such as the Home Office, Foreign Office, and Treasury, as well as the heads of the so-called superministries formed in recent years by the amalgamation of several departments. Bearing the title of Secretary of State, the latter were in charge of such huge agencies as Defence, Social Services, Trade and Industry, and the Environment. The Cabinet also included members without departments, such as the Leader of the House of Commons and the Minister in charge of Britain's negotiations with the Common Market. In addition to the Cabinet, the Government included some sixty-nine other members. A few were Ministers at the head of a department, but not in the Cabinet. A new category consisted of Ministers subordinate to the heads of the superministries, but with the status of a department head. Below them ranked the Ministers of State, who also assisted the heads of larger and more important departments in positions of considerable responsibility. Other assistants to Ministers were the parliamentary secretaries and undersecretaries, who technically are not Ministers of the Crown, since they are not appointed by the Queen. Also included in the Government were the whips, whose main function is to help the Prime Minister ride herd on his supporters in the House and who are usually given appointments without significant departmental duties. Finally, occupying a kind of twilight zone between members of the Government and ordinary backbenchers were the thirty to forty parliamentary private secretaries (P.P.S.s). Serving principally as a means of contact between a senior Minister and the backbenchers of his party, the P.P.S. should not be confused with the Minister's private secretary, a civil servant whose sphere is in the department. Although neither a Minister nor a member of the Government, the P.P.S. is subject to a more stringent discipline than the ordinary backbencher and is likely to lose his post if he so much as abstains in a vote.

Altogether, counting members of the Government and P.P.S.s, the members of the two Houses who are attached to the fortunes of the Prime Minister and his Cabinet by holding a post, official or unofficial, will probably number well over a hundred. Overwhelmingly they are in the House of Commons, constituting a substantial fraction of the majority of its 630 members. There is a power of patronage here that a Prime Minister confronted with an obstreperous party will find useful. In 1964 Harold Wilson raised the number of Ministers alone to ninety-eight, almost 50 percent over what it had been under Churchill and Macmillan.

As the scope of policy expands and the bureaucracy grows in size and complexity, there is pressure to increase the size of the Cabinet. Yet there seems to be a kind of upper limit fixed perhaps by the simple physical fact that only a certain number of people can do business around a table. Although the Cabinet numbered twenty-three by World War I, this was still its average size under the Conservative Douglas-Home and the Labourite Harold Wilson. As for a lower limit, in both world wars the size of the Cabinet has been drastically reduced to half a dozen or so. This has led many observers and even some politicians to advocate similarly small Cabinets for peacetime. If the vast, important, and highly complex business of total war can be carried out more effectively under a Cabinet of half a dozen, surely the work of peacetime government would benefit from a similar change. The trouble with this recommendation is that while the activity of a wartime government is vast and complex, its goals are immensely simplified. One word describes them, "victory," and from it a system of fairly clear priorities can be derived. Indeed, so settled were the means and ends of British government during the latter part of the war, that the Cabinet hardly met, leaving the implementation of the agreed policies almost entirely to Churchill. In peacetime the multiplicity of demands of a politically mobilized society reasserts itself, requiring that the departments representing these demands be given direct access to the authoritative decision maker. To satisfy this pressure in view of the increasing differentiation of the pattern of power is difficult. At one time just after World War II, the increase in the number of departments seemed to mean that more and more of them would not be represented directly in the Cabinet. Amalgamations leading to the creation of superministries, however, have reversed this trend, and the Cabinets of Wilson and Heath have included all ministries except three or four less important ones.

Although constitutional convention gives the Prime Minister complete discretion in deciding who the members of his Cabinet will be, his actual power is greatly circumscribed by political realities. Every Prime Minister has certain eminent party colleagues whose appointment to the Cabinet is a foregone conclusion. In the nature of the two-party system, each party has wings of opinion whose leaders must be included in the interest of harmony. It is therefore inevitable that a Cabinet will include men who want the Prime Minister's job, and given their existence, the Prime Minister will normally prefer to have them inside, blanketed by collective responsibilities, rather than outside, raising a storm on the back benches and in the country. Regional forces play little part in determining Cabinet membership. Major exceptions to this are Scotland and Wales, which, with the rise of intense Celtic nationalism, have been directly represented in recent Cabinets by their respective secretaries of state. Nor are the factors bearing on a Prime Minister's choice purely political. Sheer managerial ability can raise a man to Cabinet level, although its presence or absence is probably more important during the reorganization of a Cabinet than at the time of its formation. Competence of this order undoubtedly had a great deal to do with the exceptionally long tenure—six years—of Denis Healey as Minister of Defence under Wilson.

These constraints, then, political and otherwise, shape the "shadow Cabinet" of the Prime Minister during the time when he is Leader of the Opposition. Yet the comparison of this leadership group when the party is out of power with its successor when the party takes office, suggests the substantial freedom of choice possessed by the man who is, in Churchill's phrase, "Number One." The feelings of those who await his decision is another good measure of this freedom. "It is like the zoo at feeding time," said Lord Salisbury. "It's been terrible: I have had people in here weeping and even fainting," remarked Ramsay MacDonald in 1929. In 1945, Attlee at the last moment switched Ernest Bevin, whom he had slated for the Treasury, with Hugh Dalton, whom he had led to expect the Foreign Office. Similarly, in 1964 Wilson switched Richard Crossman, who had been shadow Minister of Education, with Michael Stewart, who had been the front-bench spokesman on housing. Moreover, what the Prime Minister can give, he can take away. Once his Cabinet has been tested by a period in office, he has even more freedom in shuffling its members or, indeed, in getting rid of them altogether. An illustration of the extreme to which a Prime Minister can go, which, even though not typical, has continued to impress Cabinet members, was the purge of July 1962, when Macmillan suddenly dismissed seven members of his Cabinet, including the Minister of Defence and Chancellor of the Exchequer.

Under the long-established conventions of Cabinet government, a party leader, when summoned by the sovereign to form a Government, makes his own decision on whether to accept. Having accepted, he selects the members of the Cabinet, which as a body speaks for the whole Government. He may shift members of the Cabinet from one office to another or dismiss them, which in a sense is merely a consequence of the fact that his own resignation brings the Government to an end. The decision to resign, or that crucial political decision of whether and when to dissolve Parliament and have an election, is his sole decision. Such is the field of his authority. Needless to say, the actual exercise of his authority is subject to multiple constraints. But as a factor in the determination of power—the ability to impose one's will on a situation—these norms of British political culture all tend toward magnifying the office, not only in its constitution but also, as we shall see, in its operation.

Collective Responsibility

A major convention of British Cabinet government is the rule of collective responsibility. In the words of a recent Cabinet Minister, collective responsibility means "that every member must accept and if necessary defend Cabinet decisions even if he opposed and still dislikes them," unless, of course, he chooses to resign.[7] It means that and a good deal more. Not only are members of the Cabinet bound in vote and speech to defend the authoritative decisions of the Cabinet system, but so also are all members of the Government and, though not so tightly, their parliamentary private secretaries. Moreover, the decisions to which they are bound are not only those of the full Cabinet. The decisions of Cabinet committees now have the same validity as decisions of the Cabinet proper. With the expansion of policy Cabinet committees have increased in number and grown in authority. From the occasional ad hoc committee of the mid-nineteenth century there has developed an array of standing committees, which in the postwar years has sometimes numbered well over a dozen, along with such ad hoc committees as may be found useful. At one time all decisions of a Cabinet committee had to go to the full Cabinet for approval. Beginning in World War II, their decisions were accepted as binding, unless a member of the committee chose to appeal the decision to the full Cabinet. In 1967 Wilson took the further momentous step of excluding appeals unless the chairman of the committee gave his assent. Although this new rule could not take away the right of a Cabinet member to bring a matter before the Cabinet, it greatly reduced appeals.

There are other decisions that, although not made by the Cabinet, have similar consequences. Some arise when the Prime Minister intervenes in a particular field, either by himself or in consultation with the Minister concerned and perhaps a few others. In September 1938 the Prime Minister, Neville Chamberlain, without prior

---

[7]Walker, *The Cabinet, op. cit.,* p. 30.

Cabinet approval, sent a telegram to Hitler to arrange a meeting and later signed the Munich agreement before informing the Cabinet. Except for one Minister who resigned, the Cabinet accepted these acts—and defended them in a four-day debate. In November 1967 the decision to devalue the pound was taken by the Prime Minister and Chancellor of the Exchequer, but was immediately reported to the Cabinet for its approval.

Not only the Prime Minister but ordinary Ministers can effectively commit the Government, a fact that may be of great importance when fields such as economic, financial, or defense policy are concerned. There is an old convention of the Constitution that Ministers are individually responsible to the House for the actions of their departments. This still holds when it comes to answering questions and expounding and defending department policy. But party discipline today is such that individual Ministers are no longer forced out by adverse votes, as they once were; they can count on the Government's rallying its majority to the defense of their decisions, even if the decisions were actually made in the depths of the bureaucracy, quite innocent of ministerial knowledge or influence. Just as politics dictates support, politics can also lead to the withdrawal of support. A case in point is the resignation of Sir Samuel Hoare over the Hoare-Laval plan in 1935. With the Cabinet's knowledge and approval Hoare, the Foreign Secretary, made an agreement with Laval, then the French Premier, approving a partition of Ethiopia as a means of appeasing Mussolini. When word of the agreement was leaked, a storm of wrathful protest swept Britain. The Cabinet bowed, repudiated the agreement, and dropped Hoare from office.

With the consequences of collective responsibility so far-reaching, it is crucial that the decisions entailing it be properly made. Collective decision making must be such as to make collective responsibility tolerable. A major question for any departmental Minister is, What questions should go to the Cabinet, or to a committee, possibly as the first step on the way to the Cabinet? There are no precise rules governing this matter. It is a political question for politicians to answer. Whatever might harm the Government politically is a general rule. Such harm might arise from parliamentary or public controversy. Hence the Cabinet has considered not only whether to apply for admission to the Common Market, but also the location of a third airport for London.

Disputes between Ministers and departments are another source of questions for collective decision, in which cases the Cabinet acts as a court of appeals. The major category naturally consists of conflicts between the spending departments and the Treasury, which has the task of preparing the estimates of expenditure for submission to Parliament. At one time the initial responsibility for determining the overall limit on expenditure and the ceilings for programs and departments was put on the Minister in charge of the Treasury, the Chancellor of the Exchequer. When a spending department refused to accept its allocation, the matter would go to the Cabinet for decision. A major battle might ensue, as in 1951 when Aneurin Bevan, Minister of Britain's newly established National Health Service and Leader of the left wing of the Labour party, clashed with Hugh Gaitskell, Chancellor of the

Exchequer and the rising star of the moderates. At issue was the provision for the Health Service, which Gaitskell sought to restrain in a time of heavy inflationary pressure. Failing to carry the Cabinet, Bevan chose to resign rather than accept the collective decision. "The Chancellor of the Exchequer," he said, when explaining his resignation to the House, "is putting a financial ceiling on the Health Service."[8]

In these conflicts the Chancellor fought from a strong position, since he was the man responsible for finding the money by taxation and other means to cover expenditure. Yet his position was tactically weak, since the spending Ministers were tempted to gang up on him in pursuit of their respective departmental interests. Recently the control of expenditure was moved further into the committee system. While no rigid scheme was established, the new arrangement was to have the sum total of expenditure determined by the small and powerful Cabinet committee concerned with economic policy and chaired by the Prime Minister. Thereafter the task of allocating the total among departments might be assigned to an ad hoc committee or committees. The effect was to confront each Minister with his responsibility for overall expenditure as well as for his department's needs, and so to prevail upon him to adopt a government-wide, as well as a departmental, point of view. As two officials closely connected with the origination of this reform wrote, "each minister would be forced to balance the claims of his own department against what would have to be foregone by all the others."[9]

Cabinet Ministers wear two hats. Each is at once the head of a department and a part of the chief executive that stands above departments. Under a unitary executive such as the American presidential system, the two roles are physically separated in such a manner that department heads in conflict appeal to their superior, the President, for a decision. It is of the essence of a plural executive such as the British Cabinet that the two roles are combined. The danger of the plural executive is precisely its pluralism, which tempts individual Ministers to forget their government-wide responsibilities. If, however, Ministers can be brought fully to recognize both responsibilities, a degree of coordination in administration and coherence in policy may be reached that is superior to that of the unitary executive system. For now the chief executive is not confronted with the problem of departmental Ministers he must watch and control. On the contrary, the chief executive consists of those Ministers who, under the British system, bring a full knowledge of departmental actions and intentions to executive decision making. The high quality of such decisions—their coherence and comprehensiveness—is presumably also a justification for the far-reaching burdens of collective responsibility.

These arrangements do have some curious consequences. They may at times oblige a Minister to declare his support for, and expound the virtues of, a policy that in fact he detests and shortly before has been tearing to pieces in Cabinet. This

---

[8] 487 *H. C. Deb.* 41 (23 April 1951).

[9] Lord Plowden and Sir Robert Hall, "The Supremacy of Politics," *The Political Quarterly*, 39 (October–December 1968), 369.

is not, however, considered to be lying to the House, but simply a consequence of the convention of collective responsibility. That convention also logically implies secrecy about disagreements in Cabinet, since revelations of such disagreements would mean that Ministers were not presenting a united front. Strict observance of the rule of secrecy would be politically intolerable for ambitious men who often have a strong and opinionated following in party and the public. Ministers therefore find ways of quietly letting their true position in Cabinet be known to the press.

Since collective responsibility is a convention binding only among members of a Government and not between a Government and Parliament, it can be relaxed by any Government. This happened in 1932, when the National Government allowed certain of its members to speak and vote against its tariff proposals in order to avoid their resignation. This Government, however, consisting of Conservatives, Liberals, and a few Labourites, was one of the rare cases in British history of a true coalition government. Its behavior was reminiscent of the practice of coalition governments formed under parliamentary systems where there are many parties. Under the French Third Republic, for instance, although there was a constitutional rule of collective responsibility, sometimes a Minister in speaking and voting might disagree with the position taken by the Cabinet. This occurred when dissension within the Cabinet became so sharp that certain Ministers insisted on the right to vote against a government bill and were allowed by the Prime Minister and a majority of their colleagues to do so without incurring the obligation of resigning from the Ministry. Likewise, in Britain before the rise of cohesive political parties, the rule of collective responsibility was followed only slackly. In George III's time Ministers spoke and sometimes even voted against policies adopted by the Cabinet. Party has clearly played an outstanding role in the development of this aspect of the British Constitution.

The New Structure of Decision Making

How to maintain the conditions for coherent policy making is an acute problem for every modern government in this day of the welfare state and managed economy. It is not a problem that admits of ideal solutions in any country. Yet it is also obvious that a system of executive decision making that originated in the eighteenth century and reached its classic form in the nineteenth should not survive the twentieth without major adaptations.

One of these has been the development of the Cabinet secretariat. Before World War I no records of Cabinet proceedings were kept, and Ministers were not permitted even to take notes on Cabinet discussions. The only exception was the Prime Minister, who wrote a personal letter to the monarch reporting decisions and the discussion leading to them. The results are vividly suggested in a famous note from the private secretary of a Cabinet Minister to the private secretary of the Prime Minister in 1882:

Harcourt and Chamberlain have both been here this morning, and *at* my Chief about yesterday's Cabinet proceedings. They cannot agree about what occurred. There must have been some decisions, as Bright's resignation shows. My Chief has told me to ask you what the devil *was* decided, for he be damned if he knows.

Action was first taken with regard to defense policy. The Committee of Imperial Defence, the first of the standing committees of the Cabinet, was created in 1903. It had only one permanent member, the Prime Minister, but the persons usually attending included the political heads of the defense departments along with the commander in chief from the military bureaucracy, while the heads of the military intelligence departments served as joint secretaries and a clerk from the Foreign Office kept minutes. As the committee's work grew and subcommittees proliferated, the committee acquired a sizable secretariat to prepare the agenda, keep minutes, and perform liaison work with other departments—notably the Foreign Office—that were interested in defense policy. In 1916, under the pressure of war, Lloyd George, shortly after becoming Prime Minister, took over this secretariat and put it at the service of the Cabinet and all Cabinet committees. By 1969 the total staff numbered 108, of whom about 45 directly serviced the Cabinet and its committees. The head of the Cabinet office, known as the Secretary of the Cabinet, like the other members of the staff, is a permanent official and ranks as one of the three top civil servants, the other two being the permanent secretaries of the Treasury and of the recently established Civil Service Department.

The bland-sounding tasks of the Cabinet secretariat in fact constitute an important element in the network of power relations within the British executive. The innocent task of preparing the Cabinet agenda can mean keeping one Minister waiting for decisions while another is given ready access, a good reason why the agenda is drawn up under the direction of the Prime Minister. The secretariat sees to it that all items of Cabinet business are properly supported by memoranda and that the memoranda are circulated to the proper people at the proper time. It makes sure that non-Cabinet Ministers whose departments are involved in an item of Cabinet business are present at the relevant discussion. Perhaps its principal function relates to the minutes, which are based on notes taken—in longhand— by the secretary of the Cabinet and two assistants. A minute (or conclusion as it is often called) summarizes the documents on which the decision has been made, sets out the gist of the pertinent statements of fact and of the general arguments urged, and concludes with a statement of the decision taken, summed up orally by the Prime Minister. After a meeting the minutes are promptly sent to departments. They are important not merely as a record, but above all as instructions telling departments what to do. These minutes from the Cabinet and Cabinet committees provide, in the words of an ex-Minister, "the whole of the civil service with their marching orders day by day." They are the means by which the government machine is set in motion and controlled. Moreover, they keep Ministers and officials constantly and accurately informed as to what department has come out on top in the current Cabinet battles, information that cannot fail to influence the outcome of emerging conflicts at the ministerial or official level.

The constant communication of this sort of information to the decision-making centers of the government is of the utmost importance to the smooth and rapid working of the Whitehall machine, as it is to any modern bureaucracy. At any given moment throughout the British administration many issues involving different departments are coming up for decision, and the knowledge of the latest Cabinet decision on policy will help direct these issues toward solution. Inseparable from this information relating to substance, however, is the further information relating to the balance of power within the Cabinet. Accurate knowledge as to how this balance is tipping, and especially as to which side the Prime Minister is taking, can save a great deal of time by discouraging subordinates from making vain efforts to appeal decisions that are bound to fail. Finally, in addition to these tasks of preparing for meetings of the Cabinet and Cabinet committees and of recording and circulating their decisions, the secretariat has the vital function of follow-up. It does this by periodically checking with departments to ensure that the authoritative decisions have been carried out.

While the secretariat consists of officials and so is subject to the authority of successive Cabinets, the system has some unexpected features. One is that while the Prime Minister orally sums up the Cabinet conclusion, the secretary actually formulates the minute that communicates this decision to departments. This minute is not subject to approval, that is, change, by the Cabinet. Nor can the Prime Minister alone order it to be changed. A well-authenticated story has it that Ramsey MacDonald once tried to get the Secretary of the Cabinet to make an addition to a minute. The official replied, "I can't do that, prime minister, unless I have a minute in writing instructing me to correct the minutes." MacDonald did not press the matter further.[10]

A consequence of the alternation of parties in power is that no Cabinet may see any minutes or other papers of a previous Cabinet of the other party. The purpose is to protect the confidentiality of discussions among Ministers and to prevent any partisan exploitation of them. For similar reasons, at Number 10 Downing Street, the papers collected by the small office that directly serves the Prime Minister will be bundled away for safekeeping when a general election changes the party in power. Likewise, no incoming Minister of a different party may see departmental papers "indicating the views expressed by their predecessors of a different party."[11] This protects the confidentiality of Ministers' exchanges with other Ministers, civil servants, and outside bodies, including foreign governments. While Ministers will not have full access to the previous history of a policy, they will, of course, know what policies were decided on, their civil servants helping them and the new Government to maintain whatever continuity may be required. Such

---

[10]R. H. S. Crossman, Godkin Lectures (Harvard University, 1970).

[11]800 H. C. Deb. 293 (28 April 1970).

arrangements are consequences of ministerial control and party government. They also mean that such entities as the Cabinet secretariat are, in the words of an ex-Minister, "a power in their own right."

Along with the growth of the secretariat, the growth of the Cabinet committee system has paralleled the expansion of policy in the twentieth century. In 1929, apart from the Committee of Imperial Defence and a small number of ad hoc committees formed from time to time for special purposes, only one standing committee of the Cabinet was in operation, the Home Affairs Committee, charged with considering items of domestic legislation. Even at this late date in Britain's modern political development most business was transacted in full Cabinet. In contrast, after World War II, the Labour Government of 1945–1951 used as many as fifteen standing committees. While the changing problems of public policy mean that old committees will die and new committees will be created, something in the nature of a basic framework seems to be establishing itself. Among the dozen or so used by the Wilson Government the principal standing committees were:

1. The Overseas Policy and Defence Committee, presided over by the Prime Minister.
2. A small Economic Policy Committee, also chaired by the Prime Minister and concerned with strategic decisions.
3. A large Economic Policy Committee, chaired by the Chancellor of the Exchequer and including all the departments concerned with economic problems.
4. The Social Services Committee, chaired by the Secretary of State for these matters.
5. The Home Affairs Committee, dealing with matters of domestic policy not under the previous committee.
6. The Public Expenditure Scrutiny Committee, which had the function of reviewing departmental estimates and allocating expenditure among the various departments.
7. The Legislation Committee, which supervised the drafting of bills, making sure they corresponded with Cabinet decisions, and dealt with that crucial and sensitive matter of rationing parliamentary time among departments and Ministers by deciding the order in which bills would be introduced into the House.

Under Wilson, the Prime Minister also met with a small group of his senior colleagues—the Management Committee or Inner Cabinet, most of whom were also committee chairmen—to discuss upcoming business and their strategy for dealing with it in Parliament and elsewhere.

In the normal course of political development the growth in scale and complexity means that the mass of government business increases and the number of departments multiplies. At the same time the problem of coordination becomes more difficult as departments are excluded from the Cabinet and the Cabinet itself is overburdened by the increase in business. Cabinet committees help to relieve the pressure on the Cabinet and to coordinate departments with closely related concerns. In a further step aiming at better coordination, several related departments in a number of cases have been amalgamated into a superministry. In the early 1950s an attempt was made to set up coordinating Ministers—"overlords" —without combining the departments they were to supervise. This did not work, since the overlord was not given the ultimate authority over, and responsibility for, the respective departments, a fact that was brought home when Parliament asked who was to answer to it for the departments. The necessity for amalgamation was finally accepted and has led to the establishment of superministries, each with a single responsible Minister at its head, but with a number of other Ministers assisting him—in the case of the huge Ministry of Technology, making a total of seven Ministers for that one department in the Wilson Government.

Under the Wilson Government the superministries included, in addition to Defence, Social Services, responsible for the work of the two former Departments of Health and Social Security, and Technology, which, as the central point of contact between government and industry, took over many or most functions of the former Department of Scientific and Industrial Research, the Atomic Energy Authority, the Ministry of Aviation, the Ministry of Power, the Board of Trade, and the Department of Economic Affairs. The Heath Government went on to create a new Ministry of Environment—concerned with housing, transport, land use, pollution, public buildings, local government, and regional policy—and to combine a somewhat reduced Ministry of Technology with the Board of Trade to constitute a new superministry of Trade and Industry. Some may think that the Treasury should be included under this heading of superministry, especially in view of the extension of its functions since the war from the traditional financial concerns to major tasks of economic policy. As the traditional coordinating department in the whole system, however, it is a staff agency with few operating responsibilities, but with a unique and powerful position in relation to other departments.

The superministries, as is intended, make possible the direct representation in the Cabinet of nearly all fields of policy—but not without problems. The Secretary of State is assisted by Ministers subordinate to him who will have a closer acquaintance with various aspects of the whole field of departmental policy. As the head of the department, however, it is he who, under the doctrines of both individual and collective responsibility, must represent the department and speak for it in Cabinet. Much as he may need help, he can bring along one of his more knowledgeable subordinates to a Cabinet meeting only with permission, which is sometimes refused.

Another aspect of the emerging pattern is the fact that the superministries tend to parallel the major Cabinet committees. In the case of the Social Services Committee, for instance, the Secretary of State for that group of fields makes a strong chairman. Needless to say, such arrangements, while strengthening coordination among groups of departments, may also fragment Cabinet authority by creating centers of power that are harder to control than their constituent parts were in their original state of dispersion and autonomy. The ability of a department to commit the whole Government becomes far more serious when it is a superministry operating out of such a complex of power.

Another significant development is the tendency to establish committees of officials parallel to Cabinet committees. Such a committee consists of civil servants from the same departments represented on the ministerial committee. Its job is to prepare issues and decisions, raising questions for action by Ministers and itself moving toward decisions in the light of existing policy. There is nothing new in the interdepartmental committee. It is inevitable where departments have a mutual concern, which may well involve conflict, that their representatives should meet and discuss a question before sending it up to Ministers. From disagreements that first emerge at this level arise many of the questions that constitute the Cabinet agenda.

Also at the official level the views and wishes of interest groups may gain access and be taken into consideration. There is nothing illicit or novel about this. Consultation between government departments and outside groups—such as trade unions, trade associations, professional organizations, and large enterprises (including those in the nationalized sector)—is an established feature of the process of identifying problems of public policy and canvassing possible solutions. Indeed, as later discussion will bring out (see Chapters 4 and 10), the National Economic Development Council (N.E.D.C.), established in 1962—which had members drawn from Government, business, the nationalized industries, and the trade unions, along with the similarly constituted score or so of little "neddies" for particular industries—institutionalized and systematized this practice of consultation for the broad purpose of achieving better economic growth.

While consultation with interests is inevitable in Britain, as in any other developed modern state, it may also add to the centrifugal forces acting on policy making. For example, land use is a subject of acute concern to interests in both the public and private sector: farmers, real estate developers, and expanding manufacturing concerns, as well as government departments interested in sites for public housing, new airports, superhighways, and so on. Before any such question can go to Ministers, there must be prolonged discussion at the official level. Yet once parties at this level reach agreement, which is necessarily intricate and weighted with compromise, it is very hard for Ministers at any level to reject such an agreed solution, let alone attempt to fabricate a new one on their own. Some close observers concluded, after watching administrative developments of the early postwar years, that by far the most important development was this tendency of the interdependent decision-making process at the lower levels in effect to commit the higher ministerial authorities. The corporatist tendencies of the modern state promoted by its ever widening intervention in the economy create major problems for coherence in policy making.

The dual role of Cabinet Ministers helps counteract centrifugal tendencies. Similarly, their officials, insofar as they try faithfully to represent their respective Ministers, will be restrained in their assertion of purely departmental or sectional interests. Moreover, the mechanics of the developing Cabinet office provide an infrastructure that can be used to guide the crucial decisions toward the center. The official committee paralleling the Cabinet committee may very well have as its chairman a civil servant from the Cabinet secretariat, whose resources for

assessing the problems before the committee and whose influence on its deliberations may be strengthened by his having a staff of his own drawn from the Cabinet
office. Thus in the Cabinet office are included not only the secretaries of the
Cabinet committees to which the official committees are correlated, but also some
of the chairmen of official committees with their staffs.

The British Cabinet, under conditions of party government, provides the essentials of an effective coordinating body—a representation of the elements to be
coordinated along with a mechanism and an incentive to unify them. As policy has
developed and the public sector has grown creating new centrifugal tendencies,
new agencies were created to strengthen the unifying forces: Cabinet secretariat,
superministries, Cabinet and official committees, the new Civil Service Department. Even when these were effective, however, they have left the main initiative
in policy making to the several departments. To make the Cabinet itself the initiating
body is theoretically possible. This would entail giving it the resources to survey
and evaluate the whole complex of government policies and to compare them with
other possible lines of action with a skill and judgment equal to that of the departmental bureaucracies. This is a tall order, but the Heath Government has moved
in this direction. It brought in teams of outsiders, mainly from business, to provide
a new overview of policy, showing the strategic relations between different policies
and helping Ministers make decisions about priorities. A small Central Policy
Review Staff (C.P.R.S.), composed of civil servants and of experts brought from
outside, was also added to the Cabinet office. Its task was to look at problems and
ideas that were not any one department's specific responsibility, to provide the
Cabinet with evaluations of departmental proposals free of the compromise that
interdepartmental committees tend to produce, and especially to work with the
previously mentioned groups engaged in shaping a system of priorities. Its potentialities can be better assessed after we have examined the scope and structure of
the public sector. (See Chapter 4.)

Prime Ministerial Government

However we may assess the Cabinet system as a structure of policy making, it is
clear that it has changed a great deal since the nineteenth century and indeed since
the interwar years. The Cabinet has adapted to the collectivist age. In large part
this has taken place in a step-by-step adaptation to a series of particular and
immediate problems, each considered in isolation and on its own terms rather than
in the context of some grand plan. This is the way in which governmental structures
normally do develop and to which the British, with their pride in empiricism and
muddling through, are especially devoted. The virtues of not trying to do too much
at one time by way of a grand plan are obvious. The danger is that a series of
uncoordinated steps, each quite sensible in itself, can set up a feedback of unanticipated consequences that is overwhelmingly negative. The paradigm of this
process of governmental counterproductivity is that proliferation of specialized

agencies in the highly developed modern polity which, although each new creation probably heightens effectiveness in one field, raises complexity to such a pitch that the government machine as a whole tends to go out of control. The central structures of policy making suffer grievously from this tendency in Britain, as in all modern states.

There are various ways in which attempts are made to offset these tendencies. One is to reduce the total level of governmental activity, that is, to reverse the trend of modernity toward a constant expansion of policy. The Conservative Government that came to power in Britain in June 1970 was pledged to such an effort. The order of possibility open to modern governments along this line was suggested by the new Chancellor of the Exchequer when he said he proposed to reduce the *increase* of government expenditure from its existing 3.5 percent per year to 2.8 percent per year. New government structures can be created and old ones can be strengthened to cope with fragmentation. In Britain the Treasury has traditionally functioned as a coordinating department, and it will be appropriate to discuss how its powers have developed when we consider problems of administration and planning.

Another line of attack is planned decentralization, which removes from central authority those categories of decision that can be taken by functional or regional units and so makes it possible for the central authority to deal with the questions that are properly its concern. This is a need that many civil servants and even Ministers have recognized for a long time and that, especially in recent years, has inspired various changes in the machinery of government. Planned decentralization makes no sense unless it is matched with arrangements to make sure that the crucial issues are brought to the attention of the central authority and that this central authority has the facilities for dealing with them. This obvious necessity has been responsible for one of the most interesting and controversial developments of the Cabinet system—the presumed increase in the authority and function of the Prime Minister.

As we have seen, the old established conventions of cabinet government regarding the constitution and resignation of a Cabinet, the appointment and dismissal of Ministers, and the dissolution of Parliament and calling of an election, give a Prime Minister wide opportunities for influencing the decisions of his colleagues, individually and collectively. They are important not so much in their exercise as in their potentiality for exercise. One is reminded of the old "fleet in being" theory, that British battleships kept the peace not by what their guns did, but by the widespread knowledge of what they could do. The norms of prime ministerial authority with regard to certain grand, but only occasional, decisions have numerous offspring in the form of more specific controls. Such, for instance, are the powers of the Prime Minister regarding Cabinet committees. As he constitutes and names the Cabinet, so also does he determine what Cabinet committees, standing and ad hoc, are to be set up and who are to be the members, including the crucial figure of chairman, with his power over appeals. If a matter is to be referred to a committee, the Prime Minister says to what committee. Similarly, he determines the agenda for the Cabinet itself, and his oral summations give the government machine its principal marching orders. That the Prime Minister says and does these things and that Ministers expect him to do them cannot fail greatly to improve his chances of winning such conflicts as may arise between him and one or several of them. One cannot fail to be reminded of the powers that Speakers have sometimes had in American legislatures, both state and national—for example, to appoint committees, name committee chairmen, and assign bills—and how they have sometimes used these powers in building formidable empires of influence.

Moreover, and this is the crucial point, when we consider the question of an increase in the Prime Minister's influence, while these controls or powers may be considered merely the logical projection of his traditional constitutional authority, they have emerged with, and relate to, a whole new system of collective decision making, as described in the previous pages. This new structure would seem to give that old authority not only a new appearance, but also a new reality. Under the classic Cabinet system the Prime Minister was obliged to win any important matter by fighting it out in full Cabinet where his opponents would be able to appeal to their colleagues in the name of the public good, party principle, personal ambition, and other familiar grounds of political motivation. Conceivably, under the new system the Prime Minister, anticipating resistance in the Cabinet, could send the matter to a committee. If he were prudent, he might even send it to an ad hoc committee with a membership selected by him especially for this purpose and with a chairman who would discourage appeals that, in any case, if pressed, would reach the Cabinet only by way of the Prime Minister. Following this procedure—to continue the speculation—the Prime Minister could presumably expect a favorable decision to go out to the government machine without the risk at any point of formal confrontation with its opponents.

What is lacking from these ominous portraits of "prime ministerial government" can be summed up in one word—politics. No one can doubt that the conceptions of legitimacy that are the basis of the British Constitution endow any Prime Minister with substantial authority. In little, his relations with his colleagues reproduce that primordial political situation, the confrontation of "chief" and "administrative staff." His prime ministerial authority enables him within limits to control and use their powers as political leaders and administrators. Within the power relationships of the Cabinet, this authority is a constant, changing only slowly over time. Yet, as we have seen, the lines of power set up by authority are supplemented (and sometimes diverted) by other, often more volatile variables. Thus what a Prime Minister can "get away with"—to use an expression that British insiders themselves sometimes use—will also be determined by his position in the party and in the country. Indeed, these variables also include highly personal relationships with colleagues, depending upon friendship and family, as well as capacities for psychological domination and subordination. In trying to get his way, a Prime Minister cannot fail to recognize, allow for, and use such factors. For example, just as his colleagues know that if he resigns the whole Cabinet comes to an end, he knows that if they—or the politically more eminent among them—resign, his premiership will be gravely discredited. Neither of these things needs to happen to make their possibility a continual influence on Cabinet interaction. Moreover, it is not just this extreme possibility that constrains the Prime Minister but also lesser and more realistic dangers. Cabinet dissension can spread to the back benches of the party, making Parliament harder to handle, and indeed to the Civil Service, creating problems of administrative control.

A closer look at a crucial series of decisions in foreign policy will illustrate this analysis. In October 1956 British troops in cooperation with French troops attempted to seize control of the Suez canal, nominally in order to protect this international waterway against the dangers of war created by an attack on Egypt launched by Israel, actually in order to deprive Egypt of control of the canal and promote the installation of a more friendly government there. When the United States prevented the British from obtaining the international financial assistance needed to get them through the crisis, the British were obliged to declare a cease-fire and ultimately to withdraw without achieving their purposes, nominal or real. This ill-fated operation was an intensely personal policy of the then Prime Minister, Sir Anthony Eden. Before World War II he had been one of the chief opponents of appeasement of the fascist dictators, and he again saw the old pattern of aggression when Nasser in breach of solemn agreements seized control of the canal with strong Soviet support. A certain edge was added to Eden's reaction by the fact that it was he who, only two years before and against the opposition of a substantial faction in the Conservative party, had made arrangements with Nasser regarding the canal highly favorable to Egypt.

Indeed, so personal was the policy that for some years after the affair, it was thought that Eden had carried out the whole thing on his own authority and without the knowledge or consent of his Cabinet. While Eden moved much planning and decision making to a small committee of more eminent Ministers and often acted on his own, he did keep the Cabinet informed and won acceptance of the fundamental decisions, only three Ministers out of a total of some eighteen dissenting from the plan for an invasion. The very fact that this was a highly personal policy, however, weakened Eden's position when the Americans behaved in so unexpected a manner. His colleagues had accepted his proposal for the use of force, but not the disastrous financial and economic situation that suddenly loomed as a consequence. This issue being raised, the Minister concerned, Harold Macmillan, Chancellor of the Exchequer, reversed his position of support for the policy and brought a majority of the Cabinet to his side. A Prime Minister with a stronger political and personal position might have been able to disregard that majority or to rally it for a prolongation of the use of force. Eden, however, was confronted not only with dissension in the Cabinet, but also with the prospect of its spreading. Two Ministers had already resigned. Some senior foreign service officers were on the verge of resignation, an almost unprecedented step. Revulsion among backbenchers threatened abstentions in parliamentary votes. Eden felt obliged to acquiesce. As a leading student of executive power remarks, "his plight speaks to the exercise of power in a collegium."[12]

We cannot expect that the British Prime Minister will have the kind of power over his Cabinet that an American President has over his. It is of the essence of the British Cabinet that a substantial number of its members will be men with strong political bases in Parliament, the party, and the country. An American Cabinet, on the other hand, rarely contains—at any rate in recent years—many men of major political stature. The political figures whom the President must continually take into account are to be found rather in the Congress, especially among the chairmen of its powerful committees.

Nevertheless, the Prime Minister like the President can provide an energizing, directing, and coordinating center for government. In operating within the new structure based on superministries and Cabinet committees, his old authority gives important powers of control. Moreover, the developing machinery on the official level centers in his office. At Number 10 he has a small office of only a half-dozen or so top civil servants but of growing importance. He is also directly in charge of the new Civil Service Department, whose major concern is questions of machinery of government. Moreover, the Cabinet office, while serving the Cabinet as a whole, is primarily at the disposal of the Prime Minister. With its network of officials undergirding the Cabinet committees, it can keep the Prime Minister informed of what is going on. Specifically, for instance, its permanent head, when briefing the Prime Minister on the agenda, can tell him just how a certain proposal originated and what has been said for and against it. The new central policy review staff will probably further strengthen the Prime Minister. While it will make available to all Cabinet members an assessment of proposals that is independent of departmental evaluations, it will operate directly under the Prime Minister, the government figure who overwhelmingly has the greatest interest in the impact and success of government policy as a whole. It is highly unlikely, however, that such mechanisms can change the essential collegiality of the Cabinet system.

---

[12]Richard E. Neustadt, *Alliance Politics* (New York, 1970), p. 95.

Three

Control of
the Public Sector

To draw a line between the polity and the rest of society is becoming more and more difficult in Britain, as in other advanced countries. Only a few decades ago it might have seemed plausible to draw that line where the bureaucracy—that is, the men and women directly employed in public administration—confronted the rest of the populace. But today the bureaucracy, huge as it has become, is only a small segment of the "public sector." Moreover, the public sector itself is intimately and purposively connected with the private sector by linkages that transmit its influence into the rest of the society, especially the economy. Export industries, for instance, while nominally part of the private sector, are shaped and conditioned by government programs in the service of broad policies to protect the balance of payments. Under British law workingmen are free to bargain collectively with their employers over wages and conditions. In fact, governments exert vast efforts to make these bargains come out in a way not too unfavorable to the general health of the economy. The so-called private sector is continually expected to carry out public purposes.

The main problem of public administration is how to make this huge machine with its multiple and many-jointed linkages an effective instrument for carrying out government policy. Whether it is effective will depend not only on the capacities of persons and structures, but also upon the policies that the central authorities have charged them with carrying out. If these policies arouse hostility, evasion, or resistance, or indeed if they fail to elicit the willing cooperation of the groups affected, the machine will not work. What people can be prevailed upon to accept from government is a major determinant of government's effectiveness. Their consent must be won. If, for instance, trade unions resolutely refuse to accept controls over the price of labor, the machinery set up to exercise this control in the service of planning will break down. The main problem of public administration thus merges with a principal question of public policy. For in a modern democratic state such as Britain a central question of conflict over public policy has been how far and in what ways state power shall be extended over the lives of individuals and groups. The general trend toward centralization and the expansion of policy has meant that more and more areas of free private activity have been included in and subjected to the pattern of power.

The main forces of modernization—democracy and science—might seem to make this trend inevitable. Yet the extent and manner of government control in Britain, as elsewhere, has been a main issue of political conflict. Moreover, the main shifts in approach have not been determined solely by the outcome of general elections. The extension or retraction of government control has been affected not only by how people have voted, but also by how they have reacted directly to attempts to control their behavior. Not only the realities of getting elected, but also the realities of governing have determined the fluctuating boundaries of the pattern of power, and the main shifts in government attitudes toward economic control have occurred not at elections but between them. As we shall see in this chapter, the problems of public administration lead straight into the central problems of politics.

Conventionally, the public sector is constituted by the central government, the local authorities, and the public corporations. The latter consist largely of the nationalized industries: the airlines, railroads, coal mines, and gas, electricity, steel, and atomic energy industries. One index of the size and influence of the public sector is monetary. In 1968 expenditure, current and capital, for the public sector came to a little over £19 billion. This amounted to 52 percent of a G.N.P. of nearly £39 billion. The impact of the public sector on investment and, so, on economic growth is suggested by the fact that it accounted for nearly 50 percent of gross domestic capital formation. In terms of employment the public sector included 25 percent of the total work force, some 6.3 million in comparison with 19 million in the private sector. Of these 6.3 million the central government accounted for 1.9 million, the local authorities for 2.3 million, and the public corporations for 2 million. In the higher-skill categories the share of the public sector increased, including about half of all university graduates and a third of all qualified scientists and technologists.

It is the departments of the central government, with their growing armies of clerical, technical, and administrative employees, that attract most attention as the embodiment of modern bureaucracy. Table 3.1 shows their increase in numbers since the eighteenth century.

This expansion in scale was accompanied by an increase in specialization, reflected in the creation of new departments. Tracing back the departments that independently or as parts of amalgamations were still operating in 1970, one finds that the following had already come into existence by the end of the eighteenth

Table 3.1 Growth of the United Kingdom Civil Service (Nonindustrial Staff)

1797	16,267	1914	280,900
1832	27,000	1939	399,600
1871	53,874	1950	664,200
1901	116,413	1960	634,600
1911	172,352	1969	889,500

DATA SOURCES: W. J. M. Mackenzie and J. W. Grove, *Central Administration in Britain* (London, 1957), p. 7; and *Annual Abstract of Statistics* (London: H.M.S.O., 1970).

century: Admiralty, Treasury, Post Office, Foreign Office, Home Office, Board of Trade, and War Office. During the nineteenth century the Colonial Office, Scottish Office, and Departments of Agriculture and Fisheries, Education, and Works were set up. In the twentieth century the pace quickened, with the following departments created up to the outbreak of World War II: Labour, Air, Pensions and National Insurance, Health, Transport and Civil Aviation, and Commonwealth Relations. Since the start of World War II the following were established: Supply, Fuel and Power, Housing and Local Government, Education and Science, Land and Natural Resources, Overseas Development, Welsh Affairs, and, in an attempt to cope with this very proliferation of specialized departments, the superministries of Defence, Trade and Industry, Health and Social Services, and Environment.

Beyond this central bureaucracy are the other agencies of the public sector, especially included under local government and the public corporations. And merging with the public sector is a set of organizations, groups, and relationships that, whether technically public or private, are in fact indispensable to the implementation of public policy. A recent government report remarks that

> the complex intermingling of the public and private sectors [has led to] a proliferation of para-state organisations: public corporations, nationalised industries, negotiating bodies with varying degrees of public and private participation, public participation in private enterprises, voluntary bodies financed from public funds. Between the operations of the public and private sectors there is often no clear boundary.[1]

Ministers and Civil Servants

To control and give direction to this huge machine means in the first place making it responsive to the policy-making center—that is, the Cabinet and Ministers—and in the second place imparting to it the capacity to carry out these policies effectively.

---

[1]Fulton Committee, *Report on the Civil Service,* Vol. I (London: H.M.S.O., 1968), Cmnd. 3638, p. 10.

The first problem is a special case of the general problem of how to establish democratic control over the instrumentalities of state power at a time when policy is becoming ever more complex and technical. Even if one assumes that popular control over Ministers can be ensured by the mechanisms of party government, one must still question whether a set of politicians with limited expertise and many distractions can effectively control the top bureaucrats who make a career of government service. In Britain the thing to fear, it must be emphasized, is not purposeful bureaucratic sabotage. During the 1930s there were observers who predicted such a conflict even in Britain if and when a socialist government—that is, the Labour party—came to power.[2] As a deduction from simple-minded Marxist premises, the argument was plausible. The upper ranks of the Civil Service are— as they were then—recruited substantially from the upper and middle ranks of British society, as Table 3.2 makes clear. If the working classes and the upper classes believed their respective interests were fundamentally in conflict, it would no doubt follow that a bureaucracy composed of upper-class personnel would try to sabotage a working-class program. In fact, when the news came through in 1945

Table 3.2 Social Composition of the British Civil Service Administrative Class, 1967 (in Percent)

Father's Occupation	
Higher Professional or Managerial	21
Intermediate Professional or Managerial	46
Skilled Worker	23
Semiskilled and Unskilled Worker	6
Other	3
	100

Education: Type of Secondary School Attended	Year of Entry into Service			
	Before 1940	1940– 1950	1951– 1960	After 1960
L. E. A. Grammar	30	29	33	29
Direct Grant	20	17	21	18
Public School or Fee-paying School	50	50	46	50
Other	0	4	0	3

DATA SOURCE: Fulton Committee, *Report on the Civil Service,* Vol. 3, Part 1 (London: H.M.S.O.), pp. 54, 73, and 85.

that Labour had won, the mood among higher civil servants was euphoric, and with their socialist Ministers they set about putting through a program of reform

---

[2]See, for example, J. Donald Kingsley, *Representative Bureaucracy: An Interpretation of the British Civil Service* (Yellow Springs, Ohio, 1944); and Harold Laski, *Parliamentary Government in England* (New York, 1939).

comparing in magnitude with those other great instances of peaceful revolution, 1832 and 1906. In their recollections no Ministers have been more eulogistic of the Civil Service: "Unequalled in all the world," declared Clement Attlee, the former Labour Prime Minister and a man noted for understatement.

To say that civil servants are loyal to the Government of the day, however, does not mean that they are merely passive tools of ministerial initiative. They have ideas about what ought and ought not to be done, and they are expected to present these ideas to their ministerial chiefs. That they have a role in making policy as well as executing policy is made clear in any of the classic formulations of their function. One of these formulations was presented by Sir Warren Fisher, a notable head of the Civil Service during the interwar years. He said:

> Determination of policy is the function of ministers, and once a policy is deter-
> mined it is the unquestioned and unquestionable business of the civil servant to
> strive to carry out that policy with precisely the same good will whether he
> agrees with it or not. That is axiomatic and will never be in dispute. At the same
> time it is the traditional duty of civil servants, while decisions are being formu-
> lated, to make available to their chiefs all the information and experience at their
> disposal and to do this without fear or favor, irrespective of whether the advice
> thus tendered may accord or not with the Minister's initial views.[3]

As Fisher made clear, the norm is that civil servants are expected to criticize Ministers' proposals and to present and argue for their own, but once the Minister has decided, the civil servant must do his best faithfully to develop the ministerial program and see that it is effectively carried out by the department. All this, moreover, is not only convention, but, on the whole, the truth about ministerial-bureaucratic relations and is not disputed in serious discussions of the topic. A more critical hypothesis—suspicion, if you like—undercuts this analysis. It raises the possibility that although the civil servant is typically an honest and obedient subordinate, the Minister may simply not know enough to initiate proposals or to criticize authoritatively what the civil servant puts forward. If so, there would be no conflict, no duplicity, no sabotage, yet a largely one-way flow of influence from bureaucrat to politician.

Certain elements in the situation make this outcome likely. The background of the typical Minister hardly gives him a profound grasp of the problems of his department. Even if he was front-bench spokesman in the relevant field when in Opposition, the absence of a full system of specialized legislative committees before which bureaucrats appear prevents him from getting a close and intimate look at what the department is doing. As a Minister he is very probably moved from department to department, the average tenure being about two years. Such mobil-ity is no doubt helpful in keeping the Minister's mind fresh and in satisfying his political ambition as he climbs the ladder of success, but it also severely limits his

---

[3]Royal Commission on the Civil Service, 1929–1931. Evidence.

experience in any particular field. Also, as the head of a department he is diverted by other duties. A recent study concluded that in the Wilson Government, the average Minister's work week came to sixty-one hours, of which he spent fifteen on departmental business, seventeen at the House, and twenty-nine in other activities. If we think in terms of conflict, this distribution of time puts a quarter-time Minister against a full-time bureaucrat. Finally, there is the fact that the Prime Minister in picking members of the Government is confined almost entirely to members of Parliament—a very narrow base for recruitment—and, moreover, is sometimes obliged to give preference to political and party popularity regardless of competence.

On the other hand, Ministers have powerful means by which to convert their immense formal authority into effective control. In the first place, they are free to call on expert aid from outside. The party research department and officials of interest groups are available to them in office as they were in Opposition. Increasingly important are professionally trained people, especially from the academic world. When the Labour Government took power in 1964, Ministers brought in a score or so of temporary officials—one Labour Minister christened them "the irregulars"—to a great extent in deliberate imitation of the Kennedy administration. The larger frustrations of that Government impeded extensive social or economic reform. Yet the use of "irregulars" received the blessing of a major report on reform of the Civil Service, and the new Conservative Government similarly brought in outside advisers from the business and professional world for the purpose of policy analysis and review.

Even more important than help from outside experts is the party mandate. In Britain, as elsewhere, party manifestoes contain their fair share of fuzzy compromises and nonoperational rhetoric. But usually there will also be a series of quite definite and intelligible pledges tucked away amidst the pompous prose. These may constitute tacit promises to an interest group or specific reforms worked out by party intellectuals and presumably reflecting party principles or ideology. In either case the brief proposal of the manifesto will probably be backed up by a position paper, perhaps published as a party pamphlet, and watched over by a group of outsiders specially concerned with its enactment. With this kind of support the Minister is in a position of incontestable superiority, as civil servants universally recognize, whatever their views of the feasibility or merits of such proposals. R. H. S. Crossman, a long-time leader of the left wing of the party and a redoubtable Minister in the Wilson Government, reported his experience in these words:

> The truth is the British civil service accepts the two party system completely. Indeed, in certain ways it's almost embarrassing. When you arrive in government after winning an election, there they are. They say, "Minister, we have been working on your manifesto; we have all the plans ready for implementing all your legislative proposals." I am well aware that as of today [this was shortly before the election of 1970] my ministry has a section which is

busily studying the Conservative manifesto, preparing for the unfortunate possibility of a turn-over.[4]

The respect was mutual. After Crossman had left office a senior civil servant said of his term in office: "It was the most productive two years in the history of this ministry. It was absolute murder for the civil servants; tears, nervous breakdowns. But things *happened.*"

The Question of Expertise

Beyond the question of whether Cabinet and Ministers can control and direct the upper level of the bureaucracy lies the far more complex and important question of the effectiveness of the bureaucracy and related agencies as instruments of state power. This raises problems relating to quality of personnel, as well as aspects of structure, in particular, types of decentralization and means of coordination.

A recent report on the Civil Service by a committee under the chairmanship of Lord Fulton severely criticized it and proposed a series of reforms, many of which are now being carried out. These proposals are worth considering in some detail, as illustrating modernization and its problems. The proposals advocated not merely greater specialization, but especially specialization based upon scientific knowledge. Concerning itself mainly with the upper levels of the bureaucracy, the Fulton Committee sought greatly to enhance the position and authority of the technically and scientifically trained person.

At the time of the report, in 1968, the Civil Service was divided into a number of classes. Those of interest to us were the generalist and the specialist classes. The former, recruited on the basis of general education and personal qualities, consisted of several levels. At the top was the Administrative class, numbering 2,700 men and women, to which about one hundred new members between the ages of twenty and twenty-four were recruited each year, usually straight from the university. Two methods were used. Method I, the older, was based on written examinations testing general intelligence and academic competence in typical university subjects ranging from Arabic to Zoology. Method II, the extended interview, came out of a system developed during World War II to select army officers and was based largely on close observation of candidates over a period of two days going through exercises that were similar to the work that a successful candidate would perform in the public service. The Administrative class consisted of six grades: assistant principal, principal, assistant secretary, undersecretary, deputy secretary, and permanent secretary. It was the elite of the system, its members enjoying the highest pay scale and virtually monopolizing the top administrative

---

[4]R. H. S. Crossman, Godkin Lectures (Harvard University, 1970).

posts from assistant secretary on up. Other general classes that should be mentioned were the Executive class, numbering 83,000 and usually recruited from young people just finishing secondary school, and the Clerical and Clerical Assistant classes, numbering 191,000, who performed the routine work of the departments.

In contrast to these general classes were the Professional classes and Scientific and Technical staffs. Numbering 132,300, these groups were recruited from people outside the Service who had already obtained some special qualification relevant to their work—for example, doctors, lawyers, scientists, architects, economists, engineers, surveyors, and supporting workers. Some of these professional and scientific civil servants, needless to say, were persons of exceptional attainments. Yet under the existing procedures governing appointments, they could not be moved to the top administrative posts unless they were first promoted to the Administrative class. This transfer rarely took place. In 1968 thirty-three out of thirty-six posts of permanent secretary were held by members of the Administrative class.

Probably the major reform proposed by the committee—and, at this writing, in the process of being put into effect—was the abolition of the system of Civil Service classes in favor of a system of grades modeled on the American practice. Already such a unified grading scheme has been worked out for the Administrative, Executive, and Clerical classes. If and when the scheme is extended to professional and scientific workers, not only will the discriminatory titles, conditions, and pay be eliminated, but also the opportunity will be opened up for scientists and other professionally trained people to move more easily into the higher administrative positions.

The rationale for this reform as stated by the committee is wholly modernist. In its view the old system expressed an old fashioned faith in the "generalist" as against the "specialist" for the task of administration. "The ideal administrator," the committee wrote, "is still too often seen as the gifted layman who, moving frequently from job to job within the Service, can take a practical view of any problem, irrespective of its subject-matter, in the light of his knowledge and experience of the government machine."[5] But, according to the committee, this will no longer do as the inspiration for recruitment, training, and promotion when the tasks of government involve highly technical operations, especially in the realm of economic and financial policy. In the committee's view these upper posts must be manned by people who have not simply a general grasp of administration, but who have professional knowledge of the subject matter of the department they are administering.

The scientific and technocratic spirit in these proposals is plain. They are also an attack upon traditionalism in British society as well as in the government Service. For the structure of classes in the Civil Service faithfully reflected the class structure

---

[5]Fulton Committee, *op. cit.,* p. 11.

of British society. The system of recruitment was geared to the educational system, which at once determines and reflects class structure. From the time more than a hundred years ago, when the Service was put on a merit basis, it was expected and certainly hoped that its upper reaches would attract the graduates of the old and elite universities, Oxford and Cambridge. Nor has Oxbridge relaxed its strangle hold on those posts, in the period 1957–1963, for example, producing 85.5 percent of the successful candidates for the Administrative class in contrast with only 14.5 percent from other universities.

Moreover, and this is closer to our concerns, although Oxford and Cambridge have greatly broadened the social sources of their student body in recent decades, the social origins of those entering the Administrative class have remained fairly narrow. (See Table 3.2.) In spite of efforts to correct the imbalance, as the Fulton Committee reported, "direct recruitment to the Administrative Class has not produced the widening of its social and educational base that might have been expected."[6]

The upper classes of British society have traditionally defended their privileges on the grounds that they perform an important political function. In Schumpeter's words they constituted that "social stratum" who "after having proved itself able to avoid an analogon to the French Revolution and to eliminate the dangers from dear bread . . . continued to know how to manage social situations of increasing difficulty, and how to surrender with some grace." The Administrative class of the Civil Service has continued to draw substantially on this social stratum. Moreover, its function has not been conceived as essentially technical. Its central concern is "the formation of policy"; it is the "policy-making" class of the Service. In the late nineteenth century the political leadership of the country maintained contact with the "other classes" as the era of social reform and collectivist policy was inaugurated. But the party and parliamentary leaders who carried out these reforms depended upon the close cooperation of their advisers in the newly reformed Civil Service. Oxford and Cambridge turned out a disproportionate share of both British Cabinets and the Administrative class, so that men who had been contemporaries at the universities often later bridged the gap between Westminster and Whitehall.

It is sometimes said that the task of the Minister is to tell the civil servant what the voters will not stand. This saying, although too negative, gets across the point that an important part of the politician's job is to reflect pressures from the people. The top civil servants also feel pressure from the people, in the people's capacity not as voters, but as citizens bearing the burdens and receiving the benefits of the modern state. The people, as individuals, as members of groups, as highly organized bodies in business and social life, can make their demands known through politicians. But they also continually make known their will as the objects of, and often the partners in, bureaucratic action. Their consent and cooperation must be secured if the vast and complex policies of the modern state are to be carried out

---

[6] *Ibid.,* p. 12.

effectively. The bureaucrat himself is the principal object of these reactions, the management of which is a crucial kind of politics. His task is to make policy effective, but since he does not have unlimited coercion at his command, he can achieve this only by making policy in some degree also responsive. He does not address himself publicly to the demands coming up through Parliament, pressure groups, and parties. But the assistant secretary who spends long hours trying to wear down a little further the hostility of trade unionists to an incomes policy or to warm up businessmen to the point of cooperation with an export drive is, nonetheless, deeply immersed in politics.

Policy making has a large and growing scientific and technical component, but it is not itself an act of applied science. Neither Ministers nor top civil servants can perform their respective functions by deduction from a body of empirically based, systematically organized, and experimentally tested propositions. The element of political judgment in the advice of the administrator takes a good mind—broad, lucid, and flexible—but it has not yet been reduced to a scientific basis. Today, as at the origins of the Civil Service in the nineteenth century, its defenders insist upon this distinctively political character of the tasks of its higher ranks. As one authority has written:

> They must temper their appreciation of technical beauty with a keen sense of their public relations. In short the Administrative Grade and its hierarchical form is necessary precisely because the work of a ministry demands a sense of public policy as well as a grasp of techniques.[7]

None of this should be taken to mean that the role of science and technology in British government has not increased and will not continue to increase. Britain,

Table 3.3 Nobel Prizes by Country and Field, 1945–1970

	Physics	Chemistry	Medicine/ Physiology	Three Fields
Great Britain	5	12	8	25
France	2	0	2	4
Germany	2	4	3	9
United States	16	11	22	49
Soviet Union	4	1	1	6

DATA SOURCE: The World Almanac, 1971.

the home of Sir Isaac Newton, is by no means inhospitable to science, as one can see from her fantastic comparative achievement in winning Nobel prizes. (See Table 3.3.) Nor are British government and business insensitive to the importance of science to economic progress. In relation to her G.N.P. Britain spends more on research and development than either France or Germany and much more than

[7]S. E. Finer, *A Primer of Public Administration* (London, 1950), p. 120.

the United States. Scientists share membership on the majority of the vast network of advisory committees that are attached to government departments. Of the top British scientists constituting the members of the Royal Society, 20 percent held full-time or part-time appointments in government or quasi-government bodies in 1970. Within the Civil Service itself, the impact of science is increasingly evident. Of the sixty or so top civil servants engaged in administration in the huge Ministry of Technology in 1968, twenty-two were scientists.

It is this last statistic that is most interesting as suggesting a possible future. People can grant that the "generalist" with his essentially political talents performs a different function from the "specialist," yet disagree about how generalists are to be produced. In the past the generalists have been trained very largely in the subjects that constituted in Britain the principal means of a liberal education—classics, history, and mathematics. But science—meaning by this both natural and social science—can also be the vehicle of a liberal education. This at any rate is the view taken by the modernist. If he is right, the shift from the traditional to the more scientific subjects that is to be expected in an increasingly technological future need not mean that the administrative generalist will disappear from the Civil Service.

Territorial Decentralization

The capacity of a bureaucratic system can be enhanced by improvements in personnel or by changes in structure. Many acute observers will say that the problem of ineffectiveness in British government results far less from the allegedly irrelevant education of civil servants and inadequate use of scientists than from overcentralization and the consequent excessive load of business on the higher Civil Service. One senior civil servant recently made these private remarks:

> I don't myself think there is any great substance in the oft-repeated stories about inadequate use of scientists and other "experts" (other than experts in government!) in our civil service system. The fashion of criticism changes, and the Fulton Report calls for economists and sociologists to unlock the door to wise decision-making.
>
> We obviously shan't have a smaller public sector in future; but I think we can readily develop ways of managing it better—basically a question of deciding which are the things which have to be decided politically and centrally, and which are the things which can be decided regionally or locally or by independent public boards or agencies.

In Britain as in the United States, amid constant praise of the virtues of local government, centralization has gone forward at an increasing rate, especially in this century. In the late sixties, however, the proposals to local government or regional bodies for planned decentralization seemed to take a more serious form. They reflected primarily the desire of central managers, both bureaucrats and Ministers, to shed some of their overload of administration. But there was also a political side. An upsurge of national feeling in Scotland and Wales—Ireland is an older and more complex story—was expressed in demands for more autonomy for these areas of the Celtic fringe. Some observers also say they detect a rise of regional feeling generally in Britain. To this extent there is political support and stimulus for these efforts of administrative reorganization, and we see a corresponding response in the promises of the political parties.

Since the British Constitution, unlike the American or German, is unitary and not federal, local governments have only the powers allowed to them by the central government. For England and Wales (the Scottish system is slightly different), the scheme laid down in a series of great reorganizing acts of the late nineteenth century still prevailed in 1971. The areas consisted of two basic sorts. There were sixty-one administrative counties, sometimes coinciding with the boundaries of the ancient shires and ranging in size from massive Lancashire with 2 million inhabitants to diminutive Rutland with only 26,000. The other basic type was the county borough, of which there were eighty-three. These consisted of all the largest cities except London and in a geographic sense were often embraced by the larger territory of an administrative county, although they constituted a separate jurisdiction. This meant that the surrounding area of a big city might be separately governed from the city itself, a separation of town from country that tended to rule out metropolitan government. London, however, the exception from the general scheme, did have metropolitan government, its 7.5 million people being governed by thirty-two borough councils and by the Greater London Council. The administrative counties were further subdivided into noncounty boroughs, urban districts, and rural districts, the latter including thousands of parishes of medieval origin, which had such splendid duties as the maintenance of public footpaths.

As in relations between an American state and its local governments, the central government may and often does use the local governments as agents for carrying out central government policies. This is not the case with all central government programs; many are carried out directly. Whitehall departments, for instance, have local offices that directly administer such matters as tax collection, pensions, national insurance, national assistance (welfare), and employment exchanges. Needless to say, the nationalized industries also have their own local agencies for performing their functions and bringing their services to the public. The traditional method of executing central policies, however, was to use the established local authorities. Since these are legally the creatures of the central government, they can in theory be put under any obligation the sovereign Parliament chooses to put them under. In fact, central departments have been given far-reaching powers of direction and control, as reflected, for instance, in the words of the Education Act of 1944, which gave the Minister the duty to "secure the effective execution by local authorities under his control and direction of the national policy." All local borrowing must have central approval. Many proposed local programs can be put into effect only with appropriate departmental approval. But the legal power of direction has been supplemented and sweetened by a system of grants-in-aid.

These normally involve the payment by the central government of part of the cost of a program and in return impose certain standards upon its form and execution. Originating in 1835, central grants to local government have grown immensely in this century and constitute a convenient measure of the pace and degree of centralization.

Table 3.4 Local Government Expenditure 1890–1968

	1890	1905	1935	1955	1968
Local Government Expenditure at Current Prices in £ Millions	50	123	428	1536	4649
Local Govt. Expenditure As Percent of Total Government Expenditure	—	51	38	25	24
Central Grants As Percent of Local Government Current Expenditure	25	32	46	54	58
Central Grants As Percent of Local Government Expenditure, Current and Capital	22	25	40	39	38

DATA SOURCES: Peacock and Wiseman, *The Growth of Public Expenditure in England,* pp. 197, 200, 208; Central Statistical Office, *Annual Abstract of Statistics* (H.M.S.O., 1970).

As Table 3.4 shows, while the absolute amount spent by local government has increased immensely, its relative importance has shrunk steadily. Local government expenditure has fallen from a half to a quarter of total government expenditure, and of this quarter something like half is supplied by and is under the control of Whitehall. It is a very different world from that of the nineteenth century, when many observers, such as the German scholars Gneist and Redlich, regarded the strength of British local government, in contrast with the centralization of France, as the secret of British liberty. Yet this method of using local authorities to carry out national policies does avoid day-to-day administrative interference and control. With regard to the police, for instance, although the central government sets standards and inspects to see that they are applied, no central department can ring up and give orders to the head of the police force in a local area, as the Ministry of the Interior can do in France.

Recent proposals for reform will not sound unfamiliar to an American. In order to relieve local authorities from their sole dependence on property taxes (called "rates"), it has been urged that they be authorized to impose new forms of taxation such as a local income tax, sales tax, or motor license fee. Also attempts have been made to bridge the gap between the big towns and their surrounding areas with regard to those functions requiring integrated planning and administration. The proposals of the Heath Government put forward in 1971 would greatly reduce the number of local authorities, reorganizing them on the basis of two new types. A type of large jurisdiction, called simply a "county," of which there would be fifty-nine, would include all areas—whether town or country—within its geographic boundaries. A second type of authority, the "district," often consisting of large towns, such as the old county boroughs, would, however, be only a second-tier unit within the larger jurisdiction. Both would, of course, have an electoral base. The counties would normally provide the large-scale government services such as strategic planning, transportation, roads, education, social services, police and fire services, while the districts would be responsible for more localized services, such as development control, housing, and garbage collection. In addition to London exceptions to this scheme would include six metropolitan counties around Birmingham, Sheffield, Manchester, Liverpool, Leeds, and Newcastle-upon-Tyne. There would still be need for wider arrangements to provide for regional planning.

The idea of regionalism has been gaining ground since the interwar years, when central departments first began to interpose an intermediate level between White-hall and their local offices and when special agencies were set up to deal with the economically depressed areas. The regional offices of central departments have become strong and well-established units of government. Less success attended the Wilson Government's establishment of eight districts for England, each with an appointive council of laymen and board of civil servants to assist with economic planning. There were uneasy relations, however, between these agencies and the local authorities, which had long seen a possible threat in regional bodies. Tension also arose with central departments, which largely rejected or ignored their recom-mendations, and the only effective districts were those with special responsibilities in relation to depressed areas. Also, while the boards and councils could initially deal with local interests by negotiation and concession, there was a tendency for these interests soon to demand some real power.

The fact that not much has been done to bring about territorial decentralization, however, does not mean that the question is closed. In 1969 a Royal Commission on the Constitution was appointed to consider "what changes may be needed in the central institutions of Government in relation to the several countries, nations and regions of the United Kingdom." In the campaign of 1970 the Conservative party committed itself even more strongly and explicitly than the Labour party to what its manifesto called "a genuine devolution of power from the central govern-ment."

Functional Decentralization

More successful have been the efforts toward functional decentralization. These have brought about the "hiving off"—a favorite word in Whitehall currently—of parts of departments in the form of independent boards or agencies. Far more than Americans, the British in the past have tended to keep government activities within existing departments. To revisit Whitehall these days is to have a mild sense of being in Washington, as more and more agencies appear alongside the old mono-liths.

These public bodies, which on the one hand are not parts of a department, yet on the other hand are not purely private, embrace a wide variety of types. Although many have emerged recently, not all are new. Public boards of a commercial character—that is, ones that engage in substantial trading operations—are well recognized. They consist of certain of the great nationalized industries, such as the two airway corporations, B.O.A.C. and B.E.A.; Cable and Wireless, Ltd.; the National Coal Board; the Electricity Council and the Central Electricity Generating Board, as well as the various area boards; the Gas Council and its area boards; and in the case of transport various bodies, including the British Railways Board and the London Transport Board. Also included under commercial boards are the British Airport Authority, the Atomic Energy Authority, the Herring Industry Board, and the Whitefish Authority; the Sugar Board; and, since it was recently converted from a department to a public corporation, the Post Office. Beyond these are a number of regulatory bodies, advisory boards, and finance corporations of which no exhaustive list, let alone authoritative classification, has yet been compiled.

In essence the idea of hiving off is to remove certain activities of the managed economy from the direct control and responsibility of Ministers, each separate operation being given—by statute if necessary—a specific objective with appropriate powers and then being allowed to carry on its own affairs free from political interference. This was precisely the idea that initially inspired the form of organization given the nationalized industries. While nationalization was inherently an act of state centralization, it was agreed by nationalizing Governments, whether Conservative or Labour, that as far as possible the new state enterprises would be given autonomy and removed from ministerial control. A generation's experience with them has brought out the possibilities and problems of the independent agency under the British system.

The National Coal Board will serve as an example. The Board is a public corporation, which means that while it has the commercial powers of a private corporation for the purposes defined in its charter, its members are appointed by the Minister of Trade and Industry, who has certain supervisory powers. When the 1,500 collieries of Britain were nationalized in 1947, their ownership was vested in the board, which manages them through forty-eight areas and eight divisions and half-a-dozen specialized departments, much as a board of directors would run a very large business. A major purpose of the structure was to give the board substantial independence in the business management of production and marketing. According to Herbert Morrison, a Labour Minister who was one of the principal architects of the public corporation, the problem was to get "the best of both possible worlds, the world of vigorous industrial enterprise without the restrictions imposed by Civil Service methods and Treasury control, and the world of public service and accountability."[8] The industry was charged with covering its costs, which would make it independent of public funds and so of the detailed controls

---

[8] Herbert Morrison, *Government and Parliament: A Survey from Inside* (London, 1954), p. 251.

over expenditure exercised over regular departments by the Treasury. The Minister was given certain specified powers, such as powers of approval of schemes for capital development, powers of appointment and dismissal of the board, and powers to investigate and obtain information. He was also given authority to issue "directions of a general nature" in matters that appeared to him "to affect the national interest." Few such general directions have been issued, but the existence of this authority in the background has made it possible for the Minister usually to get his way without formal action.

The importance of the industry makes it inevitable and desirable that the Minister accept responsibility for what one occupant of the post called the "general success or failure of the enterprise."[9] But to uphold the distinction between "general success and failure" and particular actions of the board or its subordinate parts is not easy amidst the pressures and temptations of politics. The Minister may try to accept responsibility only for general policy and not for day-to-day administration, yet Opposition M.P.s will fudge that distinction as much as possible in their desire to score points. Moreover, the same political forces that move them will tempt the Minister to interfere at the levels of both policy and administration. It is entirely understandable and legitimate that he and the board should jointly determine the target for coal production and the prices to be charged for coal. To raise the price of coal, however, can add to the unpopularity of a Government. To close a pit, although necessary for greater efficiency, may threaten a loss of votes in a local election. The basis of these pressures is the enfranchised and mobilized electorate. While the wisdom of efficient administration advises decentralization, the pressures of democracy tend to push decision making back to the central authority.

It would be far easier to control and confine these political forces if the line could be firmly and unmistakably drawn between what must be decided centrally and what can be left to the independent board. The original acts setting up the public corporations defined this line only in such broad terms as "the national interest." Several decades of effort to give precision to the respective spheres of Minister and board have not been wholly successful. A solution would consist in finding a formula for each nationalized industry or similar activity that clearly stated the objectives of the operation and, if possible, also the criteria it was to follow in pursuing those objectives. The whole process would then be self-operating, and the Minister would need to intervene only to see that the formula was being observed. Along this line annual financial targets have been established for the nationalized industries in order to clarify the old vague requirement to cover costs "taking one year with another" and in order to use the prospects of a deficit or profit as guides and incentives to managers. Attempts have also been made to reduce to rule the criteria for judging proposed capital investment and the method for setting prices. Thus far, however, several decades of experience with public

---

[9]Hugh Gaitskell, quoted in Mackenzie and Grove, *Central Administration in Britain* (London, 1957), p. 435.

corporations have failed to give precision to the respective spheres of Minister and board, and the tendency in Britain, as in other countries, is for Ministers to intervene in the affairs of nationalized industries frequently and without a wholly satisfactory rationale. The problem is twofold: to draw a firm and feasible line between the activities of center and locality and then to stick to it in the face of the powerful centralizing forces of egalitarianism and democracy.

Again, however, in recent years some political forces supplementing administrative decentralization have grown stronger. These are not only political but indeed ideological, reflecting as they do the disillusionment of some sectors of opinion with the new efforts of economic planning and control that were made in the sixties. In Britain, as in France, this disillusionment has strengthened the advocates of "a return to the market." In their proposals hiving off is not only a method for improving the efficacy of the agencies of state power. On the contrary, one should say. For these reformers see hiving off as a means of reducing state activity by moving certain activities out of government control and subjecting them to regulation by the market. One kind of proposal is to separate off certain activities that can and should support themselves largely or entirely by fees charged for their goods and services—for instance, the Stationery Office, the British equivalent of the U.S. Government Printing Office. Other agencies, such as the Royal Mint, which coins money for many governments other than the British, could be given trading funds and held responsible for using them efficiently. More controversial are proposals to hive off parts of nationalized industries that promise to be commercially viable and return them to private ownership. The Heath Government, for instance, has proposed that Thomas Cooks', the old and famous travel company, which was nationalized along with the railroads, be hived off and returned to private management.

This resurgence of faith in the market, particularly marked in the Conservative party, springs from the recent failures of central economic planning. This is not the first time that the realities of governing have revealed limits to the effort of modern government in Britain to control the economic environment.

Four

Control of
the Economy

Economic planning is a typical effort of the modern state. Its sources are various. In a real sense it can be regarded as the accidental product of the welfare state. If we think of the latter as the response of the democratic polity to the increasing demands for wider and more varied services, we can see how in due time the activities of the state will comprise a major segment of the economy. Public expenditure mounts to a quarter, a third, and even a half of the national product, with taxation in its many forms increasing similarly. In such a situation, whatever the intentions of the state toward the free market, its own activities have an overwhelming influence upon general equilibria, specific lines of production, and the prosperity of particular regions. Having these great and growing effects, the state can hardly avoid trying to calculate and control them. Not to try to plan in some degree and form would simply be a refusal to recognize reality. Thus the managed economy grows naturally out of the welfare state.

A more conventional view finds a principal source of state intervention in the inadequacies of the market. At one time the rationale of intervention was simply to make up for isolated deficiencies of the market system: to impose on industry safety regulations that the average worker would not have the economic power or perhaps the sophistication to insist upon, and to make minimum provision for incapacitation resulting from illness or old age. In Britain interventions of this sort never ceased, even at the height of laissez faire. The collectivist period properly begins when government assumes a responsibility for certain dimensions of the economy as a whole. Attempts to prevent inflation on the part of the body charged with determining the value of money go back a long way, but not until the great depression of the thirties did government in Britain begin to acknowledge that it could do something beyond balancing the budget to remedy deflation. The great Keynesian breakthrough in economic theory legitimized, broadened, and directed these efforts, as the increasing programs of the welfare state gave governments the fiscal means for carrying them out. The government now fully recognized that the market system had general as well as isolated deficiencies. This recognition was marked by the commitment to full employment assumed by all parties during World War II and expressed in the famous white paper (Command 6527) issued by the Coalition government in 1944.

As a country that imports half of its food and two-thirds of its raw materials and depends upon sales abroad to pay for these imports, Britain is even less able to trust the market to govern her relations with the international economy. During the great depression of the thirties, she broke with her historic commitment to free trade and took the first steps to control her external economic relations. During the postwar years the balance of payments with the rest of the world has been an urgent and continuing problem; periodic external crises, often rooted in internal inflationary pressures, have been the occasions for some of the more characteristic efforts at economic control.

A further phase in collectivist policy was the assumption of responsibility for economic growth, which Britain, like other advanced countries, undertook in the early postwar years. To the short-run goals of full employment, price stability, and external balance, this new task added the long-run goal of constantly increasing productivity and thus, presumably, constantly raising the standard of living. In terms of the larger purposes of political modernity, this new goal constitutes no real innovation. Laissez faire itself, as a prescription for government policy, had been directed toward it, as Adam Smith made clear when he wrote on how to increase the wealth of nations. The thrust of modernity toward the mastery of nature that was expressed in industrialization inspires the international G.N.P. race among the advanced nations today. In the pursuit of long-run economic development, as in the attempt to achieve short-run equilibria, planning is a natural stage in the unfolding of the modern spirit. Both science and democracy point in this direction.

From the viewpoint of the basic forces of modernization, planning must seem inevitable. The empirical and historical record, however, has been marked at times by efforts to withdraw from planning. In planning, as in centralization generally, there have been cycles of tightening and loosening, as spasms of *dirigisme* have been followed by spells of neoliberalism. The history of planning in Britain since the war is clearly divided into such phases. Indeed, the vocabulary used to describe these efforts changes from phase to phase. The term "economic management" itself came into vogue in Britain in the fifties, as a substitute for "economic planning," which, after the frustrations of the Labour government, was felt to imply a degree of central control that was neither feasible nor desirable.

From Planning to Management

As economic policy has shifted back and forth between planning and management, the instruments used to achieve the ends of policy have changed correspondingly. The tighter kind of control attempted during the phases of planning has involved the creation of new ministerial and bureaucratic structures to coordinate and direct the effort. Usually the new instrument proposed is a separate Department of Economic Affairs (D.E.A.). During the phases of economic management, on the other hand, the traditional department of coordination, the Treasury, is largely relied upon for central direction. As planning rises, the Treasury declines; as planning and control are again relaxed, the Treasury moves back into its position of dominance. This is not to say that the Treasury is ever effectively excluded from the major decisions on economic policy. Some would argue that its attitudes are so antipathetic and its structures so dysfunctional to planning that its presence at the center of British government has been the chief reason why planning has had so little success. A more likely hypothesis is that economic control is severely limited by basic traits of the British polity and economy and that over time the Treasury, as an instrument of central coordination, has adjusted to, and psychologically internalized, these limits. The inadequacies of the Treasury—and they are very real—reflect the realities of the economic and political context.

Britain's achievements in economic mobilization during the war raised high hopes for economic progress after the war, and, while many controls were removed, the basic scheme of planning under the new Labour Government that came to power in 1945 was derived from the wartime model. The Treasury was brought back from the obscurity of wartime, when for a time it had not even been represented in the Cabinet. During this first phase of economic policy, which lasted until the late forties, it still occupied a secondary role in planning; and the principal instrument was not the financial budget, but a manpower budget laying down the main lines of control over the economy by means of its allocation of that ultimate scarce resource, labor.

If the British workers and their unions had been willing to accept government control over where they worked, how much they were paid, or both, Labour's postwar system of physical planning would probably have been a success. To be sure, there were other pluralistic forces besides labor that put a drag on the efforts of planners to control quantitatively the various sectors of the economy. Within the government the independence of departments reasserted itself, darkening the prospects of a chain of command from central planners to departmental executors. Business and professional groups used their very considerable leverage against government control. Yet the labor force—because of its size, its human character, and its high degree of organization—remained the most important and difficult factor to control. This has been well understood by economists. "Planned production," one socialist authority had written, "implies either compulsory industrial direction or a planned wage structure.''[1] The policy of industrial conscription and labor direction that had been accepted by British workers during the war was out of the question now. During the crisis years of the Labour government, the unions demonstrated, as they have continued to demonstrate, that they would under no conditions accept a wages policy. As a result the "targets" of the manpower budget were missed again and again by huge margins. Increasingly the Government was obliged to resort to the financial budget and the use of Keynesian techniques to affect economic behavior through manipulation of the market, rather than by direct control. By the end of the Attlee regime in 1951, economic planning had given way to economic management.

While the unions would not accept a wages policy, the Government did win their consent to restraint in pushing wage claims during the brief but crucial period from 1948 to 1950. This agreement resulted from a long and complex bargaining process between the Government, organized labor, and organized capital. In response to union demands the Government imposed a capital levy on wealth and continued heavy subsidies to reduce the price of basic foods. It also secured agreement from the peak business organizations that they would limit dividends. In return the unions agreed not to press for wage increases except under a few specified conditions. This important piece of policy making was accomplished outside the parliamentary system, and no statute or other legal document marked its consummation. The essential process was informal bargaining between representatives of Government and representatives of the organized producers groups in the two main economic sectors—capital and labor. Moreover, it worked. Wage rates, which had been rising rapidly, increased hardly at all until the pressures on prices from the devaluation of 1949 made it impossible for the unions any longer to hold the line and the T.U.C. in September 1950 rejected the policy.

As the postwar years wore on, it was realized that contrary to earlier beliefs, the thing to fear was not the old plague of mass unemployment, but the new affliction of chronic inflation. To cope with this, Governments resorted to fiscal and, later, monetary policy. They also found themselves obliged, as in 1948, to deal directly —and one might say, politically—with the big, organized producers groups of the economy in an effort to hold back wage and price increases. This effort became known as an "incomes policy." The problem with which it tried to deal, the restraint of inflation, was a problem for both economic management and economic planning. To a large extent, this problem was responsible for shifts of government policy from management to planning and back again, as governments of both parties tried in vain to find a successful solution.

The second phase of economic policy extended from the late forties to the early sixties. This was a period of economic management. (To show the convergence in party positions, the term "Butskellism" was coined to describe this phase by combining the names of the two leading economic spokesmen, the Conservative

---

[1]Barbara Wootton, *Freedom Under Planning* (Chapel Hill, N.C., 1945), p. 118.

R. A. Butler and the Laborite Hugh Gaitskell.) Thanks to a favorable change in the terms of trade—that is, a fall in the prices of agricultural products and raw materials relative to prices of manufactured products—the balance of payments was deceptively healthy for some years. But the old problem soon arose again. Like Labour before it, the Conservative party attempted to strike a bargain with labor and capital to hold back the cost-based factors of inflation. Failing to come to an agreement with the unions, the Government was confronted with the alternative of disinflation, which meant using fiscal and monetary policy to reduce aggregate demand and thereby creating some degree of unemployment. This was a hard choice for the Conservatives. Under the leadership of their progressive wing, they did not attack the welfare state, as Labour had expected, but added to it. Along with the protection of this large social expenditure, the party had also committed itself to the new meaning of full employment—in effect, an unemployment rate of 1 percent or so in contrast with the 4 percent rate that the fathers of the idea had anticipated. With fear and trembling, politically speaking, the Macmillan Government disinflated, at the expense of 2.8 percent unemployment in January 1959—the highest rate since the war. But prices did level out, and the Government went into the election year of 1959 with a strong expansionist policy, which it was expected would not only bring back full employment, but also coexist with price stability as economic growth went forward.

Full employment was restored, and the Conservatives won their third general election in a row, a feat without parallel in this century. But prices far from being quiescent soon began to mount again, and as her prices went up in the world market, Britain by 1961 was again confronted with a serious balance-of-payments crisis. Several years of restrictive fiscal policy and, so, of slow growth had bought only a brief respite, followed by renewed crisis. The tools of economic management forged in the late forties and early fifties now seemed less than adequate for either the short-run task of economic equilibrium or the long-run task of economic development. It is not strange that the more austere and direct methods of economic planning should once again look attractive.

From Management to Planning

This new line of thought, rising out of British experience, was strengthened when Britons looked abroad. In France, which had just thrown off the old loose ways of the Fourth Republic for the new discipline of the Gaullist regime, long experience with the Monnet plan, a highly *étatist* system of economic control, seemed to be showing abundant results. Between 1950 and 1960 average G.N.P. per capita had risen 3.5 percent in France, but only 2.1 percent in Britain. The lesson was humiliating for the British, and it seemed clear that they, too, should adopt the more *dirigiste* methods of the French planning system.

Like the earlier move from planning to management, this shift to a new phase of planning was not mediated by the mechanisms of party government. It was the

Conservatives under Macmillan, a planner in sentiment even in the interwar years, who inaugurated the new phase. Moreover, as often happens among the highly integrated elites of British society, there was a general shift of opinion in the same direction. Like Ministers, civil servants reacted to both the failure of the old looser methods and the promise of the French model. Even more interesting and important, leading business circles, especially in manufacturing, agreed that it was time for government to move toward a more tightly coordinated and positively directed economic effort. This marked a crucial change in the attitudes of organized business. Even after the war British industry had continued to be torn between its old principle of independence of government and the new possibilities for exercising influence on government at the cost of closer association with it. Finally, in the early sixties a decision was made in favor of the latter alternative, a decision reflected in the vigorous advocacy by the Federation of British Industries of economic planning for growth based on the French model. Indeed, it was industry's acceptance of its new responsibilities in the N.E.D.C., set up by the Conservatives in 1962, that led to the amalgamation of the three main peak organizations into one comprehensive organization, the Confederation of British Industry. Nor was this new commitment merely organizational. Individual firms cooperated heartily in providing the massive information needed for the new national plans.

The unions refused to have anything to do with the National Incomes Commission (N.I.C.), a body set up by the Conservatives to give some kind of guidance with regard to prices and wages. (Indeed, its utterances were called "guiding lights.") But organized labor did send its representatives to N.E.D.C. and to the little Neddies for specific industries, which were set up in later years, ultimately reaching a total of twenty-one. N.E.D.C. was not part of the Treasury Department, but, like N.I.C., was created by the then Chancellor of the Exchequer, Selwyn Lloyd, who was N.E.D.C. chairman and the responsible Minister. Bringing in both sides of industry as well as independent members and Ministers, the N.E.D.C. also had a small but impressive staff of economists and professionally trained people and was the center from which the Conservatives launched their effort to increase economic growth.

This was essentially a feasibility study for a period of five years, based on the assumption that national income would grow 4 percent per year and identifying some of the problems, such as the necessary level of exports and the tolerable level of imports, that would arise during the period.

Labour, which took office in 1964, built on these foundations and ambitiously extended the commitment to economic planning and control. Although, as one would expect from their ideological position, they showed greater willingness to intervene in the economy, their system still remained only "indicative," that is, it relied on "pointing out desirable ends rather than on giving orders to achieve them." A new Department of Economic Affairs was established under George Brown, a top party leader, who became the chairman of the N.E.D.C. Using the N.E.D.C. as well as its own staff, the new department produced in September 1965 the comprehensive National Plan whose purpose was "to develop a coordinated, internally consistent set of projections of how the economy might develop to 1970 and thereby create expectations that would induce private economic decisions to conform to the projections."[2] Within six months inflation had brought on a new crisis in the balance of payments. The restrictive fiscal policy undertaken in consequence made certain that the estimate of 3.4 percent annual growth in productivity per capita, on which the plan was based, would not be realized. This offspring of the new phase of economic policy, produced with such great exertion by government and industry under two Governments, was born dead.

The Politics of Inflation

During Labour's remaining four years in office economic policy was devoted to a fruitless struggle with the problem that wrecked its brief and ambitious effort to plan the economy. As its failure became evident, Labour dropped the word "planning" from its rhetoric and prepared the way for the reduction in government control that the Conservatives inaugurated when they took office in 1970. The central problem was inflation, and the history of the National Board for Prices and Incomes (N.B.P.I.), one of the most remarkable creations of the Labour Government, illustrates the nature of the problem and its intractability. When Labour took office, Ministers, officials, and the incoming "irregulars" fully understood the vital need to get an operative, not merely rhetorical, agreement with the big producers groups regarding prices and wages. While the unions had refused to come to terms with the Conservatives, it seemed logical to many that Labour—with its social-democratic ideology, its organizational connection with the unions, and its long personal association with union leaders—would be able to achieve agreement, once again, so to speak, as it had done in the late forties.

For two years Parliament played a secondary role, while the Government tried to achieve its ends by voluntary means. The first stage was a "Declaration of Intent," published in December 1964, in which trade unions and employers associations agreed in principle to keep incomes in line. A few months later, the N.B.P.I. was established with a professional staff and including persons drawn from both sides of industry as well as independent members. Its main task was to look into proposed increases in prices and wages and advise the Government as to whether they were in "the national interest." In connection with activities of the N.B.P.I., the Government had the power to require early warning of proposed increases, the power to forbid such increases for a period of time, and the power to order a complete freeze. During the years 1966–1967 these efforts did reduce increases in weekly wage rates by a small but significant amount—perhaps one percentage point in a rate of 6 or 7 percent per year. But the pound could not be protected, and the devaluation of November 1967 added to the pressure on prices

---

[2] *The National Plan* (London: H.M.S.O.), Cmnd. 2764.

whose rise in turn set off a surge of wage increases. By the end of 1968 the Government had virtually given up its effort to use the N.B.P.I. to restrain inflation, and the year 1970 saw a wage explosion that by the autumn had wages rising at an annual rate of 20.8 percent and prices at a rate of 10.4 percent. It remained only for the Conservatives to abolish the board—which is not to say that it will not be resurrected by them under a new name.

Conventionally, the two main types of inflation are identified as demand-pull and cost-push. Either may result in prices rising more than productivity. In the age of full employment and the welfare state aggregate demand fed by government expenditure has often added to the inflationary problem in Britain. It may well be that Labour was slow to take the necessary measures of fiscal disinflation consequential upon devaluation. In any case, by 1970 the austerities of the new Chancellor of the Exchequer, Roy Jenkins, had deflated demand to new levels. Unemployment rose to 2.4 percent by June, and in succeeding months the Conservative Government felt obliged to keep it at these high figures. Yet the price rise continued. Its impetus now was clearly cost-push, especially the wage explosion, which resulted largely from the ability of the well-organized unions to push up wages even under these circumstances. Labour as well as the Conservative Government admitted this fundamental fact by attempting to put a rein on union power through statutory reform. Yet it is hardly the whole truth to think of the unions as organizational giants overpowering the representatives of the national interest. One of the peculiarities of the situation is that these giants often are not masters in their own houses.

One reason for the failure of the incomes policy consists in certain structural weaknesses on the side of both trade unions and employers' associations. These weaknesses throw light on the stage of modernization reached by the British polity. Today government management of the economy in advanced countries entails making bargains. If these bargains are to be kept, there must be coherent and authoritative leadership within these organizations. Yet British producer groups have long been criticized for their lack of cohesion as compared with similar groups in such countries as Sweden.

Concentration is high among unions; some 70 percent of trade union membership in 1967 was accounted for by eighteen huge organizations. (See Chapter 10.) This would seem to indicate the kind of large-scale centralized organization needed to carry out effectively the union side of an incomes-policy bargain. At the same time, however, full employment has created countervailing tendencies, shifting much significant collective bargaining from the national to the plant level. Even when national organizations did accommodate their agreements with regard to wage rates to the criteria of the incomes policy, "earnings drift" at the plant level continued to swell the forces of cost inflation. In addition to full employment this tendency was bolstered by attitudes that go deep in British culture. First among them is "a proletarian spirit that seems conservative even by the standards of a traditionalist society," as an American observer has put it. Its principal consequence was wide support for restrictive labor practices and dogged resistance to practices increasing productivity. Also, in his opinion, "a tradition of paternalism" shared responsibility for the resulting underutilization of labor. This leads management to feel, in the words of one employer, that its "first responsibility is to provide work for these chaps—to keep the shop occupied."[3] Thus, in economic as in political behavior the ancient heritage of class consciousness showed its power.

Earnings were still substantially influenced by the terms of wage settlements on the national level, hence the importance of attempting to influence the negotiations leading to them through an incomes policy. Yet the trend to decentralization, which is reflected in earnings drift, meant a real loss of authority for the national unions. In the field of trade unions, at any rate, the present stage of modernization has meant a weakening rather than a strengthening of bureaucracy and large-scale organization. Even less than in the past are the British unions appropriate instruments to control and direct one of the major regulators of the economic system —the price of labor. The Wilson Government, finding that it could control the price of labor neither by persuasion, nor by bargaining, nor by legal coercion, was obliged to give up its ambitious hopes for economic planning. The National Plan was pushed aside, and the term "planning" virtually disappeared from party propaganda. The Department of Economic Affairs lingered on until 1969, when it was finally abolished; its economic planning section was transferred to the Treasury, which again became incontestably the major instrument for control of the economy.

The Treasury

Government in Britain intervenes in the economy on a wide scale, as do governments in other modern polities. In spite of the powerful impulsion given to such intervention by the forces of modernity, there seem to be major limits beyond which such intervention is not effective. These barriers, which have appeared when twice since the war attempts to control the economy have been forced into retreat, are deeply rooted in fundamental systemic traits of the British economy and polity. The Treasury, as the traditional coordinating department of British government, reflects in structure and attitude these characteristics.

The unique function of the Treasury as the principal coordinating department is suggested by its small size in comparison with the size of other departments. In 1971 its total personnel numbered 2,369, of whom some 150 had responsibility for policy. The Chancellor of the Exchequer is the Minister responsible for the Board of Inland Revenue and the Board of Customs and Excise. Each board has a large staff and important functions, and each is itself an independent department, not part of the Treasury and not subject to its officials. The Treasury is a central

---

[3]Lloyd Ulman in Richard E. Caves, *et al.*, *Britain's Economic Prospects* (Washington, D. C., 1968), pp. 332, 335.

coordinating agency, not an operating department. When it acts, it acts through other agencies and departments. Its style in conducting these relationships tells one as much about the British political system in general as about the Treasury in particular.

For a department often reputed to be stuffy, the Treasury has adapted with remarkable alacrity to the new and ever-changing demands of the collectivist age. In particular, it has in a series of major adaptations taken on the central responsibilities for steering the economy. Yet the manner in which it carries out these new tasks of economic coordination is in keeping with its much older functions of financial coordination. These functions consisted first in controlling departmental expenditures and second in deciding how the money would be found to meet them. The latter was regarded as the exclusive responsibility of the Chancellor in the sense that, after such consultations as he chose to make, he decided what the pattern of taxation would be for the next year and revealed his decision to the Cabinet only a day or two before presenting it in his budget speech in the House.

In controlling expenditure, however, the Treasury was in constant touch with other departments. Its powers were formidable. Perhaps the most important, and certainly the most characteristic, was the requirement of prior approval. This meant that another department could undertake no activity involving expenditure in the near or distant future unless that activity had the Treasury's approval. Normally, even the planning of such an activity would not be pushed very far unless the Treasury had been consulted. This requirement of prior approval was separate from the annual review of the estimates of expenditure that the other departments submitted to the Treasury for scrutiny and approval before their presentation to Parliament, much in the manner of the review conducted by the Bureau of the Budget in the United States. The exercise of control through the requirement of prior approval meant that the Treasury was in constant, day-to-day and week-to-week contact with the spending departments and was brought into their forward planning of particular expenditures at a very early stage. As the size and complexity of public expenditure increased, this power was relaxed in detail and greater delegations of discretion were made to other departments. Yet in spite of the Treasury's great and growing concern with the total expenditure of a department, it still does not surrender its interest in individual items—for the inexorably logical reason that one cannot decide on the merits of a total figure without having a look at its parts.

Prior approval had a coordinating effect, insofar as Treasury decisions expressed the priorities expressed in Government policy. But Government policy is continually being made and modified, especially by Ministers bringing bright ideas to the Cabinet. To prevent the Treasury from being bypassed in this manner, a rule of Cabinet procedure gives the Chancellor the right to keep financial problems off the Cabinet agenda until the Treasury has had an opportunity to see and criticize them. A further and similar protection is provided by the ancient rule of the House of Commons that only Ministers can bring financial proposals before it. In contrast with American practice, this prevents legislators from presenting to the House the temptation of spending money in isolation from the responsibility for raising it. While this rule does further safeguard the right of prior approval, the comparative expenditure in the two countries does not suggest that it is any guarantee of more cautious finance.

Even this brief recital of some of the powers of the Treasury suggests the special character and style of Treasury control in its classic form. In the first place this power is negative, as indicated by the witticism attributed to Churchill that the Treasury was an "inverted Macawber—always waiting for something to turn down." The Treasury did not take the initiative—dictating to departments what they should undertake in order to fulfill government policy—but rather shaped the initiative already taken by them suggesting alternatives when possible, but essentially trusting to departments to supply innovation and expertise.

Moreover, when we glance at the ministerial superstructure conditioning the official substructure, it is plain that even this negative power must be qualified by the realities of a plural executive and its collective decision making. Aggressive ministerial spenders were not, and could not be, prevented from taking their plans to the Cabinet; and once there they might well, as sometimes happened, defeat a reluctant Chancellor. In turn these realities of Cabinet government were anticipated by the behavior of civil servants in such a way that Treasury officials— while hardly deferential—worked with departments by persuasion rather than coercion, trying to "win acceptance of policy" rather than simply to "enforce policy." The officials with whom they dealt were not subordinates but equals, perhaps themselves permanent heads of "great departments of state" and serving Ministers who, like the Chancellor, shared the sovereign authority of the Cabinet.

This reality of British government was nicely reflected in the experience of the Department of Economic Affairs under the Wilson Government. In the conception of its first chief, George Brown, the D.E.A. was a major overlord department in charge of all aspects of economic policy; the other economic departments, including the Treasury, were merely executive agencies to carry out decisions made at the center. Things did not work out this way—nor could they have, given the fact that Wilson appointed as Chancellor, James Callaghan, a major Labour party leader. The politics of the British kind of democratic leadership and the structure of the plural executive do not permit the strict hierarchical control entailed by economic planning as contemplated by some of the fathers of the D.E.A.

The New System

A main problem in establishing control over the pattern of power is to distinguish matters that must be centrally decided from those that should be left to functional or territorial authorities. This means making sure that the important matters do come before the central authority and, at the same time, that unimportant matters do not paralyze it. But how decide what is important or unimportant? How reduce this crucial distinction to some kind of operational rule or procedure? Without some rule there is a tendency for each case itself to require a central decision on whether it should be decided centrally.

One answer to the question of what ought to be decided centrally is that it depends on how much money is involved; the greater the expenditure, the more deserving it is of central scrutiny. The rule is crude and by no means excludes the need for sensitive political judgment. Actions of government entailing little or no expenditure may be very important and politically controversial—for instance, a deportation case coming before the Home Secretary, proposed legislation relating to the death penalty or homosexuality, or declarations of praise or blame with regard to foreign affairs. Still, as a rough and ready indicator of the degree of importance to be assigned to a proposed activity of government—and this is especially true in these days of the welfare state—the quantum of expenditure is the best available basis. Above all, it is operational. Looking at the proposed programs of various departments, we see a miscellany of qualitatively and physically different activities, whose relative importance is not immediately evident. No one, however, needs to be told that £100 million is a great deal more than £5 million.

As the agency whose ministerial chief's special responsibility was raising money, the Treasury also acquired the function of providing the funds for the spending departments. This latter function meant that it continually knew how much money, and in particular how much more money, departments were proposing to spend. Therefore it inevitably became the main agency through which the central authority impressed upon department activities its sense of priorities, of what was important and unimportant.

Under some systems of government control of the economy, money is a poor indicator of importance. During World War II, for instance, the main economic decisions were made in the course of framing the manpower budget, under which the total labor force was allocated among the chief industries and the fighting services; budgets were provided for critical materials, indicating what industries were to get them; and an important program was established, setting out the physical volume of various types of imports. Under this system the physical quantities of men and matériel, rather than their costs, were the key indicators, and the Treasury sank in importance accordingly. Such a system of physical planning, however, has not yet proved practicable in peacetime. As we have seen, Britain has twice been thrown back on an approach to economic control based not upon superseding the market, but upon manipulating it through the public use of, and control over, money. The Keynesian revolution in economics and the enormous development of quantitative techniques provided the foundation for this type of economic management. The old Treasury and the new economics met and merged, the Treasury becoming the main agency not only for coordinating government activities, but also for coordinating the British economic system. This was not inevitable, but depended upon two facts: First, the Treasury dealt with money, and money was the substantial means by which the new form of control was exercised; and, second, the

Treasury's style of coordination was appropriate to the needs of economic management.

Within the broad limits conditioning its style of coordination, the Treasury has developed major new capacities for dealing with economic problems. In one respect it has lost certain of its previous functions. One of the peculiarities of the British system of public administration had been that control over the Civil Service was exercised by the Treasury. This control included responsibility for overall efficiency of the public service, development of management services, settlement of pay and conditions of service, and grading of staff. In 1968 these responsibilities were given to a new Civil Service Department, which, directly under the Prime Minister, now has important coordinating functions in unified central management of the services. Otherwise, the organization of the Treasury falls into three groups. The public sector group consists of a number of divisions, each concerned with control of expenditure by several departments with related fields of policy, as well as a small division concerned with taxation. The finance group is concerned with borrowing and lending, the balance of payments, and foreign exchange. The economic management group deals with major questions of overall economic policy. It is this latter group that constitutes the major addition in structure and personnel. From the prewar years, when the Treasury was quite innocent of professional economic advice, it has developed a considerable capacity, absorbing in turn the economic section set up in the Cabinet office during the war, the central economic planning staff established under Cripps' short-lived Ministry of Economic Affairs, and, more recently, the economic planning division of the defunct Department of Economic Affairs. Indeed, it has itself become Ministry of Economic Affairs as well as a Finance Ministry.

The use of the old financial powers in the service of the new economic responsibilities is a main feature of the control of public expenditure, as it must be at a time when total public-sector spending exceeds half the G.N.P. Today, as in the past, the Treasury seeks balance among the various expenditures in the public sector. Conceptually, the standard of balance means that expenditures should be so allocated that the last pound spent on each activity produces the same amount of public good. It makes marginal amounts relevant to the decision: Is an extra £5 million on one program more worthwhile, or less worthwhile, than £5 million on another? Measurement of public good is so difficult that it is left to politicians and voters. But their judgment can be assisted by techniques of cost-benefit analysis, and the Treasury has taken many pains to develop these techniques. They are especially relevant where the purpose of the programs is largely economic, as, for instance, in a choice between further expenditure on roads or railways. A very large part of public expenditure, however, is more social than economic, including health and welfare, housing and community services, children's services, benefits and assistance, law and order. The modern democratic polity generates great pressure toward increasing such expenditures, and the welfare state includes an array of groups of consumers of welfare state benefits to whom parties and governments are acutely sensitive. Calculation of the social and human costs and benefits of such programs in comparison with their economic costs and benefits has not yet been put on an objective basis. This makes them even more highly political than the more economic programs and gives them a strong impulse toward indefinite expansion.

The tendency of overall expenditure to get out of hand in the democratic welfare state has led to what is undoubtedly the major innovation in Treasury control. This is the new system of establishing ceilings on total public expenditure and on departmental expenditures, as the premises for further decisions on the particular programs constituting these totals. The establishment of a total for public expenditure is a crucial step in economic policy making. It means deciding how the resources of the economy will be divided between public consumption and investment, on the one hand, and private consumption and investment on the other. This confrontation of prospective public expenditure against prospective national resources is the heart of the matter. Ultimately, decisions of such magnitude must be made by Ministers, presumably by the economic committees of the Cabinet and the Cabinet itself. But with its superb professional capacity, the Treasury can develop the alternatives. Each year, and looking ahead for a period of five years, it acts with an interdepartmental committee of officials, the Public Expenditure Survey Committee, to prepare the submissions for ministerial decision. Since the fall of 1970, moreover, the Cabinet and Prime Minister seemed to have in the new Central Policy Review Staff (C.P.R.S.) the resource for criticizing these submissions.

This global or deductive approach to expenditure cannot be exclusive. As already remarked, a decision cannot be made on a total expenditure without scrutinizing its components. A decision cannot be made on the total to go to public as compared with private uses unless there is some idea of what is to be achieved in each of these spheres, vast as they may be. Similarly for the allocation among departments: Their totals cannot be determined without an assessment of the items composing them. This means that, along with the new approach, the old inductive approach to the control of expenditure continues. But now, it is hoped, the old procedures are rationalized by the new discipline introduced by the economic perspective. Under the new procedure the big issues of public expenditure and the economy are looked at as a whole, over a period of years, and in relation to prospective resources.

Moreover, the way in which the components of these totals are conceived for budgeting purposes is being radically revised. Within the Treasury and bureaucracy generally, efforts are now being made to set down proposed expenditures in terms of objectives. This budgeting procedure is called "output budgeting," or "management by objectives" (M.b.O.). Its purpose is to set forth not merely what the items of expenditure will be, but also what blocks of work will be accomplished. In the old-fashioned budget many items of expenditure are scattered under different headings—personnel, materials, and so forth—while under the new system these are brought together so that they can all be seen in relation to the objective—for example, the school, hospital, or road that is to be built. The idea of such a budget is simple; its actual formulation is very difficult. But insofar as it can be done, it enables a government to decide what its main objectives are to be and how much it wishes to spend on each—for example, how much money to combat poverty in comparison with how much to clean up the environment. Such subtotals must necessarily be determined in order to provide a rational basis for the basic economic decision of how much to take for the public sector from the total national resources.

This description of the many advances in the system of economic management may sound like high praise for the Treasury. Indeed it is. One of the Treasury's severest critics of a few years ago recently remarked of its performance since World War II: "The relevant comparison is not with some absolute standard, but with institutions carrying out similar functions in other countries. On this basis the British Treasury was ahead of most other finance ministries."[4] Among these he specifically included the German, French, and American ministries.

Yet the position and role of the Treasury, like the British style of economic control, is by no means fixed. Much criticism is still directed at the way in which the annual decisions regarding taxation and other revenue-raising measures are taken. As they have been for the past hundred years, these decisions are still taken by the Chancellor of the Exchequer, who reveals them to the Cabinet only a day or two before putting them to the House of Commons in his budget speech. While he consults with other Ministers regarding specific problems affecting their responsibilities, he discusses the budget as a whole only with the Prime Minister. In effect, these crucial decisions of financial and economic strategy are pretty well excluded from the collective decision-making processes of the Cabinet system.

In this light we may again look at the potentialities of the Central Policy Review Staff set up in the fall of 1970 (see Chapter 2). On the whole, as we have seen, the initiative in policy making in British government comes from Ministers and departments, and the total figure for public expenditure arises from many departmental and subdepartmental proposals. The new methods of surveying public expenditure have attempted to impose upon these components the discipline of a ceiling derived from current decisions on economic policy. In determining this ceiling and related allocations, decision makers and their officials must view the economy as a whole.

At present the agency relied upon to provide the analysis and the policy initiative is the Treasury. But its resources are at the service of only one Minister, not the Cabinet as a whole. The true executive, therefore, while always retaining its formal authority, lacks the resources for authoritatively assessing what is proposed to it and for developing realistic alternatives. One purpose of the C.P.R.S. was to right this imbalance. Conceivably, it could become not simply a device for coordinating departmental initiatives, but rather a means of positive central direction. The total of public expenditure cannot be greatly changed from year to year; one official's estimate was that projected levels can be reduced by no more than 2½ percent

---

[4]Samuel Brittan, *Steering the Economy: the Role of the Treasury* (London, 1969), p. 313.

per year.[5] Yet the huge public sector constitutes a *masse de manoeuvre* which, if properly directed, over time could have a profound effect upon the economy. To establish control from such a perspective must be the rational administrator's fondest dream. This shift in the character of policy making would also mean a change in the locus of policy making. Positive direction from the center would severely qualify the traditional, uneasy equality among departments and their corps of officials. The superministries have attempted this with regard to groups of departments; perhaps the same could be done for all units of government. Standing at the top would be the Cabinet, or perhaps, if we follow the speculations of some observers, the Prime Minister in a new position of eminence.

To mention these possibilities against the background of the structure and spirit of British government is to suggest how radical and remote they are.

---

[5] Sir William Armstrong (permanent head of the Civil Service Department), in *First Report from the Select Committee on Procedure*. With proceedings, etc. (London: H.M.S.O., 1969), p. 33.

Five

The Authority
of Parliament

Two ruling forces of modernity are the drive for efficiency and the passion for equality. Previous chapters have been concerned with the first of these: the effort to make the machinery of state power more effective. Modern attitudes view this machinery as a means to an end, not an end in itself, and continually press to improve its service to public policy. Cost-benefit analysis—although the first bright hopes for it have become a bit tarnished—is a recent achievement of this effort toward greater effectiveness of the machinery of state power. Yet as the record of government efforts to control the British economy demonstrates, that effectiveness cannot be achieved without regard for responsiveness. As producers, whose cooperation must be won, the governed in a democracy condition in great degree what their governors can accomplish. When the British people chose, they made the severe and strictly controlled system of physical planning of World War II work admirably. Their consent had been won. The British people willed that war and victory in it with a unanimity and intensity that was expressed as meaningfully in their readiness to bear its heavy burdens as in any referendum or general election. Similarly, today, if the performance of government fails to satisfy Britons, the reasons certainly will not be found only in failures of economic science, public administration, or other branches of technical knowledge and their application. The state of the public will is far more important: how the various wishes of the public are formed, what the public expects from government, and what its members will and will not endure.

Party Government and Democracy

In the conventional view, British government displays a high degree of democratic responsiveness, and the mechanism by which this is achieved is party government (see Chapter 1). The doctrine of party government, it must be noted, is only one among many versions of basic democratic theory. As we have seen in our discussion of political modernization, the liberal period in Britain produced versions of popular government that would be hard to reconcile with party government as it is known and practiced in Britain in recent times. Nineteenth-century Liberals and Radicals were highly individualistic in their approach to politics as well as economics. In their view the basic unit of representation was not a class or community, but the individual, rational man. The importance of "conscience" was much in the minds of these offspring of liberalism and religious dissent. On their premises party discipline and strong party organization could not easily be justified. The highest respect was reserved for the independent politician in the sense not of one who was outside party but of one who was in party solely because of conscientious opinion. So while parties did develop in this period and party organization began slowly to be built up throughout the country, in the legislature cross-voting was common and party cohesion very low. The middle period of the nineteenth century was, in the words of one historian, "the golden age of the independent M.P."

In contrast, the political culture of the collectivist period attributes to party a quite different function and a far higher claim to solidarity. Independent voting in the name of conscience is looked on with a much more critical eye. Clement Attlee, the former Labour Prime Minister, reflects this change:

> In my experience a good deal of so-called independence owes more to a desire for notoriety than to conscience. There are some people who delight in a "holier than thou" attitude. I recall an old Labour M.P., Tom Shaw, saying to me, "When I was young I was always talking about my conscience, but one day I realized that what I called conscience was my own bloomin' conceit."[1]

> In the United States the doctrine of party government has never taken deep hold in either the opinions or behavior of people in practical politics. Here the older doctrines of political individualism still prevail. The contrast between the two perspectives on proper democratic behavior came out in a recent exchange between a British party leader and an American legislator. In the spring of 1970, R. H. S. Crossman, then a Minister in the Labour Government, was explaining to an American audience the meaning of the party mandate and how it bound Labour M.P.s to vote together. In the question period after the lecture, a member of the Massachusetts state legislature raised doubts about "the morality of the Member of Parliament voting in a way other than how he believes." "Doesn't

---

[1]Quoted in Alan Beattie, *English Party Politics*. Vol. II (London, 1970), p. 550.

he compromise his conscience?'' asked the earnest questioner. Crossman's reply suggests the mutual incomprehension of these two firm believers in democracy:

> . . . there is no difficulty here because the M.P. is a member of the party and the M.P. is bound, therefore, by Conference decision . . . If he doesn't like that, he's not in the party and, as for the morality, of course, his duty as a party member is to accept the constitution of the party. I can't understand what you're saying.[2]

Viewed from the perspective of party government, the role of Parliament is modest. If we think of the party program as the means by which a like-minded majority directs the course of government action, there is not much for the legislature to do beyond registering the decision of the electorate in favor of the program and providing a forum from which the competing parties can carry on their continuous appeal to the people in anticipation of the next election. Questions no doubt arise as to who is to interpret this program—the parliamentary party, its leadership, or the party outside Parliament—but the drift of the theory clearly is that all, leaders and followers alike, are instruments of the purposive partisan majority in the country. This linkage subordinates the legislature to a parliamentary majority and the parliamentary majority to a majority of the voters. A similar role for Parliament follows if, taking a more Tory view of the matter, we put less stress on program and more on the choice of a team of leaders. In this view the people have spoken by choosing a prospective Cabinet and especially a prospective Prime Minister. The task of the legislature, therefore, is primarily to support the people's choice, providing the Prime Minister with the majorities he and his lieutenants need to make laws, raise and spend money, and control the administration. M.P.s may have the important function of choosing the Leader and in a crisis of removing him. But so long as he has the post, whether in office or Opposition, he and his lieutenants appear as the center of initiative and decision.

Both versions of party government require high party unity and legitimize strict party discipline. Both tend to make Parliament merely an adjunct of a continuous electoral campaign between the parties, without any distinctive function of its own. Viewed as the product of one election, Parliament becomes an electoral college whose function is to transmit the people's choice, whether of program or leadership or both, to the seat of authority. Viewed from the perspective of the next election, Parliament is a forum of propaganda, which the parties use as part of their apparatus for winning and holding public support. The idea of party government poses the central question of the study of Parliament today: Is it merely an adjunct of party competition, or does it have a distinctive role of its own? Does it have important functions that are peculiarly parliamentary and that it performs with a

---

[2]R. H. S. Crossman, Godkin Lectures (Harvard University, 1970).

substantial degree of autonomy? After a generation or more of reporting with approval or dismay the "decline of Parliament," observers are beginning to see that it does have such a role and does perform such functions.

Sovereignty and Symbolism

References to "Parliament" in discussions such as this mean, for almost all intents and purposes, the House of Commons. In legal theory, however, the Parliament of the United Kingdom of Great Britain and Northern Ireland is not a single body, but consists of three powers: the sovereign, the House of Lords, and the House of Commons. The consent of each is normally required to give legislation its legally binding force, as indicated in the usual enacting clause of a statute: "Be it enacted by the Queen's most excellent Majesty, by and with the advice and consent of the Lords Spiritual and Temporal, and Commons, in this present Parliament assembled, and by authority of the same." The sovereign, it should be emphasized, is legally speaking a part of Parliament and in this connection should be referred to as "The Queen in Parliament" not "The Queen and Parliament." To be sure, her assent is always given to legislation that has been properly passed by the chambers—the last time it was refused was 1707—and her role in legislation, as in all acts of government, is governed entirely by the advice of Ministers responsible to the House of Commons. Likewise the power of the House of Lords, which until the nineteenth century was the dominant chamber, has been vastly reduced. Under the Parliament Acts of 1911 and 1949 it has only a brief, suspensive veto over legislation (see Chapter 6). And even this limited power is rarely exercised against the will of the Commons. In effect, therefore, the legislative power rests exclusively with the so-called lower House.

This power is very great. Legally speaking, it is unlimited. In few other regimes do we find as complete an embodiment of the modern concept of sovereignty as in the legal theory of the powers of Parliament. In the United States the power of the legislature is limited by various provisions of a written constitution, such as the Bill of Rights, most of which can be used as the basis for court action challenging laws deemed unconstitutional. Britain's unwritten Constitution sets no limits upon the legal power of Parliament. On the contrary, a central principle of the Constitution is Parliament's legal omnipotence. Whatever may be said on other grounds against a law that has been enacted in Parliament, it cannot be challenged in a British court of law as unconstitutional. In the words of Sir Edward Coke, the great seventeenth-century lawyer and judge, the power of Parliament is "so transcendent and absolute as it cannot be confined either for causes or persons within any bounds."[3] Or as DeLolme, the author of a famous exposition of the eighteenth

---

[3]Quoted in Sir Bernard Cocks (ed.), *Erskine May's Treatise on the Law, Privileges, Proceedings and Usage of Parliament.* 17th ed. (London, 1964), p. 28.

century constitution, facetiously put the matter, "parliament can do everything but make a man a woman and a woman a man." There is perhaps no more striking instance of Parliament's sovereignty than its legal power to determine its own life span, as it did during World War II by putting off a general election until the end of hostilities in Europe. The result was that—apart from changes brought about in by-elections—the same House sat from 1935 to 1945.

The expressive symbolism of the House of Commons is fully in accord with this transcendent authority. Everything about it—its architecture, officials, forms of address, tone and manner of speech, and so on—is deeply impressive, as one would expect of the "Mother of Parliaments." To understand what Parliament is and does, one must sense this expressive symbolism, if only vicariously.

Let us imagine that the reader is sitting in the visitors' gallery of the House for the first time. No doubt his first impression will concern the physical appearance of the House. Even if he does not find it attractive, he will almost certainly find it surprising. In particular, if the visitor has seen other legislative chambers, he will be surprised by the unique size and seating arrangements. From the standpoint of size, it is little more than a glorified town hall. It seats fewer than two-thirds of its 630 members, even though it makes no space-consuming concessions to members' comforts (such as providing desks and individual chairs). All members are seated on long benches, and the M.P.'s lap is the only support for papers. The chamber measures roughly three thousand square feet, while the American House of Representatives, despite a much smaller membership, commands more than four times that much space. The prevailing atmosphere of the House of Commons, therefore, is intimate—except on great occasions (e.g., before an important "division") when, with over 600 members crowding into a space designed for 346, the chief impression is one of excitement and expectancy.

The feeling of excitement at such times is further increased by the seating arrangements. In most of the world's legislative chambers, members sit in semicircular or straight rows, facing a rostrum from which members address the chamber and from which its presiding officer conducts the proceedings. The impression is of an auditorium facing a stage on which individual legislators play the star turn. In the House of Commons, however, members sit on two sets of long benches that are graded upward and *face each other*. The Speaker sits at the head of and between the rows of benches. On his right are the benches of the Government and its supporters—Ministers on the front bench (or Treasury bench, as it is sometimes called), ordinary members ("backbenchers") grouped behind them like obedient and anonymous soldiery. On his left sit the Opposition—the "shadow Cabinet" on the front bench and its own soldiery arrayed on the benches behind. The two groups face each other like football teams in a scrimmage; when members make their verbal cuts and thrusts, they inevitably appear as members of a team—not as figures temporarily elevated in splendid individuality to the national tribune.

Since the present House of Commons is only a few years old (the old House having been destroyed by German incendiary bombs in 1941), neither its layout nor its small size are accidental. Despite certain obvious discomforts, it was decided to make the new House of Commons almost exactly like the old, not alone because of attachment to the past, but because it was widely felt that the physical character of the House somehow affected the character of its proceedings. For example, Churchill, the most insistent spokesman for the small chamber, felt that the whole style of debate in the House would be changed for the worse if the House were enlarged; that the effects of meeting in a large and half-empty hall (and the House is rarely full even now) would be depressing; that the old sense of crowding urgency on great occasions would go; and even that the clean-cut two-party system would be endangered if the seating arrangements were altered.

The next thing the visitor to the House will notice is the general tone of its proceedings. It is here that he will be impressed most by the curious mixture of formality and informality. In some ways the House of Commons is the most formal of all legislative chambers. Its deliberations are governed by procedures most of which are hoary with age and many of which are pure ceremony of the quaintest sort, procedures that either no longer serve a useful function or have long since been adapted to new uses while maintaining their old form. The visitor may, for example, be in the House when it is getting dark. Suddenly the cry goes up: "Mr. Speaker, I call for candles." True, candles have not been used to illuminate the House for decades, but if a member were to say, "Mr. Speaker, how about putting the electric lights on," his request would be without effect. The rules of parliamentary procedure are the product of a long development. In fact until the nineteenth century, almost all the business of the House was covered by usage, with only a small handful of standing orders, as the rules deliberately adopted by the House to regulate its proceedings are called. Since 1832 the number of standing orders has grown immensely, but they do not constitute a complete code of procedure. The greater part of the rules of procedure are still unwritten—to be gleaned from the journal of the House, reports of debates, or the rulings of the Speaker.

If any physical evidence of the continuity of British parliamentary institutions were needed, Mr. Speaker would furnish it. He sits in his chair (on his "throne," perhaps we should say), looking like nothing so much as the frontispiece from a biography of Handel in his flowing wig, black satin knee breeches, buckled shoes and long black gown, a figure straight out of the age of squirearchy. He is an arresting figure, and not only does he look much prettier than his French counterpart, who sits in the bourgeois drabness of modern evening dress, but he is far more authoritative. To cite a simple example: If the French National Assembly gets out of hand, the President of the Assembly rings a bell, an act which often merely augments the prevailing din. But if the House of Commons becomes disorderly— which it rarely does—the Speaker almost always manages to restore order without recourse to mechanical devices. He merely rises from his chair, the rule being that when Mr. Speaker is on his feet all members must be off theirs. And only at times of riotous turmoil does he resort to the ultimate, almost unfailing, method of getting order—putting on his hat. His powers over debate, over the putting of motions and questions, and over members' conduct, are vast and to some extent arbitrary.

But even more important than his formal powers is the readiness with which his rulings are obeyed. No doubt his effectiveness as a presiding officer is in large measure due to the same factor to which the monarchy largely owes its popularity —that his political impartiality is completely established and unquestioned. He is the very embodiment of the rules of procedure and, like the rules, neutral. This neutrality is guaranteed in numerous ways. The Speaker is elected for the life of a Parliament, not for a single session, as in France, and he will be reelected, according to a convention dating back to the early eighteenth century, as many times as he wishes. Thus Speakers, like monarchs, are generally in office for long periods and acquire the usual venerability of age and experience. Although elections to the speakership may be contested by the parties, only men who have not been violent partisans are put up, and the aim is always to secure a unanimous election. Finally, once a man has become Speaker, he is divested of his political personality, so to speak, in a number of ways. Although he continues to be a member of Parliament, his constituency chores are taken care of by another member. He may vote only if there is a draw in a decision, and then only to preserve the status quo. He never takes part in a debate (absolutely never). And his seat is never contested by the other party ("never," in this case, in the Gilbertian sense; there have been four contests for the Speaker's seat since 1714).

But whatever the sources of the Speaker's power, he has it—and does not greatly need it. The normal tone of the House is orderly and polite; it is a chamber with an aristocratic past and with palpably aristocratic habits. True, the prevalent politeness is to some extent backed by rules. For example, in referring to another member, a member speaking in the House must never use his name but must refer to him by a ceremonious title. If he is a member of another party, the usage is "the honorable member for _____" for an ordinary M.P.; "the right honorable member" for a Privy Councillor; "the honorable and learned member" for a lawyer; "the honorable and gallant member" for a former officer in one of the armed services; or "the noble Lord" for the son of a great nobleman who possesses a courtesy title. If the other member belongs to the same party, the title will be varied —for example, "my honorable friend, the member for _____." These ceremonious titles are not conducive to belligerence, however much venom certain members manage to inject into them. Again, the Speaker is empowered to see that members use only decorous language. He may have obstreperous members removed by the Sergeant-at-Arms and, indeed, suspended from the House altogether. A brief but representative list of expressions ruled unparliamentary in the late-nineteenth century includes "cowardly," "a poltroon," "of remarkably fragile honour," "a bigoted, malevolent young puppy," "the reverse of the truth," "bloodthirsty," and "mendacious."

It would be a mistake, however, to suppose that the politesse of the House is merely a matter of rules. The rules and precedents are often overlooked, particularly when they are picayune. Churchill and Bevan, among others, have unburdened themselves of expressions that would have astounded the fastidious Speaker Denison in the nineteenth century. The courtesy and good humor of the House are rather a part of its spirit. They come out most clearly and under least compulsion when a member has made a "maiden speech," his first essay in the House of Commons. No matter how miserable the speech, the next speaker—whether friend or foe—will congratulate him on an eloquent and informative performance and will express the pleasure of the House in hearing it and the hope that the member will be heard from frequently on other occasions.

This courtesy toward the maiden speaker is also a rule, even though it exists merely intangibly, in the spirit of the House. It is part of the ritual by which the House never lets us forget that it is both an ancient and a solemn institution. The House, no less than the monarchy, appeals to the form worshipper, the pomp worshipper, that dwells in most of us. Yet for all its formality, it is, as the visitor will immediately sense, basically an intimate and informal place. Here, of course, is where its size plays an important part. For example, it is not unusual for the great table that supports the golden mace to support also the gangling legs of some elongated frontbencher. Members present in the House of Commons sit in almost every conceivable posture: some, like Balfour, on their shoulder blades; others reclining on their sides. And there is an almost constant coming and going, bowing in and bowing out, and conferring behind the Speaker's chair. But the prevalent informality is most notable in the speeches. British parliamentarians need suffer neither the academic pompousness of German legislators nor the incessant Fourth-of-July oratory of the Americans. The tone of the House of Commons is conversational rather than declamatory, witty rather than learned—it could hardly be otherwise. In so small a chamber, lectures and orations invariably sound ludicrous —except on the greatest of occasions or when delivered by a semilegendary figure like Sir Winston Churchill. Moreover, it cramps the orator's style to be compelled to speak in his place, with others crowded around him, rather than from a special tribune. It equally cramps his style to have neither a desk on which to put things, nor a rail on which to lean. It cramps his style not to be allowed to use a prepared speech or even special notes; the House permits only Ministers making important announcements of policy, where every word counts, to read their speeches. And not least, since all remarks in the House are to be addressed not to other members but to Mr. Speaker, a man can sound ridiculous haranguing a crowd of one. Speeches, therefore, tend to be calm. They also tend to be concise, partly because this is the tradition of the House, partly because the Speaker may immediately suppress all irrelevant remarks and tedious repetitions, and partly, no doubt, because the crush of modern business demands dispatch.

But informality is not all. The House can be a mercilessly discourteous audience, particularly if a member departs from its mores, and it is always a tough audience. A. P. Herbert, never one to tremble before a crowd, called it the "torture chamber," and with good reason. In almost any circumstance members, unless they are completely bored, will keep up a running fire of interjections. If the speeches offend the House, a merciless cacophony may break loose. The would-be orator, for example, will almost certainly be engulfed in a tumultuous rustling of papers, stamping of feet, coughing and sneezing, or, as has happened once or twice, such a continuous chorus of "hear, hear" that he cannot be heard. The House is generally courteous and calm; but it is never easy on speakers in the sense of tolerating nonsense or lack of decorum or blatant unconventionality. The atmosphere of the House, it has been said, is "gentlemanly." If so, it must also be remembered that a gentleman has been defined as a man who is never unintentionally rude.

Class Composition

Like any other democratically elected legislature, the House of Commons by no means represents all occupational and social groups in proportion to their numbers in the country. It is not, socially speaking, a "mirror of the nation." In Britain, as

Table 5.1 Background of M.P.s Elected in 1970 (in Percent)

	All Parties
Professions	46.4
Business	20.7
Manual Workers	12.4
Miscellaneous	20.0

SOURCE: David Butler and Michael Pinto-Duschinsky, *The British General Election of 1970* (London: Macmillan, 1971), p. 302. Reprinted by permission of Macmillan London and Basingstoke.

in legislative bodies elsewhere, the professions are strongly represented. They make up one-half of the membership of the Commons (see Table 5.1). The law profession, however, which accounts for only about one-fifth of all M.P.s, has nothing like the predominance it enjoys in the American Congress, where representatives with legal training often number over half the membership of the two houses. In the House of Commons businessmen and workers just about balance one another, although together they are outnumbered by members of the professions. The category "manual workers," however, deserves comment. At first glance it constitutes a sharp contrast to the heavy businessman contingent in Parliament. It would also seem to contrast with the distribution of occupations in the American Congress, where manual occupations are rarely used to characterize members. In fact, a great many of these M.P.s are trade-union officials who have not worked in a mine or on the shop floor for many years and who occupy managerial posts with responsibilities as great as, and in many ways similar to, those occupied by the businessmen with whom the conventional job description seems to set them in opposition. The miscellaneous category in Table 5.1 includes as its principal constituents farmers and journalists. On the basis of occupation the House, while including a broad representation, tends to be a middle- and upper-class body.

Class analysis, however, is more illuminating if we distinguish the parties. Table 5.2 compares the two main parties on the basis of occupation. We find the expected and substantial contrast in the representation of businessmen as opposed to workers, each category accounting for a quarter or more of the appropriate

Table 5.2 Background of Labour and Conservative M.P.s 1970 (in Percent)

	Conservatives	Labour
Professions	45	40
Business	30	10
Manual Workers	1	26
Miscellaneous	24	16

SOURCE: David Butler and Michael Pinto-Duschinsky, *The British General Election of 1970* (London: Macmillan, 1971), p. 303. Reprinted by permission of Macmillan London and Basingstoke.

party's total. The Labour party does include some businessmen. And among Conservative backbenchers, it must be pointed out, will be found two genuine manual workers. When analyzed, the professions also reveal party contrast. Although the two parties are not very different in the representation of most professions, with regard to teachers there is wide disparity: Only nine count themselves Tories, while fifty-six sit on the Labour side. In the House elected in 1966, the contrast was even sharper: nine Conservative to seventy-two Labour teachers. Lawyers are stronger on the Conservative than on the Labour benches, while, as would be expected, almost all the farmers are Tories.

Table 5.3 Educational Background of M.P.s 1970 (in Percent)

	Conservatives	Labour
Elementary	1	21
Secondary	25	62
Public School	74	17
Eton	18	1
Oxford and Cambridge	52	24
Other Universities	12	29

SOURCE: David Butler and Michael Pinto-Duschinsky, *The British General Election of 1970* (London: Macmillan, 1971), p. 303. Reprinted by permission of Macmillan London and Basingstoke.

Education tells a similar story (see Table 5.3). Labour is the party of M.P.s who started their education in the government-supported schools and one-fifth of whom never went beyond the elementary level. Those who did go to a university were not likely to go to Oxford or Cambridge. Conservative M.P.s, on the other hand, overwhelmingly went to "public" (i.e., exclusive private) schools and thence to Oxbridge. Still, the strength of university graduates on the Labour benches must not be overlooked, the totals for the two parties being not far apart: 64 percent for the Conservatives and 53 percent for Labour.

These figures on occupation and education measure what an observer in the gallery quickly senses. In terms of social origins, the Labour party in the House is a more heterogeneous and socially representative body, although tending, like parties of the Left generally, to be a party of intellectuals and union officials. The balance between the latter two categories, it may be noted, has shifted in recent years; professional people, and especially university teachers, are noticeably displacing workers. The Conservative party, in accent, manner, and dress as well as in occupation and education, has not so much a middle-class as a distinctly upper-class flavor. Perhaps the best objective clue to this is the high percentage of its members who went to Eton, a school that has produced English notables at least since the battle of Waterloo was supposedly won on its playing fields. On both sides of the House, but especially on the Tory side, sits a powerful remnant of the governing class that won the admiration of Tocqueville and Schumpeter.

Six

The Functions
of Parliament

The extravagance of the legal theory of its powers, the impressiveness of its symbolism, and the remnants of the governing class among its members only make more poignant by contrast the actualities of the position of the House of Commons under Cabinet government. For, in the words of an ex-Minister, it is the Cabinet that wields "the collective sovereign power of the state" (see Chapter 2). To be sure, the Cabinet is responsible to the House, which, if it chose, could deprive any given set of Ministers of this power and vest it in another set. But nowadays the chance of a Cabinet's losing the confidence of the House is very slight.

The Decline of Parliament

Two indexes of this imbalance of power between Cabinet and House—and also, incidentally, of the decline of Parliament—are the historical record of Cabinet defeats and the rise of party cohesion in votes of the House. On the basis of a comparison of the mid-nineteenth century with recent decades, the probability that a Cabinet will be defeated in the House of Commons has declined almost to the vanishing point. In the period 1846–1860 parliamentary independence reached its peak, the House administering eight major defeats to successive Governments. On six occasions defeat led to the resignation of the Cabinet; on the other two the Prime Minister got a dissolution of Parliament and went to the country in a general election. In these fourteen years there were five different Cabinets, each with an average life of less than three years. In 1867 Walter Bagehot stated a cardinal truth of British government at that time when he wrote that the House of Commons "lives in a state of perpetual potential choice."[1]

In the twentieth century the relationship is radically different. The last time a Government resigned because of a defeat in the House was 1923. A year later another Government suffered a defeat serious enough for it to call a general election. In each of these cases, however, the party constituting the Government had only a minority in the House and was dependent upon support from another party to govern. This was the period when the rise of Labour and decline of the Liberals had created a situation of three-party competition, which broke up the normal pattern of two dominant parties. To find an instance when a Government originally enjoying such a party majority in the House lost on a vote that caused it to resign, we must go back to 1885, when Gladstone's Liberals split over Irish Home Rule. In the present age of collectivist politics and party government, we would expect Governments to resign only as a result of defeat in a general election. This has indeed been the case in each of the changes in governing party since 1945: the resignations of Attlee in 1951, Home in 1964, and Wilson in 1970. Labour was in for six years, followed by the Conservatives for thirteen, then Labour again for six—an average for each party of about eight years.

The indexes of rising party cohesion parallel and in part explain this immense increase in governmental stability. Table 6.1 gives this measurement from the mid-nineteenth century to recent times.

Table 6.1 Party Unity 1860–1946 (Measured by Coefficients of Cohesion)[2]

Year	Liberals	Conservatives	Labour
1860	58.9	63.0	—
1871	75.5	74.0	—
1881	83.2	87.9	—
1894	89.8	97.9	—
1899	82.5	97.7	—
1906	96.8	91.0	88.4
1908	94.9	88.3	92.8
1924–1928	88.8	99.2	99.8
1945–1946		99.0	99.9

DATA SOURCE: Samuel H. Beer, *British Politics in the Collectivist Age,* rev. ed. (New York: Knopf, 1965), pp. 123, 257, 262.

---

[1] *The English Constitution,* World's Classics ed. (London, 1928), p. 125.

[2] Starting from the assumption that a fifty-fifty split in a party signifies zero cohesion, we calculate the coefficient of cohesion by dividing by fifty the difference between fifty and the percentage of party members voting on one side. Thus when 90 percent of the members of a party are on one side, the CoC is 80 percent. In this analysis abstainers are not counted. Only the votes of those who took one side or another are examined. In Table 6.1 the divisions analyzed are in nearly all cases those in which the Government of the day put on its whips, whether or not the other parties did likewise.

This measurement of party unity tells us only the extent of cross-voting, that is, when a party member deserts his party and votes with its opponents. It says nothing about threats of cross-voting, abstentions, contrary speeches, conflicts within the party caucus, and other forms of party dissidence. As we shall see, party rebellions and revolts on the back benches have by no means come to an end. Yet the immense rise in party cohesion since the mid-nineteenth century vividly indicates the transformation in parliamentary behavior between the liberal and the collectivist ages. As far as cross-voting is concerned, the independence of M.P.s has declined almost to nil, while the stability of governments has risen to new heights. In the House of Commons today we see two bodies of freedom-loving Britons, chosen in 630 constituencies throughout the United Kingdom, and subject to influences that run back to an electorate that numbers nearly 40 million and that is divided by the complex interests and aspirations of an advanced modern society. Yet day after day, with a Prussian discipline, members troop into the division lobbies at the signals of their whips and in the service of the authoritative decisions of their parliamentary parties. However we may ultimately assess the shift in the balance of power between the executive and the legislature, such behavior constitutes a profound transformation.

A third body of evidence showing the degree and manner of the Cabinet's dominance relates to its control over the business of the House. According to the standing orders and the unwritten rules, the procedures of the House presuppose on the one hand a Government—that is, not merely a number of official members, or Ministers, but a unified ministerial body having a program that it will put before and carry through the House—and on the other hand an Opposition, similarly organized and capable of exercising responsibility for sustained and systematic scrutiny of what the Government proposes and does. In historical perspective these characteristics of the present procedure of the House of Commons simply embody, at this stage in political development, the ancient bipolar conception of authority. In that conception there are two main elements in British government: One is the central, initiating, energizing element—formerly the monarchy and today the Cabinet; the other is the checking, criticizing, controlling element—the Parliament and, nowadays especially, the Opposition. This bipolar model constitutes the basic structure around which the procedure and work of the House are organized.

The standing orders of the House divide its business into two very unequal branches, private business and public business. *Private business* consists mainly in the passage of private bills, of which some fifty or sixty are enacted each session. A private bill relates to a specific locality or to an individual firm or other corporate body—for example, the authorization of some activity by a local authority. It is handled in a semijudicial manner and takes up very little of the House's time. *Public business* comes under two main headings, private members' business and Government business. *Private members' business* consists of bills or motions introduced by unofficial members, that is, M.P.s who are not members of the Government, but who may be members either of the Government party or of an

Opposition party. Private members may freely introduce bills; the problem is to get time for them. M.P.s draw lots to see in what order their bills will come up. But how much time will be allocated to these bills, or whether they will be given any time at all, is subject to the discretion of the Government, which may reduce this time by a simple resolution of the House. In the early postwar years, when the Government was carrying through large legislative programs, the time for private members' bills and motions was cut on average to as little as two days per session.

Apart from the provision made for private members' time, the standing orders of the House allot the rest of the session to the Government, which may distribute its business among these days for the most part as it sees fit. The allocation of this time for *Government business* constitutes an important part of the work of a Cabinet, the two main sources of conflict among Ministers being money for their programs and parliamentary time for their bills. It is not a committee of the House, such as the rules committee in the typical American legislature, but the Government that controls the allocation of parliamentary time, and the House learns about the allocation of time from the Government every Thursday when the Leader of the House announces the order of business for the coming week.

Historically, growing control over the time of the House and increasing allocation of time to Government business parallel the other changes that transformed the nineteenth-century Parliament. That century was marked by a continuing struggle between Cabinet and House for control over the parliamentary time table. One reason for the frequent defeats of Governments in those days was their lack of control of the business of the House. But in the course of time, and especially after the Irish members pushed to extremes their use of obstructionist tactics, the House developed means for severely controlling debate and empowered the Government with substantial control over its business.

The Cabinet's control over the business of the House is qualified by conventions, pressures, and various prudential considerations. A Cabinet may decide to provide time for private members' bills not only in order to be fair, but also in order to avoid having to take sides on a hotly controversial issue. In this way the Labour Government allowed a private member's bill abolishing capital punishment to go through in 1964 on a "free vote," that is, without the Government itself taking a stand. For similar reasons Governments have left to private members the bills easing the laws regarding divorce, abortion, and homosexuality. Moreover, apart from time spent on bills and motions, other occasions are considered to be largely at the disposal of private members: for example, the daily Question Hour—although it must be said that the actual interchanges at that time appear hardly less partisan than the set debates between Government and Opposition.

Of crucial importance are the conventions obliging the Government to set aside from its own time a very substantial part for the use of the Opposition. During the annual debate on the reply to the Queen's speech, the second part of the debate is devoted largely to amendments moved by the Opposition. Later in the session, some twenty-six days, nominally devoted to debating the estimates of proposed expenditure put before the House and called the Supply days, are made available to the Opposition for criticizing administrative policy under virtually any heading it chooses. Most important is the long-established convention that the Government will never fail to accede to the Opposition's request for time to move a vote of censure on the Government. In addition, of course, front-bench spokesmen for the Opposition, like backbenchers speaking for themselves, take part in replying to the Government in debates initiated by it.

The purpose of these examples is to show that the initiative in parliamentary business is far more widely distributed than would be expected from considering only the near monopoly of parliamentary time by Government business. One authoritative estimate, based on an assessment of where the initiative lay during the 1950s, gives the following distribution of time for the average annual session of 159 days: private members, 35 days; the Opposition, 32 days; the Government, 69½ days; indeterminate, 22½ days. Enjoying such rights to control parliamentary time, the Opposition cannot fail to be consulted by the Government when the weekly timetable is being framed. While the Cabinet makes the final determination, it does so only after consultation between Government and Opposition whips and with reasonable regard for the requests of the latter.

Criticism and Control

The forms of procedure used in the House can be classified under three headings, according to the explicit purposes for which they are used: (1) criticism and control of policy, (2) legislation, and (3) control of finance and expenditure. As the previous discussion should have made clear, the ostensible purpose of a procedural form in the House of Commons does not necessarily indicate its actual function; and as we shall see, one of the most fascinating and elusive problems in the study of that body is to determine from its proceedings at any time or over time what political functions are actually being performed. It is appropriate to look first at criticism and control of policy, since this class of proceedings suggests the oldest function of the House, the airing and redress of grievances. When medieval kings first called Parliament into existence, largely in order to enhance their revenues, the members of the lower House soon learned to demand some quid pro quo in return for their grants. The proceedings that descend from this ancient transaction will be discussed under the heading of control of finance. But the task of bringing to the executive's attention conditions that call for action and of criticizing what is proposed to be done about them has become a more general function of the House.

A major opportunity for discharging this task is provided by Question Hour, which occupies the House almost immediately when it convenes at 2:30 P.M. on the first four days of the week. The occasion makes an exciting start of the day's sitting. Members crowd in and leaders are well represented on both front benches, the Prime Minister himself necessarily being present on two days when questions directed to him are taken. Any M.P. may submit a question to any Minister regarding a matter for which the Minister is responsible, and Question Hour is one of the remaining ways in which the individual responsibility of Ministers is still expressed and enforced. The questions are submitted at least forty-eight hours in advance and are printed on the daily order paper. Ostensibly they are requests for information. But when that is the questioner's only object, he is more likely to write directly to the department concerned or to put down his question explicitly as a request for only a written answer. The questions for oral answer are the ones that raise the level of interest and partisan combat. For despite the fact that the putting of questions is left mainly to backbenchers on both sides, the scoring of party points is a main purpose, and former Ministers, although more likely junior than senior ones, will be found among the questioners.

The topics range from some very specific act, or failure to act, to major policy positions of the Government. Two recent examples illustrate the range:

> Mr. George Cunningham (Islington, South-West): To ask the Secretary of State for the Home Department, when he expects to be able to release the site of Pentonville Prison to the Islington Borough for building purposes.

> Mr. Woodhouse (Oxford): To ask the Secretary of State for the Home Department, if he will introduce legislation to amend the Commonwealth Immigrants Act 1968 to remove the clauses discriminating on racial grounds against citizens of the United Kingdom born in former colonies.[3]

While the initial question itself will often have a sharp polemical edge, it is especially the supplementary questions used to follow up the attack that have the desired effect of scoring the point, embarrassing the Minister, winning the headline, impressing the Leader, and so forth. The whole business of putting a question is conducted with rapid-fire precision: The Speaker merely barks out the name of the M.P., who thereupon rises in his place and states the number of his question on the order paper. If the supplementaries are not too drawn out, as many as fifty or more questions can be gotten through in one period. Although briefed by his civil servants, the Minister may find these few minutes a severe test—perhaps more of his verbal than his administrative ability—but still a severe test, with considerable bearing on whether his reputation goes up or down. It has been reported that a British Prime Minister, after referring sourly to the lofty unapproachability of President de Gaulle and of the effect on him of the deference of his "court," added that if the President of France had to come down to the House twice a week and stand up to a running fire of questions, this deferential attitude would surely be attenuated.[4]

Unlike the French system of interpellation, questions put in this manner do not lead to debate and a vote. If the answer given by a Minister is considered unsatisfactory, even after supplementaries, members have several methods available to prevent the matter from being buried. If they feel it urgently needs airing, they can

---

[3]Order Paper. Questions for Oral Answer (July 23, 1970) Nos. 45 and 46.

[4]Ronald Butt, *The Power of Parliament* (New York, 1967), p. 324.

attempt to get a debate under standing order nine. This rule has recently been liberalized to permit such a debate if the Speaker finds the subject "to be so pressing that the public interest will suffer if it is not given immediate attention." Such an emergency debate, which, needless to say, is a fairly serious reordering of the Government's timetable, will take place either that evening or, at the Speaker's discretion, the afternoon of the following day.

The actual form under which the debate takes place is a motion to adjourn the House. Adjournment motions are used in a variety of ways to provide opportunity for criticism by backbenchers and by the leaders of the Opposition. In the daily half-hour adjournment debate, which takes place between 10:00 and 10:30 in the evening, the topic, as at Question Hour, must be within the responsibility of a Minister, who is given notice so that a reply can be prepared by his department. Members win the right to initiate such debates partly through their luck in drawing lots and partly through the Speaker's selection of topics from those proposed by members.

Two other types of opportunity for criticism of policy are of major importance. The debate on the address in reply to the Queen's speech comes each fall at the culmination of the ceremony associated with the opening of Parliament. M.P.s and peers crowd into the upper chamber where the Queen reads a short speech— extremely short compared with a President's state of the union message. Written by the Government and announcing both its legislative program for the coming session and its policy on major questions, such as international affairs, this speech initiates a debate in the House of Commons, which starts with a confrontation of Government and Opposition and runs on for perhaps six days. Subjects for each day's debate are arranged through "the usual channels," that is, by the whips of the two parties. The last half of the debate is given over to the initiatives of the Opposition and occasionally backbenchers.

Another type of occasion on which Government and Opposition are explicitly pitted against one another is the debate on a motion of censure, or other motion of confidence. In moving a vote of censure, the Opposition will spell out the nature of its complaint, normally an allegation of some large failure of public policy. A motion of confidence may also be moved by the Government, perhaps at a time when things have not been going too well and the Cabinet feels that it must not only provide an opportunity for criticism, but also give a lead to opinion in the House and in the country. Confidence, which is of the essence of the relationship between executive and legislature under a parliamentary system, may be called in question in the course of other debates. That fateful debate of May 7 and 8, 1940, which took place as the German armies swept across Europe and which led to the fall of Chamberlain and the installation of Churchill as Prime Minister, took place on an adjournment motion. It was turned into a vote of confidence when on the second day Herbert Morrison, a leader of the Labour party, rose and declared that he was neither satisfied with Chamberlain's explanation of the Government's failures nor confident that the Government was aware of its shortcomings. Whereupon the Prime Minister, Neville Chamberlain, replied: "I accept the challenge

. . . and call on my friends to support us in the Lobby to-night."[5] In the ensuing division, while Chamberlain won, the Government's majority, usually around 240, fell to 81, when 41 members from the Government benches voted with the Opposition and about 60 others abstained.

Legislation

"The chief function of parliament," said the famous lawyer of the last century F. W. Maitland, "is to make statutes." Unquestionably, legislative proceedings occupy the House of Commons more than any other type of proceedings—perhaps as much as half of its time. In a year the Parliament will produce some fifty or sixty public acts, of which perhaps half a dozen originated with private members and the rest with the Government. There are normally five stages in the passage of a bill by the House of Commons. As in American procedure, the *first reading* is largely perfunctory. Only the title of the bill is read, and the Minister in charge (assuming it is a Government bill) names the date on which the second reading debate will take place. Here is a crucial difference from American procedure that goes to the heart of the difference between the two political systems. In the American Congress, after a bill is introduced, it is sent to a committee, whose deliberations may greatly affect its content and its fate. These procedures, reflecting the separation of powers, show the independence of the American legislature and the powerful position of its committees. To find a comparable function in Britain we would need to look at the way in which the Cabinet, or a Cabinet committee, deals with proposed legislation before it ever goes to the House.

In the *second reading* debate, to which one parliamentary day is ordinarily devoted, the House is asked to approve of the bill as a whole before it is sent to committee for detailed consideration. For this reason members may not offer amendments that change the content of the bill, but only amendments which in effect involve its total rejection. Thus in contrast with Congressional procedure, it is not in order for a member of the House of Commons to move to strike all sections of the bill after a certain clause and add new provisions. The explicit purpose of this stage is to give the House the opportunity to decide in principle whether it wants such a bill, a decision that will restrict the nature of amendments that may be offered in committee. In fact, a good many of the speeches made at this time will be concerned with only some of the bill's provisions, as members reflect their special interests and competencies and perhaps prepare the way for amendments that they will move at the committee stage. Needless to say, the Government wins its inevitable majority at the end of the day, and the bill goes to committee.

At this point, if the bill involves the expenditure of public money, an additional stage is inserted between stages two and three. The House must approve what is

[5]360 *H. C. Deb.* 1266 (8 May 1940).

called a *financial resolution,* which like any other matter involving a charge on the public funds, must be moved by a Minister of the Crown. The approval of a financial resolution should not be confused with voting an estimate of departmental expenditure. The latter is normally part of the annual financial business by which money to cover government expenditure is appropriated. A financial resolution, on the other hand, is voted only in relation to a specific bill that involves public expenditure. The financial resolution is comparable to an authorization of expenditure, in congressional parlance, while the voting of the estimate is like congressional appropriation.

The *standing committees* of the House, to which nearly all bills are now referred, are miniature Parliaments. They consist of twenty to fifty members who are presided over by an impartial chairman and led by a Minister who heads a partisan majority proportionate to the majority in the House as a whole. The proceedings, however, are far more relaxed and less partisan, and amendments, normally referring only to details of the bill, are often accepted by the Government in committee. But even when amendments are turned down at this third stage, they sometimes reappear on the Minister's initiative at a later stage.

Usually eight standing committees are appointed. In keeping with their parliamentary character, most are not assigned special fields of policy, but are simply designated by letters of the alphabet. They are constituted specially for each bill: A nucleus of members interested in or expert in the subject matter of the bill are initially chosen, along with as many other members as necessary to get the right party balance. The rise of Celtic nationalism, however, has affected the committee system of the House. The Scottish Standing Committee, consisting of members from Scottish constituencies, takes the committee stage of all Scottish bills. Enlarged to include all Scottish M.P.s, as well as a few others, this committee becomes the Scottish Grand Committee, to which Scottish estimates and the second reading of purely Scottish bills are referred. There are also Welsh standing and grand committees.

In the *report stage* the bill as amended in committee comes back to the floor of the House. On the order paper, which gives the agenda for the sitting, will be various amendments, possibly including amendments rejected in committee as well as new substantive amendments and new clauses. At this point the Speaker has the power to select the amendments to be discussed (the power of "kangaroo"), which he may use to prevent repetition of arguments already aired in committee. The Minister in charge may again accept amendments; he may also use the full party majority available to him from the whole House to reverse a change that his narrower majority in committee has failed to control.

After going through the bill in the report stage, the House then gives the bill its *third reading.* Needless to say, this does not mean that the bill is actually read before the House—some of these bills run to hundreds of pages! What happens in that a debate takes place on the Minister's motion that the bill be "read a third time." At this stage (the fifth, assuming there has been no financial resolution), debate is again presumably on the general principles of the bill. It resembles the debate on second reading, and the opportunity to amend is similarly narrowed to proposing rejection of the bill as a whole.

Legislative procedure in the House of Lords is similar to procedure in the Commons, taking a bill through the same five basic stages. The Lords' suspensive veto is almost negligible, and the principal use of the upper chamber in law making is to provide an opportunity for extended consideration of noncontroversial amendments. If the Commons will not accept a Lords' amendment and the Lords refuse to back down, the provisions of the Parliament Act of 1949 come into play. Under these provisions the bill will become law in the form desired by the Commons, providing the Commons has repassed it in the same form in two successive sessions, one year having elapsed between the second reading on the first occasion and the third reading on the second occasion. With regard to finance, the Lords' power is even slighter, since any bill certified by the Speaker of the House as a "money bill" must be passed by the Lords without amendment within one month after being sent up; otherwise, it will go to the sovereign for the royal assent without needing to be passed by the upper House.

The ultimate phase of law making, the royal assent, is signified to Parliament in a ceremony that retains a medieval charm. Normally the Queen does not indicate her assent in person, but by means of a commission signed by her and listing the bills to which she assents. Upon receiving such a commission, the Lords sends its ceremonial officer, the Gentleman Usher of the Black Rod, to signify to the Commons that its attendance is desired. When this message is delivered—and it may break into the middle of an important debate—the Speaker, at the head of a straggling line of M.P.s, goes across the Palace of Westminster to the upper chamber. The commission is then read, as are the titles of the bills, and the royal assent to each is signified by a clerk in Norman French. Assent to an appropriation bill is signified by the words, "La Reyne remercie ses bons sujets, accepte leur benevolence, et ainsi le veult." For all other public acts, the formula is "La Reyne le veult."

In controlling the legislative process, the Government has at its command several potent instruments of parliamentary procedure. These derive largely from changes made during the latter part of the nineteenth century, under the impact of Irish obstructionism, the increase in government business, and the heightening of party conflict in Parliament. In 1881, in reaction to filibustering by the Irish, Gladstone introduced the rules from which modern closure and the guillotine developed. *Closure* means that the Government can apply its majority to stop debate. It can only do this, however, when the Speaker finds that every section of opinion has had a chance to speak on the matter before the House and when not only a majority, but at least one hundred members are present and voting in favor. This instrument is available not only in the House but also in standing committee, where the Minister can use it to prevent dilatory talk and to hasten a bill on its way.

Closure itself may not suffice where a determined minority exploits its rights by arguing every amendment and every possible line of dissent. To cope with such efforts, the Government may utilize a *guillotine,* or "allocation of time order."

Such an order, which is voted by the House, is a timetable specifying precisely how much time is to be allotted to each stage of a bill, or even to discussion of groups of clauses in standing committee. The passage of such an order means that when the time allocated to a certain phase has expired—regardless of the extent or coverage of the debate—the Speaker puts the question, and the House, having given its inevitable answers, passes on to the next phase indicated in the order.

Delegated Legislation

The exercise of powers of delegated legislation is, on the one hand, law making. On the other hand, the procedures of the House that attempt to give it the means to assert its authority in this sphere of law making constitute opportunities for criticism and control. As government intervention grew with the rise of collectivism, the sheer increase in rule making, the need for flexibility in changing and adapting these rules, and the increasingly technical and complex character of the rules made it more and more difficult to keep all law making on the floor of the House. In consequence, the practice of delegating to Ministers the power to make rules with the force of law grew rapidly. By 1920 the rules and orders issued under delegated powers filled five times as many pages as the statutes passed that year by Parliament. Today the welfare state and managed economy continue to produce vast quantities of legislation in this way. The "statutory instruments" embodying such acts of executive law making number between 2,000 and 3,000 a year, and some are of very great length and complexity.

As far as parliamentary control is concerned, statutory instruments fall into four classes. With regard to some rules of minor importance, no special steps are taken to bring them to the attention of Parliament. A second class are merely laid before the House, that is, put on file in its library. A third class not only are laid before the House, but also are subject within a certain period of time to being nullified by the House's passing a "prayer," that is, a request to the Queen to quash the rule. Finally, there are those rules which do not come into legal effect until the House has taken action by an "affirmative resolution" to approve them.

In attempting to cope in some way with the mass of rules laid before it, the House has had since 1944 the assistance of the Select Committee on Statutory Instruments—commonly called the "Scrutinizing Committee." While it may not comment on questions of policy or even efficiency, the committee is charged with calling the attention of the House to statutory instruments such as those which impose charges or make an unusual use of the power originally conferred. Assisted by a small expert staff, the committee examines a large number of instruments each session, sometimes as many as a thousand. It will call the attention of the House to perhaps half a dozen; among these, however, one that is felt worthy of a debate will be found only very rarely.

Finance and Expenditure

The third category of proceedings in the House of Commons in addition to criticism and control of policy, and legislation is the control of finance. It will take up perhaps a third of the typical session. In Britain as elsewhere the financial business of the legislature consists of two sorts of activity: appropriations (supply, as the British have traditionally called it) and taxation (ways and means). The process of appropriation begins every year sometime in February when the estimates are introduced in the House. These are departmental requests for money needed in the impending financial year. They are collated and reviewed by the Treasury and presented to Parliament—in the case of the armed services, presented by the appropriate departmental Minister and in the case of other services, by the Financial Secretary to the Treasury. Ultimately the estimates are embodied in the annual Appropriation Act, which is usually not passed until some time in late July or early August.

For all this business the House has set aside a total of twenty-six days—the Supply days—which are fitted into its work schedule at various times from February until the middle of the summer. On most of these days the House, sitting as Committee of Supply, concerns itself with the estimates of a particular department. These debates, however, are not normally on financial matters, such as how much money should be provided for a department or for one of its services. Instead, the debates center on departmental policies and programs.

Thus in the past a grant to the Ministry of Housing and Local Government has been the peg on which was hung a debate over whether or not the Government was making an efficient use of manpower in its public housing program. The Foreign Office estimate has been used to set in motion a wide-ranging discussion of the Government's actions in international affairs. Before the Post Office was hived off, its estimate could be used to raise the question of increased charges for the use of telephones (which, like all telecommunications in Britain, come under the Post Office).

It is not unknown for such a debate to center on what the Opposition regards as excessive spending on a government service, such as the vastly expensive National Health Service. That these debates do not normally deal with expenditure, however, is made plain by the usual method of inaugurating them. The Opposition moves for a nominal reduction—say £100—in the amount proposed to be appropriated. A hundred pounds is negligible in a departmental program running to millions of pounds, yet by long tradition a vote on an estimate, no matter how insignificant the amount, is a matter of confidence. This means that the Government will take special care to muster a majority and that the vote itself will make no difference in policy or expenditure. At the same time, because the estimates cover practically the whole spectrum of government action, they provide a highly flexible matrix for structuring criticism. Hence, while it is no doubt convenient for the Government to be sure of its appropriations for the coming year, it is also convenient for the Opposition to have at its disposition the twenty-six days devoted to criticizing such aspects of Government policy as it chooses to select.

In any one year most of the estimates will not, of course, be discussed. Most departments, however, can expect to come under some scrutiny, broad or narrow. Debates sometimes may range widely over a department's policy during a substantial period of time; more likely, they will take up some special aspect. And indeed, a Supply day can be used for what might be called "targets of opportunity," that is, grievances such as strikes, bureaucratic gaffes, and breakdowns of public service, which are typical in the huge modern polity and which can readily be blamed on the Government of the day. Behind the ostensible purpose of these debates, which is to decide how much money should be voted for government purposes, lies the function of providing an opportunity for the Opposition to pursue its scrutiny and criticism of government action in a flexible and systematic manner.

Proposals for taxation, as we have seen in our discussion of administration, begin in the executive branch. On the bureaucratic level the center of origin would be that small division in the public sector group of the Treasury that since 1967 has had the task of coordinating Treasury work on the budget. The budget is under consideration almost continuously throughout the year by a high-level official committee of the Treasury. Final decisions are made by the Chancellor in consultation with the Prime Minister. After their decisions have received the approval of the Cabinet, the Chancellor presents them to the House in his budget speech around the beginning of the fiscal year—in Britain April 1.

The British give a narrower meaning to the term budget than do Americans, who use it to refer to both the revenue and expenditure side of government finance. Strictly speaking, when the Chancellor presents his budget, he puts before the House only his proposals for raising revenue. Since he is, however, the Minister responsible not only for prudent housekeeping, but also for management of the national economy, his presentation will be concerned with both expenditure and taxation as the basic elements of fiscal policy. Today no less than in the days of Gladstone—a Chancellor "who could lead his hearers over the arid desert, and yet keep them cheerful and lively and interested without flagging"—the budget speech is a great parliamentary and national occasion.

After the budget speech, which is likely to last two or three hours, the House immediately passes a series of tax resolutions that authorize the Government to collect all new taxes immediately. The ensuing debate, first on the budget and then on the finance bill, which is brought in to give effect to the new revenue proposals, occupy perhaps fifteen days of parliamentary time. Like the Supply days these days are distributed over the remainder of the session. The final outcome of the two processes of legislative activity is the Consolidated Fund (Appropriation) Act and the Finance Act, both finally enacted toward the end of the session, in late July or early August.

Proposed Reforms

This system of procedure regarding expenditure and taxation clearly bears the stamp of an earlier generation before Governments were greatly concerned with the economic influence of government finance on the national economy. As we have seen, under this older and narrowly financial approach, the Treasury was concerned with economy, efficiency, and a balance among department spending programs in accordance with Cabinet priorities. Like the relevant Treasury procedures, the financial procedures of the House of Commons had also developed during the latter part of the period of liberal modernization, and in spirit and form they are often identified with the great reforming chancellor, Gladstone.

On the parliamentary side the procedures of Gladstonian finance surely gave the House of Commons the opportunity to control both expenditure and taxation. The rise of party discipline, however, severely limited the significance of these procedures. Moreover, in recent years the growing use of government fiscal activity to manage the economy could not be readily expressed through them. To take a crucially important example, under these procedures all expenditure was voted on an annual basis—as if Parliament could, and did, from year to year decide what the total expenditure would be. In fact the massive programs of the modern polity —building roads, houses, schools, hospitals, and so on—mature over a period of years and can be only marginally altered by the annual financial exercise (see Chapter 4).

For more than a decade the Treasury has been adapting its procedures to this need for long-term calculation and control of expenditure as well as to other needs of economic management. Recently the House of Commons has also begun to respond, and at this writing it would seem that reforms of major importance are in the process of being made. Precisely what the new system will be cannot be predicted. Yet it is possible to suggest the general lines that reform will probably take. In the first place, M.P.s will be given the information needed to show the interplay between public finance and national economy for a period of several years. This would mean information regarding prospective government expenditure as well as assessments of the likely course of economic growth. So informed, M.P.s would be able to share with Ministers and civil servants in that confrontation of public expenditure versus national resources which is at the heart of the task of economic policy making. As a step in meeting this need, the Government is already providing the House annually with a report on the probable expenditure for the next five years. Moreover, if informed judgments are to be made, not only must a global estimate of expenditure be provided, but also some indication of how it will be allocated to the main areas of government action. This is now being done not only within the executive for its use, but also for the use of Parliament by means of the annual white papers on public expenditure.

Finally, if the House is to make intelligent use of such new and fairly complex and technical bodies of information, it will need appropriate machinery. Since 1912 it has had a committee specially charged with reviewing expenditure proposals presented to Parliament, the Select Committee on Estimates. This body was created when the House revealed its inability to control expenditure by means of its debates on the estimates. While the committee likewise found it impossible to learn enough about proposed expenditure in time to feed this information into an effective discussion, it has performed a useful service, especially in recent years, by its many inquiries into the economy and efficiency of projects involving heavy spending. This ad hoc approach, concentrating on economy, does not meet the new needs of economic policy making. In consequence a select committee of the House proposed, and the Heath Government agreed, that in place of the Estimates Committee a new Select Committee on Public Expenditure would be set up. It would consider the long-term projections of expenditure to be submitted to the House and would operate through eight subcommittees corresponding to broad fields of government activity.

These subcommittees may take the place that some reformers had expected would be filled by a new set of specialist select committees. Under the Wilson Government six such specialist committees were set up: three "subject" committees to consider science and technology, race relations and immigration, and Scottish affairs; and three "departmental" committees to investigate the ministries responsible for agriculture, education and science, and overseas aid.[6] These committees had the power to send for persons, papers, and records, but did not take part in legislation or appropriation. They took evidence sometimes from Ministers and often from civil servants. They employed specialist technical and professional advisers. Dashing the high hopes once held by their advocates, however, the new committees did not catch the fancy of the House. "It must be conceded," concluded a recent report, "that when—too rarely—their reports have been debated, the degree of interest shown by other Members has sometimes been disappointingly small." While the subject committees will probably be kept, the departmental committees will be abolished. In accord with the present high esteem enjoyed by output budgeting and cost-benefit analysis, the new expenditure committee will work through subcommittees that are neither subject nor departmental, but functional. Each of the functional subcommittees is expected, as a principal duty, to examine "the implications in terms of public expenditure of the policy objectives chosen by Ministers and assess the success of the Departments in attaining them."[7]

Conceivably, the future procedure of the House in financial affairs might take the form of a three-stage process. The new select committee on public expenditure would annually receive the two basic sorts of information regarding public expenditure and economic growth. It would examine these and make a report to the House, perhaps even going so far as to present alternative proposals regarding not only the overall size of the public-sector expenditure, but also the priorities between different main blocks. This report would provide the foundation for an

---

[6] *Select Committees of the House of Commons* (October, 1970), Cmnd. 4507, p. 4.

[7] *Ibid.*, p. 5.

annual debate, presumably in the autumn or early winter. In the second stage the House would, as at present, debate the estimates. These would be presented, however, in two forms: the conventional line-item form and an output budgeting form, conforming as far as possible to the categories of the public-expenditure projections. Clearly, if this could be done, it would greatly facilitate the kind of policy discussions that take place on the Supply days. M.P.s could see much more clearly what the actual priorities of government policy are and could more intelligently criticize the use of national resources for any objective or field of objectives.

The final stage would consist in a postaudit by a parliamentary body. There would be no great departure from the present procedure. In charge of the annual audit of appropriation accounts of the departments is the Comptroller and Auditor General, an official who is independent of the executive, holding office during good behavior and removable only by resolutions of both houses. He and his staff examine departmental accounts to check on not only their legality, but also their economy and efficiency. It is with such matters that his reports to the House are normally concerned. On this basis the Public Accounts Committee of the House conducts its own inquiry, summoning before it and examining the responsible financial officers of various departments and reporting its findings to the House. The new form of the estimates, which would be reflected in the departmental accounts, could only make the work of the committee more effective in assessing the government's allocation of its resources. While the Public Accounts Committee would continue to audit the accounts of departments, the Select Committee on Nationalized Industries would also continue to perform a similar task with regard to the accounts of the nationalized industries.

The present trend in procedural reform is bringing Parliament abreast of the executive in the way problems of financial and economic policy are conceived, much as certain procedural reforms of the Gladstonian period brought the Parliament of the Liberal era abreast of the reforms that were then creating a new Treasury. If we think of the role of American legislative committees concerned with finance—as some British advocates of reform quite explicitly do—we can also see the prospect of the new select committee's alternative proposals for spending becoming an alternative to the Government's own program. Beyond that we can see the possibility of the new committee's emerging as a kind of rival executive to the Cabinet. It is not idle to consider the prospect of such rivalry, dim and distant as it may be. Indeed, the fact that Ministers and civil servants are alert to it as a possibility is a reason why it does not eventuate. By anticipation they ward off the threat.

The point is illustrated by the fact that a quarter of a century ago a reform proposal much like the one recently adopted was rejected. In brief, the proposal was to set up instead of the estimates committee a committee on public expenditure that would work through subcommittees and would be assisted by "trained clerks," that is, specialists. Although the Labour Government was in a vigorous reforming mood at the time, it reacted to these proposals just as any other British

Government would have reacted—negatively. Herbert Morrison reflected the attitude of Labour in the answers he gave to questions from the select committee on procedure that was considering the proposal:

Q: You would never suggest that in the final resort the House of Commons was responsible to the Government of the day?

A: To the Government of the day?

Q: Yes?

A: That would be against the whole doctrine. The Government is responsible to the House. On the other hand, the Government has to try to lead the House.

Q: Then why is it, that when you get into the field of departmental inquiry, you take the attitude that the civil servant is a superior person, and that the power of the representatives of the House, the power of the trained clerks, I think you said, would be too great, and would be resented in the Departments . . .

A: Because then we get into the argument as to who is responsible for executive current administration, the Government or Parliament. I say it is the Government that is responsible. It is responsible to Parliament, but if Parliament is going to set up another duplicating set of administrative experts to take an interest in current administration, there is going to be a clash between Parliament and Government, which I think would be bad.

Parliament's business is to check the Government, throw it out if it wants to, go for it, attack it, criticise it, by all means, but Parliament is not a body which is organised for current administration—not in this country. They have had a go at it in France and the United States, and I do not think too much of it.[8]

---

[8]Select Committee on Procedure, *Third Report* (October, 1946), Minutes of Evidence, p. 111.

Seven

The Power
of Parliament

The previous chapter makes clear how very faithfully the model of party government embodies some of the most important dimensions of British political behavior. We see how the ostensible purposes of much parliamentary procedure usually
conceal quite different functions. We also see that whatever the proceedings, the
Government almost always controls the initiative and the outcome. Under any of
the three headings—control of policy, legislation, or control of finance—it could
well be argued that the function of Parliament comes down to criticism, nothing
more and nothing less. In this perspective Parliament neither makes laws nor
controls finance and policy. If a person wants to know what laws will be passed
during a coming session, he does not take a poll of M.P.s, he reads the Queen's
speech. If it says that "My Government" proposes to introduce legislation for a
certain purpose, the chances are overwhelming that by the same time the following
year a statute to this effect will be on the books. Similarly in the daily business of
the House, if we want to know what is going to be discussed during the coming
week, we cannot do better than to listen to the Leader of the House when he
announces the parliamentary timetable on a Thursday afternoon.

The Continuous Electoral Campaign

The power to criticize is no mean power. In the context of the British party system,
it means that the appeal to the electorate in the next election is constantly foreshad-
owed in the clash between Government and Opposition. The disjunction between

223

the legislative leaders of the parties and the leaders of the parties in the national election that characterizes the American system is completely bridged in the British party system. The leaders of the disciplined forces of Government and Opposition in the House are also the leaders of the party organizations throughout the country. The party battle, centering on the daily clash at Westminster, is simplified and dramatized: There is no mystery as to who is responsible, no difficulty in identifying the alternative team. Under the British party system the House is the principal forum from which the parties appeal to voters for their support in the next election. "Governing has become a prolonged election campaign," writes Bernard Crick. "Parliament," he continues, "is still the agreed area in which most of the campaign is fought" and the principal device by which "the Parties obtain something like equal access to the ear of the electorate in the long formative period between the official campaigns."[1]

This is all in accord with the doctrine of party government that finds the main functions of the legislature to be, first, to register the decision of the voters at an election, and, second, to provide the forum from which the two antagonists carry on propaganda and, it may be hoped, political education. Not that one should exaggerate the attention given to Parliament. The newspapers that carry reasonably full reports of parliamentary debates are read by only about a tenth of the adult population. About the same percentage has been identified as the "serious public," meaning those who are "very interested" in political affairs and who follow them between elections.[2] As opinion leaders such political strata perform an important function in forming the opinion that is expressed at elections. In pointing to the interaction between these strata and the continuing controversy in the House of Commons, the model of party government brings out an important dimension of the process of social choice in Britain.

Yet this view of the House and its functions is not quite right. To some critics it is correct factually but not normatively. These critics lament the decline of Parliament from its supposed preeminence in its great liberal period. They propose reforms which, although they cannot undermine the vast stability of government in this day of the collectivist party, will somehow recapture for Parliament a voice not only in criticizing, but also in influencing government policy. But this reformist perspective, like the party-government view itself, is also not factually correct as a true and rounded portrait of what goes on in the House. Any first-time visitor to the gallery of the House must feel that something very important is going on in the House itself, quite apart from the reverberations of its proceedings in the outside world. The excitement, the tension, the strain are the tip-offs. This would not be the atmosphere if the House were a mere electoral college and sounding board. On the contrary, something important is at stake, and the outcome is not

---

[1]Bernard Crick, *The Reform of Parliament* (London, 1964), pp. 25–26.

[2]Richard Rose, *Influencing Voters: A Study of Political Campaigning in 1964* (London, 1967), p. 169; and Rose, *Politics in England* (Boston, 1965), p. 89.

cut-and-dried, but uncertain and risky—hence the effort to influence the outcome, creating strain in the protagonists and tension and excitement among combatants and spectators. After all, why do so many busy and important politicians spend so much time in and around the House if nothing politically important is going on? As we have seen, Ministers spend about a quarter of their time there, which is as much as they spend in their departments in the actual business of running the government. A Minister will no doubt use some of this time speaking in such a way as to influence votes in an election several years hence. But educating the public is obviously only one of several considerations that keep him in Westminster.

We can hardly fail to sense the power of the House. To be more specific and say just where its power lies is not so easy. We must begin with a look at the parliamentary parties. The political party was the source of Parliament's new behavior, marking the transition from a liberal to a collectivist phase of modernity (see Chapter 9). It is, therefore, in the analysis of party, the instrument of the new control, that we will find the contours and limits of this control. That means, first, looking at the relations between Governments and their own backbenchers and, second, examining the interaction of the organized Opposition and the Government. Not that the individual M.P. acting on a nonpartisan basis may not at times accomplish notable things; he may remedy a grievance or secure the passage of an important law, as noted in our discussion of the activities of private members. But whether or not the independent M.P. was ever as important as some critics of Parliament believe, he is not the lever by which government is moved today and the enlargement of his powers cannot be the means to enhance the role of the British legislature. Party sets the conditions for present parliamentary activity and for any conceivable reform.

Party Organization

For an American the most interesting and puzzling aspect of the behavior of the parties in Parliament is party discipline. Party discipline refers to a system of sanctions by which the parliamentary party induces recalcitrant members, or perhaps merely slack and apathetic ones, to act in concert with its authoritative decisions. The most dramatic of these sanctions is the "withdrawal of the whip," which means that the member is expelled from the parliamentary party with consequences that may include the termination not only of his hope for ministerial promotion, but also of his parliamentary career. For the party to have at its command such severe negative sanctions may well seem to explain the phenomenal cohesion of the parliamentary parties. At first glance party discipline is to party unity as cause is to effect. The use of these powers needs to be examined against the background of party organization in the House.

While the two parliamentary parties, Labour and Conservative, differ significantly in spirit and method of operation, they have important similarities. At the head of each stands a Leader who is elected by the members of the parliamentary party, but who is also recognized as Leader of the party outside Parliament as well. When his party wins a general election, the Queen automatically makes him Prime Minister. In Opposition he is the head of a leadership group, the shadow Cabinet, which sits on the front benches of the Opposition side of the House—that is, to the left of the Speaker—and which carries on a continuous and organized attack on the Government. Along with other members who assist them—rather as other members of a Government assist the Cabinet Ministers—the shadow Government may be a sizable body. In 1965 under Edward Heath it consisted of some seventy-two persons. While Conservatives leave the selection of its members to the Leader, the shadow Government of a Labour Opposition consists not only of spokesmen chosen by the Leader, but also of certain members—the Parliamentary Committee—elected by the whole body of Labour M.P.s.

In addition to its leadership group, each party has an organization reaching into the back benches—in American parlance, a "caucus"—which normally meets once a week during the session. On the Conservative side this organization is called the Conservative and Unionist Members Committee, or the 1922 Committee. This nickname derives from the fact that the Committee was founded after the election of that year by a group of backbenchers who intended it to be—in the words of one of its founders—"a rein upon the leaders." At first exclusively a backbenchers' organ, communicating with the leadership through the traditional whips, the committee in time drew the leaders into a quite close relationship. In recent years the Leader himself has often appeared before it, even when he was Prime Minister.

The Parliamentary Labour party (P.L.P.) consists of all Labour M.P.s, both leaders and backbenchers. When in Opposition, the P.L.P. annually elects the Leader, deputy leader, chief whip, and twelve others who, with representatives from the Lords, constitute the Parliamentary Committee. When Labour is in power, it has no Parliamentary Committee, but a Liaison Committee of backbenchers and Ministers presumably keeps leaders and followers in touch. Moreover, Ministers regularly attend meetings to explain, and if necessary defend, what the Government is doing—sometimes virtually appealing for a vote of confidence.

In both parties backbenchers are also organized into a series of functional committees concerned with various fields of public policy that parallel departments or groups of departments. When Labour is in Opposition, the chairmen are usually shadow Ministers for the respective departments, an arrangement that links backbenchers and the leadership group. The committees discuss current policy questions, take votes, and make reports to the parliamentary committee. While the Conservative committees do not formally take votes, a whip is attached to each, and through him, as well as through the committee's secretary, reports will reach the leadership.

The whip is the final element in this structure, and the oldest in point of origin. He descends from the early days of Cabinet government in the eighteenth century, and his name is taken from the hunting field, where the "whipper-in" is the man who manages the hounds. The Conservative Leader always appoints the chief whip; the Labour Leader appoints his party's chief whip only when he is Prime

Minister. The chief whip is a busy man, and when his party is in power, he has eleven paid assistants, as well as a number of unpaid assistants. Of old, the job of the Government whips was "to make a house, keep a house and cheer the minister." Their primary task is still to make sure that enough party members are available in the House or nearby in the lounge, library, tearoom, or bar to enable the Minister to win the divisions necessary not only to impose the Government's will, but also to keep the wheels of British government from grinding to a halt. It is exacting work. Every two hours the Government whips report to Ministers the number of members available before each division, giving a precise count of the prospective votes on each side along with an indication of the expected Government majority.

All this takes advance planning of the business of the House and the attendance of members. In carrying out their duties, the Government whips act under instructions from the Leader of the House, normally a Minister and member of the Cabinet. In this role they not only inform members, but also persuade, cajole, and, if necessary, warn those who are indisposed to accept authoritative party decisions. But they are also most emphatically a means of communication between backbenchers and the leadership. From what they learn at party meetings and in everyday, informal contact with backbenchers, they keep the leaders informed of the views, grievances, and general temper of the party. The whips let the leaders know what their followers will not stand, a crucial reality that by anticipation deeply affects what any Government attempts.

This whole mechanism of party organization provides two crucial things: first, a means of making authoritative decisions in the name of the party and, second, a means for seeing that these decisions are known and carried out by the party members in the House. The two parties operate in much the same way when in power. The authoritative decisions on tactics and policy come from the Cabinet and are communicated to M.P.s by the whips and by Ministers at the various party meetings, as well as by ministerial statements to the House itself. In Opposition the procedures differ significantly. On the Conservative side it is understood that the Leader has the final say, although, of course, in regular meetings with his shadow Cabinet—as in his dealings with the 1922 Committee—he cannot fail to take account of political realities. On the Labour side authority reverts to the Parliamentary Labour party. The standing orders under which the party operates most of the time specify that "the privilege of membership [in the P.L.P.] involves the acceptance of the decisions of the Party Meeting." (Indeed, these words would seem to bind not only all members, leaders, and followers when the party is in Opposition, but also by clear implication members of any Labour Government as well.) At the regular weekly meetings of the party, with the Leader and Parliamentary Committee giving a lead, the major questions of the business to come before the House are debated and brought to a vote, whose outcome in turn governs the vote of the party in the House. It is not strange, therefore, if some observers find that the most interesting and important debates are not on the floor of the House but "upstairs," that is, in the party caucuses.

Party Discipline

In the use of disciplinary powers the parties also differ. The Conservative Leaders have the power to withdraw the whip, but have proved far less inclined to use that power than has the P.L.P. Although rebellions are at least as common on the Tory as on the Labour backbenches, in only one instance since World War I has a Conservative member been expelled from the parliamentary party. In the Labour party such a question can be decided only by the P.L.P., whether or not the party is in office. When the standing orders are in force, they make an exception for a member only on the ground of "deeply held personal conscientious conviction," and then only to the extent of permitting abstention, never cross-voting.[3] Matters of conscience have been held to include such questions as Sabbath observance, temperance, gambling, and conscription.

These disciplinary powers would seem to have a formidable potential, vesting the whole power of Parliament in a majority of a partisan majority. Conceivably, this arrangement could lead to that ultimate democratic horror—minority government issuing from majority rule. In fact, precisely because this ponderous mechanism does work in a context of democratic politics, its powers are far more limited than they appear to be. A purge of party rebels presents to the electorate the spectacle of a divided and quarreling party and disheartens the organized partisans of the electioneering apparatus outside Parliament. Within the parliamentary party it is a threat to others who also may at some time want room for protest. Considerations such as these severely limit the use of disciplinary powers.

But rebellion can lead to serious consequences for the individual. The classic cases go back to Attlee's first Government after the war. As tension with Russia mounted, a number of Labour M.P.s on the Left became very disturbed and sharply attacked the Government's foreign policy. In 1948 the "cannibalization" of the Social Democrats of Czechoslovakia by the Communists after the Russian-backed coup of that year did much to quiet their dissent. Still, at the time of the Italian general election in April, when the Labour Government was officially supporting the noncommunist parties in the election, thirty-seven Labour M.P.s were prevailed upon to sign a telegram encouraging the left socialist allies of the Communist party of Italy. Fifteen of the signers, when approached by the National Executive Committee of the Labour party, declared either that they had not signed, had signed under a misunderstanding, or had since retracted. Twenty-one others, having been informed that "unless they individually undertake by first post Thursday, May 6, 1948, to desist in future from such conduct they are excluded from membership in the Labour Party," gave the required pledge. The M.P. who had gathered the signatures, however, was promptly expelled from the party, as were, a year later, three others who had given the pledge but had continued with disapproved activities. Deprived of national party endorsement, all stood as inde-

---

[3] For text, see *Annual Report,* 51st Conference of the Labour Party, 1952, p. 201.

pendent socialists at the next general election, in 1950. One had strong support from his constituency party, but all were overwhelmingly defeated by official Labour candidates. To be sure, the initiative in these cases was taken by the National Executive Committee (N.E.C.), the whip being withdrawn after, rather than before, its action. Still, the ultimate fate to which withdrawal of the whip might lead was made vividly clear. It may be doubted, of course, whether the whole action made any difference to a parliamentary party that at this time enjoyed a majority of around 191 over the Conservatives and of around 128 over all Opposition parties.

The narrow limits of disciplinary powers are illustrated abundantly by their inability to calm the prolonged and fierce dissension on the Labour Left during the early 1950s. The rebels, led by Aneurin Bevan, a former Minister and a contender for the succession to Attlee, could count on a solid core of about a quarter of the P.L.P. When the issue was popular, this number could be raised to almost half. The peak of the Bevanite rebellion and influence was reached in 1954 during the struggle over the party's position toward a German contribution to the proposed European Defence Community. At the party conference in the fall of 1953, the Attlee-Gaitskell faction won a majority for a favorable response, but only because of a last-minute switch by a small trade union, and by the narrow margin of 3.3 million to 3 million votes. At a meeting of the P.L.P., a motion to support the same position passed, but only by 113 to 109. Although the party then compromised by deciding only to abstain from voting and not to support the proposal when it came before the House, six left-wingers broke party discipline and voted against it. In consequence, the party did withdraw the whip. But there the matter rested; such was the support for the rebel viewpoint in both the parliamentary and extraparliamentary parties. Within three months the whip was restored.

In the Labour party the harsh procedures of party discipline have been used only on very small groups against whom the great mass of the party in and out of Parliament will rally. When the party was unified to this extent, however, such coercions were hardly necessary. When the party was seriously divided, as in the days of the Bevanite controversy, the mechanism of party discipline did little, if anything, to heighten cohesion. In short, when these powers should have been useful, they were ineffective, and when they were effective, they were not really necessary. Perhaps the tendency to splinter, inherent in an ideological party of the Left, makes such procedures and the threat of them necessary. Yet we may suspect that Labour probably would fare no worse if, like the Conservatives, it let the power of withdrawing the whip atrophy.

Back-bench Influence

On few generalizations do former Ministers agree more than on their report of the constant, anxious, and even deferential attention Cabinets give to the opinions of their backbenchers. Reporting on his experience in the Wilson Government, Richard Crossman recalled that each Cabinet begins with a discussion of next week's business and parliamentary matters. Members of the Cabinet, being themselves members of the House of Commons, "are constantly aware of the troubles we are having over the road in the Palace of Westminster [with the Labour backbenchers] and are discussing how they should be handled, what will be the next cause of trouble. This is a constant preoccupation of a British cabinet—its sensitivity to the House of Commons."[4]

Herbert Morrison, Leader of the House under Attlee, points out a particularly important dimension of this interaction of leadership and backbenchers. After recognizing the fairly numerous occasions when overt activity by backbenchers has succeeded in causing the withdrawal or modification of a proposal put forward by the Government, he distinguishes another category of back-bench influence that is actually of greater importance, although harder to detect and evaluate—the cases where Ministers respond to backbenchers by anticipating their reactions. Ministers have many channels through which they are made aware of the opinions of their own backbenchers, and in considering projected legislation or policy, any sensible Government will take these opinions into account. Their concessions are made not merely in advance of parliamentary proceedings, but in the course of developing the proposal within the executive. "Such concessions," Morrison concludes, "of course, cannot very well be recorded in the columns of Hansard."[5]

The importance of anticipation must be kept in mind when considering the record of overt back-bench pressure on Governments. For the interaction of back-benchers and leaders takes place against a background of possibilities, often unmentioned, yet vividly present to the minds of participants and conditioning their present behavior. Writing of this background of thought among Conservatives at the time of the Suez Crisis in 1956, Richard Neustadt reports:

> The Tories had been traumatized in 1940 when abstentions on their own side yielded Neville Chamberlain so relatively narrow a majority as to impair beyond recall the public image of his Government. He went. By this route Tory Premiers have ever since feared to go.[6]

Conservative Revolts

"Over and over," wrote one Conservative ex-Minister with reference to the 1950s, "I have seen cases where the Government were forced to swallow their pride and to back down on some issue under the pressure of backbench action."[7] A few

---

[4]R. H. S. Crossman, *The Myths of Cabinet Government* (Cambridge, Mass., 1972), p. 47.

[5]Herbert Morrison, *Government and Parliament: A Survey from Inside* (London, 1954), p. 167.

[6]Richard E. Neustadt, *Alliance Politics* (New York, 1970), p. 83.

[7]Enoch Powell, "1951–1959: Labour in Opposition," *Political Quarterly* (October–December, 1959), p. 336.

examples will indicate how much importance should be attached to this pressure. In 1955 the Minister of Agriculture, Fisheries, and Food backed down on a proposed reduction of the whitefish subsidy. The reason, it appears, was that he found not only the Labour party opposing the reduction, because it harmed "the small man," but also a number of his own backbenchers. Highly critical Conservative M.P.s from the fishery constituencies met with the Minister; some M.P.s even threatened to defy the whips and vote against the statutory order making the reduction. As a result, the Minister withdrew the order and issued a new one, which changed the proposal by restoring half the cut originally proposed for the smaller vessels.

In 1957 the Government withdrew the clauses of the Electricity Bill of that year, which would have given the Central Electricity Authority power to manufacture electrical plant. The Monopoly Commission had reported that private manufacturers made a practice of fixing prices of such equipment, and the clauses in the bill were intended to enable the public corporation to act if prices were fixed against it. Pressure centering in the back-bench Conservative Fuel and Power Committee caused the Minister to accept arguments he had previously rejected and to give in to back-bench demands.

A more notable instance of such influence took place in the same year during the course of the passage of the Government's controversial Rents Bill. Under Clause Nine some 800,000 tenants renting properties at "middle class" rents were to have their rents decontrolled six months after the passage of the bill. The Labour party opposed this clause along with the whole bill. In addition a number of Conservatives were uneasy, not over the principle of decontrol, which they favored, but over the short period of notice for the tenants affected. On the other hand, the Minister, his permanent secretary, and other officials favored getting through the period of dislocation as quickly as possible. Tory backbenchers used the standing committee stage for a prolonged demonstration of their dissidence. The Minister finally agreed to extend the period of decontrol from six months to fifteen months. A short time later, when mounting outside pressure was added to parliamentary criticism, he acted to give the courts power to delay evictions for hardship.

The case of the Shops Bill in 1956–1957 also involved a good deal of pressure from outside Parliament and is a good example of how departments work out noncontroversial legislation with the pressure groups concerned. The bill, which provided for earlier closing hours in retail stores, had been prepared by the Home Office under the Labour Government and was introduced under the succeeding Conservative Government. It was supported by both sides in the industry—the retail trade associations and the shopworkers' trade unions, which had been extensively consulted in its preparation—and by the Labour party. The small independent shopkeepers, however, were opposed, and they quickly gained strong support among Conservative backbenchers. While the bill itself was introduced into the Lords, Conservative backbenchers in the Commons were loud and prolonged in their protests. After much hesitation and under a new Home Secretary,

R. A. Butler, who had "the most sensitive antennae for back-bench feeling," the bill was totally withdrawn.[8]

In 1964 the biggest back-bench revolt in the Conservative party since the fall of Chamberlain marked the hotly contested passage of the Resale Price Maintenance Bill (R.P.M.). In this case the most significant measure of back-bench influence came before the bill was introduced, when Conservative M.P.s had prevented Government action for a period of ten years and then, thanks to the fears of the Cabinet, were granted substantial concessions in the bill to be introduced. The controversy went to the heart of important issues of economic policy and Conservative party philosophy. R.P.M. is the practice by which manufacturers oblige retailers to sell their branded goods at stipulated prices. This was clearly in contradiction to the defense of competition and the free market, of which Conservatives made much in their clashes with socialistic Labour. In 1961 the president of the Board of Trade brought a proposal for abolition of R.P.M. from the Economic Policy Committee to the Cabinet. There it was defeated on the straight political grounds that it would split the party in Parliament and outside. The next year, when the Prime Minister himself brought the matter up, he was warned off by his Ministers, who were aware of the intensity of back-bench opposition.

The coincidence of two events precipitated Government action. One was the arrival at the Board of Trade of Edward Heath, a forceful and obstinate man; the other was the introduction of a private member's bill to abolish R.P.M. Faced with the need to define his own position regarding the bill, Heath prepared a Government measure for abolition. In the Cabinet his opponents, fearing back-bench reaction, forced a compromise. Opposition in the House was still intense. Some of the leading opponents were connected with interests that would be adversely affected, including a vice-president of the National Chamber of Trade and a high official of the Pharmaceutical Society. But the Opposition extended well beyond such "interested M.P.s." When Heath met with the back-bench Trade and Industry Committee, three-quarters of the hundred or so present were against his bill. He conceded nothing either to them or to the 1922 Committee. On the second reading of the bill, twenty-one Conservatives voted against the bill and fifty abstained, some twenty-five abstaining for the purpose of showing their opposition. In the committee stage Heath defeated a crucial amendment by only one vote. Finally, a few further changes—which, however, did not touch the fundamental principles of the bill—were conceded, and the bill passed into law.

Labour Revolts

After the R.P.M. revolt Heath said that if he had lost the crucial vote in standing committee he would have resigned. Much more than the resignation of a Minister and the defeat of a bill was at stake in the controversy over trade-union reform that

---

[8]Ronald Butt, *The Power of Parliament* (London, 1967), p. 227.

wracked the Labour party in the spring of 1969, as the Wilson Government approached its end. When Labour had previously been in power, under Attlee, the left wing of the party was the seat of much dissidence. The rebels, however, were never ready to push a break with the leadership to the point of risking an overturn that might bring in the Tories. Hence, their activity subsided abruptly when Labour was returned with an overall majority of only six in the election of 1950. But the rebels of 1969 were ready to face the prospect of a return of the Tories. One reason was that they represented not so much the left wing of the party as the trade-union section of the party. This rebellion bespeaks the special power of trade unions in the Labour party when the "interests of labor" are at stake, as well as the conditional nature of the power of a Cabinet and of party leaders generally in the British Parliament.

As we have seen in our discussion of economic planning (see Chapter 4), the Wilson Government was engaged for most of its existence in a largely fruitless effort to control inflation. A major branch of its policy in this field consisted in attempts to subdue the wage-push component. As it became clear that incomes policy and fiscal measures would not suffice, reform of industrial relations was seen as having a possible contribution to make. A principal source of the pressure on wages was the rising frequency of unofficial strikes at the plant level. Indeed, the typical strike in the sixties was unofficial, called by local leaders without the support, and very often even without the knowledge, of the national organization. Early in 1969 the Government presented a white paper outlining to Parliament proposals for trade-union reform, of which the principal one would give the Minister of Employment and Productivity power to impose a twenty-eight-day cooling-off period on unofficial strikes, backed by the threat of a financial penalty against unions or individuals who did not comply. In his budget speech the Chancellor made it clear that this measure was an essential of the Government's economic policy. The Prime Minister backed him up, saying it was an issue of confidence and that its defeat would lead to a general election.

From the time it was first announced the measure met with opposition in both the parliamentary and extraparliamentary party. The principal source of opposition was the trade unions. "The Labour party," Ernest Bevin once told the party conference to its face in 1935, "has grown out of the bowels of the T.U.C." As we shall see, this fact of history is reflected in the overwhelming dominance of trade-union votes, representatives, and finance at all levels of party organization outside Parliament. In addition to these general ties of dependence, some 132 Labour M.P.s had been financially sponsored by trade unions in the election of 1966, a relationship meaning that a union has paid the larger part of each candidate's election expenses as well as having contributed heavily to the upkeep of the local party. Although some left wing M.P.s supported the Opposition, the hard core of resistance to the Government was found among the "interested" M.P.s who had union sponsorship.

Before the bill was introduced, a debate on the white paper in March led to a vote in which fifty-five backbenchers, defying a three-line whip, voted against the

Government, while another forty deliberately abstained. Although Wilson and nine other Ministers were members of the twenty-eight-man National Executive Committee of the extraparliamentary party, this body voted its opposition to the white paper by a majority of three to one, including among the opponents James Callaghan, Home Secretary and Treasurer of the party. As the Government persisted, the Trades Union Congress called an emergency meeting of the whole body in June —the first since 1920—at which it, on the one hand, demanded that the Government drop the bill, and, on the other hand, as a concession to the Government, strengthened the T.U.C.'s power to suspend a member union because of unofficial and jurisdictional strikes.

Wilson rejected these concessions as inadequate to the problem, and negotiations between the Government and the T.U.C. continued into June, when the Prime Minister asked the Cabinet for authorization to go ahead with the legislation. The chief whip reported, however, that the measure had no hope of passing Parliament, almost all loyalist M.P.s having gone over to the Opposition, thanks in part to the T.U.C. concessions. From this point in the meeting the split in the Cabinet grew, until only Wilson and Barbara Castle, the Minister in charge of the bill, remained in favor. After a brief resistance, and helped by a face-saving declaration by the T.U.C. that it really would use its powers against unofficial strikes, Wilson gave in completely, and the bill was dropped.

In this instance of party rebellion, the influence of the trade unions had changed a major policy to which the Government had publicly and firmly committed itself. Crucial to the effectiveness of this influence, however, was the fact that backbench M.P.s were ready to defeat their Prime Minister and Cabinet in the House of Commons. R. H. S. Crossman, a Cabinet member at the time, summarized the whole affair in these words:

> The Industrial Relations Bill which we lost was a bill in which we were going to give the trade unions enormous concessions in return for their allowing us to introduce sanctions against unofficial strikes. The sanctions proposed were not very effective, but we lost the Bill because when the crunch came we did not take the risk of having a vote in the Parliamentary Party. So the Bill was dropped. The Parliamentary Party had defeated the Government . . .[9]

Opposition Influence

In reassessing the role of Parliament, observers have given a good deal of attention to the influence of backbenchers on their party leaders. Less new ground has been broken in the examination of the interaction of Government and Opposition. In most accounts this is still described as a clash between two unyielding partisan

---

[9]Crossman, *op. cit.,* p. 118.

bands, which may affect votes at the next election but not policies of an incumbent Government. This familiar stereotype, however, needs to be viewed with some skepticism. We cannot disregard the hypothesis that the Opposition influences the Government.

Let us grant that much of the party battle in the House is directed at the voters outside. If each of the parliamentary parties were committed to a fixed program by ideology or some form of party control, this process of appealing to the voter could have the effect of changing policy only by means of a general election. Indeed, it is fair to say that in many of the sketches of party government this is presumed to be the principal mechanism by which voters control governments. The alternation of parties is considered the essential means of changing policy. Yet if we relax the assumption that the parties are committed to fixed programs and recognize that within limits they will change their programs in order to win votes and rule more effectively, the mechanisms of interaction become far more complex and much truer to life. In this view the Government, anticipating the electoral gains of the other side, adjusts to the strong points brought forward by the Opposition—as the Opposition also adjusts to the popular programs enacted by the Government.

When examining control of the economy, we had occasion to remark that those crucial swings of British Governments back and forth between planning and management have not been mediated by the obvious mechanisms of party government (see Chapter 4). Ronald Butt, an acute student of Parliament, finds in this area an important example of the influence of the Opposition. Writing of the conversion of the Conservatives to planning under Macmillan, Butt observes that while this shift was influenced by the successful example of France,

"it also owed something to the existence of a party in Britain which would naturally capitalize on the fashionable switch-back toward planning the economy. In the climate of opinion in the early sixties, the existence of a Labour Party with a plan to control the heights of the economy without wholesale reliance on nationalisation was an incentive to the Conservatives to produce a counterbalancing policy. . . . In this broad sense, therefore, the voice of the Opposition contributes to the policy-making of Government in any given Parliament and is not simply a factor in deciding what the composition of the *next* Parliament should be.[10]

We need not suppose that British Governments have always behaved in this way. In the aristocratic period public opinion as a force for determining the outcome of elections and fate of Governments was negligible. Cabinets rose and fell on the basis of shifting parliamentary support, and when a general election did occur, the Government that had been in power was invariably returned to office. It was only in 1841 that for the first time a Government dissolving and appealing

---

[10]Butt, *op. cit.,* p. 301.

to the country lost its majority. Subsequently, during the liberal period of Parliament, Governments at times were defeated in the House and then appealed to the country, which might or might not support them. With only primitive party organizations, neither Government nor Opposition could have calculated accurately which way the opinion of voters would swing, even if it had tried. Having adopted a position in Parliament, the Government might well find itself taking its first reliable sounding of opinion the hard way, at the hustings. In time, however, the elaborate organization and communication systems of the collectivist age made it possible for Governments and Oppositions to tune their parliamentary performance far more finely to the anticipated voices of the people. The main source of the Opposition's influence on the Government took the form not of changed votes in the House, but of anticipatory reactions among Ministers. Such behavior is harder to identify and measure than cross-voting in the House or shifting majorities in the country, but it is no less real for that.

Over these same generations of transition from aristocratic to liberal politics the Opposition was becoming a more and more formidable body. Its history goes back to the beginnings of the modern age, when the medieval practice of ventilating grievances was supplemented by a new kind of opposition, which grappled with questions of policy. Toleration of such opposition was fully accepted in the eighteenth century, although the idea of a "formed opposition" in Parliament, that is, a body of men consciously acting together in opposition to the King's Government, was frowned on (see Chapter 8). Actually, the institution of an organized Opposition carrying out a systematic, united, and prolonged attack over the whole range of Government policy arose only at the end of the nineteenth century. Governments were weaker by far in mid-Victorian Parliaments than they are today. But this was not because the Opposition was stronger. On the contrary, it consisted of a coalition of shifting groups even more incoherent than the Government majority.

In comparison with the unorganized Opposition of a hundred years ago, the present-day Opposition not only provides more responsible criticism, but also exerts more influence on the incumbent Government. As we have seen, each party when in Opposition has a front-bench structure that marshals continuous and often expert opinion on its side in the House and reaches out to further support from professional sources in the party organization and associated circles in the country. Endowed by parliamentary procedure with constant opportunities for attack and counterproposal, a body so equipped and organized is a massive and formidable reality for any Government. If one is to say that Parliament has declined in the past hundred years, one must reconcile this view of the trend with the fact that the Opposition has risen to new heights of prominence and power.

If today individual M.P.s complain more about their lack of power—and perhaps they do—the reason is not far to seek. The backbencher of the present day, like the ordinary citizen, expects a great deal more for himself. A hundred years ago, in mid-Victorian days, aristocracy was still a great power in the land; between the Earl who might be Prime Minister and the offspring of even well-to-do gentry on the backbenches of the Commons the social distance was known and respected.

Neither in the society at large nor in the House of Commons did egalitarianism enjoy a good name. Today equality has become such a cult as to make backbenchers less satisfied with what may actually be a greater share of power.

The model of party government is an instructive guide to the realities of parliamentary behavior, providing we do not succumb entirely to its persuasive simplicities. The House does act as an electoral college, transmitting the outcome of an election into the establishment of a Government. It also serves as a forum for propaganda in the continuous election campaign of British politics. Yet this conventional picture is far from complete. It neglects the dynamic interplay of backbenchers, Government, and Opposition. Above all, it must be revised to allow for the fact that any Government—and indeed any Opposition—will continually adjust its program and general stance in the light of many circumstances, not the least of which is its anticipation of the next election. Shifts in public opinion may thus greatly affect policy without being expressed in changed votes. The mechanism is still that of party responding to popular control, but it does not depend on the unreal assumption of parties committed to fixed and unchanging programs.

Moreover, this interaction between parliamentary and electoral forces is only one major instance of how Parliament is continuously involved in the process of opinion formation in the country as a whole. Ronald Butt observes that "the most profound impact an opposition can make on parliamentary politics may be when it provides a focus for great national debates on matters which deeply divide or disturb the community." In his opinion the outstanding example in post-war years was the Suez affair in 1956. Noting how deeply the policy embittered the conflict between parties in the House, he asserts that "their arguments not only led, but to a great extent created, the debate in the nation." Britain's imperial power had been in decline for years. But the failure of the Suez policy was a rude shock "exposing to the Conservative Party and to the nation Britain's reduced position in the world."

> What was to be the Conservative attitude to prestige politics in the future? What new role could be found for Britain, to solace the nation for its lost world power? For good or ill, all these questions arose from the battle in the House of Commons over Suez. The schism in the nation was largely created by the schism in Parliament.[11]

The Inner Circle

To stress the linkage of parliamentary activity with opinion formation in the polity as a whole should not, however, be allowed to obscure those processes which are performed in a much narrower arena. As in the Suez debate, the force and content

---

[11] *Ibid.,* p. 305.

of various currents of public opinion may be substantially determined by what goes on in the House. But the House does not only affect the substance of opinion. It also generates, sustains, and imposes upon individuals, factions, and parties special standards of conduct and style. And these standards may be at variance with those engendered by the struggle for power in the wider arenas of electoral politics.

A gifted observer once spoke of the Chamber of Deputies of the Third French Republic as a "closed arena," a way of emphasizing the importance of the political forces generated autonomously within the chamber itself.[12] In a carefully limited sense the term can also be applied to the House of Commons. It has its own political subculture, which governs a life that is no less communal for being intensely competitive. As a human community it has its own standards of excellence and norms of conduct, as well as an elaborate system of sanctions and rewards to enforce them. The power of these sanctions cannot be doubted by anyone who has watched a pack of critics drive a Minister into a corner at Question Hour and has then seen him flinch and flounder amidst triumphant cries of "Answer! Answer!" The House of Commons owes too much to the English public school to be entirely gentle. Commenting on the trials of Anthony Barber, the Conservative Chancellor, during his first months in office, the London *Economist* spoke of "the remorseless interest of the House of Commons in seeing a man at a disadvantage brought down."[13]

If the House no longer makes and unmakes Governments, it continually makes and unmakes reputations. The House still functions as the principal arena for leadership selection in the British political system. Ability to cope with the party conference and the TV camera, not to mention such matters as sheer managerial competence, have a bearing on a politician's advancement. But perhaps, above all, he must be a "good House of Commons man," showing achievement according to the special and complex standards known to that community and to some, but not many, outsiders. For this community does blend with a small, special public, which is linked by communication centers such as the clubs of Pall Mall, the university common rooms, and the offices of the quality newspapers and weekly political journals. No self-respecting Minister or civil servant can enjoy having acts of injustice or stupidity for which he is responsible exposed to the scrutiny and comment of these circles. Nor can he be insensitive to their praise, with its hint of a footnote in history. "Fame is the spur." But while the electorate can vote power, only a more discriminating public can confer fame. Indeed, the two sets of standards, those which lead to success in the House and those which lead to success in elections, may well be in conflict. The kind of demagogy that wins votes outside may destroy a reputation in the House. The Reverend Ian Paisley could win a dominating position in Northern Ireland with his harsh appeal to religious prejudice, but in the Commons he was received with cold disregard.

---

[12]W. L. Middleton, *The French Political System* (New York, 1933), Chapter 5.

[13]*Economist* (London), Feb. 27, 1971, p. 17.

The House has its own standards, which with a real degree of autonomy it imposes on the behavior of politicians and parties.

The House of Lords

If by the modernity of tradition one means an extreme reluctance to part with any institution with a claim to antiquity, the British retention of the House of Lords is a prime illustration. This body, which originated as the great council of barons of the medieval king and which includes members with such titles as baron, viscount, and earl—not to mention bishop and archbishop and even marquess, duke, and prince—still meets regularly in its ornate chamber at the west end of the palace of Westminster and carries on a large volume of legislative and supervisory business.

Its powers, as we have seen in the discussion of legislation, have been reduced almost to nil. Yet its activities are still sufficiently important to demand brief mention. Along with other steps reforming and modernizing British government, several important changes in the composition of the Lords have recently made it a more useful body. Prior to the reforms of 1958 the Lords had some 860 members, of whom about 800 were hereditary peers; 26, bishops of the Church of England; and 9, Lords of Appeal. The last named are lawyers appointed to the House for life to permit it to discharge its functions as the highest British court of appeal, and when appeals are heard only these law lords attend the sessions. The principal reform made in 1958 was to make possible the granting of nonhereditary life peerages. The same act provided that women, who were previously barred from membership, could also be admitted as life peers. A later reform made it possible for a peer to surrender his peerage, a right exercised especially by those who wished to clear their way for a seat in the House of Commons. In 1964 an expense allowance was provided, reflecting the modest circumstances of many contemporary peers. This allowance is currently 4½ guineas ($11.28) per day. While he was Prime Minister, Harold Wilson, in accordance with his announced intention, created no hereditary peerages; and as of this writing Edward Heath has followed suit. Both, on the other hand, added substantially to the number of life peers.

Mainly by the creation of life peers, Governments have somewhat redressed the imbalance of parties in the Lords. In 1967 its membership was calculated to consist of 350 Conservatives, 100 Labour members, and 40 Liberals, with 96 Independents. Most peers do not attend, and the hard core of debate is sustained by a daily attendance of some 200, almost all of whom are life peers. While the rules of the Lords are more relaxed and the weight of business less pressing, party organization prevails in the upper, as in the lower, House. When votes are taken, party unity is strongly in evidence.

With regard to legislation, the Lords have several ways of making themselves useful. First, it need only be mentioned, they have a part to play in the enactment of private bills and review of delegated legislation similar to that of the Commons.

Second, peers may introduce private members' bills without having to surmount the kinds of obstacles that would confront them in the Commons. On the other hand, the fact that these bills have no future unless the Government is willing to give them time in the lower House keeps their numbers low. Third, the Lords retain their suspensive veto. Actually they almost never reject bills that have come from the House of Commons—however much they may criticize them—yet when they do, even their slight remaining powers may in the right circumstances make an important difference. For example, in the 1955–1956 session a private member's bill abolishing capital punishment passed the Commons, the Conservative Government of the day taking no stand, but finding time for the bill and permitting a free vote among its backbenchers. The House of Lords, however, rejected the bill. Under the law governing the Lords' suspensive veto, the Commons would have had to repass the bill in the subsequent session. The measure failed because the Government was not ready to provide the parliamentary time, although it did enact its own bill limiting somewhat the use of the death penalty.

The House of Lords is also useful as an originating chamber. As such it may save a little time in the Commons by providing the forum for the initial debates on a bill. About a quarter of all bills, and sometimes more, are first introduced in the Lords—although they may never be money bills, and usually are bills of only lesser importance. Finally, perhaps the most important legislative function of the Lords consists in its activity as a revising chamber. As bills from the House of Commons go through the upper chamber, many amendments are put. Often this is only for the purpose of enabling the mover to voice a point of criticism, whereupon he withdraws his amendment. At the same time, the legislative process of the Lords affords the Government a chance to tidy up or improve proposed legislation. Sometimes peers find legal or other flaws in bills that have escaped the scrutiny of both the executive and the Commons; often changes first suggested in the Commons are actually inserted in the Lords, after the Minister has had time to "take them into consideration," that is, to discuss them with his civil servants and the affected interest groups. And, of course, the passage through another chamber gives Ministers and civil servants a further chance to perceive and repair their own errors of omission or commission with regard to a bill.

Aside from its functions as an originating and revising body for legislation, the Lords has also created something of a role for itself as a chamber for debating large questions of the day. Recent additions to its membership have broadened the social spectrum represented. We now find in the Lords professors, journalists, and trade union officials, as well as company directors and lawyers. These talents have their opportunity in fairly frequent general debates on broad questions of public policy.

If we cannot speak of the decline of Parliament, we surely can speak of the decline of the House of Lords. It is fair to say that until 1832 the upper House was the dominant chamber. In the "balanced constitution" of the aristocratic period it enjoyed its position of parity and, moreover, thanks to the patronage of its members, a large influence over many members of the Commons. In the liberal period it still provided Prime Ministers, the last having been the Marquess of Salisbury, who retired as Prime Minister in 1902. As late as 1910 it could precipitate a constitutional crisis of the first magnitude. In that year the Lords not only rejected a finance bill that the Liberal Government regarded as especially important, but they also rejected a subsequent bill that proposed to limit their powers. In the course of their resistance, they forced two dissolutions before they gave in by accepting the limitation of their power by the House of Lords Act of 1911.

It is hard to recapture the atmosphere of an England that could permit, legitimize, and take seriously this prolonged resistance to measures sanctioned by all the norms of popular government on the part of a body whose members were overwhelmingly hereditary, Conservative, and rich. Today that England of the aristocracy and of the governing classes of the Victorian bourgeoisie has declined to the vanishing point, and with it the House of Lords. The House still provides a place for ancient ceremony, as when the Queen opens Parliament each autumn. For a moment the chamber is peopled with gorgeous costumes, animated by medieval ritual, and suffused with nostalgic splendor—for all the world to see, now that the proceedings are put on television. But as the brief ceremony ends and as these university dons, former borough councillors, and ex-civil servants turn in their rented coronets and ermine-trimmed robes, we realize that even in England things sometimes change.

Eight

The Foundations of Modern British Parties

In a highly developed modern polity like Britain, the pattern of interests matches in scale and complexity the pattern of power. As we have seen, the instrumentalities of the state penetrate deeply into British society. Spending half of the national product and employing a quarter of the labor force, the public sector also intermingles with the private sector, creating what the Fulton Committee called "a proliferation of para-state organisations" that mobilize and direct resources in the service of the purposes of the state. The field of activity in which these purposes arise, compete, and are adopted is no less extensive. In this age of collectivist politics its principal actors include political parties and pressure groups, but it should be clear from previous chapters that Parliament, Cabinet, and bureaucracy also play major roles in articulating and determining the ends for which state power will be used.

Basic Conditions of Mass Politics

A comparison covering about a century and focusing on the general elections of 1874 and 1970 suggests the immense growth of public participation. In 1874 the population of the United Kingdom, which then included the whole of Ireland, was some 32.4 million. By 1970 the United Kingdom, although its Irish portion now included only the six northern counties, had a population of 55.3 million. At the time of the general election of 1874, the registered electorate of the United Kingdom numbered under 3 million. By 1970 it had risen to nearly 40 million. A more significant indicator, however, would be the number of persons actually voting. In 1874 this was 1.6 million, or 5 percent of the population. In 1970 it was 28,-344,807, or 51.2 percent of the population.

These figures vividly reveal what is meant by the mobilization of interests and the rise of collectivist politics in the modern state. Even though the Reform Act of 1867 had extended the vote to the skilled urban workman, the participating electorate in 1874 still constituted only a small number of the members of the polity. But it is the absolute figures that are the most suggestive. With a total vote of 1.6 million, they mean that the average vote per constituency in the United Kingdom was 2,500, the size of the House at that time being 652. To be sure, just about half the seats were uncontested. Even when we allow for this, the average vote per contested constituency was only 5,000. No words could suggest more vividly the simplicity and organizational informality of the electoral process in contrast with the situation a century later when, on average, 45,000 voters took part in the choice of each M.P.

But the mobilization of interests has meant much more than simply a rise in the number of persons taking part in processes of political choice. For the typical participant there has been a great increase in the facets of his total activity involved in these processes. More of his interests, ideal and material, have become the subject matter of political discussion, electoral campaigns, and government decisions. His life has become far more "politicized." This too has meant an increase in scale and complexity of the polity.

One indicator of increased politicization can be found in the subject matter of electoral campaigns. The 1874 election turned out a Liberal Government under Gladstone and brought in a Conservative Government under Disraeli. Although Disraeli's Government did proceed to enact a series of far-reaching social reforms, during the campaign he had referred to social questions in only the broadest and vaguest way. This was before the day of party manifestoes, but in his election address to the voters of his constituency Disraeli mentioned the subject of reform, going no further, however, than to express his continuing concern with "all measures calculated to improve the condition of the people." This unexceptionable sentiment was not quite so meaningless as it seems out of its historical context. The "condition of the people" question had been given some content by Disraeli in previous utterances. But even in his famous Crystal Palace Speech of 1872, a notable declaration of Conservative purpose at home and abroad, he had stayed on the level of broad generality with regard to his domestic policy. On that topic he said:

It involves the state of the dwellings of the people, the moral consequences of which are not less considerable than the physical. It involves their enjoyment of some of the chief elements of nature—air, light and water. It involves the regulation of their industry, the inspection of their toil. It involves the purity of their provisions, and it touches upon all the means by which you many wean them from habits of excess and brutality.[1]

This reticent approach to campaign promises was entirely in accord with the Tory ideal of not tying the hands of the statesman and meant that, as a contemporary of Disraeli's remarked, "there was no special measure which he had received a mandate to carry through, no detailed policy he had advocated which the country was enabling him to execute."

In 1970 a general election also resulted in a change of Government; Labour under Harold Wilson was defeated by the Conservatives under Edward Heath. Entering this campaign, the Conservatives issued a party manifesto entitled "A Better Tomorrow," which ran to some thirty pages. Its domestic proposals took up 90 percent of the space and are far too lengthy to be more than summarized here. Their wide range and high specificity, however, are obvious from the following summary:

ON THE ECONOMY. Cuts in income tax and surtax; abolition of the Selective Employment Tax and the betterment levy; possible replacement of purchase tax by the Value Added Tax; repeal Industrial Expansion Act; reduce government involvement in nationalized industries; phase out Regional Employment Premium; no statutory wage control; forbid all unjustified price rises in the public sector.

ON INDUSTRIAL RELATIONS. Legally binding agreements between employers and unions; secret ballot and cooling-off period of not less than sixty days for disputes seriously endangering the national interest.

ON FOOD AND FARMING. Introduce import levies; keep support system at a declining cost for at least three years; keep annual review and production grants.

ON HOUSING. Abolish Land Commission; encourage council house sales; renegotiate subsidy system to concentrate assistance on worst areas and change it to provide adequate rent rebates for those who cannot afford fair rents.

ON EDUCATION. Concentrate on primary school building; local authorities to decide on secondary organization for themselves; encourage direct grant schools; raise school leaving age.

ON SOCIAL SECURITY. Introduce scheme based on negative income tax; pensions for those over eighty; improve benefits for disabled; ease earnings rule for pensions; make pension rights fully transferable; make public service and armed forces' pensions increases payable at 55.

---

[1] Quoted in W. F. Monypenny and G. E. Buckle, *The Life of Benjamin Disraeli, Earl of Beaconsfield,* rev. ed. in 2 vols., Vol. II (London, 1929), p. 530.

ON IMMIGRATION AND RACE RELATIONS. Single system of control over all immigration from overseas; limit future work permits to specific job in specific areas for specific period; assist voluntary repatriation; extra help to local authorities with large immigrant populations.

ON LAW AND ORDER. Modernize law on public order, obstruction and forcible entry; oblige those causing injury or damage to compensate victims; inquiry into law of trespass; review Official Secrets Act.

This comparison between the elections of 1874 and 1970 suggests, though it does not quantify, the multiplication and variegation of interests that have occurred during the past hundred years. As we have seen when discussing the dimensions of political development, such an increase in demands asserted in the polity also constitutes an increase in scale, quite apart from any change in the number of participants. The effect is to multiply manyfold the increase in scale and complexity brought about by the massive rise in numbers.

Such developments constitute the basic conditions of mass politics in the collectivist age. We can think of them as posing a problem: How is it possible for such a huge agglomeration to function as the main agent for determining the ends of the polity? How can so many people with so many different demands be joined together in such a way that they exercise effective, ultimate control over their government? These are the questions that come to the mind of the person concerned with testing or vindicating democratic theory. A more relaxed and analytical way of putting the question is to ask what broad model (if any) best describes how demands arise and come to be adopted in the system.

In this book the doctrine of party government has been put forward, hypothetically, as providing a model likely to reveal the main structures in the pattern of interests. It is important to realize that other models could be tried out, some of which are compatible with the party government model and some of which are not. A brief review of them will sharpen the concept of party government and may be helpful in the course of the analysis in revising the concept to fit realities.

One possibility is that mass politics tends to become what the name immediately suggests: a mere aggregate, an atomized mass without substantial structures, formal or informal, to give it shape or direction; responding with volatility and confusion to the erratic stimuli of the mass media and dangerously susceptible to the appeal of the demagogue and the Caesar. This line of analysis, which has been developed in recent decades by students of "mass society"—such as Ortega y Gasset, Emil Lederer, Hannah Arendt, and others—goes back to earlier critics of modern society, who saw in mass politics a severe threat to social and political cohesion.

Another, blander model comes from the students of pressure groups—the Bentley model. The basic units, according to this view, are a plurality of groups, normally based in the economy and usually giving rise to organizations, such as trade unions, trade associations, and professional organizations. Parties can be analyzed into coalitions of such groups, and have no significant role or influence of their own, their so-called ideologies or philosophies being reducible to composites of the particular demands of their component groups. A mechanical balancing of group forces produces decisions that constitute the pattern of policy. As it shifts, this balance produces, at best, compromises reflecting the strength of the demandant groups; at worst, immobilism and inaction when such compromises cannot be struck; and, on average, a meandering but tolerable sequence of government interventions.

Various types of elitism are compatible with these models. In Britain, throughout its various phases of modernization, party government has been associated with, and perhaps has presupposed, a governing class in some form. This association is clear, for instance, in Schumpeter's discussion (see Chapter 1). The Marxist idea of a ruling class of capitalists has been applied to Britain, as in the later writings of Harold Laski. Of interest to current analysis is the technocratic possibility. Technocracy is something more than the rule of bureaucrats—the possessors of the skills used by, and organized in, the pattern of power. Although technocracy was long foreseen, it is most instructive as a concept of analysis when taken as a product of the current, acute phase of the scientific revolution. The vast increase in scientific knowledge in recent decades, along with the institutionalization of research and the use of its findings directly in making and implementing policy, has elevated people with special knowledge to an entirely new plane of influence. The complexity and technical character of public policy—military, foreign, and domestic —makes them indispensable. At the same time, their technical knowledge—of weapons sytems, spaceships, medical science, economic problems, and so on— enables them to perceive problems and propose solutions well beyond the conception, or even the comprehension, of most citizens. Herein lies the possibility of a new kind of elite, embracing the top professionals in the public and private sectors and transcending, and possibly manipulating, the party system.

All these approaches have something to contribute to the analysis of British politics. But there are several reasons for taking the party government model as the leading hypothesis. One reason is that conventionally it has provided most American political scientists with their main instrument for interpreting British political institutions, in which, moreover, some have found a model for the reform of American politics. Although the hope, once widely entertained, of creating "a more responsible two-party system" in the United States has greatly diminished, the idea of such a party system is still put forward by some reformers as a goal and used by many teachers as a device for bringing out the distinctive traits of the American system.

A more important reason for taking seriously the party government model is that in one version or another it is the way Britons generally think they are governed. Surveys of opinion show that the electorate overwhelmingly sees elections as contests between the two main parties, enabling the victor to constitute a Government, which in turn produces a distinctive kind of policy output. "The individual elector," write Butler and Stokes, "accepts the parties as leading actors on the political stage and sees in partisan terms the meaning of the choices which the universal franchise puts before him."[2] Moreover, typically, the voter not only holds the party in power responsible for government policy, but also regards a change of party as an effective means of achieving the economic and social conditions he values. The behavior of British voters corresponds with these perceptions. In Britain there is no real equivalent for the term "independent," which many American voters use to characterize their political identity. A Gallup survey in 1966 asked British voters whether they considered themselves Conservative, Labour, Liberal, or Independent. Only 3 percent chose Independent. In the United States a similar question in a Gallup survey in 1967 drew the response "Independent" from 31 percent of the sample.

In recent history the general election of 1945 illustrates the power of party. Clement Attlee, the Labour party Leader, could not compare in personal appeal with Winston Churchill, the wartime Prime Minister, who campaigned amidst an outpouring of gratitude and respect. While the crowds turned out to cheer Churchill, however, at the polls the people voted for the Labour party and its program, sweeping out Churchill's Conservatives in a crushing defeat.

Party and Modernity

For the student of political development there is an even more weighty reason for considering party the major structuring influence on the pattern of interests. This is the obvious link between the party system and political modernity. In Britain the rise of parties coincides with the beginnings of modernization. Conventionally, the two-party system is dated from the emergence of Whigs and Tories in the conflict over the Exclusion Bills of 1679 and after, which attempted to bar the succession to James II, then duke of York, because he was a Catholic. The Conservatives of today are directly descended from those Tories and are sometimes spoken of as the oldest political party in the Western world.

The historical association of political parties and modern polities is clear. The important question is analytic and theoretical: Is there some intrinsic connection between modernity and party? Are there conditions, cultural or structural, that are inherent in modernity and that produce a party system? Conceivably, party could be a type of structure inherent either in all polities or in all developed polities, modern or not. On the other hand, they could be much more transitory than is usually thought, characterizing a certain period in the development of the modern polity, but tending to wither away or decompose at a later stage. If there is an intrinsic connection between party and political modernity, some understanding of this connection should throw light on the role parties play in the process of social choice, and on the limitations of this role.

---

[2]David Butler and Donald Stokes, *Political Change in Britain* (New York, 1969), p. 23.

Political parties are bodies of men seeking to win positions of authority in the polity. But political formations characterized by this goal can be found in most regimes, nonmodern as well as modern. Thus the baronial factions in the court of a feudal king competed for the great offices of state and other avenues of influence within a political and social system that itself remained unchanged. Modernity, however, brings into existence a new pattern of political culture and a new form of polity and, in consequence, a new structuring of the pattern of interests.

One characteristic of the new pattern of interests—and an important condition in making a party system possible—is suggested by Sigmund Neumann's observation that the rise of political parties correlates with the rise of the modern legislature. He wrote,

> It is not . . . accidental that the beginning of modern political parties is closely tied up with the rise of a parliament. When political representation broadens and a national forum of discussion develops, providing a constant opportunity for political participation—wherever those conditions are fulfilled, political parties arise. This happened in England in the revolutionary seventeenth century; in France on the eve of the great Revolution of 1789; in Germany around 1848. Even where contingent influences may create political groups of an awakened intelligentsia, as in the nineteenth-century tsarist Russia, they assume political dimensions only where some degree of participation is possible."[3]

Parliaments predate modernity and, indeed, as institutionalized meetings of the estates, were a normal feature of medieval regimes in Europe. It is the modern, not the medieval, legislature, however, that correlates with the rise of political parties, for it is only in the modern legislature, freed from medieval restraints by the conception of sovereignty, that law making on the requisite scale takes place. In the English case the essential functions of the medieval Parliament were the redress of grievances and the grant of supplies. Not that statutes were not enacted, but their scope was so limited that a whole school of medievalists has been able to maintain that the Parliament of those times should be regarded not as a "legislature" but, in accord with the term used by contemporaries, as a "court." Thus C. H. McIlwain's classic work elaborating this theme is entitled *The High Court of Parliament.*

As modernization progressed, the legislature shed these medieval restraints and law making was extended to matters that had previously been untouched. Legislation establishing religious toleration was perhaps the most radical innovation. Also, the regime itself might be modified, as it was by the great acts regulating the succession to the Crown in Britain, the Bill of Rights of 1689, and the Act of Settlement of 1701. As for the arena in which these questions were raised and decided, factions that resemble parties may form where the royal council of a sovereign monarch is the only forum in which the law-making authority can be

---

[3]Sigmund Neumann, *Modern Political Parties* (Chicago, 1956), pp. 395–396.

influenced. But a representative legislature like the British Parliament, with elections subject to the influence of groups and opinions in the country, is more likely to produce what we call political parties. In this way Tories and Whigs, originating in the struggle over the Exclusion Bill, continued to find the center of their conflicts in the Parliament, where laws were passed and money appropriated. The modern party and the modern legislature are intrinsically related.

The modern political party presupposes both the legitimacy of law making and a structure, such as a legislature, giving some significant number access to participation in the exercise of this power. The feature of modernity that is our concern, however, is political parties—in the plural. A plurality of parties is not likely to arise unless another condition obtains, namely, the acceptance of opposition on basic matters of public policy. As we have seen in discussing the rise of opposition in Britain, modernity does involve this condition, legitimating disagreement that extends beyond mere presentation of grievances to principles of public policy. Under the Tudors this condition did not obtain, the initiative and determining influence in "great questions of state" being reserved for the monarch. By the early eighteenth century it was entirely legitimate for members of Parliament to criticize and oppose even those proposals brought forward by the sovereign's Ministers, and by the late eighteenth century such opposition was common. Such acceptance of differences of opinion over the common good seems inherent in the premises of modernity. Modernity departs fundamentally from any notion of a final and fixed social order buttressed by tradition. The voluntarist spirit, as it makes will the source of law, thereby also opens the way to the toleration of different conceptions of authority and purpose (the common good) within the ruling community. Scientific rationalism would seem even more influential, given its adaptability to the notion of the piecemeal discovery of truth.

Modernity legitimizes differences of opinion over the common good and creates the expectation that such differences are inevitable and even desirable. Toleration of opposing views comes to be founded on the belief that controversy is a necessary part of the rational discourse from which public policy should emerge. Such a premise is essential to the eighteenth-century idea of parliamentarianism, the notion that the legislature is a forum for deliberation where decisions are made by mutual persuasion among men with diverse viewpoints. This notion of the common good as something arrived at by rational discourse and mutual persuasion is central to Edmund Burke's conception of the role of the legislature and its members. In his speech of 1774 to the electors of Bristol—the voters of his constituency—he declared that Parliament was not "a congress of ambassadors from different and hostile interests, which interests each must maintain as an agent and advocate against other agents and advocates." It was rather "a deliberative assembly of one nation with one interest, that of the whole—where not local prejudices ought to guide but the general good resulting from the general reason of the whole." In consequence, he continued, while a member of the legislature ought to give "great weight" to the wishes of his constituents, he ought never to sacrifice to them "his unbiased opinion, his mature judgment, his enlightened conscience."[4]

This passage breathes the orderly reformism of which Burke was the first philosophic champion and for which British politics became noted. It involves a crucial prerequisite of party government: the acceptance of opposition and criticism on matters of public policy on the grounds that controversy is a legitimate phase in the determination of truth. This premise of the party system did not suddenly appear, but unfolded slowly as men grudgingly accepted opposition as inevitable, then as tolerable, and finally as desirable and even indispensable. Yet the essential doctrine—the idea of the piecemeal discovery of truth mediated by argument— goes back as far as Milton's *Aereopagitica* (1644) and runs through modern political thought to its classic formulation in John Stuart Mill's essay *On Liberty* (1859). Its crucial importance as a cultural premise of the party system and of party government can be seen if we consider the practical tendencies of the contrasting view that there is one Truth, fixed, permanent, and neither needing nor permitting criticism. This is not only a premodern idea; it also finds lodging in the utopian strain of modernity, which sees in one great truth the definition and justification of a final and unchangeable political and social order. The natural vehicle of this belief is the one-party state.

In these ways modernity lays the foundations, cultural and structural, for the rise of political parties. Yet the actual existence of parties was bitterly resisted for many decades. Even in the late eighteenth century, the Fathers of the American Republic rejected with abhorrence the prospect of such bodies arising in this country, condemning them as "factions" and seeing in them a great threat to popular government. Modern as these men were in spirit and ready as they were to accept and tolerate differences of opinion, they thought government could and should be carried on without the emergence of organized bodies of partisans.

Likewise in Britain, although individual opposition had long been tolerated, the idea of a "formed opposition" was repugnant to common opinion in the aristocratic polity of the late eighteenth century. Some voices had been raised in defense of parties, but the first powerful case was put forward by Burke in 1770. In his *Thoughts on the Present Discontents* he defended parties, largely on the pragmatic grounds that if men are to act effectively they must act in concert. Moreover, he defined what he was defending in a classic formula: "Party is a body of men united, for promoting by their joint endeavors the national interest, upon some particular principle in which they are all agreed."[5] The legitimacy of the modern political party cannot be logically deduced, so to speak, from the premises of modernity. But assuming conduct oriented by the norms of modernity, and given the structural fact of a legislature with its growing political community outside, political parties were a natural, if not inevitable, consequence.

This discussion of the connection between modernity and party is important

---

[4] Edmund Burke, *Writings and Speeches,* Vol. II (Boston, 1901), pp. 89–98.

[5] *Ibid.,* Vol. I, p. 110.

because it tells us something about the nature of political parties. They have been defined in many different ways: as nothing more than groups of men who seek to win power, differing only as "ins" and "outs"; as mere coalitions of special interest groups; as combinations seeking only to acquire and distribute patronage; and so on. These definitions point to traits that can be found in most political parties in the modern world. No doubt some political formations called parties are exhaustively characterized by such definitions. But to start from the cultural and structural dynamics of modernity shows that inherent in these dynamics is a distinctive kind of political formation. These dynamics tend to produce political formations consisting of bodies of men acting in support of different conceptions of the common good and in conflict with one another. In short, modernity tends to produce as a regular feature of the polity organized opposition over important matters of public policy. It is not necessary to say that such political formations must inevitably arise or that they cannot be offset; the example of the modern dictatorship shows that this is not so. The essential point is that political formations as characterized in the Burkean formula have grounds that are deep seated in modernity.

Party and Development

Political parties are intrinsically connected with change. Moreover, they reflect the fact that change in the modern period takes the form of development. In the context of the present analysis, the important characteristic of modern development is that it is marked by a series of stages that show a trend. This is a distinctive mode of change. It does not apply to change that consists in a mere continual repetition of the same forms of behavior. It does not apply to change consisting of a succession of discrete and dissimilar moments without connection. Moreover, it is incompatible with a mode of evenly incremental change in which each moment is, so to speak, equally a "stage" and a "transition." This last distinction is crucial since it involves the question of whether the "stages," "periods," and "eras" that students of development find in historical change correspond to realities or are simply imposed upon a continuous flux for the sake of making it more intelligible. Quite possibly some stretches of historical change must be so treated; they are merely prolonged transitions that cannot be divided into periods. But other stretches of historical change do satisfy this requirement of the concept of development.

The course of political modernization in Britain, for example, falls into three or four stages, which do not merely serve the convenience of the student, but reflect realities in behavior and attitude. This means that certain times are times of relatively full realization of a given political order and other times are times of transition between such periods of realization. The seventeenth century, especially the earlier part, was a time of transition to modernity, and the aristocratic polity flourished in the eighteenth century. In the nineteenth century the liberal order in economy and polity achieved a kind of fulfillment, although, of course, elements from the previous stages strongly survived. Moreover, within this liberal and individualist period, it makes sense to distinguish two phases: an earlier one marked in the polity by narrow suffrage and a policy of laissez faire, and a later phase of Radical democracy, when the active political community was greatly enlarged and when substantial though piecemeal interventions in the economy by the government were sanctioned. The twentieth century, which has become collectivist both in public policy, with the rise of the welfare state and managed economy, and in political formations, with the emergence of distinctive forms of political parties and pressure groups, constitutes the fourth stage of political modernization.

The significance and distinctiveness of this kind of historical change is illustrated by a striking characteristic of modern British political history. This is the recurrence, toward each mid-century, of a marked lull in political conflict. In the 1950s this decline in party conflict was so marked that many people spoke of "the end of ideology." Certainly, there was a great change from the interwar period, when even a moderate such as Clement Attlee could declare that "the issue before the country is Socialism versus Capitalism—and Socialism is not a matter of degree." By the 1950s, although not without bitter resistance from within, Labour had receded from its old premise of wholesale nationalization and comprehensive planning; while the Conservatives, to the surprise of everyone but themselves, had accepted the welfare state with its heavy burdens of taxation and the managed economy with its broad intervention in the private sector. The two leading spokesmen for the Conservatives and Labour, R. A. Butler and Hugh Gaitskell, respectively, had such similar views of both means and ends that the term "Butskellism" was coined to indicate their consensus. Compared with the interwar years, British politics in the 1950s showed a great decline in class antagonism. The questions dividing the parties became marginal, statistical, quantitative—questions of "more" and "less" rather than great social theories in conflict. Correspondingly, general elections consisted not of pitched battles between opposing social philosophies, but of small raids on interest groups. One American journalist wrote of the general election of 1951 as "the lull before the lull."

A quite similar pattern of consensus in attitude and behavior characterized the earlier mid-century lulls. After the "roaring forties" of the nineteenth century, the fifties led to that period of calm and balance that some historians have called the "Victorian compromise." Chartism with its menace of working-class violence and even revolution had withered away. The main pillars of aristocratic economic privilege had been pulled down with the repeal of the Corn Laws. Prosperity abounded under the new regime of laissez faire. As for politics, the parties were at a low point of cohesion, and, indeed, a kind of multipartism reigned in Parliament. In 1859 Lord Derby, the Prime Minister, declared that although he was not ready to say that parliamentary government itself had come to an end, with regard to a two-party system in which leaders commanded the votes of their followers and exercised a species of parliamentary discipline, "those days are gone, and are not likely to return." In sharp contrast with the bitter contention raised before 1832 by the issue of extending the franchise, now the prospect of giving the vote to the skilled urban workman merely excited a sluggish competition between the parties, which was won almost by accident by the Conservatives when they succeeded in passing the Reform Act of 1867.

The 1750s succeeded a time of no less instability and bitter party combat, although perhaps at further remove. The furious strife of "the great parties" of the late seventeenth century—to use Burke's characterization—bequeathed to the early eighteenth century a period of party combat that involved vital questions of foreign policy, the position of the Church of England, and, most ominous of all, the question of a Jacobite succession. As late as 1746 Bonnie Prince Charlie, the son of the Stuart pretender, was able to land in Scotland, invade England, and keep the field for a year. But the Tory party, which had already lost its capacity for coherent political action, was hopelessly compromised by "the Forty-five." It lingered on as a collection of country squires and a disembodied tradition, while the Whigs, broken into aristocratic "connections," fought one another and monopolized successive Governments. It was an issueless politics, in which the active political community accepted with hardly a question the aristocratic polity and the mercantile system for protecting and fostering British agriculture, industry, and, above all, commerce. So quiet were the times that at the opening of Parliament in 1753, the King's Speech, after requesting supply, had nothing further to recommend to the attention of the assembled houses than the increase in the "horrid crimes of robbery and murder." Quite naturally, when we take a detailed look into the politics of these years, we find only a politics of interest and connection, not of party or principle. This is also true of similar moments in other stages of political modernization. As in other periods in which party and party conflict decline, the reason in the mid-1700s was not an "end of ideology," but rather a "consensus on ideology." After long contention a certain political and economic order had been established that was widely accepted in the active political community.

Each of these periods of consensus marks the realization of a certain identifiable political order, possessing in each case a distinctive political culture and distinctive patterns of power, interest, and policy. For the student of political parties the important fact is the connection of party with such an order. On the one hand, party has been a main instrument in the establishment of this order. The party struggle preceding the period of consensus and realization involved changes in attitudes and behavior that helped constitute the new order. In this way party is an important means of political development, and the party struggle an important arena of political modernization. At the same time, a party that has contributed to the establishment of an order becomes identified with that order and, as the party of the status quo, defends what it had so large a part in bringing into existence (not that parties ever fully realize their initial visions). Societies and polities cannot be fabricated de novo; and an established order includes many elements and shades of meaning proceeding from sources other than the conscious orientation of a political party. The party of the status quo acquires a commitment to an order with complex origins.

Without trying to assign causal primacy to either, we can see the connection between modern development as a mode of change and the modern party as a type of agent of change. The Burkean party is characterized by a distinctive conception of the common good (authority and purpose), which is supported by a body of men acting in concert during some substantial length of time. The action of such an agent of change is one reason why modern political development is marked by stages, a mode of change in which a distinctive order rises, flourishes and is transformed in a new transition. Likewise, the fact that there are such established orders constitutes a source of the conceptions of the common good that are characteristic of the Burkean type of party. When historical change consists in mere flux, or in a succession of discontinuities, this type of political formation cannot function. It is appropriate that Burke, with his strong sense of modern historical development, should also have perceived the type of political formation it entails.

To summarize the analysis up to this point: The cultural and structural conditions of modernity that give rise to British political parties are threefold. First, the emergence of sovereignty—the power and legitimacy of law making—and the vesting of sovereignty in a body with substantial participation creates the objective possibility that differences may arise over the nature of the common good among the active members of the polity. To legitimize law making does not, however, necessarily legitimize controversy over law making and the toleration of opposition to those chiefly charged with it. Modern attitudes provide this second prerequisite of parties by sanctioning efforts for change based on changing human wishes and new perceptions of truth. Third, there is a structural interdependence between the character of modern development and the organization of opposing viewpoints. As we have just seen, organization means that these viewpoints are advocated over a period of time and that they constitute coherent outlooks on the political and social order. The opposition of early modernity took an organized form because it was confronted by an established order: that is to say, by social and political arrangements that endured over a substantial period of time and themselves constituted a coherent polity and society. At the same time, throughout modern political development an important reason why such established orders have been brought into existence has been that they were sought and maintained by political parties organized around conceptions of the common good.

Party, Pressure Groups, and Class

To understand the conditions that must obtain if parties are to come into existence does not tell us what the parties stand for or what their aims are. Understanding the prerequisites of the party battle does not explain its content and issues. To shed light on this question, it is plausible and conventional to look to influences from the environment of the polity, especially the economy. One of the most striking characteristics of modernization is a rapid and immense increase in the power of the state. Historically, this increase in power has proceeded largely from development of the economy. It can hardly be doubted that so dynamic a sector of modern society has a profound effect on the polity. In European history the classic instance is the impact of industrialization, which brought into existence powerful new classes, the commercial and industrial bourgeoisie, who through several turbulent decades disrupted and transformed—often by revolutionary violence—the old political and social order of the aristocratic and monarchic age.

The relationships of economic groups and the polity in the course of economic modernization can be stated in general form. Economic development proceeds through specialization. Advances in technology produce new divisions of labor with corresponding innovations in capital equipment and land use. As the new skills and techniques are put into practice, new occupational groups come into existence. The specialization that brings about the increase in productive power of the modern economy means at once greater differentiation, making a more complex economy, and new occupational components, constituting the new strata of the changing economic order.

These new strata are a principal basis of the growing power of the modern state. Their skills and resources are increasingly mobilized as the modern state extends its control over the environment. They provide personnel for the bureaucracy, civilian and military, and their growing wealth enlarges the resources on which the state may draw by taxation. At the same time, the emergence of new strata also brings about changes in the pattern of interests. Conflicts between strata arise— for instance, the classic conflict between older agrarian interests and a new and growing group of middlemen in an expanding economy. There is also a possibility of conflict between the activities of new strata and the established policies of the state, such as the restrictions in the early phases of modernity upon the movement of labor and goods. From such situations, which recur continually in the course of modernization, new demands on the polity arise. Emerging strata, their economic power perhaps enhanced by organization, attempt to use state power to protect and promote their interests in relation to other strata and to state policy itself.

This brief sketch, which puts into historical perspective the familiar interest-group model of politics, reveals a great deal about the politics and political issues of modernizing states. In the British case each of the main stages of political development coincided with a distinct economic order. The aristocratic age was a time of agrarian predominance and of rapid commercial progress. The nineteenth century was, of course, the era of industrialization, while the collectivist era in politics and government came when the fully industrialized economy was massing its growing productive power in large corporate organizations. Each of the economic orders had a pattern of economic interest groups, old and new, many of which became pressure groups attempting to use state power to promote their ends. Among the influential actors in modern British politics, we cannot fail to include the capitalist farmers, enclosing landlords, stockjobbers, and merchants of

Whig England; the manufacturers, traders, shipowners, railway directors, and banking and insurance companies of the Victorian era; the trade unions, trade associations, and professional organizations of the contemporary welfare state and managed economy. When interest groups take an organized form, they are commonly called pressure groups. In this sense British politics has never been without pressure groups.

To grant the importance of interest groups does not show their connection with political parties and certainly does not imply that parties can be regarded as mere coalitions of interest groups. On the contrary, the two types of political formation, parties and pressure groups, are radically different. There are various important differentiae, but one significant behavioral index is their use of quite different channels of access. In each of the main stages of British political development, the political behavior of the special interests has usually constituted a mode of representation distinct from that of the political parties. In the collectivist polity, for example, the great producers groups of the present economy, organized in specialized associations and affiliated in wider groupings, have developed a system of access to policy making that bypasses parties and Parliament and goes directly to the executive. Close and continuous relations between these groups and the departments and subdepartments of the bureaucracy have created what may be called a system of functional representation, in contrast with the system of parliamentary representation dominated by the political parties. A similar contrast can be found in the political orders of the earlier stages of political modernization.

The connection between party and economy becomes clearer if we look at those broad categories of interest groups constituting classes. Even in England, where the connection between class standing and party affiliation is today, and no doubt has been in the past, exceptionally strong, the correlation is not perfect (see Chapter 11). Nevertheless, during the past generation quantitative studies of the question have shown that two-thirds of the working-class vote has regularly gone to Labour, while an even larger fraction of middle-class voters have supported the Conservatives. A similar connection between party and class can be found in the past. It was the British working class that overwhelmingly provided the leadership that founded the Labour party and guided it through its first decades. In the early nineteenth century the manufacturing and commercial classes lent their support largely to reform, although for a long time they accepted the leadership of aristocratic families that espoused the Liberal cause. During the fierce party fights of the late seventeenth and early eighteenth centuries, the bulk of the aristocracy, which, of course, had its economic base in vast landholdings, were Whigs, while the Tories drew their strength from the lesser landowners and the gentry.

A class consists of a number of similar occupational groups, performing as a whole a major economic function. When such a class has provided the spearhead for political innovation, it has usually been helped by the fact that it embodies new advances in technology. Such was the case with the landholders who benefited from the agricultural revolution of the seventeenth and eighteenth centuries, the manufacturers who emerged during the Industrial Revolution, and the trade union leaders who utilized the new techniques of organization developed in more recent times. In this sense the innovating class commands growing economic power, which it may use in its contest for political change.

As science and technology advance they endow certain groups with new and exceptional power over nature and society. Such were the manufacturing classes of the Industrial Revolution; such too are the managers and professional classes of today's collectivist economy. Their growing skills and resources are means that these groups can use to try to better their position in the polity. But as these examples suggest, the important fact is not whether the rising class is based in the polity or in its environment, in the public or the private sector. Technological development can produce new classes and prepare the way for class conflict in a socialist as well as in a liberal economy.

In the course of modernization, however, technological development has not done more than prepare the way for class conflict and political innovation. What values a new class will champion when it enters politics, or indeed whether it will make an effort to enter politics or passively accept its old status, depend as much on political as on economic variables. The classes that have led the way in British political development have not been simply pleaders for the particular interests of their component groups, but have advocated broad conceptions of the common good. As objectives of political action, a plea for a particular interest and a conception of the common good are quite different. Intrinsically, the difference resides in the fact that a conception of the common good, however biased, makes provision for many interests, while the objective of the particular interest is essentially "more" for the relevant group. In consequence, a conception of the common good provides a normative basis for restraining and directing the interests of even the more favored classes. To be sure, special interest groups and their advocates may also be members of larger political groupings, such as political parties, not to mention the national political community itself. As such their attitudes and behavior will also be affected by norms of the common good. But in the modern polity the function of advocating particular interests becomes differentiated from the function of advocating conceptions of the common good. This is a major reason for distinguishing between pressure groups and political parties.

In periods of innovation, one reason the innovating classes have been able to bring along substantial allies from other groups is that they have appeared as champions of broad perspectives. Burke's conception of a hierarchic society, for instance, expressed not merely a norm of inequality, but also a belief that hierarchy should and could in the long run guarantee the rights and interests of all. In this view the aristocracy without question occupied the peaks of authority and privilege, but there was also allowance for other classes, including those Whig allies, the mercantile and commercial classes. When Burke spoke of "the strength of the nation," he listed the elements seriatim: "the great peers, the leading landed gentlemen, the opulent merchants and manufacturers, the substantial yeomanry."[6] In terms of economic policy, the Whig polity made commerce "the dominant factor" in the existence and well-being of Britain, and the mercantile system, which was designed especially to promote British commerce, had as firm a grip on the minds of the great landowners as on the minds of its more immediate beneficiaries in the commercial classes. These Whig aristocrats were among the first and most vigorous of the modern nation-builders, and they entertained aspirations for national and imperial development ranging far beyond their own direct concerns as landed magnates.

Party and the Intellectuals

As in the case of the Whig aristocrats, the conceptions of the common good that have informed party activity throughout British political development have by no means been mere reflections of the economic positions of the classes adopting them. The mobilization of interests through which new groups have been drawn into the active political community has been a response to many factors besides technological advance. Above all, it has been profoundly affected by that complex process by which, on the plane of thought and opinion, the implications of the premises of modernity have been explored and put before the public by the intellectual classes of the time.

Along with the process of economic modernization has gone the process of cultural modernization. Both proceed from the same premises, but they do not always lead in the same direction. Industrialization, for instance, is one of the most obvious and direct consequences of modern attitudes. Yet it does not necessarily require democracy and liberty in the political system. On the contrary, the nature of the individual enterprise, as well as the economy as a whole, might well seem to make a hierarchic and authoritarian system of control far more appropriate. Such indeed was the opinion of some early observers, such as St. Simon, an opinion which the experience of both Czarist and Soviet Russia as well as that of many newly developing countries has not disconfirmed. Therefore, if the period of industrialization in Britain and generally in Western Europe was a time of rising democratic forces, the reason is to be found not in the economic process, but in the profound changes taking place in the climate of opinion.

In giving a character to this change, the role of the intellectual classes was preeminent. As we have seen in looking at the rise of free-trade sentiment in Britain, the economists were in the field decades before the groups whose interests were involved began to respond (see Chapter 1). With reference to the great age of reform generally, a major portion of the legislation was inspired by Benthamism, and not a little was actually drafted by Benthamites. In earlier as well as later times, men who explore, articulate, and publicize ideas about the political and social

---

[6] *Ibid.*, p. 492.

order have played an important role in the development of British political culture. From its earliest days, when John Locke was secretary to Shaftesbury, the founder of the Whig party, to its days of ascendancy, when Edmund Burke was secretary to the Marquess of Rockingham, the Whig aristocracy had close connections with an intellectual world, ranging from philosophers and poets to the pamphleteers and scribblers of Grub Street.

Similarly, as Schumpeter has emphasized (see Chapter 1), in the critical moments during the rise of the working-class political movement in Britain in the late nineteenth and early twentieth centuries, a small band of socialist intellectuals played a highly influential role. Years before there was a Labour party, the Fabian Society, founded in 1884, set out to "permeate" influential public opinion with their version of socialism. The active membership in those early days was drawn from such quarters as belles-lettres, journalism, education, and the Civil Service. While the Society never committed itself to a single program, perhaps because it recognized the difficulty of getting precise agreement among such lively minds, it was responsible for shaping in fundamental ways the great political movement that arose after the founding of the Labour party at the turn of the century. It rejected revolutionary methods in favor of parliamentary ones, although that choice was probably already implicit in the constitutional and law-abiding commitments of British trade unionism. Its brass-tacks, problem-solving approach, much akin to the practical spirit of the Benthamites, also found a home in important circles of the Labour party.

Perhaps the Fabian Society's most distinctive contribution, however, was to propagate and give operational meaning to the conventional socialist idea of "common ownership" of the means of production. The idea of common ownership was not a necessary outgrowth of the economic conditions of the working class in industrialized Britain. In the United States similar conditions have consistently failed to produce any such political upshot. American working-class politics has taken a social-democratic turn, as in the New Deal, but it has never been in any significant way what is called "socialist" in the conventional European sense. Moreover, not only did the Fabian intellectuals adopt and propagate this idea, they also brought it down to earth in their proposals for a program of bureaucratic nationalization of the principal industries.

In any society the intellectual class is of crucial importance. Its essential concern is with the more general principles that underlie the norms and beliefs followed in the everyday conduct of the society. Through schools, churches, newspapers, and similar organs, intellectuals function as important agents in the cultural socialization of each generation, "infusing into the laity attachments to more general symbols and providing for that section of the population a means of participation in the general value system."[7] Some also devote themselves to the elaboration and

---

[7]Edward Shils, "The Intellectuals and The Powers," *Comparative Studies in Society and History,* 1 (October 1958) (The Hague), p. 7.

development of alternative potentialities of the cultural heritage; criticizing received beliefs and drawing out new models of the social and political order. This process of shaping the tastes, preferences, and ideals of each generation and all classes is crucial to the process of demand creation, which conditions fundamentally the development of both the economy and the polity. It enlists some of the most powerful minds and irrepressible individualities of each age, and from it have issued major perspectives on which political parties have been founded and by which the development of the polity has been driven forward.

Nine

The Modernization
of British Parties

The premises of modernity have provided the basis for a wide-ranging and complex elaboration of political and social values. The modern spirit itself, with its emphasis on invention and innovation, legitimizes and stimulates this work of intellectual development. The resulting history of political attitudes, whether in formal theories or in the operative ideals of public opinion, is rich and complex beyond the scope of any typology. Ancient prejudices hang on, and the eccentric products of wayward circumstance and imaginative genius continually disrupt our simplifying models. Fully recognizing the extent to which abstractions distort reality, however, we may use a simple four-cell diagram to show some of the main political values entertained by British political parties in the course of modernization.

Values and Party Development

Voluntarism and rationalism respectively provide themes of will and control for elaboration. Thus modern conceptions of authority vary along an axis of greater or less equality, while modern conceptions of purpose can be classified according to whether they make the locus of control the individual or the state. These two dimensions, inequality-equality and collectivism-individualism, create four cells into which the central values of the principal parties of innovation can readily be fitted. The arrows show the line of chronological succession. (See Figure 9.1.)

Looking at conceptions of authority alone (see Figure 9.2), we can ask of any

Figure 9.1 Modern Political Values

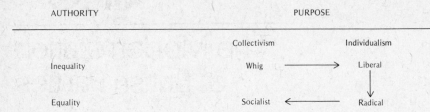

political order how the common interest and particular interests, respectively, are given representation. The collectivist category provides variations on the theme of functional representation, while the individualist category includes various kinds of voluntary association as the means of access for particular interests. Along the equality-inequality axis, modes of representation of the common good are classified according to whether they are more or less direct. Into the four resulting cells the four main conceptions of authority can again be fitted.

Figure 9.2 Conceptions of Authority

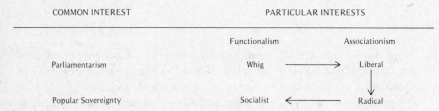

Missing from these diagrams is a major and, indeed, the senior actor in British party history—the Tory party. The Tories are absent because our classifications have dealt with variations of modern political values. The Conservative party, however, is an older and more complex entity.

Its origins go back before the modern period, at least to Tudor England, when the ideal of the hierarchic, corporate, and Christian society, although challenged by the first stirrings of modernity, still inspired the established order. This order, reduced to the status of a party during the transition to modernity in the seventeenth century, has nourished the heart of British Conservatism to this day. While retaining its Tory heart, however, British Conservatism has endured many massive infusions from other political bodies. Typically, these are former innovators who, having become attached to an order that they had a hand in creating, find themselves challenged by champions of further change and so move over to the Conservatives, the traditional party of any established order. Thus, under the impact of the French Revolution, the Tory party, hardly more than a scattering of backbench squires, emerged as the dominant party of the Younger Pitt because of an accession of Whigs. In the nineteenth century steps toward popular government and less inequality continued to push aristocratic names into the Conservative ranks. Toward the end of the century, as the Radical tide rose in the Liberal party, financial, commercial, and industrial wealth moved strongly toward the Conservatives; for instance, the number of businessmen greatly increased among Conservative M.P.s. With the rise of Labour, in turn, the Conservatives picked up further support from Liberal voters, perhaps the larger part of them. During the post-World War II period it was shown that when Liberal voters moved to other parties, support was two-to-one in favor of the Conservatives.

As a result of this long accumulation and complex inheritance, the Conservative party is much harder to understand than its younger and simpler competitors. It is right to stress its ancient heritage—for example, its disdain for equality and its readiness to accept collectivist measures for the sake of security. At the same time there is both a strong Liberal tradition and a strong businessman's stratum in the party, which can be used to rationalize and support a sharp turn away from government intervention and toward use of the market. Moreover, when we recall that the Radical current in the Liberal party included a high regard for the "little man," the powerful support that many Conservative backbenchers gave to Retail Price Maintenance, against the free market and in favor of the small shopowners, makes ideological as well as electoral sense.

But the term ideological can be applied to the Conservatives in only the most tenuous sense. An array of diverse and contradictory perspectives inhibits simple theoretical formulations of purpose. Conventionally, the Conservatives have been regarded as the party that has no ideas but which can govern. Its diverse heritage helps account for both characteristics. The absence of ideology makes it more flexible, with the result that Conservatives have sometimes been able to perceive and to adapt to circumstances that baffled their more single-minded rivals. But this ability to govern is also something more positive than mere flexibility. Putting it a bit formally, we might call it a multiple capacity for perception deriving from a complex tradition. In any case it is not accurate to think of the Conservatives as nothing more than the party of the status quo. On the contrary, they have often been agents of modernization. While not propagators of grand theory, they have often been the authors of the concrete measures by which modernity was forwarded. The roll of innovative British statesmen would be sadly incomplete if it did not include the Tory names of Pitt, Canning, Peel, Disraeli, Neville Chamberlain, R. A. Butler, and Harold Macmillan.

One effect of these ambiguities of Toryism has been to complicate the pattern of party development. The basic mechanics of the process are clear: A party of innovation having close ties with an economic class mobilizes a coalition that is instrumental in establishing a new order in politics and policy; in due course the innovators defend this order against the challenge of a new party of change. But the peculiarities of the British party of order, the Conservatives, mean that frequently it too has been responsible for significant innovation. Thus in 1846 Peel completed the major work of liberalizing British economic policy by repealing the Corn Laws, although he split his party in the process. A generation later the Conservatives, under Disraeli, often took the lead during a new phase of social reform that was reflected in the rise of Radical influence on the Liberal side. During the interwar period Conservatives laid the foundations of government control on which the managed economy of the present day was built. In the early 1950s under the influence of Butler, the Conservatives not only accepted, but in significant ways expanded, the welfare state they had inherited from Attlee's Labour Government. In the early 1960s Harold Macmillan initiated a new effort of economic planning, which the Wilson Government accepted and built on. In 1971 Edward Heath's Conservatives led Britain into the Common Market against resistance strongly represented in the ranks of Labour.

It would be entirely out of keeping with the Tory spirit to see in this behavior anything exceptionally high-minded. The motive is often simple prudence. As Disraeli said, "The palace is not safe, when the cottage is unhappy." Or as Quintin Hogg warned a Conservative gathering in 1944, "If you do not give the people social reform, they are going to give you social revolution." But among people with power such good sense and prudence are not so common that they can be taken for granted and require no explanation. A major reason in British political culture is the tradition of a governing class, and although the essence of this class is that it has provided leadership for all parties, it has usually had its main strength among the Tories.

The basic values of British parties derive from two sources: the premodern order of Tudor England enshrined in the traditions of Toryism and the developing themes of modernity. These values appear in history in rough order of succession, both as party viewpoints and as the rationales of successive stages of political development. These stages can be characterized as Old Tory, Old Whig, Liberal, Radical, and Collectivist, each of which can be identified with a political party. But although these values and their corresponding political formations and political structures did emerge in succession, they also appeared in rudimentary but recognizable form at the very start of modernization. Each of the five main types of political formation has an analogue among the principal factions that appeared during the political struggles of the English Civil War in the seventeenth century. In the constitutional royalists we may find the first Tory party. Rejecting the frantic personal government of Charles I, their inspiration was the Tudor regime, and like Tories in other generations they had support in all classes of the population. As is common in civil wars, the opposition split and splintered. The aristocratic leaders of Parliament and its armies prefigured the later Whigs. A distinct current of opinion was also recognizably liberal. In *Aereopagitica* (1644) Cromwell's secretary, John Milton, first stated the doctrines of free speech and individual self-development to which, two hundred years later, John Stuart Mill gave classic expression in secular form.

In the struggle that broke out within the parliamentary forces in 1647 after their victories in the first civil war, the clash of democratic with liberal viewpoints is reminiscent of many later conflicts. The Levellers stood for a kind of radicalism, which, although suppressed, broke out again in the American colonies and among the democratic forces of nineteenth-century liberalism. Socialism also had its precursors in Winstanley's "Diggers," who aimed at the abolition of private property in land and the establishment of communal cultivation on a democratic basis.

In cultural history ideas and attitudes often emerge in new and original forms from successive contexts. No doubt this has been true of many of the proposals and points of view that have been put forward in the course of British party development. But the fact that the main perspectives appeared almost simultaneously at the beginnings of modernity suggests a different process. During the modern period the actions and reactions of leaders and groups have not been completely indeterminate and open, but have been contained within the possibilities of a certain cultural complex. This political culture includes both a premodern heritage and the basic premises of modernity, voluntarism and rationalism. As we have seen in Figure 9.1, these premises have various implications; they can be embodied in a number of conceptions of authority and purpose, which are made specific by their place on an equality-inequality axis and on a collectivist-individualist axis. The four resulting potentialities of political modernity correspond to the four main currents of oppositionist opinion in the Civil War. With Toryism they constitute the principal values that were expressed in later party and political development. The modernization of British political culture has been driven forward by the elaboration, systematization, and criticism of these potential patterns of value by the intellectual classes.

Whigs and Tories

A trend toward equalizing power and the conditions of life has marked the evolving aspirations of modernity. But when English parties first burst forth from the political struggles of the Restoration monarchy, it must not be thought that the Whigs, although the party of innovation, were more egalitarian than the Tories. In the late seventeenth century they were overwhelmingly the party of the great aristocrats, and for all their connections with merchants and Dissenters, their vision of the polity and society was as hierarchic as that of any medieval baron or Tudor lord. Nor, in spite of their connection with Locke, were the Whigs rugged individualists. Their conception of the society was not only hierarchic but corporate. Individuals were seen as members not only of the various ranks and orders of men, but also of the local communities of village and household, borough and shire, and it was such bodies rather than isolated individuals that were regarded as the legitimate bases of representation in Parliament. Thus Burke, writing at the height of the Whig ascendancy, attacked the philosophy of natural rights because it proposed "personal representation" and failed to recognize "corporate personality." For many years one of the charges against parliamentary reformers was that they championed "individual representation," which, in addition to its suggestion of universal suffrage, also implied equal electoral districts in place of the ancient, unified communities of the old system.

In their conceptions of authority the conflict between Whigs and Tories centered on the role of the monarch. In the Tudor regime the right and duty of representing and protecting the common good had been vested in the monarch. In practice this meant that the initiative and decisive influence in the great questions of public policy were the Crown's preserve, entrenched in its prerogative. Elizabeth denied to the Commons the initiative in questions concerning foreign policy and war and peace; the royal succession; the religious settlement and the church in general; and all exchequer matters and the royal administration, including even grants of monopoly by royal patent. While the monarch often did need the consent of Parliament with regard to such matters, the main concern of the Commons was special and local interests. In the sixteenth century the medieval notion that M.P.s were delegates or attorneys for their constituencies was still very much alive. Their principal function was to bind their constituencies to make good the grants of supply to the monarch. In return they secured the redress of grievances.

In the Whig Parliament of the eighteenth century M.P.s continued to represent the many corporate interests of the nation and the empire, which made great use of private bill procedure as a mode of access to power. The great contrast was that Parliament now was not only the focus of such functional representation, but also the body charged with deliberating on and determining the common good. As Burke said in a famous phrase, it was "a deliberative assembly of one nation with one interest, that of the whole—where not local prejudices ought to guide but the general good resulting from the general reason of the whole."[1] This did not mean that the monarch was excluded from government. Parliament meant—more precisely—the King-in-Parliament. Yet the difference from Tudor theory and practice was revolutionary: From being the principal representative of the community as a whole, standing above and apart from its three estates—Lords Spiritual, Lords Temporal, and Commons—the monarch now became only one of the three estates, King, Lords, and Commons.

Moreover, and here we get to an even more important difference, this Parliament was sovereign. In Blackstone's words, which stated the Whig orthodoxy, it was "a supreme, irresistible, absolute, uncontrolled authority" whose actions "no power on earth can undo."[2] It was from the era of the Civil War that this notion of a unified and unlimited authority in the state had emerged. Sovereignty had not been a medieval nor even a Tudor idea. Nor for all their talk of divine right was it a Tory doctrine. On the contrary, the old system of religious belief that gave royal authority a sacred foundation at the same time limited the power of kings, as it did all human authority. During the struggles of the later Stuarts the Tories were perfectly consistent, believing in divine right and, at the same time, fearing arbitrary power in the state as represented by a Parliament untrammeled by fundamental law. In the Tory conception of social purpose as well, the religious theme was strong. The old idea of a Christian society unified in its transcendental aim by

---

[1] Edmund Burke, *Writings and Speeches,* Vol. II (Boston, 1901), pp. 89–98.

[2] Sir William Blackstone, *Commentaries on the Laws of England* (1765), Bk.I, Ch.II, Sect. 3.

identical membership in church and commonwealth lingered on. The rallying cry of Toryism was "The Church in danger!"—whether from papists or dissenters. In the first decades of modern party struggle, Tory strength was great in the church and among the lesser gentry, though weak in the peerage and among the mercantile classes.

In comparison, Whiggery was markedly secular. This meant that in religious matters the Whigs were tolerant, not to say indifferent, although they could distinguish Protestant dissenters from Catholics, who might well have French connections. But their secularism was also something positive: a conception of national and imperial development that employed the instruments of state intervention at home and diplomacy and war abroad to forward colonial and commercial aggrandizement. Judged by later standards, the mercantile system and its bureaucratic instruments were unbelievably disorderly and inefficient. Yet they represented a conscious and vigorous collective effort to use the state to enhance the wealth and power of Britain, and under this policy the first British Empire was created. Led by their great aristocrats, the Whigs were strong among nonconformists, merchants, moneylenders, stock companies, friends of the Bank of England, and the mob of London.

Liberals and Radicals

Individualism informed both the Liberal vision of social purpose and the Liberal conception of how power should be organized and exercised in the state. In both politics and policy the new age of the nineteenth century broke with the immemorial corporatism of English society and government. Like the Whigs, the Liberals were committed to parliamentarism. The member of the legislature was not a delegate sent merely to reflect the will of the people; he was a representative charged with deliberation on the common good. To this extent the Burkean conception of representation maintained its sway. When we ask *what* was represented, however, a gulf opens between the Whig and Liberal views. For the Liberals gave a new stress in their political thought to the representation of individuals, rather than corporate bodies, ranks, orders, or "interests." In their politics, as their economics, the source of action was the rational, independent man.

In this individualism strong egalitarian implications can be found. From it clearly followed the notion of electoral districts containing equal numbers of voters in contrast with the inequalities of representation based on communities, such as the old boroughs and shires. Moreover, in its ultimate vision of society, Liberalism was radically classless. It was an attack upon aristocracy and hierarchy as well as corporatism. The new order of freedom for which Liberals fought would break down privilege and relieve oppression, the twin sources of hierarchy, and enable each man to make his own way in the world. Although no doubt limited in its values and biased by its class connections, the Liberal idea was nonetheless a conception of the common good. It not only drew a large following from among the rising classes of manufacturers and traders; it was also given leadership by members of the aristocracy and gentry and wide support by the growing proletariat of the cities. It was such a coalition, as we have seen, that put through the great reform of 1832.

Inequality of power, however, was strongly justified on Liberal grounds. Parliamentarism itself puts the power of decision in the small body of the elected, not the large body of electors. Moreover, in seeking to identify rationality and independence among the people, Liberals found a rough-and-ready index in the possession of property. Quite consistent with individualist premises, Macaulay argued against the democrats that it was not by numbers, but by "property and intelligence" that the country should be ruled. As we have seen, although the property qualification was modest, the act of 1832, in practice, enfranchised only 3.3 percent of the population of Great Britain.

As Radical democracy gained strength in the last half of the nineteenth century, a fundamentally different conception was put forward defining how the common good was to be determined. Breaking with Liberal parliamentarism, the Radicals put the ultimate power of decision in "the people." This did not mean simply a miscellany of rational, independent men, but rather a body of individuals bound together by a unified and authoritative will that was sovereign in the polity. In America the doctrine was termed "popular sovereignty" and came into wide acceptance in the days of Jacksonian Democracy. In both countries it meant in practice that all men were qualified to be voters, that so far as possible all decisions should be referred to the voters, and that when there was disagreement, the majority should prevail.

Liberal hostility toward corporate representation was carried on, and indeed intensified, by the Radicals. Opposed to "the people," in the Radical view of the political universe, were the "special interests," or the "sinister interests," to use the Benthamite phrase. "The interests are always awake," said Gladstone in his last and democratic phase, "while the country often slumbers and sleeps." In fact, no developing modern economy can do away with particular interests, certainly not one where, as in Britain in the nineteenth century, a rapid differentiation of the economy was driving it forward to unprecedented productivity. The interest groups so brought into existence often did associate. The Industrial Revolution had only fairly gotten under way when in 1798 manufacturing groups organized as the Chamber of Manufacturers of Great Britain. True to Liberal norms, such bodies were associations, not communities; they were sets of individuals voluntarily joining together for specific and limited purposes, not solidary groups satisfying comprehensive social needs.

Even more characteristic of the Liberal mode of representation of particular interests was the direct presence in Parliament of representatives of these interests. In a sense this was a by-product of the Liberal idealization of rational independence. For the candidate this norm implied a lack of strong ties with party or patron and so necessarily some substantial wealth of his own. "It is because I have made a fortune and am independent that I come here to ask for your suffrages to send me to Parliament," said George Hudson, the Railway King, to the voters when he first stood for election to the House in 1845. As his later actions at Westminster showed, he meant anything but independence of his vast railway interests.

But the Liberal period saw a mobilization of interests that was less directly dependent upon the developing economy and more important for the future development of party organization. The early nineteenth century was increasingly a time of reformist agitation, which, moreover, characteristically took the form of voluntary associations aimed at influencing Parliament in favor of some specific policy or piece of legislation. These were pressure groups, but more often working for a cause than for a special interest (see Chapter 1).

The Radicalization of Liberalism

In the course of the nineteenth century there took place a certain Radicalization of party organization as the techniques of voluntary association used by these pressure groups were adopted by political parties. During the period of Whig consensus the "aristocratic connections" that competed for office and patronage had worked out many of the structures and practices of party government. For example, the whips descend from the aristocratic period, as does the custom of Ministers sitting to the right of the Speaker in confrontation with their opponents to his left. In the nineteenth century British parties not only received a new infusion of principle from the rise of Liberalism, but also gradually acquired new forms of organization, as the franchise was extended, communications improved, and policies touched larger sections of the population.

The culmination of the Radicalization of party organization was the creation of the extraparliamentary party organization embracing what was, for the time, a mass membership, emphasizing a party program, and attempting to influence or even control its M.P.s. The leading example is the National Liberal Federation (N.L.F.), which was launched in 1877 and which was a quite self-conscious fusion by Liberals of the Radical stamp of the pressure groups that were forwarding their various causes. Radical sentiments strongly marked the rhetoric of its founders and legitimized its efforts to give its mass membership a voice in candidate selection, program making, and parliamentary action itself. While the agitation for the first and second reform acts had come very largely from nonparty associations, the Reform Act of 1884 followed the launching of a movement for further reform by the N.L.F., which carried out on a large scale the work of spreading propaganda, organizing meetings, and winning support for the measure. Although the federation, with its annual conference and its concern with program making, at times exercised influence, it never acquired in theory or practice the right to dictate to Liberal M.P.s.

In the earlier part of the century the Liberals had little organization in the country apart from small local associations, and the initiative in the reforms of that period very often came from pressure groups and other voluntary political associations. While not strictly part of the Liberal party, these were part of the Liberal movement that remade the British polity in a new image. With the foundation of the N.L.F. this complex of disconnected elements became part of an integrated whole.

In matters of party organization, the Conservatives demonstrated their usual adaptability. Defeated in the crucial battle of 1832 and permanently split by the events of 1846, they were generally in eclipse during the period of mid-Victorian Liberal consensus. As the franchise was extended and mass democracy was achieved, however, the Conservatives moved toward a position of dominance that has been without parallel in modern times and which on the whole was increasingly confirmed in the course of the twentieth century. As we have observed, this was in part owing to their leadership in some spheres of social reform. The Tories also were quick to pick up the new methods of organization. Indeed, their extraparliamentary organization, including local associations and a large membership, was founded in 1867, ten years before the Liberals acted. Like the N.L.F., this organization also had a representative organization affiliating local associations and staging an annual conference, which after 1885 also began to debate and pass resolutions concerning public policy. Unlike the N.L.F., however, it did not claim nor exercise any power over party policy, the party bureaucracy, or the behavior of M.P.s. Explicitly, it acknowledged that, as ever, the parliamentary party and especially its Leader were the source of party policy.

In the mid-1880s the Liberal consensus was rudely shattered and a new era of party conflict inaugurated. In the House of Commons the new era showed itself in sharp contrasts in behavior. After a long period of slackness and decline, party cohesion rose sharply, reaching present-day levels in the 1890s (see Chapter 6). The Opposition, which had been typically desultory and ineffective, pulled itself together to mount a persistent, organized attack upon the Government (see Chapter 7). There was an abrupt end to the easy agreement between the two front benches that had prevailed in the period of consensus and that had enabled Governments to rely on support from the other side when confronted with revolt on their own. Now the leaders of both parties were obliged to rely almost exclusively upon their own backbenchers, as in the party politics of contemporary Britain.

A new set of issues and attitudes arose along with the new patterns of behavior. The transition to the new stage of party development had been sharply marked in 1886 by Gladstone's introduction of his proposal of Home Rule for Ireland, which split the Liberals and led to a party realignment and a new bitterness between the two sides in the House and in the country. But in the previous decade or so, the rise of radicalism had already heightened tension within the Liberal party and had prepared the way for the renewed outburst of strife. Although wealth was moving to the Conservatives, the Radicals were not much concerned with economic or social reform. The strong political cast of their program is clear in some of their principal proposals, such as the abolition of plural voting, payment of M.P.s, shorter Parliaments, and reform of the House of Lords. Home Rule, which headed their list of proposals, expressed the quintessentially democratic doctrine of self-determination. Their demand that the Church of England be disestablished in

Wales, which was now largely nonconformist, reflected not only the religious sentiments of large sections of the Liberal party, but also the democratic principle of self-determination in cultural matters.

Far from supporting the leadership, the Radicals used the extraparliamentary organization of the N.L.F. to develop their program and to support left wing dissidence in the House. In time, as Hugh Berrington has observed, the party educated its leaders, and many of the policies of the Liberal Government that won the sweeping victory of 1906 sprang from proposals brought forward in the party conference in previous decades.[3] Although briefer than the period of Liberal dominance, the period of reform dominated by the Radicals before World War I was as significant as that dominated by the Liberals after 1832. Its culmination was the fierce struggle of the "Lords against the People" in 1910–1911 that led to the reform of the upper House.

The Collectivist Period

It is crucially important to see the Radical phase as a distinct stage of British political development. The reason is to make clear the beginnings and nature of the collectivist period and its political formations. Some writers have assumed that tight party cohesion, sharp parliamentary conflict, mass parties, and programmatic politics arose only when the working class emerged as the base of a socialist political party. All these traits, on the contrary, first characterized the Radical period. Deductively we might think that because of its conditions of life, the working class will produce a more solidary political organization than the individualist middle class. In the course of time this proved to be true. But in the early 1900s the cohesion of the Labour party in Parliament was less than that of the Liberals. One clue is suggested by the fact that the Labour party in these days was not explicitly socialist; on the contrary, its M.P.s, apart from their commitment to the "interests of labour," were enthusiastic Radicals, strong in their support of reforming Liberal Government. The characteristic solidarity of the Labour party in Parliament appeared only after it took on a commitment to socialism. On the Labour side of the House, the index of party voting—that is, votes in which 90 percent or more of the members of a party voted on the same side—rose from 80.4 percent in 1906 to 97.3 percent in the period 1924–1928.

As for harshness of conflict, when we consider the modern period as a whole, it is evident that the intensity of British political conflict has steadily declined. In what was said and done, as well as what was at stake, 1688 and, indeed, 1714 —with its Jacobite invasion in the next year—put the inauguration of the Whig ascendancy at one extreme. The struggle over the Reform Bill of 1832 is perhaps

[3]"Partisanship and Dissidence in the Nineteenth-Century House of Commons," *Parliamentary Affairs,* 21 (Autumn, 1968), 372.

matched in bitterness by the conflict over reform of the Lords in 1910–1911. In both instances two general elections were called and the monarch had to resolve the crisis by threatening to swamp the upper chamber with new peers. Yet the general election of 1906 that brought the Radicals to power was placid compared with the election of 1830, that led to Grey's reforming Government. And in comparison with the turbulence that accompanied these earlier shifts in political power, we hardly recognize 1945, when a Labour Government, assuming office with a socialist program and, for the first time, with a parliamentary majority, proceeded to put through a series of sweeping reforms to which the Conservatives adapted without missing a step.

Overall the correlation is clear: After Labour introduced a politics that was far more ideological than any that had gone before and that was, for the first time, explicitly based on class, British party conflict came to be conducted with more balance and decorum than ever before. Perhaps the reason for this was the long-run decline of religious issues in politics and the rise of economic questions to the place of main importance. Economic matters can be argued rationally—they are quantifiable and instrumental—but religion touches ultimate values.

The political culture of the collectivist period shows the continuing power of the modern thrust toward equality. This is especially apparent in the ideology of the welfare state, which affirms the need to reduce, or even abolish, economic inequality. The old Radical political ideals also won ever wider acceptance, and democracy was continually broadened in a series of acts between 1918 and 1969 that abolished the last restrictions on manhood suffrage, extended the vote to women on the same basis as it was held by men, abolished the plural votes that some property owners had retained, reduced still further the power of the Lords, and finally, in 1969, gave the vote to eighteen-year-olds.

What was especially new about this time, however, was less its egalitarianism than its collectivism. This new outlook characterized attitudes toward both policy and politics. With regard to control of the economy, the state rather than the individual was seen more and more as the center of power. With regard to participation, a new and enhanced status was attributed to producers groups, and, by socialists, to the main economic classes, workers and owners. These further steps in cultural modernization took specific form in conceptions of authority that made party government and functional representation, respectively, the means by which the common interest and particular interests were to be represented.

Even more sharply than in the past, the development of this period was marked off and shaped by the rise of a new political party. Labour was the party of innovation, and its ideas and actions are the least ambiguous expression of the new attitudes. "The Labour Party," Ernest Bevin once said, "has grown out of the bowels of the T.U.C." Founded in 1868 during the period of the Liberal consensus, the Trades Union Congress affiliated the rising national unions of craftsmen and acted as their lobby before Parliament. Extending its membership to include the newly organized unskilled workers in the 1880s, the T.U.C. decided to strike out on a more independent line when in 1899 it voted to initiate a separate political party. At first calling itself the Labour Representation Committee, the new organization took the name Labour party only in 1906. In these Parliaments before World War I, however, Labour was little more than a coalition of trade unions acting as a pressure group within the vaster Liberal movement. Socialists were affiliated with the party through two small organizations, the Fabian Society and the Independent Labour party. But Labour did not explicitly declare itself socialist until 1918.

Two momentous changes were made that year. First, the party gave itself a national constituency organization. Previously, it had been merely a federation of unions and socialist societies; now it established local organizations in parliamentary constituencies. Also, for the first time the party gave itself a program that explicitly committed it to a "Socialist Commonwealth," based on "the common ownership of the means of production." These two steps served to separate it once and for all from the Liberals. Thereafter Liberals might cooperate with Labour, as when they supported the minority Labour Governments of 1924 and 1929–1931. But Labour was never again the junior partner, nor did parliamentary support become coalition or coalescence, although Liberal leaders of the Radical stamp have often dreamed of some such party realignment.

To a greater degree than any other major party in British history, Labour developed an ideology. This was natural in a party in which intellectuals enjoyed a position of such exceptional importance. For in Britain, as on the continent, intellectuals were highly influential in giving a socialist orientation to the working-class political movement, which in turn was very hospitable to them. In their conceptions of authority, the socialists of the Labour party, like the Radicals, rejected parliamentarism and accepted popular sovereignty, expressed through the verdict of a majority in favor of a party at a general election. But because of their collectivist views they gave to party government a far firmer foundation than the individualist Radicals had. Their approach to policy legitimized a greater degree of cohesion and discipline. Even when the Radical sought so to reform the economic and social system as to eliminate privilege and promote equality, the system he supported was still an individualist system and the reforms he proposed were acts of piecemeal intervention and redress. The socialist, on the other hand, whether believing in wholesale nationalization or only in a managed economy, held that the main decisions of economic policy must be made by a government that would consciously harmonize the decisions with one another in space and time. From this necessity flowed a new and compelling sanction for party unity and party discipline.

This need is evident, but how can it be reconciled with the wide democratic participation that inevitably, it would seem, intrudes a lively, not to say chaotic, pluralism into decision making? The socialist's answer springs from his conception of the class nature of society. In his view political divisions derive from economic class divisions of which, in an industrialized economy, there are essentially two— workers and owners. Such fundamental duality subsumes the complex pluralisms of occupational and other economic groups. Moreover, it roots the solidarity of the party not merely in a meeting of free minds but in objective membership in a class with an overriding class interest. Here are firm grounds for joining and sticking with the party of your class and for reprobating any breach of solidarity. Behavior corresponded with these beliefs. In the great interwar crisis of the party in 1931, when the three top leaders of the Labour Government confronted with economic crisis tried to take the party into coalition with Conservatives and Liberals, the party inside and outside Parliament, almost without exception, rejected their leadership. Although deserted by its three top leaders, the party—in contrast with the Conservatives in 1846 or the Liberals in 1886—did not split. In behavior as in attitudes, the Labour party was a new and distinctive type of political formation.

From Labour's collectivist premises a theory of democracy by party government follows. The working class is seen as having a system of interests and aspirations that are reflected in the party's social philosophy and articulated, as the times require, in its program. Democracy is interpreted to mean, primarily, periodic contests between two such programmatic parties. At such times the voter has a choice that is meaningful in two senses: He has a choice between two coherent and distinctive programs. Moreover, he knows that the victorious party will have the cohesion to carry out the program to which it is pledged. Its "mandate" will be honored. With regard to the inner procedures of the party, there too democracy must prevail. Only the mass membership, representing the authentic voice of the working class, can be entrusted with the task of framing the party program. Discretion as to details, timing, and so forth can be left to the parliamentary leadership. But the decisive will and main thrust of ideas must come from the rank and file.

This whole set of ideas involves difficulties. It cannot be easy to reconcile intraparty democracy with the need for a viable and coherent government program and the doctrine of the mandate with the unpredictability of history. Yet this in general has been the party's official theory of itself, as expressed in the plain words of its constitution, in what speakers at conference say about its powers, and in the public utterances of party leaders. Two-party competition, tight cohesion among partisans, a program deriving from a comprehensive social philosophy, party allegiance founded primarily upon economic class and giving the party a mass membership, a party structure providing for intraparty democracy, especially in framing the party program: such are the main elements in the socialist conception of party government.

Functional Representation

Political equality and popular sovereignty constitute strong links in the Radical past with the socialist conception of authority. The new views of how particular interests should be represented, however, broke sharply with the older individualism, as the associationism of both Liberal and Radical outlooks gave way to a new version of functional representation. This term refers to any conception of authority that finds the community divided into various strata, regards each of these strata as having a certain corporate unity, sees each as performing a function in the society, and holds that they ought to be represented in the polity. The idea is medieval in origin and in British political development has taken various forms as the constituent strata have been differently constituted—estates, ranks and orders, interests, classes, and occupational groups.

At the turn of this century there were signs, on both Left and Right, that opinion was shifting toward a new functional pluralism. The same part of the party constitution, the famous Clause IV, which committed the party to "common ownership," went on to voice the syndicalist demand for "the best possible obtainable system of popular administration and control of each industry and service." For a time the guild socialists agitated in favor of a form of syndicalism; even after their propaganda subsided, the idea of workers' control, which they had done much to foster, influenced the trade unions, not being finally put to rest until after Labour took office in 1945. By that time other channels of access had been firmly established for trade unions and other producers groups.

During the interwar years there was growing recognition from other sources as well as Labour ideology of the need for and legitimacy of associating representatives of interest groups with government administration. The National Health Insurance Act of 1924, for instance, provided for the representation of specific interests —such as the medical profession and suppliers of drugs, medicines, and appliances —on the various committees charged with administering the system of social insurance. World War II involved a vast increase in the direct presence of producers groups in government as trade unions, trade associations, and similar groups were used to guide and implement the vast war effort. During postwar years the representation of interests had become so normal and expected that it was a rare and serious charge that the Government or a department had made policy without consultation with the relevant bodies. A major expression of the new role of organized interests was the position given them on bodies concerned with economic planning. At the highest level these included the Economic Planning Board, the National Production Advisory Council on Industry, and from 1962 on the ambitious effort represented by the National Economic Development Council and its score or so of similar bodies for particular industries (see Chapters 4 and 10).

Labour and Socialism

The influence of class thinking on the structure and behavior of the Labour party is easy to illustrate. If we turn to the party's conception of purpose, the question of the meaning and seriousness of its commitment to socialism raises harder questions. We do not have the kind of survey data that would enable us to say, for example, with regard to the roughly 200,000 individual and 2 million trade-union members in 1928, how many would have said they believed in the abolition of capitalism and the establishment of a socialist economy based on common ownership. We do know, however, that the imagery of socialist doctrine—common ownership versus private ownership, cooperation versus competition, planning versus the market, economic security and equality versus individual effort and reward—informed the huge mass of party utterance in the decades after the commitment of 1918. In conference debates, party programs, parliamentary speeches, and countless public meetings there was expressed a reasonably coherent and wide-ranging socialist ideology.

Moreover, we also know that during this time a massive program was developed, comprising a long list of major structural reforms, which, when the party won power, were put into effect speedily and almost without exception or change. In the campaign of 1945 Labour presented a manifesto entitled "Let Us Face the Future." It had been debated and approved at its party conference and was packed with pledges that had been accumulating over the years and that were derived from many different groups within the movement. While in power the Attlee Government of 1945–1951 based its legislative program squarely on the manifesto, and for virtually every paragraph of pledges in the statute book, a corresponding act can be found. Fulfilling its pledges of nationalization, the Government passed the following:

The Bank of England Act of 1946
The Electricity Act of 1946
The Coal Industry Nationalisation Act of 1946
The Civil Aviation Act of 1946
The Transport Act of 1947
The Gas Act of 1948
The Iron and Steel Act of 1949

As pledged with regard to the social services, Labour passed the National Health Service Act of 1946, which nationalized almost all hospitals and set up a free and comprehensive health service. Also, the social insurance system was consolidated and extended by the National Insurance Act of 1946, which provided sickness, unemployment, and retirement benefits as well as maternity grants, widows' pensions, and death grants, and by the Industrial Injuries Act of the same year, which dealt with workmen's compensation. With regard to farming, the Agriculture Act of 1947 established a new system of "assured markets and guaranteed prices." In harmony with its promises in the field of taxation, Labour maintained from wartime, and in some respects sharpened, a steeply progressive scheme of income taxation. Other major reforms included the Housing Acts of 1946 and 1949, the Rent Control Act of 1949, the Children Act of 1948, and the Town and Country Planning Act of 1947.

Even this brief summary conveys a sense of the very great effort and achievement of the Labour Government, especially in its first years. This achievement is emphasized, first, as an illustration of party government. More particularly, it was party government very much in accord with the socialist model, the new pattern of policy being derived from a party program that had been legitimated by intraparty democracy and that had originated not from an elite, but from a plurality of initiatives. Second, Labour's achievement constituted the establishment of the

British welfare state. To be sure, the origins of many social services can be traced back to the Radical period, precedents for nationalization can be found in the interwar years, and in originating or developing both sorts of reform, Conservatives played an important role. But Labour's achievement, like its promises, were distinctively different from what the Conservatives offered or would have done. If there was one central point of difference, it was the magnitude of government expenditure. When the Conservatives did face the task of adaptation to Labour's reforms, this prospect of huge continuing expenditure was the bitterest pill. Moreover, as we have seen (see Chapter 4), the expenditure of the welfare state does much to determine the nature of the managed economy. It means that the economy will be profoundly affected by what government does, and, moreover, it tends to ensure that the instruments that government will use to control the economy will be primarily fiscal.

In this sense the new order of the postwar welfare state and managed economy in Britain was very much the creation of the Labour party. Even more than in previous transitions party was the principal agent of political development. Labour did not at that time or in later years, fulfill its original vision of the Socialist Commonwealth. But it is hardly unusual for parties of innovation to be diverted from their early ideals and to find history harder to control than they had imagined.

Conservatives and Collectivism

The Conservative party has found it easier to adapt to the new issues raised by the Labour party, to the establishment of the welfare state, and to the conditions of the collectivist period generally than to some other periods of innovation in the past. Its flexibility has not been flaccid, however, and many values of Toryism have been maintained in the attitudes that shape and justify the Conservative version of functional representation and party government. Some of its older traditions facilitated the break from individualism.

As L. S. Amery, a leading Tory intellectual, observed in 1947, when urging a reform of Parliament that would include functional representation, that conception has a history in Britain going back to the medieval House of Commons when the knights of the shire represented agriculture and the burgesses a variety of localized industrial and commercial interests.[4] Generally, in the rise of the new pluralism in political thought, while the main thrust came from the Left, the Right also produced its advocates. Among them were Ruskin and his follower A. J. Penty, with their ideas for the revival of the guild system. The Conservative version of functionalism also included the proposals of the Whitley Commission in 1917 that joint industrial councils comprising both employers and workmen be established to review and improve industrial relations. Also, as we have seen, the interwar period saw an

---

[4] L. S. Amery, *Thoughts on the Constitution* (London, 1947), p. 64.

increasing association of organized producers groups with government administration.

Far more interesting have been the ways in which Conservative attitudes and party organization have adapted Tory conceptions of hierarchy to the conditions of democracy and mass politics. The essential logic is the same as that set forth by Amery, in his interpretation of the British Constitution (see Chapter 1). In that view he attributes a wide scope of independent authority to a "central governing, directing, and initiating element" in government. The role of the voter, on the other hand, is "essentially passive," consisting not in initiating proposals, but in choosing between the two alternatives presented to him at a general election—two alternative sets of proposals, but above all two alternative sets of leaders. Analogously, in a political party there is a real function for a mass membership and an elaborate extraparliamentary organization, but it is essentially to win votes for the leaders, rather than to tell them what to do. Toryism likewise supplies powerful sanctions for party unity in support of the Leader, since this merely translates into a contemporary context the old imperative that order necessitates authority. Thus contemporary conservatism rationalizes a theory of party government appropriate to the politics and policies of the collectivist age.

In the background of Tory thought on authority, class looms large, as it also does for the Socialist, although with quite different meaning. While the Socialist sees classes as economic units that divide the polity horizontally, the Tory sees classes as integrating the polity vertically. Effective leadership requires special talents that will always be confined to a few. A function of the Conservative party is to cultivate, offer, and support such leadership. When it does, it can count on Britons —or at any rate Englishmen—to recognize its claim to their suffrage.

Such expectations have not been disappointed. When Disraeli extended the franchise in 1867, he acted on the belief that "the wider the popular suffrage, the more powerful would be the natural aristocracy." During the following years of Radical and Socialist influence—from 1886 to 1971—Conservatives have held office for three-fifths of the time, or some fifty-two years out of eighty-five. This would have been impossible without a massive following among the lower classes. During the postwar period, survey data show that fully half the Conservative vote has come from the working class. Moreover, among these working-class Tories it has been possible to identify and measure a large fraction—perhaps as much as 25 percent of the total Conservative vote—to whom, precisely as in Tory theory, class in seen as an integrating, not a dividing, force and the Conservative party as the special seat of superior ability.

Needless to say, Conservatives today are more reticent in advancing this claim than they were at the founding of their national association in 1867, when the chairman could say without fear of offense to the many workingmen present that "we all of us believe that the Conservatives are the natural leaders of the people." Yet the party cries of the Conservatives still reflect their old self-confidence. In the general election of 1970, while Labour quite expectedly sought to raise fears of Tory landlords, bankers, and other capitalists, the Conservatives pictured themselves as "the party who can," which had not only compassion (conceded to Labour), but also competence. It came down to "Trust us," and at the polls millions of Britons renewed their ancient fealty.

Tory tradition also could be utilized to justify Conservative adaptation to Labour's welfare state. In arguing for the party statement that accepted Labour's main reforms, Anthony Eden, then heir-apparent to Churchill as Leader, could say to the party conference in 1947:

> We are not the party of unbridled, brutal capitalism and never have been. . . . we are not the political children of the laissez-faire school. We opposed them decade after decade.

Justified by such old traditions of state power and collective responsibility and moved by electoral necessity, Tory leaders moved rapidly during the late 1940s to accept Labour's main reforms. At the same time, as we have seen (see Chapter 4), the Labour Government, frustrated in its efforts at physical planning, shifted toward major reliance on the tools of fiscal policy. The result of this typical movement of parties in a competitive two-party democracy was a broad agreement on social and economic policy between the two antagonists, which ushered in one of those phases of consensus and political calm that have been recurrent in British political development. This was the period of Butskellism, when the community of views between the two leading economic spokesmen for the Conservative Government and Labour Opposition vividly illustrated the convergence of the two party positions.

The Collectivist Consensus

During the late 1940s and early 1950s a pattern of politics and policy became established that had new and distinctive traits. Its origins could be found in earlier years, especially the interwar period, but in the first years after World War II, this pattern achieved a kind of fulfillment that is reminiscent of other periods of consensus and stability in British political development. While changes continued both in politics and policy, the basic elements showed strong continuity through some two decades.

While the main stress here will be on domestic policy, it may be noted in passing that a strong movement toward interparty agreement also marked the views of the two parties on defense, foreign, and imperial policy. Labour had come to power with rosy hopes of easy and fruitful cooperation with the Soviet Union. These hopes that "Left can talk to Left" were dashed by the rigidities of Stalinist Russia. But not only did a "socialist foreign policy" prove unfeasible; the expectations of collective security under an effective United Nations were also disappointed. A Labour Government, therefore, found itself compelled to resort to the detested tactics of balance of power, backed up by military force and directed to the service of vital national interests. A socialist Foreign Secretary, Ernest Bevin, was a leading agent in the establishment in 1949 of N.A.T.O., which became, and has remained, the cornerstone of British defense policy.

In imperial policy we would expect sharp differences between the parties. It was not long ago—in 1953—that a young lady addressing the annual conference of the Conservative party could speak of the Empire as "the greatest and most romantic force for good that the world has ever known and is ever likely to know." But not only did the Conservatives accept the Attlee Government's abrupt grant of independence to India; they also pursued a highly conciliatory policy toward the resurgent Egypt of Nasser in the early 1950s. When Nasser seized the Suez Canal, the British military response precipitated a sharp and very bitter division between the parties in Parliament. The rank and file of Labour voters, however, were more ambivalent, which did much to prevent the issue from being pressed persistently by the leadership. Not long after this last imperial fling, it was the Conservative Macmillan who, in his "Winds of Change" speech of 1960, inaugurated a policy that led to rapid and complete independence for Britain's remaining colonies in Africa. Thereafter, partisan arguments sometimes arose regarding the size of Britain's small military commitment "east of Suez" or Rhodesian independence or the sale of arms to South Africa. But although they reflected real differences of sentiment and approach, they did not disrupt an overwhelming agreement toward colonial and postcolonial problems.

The weightiest differences in foreign affairs have arisen over British membership in the Common Market. Neither party has been perfectly consistent in its position. In Opposition the Conservatives under Churchill welcomed the first initiatives toward European union, but once in office stayed aloof until, rather late in the day, they saw that the Common Market was a reality moving from strength to strength. As Macmillan attempted to gain entry, Labour under Gaitskell committed itself to sharp opposition. In spite of this commitment and although de Gaulle had vetoed Macmillan's effort in 1963, the Wilson Government reversed itself in 1967, only to meet with another rebuff. Once again in Opposition, Labour drifted rapidly back into its old position of resistance, leaving to the Tories under Heath the history-making task of taking Britain into Europe.

The consensus on policy and its intrinsic relation to the new pattern of politics can best be illustrated by reference to certain central features of Britain's postwar welfare state. That term has a varied usage. In this work it does not include the system of coordination and control of economic policy that was discussed under the heading of the managed economy, but rather the system of social services. This consists of not only the complex of programs centering on unemployment, sickness, and old age, but also public housing, education, and the momentous commitment to economic security embodied in the pledge of full employment. It was Labour's ambitious efforts in these areas that created the immense financial burden, the acceptance of which by the Conservatives constituted so important a step in British political development. Moreover, once in office the Conservatives not only maintained, they increased welfare expenditure. Looking specifically at expenditure on welfare grants to persons and welfare expenditure by all public authorities, we find a doubling of expenditure under the Conservatives in the fifties. From £1,537 million in 1950, the sum rose to £3,171 million in 1959. The increase was not only absolute, but also relative to personal income. As a percentage of personal income, these expenditures rose from 13.9 percent in 1950 to 16.1 percent in 1959.

The connection with the new politics comes closer to light when we look at the specific items comprised in these totals. They included national insurance benefits, consisting of retirement pensions, widows' and guardians' allowances, death grants, and unemployment, sickness, maternity, injury, and disablement benefits. They also included postwar credits, war pensions, service grants, noncontributory pensions, public assistance grants, family allowances, industrial services for the disabled, and expenditure on education, child care, and the national health services. Another important welfare expenditure not included in the above totals consisted in the housing subsidies, which also rose steeply under the Conservatives from £72 million in 1950 to £116 million in 1959.

It will be no surprise to the American reader that there is a strong tendency for each item in this multiplicity of programs to acquire a body of political supporters consisting of those who benefit from it. As consumers of these programs they have an interest in seeing them expanded and certainly in preventing them from being reduced. It is in the nature of the welfare state to produce a host of such consumer groups whose material self-interest is affected by some measure of government action, actual or prospective. The programs of services producing the "social dividend" are the more obvious examples. But groups are also brought into existence by the "social burden" of the welfare state, especially the various tax programs with their varying incidence on different categories of persons.

Consumer groups are important actors in the system of group politics that the welfare state calls into existence. Such a group politics is by no means incompatible with strong and active parties. Indeed, the two sorts of actors tend to complement one another, the party, under the severe political pressure of competition from its rival, vigorously seeking out groups with actual or potential demands that it may offer to satisfy. Where two parties are fairly evenly matched in electoral support, as in Britain in the postwar period, the resulting process of "bidding" for the votes of consumers groups becomes a principal pattern in the new scheme of politics. Thus the policy statement that was issued in 1958 by the Labour party, in its desperate bid to avoid defeat for the third time in a row, was entitled *Your Personal Guide to The Future Labour Offers YOU* and was conveniently thumb-indexed with references to "Your Home," "Education," "Health," "Age Without Fear" and so on, as if to enable tenants, workers, patients, youth, and other groups to turn directly to the promises beamed to them.

If such consumer groups occupied the center of the political stage in party conflict and won their representation through their voting potential in elections to Parliament, there was also another aspect of group politics that was no less important to the system of the collectivist consensus. The groups in this field were the producer groups of Britain's highly industrialized economy, usually appearing in their organized form as trade unions, trade associations, and professional bodies. It is these groups that won a certain legitimacy from the new acceptance of functional representation. As we have seen in our discussion of the bureaucracy and the managed economy, they also acquired a high degree of institutionalized access. Not only did the new functional pluralism of twentieth-century political culture legitimize a wide role for them as groups to be consulted. The realities of the managed economy meant that the producers who carried on the work of the various economic sectors had to be brought into close cooperation with government. Such groups possessed the expertise and skilled knowledge that government agencies had to command in order to know how to formulate and carry out their policies of intervention. Moreover, the dependence of government upon these sectors for successful implementation of a policy—for example, an export drive or an increase in productivity—meant that their hearty cooperation had to be won if the policy was to be carried out. These facts, as we have seen, often tended to give the producers groups far more than a merely advisory role.

In sum, just as there was a dual aspect to domestic policy—the welfare state and the managed economy—there was a dual aspect to the new system of politics— on the one hand, the politics of parties and consumer groups; on the other, the politics of Governments and producer groups. The two branches of politics, like the two aspects of policy, were not physically separate. The programs of welfare expenditure, for instance, were also instruments of economic management. Depending, however, on how the political situation was viewed—from the perspective of the managed economy or that of the welfare state—the flow of influence was seen to come, respectively, from producers or consumer groups. The two perspectives on the flow of power direct attention to the following relationships: (1) controlled economy: producer groups: functional representation: bargaining for cooperation and (2) welfare state: consumer groups: party government: bidding for votes.

The Relevance of Party Government

At the start of this discussion of British parties (see Chapter 8) it was stated, as a hypothesis, that the model of party government best identified the main structures of the pattern of interests in the age of collectivist politics. No final assessment is possible until we have looked more closely at the past few years—the task of the next chapter. But at this point an intermediate summary is in order.

During modern times parties have been major agents of political development in Britain. While they have often been coalitions of interest groups, they have also usually been more than that, representing conceptions of the common good and showing distinctive views of authority and purpose in the way they think, approach power, and try to change society. In this sense the interest-group model, while instructive in all periods of modernization, is incomplete without recognition of the role of party. This is not to say that party government, as presented in contemporary models, applies throughout the modern period. On the contrary, it is clear from the previous review of party development that a principal feature has been increasing differentiation. As in other modernizing processes, there has been specialization with respect to parties and the party system. Parties have become more clearly distinguished from, and independent of, other social systems, such as family, church, and economy. At the same time they have developed their own systems of communication and control in such a way that their differentiation from other elements of British society has been accompanied by an increasing formalization and rationalization of internal processes. From this process have emerged the highly organized, strongly cohesive, programmatic parties on which the contemporary models of party government are based.

When assessing the role of party, we must note the phase of the political cycle from which data are chosen. According to the concept of party government, parties are important instruments of social choice. Between their promises there is supposedly a significant difference, which in turn is reflected in the character of the policy followed by the party preferred by the electorate. In the 1950s and 1960s, however, there was so marked a convergence in what the parties promised and, even more, in what they did when in office, as to raise serious doubts about these suppositions. A virtue of the historical approach is that it puts such questions in context. In the light of recurrent cycles in British party development, it is not surprising that a period of transition, marked by sharp party strife, should be followed by a time of consensus, when party tensions relaxed and a new group politics supervened. It is in such a cycle that social choice has often been expressed and parties have done their work. This historical approach prevents the lesser role of the Labour party during the phase of consensus from obscuring its functions, first, as a challenge to which Liberals and Conservatives were obliged to respond during the interwar years, and, second, as the principal founder of the welfare state in a burst of innovation after World War II. Seen in this light, the model of party government makes good sense.

Ten
The Continuities of Collectivist Politics

During the postwar period in Britain new patterns of politics were established with a character sufficiently distinctive to justify speaking of them as the system of the collectivist consensus. The first question suggested by this observation is, Do the trends of the late sixties and early seventies show any significant departures from that system? At issue are continuities or discontinuities in functional representation and party government. But inseparable from the developmental approach of this book is a second question concerning how these trends might shape the future of British politics. The history we have looked at suggests that consensus does not last, that it is usually broken up by party realignment, and that new class divisions and new issues then arise during a time of renewed party contention and political transition. These are only possibilities, not laws of political development. They do serve, however, to focus attempts at interpreting the severe challenge to which the collectivist system is being subjected.

Functional Representation

Functional representation is inherent in the highly developed modern polity. Such a political system will mobilize a large share of the resources of the society in an effort to control the social and the natural environment. This mobilization of power at once subjects the resources of the society to greater government control and gives those in immediate command of those resources a new opportunity to influence government. "The greater the degree of detailed and technical control the government seeks to exert over industrial and commercial interests,'' E. P. Herring wrote many years ago, ''the greater must be their degree of consent and active participation in the very process of regulation, if regulation is to be effective or successful.''[1] The essential political point of this analysis should be kept distinct from a more familiar observation regarding economic modernization. It is well recognized that when technological development brings into existence new producers groups that perform specialized functions in the division of labor, their control over these functions makes it possible for them to organize in order to use concerted action to win advantages from other groups in the economy. Thus, in the past groups of skilled workmen have organized into craft unions in order to bargain with employers. But the managed economy introduces a further source of power for producers groups: The mobilization of their talents by the polity subjects them to the state and, at the same time, gives them influence over it.

Such dependence of controller upon controlled arises not only between the public and private sectors of the modern mixed economy, but also within the public sector. For example, central planners may find themselves obliged to make concessions in order to win the cooperation of the managers of nationalized industries. Indeed, some observers of nationalization in Britain have concluded that public ownership may make an industry even harder to control than when immediate power over its resources was dispersed among many owners. Similarly, within a fully socialized economy top controllers are confronted with the possibility that the bureaucrats in charge of specialized sectors may muster their skill and expertise to show that proposed tasks are impossible and, if coerced, may carry out orders only grudgingly and inefficiently. A major function of the totalitarian party is as an agency of indoctrination and surveillance to reduce the size of this problem. But in a free country the need to bargain with those being controlled is constantly heightened as the managed economy grows.

The root of the power of these functional groups is twofold. First, they constitute bodies of people performing specialized functions who acquire the capacity for unified action by being organized. As we have seen, their power arises whether their organization is part of the public or private sector. Second, the function being performed has come into existence with developing technology and consists in the exercise of specialized skill and expertise. When a government mobilizes these resources in the course of extending its management of the economy, it becomes heavily dependent upon the advice of those in command of the relevant skills and expertise. Advice includes sheer information, for instance, statistical data, without which neither the regulation of a particular trade nor the control of the economy as a whole would be practicable. But the advice government seeks from producers consists also of their technical knowledge and judgment. No Ministry of Economics could have a staff large enough and specialized enough to enable it to make and administer policy without the advice of the producers in the sector concerned.

---

[1] E. P. Herring, *Public Administration and the Public Interest* (New York, 1936), p. 192.

"The form and functioning of British Government," S. E. Finer has written, "are predicated upon the assumption that it will be advised, helped and criticized by the specialist knowledge of interested parties."[2]

Trade Unions

Organization presumably enhances the capacity of a group of people for unified action. Moreover, it is plausible to argue that the more concentrated the organization the better the chances for unified action. Some dimensions of concentration can be measured. One is density, that is, the percentage of eligibles, such as individuals or firms, that have been organized. But if there are many organizations, a high degree of density is compatible with a low degree of unity. Another dimension of concentration, therefore, is amalgamation, that is, how far those organized have been brought together into one body—whether by outright merger, by federation, or by other arrangement. Over time the trend among producers groups in Britain has been toward an increase of concentration in both dimensions.

In the case of trade unions the increase in concentration provides a good indicator of the transition to the collectivist phase of political development. From 1892 to 1953 membership in all trade unions in the United Kingdom rose from 1,576,000 to 9,524,000, an increase from 11 percent to 42 percent of the total employed population. In 1967 the total was 9,967,000, or 38 percent of an employed population of 25,986,000. In the United States that same year union membership was only 23 percent. Amalgamation, which set in strongly after World War I, has reduced the number of separate unions and produced the huge organizations of recent decades. Between 1938 and 1967 the number of unions in the United Kingdom was cut by half, and by 1967, 70 percent of union membership was concentrated in eighteen unions with over 100,000 members each.

These trends are not steady but show significant changes in rate, as can be readily seen in the figures for unions affiliated with the Trades Union Congress. A sharp increase in T.U.C. membership reflected the organization of unskilled workers in the late 1880s, but from the late nineteenth century until the years before World War I there was hardly any growth in union membership. Then came the years of rapid change, when the unions reached a new plateau of strength and the Labour party struck out for sovereign power. As Table 10.1 shows, between 1911 and 1920 T.U.C. membership more than tripled, and although it fell during the years of slump, it remained more than twice what it had been before the war. In the same years, around World War I, a sharp trend toward amalgamation set in, the average size of affiliated unions rising from 8,000 to 30,000 between 1911 and 1920. A third indicator of profound change consists in the data on strikes in Table 10.2. As Table 10.2 shows, a wave of industrial action began just before World War I and rose to a peak in the years after it. The high point was, of course, 1926, the

---

[2]"The Political Power of Private Capital," Part II, *Sociological Review,* new series, 4 (July 1956), 14.

Table 10.1 T.U.C. Membership, United Kingdom, for Selected Years Between 1868 and 1970

Year	Number of Unions	Membership (in Millions)
1868	—	.118
1889	171	.885
1890	211	1.470
1911	202	1.662
1920	215	6.505
1938	216	4.460
1946	192	6.671
1952	183	8.020
1969	155	8.875
1970	150	9.402

DATA SOURCE: T.U.C. *Report* (London, 1970), pp. 544–546.

Table 10.2 Strike Data (annual averages) United Kingdom, for Selected Years Between 1892 and 1970

Years	Total Striker-days (in Millions)	Number of Strikes
1892–1896	13.3	760
1907–1911	7.2	570
1912–1916	13.2	890
1917–1921	31.8	1120
1922–1926	41.8	570
1927–1931	4.4	380
1937–1941	1.6	1020
1947–1951	1.9	1590
1952–1956	2.5	2100
1957–1961	4.6	2630
1962–1966	2.5	2260
1967	2.8	2120
1968	4.7	2380
1969	6.8	3020
1970	9.5	4000

DATA SOURCE: Professor H. A. Turner, Cambridge University, England.

year of the General Strike. In absolute as well as in relative terms, the figures for days lost in strikes have not been approached even in recent years of industrial unrest. As the data suggest, it was the second and third decades of the twentieth century that saw the emergence of the typical problems and principal actors of the collectivist age.

Labour's peak organization, the T.U.C., has not had a serious rival since its founding in 1868 and has successfully weathered the various surges in union growth without disruptive splits such as the one between the A.F. of L. and the C.I.O. in the United States. From 1894, when T.U.C.-affiliated membership included 65 percent of all unionists, the T.U.C. has increased that proportion—with some ups and downs. In 1953 it reached 85 percent, and in 1967, T.U.C. membership included 88 percent of all unionists in the United Kingdom. Moreover, in spite of the decline of old industries, such as shipping, textiles, and mining, the T.U.C. has maintained—but only maintained—its membership relative to the economy as a whole. In both 1952 and 1969 T.U.C. membership was 34 percent of the total working population of the United Kingdom. Within the T.U.C. itself amalgamation has created a few giants. In 1970, the six largest unions embraced just about half the total affiliated membership (see Table 10.3).

Table 10.3 The Big Six in the T.U.C. (1969)

Transport and General Workers Union	1,531,607
Amalgamated Union of Engineering and Foundry Workers	1,131,252
National Union of General and Municipal Workers	803,653
National and Local Government Officers' Association	397,069
Electrical Electronic Telecommunication Union	392,401
Shop, Distributive, and Allied Workers	316,387
	4,572,369

DATA SOURCE: T.U.C. *Report* (London, 1970), pp. 792–829.

Even more important in the context of Britain's present economic problems, the two largest unions, the Transport Workers and the Engineers ("machinists" in American terminology), were headed by Jack Jones and Hugh Scanlon, respectively, both leaders in the left wing of the Labour party and in the trade union movement and both strongly disinclined to accept or implement an incomes policy, whether administered by a Labour or by a Conservative Government.

In view of the high degree of concentration in the peak organization and in its member units, the T.U.C. might seem to be well fitted structurally to coordinate and unify action on the part of the industrial working class. One of the needs of the managed economy, as we have seen, is efficient, reasonable, and authoritative producers groups that are capable of making and keeping bargains with government on behalf of large sectors of the economy (see Chapter 4). In this respect the T.U.C. has performed poorly. Perhaps the most crucial test came in the period 1964–1966, when a Labour Government attempted to cope with the wage-cost aspect of inflation through voluntary arrangements carried out in cooperation with the T.U.C. In spite of promises and good intentions, the T.U.C. was unable to act effectively and the voluntary policy had to be superseded by drastic legal action (see Chapter 4).

This weakness of the T.U.C. as a coordinating and directing body is of long standing, and many critics have urged the strengthening of its powers, especially those of the General Council, a representative body of thirty-nine that manages affairs between the annual congresses. But the inadequacies that plague the British labor movement today also have a more recent origin. As we have seen in discussing the politics of inflation, individual unions themselves have suffered a loss of authority (see Chapter 4). The leadership of national organizations and national officers has been severely challenged by the rise in power and activity of shop stewards at the workplace and by an upsurge of local bargaining between workers and employers. Local leaders have shown they can sometimes override national officers, as, for example, during the dock strike of the summer of 1970, when the militant leader of the Transport Workers found he was not militant enough for the local leadership, which obliged him to go back on terms he had found acceptable and to champion the stiffer demands pressed on him from below.

The great rise in unofficial, or wildcat, strikes is an indicator of this disruptive localism. As Table 10.2 shows, while the number of striker-days lost is still well below what it was during the great upsurge of unions fifty years ago, the number of strikes now vastly exceeds the number then. It is as if that earlier wave of industrial action reflected the rise of a united working class, while the myriad and uncoordinated actions of the present result from its decline and decomposition. In any case, it is surely an error to think of the deepening economic problems into which Britain was forced by wage-cost inflation in 1970 and 1971 as resulting simply from the irresponsibility or radicalism of national labor leadership. There is good reason to believe that many national leaders, and especially those prominent in the T.U.C., wished to moderate the self-defeating pressure for wage increases, only to find themselves confronted with a crisis of authority within their organizations that undermined their power. At the time of its 1970 meeting, a by-no-means unsympathetic journalist remarked on "the fact that with the rank-and-file running wild, the T.U.C. is facing the gravest crisis of authority in its 102-year history; that Britain is now the victim of the worst strike figures on record; and that it is high time the unions answered the hoary question: What are we here for?"[3]

Trade Associations

During the latter part of the nineteenth century, a new element was introduced into British politics through the formation of nationwide organizations based on a productive function. If trade unions were the leading example, trade associations, linking business firms, followed close behind. Their purposes were to represent employers in relations with trade unions and to provide various economic services for their members; but as government intervention in the economy grew, they also came to advocate business interests at Westminster and Whitehall. Like labor, business organization leaped forward in the years of collectivist transition, around World War I. The Federation of British Industries, which was founded in 1916 and which by the end of its first year included 62 associations and 350 individual firms, had grown by 1925 to include 195 associations and 2,100 firms.

The trend to concentration has been continuous. By the 1950s trade associations in the industrial sector were virtually all-embracing, with 90 percent of the larger firms and 76 percent of the smaller belonging to one or more of the 1,300 industrial

---

[3]David Haworth, *The Observer* (London), Sept. 13, 1970.

trade associations. But as business has lagged behind labor in organizing for economic and political purposes, so also has it, on the whole, displayed a relatively lower capacity for unified action. The T.U.C. was founded in 1868, but it was not until almost one hundred years later, in 1965, that British industries finally established a single peak organization, the Confederation of British Industry (C.B.I.). British commerce was and is separately organized from industry. The Association of British Chambers of Commerce, founded in 1860, had grown by the 1950s to include some one hundred constituent chambers, with 60,000 members, which still left a large number of retail merchants federated in another organization, the National Chamber of Trade.

In the industrial sector, the first solid success in interindustry organization came during World War I. This move toward amalgamation still left three organizations in the field: the Federation of British Industries (F.B.I.), which tended to group the larger firms; the National Union of Manufacturers; and the British Employers' Confederation, an overlapping body whose affiliates dealt with labor relations. It was in effect these three bodies that were finally merged in 1965. Of the 108 organizations belonging to the C.B.I., 33 operated solely as employers associations and 75 combined the functions of employers' associations with those of trade associations. After 1965 amalgamations joining the two functions continued. Compared with some other central business organizations, however, the authority of the C.B.I. is weak. In contrast with the Swedish Employers' Confederation, for instance, it does not itself take any part in collective bargaining nor lay down the lines that associations or firms are to follow in negotiating industry agreements.

Like British labor, British business organizations, while having relatively comprehensive membership coverage, have been criticized for not having stronger and more coherent central authority. The Engineering Employers' Federation, which deals with the machine-tool industry, a crucial sector in the British economy with regard to exports and productivity, has been taken to task by a Royal Commission for an old-fashioned structure that "still has no formal place in its constitution for the large companies owning many factories which have come to play so important a part in the industry."[4] Similarly in the Federation of British Industries, the largest manufacturers were underrepresented in its governing body, the Grand Council. When a significant divergence of opinion arose between the larger and smaller firms this differential noticeably affected F.B.I. policy. Such was the case in the early sixties, when big business in Britain on the whole was strongly urging on the Government the merits of membership in the Common Market, while the smaller firms hung back. As a result the F.B.I. posture was a good deal more cautious than the consensus among the larger firms would have justified. As for the recently established Confederation, although its creation represents a major step toward more coherent organization for British business, the new body still has even less

---

[4] *Royal Commission on Trade Unions and Employers' Associations, Report* (London: H.M.S.O., 1968) Cmnd. 3623, p. 21.

authority over its affiliates than the T.U.C. has over its member organizations.

As public policy expanded in this century, business groups, like other producers groups, were drawn into closer contact with government. Government initiative during World War I led to the creation of some trade associations and the establishment of regular contacts with many that continued into peacetime. Total mobilization during World War II vastly extended these contacts and burdened them with vital functions in the wartime economy. Many trade associations were embodied in the government machine and charged with administering specialized sectors of the economy under a system of detailed physical planning and control. At the same time, trade unions were brought into full partnership with government and business. At every level and in most spheres of policy, labor as well as business representatives were included on committees directly associated with the administrative machine. This tight system of planning did not long survive the war, but the arrangements bringing producers groups and government departments together in regular, institutionalized contact did survive. The present arrangement by which every section of industry and every firm has a "sponsoring" department in Whitehall with which it exchanges information and advice, and which it may influence or be influenced by descends from that time.

The system of consultation reached a culminating point with the establishment of the N.E.D.C. in the 1960s (see Chapter 4). The main council, as well as the councils for specific industries, which ultimately numbered twenty-one, included independent experts and representatives from business, organized labor, and government. The main object was to raise the rate of economic growth, and these producers' representatives were brought directly into the government machine, since it had been learned that without their cooperation this primary goal of public policy could not be achieved. During the more ambitious phase of N.E.D.C. planning, an overall rate of growth would be set, as well as growth rates for particular industries, after which the industries would be brought into consultation to determine whether and how these goals could be achieved. After the inflationary crisis of 1966 forced the Government to lower its sights, the industries were asked to work toward more realistic assessments. In February 1969, for instance, the Government produced a "green paper"—the color signifying that its proposals had not yet been adopted, but were only up for discussion—which stated its tentative view of the prospects for the economy up to 1972. The main council then selected particular industries for detailed consultation. Among these were seven covered by industry councils, mechanical engineering, motor manufacture, machine tools, electrical engineering, electronics, chemicals, and paper and board. The specific reports, which came back to the main council in December 1969, provided the foundation for an economic assessment that was made available to government, industry, and the general public. It is said that the Treasury subsequently readjusted its forward view in the light of these commentaries.

The system was useful to the government as a way of winning the consent of industry to its programs. Moreover, it made use of the talents of each industry in criticizing its own performance—in the words of one insider, it was a case of "industry talking to itself." The better trade associations were helpful in this respect. Thus a voluminous report on the wool industry showing that many small firms would not be able to survive had a bearing on government policy toward mergers. The associations were also used to nominate members of the industry councils and to exert moral influence on firms to get cooperation. On the industry side, associations and individual firms found the councils effective in relations with government. Sheer information of what government is going to do over a period of time is crucially important to firms and industries when the public sector is as large as it is in Britain today. An industry might also have specific requests for government action with regard to export guarantees, manpower-training programs, or other forms of government aid. Its contact was usually with its sponsoring department, which was normally a member of the industry council and would take up the matter with the department from which action was desired. If the relationship did not involve bargaining in the sense of negotiation leading to an explicit, binding agreement, it did lend itself to lobbying, in that one party might indicate what it was prepared to do providing the other would reciprocate in some way.

Although the British effort had been in some degree modeled on the French method of planning, the N.E.D.C. system was a good deal less etatist than the French Commissariat du plan. The reason is not because the organized interests were too tough and hard-nosed. On the contrary, British planners even in their more ambitious moods (except in wartime) seem to follow the same consensus-seeking, rather easy-going methods as do the central authorities of organized business and labor. As an eminent civil servant frequently used to remark: "The British like a great deal of rather weak government."

Party Government

Judging by the first year of the Heath Government, the policies of its two main parties are marked by a new divergence. The novelty of this development appears when we look back at the two previous changes of the party in power during the postwar period, the first in 1951 and the next in 1964. In each of these transitions a high degree of continuity in government policy was displayed. By showing that it accepted the welfare state and the managed economy developed by the Labour Government, the Conservative party under Churchill and his successors confirmed the consensus that had been emerging in the late 1940s. A decade later, deepening economic problems led the Conservatives to take fundamentally new initiatives with regard to control of the economy. But again when the Opposition took power in 1964 these initiatives were maintained and developed, with Labour building on Conservative foundations in making its ambitious attempt at national planning and wage-price control.

Party Policy

There was, however, far less continuity between the policies of the Heath Government and its predecessor. With regard to both main branches of domestic policy, the Conservatives broke sharply with Labour. In the field of economic control, the Prices and Income Board was abolished and the Ministry of Technology was replaced by a smaller and less active Ministry of Trade and Industry. In their effort to control wage-push inflation, the Conservatives put their main reliance upon control of the public sector. In this role, according to their view, government, as the employer of a quarter of the work force, has the power to resist inflationary wage settlements on a wide front, at once relieving pressure on the economy and setting an example for employers in the private sector. This policy led to sharp confrontations with the unions, in particular to serious strikes by electricity workers and postal workers in pursuit of wage claims. Among other agencies of economic control the N.E.D.C. was retained, as we have seen, but in the modest role of a channel of communication rather than as a means of planning. In the field of economic control generally, the Heath Government diverged not only from the practices of the Wilson Government, but also from the initiatives of the Conservatives in the early 1960s.

The main thrust of Conservative policy, however, was to restrain public expenditure. This question had been crucial from the moment when the Conservatives, while in Opposition during the Attlee Government, took the essential step of adapting to Labour's revolution by accepting the huge new financial burden it entailed. Thereafter, on social (and political) grounds, welfare state expenditure was protected even in times of economic stringency during the fifties and sixties. The new approach of the Heath Government affected social policy, but its grounds were economic. What might be called the "official" Conservative view of Britain's economic problem under the Wilson Government was that Labour allowed expenditure to rise excessively, financing the new burdens by additional taxation, which reduced incentives for more efficient enterprise and added to inflation by raising the tax component of costs and reducing take-home pay. As a percentage of G.N.P., all taxes (meaning central and local taxes and national insurance contributions) fell slightly in the thirteen years of Conservative rule, 1951–1964, from 37.4 percent to 33.2 percent, only to rise steeply to 44.2 percent during the next five years under Labour. In this same period public expenditure rose from 44 percent to 51 percent of national income. From this perspective, the new divergence between the parties goes back to the middle sixties, when Labour, carrying out its generous campaign pledges, introduced a new rate of increase in public expenditure and taxation.

When Conservatives are asked what expenditures they would cut in their campaign to stimulate the economy, questions of social policy again come to the fore. Some of the things their leaders have said, supported by emerging trends of recent policy, suggest a rationale that sets off the Conservative view from the Labour view and indeed touches fundamental positions in the conflict between socialist and nonsocialist thought. Very simply put, this difference in social policy centers on the question of selectivity versus universality in welfare services. Broadly speaking, Labour's approach in setting up the services was that they should be available to everyone on the same basis. National insurance contributions and benefits would be identical for all. National health services would be free to all. Even public housing would be open to all—without a means test to determine need. The conception of universality expressed in these policies can be seen as derived from the socialist notion of equality. The rationale of selectivity derives from the quite different premise that welfare services should provide not for everyone but only for those in need. Such programs would be "poverty programs" in American terms, directing expenditure to the poor leaving the provision of such services for people who can afford to pay for them largely to the market and to free choice.

The sharp distinctions implied by this definition of the issue cannot be fully expressed in actual government programs. Yet not only in Britain but in Europe generally, there has been a trend toward selectivity in social services. Sometimes the goal is referred to as a "two tier system," in which certain basic and heavily subsidized services will be supplied to the poor, while those better off are charged more for them, or are left free to make their own arrangements in the private market. In Britain, old-age pensions have been shifted from the universalist basis of the National Insurance Act of 1946, which provided everyone with the same benefits, to an earnings-related basis that provides that people will pay according to income and will be pensioned according to earnings. Initially put forward by Labour, this idea was carried out on a small scale by the Conservatives in the early sixties and then, under the Wilson Government, developed into a far-reaching pension bill that failed of enactment in 1970 only because of the dissolution of Parliament. The Conservatives have also proposed taking further steps toward a two-tier system by enlarging the provision for old age that would be made through private schemes. One barrier to this has been the fact that private pension plans often cannot be transferred when the employee changes employers. An item in the Conservative election program of 1970 proposed that the government take steps to make such plans transferable.

In regard to housing, the Heath Government moved to end subsidies to tenants who could provide for themselves and to relate public expenditure more closely to need. A start was made by charging those who could afford it a more economic rent for public housing. The sale of council houses to tenants was encouraged. On the other hand, the scheme for rebating rents to poorer families was extended to all tenants in public housing and for the first time to tenants in private housing as well. In the national health service, similar changes were made. Characteristic was the decision to increase the charge for prescriptions, but at the same time to extend further the exemption from payment for poorer families. A new family-income supplement scheme was announced, which similarly reflected the Government's concern with the poverty problem. This scheme provided cash payments to families who had members employed in full-time work, but who, nonetheless, were below the poverty line.

Savings on social services constituted a substantial part of the reductions the Conservative Government made in the plans for future expenditure that they had inherited from Labour. Other reductions were made in industrial and agricultural subsidies. As pledged, these prospective savings were promptly converted into tax reductions. Moreover, the first major reduction bore not on the sales tax but on the income tax. In the fall of 1970 the standard rate—a rate paid on taxed income before the scheme is graduated by the imposition of a surtax—was reduced for the first time in eleven years and brought back to where it stood before Labour raised the rate in 1964. The provision of greater incentive to taxpayers to increase their earnings was given as a principal reason for the change. Corporation tax was also reduced, and while depreciation allowances were improved, Labour's scheme for investment grants to business was abolished. Conservatives, reviewing their first steps, claimed that by the end of four years their new policies would mean a reduction in annual public expenditure of a billion pounds, obviating the need for tax increases of some 300 million and making possible tax reductions and, hopefully, more economic growth.

In their complex tradition, the Conservatives can no doubt find justification and precedent for these new departures. Yet objective circumstances as well as party outlook account for the discontinuities, just as they had much to do with the strong threads of continuity in the transitions of 1951 and 1964. British parties are confronted with the realities of getting elected and the realities of governing. Typically at the time of a previous transition, the pattern of policy worked out by the incumbent party gave promise of being adequate to these realities, so it was natural for the successor party to shape its innovations within the outlines of existing policy patterns. The frustrations and failures of the Wilson Government provoked a very different reaction from the Opposition. Circumstances that for over two decades had forced the two parties toward one another now reversed the direction of pressure, initiating a new phase of significant party strife. The parties showed that they were still functioning as instruments of social choice. This is not to say that the pressure of Britain's problems may not force further and unexpected shifts in party positions. These problems, in the private words of one high Conservative, are "almost intractable."

Party Structure

The structures of the two parties consist of very similar elements. The parliamentary side of a party includes the Leader, his circle of lieutenants, and the backbenchers, who are organized into a parliamentary body that acts as a unit and also divides into functional committees. The extraparliamentary side consists of the mass membership distributed among constituency parties—and in the Labour party, certain functional bodies such as trade unions; the annual conference and other intermediate representative bodies; and the party bureaucracy, which takes care of such matters as public relations, research, finance, and organization and which is linked with a body of professional agents serving the local parties. The interesting questions are, What are the relationships among these elements? and in particular, Are there such differences between them as to distinguish Labour and Conservative types of party government?

In theory, there are important distinguishing differences. As we have seen in Chapter 9, differing party conceptions of how authority should be structured and exercised in the larger polity also inform their respective public images. Both socialist democracy and Tory democracy have yielded versions of party government, but one has stressed the role of party adherents in giving direction to the party and its representatives in power, while the other has stressed the necessity for a leadership that will generate the initiative for a governmental record to be submitted to the voters for approval or disapproval. In actual practice there has been a convergence in structure as marked as the convergence in policy. In the first decade of this century the political ways of the two parties were as different as their leaders were distant in social origins. The Conservative Leader Arthur Balfour was a Cecil and the nephew of the Marquess of Salisbury, who had himself only recently relinquished the party leadership. J. Ramsey MacDonald, the illegitimate son of a Scots miner, held the post of secretary of the Labour party, which did not yet have a Leader in the traditional sense. Balfour was known to have remarked that on questions of public policy he would as soon take advice from his valet as from the annual conference of his party. The parliamentary work of the handful of Labour M.P.s, on the other hand, was dominated by the initiatives of the extraparliamentary party and the trade unions. Since that time the parties have come to look much more alike, and it is not irrelevant to note that the social origins of their two leaders are also hardly distinguishable. Wilson's father was a works chemist—a salaried technician—and Heath's a carpenter who built up a contracting business, thus enabling the press to refer to the present Prime Minister as the first Tory Leader from the working class.

With regard to the parliamentary parties, a growing similarity (see Chapter 7) has resulted from adaptation by both parties. Most notably, the Labour Leader has come to occupy a position of authority in relation to his lieutenants and backbenchers greatly resembling the present-day Tory model. That change, however, must be considered in connection with the fact that in back-bench organization and activity the Conservatives have in many respects imitated Labour. There remain traces of their differing origins. The Labour Leader must annually subject himself to reelection, a procedure that, although it is a formality when he is in office, may occasion a serious challenge when the party is in Opposition. The Conservative Leader, in contrast, while probably having no more secure tenure, retains his post without need for renewal, although he is subject to challenge. As we have seen in Chapter 7, these structural differences in the parliamentary parties become most significant if we compare the behavior of the parties in Opposition. The formal recapture by Labour backbenchers of the power to determine the party's parliamentary stand gives them more effective and continuous influence on the leadership. In contrast, the Conservative Leader, in Opposition and in office, remains the authoritative voice of party policy; and, while he must carry his backbenchers with him, he is not obliged to subject his proposals to the formal vote of a party caucus, which may accept, amend, or reject them or put forward its own.

It is, however, with regard to relations with the extraparliamentary party that the main differences in Labour and Conservative methods and spirit appear. In this respect, Conservative M.P.s and their leaders enjoy significantly more of that independent authority that in the classic Tory view of the British Constitution attaches to the governing powers (see Chapter 1). In a crucial sense this is simply a result of the contrasts in formal organization. Under the neat, written constitution of the Labour party drawn up by the Fabian Sidney Webb in 1918 and hardly changed since then, there are two sorts of members of the party, affiliated and individual. The affiliated members are organizations, mainly trade unions but also a few socialist, professional, and cooperative societies. The individual members belong to the party through local parties set up in the parliamentary constituencies. Both sorts of members are represented at the annual conference. In 1968, out of a total membership of 6.1 million, the sixty-eight trade unions accounted for 5.4 million and the 656 local parties for 701,000. Accordingly, at the conference of 1969 the union delegates cast about 90 percent of the votes. The unions affiliated with the Labour party do not, of course, include the whole of the British working class or the whole of British organized labor. From a total of 25.6 million wage and salary earners in the United Kingdom in 1970, over 10 million were trade union members, of whom some 9.4 million, in turn, were affiliated with the T.U.C. Yet the party does have the big batallions of organized labor. At the party conference each union casts its vote as a unit—in Britain this is called a "block vote," in the United States it would be called "voting by the unit rule"—so when Jack Jones rises to speak on economic policy or on the Common Market, the leadership listens attentively to the head of a union that pays affiliation fees on 1.5 million members, makes proportionately large contributions to the special funds collected for fighting general elections, casts almost 25 percent of the total vote of conference, and disposes of resources of manpower in the economy at large that are indispensable to the success of any Government.

The formal organization of the Conservative party confronts its leadership with no such concentrations of political and economic power. In contrast with Labour's arrangements, Conservative membership is wholly individual. Organized in local associations based on the parliamentary constituencies, the members of the National Union of Conservative and Unionist Associations—to give the extraparliamentary organization its proper name—annually send "representatives" (they stress this Burkean term in contrast with the Labour term "delegate") to the conference. The less-weighty character of this gathering is suggested by its greater numbers—usually some 3,000 or 4,000 compared with Labour's 1,000 or so—which make serious debate and decision making very difficult, and by the fact that regardless of size, each local association sends the same number of representatives. Industrial Britain is present, as the sprinkling of working-class accents certifies. But overwhelmingly the representatives are solid middle class. Noticeably absent among employers and managers are the opposite numbers of the big trade union leaders. Although the leaders of finance, industry, and commerce are no less partisan in their political preferences and although wealthy men have continued to be a major source of the huge (by British standards) party funds collected by Conservatives, the "top people" from these economic worlds play virtually no part in the public gatherings of the Conservative party.

This disparity in formal representation of the economic powers aligned with the two parties also applies to other elements in their coalitions. The intellectual wing is far more articulate and influential at the Labour conference. It is probably also fair to say that members of Parliament are present in larger numbers and are more active at the Labour conference than at the Conservative one. Given these differences in the "real forces" represented, it is inevitable that conference and the extraparliamentary party in general will have much more influence in the Labour party than in the Conservative party.

The formal allocations of authority in the two parties accord with these realities. Although the Labour constitution, written fifty years ago, still retains its original provision that "the work of the Party shall be under the direction and control of the Party Conference," the extraparliamentary party has retreated deeply from its old practice of "instructing" the parliamentary party. Controversy raged bitterly in the late fifties over the constitutional standing of conference decisions, when conference and leadership adopted conflicting views of British nuclear policy. At the conference of 1960, conference defeated the leadership by adopting a proposal committing the party to unilateral disarmament and virtually a rejection of N.A.T.O. Rather than accept this decision as party policy, the Leader, Hugh Gaitskell, mounted a massive campaign to reverse the decision, which he successfully accomplished at the 1961 conference. One could argue that Gaitskell's resistance showed that conference was not sovereign or, conversely, that his insistence on getting it to reverse itself showed that he did recognize its authority. More interesting, however, was the fact that in accomplishing his end, he deeply compromised his own initial position on major points. Whatever we may say about the authority of conference, this episode showed its great influence on the declared policy of the parliamentary leadership.

To compare the other representative bodies of the two parties is to see the same contrast. On the Conservative side these bodies in theory are only advisory to the Leader and in fact do not significantly influence the positions of the parliamentary party on public policy. The Central Council, which is technically the governing body of the National Union, is only slightly smaller than the conference and meets twice yearly. There is also an Executive Committee, which meets each month and which has a small General Purposes Subcommittee whose membership, like that of the Executive Committee, is largely ex officio. Quite independent of the National Union is the Conservative Central Office, which is responsible to the Leader, who appoints its principal officers. While the chairman of the Central Office is usually a prominent politician, since its reorganization after the defeat of 1964 it has had a permanent head in its deputy chairman, Sir Michael Fraser, who is not only an administrator, providing a center for the large and competent staffs of the party bureaucracy, but also an idea man, sometimes known as "the fount of all knowledge and the supplier of all briefs."

In contrast, the National Executive Committee (N.E.C.) of the Labour party has a position of large, formal authority and substantial influence. Its election by the conference ensures that the real forces present there will also be represented in the committee. The twenty-eight members are chosen as follows: twelve elected by the trade union delegates; one elected by the affiliated socialist societies; seven elected by the constituency delegates; five women elected by conference as a whole; party treasurer, elected by conference, ex officio; party Leader, chosen by parliamentary party, ex officio; and deputy party leader, chosen by parliamentary party, ex officio. Half or more of the members are usually M.P.s, and normally the N.E.C. and the parliamentary leadership, who meet together each month whether the party is in office or in Opposition, work in harmony. Yet the N.E.C. can be a source of difficulties. Not the Leader but the N.E.C. has control of the party bureaucracy, a power which it asserted vigorously in the later days of the Wilson Government by rejecting the Prime Minister's choice for party secretary. It has the power to withhold endorsements from parliamentary candidates, to disaffiliate local parties, and to expel individuals (see Chapter 7). It can take a stand on public questions that differs from the position of the parliamentary leadership, as it did in the spring of 1969, when it declared against the trade union legislation to which the Labour Government itself was committed. Its power in relation to the campaign manifesto gives it an opportunity to influence public policy that is deserving of more extended discussion.

Manifesto and Mandate

When we try to assess the influence of the extraparliamentary party organization, we can focus our question by asking what role that organization had in framing the formal pledges of the campaign and how far these pledges controlled government policy when the party held office. In short, who prepared the manifesto, and did it mandate the victorious party?

The Labour constitution provides that conference shall draw up the party "programme" and that party members, conference delegates, candidates for Parliament, and members of Parliament must "accept and conform" to it. More to the point, the constitution also provides that the parliamentary committee and the National Executive Committee shall jointly decide what items from the programme shall be included in the manifesto issued on the occasion of a general election. Judging by what went on during the last significant phase of policy making by the party, this constitutional formula is still a good guide to what actually happens. In 1961 conference debated and approved a lengthy statement of home policy, *Signposts for the Sixties,* which had been drawn up by the National Executive Committee and which, keying its appeal to "the scientific revolution," stressed economic planning and expansion, land use, social security, educational equality and tax reform. Three years later the election manifesto, *The New Britain,* did draw heavily in tone and in content upon the earlier and longer document.

To identify the sources and influences that were actually responsible for the ideas embodied in these documents is a more complex matter. The pledges did not originate with conference, if by "originate" is meant that they derived from the resolutions put forward by local parties and trade unions. Those energies of the party were brought into play by the struggles between Left and Right over such great symbolic issues as nuclear policy. With regard to these issues, conference did leave its mark on the manifesto. The compromise to which the leadership had been forced in nuclear policy was reflected in the manifesto's virtual pledge to give up "the independent British deterrent." The proposal to renationalize the steel industry went back to repeated confirmations in party pronouncements dating from the interwar years and carried out by the Attlee Government. Although many of the revisionist leaders of the party regarded public ownership as irrelevant to Britain's problems and to socialism, it would have been impossible to omit this pledge, such was the strength of favorable sentiment in the party generally and in conference in particular. (Incidentally, it is worth noting that although the Conservatives had reversed the earlier act of nationalization, they omitted any mention of renewed denationalization in their 1970 manifesto and seemed to be ready to let public ownership stand, subject only to marginal measures of hiving off.)

The initiatives in framing the new policies came from the higher echelons of the Labour party, but they were diverse. The broad thrust to modernize the party and to get away from the old "cloth cap" socialism, with its rigid pledges of universal nationalization, was widely supported among the parliamentary leaders. The actual proposals owed a great deal to the Research Department, which at that time was headed by Peter Shore, an exceptionally imaginative reformer and later a Cabinet Minister. Some of the more complex and technical proposals came from outside experts. For example, the reform of old-age pensions in such a way as to break from the old flat-rate scheme and relate payments to the previous earnings of pensioners was largely developed by Richard Timuss of the University of London and a group of his co-workers. The task of drawing up what proved to be the decisive document, *Signposts of the Sixties,* was given by the National Executive Committee to a subcommittee consisting of four M.P.s and three trade unionists. It was not a Radical body, but under the chairmanship of Harold Wilson, then still nominally a leader of the Left, it modified the original draft from the Research Department so as to produce a thoroughly revisionist statement, which it was hoped would appeal to the growing proportion of white-collar workers in the economy. In the years leading up to the election of 1964, the parliamentary leadership was fundamentally united in its outlook and, within broad limits set by party opinion, had its way in determining policy positions.

As for the extent to which a Labour manifesto can mandate a Labour Government, the experience of the Wilson regime is instructive. In spite of the compromise of 1961 that Britain should "cease the attempt to remain an independent nuclear power"[5] and the virtual pledge of 1964 against an "independent British deterrent," after six years under the Wilson Government, Britain still had her own nuclear armament. Broadly, foreign policy and related questions of defense have not shown themselves to be likely subjects for programmatic commitment. The principal reason is that pledges of action and achievement in foreign affairs are not wholly subject to the control of the sovereign nation, but also depend for their success upon the vagaries of other powers as well. That was the bitter experience of the Attlee Government, which took office committed to warm relations with Russia. Under less tragic circumstances, Harold Wilson learned the lesson again when his bid to enter the Common Market was abruptly vetoed by de Gaulle.

When we compare the pledges of the manifesto with the record of government action in various fields of domestic policy, however, their conformity is impressive. R. H. S. Crossman has said:

> One of the things which most interested me in 1964 was to see the way in which the Mandate was honoured, sometimes embarrassingly. There were one or two parts of the Mandate which I always thought were doubtful. We set about carrying them all out—good, bad, indifferent.[6]

As pledged, a vast system of national economic planning was established; steel was renationalized; a Ministry of Technology was set up; regional planning was developed; a capital-gains tax was enacted; retirement, sickness, and unemployment benefits were increased; health-service charges were abolished; rent decontrol was halted; expenditure on housing, education, and hospitals was increased; a commission was set up to acquire land for public housing; and comprehensive public education was encouraged instead of the segregating of students according to ability. The promises were not as specific, numerous, or radical as those made in the famous manifesto of 1945. Yet the record of performance compares favorably. Since such action usually costs money, the mandate was in large part responsible for the steep rise in taxes from 33.2 percent of the G.N.P. in 1964 to 44.2 percent in 1970. As the party boasted in a review of its record, "public expenditure levels in the social programme have been raised by up to 70 percent in five years."[7]

When we turn to the party's promises on what their policies would accomplish, however, the failures begin to mount up. Inflation was not controlled, nor the pound defended, nor economic growth stimulated, nor unemployment avoided. As in Attlee's time, the party found that it was far easier to expand government services than to control the economy. Indeed, the two aims often came into conflict. As one junior Minister later remarked, "We carried out our mandate on social policy so faithfully that we were unable to carry out our promises with regard to the economy."

---

[5] *Labour Party Conference Report* (The Labour Party, 1961), p. 8.

[6] R. H. S. Crossman, *The Myths of Cabinet Government* (Cambridge, Mass., 1972), p. 96.

[7] *Labour Party Conference Report* (London: H.M.S.O, 1969), p. 385.

The function of manifesto and mandate in the Conservative party can be described more briefly, because the process is not complicated by doctrines such as Labour's powerful belief in intraparty democracy. The parliamentary leadership does have a freer hand. Yet since World War II the party has made increasing use of policy statements and shown increasing concern with election manifestoes. In 1945 the closest thing to a program or manifesto produced by the Conservatives was a brief message entitled "Mr. Churchill's Declaration of Policy to the Electors." But in the wide-ranging party reorganization that followed its crushing defeat in the 1945 election, the policy statement authorized by the Leader, published in pamphlet form and distributed by the millions, became a major feature of Conservative propaganda. Since that time great energy and attention have been given to the development of policy ideas, both as a means of winning elections and as a basis for governing the country. After the defeat of 1964, the party launched an elaborate review of policy. As many as thirty-six groups were put to work, drawing their members from Parliament, business, and the universities, and utilizing the services of the Research Department. In a new departure, Heath submitted a statement of policy to the conference in 1965, but only for discussion not for approval or disapproval, and no votes were taken. This document showed the new directions of Tory policy that were to be associated with Heath's leadership. It did not mention economic planning or an incomes policy, both of which had been stressed previously by Conservatives, but instead emphasized tax reduction, trade union reform, selectivity in social services, and the Common Market. From it were drawn the main themes of the manifestoes of 1966 and 1970. In the prolonged policy-making exercise leading up to the election of 1970, the voice of the Leader predominated. "He got his own way in policy and he got his own men where he wanted them," was the way one insider summed up the results.

During the first year of the Heath Government, as we have seen, the Tories sought to carry out their campaign pledges with almost doctrinaire rigor. "I take election promises seriously," remarked Heath after a year in office, "and we have been at great pains to fulfill them. I find that many of my colleagues bring a copy of the election manifesto to Cabinet meetings. At the last count we found that we have already redeemed 79 election pledges."[8] One reason for this emphasis was a recognition of the political advantage of promise keeping, and in the spring of 1971 Conservative publications continually directed attention to the correspondence of government action with pledges of the manifesto. While Tory values endow Conservative leaders with a wide sphere of independent authority within the party and within the polity, the leaders' judgment of electoral consequences may cause them to behave like adherents of mandate theory. In the case of Prime Minister Heath, moreover, the system of elaborate program making and his campaign pledges strengthened his hand when he won power. The whole business had been conducted under his close supervision and control and very much reflected

---

[8] *The Sunday Times* (London), June 20, 1971, p. 10.

the new direction he wished to give Conservative and British policy. Supported by party and by public approval of his proposals, Heath's leadership in policy making was strengthened against fractious Ministers, civil servants, and backbenchers. In this curious manner the democratic mandate enhanced Tory authority.

Eleven

The Challenge to
Collectivist Politics

The previous account reveals changes from the collectivist system, although hardly a profound breach with it. Functional representation has declined from what it was in the fifties and early sixties. Certainly, party conflict has revived as the deepening problems of the economy have been met by a pronounced and even ideological differentiation of party positions. If we look toward the grass roots rather than the commanding heights of the polity, however, mounting evidence suggests more important developments. It does not indicate a clear and indubitable outcome. Yet the signs of qualitative change are too strong to permit us to overlook the question, Is British politics undergoing a system change comparable to the major transformations that marked earlier phases of party modernization?

The flaring up of party strife may simply be a renewal of conflict between two old antagonists who will remain essentially unchanged in an unchanging party system. On the other hand, it may constitute the kind of breach of consensus that in the past has led to the emergence of quite new structures and issues and the transition to a new phase of party development. It is useful and necessary to ask this broad question, for when a state of affairs has lasted a generation or so and we have gotten used to it, it is very easy to assume in the very questions we put to the facts that no major change in that state of affairs is taking place. Yet past history warns against this assumption as applied even to slow-moving, phlegmatic England and forces one to keep in mind that these present changes may not be merely a variation within the collectivist system, but rather a departure from it.

Indicators of such possibilities are of three sorts: strong evidence of organizational decomposition with regard to both parties, a new volatility in voting behavior suggesting the breakup of old class solidarities, and the emergence in substantial numbers of nonparty political groups stressing decentralized and participatory reforms.

Party Decomposition

Signs of party decomposition abound in Western democracies. In the United States in recent years, party identification has dropped sharply and ticket splitting has risen to new heights. Similar evidence of loss of support for parties can be found in France and Germany and, ironically, may be a necessary condition for the recent trend toward a two-party system in each country. In Britain one major indicator has been a decline in the mass organization at the local level.

The term "mass organization" itself deserves some analysis, since, taken literally, it has seriously misled many students of British politics. Each of the parties includes a network of local organizations based on parliamentary constituencies and containing individual dues-paying members. Each party has branches in the wards or polling districts where electioneering for local as well as parliamentary candidacies is conducted. On the Conservative side, an annual general meeting open to all members elects the officers of the association, who, with representatives from the branches and certain others, constitute the governing body, the Executive Council. One of the most important tasks of the association is to hire an election agent who is trained and certified by the Central Office and who will supply professional knowledge of Britain's complex election laws and of techniques for conducting campaigns and winning elections. A party bureaucrat, the agent is little concerned with policy and looks forward to a career as an organizer rather than as a candidate or boss.

In selecting its parliamentary candidate the local association also acts under some guidance from the Central Office. The National Union will suggest names of likely possibilities. (It should be remembered that in Britain the candidate does not need to live in his constituency, and about half the M.P.s come from outside.) Before final adoption of its choice at a general meeting of the association, the approval of a central committee of the Union and the parliamentary party must also be obtained. Actually, approval is virtually automatic, and in their selections the local associations show that the "complete autonomy" attributed to them under the party rules is no misnomer. An American, thinking of his own political system, will not find this autonomy strange, but he will be thoroughly baffled by the absence of open public competition. The solicitation of support by aspirants must be done modestly, quietly, and certainly not through public meetings or campaigning among party members to win their support. The main work is done by the Executive Council and its small selection committee.

Quite similar is the Labour-party variation on the basic structure, which goes back to the nineteenth century and, indeed, was adapted from American innovations in party organization. One difference is that the governing body, usually called the General Management Committee, includes delegates not only from the wards, but also from branches of other organizations, especially trade unions. This body elects an executive committee and other officials, including a secretary who is often the election agent.

This structure, as its Jacksonian antecedents suggest, could make possible wide participation and lively competition within the local parties. British parties have indeed mobilized the electorate to the extent that remarkably large numbers regularly pay dues. In 1969 the Conservatives estimated their individual members numbered 2,225,000, while Labour reported 701,000. This does not necessarily reflect great commitment. In the Conservative party the minimum annual subscription is still only 2s. 6d. ($.34). In the Labour party it is 12s. ($1.44), of which one shilling goes to the national party. In effect a delegate committee of perhaps a hundred persons in each local party runs its affairs. This applies even to the selection of a parliamentary candidate, a practice made more remarkable by the fact that three-quarters of the seats are safe, making selection by the local party committee in those cases tantamount to election. The same restraint is carried over to the readoption of an incumbent M.P. Unlike the American congressman, who often has to face a sharp primary contest for renomination, the M.P., once elected, is virtually certain of readoption by his local party at the next election; and challenges, while technically possible, are virtually unknown. Objectively, the structure of British parties makes possible the kind of wide participation and open competition that characterized American parties in the days of the delegate-convention system. Subjectively, however, the norms of British political culture rigidly rule it out.

While the reports of membership given by the parties cannot be taken as enumerations of committed activists, the movements of these figures are indicators of the changing strength of the local party organizations. Taken in this light, the recent trends in party membership reflect severe decline. Membership in the Conservative party, which had numbered 1 million in 1946, and rose to 2.8 million in 1953, sank to 1.5 million by 1969. On the Labour side, the data point to an even deeper slump. From 1928, when it was first reported, individual membership mounted steadily (except during the war years), reaching a peak of about 1 million in 1953. Then the figures began a steady decline that in fifteen years reduced them by 30 percent and has shown no sign of being reversed.

Equally serious is the failure of the trade union section of party membership to grow. Although the figure for trade union membership is in a sense nominal, representing the decision of unions to allocate certain sums from their political funds to the Labour party, a lessening of the will or the ability to increase these contributions signifies a serious loss of momentum. The work force in Britain grows, but the Labour party, like the unions, embraces a diminishing share of its members and of their resources and support. The consequences are sharply focused by the decline in the number of agents. While Labour has never been able to maintain a corps of agents as well paid or as numerous as those in the Conservative party, in 1951 it managed to field 296 full-time agents in Great Britain. By the election of 1970 this number had fallen to 141, in contrast with 396 on the Conservative side.

Class and Voting

The body of party activists has declined in number and performance, especially on the Labour side. Serious as this is for the so-called mass party, its meaning becomes apparent only if it is seen as one expression of a deep-running shift in political sentiment. Another indication is the way British voting behavior in recent years has departed sharply from the established patterns of the collectivist system. The essentials of that pattern were a very high correlation of class and party and, in consequence of this, a steady attachment of two great class-based blocs of voters to their respective parties.

A few years ago a writer authoritatively summed up the consensus among political scientists: "Class is the basis of British politics; all else is embellishment and detail."[1] What this means can be most readily seen in data taken from the Gallup surveys. These surveys divide the electorate into four social classes: upper middle class (6 percent), middle class (22 percent), working class (61 percent), and very poor (11 percent). Table 11.1 shows the strong and persistent correlation

Table 11.1 Class and Voting, Great Britain (in Percent)

	Upper Middle Class		Middle Class		Working Class		Very Poor	
	1950	1966	1950	1966	1950	1966	1950	1966
Conservative	79	79	69	66	36	34	24	19
Labour	9	5	17	14	53	46	64	51
Liberal	10	6	14	7	11	5	12	5

DATA SOURCES: Henry Durant, "Voting Behaviour in Britain, 1945–1964," in Richard Rose (ed.), *Studies in British Politics* (New York: St. Martin's, 1966), p. 123; and *Gallup Political Index, 1966* (London: The Gallup Poll).

between class and party preference. More than half of the two lower classes have regularly voted Labour, with the figure for the very poor occasionally touching two-thirds. The two upper classes are much the more partisan, giving two-thirds to three-quarters and more of their support to the Conservatives. In all advanced countries class is one of the weightiest factors affecting electoral behavior, but comparative study has shown that it is exceptionally important in Britain. Compared with three other English-speaking countries—the United States, Canada, and Australia—Britain has the highest level of class voting. Table 11.2 shows the contrast with the United States.

---

[1]Peter Pulzer, *Political Representation and Elections: Parties and Voting in Great Britain* (New York, 1967), p. 98.

Table 11.2 Class and Voting Preference, U.S. and Great Britain (in Percent)

	United States (1960)		Great Britain (1959)		
	Republican	Democratic	Conservative	Labour	Liberal
Nonmanual	55	45	72	19	9
Manual	40	60	27	63	10

DATA SOURCE: Robert R. Alford, *Party and Society* (Chicago: Rand McNally, 1963), pp. 348, 352.

A more sophisticated analysis of the relationship has been presented in a recent study.[2] It shows that British voters tend strongly to think in terms of two classes, the working class and the middle class, and to use occupation rather than wealth, education, or other marks of status as their basis for assigning individuals to one or the other class. When occupations are ranked according to prestige, they tend to fall into two broad groupings, the working class and the middle class. The line between the two groupings, however, does not fall precisely between manual and nonmanual occupations, which is the boundary commonly used in correlation studies. The British voter himself tends rather to draw the line within the area of nonmanual occupations. Those in nonmanual occupations with supervisory tasks, such as draftsmen, local government officials, and secretaries with subordinates, are assigned to the middle class, along with the lower and higher managerial occupations. But on the working-class side of the cleft are those in routine non-manual occupations, such as policemen, shop assistants, and transport inspectors, along with skilled and unskilled manual workers. The importance of this classification becomes apparent when party identification is related to occupation. The lower nonmanual workers, although generally regarded as working class by British voters themselves, prove to be much more strongly Conservative than the voters in the manual occupations (see Table 11.3).

Table 11.3 Party Self-Image by Occupational Status, 1963 (in Percent)

	Higher Managerial	Lower Managerial	Supervisory Nonmanual	Lower Nonmanual	Skilled Manual	Unskilled Manual
Conservative	86	81	77	61	29	25
Labour	14	19	23	39	71	75

SOURCE: David Butler and Donald Stokes, *Political Change in Britain: Forces Shaping Electoral Choice* (New York: St. Martin's, 1969), p. 77. Reprinted by permission of St. Martin's Press, The Macmillan Company of Canada, and Macmillan London and Basingstoke.

Like the Gallup data, Table 11.3 shows the strong correlation between class and party preference, Conservative strength increasing and Labour strength decreasing

---

[2]David Butler and Donald Stokes, *Political Change in Britain: Forces Shaping Electoral Choice* (New York, 1969), Chapter V.

as we move up the occupational scale. But it is also evident that even in class-bound Britain there are marked deviations from a strict class-party correlation. At the upper end of the occupational scale, among the managerial groups, Labour has a significant following. We find here those "middle-class radicals" who have been important and influential in the Labour party since the great days of the Fabian Society. From the interwar period, when the reorganization of the party opened up individual membership to them, they have provided a disproportionate share of Labour M.P.s and Labour Cabinets. In the postwar period, their role increased. While Ministers from working-class backgrounds provided half the membership of Attlee's Cabinet, by October 1969, in the Wilson Cabinet, there were none. Similarly in the House of Commons, one of the most striking changes has been the increase in the number of Labour M.P.s from middle-class backgrounds, especially teachers and university lecturers (see Chapter 5).

In a more general sense, this political splitting of a higher class has been of crucial importance to the operation of the British polity. A necessary condition for the functioning of the governing class has been the fact that substantial numbers of people from a higher class have supported and given leadership to the parties of innovation that drew the bulk of their support from lower social strata. Whigs, Liberals, Radicals, and Socialists have numbered them among their leaders.

We might think it more peculiar, and therefore especially deserving of study, for a member of the middle or upper class to side with a socialist party than for a member of the working class to accept the leadership of a party strongly based in the professional and managerial elites. Nevertheless, it is not the middle-class socialists but the working-class Tories who have attracted more attention from political scientists. As the Gallup data show, Conservatives have continued to win the support of a third of the manual workers. This comes to about one-half the total Conservative vote. Today, as in earlier decades of British democracy, the working-class Tories have been essential to Conservative success. Among these millions, the figure of principal interest has been the deference voter. The term "deference voter," like the motivation it tries to capture, is complex. It derives from the comments of nineteenth-century observers, and the tone of the relationship is caught in such nineteenth-century portraits of interclass harmony as those of Gurth and Ivanhoe or Samuel Weller and Mr. Pickwick. In the motivation of the deference voter there is sometimes an element of pure ascription: the notion that the right to rule belongs to certain persons simply because of who they are—"They're my guv'-nors," as working-class Tories sometimes still say. But the deference voter normally does not disregard consequences. He identifies the people to whom he defers by certain well-known signs of class status: accent, upbringing, occupation, and education, not to mention handwriting, table manners, and time of dining—a whole style of life. At the same time, he thinks instrumentally, taking upper-class status as a probable indication of superior political competence, as these responses illustrate:

They [i.e., the Conservatives] have some of the best brains in the country. They are altogether more successful and brainy than the Labour, and they have a great deal of experience behind them. They've a tradition of governing and leadership behind them for generations.

They have been brought up to rule, to take over leadership. They have been educated to a certain extent to take over. They have no axe to grind for themselves. They look out for other people.

The Tory people are the brains of the country. They know how to get things done. Everyone of them is a man you can look up to and respect.[3]

The peculiarity of the deference voter is that he finds the guarantee of Tory competence in upbringing or, as he often says, in "breeding." In popular form, this is precisely the theory of Tory democracy, with its premise of a governing class brought up in a tradition of public service (see Chapter 9). The distinctiveness of the deferential outlook appears in contrast with the attitude of other working-class Conservatives, who are sometimes called "secular" or "pragmatic." The latter also hold the Tory party to be of superior competence, but their judgment is based not on the superior upbringing of the Tory politician, but on his demonstration of ability by achievement in business, government, or other spheres.

The attitudes of the deference voter descend from Britain's distant past and reflect the adaptation to the institutions of democracy of the premodern belief that inequality and hierarchy are necessary conditions of social order. In accord with the historical origins of their attitudes, deferential voters accept the existence of class stratification; but instead of seeing class as a divisive force, they regard it as an integrating one. Whereas the socialist working-class voter is likely to see class as dividing society horizontally and separating parties, the deferential working-class Tory sees it as vertically uniting one level of society with others. Deferential voting is thus one kind of class-based voting. Numerically it has constituted perhaps a quarter to a half of the Conservative vote among the working class. As class declines as an important political force in British society, not only will working-class support for Labour be affected, but so also will this large bloc of support for the Conservatives.

The New Volatility

The correlation between class and party preference (or voting) remains high, as shown by the data for the general election of 1970 in Table 11.1. Yet there are many powerful indications of a severe weakening of class as a force determining political attitudes. In a study of groups of voters who had entered the electorate

---

[3]Robert McKenzie and Allan Silver, *Angels in Marble: Working Class Conservatives in Urban England* (Chicago, 1968), p. 109.

at different times in the past, Butler and Stokes found that among both working-class Labour voters and middle-class Conservatives the belief in politics as a conflict of class interests increased for each successive age-cohort (groups of persons born during a certain period) of the interwar and wartime years and declined markedly among those who first entered the electorate after 1951. Perceptions of difference between the parties followed the same trends, the proportion of respondents seeing a "good deal" of difference declining in the postwar period.

Table 11.4 Don't Know Percentages in Gallup Polls

Year	Average
1947	11
1948	15
1949	15
1950	9
1951	12
1952	11
1953	12
1954	13
1955	13
1956	16
1957	17
1958	17
1959	16
1960	16
1961	16
1962	17
1963	17.5
1964	17
1965	15.5
1966	15
1967	16.5
1968	21
1969	22.5
1970	17.5
1971 (first six months)	18.5

DATA SOURCE: *Gallup Political Index, 1947–1971* (London: The Gallup Poll).

In this connection the number who replied "Don't Know" when asked what party they would vote for in a general election is also significant. As Table 11.4 shows, the "Don't Knows," after rising gradually in the postwar period, took a sharp surge upward during the late 1960s. This suggests a weakening of attachment to party and, given the strong class orientation of British voters in the past, supports the notion that class is losing power as a determinant of party preference. Likewise, the steady decline in turnout at general elections, which fell from 84 percent in 1950 to 72 percent in 1970, is compatible with a decline in partisan attachment. The bearing of turnout on the role of class appears especially when it is noted that turnout fell markedly in solid working-class areas, particularly mining areas, while it rose slightly in almost all other types of constituency. The contrast with political behavior a decade or two ago is suggested by the 1960 Gallup poll, which concluded that no more than 20 percent of the electorate had ever changed parties and that of those who did change, most were Liberals.

With these declines in class-based political attitudes and partisan identification has gone a striking increase in electoral volatility. The voters, who seemed in the forties and fifties to change their party support only slowly and infrequently, now shift rapidly back and forth among the parties and "Don't Knows." Not long ago, once a Government had won power, it could count on enjoying wide public support for a period of years. In the emerging pattern, by contrast, a Government barely takes power before its public support begins to slip away and by-election defeats erode its majority. Moreover, changes of opinion among the electorate may be even greater than the shift away from one party indicates. This effect has been brought out by surveys conducted by the Conservative Central Office, which, especially since the mid-sixties, has made an extensive and highly professional use of survey research. Between the 1964 and 1966 general elections, the Conservative vote dropped from 11.6 million to 11 million. This small net change, however, was the result of large movements back and forth between the parties. Apparently, some 3.5 million Conservative voters moved away from the party, while some 2.9 million who had not supported the party in 1964 shifted over to the Conservative column. Overall, some millions of voters had changed parties.

The new volatility of British political opinion is also brought out in other survey data. One measure is the monthly change in the ratio of support for the two parties as shown in the Gallup surveys. When, for instance, the survey for one month shows Conservative support as 35 percent and Labour support as 30 percent and for the next month as 37 percent and 29 percent respectively, the Conservative lead has moved from 5 percent to 8 percent, constituting a change of 3 percent over these two months. In the early postwar years these changes were moderate. But between 1948 and 1970 the yearly average rose from 2 percent to 6 percent.

The raw data themselves indicate that something quite unusual has been happening in British politics. The Gallup monthly surveys measuring support for the parties were begun in 1947. On a graph the curves of support for the two main parties show a new pattern emerging in the sixties. While for the earlier postwar period the curves are relatively flat, for the sixties the slopes become markedly steeper, indicating large shifts of support up and down in short periods of time. Whether the central tendency of support for a party over a longer period of time, such as a year, was up or down, the dispersion of support around that tendency at shorter intervals had clearly increased. A conventional method of measuring such dispersion is to calculate the standard deviation. When this is done for the monthly data for each year, as in Table 11.5, volatility becomes vividly apparent, especially for the Labour party in the late sixties. On the Conservative side volatility showed some slight rise in the sixties, although the main increase took place in 1957 and 1958, when the party was in power, and just before the general election of 1959. Since 1965, on the other hand, Labour support in its up-and-down

Table 11.5 Index of Party Volatility Standard Deviations for British Gallup Polls

Year	Labour	Conservative
1947	6.86	4.91
1948	1.30	2.50
1949	2.33	4.07
1950	2.50	1.25
1951	6.02	2.27
1952	4.16	2.45
1953	1.25	1.45
1954	2.34	1.90
1955	0.74	2.24
1956	1.97	2.61
1957	2.36	11.34
1958	1.64	15.85
1959	1.46	6.47
1960	3.44	0.68
1961	1.80	4.72
1962	2.66	3.00
1963	1.81	1.35
1964	3.73	4.10
1965	8.04	6.24
1966	12.59	2.75
1967	14.48	6.39
1968	12.75	7.35
1969	14.90	4.53
1970	8.42	2.96
1971 (first six months)	7.31	7.08

DATA SOURCE: *Gallup Political Index, 1947–1971* (London: The Gallup Poll).

movements showed a volatility unmatched in the previous generation. Indeed, it was the volatility of the electorate that was responsible for the fact that almost all public opinion polls erred in their forecasts of the winner in 1970. Contrary to previous experience, the campaign did significantly affect voting intentions, and a late swing to the Conservatives just before polling day was missed by nearly all surveys.

Bases of Class Behavior

The most striking aspect of the general election of 1970 was not the Conservative victory in the face of contrary predictions by the polls, but rather the wide, wild swings of voter opinion between the parties in the years before the election— which, moreover, have continued after it. During the campaign, a Labour party agent of a London constituency was asked about this new volatility. "People don't vote the way they used to," he replied. "They don't vote like their fathers. They don't vote as members of a community or a class, but as a matter of individual choice." Normally in the past, in Britain perhaps even more than in other modern polities, a massive array of influences and institutions has corseted the individuality of the voter: family, neighborhood, class, church, pressure groups, parties, and so on. In this way political opinions and party preferences have been stabilized and indeed made heritable, and political leaders have been provided with those cohesive majorities that are necessary for steady and coherent governance.

As modernization proceeds, these old protective influences break up and fall away, leaving the individual voter isolated and unsupported, an atom in the mass electorate. Left to rely upon his own "private stock of reason"—to quote Burke's admonitory phrase—and whirled along by the forces of electronic communication, he will inevitably swing back and forth in his judgment of men, governments, and parties.

A new atomism in British society appears to be producing a new individualism in British politics. Negatively stated, the change appears especially as a decline in class solidarity, affecting both party activists and party voters. Local organization flags as activists fail to maintain old levels of effort and recruitment. Party voters generally draw back from their old allegiances—or, in the case of new voters, fail to develop the deep attachments felt by their fathers—and easily and frequently switch their political preference. While these changes also affect Conservatives, they are especially vivid on the Labour side. Not just the party, but also the trade unions are affected—the whole of what was called "the Movement." Like the party, unions are also faltering in recruitment and losing the loyalty of those who do remain members. Strikes tend to be numerous, small, and locally inspired. The push they give to price rises does at least as much harm to workers generally as to the profit makers, and it certainly does more harm to the unorganized and the poor. It would appear that while the great wave of industrial action in the first and second decades of this century reflected the rise of a united working class, the myriad uncoordinated strikes of the present phase result from its decline and decomposition (see Chapter 10).

Such a development seems natural and logical when we project some of the inherent tendencies of modernization. The concept of class is complex and ambiguous, but in political analysis it has commonly been used to identify certain sorts of social and economic conditions that promote concerted action among a number of people. As we have seen, in Britain two broad groupings of occupations can be identified whose members tend to vote similarly. Occupation has been an excellent indicator of the class to which a person will be assigned by himself and by others and of how he will vote. When we ask, however, what it is about an occupation that has led people to assign it to one class or another, no simple answer appears.

One influential aspect is standard of living. A person's occupation is a good rough index of his income and thus of what he can buy in the way of food, clothing, housing, education, and recreation. In this respect a qualitative change has transformed the standard of living of all occupational groups and classes in Britain, as in other Western countries, as a stage of unprecedented productive power has ushered in the age of affluence. Slums can still be found, and serious destitution afflicts many families. But the massive squalor of working-class London that horrified the reformers of the late nineteenth century, and which could still be found in spots during the interwar years, no longer exists. Moreover, the welfare state has supplemented the rise of affluence by creating a new level of security explicitly guaranteed by the society as a whole. Marked differences in standard of living remain, but the old inequities in material style of life between the working class and the middle class have been blurred and reduced.

During the 1950s, as real income in Britain rose an average of 3 percent a year under a Conservative regime and automobiles, refrigerators, and TV sets were acquired by families of all classes, Labour continued to lose, in four successive elections receiving a steadily declining percentage of the two-party vote. Some observers not unnaturally found in the new levels of consumption the roots of a political *embourgeoisement* that was turning the working class away from the old "cloth-cap" socialism. This view of the new political realities inspired the rise of revisionism under Hugh Gaitskell and, after him, Harold Wilson. The victories of the mid-sixties appeared to vindicate the revisionist analysis.

It may be doubted, however, that a social sentiment as strong as class identification can be greatly affected by a mere change in consumption levels. Another basis of class is often found not on the consumption but the production side of economic relations. In the Marxist view class distinctions are related to the mode of production, the owners of private property being set off from, and opposed to, the nonowners. This foundation for concerted behavior on the part of opposing classes, however, has also been greatly eroded in the collectivist phase of modernization. Ownership has become widely diffused. The control of economic enterprise has shifted into the hands of men who are not owners, but managers, while on lower levels the workers have formed unions and have dealt collectively with management. Thus the sharp distinction between owners and nonowners has been lessened by bureaucratization, and a degree of industrial democracy has moderated the conflict of interests and institutionalized its management.

Already during the early decades of this century in Britain, the rise of organized labor and organized business was marked by these tendencies. Also the huge growth of the public sector has absorbed from the private sector many of the conflicts between levels of a bureaucratized economy. At the same time, technology has further diminished distinctions among the various strata of employees by increasing the proportion of nonmanual to manual workers. In manufacturing alone, for instance, between 1954 and 1964 administrative, technical, and clerical workers rose from 18.4 percent to 23.1 percent of the work force.

A third and more fundamental basis of class distinctions is power: the ability of one person to impose his will upon another person. The concept is broad. It includes the ability to control others that results from shared conceptions of authority, as in the political system, or from other legitimizing beliefs, such as the right of the employer to hire and fire. It also extends to control based on physical force, economic benefits, or psychological identification. Income and property as determinants of class are specific forms of the broad category of power. Income is power over the labor and products of others, and property in the means of production is power to organize the labor utilizing them. Degree of power is a major determinant of the schemes of social evaluation expressed in popular conceptions of class. It is significant that in distinguishing between the two main classes, British respondents draw the line not precisely between manual and nonmanual occupations, but between the nonmanual occupations with and those without supervisory duties.

The possible foundations of a class system are as subtle and numerous as the forms of power. Seen in this light, the elimination of class may seem an endless quest, each new stage of equality being achieved only to reveal a new dimension of domination and subjection. To eliminate private property and equalize incomes would not necessarily eliminate class, because great differences in power might remain. Indeed, under some circumstances these steps might intensify class distinctions and class conflict—if the new polity were founded on dictatorial bureaucratic socialism, for example.

Income, property, and power in their protean forms help account for class-based behavior. They are sometimes referred to as "objective" bases of class, a term that is permissible only if it is recalled that social relationships are never objective in the sense of being purely physical patterns, but always involve meaning. Keeping this in mind, we may identify another aspect of class that is relatively more subjective. This consists in a culturally conditioned mode of perceiving the objective relationships of affluence, ownership, organizational position, and domination and subjection. With respect to this cultural aspect, societies may differ greatly even though they resemble one another in economic structure. Thus although both countries are highly industrialized, the sense of class is much stronger in Britain than in the United States. In Britain a "sense of degree" has long been a powerful ingredient of the social outlook normally passed on to each generation. This difference in the "inner eye" of the Briton means a greater readiness, as compared with an American, to perceive social stratification and to identify with a class. As an influence on behavioral solidarity and conflict the effect is to reinforce other bonds arising from objective factors and to enhance class-based action in economic and political life.

Modernization and Class

Modernization has a bearing on this potent force in British political life because of its patently premodern origins. From one era to another the sense of degree has taken different concrete forms, and the various categories of persons in society have differed in numbers, in functions, and in relations with one another: from the "sundry estates and degrees of men" of old Tory times; to the "ranks, orders, and interests" of the eighteenth century; to the "upper, middle, and lower classes" of

Victorian days; down to the occupational hierarchy of contemporary collectivist Britain, where the leading positions of the various bureaucratic sectors constitute not an estate, or governing, class, but "the Establishment." Throughout,
however, the ideas of hierarchy and degree and the sentiments of deference
and noblesse oblige have powerfully shaped political, economic, and social relations.

The thrust of modernity has been mixed, but on the whole contrary to inequality
and class. In their structures of control, industrialization and bureaucratization have
often created new objective references for the class system. New hierarchies of
capitalist and entrepreneur in the nineteenth century and of technocratic and
managerial elites in the twentieth century constitute realities on which the inherited
expectations of the Briton can crystallize. On the other hand, modernity has
mobilized ever new levels of the populace and has drawn them into political
participation. Upbringing is being supplanted by education as a basis for advancement and for judging capacity. Mobility is undermining the family and neighborhood foundations of working-class culture. Above all, voluntarism, with its
increasingly democratic and egalitarian tendencies, works against distinctions and
identities based on social evaluation. Abstractly, its goal is a single, universal class
of equal and independent individuals.

The upshot of modernization, it should be repeated, is to undermine not only
the distinctions but also the identities of the class system. The solidarity of the
working class on which the Labour movement in its political and economic forms
was founded derived both from the objective structures of nineteenth-century
capitalism and from the attitudes of premodern traditionalism. The current phases
of modernization weaken both the modern and the premodern bases of class.
Affluence and bureaucratization, democratic participation through party government and functional representation, and not least the advance of the rational,
egalitarian spirit in British political culture have been loosening the bonds of class
as both a horizontal and a vertical force of integration. The new volatility of
electoral behavior is a natural expression of this new atomism in social structure.

To say that modernity dissolves the hierarchical and corporatistic heritage of
medievalism is merely to point again to what deeply alarmed the earliest critics of
modernity. Burke feared the tendencies of his time to destroy the organic unities,
"the little platoons" and the great "establishments," that helped both to preserve
order and to satisfy the human heart. At the start of the nineteenth century Auguste
Comte was no less alarmed by the prospect of disintegration, as the increasing
division of labor in both the economic and moral spheres threatened, in his eyes,
to "snuff out the spirit of togetherness." Later Emile Durkheim saw society becoming a "dust of individuals," while the Fabian Graham Wallas feared the lack of
"sufficient cohesive force" in modern society. In the British polity class has been
such an integrating force and a principal aspect of "the modernity of tradition."
In the course of development, however, modernity may come to overbalance
tradition so far that the old solidarities are set on the way to final dissolution.

The Liberal Revival

Along with party decomposition and heightened electoral volatility, certain new forms of political action have suggested possible future patterns of organization and purpose. As attachment to the two major parties flagged in the sixties, new modes of action attracted support. Leading the way was the Liberal party which enjoyed a vigorous but brief revival that elaborated themes that came to be strongly reflected in the new politics of reform of the late sixties and the early seventies.

As tends to happen when a successful party of innovation is confronted by a new challenge, the Liberals, after their great Radical victories before World War I, being faced by the powerful upsurge of socialism, rapidly lost electoral and financial support to the Conservatives. By 1935 the new party dualism of Labour versus Conservatives as well as the new issues of collectivism had been decisively established (see Appendix E). During the height of the collectivist period, the Liberal members of the House were reduced to half a dozen, while observers, hard put to explain even such tenuous survival, impatiently awaited the party's final demise. Then quite unexpectedly, beginning in the very late fifties and continuing with increasing strength through the early sixties, the Liberals staged a strong recovery. By 1964 their vote for Parliament had risen to 3 million, four times what it had been in the mid-fifties. At the same time they also made striking gains in local elections, probably quadrupling their representation on local councils of all categories. Moreover, the number of seats won at Westminster and in localities was never proportionate to the strong surge of favor recorded in opinion surveys. At one point in 1962, the Gallup survey showed that with the support of fully 30 percent of the sample the Liberals by a slight margin outpolled both the big parties.

While Liberal strength soon sank back to its previous level, the revival brought forward a distinctive critique of collectivist policy. As Liberals themselves insisted, they were not merely a third party poised between Conservatives and Socialists, but rather, as the representatives of the individualist position, the sole alternative at an opposite pole from the two great adherents of collectivism. Thanks in no small part to Jo Grimond, the politically magnetic and intellectually distinguished head of the party during the revival, this emphasis was embodied in constructive criticism that did much to transform the terms of political discussion in Britain.

The new ideas put forward by the Liberals centered on two serious and virtually inherent deficiencies of the managed economy and welfare state. These have occupied earlier pages of this study, so they need only be briefly mentioned and related to the problem at hand. First, the managed economy, by making national economic efficiency its chief goal, must often downgrade local economic and social values. In 1963, for instance, the so-called Beeching Report, charged with making proposals to reduce the deficits of the British railroad system, recommended that most lines that were not paying their way be closed down. It so happened that the major portion of the railroads of both Scotland and Wales were in this position, the upshot being that when the recommendations were carried into effect, much hardship was suddenly visited on many rural areas in the Celtic fringe.

Yet given its terms of reference the report made good sense. In this way what may appear to local eyes as overcentralized and bureaucratic government is less a matter of choice than a natural consequence of the basic goals and structures of the managed economy. Moreover, these situational forces are supplemented by political pressures. Producers groups usually have a national coverage and act through centralized structures that find parallel organizations in central government departments to which the groups have ready access and in which they find similar national viewpoints.

The flaw in the welfare state consists in the dysfunctions of universalism. Modern egalitarianism, as in democratic socialism, leads to schemes for flat-rate benefits, available to all free of means tests (see Chapter 10). Ironically, however, the commitment to universalism may result in many of the most needy being excluded, while benefits go to those not greatly in need. In 1965 the Milner Holland Committee reported that this was the overall effect of the British system of housing subsidies; council tenants of public housing and owner-occupiers received substantial aid even though not poor, while private tenants, who included a far higher percentage of the poor, received no such help. Here again the political factor is important. Benefits directed only to the few poor may be unpopular with the taxpaying majority, while a scheme that spreads benefits to the many not in need is likely to be well-received. As a result, an arrangement intended to tax the majority for the sake of the needy minority becomes one in which the majority tax themselves for their own benefit.

With regard to both deficiencies of British policy, the Liberals took a strong initiative, putting forward their ideas as early as 1962 in a series of well-argued pamphlets on tax reforms, industrial organization, education, consumer protection, social policy, and reform of local and regional government. Their bias toward dispersion of power was reflected in their support for copartnership in industry and plant bargaining in industrial labor relations. Their faith in local self-government, an ancient Liberal orthodoxy, was expressed in detailed proposals to strengthen local government and promote devolution. While favoring greater equalization of opportunity in their tax, education, and consumer reports, their housing proposals reflected their concern to get at this aspect of the problem of poverty by a selective approach.

Their revival tells us something important both about the Liberals and about the present tendencies of British politics. One reason the Liberals were especially sensitive to these deficiencies of the welfare state and managed economy was that they had never in the first place fully accepted the collectivist system. Odd as some of their policy proposals had been at times—and as a minor party anxiously looking for supporters they did tend to pick up some freakish allies—they retained a basic allegiance to the political, economic, and especially moral aspects of their nineteenth-century individualism. One of the most striking traits of Liberals, as their attitudes have been revealed in opinion surveys, is their rejection of class. They reject class both as an analytic concept explaining behavior and as a normative concept indicating to the individual where his social allegiance should lie. Moreover, the party enjoys a remarkably even spread of support among all strata, in contrast with the polarization of support for Conservatives and Labour. "In marked contrast to the intimate ties between class and Conservative and Labour support," as Butler and Stokes remark, "support for the Liberals was remarkably unrelated to class self-image and to occupational grade."[4] Like their great Victorian predecessors, individualist in outlook and hostile to class, the Liberals carried these older values into the collectivist age and, as the orthodoxies of that age began to weaken, came into their own. They had endured long enough to become relevant once again—but only for a moment.

The New Politics of Reform

It is a seldom-examined cliché that small third parties are a source of new ideas in a two-party system. In the case of the Liberal revival this did happen. During the sixties the big parties put forward on their own many of the proposals being urged by Liberals, partly in response to the same conditions, but also partly in imitation of the Liberal lead. "The Grimond decade," wrote *The New York Times,* "will be remembered . . . as a time when the Liberals sowed for others to reap; when their efforts in several key areas had enough impact to persuade both Tory and Labour Governments to steal their policies."[5] One fully intentional result was that the Liberal appeal was blurred and weakened in favor of the two main parties.

Also influential in offsetting the Liberal appeal was the development of initiatives often launched by the Liberals by a host of new reform groups outside the two-party system. Such groups, which are sometimes termed promotional or cause groups to distinguish them from the interest-oriented groups that people the structures of functional representation, have occupied a large place in British politics since their first appearance as the earliest movers of nineteenth-century liberalism (see Chapter 9). Yet it is fair to say that recent years have seen an increase in their numbers and activities, especially a shift to concern with the gaps and the deficiencies of collectivist policy. They include such well-known organizations as the Howard League for Penal Reform, the National Council for Civil Liberties, and the National Society for the Prevention of Cruelty to Children. One of the more notable has been the Child Action Poverty Group. Founded in 1965, it took the Wilson Government severely to task for the fact that the problem of family poverty had actually worsened under Labour's rule. The group's influence was acknowledged when the Government adopted its proposal to help the very poor by increasing family allowances for all families and then "clawing back" a large portion of the sum distributed by taxing those who were better off. The problem of homeless people in the welfare state led to the founding in 1966 of SHELTER by an explosive

---

[4]Butler and Stokes, *op. cit.,* p. 79.

[5]January 18, 1967, p. 42.

young New Zealander named Des Wilson. Within three years, it became one of the largest charitable organizations in Britain, raising £2 million and itself providing housing for some 3,000 families. During the sixties there was also a proliferation of small, local voluntary associations. In 1960 the first Association for the Advancement of State Education was set up; by 1966 there were 120. The Councils for Social Service, which had long existed as coordinating bodies for local social-service organizations, showed a vigorous new life. In the early sixties, membership in the National Union of Students, the official and long-established student organization, grew rapidly from 150,000 to nearly 400,000. At the same time advocates of "student power" produced the Radical Students Alliance.

Writing of the new politics in general, one Labour observer recently commented,

> Thousands of such pressure groups or action groups have come into existence: community associations, amenity groups, shop-stewards movements, consumer societies, educational campaigns, organisations to help the old, the homeless, the sick, the poor or under-developed societies, militant communal organisations, student power, noise abatement societies, and so on.[6]

Local self-assertion against central government achieved its sharpest form in the sudden surge of Celtic nationalism. The Scottish National party, championing ultimate independence from Westminster, had only modest success after its founding in 1928, polling less than 1 percent of the total vote in Scotland by 1959. In the next decade, however, membership in the party rose from 2,000 to 135,000; and in the election of 1970 the party won 11.4 percent of the total Scottish vote, although this gave it only one seat in Parliament. The change in outlook and sentiment that accompanied this change in voting behavior is illustrated by the drastic shift in rhetoric of the Scottish trade-union movement. From the time of its foundation in 1897, the Scottish T.U.C. had disdained nationalist sentiment and had used the standard rhetoric of all-British working-class solidarity and socialist centralism. Then abruptly in the sixties Scotland and its problems shifted to the center of the Scottish T.U.C.'s deliberations.

Plaid Cymru, the Welsh Nationalist party, founded in 1925, also grew rapidly in the sixties, by 1970 its membership reaching 40,000 and its vote in the general election 11.5 percent of the total in Wales. It may also be noted that the Cornish Nationalists, known as Mebyon Kernow, or Sons of Cornwall, were represented by a candidate who won 2 percent of the vote in his constituency, while a hotelkeeper championing more local self-government for the Isle of Wight won 2.8 percent of the vote there under the banner of the Vectis Nationalists—Vectis being the Latin name for the island.

---

[6]Anthony Wedgewood Benn, *The New Politics: a socialist reconnaissance,* Fabian Tract 402 (London, 1970), p. 9.

Conclusion

After a period of stability, the British polity is changing, perhaps in quite fundamental ways. Already this development has impaired the performance of government. The decline of class and of the complex of traditional sentiments that have been associated with class have had a disintegrating effect in the spheres of both authority and purpose. The solidarity of support for the parties has been weakened. A new volatility deprives Governments of the time and toleration needed to develop new lines of policy and put them into effect. Such a loss of authority weakens party government as a means of social choice and popular control.

The loosening of these traditional bonds of social cohesion also affects the moral coherence of the parties. Vernon Bogdanor has written that the fragmentation of socialist ideology is in part "a reflection of the erosion of the social base of the Labour Party, the manual working class." When the party was formed, this class was

> sufficiently united in its aims to provide a broad and coherent basis for a common policy. But with the weakening of class feeling, the social base of the Labour Party has become eroded. And with the erosion of the social base, the politics became eroded also. The Labour Party thus ceased to provide an agenda for radical change. On the central issues which faced it in office—on devaluation, on the maintenance of military bases East of Suez and on the Common Market—the Labour Party found itself divided. It could be held together only by the tactical skill and the political ambiguity of Harold Wilson. [7]

As history produced the parties that flourished in the collectivist age, history may transform them in the future. That ancient and essentially political distinction between classes founded upon domination and subjection will surely persist and, given the technocratic trends of modernity, may become even more marked and significant. Yet modernization has weakened many of the bases of the two-party system, and the new political initiatives of recent years may prefigure a looser, more diffuse, more individualist system for expressing different views of the common good. These neo-Victorian pressure groups must remind one of a time when parties were far less cohesive, monopolistic, and authoritative than they are today.

In content as well as form the new politics brings an echo of the past. The attempt on both the Left and the Right to decentralize and give expression to local and regional aspirations appears to be another individualist phase of the recurring individualist-collectivist cycle in British political development. Along with this turning away from collectivism, the issues of the future may include a new expression of the ideal of equality, which accepts the security brought by the welfare state but qualifies the consequences of its universalism and bureaucracy.

---

[7]Vernon Bogdanor, "The Labour Party in Opposition, 1951–1964," in Vernon Bogdanor and Robert Skidelsky (eds.), *The Age of Affluence, 1951–1964* (London, 1970), p. 114.

Radically new and postmodern issues might arise. The framework of values developed by the party system over the past 300 years came into existence at the same time as the modern nation-state (see Chapter 9). Moreover, while the national question has at times caused bitter and even violent struggles, the main conflicts of political development have presupposed a "united kingdom" and a sovereign state. The prospect of Britain's entry into the Common Market, however, raises the question of whether this step may not create a new dimension of political controversy and party division. On the class conflict that has been such an important focus of British party conflict, entry into Europe may intrude a center-periphery division, the lines of party conflict being drawn between those who favor and those who oppose further integration of Britain with Europe and of the constituent nations into one polity. If so, a qualitatively new issue would be introduced transcending the boundaries that for some 300 years have limited the party battle to the arena defined by the coordinates of equality-inequality and of collectivism-individualism.

Epilogue: Northern Ireland

Northern Ireland—or Ulster, as the region has been called since the Middle Ages —is an apt theme to provoke final reflections on British government and politics. It challenges collectivist politics by refusing to conform to the categories of class-based political behavior. It challenges British politics as a severe test of the ability of British leaders and institutions to solve a fundamental problem. For the political scientist Northern Ireland is a challenge to the British political system, because it raises the question whether Ulster should be considered a part of that system for the purposes of political analysis.

Before the United Kingdom government in London imposed "direct rule" in March 1972, the government of Northern Ireland was the most striking example of territorial decentralization in the British political system. Its authority was based on an act of 1920 that gave Ulster wide powers of Home Rule. The act distinguished between "reserved powers," dealing with such questions as defense, treaties, and nearly all taxation, which continued to be matters for the London government, and the remaining powers of government, called the "transferred powers," which included jurisdiction over health, education, welfare, employment, agriculture, commerce, transport, and a small range of taxation. To exercise these transferred powers, a government was set up in Belfast with its administrative center on the outskirts of that city at Stormont Castle, from which was taken the name by which the regime was commonly known.

In the British manner, the Stormont government included a responsible Cabinet and a bicameral legislature, consisting of a House of Commons with fifty-two members and a Senate with twenty-six. Since Ulster was ruled in some fields of policy from London, its six counties were also divided into constituencies of the United Kingdom Parliament, to which twelve members were sent. The Stormont regime, one might say, was an intermediate tier of government between the usual array of local authorities and the central government in London—rather like an American state, except for the crucial fact that London retained the supreme authority to alter or abolish these arrangements.

This exceptional regime was established because the Protestant majority of the North refused to join the Irish Free State—later called the Republic of Ireland, or *Éire*—which was set up by the overwhelmingly Catholic South of Ireland after a long and violent struggle against British rule. With Protestants outnumbering Catholics about two to one, the Ulster polity divided sharply along religious lines, and the Ulster Unionists, the political arm of the Protestant majority, never had less than forty of the fifty-two seats in the lower house. Moreover, knowing that many or most Catholics wished to see a united Ireland, the Unionists took further steps, such as gerrymandering and limitations on the franchise, to reduce Catholic political power in local government and at Stormont. In the case of Ulster, the result of territorial decentralization of government was not to increase democracy, but to diminish it.

The politics of Ulster departs sharply from the collectivist model that prevails generally in the rest of the United Kingdom. In Northern Ireland voting follows the lines of religious cleavage, and these lines cut across class divisions. Protestants tend to outnumber Catholics in the better-paying and more prestigious occupations, but members of both religious communities can be found in all social and economic strata. As Richard Rose points out, "there are more poor Protestants than there are poor Catholics."[8] If Ulster voters behaved as British voters do, Northern Ireland would be a promising field for socialist politics. But in fact the Northern Ireland affiliate of the Labour party was never able to win more than four of the twenty-two industrial constituencies of the Stormont Parliament. Nor have the more radical efforts of recent years—as symbolized, for instance, by the fiery Bernadette Devlin—been any more successful in building a substantial political following on a working-class appeal. On the contrary, working-class Protestants, like Protestants of the professional and managerial classes, have voted overwhelmingly Unionist in elections to the Stormont Parliament and to the London Parliament, where the eight Unionist M.P.s accept the Conservative whip. Similarly, the Orange Lodges, a social organization of militant Protestants, include members from all classes.

Judging from behavior as well as rhetoric, it is obvious that the religious cleavages of Ulster are important to its political divisions. Yet this religious background provokes almost as many questions as it answers. One problem is that the correlation between religion and political affiliation that prevails in Ulster does not carry over to other parts of the United Kingdom. In various parts of Britain there are substantial numbers of Catholic voters. But in contrast with their coreligionists in Ulster, they fit fairly easily into the collectivist model, tending for the most part to

---

[8]Richard Rose, *Governing Without Consensus: An Irish Perspective* (London, 1971).

vote Labour (along with millions of Protestants), in accordance with the high percentage of manual workers among them.

It is tempting to say that in Ulster religion is merely an indicator of a deeper cleavage, which centers on nationality. From the 1920s the principal opposition party in the Stormont Parliament has called itself "nationalist" and has aspired to unity with the South. In its constitution Dublin claims to be the legitimate government of the whole island, including Ulster. Certainly, the Catholics of Ulster claim passionately that they are Irish in nationality—and hence, should be under an all-Ireland government. But again there is a difficulty: Ulster Protestants also claim Irish nationality, and not unnaturally, since their ancestors came to Ireland more than three hundred years ago. This claim to a common nationality, it would seem, should be a bond of unity between Catholics and Protestants. And indeed it was during the eighteenth century, when men of both religious persuasions resisted the British and many worked and fought together for a united, secular, and republican Ireland. Today, however, the Protestant Irishmen of Ulster say that they are also British in nationality and look to Britain for their security.

The pursuit of security is an important clue to the political behavior of Ulstermen generally. On both sides of the barricades, fear moves people to their depths. We may ask what real reason there can be for such fear. No doubt the Unionists have used their political power in discriminatory ways. Scandalous instances of discrimination in the assignment of public housing have been brought forward by Catholic spokesmen. Belfast's development efforts have favored the industrialized Protestant East over the more rural and Catholic West, and unemployment has been higher among Catholics than Protestants. Yet Catholics in large numbers do enjoy the benefits of subsidized public housing. Ulster has adopted nearly all the social services of the British welfare state—with the help of substantial British financial aid—and Catholics share these on the same terms as others. On their side, Protestants fear the influence of the Catholic Church on any government of a united Ireland, with all this might mean in the form of censorship and church interference with the rights of privacy in such matters as contraception.

Yet even if we grant that there is substance to the fears each side entertains toward the other, the effects must still seem unbelievably out of proportion to the causes. The objective realities are simply inadequate to explain the bitterness and bloodshed of the past few years, not to mention that in previous generations. For this sort of intercommunal rioting and homicide, down to the very patterns of street fighting in the very same streets, has been a recurrent feature of the life of Belfast for a hundred and fifty years. Indeed, this terrible heritage from the past, sustained by myth and legend and renewed each generation by traumatic experience, is a principal key to understanding the tragedy of the present. Every observer of Ulster's passion has emphasized the power of history, and any observer of the TV clips of the rioting can see how that power is perpetuated. From the age when he is first able to throw a stone and utter a curse, the child brought up in this discord acquires a sense of identity as one who attacks and is attacked by Protestants/Catholics. Attitudes that have their genesis in these formative years do not need reasons in order to continue producing their terrible effects. In short, the sheer fact that Ulster Catholics and Ulster Protestants have fought one another so bitterly for so long is a principal explanation of why they continue to fight today.

A background of concrete social interaction can, of course, have a happier consequence when it has followed patterns of harmony and cooperation. Such a historical background has helped give the British system that strong sense of national community that has enabled it to sustain the shocks and discords of modern politics. But Ulster does not belong to this community and the political system founded upon it. Nor does Ulster belong to the community that sustains the polity of Southern Ireland. History that has made nations of both Britain and Éire has made of Ulster a kind of anti-nation with a hopelessly divided regime.

Select Bibliography

Basic Factual Information

Annual Abstract of Statistics. Annually revised. London: H.M.S.O.

The Annual Register of World Events. Annually revised. London: H.M.S.O.

Britain: An Official Handbook. Annually revised. London: Her Majesty's Stationery Office (H.M.S.O.).

Butler, David, and Jennie Freeman. British Political Facts: 1900–1968. London: Macmillan, 1969.

National Income and Expenditure. Annually revised. London: H.M.S.O.

British Constitutional and Political Development

Amery, L. S. Thoughts on the Constitution. 2nd ed. London: Oxford University Press, 1953.

Bagehot, Walter. The English Constitution. 1st ed. London: Chapman and Hall, 1867, and subsequent eds.

Birch, A. H. Representative and Responsible Government. London: Allen and Unwin, 1964.

Chrimes, S. B. English Constitutional History. London: Oxford University Press, 1965.

Feiling, K. G. History of England from the Coming of the English to 1938. Oxford: Clarendon Press, 1950.

Guttsman, W. L. The British Political Elite. London: Macgibbon and Kee, 1963.

Keir, D. L. The Constitutional History of Modern Britain. 7th ed. London: Adam and Charles Black, 1964.

Marsh, D. C. The Changing Social Structure of England and Wales. London: Routledge, 1965.

Taylor, A. J. P. English History 1914–1945. Oxford: Oxford University Press, 1965.

Cabinet and Prime Minister

Crossman, R. H. S. The Myths of Cabinet Government. Cambridge, Mass.: Harvard University Press, 1972.

Daalder, Hans. Cabinet Reform in Britain 1914–1963. Stanford, Calif.: Stanford University Press, 1963.

Jennings, Sir William Ivor. *Cabinet Government.* 3rd ed. Cambridge, England: Cambridge University Press, 1959.

King, Anthony, ed. *The Prime Minister.* London: Macmillan, 1969.

Mackintosh, John P. *The British Cabinet.* 2nd ed. London: Stevens, 1968.

Morrison, Herbert. *Government and Parliament.* London: Oxford University Press, 1954.

Walker, P. G. *The Cabinet.* London: Jonathan Cape, 1970.

Civil Service and Administration

Campbell, G. A. *The Civil Service in Britain.* 2nd ed. London: Duckworth, 1965.

Chester, D. N., and F. M. G. Willson. *The Organisation of British Central Government 1914–1964.* London: Allen and Unwin, 1968.

Clarke, J. J. *The Local Government of the United Kingdom.* 15th ed. London: Pitman and Sons, 1956.

Cohen, E.W. *The Growth of the Civil Service 1780–1939.* London: Allen and Unwin, 1941.

Dale, H. E. *The Higher Civil Service.* London: Oxford University Press, 1941.

The Fulton Committee. *Report on the Civil Service.* Vol. 1, Cmnd. 3638. London: H.M.S.O., 1968.

Griffith, J. A. G. *Central Departments and Local Authorities.* Toronto: University of Toronto Press, 1966.

Mackenzie, W. J. M. and J. W. Grove. *Central Administration in Britain.* London: Longmans, Green, 1957.

Report of the Royal Commission on Local Government in England. *(Maud Report.)* Vol. 1, Cmnd. 4040. London: H.M.S.O., 1969.

Public Enterprise and Economic Planning

Beer, S. H. *Treasury Control: the Coordination of Financial and Economic Policy in Britain.* Rev. ed. Oxford: Clarendon Press, 1957.

Brittan, Samuel. *Steering the Economy: the Role of the Treasury.* London: Secker and Warburg, 1969.

Caves, Richard E. et al. *Britain's Economic Prospects.* Washington, D. C.: Brookings Institution, 1968.

Control of Public Expenditure (Plowden Report). Cmnd. 1432. London: H.M.S.O., 1961.

Dow, J. C. R. *The Management of the British Economy 1945–60.* Cambridge, England: Cambridge University Press, 1966.

Eckstein, Harry. *The British Health Service: Its Origins, Structure and Achievements.* Cambridge, Mass.: Harvard University Press, 1959.

Grove, J. W. *Government and Industry in Britain.* London: Longmans, 1962.

Hall, Mary P. *The Social Services of England & Wales.* London: Routledge, 1969.

Shonfield, Andrew. *Modern Capitalism: the Changing Balance of Public and Private Power.* London: Oxford University Press, 1965.

Parliament

Butt, Ronald. *The Power of Parliament.* London: Constable, 1967.

Crick, Bernard. *The Reform of Parliament.* London: Weidenfeld and Nicolson, 1964.

Finer, S. E., H. B. Berrington, and D. Bartholomew. *Backbench Opinion in the House of Commons, 1955–1959.* London: Pergamon Press, 1961.

Hansard House of Commons Debates. London: H.M.S.O., daily, weekly, and annually.

Jennings, Sir Ivor. *Parliament.* 3rd ed. Cambridge, England: Cambridge University Press, 1957.

May, Sir Thomas Erskine. *Treatise on the Law, Privileges, Proceedings and Usage of Parliament.* 18th ed. London: Butterworth, 1971.

Richards, Peter. *Honorable Members.* 2nd ed. London: Faber, 1964.

Young, Roland. *The British Parliament.* London: Faber, 1962.

Parties, Interest Groups, and Electoral Behavior

Beattie, Alan, ed. *English Party Politics*. 2 vols. 1600–1906 and 1906–1970. London: Weidenfeld, 1970.

Beer, S. H. *British Politics in the Collectivist Age*. Rev. ed. New York: Vintage Books, 1965.

Blondel, Jean. *Voters, Parties and Leaders: The Social Fabric of British Politics*. Harmondsworth, England: Penguin Books, 1963.

Butler, David, and Michael Pinto-Duschinsky. *The British General Election of 1970*. London: Macmillan, 1971.

Butler, David, and Donald Stokes. *Political Change in Britain: Forces Shaping Electoral Choice*. New York: St. Martins Press, 1969.

Eckstein, Harry. *Pressure Group Politics: the Case of the British Medical Association*. Stanford, Calif.: Stanford University Press, 1960.

Finer, S. E. *Anonymous Empire: A Study of the Lobby in Great Britain*. 2nd ed. London: Pall Mall Press, 1966.

Lieber, Robert J. *British Politics and European Unity: Parties, Elites and Pressure Groups*. Berkeley, Calif.: University of California Press, 1970.

Manzer, R. A. *Teachers and Politics*. Manchester, England: Manchester University Press, 1970.

McKenzie, R. T. *British Political Parties: The Distribution of Power within the Conservative and Labour Parties*. 2nd ed. London: Heinemann, 1963.

———— and A. Silver. *Angels in Marble: Working Class Conservatives in Urban England*. Chicago and London: University of Chicago Press, 1968.

Nordlinger, Eric A. *The Working-Class Tories: Authority, Deference and Stable Democracy*. Berkeley, Calif.: University of California Press, 1967.

Ranney, Austin. *Pathways to Parliament: Candidate Selection in Britain*. Madison, Wisc.: University of Wisconsin Press, 1965.

Rasmussen, J. S. *The Liberal Party: A Study of Retrenchment and Revival*. London: Constable, 1965.

Rose, Richard. *Influencing Voters: A Study of Campaign Rationality*. New York: St. Martins Press, 1967.

Self, P., and H. Storing. *The State and the Farmer*. Berkeley, Calif.: University of California Press, 1962.

Wootton, G. *The Politics of Influence: British ex-servicemen, Cabinet decisions and cultural change (1917–57)*. Cambridge, Mass.: Harvard University Press, 1963.

Academic Journals

The British Journal of Political Science

Government and Opposition

Parliamentary Affairs

The Political Quarterly

Political Studies

Public Administration

3

The French
Political System

Suzanne Berger

One

The Tradition of
Modernity in France

France was the first modern state. Secularization and political democracy may have appeared earlier in the United States, national bureaucracy and rationalized central administration may have been accomplished earlier in Prussia, and national political integration may have proceeded furthest in Britain. But it was in France that these processes of political modernization first coincided at the end of the eighteenth century to produce a state unlike any that Europe had ever known. The Revolution of 1789 was in this sense a modernizing revolution. It did not create the nation or the bureaucracy or even the urge to secularism and democracy—these had all existed in some form before the Revolution, as they had existed in the other European states. What the Revolution accomplished was to build a political system in which all these processes of modernization could be institutionally expressed and organized. What was new was not the values themselves, but the creation of a state to enforce them for the entire society. In the years of political struggle to restore the political system of the Revolution, the parties that contended understood that the battle over the legacy of the Revolution was the battle between political traditionalism and political modernity. Now, almost two hundred years after the Revolution, the values embodied in the Revolution have themselves become a tradition. Both Left and Right of the Fifth Republic draw on this legacy. And if in Britain contemporary politics show the modernity of tradition, French politics today represent the tradition of modernity.

France, Britain, the United States—all modern states—have developed different political institutions, values, and problems. If the processes of political modernization destroyed and eliminated the old political system and created a wholly new

333

one in its place, we would expect all modern states to be more or less identical. But in fact, political modernization does not clear the political terrain of all vestiges of the past and raise a new house on bare earth. Rather, modern states have been built on top of and with the half-collapsed, half-standing institutions of the past. States differ, however, in *how much* and *what* they preserve of the past. In the United States, for example, the legacy of the nation's beginnings is liberal, individualistic, and participant. In France the past is the society and politics of the "old regime": traditional, hierarchical, and static. With different pasts to build on, France and the United States, both modern industrial societies, developed political systems that are and most likely will continue to be very different.

Modern states differ not only because they build on different bases, but also because they make different choices about how much of the past to preserve in the modern political system. The French political elites, confronted with the issues of modern politics, made decisions that did not radically eliminate the old political values and institutions, but rather embodied them in the new order. France modernized by fusing elements of traditional and modern political systems into the state. In France, therefore, political modernity and political traditionalism coexist. The result is a state with certain great strengths and capacities. France, better than many other industrial nations, has been able to accommodate great social and economic change while protecting the fabric of society. The notions of social prestige, the values of social conservatism and familism, and the class structure that modern France inherited from the old regime all worked to slow down the process of industrialization and to ward off some of its harshest consequences for the social groups that in other countries suffered most. At the same time, the coexistence of competing values and institutions in politics has been the source of major strains and disruptions.

To understand why the French elites systematically preferred a solution that preserved significant parts of the traditional state and society, we would have to examine the social situation and aspirations of the elites themselves. But here we are primarily concerned not with why the elites chose to maintain traditional values and structures, but with the consequences of those decisions.

The decisions of the elites about how to integrate the remnants of the old polity and society into modern France—about how to modernize state and society— covered a wide range of different issues. The passionate debates over state subsidies to Church-run schools were in reality debates over the place of the Catholic church in a modern state. Legislative argument over the inheritance laws and laws governing corporations turned on different appreciations of the values of the family and the needs of modern industry. The political battles over agricultural tariffs were in fact battles over whether the state should protect a traditional sector of the economy even at the expense of industry. As the Radical party declared in 1934 in favor of preserving the traditional countryside in modern society:

Though the economic function of agriculture is important, some people have contested the utility of maintaining it because of its high costs. It is pointless to pose the problem in economic terms. The social benefits that the peasantry provides the nation are vital to national life and irreplaceable: no matter what their cost is, it must be paid.[1]

The choices that were made in all these cases where the stakes were the mix of traditionalism and modernity that the state would authorize have been profoundly important, for they have determined the major problems of contemporary French politics. The decisions of the elites about how to achieve national political integration are particularly important in this respect, for they relate directly to the two major weaknesses of the French state today: the contested legitimacy of government and the crisis of relations between citizens and the state.

The goal of national political integration is in certain respects imposed on all modern political systems, but there are more ways than one to organize power territorially, to integrate the national economy, and to create a political community. The French political elites had available to them several possible courses of action for achieving territorial integration, economic integration, and a certain integration of the political values of the national population. The alternatives they chose were decisive for the future of the state.

Territorial Integration

The territorial definition of France was a matter solved before the other problems of modernization moved onto the agenda of national politics. Through centuries of annexation, conquest, and royal marriages, the French monarchs had carved out a nation whose boundaries were by and large fixed at the beginning of the eighteenth century. After a period of rapid territorial expansion and contraction during the Revolutionary and Napoleonic wars, the Second Peace of Paris (November 20, 1815) defined the territory of France and settled Frenchmen within boundaries that they acknowledged as the legitimate confines of France. By the time when mass political participation and political parties were developing, the French generally agreed on who was and who should be French. The only outstanding territorial problem was the annexation by Germany of two provinces, Alsace and Lorraine, in the settlement of the Franco-Prussian War (1870–1871). Though this amputation of French territory generated different ideas about foreign policy and military preparation, it did not provide a basis for fundamental political alignments. Unlike Germany, where territorial questions provided a major axis of political division in the modern political system, France rarely experienced serious domestic political conflict over the territorial dimension of national power. The single major exception was the dissension over Algeria. In the conflicts that divided the French political elites over granting independence to Algeria, the Algérie-Française group opposed independence on the grounds that Algeria was not a colony but, rather,

---

[1]Cited in Serge Mallet, Les Paysans contre le passé (Paris: Seuil, 1962), p. 15.

an integral part of French territory. Despite the bitterness and violence of the controversy, once Algerian independence was granted, in 1962, the political groups that had mobilized around this territorial issue disappeared quickly.

Even after the territory over which the state should extend its authority was determined, the distribution of the state's power in this territory was still open for decision. The question of territorial integration involves a resolution of the question of how a state will exercise political power in the nation as a whole: how it will divide power and authority between the center and local and regional governments. By choosing a particular blend of centralization and decentralization, the state shapes the outcomes to three other political questions: How much political liberty will there be in the state? What kind of political participation will citizens experience? How will the barriers to political community that derive from the diversity of local situations, needs, and desires be overcome?

The relevance of the territorial organization of power to political freedom has been one of the recurrent themes of modern political theory. The writers of the American constitution were deeply concerned with this issue, and they believed that the federal system they adopted would best protect the freedom of individuals and groups, even though they recognized that federalism might not maximize the efficiency and effectiveness of the state. In France the theorist most concerned with this issue was Alexis de Tocqueville (1805–1859), whose studies of the Revolution of 1789 and notes on the Revolution of 1848 were reflections on the problems of freedom in a democratic society. Tocqueville observed that the process of democratization at work in France in the nineteenth century had as its principal outcome the destruction of intermediary groups between the individual citizen and the state. In the aristocratic old regime these intermediary groups were formed on the basis of birth and privilege, and they exercised many functions that today are considered political. The administration of justice, the levying and collection of taxes, and police functions were in the hands of private individuals or corporations, acting not as agents of the state, but rather, as the privileged wielders of rights that they had inherited or purchased. The central state could neither hire nor fire these secondary political actors; it could control them only by dispossessing them: only by "nationalizing" the power and authority exercised by these private groups. The centralizing monarchs had throughout the eighteenth century attempted to gain control of these autonomous centers of power, for example, by revoking the charters of autonomous municipal corporations. But the greatest pressure for the destruction of these intermediary groups came from the forces that sought a greater democratization of society and, therefore, tried to destroy aristocratic distinctions. The leveling of political privileges based on class and birth concentrated political power in the hands of the central government, which gradually became the sole repository of power and authority in the nation. As Tocqueville commented:

> The State has everywhere resumed to itself alone these natural attributes of sovereign power. In all matters of government the State tolerates no intermediate agent between itself and the people . . . all these various rights, which have been

successively wrested, in our time, from classes, corporations, and individuals, have not served to raise new secondary powers on a more democratic basis, but have uniformly been concentrated in the hands of the sovereign. Everywhere the State acquires more and more direct control over the humblest members of the community, and a more exclusive power of governing each of them in his smallest concerns.[2]

The state intervenes more and more in spheres of life once regulated autonomously by the individual or for the individual by some other group—family or class or corporation. This expansion of the central government into the sphere of personal liberty goes virtually unchecked, Tocqueville argued. The only effective obstacle to the extension of power is the resistance of another power, and in France democratization has removed those groups which once checked the power of the central state: the aristocracy and the feudal guilds and corporations. In Tocqueville's words:

> The circumstance which most contributed to secure the independence of private persons in aristocratic ages, was, that the supreme power did not affect to take upon itself alone the government and administration of the community; those functions were necessarily partially left to the members of the aristocracy: so that as the supreme power was always divided, it never weighed with its whole weight and in the same manner on each individual. Not only did the government not perform everything by its immediate agency; but as most of the agents who discharged its duties derived their power not from the State, but from the circumstance of their birth, they were not perpetually under its control. The government could not make or unmake them in an instant, at pleasure, nor bend them in strict uniformity to its slightest caprice—this was an additional guarantee of private independence.[3]

Tocqueville recognized that it would be impossible for an aristocracy to serve this role in a democracy, but he argued that there are functional equivalents to an aristocracy that a democratic nation might use. Freedom, he suggested, can be preserved in a democracy only by organizing separate, autonomous, and therefore competitive centers of political power. On his travels in America he had observed that voluntary associations of like-minded citizens, an independent judiciary, the press, and state and local governments were performing essentially the same function in checking the central government that the aristocracy had played in France during the old regime. What Tocqueville hoped for in France was the development of independent local institutions that would both provide citizens with political experience at the local level that they would carry over into participation in the state and, at the same time, check the powers of the central government.

---

[2] Alexis de Tocqueville, *Democracy in America* (New York: Schocken, 1961), Vol. II, pp. 363–364.

[3] *Ibid.*, pp. 386–387.

There have been many in France to challenge the premise of Tocqueville's thesis that the chief danger to freedom lies in the action of the central government and that the most important way to increase an individual's freedom is to expand the sphere in which he is not touched by the state. To the contrary, it has been argued that a strong state is the best guarantee of individual liberty and that action of the state may increase freedom and state inactivity reduce it. In France, the idea that centralization and liberty are directly related is best expressed in the Jacobin tradition. The Jacobins were a radical, activist faction that formed during the French Revolution, under the leadership of Maximilien Robespierre and Louis de Saint-Just. While other political factions saw the loosening of the grip of the central state in the wake of the Revolution as an opportunity for enlarging the liberties of local and provincial governments, the Jacobins sought to strengthen the authority of the central state. In the initiatives and independence of local centers of power, the Jacobins saw threats to the unity of the nation. And on this unity depended the freedom of the individual citizen. For the Jacobins justice required that the republic be one and indivisible. Laws must be the same for every citizen in every part of the nation. And if substantial discretion and autonomy were left to local authorities, this result would not be achieved. The citizen who lived in Lozère would be obeying laws different from those that governed the citizens of another department. The Jacobin conception of political justice implied, therefore, that only the central government should legislate.

Centralization receives political support in France not only from the Jacobin Left but also from an important section of the Right, which continues the legacy of the centralizing monarchs. Indeed, centralization has become a key tenet in the tradition of modernity shared by both Left and Right in contemporary France. In the recent debate over the creation of regional governments, the Communists referred to this tradition when they charged that dismantling the state would open France up to the greed of foreign monopolies and concluded that "to organize the region must not mean creating fiefs as was done in the past for barons. Political power can only be national and the law can only be the same for all Frenchmen, whether Bretons or Alsatians."[4] A Gaullist deputy, attacking the same regionalization proposals, wondered rhetorically whether the government should not put the regional advocates on trial for treason *("atteinte à la sûreté de l'Etat")* and appealed to Frenchmen of the Left and Right to defend the nation—"the sole political entity."[5] The Gaullist parliamentary group discussed regionalization and resolved: "In restoring the State, General de Gaulle gave strength back to the nation. We consider therefore that any attempt to disaggregate the State would lead to disaggregation of the nation."[6] At the heart of the conflict among French political elites about how to organize power in the nation lies the profound disagreement about

[4] *Le Monde,* January 6, 1971.

[5] *Le Monde,* December 8, 1970.

[6] *Le Monde,* January 8, 1971.

freedom in a modern state that is expressed in the conflict between the Jacobin thesis that centralization supports and increases the political liberty of citizens and Tocqueville's thesis that only decentralization of power can preserve freedom in a democracy.

The second issue at stake in decisions about the division of power between central government and local and regional governments is political participation. One of the principal concerns of contemporary political science has been the impact on the state of different patterns of civic participation. Whether citizens participate, how much, and in which kinds of organizations are all questions of critical importance for the state. The recruitment of new political leadership draws in large measure on the network of secondary political groups. The capacity of the state to manage the problems of society requires a chain of intermediary organizations capable of channeling social needs, desires, and information up to national centers of power and carrying back state policy. And finally, the stability of the political system as a whole depends on maintaining a delicate equilibrium whereby participation is neither so intense that the fate of the state hangs constantly in the balance nor so weak that the mass of citizens remains apathetic, passive, and uninvolved in politics and the regime can find no popular support.

The relationship between participation and the organization of the state is not, however, one-way. Participation does shape national politics, but at the same time national politics shapes the kind of participation that is possible and likely in a given state. In this regard the decisions on centralization are critical, for the degree to which power has been concentrated at a single central point or dispersed through the nation determines whether there will be participation, how it will be organized, and when it will occur. In France, for example, the Ministry of Education makes virtually all decisions about education everywhere in France, down to the scheduling of subjects in each school day. With power concentrated in Paris, what sense does it make for parents in a town to band together in a P.T.A. to try to influence local educators? Why participate in local voluntary educational associations when the power to change the school is not located on the local level? Why form local civic associations when the municipality has so little discretion in the use of its funds that virtually all matters must proceed through the prefecture, the departmental headquarters of the central government? Why belong to a local historical sites association when it is the Fine Arts bureaucracy in Paris that will decide what kind of tile must be used to roof an old church? Why participate at all in local groups when the questions that matter most to a community are by and large decided in Paris, far beyond the reach of local groups and local participants?

When local or regional governments have the political power and fiscal resources to resolve certain of their own problems, they provide targets for citizens who find opportunities within their reach for influencing politics. In France the pattern of centralization has made such opportunities scarce. The weakness of participation at the local level that results from this has two important consequences. Democratic politics requires that the political system provide experiences of conflict and compromise, discipline for group ends, and leadership and followership—in sum, a political education, both for political activists and for the interested but less active citizenry. This education, as well as the more specific skills of administration and planning that are the prerequisites of effective intervention in contemporary politics, can only take place through actual participation. By limiting the possibilities for participation, the French state has reduced the reservoir of civic experience and left only a small pool of political militants from which the state may draw to replenish its ranks. By controlling or eliminating the possibility for local initiative, the state does limit the risk of having incompetent or corrupt local officials, but at the same time it stunts the growth of responsible local leadership by depriving men at the local level of the resources for attaining their goals. By centralizing power at the top, the "republic one and indivisible" assures that the rules are the same everywhere. But this means that there is little chance that the rules can ever be changed.

The difficulty of bringing about political change is, indeed, the second consequence of the scarcity of opportunities for participation at the local level. The virtual impossibility of bringing about any significant change on local or middle levels of the system engenders frustration and apathy about politics and support for political ideologies and parties that aim at a total capture of the state and total transformation of the social system. Civic passivity and revolutionary politics are in a sense two sides of the same coin in France. Men feel either that change is impossible, and they become cynical and apathetic, or else they come to feel that the only way to change anything at all is to change everything: to capture the central government. If to influence local school policies, one must reach out and change the Ministry of Education in Paris, then the logical instrument of political action is the political party with a global political strategy, not the limited-purpose interest group. The centralization of France has, therefore, provided a permanent incentive for organization in ideological political parties with plans to transform the state and society and a permanent disincentive for groups with more limited and, potentially, more parochial concerns.

The decisions that the French made about the distribution of power in the nation have had a third set of consequences for politics. The division of power between the center and local or regional authorities is a matter that affects not only the liberty of citizens and their opportunities to participate but also how the country will be governed. It is difficult to imagine any country so simple and homogeneous that all decisions could be made in the capital. The diversity of needs and situations always requires that some discretion be left to men on the spot to appraise and act on the problems of the locality. As societies become modern, their complexity and diversity increase, so it becomes more difficult to concentrate power at any single point in the system.

As the modern state has assumed responsibility for the regulation of social and economic problems once left to the initiative of private groups, it has discovered the need for more information and for a kind of information that cannot simply be channeled up to the top. If the problem were only one of transmitting facts, advances in the field of computer technology might promise to make a completely centralized state possible. The fact is, however, that managing a modern economy requires not a set of discrete decisions but, rather, a process of decision making during which modification and adaptation of policies is continuously taking place in response to feedback from earlier decisions. Examples are easy to find, both in the economy and society. The development of a prototype aircraft, for example, like the setting up and administration of a welfare program, involves a series of complex decisions requiring judgments by persons directly in contact with the problem. Whenever such matters have to be referred to higher authority, the results are technological stagnation in the first case and tensions and pressure for self-rule and community power in the second. As the goals that are pursued through political institutions multiply, excessive centralization of power is more likely to paralyze the state than to increase efficiency.

While it is not possible for a modern state to govern society from the capital, there are more ways than one of moving political decision making closer to the problems. One method is decentralization: to give the authority for making a decision and the resources to carry it out to a body that is independent of the central government. In the United States, for example, decisions on education are ordinarily taken by state or local authorities and financed by their own fiscal resources. The independence of these subnational bodies is ensured in two ways. The state or local official has his own political base, for he has been directly elected and is not appointed by or responsible to the national government. And whereas in France, a local official can be recalled by the national government, the American President and Congress have no authority to remove a mayor or governor. The independence of American local government is the result, moreover, of its independent fiscal resources. State and local governments have the authority to levy taxes, within limits that they set for themselves and that are outside the purview of the national government. Just how different France is and the consequences of the differences will be discussed in Chapter 5. Here we intend only to suggest that moving power and authority closer to the problems, which in the United States (and in Britain and Germany to a lesser extent) is achieved by a decentralization of political power, in France is accomplished by another method: deconcentration. Deconcentration is the delegation of the power of the central government to one of its agents, who exercises this power in the region or locality. Rather than making local decisions in Paris or giving local officials the authority and resources to make their own decisions—the decentralized solution—the national government delegates its authority to one of its own representatives in the locality. In the words of one of Napoleon III's ministers, "Deconcentration means striking with the same hammer, after shortening the handle."

There have been three ways of shortening the handle in France, three different agents of the center who make decisions in the localities: the prefect, the representative of the government ministry, and the mayor. The most powerful of these is the prefect, who is the direct arm of the state, representing both the government and the Ministry of the Interior. Between the communes and the national government there is only one other governmental level: the department. There are ninety-five departments in France; in each of them executive power is exercised by a prefect. While the prefect formally shares power with an elected departmental council *(conseil général),* his legal prerogatives as well as the department's financial dependence on the central government give the prefect the real power in the department. The second set of state agents are the representatives sent out to the departments by the government ministries. They report both to the prefect, who is supposed to coordinate their local activities, and also back to their ministries in Paris. The third representative of the state is the mayor, who is the local agent of the Ministry of the Interior and thereby directly responsible to the prefect. Mayors are elected, but their dual role limits their independence; many of their decisions have to be approved by the prefect, who may, in fact, revoke them. As in the case of the departmental council, the power of the mayor is severely constrained by the limited possibilities of obtaining financial resources, except by recourse to the state.

The consequences of administering the country with deconcentrated rather than decentralized authorities are important. There are obvious advantages, the most important of which are associated with the uniformity that such a system can ensure. The common education and outlook of the prefects, as well as their common dependence on central authority, tend to produce the same kinds of decisions in all parts of the country. In France situations like those that arose in the United States when Southern governors defied the rulings of the Supreme Court on school desegregation would be inconceivable. The checks and controls with which the central government surrounds local officials also make municipal corruption of the kind that is common in the United States a rare occurence in France.

At the same time, however, the reliance on deconcentration instead of decentralization has heavy costs. In terms of its impact on citizen participation, deconcentration has much the same effect as the centralization of power. It limits the field for local initiative and deprives local leaders of political experiences that might prepare them for national politics. With respect to the quality of decisions, the reliance on a restricted set of state agents makes innovation difficult, for in areas where prefects or mayors lack expertise, they must fall back on formal rulings and precedent. A decentralized system, in contrast, is much less restricted to a given set of formal authorities; according to the needs of the situation, local authorities may create new bodies to deal with new problems. The diversification of urban problems in the United States has thus produced a multiplication of new governmental bodies: model-city boards, metropolitan districts, commissions, interstate commissions, port authorities, and so forth. In France, in contrast, there has been little institutional innovation because of the limits set by the hierarchical system in which authority is exercised. The institutional rigidity of the system makes it difficult to cope with new problems.

Economic Integration

Compared with her European neighbors, France attained a high measure of economic integration at an early stage in the process of political modernization. In contrast to Germany, where well into the nineteenth century a multitude of autonomous jurisdictions and sovereign powers posed barriers to trade, in France, the Revolution of 1789 tore down the last legal barriers to free exchange throughout the nation. Indeed, the obstacles to intranational trade had been severely weakened even before the Revolution, and the Revolution provided the final push that cleared the ground of the privileges with which provinces and cities, guilds, and corporations had protected monopoly rights.

The problem of establishing national markets for labor and capital and a set of national prices for goods is not solved merely by destroying the legal and political obstacles to exchange, however. To create a free flow of men and goods through the nation, an infrastructure of transportation and communication networks must be set into place. Despite the political turmoil of the half-century after the Revolution, the successive regimes carried out a vast program of building highways, secondary roads, and canals. Though regions at the periphery continued to experience difficulties in reaching urban markets, nonetheless the situation of the outlying provinces of France was far from that of the isolated regions of Italy, for example. In Italy, even after national unification, the differences between the traditional economy of the South and the modern industrial economy of the North survived, indeed increased, so that today economists often consider these two parts of the nation as separate economies in order to analyze the Italian economic system. In sum, national unification may be a necessary, but is not a sufficient, condition of economic integration.

France by the middle of the nineteenth century had achieved economic integration, but she had done so in a way that left two problems outstanding. First, the pattern of industrialization in France left intact many of the institutions of the traditional economy. These "feudal remnants" not only survived industrialization but were often reinforced by it. The case of agriculture is revealing. The modernization of farming with the use of machines, fertilizers, and scientific methods of cultivation and the appearance of large capitalist farms in the Paris Basin did not eliminate the large numbers of small and medium-sized peasant farms. Instead, the peasant farmers used modern technology to support their traditional enterprises. When fertilizers increased farm yields, the peasants used the new surpluses to maintain a large population on the family farm. When machines became available, the farmer who was losing his workers to the cities could continue to run his farm in much the same way as before, by simply replacing the farm laborer-turned-factory worker by a tractor or thresher. The modernization of agriculture was a process that did not rule out the survival of a large peasantry. Economics and technology, in short, left open several alternative solutions for the countryside. What was decisive were the policies of the French state, which encouraged the preservation of a large traditional peasantry.

The price of this choice was high. In order to permit the peasant on a small, inefficient farm to survive, the government supported agricultural prices at a high level. The state had to abstain from programs of modernization of farm structures, because the immediate result of policies to increase average farm size or encourage crop specialization by the more productive farmers would have been to reduce the number of farms. A fundamental transformation of the agricultural system that would have made French agriculture more productive would have sacrificed the traditional peasantry. This the state refused to do, and as a result, the price of food remained relatively high in France, perhaps slowing the rate of industrial growth.

Why did France choose to maintain the peasantry? More generally—for the cases of small commerce and business are like agriculture—why were traditional sectors of the economy preserved in the process of economic integration and modernization? The answers to these questions are political. The elites of France believed that the preservation of traditional structures alongside modern industrial structures was necessary for the political stability of the nation. The political equilibrium on which the governments of the Third and Fourth Republics were based was one in which industrial interests shared power with the representatives of the traditional sectors of the economy. In order to support this political balance, the economy could not be dominated by the interests and values of the modern industrial sector alone. Indeed modern industry itself, having grown up in the protective fold of a system that muted competition and rewarded values other than those of economic rationality, was not eager to eliminate traditional firms. These considerations were strengthened by the realization that dismantling the traditional countryside, for example, would trade peasant electors for working-class electors, thereby increasing the clientele of the socialist parties.

What are the consequences of the decision to maintain the traditional sectors of the economy alongside the modern sectors? The problems that France faces today in adjusting her economy to the competition of the other members of the European Common Market are in large measure a result of these political decisions of the past century. The family businesses of France are no match for the foreign firm that can draw on outside capital to finance its investments and on the expertise of trained managers to run the business. The small French farms have trouble competing with modern Dutch agriculture. The solutions that the state once developed for the economic integration of the traditional sectors of the economy become less and less viable as France is opened up to the competition of other producers. In the last decade in France there has been a new awareness of the costs of maintaining the less productive sectors of the economy, resulting in series of proposals for modernizing the most important of them: the nationalized industries, agriculture, and the railroads. Aside from the economic problems that such proposals raise, there remains the political dilemma: Can the regime afford to diminish the reservoir of traditional voters, from whom it draws support? The question of how to modernize the French economy without destabilizing the political system thus remains one of the most important issues in French politics today.

The historic pattern of economic integration has left another serious problem on the agenda of contemporary politics: regional disparities in economic development. The communication and transportation networks that made economic integration possible serve certain regions of France far better than others. The western periphery—Brittany and the Vendée—the Massif Central, and the departments in the Southeast are regions whose contacts with the rest of France are difficult. Highways and railroad lines are not only less densely distributed in these regions, relative to the rest of France, but they are also less modern. The same is true of telephones: In the region around Paris, 21 percent of the population have telephones, while in the Breton department of Côtes-du-Nord, for example, only 5 percent have.[7]

The problem of the "French desert," however, is a product not only of poor infrastructure but chiefly of the centralization of economic activity in a few regions and the underdevelopment of the rest of France. There are two comparisons that reveal the magnitude of regional disparities in France today: the contrast between Paris and the rest of France, and the contrast between the rich, industrial France northeast of a line from Mont-Saint-Michel to Arles and the poor, more traditional France southwest of it.[8] Political centralization in France is paralleled by a concentration of economic control and of working population in and around Paris. Over half the head offices of important firms in 1962 were located in that area—a degree of economic control out of proportion to the total amount of economic activity in the region, since only a third of the working population was located there. In contrast, the industrial region around Lyons, which has a work force half as large as that of Paris, has only one-seventh as many very large firms based in the area. As Kevin Allen and M. C. MacLennan concluded from their study of French regions: "The effects of this concentration in economic, social, administrative and political terms is observably large and as a result the area of influence of the Paris region is vastly superior to that of any other urban centre in France."[9] One measure of this predominance is the difference between family incomes in Paris as compared with the rest of the country. Household incomes (excluding social security benefits) in 1962 in Paris were 50 percent higher than anywhere else in the country. Wages and salaries in industry, agriculture, and services are highest in the Paris regions, while in the West, Southwest, and Massif Central they often do not reach even half the Paris level. Indeed, these three regions lag behind the rest of France on virtually all measures of standard of living, industrial strength, and modernization.

The differentials between "rich" France and "poor" France pose both economic and political problems. Because of the concentration of economic activity in the area around Paris and the facilities for easy communication and transportation,

---

[7]Yves Durrieu, *Régionaliser la France* (Paris: Mercure de France, 1969), p. 124.

[8]Kevin Allen and M. C. MacLennan, *Regional Problems and Policies in Italy and France* (Beverly Hills, Calif.: Sage, 1970), p. 125.

[9]*Ibid.*, pp. 143–144.

businesses prefer to locate there, rather than in regions like Brittany, where the traditional basis of the economy, agriculture, is in crisis and industrial jobs are badly needed, but where industry is weak and infrastructure poor. Industry continues to expand in Paris, creating problems of housing, schools, and urban transport, while in the provinces the people leaving the farms find no jobs in their own region and are forced to migrate to the big city. As Paris and a few other modern, industrial regions grow, the disadvantaged regions lose traditional sources of employment and find no new industries to replace them.

Regional disparities are not new in France, but political awareness of them is. Problems become political issues only when groups mobilize around them, define them in terms that relate to the other issues on board, and introduce them into the process of political decision making. The groups that might have picked up the problem of regional disparities and challenged the economic policies creating and reinforcing such disparities were the opposition political parties. But in France opposition to the economic policies of the government has been organized by left-wing parties whose doctrines focus on class, not on region. The Socialists and Communists have been sensitive to the impact of state economic decisions on the fortunes of given social classes. In legislative debates on the national Plan, for example, the Communists examine proposals for their effect on workers and present analyses of their opponents' position and their own in class terms. The impact of state decisions on regional differentials has been a question in which no major political group has been interested. As a result, regional problems have not surfaced as political issues.

This has begun to change, however, in the last few years. The awakening of political interest in regional problems has a variety of causes: increased desire for participation in local and regional affairs, an exacerbation of the economic difficulties of the underdeveloped regions as agriculture and traditional industries decline, and a new concern with domestic problems now that France's colonial involvements have come to an end. Whatever the outcome of the recent discussions of reform proposals to create regional governments and whatever the effects of the increased level of demands for national assistance to backward regions, the significant facts are that the region has become a political issue and that political groups are beginning to align themselves on positions of support and opposition with respect to various regional projects. One political party, the Radicals, made regionalization the banner of its platform in a recent campaign before municipal elections. And groups advocating regional platforms are springing into life in the provinces. The problems of the regional distribution of economic activity and of the place of traditional sectors in the economy are political problems that derive above all from the policies the government pursued to achieve economic integration and growth. The process of economic integration, like that of territorial integration, required choices on the part of the French state. The pattern of these choices has in significant measure determined the agenda of contemporary French politics.

Integration of Political Values

Economically and territorially, France was more integrated than many other European states at comparable stages of political modernization. In one critical respect, however, France was profoundly divided. Despite the new ties that the economy created among Frenchmen in all parts of the nation, despite the new possibilities for communication and social intercourse, the area of political consensus in France was apparently diminishing and not expanding at the beginning of the twentieth century. The French in this period were deeply divided over the values and goals of the political system. It seems as if the increasing awareness of the importance of the state that social and economic integration fostered led to less agreement than had existed before about the purposes that the state should support.

The politicization of the French population proceeded through the nineteenth century in two broad stages. First, wide sections of the population became increasingly conscious of the significance of the state in affairs of everyday life. For millions of peasants, isolated from the centers of national power, the decisions of the state to tax or to conscript or to interfere in the running of the parish church were the first demonstrations of the importance of the state for private life. Once individuals blamed their troubles on private failings or on the decisions of local elites. Now, increasingly, they perceived the central government—Paris—either as the source of the problem or as capable of providing a remedy for it. The links between private, everyday life and the state became more and more visible.

As individuals all over France became aware of the impact of the state on local and personal affairs, the politicization of the population moved into a second stage. Common, national perceptions of what the major political issues were began to emerge, and people in all parts of the country began to see themselves as allies or enemies in a common cause. The development of a set of political issues that people in all regions regard as salient and central is a gradual process and one that is neither unilinear nor irreversible. Political modernization tends to promote the emergence of issues that carry the same political meaning and weight throughout the nation, but in even the most developed countries there are issues more important for certain regions or groups than for others. In the United States, for example, despite a very high degree of political modernization—however measured—it is only recently that the "nationalization" of political issues has proceeded to a point where racial questions begin to have the same political salience in North and South.

The organization of national political life around common issues in no way assures a greater measure of political integration. Indeed, political conflicts and tensions that were scattered and defused by their uneven relevance for different groups and regions may become embittered when they are perceived in the same terms in all parts of the country. Apparently this is what happened in France. As all sections of the country began to see the principal issue at stake in politics as the Church-state issue, the measure of political consensus that had already been achieved was undermined by new polarization over secularism. Politicization of the French coincided with the emergence of the Church-state issue, and this was to have profound consequences for modern France.

The Church-state issue involved three distinct relationships between the Catholic church and the French government: institutional and social, international, and ideological—relating to the control of the beliefs and loyalties of Frenchmen. The institutional aspect of the problem was by and large resolved by the Revolution of 1789. In the social system of the old regime, the Church was one of the feudal orders. It possessed important political, fiscal, and judicial privileges. It had independent economic resources from the tithe and from its own rural and urban land holdings. The clergy paid no taxes but, rather, voted subsidies to the state. The higher clergy were secular lords; in 1789 all of them were of noble birth. The local priests were in effect the local governmental officials, since they kept parish records, conducted marriages, ran the schools, and organized poor relief. On the institutional level, the Church suffered the expropriation in the Revolution that was the fate of the other feudal orders. Indeed, the priests' initial enthusiasm for the Revolution led them to encourage the notables and the higher clergy to renounce voluntarily their feudal privileges. It was the Bishop of Autun—later known as Talleyrand—who proposed that the state take over Church land in exchange for paying the priests a salary and assuming the expenses of the Church. By the end of 1789 the Church had lost all the institutional privileges that it had enjoyed as a feudal order.

In its international aspect the Church-state problem centered on the relations of an external sovereign power—the pope—with Catholic clergy and believers who were French nationals. The conflict had its origins in the struggles between monarchs and popes over the control of the Church in France, and it revived with new violence after the revolutionary assemblies attempted to integrate the Church into the republic by making priests subject to elections and requiring them to swear oaths of allegiance to the state. To the French Republicans, the Catholics appeared to be the agents of a foreign and hostile power that, in the hope of restoring the monarchy, sided with the countries that attacked France. However, not only Republicans regarded the hold of the pope on French citizens with deep misgivings. None of the regimes after the Revolution—neither Napoleon nor the restored monarchs—ever agreed to restore to the Church the autonomy it had enjoyed before the Revolution. The Napoleonic Concordat did recognize the Catholic church as the religion of France, subsidized churches, and allowed priests to resume teaching in primary schools—since the state in any event did not have enough teachers. But in matters that Napoleon considered critical to the state, like higher education, he refused to let the Church intervene, declaring that "priests do not have that national spirit, the independence of opinion that teachers of a great nation need." The battle over which rights the Catholic church was entitled to exercise in France continued through the nineteenth century, focusing on the activities of certain orders, like the Jesuit order, that were particularly associated with the pope, and on control of educational institutions. These struggles led to the 1906 decision of the Chamber of Deputies, against the bitter opposition of French

Catholics and the Pope, to separate Church and state. The state would no longer recognize Catholicism as the state religion, pay the salaries of priests, or subsidize Church schools. Church buildings, which had been the property of the state, were to be turned over to lay Catholic groups.

The violent reaction of the Church to this "expropriation" was the culminating point in a long attack on the Third Republic. In the course of the nineteenth century the Church had become the mainstay of all the elements that wished to overthrow the republic and reinstate the old regime. The other groups of the old regime—the king and the nobles—were too weak and too divided to organize effective opposition to the republic. The monarchists after 1830 could not agree on candidates for the throne. Moreover, while the monarchy ruled it had not needed and had not built a base of popular support, so that once universal manhood suffrage was instituted the monarchists had increasingly to rely on the Church for mobilizing support. The Church, in short, was left holding the bag of reaction. On a succession of issues that were the life crises of the Third Republic—the attempted coup d'état of General Boulanger, the Dreyfus case—the Church lined up with the enemies and attackers of the republic, even when no direct interest of the Church was at stake. By the end of the nineteenth century the defense of the Catholic church had become inextricably tied up with the defense of all the conservative, old regime interests.

The highest Church officials publicly denounced the republic; local priests actively worked to elect antirepublican candidates. One priest declared before the 1901 elections,

> In the next election, from one end of this land to the next there will be only two candidates: Jesus Christ and Barabbas; Jesus Christ in the person of the Catholics, or as a second choice, of those candidates who will defend Christian freedoms; and Barabbas under different names: Barabbas, the anti-clerical, Barabbas, the Freemason, Barabbas, the revolutionary, Barabbas, the anarchist, Barabbas, the communard. Are you going to vote for Barabbas? . . . To battle under the shield of Saint Michael, the guardian angel of the country, the enemy of the Revolution. He conquered the revolution in heaven by defeating the chief revolutionary: Satan! Forward with Saint Michael against the Revolution!

The republicans responded in kind. Emile Combes, a Radical premier, declared during a legislative debate in 1903 on whether priests should be allowed to teach:

> It is the spirit of olden days, the spirit of reaction, which makes these religious orders rise up out of the debris of the old society like a living negation of the fundamental principles of modern society. The spirit of modern society, the spirit of the Revolution must relegate them forever to a past definitively condemned by the doctrines and morality of democracy.

Pope Leo XIII finally recognized that the Third Republic was not likely to collapse under the Church's attack and that the interests of Catholics would be protected best by participation within the framework of the system. The acceptance of the republic (1892) did not, however, mean that the Church-state crisis was resolved, for in its third aspect the problem remained as acute as before. The issue that remained was that of the control of belief. In the old regime virtually no conflicts arose between the monarchy and the Church over men's loyalties. The monarchy neither required nor could have tolerated popular participation: it needed subjects not citizens. The attitudes, beliefs, and opinions that men held on political matters were a matter of little concern to the state. Since the state did not need citizens as participants, it did not need to educate them in a particular set of beliefs.

The passive, apolitical conduct, the parochial loyalties, and familistic attachments of average Frenchmen were, one might say, the political culture of the old regime. Whether or not the Church controlled education, then, was largely a matter of indifference to the state, since the state did not need to use the schools to inculcate a set of civic beliefs and allegiances. Modern states have important interests at stake in the educational process, both because it turns out citizens and because it provides the skilled personnel needed for the government and for the economy. The monarchy needed neither of these products, and so the clergy's exclusive control of the institutions in which beliefs and loyalties were transmitted went unchallenged by the state.

The Revolution of 1789 brought about a radical change in the conception of the authority of the state, and as a result, the Church's monopoly on Frenchmen's beliefs came under mortal attack. The new state of the French Revolution depended on the active political participation of a nation of citizens. To make men citizens they had to be educated in a new set of civic virtues and sentiments. As Robespierre and the Jacobins understood well, the survival of the republic and of the new system of politics depended on the political commitment of common men who would participate in politics not only or primarily for self-interested reasons but also because of a desire to serve the public good. The revolutionaries saw that citizenship requires an understanding of the state not only as a mechanism for dispensing goods to individuals but also as the basis of the good life. The state is the instrument with which to implement values in society. As Jean Jacques Rousseau had argued before them, men can be good only when they live in a good state, and, conversely, to build a good political community requires a high degree of moral commitment from citizens. Once political leaders reasoned this way, the morality and beliefs of private individuals became a matter of the greatest importance for the state. What the state sought from its subjects was no longer limited, as under the monarchy, to passive, obedient conduct; it required the active, willing, moral commitment of the citizen. The purpose of legislation, declared Robespierre before the Convention, should be the reinforcement of all those values on which the republic is based:

> Everything that stirs up love of country, that purifies morals, that elevates the spirit, *everything that guides the passions of the human heart towards the public interest* should be voted or established by you. Everything that tends to focus feelings on narrow personal matters, or to arouse a fascination with the

trivial and a disdain for what is important, such things should be rejected or repressed by you. *In the system of the French Revolution, all that is immoral is impolitic, all that is corrupting is counter-revolutionary.* [Italics added.]

In other words, the attitudes, beliefs, and "passions of the human heart" have become critical for the state. The state can no longer afford to ignore the ideas and feelings of men. Rather, the government must legislate in such a way as to produce in men the attitudes and beliefs that will make them good citizens and make the state a good state.

What can the state do to foster civic virtues in its citizens? Robespierre, like Rousseau before him and the school teachers of the Third Republic after him, believed that what was needed was a kind of "civil religion," a set of beliefs that would attach men to the notions of justice, brotherhood, and equality with the same conviction and fervor with which they had once held religious beliefs. The principal institution for accomplishing this end was public education. As Robespierre explained in a 1794 speech,

Public education must be stamped with high aims, corresponding to the nature of our government and the sublimeness of the destinies of our Republic. You realize the necessity to make education common and equal for all Frenchmen. We are no longer going to educate "gentlemen" but citizens. Only the nation has the right to raise its children.

The new values, conception of citizenship, and radically expanded scope of state authority all required that the monopoly control of belief that the Church had held until the Revolution should be "nationalized" by the state. Where once the Church had formed the beliefs and worldview of men, now the state needed to do so in order to make citizens.

In the conflict that ensued between Church and state over the loyalties of Frenchmen, the chief battlefield was the school. Through the first half of the nineteenth century the Catholics tried to reestablish their right to run secondary schools. After the establishment of the Third Republic they were beaten back to a defense of their position in primary education. And in 1906 when the separation of Church and state was voted by the Chamber of Deputies, the state finally ended all support to Church schools.

The political passions over the "school question" fed into a political system that was already polarizing into two camps, indeed into two Frances: secular republican France and Catholic France. The political groups that stood for a secular republican France identified themselves by a common set of ideological ancestors, a common set of ideas, and a common institution: the public school. The revered ancestors of republican France were the Jacobins, the revolutionaries of 1830 and 1848, and the founders of the Third Republic. As for a common enemy, in the words of Léon Gambetta, one of the fathers of the Third Republic: "Clericalism, there's the enemy!" At the core of republican political doctrines was a philosophy about the character and purpose of public education, expressed in the term *"laïcité."* In

English *laïcité* would have to be translated as neutrality or secularism, but the operational sense of the term in France was the exclusive control of education by public institutions. Indeed the defenders of *laïcité* argued that the public school should not and could not be simply neutral in its teachings on Catholicism and the old regime, for example, since these latter were false beliefs and evil institutions.

The camp of Catholic France was organized around different values and different institutions. The values were those of authority, hierarchy, and order; the institutions were family, Church, and the Catholic school. In the view of the Catholics, the values, beliefs and minds of the young ought to be shaped by the Church. Even a neutral school—and the Catholics denied that the *laïque* school was neutral— is in principle bad, for in their view, life itself is not neutral but pervaded by values that a child should be taught to recognize and respect. As Pope Leo XIII declared —and Catholic France concurred—"The school is the battlefield where it is decided whether or not society will remain Christian."

By Catholics here we mean political Catholics: those individuals and groups who were politicized by the range of conflicts that arose between Church and state and who were mobilized by these conflicts on the side of the Church. In the religious sense, of course, the vast majority of all Frenchmen were Catholics—born, married, and buried in the Church. Not only the defenders of Catholic schools but also the Radical politicians of the Third Republic baptized, confirmed, and married off their children in the Church. The Catholics, politically defined, were a subset of religious Catholics who were made aware of the impact of politics on their lives principally through the impact of state decisions on the religious institutions to which they belonged and whose response to this impact was to line up on the side of the Church. Whether or not there *are* Catholics in this sense in a given country depends on the course of political development in the state—on whether there is political mobilization around the Church-state issue. It is not a simple function of religious practice.

Mass political participation, then, developed in France at a time when the burning questions in politics turned on the issue of which values and beliefs were so important to society and the state that the state should be able to mold them and which values and attitudes were primarily religious and thus fell into the province of the Church. The political issue that first politicized the French was secularization. The violence of the conflict and the irreconcilability of the opposing positions led to a polarization of the political system into the two camps that have been described above as republican France and Catholic France. The parties and coalitions of Left and Right were organized within these camps. Between the two camps there was no shared ground, or at least, during the height of the conflict at the turn of the century political groups behaved as if there were none. The ideological character of the issue at stake meant that conflict on this one issue extended to a wide range of other phenomena.

What occurred in France at the turn of the century was a hardening up of the lines of fissure in the system and a division of the parties into a Left camp and a Right camp, each defined primarily by its position on the Church. These political allegiances and alignments have proved remarkably resistant to subsequent changes in French society. As Chapter 3 on the party system will describe, various axes of political division have been created alongside the Church-state axis, but the latter continues to exert a significant influence on contemporary political life in France.

The political choices that were made when the central issue in politics was conflict over the values of the national community have willed a difficult legacy to modern France. Like the solutions that the state developed to integrate the nation economically and territorially, the policies of political integration created new problems and left others unresolved. The ideological character of politics, the contested legitimacy of the Constitution, the challenge of protest that is not only antigovernment but antiregime—these and many other problems on the agenda of France today derive directly from decisions made along the route to political modernity.

Two

Political Legitimacy and the Constitutional Order

The government and institutions of the French political system today are called the Fifth Republic, because the constitution under which the French have lived since General de Gaulle's return to power in 1958 is the fifth of the republican constitutions that have been tried in France. France since the Revolution of 1789 has been governed by two monarchical systems (the Bourbon and Orleanist) and two imperial systems (those of Napoleons I and III), as well as by the four republics that preceded the Fifth Republic: the First, Second, Third, and Fourth Republics of 1793–1799, 1848–1852, 1870–1940, and 1946–1958. Why have there been so many fundamental changes in the organization of the French state? Why have the French been unable to define neutral "rules of the game" that all participants in the political process could accept? Under what conditions might the French finally agree on a constitutional framework within which all political groups could pursue their goals? Does the constitutional settlement of the Fifth Republic have wide enough support so that political groups will turn from challenging the regime to working within it? The unstable and often violent history of French politics since the Revolution of 1789 suggests that these are the questions on which the future of France depends.

A constitution is a set of fundamental rules defining the scope, distribution, and exercise of political authority in a society. In every stable political system, there exists some general agreement on the extent of state power, on who ought to wield the power of the state, and on which constraints ought to limit the state. These national decisions on the rules of the political game are constitutional decisions, and they may be embodied in a formal constitutional document, as in the United

States, or simply understood and agreed upon, as in Britain. The problems that arise in a state about the legitimate use of power are so numerous and complex that no single constitutional law could possibly settle all points in controversy. What constitutions do attempt to resolve are the *fundamental* rules of the political game—the basic framework within which political action and conflict will take place.

The history of even such relatively stable states as the United States and Britain shows that what is constitutional is never decided once and for all in a nation. Political values change, and the constitution, too, is forced to adapt, insofar as the national consensus it once represented no longer exists. Such constitutional adjustments are easy when there is general national agreement on new rules for the political game, as, for example, in the recent United States decision to admit eighteen-year-olds to full participation in politics. But the same question of who has a right to share in political power was far less simply resolved on previous occasions in American constitutional history, when other groups demanded a change in the framework of the state. The civil rights of women and of black Americans were not generally acknowledged, and the struggle to amend the Constitution to recognize their rights to full citizenship was a long one.

In France, however, the basic problem has not been the constitution's responsiveness to changing political values but, rather, the inability to find a constitutional settlement that could reconcile the conflicting and mutually exclusive sets of political values held by the major participants in the political process. Frenchmen have held different views on the fundamental questions of politics: In which spheres of private and social life may the state legitimately intervene? What should be left to the initiative of individuals and groups? What rights does the individual have, even against the state? What can the state demand of citizens? On matters that are subject to authoritative decision, who in the state has the right to act? local or national officials? bureaucrats or politicians? Parliament or President? How should these various authorities be related? And when political authority does act, what are the means and procedures that should be employed? These are the issues that constitutions try to resolve so that within an agreed-upon set of rules, citizens and groups can pursue their goals without at each point challenging and endangering the very existence of the state. Each of the French constitutions has embodied a certain set of answers to the above constitutional questions, but in every case significant opposition to the constitution has persisted and weakened the stability of the system.

The fault lay not with the men who wrote the constitutions but with the politicians, who failed to create a national consensus on the organization and exercise of political power. In stable political systems the area of constitutional agreement is broader than the constitution. In the United States, for example, the country's sense of what is constitutional includes not only the document bearing that title but also the Supreme Court's interpretations of the document. In Britain there is no single written constitutional document; what is referred to as the constitution are all the laws and political conventions regarded as basic for the political system. In contrast, the problem in France has been the persistence of profound disagreements over what the state should be and how state power should be exercised along with the absence of an area of constitutional consensus wide enough to accommodate the major political forces of the nation. In this broad sense, despite almost a dozen constitutional documents, France has always lacked a constitution.

Constitutional Traditions in Conflict

The search for a constitutional framework acceptable to the major political groups of the nation has been a central problem of contemporary French politics. One of the principal obstacles has been the profound mistrust that permeates the political community. The intensity of the political conflicts over secularism, over socialism, and over Gaullism created camps of permanent enemies in politics (see Chapter 3). No group was willing to contemplate the possibility of its mortal enemies taking power, and so each one took advantage of its periods in power to refashion the constitution in such a way as to reduce its opponents' chances in politics. The laws on elections were prime targets of such maneuvers, each side trying to write an electoral law that would maximize its chances and diminish those of its rivals. The parties with strong national organizations always tried to obtain elections with proportional representation; the parties based on local notables always tried to use single-member districts. The Gaullists upon their return to power in 1958 restored the latter system and were richly rewarded for their pains: In the 1958 legislative elections the Gaullist party, with less than 18 percent of the vote, won 40 percent of the seats in the National Assembly, while the Communists, who received 19 percent of the vote, won only 2 percent of the seats. The electoral system is only one case of many in which legal arrangements have been used by the political parties in order to increase their power at the expense of opponents. The constitutional questions of whether to have a second house in the legislature, whether to strengthen the presidency, and how to distribute power between central and local governmental authorities have been treated by the political groups in the same way: as potential weapons in political battle. The constitution, far from limiting the terms of political conflict, has been simply one prize among others of political warfare.

Chapter 3 describes the issues dividing the political parties and suggests some of the reasons why the nature of partisan conflict in France has made it impossible to define any set of rules of the political game that appear neutral and fair to all participants. Here we shall consider the political values that figure in controversies that are directly related to the constitution. The different conceptions of authority that divide French political groups have been expressed in two opposing constitutional traditions, each with its own institutions, personnel, and typical political practices. These two constitutional models are the parliamentary and the presidential. In the parliamentary constitutions like those of the Third and Fourth Republics, the legislative assembly is the sole representative of national sovereignty, and governments are formed and changed at the will of this body. Those groups in French history who have supported parliamentarism have had in common the belief that political institutions should be structured, above all else, to maximize the values of representative democracy. Representative democracy has meant different things to different political groups in France. For the Jacobins and those who followed in their ideological footsteps, those institutions were best in which there was the most direct democracy and the least delegation of authority. The people were sovereign, and the best representative assembly was one that most closely reflected and expressed the will of the people. For other groups, like the conservative republicans of the Third Republic, the best system was one in which the system of representation allowed the people to choose a legislature whose collective will was the sovereign expression of France. The Parliament itself embodied national sovereignty. As Paul Reynaud, a former Prime Minister, declared in the National Assembly in 1962, "Here and nowhere else is France."

In what we will call presidential constitutions, the chief of state derives his effective power and authority from sources independent of the legislature. The chief executive—whether President in the Fifth Republic, head of state in the Vichy regime, or emperor in the Second Empire—is not responsible to the legislative assembly, and the assembly itself is in significant measure dominated by him. The most important value associated with this constitutional tradition is that of the political unity of the nation. Beyond the reach of political parties, contending interest groups, and opposing ideologies, above the forces that divide France, the chief of state defends the unity of the nation. According to the supporters of presidential constitutions, only a strong and unitary executive can develop coherent policy for the country; only he can bring the nation intact through periods of crisis. Government should not be entrusted to an assembly, for this would only transmit the divisions in the society and the conflicts among political groups into the state and thus make any stable political authority impossible. Political order is the prerequisite of all other political values, and in France the only way to assure political order is to organize the power of the state in a system that provides a strong executive, the supporters of presidential government believe.

On paper, most French constitutions have been mixed constitutions and have attempted to incorporate some elements of both models. The Constitution of the Fifth Republic, for example, has many features of a parliamentary regime. But in practice the mixed constitutions have always served to establish the predominance of either Parliament or head of state, and there is no precedent in French political history for the effective sharing of powers between the legislature and the President that characterizes American political practice. The failure to reconcile the competing ideals of authority of these two constitutional traditions has meant that a parliamentary regime seems illegitimate to the supporters of strong executive power and, conversely, that a presidential system like that of the Fifth Republic is unacceptable to the proponents of government by legislative assembly.

Parliamentary Democracy

A parliamentary constitution is, quite simply, one that uses a representative assembly to produce a government out of the assembly, to check and control the government, and to change it. Who holds executive power, how this power will be exercised, and when it will change hands are all decided by the legislature. As rapid comparison shows, a parliamentary system organizes the state very differently from a presidential system in all three respects. In a presidential system like that of the United States, the legislature has no say on who is to hold executive power, for this is settled by direct popular elections. In checking and controlling government, the Congress has a large but not exclusive role, for the Supreme Court, too, shares this function. Moreover, in a presidential system the checking of power is a two-way street: The Congress may amend or reject the President's bill, but he may veto theirs. In determining when and how the government changes hands, the legislative assembly in a presidential system plays no role at all; executive power is regulated by fixed terms of office. The Prime Minister of the French Third Republic could fall from power any day; the presidency of the United States changes hands only at regular four-year intervals.

In parliamentary systems, governments are created, checked, and changed by the legislative assembly. *How* this happens varies greatly from country to country. In Britain since the thirties the electoral system and the strength of the two major parties combine to produce legislatures in which one of the parties has always been strong enough to form the government alone. In the French Third and Fourth Republics, in contrast, governments were produced not by the clear mandate of election results but by parliamentary coalitions. The two principal reasons for this were the multiplicity of political parties and the effects of the electoral system (see Chapter 3). No single party in the Third and Fourth Republics ever won a majority of seats in the National Assembly, so in order to form any government at all, several parties had to ally. The governments lasted only as long as the parliamentary coalitions on which they were based, and in France this was on the average a very short period. From the first government under the Constitution of the Third Republic to the last government under the Fourth Republic (1876–1958) France was ruled by 119 governments.[1] The average life of a government was eight months. Weeks might pass between the time one government was voted out and a new government could be formed, and, in fact, for almost three months out of the last year of the Fourth Republic France was without a government.

There is no reason why parliamentary coalitions cannot produce stable and long-lived governments. Though governments based on a single party are inherently more cohesive, the examples of Sweden, where the Socialist and Center parties ruled together for many years, of West Germany, where the Social Democrats and Christian Democrats formed a government that lasted three years, and

---

[1] François Goguel and Alfred Grosser, *La Politique en France* (Paris: Seuil, 1970), p. 36.

of other European parliamentary democracies show that governmental instability is not the inevitable product of multiparty coalitions. Therefore, to understand why the French parliamentary system in the Third and Fourth Republics was unable to create stable governments, we must look for factors other than the multiplicity of parties.

If the French political system is compared with the political systems of those European countries where the parliamentary system has produced strong, stable governments, two important differences stand out. First, coalition governments are stable when the parties composing them are able to discipline their members. In France, however, the parties of the Third and Fourth Republics that participated most often in governmental coalitions were the parties with the weakest party discipline. The parties that were reservoirs of the *ministrables,* the deputies most eligible for ministerial careers, were loosely knit groups of local political notables, banded together in a national party whose structure was shadowy and control over its members nonexistent. The governmental parties of the Fourth Republic (the Socialists, the M.R.P., the Radicals, and various Center parties) were more disciplined than the typical governmental parties of the Third (the Radicals, Radical-Socialists, moderate Republicans, Left Republicans, and Center parties), but nonetheless, in every crisis of the Fourth Republic, the Prime Minister had always to worry first about whether he could carry his own party along with him as well as whether he could satisfy the other parties of the coalition. The Prime Minister often could not control the policies of Cabinet ministers of his own party, for in the absence of any effective party discipline, he could discipline a member of the Cabinet only by threatening to dissolve the government. The weakness of party discipline contributed even more directly to governmental instability by making it possible and indeed profitable for members of the government to abandon it at an opportune moment in order to be "eligible" for participation in the next government. The minister who defected was not often punished by his party, and he was frequently rewarded by the system for having known when to jump off a bandwagon that had run out of steam in order to jump onto the next one.

The second point of difference between the parliamentary systems successful in creating stable governments and the French system is the set of attitudes and expectations regarding executive power that have developed in political culture and political practice. In Britain parliamentary tradition and political culture support a strong executive. Although the government is ultimately dependent on and responsible to Parliament, Parliament acknowledges and accepts the authority of the government and the desirability of according it substantial powers. In radical contrast, French political culture and parliamentary tradition are deeply antagonistic to the notion of strong and autonomous executive authority. One of the strongest themes of French political culture is profound mistrust of the state and hostility toward the exercise of power. As François Goguel and Alfred Grosser have written, the French look at their participation in politics as a way of weakening the State, rather than reforming it or getting it to serve their interests and preferences. It is this hostility towards the State, this tendency not to understand its role and to distrust those who work for it which is the clearest evidence today of the traditional political behavior of Frenchmen.[2]

A survey carried out in 1970 on the attitudes of a representative sample of Frenchmen discovered that attitudes about the state are a mixture of resentment and expectation.[3] Almost half of those interviewed believed that the state defends the rich rather than the poor; a third found it unjust. Most described the state as an organizational labyrinth, impossible to understand or to influence unless one is an expert (73 percent of the sample). Each felt that he was powerless in dealings with the bureaucracy and that "others" were receiving special favors that were denied to him. But at the same time that the citizen distrusts the state, he expects much from it. For 64 percent of those surveyed the most important function of the state is to provide economic and social security. The state should protect the citizen against the risks of unemployment, inflation, old age, sickness, and dislocation due to transformation of the economy. Only after this cardinal demand for state protection did the group interviewed mention demands for state action to maintain public order, to regulate economic activity, to assist underprivileged groups in society, and to defend France in the international arena.

Both for public opinion and for the political elites many of the ambivalent feelings about the exercise of state authority are centered on the role of the executive. When Frenchmen were asked "What is it that for you best symbolizes the state?" the largest number (25 percent) answered "the President of the republic"; the second largest group (23 percent) replied "the government." It is not surprising, therefore, that in the parliamentary republics the general societal mistrust of political authority combines with the doctrine of parliamentary sovereignty to focus hostility on the executive. Where the British Member of Parliament expects to support the policies and, more generally, the authority of a government formed by his party, the French deputy regards with suspicion even a government for which he has voted and jealously watches for any encroachment of the executive on the assembly's sovereign prerogatives. The notion that Parliament should consider its main function as blocking and checking the executive, rather than collaborating with him, was best expressed in the political ideas of Alain, the penname of Emile Chartier, who commented on the politics of the Third Republic. As Alain saw it, the principal problem of politics is to defend individual liberty against forces that constantly seek to exploit and enslave men. In modern society these forces are the great economic and social powers; the political elites are nothing but the political arm of these oligarchies. Power, like wealth and status, corrupts those who possess it: "No elite is worth anything, for it is destined to

---

[2] Ibid., p. 26.

[3] Le Monde, October 10, 1970.

exercise power and therefore destined to be corrupted by the use of power."[4] Even when the rulers are elected by the ruled, the latter end up being exploited by the men they have chosen. As Alain wrote:

Universal suffrage does not really create democracy . . . A tyrant can be elected by universal suffrage and that does not make him any less a tyrant. What matters is not the origin of power, but the continuous and effective control that the ruled exercise over government.

. . .

In every constitution there are monarchic, oligarchic, and democratic elements, more or less in balance. The executive is inherently monarchic. In action one man must always command, for everything can not be decided beforehand . . . The legislating function, which includes the administrative, is inherently oligarchic, for in order to run an organization, scientists, lawyers are needed . . . What then is Democracy if not the third element that I call the Controller? It amounts to the power, always in vigor, to depose the Kings and the Specialists immediately, if they do not serve the interest of the majority. For many years this power was exercised through revolutions and barricades. Today it works through Parliamentary Motions of Confidence. Democracy is in this sense a perpetual struggle by the ruled against abuses of power.[5]

There is something new in politics these days, democracy, which is nothing other than the organization of resistance against these formidable powers, against the rulers. A representative assembly can neither substitute itself for these powers, nor choose them, but in the name of the people, it can refuse to obey them.[6]

The deep suspicion of executive power that found expression in Alain's conception of resistance—putting obstacles in the path of executive action—as the proper function of the legislature was an important element in the political culture and parliamentary practices of the Third and Fourth Republics. Political personalities who seemed likely to become strong executives were feared and resented by the deputies, and they were systematically kept out of governments—until, of course, a crisis arose that could not be handled by the usual parade of ministers. The long periods of political "exile" of Georges Clemenceau, who later served as Prime Minister during World War I, of Pierre Mendès-France, to whom the National Assembly finally had to have recourse to extricate France from the Indochinese war, and of Charles de Gaulle, whom the Assembly called back only when civil war seemed imminent, exemplify the fate of strong leaders in a political system hostile to executive authority.

Even when the Assembly was willing to elect a Prime Minister, it had an armory

---

[4] Alain, *Elements d'une doctrine radicale* (Paris: Gallimard, 1933), p. 11.

[5] *Ibid.,* p. 152.

[6] Alain, *Propos de politique* (Paris: Rieder, 1934), p. 183.

of weapons with which it could prevent him from carrying out his program. The parliamentary commissions that considered a bill before it was voted on in the Parliament could amend the government's project in any respect, so that the bill Parliament debated was no longer the government's, but the commission's draft. Even the budget could be amended by the deputies. Though various rules were adopted that prohibited amendments increasing public expenditures, in fact the deputies found ways to circumvent these limitations on parliamentary sovereignty. The Parliament, moreover, set its own agenda, so that the timing of debates on issues the government considered critical was at the discretion of the legislative assembly, not the government. The ultimate weapon was the threat to vote down the government. Despite the various attempts (particularly in the Constitution of the Fourth Republic) to tie the assembly's hands by prescribing more stringent requirements for defeating a government, these provisions, which might have strengthened governments by increasing their longevity, remained dead letters. Neither the Third nor the Fourth Republic was ever able to accommodate stable and effective government and the exercise of parliamentary democracy. Unwilling to live with strong governments, the French Parliaments denied the state the means required to act on the great problems of contemporary societies. The backlog of unresolved problems and the social tensions and frustrations they engendered burdened weak governments, which sought to evade making decisions for fear of falling from power.

The counterpart of the weak governments of ordinary times were the "savior" governments of times of crisis. When domestic pressures or problems in the international arena became too insistent to be handled by inaction, Parliament abdicated power into the hands of the executive. The "savior" governments of Clemenceau, who stepped in to organize France for war, of Raymond Poincaré, who rescued the economy in the interwar crisis, of Henri Pétain, called to head the government after the military collapse of 1940, and of de Gaulle in 1958 were the necessary concomitant of a parliamentary system that deprived governments of the authority necessary to rule the state.

Another way of stating the problem of French parliamentarism is to say that the three functions carried out by the legislative assembly—creating, checking, and changing the government—were so confused that governments were never able to acquire sufficient authority so that the checking and controlling of the Parliament did not amount to sabotaging the minimal life requirements of government. In France the normal mode of checking a government was changing it. Ministerial crises, followed by a rotation in the personnel of the government, not popular elections, were the dominant mechanism for changing the wielders of power. Ministerial instability as a mode of political change depends on the existence of a broad spectrum of political groups from which new governments can be drawn. In the Third and Fourth Republics the size of the pool of Cabinet-eligibles was always limited by the existence at both ends of the political spectrum of antiregime parties. The parties of the extreme Left and extreme Right were not an Opposition, in the British sense, for the political alternatives they proposed were not only a different set of policies from those of the government in power but also a different constitutional framework. What the monarchists and the Communists in the Third Republic or the Gaullists in the Fourth Republic challenged was the regime itself. They offered not alternative governments but alternative states. In face of this threat to the political status quo, the other political parties, despite great differences among themselves, could usually agree on a strategy toward the antiregime parties. They were to be isolated in their political "ghettos," and all means were good that avoided increasing their numbers. This meant avoiding recourse to elections, for the citizens might return more of the extremes, thus making it more difficult to form governments.

Ministerial instability as a mode of regulating political change worked reasonably well in France as long as the Center that provided the personnel of power remained broad and solid. When all political change takes place by shifts among the Center groups and by varying the weights of these groups in different governments, the political system becomes rigid and unworkable if the Center is reduced by the growth of the extremes. This is what happened in France at the end of the Third Republic. The old formulas for making governments failed because they depended on a broad Center that no longer existed.

Ministerial instability as the mechanism of political change had certain advantages for a country as profoundly divided as France was in the Third and Fourth Republics, for it made government possible. By making nonelectoral change the dominant mode of change in the system, the government was insulated against popular pressures, which in some periods at least were so intense and so polarized that no government could have satisfied them. The price of such protection was very high. Isolating the process of political change from the pressures of the electorate and the threats of the extreme parties cut Parliament off from the nation and tended to make it a closed arena. The walls that defended Parliament against the outside world, that made it, in Nathan Leites' phrase, a "house without windows," kept out the stones and the burglars, but they also kept out the winds of change in the country.

All institutions tend to acquire a life of their own: to develop a system of values and a set of roles that define the social system of the institution. In some degree all institutions socialize their members by making acceptance of the "rules of the game" the prerequisite of success within the system. And as has been observed in many legislative assemblies in various countries, one of the roles that a deputy plays is that of member of the parliamentary social system, among such other roles as member of his party, representative of his constituency, representative of particular interest groups, and so forth. What is striking in the French parliamentary system is that the values and roles associated with membership in the legislature have been so powerful as to rival, if not outweigh, all other allegiances. The behavior of the French deputy has been heavily conditioned by the single role of member of Parliament, and he has often been willing to sacrifice the goals of party or constituency in the service of parliamentary goals. As Robert de Jouvenel ironically put it, two deputies, one revolutionary, the other reactionary, have more in common than two revolutionaries, one of whom is a deputy and the other not.

Changes in governments and shifts in parliamentary alliances thus often reflected not conflicts over issues and interests, but maneuvers aimed at increasing the participants' success within the parliamentary arena. Ministerial instability can be explained in part as a product of the internal politics of the legislative social system. Deputies were eager to vote down a government because that opened new possibilities for entrance into the next government. The governments themselves resigned too easily, for each minister was already thinking of his place in a future government. The rewards of the system—Cabinet posts—were reserved for deputies with certain talents: flexibility, a capacity to arrange compromises and avoid divisive choices, and weak allegiance to party. The qualities that made for success in the parliamentary arena were not, however, characteristics that produced national political leaders. Indeed those deputies who tried to use their position in the legislature as a base for appeal to the nation or, conversely, who tried to mobilize popular support in order to maximize their strength in Parliament were punished —deprived of possibilities of participation in governments—by the rules of the parliamentary game.

To many in the nation, Parliament seemed a system in which internal maneuver and success mattered more than output and in which the friction of the machine consumed all energy. A large part of the electorate came to hold the entire parliamentary world in contempt. Cutting the Parliament off from political pressures had simply displaced the locus of political conflict. Peasants, policemen, industrial workers, and others protested in the streets. Growing frustration about the difficulties of reaching across the barriers that shielded Parliament from public pressure and about the ineffectiveness of the institution fed extremist parties that remained outside the cozy parliamentary world. In the Third and Fourth Republics antiparliamentarism was an important theme not only for the antiregime parties but also for broad sectors of public opinion.

Diagnoses and Remedies

Why did parliamentarism work in Britain to produce both representation and expression for the major social groups and stable political authority while it failed in France? There are three approaches to this problem, each diagnosing a different disease and prescribing a different medicine for France. One explanation focuses on the role of the parliamentary institutions themselves. Those who hold this view believe that the principal determinant of governmental stability and effectiveness is political structure, so that one set of institutions may produce instability in a country where another set of arrangements would promote effective government. Some defenders of the parliamentary model argue that the institutions of the Fourth Republic might have worked if the deputies had actually observed the rules. The Constitution of the Fourth Republic contained, for example, a number of requirements for special majorities to defeat governments, but these stipulations were never followed, and governments continued to fall on simple majorities in ordinary debates. Similarly, the deputies themselves voted to limit their powers to amend budgets, but these provisions, too, were often disregarded. If not the parliamentary structures of the Third or Fourth Republics, then another set of parliamentary institutions can be devised to produce representative and effective political authority. Such is the view of Mendès-France, who rejects the presidential model of the Fifth Republic and urges a return to a reformed parliamentary system with guarantees both for more effective links between the electorate and the Parliament and for stronger executive power.[7]

Attributing the same crucial role to institutions, the critics of the parliamentary model charge that the weakness and instability of the Third and Fourth Republics were due to inherent defects of parliamentary institutions. Michel Debré, the major author of de Gaulle's constitution, wrote a book during the Fourth Republic on the failures of the regime, *The Princes Who Govern Us (Ces princes qui nous gouvernent)*. He asked rhetorically whether the troubles of the system were simply reflections of the troubles of the nation and then proceeded to argue that the political divisions of France were created by the parliamentary system. Parliament is not the legitimate expression of the nation, he noted, but only the product of a particular electoral system and of a constitution approved by only one-third of the electorate, of which one-half were Communists. Neither Britain nor the United States are any more united than the French, Debré argued. If their governments are more stable, it is because they have known better than to build their divisions into their governments. To achieve unity, a strong executive, a state with authority, France needed new institutions. Debré's critiques of the parliamentary regime were blueprints for the Constitution of the Fifth Republic, in which he at last had the opportunity to give France the institutions that he believed would produce strong government.

There are other observers of French politics who believe that the weakness of the parliamentary state reflected not so much bad institutions as the existence of profound political divisions in the country. The rigidity of class distinctions in France, the low level of civic education, the ideological quality of political conflict, the burden of the problems the state faced—these were some of the causes that have been suggested for the breakdown of the parliamentary regimes. As Philip Williams explained the fall of the Fourth Republic:

> The personal and factional intrigues of the deputies merely aggravated a far more serious situation: it was the lack of a majority in Parliament (because there was none in the country) which made unstable government inevitable. As if this were not enough, France was the only country which had both a great empire and a strong Communist party. Without the Communists the shrivelled democratic Left and progressive Centre could not muster a majority for decolonization; but with Communist support came fears for domestic stability and international

---

[7]Pierre Mendès-France, *A Modern French Republic* (New York: Hill & Wang, 1963).

tranquillity which alienated Centre votes and in turn made it impossible to find a majority.[8]

The parliamentary regimes of France were weakened by the range, depth, and concurrence of the problems they had to solve. The combined weights of economic reconstruction, rearmament, and decolonization were an intolerable burden for a state whose very legitimacy was contested by substantial political groups. Are there any constitutional arrangements that could produce strong and representative government in a country where a substantial proportion of the electorate supports antiregime parties? Would institutional changes attenuate the ideological conflicts that make political compromise so difficult in France? According to this analysis France needed social and economic reforms and also a reform of the political system as conceived in the largest sense: more civic participation, internal restructuring of the political parties, and decentralization. To change only the organization of power at the national level would simply not get at the roots of France's political troubles.

The future of parliamentary institutions in France may, however, depend on considerations quite different from those on which the institutionalists and the political reformers have focused. The significant question may be whether Parliaments, no matter how organized, are competent to deal with the typical problems of modern politics. As long as the main substance of parliamentary work was the production of legislation of a general, regulatory nature, legislative assemblies seemed to be adequate instruments for the conception and control of policy. Before World War II the political elites of the governmental parties rarely conceived of law as an instrument for transforming and developing society and economy or as an instrument for reducing inequality. Both the liberals and the Jacobins believed that the law should have an equal impact on citizens and that so long as discrimination was not deliberately legislated, it would. After the war this conception of the task of the state changed drastically. Demands arose from all sectors of society for the state to play a more active role in the economy in order to control fluctuations in economic activity and in order to encourage economic growth by selectively supporting certain industries and by promoting investment and innovation. A broad segment of public opinion demanded that the state intervene to reduce the inequalities of French society: inequalities among different individuals and social groups, among backward and advanced regions, among different sectors of the economy. The policies of economic planning and the social legislation that responded to these demands required very different political skills from those possessed by the deputy. No special expertise had been required for decisions on periods of conscription, for example, or on state aid to Church schools, or on subsidies for winegrowers—typical parliamentary issues of the Third Republic. Nor had the casual, ad hoc, piecemeal intervention of the state in the

---

[8]Philip Williams, *The French Parliament (1958–1967)* (London: Allen & Unwin, 1968), p. 17.

economy before the war required coherent long-term legislation. When the work of government became more technical and complex, the deputies had difficulty understanding the problems before them, let alone proposing effective means for dealing with them.

As the tasks assumed by the modern state have multiplied in number and complexity, power has shifted from the hands of parliamentarians to experts in the administration, to the "technocrats." Not only in France, where the parliamentary system worked badly, but also in Britain where it worked well, the locus of decision making moved from parliamentary arenas into the ministries. The specialists, the bureaucrats, and the representatives of special interest groups have come to play a more important part in making policy, and the politicians a less important part. Not only in France, where Parliament has few resources for obtaining the information and the expertise necessary for presenting alternatives to the government's proposals, but even in the United States where Congress has organized specialized committees, hearings, and technical assistance for the legislator, the President's access to expertise and an organization inherently better suited to the conduct of such state business as foreign affairs has apparently given the executive and the administration an insuperable advantage over the legislature. The question is whether in any modern state a legislative assembly will be able to carry on the work of government in a way that was possible when the problems of politics required less specialized knowledge, technical competence, and long-term planning and organization to resolve them.

Presidential Democracy

The Constitution of the Fifth Republic was written in reaction against the constitutional pattern of the parliamentary system. When General Charles de Gaulle agreed to form a government in May 1958, after a revolt of the French settler colony in Algeria and the disobedience of army units had sapped the authority of the government in office, the parliamentary system appeared to have confirmed the worst prognostics of its critics. Cabinet instability had increased as the problems of decolonization in Algeria became meshed with the internal divisions of the political parties, and for long periods in the last year of the Fourth Republic, no government could be formed and the country's affairs were left in the hands of caretaker governments. Every day turned up new evidence of the government's inability to control the army and the bureaucracy. While governments stood by impotently, Paris police demonstrated against Parliament; colonial administrators conspired with the French community in Algeria to ignore orders from Paris and to carry out their own policies; and the army in Algeria supported insurrectionist projects of civilians opposed to decolonization. The parliamentary system appeared incapable of creating a government with enough cohesion to formulate an Algerian policy and enough authority to oblige the army and the bureaucracy to carry it out. As a condition of his forming a government, de Gaulle demanded that the parties agree to a vote on a new constitution. Pressured by the collapse of the authority of the state and the rapidly deteriorating state of affairs in Algeria as well as by a loss of confidence in their own capacity to reestablish order and preserve the republic, the party leaders acceded to de Gaulle's conditions. De Gaulle was at last free to write the constitution with the strong executive power that he had always advocated for France and to get rid of the parliamentary system of the Fourth Republic, which he had attacked from the beginning.

The Constitution of the Fifth Republic was drafted by a small circle of de Gaulle's trusted political associates, with Michel Debré, the future Prime Minister, in charge; then submitted to a Constitutional Advisory Committee, composed primarily of members of Parliament; then presented in a national referendum to the French. In all essential respects the document embodied the constitutional system that de Gaulle had been urging on the French since the war. Indeed, one of de Gaulle's early postwar speeches, at Bayeux in 1946, presented a virtual blueprint of the Constitution of the Fifth Republic. De Gaulle declared in 1946:

> It is obvious that executive power should not depend on the Parliament, based on two houses and wielding legislative power, or else there will be a confusion of responsibilities in which the Government will become nothing more than a cluster of [party] delegations. . . . The unity, cohesion, and internal discipline of the Government of France must be sacred objects, or else the country's leadership will rapidly become impotent and invalid. How can such unity, cohesion, and discipline be preserved if the executive power emanates from another body, with which it must be balanced, and if each member of a Government which is collectively responsible before the national representative body is but the emissary of his party? The executive power should, therefore, be embodied in a Chief of State, placed above the parties, elected by a body that includes the Parliament but is larger than it . . .
>
> It is the role of the Chief of State to consider the general interest in his choice of men, while taking into account the orientation of the Parliament. It is his role to name ministers, and first of all, the Prime Minister, who will direct the policy and work of the Government. It is his role to promulgate laws and make decrees, for they obligate the citizens to the State as a whole. It is his task to preside over the Cabinet and, there, to defend the essential national continuity. It is his function to serve as an arbiter, placed above the political circumstances of the day, and to carry out this function ordinarily in the Cabinet, or, in moments of great confusion, by asking the nation to deliver its sovereign decision through elections. It is his role, should the nation ever be in danger, to assume the duty of guaranteeing national independence and the treaties agreed to by France . . .

The main points of the Bayeux speech were themes that drew on an old constitutional tradition that was based on a strong executive. Like other critics of the parliamentary model before him, de Gaulle denounced government by legislative assembly as destructive of national unity and strength. According to antiparliamentary analysis, government by assembly meant government by the political parties.

Instead of creating a mechanism for representing and defending the public interest, government by the parties meant perpetual conflict among partial and partisan interests. The authority of the state was destroyed in these contests. The executive was a weak creature, dependent on the will of changing assembly votes. In ordinary times the government was so dependent on the interest groups and political parties that it was incapable of any independent initiative. In times of crisis, the government was so weak that the country was likely to fall into the hands of authoritarian rulers (as had the First, Second, and Third Republics, de Gaulle pointed out in the Bayeux speech). It was with a view to overcoming these political weaknesses, problems that according to the Gaullists derived from the parliamentary system, that the Constitution of the Fifth Republic was conceived.

The constitution established three fundamental political authorities: the President, the government (Prime Minister and Cabinet), and the Parliament (National Assembly and Senate). In theory, the constitution sets up a mixed parliamentary-presidential system, for the government remains responsible before the legislative assembly (unlike a pure presidential model), while the chief of state has substantial powers that are not subject to parliamentary control (unlike a pure parliamentary model). In fact, the political practices that have developed on the basis of the constitution in the past decade have produced a presidential system in which Parliament plays a secondary role. Though the powerful personality of de Gaulle, the first man to hold the presidency, may account in part for the predominance of the President in the system, the experience of the second President of the Fifth Republic, Georges Pompidou, shows that levers of power that the constitution provides to the presidential officeholder allow even a less forceful individual than de Gaulle to dominate the political system.

The Parliament

If the President has emerged as the central political figure of the Fifth Republic, it is in large measure due to the changed role of the National Assembly and the Senate in the political system. The curtailment of the power of these two legislatures (together called the Parliament) has made it possible for the President of the republic and the government to enlarge the substantial grants of authority that they are given by the constitution and to establish a position of predominance in the state. In the parliamentary regimes of the Third and Fourth Republics, Parliament chose governments, controlled them by controlling their legislative programs, and changed them. In the Fifth Republic, Parliament still participates in carrying out these three functions, but it must share its power with President and government. The powers it continues to exercise are clearly circumscribed by the constitution.

Forming a government, once the exclusive prerogative of the Parliament, has now become one of the powers of the President of the republic. The President names the Prime Minister and on his suggestion chooses the ministers. The constitution does not require the Prime Minister to present his program to the National Assembly for a vote of confidence, and though some of the governments of the

Fifth Republic have done so, others have not. The role of the Assembly in the choice of the government has thus been reduced to a right to defeat the government by passing a motion of censure. Even this possibility has been sharply decreased. The new constitutional rules require that a motion of censure initiated by the Assembly first receive the signatures of one-tenth of the members of the Assembly; that the vote on the motion be delayed for forty-eight hours; and then that the motion receive a majority of all members of the Assembly (not only of those voting) in order to pass.

In a second respect as well the National Assembly has lost power in the formation of the government. The governments of the parliamentary republics were composed of members of the legislature, and when the governments fell, the ex-ministers resumed their jobs as deputies. The Constitution of the Fifth Republic, in contrast, requires a deputy who enters the government to give up his parliamentary mandate. Every deputy now stands for election with a "substitute," who takes the Assembly seat of a deputy named to the government. When the minister leaves the government he cannot resume his Assembly seat. The intention behind this new rule was to prevent ministers from resigning from governments with the hope of bringing them down in order to serve in new ones—one of the practices of the parliamentary regimes that, in the view of the framers of the Constitution of 1958, had contributed to Cabinet instability. The ex-ministers of the Fifth Republic have sometimes circumvented the requirements of the new rules by having their substitutes resign so that a by-election can be held and the ex-minister can run for his seat again. The violation of the spirit of the new requirement has not, however, revived the old patterns of ministerial indiscipline. In addition to the constitutional rules that sever the members of the government from the Assembly, a new political practice has contributed to weakening the influence of the Assembly on the government. In violation of the unwritten rules of the parliamentary system, de Gaulle named men to the government who had never been deputies at all. Some were high civil servants; others had experience in the private sector. The most prominent of these "technicians" was Georges Pompidou, now President of the republic, who was a bank director in 1962 when he was named Prime Minister by de Gaulle. This trend has been reversed in the last five years, and all of the members of the governments chosen by Pompidou were members of the Assembly. Many of them, however, had come into government as technicians and had subsequently run for office.

Of all the functions that Parliament had performed in the Third and Fourth Republics, that of controlling the legislative process was the one most profoundly modified by the Fifth Republic. Where the parliamentary constitutions were silent, the legislature was free to act. The Constitution of 1958, in contrast, describes and delimits with considerable detail the part that the legislature may play in the legislative process, and the Parliament may not exceed the grants of power specifically accorded it by the constitution. The main feature of the new division of power between Parliament and Government in the legislative process is a distinction between "laws" and "regulations" (Articles 34 and 37). The Parliament is entitled to deliberate and vote only on laws, a category described in the constitution as including legislation concerning civil liberties, political rights, crimes, taxes, elections, and nationalization of industry. Into the category of law also fall the "basic principles," though not the detailed provisions, of legislation on defense, local government, education, property, work, and social security. The subjects which are the object of law and to be deliberated and voted on by Parliament are thus strictly delimited, and all other subjects are constitutionally defined as the objects of regulations, which are proclaimed by the government without the participation of Parliament. In cases of dispute over whether a bill falls into the domain of law or the domain of regulation, the Constitutional Council decides. The constitution also allows the government to request authorization from Parliament to make by ordinance decisions that would normally fall into the domain of law (Article 38). According to the constitution, these ordinances must be ratified by Parliament, but in practice the government has used this power to handle politically touchy matters, like the licenses of liquor distillers, and often has either delayed for long periods before obtaining parliamentary ratification or has failed to obtain it. Finally, the constitution limits the role of the Parliament in the budgetary process by specifying that only the government may introduce a bill that would increase public expenditures or decrease public revenues.

The first consequence of these limitations on the domain of Parliament has been to reduce the burden of parliamentary work. Nine-tenths of the bills introduced in the last year of the Fourth Republic would be considered regulations by the new rules and would never appear before the Parliament at all. In principle, the Parliament can devote more of its time to consideration of the most important pieces of legislation, instead of dispersing its efforts on minor bills. In fact, the Parliament often finds itself in much the same rush as before. The constitution fixes the dates of the parliamentary sessions, allowing the Parliament to meet only six months a year, far less than the average session of the parliamentary regimes. The constitution also specifies that the Parliament may spend no more than seventy days on the budget, or else the Government may enact the budget by decree.

Even more important has been the impact of the constitutional limitations of the Parliament's role on the relationship between Parliament and government. Parliament has been weakened not only by having had its business strictly defined, but also by having had spelled out in the constitution how its business is to be conducted. Bills go first to committees of the National Assembly or Senate for discussion and possible amendment and then are reported out for discussion and vote. In the Third and Fourth Republics the committees were powerful actors in the legislative process; the bill that reached the Assembly was not the bill that had originally been introduced but the bill as amended by the committee. The government had no power to require the Assembly to consider the original governmental proposal. In the Fourth Republic, there were nineteen committees, each one closely associated with one or more ministries. Deputies representing particular economic interests served on the committees linked up with the ministry most directly concerned with those interests, and from this network of interests, pressures, and influence a governmental bill often came out mutilated. In order to prevent this collusion between the interest groups, the committees, and the ministries, the framers of the Constitution of 1958 specified that there would be only six standing committees in the Assembly, each having jurisdiction over a broad range of different subject matters. Since every member of Parliament serves on a committee, the committees have become for the most part unwieldy bodies from which it is unlikely that a common outlook could emerge and which would be unlikely to unite and present a solid front against a governmental project. The deputies are distributed among the committees in such a way that the political parties are represented in each committee in proportion to their strength in the legislature. The constitution also provides for setting up special committees to consider a single bill, and this has been done occasionally. The experience with these special committees showed, however, that since they were composed of deputies with a strong interest in a particular measure, the committee was able to formulate a common position and resist government propositions far better than the large all-purpose standing committees could. The special committees, in short, turned out too much like the old regular committees of the Fourth Republic, and the government now tends to avoid creating them.

After the committee reports out the bill, it moves to the National Assembly for debate and vote. The government decides the order in which bills will be presented, and so the Parliament is no longer "master of its agenda," as the expression of the parliamentary regimes put it. The organization of parliamentary time is now determined by the government's legislative priorities. A private member's bill must in effect be accepted by the government if it is to be discussed at all. The only time in the parliamentary schedule that the government does not control is oral question day, one session per week that the constitution sets aside for questioning of the government by the deputies. In the parliamentary republics, questions followed by a vote of confidence on the government's reply were one of the great weapons of the Parliament against the government. But in the Fifth Republic, the Constitutional Council has ruled that votes on motions introduced in question sessions are unconstitutional, and so the government is protected against the harassment of any votes of confidence it does not itself initiate, with the exception, of course, of the motion of censure.

In debate on the floor the government enjoys a kind of constitutional protection against its adversaries that gives it great tactical advantages. First, the timing of the debate is at the government's discretion. The text of the bill that the legislature discusses is the government's, with only those committee amendments that the government has chosen to accept. The government's program no longer suffers the fate of the government bills of the Third and Fourth Republics, which often emerged from committee in a form unacceptable to their original authors, who had no recourse against the committee except to get a deputy to introduce amendments to the committee product on the floor in order to restore the original bill. Once the debate is in process, the government may reject consideration of any amendment that was not presented before the committee. The penultimate weapon of the government is the right to demand that the legislature vote on the whole bill and not vote separately on individual clauses and amendments. The "package vote" allows the government to force the legislature to agree to a bill whose general purposes they accept, even when particular provisions would be rejected if ordinary legislative procedure were used.

Finally, the government can force the legislature to accept a bill by declaring its passage a matter of confidence. In such a case the bill passes unless the opposition can present and pass a motion of censure. This means that the bill on which the government has staked its existence passes unless an absolute majority of the assembly opposes it. Since a motion of censure requires a vote of the majority of all members of the National Assembly, those who abstain or are absent in effect count for the government. The opposition has been able to muster the necessary majority to defeat the government only once in the course of the Fifth Republic. In October 1962 the government of Georges Pompidou was censured after de Gaulle proposed a referendum on a constitutional amendment for the direct popular election of the President of the republic. De Gaulle had bypassed the Parliament, which according to the Constitution of 1958 (Article 89) must vote on proposed constitutional amendments before they are submitted to referendum. After the vote of censure, Pompidou resigned; de Gaulle dissolved the Assembly; called new elections; and the new legislature gave a vote of confidence to the new Pompidou government.

The third major function of the legislative assembly in the parliamentary system was to change governments. In the Fifth Republic, the National Assembly still exercises this function, but in a fashion that is circumscribed by the constitution. Although the President names the Prime Minister, he cannot recall him. He can only accept his resignation. Only the National Assembly can oblige the government to resign by defeating it on a motion of censure or on a vote of confidence initiated by the government itself. The result has been continuity in the office of Prime Minister. As of July 1972 only five men have served as Prime Minister in the Fifth Republic: Michel Debré, Georges Pompidou, Maurice Couve de Murville, Jacques Chaban-Delmas, and Pierre Messmer. The phenomenon of ministerial instability has not, however, disappeared. Even in the absence of effective parliamentary pressures to change the composition of governments, the government has felt it necessary to change its politics by changing its personnel. The Ministries of Agriculture and Education, for example, have each had three different ministers over the past four years.

The constitution has modified not only the functions performed by the Parliament but also the relationship between the two houses, the National Assembly and the Senate. The National Assembly, with 487 deputies, is essentially the same body as the Assembly of the Fourth Republic. The Senate (283 senators), however, replaces the second chamber of the Fourth Republic, the Council of the Republic, and has more power than its predecessor, which could amend or defeat a bill the Assembly had voted only by an absolute majority. Senators are elected by indirect suffrage—the representatives of local and departmental governments elect them —and they serve nine-year terms. The role of the Senate in the legislative process depends on the government's decision. If the government does not intervene, both the National Assembly and the Senate play the same part in the passage of legislation. Bills must pass both houses; any differences between the houses have to be ironed out in a conference committee composed of members of each house and then submitted to both chambers for final vote. However, when the Senate and the National Assembly do not agree, the government has the option of sending the bill to the National Assembly for final determination. The Senate then does not participate in the decision. In other words, the Senate cannot oppose the National Assembly effectively, if the government supports the Assembly. The Senate is clearly secondary to the National Assembly in other respects as well. Only the National Assembly may defeat the government with a motion of censure, and Prime Ministers have presented their programs for votes of confidence only in the Assembly. The Senate thus plays no part in the formation or defeat of governments.

The Senate has been losing power throughout the course of the Fifth Republic. After a constitutional amendment providing for direct election of the President was passed in 1962, the Senate was left as the only national political authority that did not emanate directly from national popular elections. The Senate's electorate of local officials is disproportionately rural, small-town, and provincial; and the senators are in large numbers men who were once the deputies of the Fourth and even Third Republics. Particularly in the early years of the Fifth Republic, the senators were the most active opponents of the government's programs and, as mentioned above, the government frequently had recourse to the National Assembly to overrule the Senate. The Senate was discredited in the eyes of the Left as an inadequately representative body; it was discredited in the eyes of the Gaullists as an obstructionist stronghold of the political forces opposed to the Fifth Republic.

It was therefore a great surprise when in April 1969 a national referendum defeated General de Gaulle's proposal that the Senate be replaced by a body that would include representatives of economic and social groups as well as of territorial units. The Economic and Social Council would essentially have been merged with the Senate, and delegates from the professions, the unions, business, commerce, and family associations would have sat in the new assembly alongside the representatives of local governments. The reform would have changed not only the composition of the body, but its powers as well. The new Senate would have had the right to present an opinion on laws, but not to vote on them. The transformation of the Senate was tied to a project establishing regional authorities throughout France. The authors of the reform intended that the new governmental bodies be organized in such a way that they could not be used by the political parties or the traditional political elites as bases of power from which to challenge the government. The mode of selection of the members was supposed to ensure that the "real" forces of the nation, the economic and social groups, presumably less partisan and more concerned with finding solutions to problems within the framework of the existing system, would dominate in the new assemblies at the regional and national levels. Political groups that had been in favor of decentralization and regionalization all along were not enthusiastic about the government's proposal, because they found it inadequate, and they pointed out that it would probably allow the old local notables to take control of the new regional authorities. On the other side, the traditional political elites also opposed the reform, for they felt it endangered their position in local politics. The great opponent of the reform was the Senate, whose members fanned out into the country to lead a campaign to vote no in the referendum. De Gaulle announced before the referendum that if the vote were negative, he would resign his office.

Despite the transformation of the regional referendum into a vote of confidence for de Gaulle, 53 percent of the voters cast their ballots against the proposal, defeating it. It would be impossible to conclude that this vote measures popular support for the Senate, because a variety of other factors clearly influenced the outcome, most important of which were dissatisfaction with the regional aspects of the reform and the widespread feeling that since there was a likely successor to the presidency (Pompidou), de Gaulle's ultimatum could be ignored without imperiling the stability of the regime. From a comparison of voters who supported de Gaulle in the 1962 referendum (on direct election of the President) with the supporters in 1969, it appears that the groups defecting were drawn heavily from the traditional sectors of French society. Though the role of the Senate may be "altogether secondary" (de Gaulle's phrase) and the institution itself may appear to groups from the modern, urban centers as a dead weight from the past, for a significant part of the country the Senate represents "a certain France." The groups who feel this way are still strong enough to protect the institution.

The Government

The government includes the Prime Minister, ministers he names to the Cabinet, and state secretaries. In a certain sense, the President of the republic is also a member of the government, since he presides by right over the meetings of the Council of Ministers. Anyone who read only the sections on the government in the Constitution of 1958 would have a hard time predicting the role the government has actually played in the Fifth Republic. The constitution states that "the Government determines and conducts the policies of the Nation. It disposes of the administration and armed forces" (Article 20). "The Prime Minister directs the action of the Government. He is responsible for national defense. He assures the execution of the laws" (Article 21). These rather vague descriptions of the role of the government and the Prime Minister left open the most important question: Would the executive power be exercised primarily by the Prime Minister and government or by the President? The history of the Fifth Republic has answered the question in favor of the President. The Prime Ministers have been the trusted and hand-picked associates of the Presidents. Major policy decisions under Pompidou as well as de Gaulle have been made by the President and carried out by the Prime Minister.

Historical circumstances, rather than the structures laid out in the constitution, explain the development of the political system in a direction that strengthens the

President and weakens the Prime Minister. Charles de Gaulle, the first President of the Fifth Republic, was an exceptional figure, whose role in French history conferred an extraordinary prestige and authority on his person. (See the section "The President" in this chapter.) Both because of his personal authority and because of his own conception of the presidency, de Gaulle was bound to dominate the relationships with his Prime Ministers. Though Debré chafed in the role when he was obliged to carry out Algerian policies with which he was hardly in agreement and Pompidou apparently did not espouse some of the policies he had to present after May–June 1968, neither of the two men ever challenged the President's right to make the major policy decisions.

De Gaulle's power and prestige were so great that he might have dominated all state policy. In noncrisis periods, however, he concerned himself primarily with foreign policy. Here de Gaulle made decisions alone, often announcing his policies only after the fact to the Council of Ministers. Sometimes he did not even trouble to do that, and the government learned of the decision from the newspapers, as on the occasion when he came out for independence for Quebec while on a trip to Canada. De Gaulle's exclusive control of foreign affairs supported the development of an extra-constitutional distinction between a "reserved sphere" in which the President may act and a residual parliamentary and governmental sphere. Into the President's sphere, as defined by de Gaulle's interests, fell foreign policy, defense, and constitutional matters. "All the rest" he ordinarily left to the government. The distinction had the effect of shearing the Prime Minister of powers that according to the constitution were his, if not to exercise alone, at least to share with the President. The constitution does not give the President a monopoly of the conduct of foreign policy, though it does grant him the right to "negotiate and ratify treaties." Nor does it give the President a predominant role in amending the constitution. On the contrary, the constitution specifies that constitutional amendments must be initiated by the President and the Prime Minister together and voted by both houses of the Parliament. Because of de Gaulle's exceptional authority, the President was acknowledged to have an exclusive right of decision on these questions that is nowhere recognized by the constitution. With the passing of the presidency from de Gaulle to Pompidou, the boundaries between the reserved sphere and the rest have become blurred. Nonetheless, the distinction has not altogether disappeared. It was revealing in this regard that Pompidou, not Chaban-Delmas, met Edward Heath, the British Prime Minister, to discuss British entry into the Common Market and, more generally, that it is Pompidou who makes foreign policy decisions.

The third historical circumstance that worked to make the Prime Minister a less powerful figure than the letter of the constitution might suggest was the strength of the Gaullist party in the legislature. At least in the early years of the Fifth Republic, this factor of Gaullist party dominance, like the development of a reserved presidential sphere, depended on the extraordinary esteem in which de Gaulle was held by the French electorate. A vote for the U.N.R., the Gaullist party, was in the minds of the voters a vote for de Gaulle. The significance of this for the role of the Prime Minister was that his majority was in fact a majority held together by the President. The Prime Minister had no power base independent of the President, and had he attempted to challenge the President, he would not have been able to rally his parliamentary majority behind him. This phenomenon has two components: The Prime Minister is weakened because his party has a double allegiance, to him and to the President, and even further weakened because, in the final analysis, his party supports him *because* he is the President's candidate.

It might have been anticipated that after de Gaulle, the tight embrace between the party and the President would loosen up and that in a more fluid situation the Prime Minister would be able to liberate himself from dependence on the President and to develop more autonomous relations with the legislative party majority. In fact this has not happened. Even a man like Pompidou, with none of de Gaulle's charismatic relationship to the French and with no glorious historic role to recommend him, has been able to take hold of the party and to keep the Prime Minister in almost the same dependent role as that which Pompidou himself had experienced during his terms as Prime Minister. Only six weeks after Chaban-Delmas had received a large vote of confidence from the National Assembly, Pompidou requested his resignation (July 1972), once again demonstrating where the real power in the regime lies. Perhaps a man less popular with the U.N.R. than Pompidou might not have the same authority with the majority in the legislature, but it seems more likely that in modern states all those factors that focus attention on a single leader—elections, television, press—will work to make the President and not the Prime Minister the real leader of the majority.

What if the Prime Minister were of a different party than the President? If the legislative elections returned a National Assembly whose party composition was such that the President could only name a Prime Minister of a party other than his own, what powers might the Prime Minister exercise by virtue of functions assigned him in the constitution? The constitution grants the Prime Minister several important powers that he may use even without the agreement of the President. The most important of these is the right to make policy and enact decrees on any subject except those specifically assigned by the constitution to the Parliament. When a bill falls into the category of regulations, not law, the government may act without the approval of Parliament or President. Moreover, in many of the laws that do require the consent of Parliament there is provision for enabling legislation, and this is prepared by the government and cannot be rejected by Parliament. The constitution also grants the Prime Minister important weapons for controlling his own government and for dealing with Parliament. Because it is the Prime Minister who is empowered to enact regulations, he may refuse to sign the decrees prepared by his ministers. The Prime Minister may summon Parliament to meet in special session. The decision to convene a conference committee of deputies and senators to resolve differences over the passage of a bill is his. With few and rather unimportant exceptions the other powers of the government can only be exercised together with the President.

The President

The constitutional document of 1958 did not create a presidential system. Indeed, most observers of the French political scene described it as a modified parliamentary system, which would revert to traditional parliamentary practices once de Gaulle left the presidency. The Constitution of 1958 places the President in much the same position as the Prime Minister: with few powers that he might exercise without the agreement of either government or Parliament. Those powers are, however, extremely important. The President may dissolve the National Assembly and call new elections at any time, except if he has already done so within the year. If the legislative elections return a National Assembly whose political composition makes it impossible to form a government, if a government pursues policies he disapproves, or if the Assembly refuses the Prime Minister he has named, then the President may appeal to the electorate. The risk he runs is that, like the first President of the Third Republic, Marshal Marie de MacMahon, who dissolved a chamber he found too republican only to have the electorate return more of the same, he may find himself obliged to give in or resign. The one dissolution of the Fifth Republic followed the 1962 censure of the Pompidou government, and it did serve the President's cause, for new elections brought back an Assembly with more loyal Gaullists.

The second major set of presidential powers are the emergency powers he may exercise "when the institutions of the Republic, national independence, the integrity of national territory or the application of international commitments are threatened in a serious and immediate fashion and the normal functioning of public institutions is interrupted" (Article 16). In such circumstances the constitution authorizes the President to take whatever measures he deems necessary to meet the emergency. The only checks on the very broad grant of powers extended by Article 16 are the requirement that the President consult with the Prime Minister, the Presidents of the two houses of Parliament, and the Constitutional Council and the provision that Parliament remain in session during the period of exercise of these special powers. In the final analysis, these checks do not constitute an obstacle to the President's exercising his own judgment both as to whether an emergency exists, which requires the use of the special powers of Article 16, or as to what ought to be done during the emergency. Indeed the only formal limitation on the vast powers implied by the phrase "whatever measures circumstances require" is the qualification that the President's decisions must be motivated by the intention to allow the basic public institutions to operate as soon as possible.

Article 16 was invoked once during the Fifth Republic—in April 1961, when French generals in revolt against a policy leading to Algerian independence threatened to invade the French mainland and take over the government. De Gaulle declared a state of emergency. Even though the Military *Putsch* was defeated a few days after Article 16 had gone into effect, de Gaulle continued to exercise the special powers of Article 16 for another five months.

In other respects as well, de Gaulle interpreted his own powers under Article 16 broadly and the checks that other groups might exercise, restrictively. Parliament, as the constitution required, met during the period of special powers, but de Gaulle refused to allow them to legislate. On another occasion, when Parliament in 1960 had tried to defeat the government over a bill creating an independent nuclear force, de Gaulle was apparently willing to contemplate using Article 16 if the motion of censure passed, though whether a parliamentary veto on nuclear armaments would have created a state of emergency was highly debatable, to say the least. The constitution provides no effective check on a President who would choose to use Article 16 in an arbitrary or dictatorial fashion, and the only real controls are the President's own respect for democratic process and the possibilities of extra-constitutional resistance to the President's special powers by other public bodies.

The third set of powers that the President may exercise alone—without the agreement of government or Parliament—concern the administration of justice. The President names three of the nine regular members of the Constitutional Council; and he has the right of pardon.

Beyond these powers the President can act only in collaboration with other political bodies. Even to call a referendum, which the President alone may do, requires that either the government or the Parliament propose it to him. Since 1958 the referendum has played a very important role in strengthening the presidency. De Gaulle used it when he critically needed support for a decision disputed by parts of the political elite, at such times calling a referendum and declaring that he would resign unless the sovereign will of the people confirmed his policy. Referendums were held in September 1958 on the new constitution; in January 1961 to approve the policy of self-determination for Algeria; in April 1962 to approve the Evian agreements that ended the Algerian war; in October 1962 to ratify a constitutional amendment for the direct election of the President; and finally in April 1969 to decide on regional governments and reform of the Senate.

The device of the referendum allows the President to present an issue to the public in terms that often simplify complex matters by demanding a yes or no answer from the voter. By staking his office on the outcome of the referendum and threatening the public that without him the political system would return to the disorders of the Fourth Republic, de Gaulle was able to win massive public approval in the referendums. In each case except the last one, de Gaulle was supported by a large majority of the electorate, and he was able to push through policies that powerful groups in the political elite opposed. Once the President had behind him a successful referendum vote, it was—and will be—virtually impossible for any of the other branches of government to block his projects, for the expression of public sentiment in the referendum has the weight of popular sovereignty. For example, when the President of the Senate requested that the Constitutional Council rule on the constitutionality of the 1962 amendment for direct election of the President, a change that had been ratified by referendum but not previously approved by the Parliament, the Council refused to consider the case. The Council argued that while it had the right to judge the constitutionality of laws voted by Parliament, it should not consider those passed by referendum, since such decisions are "the direct expression of national sovereignty."

All other acts of the presidency can be taken only in close cooperation with the government. Since this is the case, why has the Fifth Republic developed into a presidential and not a parliamentary system? The reasons for the predominance of the President in the Fifth Republic derive not from the letter of the constitution but from two other sources: de Gaulle's conception of the presidency and the constitutional amendment providing direct election for the President. The political system of the Fifth Republic is in many respects the creation of a single man, Charles de Gaulle. De Gaulle came to power in 1958 supported not only by overwhelming public approval of the constitution he proposed, but also by widespread and profound public respect for the historic role and political figure that de Gaulle represented. For Frenchmen, de Gaulle was the man whose refusal to accept defeat in 1940 had preserved French honor and the integrity of the French nation for the future. De Gaulle had saved France once, by leaving France for England in 1940 and organizing armed forces that served with the Allies and aided in the liberation of France in 1944. He saved the country a second time, when he agreed to form a government in 1958 to avert civil war. In his own mind, as well as for what may have been a majority of Frenchmen, de Gaulle had a double legitimacy: not only the legitimacy that election conferred, but a legitimacy that flowed from a historic destiny in which de Gaulle had embodied and defended France.[9] De Gaulle commanded a kind of religious respect and admiration from his closest political associates as well as from the public. Without understanding this, it would be impossible to understand how, with a constitution that gave as many levers of power to the Prime Minister and government as to the President, de Gaulle was able to impose his will on the entire political system and to orient according to his own ideas not only the content of policy but the institutional development of the regime. Few jurists would have accepted de Gaulle's interpretation of the constitution when he declared in 1964 that "the indivisible authority of the state is entirely entrusted to the President by the people who have elected him and all other authority, whether ministerial, civil, military, judicial is conferred and maintained by him." But the political practice of the Fifth Republic proceeded as if the constitutional system were indeed such as de Gaulle described it.

The place of the presidency in the political system bears the stamp of de Gaulle's conceptions of how the French state ought to be organized if France is to play the great role that is her rightful part in world affairs. Already in his Bayeux speech, de Gaulle had shown a clear preference for a political system in which the President would be dominant. Political unity, he argued then, can be preserved only when the executive power of the state is in the hands of a single authority, responsible before no group but the nation itself. The Constitution of 1958 assigned

---

[9]Maurice Duverger, *Institutions politiques et droit constitutionnel* (Paris: Presses Universitaires de France, 1970), p. 741.

functions to the President that seemed substantially less broad than those de Gaulle had outlined at Bayeux. In part de Gaulle may have felt it necessary to reassure the traditional political elites about the democratic and republican character of the constitution he was proposing by limiting the powers of the presidency. And he may also have felt certain of being able to accomplish what was necessary by force of his own authority, even with a constitutional grant of power that fell beneath his ultimate hopes. De Gaulle's experience in office confirmed that his own prestige and authority gave the presidency the preeminent role in the system that he felt necessary to political stability. The problem was whether his eventual successors, who would not bring the same authority with them to the office, would be able to govern with the same set of constitutional powers. The question became a pressing one after an assassination attempt. And when de Gaulle decided on the 1962 referendum to ratify the constitutional amendment for direct election of the President, it was not because his own authority in the office was insufficient for his purposes but, rather, to strengthen future Presidents.

The direct election of the President has fundamentally changed the nature of the constitutional system. In the Constitution of 1958 only the National Assembly depended directly on universal suffrage, and this legitimated a claim to supremacy over Senate and President, both of which were chosen by indirect suffrage. The President was elected by an electoral college that resembled the Senate's: local and provincial officials, deputies, and other high officials in the state. The President was thus dependent on the traditional political elites for election. In an age of mass politics, direct elections confer a democratic legitimacy to authority that no other method of selection or election can. The President of the Constitution of 1958 could appeal to the national electorate only by the referendum or by dissolving the National Assembly and calling new legislative elections. Both these methods could be used in only rather limited circumstances; neither of them provided the President with the kind of national confirmation of his authority that direct election of a man confers. By changing the mode of election, then, de Gaulle was able to provide the President with a claim to represent national sovereignty that, except for its lack of tradition, was as strong as the National Assembly's claim.

The result is a mixed system of authority in which, as long as President and government are of the same party, the presidential elements are likely to dominate. As Pompidou described the system in 1964:

> France has now chosen a system midway between the American presidential regime and the British parliamentary regime, where the chief of state, who formulates general policy, has the basis of his authority in universal suffrage but can only exercise his functions with a government that he may have chosen and named, but which in order to survive, must maintain the confidence of the Assembly.

Despite the predominance of the President, the system will work only when the President and the government can work together, for each one has sufficient powers to block the functioning of the state.

The Constitutional Council

Until recently, the Constitutional Council would not have merited more than a mention in a description of the functioning of the Fifth Republic. Though the powers granted the Council in the constitution seemed to lay out a role as broad as that exercised by the American Supreme Court in determining the constitutionality of legislation, the history of the Constitutional Council has justified none of the expectations (or fears) of strong judicial authority. The very composition of the court assured that the government would find a very sympathetic hearing in it. Three of the nine regular judges are named by the President, three by the President of the Assembly, and three by the President of the Senate; the nine judges serve nine-year terms. Former Presidents of the republic serve as lifetime members. The main substance of the court's activity has been settling conflicts between the Parliament and executive over the boundaries of law and regulation (see the section "The Parliament" in this chapter) and deciding the outcomes of disputed elections. In virtually all important decisions, the Constitutional Council upheld the authority of the executive. It refused to determine the constitutionality of the 1962 referendum vote on direct election of the President; nor would it decide whether Parliament should have the right to present a motion of censure when meeting in special session during the exercise of the special powers of Article 16 (1961).

The Constitutional Council seemed so compliant an auxiliary of executive authority that no one could have anticipated its ruling against the government in July 1971 on the constitutionality of a law regulating voluntary associations. The government had presented a bill to Parliament that modified the 1901 law on the freedom to form associations. The 1901 law automatically granted legal recognition to any group requesting it. In 1936 when the activities of right-wing and fascist groups had threatened the republic, legislation had been passed that gave the government the right, subject to judicial review, to dissolve groups whose acts endangered the state. After the May–June 1968 student and worker strikes, the 1936 legislation had been used rather freely by the Minister of the Interior to close down left-wing associations and ban their newspapers. Now the government was requesting legislation that would allow it to refuse the right to form an association to any group that was considered to be simply a revival of an organization previously dissolved. Such a change would have amounted to prior censorship and, as such, a serious limitation of the freedom of association guaranteed by the 1901 law. The National Assembly passed the bill, but the Senate refused it, and the government used its right to return the bill to the Assembly for final deliberation. The President of the Senate then requested that the Constitutional Council determine the constitutionality of the bill. The Council accepted the case and declared parts of the law unconstitutional because they limited freedom of association, a right protected by the preamble to the Constitution of 1958. This case of judicial protection of civil liberties against the executive has hardly established a precedent for wide use of the powers of judicial review by the court. What is important about the case is that in a political system with few effective checks on the power of the executive when President and government agree, the court may be the only institution that can defend fundamental liberties. One question is whether the court would be willing to play this role, and here it would be premature to draw conclusions from a single case. The other, and more fundamental, issue is whether such an exercise of judicial authority would be considered legitimate in a political system where authority that does not derive from popular sovereignty has little sanction in republican political tradition.

Three

The Development of the Party System

For anyone raised in a country with a two-party system, the multiplicity of French political parties seems both unnecessary and unsuited to the purposes of modern politics. Why are there six major parties when a simplification of the party system to two or three would better serve the functions of governing and organizing opposition? Why are parties with interests and programs as close as those of the Radical-Socialists and the Center parties or as those of the two Socialist parties unable to unite or even to form stable coalitions? How do parties formed at the time of the passionate conflicts between partisans of Church and state survive even when the issue that created them has almost vanished from the political scene? And even more difficult to fathom, what shifts in French society or changes in the policies of the state might promote the emergence of a new party system?

First, how can we explain the multiplicity of parties and account for the particular parties that occupy the political arena in France today? There are several explanations of why a country develops either a two-party or a multiparty system. One theory emphasizes the importance of electoral systems. The single-member district, one round of balloting, winner-take-all elections of the United States and Britain apparently disadvantage third parties, which receive far fewer legislative seats than the number to which they would be entitled were their share of the national assembly calculated as a proportion of the total national vote. Instead of being added up nationally, however, votes in the United States and Britain are counted in single-member districts, in each of which the third (or fourth) party is most likely to be swamped by the two big parties. In France, on the other hand, the two rounds of balloting, multimember large districts, and proportional representation that have been used in various combinations at different times allow smaller parties a better chance for representation and survival, for these parties can add up their votes over a wider territory. When, for example, elections are held in single-member districts, a party that wins one-third of the votes in several constituencies wins no representatives at all. If, as has often been the case in French elections, these small constituencies were combined into larger, multimember electoral districts, then such a party would have won one-third of the seats at stake.

France has experimented with several electoral systems, and each one has apparently strengthened and weakened different parties. In 1951 a reform of the method of calculating proportional representation provided incentives for the Center parties to ally and reduced the representation of the parties of the extreme Right and Left. In order to weaken the parties at both ends of the political spectrum, General de Gaulle when he came to power in 1958 returned to a single-member district system, with no proportional representation. This system, with two rounds of balloting, is the one used today in French legislative elections. American and British electoral rules have never been tried in French elections, so one can only speculate about whether their adoption would reduce the number of parties. The procedure adopted in 1965 for electing the President of the republic does force the voters to choose between the candidates of two parties on the second ballot. The two presidential elections that have been held with this system (1965 and 1969) apparently strengthened the largest parties and weakened the smaller ones, but it is still premature to draw conclusions about the impact of this electoral constraint on the French party system.

Other explanations of the multiparty system have identified ideology as the cause of the proliferation of political parties in France. Ideological stakes, or values, are less susceptible to compromise and accommodation than are economic stakes. While it is possible to negotiate political agreements that partially satisfy each of several groups' claims to a larger share of the national pie, it is difficult to imagine a political agreement that divides up absolute values. Workers seeking wage increases of 15 percent may be satisfied with a settlement that gives them 10 percent; but workers who want nationalization of the factory they work in must be either entirely satisfied or wholly dissatisfied, for a factory cannot be half-nationalized.

In spheres involving other values than economic ones, the point is even clearer: What compromise could satisfy both those who want the state to recognize Catholicism as the state religion and those who want a secular state? In sum, in countries where men find it more important to express and defend certain values than to obtain satisfaction of material interests, political compromises may be difficult to arrange. Considerations of political effectiveness and the hope of winning partial victories, which lead some groups to ally or to coalesce in larger, stronger, though less homogeneous organizations, weigh much less heavily in the calculations of political groups that are primarily concerned with defending ideological values. Ideological groups have fewer incentives to ally and many more reasons to protect jealously their independence and autonomy—for only in so doing can they continue to express the values for which they were founded. The strength of ideological factors in French politics may keep alive numerous political groups, even though the economic and social interests they represent are neither widely divergent nor irreconcilable.

Whatever the explanation of the multiplicity of French parties, however, it cannot account for the particular parties that have emerged in France. Despite changes in labels, splits, and regroupings, there has been a remarkable continuity in the major party organizations over the twenty-five years since World War II. Six political formations—Communist, Socialist, Radical, Christian Democratic, Independent, and Gaullist—have managed since the early years of the Fourth Republic to weather the vicissitudes of electoral swings, the arrival of new generations in politics, and even changes of regime to survive into the seventies.

Why this should be so is difficult to understand. One possibility is that each of the six parties represents a distinct social group, cluster of interests, or class and that the particularities of the party reflect the special characteristics of the group it defends. If such a theory were true, we could explain why these six political parties emerged and continue to exist and could predict that these parties would change when the interests of the social group they represented changed. Unfortunately, this answer does not help decipher much of the French political puzzle. Examination of the social bases of support of the political parties shows that each of them draws significant support from various social groups. The Socialist party, for example, gets 33 percent of its vote from blue-collar workers, but also 15 percent from peasants, 19 percent from white-collar workers, and 10 percent from businessmen and members of the liberal professions (see Table 3.1). The Independent Republicans, whose politics are at the other end of the political spectrum from the Socialists, have virtually the same pattern of electoral support. Even the Communist party must appeal to various classes: Only 51 percent of its votes come from workers. The characteristics of the social groups that provide supporters for a party may explain some aspects of the party's physiognomy and program, but the mesh between given social and economic groups, on the one hand, and a given party, on the other, is not close enough to answer the question of why, of all possible parties that might represent the interests of French society, these six have emerged.

Political sociology of the parties provides only part of the explanation of why Communists, Socialists, Radicals, Christian Democrats, Independents, and Gaullists are the main political actors in France. A method that might be called political archaeology, that is, using historical research to unearth the successive strata that underlie the contemporary political system, is the approach we must take in order to understand why these parties exist today and why they behave as they do. Just as the archaeologist discovers in his work that each civilization superimposes its structures on those built by previous generations, using the creations of the old society at the same time that it covers them up with its own creations, the political scientist studying the French party system discovers that the parties today represent superimposed layers of different political periods. Each party was built with the ideals and interests of a particular period, and its structure and ideology reflect the major problems and conflicts of the moment of its founding. Parties created at

Table 3.1 Distribution by Sex, Age, Profession, and Monthly Income of the Electorates of the Major Political Parties in 1965 Survey, in Percentages

Voter Characteristics	Communist	Socialist	Radical	M.R.P.	C.N.I.	U.N.R.	Indep. Rep.
Sex							
Men	61	63	64	47	55	48	49
Women	39	37	36	53	45	52	51
Age							
20–34	33	27	25	29	26	24	32
35–49	32	28	26	27	28	27	29
50–64	23	27	32	26	28	27	25
65 and older	12	18	17	18	18	22	14
Profession of Head of Family							
Farmers	8	15	17	25	20	13	17
Businessmen, shopowners	5	6	14	9	13	11	9
Liberal professions, upper white-collar workers	2	4	4	4	8	5	7
Employees, average white-collar workers	17	19	18	14	15	20	17
Blue-collar workers	51	33	25	25	20	27	31
Without profession	17	23	22	23	24	24	17
Monthly Income (francs)							
Less than 500*	13	17	16	23	15	16	20
500–799	22	22	25	20	20	20	20
800–1249	32	29	28	25	23	26	26
1250–1749	18	17	14	15	16	17	16
More than 1750	11	9	11	8	17	14	11
Nondeclared	4	6	6	9	9	7	7

*$1.00 = 5.4 francs.

DATA SOURCE: *Sondages* No. 2 (1966), pp. 13–14.

different stages of French political development represent, therefore, different kinds of concerns. For this reason the conventional presentation of parties, which strings them on a single Left-Right axis (as above, where we listed Communist to Independent Republican), is misleading for it mistakenly suggests that these parties have different answers to the same set of questions. Not only the answers, but the questions or issues to which each party is oriented are different. Only an excavation down to the origins of the party and an exploration of its historical role and meaning can determine the issues around which the party is organized.

The parties, however, do not *only* reflect the problems on which they were founded, for in order to survive in a changing political environment, they have had to confront new issues and new demands. In some measure, of course, parties can control which issues and demands are admitted into the arenas of political decision making. Even very severe economic and social problems remain "nonissues" politically until a group is able to link the problem to other public discontents and desires that depend on authoritative decision. For example, whether or not regional inequalities become a political issue in France or simply remain an economic fact may well depend on whether one of the parties picks up the problem and translates it into political terms. While the reactions of the parties to a new problem may determine the timing of its entrance into politics and shape the way it is politically perceived by elites and the public, it is unlikely that parties can forever block the political consideration of significant problems. A party unwilling to take up a set of new demands must always consider the potential costs of having another party do so. In the fall of 1970, for example, when the Gaullists refused to respond to demands for regional organization, the Radical party made regionalization the banner of its program, and the Gaullists hurriedly "restated" their position in order not to lose too much political capital. In periods when all the parties have tacitly collaborated in excluding certain demands from politics, new parties have arisen to advance these claims. The founding of the Socialist party at the end of the nineteenth century, for example, owes much to the attempts by the existing parties to keep the demands of the working class out of the political system.

To avoid these risks and to widen the basis of their appeal, the political parties have shifted their interests and ideals in response to the demands of new times. Each party now represents both the structure and ideology of its origins and the successive layers of response to new political problems. Each major issue to which the party responds generates particular categories and party institutions and brings into the party special kinds of leaders and followers. In an "archaeological" slice into a French political party, we can identify the men and issues of different political periods, all of whom coexist in a single party organization. The programs of the present Christian Democratic party *(Centre Démocrate),* for example, express certain values developed in the nineteenth- and early twentieth-century conflicts between Church and state, include other issues that emerged in the struggle between socialist and antisocialist forces in the early and mid-twentieth century, still other items that derive from the European orientation of the Christian Democrats in the early postwar period, onto all of which are added the political choices of this group during the Gaullist governments of the past decade. To each of these layers is attached a particular set of political personnel and a certain part of the Christian Democratic electorate.

The process of political change in the parties is one of accretion and erosion, not one of radical elimination. The layers below do not disappear but shape the topography of the layers on the surface. The men who entered a party thirty years ago to defend particular values are aging, and their influence and power are gradually declining; but during their long reign they will have stamped both the party institutions and the new generation of party men in their mold. The Christian Democrats, despite the virtual identity between their views on matters of current politics and the views of other political groups, cannot, or rather, choose not, to merge with other groups, because Christian Democracy remains different from even those parties whose current choices it shares. *What* are different are the men, the constituents, the institutions, the political instincts, and the political categories built up over the years of organizing around the issues of different periods.

Many conflicts of interests and ideals have shaped the behavior of French political parties. Three of these conflicts, however, have had such a massive impact on French politics in general and on the values and orientations of the parties in particular that the political crises that generated them must be discussed at some length.

The Crisis of the National Community: The Church-State Conflict

The appearance of mass political parties in France in the first decade of the twentieth century coincided with the crystallization of political conflicts around the issue of relations between the French state and the Catholic church. In the years in which party organizations were developing a mass base, the dominant political elites were lining up on the side of Church or state. The laws up for decision in Parliament, the pressures from citizens, the passions of the press—all these political forces pushed the naissant parties to focus on the issues that involved the role of the Catholic church in the state. The political parties were polarized into two camps: a Left camp of the supporters of a secular (laïque) France and a Right camp of the partisans of a Catholic traditional France. For most Frenchmen, Left and Right came to mean anticlerical and clerical.

When new problems arose in politics, they were looked at through glasses tinted by the colors of this particular battle. The passions and ideas, alliances and enmities generated by the alignment of party politics on the Church-state crisis continued to orient the political understanding of Frenchmen long after the moment of acute crisis had passed. We shall discuss later why the French system is so slow to generate new ideas and political alliances; why, in this particular case, clericalism and anticlericalism remain powerful organizing concepts in French politics, even when the passion and substance have evaporated from the issue that once gave the concepts their meaning. Here we intend only to emphasize that, despite public apathy about the one remaining significant issue of public policy in the Church-state area—the question of state subsidies to and control of Church-operated schools—party divisions based on the Church-state controversy persist and structure the political behavior of Frenchmen.

Today, some sixty-five years after the parliamentary decision to separate Church and state was supposed to have "solved" the problem, the division between Left and Right voters in many regions of France continues to be the same as the division between those who send their children to public schools and those who send their children to Church schools. In Finistère, a department in western France, for example, the correlation coefficient between the proportion of children in Catholic schools and Right votes is .791. Even when party labels and attachments change, the political attitudes expressed may remain the same. For example, in large parts of central France, the Left electorate switched its vote after the war from the

Radical and the Socialist parties to the Communist party, but apparently the political meaning of the vote remained the same: anticlericalism. Even in regions where other political conflicts and alliances have replaced Church-state as the dominant axis of party struggle, the Church-state categories continue to account for a diminishing but still significant part of the vote.

What have been the consequences of the organization of French politics on an axis of conflict whose poles were set by the Church-state issue? First, the weight of this issue has contributed to the ideological character of French political life. As was pointed out before, parties that care more about defending ideal values like the ones central to the Church-state crisis—faith or reason, tradition or science, moral order or moral improvement—will be parties unwilling to seek out compromises. Ideological politics generates inflexible stances by the parties, not only because of the indivisible nature of the goals that are pursued but also because of the high emotions that the issues evoke. What issue of pragmatic, interest-based politics can arouse passions as intense as those of the Frenchmen who felt, in one camp, that attending public schools endangered the religious salvation of their children and, in the other camp, that all chances for political community and moral progress depended on each little citizen's receiving an equal, identical, hence public education?

And once such feelings are created by politics, how can men so bitterly opposed on one issue shift alliances when other issues, secondary by their definition to the dominant conflict, are raised? The second consequence, indeed, of the organization of political life on the Church-state axis was the freezing of party alignments and, in general, the paralysis and stagnation of the party system. Within the camp of the clerical Right there have always been groups that believed that private property and the market economy should be replaced by an economic system based on different social values that would better protect the right of all classes to a decent living and to participation in the decisions that affect their working lives. These "socialist" groups within the Catholic camp, however, have not been able to get together with elements within the anticlerical Left who share their views on economic matters, any more than Left-wingers with conservative property views have been able to ally with those on the Right with the same economic ideas. In both cases what divides Left and Right has mattered more than the issues on which groups within the camps agree, and so, despite temporary and unstable alliances across the boundaries of Left and Right, there has been no fundamental reform of party alignments. In 1965, for example, when Gaston Defferre, a conservative Socialist, tried to form a federation of the M.R.P. (Popular Republican Movement), the Socialists, and the Radicals, three parties representing constituencies with similar or overlapping social and economic interests and with moderate political programs, the proposed alliance foundered on old ideological obstacles, prominent among which was the school question. Despite the convergence of interests, despite the incentive to alliance provided by a forthcoming presidential election, the M.R.P. on the Right and the Radicals and Socialists on the Left could not break out of the mold set by historic political controversies.

The third major consequence of the organization of the parties along the Church-state axis of conflict has been the difficulty of inserting economic and social demands into the political process. Parties set up for the expression of the ideological values centered on secularism and religion are poor instruments for the aggregation and defense of economic interests. An interest group that wished to promote its demands in the parliamentary arena found parties oriented by ideas that had little to do with social and economic concerns. An agricultural group in the thirties, for example, when looking for a party to support its demands for higher food prices, found that the party system provided only left-wing and right-wing, that is, anticlerical and Catholic, parties and that choosing one or the other of them immediately classed the interest group in the camp of Left or Right. Thereupon the group lost whichever of its members belonged to the opposite electoral camp, without any guarantee that the party it chose would or could promote the group's demands.

In no political system can interest groups support a party with any absolute assurance that if the party wins power the group's demand will become policy. But in France the interest group's weighing of the potential risks and benefits of supporting a party dipped far towards the side of costs. Until the Fifth Republic, French governments were coalitions of various parties, in which no single party could impose its program. Moreover, the economic and social items in party programs were likely to have low priority. The interest group might well find that the party on which it had banked furthered ideological demands at the expense of satisfaction of social and economic demands.

Confronted with the inadequacy of the parties for identifying, organizing, and presenting economic and social demands in the arenas of political decision, some groups sought access to power outside the party framework. Interest groups tried to work directly with the state bureaucracy; others tried to establish corporative associations that could satisfy the needs of members without resort to the state; still others used violent tactics in order to force their demands into the political process. These attempts to bypass the parties produced successes that were generally directly proportional to the specificity of the group's demands and to the restricted nature of the group's clientele. A wheat producers' group whose members had large farms specializing in a single crop and whose only demand was for higher wheat prices might successfully pursue its demand, even without a party to back it up. On the other hand, an agricultural group representing owners of both large and small farms of various kinds and having a variety of demands for price supports and state assistance to "improve the lot of the peasant class" was unlikely to obtain satisfaction, because the diversity of the situations it tried to defend required a reconciliation and aggregation of interests beyond the capacity of an interest group.

Which political functions can be handled by interest groups and which can be managed only by political parties varies from country to country. But in France it is clear that the ideological character of the parties has made them such poor instruments of interest aggregation that interest groups have been forced to take on tasks that only a party could manage successfully. As one result of this, certain social and economic categories have been poorly defended in politics. Another consequence historically has been the organization of new parties in order to promote interests that existing parties ignored.

The Crisis of Socialism: Class Against Class Conflict

Among the social groups whose interests were systematically excluded from the political arena by the division of the parties into a republican, secular Left and a traditional Catholic Right was the working class. The economic, social, and political demands of the growing work force employed in industry were demands that neither Left nor Right at the turn of the century undertook to translate into projects for public action. The unwillingness of the political parties to incorporate the demands of the working class reflected in large measure the bourgeois composition of the political elites of both Left and Right parties and their broad consensus on preserving the social and economic status quo. The social consensus of the political elites provided a stable foundation for the political system, so that, despite ideological disagreements on political authority, all groups rallied to the defense of traditional social and economic institutions and supported only changes that could be accommodated within the social status quo.

To explain why the parties excluded the demands of the working class, it is not enough to show that the elites of all parties, Left and Right, were drawn from bourgeois society. In Britain, for example, the evolution of the Conservative party shows that a party based on traditional elites can incorporate the demands of other social classes and respond by adaptation to new problems. The inability of the French political parties to recognize and include working-class social and economic demands was the result not only of the conservatism of the political elites but also of the kind of politics that had developed during the Third Republic. The structuring of partisan conflict and of the parties themselves by the issues of republicanism, the Church, education, and the legacy of the Revolution of 1789 had created political categories with which it was virtually impossible to identify, let alone organize to meet, problems caused by social and economic needs and change. The struggle to introduce these demands into the political system produced new party organizations and a new axis of conflict, whose poles were the interests and values defended, on one end, by the propertied classes and, on the other, by the industrial proletariat.

The conflicts over the organization of production and the distribution of the rewards of production which divided these two camps became crystallized in a confrontation between the Socialist party (or parties) and the opponents of socialism. This conflict, like the crisis of political authority expressed in the Church-state conflict, had its origins in the nineteenth century. Indeed, its outlines can be traced in some of the later phases of the Revolution of 1789. Despite the active and increasingly autonomous role of industrial workers in the revolutionary movements of 1848 and 1871, however, the development of working-class political organizations was slow. Until the end of the nineteenth century, socialist and working-class groups were intellectual circles or workers' mutual assistance societies, with small followings and, often, short lives. The lengthy maturation of the working-class movement reflected the slow pace of French industrialization and the predominance in the industrial, as well as commercial and artisanal, sectors of small-scale family enterprises in which trade-union organization was difficult. The variety of industrial structures was matched by a great diversity of working-class statuses, situations, and attitudes, and this, too, inhibited the growth of mass organization. The fierce political repression following the Paris Commune of 1871, in which the revolutionary leaders were killed or sent into exile, further retarded the development of working-class political organizations.

The French Workers' party *(Parti Ouvrier Français),* organized in the last decade of the nineteenth century, was the first French party focusing on working-class demands that mobilized a mass following. This party differed from the other parties of Left and Right in three important respects. Unlike the traditional parties, whose organizational structures were thinly developed and, indeed, barely existed except at election times, the French Workers' party created an organizational network that made possible continuous party activity engaging the energies of supporters at all levels of the group. In contrast to the other parties, which made little effort to recruit members and whose typical members were local notables interested in winning elections, the new workers' party had a high ratio of members to electors. Sixty percent of its members were industrial workers. Finally, unlike the other parties, whose doctrines were statements of position on the legitimacy of the republican state, the workers' party declared its adherence to Marxism and announced that the battles it would fight would be those of the working class, for whom the old political categories no longer defined the terms of political commitment.

For this party and for the unified Socialist party, which in 1905 absorbed it along with other socialist factions, it was often difficult to reconcile defending the working class, and the working class alone, with defending the republican, secular political values also held by socialists. The Socialist party came on the political scene at a time when it was already occupied by other actors and when another political drama was already being acted out. Today as at its founding, the great question for the socialist movement is its relationship to these other political actors. Unable to wipe the slate clean and to write their own terms for partisan conflict, the socialists have had to operate in a political world they did not make. In simplest form, the debate among socialists has revolved about the question of whether socialists should remain bystanders in political quarrels that do not directly affect the interests of workers as workers or whether socialists should actively line up with the republican Left, since workers are citizens as well as workers and citizens have an interest in preserving a particular kind of political regime.

The question was not an abstract one, but a matter of practical politics. Should socialists run candidates in legislative elections, particularly when this meant appealing for votes to other sectors of the population than workers? When a Socialist candidate came in after another Left candidate on the first round of balloting, should the Socialist candidate stay in the race on the run-off ballot at the risk of splitting the vote of the Left and letting the Right win? What part should the Socialist deputy play in Parliament? Should he support projects of the nonsocialist Left? or vote for a nonsocialist Left government? or accept office in a Left government? On each of these questions the socialist movement was torn by bitter conflicts between those who believed that the political system could evolve toward socialism through reforms and those who argued that the ruling classes would never peacefully relinquish power and so the state would have to be captured in a revolution.

The reformers, like the great socialist leader Jean Jaurès, believed that the socialist society they desired would emerge from a long process of historical evolution. The political traditions and accomplishments of the French Revolution and of the republican, secular Left through the nineteenth century would be extended into the economy and society, and the idea of participatory democracy would be widened to include the working class. These socialists saw themselves as an integral part of the Left and as its most advanced wing. They conceived their role as two-fold: first, to represent and defend the proletariat and, second, to ally with, encourage, and prod all that was progressive in France in order to speed up the process of change. These socialists therefore advocated a wide participation in parliamentary politics and a general policy of support to the nonsocialist Left in all matters except those where the interests of workers were directly at stake. They kept "republican discipline": In elections they withdrew after the first ballot in favor of the Left candidate most likely to win; in Parliament they voted for Left governments.

In opposition to the strategy of "republican discipline" other socialists advocated a strategy of nonalliance with the bourgeois Left, a "class against class" strategy, in the phrase of the Communist leader Maurice Thorez. These were socialists who refused to align themselves along the axis of conflict of the traditional Left and Right and who defined Left–Right as the distinction between the working class and the bourgeoisie. The categories that provided their guidelines for political action were those generated by the battle for socialism, not by the battle for "bourgeois" political democracy. These socialists (and the Communists after the founding of the Communist party in 1920) broke with republican discipline and maintained their candidates alongside other Left candidates in run-off elections so that working-class interests could be expressed.

Even the staunchest advocates of class discipline against republican discipline could not always avoid lining up on old battlegrounds and allying with nonsocialist Left groups in support of republican values. As the threats of Nazism abroad and the extreme Right at home grew through the thirties, the Communist party shifted and began to urge an alliance among all Left parties to defend democratic liberties. To achieve this "Popular Front," the Communists loyally observed republican discipline in the 1936 elections and supported the Left government elected by the new legislature. Again during the period of wartime resistance to the Germans, the Communists found it politically desirable and necessary to broaden their alliances beyond the boundaries indicated by the terms of class struggle to fight a battle that they defined in national and liberal terms. To build a "national front" to win the war and restore the French republic and national independence, the Communists looked even beyond alliance with the Left to the Catholics. The Communist poet Louis Aragon dedicated to two fallen Resistance heroes, a Communist and a Catholic, a poem memorializing the single cause of the soldier who believes in heaven and the soldier who does not: "Only a madman would think of his quarrels in the heart of a common battle."

In periods other than those of national crisis the Communist party has sometimes found it expedient either to behave as the most extreme part of a Left camp defined by old republican categories and to ally with all Left parties or to present itself as the pivot of class alliance against bourgeois parties and to ally with socialist Left parties. Each of these two strategies is a departure from the strict class against class strategy by which the Communists define their party as the sole representative of the proletariat and as the ally of no other party. Whichever of these three political strategies is in force determines the election policy of the party, its willingness to negotiate joint action with the Socialist party and the non-Marxist Left, and its nationalist or internationalist orientation. The Socialist party is similarly torn between the imperatives of republican discipline and class against class struggle. The burning issues before the Socialist party in the past decade—whether to ally with Communists or Radicals, whether to merge the party in a broad Left federation— all reflect this tension. The Radical party, too, is torn by the contradictory implications of different political goals: By their republicanism they are pulled toward alliance with the Socialists (and potentially with the Communists); by their conservative economic interests, toward alliance with the Center parties.

The political alignments that emerged in conflicts over economic and social values have not replaced those that developed during the crisis over Church-state relations. One system of political institutions and political categories has been superimposed on another but has not supplanted it. There is, indeed, not only a competitive but also a symbiotic relationship between the two traditions; each derives a measure of strength and influence from the other. The Communist party, for example, enrolls as members not only Frenchmen who see the party as the political arm of the proletariat in the struggle against the bourgeoisie but also those who see the party as the most advanced sector of the Left and, hence, as the legitimate heir of the Jacobin revolutionary tradition. The Radicals appeal not only to members of the middle class but also to those voters of all classes for whom anticlericalism remains an important issue. This crosscutting of issues explains in part why all parties recruit a significant proportion of their voters from all classes (see Table 3.1). It also helps to account for the resilience of the old ideologies. The parties breathe life into the old political categories by their efforts to appeal to the widest likely constituency. Thus the Radicals try to keep anticlericalism alive because it secures them a part of the electorate that they would probably lose if elections were battled out on economic and social policy alone.

The Crisis of Government: Majority-Opposition Conflict

To these two political strata—the forces mobilized around the Church-state issue and around the socialism-antisocialism question—with their characteristic values and quarrels, pairs of allies and enemies, the Fifth Republic has added a third layer of political forces. The alignment of political parties in the Fifth Republic has increasingly taken place along an axis of conflict, at one pole of which is the majority party, the Gaullist Union of Democrats for the Republic, with the Independent Republicans and several Center groups gravitating around it; at the other pole is a collection of Left and Center parties, united only by their nonparticipation in the governmental majority. The emergence of a majority camp and an opposition camp may be the single most important political development of the Fifth Republic: one that might fundamentally alter the characteristic patterns of power and representation in French national politics.

If two stable and coherent political coalitions emerge, one majority, the other opposition, it might presage the disappearance from French politics of the features that have resulted from a multi-party system with a high degree of ideological strife. In the Third and Fourth Republics governments were short-lived coalitions of different parties, drawn from a reservoir of potential governmental parties. Excluded from this pool were the parties of the Left and Right extremes, which formed a permanent opposition whose rejection of the political system was so comprehensive that their conditions for participating in power amounted to nothing less than a transformation of the regime. Alongside the permanent opposition parties and often collaborating with them to bring down governments was the temporary opposition: parties "eligible" for government but not included in the current line-up of ministers. When a government fell, its successor was formed by members of parties that had not participated in the last government and by members of the last government who had jumped off the bandwagon at an opportune moment for climbing onto the next one. The absence of a clear distinction between governmental and opposition parties strongly contributed to the instability of government, because at any time a government might be undermined by having its own members prepare to join the successor government. Just as important, it never was clear just which parties would replace the parties in power if they were voted out. By mixing the functions of government and opposition, neither could be effectively performed. The apparent opportunism of the ruling parties, the absence of clear political alternatives, and the string of short-lived governments all fostered a public cynicism and apathy about government that further undermined the efficacy of the state.

The polarization of the parties into a majority and an opposition would affect the prospects of governments in several ways. First, the existence of stable majority and opposition coalitions would mean that the political composition of governments would be decided in most cases directly by the results of the legislative elections, instead of by negotiations among the parties after the elections. The government would thus be strengthened by a direct popular mandate. At the same time, the opposition would be encouraged to present alternative sets of policies to the electorate, for each of the two groups competing in the election would present itself as a possible government. Second, the hands of government would be strengthened with respect to its own members by the hardening of the distinction between government and opposition parties. The parties that participate in government by a stable majority coalition have virtually no incentives to sabotage the government, for they have little or no chance of participating in the successor government that would be formed by the opposition. Party discipline is thus strengthened. Just as British Labour party M.P.s know that in voting against their government they risk bringing the Conservatives in, so the Gaullist deputies have been restrained in their criticism of government by the risk of helping the opposition to power. Such a constraint on the members of the governmental coalition is operative only when the defectors cannot hope to join the opposition government and only when the threat of the opposition's taking power is a credible one.

Not only the task of governing but also that of organizing opposition to government would be facilitated by a realignment of parties into majority and opposition camps. The existence of a solid majority has incited the parties outside the governmental coalition to coordinate their strategies with respect to the majority and even to try to unite their organizations. Where the previous party system rewarded with power those parties capable of maximum flexibility with regard to their allies, the new system forces the opposition parties to form stable alliances if they are to have any chance at all of participating in government. The access to power now runs along a route whose itinerary forces parties to contest elections that they can win only if they consolidate forces. Not only the run-off ballot in legislative elections but also, since 1962, the direct popular election of the President of the republic has provided incentives for the parties of the opposition to unite.

There have been two important attempts during the Fifth Republic to merge opposition parties. In 1965 Gaston Defferre tried to establish a federation of the Socialists, Radicals, and Christian Democrats (M.R.P.), but the proposal failed because of the old ideological issues. In the same year the Socialists, Radicals, and several of the new political clubs agreed to an alliance (Federation of the Democratic Socialist Left) in support of a single Left candidate, François Mitterand, against de Gaulle in the presidential election. After the election, the Federation tried to integrate its three constituent groups into a single party. For a time, the thrust to unity was powerful enough that the members of the Federation settled on a single Federation candidate in each district for the 1967 legislative election, formed one parliamentary group, and agreed on a schedule leading to unity in 1969. By 1968, however, the old ideological tensions in the Left had rent the fabric of agreement: One group in the Federation wanted alliance with the Communist party; another faction sought political rapprochement with the Center. The May 1968 crisis, the June legislative elections, and then the Soviet invasion of Czechoslovakia in August 1968 exacerbated these points of stress, and by the end of 1968 the Federation had collapsed into its constituent parts. As this is being written the parties of the opposition are once again embarked on a search for unity.

The question of whether these new negotiations will succeed is part of the more fundamental issue of the conditions under which the majority-opposition axis of conflict might come to structure partisan conflict in France. The trends in this direction have precedents in the Third Republic, during the long reign of the Radicals. But never prior to the Fifth Republic has it seemed likely that the confrontation between majority and opposition could replace the other axes of conflict as the dominant organizing principle of party alignments. Speculations about the future of French politics, therefore, depend on an assessment of the forces at work in the consolidation of the majority and the opposition.

One obvious factor in the emergence of the majority-opposition axis is the strength of a single majority party, the Gaullist Union of Democrats for the Republic. In all the legislatures of the Fifth Republic, the Gaullist party has been able to command a majority. In the 1958, 1962, and 1967 Assemblies they needed the support of their regular allies, the left-Gaullists and the Republican Independents; in the 1968 legislature, for the first time in French party history, they won an absolute majority of the seats.

Never before has a French government been able to rely on a parliamentary majority based on a single party. Never before has being in government provided the occupiers of power with so many opportunities for strengthening their party. These opportunities are the product of both the changed structure of government and administration and of the new tasks of the state. The enlarged role of the presidency in the political system means that when President and parliamentary majority are of the same party (as they have been throughout the Fifth Republic), that party has access to the political resources controlled not only by the Parliament but also by the executive and administration. The growing intervention of the state in society and the economy has increased the number of decisions about the allocation of resources that are made within the bureaucracy and has shifted power from Parliament to the administration. When a deputy, for example, tries to find funds for school construction in his district, he no longer presents his demand in Parliament but must convince the experts in the planning divisions of the bureaucracy. Small shopkeepers resentful of the encroachments of supermarkets seek redress—most recently in the form of a special tax on supermarkets—from the Finance Ministry. Peasant organizations that once lobbied in Parliament for tariff legislation and subsidies now must apply to administrative commissions that regulate agricultural markets.

In consequence, control of the bureaucracy is more than ever before the key to control of the resources distributed by the political system; and the majority party, by its relationship to the presidency as well as its parliamentary rule, has privileged access to the bureaucracy. The mayor of a poor mining town expressed the growing sentiment that majority deputies bring in more for their districts than opposition deputies do when he said, "I don't care whom we elect from this area as long as he's in the majority so we can get funds." U.D.R. candidates promise the voters in electoral campaigns that they can "do more" for the district than the opposition, and in fact they can. The rewards of politics are, in sum, increasingly distributed in a way that supports the "majoritarian phenomenon."

On the side of the opposition, the prospects for party unification appear dimmer. As the failure of the Defferre project and the collapse of the Federation of the Democratic and Socialist Left have shown, the survival of old ideological disputes continues to divide the parties of the Left. Even if the quarrels of the past should fade in face of the united majority, there is one obstacle to Left unity that is unlikely to disappear—the Communist party. The Communist party is "not a party like the others." Its internal structure, policies, and relationship to the Soviet Union are as many reasons why it is virtually impossible that the Communist party would agree to any fusion of its organization with other Left parties. Short of fusion, even alliances that would extend beyond election periods and be based on joint action for common objectives have so far not been achieved.

Yet the Left cannot simply circumvent the Communist party in projects for organizing an opposition camp. The Communist party is the largest party on the Left and wins about a quarter of the votes, a bloc second in size only to the Gaullist electorate. Indeed in the 1969 presidential elections the candidates of the non-Communist Left parties received a total of only 9.8 percent of the vote, while the Communist candidate won 21.5 percent. The politicians of the non-Communist Left have explained their poor showing by failure to agree on a single candidate, but the election results suggest still another possibility: The Communist party, as the largest party in the opposition, may be in the best position to profit from an alignment of party politics along the majority-opposition axis. If, instead of using their votes to choose the party that best expresses their ideological preferences, French electors increasingly use their ballots to express support for the government or opposition to it, then the party that offers the most powerful opposition may be the winner. The Communist party candidate can claim to "do more" in opposition for many of the same reasons that the Gaullist candidate can promise to "do more" in government: because of the size of the party, the discipline of its members, and its control over other powerful sectors of society (in the case of the Communist party, for example, over a substantial sector of the labor movement).

The crystallization of party politics around the poles of majority and opposition camps might lead to a merger of Left parties, but it might alternatively produce a consolidation of the Left around the Communist party and a withering away of the non-Communist Left parties. The second possibility—the emergence of the Communist party as the dominant or single opposition party—cannot be ruled out, and this throws into question the future of French politics. In other states where the political parties alternate in government and opposition, the programs of the parties are more remarkable for their similarities than their differences. If the Conservatives replace Labour in power, the Republicans replace the Democrats, or the Social Democrats replace the Christian Democrats, certain policies may change, but no fundamental transformation of the state or of its programs is likely. If the opposition party were the Communist party, as is not unlikely in France, the same condition would not obtain. Is a regular alternation in power of majority and opposition parties possible when the dominant opposition force is an antisystem party? Is the simplification of party politics into majority and opposition desirable if it means that the only alternative to the government is the Communist party? Or is the assumption that the strengthening of the Communist party would have destabilizing effects on the political system an assumption that is itself a product of the old ideological party politics? The Communist party has operated outside and against the political system in the past, but will it continue to do so in the future? Or might the role of opposition encourage the forces within the Communist party that tend to make it a party "like the others," a party willing to accept the rules of the political game, which imply the continued existence and competition of other parties, and willing to bring about the changes it desires within the constitutional framework.

The Parties

The future of the party system in large measure depends, as the preceding discussion suggests, on the parties' capacity for adaptation and innovation. It is no simple matter to assess the possibilities of change within a given party. Who in 1969 could have foreseen that a dynamic, ambitious leader would be able to revivify the almost moribund Radicals? Who now can predict whether the proposed reforms will in fact change the party and attract new members and voters or whether, like so many times in the past, the reformers will be defeated or absorbed? The evolution of the parties, however, is also determined by more permanent factors than the emergence of charismatic leaders or the impact of catastrophic political events. The historical development of a party, the social and economic composition of its leaders and followers, the procedures and institutions it has created to govern itself and those it uses to make policy, the regional bases of the party's power, the pattern of its influence in other organizations and sectors of society— these factors and others we will suggest in describing the state of French parties in 1972 are the factors that shape the party's future. They are, at the same time, "shapable" by the party leadership. In sum, to describe a party is to specify the factors that by their persistence, weight, and inertia are in the process of creating the party's future. It is, at the same time, to recognize that men can shape and reform their institutions. As Marx said, men make their own history, but within limits. The following discussion of the major political forces should suggest both the possibilities and the limits that condition the development of the parties in France.

The Communist Party

The Communist party operates both within the political system and outside and against it: this is what is meant by the phrase that the Communist party is not a party like the others. On the one hand, the party performs important functions for the stability of the political system, legitimating the state by its participation in it and integrating into the political process those social groups that once were isolated and excluded from politics.[1] Since its founding in 1920, the party has shifted from a revolutionary conception of its relationship to the state, which implied total rejection of the system and no alliances with other political forces, to a conception of its political role as one of defending working-class interests and democratic liberties within the constitutional framework. This evolution is neither complete nor unidirectional: The party as a revolutionary organization and the party as opposition critic are conceptions that coexist within the Communist party and within the minds of the electorate.

In its role of "tribune of the people," the Communist party has made the defense of the working classes the principal object of its activities in politics. In fact, the Communist party has extended its support not only to industrial workers but to virtually all groups whose interests have suffered from the industrialization and modernization of French society—to the victims of capitalism, according to the diagnosis of Marxism. A 1966 survey suggests that for most Frenchmen the "tribune function" of the Communist party is its defining characteristic. Forty-one percent of those interviewed saw the party as above all the party of the workers, in contrast to 17 percent who defined it as the largest force on the Left, 7 percent who defined it as a party seeking revolution, and 27 percent who described it as the party of the discontented. The role of tribune is compatible with a large measure of acceptance of the values espoused both by those in power and by the non-Communist opposition. The Communist party has since 1934 affirmed its allegiance to the patriotic ideals of the French republican tradition. Indeed, in recent years various statements by the party suggest that it may have accepted the values of political stability and strength central to the Gaullist conception of the Constitution of the Fifth Republic. At the very least, the party's opposition to the institutional arrangements of the Fifth Republic has been greatly reduced. And in negotiations with other Left parties the Communist party has agreed to maintain the essential features of the constitutional framework and to work within it to develop a "real democracy."

The manner in which the Communist party pursues its goals in politics, like the definition of the goals themselves, has contributed to the legitimation of the very political system that at other times and in other ways has been the object of the party's attack. The Communist party sets a high premium on electoral victory and, with more success than any other party, encourages its party members and electors to participate actively in electoral campaigns. Communists participate in government at all levels: as mayors and municipal councillors, as members of departmental councils and of regional development commissions (C.O.D.E.R.), and nationally as deputies and senators. Whatever the purposes and intentions of the Communists, their active political participation in the system has had the *effect* of institutionalizing and legitimating the structures of government. By enmeshing

---

[1]This interpretation draws on that of Georges Lavau, "Le Parti communiste dans le système politique français," in F. Bon et al., Le Communisme en France (Paris: Colin, 1969).

Communist officials and electors in a network of choices among alternatives possible in the current regime and by involving them in activities within political institutions, the party in fact strengthens the political system—perhaps unintentionally, as Georges Lavau points out, but inevitably. The party's participation in the electoral process, the responsible and prudent way in which its members exercise public authority wherever they hold office, and the party's willingness to negotiate alliances with other parties are all fundamental indications of the extent to which the party now conceives its role as one of bringing about change by working within the system in alliance with other political groups. No evidence better illustrates this point than the party's response to the student uprising and the workers' strikes of May–June 1968. The party not only made no effort to exploit the political situation and come to power but, on the contrary, deployed its energies and its cadres in an effort to control the movement and, quite simply, to restore order. The bitterness of the student revolutionaries about the party's betrayal as well as the legendary outburst of a factory owner who, when his establishment was occupied by Maoists, exclaimed that only the Communist party could save him, both testify to the measure of integration of the party within the political system.

In three critical respects, however, the party has not accommodated itself to the system and continues to maintain structures and policies that challenge the legitimacy of the state. First, the relationship of the French Communist party to the Soviet Union, while no longer the virtually automatic subservience of Stalinist years, remains one in which the national policies and goals of the French party can be and are overruled in the interest of defending the national policies and goals of the Soviet party. In the case of the Soviet invasion of Czechoslovakia, for example, although the French Communist party at first publicly condemned the invasion, it eventually lined up with the Soviet Union in agreeing that the matter should not be discussed at a meeting of the various Communist parties. The domestic costs to the party were very high: intensification of tensions within the party between liberal and conservative elements and an embittering of the party's relations with potential allies that left the party back in the political ghetto from which it had been slowly emerging. The party's willingness to incur these costs is a dramatic example of the virtually uncritical approval it bestows on the policies, institutions, and politics of the Soviet Union and the East European Communist states. The special attachment of the Communist party to the Soviet state raises suspicions about whether, if the Communists came into power, they might prefer Soviet interests to French interests. At the very least, the actions of the Communist party create enough ambiguity on this score to make this one of the principal obstacles to alliance with the Left and a stumbling-block for electors who might otherwise vote Communist.

Second, the organization of the French Communist party continues to be shaped by other imperatives than those of operating successfully within the political system. The secrecy with which the party veils its proceedings, the very limited scope of democratic procedures in the internal governance of the party, and the restriction of possibilities for members to express dissent or organize within the party to change it—all these features of party organization suggest that the party has not given up its revolutionary aspirations. The Leninist structures of the party and its rules of discipline seem more suited to a goal of capturing the system than of winning power within it. For example, despite the party's active participation in elections, it continues to support and indeed to prefer organizing members in cells at their place of work, rather than in their neighborhoods, although neighborhood organization would be more consistent with the goal of winning power through elections. While the party justifies the discipline of democratic centralism and hierarchical structures as necessary for revolutionary organization, some of its critics point out, to the contrary, that the party uses its rules and institutions to stifle political initiatives that might lead to revolution. Roger Garaudy, a leading party intellectual until his expulsion for dissent on Czechoslovakia and for the "heresy" of proposing new political alliances of workers, technicians, and intellectuals, has argued that the absence of party democracy serves conservatism and not a program of revolution. But even if these critics are right about the nonrevolutionary character of the party, it is difficult to imagine that the Communist party could ever be a full participant in the state as long as the norms of its internal governance are so radically at variance with the pluralist, democratic rules it professes to support for the political community as a whole.

Finally, in the programs advocated by the party and in the criticisms it offers of the current government, there is an ambiguity about its ultimate aims that makes it impossible to see the party as one like the others, only more radical. As Georges Lavau has pointed out, the party's criticism of the government differs from that of the other parties not only in frequency and intensity but in nature, for it links its critique of particular policies and decisions to an analysis of the system as a whole: ". . . it integrates the critique of political choices into a critique of values, social structure, and economic relations. Its opposition therefore has altogether a different dimension than that of any other party."[2] In other words, the party's opposition to any single action of the government seems to imply a total rejection not only of the item under attack but of the regime and of the economic and social system on which it is based. The question then arises of what the party proposes to put in their place. The Communist projects for the future of state and society are in a state of flux, which can be interpreted either as evidence of a fundamental change in party positions or as simple tactical moves. If the Communist party came to power, would they permit other parties—and which other parties—to operate? Would they allow themselves to be voted out of office? What would be their foreign policy? What changes would they promote in the economic and social systems? The party has answered these questions many times—but not always in the same way and often with statements that leave room for doubt about the party's ultimate intentions. Such ambiguities lend credence to those willing to believe that the party has not renounced its revolutionary projects, and they

---

[2] *Ibid.,* p. 57.

reinforce the fears of even those groups on the Left willing to consider political rapprochement with the Communist party.

Members and Electors

To assess the prospects of change within any party requires knowing who votes for it and who the members are. The Communist party is no exception. Although its decisions appear to emanate from on high, in fact, like other parties, the Communists are constrained in their choice of policies by the nature of their constituency. We know too little about the political process within the party to be able to describe how these constraints operate: how pressures and interests of the members and electors are transmitted to the decision-makers. But we can look at the characteristics of the membership and electorate in order to estimate the kind of demands that the party must meet.

The voters of the French Communist party are the most faithful of all party electorates. While the votes for the other parties have fluctuated wildly in the period 1945–1968 (the M.R.P., for example, hit a peak of 23 percent of the registered voters in 1946 and fell to 6 percent in 1962), the Communist party has won over 20 percent of the registered voters in five of the nine postwar legislative elections and has never fallen below 14 percent in the other four.[3] While the Communist vote suffered a sharp decline in the first elections of the Fifth Republic, its successes in the 1967 legislative elections and in the presidential election of 1969 suggest that the party may be on the way to recovering its Fourth Republic level. This continuity reflects two stable phenomena: the geographic concentration of the Communist vote in three regional "bastions," north of Paris, the Center, and Provence, where the long, solid implantation of the party has buffered the Communist electorate against the impact of Gaullism; and the fidelity of the individual Communist voter, who changes his vote less often than the typical voter of any other party.

The imperviousness of the Communist party vote to changes in the fortunes of the international Communist movement and in domestic politics may reflect still another factor: that Communist voters see politics as class conflict and consider their votes primarily as instruments for affecting the balance of social and economic power. One-third of the working-class votes Communist, and half of the Communist voters call themselves members of the working class—although only 46 percent of them would be so defined by objective criteria. In fact a Communist voter is more likely than any other voter to define himself in terms of class.[4] But the immunity of the Communist voter to change is relative and perhaps wearing off: In the 1958 elections that confirmed the position of General de Gaulle and estab-

---

[3]Jean Ranger, "L'Evolution du vote communiste en France depuis 1945," in Bon, *op. cit.*, p. 212.

[4]*Ibid.*, pp. 223–224.

lished the Fifth Republic one-third of the Communist electorate defected to vote in the new regime.

The subjective class definitions of the Communist voter are reinforced by party policies, which give highest priority to winning working-class voters and members. In this effort the party has been increasingly successful, for the proportion of workers in the Communist electorate has risen from 37 percent in 1948 to 46 percent in 1966.[5] This evolution parallels the growth of the blue-collar population within the nation, as has the rise within the party of the numbers of white-collar workers and employees of the public sector. The composition of party membership has adjusted to the long-term shifts in the composition of the national population. As a further illustration of this adjustment, at the same time that the agricultural population has declined, the number of rural electors of the Communist party has also declined. In sum, the party has proved adaptable enough to weather the decline of its old constituencies and to appeal to the rising classes of the population.

More than any other French party, the Communist party is a membership organization, not only an electoral association. The party has about 300,000 dues-paying members, a number greater than the memberships of all other parties combined. The social composition of Communist party members is virtually the same as that of its electors. In contrast to the stability of the electorate, however, the membership of the party declined massively in the postwar period, and in 1966 there was only half the membership of 1947.[6] The membership has spurted again in recent years (1968–1970), so the trend may be reversed. Not only the total membership, but the individuals composing the membership have changed drastically. Only about half of the members of the party in 1966 had belonged for over a decade, showing a rapid rate of turnover. The same is true of occupants of high party office: half of the members of the central committee have joined that body since 1961.[7] In sum, the recruitment of new members and leaders and the capacity to attract votes from the classes in the population that are expanding suggest a considerable potential for change within the party at the same time that the rigid party structures make such change difficult. In 1970 for the first time, the party tried out a new style of open meeting in which the public was invited to meet and quiz a Communist leader, "face-to-face." This open give-and-take remains so far restricted to the party's contacts with nonmembers, and the more fundamental question of whether the party will reform its own internal system of authority has not yet been answered.

---

[5] *Ibid.,* p. 243.

[6] Annie Kriegel, *Les Communistes* (Paris: Seuil, 1968), pp. 31, 37.

[7] Guy Rossi-Landi, "Le Parti communiste français: structures, composition, moyens d'action," in Bon, *op. cit.,* p. 207.

The Socialist Party

While the Communist party has recovered from the massive decline of the first years of the Fifth Republic and stabilized its electorate and membership, the non-Communist Left has gone from crisis to crisis. Today what is at stake is the viability of those Left parties which neither systematically reject the legitimacy of the regime, as the Communists do, nor consider themselves potential members of the government majority, as the Center does. In a political system with a majoritarian government party and an opposition in which the Communist party is the major force, is there political "space" for non-Communist Left parties? The answer depends in great measure on the fortunes of the Socialist party, for whether acting alone or as a partner in the Federation of the Democratic Socialist Left with the Radicals and the political clubs, the Socialist party is the pivot of all political strategies of the non-Communist Left.

The Socialist party like the Communist party draws its doctrines from the Marxist heritage. Like the Communists, the Socialists declare that political democracy and economic democracy are inseparable and that planning and nationalization of the means of production—or at least of the key sectors of the economy—are required to transform the regime into a real democracy. The path from Marxism diverges, however, once the Communists and the Socialists try to go beyond this general agreement on national control of the economy. While the Communist path from Marxism links up with the experience of the Soviet Union and the international Communist movement, the Socialist path connects and merges with the tradition of the national French Left, going back to the Jacobins of the French Revolution. The two great Socialist leaders, Jean Jaurès and Léon Blum, conceived their political lifework as a reconciliation of socialism and French national traditions. What emerged from these syntheses was a socialism based more on a new humanism than on economic materialism. This revisionist interpretation of socialism was contested within the party by the orthodox Socialists led by Guy Mollet, who argued that the fundamental social reality remained that of class struggle.

Mollet defeated Blum in the intraparty power struggles after World War II, but with the perspective of twenty-five years it is clear that revisionism has triumphed. Both in theory and in practice the Socialist party of the seventies has given up revolution as a goal. While the Communists continue to define political power in a socialist state as "the power of the working class and other parts of the working population," the Socialists explicitly reject any exercise of public power that is not based on democratic elections: Legitimate socialist authority is for them "the power of the majority expressing itself by means of universal suffrage, freed from the limitations that are imposed on it by the domination of the capitalist class." (The two definitions of power in a socialist state are from a joint communiqué of the Socialists and Communists, which sums up conversations between representatives of the two parties.)[8] While the Socialists have lost a revolutionary vision of the

---

[8] *Le Monde,* December 12, 1970.

transformation of capitalist society and the creation of a socialist state and society, they have not replaced it with any other. The Socialists continue to call for a new society "of justice and liberty" and claim that this requires a "fundamental transformation of social structures," but what they intend to put in the place of the old social and political system remains vague. Not only do they lack a blueprint for the construction of socialist society, but also, in giving up strict Marxist categories of class analysis, they have found no other terms for the systematic analysis of the problems of French society today.

No area better reflects the uncertainties of the Socialists than their alliance policies. The question of whether to ally with groups to their left, principally, the Communist party, or to their right, principally, the Radicals goes far beyond the issue of winning elections to the question of what kind of France the Socialists desire. The vagueness and uncertainties of Socialist programs are thus perfectly mirrored in the party's shifting alliances. In the course of the Fifth Republic, the Socialists have moved from an initial position of qualified support for the regime to a position of all-out opposition. Guy Mollet had ensured de Gaulle's legal return to power in 1958 by convincing a majority of the party to vote for de Gaulle's investiture as Premier, in order to avoid political crisis and a military dictatorship. The divisions within the Socialist party over de Gaulle led to the succession of its left wing, which regrouped in a new party, the Unified Socialist party (P.S.U.).

As the Socialists shifted into total opposition to the government and elections revealed the weakness of the Left, torn by its own divisions and reduced by the electoral successes of the Gaullists, the Socialists began to move toward alliances with the other opposition groups. The Socialists joined with the Radicals and the Convention of Republican Institutions (C.I.R.) in the Federation of the Democratic Socialist Left (F.G.D.S.), and in the years 1965–1968 the divisions of the non-Communist Left seemed to have been overcome by the common desire to return to power. (See the section "The Crisis of Government: Majority-Opposition Conflict" in this chapter.) The F.G.D.S. seemed the first step toward the fusion of the Socialists and the rest of the non-Communist Left into a single party. At the same time, negotiations between F.G.D.S. leaders and the Communists on a common political strategy against the Gaullists and on electoral arrangements to reduce the competition among Left candidates succeeded so well that the 1967 legislative elections increased Left strength in the National Assembly by half. The unity of the Left seemed closer than ever before.

Two political crises coincided to shatter this perspective: the events of May 1968 and the Soviet invasion of Czechoslovakia in August 1968. The differing responses of the Left parties to the student and worker strikes and governmental crisis of May–June divided the Federation internally. Czechoslovakia revived the non-Communist Left's fears that neither the Soviet Union nor the relation of the French Communists to the Soviet Union had fundamentally changed, and negotiations between these two parts of the Left collapsed. From all the debris of shattered hopes for Left unity, one new institution emerged: a reformed Socialist party. The prospects of a single non-Communist Left party had not materialized, but in the long process of negotiation and discussion with other groups on the Left, the Socialist party had changed. The balance of power among rival factions had shifted to younger men, less marked by old quarrels and more willing to open up for discussion the problems of organization and doctrine that were paralyzing the Socialist party. The 1969 congress changed the party name from S.F.I.O. (French Section of the International) to Socialist party, and Guy Mollet was replaced as party secretary. Several groups from the C.I.R. agreed to join the Socialist party. Two years later, at the 1971 congress, the Socialist party chose the leader of these new recruits, François Mitterand, as party secretary. The Socialist party resumed negotiations with the Communists, and in June 1972, with the prospect of legislative elections within the coming year, they signed an agreement on a common program.

Members and Electors

The new Socialist party has a long row to hoe, if it is ever to recover the strength and sense of purpose that the old Socialist party lost in the course of the Fourth and Fifth Republics. Between 1946 and 1958 the Socialist party lost two-thirds of its members and three-fifths of its Assembly seats. In its old regional strongholds the Socialist party found itself contested and often replaced by Communists. Today the Socialists are still strong in the industrial North and in a few departments of the Center, Southwest, and the Midi. But in these regions, too, there is stiff competition from the Communists and, increasingly, from the Gaullists.

The problems of reconstructing the party are complicated by the characteristics of the Socialist party's membership and electorate. A national survey of Socialist party membership shows that more than a quarter of the members hold government jobs at some level. A fifth work in traditional sectors of the economy: commerce, agriculture, and artisanal occupations. Another fifth of the membership are retired or "without a profession" (principally housewives). The Socialist party membership is, moreover, an aging population. A 1969 study of the members in one of the most modern departments of France, Isère, found that 41 percent of the members had joined the party before 1940 and only 28 percent after 1958.[9] Sixty-one percent of the members were over fifty. The occupational distribution of the members and their age suggest that the party may find serious obstacles to reform in its own membership. The party rules requiring that a man be a member for five years before becoming eligible for election to office can be rescinded, but potential recruits to the party may still find the party impervious to innovation and reform because of the predominance of old and conservative members.

---

[9]André Bernard and Gisèle Leblanc, "Le Parti socialiste SFIO dans l'Isère," *Revue française de science politique* (June 1970).

The Radical Party

The Radical party, founded in 1901, was the first modern French political party. The first Radicals counted in their numbers men who had been the founding fathers of the Third Republic, and the history of the Radical party is inextricably linked to that of the Third Republic. The triumphal moments of the republic were the highwater marks of the Radicals, and after the debacle of 1940 the Radicals were never again to recover the strength that had been theirs in the first third of the century. Discredited by their part in the defeat of France and the fall of the Third Republic, the Radicals were sullied again in the regard of public opinion by their participation in the Fourth Republic. The elaborate parliamentary negotiations and rituals that produced and destroyed governments seemed proof to the public of the incoherence and incompetence of the old parties in the face of political crisis. And although greatly reduced in numbers and torn by internal divisions, the Radicals had come to play a critical role in the Fourth Republic. With the appearance of large permanent opposition groups—the Communists and the *Rassemblement du peuple français* (R.P.F.)—the parties that formed the governmental coalitions came increasingly to rely on the support of the small but pivotal group of Radical deputies. It was a Radical Premier, Pierre Mendès-France, who extricated France from Indochina; and conservative Radicals, like André Marie and Henri Queille, bailed the system out when combinations of parties and men from the major groups failed to produce governments that could get parliamentary approval.

The decline of the Radical party is attributable not only to its experiences in power but also to its inability—or unwillingness—to adapt the party program to contemporary problems. The Radicals' long advocacy of republicanism and anti-clericalism seemed less and less relevant to generations for whom the burning questions of the Third Republic were settled matters. Even the Radicals appeared to lose interest in the old issues—some of them voted for state subsidies to Church schools—but the party did not develop any new platforms. The most serious attempt to reform the party was the work of Mendès-France in the mid-fifties, but he failed to rally the majority of the party to his ideas and was finally expelled. Even during the period of alliance with the Socialists and the Convention of Republican Institutions in the Federation of the Democratic Socialist Left, the Radicals hung on to their old doctrines and party structures. When the Federation collapsed, the Radicals emerged weakened but essentially unchanged. As the latest of the would-be reformers of the Radical party, Jean-Jacques Servan-Schreiber, has commented,

> Since the end of World War II, the substance of politics has shifted, . . . to what politics is about today: economic and social matters. Our times are demanding in that very area where Radicalism has never really developed its convictions, where its ideas are vague, its attitude ambiguous and often weak.

Servan-Schreiber's plan to reform the Radical party dates to the fall of 1969, when he was elected secretary general of the party and given the mandate to prepare a new party program. The document that he drew up had a dramatic impact on public opinion as well as on the party membership, for it attacked and proposed radical solutions for some of the sacred tenets of French society. The debate over the platform centered on two propositions: to control the rights of heirs to manage property they inherit by limiting the rights of inheritance and to break down the bureaucratic structures of an overcentralized state by creating regional governments and giving them rights of decision in matters once reserved to the national government. The "attack on property" implied in the limitation of inheritance rights stirred up such bitter controversy in the party that Servan-Schreiber's proposal was first watered-down, then put on the shelf politically. The arguments for decentralization, on the other hand, immediately elicited support from a wide range of individuals and groups. The defeat of the 1969 constitutional amendment on regional organization had left the advocates of regionalization in disarray, and the case for decentralization that Servan-Schreiber argued in the course of his electoral campaign for the National Assembly rallied many outside the Radical party who supported regional organization.

It is too early to tell whether Servan-Schreiber will be able to attract enough new men to the Radical party or to convince enough old members of the value of his ideas to succeed in his effort to make the party the instrument of a modern political program. The party remains bitterly divided on Servan-Schreiber's methods, his ideas, and his personal style. Even on the issue of decentralization, which promises to be the plank with which the party could exert the widest appeal, many Radicals are in deep disagreement with Servan-Schreiber's goals. Whether Servan-Schreiber succeeds in reforming the party or is defeated and disavowed as a long line of potential reformers before him have been, the future of the Radical party is clearly dependent on the fortunes of the other parties. The fundamental question is what role a small party like the Radicals can play in a political system whose central axis is the conflict between a governmental coalition and an opposition dominated by the Communist party.

Union of Democrats for the Republic

The U.D.R. (or U.N.R. as it was first called) was born in October 1958, a few days after a national referendum had given an overwhelming majority to the Constitution of the Fifth Republic. Like the *Rassemblement du peuple français* (R.P.F.) and the Social Republicans, the Gaullist parties of the Fourth Republic, the U.D.R. was formed to support the actions and policies of Charles de Gaulle. These parties all had the same point of departure, the arrival in London in June 1940 of the first groups of Frenchmen to respond to General de Gaulle's radio appeals to refuse to acknowledge the defeat of France and to continue the war against Germany. The original supporters of de Gaulle—*les compagnons*—have formed the hard core of all the postwar Gaullist parties, but their small numbers have been enormously swelled by later recruits: those who joined de Gaulle during the course of the war; those who came aboard in the R.P.F. period (1947–1953); and, the largest contingent of all, those who became Gaullists after de Gaulle came to power in 1958.

Diverse, even contradictory, motivations made men Gaullists, but for virtually all of them, joining the party or voting for it involved a commitment to the personal authority of General de Gaulle. Leadership is always an important element in a party's appeal, but the difference that Mollet made for the Socialists, Waldeck Rochet or Thorez for the Communists, or even Servan-Schreiber for the Radicals is not only quantitatively but qualitatively different from the significance of de Gaulle for the U.D.R. Political scientists may quarrel over whether de Gaulle was a true charismatic leader, but it is indisputable that in de Gaulle's relationship to his voters and party members there was a powerful emotional component that cannot be reduced to interest or utility or constitutional legitimacy. The paternalism of an authoritarian leader may elicit the same kind of trust from the people that de Gaulle received from the French, but de Gaulle to the French was not the figure of a loving father. He was the symbol of an austere and demanding civic virtue. The trust that Gaullist followers invested in their leader evoked their active participation in his purposes, not the passivity of the subjects of a traditional authoritarian ruler. Voters and party members who accepted de Gaulle's identification of himself with France and who believed that he had a superior understanding of what the public interest required were politically changed or energized by these beliefs, though the swings in de Gaulle's popularity and electorate show that changes wrought by charisma are not always lasting.

So closely has the existence of the U.D.R. been linked to the person of de Gaulle that his retirement from the political scene in April 1969 and his death in November 1970 have raised the question of the party's long-term survival. The problem of the future of the party "after de Gaulle" has indeed haunted the U.D.R. from its early years. Gaullists feared—and others hoped—that the party's hold on the electorate was only a reflection of popular support for de Gaulle and that once he withdrew from politics, the voters would return to their old political attachments. The leader of the Christian Democrats in 1964 expressed a commonly held opinion when he described the Gaullist regime as linked to the existence of a single man and predicted that the Gaullists could not survive de Gaulle:

> The majority in Parliament is only a shadow, projected onto the electorate, of a power established at the summit, which exists in complete autonomy . . . The parliamentary majority is a group condemned to dispersal as soon as the top no longer maintains it.

Not only the party's appeal to the electorate but also the cohesion of the party itself depended on de Gaulle's appeal to men of very different political persuasions. De Gaulle's authority often seemed to be the only cement holding together the opposed factions of the Gaullist movement—those Gaullists who favor increased state intervention and planning in the economy and the Gaullists who want to liberalize the economy and encourage large modern enterprises; those who want to modernize French society and those who seek protection for traditional social groups; those who advocate regionalism and decentralization and those intent on preserving the power of the central state. Since de Gaulle's retirement these tensions have broken out into the open more frequently, revealing at one time the different social conceptions of President Pompidou and Prime Minister Chaban-Delmas, at another time the conflicts between "law and order" Gaullists who favor a hard line on extreme-Left political activists and liberal Gaullists who disapprove of using extraordinary police and judicial procedures. One measure of the U.D.R.'s chances for unity without de Gaulle will be Pompidou's success in containing these clashes within the party and buffering his government against the struggles for power among the different political tendencies of the Gaullist movement.

The party's dependence on de Gaulle has been one aspect of its fragility; the weakness of party structures, the other. As Jean Charlot described the party in 1967: "It is first a team of cabinet ministers, then a central committee for selecting candidates to run in legislative elections, then the largest parliamentary group in the National Assembly and then—only last—a party."[10] After four years of Gaullist power, the party had only 50,000 members. It is hardly an exaggeration to say that the party existed only at election time. De Gaulle's political preeminence made it close to impossible for the party leadership to develop any independent authority in the political system. The party was obliged to swallow and defend each of de Gaulle's initiatives, without the possibility of advance discussion. The U.N.R. deputies with good reason were called the "unconditionals"; they ratified government decisions on which they had little influence.

The party's inability to bring pressure to bear as a party on the principal centers of power was one source of weakness. The party's relationship with de Gaulle hindered its development in a second way: While it drew its strength from association with him, de Gaulle refused to act as party leader or even to take an active part in party life. At times he seemed to have the same contempt for the U.D.R. as for the parties of the Fourth Republic.

Members and Electors

What is problematic in the future of the U.D.R. is not only its dependence on the Gaullist legacy and its underdeveloped party structure, but also the ambiguity of its politics. One factor in this that has already been mentioned is the great diversity of political tendencies within the U.D.R. In a country where political parties maintain a high degree of ideological homogeneity at least among members, what is the future of a party whose members are economic liberals and planners, Jacobins and Girondins, nationalists and Europeans? The political strategy of the party leadership after de Gaulle seems in fact to be increasing the heterogeneity of the party, for in the effort to extend U.D.R. power on the local level, the party has coopted local politicians to run on U.D.R. lists in the municipal elections. These new party members come from the traditional parties and have none of the experiences in

---

[10]Jean Charlot, L' U.N.R. (Paris: Colin, 1967), p. 23.

the Gaullist movement that provided the first generation of U.D.R. members with a common outlook on politics.

If one turns from the party membership to look at the Gaullist electorate, still other questions arise about the political base of the U.D.R. The Gaullist electorate is, basically, the electorate of the old Catholic Right parties. Geographically, the strongholds of the U.D.R. in eastern and western France and in the Paris Basin coincide with the old electoral fiefs of the Right. The gains of the U.D.R. have been at the expense of Center or Right deputies, although in the 1968 elections Gaullists took a few seats won by the Left in 1967.[11] On the level of individual voters, one can best predict who will vote Gaullist by knowing, not income levels or profession (one-third of the workers vote Gaullist—the same proportion as for the Communists), but whether an individual is a practicing Catholic. Surveys have found that Frenchmen who declare they have ''no religion'' vote in overwhelming numbers for Left parties; those who define themselves as religiously observant vote Gaullist.[12] The character of the U.D.R. electorate, added to the defeat of the left Gaullists in the party power struggles, have clearly stamped the party as a party of the Right.

Is the U.D.R. then only the old Right, galvanized and unified by General de Gaulle? Or has the U.D.R. taken electors from the Right to make a new party— neither Left nor Right but majoritarian and governmental? Has the alignment of politics along a majority-opposition axis of conflict created a party geared not to the representation of group interests or to the expression of ideology but to producing and supporting a government? If so, the U.D.R. may be the expression of a fundamental reorganization of the French party system. What appear to be its weaknesses in comparison with the other parties may in fact be structural differences between a party that conceives its role in terms of winning elections and governing and a party that conceives its role in terms of a coherent ideology. For example, the relatively low members-to-electors ratio of the U.D.R. may not be a sign of weakness but, on the contrary, evidence that the U.D.R. is a new kind of party organization—a party of electors—in a political arena where the traditional actors have been parties based either on notables (Radicals, Independent Republicans) or on party workers and mass memberships (Socialists, Communists).[13] The Democratic and Republican parties in the United States and the Labour and Conservative parties in Britain are examples of parties of electors based on broad, general communities of values, rather than on agreement on precise doctrines. They are open to men from different milieus and with diverse stakes in political participation.

What is the evidence for considering the U.D.R. as the dominant party of a new

[11]François Goguel, ''Les élections législatives des 23 et 30 juin 1968,'' *Revue française de science politique* (October 1968), p. 839.

[12]Jean Charlot, *Le Phénomène gaulliste* (Paris: Fayard, 1970), p. 72.

[13]*Ibid.*, pp. 63 ff.

majority-opposition party system? First, the U.D.R. pulls its electors from all groups in French society, in proportions that are the same as the proportion of the group in the population. No French party relies on a single class for its voters, but the U.D.R. reflects more faithfully than any other party the diversity of the French population. The U.D.R. claim to represent the nation—to be equally available to all electors—has some foundation in the composition of its electorate. This claim runs counter to the goal of the old parties, which tried to mobilize particular classes of the population and in whose electorates those classes are therefore "overrepresented."

This U.D.R. strategy has been rewarded with electoral success. From November 1958 to March 1967 the Gaullists doubled their electorate. In the legislative elections after the May–June 1968 events, one out of three voters cast a ballot for a Gaullist. This second kind of evidence of the majoritarian, governmental character of the U.D.R. is strengthened by the fact that the U.D.R. legislative electorate is rather distinct from de Gaulle's presidential electorate. The legislative elections of 1967 and 1968 showed that the voters casting ballots for the U.D.R. were not the same as those who voted for de Gaulle himself, although there was much overlap between the two groups. Indeed the U.D.R. electorate was independent enough of de Gaulle's electorate to survive when the latter disintegrated. In the April 1969 referendum the electorate turned down a proposal on which de Gaulle had staked his political office and then proceeded (June 15, 1969) to elect Georges Pompidou President with the same majority that had been supporting U.D.R. legislative majorities.

Finally, the pattern of alliances that the U.D.R. has concluded with other parties supports the case for treating the U.D.R. as the typical party of a majoritarian party system, rather than as a weak version of the parties of the old multiparty system. The party alliances that formed the basis of the governments of the Third and Fourth Republics were fragile and short-lived creations. Typically, the parties that were the pivots of government—the Radicals in the Third Republic, the Socialists in the Fourth—were elected with support from one set of allies and then in Parliament formed governments with other groups of allies. The Radicals of the Third Republic, for example, typically got themselves elected with help from the Socialists and even the Communists to their left and formed governments with Centrists and conservatives to their right. The electorate did not get to choose between alternative governmental coalitions but only between parties representing different ideologies and interests. The alliances of the U.D.R., in contrast, have created a true governmental coalition.

The "contract of the majority," in Valérie Giscard d'Estaing's phrase, which links the Independent Republicans to the U.D.R., is an alliance that differs greatly from the party alliances of the past. At critical moments for the government the U.D.R. has always been able to count on Independent Republican support: in 1965 when de Gaulle was opposed in the presidential election by a Centrist candidate (Jean Lecanuet); in May 1968 when the life of the regime was at stake; in April 1969 when the great majority of Independent Republican deputies supported de Gaulle in the regional referendum; in June 1969 when they backed Pompidou for President against the Centrist Alain Poher. In legislative elections the group has negotiated electoral agreements with the U.D.R. so that Independent Republican and U.D.R. candidates do not compete in the same districts (the arrangement of 1967) or at least step down in each other's favor on the second round of balloting (the 1968 arrangement). For the first time, then, the U.D.R. and the Independent Republicans present themselves to the voters as a government. The Center may be retracing the route of the Independents, with the 1969 split between Centrists who supported Poher and those who lined up for Pompidou and with the subsequent entry into the government of the Pompidou supporters. The composition of the government in spring 1972 reflected a coalition of U.D.R., Independent Republicans, and Centrists that elected the President and that will, in all likelihood, fight the next legislative elections together.

The Center: Democratic Center and Progress and Modern Democracy

The Center groups of the Fifth Republic are the heirs of the Popular Republican Movement (M.R.P.), the Christian Democratic party of the Fourth Republic, but the legacy has been greatly diminished by the claims that rival heirs have successfully pressed for the votes of the old Catholic Right. The Popular Republican Movement was one of the three great political parties of the early postwar period (the other two having been the Socialists and the Communists). The founding of the Gaullist party and the revival of traditional Right groups and of the Radicals all drew on the reservoir of conservative voters who had voted M.R.P. in the immediate aftermath of the war, when the parties of the traditional Catholic, clerical Right were absent from the political scene. At the same time that the M.R.P. was losing voters and members to the new Right parties it lost its Left wing as well, for the predominance of the right in the national leadership rapidly disillusioned the progressive Catholics who had hoped to transform the M.R.P. into a socialist party. The advent of the Fifth Republic in 1958 completed the debacle: The M.R.P., which had had 169 deputies in the 1946 National Assembly, had only 64 in the first Assembly of the Fifth Republic.

The decline of the M.R.P. continued in the Fifth Republic, and by the early sixties the party organization was virtually moribund. The survivors have now gathered in two groups. The Democratic Center (Centre Démocrate) was formed from the groups that supported the 1965 presidential candidacy of the former M.R.P. leader Jean Lecanuet. Despite Lecanuet's reasonably good showing in the presidential election, the Democratic Center proved no more successful than the M.R.P. had been in stemming the shift of Right voters to the U.D.R., and the number of deputies elected from this group continued to decline. Too small to form an independent parliamentary group, the Democratic Center deputies in 1967 joined with deputies from the National Center of Independents and Peasants and an assortment of Republican and Radical deputies to form a single Center parliamentary group: Progress and Modern Democracy. The leader of this group is Jacques Duhamel, who emerged as the dominant Center politician after Lecanuet failed to be reelected to the Assembly.

The tensions between the Democratic Center led by Lecanuet and the parliamentary group Progress and Modern Democracy led by Duhamel have now gone beyond intraparty rivalry. Each of the two groups pursues an independent strategy with regard to the Gaullist majority. During Pompidou's campaign for the presidency in 1969, he proclaimed his intention to "open" the majority to other political forces. The first to respond to this "opening" were the leaders of Progress and Modern Democracy, who supported Pompidou against a Centrist presidential candidate. Despite rumblings in the U.D.R., where devoted partisans of de Gaulle accused Pompidou of having sold out the Gaullist legacy, Pompidou kept his promise of broadening the basis of the governmental majority and gave three ministries to Progress and Modern Democracy deputies. The Progress and Modern Democracy group has thus become part of the majority, alongside the U.D.R. and the Independent Republicans, while Lecanuet and the Democratic Center remain in opposition.

What distinguishes the Center from the other groups in the majority? According to Jacques Duhamel, the Center's leader, the difference between his group and the U.D.R. is "something undefinable, yet essential. A certain way of acting, and a guarantee of what I would call tolerance." The "undefinable" difference is certainly nourished by the separate histories of the Catholic Center party and of the Gaullists. But in the final analysis, the refusal of the Center to merge with the U.D.R. seems to have more to do with the political advantages that the Center hopes to secure by serving as a pivotal, and autonomous, group within the majority than with any profound political differences between the Center and the U.D.R. Political groups close in doctrine to the U.D.R. now have a clear interest in joining the majority; but the structure of political incentives does not yet provide a clear advantage to those groups who throw off their organizational independence to join the U.D.R. As long as the Center retains important local bases of power and as long as the U.D.R. still sees advantage in extending its base of support by coopting groups as well as appealing to individual electors, the Center like the Independent Republicans will probably continue to remain independent partners within the majority coalition.

The Independents: Republican and Peasant

The advent of the Fifth Republic in 1958 brought the Independents and Peasants into the National Assembly in force, with a number of deputies second only to the Gaullists. The National Center of Independents and Peasants was formed to regroup moderates and conservatives and was one of the most important political groups of the Fourth Republic. The success of the Independents in maintaining and increasing their strength in Parliament in the 1958 elections when all other parties suffered important losses to the Gaullists seemed to augur well for the future of the group. Indeed, in the early years of the Gaullist republic the Gaullist party seemed so fragile an organizational creature that the Independents could reasonably hope to win a lion's share of the electoral benefits of a conservative regime. Once de Gaulle had resolved the Algerian crisis, which had brought the Gaullists to power, those conservative forces which were more deeply entrenched in local politics might well inherit the kingdom.

These hopes gradually faded as the Gaullist party showed its strength and disagreements broke out between de Gaulle and the conservatives. In the first years of the Fifth Republic relations between the government and the Independents and Peasants had been good: the Independents supported the government in Parliament, and the most prominent member of their group, Antoine Pinay, served as Finance Minister from 1958 to 1960. After 1960, however, as the government shifted its policies in Algeria toward independence and defined economic orientations that disadvantaged traditional sectors of the economy, the political support of the Independents became more problematic. The parliamentary support of the Independents and Peasants deputies became increasingly less dependable. Finally, in 1962, a majority of them lined up against the government in a vote of confidence on the issue of the election of the President of the republic by direct popular vote. The pro-Gaullist minority split off and formed a separate parliamentary group, the Independent Republicans. Led by Giscard d'Estaing, this group has become the regular, permanent ally of the U.D.R. With its growth from thirty-three deputies in 1962 to sixty-two deputies in 1968, it now constitutes a significant part of the majority. While the fortunes of the Independent Republicans soared, the National Center of Independents and Peasants declined rapidly on the national level, though its members continue to control a significant amount of power on the local level.

The Independent Republicans are a party in the old conservative pattern, based on networks of local notables whose formal organizational commitments are loose and casual: "no membership, no party card, no organized recruitment." In fact, it was four years after the 1962 split before the Independent Republican parliamentary group established a national organization. Most of the political activity of the Independent Republicans is still concentrated not in the national organization or its regional sections but in a network of "Futures and Realities" clubs, sponsored by the Independent Republicans. The party has attracted much of the old conservative clientele, but at the same time it has attempted to carve out a distinctive constituency in the new middle class by describing itself as the party of progress, dynamism, youth, and technological innovation. Its economic liberalism is a new theme on the French Right, one calculated to bring into the party the managers and upper-level employees of the modern industrial sector of the economy. Even if the party succeeds in broadening its electoral base, the fate of the Independent Republicans, like that of the other small parties, depends on the major parties. In the last analysis, the future of the Independent Republicans remains linked to the future of the Gaullist majority.

Four

The Changing Politics of Policy Making

France like other modern industrial states has experienced major changes in the process of policy making over the last thirty years. The relative power and influence of the groups and institutions that have been described in earlier chapters have been significantly redistributed, and the changes in the French political system from 1952 to 1972 have been far greater than any comparison of the formal constitutional powers of institutions would suggest. The roles that Parliament, President, the bureaucracy, political parties, and interest groups play in policy making have altered in ways that are critical for the process and output of politics.

These changes are in part the product of the new tasks the state has undertaken in the management and development of society and economy. To consider only the vast extension of the state's role in the economy, one recent study found nine goals that have become the objects of economic policy in European states:

> . . . Price stability, a satisfactory balance of external payments, full employment, fairer distribution of income and wealth, adequate provision of social goods, a substantial rate of growth of GNP, balanced development of the country's regions, restriction of the growth of money incomes to that of productivity, and sufficient competition between firms and equal competitive conditions.[1]

---

[1] Malcolm MacLennan, Murray Forsyth, and Geoffrey Denton, *Economic Planning and Policies in Britain, France and Germany* (New York: Praeger, 1968), p. 26.

418

If such an inventory of goals of the economic policies of European industrial states had been drawn up before World War II, only one of the objectives would have been included: managing the balance of payments. Certain of the other items were occasional objects of political concern: States tried to provide or encouraged private industry to provide the infrastructure necessary for economic growth; in periods of economic crisis states tried to maintain price and employment levels; occasional efforts were made to aid backward regions. But by and large these goals were the object of only sporadic state action, and the policies formulated to attain them were short-term and piecemeal, based neither on overall objectives for the economy nor on coherent strategies. It was only after the war that the economic goals listed above—or some combination of them—became the regular operative objectives of state policy. As a result, the policy-making institutions of the state had to be reorganized to make it possible to achieve these new purposes.

The second source of innovation in the institutions and processes of policy making has been changes in the conceptions of tasks already performed by the state. Problems once regarded as political, in the sense of involving choices between competing sets of values, have come to be considered and treated as administrative and technical; at the same time, problems that were once seen as administrative matters have acquired political saliency. Some observers of European politics suggest that there is a long-term shift in the content of the politics of developed societies away from the divisive issues of ideological politics and toward issues in which technical competence, special knowledge, and the adjustment of material interests are more salient than value conflicts. From the mid-fifties to the mid-sixties this "end-of-ideology" theory seemed quite a convincing explanation, for the politics of both Europe and America were geared to problems that generated little ideological heat. With the reappearance in the past few years of profound conflicts over the purposes of state action, political values, and social structure, it has become clear that the end-of-ideology theory was only a partial and incomplete explanation of trends in industrial societies. At the same time that certain problems were being depoliticized, others were becoming political. The organization of higher education, for example, once a matter of almost purely administrative concern, has become a highly charged and politicized question in most European states. Political groups now regard the values at stake in the reorganization of the university as crucial to their conception of the legitimate relationship between state and society. The transfer of problems between the sphere of politics and the sphere of administration has thus moved in both directions. The rate of circulation between the two spheres has been greatly accelerated in modern states. It is this rapid transformation of the content of politics, rather than the end of politics or its radicalization, that best describes what is happening in European states. With these changes have come changes in the personnel and methods of decision making.

Strategies of Reform

The new tasks of the state and the changing conceptions of political issues have been two major sources of strain and tension for traditional policy-making institutions in France. The inadequacy of a decision-making process developed in the nineteenth and early twentieth centuries for dealing with the issues of postwar France has provoked many and diverse problems, which no single institutional reform could remedy. The French have tried to adapt the policy-making process by using three different strategies of institutional reform: transforming old institutions by bringing in new blood and creating new rules; creating new institutions alongside of and often in competition with the existing ones; and transferring the power of decision from political to administrative elites.

Attempts to bring about change by reworking old institutions are subject to familiar pitfalls, and the French reforms that have followed this first strategy have not often been successful. The values and personal interests that become attached to a given set of institutional arrangements create resistance to innovation within an organization and make it difficult to change established patterns of behavior. For example, to modify the authoritarian aspects of the French public school system, the Ministry of Education might order school principals to meet with parents and students to discuss the curriculum. But the principal's job expectations, his sense of social prestige, and his feelings about what is right in a school have become so inextricably connected to a certain way of performing his job and dealing with others in the system that such a directive would probably not have much impact.

There are two approaches that would make it likely that the school principals would try to change the system within which they work. One would be to provide incentives by rewarding principals who implement such changes and penalizing those who persist in the old ways. This would require, of course, that "someone" check up on each principal and that this person have authority to administer rewards and penalties according to the principal's performance. This "someone" in the French system can only be central authority, for to institute any other system of controls would require serious modification of the distribution of power between the central state and local authorities. In other words, power is distributed in such a way in France today that only the center can exercise effective controls. The effectiveness of reform measures that require the people already in place to obey new rules thus depends on the effectiveness of centralization. It is easy, however, to imagine the kinds of reforms that can never be carried out if they need the supervision of the central administration. The reform to democratize the school system suggested in the example above would be vitiated in its very principle if implementation required an inspector from the ministry to check on the exercise of local autonomy. The only "controllers" who could in fact assure that the principal shared his power with other participants in the local system would be local controllers, but centralization does not allow this in France.

The second way to get the principals to change the system would be to replace the principals with new ones who had been educated in the spirit of a more democratic school system. Reforming institutions by infusing them with new blood was in fact the idea behind one of the most important efforts at innovation in postwar France: the creation in 1945 of a National School of Administration, E.N.A. *(Ecole Nationale d'Administration)*. Until then, the higher civil servants were predominantly men who had graduated from a few private universities or from law schools. Their education had provided them with essentially legalistic interpretations of the problems the state confronted, and it had left them poorly prepared to understand the complexities of economic and social policy. The institutions in which they had studied recruited students almost exclusively from the bourgeoisie, and this, as well as the private character of the institutions, predisposed many of the graduates toward a rather unsympathetic view of any extensive state intervention in the economy and society. E.N.A. was founded in order to develop a class of top-level civil servants who would be both committed to an active public sector and competent to manage it. The graduates of E.N.A. were to be the main reservoir for all top posts in the administration: the ministries, the state banks and industries, the diplomatic service, the prefectoral service, and the administrative courts *(Conseil d'Etat)*. The new school was supposed to provide all higher civil servants with a common general education in the subjects relevant to the needs of a modern state: economics, sociology, political science. Book learning was to be supplemented by periods of apprenticeship in various public institutions. And the recruitment of the top civil service was to be broadened by an entrance examination system that would open E.N.A. up to students of diverse class origins. (As it turned out, E.N.A., like the schools that preceded it, draws its students almost exclusively from the Parisian bourgeoisie.)

The result of restricting entry to the higher civil service to E.N.A. graduates has been to introduce important changes into the operation of the state bureaucracy. The mentalities of the old-style bureaucrats and of the E.N.A. graduates were so different that in the school's first years of existence its graduates met hostility and resistance in their assigned positions. The social science training of the E.N.A. graduates gave them not only new methods but also new conceptions of the role of the state, and it was this difference in values as much as any differences in skills that set off the young bureaucrats from the old. The E.N.A. men succeeded in imposing their methods and values on the bureaucracy because of numbers—by 1969, 1800 higher civil servants had passed through E.N.A.—and because the old E.N.A. graduates were continuously reinforced by the new classes arriving each year in the bureaucracy.

One of the problems of trying to change an old institution by bringing in new blood is that the system often absorbs the new men and socializes them in the old ways. Would-be reformers find that they can be successful in an institution only by conforming to the norms of the system; thus they are swallowed up by the very institutions they are supposed to change. A good example of this was provided by the Parliament of the Fourth Republic. After the Liberation a generation of men with little or no previous parliamentary experience was elected to Parliament, and they brought with them new political aspirations, values, and the experience of working in the Resistance with men of different political beliefs. Despite this background, after a few years the new men found themselves involved in the same parliamentary game that had paralyzed the Third Republic. It became clear that the new deputies had been socialized by the old system. E.N.A., on the contrary, succeeds because it injects a new class of graduates into the bureaucracy each year, thus ensuring that the top levels of the administration will eventually be controlled by its men and reinforcing the commitment of E.N.A. graduates already in the system by surrounding them with other E.N.A. alumni.

The contrast between the cases of the Fourth Republic deputies and E.N.A. shows both the possibilities and the limitations of bringing about change in a system by introducing persons with new ideas and values. It works well only when a continuous flow of the new men pours into the institution—a one shot injection of new blood is hardly likely to dilute the strength of the old values and practices enough. In industrial societies schools are virtually the only institutions that can reproduce a constant supply of men with given values and skills. This means that the strategy of reform that depends on introducing new men into institutions requires an educational system already transformed by the values that are to be introduced into the bureaucracy. This is one profound reason for the central place of education in political conflicts in France today. In the organization of schools and universities and in their curriculums and procedures, all political groups in France perceive values that will mold the content and process of politics.

The second approach that has been tried in France to reform the methods and institutions of political decision making is the creation of new institutions, sometimes to replace the old ones, far more frequently to coexist with them. No case better exemplifies the possibilities of this strategy than the General Planning Commissariat, established in 1946 alongside the Ministry of Economy and Finance. While the Ministry of Finance continued to perform the traditional economic functions of the state—raising and collecting taxes, preparing the annual budget, supervising the accounts of the public sector—the new Planning Commissariat was entrusted with responsibility for defining and achieving many of the new economic goals of the state. As suggested above, these new goals required long-term projection of the needs and resources of the country and coherent plans of action for attaining them. Whether it was the state's concern with achieving a certain rate of economic growth, the desire to relocate industries in order to promote a more even distribution of economic activities across national territory, or the selection of economic targets requiring transformation of certain industries, it was clear that the traditional personnel and structures of the Ministry of Finance would not be able to handle the new tasks. The General Planning Commissariat was given the job of projecting needs and resources, relating them to rates of economic growth, and specifying the changes in supply factors, in the production process, and in demand that would be necessary to reach given economic objectives. These economic projections were drawn up in five-year national plans. The Planning Commissariat was responsible not only for developing the plans but also for involving in their preparation the economic actors on whose decisions the success of the plan depended. The Planning Commissariat organized commissions in which industrialists, trade unionists, representatives of agriculture, commerce, consumers, and others deliberated with the planners on national goals and means to reach them. By broadening participation in the elaboration of the plan to include the economic decision-makers themselves, the planners were able to gauge the climate of the economy and, at the same time, to provide business and labor with information about the state's intentions and about the evolution of the economy. Communication and information facilitated a voluntary coordination of the economic choices of thousands of private decision-makers and made it possible to develop the national economy in particular directions without authoritative controls. The plan objectives were binding on the economic decisions of the public sector, but the plan could only encourage (by subsidies and other aids) and could not force private industry to carry out the plan. The delicate negotiations between private and public sectors and among different interests within the private sector and the conceptual problems of specifying economic objectives for a five-year period and of relating the goal of economic growth to goals of price and wage stability or favorable balance of payments are among the difficult tasks that the Planning Commissariat has undertaken. Such tasks would be more difficult for an organization like the Ministry of Finance, working within a tradition of bureaucratic secrecy, compartmentalization of activities, and suspiciousness of direct contacts with the public and constrained by the intellectual formation and values of its personnel.

New institutions are, however, no universal panacea. The Planning Commissariat is a small organization and so the problems of staffing it are not major. When, however, the state creates new institutions that require large numbers of personnel, the difficulty of finding men with the skills and perspectives needed for the new institutions is a serious obstacle to change. For example, one of the reasons for the failure of the regional councils (C.O.D.E.R.) was that their members were drawn exclusively from established local elites and retained their loyalties to the organizations from which they came. Another problem new institutions face is coexistence with other groups. The Planning Commissariat, for example, has been involved in the kind of competitive relationship with the Ministry of Finance in which each institution has increased its power and influence often at the expense of the other.

For the political system as a whole, this competition among institutions may be highly desirable, for it provides flexibility and the organizational possibility of innovation. Different kinds of institutions generate different policies, and the presence of competitive institutions increases the chances that the public and the political decision-makers will be offered alternative policies from among which to choose. The overlap of institutional responsibilities also makes it more likely that when the executive changes course, he will be able to have his new policy carried out by the bureaucracy. For example, the governments of the Fifth Republic set a higher priority on price and wage stability and on maintaining a favorable balance of payments than the Fourth Republic governments, which had on the whole chosen rapid economic expansion even at the expense of inflation and foreign indebtedness. This shift in economic goals was accompanied by—and facilitated by—a shift in the relative power of the branches of the bureaucracy in which economic policy is developed. The Ministry of Finance has recovered the position of unchallenged predominance that had been contested by the Planning Commissariat during the Fourth Republic. The Planning Commissariat is now obliged to accept goals quite different from those it would itself propose and, indeed, to adapt to a political situation in which planning has declined in importance as a policy-making process. The availability of both the Ministry of Finance and the Planning Commissariat allows a freedom of action and choice to the executive that would be far more difficult to obtain were he dependent on a single economic agency.

Politicians or Technocrats?

The third strategy of reform has been to transfer the power of decision from politicians to bureaucrats with special expertise, the "technocrats." In this context, the most useful distinction is between decision-makers whose access to power is determined by election, the politicians, and decision-makers, the technocrats, whose route to power is the acquisition of certain skills or, more precisely, certain diplomas. The paths to power for a French politician have changed over time. There are two classical patterns: the path of the local notable, who starts as mayor or municipal councillor in his commune, then is elected to the departmental council, and finally seeks election as deputy; and the path of the party man, whose political career takes place within the organization of a political party and who is chosen by the party to run in a district as a representative of the party, not as a local son. In the Fifth Republic, a third pattern has evolved. Someone who exercises national power by virtue of his technical skills goes back and seeks election, presenting himself to the electorate not as the best informed representative of local interests nor as the representative of particular political conceptions associated with a party, but as a man who, because of his national power position, can "do more" for the solution of local problems than any local son or party man could. These three routes to power, despite divergences, all converge on a single point: election.

Winning elections requires the mastering of certain skills and the development of certain qualities. Politicians must be able to translate public issues into terms the average citizen can understand. In part this means that the politician has to be able to relate national concerns to private, local stakes. The Normandy farmer may not understand or care much about the fate of the Atlantic alliance, the future of the Commonwealth, or supranational or federal political structures for Europe—all questions at stake in the admission of Britain to the Common Market—unless politicians explain that each of these questions involves matters that are of direct personal concern to his livelihood and community. It was indeed because politicians had succeeded in convincing the peasant electorate that the Common Market was the solution to its economic problems that de Gaulle's threats to paralyze the Common Market in order to stop supranational projects turned peasant electors who had previously voted for de Gaulle to rival presidential candidates (1965). Likewise, someone whose power depends on winning votes is apt to be more sensitive to the local fallout from national decisions than the technocrat, who does not have to confront the public in face-to-face relationships. The social impact of national policy and the reactions of the public are factors that usually weigh heavily in the calculations of those who exercise power by virtue of elections. Such persons are more likely to consider individual and social costs than are men who reach power by other routes.

There are fewer points of access to the road to power for a technocrat than for a politician, and only those who have attended one of the *grandes écoles* (literally, the great schools) have a significant chance of rising to the top. Indeed as Jean Meynaud has pointed out, the most economic description of a French technocrat is a graduate of E.N.A. or *Ecole Polytechnique* (which educates engineers and scientists). The diplomatic service, the most important ministries, the state banks and industries of the public sector, and the other *grands corps* of the state are recruited almost exclusively from among the E.N.A. and the *Ecole Polytechnique* graduates.[2] Not only are the top jobs in the bureaucracy filled by the graduates of these schools but also, particularly since the advent of the Fifth Republic in 1958, these technocrats sit in the top levels of government. Charles Debbasch in his study of the role of the bureaucrat in the Fifth Republic *(The Rule of the Bureaucracy)* reports an item in a local newspaper with a revealing error. The article reads: "Mr. X has returned to Cogolin for vacation. We know that he is a student at E.N.A., a school that prepares its students to become, among other things, prefects, *ministers,* etc. We wish this brilliant student a good vacation."[3] [Italics added.] The reporter's mistake in thinking that the National School of Administration turned out cabinet ministers is understandable. In the first governments of the Fifth Republic, 40 percent of the ministers were technocrats, not politicians. In the first ten years of the regime, six ministers were graduates of E.N.A., four of *Ecole Normale Supérieure* (which prepares university teachers), and three of *Ecole Polytechnique.*[4] Though the number of nonpolitician ministers has declined in subsequent governments, the number of technocrats in the top staff jobs of ministerial cabinets remains very high. In the Third Republic the ministers usually chose other politicians to serve on their staffs. Technocrats began to appear on the staffs of the Fourth Republic ministers, and in the Fifth Republic they have come to have a virtual monopoly of these posts.

Though the shift of power from politicians to technocrats began in the Fourth Republic, it is under the Fifth Republic that this change in the cast of political decision-makers has been most dramatic. The numbers of bureaucrats exercising

[2]Jean Meynaud, *La Technocratie* (Paris: Payot, 1964).

[3]Charles Debbasch, *L'Administration au pouvoir* (Paris: Calmann-Lévy, 1969), p. 91.

[4]*Ibid.,* pp. 50, 57.

functions previously exercised by men who had been elected to office has greatly increased. The issue is not, however, one of numbers alone, but of the relative influence of politicians and technocrats in the process of policy making. It would be impossible to design an index of influence that would allow us to sum up the respective powers of the two groups in the political system as a whole, for there is no common denominator of power that would enable a researcher to match the increased power of an elected official (the President) in foreign-policy decisions against the increased power of the technocrats in economic matters. In most areas of policy, with the exception of defense and foreign policy, case studies of decisions made fifteen years ago and today suggest that the power of the technocrats has increased relative to that of the politicians.

If the politicians' route to power develops certain qualities and skills, the technocrats' route rewards certain kinds of competence. The process of recruitment for the *grandes écoles* selects persons who can meet high standards of intellectual accomplishment and who share the cultural norms of the Parisian upper-middle class. The student from working-class or peasant origins who makes it into E.N.A. is a very rare case; the student from the provinces is almost as uncommon. The education that students receive in E.N.A. and the *Ecole Polytechnique* develops a world view quite different from that of the politician, for it presents the standards of rationality and growth as the highest priorities of state policy. For technocrats even more than for politicians, who are obliged to meet their provincial constituents regularly and to deal with their problems, Paris and the central government are the hub of the political universe. The technocrat identifies the central state with the public interest and tends to see local objections to national decisions as motivated only by private, selfish, or parochial interests. The technocrat's education has taught him that the public interest is best served by rational, coherent policy making, and so he is likely to regard processes of negotiation and compromise among interests with a certain contempt. The technocrat who works in the provinces sees himself as the emissary of the center, and it is unusual for him to develop loyalties to any local institutions.

One of the new themes of opposition parties in France today is that the state has been taken over by technocrats who disregard the human aspects of politics and try to impose policies that are perhaps economically justifiable but which have social costs that are not taken into consideration. Like some Americans who see the United States as controlled by a military-industrial elite which is politically irresponsible—that is, unchecked by popular election and insensitive to human and social needs—the French critics of technocratic power argue that rule by technocratic elites has resulted in a virtual disenfranchisement of their population.

The rise to power of the technocrats is only one part of a more general phenomenon: the transfer of policy making from arenas of power in which politicians and political criteria are dominant to arenas of power in which technocrats and technical criteria are decisive. How can we explain this shift in French politics? In part the answers lie in factors that attained their most developed form under the Fifth Republic, but whose origins preceded it. The changes in the tasks of the state and in political beliefs and values enhanced the role of the technocrats. Even when the knowledge required to tackle one of the state's new tasks was not of a highly technical nature, the presumption was established that, in whatever concerned the economy, there was a "best solution" and an expert was the man to find it. As one French politician put it, "there are not ten best ways to collect garbage." This remark is striking for Americans, whose experiences in local government suggest that there is no best way to collect garbage, only ways with different costs and benefits for different social and political groups. In other words, in France it was not only and perhaps not primarily *what* the state tried to accomplish that led to the triumph of technocrats over politicians, but *how* the state and the major political groups in the nation defined the problems and the methods to resolve them. Despite signs of rising public resentment against technocratic power and of frustrated aspirations to participate, the notion still prevails in France that for a broad range of economic, social, and political matters, only a person with the special education of a technocrat is competent to make decisions.

A second major factor that has contributed to the shift of policy making from political arenas to technocratic arenas is the Constitution of the Fifth Republic. As Chapter 2 described, the constitution specifies the subject matter on which the Parliament may legislate, thus limiting the powers of Parliament and increasing those of the government, which may act by decrees on any subject not specifically assigned to the Parliament. This distinction between the domain of law, in which Parliament legislates, and the residual domain of regulation, in which the government is free to act, has removed a vast number of decisions from the arena of policy making in which politicians dominate and has transferred them to the bureaucracy. Two other provisions of the constitution have had the same effect. One is the clause enabling the government to request that Parliament allow it to act by ordinance on matters that ordinarily are the subject of laws. The Parliament, for example, authorized the government to issue ordinances on the control of various "social diseases": alcoholism, homosexuality, and prostitution. According to the constitution, such ordinances should return before the Parliament for a vote. In fact, frequently the government has either not presented the ordinances to Parliament or has presented them after such long delay that the principle of parliamentary review and control has been subverted.

Finally, even when a bill is passed by Parliament, the government and bureaucracy often have wide scope for modifying the bill's provisions or delaying the bill for an indefinite period. Though Parliament determines the basic framework of legislation on national defense, local government, education, property law, and social security, the government determines the details of the legislation. This gives the government great latitude, which it frequently exercises in directions quite independent of the legislature's intentions. When, for example, the Parliament passed a law in December 1967 legalizing and regulating the dissemination of birth-control information, the government delayed fourteen months before issuing any measures that would enable the law to go into effect, despite the law's explicit requirement that the government act within six months. Four years later, many of the law's most important provisions still remain dead letters, because of the government's failure to act. There are many similar cases. Parliament passed a law on health insurance for self-employed persons in the middle of 1966 that was to go into effect in January 1967. Two years passed, and, as a wave of protest arose from shopkeepers and professionals affected by the legislation, it became clear that the government was not going to apply the law. Indeed, the government returned to Parliament with a new project, significantly modifying the law already passed but never applied, and this modified bill finally went into effect in January 1971. Although the constitution gives Parliament the right to decide basic principles of social security, the government was able to use its right to draw up the enabling clauses as a device to stall for four years. One can only conclude that the bureaucrats, not the deputies, were in the long run the decision-makers.[5]

Many of the problems that have been transferred from Parliament to the government involve political decisions, in the sense that the criteria by which they will be decided are only secondarily technical and are above all related to interests and values. In the example above regarding health insurance for the self-employed, the ministry took four years not to work out the technical details of implementation but to reach a political arrangement among the interest groups. But decisions removed from Parliament to the government—even political ones—will be made by men who are not themselves politicians. As described above, a minister's top advisors and the higher civil servants in the permanent administration of the ministry have both followed the same career pattern: through the *grandes écoles* and not through elections.

Policy Making in the Fifth Republic: The Cases of Agriculture and Labor

Both the locus and the personnel of the policy-making process have undergone major changes in France in the past two decades. Though some of these changes antedate the Fifth Republic, the impetus provided by the new constitution and by the massive influx of technocratic personnel into the top levels of government make it reasonable to consider 1958 a watershed. We have described above some of the most significant changes in the political system and how they were brought about. What remains to be considered is the difference these changes in the process of policy making have made in the output of the political system. The most useful way to approach this problem is to take an area in which the state has intervened regularly and to examine the policies produced by two different systems of decision making. The two areas we have selected—agriculture and labor—have been problematic for the governments of both the Fourth and Fifth Republics. Legislation in both areas affects a significant proportion of the working population and arouses the activity of powerful interest groups. In these areas, unlike foreign

---

[5] *Le Monde,* August 13, 1971.

policy or defense decisions, a broad range of different political groups and institutions—parties, interest groups, Parliament, prime minister and government, President—are involved, and no single force is decisive.

In the Third and Fourth Republics the fundamental decisions on agriculture were made in Parliament. The conception of the state's role in agriculture that most political groups shared was primarily social and political and only secondarily economic. The state intervened in the agricultural sector primarily to maintain a large peasant population in the countryside. The political stability of France was believed to depend on keeping a balance between rural and urban worlds, and the countryside was the reservoir of the conservative electors that counterbalanced the socialist workers of the cities. As industrialization gradually shifted this balance, the political elites tried to maintain the rural-urban equilibrium by advantaging rural electors through malapportionment of legislative seats and by devising an agricultural policy that would preserve the traditional countryside. The political elites realized that agriculture needed to be modernized enough to survive in an industrial economy. Therefore various technological improvements, like fertilizers and machines, were introduced, and organizations such as purchasing cooperatives and farm banking and loan associations that would make the peasantry less dependent on the city were encouraged. At the same time, the modernization of the countryside could not be allowed to go too far, for any substantial increases in productivity would require transformation of farm structures and ultimately a decrease in the farm population.

What resulted from this conception of the goals of agricultural policy was a patchwork quilt of subsidies, credits, piecemeal reforms, and political crumbs, tossed out to districts largely in function of the electoral needs of the deputies of the area and the strength of a few agricultural interest groups representing the large producers. Even the general farm legislation of the Fourth Republic was not based on any long-term plan for the development of agriculture or on any deliberate set of choices about the internal restructuring of the countryside. The great agricultural bill of the Fourth Republic was one providing that the prices of all major agricultural commodities be hitched to an index of industrial prices *(indexation)*. This bill exemplified all the weaknesses of agricultural policy in the Third and Fourth Republics. It did not consider the impact of across-the-board price increases on the development of the agricultural economy. (Should the state be encouraging surplus crops as well as the crops of which Frenchmen were consuming greater quantities?) It did not attempt to deal with the more profound problems of the countryside on which prices had only a marginal effect. (What difference would higher prices make to a peasant who farmed only ten acres and whose yields were low? What solutions would transform unproductive agricultural structures—the real cause of poverty in the countryside?) Finally, like so many other pieces of agricultural legislation of the Third and Fourth Republics, the law on *indexation* did not take into account the impact of these decisions on the general economy. (Would inflation result from generalizing all price increases through the chain of escalator clauses?)

The role of the bureaucracy in the conception and execution of agricultural policy was jealously limited by the deputies, for control over agricultural policy represented both the ammunition for elections and the essential instrument for preserving their electorates. Moreover, given the aims of the state in the agricultural sector, the decisions involved turned on political rather than technical criteria, so the bureaucrat's special expertise was not critical. The locus of agricultural policy making, then, was Parliament, and this had important consequences both for the kinds of policies that the system could produce and for the political forces and interest groups that participated in the development of policy. The concentration of agricultural decision making in Parliament advantaged certain types of agricultural organizations and certain groups of producers and supported the development of particular kinds of linkages between the countryside and the state.

The election of peasant deputies provides one example of how the structures of policy making determine the way groups organize to defend their interests in politics. When Parliament was the locus of decisions on agriculture, candidates who ran for election on peasant lists might convince the rural electors that sending "one of their own" to Parliament might bring back state aid to the district. If it is Parliament that decides who gets what from the state, it is clear that would-be recipients should find ways of getting their representatives into Parliament. At one point during the Fourth Republic this simple logic propelled forty-seven deputies elected on peasant platforms into Parliament. Just as important, the deputies who came from agricultural constituencies, having been elected as Socialists or Radicals or on some other party list, organized themselves once they reached Parliament into an agricultural parliamentary group *(amicale agricole parlementaire)*. These so-called study groups of deputies representing particular interests had no formal constitutional status, but they were nonetheless among the most important forces in the political system. It was within the agricultural parliamentary group of deputies drawn from almost all the parties, rather than within the individual parties, that essential decisions on agricultural policy were debated. A hundred deputies belonged to the agricultural group in the last years of the Fourth Republic, and at several critical junctures the group had a significant part in overthrowing governments.

Agricultural interest groups, too, organized in ways that reflected the predominant role of the Parliament in policy making. The most important agricultural organization of the Fourth Republic was the F.N.S.E.A. *(Fédération National des Syndicats d'Exploitants Agricoles)*, a federation with branches in every department and a national membership of almost a million in 1953. Although the strongest agricultural producers had organized specialized interest groups to defend their crops—this was the case for wheat, wine, and sugar beet growers—the great majority of farmers were represented only by the F.N.S.E.A. Why should this all-purpose farm organization, rather than specialized interest groups, have provided the major link between the countryside and the state? The answer is a complicated one, for many factors contributed to the predominance of the F.N.S.E.A. It is clear, however, from the decline of the F.N.S.E.A. in the Fifth

Republic that one important aspect was the parliamentary setting in which agricultural decisions were made. The F.N.S.E.A. was able to arrange compromises among a large number of diverse and contradictory agricultural interests and to present a platform to the Parliament that it could call, without challenge from any other agricultural organization, the demands of the countryside. In other words, the F.N.S.E.A. performed a function for Parliament that neither the political parties nor the Parliament itself could perform very well. Since the political parties were aligned on ideological positions that were largely irrelevant to the problems of the countryside, they were poor instruments for the aggregation of economic interests. Parliament itself was badly organized for the integration of diverse interests into a single policy, and the agricultural parliamentary group only partially filled the need for institutions to organize the terms of debate over agricultural problems. Thus the F.N.S.E.A. served an essential function of mediation between various rural interests and Parliament in presenting a list of demands that focused political discussion. That the F.N.S.E.A. did not perform this function very well did not matter much as long as the only aims of the state were to produce discrete bits of assorted assistance to the countryside.

The Fifth Republic dismantled this system in which the goals of state policy, the organization of interests, and parliamentary power were mutually reinforcing elements. One of the first acts of the new government was to repeal *indexation* because of its effects on the general economy, and Michel Debré soon gave notice to the political elites that the government would not pursue a traditional agricultural policy based on prices. In May 1960 Debré appeared before Parliament and presented the principles of agricultural legislation aimed essentially at reforming land structures and developing new marketing systems for agricultural goods. The Parliament passed this framework law, but before it could go into effect the government had to draw up enabling legislation. Two years after the passage of the law the government had barely begun to do so: Only four out of thirty enabling decrees envisaged had been issued. At this point, in the spring of 1962, the Minister of Agriculture, Edgard Pisani, appeared before Parliament with a proposal for a law to "complement" the 1960 legislation. It would be more accurate to describe the new bill *(loi complémentaire à la loi d'orientation agricole)* as replacing the previous bill, rather than filling it in. The new document went far beyond the previous one in proposing a program of long-range structural reforms in the countryside. The bill gave a state land agency the first option on all farmland purchases and restricted the purchase of land by persons not engaged in agriculture. It created a fund for pensions for old peasants who were willing to leave their farms so that they could be regrouped with neighboring ones in order to improve the productivity of farm structures. Job training was to be offered to young peasants who wished to leave the countryside. The bill also significantly strengthened the marketing groups that had been created by the 1960 bill, giving producers' groups the right to extend their rules to unorganized producers as well as to members. In sum, this was a coherent project for the development of the agricultural economy, one that took into account the need for reforming the internal structures of the countryside as well as the need for organizing agriculture's relations with the rest of the economy.

The new bill was drawn up by technocrats in the Ministry of Agriculture, and neither the political parties nor the national farm organizations were involved in the process.[6] Indeed, the project was leaked by the press before it had even been discussed in the Council of Ministers. The bill emerged onto the political scene at a time of violent peasant demonstrations against the government. To protest against the collapse of the artichoke market, Breton peasants had dumped 300 tons of artichokes in the streets of Saint-Pol-de-Léon; elsewhere, peasants protested against the purchase of land by people from the cities. Pressure mounted for the government to take some action to satisfy the rural population, whose demands had become embittered, first by the repeal of *indexation* and then by disappointment over the abortive 1960 legislation. The national farm organizations lined up behind the Pisani bill and announced that if Parliament did not pass it, they would call a massive strike and series of demonstrations. The project, after amendment by the Council of Ministers, was finally presented to the National Assembly on July 4, 1962. Instead of being passed to one of their six standing committees, a special commission was formed to consider it. The parliamentary session was supposed to finish on July 23, and this meant that deliberation on the bill both in committee and in the two houses was extremely rushed. As one observer noted, "The deputies and senators, already furious about having been ignored during the phase of drawing up the project, became more and more hostile to the procedure followed by the Minister and to the pressures that the agricultural organizations brought to bear on the Parliament."[7] Even the U.N.R. deputies protested about the pressures to which they were subjected and about the bureaucracy's infringement on the rights of Parliament. Finally, the Minister agreed to several amendments to critical provisions, and the bill passed. At every stage in this process the critical actor was the Minister of Agriculture. The key decisions had been made in the ministry, and though the minister was obliged to compromise on some points both in the Council of Ministers and in Parliament, the essential lines of policy remained those that had been drawn by the bureaucracy. This case, which is a typical example of policy making in the Fifth Republic, shows how greatly political practice has changed since the Fourth Republic: the bureaucracy has become the locus of decision making, and Parliament ratifies policies that it has not designed.

The shift in the locus of policy making from Parliament to the ministries has had important consequences for the other participants in the political system. In the case of agriculture, the first to profit from the new power situation was a young peasants' association, the "young Turks" of the national farmers movement, who

---

[6]Gaston Rimareix and Yves Tavernier, "L'Elaboration et le vote de la loi complémentaire à la loi d'orientation agricole," *Revue française de science politique* (June 1963), pp. 389–425.

[7]*Ibid.*, p. 403.

had been advocating radical changes in agricultural policy for years. The young peasants had no allies among the established parliamentary elites, and as long as agricultural decisions were made in Parliament, they had virtually no chance of having their views influence policy. When bureaucrats became the real decision-makers, the young peasants were able to gain a hearing for their views that numbers alone would never have assured them. In part their success was due to the fact that their position was closer to the government's than that of any other agricultural group. But more generally, the young peasants' chances of success were greater in this system because as a small, well-organized group with a coherent set of demands they were better able to negotiate with the technocrats than with politicians. Correspondingly, the relative failure of the F.N.S.E.A. in dealing with the new governments was due, in part at least, to its inability to switch from a logic of persuasion, in which the terms were political, to negotiations with technocrats, who saw the countryside in economic terms.

The biggest winners in the new system, however, have been the specialized interest groups. In dealings with the government, the specialized producers' groups have profited from advantages that none of the general farm associations possess. The interest groups have experts who can discuss agricultural policy with the technocrats with the same economic competence. While the general farm associations are represented in discussions with the government by their elected officials, men who must travel in from the provinces each time they want to take up a problem with the government, the interest groups have permanent staffs in Paris, who meet regularly—both professionally and socially—with their counterparts in the bureaucracy. Indeed, the experts who work for the agricultural interest groups and the technocrats in the Ministry of Agriculture and the Planning Commissariat have often attended the same schools; their common education has given them similar outlooks on the problems of the countryside. They are likely to come from the same social milieu and to share a circle of well-placed friends and connections. The peasant leader from the provinces, who may have completed only the minimum years of schooling, has no friends in Paris, and often feels socially inferior to the men he deals with in government, belongs to another social world.

The question is not only one of men but of goals and organizations. The interest group is advantaged in its relations with the bureaucracy by the limited character of its demands and by the nature of its constituency. The representative of the wheat farmers' association can identify a given number of points in the bureaucracy where he must apply pressure in order to advance the demands of his members, and he can present a set of discrete proposals. The representative of the general farm association, on the other hand, has no obvious interlocutor short of the Minister of Agriculture, and the goals he defends are frequently of a global nature—a standard of living for peasants equal to that of other groups, for example —that cannot easily be broken down into the concrete measures the bureaucracy can manage. The general farm association was geared in its goals and organization to operating in a parliamentary arena, and it finds it difficult to adapt to the bureaucratic arena. The same is true of the relative strengths and weaknesses of the interest group and the broad, all-purpose farm organization in dealing with the institutions of the European Common Market. The shift in agricultural policy making from Paris to Brussels has reinforced the shift from politicians to bureaucrats, and in this new arena the F.N.S.E.A. finds itself unable to exploit the political resources that once weighed so heavily in the French parliamentary context.

The debate over agricultural policy was once carried out by representatives of peasant groups with deputies; today, with bureaucrats. Direct negotiation between interests and government bypasses the mediation of political party, and the institutional setting of policy making in France comes increasingly to resemble the British model. The latest change in the system, indeed, borrows directly from the British political system. In the summer of 1971 the Minister of Agriculture announced that each year the government would meet for a roundtable discussion with representatives of the major agricultural associations to discuss questions of prices, investments, markets, social security, and modernization of the agricultural economy. There are differences between the first French roundtable and the British annual price review: In Britain representatives of all ministries concerned with agriculture participate, while in France only the Ministry of Agriculture was represented, despite the great importance of the Ministry of Finance for decisions made in the agricultural sector. Moreover, the British negotiations are prepared by lengthy studies, and they focus primarily on the evolution of agricultural revenues—a topic the French government refused to place on the agenda. Despite differences, the procedure has the same impact in both cases: to establish a privileged relationship between certain agricultural groups and the government (the Communist peasant movement, for example, was excluded in France) and to exclude from agricultural decisions the representatives of general political groups.

The Fifth Republic has not only supported the making of public policy by negotiation among organized interests but it has tried to generalize this mode of decision in the economy. After 1968 the government has set as one of the state's highest priorities the establishment of a *politique contractuelle* (a policy of contracts) as the mode of conflict resolution and regulation of relationships between labor and business. The *politique contractuelle* is a policy of industrial relations by negotiated settlement between labor unions and industrialists (in the private sector) or between the unions and the directors of the nationalized industries and the public services. The idea of regulating industrial relations by negotiated agreements is a relatively old one in the United States, where collective bargaining is the normal procedure for settling questions of wages, hours, working conditions, fringe benefits, and job security. In France, however, the traditions and values of both labor and business have been profoundly antagonistic to the idea. On the part of business men, there has been deep resistance to sharing power in the factory with the unions. Any system of collective bargaining requires that the union have the ability to check on the execution of the agreement, and for this the union must have a recognized status in the factory. The industrialists have been reluctant to grant this. Before 1968 unions were not allowed to hold meetings in the factories;

union representatives had no right to meet with individual workers or to discuss problems with representatives of management. In many factories workers who were known to be members of the unions were harassed, and if they were found conducting union business, they faced being fired.

Despite the important political differences that divide the major French labor federations, they all share a tradition that regards with deep suspicion even the amount of collaboration with management that is implied in collective bargaining. The three largest federations of industrial workers are the *Confédération Générale du Travail* (C.G.T.), which is closely linked to the Communist party, the *Force Ouvrière* (F.O.), which has affinities to the Socialist party, and the *Confédération Française Démocratique du Travail* (C.F.D.T.), which was once a Catholic association and now is a Left-wing group whose sympathies go to the United Socialist party, the Socialists, and the political clubs. Of the three, it is the C.G.T. that is most hostile to any system of negotiations in which labor commits itself to agreements with management. The C.G.T. has adopted the Marxist interpretation of industrial relations that sees grievances, strikes, and settlements as mere episodes in a class struggle whose ultimate purpose is to replace an industrial system based on capitalist control of the means of production by socialism. For this reason the C.G.T. and, in lesser measure, the C.F.D.T. and the F.O. are reluctant to commit themselves to any contract that implies an obligation to refrain from a strike before the expiration of the contract; the unions wish to retain their freedom to take up the class struggle at any time that appears advantageous for the cause of the workers. In the unions' view, collaborating with management in a settlement consolidates the industrial system, thus reinforcing the economic and political status quo. And in a situation where the unions have so little power to oblige managers to respect the contract, why should they commit themselves?

For very different reasons, therefore, both management and unions opposed a system of regulating industrial relations by contractual agreement. The issues that in other industrial states are decided by collective contracts are in France often decided unilaterally by management. When workers do go out on strike, the agreement that ends the strike has usually been one that management alone signs. In the public sector, before 1968 industrial relations were conducted in essentially the same fashion, except that the ultimate power of decision on questions involving the wage bill of the enterprise belonged to the Ministry of Finance, not to the management. Thus, in both private and public sectors the body of regulations governing management and labor was underdeveloped. Negotiations were regarded by all parties, not as the mechanism for reaching authoritative decisions that would bind all participants, but as one instrument among others in a basically conflictual situation.

The crisis of May–June 1968 brought to the fore factors that made management, state, and labor reconsider their opposition to regulating industrial relations by negotiations. For the managers of private industry and for the labor unions, it was the need to reestablish control in a situation where wildcat strikes, the politicization of thousands of nonunionized workers, and the establishment of plant committees outside the aegis of the unions had led to a general breakdown of the existing system of relationships between workers and managers in the plant and workers and unions. Once order was restored, the pressures on the unions and business for change were lessened, but the state had thoroughly committed itself to a reform of the industrial relations system. Already as part of the Grenelle agreement negotiated during the crisis, the state and industry had recognized the unions' rights in the factory, and one of the first major pieces of legislation in the wake of the May–June events was a law recognizing the right of union organization in all factories hiring more than fifty employees. Minister of Social Affairs Maurice Schumann, in presenting the bill to Parliament, described it as a step toward a new system of industrial relations. In suggesting that the managers should recognize the union leaders as their "natural interlocutors," he showed that the government considered the bill as a necessary element of the *politique contractuelle*.

The government's next steps were to reorganize the process of decision making in the public sector so as to make possible direct negotiations between the directors of the state firms and the unions. Until then, the directors had had very little power to negotiate agreements, because ultimate responsibility for the decision rested in the ministries. After 1968 the authority needed to run state enterprises was increasingly devolved from the ministries to the management. In the labor disputes that have since arisen in the nationalized electricity agency (E.D.F.), in the state railroads (S.N.C.F.), and other public services, the directors themselves have had substantial powers to decide questions at stake, including wages. At the same time, the government tried to encourage the unions and the directors of the public sectors to settle their grievances with contracts that both parties would sign. The state, indeed, was willing to pay dearly to achieve this result, and the contracts that E.D.F. and the S.N.C.F. offered to the unions contained significant concessions on such union demands as guaranteed increases in real wages. The government, moreover, was willing to abandon clauses in the contracts that the unions found unacceptable, the most important of which was a clause limiting the right to call strikes. The unions were initially hostile to the contracts, and the C.G.T. refused to sign the first agreements. Gradually, however, this resistance has weakened, largely because of the government's substantial concessions, but also in part because the unions themselves have an interest in negotiating agreements in which their right to participate in certain plant-level decisions is recognized. Since the fall of 1969 forty-two agreements have been signed in the public sector, and some of the later ones have even received the signature of the C.G.T.

In the field of industrial relations, then, as in agriculture, the state is trying to establish a system of policy making by negotiation between organized interests and the state. Formidable obstacles still remain, for neither the trade unions nor industry have given up the values and stakes that derive from a long history of noncooperation.

Return to Politics?

In France since the Fifth Republic policy making has moved out of the political arenas of party and Parliament and into arenas where the participants are interest groups and technocrats. As the cases of agriculture and labor suggest, this is the result of replacing the traditional forms of political conflict by a process of negotiation between organized interests and government. In agriculture, negotiation between the Ministry of Agriculture and the agricultural groups replaces the defense of agricultural interests in Parliament. In the nationalized industries, negotiation between the director of the firm and the labor unions replaces a procedure in which the politicians in government decided on the wage bill for workers in the public sector. These changes in the personnel of politics, the shift in the locus of policy making, and the transformation of the process of resolving conflicts have apparently removed the flesh and blood from traditional political issues, leaving their bones to be picked over by the political parties while the real problems of the nation are resolved by interest groups and government.

Yet in the last five years there have been increasingly frequent signs of the fragility of government by collaboration of bureaucracy and organized interests. The most significant evidence in this respect has been the increase in political activity and even political violence by groups that are not represented in the circles of decision making. These groups are an extremely diverse lot. There are social categories like the small shopkeepers, whose organizations are too weak or whose demands are too opposed to governmental policy to gain a seat at the roundtables where technocrats and interest groups negotiate. For years small shopkeepers felt oppressed by official policies favoring lower price margins in commerce, increased competition, and supermarkets. Unable to find channels of political expression, the shopkeepers' dissatisfaction broke out in a wave of demonstrations and tax strikes. Government offices were besieged by angry shopkeepers, and several tax collectors were kidnapped for brief periods by a commando group inspired by Gerard Nicoud, leader of a new group that denounced the regular merchants' association for having sold out to the government. In other sectors of society, too, individuals whose firms or farms were small, poor, and less productive than the average and who saw themselves as the victims of the state's modernization policies began to break away from groups that had traditionally represented their interests to form their own organizations. In agriculture, for example, the M.O.D.E.F. *(Mouvement pour la Défense des Exploitations Familiales),* an organization that once had had little influence beyond a few Communist strongholds, began to pick up members in poor regions all over France and to challenge the organizational monopoly of the F.N.S.E.A. The M.O.D.E.F. described its goals as defending the family farm and the small peasantry against the technocrats and big agricultural interests.

The major challenges to the state have come from groups that are badly represented by the interest groups that have access to the processes of decision in government. In part, this is because the interest groups themselves are controlled by the more prosperous and modern economic groups: it has been the wheat farmers and not the dairy farmers that dominate agricultural syndicalism; the skilled workers and not the *smigards* (workers earning the minimum legal wages) that are the main core of the labor movement. But even more important, the disaffected social groups are those that cannot be defended well by interest-group politics. What the small peasant or the small shopkeeper demands is not so much the satisfaction of particular economic grievances but a change in the fundamental political choices of the state. An interest group is a vehicle poorly suited to the expression of this kind of demand. And the political parties, which are structurally capable of mediating such demands by expressing them in alternatives to governmental policies, have not done so. The political parties' failure to perceive and organize the demands of those groups that have not been integrated into the policy processes of the Fifth Republic has had two serious consequences. Inability to locate the specific sources of stress in the political system of the Fifth Republic has contributed to the stagnation and decline of the opposition parties, which seem to cling blindly to old political issues while new ones escape their notice. At the same time, the political parties' failure to provide a channel for the expression of the political grievances of groups that are badly represented in the current political system leave such groups stranded. As one peasant leader from a poor region put it, "Between the government and us there is a great vacuum." The groups outside the system have come to feel that the only way to move or change the government is through what peasant syndicalists call "direct action": demonstrations, strikes, violent acts. In the absence of political parties able to funnel the needs and desires of social groups into the centers of political decision, dissatisfaction and grievances are bottled up in society and spill over into extralegal forms of political action.

No event better illustrates the explosive potential of the frustrations and unmet demands of groups excluded from the policy process than the abortive revolution of May–June 1968. What the massive demonstrations of students and workers showed was the system's inability to satisfy a broad range of economic, social, and political demands. Some of these reflected a desire for a vast transformation of the values of society and politics: for reducing or eliminating authority and hierarchy; for increasing participation and the possibilities for self-expression; for social equality. Perhaps no political system could satisfy such demands. In this sense it is no special limitation of the French state that it was unwilling to undertake changes that would have amounted to a revolution in values and social structure. What does reveal the weaknesses of the French political system is that even demands that could have been satisfied within the framework of the political and social status quo were not met and that it took the revolutionary movements of May–June 1968 to push through improvements in the standard of living and working conditions that might well have been obtained by normal political processes. In sum, the May–June 1968 events demonstrated the existence of widespread dissatisfaction that the policy-making processes of the first decade of the Fifth Republic were unable to meet.

Since May–June 1968, there has been a swing back toward politics as the government has ventured out of the closed arena to which only the organized interests and the technocrats had access and has reached out to the traditional political intermediaries. Within the government itself politicians are playing a more important role, and recent policy declarations on agriculture, for example, or on small commerce show increased attention to the political aspects of economic modernization. Circumstantial factors like the municipal elections may have contributed to this shift. And Pompidou's need to consolidate the Gaullist electorate in the absence of de Gaulle certainly accounts for some of the government's new interest in traditional political forces.

These shifts in the policy-making process of the Fifth Republic are too new and too tentative to permit the conclusion that major changes are at stake. The present situation is one in which several modes of decision making and, indeed, several different policies coexist in certain critical policy areas. For example, the government has allowed small shopkeepers to participate in decisions on building new supermarkets by establishing departmental commissions on which all forms of commerce are represented and giving these commissions the right to advise the prefect on proposals for new supermarkets. At the same time, however, the technocrats apparently retain their rights of decision in the matter, for any request to build a supermarket that is refused by the departmental commission is automatically referred to a national commission in Paris, on which only representatives of the ministries sit; and this commission may accept the project even over the local rejection. The government now uses both political and technocratic criteria, personnel, and processes of decision; and though the balance has apparently shifted recently, it is too early to take the measure of the changes. Not only for students of French politics but for anyone interested in the politics of industrial societies, the outcome of this uneasy coexistence between political and bureaucratic processes of decision is a matter of great importance.

Five

Local Governments in a Centralized State

In the past decade in France, as in other advanced industrial societies, the problems of local governments have burst into national politics. Population movement from countryside to city, increased birth rates, racial tensions, the relationships between metropolis and surrounding communities, the desire of citizens to have a larger say in local political decisions—all these and many other factors have pressed with increased force on existing political structures and have produced a new awareness of the need for reform in the institutions of local government.

In France three of these factors have been particularly important. First, the years since World War II have been decades of unprecedented mobility in France. Over a six-year period (1962–1968) one out of every fifteen Frenchmen changed the region in which he lived, and an even higher proportion moved from one town to another within the same region. One part of this vast population movement can be accounted for by the shift in employment from agriculture to industry. Between 1954 and 1968 the proportion of the work force employed in agriculture dropped from 31 percent to 17 percent. Since few of the former farmers can find work in their regions that allows them to continue living on their farms, change in employment is usually accompanied by a change in residence. Western France and central France, regions with large agricultural populations and little industry, are being drained, while new residents continue to feed into the urban populations of Paris, the industrial northeast, and the southeast. Another part of the population movement in this period was created by the decline in traditional industries—mining, shipyards, textiles—and the relocation of workers to regions of France with modern industry. Thus in the period 1962–1968 the departments of Nord and Lorraine, whose traditional industries were in crisis, lost heavily, while the departments of the Rhone-Alpes region around Grenoble and Lyons, where modern industries have developed, gained substantially.

The impact of internal migration has created different problems for growing and declining communes. The commune is the basic political unit in France; all parts of the country, rural and urban, are organized in communes. There are close to 38,000 communes; less than 10 percent are urban by French census definition, that is, have more than 2,000 inhabitants (see Table 5.1). As population has moved out of rural areas into cities, the proportion of small communes has increased.

Table 5.1 Distribution of Communes by Population, 1968

Population	Number of Communes	Percentage of Number of Communes	Percentage of Number of Inhabitants
100,000 and over	37	0.1	19.0
30,000–100,000	160	0.4	15.5
10,000–30,000	482	1.3	15.9
5,000–10,000	642	1.7	8.6
2,000–5,000	1,938	5.1	11.5
1,000–2,000	3,618	9.6	9.7
0–1,000	30,831	81.8	19.8

DATA SOURCE: Jean de Savigny, *L'Etat contre les communes?* (Paris: Seuil, 1971), p. 187.

In 1968, 24,007 out of the 38,000 communes had fewer than 500 inhabitants, and these small towns experience increasingly greater difficulties in maintaining an infrastructure of public institutions and services with a dwindling pool of taxpayers. The case of the commune of Sacquenville, population 353, is typical. The town must provide school facilities, running water and electricity, public baths, fire-fighting equipment, road maintenance, and salaries for its municipal employees. In order to create facilities that might attract new people to settle in the commune, the town must make substantial investments. Since it cannot do so with its own already overtaxed resources, expansion depends on the town's borrowing money or obtaining subsidies from the state. Even so, Sacquenville is lucky, for it is not far from Paris, and the town can expect that if it improves public facilities and services, it will be able to draw in new residents as the Parisian population spreads out into surrounding areas. French small communes that are not in the immediate vicinity of a large urban center face long-term decline, while at the same time they must try to satisfy their citizens' rising expectations with a shrinking reservoir of resources.

Cities confront another order of problem. The metropolitan areas of France have grown rapidly in the past two decades. The population of metropolitan Grenoble, for example, rose from 262,000 in 1962 to 352,000 in 1968, while in the same period Marseille's population expanded from 639,000 to 964,000 and other large cities experienced comparable rates of growth. Schools, housing, public services, transportation, cultural facilities, indeed, new districts of the city must be provided for the new residents. At the same time, the old residents pressure local governments to improve the quality of the public goods that they use. The problem for local finances that the massive influx into the cities raises is obvious; but there are other costs of rapid growth that are just as difficult to meet. The institutions of local government and administration were designed to service a much smaller population, and the new tasks strain their capacity to manage community affairs. When local administration cannot cope with the magnitude of needs that a large urban population generates, the burdens are shifted off onto national government, thus transforming the relationships between local government and the state.

The second factor contributing to the French urban crisis is the increased importance of problems that cannot be resolved by an individual commune but only at a regional level. There have always been good reasons for a French commune to cooperate with neighboring communes in the provision of such public services as schools, the bussing of school children, or the provision of running water and electricity, since "intercommunal syndicates" could provide such services at considerable savings to the individual towns. Today, however, communes find themselves faced with problems that they could not solve themselves, even if they had the money to do so. When, for example, the city of Grenoble tries to attract new industry, it must be able to count on neighboring communes to provide the housing for new workers, since there is little free land in the city proper. Grenoble must be able to guarantee the potential industrial developer that facilities will be built to house and transport the needed work force to the new enterprise. For this, Grenoble and the surrounding towns have to agree on a long-term plan for the development of the region. The same need for regional policies arises whenever a commune wishes to develop facilities whose benefits will accrue in large measure to those who live outside the commune itself but in the region. Housing as we have seen is one public good whose external economies may be as important as the values received by those within the community. Transportation systems are another public good whose benefits usually are enjoyed by people in a larger area than that covered by a single commune. Industrial development, too, requires a commune to make expenditures for infrastructure in order to reap a reward that cannot be kept within the confines of the political unit that has footed the bill. The patterns of urban expansion and of industrial growth have increased the number of public services whose impact is regional and have thus created new pressures for regional policy and for regional political action that cannot be met by any simple extension of the old "intercommunal syndicate" model of cooperation.

Along with the shifts in the national distribution of population and the emergence of regional problems, a third factor has weighed heavily in the current debate over local government in France: the growing desire for participation in local politics. In one sense, the new demands for civic participation in city government can be explained by the shifts in population out of small towns into larger cities. In a small town, the size of the population, the scale of the problems, the relative simplicity of the issues at stake, and the visibility and accessibility of the political elites facilitate political participation. Information spreads quickly in a small community and citizens are usually well-informed about the issues at stake in the town. They are, moreover, in a better position to influence political decisions than is the typical city-dweller, for in a small town most people have a good chance of knowing a local politician or of having access to one through friends and relatives. In French cities, in contrast, citizens both need more from local government and have fewer opportunities to express their needs than in the small town. The citizen of a city with a population of several hundred thousand has little chance of knowing a local politician and has difficulty in finding any channels through which he can influence political decisions. The decisions themselves are more complex and, so, are often made by technicians and bureaucrats, rather than by elected officials. The plight of a group of Grenoble citizens who unsuccessfully knocked on the doors of city officials and bureaucrats to complain that water pressure was insufficient to get water up to their fourth-floor apartments is typical. The response of these frustrated Grenoble citizens to the unresponsiveness of city government was to organize a civic reform group and to run candidates in the next municipal elections. This was a most untypical occurrence in France at the time the Grenoble civic associations began in the early 1960s, but such an organizational response is now spreading throughout France. The demand for wider participation in local politics has contributed in the past ten years to the flourishing of neighborhood committees, city-wide civic action groups—the G.A.M.s *(groupes d'action municipale)*—and to a national federation of civic groups. Though the creation on a wide scale of these new groups in the cities marks a significant change, the obstacles that in the past inhibited the growth of voluntary associations in France continue to block the expansion of these new organizations and to reduce their capacity to serve as vehicles for the participation of citizens in local politics. How to make possible wider participation in the affairs of city government remains on the agenda of unsolved problems in France.

These issues are of course not unique to France. Other industrial states are under pressure to accommodate larger urban populations and to satisfy growing demands for civic participation. French cities and regions confront difficulties that are virtually identical to those of the cities of Britain or the United States or Germany, but the political and social structures, values and expectations, and historical experiences that French, Germans, British, and Americans bring to the resolution of these problems vary greatly. The questions we wish to consider for France are, What resources does the political system offer for working out these problems, and what obstacles does it present? and How do these resources and obstacles shape policy outcomes?

Structure of Local Government

The political framework within which French cities deal with the changing needs and demands of their populations is built on three levels of government: the commune, the department, and the national government. These are the only political units in France that are governed by elected bodies and that have the right to legislate for their citizens. Other political units are only administrative entities (the cantons and arrondissements) or territorial groupings to facilitate planning (regions). The three-tier distribution of political power was fixed in its essential features by the end of the nineteenth century. The basic legislation on municipal government is a law passed in 1884, whose fundamental principles still regulate the exercise of political power at the local level. The 1884 law specified that the commune should be governed by an elected municipal council and a mayor, chosen by the municipal council. The number of members on the municipal council now varies according to the size of the commune's population, and the mode of election in municipal elections also differs according to population size. Aside from these and a few other differences that concern the relationship of the commune to the state, French communes are all organized in essentially the same way.

The mayor and municipal council deal with two kinds of decisions: decisions about how to carry out and finance services that the state requires local governments to perform and decisions about which priorities should orient policy in the sphere in which communes are free to allocate resources as they choose. Local governments are obliged by law to allocate sums in their budgets for such items as salaries of municipal employees, the upkeep of schools and town buildings, debt service, and various kinds of social assistance. These obligatory expenditures of local government are specified by national legislation. Should any municipal council fail to provide for them in its budget, the state will rewrite the local budget to include the obligatory expenses and to include tax revenues to cover them. After the municipal council has satisfied its legal obligations, it is in principle free to legislate in any sphere as it chooses, except where national law expressly prohibits local action. This seemingly wide mandate is, however, subject to two constraints, one budgetary and the other political. The state must approve the decisions of local government, and it may veto not only those local decisions that are illegal but also those that it judges unwise. If the commune wants to borrow money to finance new investments, if it adds a new tax, or even if it wishes to name a street after a man—to consider only a few examples—the state can refuse to authorize the commune to carry out its decision.

The state exercises checks over local government through the mayor, the prefect, and the departmental representatives of the ministries. The mayor is an elected official, but he is also the representative of the state at the local level. This is because the commune is not only an autonomous self-governing unit, but also the basic unit of the central-state system. As an agent of the state, the mayor is responsible for public order in the commune and for carrying out certain administrative tasks set by the state, for example, the collection of statistics. In this role of state representative at the communal level, the mayor is directly responsible to the prefect, who is his superior in the administrative hierarchy of the state. The mayor in these functions is not responsible before either the municipal council or the local citizenry.

The prefect is the representative of national government in the department. He embodies the authority of the state at the local level, and as Jean-Pierre Worms has pointed out, Frenchmen credit him with the same omnicompetence and omniscience that they expect from the state:

> . . . they feel that somehow everything depends on him. They blame him for everything that goes wrong, and it's to him they look to improve things. The logical destination of every petition or demonstration is the prefecture.[1]

When peasants in the sixties protested the level of agricultural prices set by the state, they naturally singled out the prefect as the object of their wrath; the buildings of the prefecture are the most common target of the rocks and eggs of political demonstrations. The prefect's wide-ranging powers over local government fall into two broad categories: control of the legality of local governmental decisions and review of the substance of the commune's decisions in policy areas where the commune is not bound by national legislation. The prefect examines the decisions of municipal councils to assure that they are legal and that they satisfy the obligations that the state places on local governments. The prefect may refuse to approve a communal budget, and he has the authorization to write in any obligatory expenditures for which the council has failed to provide.

The prefect's powers extend, however, beyond controlling the legality of municipal acts. On behalf of the central government, the prefect exercises a tutelage authority over local governments. Much of the commune's legislation cannot go into effect without the prefect's approval; some communal decisions depend on prior consent of tutelage authority. As "tutor" of the commune, the prefect has wide powers. Indeed, under specified circumstances he may suspend a mayor or municipal council. These powers are rarely used, but their existence creates a system of incentives for local government in which avoiding any decision that the prefect might not approve is an important goal. As Marie-Françoise Souchon concluded from her study of two small communes,

> [T]he tutelage authority has little need of its powers. The mayors make it a point of honor to present a budget beyond reproach. The red marks [the prefect's comments] in the margin are extremely rare and mostly are notes to the effect that the matter should be taken up in a special meeting of the municipal council. If their budgets came back covered with corrections, the mayors would feel

---

[1]Jean-Pierre Worms, "Le Préfet et ses notables," *Sociologie du travail,* 3 (1966), p. 252.

really guilty. The idea is quite unthinkable and they would never dream of presenting anything but a balanced budget.[2]

By anticipating the responses of the prefect, local officials avoid conflict with tutelary authority, but a "safe" policy of limited initiative and minimal risks may not be the best one for developing the commune.

In recent years the number of decisions that the commune may take without prior consent of tutelary authority has been increased. The Parliament voted in 1970 to eliminate the procedure that required a commune to await the approval of the prefect before putting its budget into effect. Now a commune's budget will automatically go into effect fifteen days after it has been submitted to the prefecture, on condition that the budget is balanced. The prefect's prior approval is no longer required before the municipal council can dispose of property belonging to the town or negotiate loans. These changes have, however, simplified only a tiny fraction of the administrative procedures through which the state regulates the behavior of local government. And the growing financial dependence of the commune on the state means that whatever independence the commune has won for disposing of matters within its own resources has been lost many times over in the controls and review the commune must accept every time it receives money from the state. Jean de Savigny has spelled out what state controls mean for a commune that decides to build a new secondary school:

1. The subprefect must certify that the project fits into the state plan for school development in the area.
2. Before the commune can buy any land for the school, the regional prefect must give his consent.
3. The purchase of land must also be reviewed by the ministerial services that deal with land-use and then by a commission on buildings and architecture.
4. Technical agencies of the state control whether the project meets standard specifications.
5. The prefect, the regional prefect, and the central government review the project and grant a subsidy if the project has been written into the triennial plan of the Ministry of National Education.
6. A state bank *(Caisse des dépôts et consignations)* examines the dossier before granting a loan.
7. An accountant checks up on the mayor's statement of expenses.
8. Technical agencies of the state will check the progress of construction.
9. The same services will check the completed building.
10. The *inspection des finances* (one of the *grands corps* of the state) may review the financial aspects of the project.

---

[2]Marie-Françoise Souchon, *Le Maire: élu local dans une société en changement* (Paris: Cujas, 1968), p. 160.

11. A national administrative court *(Cour des Comptes)* may also examine the books.
12. On the request of a citizen, a judicial review of the process may be held.[3]

Although the 1970 relaxation of the prefect's authority over the commune's acquisition of land has made part of this process easier than in the past, the commune still needs the consent of the prefect and of the ministries concerned for many aspects of the project.

In principle, the prefect coordinates the activities of the representatives of the ministries operating in his department, so that the various state agencies do not work at cross-purposes. The representatives of the ministries in the departments, therefore, report not only to their own central offices back in Paris but also to the prefect, and at the point of intersection of these two hierarchies—that of the administrative system headed by the prefect and that of the ministry itself—there are frequent conflicts of influence and interest. The prefect himself belongs to two chains of authority: His superior in the administrative hierarchy is the Minister of Interior, but the prefect represents the government as a whole, not only the Ministry of Interior. The trend of recent legislation has been to strengthen the prefect's control over the ministries' activities in his department, but certain of the most important state agencies still act with great autonomy on the local scene. The state highway agency, a corps of civil engineers *(Ponts-et-Chaussées),* is perhaps the most powerful of the state technical services operating at the local level. This agency not only draws up the plans for communal infrastructure and distributes state subsidies for public-works projects but also executes these projects and is remunerated for its services as any firm of private entrepreneurs might be. Local officials are dependent on the technical agencies of the state, like the *Ponts-et-Chaussées* or *Génie Rural* (rural engineers), and on the agricultural services for technical advice, for subsidies, and for assistance in carrying out projects.

Though the political tutelage of the prefect may be declining, the tutelage that these technical services of the state exercise over local governments is increasing. The prefect exerts pressure on the technical agencies of the state to coordinate their operations through his office, and he will in cases of conflict mediate between local governments and the ministries. Nonetheless, local officials ordinarily have to contend with the prefect and the departmental representatives of the ministries as two separate authorities, each of which controls resources critical for the commune.

The second tier of French government is the department. There are ninety-five of them, each governed by a departmental council *(conseil général).* The department is administratively subdivided into cantons, and each canton elects one member to the departmental council. The boundaries of the cantons, like those of the departments and communes, were fixed at the time of the French Revolution and have changed little since then. The canton of Pont-l'Abbé with 23,577 people

---

[3]Jean de Savigny, *L'Etat contre les communes?* (Paris: Seuil, 1971), p. 187.

and the canton of Le Faou with 4,703 are both represented by a single member in the departmental council of Finistère. The inequalities in representation at the departmental level support the predominance of rural small-town interests, for the large urban population of a city is often bottled up in a single canton. Rural cantons far outnumber urban ones; more than half of French cantons have fewer than 10,000 inhabitants. The government now proposes to carve out 400 new cantons in urban areas, and so the urban population may be better represented in departmental government in the near future.

The departmental council, like the municipal council, has a certain number of functions that the state requires it to perform and, beyond these obligatory expenditures, a wide measure of discretion. The departmental budget supports most of the road building and repair in the department, and it contributes heavily to other improvements in departmental infrastructure. Schools, agriculture, social services, and welfare are all subsidized by the department. As in the case of the communes, the activities of the department come under the surveillance of the state. National laws forbid certain kinds of expenditures in the departments and narrowly restrict the department's initiatives in the field of taxation. As the tutelary authorities of departmental government, the Ministers of Interior and Finance and the state administrative court (Conseil d'Etat) exercise a control over departmental decisions that is comparable to the prefectoral tutelage of the communes.

The department like the commune is both a self-governing body and an administrative level of the state. Indeed, in the case of the department, the chief executive of government is not an elected official, but the prefect. The departmental council does not choose a "governor"; this role is performed by the prefect who occupies at the departmental level the position that the mayor has in the commune. This means, at one end of the legislative process, that the prefect prepares the agenda and the budget on which the departmental council debates and votes and, at the other end of the process, that it is the prefect who is responsible for the execution of the departmental legislation. The Constitution of the Fourth Republic provided for an independent executive for departments; but the enabling legislation was never passed, and the prefect remains the chief executive of the department.

From an administrative chart it would appear that since local political authorities are under the control of the prefect, he could marshal them to whatever ends he chose, just as a general can move around the troops under his command. The reality of local politics is quite different. The powers of the prefect over local government, his access to the resources controlled by national government, and the prestige he has as representative of the state all give him great leverage on local elites, but they, in turn, control power resources that are critical to the prefect.[4] First, the success of most of the prefect's plans depends on the cooperation of other political groups, since he cannot force a commune or the department to carry out any projects beyond those required by national legislation. Two-thirds of the

[4]Worms, op. cit.

capital improvements expenditures of the state are spent at the local level, so that the prefect needs to work out some agreement with local elites if he wants to implement programs that will contribute to the economic development of the department. Some of the resistance he meets can be explained by the social conservatism of local notables, who are largely drawn from small-town and rural milieus. Other conflicts that hinder the implementation of his projects arise from the unwillingness of some local groups to pay the price of a benefit that will extend to a larger group. In the fall of 1971, for example, the regional prefect of the Rhone-Alpes area warned local elites of the disastrous consequences for the region of refusing to allow an oil refinery to establish a plant outside of Lyons. Two communes had already refused the refinery, one because of the protest of wine-growers, the other because of the outrage of nature-lovers, and now the population of the commune that had been selected as the third site seemed likely to add its refusal. In order to protect the general interest of the region, the prefect must often, as in this case, persuade local elites to support changes in their own environments. A prefect who wishes to move up in the administrative hierarchy of the state today needs to show that he is a dynamic entrepreneur for the state's social and economic goals. And to acquire the record of accomplishments that will further his career, the cooperation of local political groups is indispensable.

Even more important, the prefect needs local notables to serve as relays in his relations with the population. The traditional role of the prefect was to maintain order, to resolve conflicts, and to defend a general interest that was defined as the social and political status quo of the department. Although new and more dynamic functions have been added to this traditional political role, a prefect is still judged in Paris by how well he preserves law and order and the existing relations among social groups. Nothing is more injurious to a prefect's reputation than to lose contact with major groups in the department and to find that they refuse his mediation in conflicts. If he has maintained good relations with local notables, the prefect can rely on them to inform him of the political climate of the department, thus enabling him to act before conflicts break out into the open. When a prefect's relations with the notables are close, he can even count on them to channel political protest in ways that will minimize its damaging effects to his own reputation. In the fifties, for example, the leaders of the peasant syndical associations usually discussed arrangements for a demonstration with the prefecture, and the prefect was able to organize police forces, detour traffic, and generally arrange to avoid incidents embarrassing to state authority. The mark of the peasants' growing bitterness in the sixties was that they broke off relations with the prefect and chose forms of protest that exposed his political vulnerability. The peasant invasion of the subprefecture buildings in Morlaix in 1961 was a symbolic act that expressed the peasant leaders' refusal to continue cooperation with public authorities unless more peasant demands were satisfied.

In order to maintain good relations with the notables and thereby keep open his channels to the population, the prefect has to be willing to bend to local pressures and to meet outstanding grievances. This may require that he interpret national legislation "flexibly" and that he satisfy local demands even at the expense of national policy. The prefects, for example, usually accept the recommendations of the departmental advisory commissions on new commercial development, even though this frequently means refusing building permits to supermarkets, that is, hindering modernization of the commercial infrastructure. The prefects "pass the buck" to Paris, knowing that the Minister of Equipment will override their veto. By accepting the advice of local notables, however, the prefect prevents himself from getting involved in a conflict with local elites in which his own political capital would be expended and his capacity to serve as an arbiter among various social groups reduced.

Finally, the prefects need the local elites' support to protect them against pressures from Paris. As Worms has suggested, both the prefect and the local notables have common stakes to defend against the intervention of the state:

> It is obvious that if the prefect does not want his authority in the department to be subject to all the fluctuations in coalitions, policies, governments and regimes, he must maintain an important margin of autonomy in his dealings with the government. The need to calm the feelings of his citizens, to prevent them from "blowing up France" is a good argument for negotiating such a margin of freedom.[5]

To preserve his freedom of action vis-à-vis the central government, the prefect must be able to count on the support of the local elites, and to develop and protect this solidarity of interests, the prefect must be willing to make important concessions to local political groups. In sum, the relationships of prefect to local political elites are ones of mutual dependence. Each party needs the other; each is in some measure able to control the actions of the other.

Local Finances

The independence of local governments depends not only on the political relationships that link them to the center but, just as importantly, on their level of economic activity and on the resources available to finance activities. If one compares American towns and states with French communes and departments, it is clear that American local governments are both more active relative to the national government and have more of their own resources with which to finance their projects than French local governments. As Table 5.2 indicates, the proportion of public expenditures (nonmilitary) carried out by local and state governments in the United States is double that of the federal government; in France the proportion is reversed. In both countries the growing expenses of local communities have forced

---

[5] *Ibid.*, p. 271.

Table 5.2 Public Expenditures (Nonmilitary), 1967, in percentages

	United States	France
National government	34	72
States	23	–
Departments	–	8
Local governments	43	20

DATA SOURCE: Jean de Savigny, *L'Etat contre les communes?* (Paris: Seuil, 1971), p. 64.

them to turn to the national government for assistance in financing their plans. In France about 70 percent of local investments are financed by state subsidies and loans. (Communal budgets are divided into two sections: operating expenses and investments. Investments account for about 40 percent of the typical communal budget.)[6]

The economic dependence of the communes on the central government results from their extremely limited possibilities of financing expenditures beyond operating expenses with tax revenues. Of the taxes that local governments in France may levy on their citizens, only four taxes (familiarly known as the *"quatre vieilles"*) produce significant amounts of revenue; the others—a dog tax, a tax on hunting grounds, for example—are mostly trivial. The *quatre vieilles* date to the French Revolution and, while they have been amended and patched up over the years, there has been no reform of local taxes to permit local governments to tap selectively the potential sources of income for the community. *Who* shall be taxed and *how* the burden of taxation should be distributed among various groups in the community are questions that are out of the reach of local government. The four taxes that form the basis of local taxation are property taxes, an occupancy tax, and a tax on commercial establishments. These taxes used to be collected by the central government and were the principal source of national revenues. In 1917 when the income tax was adopted, the state ceased collecting these four taxes, but they were maintained as the basis for calculating local taxes. Essentially the process is the following: Taxable property is assessed. The state calculates what it would have collected if it were still collecting taxes on this basis. Then this fictive sum is divided by one-hundred, and the product is called the *centime*. Each commune figures out how many *centimes'* worth of tax it must collect in order to balance its budget. The *centimes* currently provide about 55 percent of local revenues.

The infinite complications of this tax system built on a no-longer existent national tax involve four essential problems. First, the property evaluations are so out-of-date that they bear little relation to the current distribution of wealth in the community. In 1959 the government decided to replace the four old taxes with new local

---

[6]De Savigny, *op. cit.,* p. 64.

property taxes that would no longer require the fiction that the central government still collected the old taxes. But to implement the new property taxes, property had to be reevaluated—a mammoth task that twelve years after the passage of the reform has still not been completed. Even after the reevaluation, when the new taxes will go into effect, the communes will still face the problem of being largely restricted to property taxes. Since the values of land and buildings are only poor reflections of the economic activities of the community, important sources of revenue remain outside the tax-reach of local governments. Even when the 1959 tax reform replaces the current system, local governments will still have only limited possibilities of redistributing the tax burden among different groups in the community. They will be able to raise (or lower) the rate of the tax (just as today they may increase the number of *centimes*).

Finally, basing communal finances on property taxes creates great inequities among regions and among communes. De Savigny has noted that as television, travel, and publicity make people aware of the goods and services that some areas have, they demand that their towns, too, provide these goods:

> . . . Citizens from rural areas or from the backward regions refuse to accept a situation in which they do not have the same facilities as their compatriots in the big cities: running water, swimming pools, blacktopped roads, tennis courts, youth centers—all the equipment or collective services that once were the privilege of certain towns and that now have become a universal demand.[7]

In order to acquire these goods, the poor communes with fewer taxable resources must tax more heavily. The highest taxes are, in fact, paid by the citizens of the poorest regions. Taxes on properties with the same value are 40 percent higher in western France than in the region around Paris.

After the *centimes,* the next major source of tax revenues for local governments is a tax on value-added (T.V.A.) collected by the national government and redistributed in part to local governments. The basis of this redistribution is as complex and involves as many legal fictions as the calculation of the *centimes.* The state gives each commune as much as it would have collected if the commune were still levying a local tax on commercial transactions—a tax that disappeared in January 1968! The replacement of the old local tax by a nationally-distributed tax has meant a loss of local autonomy. Formerly, a mayor who was enterprising enough to attract new business to his commune could hope to benefit from increased tax revenues. Today, his initiative has relatively little pay-off for the commune's finances. Both because local governments are engaging in new activities and thus need grants and loans from the central government and because a significant part of local taxation has shifted to a nationally-collected tax, local officials feel that they are losing control over the resources necessary to run their towns.

---

[7] *Ibid.,* p. 180.

New Communes? New Regions?

Despite the rapid increase in recent years of local tax rates and despite fiscal reforms, it is clear that communes and departments are unable to finance the growing needs of their populations. The response has been for local governments to resort more and more frequently to state subsidies and loans, whenever they wish to develop new infrastructure. In consequence, local governments have become dependent on the state for their development, and political leaders at this level see the possibilities for initiative constrained by the declining pool of local resources. Their plight resembles that of local officials in other countries, but the obstacles they have to overcome in order to maintain some measure of autonomy are in certain critical respects specific to France.

One set of these obstacles we have already described: the multiplicity of tiny governmental units at the local level. The economies of scale of providing municipal services to people living in larger units as opposed to smaller units appear to be such that towns with fewer than 5,000 inhabitants are unable to satisfy efficiently the basic needs of their populations. Since 98 percent of the French communes with about half of the national population fall into this under 5,000 inhabitants' category, it is obvious that they are facing increasing difficulties in simply financing operating costs, to say nothing of financing investments. It is possible to imagine a redistribution of national wealth that would enable the smaller, poorer communes to profit from some of the financial resources of the more prosperous regions, but it is difficult to conceive of a redistribution of wealth that would allow each of the currently existing communes to develop and maintain a full panoply of municipal services at a level equal to that enjoyed by the citizens of larger communes.

One solution would be to regroup existing communes in order to form viable units of local government. In other European countries, Sweden notably, this method has been used with success to create larger communes out of a multiplicity of small governments. In France, however, the efforts of the state to encourage local mergers have to date been largely hortatory and have had little effect. By 1970 only about 2 percent of the communes had carried out such fusions with neighbors. In the fall of 1971 the government for the first time announced a series of measures intended to pressure the local elites into mergers. Departmental commissions are to be set up to recommend changes in the communal map of the department to the prefect. The prefect then refers any proposals for fusion to the municipal councils of the towns concerned. If the municipal councils do not accept the proposed merger, the prefect may call a referendum on the proposal in the commune.

Despite these new measures, it seems unlikely that there will be major changes in the communal map of France. Local notables of all parties are almost unanimously opposed to the notion of losing local political autonomy—which they perceive as the most immediate consequence of joining forces with neighboring communes. Just as important a motive for the local officials' hostility to communal mergers—though one less openly avowed—is the fear of losing political office. As a popular French saying expresses it: "My glass may be small but it's my glass *(Mon verre est petit, mais je bois de mon verre)*. The French mayor's commune may be small, but it is the only commune he has, and he is unlikely to become mayor of another one. Even Gaullist deputies registered strong protests when the Minister of Interior proposed the communal merger legislation to Parliament, and the enabling legislation that was ultimately enacted had far fewer teeth than that which had been proposed originally.

On the side of the state, the one political actor on whom the success of the entire scheme depends has many reasons to avoid energetic measures. The prefect is the man designated by the reform bill to prod local elites into action by wielding the threat of communal referendums if they fail to carry out mergers on their own. But the prefect knows well that any such threats would embroil him in bitter conflicts with local political leaders and that, in the course of such fights, his own political resources would be eroded. Since Paris still judges the prefect primarily on his ability to maintain law and order in the department and only secondarily on his success in stimulating social and economic change, the prefect's sense of self-preservation will dictate that he tread lightly, if at all, on the sensitive toes of local leaders. Finally, as Worms has pointed out in his study of French local governments, the power of the prefect depends in part on the small size and scale of the governmental units with which he deals. The prefect reigns over a sea of tiny communes, no one of which has the political or material resources to contest his rule. Were the communes reorganized into larger units, the prefect would most likely find his dealings with local leaders becoming relations between equals, just as the mayors of large cities today exercise considerably more independence in their negotiations with prefects than do the mayors of small communes. To the extent that the prefect's power position depends on the multiplicity of small communes, he is unlikely to play an active role in urging communal mergers.

Reform at the level of the department has been a major political issue in recent years in France. In 1969 de Gaulle proposed a reform in which the departments would be grouped into regions, each of which would be governed by an assembly that would exercise certain powers currently held by the departments. This proposal was linked to a reform of the Senate and was defeated in a national referendum. Despite the failure of the referendum proposition, the regional issue was far from dead. Jean-Jacques Servan-Schreiber, the head of the Radical party, launched a new political debate on regional organization in 1970, proposing a transfer of power to the region from both the central state and from the existing departments. Servan-Schreiber's proposals were enthusiastically welcomed by certain local elites, who saw in them a way of preserving local and regional autonomy by building governmental units on a scale adequate to manage the problems of a modern society. Others attacked the reform as irresponsible because it would splinter the authority of the state and create regional enclaves of power that would not be responsive to national needs.

Although the passions of the 1970 debate have abated, the fate of the departments is still on the agenda of politics. In the 1970 debate over the Servan-Schreiber proposals, Pompidou promised that the government would introduce a regional reform bill—but one that would be based on the region as a "union of departments," that is, one that would not create an autonomous level of political power. A year later, the council of ministers approved a regional reform, to be voted on by Parliament (and not by national referendum). The reforms proposed are but a pale shadow of the ideas that have been raised in the course of the long debate over regions. The powers of the new regional assemblies are to be dispensed by the central government (through the *Conseil d'Etat*), making the region dependent on the center both for its grant of authority and for its resources. There will be two deliberative assemblies in each region, one with representatives of social, economic, and cultural associations, the other with the elected officials of the departments: deputies, municipal councillors, departmental councillors. The region will have neither its own elected representatives nor its own elected executive.

Given the problems departments face not only in raising the resources necessary for economic development but also, and most important, in coordinating their activities with other departments in the same region, it is hard to understand why the government's proposals stopped so far short of creating regional political authorities with independent and representative assemblies. As long as a regional assembly is made up of the elected officials of other organizations—whether municipal councillors, departmental councillors, or deputies—and has no elected membership of its own, it is unlikely that the group will acquire a clear identity of its own. As the abortive experience of the C.O.D.E.R.s (the regional assemblies created in 1964) suggests, such officials are likely to retain their primary allegiance to the constituencies that elect them and to the institutions to which they are elected. For the regional assembly to acquire the power and authority necessary to establish the priority of regional needs over the particular needs of communes and departments, the regional representatives should identify their own political futures with the future of the region. To achieve this, representatives might be elected by constituencies whose boundaries did not coincide with the constituencies of other political institutions, or else, from the same districts a distinct set of regional representatives might be elected whose primary attachments would be to the regional assembly.

The explanation of the weakness of the proposed regional reform apparently lies, on the one hand, in the government's unwillingness to renounce the power that it derives from centralization and, on the other hand, in the local elites' reluctance to lose the power they exercise in the department to a regional authority, even though they would have a chance of increasing their net power through participation in regional government. It is striking to note that in a 1968 survey of the opinions of local elites on regional government, only about half of them felt that the region should have fiscal resources of its own. Most of them said the prefect should be the executive of the region, only 1 percent of the survey opting for direct election of the regional executive. And 67 percent declared that the departments should be maintained with all their present rights.[8] In sum, neither national political leaders nor local notables seem ready to support a significant shift of power and resources to regional political authorities. The latest proposals, like earlier efforts, are not likely to produce major changes in the distribution of power in France.

The Politics of Local Governments: Cases of Change

The analysis of the problems of communal and regional reform suggests that the behavior and attitudes of local political leaders are among the most important obstacles blocking change in local politics. The conservatism of local notables cannot be explained by their political party affiliations. Left-wing mayors seem on the average no more amenable to innovation than Right-wing mayors. Indeed, the political ideas that predispose local elites to resist change bear little relation to the traditional political ideologies of Left and Right. Insofar as the conservatism of local leaders derives from political beliefs and ideas and not merely from the desire to maintain their power by maintaining the status quo, the relevant ideology is what Mark Kesselman has called the "rhetoric of *apolitisme*," the notion that the tasks of local government are really not political at all.[9]

For most local elites, running local government is a question of *bon gestion*, good administration. As they see it, few if any of the decisions a mayor and council have to make determine the fundamental political priorities in a town. Left-wing politicians tend to think that this is because the real choices on values are made elsewhere—either by the state or by large industrial enterprises. Socialist and Communist doctrines, and Left ideologies generally, see the central government as the decisive arena of political decision and local communities as essentially dependent on forces that lie outside their control. As one Communist mayor said, "What really counts is national politics. The possibilities of municipal action are 99 percent dependent on national decisions." And the reply of a Communist deputy when asked to list the problems of his department was the same: "Local problems cannot be regulated outside the national context. The important issues—fiscal reform, democratic participation in factories—can only be treated in a national context." In sum, for the traditional Left nothing of real importance can be changed in local politics without a change in national politics. There are two implications of this premise for Left political action at the local level. The Left sees local politics as a lever with which to move national politics. In municipal elections, for example, Left parties present platforms in which local problems are linked to national issues: A typical Left program proclaims that the need for housing, schools, and roads

---

[8]Ministre délégué auprès du Premier Ministre chargé du plan et de l'aménagement du territoire, *Résultats de la consultation sur la réforme régionale* (Paris: Imprimerie de l'Assemblée Nationale, November 25, 1968).

[9]Mark Kesselman, *The Ambiguous Consensus* (New York: Knopf, 1967).

cannot be met so long as France wastes national resources on nuclear armaments. The second consequence is that once a Left government is elected in a commune, it tends to define its tasks in much the same way that the Right would: as good city management. If the fundamental choices are beyond the reach of local officials, the best they can do is to administer well within the framework of the system. In fact, there appear to be few systematic differences between Left and Right municipalities. Even Communist town governments appear to differ little from others.

The Right comes to the same conclusions about what can be done in local government—but from very different premises. The state, in the view of the traditional Right, has invaded the proper sphere of activities of local government, draining the resources of towns, substituting itself for local officials in decisions that should have been left to local people, and drastically reducing the margin of autonomy of communal government. As a result, local officials are not able to do much: The authority for communal affairs has been transferred to the state, and the resources for local action must be begged from the center. Both Left and Right, then, starting from different ideological premises about the proper relationship of local to national politics, conclude that in the current state of affairs the only role for a local official is essentially one of a good manager. They tend to agree that, as the official we quoted before said, "there are not ten ways of collecting garbage" but only one best way and to concur that the job of local officials is to find that best way and to make it work.

The political conservatism of local elites is apparently linked to a particular understanding of their place in the national political system. Local officials see themselves as so dependent on the center that they feel they cannot accomplish any significant changes unless such reforms are propelled and promoted by the state. Confined by this vision to limited and traditional policies, local political leaders find their public apathetic and unavailable for any act of participation beyond voting. Indeed, local elites have no reason to seek mass participation, for the system they seek to preserve requires only the involvement of a small group of participants, drawn principally from the political parties. The sources of local conservatism are, of course, not only elite perceptions. As the preceding sections on the structures of local government and local finances have shown, the possibilities for political initiative on the local level *are* severely constrained. The realities of power and the ideologies of centralization mutually reinforce each other in France, and the passivity and resistance to change of the local elites are the product of this system.

As long as the vast majority of Frenchmen lived in small towns and the population grew very slowly, this system was a stable one. Today, under the pressure of the new demands on local governments, it is beginning to crack, and new models of local politics are appearing in France. The first and most important changes have been in the politics of large cities. The political leaders of cities have always had more autonomy than the officials of small communes. Their finances afford more room for maneuver, and the importance of their populations and resources make it impossible for prefects, or even the national government for that matter, to ignore their demands. The pressure of population growth and mobility and the demands for increased opportunities for political participation are felt with maximum force in the cities. It is here that the conservatism of local elites has begun to crumble.

The case of Grenoble is exemplary.[10] Until 1965, the city had been governed by a succession of Socialist and moderate governments, whose policies had been essentially the same, despite differences in political style and rhetoric. As the city's population grew rapidly, the political elites tried to adapt to the new situation with a series of improvised measures that were uncoordinated and that dealt with each crisis as it arose. New neighborhoods were built on the outskirts of the city without transportation or other public facilities; the city expanded without any overall plan. The concern of the political leaders of both Left and Right was to manage the city well, as the French saying expresses it, as a father would manage family affairs (gestion en bon père de famille). For the Grenoble city fathers this meant, above all else, that the city should avoid raising taxes and incurring debts and that development and expansion should be financed by accumulated surpluses, just as the prudent family head buys with his savings and not on credit. The model of family management has been a compelling one for local elites all over France; gestion en bon père de famille is the operational logic of local conservatism. A local reformer from a town near Grenoble related that the proudest accomplishment of the Socialist mayor of his commune was that for a four-year period there had been no increase in the centimes. The local hospital was falling into ruin for lack of repairs, but the mayor who was the chairman of the hospital commission boasted that the ledgers of the hospital were in the black. With this model of political action, it is no wonder that problems accumulated in Grenoble and that governments became increasingly less able to meet new demands within the framework of the old system.

Change came from citizens organized in a civic association, the G.A.M. (groupe d'action municipale), who were frustrated by their efforts to obtain satisfaction for what were originally very minimal demands. The current reform mayor of Grenoble, for example, became interested in local politics as a result of his attempts to get the city to adjust water pressure so that his upper-floor apartment would have a regular water supply. The G.A.M. drew on people with very diverse political sympathies: from Catholics to Left Socialists. What they all had in common was the belief that the traditional political parties were failing to provide programs for local political action that could mobilize the energies of wide circles of interested citizens who were finding no channels for expressing their grievances and goals. The G.A.M. provided an organizational framework, not only for individual citizens, but also for a number of neighborhood associations that had been organized over a ten year period. The G.A.M., like the neighborhood associations, refrained from

---

[10]See Suzanne Berger, Peter Gourevitch, Patrice Higonnet, and Karl Kaiser, "The Problem of Reform in France: The Political Ideas of Local Elites," Political Science Quarterly, 84 (September 1969), pp. 436–460.

taking positions on national political questions, for while its members could agree on approaches to local problems, they continued to hold very different positions on national controversies. The originality of the G.A.M., according to one of its Grenoble leaders, was to start with the daily local preoccupations of citizens and from these preoccupations to work up to an understanding of the political system as a whole. The traditional parties, he argued, start with national political doctrines and work down, whereas the G.A.M. begins on the local level and moves from local realities to the discovery of politics. In the future, he suggested, the G.A.M. members may realize that local problems cannot be resolved beyond a certain point without changes in national priorities—for example, that enough housing cannot be built if France is simultaneously trying to build a nuclear force. But for the time being, at least, a group based on common local objectives can make major changes in local government by working together in politics.

The Grenoble G.A.M. came to power in the municipal elections of 1965 and was reelected in 1971. The record of the G.A.M. mayor and town council suggests that there is far more leeway in the structure of local government than most communes have been willing to use and that a change in the values of those in power can have a significant impact on the output of local government, even in the absence of important changes in the resources available to the town or in the relationship with the state. What has the G.A.M. done that previous governments had not? First, the mayor and city council have committed themselves to long-range planning for the city. In order to make this possible, they created an urban planning commission (agence d'urbanisme) so that the information necessary for planning—surveys, sociological investigation, economic forecasting, feasibility studies—are directly available to the city, and the city will no longer have to rely on agencies of the national ministries to provide technical assistance for local projects. As we have seen, part of the dependence of communes on the state stems from their inability to deal with the complex problems at stake in running a city, and to the extent that the city can develop its own sources of expertise, it can liberate itself from the heavy hand of the state.

Recognition of the need to plan the future of the city had led the Grenoble reform government down another path rarely taken by their predecessors: the path of cooperation and coordination with neighboring communes. The G.A.M. government was willing to make considerable sacrifices to overcome the hesitations and suspicions of its potential partners. In order to convince the governments of the twenty-one communes of the metropolitan Grenoble area to meet regularly in a "intercommunal syndicate" that would plan the future of the region, Grenoble agreed to an equal representation in the syndicate—though Grenoble would have only as many representatives as a commune of 500 inhabitants. Grenoble, moreover, agreed to finance a major part of the expenses of an urban planning commission that would serve the entire area. The mayor considered these concessions an acceptable price to pay for obtaining one of his principal objectives: to open up new prospects for the development of the city. Since land is limited in the city proper, expansion depends on the capacity of the neighboring communes to absorb, house, school, and transport new populations. In sum, progress in this situation required coordination of Grenoble's plans with those of other towns in the area, hence a loss of independence vis-à-vis the surrounding communities. The alternatives were economic stagnation or reliance on the state to make plans for the metropolitan area. By its willingness to cooperate, even at the risk of losing autonomy, the new Grenoble government won increased power for resolving problems without recourse to the state.

Finally, the G.A.M. method of local government has given high priority to encouraging the participation of citizens. The neighborhood associations that were a constituent element in the alliance of political forces that founded the G.A.M. continue to play an active role in the politics of the new government. The G.A.M. government has experimented with various ways of encouraging citizens to participate, from diffusing more information about the issues before the town council to creating working committees on special urban problems on which representatives from civic associations as well as members of the city council sit. Members of the neighborhood associations have such good access to the mayor and the municipal council that the representatives of the traditional parties, which are the electoral allies of the G.A.M., complain about their exclusion from power and about the preference given to nonparty organizations. Grenoble, however, is far from having resolved the problem of creating enough channels for participation in the affairs of a large urban center. Despite greater information on decisions before the city council, the number of citizens attending council meetings remains small. Despite the existence of neighborhood associations in most parts of the city, the majority of the participants are middle class; the working class continues to rely on the unions and parties that have been its traditional representatives in politics.

The collapse of the old urban consensus is producing experiments in local government in cities all over France. By the end of 1970 there were 100 G.A.M.s, half of which were located in cities of over 30,000 inhabitants. This means (see Table 5.1) that about a third of the cities over 30,000 have a G.A.M. in operation, even if not in power; still other cities have broken out of the traditional pattern without using the G.A.M. organizational model. Statistics on the G.A.M.s, moreover, probably underestimate the extent of change in communal France, for the G.A.M. is a model that is not very useful in small communes, yet many small communes have been engaged in much the same processes of political transformation as the cities with G.A.M.s. A study of towns in the area of Grenoble showed that even in towns whose populations were stable and whose traditional economic base—mining and agriculture—was declining without replacement by more modern industries, some of the same phenomena observable in Grenoble were at work. In a mining town, for example, whose previous mayor had resisted any change that would raise the *centimes,* a coalition of conservatives and Left Socialists (P.S.U.) formed a new government. The old mayor had relied completely on the mining company, a nationalized industry, to resolve all problems of housing and employment. The reform government broke out of this dependence on the state and began to solicit new industries for the region and to raise the tax rate in order to improve the hospital and provide industrial infrastructure.

No case demonstrates better how much even a commune with a small population and limited resources can accomplish once traditionalist local ideology is abandoned than Crolles, a town of 2,000 people in the Grenoble region. Crolles is one of the poorest communes in the department of Isère. The population is mostly composed of workers and peasants. M. Jargot, the mayor of Crolles since 1953, has been the moving force behind the major changes in the commune. By his own account, the reason that Crolles has acquired more power and more independence from the state lies in the patterns of participation and communication that the commune has developed over the past two decades. Every year, the municipal council convokes the town's population to meet and debate the priorities for municipal action. When the town decided to establish an industrial zone in order to attract new industries to settle there and provide jobs, Jargot called together all the peasants in the area. After long discussions they agreed to sell some of their lands in the zone and to sell them at a fixed price. The town could then approach industries and offer them a site, without having had to purchase the land itself. At the same time, Crolles hired its own experts to draw up plans for the industrial zone. By involving all those affected by the decision in discussions and negotiations, Jargot was even able to convince a group of citizens whose taxes were disproportionately—though legally—lower than those of other citizens to make voluntary contributions to the commune.

Crolles like Grenoble has enlarged its resources by cooperation with groups outside the commune. By taking the initiative of uniting fifty-two communes in its region in a study commission, Crolles has been able to share the costs of technical expertise and economic studies for which most small communes must depend on the state. In order to raise the funds to build a community center, Crolles negotiated contracts to rent the building to various departmental groups that need occasional facilities for training programs, summer camps, and so forth. In effect, Crolles has been able to decide on and pay for a major investment by itself.

What are the limits of municipal reform? The financial resources available to the commune and the centralized system of power in which the commune must operate are, as we have seen, major obstacles to change in urban France. When the fiscal reform of 1959 at long last goes into effect, the basis of taxation in communes will be rationalized, but the tax revenues available to the communes will not be substantially increased. Neither the new legislation on communal mergers nor the new regional reform proposals are likely to alter significantly the structures of centralization. Thus at least in the immediate future even communes with reform governments are likely to come up against serious constraints on their power and independence whenever they attempt major undertakings.

Just as important as the constraints imposed by limited resources and by the system of centralization are the difficulties that the political party system poses to the transformation of local politics. French political parties continue to be oriented to issues that are by and large irrelevant to the questions at stake in modern urban centers (see Chapter 3). Church-state, socialism-antisocialism, majority-opposition realignment of national politics—these are axes of conflict with important consequences for local politics, but they do not express well the choices among values, interests, and groups that are salient today in France's cities. The coalitions that have emerged in communes that are breaking with the old patterns of local government reflect this lack of fit between the traditional political parties and the new problems of the cities: In the mining town, the reform government was based on conservatives and Left Socialists; in Grenoble, the G.A.M. allied with Socialists and progressive Catholics; in Crolles, Jargot's alliance depends on Communists and Catholics. The problem is that in many towns the lines of partisan division remain so important that a local coalition built with elements of traditional Left and Right parties is still impossible. The strength of the traditional political parties—based on the party organizations, the partisan affiliations and beliefs of the population, and the monopoly on local power held by party men—continues in many parts of France to be the major obstacle to the emergence of new coalitions at the local level.

At the same time, the eclipse of the political parties is not a solution either. Local politics in France has depended on a reservoir of political activists and interested citizenry that are mobilized by political parties, and according to local reformers, the decline of the parties has produced a general decline in political interest. Jargot, in attempting to explain the lack of political awareness among Crolles' youth, argued that it was essential to rebuild party organizations "for youth today find nothing: no structures, no traditions, nothing. Our generation inherited a Communist Party; we inherited the Church; we inherited political structures."

As individuals spend more of their lives within the walls of their own houses, watching television sets or involved in family-centered activities, where once they spent more of the day with others, in the factory, in cafes, in clubs, and at party meetings, the existence of structures that promote collective activity becomes more critical than ever before. A renewal of the values and understandings that orient French political life at the local level depends on the emergence of groups that can perform for citizens the role that the traditional parties once played in educating them for participation in national politics. The neighborhood associations and the G.A.M.s are to a certain extent developing as alternative centers of political life in the cities and are thus performing the functions of political parties. But the strength of the new local organizations depends in part on their narrow definition of political objectives. They confine their concerns to matters that lie within the city, and they interpret their task essentially as one of maximization: of the city's resources, of the efficiency of government. Despite their desire to encourage more participation, they continue to define the job of government in largely technocratic, administrative terms. When they move beyond efficiency, they rediscover the political differences that separate their members.

Finally, a reform of the political parties is needed if changes in local politics are to have a significant impact on national politics. The channels of communication —the political parties—must be cleared of the debris of past quarrels and refitted for the conflicts of interests and values of contemporary French society. Nothing is more revealing of the limits of reform at the local level than the sense of isolation and powerlessness in the national system experienced by even the most successful of the new mayors. As Jargot at Crolles concluded,

> We accomplish something at Crolles; in Grenoble they accomplish something, but there is no system to connect these developments into national politics. Parties are necessary to break out of our isolation, and in the sense that they are weaker now than twenty years ago, perhaps we have regressed. On the other hand, we have more power than ever before: power to run our communes, to direct the economic evolution of our regions, whereas in the past our power was mainly one of demanding things. Now we have the power to govern, but we have become administrators, and we are no longer political men.

Six

The Legacy and the Future

Today in French politics two problems emerge as central: conflicts over the legitimacy of the government and a crisis of relations between the state and the citizen. Both contribute to the instability of the French political system. Both derive from patterns of political development in which the choices of the elites to preserve a significant part of the past in the new political system required particular solutions to the problems of political integration. Political modernization, in sum, was achieved at the cost of building permanent sources of tension and conflict into the modern French state. Despite important changes in French politics over the past three decades, these tensions and conflicts continue to turn on the issues of legitimacy and citizenship. These two issues have recurred frequently in these pages, for they have woven a net of frustrations and contradictions in which rulers and ruled, government parties and opposition parties, bureaucrats and citizens alike find themselves caught.

The legitimacy problem—that is, the failure to obtain agreement from most citizens on which rules should regulate the distribution and exercise of political power—reflects the survival of diverse and conflicting conceptions of the purposes the state should pursue and the means it may use to reach them. These ideas have been embodied in different constitutions, and the succession of regimes since the Revolution mirrors the triumph and defeat of different ideas about the state. Still today there is strong disagreement over whether the state should be ruled by a strong President, as the constitutional practice of the Fifth Republic provides, or by an assembly of deputies. Those who support the latter solution draw upon the constitutional traditions of the past and look forward to a political future in which their "rules" would once again determine the organization of power. Were it only a matter of efficiency and the rational organization of the government's business, the supporters of government by assembly might well agree with the advocates of presidential government that the Constitution of the Fifth Republic is best for France. But the question of the constitution goes far beyond institutional effectiveness to the issue of who has the right to decide what political institutions should do. Who should rule? Whose interests should be represented, and how? What limits should regulate the exercise of power? Each of the French constitutions has provided a different set of answers to these questions. The legitimacy of the state established by the Constitution of the Fifth Republic is challenged, however, not only by Frenchmen attached to the values and institutions expressed in past constitutions, but also by groups of Frenchmen like the Communist party, for example, who reject old constitutional traditions and demand a radical change in the rules governing the distribution and exercise of political power in the nation.

In all nations there are conflicts over the *content* of state policy. In France, however, the absence of consensus on the state means that not only the substance of political decision but also the decision-making structures themselves are contested. The Communists, for example, challenge not only the legislative proposals of the Gaullist government but also the government's right to exist. In Britain, in contrast, no matter how bitter the opposition to particular governmental policies, no significant group questions the government's right to make policy. Despite the angry trade-unionist reaction against the Conservative government's plans to regulate unions, for example, neither the unions nor the Labour party ever denied that the government had the authority to pass and carry out such legislation. In France the line between opposition to a policy and opposition to the regime remains blurred and unfixed. History provides many examples of dissent over policy spilling over into a battle against the government that ends with the fall of the regime. The Fifth Republic, indeed, came to power as a result of opposition to the Algerian policies of the previous governments that escalated into a revolt against the government itself. What makes French politics unstable and French governments weak is not so much the inability of various groups to agree on policy as their inability to agree on who has the right to make policy or on how the rulers should be changed.

The second major problem of modern French politics is the crisis of relations between citizens and the state. The legitimacy problem describes a situation in which a certain part of the nation refuses to recognize the legitimacy of the government. But in France even those citizens who do acknowledge the legitimacy of the regime frequently regard the state with a mixture of cynicism, hostility, and apathy that makes them unwilling to participate beyond the act of voting or to provide much support for the personnel or institutions of politics. The state is frequently perceived as a distant and foreign force; it can be cajoled for favors, but not fundamentally redirected to new ends; it can be captured but not controlled. The feelings of inefficacy and cynicism reflect the citizen's belief that there is no way to make his voice heard.

Objectively, an individual citizen in any country is relatively powerless to change the course of government in a direction of his choosing. In France, however, the citizen's sense of impotence is magnified by the weakness of the intermediaries that might assist the individual in his efforts to reach the state. The problem is not only one of perceptions and attitudes. Political parties, interest groups, and civic associations do exist in France, but they have developed in ways that make them ineffective at linking the needs and desires of individuals and localities into national politics. There is a vicious circle at work here: intermediary associations are weak because citizens do not support them; citizens refuse their participation because of the inadequacy of the organizations available to them. Today in France major reforms are proposed to transform the structures of politics. Parties and voluntary associations, local and regional governments are in a state of ferment and change. Where this change will lead, whether it will go anywhere at all or simply be absorbed by the old system, depends on how the relationship of citizen to state is modified. The central question here, as in any analysis of the prospects of political reform in France, must be whether the French can find new solutions to the old problems of building a political community.

Select Bibliography

For the reader who wishes to investigate particular events or problems in contemporary French political life, the best starting point is the annual publication *L'Année politique* (Presses Universitaires de France), which describes in chronological order the major political (domestic and foreign), social, and economic events and decisions of the year. It also includes some important official speeches, documents, and election returns. Beyond this, one should consult *Le Monde,* probably the best French newspaper. For primary information, the basic source is the *Journal officiel de la République française,* in which the debates of the Parliament and laws, decrees, and ordinances are published. Two government agencies publish regular and occasional documents of particular interest to scholars of French politics. The *Documentation française* produces studies on various aspects of French life; the Institut National de la Statistique et des Etudes Economiques (I.N.S.E.E.) issues publications on economic problems each year which include a short volume with critical economic, demographic, and political statistics, *Tableaux de l'economie française.*

Studying French politics requires an understanding of the social and cultural context in which political phenomena are embedded. Two perceptive studies of French villages, Laurence Wylie's *Village in the Vaucluse* (New York: Harper and Row, 1965) and Edgar Morin's *The Red and the White* (New York: Pantheon, 1970), explain the values and structures of local life in ways that illuminate the national society. John Ardagh's *The New French Revolution* (New York: Harper and Row, 1969) describes the ferment in French society over the last decade and, particularly when read together with an account of France in the immediate postwar period, such as Herbert Luethy's *France against Herself* (New York: Meridian, 1957), shows how rapid the process of modernization has been in certain sectors of French life. Michel Crozier in *The Bureaucratic Phenomenon* (Chicago: University of Chicago Press, 1964) and *La Société bloquée* (Paris: Seuil, 1970) has analyzed the obstacles to change and to participation that derive from the French style of authority and from particular cultural norms. Also valuable for understanding change in French society are chapters by Laurence Wylie and Jesse Pitts in Stanley Hoffmann et al., *In Search of France* (Cambridge: Harvard University Press, 1963).

For the history of France from the Revolution of 1789 to the Fifth Republic, there are several good overviews: Gordon Wright, *France in Modern Times, 1760 to the Present* (Chicago: Rand McNally, 1962); Alfred Cobban, *A History of Modern France,* 3 vols. (Baltimore: Penguin, 1963); and David Thomson, *Democracy in France,* 5th ed. (London: Oxford University Press, 1969). Stanley Hoffmann's essay "Paradoxes of the French Political Community" in *In Search of France* is a brilliant analysis of French politics from the Third to the Fifth Republic. On the Third Republic, Thomson, *op. cit.;* W. L. Middleton, *The French Political System* (New York: E. P. Dutton, 1933); and François Goguel, *La Politique des partis sous la troisième République* (Paris: Seuil, 1946) provide good political histories. Robert de Jouvenel, *La République des camarades* (Paris: Grasset, 1914), describes the rules of the game of Third Republic politics. On the Fourth Republic, the best study of the whole period is Philip Williams's *Crisis and Compromise: Politics in the Fourth Republic* (Garden City: Doubleday Anchor, 1960). On the founding of the Fourth Republic, see Gordon Wright, *The Reshaping of French Democracy* (New York: Harcourt, Brace, and World, 1948). On parliamentary politics in the Fourth Republic, in addition to Williams, *op. cit.,* see also the provocative argument of Nathan Leites, *On the Game of Politics in France* (Stanford: Stanford University Press, 1959), and Duncan MacRae, Jr., *Parliament, Parties and Society in France, 1946–1958* (New York: St. Martin's Press, 1967). The political history and accomplishments of the Fourth Republic are dealt with in Raymond Aron, *France: Steadfast and Changing* (Cambridge: Harvard University Press, 1960), and Jacques Fauvet, *The Cockpit of France* (London: Harvill, 1960). On the end of the Fourth Republic and birth of the Fifth, Philip Williams and Martin Harrison, *De Gaulle's Republic,* 2nd ed. (London: Longmans, 1962), should be consulted.

The origins of the Fifth Republic must be located in political projects developed by Charles de Gaulle in speeches and writings during the Fourth Republic. De Gaulle's account of his wartime role and participation in the first postwar government is contained in *The Complete War Memoirs of Charles de Gaulle* (New York: Simon and Schuster, 1968). Indeed, one might profitably go back to a statement of his political views in a book written before the war, Charles de Gaulle, *The Edge of the Sword* (New York: Criterion Books, 1960). Also on de Gaulle, see the biography by Jean Lacouture, *De Gaulle* (New York: New American Library, 1966), and two essays by Stanley Hoffmann, "De Gaulle's Memoirs: The Hero as History," *World Politics,* XIII, no. 1, and "Heroic Leadership: The Case of Modern

France," in Edinger, ed., *Political Leadership in Industrialized Societies* (New York: Wiley, 1967). The incorporation of Gaullist ideas into the Constitution of the Fifth Republic has been analyzed by Nicholas Wahl in "The French Constitution of 1958: The Initial Draft and its Origins" in *American Political Science Review,* LIII, no. 2, June 1959.

On the institutional evolution of the Fifth Republic, the best source is Maurice Duverger, *Institutions politiques et droit constitutionnel,* 11th ed. (Paris: Presses Universitaires de France, 1970). Although focussing primarily on Parliament, Philip Williams, *The French Parliament, 1958–1967* (London: Allen & Unwin, 1968), provides an excellent account of the operations of the major institutions of the Fifth Republic. Both for general analysis of French politics through recent years of the Fifth Republic and for a good selection of documents, one should read François Goguel and Alfred Grosser, *La Politique en France,* 4th ed. (Paris: Colin, 1970). In English, a good overall picture of politics in the Fifth Republic up to 1968 is Henry W. Ehrmann, *Politics in France* (Boston: Little, Brown, 1968). The great crisis of the Fifth Republic—the student-worker strikes of May–June 1968—has been analyzed in well over a hundred books. For a sympathetic Left account of the events, read Daniel Singer, *Prelude to Revolution* (New York: Hill and Wang, 1970), and a collection of programs and tracts written by participants in the "revolution" and edited by Alain Schnapp and Pierre Vidal-Naquet, *The French Student Uprising: November 1967–June 1968* (Boston: Beacon Press, 1971). For a conservative critique of the goals of the students, see Raymond Aron, *The Elusive Revolution: Anatomy of a Student Revolt* (New York: Praeger, 1964).

On political parties and interest groups in the Fifth Republic, there has been relatively little work in English. The Communist Party has been perceptively studied in Frédéric Bon *et al., Le Communisme en France* (Paris: Colin, 1969), and Annie Kriegel, *Les Communistes* (Paris: Seuil, 1968). On the non-Communist Left, see Harvey J. Simmons, *The French Socialists in Search of a Role, 1956–1967* (Ithaca: Cornell University Press, 1970), and Frank L. Wilson, *The French Democratic Left, 1963–1969* (Stanford: Stanford University Press, 1971). On Gaullism and the U. D. R., Pierre Viansson-Ponté, *The King and His Court* (Boston: Houghton Mifflin, 1965), provides sketches of the leading figures of the regime. The leading scholar of the Gaullist party is Jean Charlot, who has written *L'Union pour la nouvelle République* (Paris: Colin, 1967) and *Le Phenomène gaulliste* (Paris: Fayard, 1970). The Right is analyzed in René Rémond, *The Right Wing in France from 1815 to de Gaulle* (Philadelphia: University of Pennsylvania, 1968). Gordon Wright describes the changes in agricultural syndicalism from Third to Fourth to Fifth Republics in *Rural Revolution in France* (Stanford: Stanford University Press, 1964); and agricultural groups in the Fifth Republic are the subject of Yves Tavernier *et al., L'Univers politique des paysans* (Paris: Colin, 1972). Business groups have been studied by Henry W. Ehrmann in *Organized Business in France* (Princeton: Princeton University Press, 1957); labor unions, by Jean-Daniel Reynaud, *Les Syndicats en France* (Paris: Colin, 1963).

There are several good studies of economic policy and planning in France. On planning, see John Hackett and Anne-Marie Hackett, *Economic Planning in France* (Cambridge: Harvard University Press, 1965); Stephen Cohen, *Modern Capitalist Planning: The French Model* (Cambridge: Harvard University Press, 1969); and Malcolm MacLennan, Murray Forsyth, and Geoffrey Denton, *Economic Planning and Policies in Britain, France and Germany* (New York: Praeger, 1968). The role of the French state in promoting the development and reorganization of industry is analyzed in John H. McArthur and Bruce R. Scott, *Industrial Planning in France* (Boston: Division of Research, Graduate School of Business Administration, Harvard University, 1969). The problems of regional policy are discussed in Kevin Allen and M. C. MacLennan, *Regional Problems and Policies in Italy and France* (Beverly Hills: Sage, 1970), and Niles Hansen, *French Regional Planning* (Bloomington: Indiana University Press, 1968). Robert Gilpin, *France in the Age of the Scientific State* (Princeton: Princeton University Press, 1968), examines obstacles to technological innovation in France and the state's policies in research and development. French educational policy is described well in Organisation for Economic Co-operation and Development, *Reviews of National Policies For Education: France* (Paris: O. E. C. D., 1971).

On local and departmental government, the two basic sources in English are Brian Chapman's *Introduction to French Local Government* (London: G. Allen, 1953) and his *The Prefects and Provincial France* (London: G. Allen, 1955). F. Ridley and J. Blondel, *Public Administration in France* (New York: Barnes and Noble, 1965), deals with the field administration of the ministries as well as local government. Mark Kesselman has studied politics in small French towns in *The Ambiguous Consensus: A Study of Local Government in France* (New York: Knopf, 1967) and Suzanne Berger, Peter Gourevitch, Patrice Higonnet, and Karl Kaiser in "The Problem of Reform in France: The Ideas of Local Elites," *Political Science Quarterly,* LXXXIV, no. 3, September 1969, have analyzed the political ideas of groups in the large modern city of Grenoble.

4

The German
Political System

Guido Goldman

One

Tradition
Against Modernity in Germany

The development of Germany, as compared with that of other European states, has been unusual in a number of significant ways. No other European polity has had as unstable a past, characterized by as many different political systems or such constantly shifting and impermanent boundaries. No other nation has been as uncertain about its nationhood or confronted by as many geopolitical dilemmas that have led so often to conflict in its external affairs. Nowhere else has modernization raised as many internal problems or resulted in a phenomenon resembling the "German Question." That question has been posed in countless different ways, but always with emphasis on some deeply flawed and unique aspect of German development that might explain the pathology of German history.

Yet, not only as measured against its own past, but also when compared with other Western democracies, the Federal Republic of Germany today appears to be a highly successful modern polity. In terms of the stability of its political institutions and party system, its social composition, economic growth, and political style, the Federal Republic seems to be functioning well as a liberal, constitutional, democratic, modern system. It is broadly similar to Britain and France and in some ways may, in fact, be working better. How can we account for this current success and for the striking failures of the German past? What is it that has changed, and to what degree is this change fundamental and likely to endure? These are vital questions that must be answered, and they require first some consideration of the historical context from which the Federal Republic emerged.

Nowhere is the study of history more relevant or fascinating than in the case of Germany. The Federal Republic is barely two decades old and not fully sovereign at that. It is a sizable fragment of the larger Germany that once existed and faces a second state, the German Democratic Republic, which contests its claims to legitimacy. The Federal Republic was formed under conditions of total defeat and occupation, as one of the few "post-totalitarian" societies that the world has known. Perforce it traces its heritage to several different antecedent regimes. Permanence is not a characteristic of the German experience.

The most distinctive feature of the problem of Germany's statehood is the prolonged fragmentation of the German people. This fragmentation, originally the consequence of the Thirty Years' War and the Treaty of Westphalia, coincided with the onset of political modernization. Therefore, while sovereignty and bureaucracy emerged in Germany at about the same time as they did in France, Germany lacked a comparable central authority and state structure. This was critical, for it meant that to prevent external domination an inherently weak multitude of several hundred states would require strong military force. In part this accounts for the abnormal predominance of military men in the period of early modernization, especially in Prussia, the largest and most powerful of the north German states.

The primacy of security was not solely a consequence of the division of Germany into so many small units. It derived as well from Germany's strategic location in the center of Europe and from the potential size of its population. It is no surprise that the study of geopolitics is of German origin. Geographically, Germany was confronted by a double dilemma. Divided and weak, it could easily be threatened by aggression from all directions. Consolidated and strong, on the other hand, and especially as a unitary state, Germany could—and in later periods would—dominate and overrun those contiguous areas, primarily in the east, which were weak and fragmented themselves. A powerful, aggressive Germany could compel its neighbors to act in collusion. The risk of *Einkreisung* ("encirclement") created special strategic problems for Germany and reinforced the grip of its military element.

In this context the process of German unification could have highly destabilizing consequences for the European state system. These could be even further exacerbated if German aspirations for national integration ranged too far into eastern Europe, where there were few natural or clear ethnic boundaries. German settlements were scattered along the entire eastern Baltic, throughout the Polish territories, and south into the Balkans to the Black Sea. Furthermore, it remained possible that a unified Germany might embrace Austria and the German portions of the Hapsburg Empire. Thus, a nation-state of all German-speaking peoples in central and eastern Europe would create the demographic basis for German preponderance in Europe—which is exactly what happened under the Third Reich.

But instead of becoming preponderant and strong, the German states long remained divided and weak, dominated in the north by Prussia and in the south by Austria. It was not until the early nineteenth century that the movement toward national unification began to gain force. This was a gradual process that lasted through the first seven decades of the century, the result in large part of Prussian-led military campaigns.

The way in which unification came about is significant in several ways. First, because it was associated with war against the French, beginning with the defeat of Napoleon and culminating with the Franco-Prussian War of 1870, the movement toward unification easily became identified with the rejection of the Napoleonic concepts of freedom, democracy, and republicanism. Nationalism in Germany tended to turn in an anti-Western direction. England and France were to be envied but not emulated. And many of the values that accompanied modernization in these two countries failed to find acceptance in a Germany that lacked confidence in its own unity and, therefore, substituted this as a goal in place of political reform.

Prussia was the only military power that could lead a successful series of campaigns to achieve German unity. Unification was, in the words of A. J. P. Taylor, "the conquest of Germany by Prussia." Austria, the sole potential countervailing pole, was left out. The result was that the highly efficient but emphatically conservative military and bureaucratic machine that ran the Prussian government and protected feudal interests would initially dominate a unified Germany as well.

The strength of Prussian conservative and authoritarian forces goes far toward explaining the failure of liberalism to emerge as a powerful force in nineteenth-century Germany as it did in Britain and France. The three prime components of the Prussian conservative state were the monarch, the military, and the bureaucracy, of which the last was perhaps the most distinctive. It was the Prussian bureaucracy that had in the early part of the century carried through a governmental "revolution from above" that more than anything else forestalled social and political revolution in Germany. The administrative reforms of Stein and Hardenberg streamlined the prevailing system of political absolutism and modified its most abusive features. The result was a talented and efficient, if still privileged and oligarchic, civil service, the mandarin core of the much-heralded Beamtenstaat, and the civilian compeer of its military establishment.

Both the civil service and the military were class-dominated, the special domain of the landed aristocracy. Titles abounded throughout the higher echelons of the bureaucracy and the officer corps. In the Second Reich ambassadors and state secretaries were still political fiefs of the large landowners and as late as 1914 all but three of the two dozen generals commanding army corps were noblemen. This reflects the tenacious grip of the small, aristocratic Junker class on the political system of Prussia and, thereby, on the Second Reich. It was a critical but also a curious phenomenon. That a preindustrial aristocratic elite could retain so much power during the period of intense industrialization and rapid modernization experienced by Germany after 1850 requires explanation.

One reason was the strategic placement of the Junkers. Concentrated in eastern Prussia and owning vast estates, they had used their wealth and cohesion to dominate the military and the bureaucracy in Prussia, and they employed these bodies as instruments to limit the prerogatives of royal absolutism. Grain growing largely bypassed the towns, which remained weak and did not develop an elaborate form of commercial agriculture. This meant that in Prussia the landed aristocrats themselves laid the foundations for the political system. They did not, as in England, have the substantial assistance of a mercantile class. This is not surprising. What is unusual is that the Junkers were then able to preserve their position. The reasons for this are twofold. First, Germany at the outset of industrialization was still fragmented; and second, the middle class, which had remained weak, strove to do too much and was then, because of the intense impact of rapid industrialization, confronted with too many problems at once. The failure of the German bourgeoisie to effect meaningful political reforms that would have challenged the position of the Junkers was most responsible for the defeat of liberalism in nineteenth-century Germany.

That the German middle class was relatively weak at mid-century was primarily due to the fact that industrialization came late to Germany. Industrialization did not really begin to take hold on a significant scale in Germany until the 1840s and 1850s. This meant that in 1848, when the German political system was first challenged by liberal forces, the bourgeoisie lacked numbers and financial strength. But while they were not yet strong, the liberals sought to achieve a great deal. They hoped to establish a constitutional system to safeguard individual rights against authoritarianism and, at the same time, to press on toward national consolidation. The continued fragmentation of Germany was a critical deterrent to the liberals' aspirations. In order to overcome it, they would require the cooperation of the monarchs, who opposed their political liberalizing aims. Confronted with a choice between a liberal political system and national integration, the bourgeois forces opted for the latter, which was of much greater economic importance. Unity was substituted for freedom as a goal, which led, as Leonard Krieger has shown, to the fateful divorce of the ideals of liberty and self-government in Germany. Nationalism survived where liberalism did not. Basically, the bourgeoisie allowed Prussia to erect the Second Reich on the ruins of freedom, but with the support of those forces which in England and France were the foremost advocates of freedom. As Engels foresaw in 1851, the German middle class proved to be too weak to overcome the division of Germany and still remain politically effective. It became reconciled under Bismarck to the old ruling order; and herein lies the essential reason why that ruling order, Junker-dominated and authoritarian as it was, persisted largely intact in the period of rapid industrialization, without the liberalizing transformations that occurred in both England and France.

Industrialization

This reconciliation of German liberalism with an authoritarian state and conservative social order was intensified in the years after unification by the effects of rapid industrialization. Because industrialization and national integration coincided, the middle class had considerable incentive to support a powerful and expanding state, which seemed to be the instrument and guarantor of the unity so vital for sustained economic growth. The commercial rewards of Prussian hegemony were enormous for the middle class. Not only did it achieve an enlarged national market, but the state intervened in countless ways to further national economic growth.

In part this was the consequence of the German concept of backwardness in the latter part of the nineteenth century. A vigorous desire to "catch-up," to narrow the gap and eventually overtake English and French industrial output, infused German thinking. A tremendous sense of national economic purpose, reflected in the search for new markets and colonies, in tariff protection and government subsidies, and in the direct role of the state as an entrepreneur and consumer of industrial products, characterized German industrialization.

What this meant is that a state still dominated by preindustrial men of a narrow, landed, aristocratic caste and that adapted itself to industrial purposes was able to escape the liberal pressures for fundamental reform, which typified the English and French experience. In a sense the advantages of backwardness, which Veblen first identified, accrued not only to the economic sector, where late industrialization meant initial access to already refined machinery and methods of production. They also enabled Germany to modernize industrially without undergoing an equivalent social transformation, such as that which created the conditions for an industrial age in Britain. In England the middle class sought to weaken and control the state, but in Germany the impact of rapid industrialization created a very different pattern. There the middle class needed a strong state for its protection, both economic and political.

This need was intensified by the speed of economic growth. Nowhere else during the nineteenth century did industrialization result in the enormous increase in output that occurred in Germany during the four decades following 1870. The indexes of this industrial growth are extraordinary. In less than half a century, Germany became a leading industrial power. Its iron and steel production doubled each decade and by 1910 exceeded that of England. Coke output increased fivefold during the quarter of a century before World War I. In chemical production, electrical-equipment production, railroad construction, machine-goods manufacture, and shipbuilding, Germany grew faster than had any other country in history.

But such growth also caused enormous dislocations. Companies grew too swiftly, became too large, and were, as a result, often poorly financed and prone to overproduce in years of economic recession. Amalgamations, trade associations, and cartels sprang up, each seeking to reduce the risks of a free marketplace. Tariff protection, achieved through the alliance of a vulnerable young iron industry and an inefficient farming system, created artificial defenses against foreign competition. Then, when the domestic market became saturated with German steel or German rye, the government bought or subsidized. These were the concessions that the government was prepared to make to industry, and they were accepted instead of meaningful political reform, especially by the small band of captains of industry who controlled the largest firms. It seemed as though the state could forestall the success of liberal politics by offering economic prosperity in lieu of political concessions. But if profits mollified an otherwise reform-minded middle class, rapid economic growth also created social and political conditions that led that class to fear any radical move against the government.

One of the salient destabilizing features of intensified industrialization in Germany was the sudden sharp expansion of the urban proletariat, whose own efforts to organize politically threatened the position of much of the bourgeoisie. In 1871, at the founding of the Reich, only one in three Germans lived in a town of more than two thousand inhabitants. Forty years later some 60 percent of a rapidly growing population was urban, and the concentration of population in large industrial cities was striking. The population of Berlin almost tripled, and those of the Ruhr and Saxon cities, where industry was most developed, grew even faster. The number of industrial workers doubled during the quarter of a century before World War I, many of them employed in the giant firms that typified German capitalism.

The swelling ranks of urban labor were a source of great unrest in the rigid German political system and led many of the middle groups to rethink their political attitudes toward the state. Germany had missed the middle-class liberal revolution; now it was confronted with the prospect that once the status quo was undermined, labor, and not the bourgeoisie, might be the prime beneficiary of change. Fear of this created a greater propensity for conservative attitudes on the part of the middle class as industrialization advanced. It also fed middle-class determination to assure economic prosperity—no matter what the political cost—so that labor, too, might be compensated through economic rewards for the political concessions that were withheld.

Herein lay the roots of a benevolent social-welfare policy, the so-called *Sozialpolitik* of the Second Reich, which was implemented through state action, with the wide-ranging support of the industrial and commercial segments of the middle class. It was to be the counterpart for labor of the protection offered to German industry, and it resulted in some of the most far-reaching labor and welfare legislation of the nineteenth century. Junker-dominated, conservative Germany inaugurated health and old-age insurance, introduced labor courts and social security, and sought to remedy the worst abuses of factory and shop. Social paternalism in the Second Reich seemed to be an enlightened and progressive policy. In fact, it was motivated by the same consideration that had prompted bureaucratic reorganization earlier in the century: that it would be better to reform from above than to risk revolution from below. This was a strategy designed to maintain the grip of an astute feudal class on the machinery of state power.

For the working class, conditions were comparatively good. Despite frequent recessions and an ever-increasing labor supply, unemployment rarely rose above 2 percent. Real wages rose more rapidly in Germany than elsewhere, while the cost of living was effectively held down. The trade-union movement, long proscribed and still politically docile, was nevertheless highly centralized and well led. It began to flourish around 1900, seeking and often obtaining substantial economic and social gains within a system that appeared to be increasingly prosperous, if politically backward.

But if the indexes of growth were impressive and the benefits to the participants substantial, this was still an unbalanced and structurally unsound economic system. Industrialization had wrought a curious pattern in Germany, quite different from the economic pattern in England or France. Companies were larger, the role of the great entrepreneurs more powerful. Yet even the most successful and sizable industries lacked self-confidence, for they had grown large and rich under highly artificial conditions of state intervention and protection. They doubted their own capacity to thrive without special favors from the state. Furthermore, industrialization had failed to eradicate the power of landed interests or to curb the practice of bestowing high offices in the civil service and the military on members of the aristocracy. Raymond Aron has questioned whether this was capitalism at all. Certainly it was a system that was not congenial to the development of a self-assured bourgeoisie that could assert itself and press for political reforms. Rather, it served to strengthen an authoritarian state structure and to produce what Ralf Dahrendorf has termed a "faulted nation." Industrialization failed to move Germany toward modernization, but rather produced what he has defined as "an industrial feudal society with an authoritarian welfare state."[1]

The Faulted Nation

This "faulted" quality was vividly reflected in the political institutions of the Second Reich. The federal parliament, the Reichstag, remained a weak and ineffective institution. Although members were elected by universal suffrage, they remained unsalaried until 1906, and they had little power in controlling state action. Constituencies were arbitrarily drawn, the largest containing twenty-five times more members than the smallest. There was no federal cabinet as in England or France. Instead, the Reich was ruled by the Chancellor, who also headed the Prussian government, and by the senior civil service and the authority of the crown. The Chancellor was not a member of the Reichstag, nor was he dependent upon a stable majority within it. There was, in fact, no real sense of government and opposition, and the political parties, of which there were many, remained badly splintered, reflecting the various social and regional cleavages that prevailed in a state so recently united and undergoing such rapid economic change.

Perhaps the most important of these cleavages was the one separating Protestant and Catholic, which resulted in the organization of a separate Catholic party. This development not only further exacerbated the fragmentation of party politics; it also contributed to the complexity of establishing coalitions, since the Center, the party which consistently commanded one-fourth of the vote, lacked a homogeneous base, except with reference to cultural and religious issues. The Center was one of the two parties to achieve a mass constitu-

---

[1]Ralf Dahrendorf, *Society and Democracy in Germany* (London, 1967), p. 64.

ency in Germany. The other was the Social Democratic party, which, although persecuted by Bismarck, was able by 1912 to gain the largest vote in the Reichstag elections.

Aside from these two, conservative and liberal parties were splintered and narrowly based, dominated by agrarian, industrial, and commercial forces. In a system where parliament meant so little, these parties were unable to promote broad issues, to develop strong personalities, or to produce real leadership. Special interests prevailed, sometimes operating through the parties, but often circumventing parliament and the party system altogether. Instead, a direct process of influencing government action through the representations of lobbyists or national associations or through the personal contacts of business, industrial, or agrarian leaders determined the nature of politics.

But worst of all, this system was extensively dominated by Prussia. In the words of Arthur Rosenberg, an outstanding historian of the period, "Prussia ruled the Empire." The Prussian system of government was in fact a travesty of the modern state. Its electoral system was so weighted that wealthy, and especially landed, interests could control the state parliament and reinforce their grip upon its government. This was of great significance because Prussia comprised two-thirds of the territory and three-fifths of the population of the Reich. In Prussia were located the most industrialized parts of Germany, many of its largest cities, and its capital, with all the intellectual and cultural ferment concentrated there. Here were the most modern parts of Germany, and yet these were saddled with the most conservative political system. Although Prussia became the stronghold of Social Democracy, this was not reflected in its political institutions.

Here was a frozen and rigid system. It was built upon repression and privilege, meeting special needs and protecting vested interests. Economically the system seemed to work, but socially and politically it did not. It had no capacity to adapt and to allocate power and responsibility to the new forces created by rapid economic change. It was as though Germany had experienced only half a revolution, the industrial half. As a result, too many preindustrial preserves remained at the helm. And as time passed, those who ruled without mass support became aware of their own precarious position. The reforms that had been introduced gradually in England and France and that were overdue in Germany would have swiftly led to the displacement of the German ruling class.

This situation was further distorted by Bismarck, who as Chancellor for almost two decades forged the political foundations of the German Empire. A brilliant strategist, skillful manipulator, and forceful personality, he was able to integrate highly heterogeneous forces without making any fundamental or irreversible concessions to them. Thus, despite his apparent achievements, Bismarck practiced a kind of politics of postponement. Social and political cleavages were never reconciled, but rather played off against each other. It was an extraordinary holding operation, a delicate balancing of complex and conflicting forces during a period in which national gains had been achieved that did not yet excessively threaten the other European powers. Bismarck, therefore, was able to utilize the successes of foreign policy for domestic effect. This was a dangerous precedent to set for the future. Dangerous also was the deceptive notion of the strong man in German history, exemplified first by Bismarck and again later by Ludendorff, Hindenburg, and Hitler.

All this posed formidable and eventually insuperable problems for Bismarck's successors. It is not enough to say that only a strong, cunning, and competent Chancellor like Bismarck could operate this system, for it is likely that given the enormity of Germany's problems, no other man, not even a second Bismarck, would have succeeded later on. But in fact, Germany was governed extremely poorly in the years after Bismarck. This was due less to the ineptitude of the several Chancellors than to the exceptional incompetence and capriciousness of Kaiser Wilhelm II—"the irresponsible maniac on the throne."[2]

The system that had seemed to work well under Bismarck soon began to show serious strains. Overproduction in heavy industry and the dire predicament of a chronically depressed and highly inefficient agricultural system led the government to remedies that threatened to undermine the precarious stability of Europe. Tariffs protecting rye and iron were not enough. Immense armament development and naval shipbuilding to absorb surplus steel and an aggrandizing colonial and Eastern policy to assuage the thwarted frustrations of a failing landed aristocracy were poor substitutes for long overdue structural reforms.

These measures were complemented by an increasingly jingoistic, romantic nationalism, which sought through the propagation of grandiose imperial notions to align a divided nation behind its hapless leaders. When Bismarck had effectively atomized domestic opponents, he had given them all something valuable, namely a united Germany. But subsequently, German leaders could not safely continue to utilize nationalism and foreign policy as an outlet for domestic pressures and a unifying ideology for conflicting groups. Germany after 1871 could afford neither a great victory nor a great defeat in foreign policy. The former would fatally upset the balance of Europe; the latter would bring the anachronistic German government tumbling down.

Yet this was not adequately understood by the Imperial government. It sought instead to "divert the pressures created by special interest groups to the outside in the sense of a 'social imperialism' designed and used to substitute expansionism for domestic democratization."[3] Social imperialism seemed the only alternative to social reform. The power of irrational, racist, pseudopopulist rhetoric served to mobilize patriotic and often bellicose sentiments. Curiously antimodern and anti-Western concepts of German nationhood and national destiny gained in force as a reaction against purportedly Western capitalism. *Uberfremdung,* the idea of excessive foreign influence, was a strange but useful concept with which both to repudiate these painful processes as not authentically German and to further the

---

[2] Alexander Gerschenkron, *Bread and Democracy in Germany* (New York, 1966), p. 88.
[3] Karl Dietrich Bracher, *The German Dictatorship* (New York, 1970), p. 19.

autarkic ambitions of the Junkers and the great industrialists. It helped to identify a foreign source for the dislocations that ailed Germany, much as the Jews would be castigated later as alien internal pariahs. Feelings of domestic anxiety and external inferiority combined to feed the shrill nationalism of the Pan-Germans, who sought that "special mission" for Germany which Johann Fichte, the eighteenth-century German philosopher, had first proclaimed.

Industrialization could not alone resolve the problems afflicting Germany. It had created the economic benefits that enabled the old order to defend its position and to deflect the middle class from its rightful political purposes. As a result, parts of the bourgeoisie became feudalized, accepting the values of the landed aristocracy rather than defeating its social and political prerogatives. Without concomitant political and social reforms, industrialization produced deeply antimodern currents in Germany; and the greater the tension between economic change and political and social rigidity, the more this reactionary, nationalistic, and antimodern way of thought came to the fore. The vigor and velocity of economic change collided with the continued social stagnation and political inertia. A country that risked only half a revolution could not become modern. As Ralf Dahrendorf has said so well, "What is remarkable about Imperial Germany is that throughout the industrial revolution it managed to miss the road to modernity."[4] It took another road instead, and that, unfortunately, was one that led to war.

War

For Germany, as for Austria and Russia, World War I was fought largely for domestic reasons: to defend an outdated political system and a petrified social structure. Consolidation of the old order might have been achieved had the war been swiftly won, as was anticipated by those who began it. But a prolonged and finally total war was destined to have just the opposite effect, to hasten the crumbling of that old order. Thus World War I served radically to transform the political and social system of Germany in a way that few had foreseen.

Germany, like all the other participants, was ill-prepared for the war. But it had at once to confront two special problems: conflict on several fronts and the impact of a naval blockade. This meant that a larger percentage of the population was inducted into military service, reducing the manpower available for domestic production at a moment when conditions of extensive self-sufficiency were forced upon the system. Before the war, about one-third of Germany's food and much of its raw materials had been imported. Faced with sudden autarky, the government had to impose wide-ranging economic controls. This meant that the impact of the war on civilian life was more extensive in Germany than elsewhere, a situation that was to have profound effects upon the pre-World War I system.

---

[4]Dahrendorf, *op. cit.*, p. 64.

The first consequence of the war for Germany was a transformation of the army. Mass mobilization and early battlefield losses diluted the Junker predominance in the military services. Military effectiveness replaced social origin as the prime determinant of promotion. A new kind of army emerged, determined to extend its control over the entire country and to achieve maximum war production, if necessary by dictatorial means blended with social and economic concessions. In the Reich the army had never reported directly to the Chancellor, but rather to the Kaiser himself. During the war its supremacy became total. By 1916, the Chancellor was its mouthpiece, the Kaiser but a figurehead. Field Marshall Hindenburg took over military command, and General Ludendorff, his brilliant chief of staff, assumed effective control of the country. It has been said that "this day marked the downfall of the Bismarckian Empire and the beginning of the German Revolution."[5] While the war brought Lloyd George into office in England and Clemenceau in France, in Germany it produced a military dictatorship.

But it was a dictatorship supported by industry and organized labor, each of which secured from it important gains. For industry there was mass production, scant control of profits, and the promise of postwar annexations. And for the unions, the war brought de facto recognition and substantial labor reforms that laid the foundations for the right to collective bargaining and the right to strike that would be granted in the postwar period. Under Ludendorff "the army became an agent of revolution from above in order to prevent revolution from below, an agent linking the old order and the new."[6] The decrees of 1916 imposed a kind of wartime socialism. Controls were placed on all civilian labor. Workers were trained for defense industries and could not freely change their place of employment. Unutilized machinery was seized for military production, and strict rationing was extended throughout the country. In war, even more than in peace, the German state gained powers that far exceeded those of other governments at the time.

The ethos motivating these innovations was not to make Germany more modern, but rather to heighten wartime efficiency. They were accompanied by no meaningful political reforms. The old ruling order, now beyond rescue or renovation, had been replaced by a military government, which made no effort to broaden its base, to share its power with parliament, or to secure popular support. The Reichstag, increasingly disturbed by the means and ends of the military, was unable to assert its will. There was no outlet for the rising political discontent. As a result, German society became radicalized.

The agent of this radicalization was the war itself. As it continued, it imposed enormous hardship on the civilian population. Average caloric consumption fell to 1,000 calories per day, and almost half a million people died of starvation. Despite controls, the price of food and clothing rose sharply in the absence of adequate

---

[5] Arthur Rosenberg, *Imperial Germany* (Boston, 1964), p. 123.

[6] Gerald D. Feldman, *Army, Industry, and Labor in Germany 1914–1918* (Princeton, 1966), p. 38.

supplies, and real wages fell. Financed through inadequate loans rather than tax increases, the war eroded the convertibility of the mark and fed an inflation that impoverished important sectors of the lower middle class. While peasants were uprooted through military service and thereby subjected to new political influences, the trade unions began to lose their grip on the industrial working class. Through induction more than 60 percent of the 2.5 million members of the free trade unions were removed from the labor force. In their place, women, adolescents, the handicapped, and others not previously employed worked long and hard hours in German factories. As labor dissatisfaction mounted, the unions, which had won de facto recognition from the army and the bureaucracy, began to lose the control of their own constituencies. By 1917, strikes, officially proscribed by the union leadership, began to surface, first in the vital munitions industry and soon elsewhere.

This specter posed inordinate problems for the military regime. In the absence of victory there was no turning back to the old system. Domestic suffering required that there be some sizable and visible gains to justify the costs of the war. The prospect of German annexations and a punitive peace, which was given a boost by the terms of settlement by which Russia left the war, seemed the only way in which the military and industrial order in Germany could survive the war. So all efforts to seek a compromise peace, such as that sought by a majority of the Reichstag in the summer of 1917, were rejected by the generals and the leading industrialists. The war of annexation was continued, and with it, in the absence of victory, the certainty that the rulers of a postwar Germany would no longer be the same.

Defeat came in the late summer of 1918. As the final western offensive in France collapsed, the generals at last registered what others had known before—that victory was unobtainable. Now, as their own forces threatened to mutiny, they panicked. The Kaiser, so long the instrument of military will, was pressed to sue for peace and to attempt yet another revolution from above to preempt a domestic uprising that could overthrow the entire political order of Germany.

Revolution

The events of October were momentous. Ludendorff was replaced, and the Reichstag began to assert itself, suddenly aware of the vast power available to it in the vacuum created by the military collapse. Sweeping constitutional reforms were passed with desperate speed, the most significant of which made the Chancellor responsible to parliament. Prince Max of Baden, a south-German liberal, was installed as Chancellor, and soon after the Kaiser abdicated, largely on the expectation that this would bring better peace terms from the victorious democracies.

In the same month the leaders of industry negotiated a far-reaching agreement with labor, seeking through expedient concessions to consolidate the vested interest of the unions in preventing a revolutionary overturning of the entire system. This agreement brought great gains for organized labor, including full recognition by a previously hostile industry of both the right to collective bargaining and the eight-hour work day. In defeat the industrialists jettisoned their traditional alliance with agriculture and the authoritarian state, hoping to forestall a workers' revolution through emergency concessions to labor. This strategy was shrewd and proved efficacious. For the union leadership, itself fearful of insurrection, the benefits of a partnership with industry were substantial and more than fulfilled their prewar aspirations. Gerald Feldman, the foremost scholar of these events, has written that "the political and social equality of the working class was tentatively won in war and was finally sanctified in defeat, and therein lay one of the great tragedies of German democracy."[7] For the moment of defeat was fleeting, and the concessions to labor that industry voluntarily sanctified were all too easily reversed as political conditions changed in the years ahead.

The events of October, which established collective bargaining and parliamenta-rism in Germany, were followed by more revolutionary developments. It was too late for an experiment in constitutional monarchy. The tide of revolutionary fervor was swelling in almost all urban areas and among the restive and embittered armed forces. Guided in part by the Russian experience, workers and soldiers formed councils throughout Germany, and in Munich the municipal government was overthrown and a revolutionary republic established. As the flames of revolution spread, so did the apprehensions of the Social Democratic leadership, which believed in an evolutionary course based on the October constitutional reforms. Forced into action by the swift pace of these events, the Social Democrats resolved to contain the revolution by placing themselves at its helm. On November 9 Friedrich Ebert, a former saddle maker and now chairman of the party, proclaimed the founding of the German Republic. The old government system of Imperial Germany was thereby overthrown, but popular pressure for a more fundamental social and economic revolution was brought under control and soon to a halt.

In order to understand the abortive nature of the revolution of 1918, two phenomena must be understood. One is the nature of the Social Democratic party (S.P.D.); the other is the complex of critical problems confronting any regime, revolutionary or otherwise, in the wake of sudden military defeat and which faced the German government at the approach of winter in 1918. After years of persecu-tion under Bismarck Social Democracy had emerged as a formidable force in German politics by the turn of the century. As a party, the S.P.D. had been rent by deep ideological divisions and serious tactical disputes. Gradually its more revolutionary prescriptions had been subordinated to a revisionist and evolutionary program that envisaged piecemeal progress toward a majoritarian and constitu-tional socialist system. While the dilemmas of democratic socialism in a nondemo-cratic state had been great indeed, this kind of moderate socialism had made important strides in the last decade before the war. By 1912, with 110 seats in

---

[7] *Ibid.*, p. 7.

Parliament, the S.P.D. had become the largest party in the Reichstag, commanding about 34 percent of the vote in the national elections of that year.

These gains were matched by an impressive growth in the strength of the trade unions, which occupied a critical role within the party. The unions had done well in terms of securing substantial wage and social security benefits for their members, and they tended on the whole to oppose radical political action, such as the use of the strike for noneconomic ends. Both the party and the unions had developed elaborate and powerful bureaucracies, each of which had a stake in securing further piecemeal concessions within the system and in quelling the more radical and rancorous of their own constituents. Although neither shared in the prewar ruling system, both the party and union leadership had surprising respect for state authority. They had the ingrained German reverence for the law and for that unquestioned ascendency of the state known in German as *Obrigkeit.* Despite the gulf that separated the state and society from the party and the unions, each replicated the authoritarianism endemic in prewar Germany, personified in figures such as Karl Legien, who led the free trade unions for thirty years, or August Bebel, or Friedrich Ebert, whom Carl Schorske has aptly named "the Stalin of German Social Democracy." This leadership was deeply compromised by the war, for which the party had unanimously voted credits in 1914 and during which the unions had collaborated so extensively with the military and industrial establishment.

But the war had exacerbated the old tensions within the party. While only fourteen of its Reichstag members had voted in caucus in 1914 against the war credits, the prolongation of hostilities and the domestic impact of war controls strengthened the radical elements within the S.P.D., who bolted from the majority two years later to form their own party, the so-called Independent Socialists (U.S.P.D.). This faction, though small in number, contained some of the foremost theorists and personalities within the Socialist camp, among them the well-known revisionist Eduard Bernstein and his former adversary, the aging Karl Kautsky. The Independent Socialists were in turn outflanked by new groups on the Left, the most important of which, the Spartakus League, claimed the brilliant leadership of Rosa Luxemburg and Karl Liebknecht.

The radical activity of 1918 was disconcerting for the S.P.D., which was fearful lest the events of the Bolshevik revolution of the previous year by reproduced in Germany. As is so often the case among long-time opposition parties, the S.P.D. was perhaps most conscious of the dangers posed for its aspirations by its own radical secessionists. The turmoil unleashed by the sudden defeat of 1918, for which the German public was entirely unprepared, raised the specter of a violent urban insurrection. This was a prospect that the S.P.D. could not but oppose, in view of its past course and present situation. A party that had rejected revolution so fundamentally in the past could not in 1918 lead a revolution. It could only deflect it, seeking to channel the momentum for change into a transformation of the political system, which would, with the passage of time, provide the electoral support for a gradual restructuring of the social and economic foundations of Germany. For a party that had gained more than one-third of the vote in the last prewar election, this concept of democratic socialism made reasonable sense.

Aside from the fear of popular revolution, the Socialist leaders faced very critical practical problems once they established themselves as the government. Germany, under its military tutelage, had fought the war until it could fight no more. Not only were the armies broken, but civilian supplies were largely exhausted. Shortages were particularly critical in clothing, fuel, and food. The ceasefire was called in October, and the armistice signed a month later. Without sufficient supplies of coal and food, civilian deaths in the postwar winter of 1918 could well have exceeded half a million, the total number that succumbed to starvation during the four years of conflict. More than 6 million soldiers were to be demobilized and the vast war industries shut down, each adding to the million men already jobless. With so much of the population exhausted and undernourished, the new government gave special priority to the kind of economic measures that might provide immediate relief, rather than to those that would reallocate the ownership of German economic resources.

But the Socialists were not well equipped to pursue this course. As an outcast in the old system, the S.P.D. had never effectively shared in the responsibility of government and was entirely untrained for the task that now lay before it. This led to a rather unusual accommodation between the leaders of the new government and the personnel of the old, typified by the continued tenure in office of members of the established bureaucracy and judiciary. Lacking a reservoir of trained talent and imbued with an excessive awe of the professional expertise required to discharge government functions, the S.P.D. leaders appealed to all civil servants to remain in their posts. This move was based on the false assumption that they would remain nonpolitical experts, serving the republic as loyally as they had the monarchy. Fewer than 11 percent of the Prussian civil servants holding high posts were removed from office in 1918. No attempt was made to democratize the bureaucracy until the abortive counterrevolutionary events of the spring of 1920 punctured the naïve illusion of the S.P.D. leaders. It was their failure to purge the old imperial civil service that Hugo Preuss, the prime architect of the Weimar constitution, later saw as the essential flaw of the Weimar system.

This reconciliation of the Socialists with the incumbent bureaucracy was matched by their accord with the military. On November 10, just one day after proclaiming the republic, Ebert, chairman of the newly constituted Council of People's Delegates, secured the support of the army. As Hindenburg reported to his staff colleagues, it was a pact ostensibly designed "to prevent the spread of terrorist Bolshevism in Germany."[8] This effort to ensure against leftist agitation was to result in the brutal suppression of the Spartakist rebellion two months later and in the assassination of the two most intellectually gifted German revolutionaries, Luxemburg and Liebknecht.

For Ebert and his associates the politics of the street offered no solutions for the

---

[8]Golo Mann, *The History of Germany Since 1789* (New York, 1968), p. 333.

problems facing Germany. In their view an uprising of the militants could only divide the forces of the Left and stir a right-wing reaction. The six-man Council of People's Delegates, which initially included three Independent Socialists, saw itself as a provisional government preparing the way for a popularly elected Constituent Assembly that would draft and ratify a new constitution. Germany would gain a new political order, based on a democratic parliamentary system. Such a National Assembly was elected in January 1919; and until it could begin its deliberations in the town of Weimar, free from the turmoil of Berlin, the council set about dealing with the economic and political emergency confronting Germany. It attempted to cope with the looming economic breakdown, to prevent the dismemberment of the Reich, and to deal with the victorious allies, whose terms for a peace settlement were not yet known.

This meant that structural reforms were to be postponed until some stability had been restored to the economy, the immediate crisis had passed, and the National Assembly had set up the political and constitutional framework for more far-reaching economic and social measures. But it also meant delaying action and thereby losing a great deal of the momentum for change available in the winter of 1918. With a preliminary agreement between the unions and industry in their pocket, the Socialist leaders felt they could wait for more quiet times before attempting the rigorous task of reallocating the ownership of assets through nationalization and land reform. As a leading Socialist and future Chancellor, Hermann Müller, put it: "One can only socialize when there is something to socialize."[9]

But this disregarded the massive support for nationalization that existed in the ranks of labor and among the workers' and soldiers' councils that winter. The Socialist leaders rather naïvely assumed that such seizure of industrial assets would be possible in the years ahead. For them reconstruction was to precede the redistribution of resources. This view was based on the assumption that the elections would produce a majority to support such basic economic reforms. But the elections never did. Socialism never gained a majority in Germany, although it did win 46 percent of the vote in January 1919. The exigencies of that first republican winter and the temporizing of the S.P.D. gave German industry and agriculture a reprieve from the expropriations that they expected and that the Social Democratic party program had promised. This was one of the most ominous and costly miscalculations of the S.P.D. when first it came to power, and one which would in time permit the restoration of the key components of the old order: the Junkers, the army, and industry.

Once again Germany experienced only a partial revolution. This time it was really an unfinished enterprise, for the Socialists had meant to change a great deal more than they were actually able to change. With so much of its prewar social and economic foundations left intact, Germany was once again to miss the path to modernity.

---

[9] Hermann Müller, *Die November Revolution—Erinnerungen* (Berlin, 1928), p. 198.

Two

The Nazi Conquest
of the Weimar Republic

Given the arrested revolutionary events of 1918, everything hinged on the success of the political institutions of the new republic in which the Socialists placed their initial hopes. But these institutions, unfortunately, were also deeply flawed at the outset.

The Weimar Republic

The Weimar Republic was an improvised system. Conditions of military defeat and domestic upheaval were hardly conducive to the creation of a complex and fragile system of parliamentary democracy. The Weimar constitution was a highly complicated instrument, reflecting in part the many compromises struck by the contending political forces represented in the National Assembly, where the Socialists did not command a majority. The fifty-six articles governing civil liberties were too extensive for a population as heterogeneous as that of Germany, and in the subsequent years of crisis these liberties were all too often abused. And the constitution was far too easily amendable. Two-thirds of a quorum of two-thirds of the Reichstag could ratify an amendment, which theoretically permitted fewer than half of the elected members to alter the constitutional foundations of the system. Like so much else that happened at the birth of the republic, this did not suggest a strong sense of permanence.

The federal structure of the state was retained, with Prussia still paramount. The old restrictive and weighted Prussian electoral law was swept aside, which was a decisive change, for it assured Socialist control of this pivotal state. However, the electoral system of the republic was poorly designed. Absolute proportional representation combined with huge districts, each with some fourteen or fifteen representatives, proved corrosive of party stability and coalition government. It meant that all minorities, even those not regionally concentrated, could find representation, which accounts for the profusion of parties in Weimar Germany. There was no incentive for interests to gather or for groups to coalesce. The constant threat of secession made the larger parties subject to the dictates of their most willful members. This served to strengthen the influence of the interest groups, whose power was further enhanced by the frequency of costly elections, which they alone could finance. The political prerogatives of business, agriculture, and labor grew powerful within these parties, because their leaders were able to secure safe parliamentary seats through their high placement on the party-determined election lists.

Control of these lists in the huge districts reinforced the ascendency of party bureaucracies and diminished the opportunities for strong leaders to emerge, a factor that helps explain the importance of mayors, controlling their own large urban constituencies, in Weimar politics.

A pattern developed of self-serving parties unable to identify themselves with the national interest. It reflected and accentuated the divisions in German society. *Parteipolitik* gained a disreputable image, while those forces or institutions which seemed to stand above parties grew more attractive. Parliament and cabinet government were not among these.

The men who made the Weimar constitution, long frustrated in their parliamentary aspirations in the Kaiserreich, sought to make the Reichstag supreme. The Chancellor and his cabinet ministers were dependent upon its confidence. But the fragmentation of political interests reflected in the proliferation of parties and the stark decline of those willing to share in a majority government made it increasingly difficult for such confidence to be obtained. As a result, the republic was governed for ten of its fourteen years by minority cabinets, and even these proved stronger than the majority coalitions, which had to satisfy too many divergent interests to rule effectively. In the seven elections to the Reichstag, only once did the incumbent parties actually gain in votes. For example, before 1924 the S.P.D. as a government party always lost votes, some of which it then recouped during the next four years, when it remained out of office. It is always destructive of stable parliamentary government when electoral opportunities consistently reward the opposition.

What dominated all the regimes in the republic was not so much parliament itself as the party factions within it. They alone made and reshuffled most of the coalitions. Of the eighteen Weimar cabinets, only three fell because the Reichstag formally voted nonconfidence. Far more often collapse came because one party deserted the coalition, often at the behest of a major interest group. Basically, from 1920 there was what has sometimes been called "a second government in the Reichstag." It was not sufficient for the cabinet to decide on a specific piece of legislation; it then had the far more complex task of obtaining the consent of a legislative majority. Not infrequently a party actually represented in the cabinet reversed itself on the floor, a practice which found its absurd extreme when Chancellor Müller subjected himself to his party's parliamentary preference and voted against a law introduced by his own government.

It was the leaders of the parliamentary party groups more than the Chancellor who determined who would serve in the cabinet. Bargaining, often in moments of crisis, could be intricate and prolonged. The result was that the cabinet rarely had a strong parliamentary mandate. Agreement was usually reached only on several initial issues; and as new problems arose, these coalitions were quickly undone. Six of them lasted less than half a year, and none survived for more than twenty months. Even in those of longer duration, the ministers held too much personal power vis-à-vis the Chancellor. Frequently specific ministers would remain in office as Chancellors came and went. These ministers, figures such as Gustav Stresemann of the Foreign Office, Otto Gessler of Defense, or Heinrich Brauns, the Minister of Labor, possessed more distinct and independent influence within the cabinet. This was matched by the importance of the Finance Minister, who was given extensive budgetary powers that further circumscribed the authority of the Chancellor. In short, there were so many constraints and channels of dissention that it proved extremely difficult for a Chancellor to assert himself and to assume effective leadership of his own regime.

This development had not been foreseen by those who forged the new parliamentary system in 1919. At the time broad consensus had been achieved by the three major parties, the S.P.D., the Center, and the newly formed Democrats, who together comprised the so-called Weimar coalition that had won more than three-fourths of the seats in the National Assembly. But these three parties, the intended pillars of the young republic, secured less than 44 percent of the vote in the very first Reichstag election, in June 1920, and the coalition never again commanded a majority in the chamber. The demise of the parliamentarism that was to be the foundation of the Weimar system was registered early. Oswald Spengler, the German philosopher so widely hailed for his prophetic wisdom, predicted with cynical self-assurance that "parliamentarism would always remain alien to Germany."[1] While it was the Right that was most responsible for undermining parliament, the system itself proved so unworkable that conservative observers gained acceptance for their notion that Germans had no natural propensity for a parliamentary regime.

This reflected the early polarization of politics that beset the Weimar Republic. Antisystem parties were soon to score stunning electoral successes, culminating in the extraordinary victory of July 1932, in which the National Socialists and Communists together secured an absolute majority in the Reichstag. But the German parliament had long since abdicated its constitutional grip on power and authority,

---

[1] Oswald Spengler, *Preussentum und Sozialismus* (Munich, 1924), p. 64.

and the President and the bureaucracy, aided by the renascent officer corps, emerged as the actual rulers of the republic. These forces were to prove themselves dependable instruments for the defense and restoration of the old order long before Hitler seized control.

The office of the presidency had been much debated in the Constituent Assembly. It was modeled very much on the French presidency, but was designed to be immune from the institutional weakness of its Gallic counterpart. Partially as the result of the insistent prodding of Max Weber, who saw the need for a strong and charismatic, integrating national figure to offset the pluralism represented in parliament, the President was to be directly elected, either by a majority on the first ballot or by a plurality thereafter, for seven years, a comparatively long term. He was to be the strong man, standing above the parties in the new political system. This was a somewhat naïve notion, for his powers were in fact immense and, with the demise of parliament, came to be used in extremely partisan ways.

The President appointed the Chancellor and, upon his recommendation, the cabinet ministers, each of whom had to resign if the Reichstag withdrew its confidence. In such a case the President had the power to dissolve parliament and to call new elections. In the Weimar Republic the Reichstag never sat for its full four-year term. Each election but the first was the result of a dissolution. Indeed, the electorate could be asked to vote far too easily and too often. The President had the power to refer any legislation passed by the Reichstag to a national referendum. He could do so as well in the case of legislation on which the Reichstag and the Reichsrat, the weaker, second chamber, in which state governments were represented, failed to find agreement. Conversely, a popular referendum was required whenever at least 10 percent of the voters desired it. In 1919 Eduard David, the veteran Socialist leader, had proclaimed this "the most democratic democracy in the world." But the constant plebiscitary implications of these provisions served to undermine the legitimacy of parliament and to strengthen instead the autocratic powers of the President.

These powers, especially under conditions of declared emergency, were awesome indeed. Article 48 of the constitution provided that where public safety and order required it, the President could, with the countersignature of the cabinet, suspend fundamental rights and decree emergency measures without parliamentary approval. Given the frequent paralysis of parliament and the recurring crisis that confronted the republic, this article was used more than 250 times. Initially, under President Ebert, it was invoked to suppress insurrection and to cope with the acute economic problems at the height of the inflation in 1923. In later years it was often employed to defend the republic against its domestic extremist enemies.

As the incapacitation of the Reichstag increased, so did government by presidential order. Between March 1931 and May 1932 the Reichstag was in session for only six days. It produced two statutes during those fifteen months, while more than sixty measures were decreed under Article 48. But the complexion of the cabinet and of the presidency had changed. The cabinet was now populated by undemocratic men and dominated once again by the Junkers. The tragedy of this vital constitutional provision, as Clinton Rossiter has written, is that thereby "Article 48 became the possession of men who despised the whole idea of Weimar democracy. The Rock of the Republic was converted by Hindenburg and Papen into a bridge leading to despotism, and over this bridge marched Adolf Hitler to his evil power."[2]

Economic Dilemmas

Perhaps even more than all these institutional failings, the economic crises afflicting the republic undermined its foundations and made possible the return to power of the Junkers and the industrialists. From its inception, the Weimar Republic faced dire problems. The peace settlement signed at Versailles contained harsh terms. Germany lost 10 percent of its prewar population, 15 percent of its arable land, all of its colonies and foreign investments, and most of its fleet and railroad stock. It was saddled with a heavy, indeed, a hopeless, reparations burden. Its losses, together with the unsound financing of the war, led to a hyperinflation that had disastrous domestic consequences. At the beginning of the war the mark had stood at 4.2 to the dollar; by January 1919 it had fallen to 9; and then four years later, when the French occupied the Ruhr, it tumbled to 18,000. By the end of 1923 the mark was in fact worthless.

Inflation wiped out the savings of the middle class and pauperized those on fixed incomes. This was critical, because it was the middle class that was growing most rapidly and which therefore could have provided the votes needed by the liberal parties to assure a majority for the democratic Weimar coalition. In 1913, the last prewar year, 43 percent of all German taxpayers had personal assets of less than 50,000 goldmarks. By 1923 this figure had almost doubled to 83 percent. For a frugal, expanding middle class in a precarious social position, the loss of its savings was a traumatic experience that sharply eroded its confidence in the republic.

However, the inflation benefited the landowners and heavy industry. Indeed, it rewarded anyone who held real assets, and especially those who held such assets on credit. The enormous loss of the value of the mark eradicated much of the farmers' debt on their land, which shrank from more than 17 to less than 3 billion goldmarks. Even more striking were the gains for the iron industry, which used its postwar government indemnity to buy back the mines it had lost in Lorraine and which expanded its holdings throughout Germany by means of the loans that were easily available to industry at that time. Thus, the two economic groups that had cared least about the republic initially found their power substantially augmented, especially in the absence of effective profit controls.

Ironically, the problems for each mounted during the period of stabilization and

---

[2]Clinton Rossiter, *Constitutional Dictatorship* (New York, 1963), p. 60.

rationalization that followed the inflation. Agriculture started to slip into what was to become chronic depression. As cheap grain imports from eastern Europe and the United States flooded the German market, prices fell, which produced pressure for government subsidies and protection. From 1925 on, more than half of the farms in Germany operated at a loss, a situation that fed the exodus from the countryside to the cities. The urban population of Germany grew by almost 30 percent during the Weimar Republic, a development which gravely exacerbated the impact of the mass unemployment brought on by the Depression in the early thirties.

The hardships of agriculture tempered any pressure for wide-scale land reform. The Socialists had not pressed for a breakup of the giant Junker estates in 1919, in part because they lacked a developed agrarian program, but also because their more orthodox theorists believed large-scale management to be more efficient and progressive. By the late twenties, the agrarian interests were again sufficiently entrenched within the system to cull special favors from the government. Although some state-initiated resettlement began, the key components of government policy were protection and subsidy rather than the basic restructuring and reduction of agricultural production that was long overdue.

Industry, too, was able to obtain special concessions. Plans for even a partial nationalization of its assets had died an early death. Instead, the Socialists and left-wing Catholics of the Center party sought in the first years of the republic to extend government regulation and taxation. However, the redistributive impact of the government's measures, imaginative though they were, were vitiated by the effects of inflation.

The inflation, which lasted through 1923, had two unusual consequences for industry. Because of the way in which it occurred, the inflation served both as a financial stimulus for the domestic consumer market and as a substitute for a tariff against imported goods. When these two artificial forces disappeared, German industry suddenly found itself with inordinate excess capacity. The result was a further concentration of ownership, with many firms combining to maximize efficiency, and a pattern of increased cartelization to ensure a more stable and less competitive demand. By 1925 one out of ten workers was employed in a giant firm employing more than 1,000 people. In heavy industry, this pattern was much more accentuated. More than 65 percent of all miners and about 55 percent of all ironworkers were on the payrolls of these mammoth companies, the largest of which—the United Steelworks—had well over 200,000 employees. While middle-sized firms suffered, the power of the Ruhr industrialists grew preponderant, and they succeeded in thwarting the attempts of the government to regulate iron and steel production. The Ruhr ironworks were handsomely indemnified for losses sustained during the French occupation of 1923, but the ironworkers, who had suffered more, received no compensation. When firms found themselves in extreme distress due to conditions of excess supply, the state intervened with its so-called cold socialization, rescuing these companies by purchasing them.

Such collusion between government and industry seemed a natural outgrowth of the pattern of extensive state involvement in the economy that had developed since the onset of industrialization. The state served as banker, regulator, customer, and, where necessary, entrepreneur of industrial production. An attitude and policy that sought the maximization of output blended well with the effort to increase social welfare and to raise consumption. These were the fundamental, rather apolitical, aspirations of the trade unions. For them the gains scored during the war were augmented by new achievements. The introduction of unemployment insurance in 1927, the provisions for organized government mediation of wage disputes, and the establishment of shop councils in factories were complemented by important consumer benefits. The construction of low-cost housing, the provisions for rent control, the subsidies for bread and for railroad transport, and the rapid enlargement of municipal facilities were all hailed as important achievements. And so they were while the economic boom of the mid and late twenties lasted. Production in the chemical industry increased by one-third in the four years following the stabilization of the mark in 1924, a gain outpaced by that of the iron industry. By 1928 real wages had finally regained the level of the last prewar year, while the ranks of unemployed, enlarged by those who had abandoned the land, held below the half-million mark.

But none of these gains were irreversible, nor were they the result of basic structural reforms. They were the benefits of a booming economy; and once that boom abated, it soon became evident how ephemeral the changes were. Economic power had been left in the hands of a resurgent industry and an ailing agriculture. Too many underlying economic patterns had been left intact. When the Depression came crashing down upon Germany, the forces of the old order were still there, seeking to reassert themselves.

In this enterprise they had potent institutional allies. The President was in their camp, and the bureaucracy and the army had not been purged. The expertise and social prestige of the civil service had been its great defense. As cabinet ministers had come and gone—some twelve dozen in the fourteen years of the republic—the senior state secretaries who remained in office had gained in power. So had the army, despite, or perhaps even because of, the allied restriction limiting it to 100,000 men. That limitation had ensured that the nucleus of the old officer corps would be retained and that only the conscripted citizen would be eliminated. Indeed, this much smaller army had a more aristocratic officer corps than before the war; in 1927 twice as many officers as in 1913 were themselves sons of former officers. And many of those who had been forced into early retirement, knowing little other than army life, flocked to the Free Corps and to the other paramilitary units that abounded in Germany. These were the forces of potential counterrevolution. And in the late days of the republic they controlled Field Marshall von Hindenburg, the senile, octogenarian President who symbolized the crippled state of democratic politics in Germany.

With all its faults, and after having suffered so much stress earlier, the Weimar

Republic was unable to withstand the effects of the Depression. The crash that began in America in the fall of 1929 struck the German economy with inordinate severity, because much of the boom had been financed from the United States. Furthermore, the entire structure of German credit was unsound. Foreign indebtedness totaled more than 17 billion goldmarks, far higher than elsewhere in Europe, and far too much of it consisted of short-term loans that had been used for long-term investment. This problem was aggravated by the inadequate ratio of their own capital to borrowed capital in the German banks. The dangers of an acute liquidity crisis, with all its multiplying effects, were enormous. Banks began to fail, and businesses contracted severely. In this situation the German government, wary of huge budgetary deficits reminiscent of the earlier inflationary period, began to cut spending and to pursue a deflationary policy. Half of the federal budget of 1930 had originally been earmarked for social costs alone. These were now sharply reduced, especially the recently established unemployment insurance. Thus, at the very moment when every third worker was in danger of losing his wages, funds were withdrawn from support of the jobless.

By 1932, with almost 7 million out of work and civil servants on reduced salaries, the average weekly income of the German family had fallen 60 percent from its level of four years earlier. Industrial production shrank to half its 1929 level, while exports fell by more. In the wake of this economic calamity, many of the major gains of labor in the country that had innovated such broad programs of *Sozialpolitik* were swept away. It was the working man and the middle class that fared the worst.

The industrialists suffered less. Prices of industrial products and raw materials, carefully controlled by cartel agreement and protected through tariffs, fell less within Germany than they did abroad. And for agriculture, whose depressed condition dated back to the mid-twenties, special emergency relief measures were pressed through by presidential order to save the estates of Hindenburg's Junker neighbors.

As banks faltered and firms closed down, the level of discontent and mass agitation mounted. The chief beneficiaries were the extremist, antisystem National Socialist and Communist parties, which together scored spectacular electoral gains. The revolutionary potential of the ferment that gripped Germany raised a frightening specter for the conservative leaders of the old order, who hoped still, through the army, the bureaucracy, and the President, to exploit the crisis in order to restore some form of the *ancien régime*. But von Papen, the shameless agent of these forces, could not restore a conservative system. The social panic that Theodore Geiger first diagnosed had spread too far among the middle class. And so it was that the conservative leaders, who still controlled vital instruments of state power, made their fateful alliance with National Socialism, a movement that they thought would serve to protect them from a fearful social upheaval.

Collapse into Fascism

The reactionary hope expressed by the alliance of the conservatives with the National Socialists was evidence of how far Germany had strayed from the path to modernity. The industrial process, without the tempering influence of basic social change, had led the old order to embrace a fascist solution in a last attempt to thwart the social revolution now so long overdue.

In this attempt the conservatives badly misjudged Nazism. For Hitler's movement, despite all its promises and wooing of the old order, was emphatically not conservative. To be sure, the movement was an effective force for preventing a violent revolt of the working classes. Its xenophobic nationalism and pseudosocialist rhetoric could serve as a surrogate for the social revolution sought in a mood of growing despair by the lower urban strata. National Socialism could deflect mass discontent from the social revolution so feared by the old order. But in doing so, it would also destroy the underpinnings of that order.

This was a radical and revolutionary movement. It was revolutionary not so much because of its theoretical prescriptions, which were carefully honed to appeal to many different dissident groups. Rather it was the Nazis' quest for total power, their inability to treat any group as inviolate, their need for social self-justification, and their willingness to use new techniques of terror, manipulation, and control that were to provide the revolutionary impulses of their regime. Von Papen and the generals, Hugenberg and the business leaders of the Harzburg Front, and the indomitable Junkers, who had made Hindenburg their spokesman, helped Hitler to gain control of the state, a step of incalculable significance and profoundly revolutionary consequence. Their fear, archaic privilege, and petty self-interest helped pave the way for the revolution. The conservatives were its unwitting handmaidens. Not only did they help to undermine the republic, but it was they who enabled Hitler to come to power legally.

This route to power was a great asset for the Nazis. The image of legality permitted them to use the powers of the existing system for its own destruction. Given the legalism and respect for officials and authority in Germany, this made a great difference. Once Hitler was installed as Chancellor, he was able through swift and skillful manipulation to wrest awesome dictatorial powers from a Reichstag that no longer believed in its own capacity to govern. With these powers applied from above and the terror produced by the Nazi organizations from below, the National Socialists rapidly liquidated or restructured virtually all the institutions of the Weimar Republic.

All parties but the N.S.D.A.P. were eliminated by the summer of 1933, thereby reducing the Reichstag to a fiction and elections to a sham. The Reichsrat was abolished and the separate states, or Länder, brought under rigid central control, a move designed to prevent regional resistance to the authority of the new national government. Upon Hindenburg's death the offices of President and Chancellor were merged. The bureaucracy and judiciary were pruned of their more democratic elements. Similarly, the universities were swiftly purged of those faculty members who dared voice opposition to Nazi rule.

In fact there was very little opposition. This was due to several reasons. On the extreme Left, the Communists adhered to Moscow's fatal misreading of National Socialism, which saw in Nazi rule a hastening of the collapse of capitalism in Germany. As for the middle class and the farmers, the Nazis offered them extravagant promises of radical concessions. And the unions and the Social Democrats were paralyzed by fear, by inner divisions, and by preoccupation with the overwhelming economic and social consequences of the Depression. It was the unions and the Social Democrats whose failure to act was most grievous. Both recognized the Nazis for what they were. In many respects the S.P.D. and union leaders were as petty and self-interested as their conservative adversaries. This was manifest in the way in which they withdrew from the last Grand Coalition in March 1930, which felled the government of Hermann Müller, the last Social Democratic Chancellor for almost forty years. It was even more apparent in their failure to react to the arbitrary removal by Chancellor von Papen of the Prussian Social Democratic government in July 1932. With 6 million unemployed, the unions had ruled out a general strike; and the Socialist incumbents refused to defend themselves, although the entire Prussian police force would doubtless have acted loyally on their behalf. By 1933, aside from their courageous vote in the Reichstag against the Enabling Act, the Social Democrats, abetted by the political conservatism of the union leaders, were no longer able to mount an effective counteroffensive. They could only hope to survive Nazi rule by going underground, by emigrating, or by ceasing all political activity.

Nazi rule was to last much longer than most of those who failed to resist its early acts had expected. Its consolidation was extraordinarily swift and its capacity to atomize opposition unusually effective. Within a year the only remaining source of potential opposition was the army. But the army, as well as industry, did well under the new regime. Although the army's autonomy of action was circumscribed, Hitler initiated a program of vast rearmament and reintroduced mass conscription, acts which drew the support of the generals. Furthermore, the purge in 1934 of the more radical elements within the N.S.D.A.P., of its socialistic cohorts and militant revolutionaries, assuaged the army's early anxieties about the scope of the Nazi program. In this early move Hitler favored the generals against his own paramilitary S.A. leaders. It was only later that the S.S. gained supremacy over the army, or rather, within it, but by then Germany was already embarked on the road to total war.

The consolidation of Nazi rule was aided by the fact that the German economy had reached its lowest point by mid-1932 and was now on the upswing. Industrial production rose more than 20 percent in the second half of that year. This reversal in the downward trend was bound to benefit the Nazis, who, in the following year, could take credit for the recovery. The fact that recovery had begun well before the Nazis came to power was quickly forgotten. Unemployment, which had peaked in 1932, fell sharply after 1933, thereby bringing the new regime important labor support.

This improvement was also the result of Nazi economic policy. Its three foremost goals were job creation, the extension of state control, and rearmament. Unwittingly, the government practiced a kind of Keynesianism, but for reasons that had little to do with economic theory. Rather, the Nazis realized that in the absence of any socializing program labor could be placated through the creation of new jobs, an aim which served as a natural complement to the rearmament that was planned for Germany. This in turn offered major benefits to industry, which began to reachieve full production levels by 1937. Indeed, industry fared particularly well during the first four years of the Third Reich. Not only had the Nazis prevented a left-wing revolution, but they produced the conditions for increased output without confiscating any industrial assets.

Instead, the state enlarged its control over the economy. State control had always been sizable in Germany and had increased during the Depression years, when many firms and virtually the entire banking system had been rescued through state takeover. The Nazis continued this trend, however, not so much through nationalization as through stringent regulation. Planning was introduced with the aim of maximizing output and minimizing dependence on foreign trade, which had heretofore played a major role in the German economy. The results were prodigious but costly. Production increased enormously, but so did the dislocations and imbalances within the economy. Germany in the late thirties seemed to be replicating its experience in World War I, when it found itself suddenly cut off from foreign markets and sources of supply. However, this time the barriers were self-imposed, a consequence of the autarky that was sought as an inevitable part of the preparation for war.

Production doubled in the first five years of the Third Reich, primarily in the industrial sector, where massive investment and state contracts were concentrated. Consumer output, by contrast, lagged far behind. By 1938 it had risen only 16 percent above the level of ten years before, while the population had increased by almost 8 percent. The severe restrictions on imported goods meant continuing shortages of basic consumer produce, especially textiles and certain foodstuffs. While consumption suffered, so did wages. Real wages in 1938 barely exceeded the rates of a decade before, and this despite the fact that there was no unemployment but rather a labor shortage. And the stunning display successes that were ostensibly meant to benefit the working class—such as the Volkswagen and the Autobahn—were not really available to the working population at all.

In short, Nazi economic policy did not substantially raise the standard of living above the peak levels achieved in the Weimar Republic. The eminent German economist Gustav Stolper has estimated that in 1937 gross per capita income was below that of 1928. It was only by comparison with the acute depression of the early thirties that the consumer and laborer did well, but the vivid memory of that deprivation created a lower horizon of expectation and diminished pressure for a greater consumer orientation. This was a basic advantage that the Third Reich had over its predecessor, the Weimer Republic.

The emphasis on full employment, autarky, and rearmament led to inflationary developments, which brought the imposition of stringent wage-and-price controls by 1938. The methods of financing of the recovery and of the war was in no sense adequate to the task. Only through strict rationing and ceilings, and even more through the artificial segregation of the German economy from world markets, was the inflationary impact of the Nazi financial policies disguised and withheld from the German population. Without an effective market mechanism, the scarcity of labor and of raw materials in the late thirties was never efficiently resolved. There was a ruthless intraindustry competition for each, which was further exacerbated as the German armies swelled, depleting the domestic labor force.

In no sense was this a sound economy. But it was one that had come to believe in its own myths, primarily that without a successful war Germany could not prosper. In part this myth was reflected in the primitive Nazi notions about *Lebensraum* and in the romantic and irrational cult of colonial aspirations. It was institutionalized during the war, through Germany's systematic plunder of the resources of occupied territories and through its ruthless exploitation of millions of slave laborers. These were morally outrageous, stopgap measures to contend with some of the gross inefficiencies of a partially mismanaged economy. These measures were compounded by the endless rivalry among the many agenices of the state and between party and police power, all of which had important economic prerogatives.

Indeed, economic policies were always subordinate to some other, primarily political purpose in the Third Reich. For a system seeking self-sufficiency, what could be more costly than the extermination of its Jewish intelligentsia and commercial leaders? An efficient system of state labor deployment was not introduced until 1939, and the kind of tough, central planning required for the war effort was not imposed until Albert Speer, partially by accident, was charged with planning responsibility in 1942. The very success of his effort, which was startling and is often cited to refute the efficacy of the allied strategic bombing, demonstrates how poor performance in many sectors had been before.

The Nazis aspired to build an invincible war machine. They succeeded in large part because their enemies abroad failed to do anything meaningful at all until it was very late. But there was no coherent economic vision that extended beyond recovery and rearmament. As Tim Mason has put it, "the needs of the economy were determined by political decisions, principally by decisions in foreign policy, and the satisfaction of these needs was provided for by military victories."[3] Without war the economic policies of the Third Reich lacked a rationale, and without victory the Reich had no hope of any enduring success. Under these conditions the German economic recovery of the thirties was but a great sacrifice on the path to ultimate self-destruction.

The primacy of politics also prevailed in the social sector. Here Nazi efforts

---

[3]T. W. Mason, "The Primacy of Politics—Politics and Economics in National Socialist Germany," in S. J. Woolf, ed., *The Nature of Fascism* (New York, 1968), p. 189.

proved much more radical and far ranging. Social policy was based on three basic motives: First, there was the need to pulverize traditional group loyalties in order to thwart any pluralistic competition for the monopoly of power sought by the N.S.D.A.P. Second, social policies had to be designed to reintegrate atomized groups and individuals and thereby to secure their compliance, maximize output, and build solidarity for the imminent war effort. Third—and perhaps most important—it was necessary to reorganize society in such a way as to justify the position of the new elite, which was composed largely of déclassé, marginal men.

What resulted was an ambiguous complex of programs and a bizarre mixture of old and new. A comprehensive effort was initiated to level society, to break traditional ties and to replace these with new loyalties to party, state, and the Führer. The instrument of this policy was *Gleichschaltung,* or "coordination." In theory this meant that each member of society would lose his social status, regional affiliations, and religious allegiance and become equal in kind, if not in rank, with all others in the Reich. This policy was pursued not to achieve some greater egalitarian equity, but to ensure that the entire population might yield to the supreme purposes of the state and its leader. To this end an ideology of racial nationalism proved efficacious, for it excluded relatively few and yet provided sufficient pariah groups, primarily Jews and aliens, to create a sense of social differentiation between the full-fledged members of the new Reich and the outcasts.

Countless new organizations were established to replace the many that had been proscribed. Labor, women, youth, farmers, shopkeepers, indeed, virtually every segment of society was meant to be restructured. Even the most basic units of social life—the family, the church, and the school—were subjected to the sweep of radical reform. But the proliferation of new organizations and the verbiage of social transformation were deceptive. Several groups were relatively immune from this process. Businessmen, except Jews; the landed aristocracy; the civil service; and the senior army officers were not compelled to change very much so long as they allied themselves with Nazi purposes. Resistance was not tolerated, but neither was change required of all groups. The burdens of Nazi social policy were distributed very unequally. Thus, it is fair to conclude as Franz Neumann did, that National Socialism still preserved many of the features of a class society and that, in fact, the traditional, conservative classes fared a great deal better than did the others.

This was partly the result of the fact that Hitler never developed a very consistent economic and social theory. It was also the consequence of the fact that the Third Reich only lasted for twelve years and for half of this period was totally preoccupied with waging war. Indeed, contrasted with the comparatively slower pace of events in the Soviet Union or Italy, its social policies took hold with remarkable speed. But as Karl Dietrich Bracher, an outstanding scholar of National Socialism, has shown, the result was that "traditional and revolutionary elements continued to exist partly fused and partly as rivals."[4] These rivalries in turn multiplied as

---

[4]Bracher, *op. cit.,* p. 235.

the new agencies established in the Reich began to compete with each other.

Foremost among them was the N.S.D.A.P. Here was a radical party composed predominately of middle and marginal strata within society and which had to justify its position as a new elite. Much of the social policy that was implemented, or at least enunciated, was intended to buttress the position of the new groups that came to power through the party. Many of these groups were composed of members from lower-middle-class backgrounds and from outlying regions within the Reich or beyond its boundaries. They were outsiders, alienated men, whose sudden success represented, as Neumann first put it, the spectacular rise of the plebian. And they were young. In 1934 65 percent of the N.S.D.A.P. members were under forty, which was the median age in the first Nazi cabinet. Hitler in 1933 was younger than John Kennedy had been at the start of his presidency.

This social group needed to justify its claims to rule the Reich. It was this purpose more than any other that defined its social policy. Basically this was a negative motivation. There was no way to explain why this particular petty bourgeois constellation of men should hold the exclusive right to rule. Unable to devise a class doctrine, it sought to identify with the largest category, the ethnic nation, and to designate society as a classless entity. The result of all this was that the Third Reich achieved what David Schoenbaum has termed "a dual structure of society." Individuals and groups moved both in their traditional worlds and in the new world forged by the Nazis. It was not so much that a new class was produced but that old ones were weakened.

Ralf Dahrendorf has argued that "National Socialism was not an historical episode but the German revolution."[5] If so, it was only a revolution in the negative sense of destroying. It was, as Hermann Rauschning has called it, "a revolution of nihilism." In the course of German history, and particularly with respect to the politics of the Federal Republic, this was a critical phenomenon. For what Hitler did was to remove many of the illiberal forces that had stood in the way of modernization and democracy in Germany.

This was at best only half a revolution. National Socialism itself was not primarily a modern movement. It retained far too many irrational, romantic, and explicitly antiindustrial themes and aims. Basic conflicts, such as the one between its agrarian ideals and its industrial performance, were never resolved. Its incredible racial policies and practices were a throwback to the most primitive level of mankind. And even if Dahrendorf is right, that "Hitler needed modernity, little as he liked it,"[6] it remains true that only through defeat, occupation, and a gradual reconstruction of German political life, could modernization lead to a liberal, democratic, and pluralistic political system. If National Socialism weakened the underpinnings of the old order and hastened the process of modernization, it installed in its place a despotism that could only be removed by massive foreign intervention. It was the

---

[5]Dahrendorf, *op. cit.*, p. 416.

[6]*Ibid.*, p. 404.

events after 1945 that laid the basis for a new political and social order. Through their policies and by their defeat, the Nazis, at a horrendous cost, had pulled down the foundations of authoritarianism in Germany. In a way their defeat in 1945 wiped the slate clean as the defeat of 1918 never had. For the first time since industrialization had come to Germany, there could be a new beginning.

Three

The Allied
Interregnum

The new beginning in German politics occurred under conditions of extreme deprivation and adversity. The devastation wrought by the war and by the despicable racial and political practices of the Nazi regime was on a scale unprecedented in modern European history. The German extermination camps had annihilated millions of Jews and other peoples. The regime's fierce totalitarianism had forced thousands into exile, had decimated the German intelligentsia, and had destroyed the foundations of civilized life for most of its population. These twelve years of domestic holocaust and the havoc produced by a total war fought to its futile and utter end had, by 1945, consumed all the resources of the German nation and left monumental wreckage in its wake. Although the Poles and the Russians and certainly the Jews had suffered more, Germany was now the desperate victim, a broken country at its "zero hour."

Almost 4 million German soldiers had been killed in action, and perhaps half that number of their civilian compatriots had perished in the concentration camps, as victims of Allied bombing, or from want of food and medical care. Some 5 million homes had been either partially or totally destroyed, and twenty million Germans were homeless. Twelve million German soldiers were prisoners of war, and a like number of civilians were destitute and adrift—belonging to a new postwar category of "displaced persons." Germany's transportation system was virtually ruined. Five thousand railroad and motorcar bridges had been destroyed, 90 percent of German harbors were inoperative, and some 50 thousand tons of wreckage were strewn in the Rhine.

In 1946, when figures on the ravages of war were first tabulated, economic production stood at one third the level of ten years before. Indeed, it has been estimated that no less than one third of all the assets of Germany were consumed or destroyed during the war. And this was before Germany had even begun to bear the cost of the reparations that were to be imposed by the victors in their vain attempt to gain some indemnity for the prohibitive cost of the war. The losses in German property rights abroad totaled at least $1 billion, and the value of the goods surrendered to the Allies at the war's end (such as the remains of the German commercial fleet) or sequestered by them immediately after the war, exceeded this amount.

Human suffering was extreme. Food was in particularly short supply and was to remain so for the first two postwar years. The coalmines were barely operating and fuel was scarce. Virtually nothing remained of normal life. There were no theaters, no newspapers, and few schools or hospitals. And amid this material deprivation, those who survived suddenly experienced the frightful shock produced by the allied liberation of the concentration and death camps. The pointlessness of the war, the burden of having fought it for so long, the sudden self-elimination of the Führer and many of his cohorts, and the vengeful brutality of the invading Russian armies (whose own losses had greatly exceeded those of the Germans), combined to create a mood of abject pathos, of guilt mixed with fear, as Germany was confronted with the evident depravity of its past and the despair of its uncertain future.

This postwar situation was unlike any other in German history. The stark contrast with the events that had followed World War I was manifested in many ways, and the substantial difference between these two postwar experiences is important in explaining the subsequent fate of the political systems that emerged from them. Each system was deeply affected by the conditions prevailing at its birth, and after World War II these were to be much more fortuitous for the growth of a stable, modern, and democratic entity—at least in part of Germany.

What were these differences? First, as we have seen, the domestic devastation experienced in the second defeat far exceeded the suffering in 1918. This time the Allied victory was clearly visible. Peace had come not through surrender, but through total physical exhaustion. This meant that the impact of the last stages of the war was far greater for the civilian population, but it also precluded the acceptance of any notion of a "stab in the back," such as had grown popular in the Weimar Republic as a slogan of the Right against those who had sued for peace or signed the Treaty of Versailles at the end of World War I.

This time most Germans shared a sense of their own responsibility for the events that had brought their country the debacle of total defeat. This perception was strengthened by the sudden demise of the Nazi leadership by suicide, escape, or Allied incarceration. Not only was there no nostalgia for the old regime, but that regime itself vanished. Despite the millions who had been members of the N.S.D.A.P., hardly anyone in June 1945, believed in a continuation of Nazi rule. In 1918 many had opposed the removal of the Kaiser and subsequently had yearned for a restoration of the imperial government. But after World War II there was no comparable movement or sentiment. The Nazi experience had been too horrendous, and its restoration was too unthinkable. The fact that there was no turning back created a mood that was much more amenable to a fundamental transformation of the political system as well as an inclination to endure very substantial social and economic changes in order to ensure a new beginning.

The posttotalitarian situation was unique. Essentially, the slate had been wiped clean. The Nazi rulers had gone and had left a political vacuum at the helm. And with the removal of Admiral Doenitz and his regime by the Allies, Germany was left with no successor government. Initially, there were few indigenous claimants for the right to constitute a national regime. Nor had the many émigrés who now returned to Germany formed a government in exile. Instead, it was the Allied military commanders who now organized the new administration of Germany. The responsibility for decision making in these difficult years was to be shared with the victors. This meant that at its weakest hour, when the opportunities for any successful national political action were so severely circumscribed, no German party had alone to carry the burden of negotiating with the victorious enemy, as the Weimar coalition had been compelled to do—at great cost to its domestic image and support—in the period following 1918.

Indeed, the occupation of Germany may have been the most salient difference between the two postwar experiences. In 1945 Germany was divided into four zones of occupation. It lost substantial territory in the east, and temporarily in the west, without being asked, as it had been at Versailles, to acquiesce formally to such postwar punitive measures. In fact, it was never asked to sign a formal peace treaty; the matter was postponed time and again by Allied disagreement. This meant that the initial losses of sovereignty and terrain could to some degree be disguised as provisional, thus incurring far less outspoken German protest at the time of the losses.

The Occupation also raised the specter of the fragmentation of Germany. From the beginning each of the four powers pursued somewhat different policies in its zone and discouraged interzonal German political activity. This meant that local politics, namely the governance of the towns, the municipalities, and the states, or *Länder,* into which each zone was subdivided, became the first arena for postwar German politics. Prussia was eliminated as an entity, subdivided among several zones and shorn of its easternmost provinces, which were either ceded to the Soviet Union or transferred by unilateral Soviet action to Polish jurisdiction. If Germany was to reemerge as a national unit, the benevolent support of the occupying authorities was essential. The new German political leaders would have to cooperate with the victors and temper any nationalistic impulses, which could only inhibit Allied acquiescence to national integration. In each zone, therefore, the new local leadership sought to adapt its policies to those of the occupying power. There was no forum for a national protest movement such as characterized early Weimar politics.

The conflicts that soon emerged among the Allies created new opportunities for German political action. In contrast to 1918, there was no enduring, monolithic solidarity on the part of Germany's wartime enemies. As the Cold War developed and new international divisions superseded the wartime antagonism, German politicians were able to identify positively with the Allied power ruling their zone, thus removing themselves more rapidly from the pariah status of a vanquished enemy. Only for a year or two did all Germans share a common enmity toward all the Allies. By 1947 the division of Germany into two camps, one Soviet, the other Western, created a new belligerence that removed the immediacy of the one that had accompanied and then followed the war. Both camps became the exposed forward lines of confrontation in the Cold War, and in that context each found itself the object of new Allied priorities in which each government sought to consolidate that part of Germany in its domain, rather than to weaken and punish it further. The primacy of anticommunism in the West and of preventing further Soviet encroachment in Europe created the conditions for the emergence of a West German entity that would soon find itself embraced as an ally by the very powers that occupied it. If the Occupation served as a kind of catharsis, the Cold War brought the opportunity for swift reacceptance by the Western Allies of their German charges.

The process was facilitated by the rather enlightened policies pursued by the Western occupying powers. The brunt of the Allied denazification proceedings and reparation measures was borne immediately after the war. Germany was spared the continuous and prolonged negotiation with the Allies over its reparations debt that had so deeply undermined the capacity of the Weimar regimes to construct a credible foreign or financial policy. The bulk of its payment agreements, including the unprecedented commitment to render restitution and indemnification to its Jewish and other civilian victims, were promulgated after the German economy had begun to recover its strength in the 1950s. Further jurisdiction for denazification was passed on to German authorities by the Allies in the late forties, although here, perhaps, the resulting postponement and somewhat dilatory prosecution were less commendable.

But even in the first years after the war, when harsh measures were imposed by the Allies, they were the dictates of an occupying authority, responsibility for which did not have to be shared by an indigenous government. It was far better to press hard in the beginning, when German perceptions of their own responsibility for the evils of the war and the Nazi system were still fresh and when the Germans' desire to repudiate their own past was still strong, than to adhere to a sustained policy of punishment and retribution over a long period. And by imposing severe measures at the outset, the Allies facilitated a restructuring of German political life, which was vital for the success of the political system that developed in the years that followed.

The Cold War

Originally, there was broad agreement among the Allies on the nature and purposes of postwar policy in Germany. The wartime terms were quite unsparing. At Casablanca, Roosevelt ennunciated the Allied aim of seeking an unconditional German surrender. Several months later, at Quebec, he secured Churchill's reluctant acceptance of the punitive measures envisaged in the Morgenthau Plan (named for the United States Secretary of the Treasury), which did not, it should be said, have the support of the foremost German experts in the Roosevelt administration. Under this plan German industry would have been substantially dismantled and the country would have reverted to an agricultural economy, the hope being that economic impotence would ensure its future political docility. This rigid anti-German sentiment found expression in the initial decrees of the American military command, especially in the basic document of the early Occupation, Joint Chiefs-of-Staff Directive (J.C.S.) 1067. The British never fully shared this view, although the concept of a Europe free of German industrial competition was not unattractive to them. Soviet policy sought to combine three aims: to obtain maximum territorial and industrial reparations, to keep Germany permanently weak, and to further pro-Soviet and Communist forces within Germany as a whole. Except for the last of these, the French position did not differ substantially from that of the Soviet Union when, in 1945, France was finally invited to join the tripartite European Advisory Commission that was to make policy for postwar Germany.

Each of the Allies obtained a separate zone of occupation. After the territorial losses in the east, the placing of the Saar under French administration, and the separation of Austria, what remained of Germany was divided four ways. The French zone, which was belatedly carved out of the territory earmarked for United States occupation, was far smaller than the others but directly contiguous and, therefore, more vital, to France. Each Allied military command was supreme within its own zone, but initially, mainly at Soviet insistence, some effort was made to promote a central administration. This was to be overseen by the Allied Control Commission, which was to deal with problems affecting Germany as a whole and with the administration of Berlin, which was itself subdivided into four Allied sectors.

But it was soon clear that no central political authority was to govern Germany. Once the war ended, the Allies quickly lost their common approach to the problem of Germany. The French held out from the start against any unitary regime that might hasten the rebuilding of a powerful Germany and jeopardize as well the eventual absorption by France of the Saar region. A series of unilateral Soviet actions in Germany and Eastern Europe led the United States to a swift departure from the spirit of Yalta. At the Yalta Conference, the Soviet Union had been assured of sweeping territorial gains in Eastern Europe. But even before the war ended, in April 1945, the Russians announced a unilateral pact with the newly imposed Polish Communist regime, ceding to it the administration of the territory to the east of the western Neisse River, which contained some 26,000 square miles and a

German population of over 3 million. This act, which remained a subject of controversy for years, was vigorously protested by the Western Allies. It was a harbinger of the discord and distrust that was soon to come.

By the time of the Potsdam Conference, in the summer of 1945, disagreement among the Allies was already manifest. Although the four Allies still agreed to pursue a common policy, each adopted its own priorities in its zone of occupation. The Soviets moved swiftly to institute wide-ranging economic reforms, to extract maximum reparations, and to structure the reemergence of local German politics in their zone in such a way as to favor the pro-Communist forces. These events, combined with the pattern of Soviet policies elsewhere in Eastern Europe, quickly caused the United States to alter its approach in Germany. The views of the men in the field—of General Lucius Clay and his advisers Robert Murphy, Lewis Douglas, William Draper and others—began to prevail over those of the Washington officials who had devised the first plans for the Occupation. Two factors fed the revision of American policy. First, there was the mounting concern about Soviet actions and intentions. Second, there was the dire economic and financial condition of Germany. The notion that Europe might again become strong while Germany, at its heart but at the same time the exposed flank of the western camp facing a Soviet-dominated East, remained weak did not seem realistic. Thus it was not long before the severe tone of American policy toward Germany was tempered. Within the first year of the Occupation, concern for the economic rehabilitation of Germany, or at least its western zones, began to replace the punitive and debilitating spirit of the first postwar plans. General Clay lost little time in suspending the delivery of reparations from the American zone to the Soviets. And his administration undertook effective steps to create the conditions for a more stable development in the western zones.

This change of policy was matched, as much as it was provoked, by Soviet actions in its zone of occupation. The Soviets pressed on with basic land reform and nationalization of industry and with a harsh program of industrial disarmament. Some 1400 factories were dismantled and their equipment shipped east to the U.S.S.R. Within three years of the end of the war less than 40 percent of the means of production in the Soviet zone were left in private hands. This course was unacceptable, for both ideological and political reasons, to the Western Allies. So was the Soviet-dictated subjugation of the non-Communist political parties in the eastern zone. The events in Hungary, Poland, and, subsequently, Czechoslovakia, were ample evidence of Soviet unwillingness to tolerate the evolution of free democratic political movements in Soviet-occupied Europe. This pattern, above all, convinced the Western Allies to change course in their German policy: to rebuild and defend their zones, thereby forestalling the further expansion of Soviet influence and potential control into Western Europe.

The conflict that was developing among the Allies was reflected in the growing disagreement at the several conferences on Germany that convened during 1947. The meeting of foreign ministers in Moscow in March of that year registered the hopelessness of achieving any economic unity among the four zones, let alone political cooperation. By December, when the ministers met again in Moscow, the division of Germany into two camps seemed imminent. And, indeed, it was. Within three months the Soviet representatives had left the Allied Control Commission. With the introduction of a single currency in the three western zones in June 1948, the rupture was irreparable. The Soviets responded with the blockade of Berlin, which was located without adequate access agreements deep within the Soviet zone, and began to lay the foundations for a separate state, the German Democratic Republic, which was proclaimed a year later.

These developments strengthened the determination of the Western Allies to establish a single entity comprising their three zones. Initially, the French were reluctant to adopt this course of action, fearful of any central German authority that might again become a power on the European continent. It was only when the French fear of the Soviet threat became greater than its fear of Germany that Paris acceded to the Anglo-American plans to press on with a coordinated policy encompassing each of the three western zones. By 1948 this process had gained powerful momentum.

Reemergence of German Politics

The reconstruction of German politics had begun at the local level. Local authorities were established in 1945 in the towns and municipalities and at the county and district level. But the key entities for German political administration became the states, or *Länder,* into which each of the zones of occupation was divided. Their boundaries, except in the cases of Bavaria in the south and the city-states of Hamburg and Bremen in the north, had little historical or cultural continuity with the past. On the whole they were rather artificial creations, but they soon gained a vested and enduring stake in their own continuance. There were four *Länder* under American occupation, three in the south (Bavaria, Württemberg-Baden, and Hesse) and one, the port city of Bremen, in the north. Together they contained some 17 million people, which was also the population of the Soviet zone in the east. The British zone was larger and potentially more wealthy. To promote inter-Allied harmony and as a concession for British acceptance of the Morgenthau Plan at Quebec, the Americans had reluctantly allocated the more populous and industrial northern zone, including the Ruhr, to England. Here, too, there were to be four *Länder,* descending from the agricultural border area of Schleswig-Holstein in the north, through Lower Saxony and the city-state of Hamburg, to the giant industrial *Land* of North Rhine-Westphalia in the south. These areas had a combined population of some 22 million Germans.

The French zone, carved out at a later date during the war, was smaller than these, containing far less territory and a population of only 6 million. Here the *Land* boundaries separating Rhineland-Palatinate, South Baden, and Württemberg-Hohenzollern were highly arbitrary and artificial. Indeed, the entire southeastern subdivision of the old states of Baden and Württemberg made relatively little sense and was to be a source of some difficulty and of subsequent revision in the years ahead. But perhaps most significant for the French was the hope of absorbing the Saar, with its vast coal resources, into France. The administration of the Saar had been a subject of prolonged and bitter dispute between France and Germany after World War I. This time the French were encouraged to believe that the permanent economic union of the Saar with France would be a safe final solution to this thorny but vital problem. In fact, the population of the Saar initially, in 1947, voted to favor such economic union, a move that helped to forestall punitive industrial measures by the French occupying forces. But this was to be only a provisional arrangement. In time the Saar became subject to the international agreements relating to coal and steel production in western Europe; and by the mid-fifties it was returned to West Germany, in accord with the changed preference of its people and with the benevolent acquiescence of the French.

German *Länder* governments were quickly organized in 1945 and 1946 in the western zones of occupation. The Minister-Presidents, or governors, who were at first appointed and then elected in the *Länder,* played an important role in the reorganization of German politics in the postwar period. Figures such as Fritz Schäffer and Hans Ehard in Bavaria, Rheinhold Maier in Baden, Wilhelm Kaisen in Bremen, Hinrich Kopf in Lower Saxony, and Karl Arnold in the largest *Land,* North Rhine-Westphalia, had a significant and lasting impact on the shape of political life and the definition of the political system that emerged in the West. The Americans and British pressed on in 1946 to establish the first zonal German authorities, the *Länderrat* in Stuttgart in the United States zone and the *Zonenbeirat* in Hamburg for the British occupied areas. By the end of that year, in view of the worsening economic situation in Germany, the first interzonal authority was created, the so-called Bizonia, whose jurisdiction extended over all the British- and American-occupied territories, except for Berlin.

The Bizonia, or United Economic Region, as it was officially called, was soon to serve as a kind of German quasi-government, with several institutions of its own, including, by 1948, an Economic Council, an indirectly elected *Länderrat,* a High Court and a Central Bank. At first its jurisdiction was to be limited to social, economic, and financial issues, and its legislation, like all laws promulgated in occupied Germany, was binding only upon Allied approval. Although the French still opposed the establishment of authentic, indigenous zonal authorities—let alone interzonal ones—the Bizonia was in fact the real predecessor of the Federal Republic, which was proclaimed, with French agreement, in the summer of 1949.

The Allied powers also encouraged the development of nonfascist German political parties. With the collapse of the Third Reich, the S.P.D., many of whose leaders had been in exile or imprisoned in the Nazi camps, at once reestablished itself. So did the Communists, the K.P.D., whose leadership returned from Moscow and began to organize throughout Germany, but with greatest effect in the Soviet zone. Fragments of the old Center party, which had been strong in Catholic areas before 1933, became active and began to combine with other liberal and conservative forces to launch a new party, the Christian Democratic Union, or C.D.U., whose structure remained highly centrifugal and federal, varying in composition and policy from *Land* to *Land* and from zone to zone. In Bavaria, the first of the *Länder* to organize a government and the *Land* with the strongest sense of its own past, the party took a different name, the Christian Social Union, or C.S.U., and a separate organization, a distinction that has continued to this day. Christian Democracy, with its stress on social concerns, was a novel product of World War II, which created such great human suffering in Germany and elsewhere that a concept of social reconstruction in place of individualistic priorities held wide appeal. Indeed, Christianity was one of the few credos to survive totalitarianism and war in Germany, and the early debates within the C.D.U. suggest how far toward a collectivist ethic thinking in Germany had moved.

For the future of these parties and the many smaller ones that emerged, the growing division in occupied Germany and the constraints imposed by the Soviet Union on democratic processes in its zone were of great significance. Following the Communist electoral setbacks in Hungary and Austria in 1945, the Soviets forced an amalgamation of the S.P.D. and the K.P.D., doubtless fearing that the popularity of the former would totally overshadow and outdistance the appeal of communism in Germany. In the October 1946 Berlin elections, the last to be carried out on a citywide basis, the new, merged Socialist Unity Party (S.E.D.), which was Communist-dominated, secured less than one-fifth of the vote. Even in the old Communist stronghold of Wedding, where the K.P.D. had gained 60 percent of the vote in 1932, the new S.E.D. obtained less than 30 percent in 1946. This only strengthened the Soviet intention to suspend the free electoral process. And although the noncommunist parties continued to be officially sanctioned in the Soviet zone, the occupying government made certain that no party would be in a position to challenge the primacy of the S.E.D. in that zone.

This meant not only that free elections and a democratic political process would be barred from the Soviet zone. It also meant that the postwar S.P.D. was to lose a very large part of its former constituency, for its strength before 1933 had been concentrated in many areas that were now under Soviet rule. Prussia, for example, had been predominately Protestant, and a stronghold of socialism. For the new Christian Democratic movement the divison would also be significant. Many of its most liberal and progressive figures, such as Jakob Kaiser and Ernst Lemmer, had their base in the eastern zone, which was lost to them after 1947. The result was that more pro-Western, traditional, and socially conservative forces within the C.D.U., perhaps best personified by the remarkable Konrad Adenauer, were able to firm their grip on the party and found themselves the beneficiaries of the partitioning of Germany. The removal of the Soviet zone meant that the political arena for the C.D.U. in what remained of western Germany would contain a substantially higher percentage of Catholics than had any single German state since unification. Also, the partition that grew from the Cold War was bound to reward those political leaders who espoused a more outspokenly pro-Western policy. No figure was to conform better to Western needs and aspirations than Adenauer himself, as did the party that he forged so much in his own image.

By 1948 the Western powers had resolved to establish a West German state.

From February to June of that year representatives of the three Western Allies and the three Benelux countries met in London despite vigorous Soviet protests. The six-power conference initially planned to improve Bizonia and to seek effective French cooperation with it. But in view of the worsening East-West relations, the conference went much further. In the end it recommended measures to further European economic integration and to found a West German state. In addition, it called for an International Control Authority for the Ruhr and for stringent military controls to minimize the fears of the French and the Benelux countries regarding the potential resurgence of German power.

The west German Minister-Presidents and the mayors of Bremen and Hamburg were called upon to convene a Constituent Assembly to draft a constitution for the new state. Initially they were somewhat reluctant to do this, fearing that such action would perpetuate the divison of Germany. A compromise formula was struck. The German body was termed a Parliamentary Council, with its purpose defined as that of drafting a Basic Law, which sounded less permanent than a constitution. Like so much else that characterized the birth of the new state, such gestures to its ostensibly provisional nature were intended to assuage the opposition of those who still hoped that Germany might remain undivided.

The membership of the Parliamentary Council comprised sixty-five delegates from the eleven *Länder,* each elected indirectly by the several *Landtage* or *Bürgerschaften,* which were the supreme legislative and electoral organs in each *Land.* Berlin, whose status was to remain special, was entitled to send five observers. It was in this body that the first parliamentary parties were formed. The S.P.D., which was more effectively organized on an interzonal basis, and the C.D.U.-C.S.U., which remained more federal in structure, each had twenty-seven delegates. The liberals were represented by five members, and three smaller parties, including the Communists, had two apiece. At the first meeting of the Parliamentary Council, on September 1, 1948, Adenauer, the chairman of the C.D.U., was elected president of the council.

The deliberations of the Parliamentary Council, which met in Bonn for many months, were long and often heated. The terms of the Basic Law that it drafted with Allied counsel and approval laid the foundations for the new state that was soon to be proclaimed. On the whole, the document and the process that produced it were remarkably successful. In contrast to the proceedings in 1919, the legal framework for the new republic was laid with greater deliberation and under far less disruptive domestic conditions. To be sure, there were forces within Germany that remained disappointed with the structure devised for the new state. Indeed, for substantially different reasons, two *Länder,* Bavaria and Lower Saxony, initially did not want to ratify the document. But once their protest had been registered, they, too, acquiesced, for this was the path toward the regaining of German sovereignty. Here was a basic difference from the constitutional process of the Weimar Republic. In 1949 there was little scope for a nationalist outcry against the constitutional movement toward a new republic. National self-assertion for Germany meant one of two choices: Either it would respond positively to the opportunity to participate in the establishment of a new West German state, no matter how limited its sovereignty or how unsatisfactory its structure; or it could seek a political framework for Germany as a whole. The latter meant cooperation with the Soviets. And in the wake of all that had happened in the Soviet zone and in Eastern Europe and in the aftermath of the Berlin blockade, this course was not readily available to West German politicians, however much some might have preferred it. West Germany would either remake itself in the image of, and under the continued tutelage of, the Western powers, or it would remain weak and without an effective voice in its own future.

And so it was that sovereignty began to flow back to Germany—but to a Germany that was to remain divided. The Basic Law was promulgated in May 1949. Elections for the first parliament were held that summer, and a cabinet was established, headed by Konrad Adenauer, in mid-September. With the formal establishment of this government, Allied military administration of West Germany formally came to an end. To be sure, the Western powers reserved for themselves very extensive rights with regard to essential German affairs. It would take years before the new republic could manage its own foreign policy, and even then, only under major constraints that remained as consequences of its curious birth. But the conditions at the time of the establishment of the new regime were auspicious in at least one respect. The Allies, who had been the bitter wartime enemies of Germany, stood prepared to embrace this new political entity. This was an advantage that had not been available to the Weimar Republic in its early years, much to its subsequent detriment.

The establishment of the Federal Republic came at a timely moment in history. The Cold War had divided Europe, but brought its Western components closer together. European integration and the muting of national antagonisms provided Germany with a great opportunity. So did the task of domestic reconstruction. The worst years of German economic and social upheaval had passed. They had been endured under occupation. Conditions within Germany at the time the new regime assumed power were still dismal and onerous; the point of departure by which its success would be measured stood at a very depressed level. Thus the strength of Germany's recovery would seem all the greater compared with the abject misery of the postwar years, years in which there was no national German government to share the responsibility for the harsh conditions within the country. The Allies had carried the burden during these difficult years. After four years of Allied rule, 1949 was a fortuitous year for the Germans once again to begin to manage their own national affairs.

What happened in West Germany was replicated in the Soviet zone. Here, too, a provisional constitution was drafted. Controlled elections were held and a separate state, the German Democratic Republic, was proclaimed in the summer of 1949. But this was a highly artificial construction, far more the product of Soviet will than of any authentic indigenous political process.

The division of Germany was a consequence of Hitlerism and a lost war as well as a reflection of the starkly transformed political and military situation in Europe.

Although this division was untoward, it facilitated the task for the West German leadership of regaining acceptance abroad. A divided Germany was weaker than a unified nation and, therefore, the source of less fear and resentment on the part of its western neighbors. The existence of the German Democratic Republic was also to serve a useful purpose, for it was to become the prime target of the animosity of the Western powers. If the G.D.R. represented the "bad" Germany, then the government in Bonn could far more easily find acceptance as the "good" Germany, a role which became all the more available to it as the Cold War intensified.

All this created unusual opportunities for Adenauer. This extraordinary and venerable figure, who had first been a contender for the German chancellorship in 1921, saw and seized these opportunities and thereby greatly expedited both the acceptance of the Federal Republic by the Western Allies and their relinquishing to it of many of the powers that they still retained in 1949. Although Adenauer stood as a singular symbol of the continuity of the new Germany with elements of the past, his tenure did not signify a restoration of the old groups. For much had changed in West Germany, especially during the Occupation. The social bases of politics and the ideological setting in which the political system evolved had been basically transformed. The years of defeat and the Allied interregnum had furthered the social revolution in Germany. The many obstacles that had stood in the way of social modernization had receded as a result of Germany's experiences during these years. What had begun during Hitler's pernicious rule had been substantially extended during the Occupation. Germany, at the launching of the Federal Republic, at last had the opportunity to emerge as a modern nation.

At first the Allies, and particularly the Americans, had sought a radical transformation of the socioeconomic bases of German society. This was in part the ethos and purpose of the Morgenthau Plan and J.C.S. 1067. Denazification, demilitarization, and industrial decentralization were to be the instruments through which the German elite was purged from its powerfully entrenched position. In the first two postwar years these policies were widely applied. By the end of 1946 almost 1 million individual denazification cases had been processed in the United States and British zones. All military installations, machinery, and appliances and even some civilian aircraft facilities were systematically dismantled. Most industries linked with war production were banned. The production of ocean-going ships, airplanes, heavy machine tools, synthetic rubber, aluminum and magnesium, and many other goods that had potential military application was prohibited. The level of output in many other industries was severely restricted. According to the Level of Industry Plan introduced in 1946, which represented a softening of J.C.S. 1067 in the United States zone, steel and basic chemical production was to be limited to less than one-third the output of 1938. The volume of trade was to be reduced to three-fifths of the level achieved ten years before. Many of the giant firms that still remained were broken up. The twelve largest coal and steel producers were divided into twenty-eight firms, and I.G. Farben, the mammoth chemical company, was parcelled into four separate units. Likewise, the huge banks and industrial cartels were carved up, although many of these would soon recombine.

These measures, which were invoked with stringent severity at first, were soon tempered by the unforeseen gravity of economic conditions in Germany in 1947 at a time when Soviet intentions began to be viewed with greater alarm by the Western powers. While many Socialist and anti-Nazi figures in Germany called for more basic economic reforms, including the nationalization of industry and fundamental land reform, the occupying authorities recoiled from such sweeping and ideologically unpalatable policies. As Lewis Edinger has observed, "the Western occupation powers rejected the price of such drastic changes when they resolved that economic recovery had to take precedence over 'political reconstruction'."[1]

But it was not such pragmatic considerations alone that motivated Allied moderation in the economic sphere. Ideological predilections accounted for the American vetoing of the socialization clause in the Hessian state constitution. Similarly, the American Occupation authorities blocked measures requiring labor codetermination in industrial management, even though they were supported by both the C.D.U. and the S.P.D. Ostensibly, the Americans argued, such procedures would strengthen Communist representation in German factories and would excessively hamper management. In fact, they smacked too much of socialism for the Americans to accept. It was only in the British zone, which was, to be sure, the industrial heartland of western Germany, that such social and industrial innovations made some headway, securing the benevolent, if limited, support of the Labour government in England.

The Western powers sought to break the power of the old groups, but not to institutionalize socialist experiments. They rejected any extensive redistribution of property in their zones. Land reform was never seriously attempted. This was not so critical in the West, because the large estates were located primarily in the Soviet zone or east of the Oder-Neisse boundary, under Polish or Soviet rule. The division of Germany and the radical land reform instituted in 1945 by the Russians had eliminated the Junkers as a force in German politics. But even under Hitler they had hardly played a role. The day of landed feudal politics had already passed in Germany.

While economic reforms fell far short of a basic transformation of the system in western Germany, social change in the years of occupation ranged quite far. This was partly the result of a deliberate Allied policy to reconstitute a democratic, posttotalitarian elite. This was a kind of "artificial revolution," an exercise in controlled revolutionary change. Its impact was most substantial among the political elite. The entire higher echelon of German government, first at the *Land* level and later at the federal level, was totally restructured. The new government and party leadership was partially recruited from among figures who had entered

---

[1]Lewis J. Edinger, "Post-Totalitarian Leadership: Elites in the German Federal Republic," *American Political Science Review,* 54, 1, 1960, p. 77.

politics in the Weimar Republic only to withdraw or emigrate after 1933. But most of its members had entered political life for the first time in the postwar period. Only 6 percent of the members of the first Bundestag, the lower federal house elected in 1949, had sat in the Reichstag before 1933, whereas well over 40 percent had served in the Bizonia economic council or in the Parliamentary Council that drafted the Basic Law.

The recruitment of a new political elite was matched by the new leadership, part of which returned from exile, in the trade unions and in the higher tiers of the postwar civil service. For much of the bureaurcracy this restructuring meant only a temporary occupational displacement, but even so, the regaining of old positions often required a frank repudiation of any previous antidemocratic sentiments. As Wolfgang Zapf, an eminent German sociologist, has shown, the general turnover in the West German elite structure was far greater during the 1945–1949 period than in either 1919 or 1933. To be sure, there were sectors that had relative immunity. One was the church leadership, which had remained rather apolitical; another, curiously, was the very highest level of big business, where, despite the prosecution of Krupp and Flick at Nuremberg, substantial continuity of ownership was maintained, reflecting the American predilection for private property and the priority attached to economic recovery, which complicated any commitment to reallocate industrial resources.

But the overall pattern was highly significant. Hitler and the Occupation together eradicated the grip of the old, preindustrial groups on German society and politics. The experience of Fascist dictatorship and war had made right-wing, antidemocratic politics an unattractive, indeed, a hopeless, option in postwar Germany. Totalitarianism followed by defeat had largely leveled society. The Occupation removed many among the remaining elite. Gradually, as German politics reemerged, great opportunities became available for those who sought to enter politics. The sudden rise of political newcomers was facilitated by the policies of the Allied interregnum. Through the effect of Allied policies Germans really were "forced to be free," as John Montgomery, the American political scientist, has shown. In many ways this phenomenon was a byproduct of other aims. John Gimbel has argued "that the politics of the American occupation were governed largely by a range of interests rather than by the attempt to democratize Germany."[2] These interests included anticommunism, the effort to reduce occupation costs, cooperation with the French, the defense of free enterprise, and containment of the Soviet Union.

But nonetheless, the Western Allies did lay the foundations for a democratic political process. They did this in part by assuming responsibility for the governance of Germany in its worst and weakest hour and then by gradually nurturing the rebirth of German political life and the structuring of stable institutions conducive to a democratic process. Their economic measures were half-hearted and often

---

[2]John Gimbel, *The American Occupation of Germany* (Stanford, 1968), p. 249.

inconsistent, their social revolution artificial, but sweeping in its impact. Without the Occupation the development of a new national government would have been far more painful and contentious. Despite the many mistakes and missed opportunities of this period, Germany was given a chance to refind itself after the horrors of Hitlerism and the war. Psychologically, it had been shaken by the Fascist experience from its propensity to substitute authoritarianism for individual freedom; economically, it had been leveled by defeat; and socially, it had been substantially reshaped during the Occupation. The four years of Allied rule were critical for the new beginning which found its constitutional expression and institutional form in the Basic Law and the establishment of a federal government in 1949, thirty tumultuous years after republicanism and revolution had first been attempted in Germany.

Four

The Constitutional Order

The political institutions of the Federal Republic appear to have functioned remarkably well over the past two decades. In part this was the result of the fact that the most difficult decisions were all made before the republic was established. As Alfred Grosser has suggested, "when the new state was born, the period of dramatic changes was already over."[1] This was in sharp contrast to the experience of the Weimar Republic, which had to confront the most painful choices during its very first years and which emerged from this process weak and divided. Indeed, the example of Weimar and of the bitter disputes that accompanied its birth helped to shape a much more stable and balanced system in 1949.

The drafting of the Basic Law and the founding of the new state were highly deliberate and relatively harmonious processes. Several factors were conducive to promoting a broad consensus in place of the debilitating discord that prevailed in 1919. First, the constitutional process promised to restore substantial sovereignty to German institutions. This served as a powerful incentive for consensus among the competing aspirants and groups in the German political arena after 1945. For the restoration of sovereignty required Allied acquiescence, which, in turn, depended upon some fundamental agreement among those German representatives who participated in the drafting and ratification of the Basic Law.

Many Germans may have felt reluctant to participate in a process that would restore limited sovereignty to only a part of postwar Germany, leaving it perma-

---

[1] Alfred Grosser, *Germany in Our Time* (New York, 1971), p. 77.

nently truncated and divided. To minimize this possibility, the constitutional vocabulary emphasized the provisional nature of the document. Its preamble clearly stated that the Basic Law was "to give a new order to political life for a transitional period" and further stipulated that the Parliamentary Council had "also acted on behalf of those Germans to whom participation was denied," namely, those in the Soviet zone.

In addition, through the Occupation Statute, which came into effect simultaneously with the Basic Law, the three Western Allies reserved for themselves extensive rights and responsibilities. This meant, on the one hand, that the prospect of reunification could be kept alive, while on the other hand, important incentives were maintained for the new German government to continue to seek cooperation with the West in order to regain the many residual powers that the Allies retained. All this helped to broaden support for the new constitutional order.

Curiously, the legitimacy of the new regime was never substantially challenged. The Parliamentary Council had only been indirectly elected. Authority had devolved on the new German government more from above, that is, from the Allied Occupation, than from a clear electoral mandate. But this had its advantages, for it meant that many of the basic issues that defined the nature of the new system could be removed in the beginning from the potentially contentious area of electoral politics. And because an agreement with the Soviet-controlled eastern zone was regarded as an unappealing and unrealistic alternative by most West Germans in 1949, the course of cooperation with the Western Allies seemed natural and desirable, and, therefore, more legitimate. When it was challenged in subsequent years by some of the S.P.D. opposition, the German government was always able to point to its further gains in authority and jurisdiction, which the Allies swiftly increased in the period after 1949. It proved difficult and unrewarding to rouse electoral sentiment against a process that continued to restore vital powers to the West German state. The early nationalism of the Left, which sought reunification in place of the Western alliance, was thus undermined by the growing national power of the German government that it opposed. This meant that, in contrast to the situation in 1919, it was not possible to foment national aspirations in an anti-Western direction and thereby question the legitimacy of the new regime.

Other factors helped firm the legitimacy of the new state. This time there was no nostalgia for an old order. This meant that the new system, no matter what its faults, was not subject to attack from quarters, primarily on the Right, that sought the restoration of an *ancien régime*. Second, although many of the figures who shared in the launching of the Federal Republic were relatively new to political life, most of them were imbued with a vivid sense of the institutional weakness of the constitution that had been drafted thirty years before. It was as though "the specter of Weimar stood at the cradle of the Bonn Basic Law."[2] So did that of the Third

---

[2]Friedrich Karl Fromme, *Von der Weimarer Verfassung zum Bonner Grundgesetz* (Tübingen, 1960), p. 210.

Reich. Thus there was a very explicit effort to forge institutions that would be free from the failings of the Weimar system and to codify individual rights that would prevent the abuses of a dictatorial regime. There was little outright euphoria over democracy or republicanism as such, but rather a prudent awareness of their potential deficiencies. This cautiousness created a much more sober and enlightened atmosphere for the drafting of the Basic Law and served to scale down expectations, which, in turn, meant less disappointment of the sort that could be channeled into antisystem opposition.

The Basic Law

The greatest shortcoming of the Weimar institutions was their vulnerability to breakdown under conditions of stress and internal discord. Rather than building consensus and ensuring stable government, the Weimar constitution extended ostensibly democratic prerogatives that actually undermined effective parliamentary government. The Basic Law sought to remedy this defect. It strengthened the role of parliament, especially in its capacity to produce government-sustaining majorities, and it substantially enhanced the authority of the Chancellor and his cabinet. The broad powers of the presidency and of the mass plebiscites that afflicted the later years of the first republic were sharply reduced. Essentially, the practice of continuous, direct democracy, which had been enshrined in so many ways in the 1919 constitution, was now blunted. In the Federal Republic the national electorate would, barring unusual circumstances, go to the polls only once every four years and then only to elect its parliamentary representatives. All other elections, either for Chancellor or President, would be indirect. And given the considerable difficulty and, therefore, unlikelihood of midsession parliamentary dissolutions, the elimination of frequent referenda, and the absence of by-elections, the voter would not again be asked to express his direct preference within the four-year interval, except at the local and *Land* levels—and the effect of those elections on national politics would remain somewhat muted.

While the direct expression of the voter was thus reduced by the Basic Law, the individual rights of the citizen were enumerated with great care. Here the relevant historical experience was that of the Third Reich, with its oppressive flaunting of all human liberties. The first nineteen articles of the Basic Law precisely state the fundamental and inalienable rights of the German citizen. They cannot be amended. Many of them enunciate rights that were grossly abused by the Nazis. Any form of national, religious, racial, or sexual discrimination is proscribed (Articles 3 and 4). The extradition of German citizens to foreign countries is prohibited, and the withdrawal of citizenship is ruled out when such loss would result in a German's becoming stateless (Article 16). Freedom of speech, movement, assembly, and association are guaranteed, except where they might be abused "in order to attack the free democratic order." In such a case their suspension requires an affirmative ruling of the Federal Constitutional Court (Article 18).

The Judicial and Legal System

The Federal Constitutional Court is a major new innovation of the Federal Republic. It serves as the guardian of citizens' rights, as the arbiter of the federal system, and as the ultimate judge of the constitutionality of parliamentary legislation and acts of government and of the democratic legality of German political parties. No similar institution exists in Britain or in France, nor did the Weimar Republic have an equivalent body. Its Federal Constitutional Tribunal remained weak, intended primarily to adjudicate disputes among the *Länder* or between a *Land* government and the national regime. Yet it was precisely the conservative predilection and the often antidemocratic bias of the overall Weimar judiciary, most of which had been appointed before 1918, that helped to undermine the democratic ethos of its constitution. Political justice was a dangerous precedent in a country that traditionally ceded such awesome power to the rule and interpretation of law. And so, in 1949 an elaborate machinery was devised to create a supreme judicial body that would protect the individual rights and democratic processes that were codified in the Basic Law.

A special procedure of selection was devised for the Federal Constitutional Court. Article 94 of the Basic Law stipulates that half of the members shall be elected by the Bundestag and half by the Bundesrat, the two houses of the federal parliament. Subsequent legislation in 1951 provided that eligible candidates over forty years of age were to be selected from two lists, one containing all judges with at least three years of prior service who were willing to be nominated, the other including candidates who were proposed by the federal government, by a *Land* ministry of justice, or by one of the party groups in parliament, but restricted to nominees who were suitably trained in law. The eight members of each of the two chambers of the court would be elected from the two lists. Three would be elected from the first list to serve for life; five would be elected from the second to sit on the court for an eight-year term, after which they would remain eligible for reelection. Compared with the arbitrary process of selecting Supreme Court justices in the United States, this carefully balanced and complex procedure provides a more systematic and professional means of recruitment for the highest court.

The scope of the court's mandate for legal interpretation is quite broad. The court has been a very active participant in the shaping of the federal political system. It has made decisions in a great variety of fields. Some of its judgments have been narrow, legalistic, and merely technical. Others have had sweeping political impact, especially its two rulings in the 1950s banning the right-wing Socialist Reich party and the Communist party. It has often intervened in electoral matters when called upon to do so and can, through the rendering of advisory opinions, greatly influence the content and direction of intended legislation or government action. Judicial review in this form was previously unknown in Germany.

In addition, the court can act on constitutional complaints brought to it by German citizens. It is the body that would try the President of the Federal Republic if impeachment proceedings were brought against him by the parliament, and it would also sit in judgment on any member of a federal court accused of an impropriety by a two-thirds vote of the Bundestag. It is the arbiter of all disputes between the various organs of the Federal Republic, including those among the *Länder* or between a *Land* and the federal government.

With such wide powers, it is not surprising that the court has been subject to occasional criticism. For one thing, its operating procedure is governed by directives of parliament and its statutes have been often revised, which has created some confusion and an impression of frequent departure from established practice. Second, it has failed to impress itself on public awareness; few in Germany know the name of its president. Also, at times its rulings have ranged far into the political realm, which, combined with its power to render an advisory ruling, could involve the court very actively in the political process. Rather than remain a mere legal referee, the court has assumed on occasion the role of definer of the rules of the game. As such it tends to become an important factor in the calculations of the other actors—parliament, the parties, the federal executive, and the *Länder* governments—in determining the positions that they choose to take. This might provoke controversy reminiscent of the politically biased justice characteristic of the German past, which would diminish the stature of the court as the ultimate arbiter, constitutional voice and protector of individual rights. Yet despite such criticism, the court has been a successful innovation within the federal system, so much so, that Alfred Grosser has termed it "the most noteworthy of the Federal Republic's institutions,"[3] especially when contrasted with the comparable institutions in Britain and France.

The judiciary as a whole plays a much more important role in Germany than in either of these two democracies. The German legal system is more complex and elaborate, the number of judges far greater. Despite its federal structure, Germany has a single, integrated legal system. The application of law is uniform throughout the republic and does not vary among its units, in contrast to the pattern in the United States, with its parallel structures of state and federal courts.

In Germany, however, there is a dual system of a different sort separating the regular and the special courts. The regular court system for trying civil and criminal cases is organized as a single hierarchy ranging from the local and district courts at the lowest level to the Federal High Court (Bundesgerichtshof) in Karlsruhe at the apex. This high court serves as a supreme appeals court in civil and criminal cases and holds the right of original jurisdiction in matters of treason or conspiracy. Its several sections, which contain over one hundred judges, also review decisions throughout Germany in an effort to assure the uniformity of the law throughout the country, a task that the Basic Law originally intended for a special supreme federal court. Such a court has, however, never been established and the constitutional provision for it was deleted in 1968 by an amendment to the Basic Law.

---

[3]Grosser, *op. cit.*, p. 92.

The special courts are a more unusual phenomenon in Germany and derive from an old tradition. Judicial agencies to settle administrative claims against state and local governments have existed since 1872. Most of these were eliminated during the Third Reich but since 1949 have been reconstituted as administrative courts, with the Federal Administrative Court (Bundesverwaltungsgericht) established in Berlin. The special courts for finance and labor were created during the Weimar Republic. The Federal Finance Court (Bundesfinanzhof) was reestablished in 1950 in Munich, together with the Federal Labor Court (Bundesarbeitsgericht) in Kassel and the Federal Social Court (Bundessozialgericht) in Essen, the latter to deal primarily with social security and welfare disputes. Each of these heads a pyramid of lower tribunals that extends downward through the *Länder* to the district level.

This maze of courts has created a host of judges—there are more than five hundred in the city of Hamburg alone! The procedure for their selection emphasizes special training and examination and early appointment to lifetime employment in the judiciary. This practice differs sharply from that in England and the United States, where many practicing lawyers are elevated to the bench. In Germany, law students nearing the end of their studies may opt for specialized training for the judiciary, which, together with probationary experience, may require an additional seven or eight years of preparation. Movement through the courts, from the lowest level upward, is part of career advancement. There is little room, except in the case of the Federal Constitutional Court and some of the special administrative and financial courts, for those outside the judiciary to make a late entry at a senior level.

This accounts for the special perspective of the German judiciary. In view of their numbers, judges do not find themselves in a particularly exalted position. Because of their training and civil service status, many view themselves primarily as administrators of the law. Great attention is given to technical detail and less to fundamental principles of jurisprudence. In view of the enormous number of lawyers in the German civil service, it is not surprising that a kind of exacting legalism, with its conservative and noninnovative implications, has characterized a good deal of government administration and judicial review.

In Germany written law has far more weight than in Britain or France. In part this is the consequence of the Germans having experienced so many different systems over the past century. Tradition and precedent may be suitable for the British legal system, but in Germany, each political system has produced legal precedents which might be highly unacceptable today. Furthermore, in view of the extraordinary abuse of legal sanctions under the Third Reich, general proscriptions of the kind found in French law, even if only rarely applied, would not be suitable in Germany's case. These historical factors help explain why German law is so explicit. It is a system in which action tends to be judged by reference to what the lawbooks actually license or forbid, rather than in an informal context of consent and restraint.

The enumeration of individual rights is, therefore, more specific and more elaborate in the German system. The Basic Law is especially precise in defining the social rights of German citizens. In part this derives from the German concept of the social-welfare state, and many of the articles have been taken directly from the Weimar constitution. According to Article 6 of the Basic Law, "marriage and the family shall enjoy the special protection of the state." It is further stated that children born out of wedlock must be provided with equal opportunities—although this clause may have reflected the special problem of postwar fraternization between the occupying armies and the indigenous population!

Education falls under stringent state regulation, although the Basic Law ceded primary jurisdiction to the *Länder* governments in an effort to take into account the differing denominational concentrations in the various states. Through Article 9, the Social Democrats were able to secure their right to form trade unions and to bargain collectively. But they were less successful in pressing the cause of nationalization of land and industry. Article 14 safeguards the right to private property and severely circumscribes the state's power to expropriate it, reflecting the antisocialist attitudes of the American Occupation authorities and leading commercial and industrial forces within Germany after the war.

As a whole, the German bill of rights ranges further than comparable documents in France, England, or the United States. But then none of these countries had a totalitarian past. To be sure, some of the provisions of the Basic Law have been modified by amendment or by the stipulations of the German penal code. For example, although Article 4 originally banned military service, conscription was subsequently introduced by an amendment in 1956. And while Article 10 specifically provided for the secrecy of the mails and telecommunications, the Allied powers retained rights of censorship and wiretapping until 1968, when these were terminated (or at least transferred to German authorities) with the adoption of special emergency legislation.

The constitutional amendments dealing with a state of emergency *(Notstandsverfassung)*, which were passed after some bitter debate in 1968, brought to an end the process whereby the Western Allies surrendered their residual powers to the German government. The only rights and responsibilities retained by the Allies were those dealing with Berlin or "Germany as a whole," which is to say, reunification and a peace settlement. Revisions of the original Occupation Statute of 1949 had come swiftly. In March 1951, the federal government was given authority to establish its own Ministry of Foreign Affairs. The entire statute was replaced by the Convention of 1955, which came into effect with German ratification of the Paris agreements of the year before and which paved the way for German participation in N.A.T.O. The Allied High Commissions were now replaced by embassies, and relations between the Federal Republic and the former occupying powers were virtually normalized.

However, the Convention of 1955 still ceded to the three powers certain rights of control and intervention, ostensibly to safeguard their armed forces on German soil, in a situation of external threat or domestic subversion. If such an emergency were to develop, the Allies were entitled to reassume many of the sovereign rights that they had yielded to the German government. The legislation of 1968 satisfied the Allies' proviso that this right of intervention should lapse once the Federal Republic had adopted satisfactory emergency measures of its own. It became a sensitive internal issue, because many groups in Germany, especially among the trade unions and the extraparliamentary opposition (which had surfaced in the late sixties), saw such legislation as being dangerously reminiscent of previous emergency provisions in the Weimar constitution, which had been all too easily abused in times of domestic stress. The legislation provided for the suspension of certain processes and rights if one of three threatening situations were to develop. In two of these, a vote of two-thirds of the members of both houses of parliament was required before special emergency measures could be invoked. It was only in the third instance, the so-called internal state of emergency *(innere Notstand),* that no formal finding of parliament was required. Since this emergency condition itself was defined in somewhat ambiguous terms, and in view of the anxiety with which German authorities and the German people tend to respond to unrest and disorder, it was this provision and its potential implications that aroused the most intense controversy.

An important incentive for the passage of the emergency amendments was the suspension of the continued Allied right of intervention. Once this had occurred, the Western Allies retained for themselves only the special rights and responsibilities relating to Berlin and Germany as a whole, including the unification of Germany and the peace settlement, which had been included as Article 5 of the Convention of 1955. While there has been little movement toward German unification, the status of Berlin has changed substantially over time, emerging as an anomaly in the present-day German system.

Berlin

Fundamentally, the division of Berlin was effected, although not formally recognized by the Allied powers, by the end of 1948. In view of this development, the Parliamentary Council clearly intended to incorporate West Berlin as a full-fledged *Land* into the Federal Republic. Because of the complex problems of access to the city, located deep within the Soviet zone of occupation, the Western Allies were eager to give emphasis to their own continued jurisdiction over it. For this reason they took steps to discourage or prevent the unqualified inclusion of Berlin within the new federation. While Article 23 of the Basic Law listed greater Berlin as a *Land,* the Allies vetoed paragraphs 2 and 3 of the first article of the Berlin constitution of 1950, which provided that "Berlin is a Land of the Federal Republic of Germany" and that "the Basic Law and other legislation of the Federal Republic of Germany applies to Berlin."

This meant that federal law could not be applied automatically in West Berlin, but had, in effect, to be adopted by special enactment. It also meant that the direct elections to the lower house of the federal parliament, the Bundestag, could not be held in Berlin as elsewhere. Instead, the city was to be represented by a delegation indirectly elected by the Berlin assembly, as though this special process would somehow diminish the formal linkage between the city and the institutions of the Federal Republic. Furthermore, the Allies ruled initially, and again as recently as 1966, that the Berlin delegates, twenty-two of whom sit in the Bundestag and four of whom are members of the federal upper house, the Bundesrat, could not vote in plenary sessions of these chambers nor participate in the election of the Chancellor, a stricture that reduced the votes available for an S.P.D. candidate, since the Social Democrats command a substantial majority in Berlin. Also, the right of conscription, introduced in the rest of the Federal Republic in 1956, has never been extended to Berlin.

Yet in virtually all other respects West Berlin is fully integrated into the federal system. Its delegates to parliament may vote in committee sessions and do participate in the election of the officers of both chambers. Indeed, in 1957, Willy Brandt, then mayor of the city, served as president of the Bundesrat and, as such, officially stood in as head of state for the President of the Federal Republic, Theodor Heuss, while he traveled abroad. Four years later and then again in 1965 Mayor Brandt actually campaigned as the designated candidate for the office of Chancellor of his party in the federal elections for the Bundestag.

Not only has West Berlin functioned very much as a *Land* within federal politics, but it has also remained, until recently, the symbolic capital of a future reunified Germany. This image has long been actively promoted by the West German government, and it facilitated the choice of Bonn, rather than Frankfurt, as the initial capital of the Federal Republic, which placed the government center in the Catholic Rhineland rather than in an urban socialist stronghold.

Since 1954, every federal convention for the election of the President has met in Berlin, most recently in 1969, over loud Soviet protest. In October 1957, the new Bundestag formally opened its deliberations in Berlin. Each year until 1970, several of its committees met periodically in the divided city, thereby striving to keep alive the image of the traditional capital in Berlin. The Federal Administrative Court is located there, as are a number of federal agencies, especially those administering the vast social security and insurance programs. As a result, more than 20,000 federal government employees work and live in Berlin, an important economic stimulus for the city. In addition there is the huge federal subsidy that is provided by Bonn from special revenues derived from all the other *Länder* and which, by 1971, totaled over 9 billion marks.

The complexity and ambiguity of this pattern of relationships reflects the special political, economic, and geographic problems of Berlin. Although the problem of access and the right of West Berliners in Eastern Europe to be represented by consular representatives of the Federal Republic has been eased by the Berlin Agreement of 1972, the strange web of special ties and peculiar arrangements will persist for some time, pending, at a minimum, some resolution of the division of Germany. No unit within the federation poses greater problems for the central government than does Berlin. Yet precisely because of these problems, the role of the federal government is probably more substantial in Berlin than in any other

Land. Ironically, the very fact that Berlin is not fully represented in parliament, combined with its growing economic dependence on federal support, has made it more subordinate to Bonn than any of the other *Länder.*

The Federal System

If the arrangement in Berlin seems anomalous, German federalism as a whole is a rather curious and complex web of relationships. In view of German history, this should come as no surprise. Germany has always been plagued by a federal problem. The Constitution of 1871 gave expression to the centrifugal forces at the root of the newly unified state. But with the predominant position of Prussia assured, German federal experience, at least until 1933, tended to focus on the problem of Prussian supremacy. During the Weimar Republic it was generally thought that Prussia could dominate the rest of Germany. As the Prussian government invariably featured the Social Democrats as its largest party, Catholic opinion outside Prussia viewed any accretion in central authority with marked apprehension. This especially typified the attitude of Bavaria, which, throughout the Weimar years, was partially represented in Berlin by its own political party, the Bavarian People's party. But it also characterized thinking in Catholic portions of Prussia itself, especially in the Rhineland.

The actions of the Third Reich, which virtually did away with the *Länder* and invoked a monolithic centralism, only served to strengthen these Catholic sentiments, which came to play a vital role in determining the role of federalism in the Basic Law. By 1949 the problem of Prussia had been removed by the division and territorial reduction of Germany. But the prospect of a unitary state remained an anathema to the Catholics, and especially to the Bavarians, who again swiftly reestablished their own regional parties. One of these, the Christian Social Union (C.S.U.), stands today as the largest party in Bavaria, although it is directly affiliated with the C.D.U. at the national level.

The Social Democrats in 1949 very much favored a strong central government, for a number of reasons. First, given the enormous scope of the economic reconstruction deemed necessary, the S.P.D. was eager to avoid regional obstacles to national planning. Second, as a unified and centrally directed party itself, the S.P.D. did not want to cede substantial powers to local and *Land* groups. The strength of Social Democratic support was certain to be in the cities and not in the rural areas. Yet it was likely that the latter would gain a substantial grip on several *Land* regimes and thereby find effective representation of their economic interests and more conservative outlook. This is, in fact, what occurred. Besides the three "city-states" of Berlin, Bremen, and Hamburg, the S.P.D. commanded a consistent majority in only one other *Land,* Hesse, during the first fifteen years of the Federal Republic.

In the dispute over the role of federalism in 1949, the Christian Democrats obtained important support from the Allies. The French feared a recrudescence of a strong, centrally governed West German state, and the Americans believed in the virtues of their own federal government, although the pattern in Germany was to emerge quite differently. Furthermore, that each Ally was sovereign within his own zone of occupation meant that each tended to identify with the local, *Land,* and zonal German authorities who had been installed or elected during the four year Occupation period. Thus, it was to be expected that the Basic Law would recognize the fairly far-reaching powers of the *Länder,* despite the fact that they were so arbitrary in design, unequal in size, and unrepresentative of any historical experience.

Thus, the Basic Law prescribed in substantial detail the means whereby a territorial restructuring of the *Länder* might be undertaken. Indeed, Article 29 proclaimed that "the division of the federal territory into Länder is to be revised by a federal law with due regard to regional ties, historical and cultural connections, economic expediency and social structure. Such reorganization should create *Länder* which by their size and capacity are able effectively to fulfill the functions incumbent upon them." The Allies were not happy with the broad implications of this article and sought to postpone its implementation until a peace treaty, which might necessitate a restructuring of all Germany, had been signed. But they did support Article 118, which called for a reorganization of three small states in southwestern Germany whose boundaries were particularly artificial and inconvenient, largely because they had been constituted in order to allocate territory for French administration out of the American zone of occupation. In 1951 a restructuring did occur, and a single state, named Baden-Württemberg, took the place of the three that had been formed when the Federal Republic was first established.

This proved to be the only change within the original *Länder* division of the Federal Republic. The only other alteration in the structure of the Federal Republic occurred in 1956: the reabsorption of the Saar as a *Land* in the federation. Previously, the Saar had been administered by the French, originally with the aim of annexing it to France. But the French proved enlightened and fair in responding to the preference of the indigenous Saar population to amalgamate with West Germany instead. And so, this economically vital, though small, region, which had been a source of so much controversy in the twenties and thirties, was restored to German rule, thereby becoming the eleventh *Land* of the federation.

Elsewhere there was no territorial revision. Each *Land* had, by 1949, too strong a vested interest in its own survival to countenance its own demise. This meant that West Germany was saddled with a rather unbalanced federal system. The discrepancy between the large states like North Rhine-Westphalia and Bavaria and the very small *Länder,* such as Bremen or the Saarland, is considerable. To some degree, North Rhine-Westphalia has emerged as the new Prussia, with its huge population of 14 million, great industrial resources, and proximity to Bonn. Yet in contrast to Prussia, no strong state identity has developed here. The artificiality of most of the *Länder* boundaries has forestalled the growth of regional loyalties. So has social and territorial mobility and the massive influx of refugees from the East. A much smaller proportion of present-day Germans now live in the *Länder* in which they were born, so that the resulting ties between the local populations and their state governments are much weaker than they were in the past.

The fact that most of the *Länder* trace their origins to the postwar period—that is, to just before the establishment of the federation—has meant that the central government could cede far greater powers to them without risking a serious diminution of its own authority. Perhaps the sole exception to this pattern has been Bavaria, and Bavarian politics have posed special problems of their own. But even there separatist tendencies, reminiscent of the German past, are unlikely to develop. Regional particularism is intersected by too many other interests to remain a formidable factor in German political life.

In part this is the result of national party politics, which has discouraged regional priorities. The S.P.D. has traditionally favored a strengthening of central authority. As the opposition at the federal level for the first twenty years of the Federal Republic, it could thus hardly champion local and *Land* grievances. And the C.D.U. has been rather loathe to do this, too, first because it has constituted the federal government for so long and also because a movement in this direction might intensify the centrifugal forces within its own ranks. The easy movement of leading political figures from office at the national level to office at the *Land* level and vice versa has also muted conflict. All too often a state Minister-President (or governor) has moved to a cabinet position, or a leader within the federal opposition has seized an opportunity to further his career and build up a political base by shifting laterally into a key *Land* ministerial post.

This pattern suggests the curious kind of horizontal or functional federalism that exists in the Federal Republic. The states and the federation do not operate in separate spheres. Rather, their prerogatives and practices are interdependent within a single system. This pertains to both legislative and executive functions. As John Ford Golay has put it, "legislative and policy-making power has been concentrated at the center, with the officials of the state governments participating directly in the exercise of that power."[4]

How does this system operate? The Basic Law suggests a compromise between central and regional powers. It distinguishes three types of legislation: exclusive, concurrent, and residual. The federation has exclusive jurisdiction to legislate in matters involving foreign affairs, nationality, passports and immigration, currency, customs, the federal railroads and air traffic, postal and telecommunications services, the legal status of federal employees, copyright, and cooperation between the federation and the *Länder* in criminal matters. Article 71 provides that "on matters within the exclusive legislative powers of the Federation, the *Länder* have authority to legislate only if, and to the extent that, a federal law so authorizes them."

A further twenty-three subjects are enumerated in the Basic Law as falling under

---

[4]John Ford Golay, *The Founding of the Federal Republic of Germany* (Chicago, 1958), p. 28.

the concurrent jurisdiction of both the federation and the *Länder*. This includes civil and criminal law; law of association and assembly; affairs of refugees; public relief; war indemnities; economic law; labor law; and legislation affecting expropriation of property, ocean and coastal shipping, road traffic, and a number of other items. Article 72 authorizes the *Länder* to legislate on these issues "as long as, and to the extent that, the Federation does not use its legislative power." It stipulates the right of the federation to legislate if the matter cannot be dealt with effectively by the *Länder* or would thereby prejudice the interests of the *Länder* and where "the maintenance of legal or economic unity, especially the maintenance of uniformity of living conditions beyond the territory of a *Land,* necessitates it." This last proviso actually gives the federation a very broad mandate to act on matters listed under the heading of concurrent legislation.

Under the terms of Article 70 all residual powers of legislation, that is, those that are not enumerated in the Basic Law, fall under the jurisdiction of the *Länder*. The primary domain for such state action is in the realm of cultural affairs. It is in matters of education, religion, and cultural life that the *Länder* have the most substantial independent prerogatives for separate legislation. As a result, it is often the Minister of Culture at the *Land* level who is, next to the Minister-President, the most important figure in a German state government. Such certainly was the case in the long incumbency of Alois Hundhammer as Bavarian Minister of Culture. In many ways he was the dominant figure in Bavarian politics throughout the 1950s.

More recently a kind of professionalism has crept into the *Land* administrations, especially in the selection of the various Ministers of Culture. Academic figures such as Bernhard Vogel in Rheinland-Pfalz, Hans Maier in Bavaria, and Peter von Oertzen in Lower Saxony, all of whom held their positions in 1972, play a vital role in the politics of their *Länder*. This reflects the importance of the cultural prerogatives that rest with the states and explains the resistance of the *Länder* governments to any intrusion of Bonn in this sphere. It was not until 1962 that a federal Ministry of Science was organized, and recent efforts to broaden its scope have been steadfastly resisted by the states. Instead, they have sought to coordinate an effective national policy for higher education and research by establishing an interstate conference of *Land* Ministers of Culture, which meets periodically to harmonize approaches and goals. Nonetheless, federal encroachment even in this preserve has ranged fairly far, especially with the appointment in 1969 of a nonpartisan expert, Hans Leussink, as federal Minister of Science.

There has, in fact, been a continuous decline in the importance of the *Länder* in direct lawmaking. Today the division of the legislative function between Bonn and the eleven state parliaments is more symbolic than real. However, this is not seen as a problem. The shift from *Land* to central responsibility in certain areas of legislation has not been met by strong local resistance. The movement toward centralization in Germany, much like the movement toward regionalism in France, is accepted as necessary to offset the exaggerations in the political system. For most

German state officials this process has seemed an inevitable consequence of the growing number and complexity of issues, which clearly require both a nationwide approach and a national solution.

Also, the *Länder* retain and exercise very far-reaching powers in the implementation of all laws, including federal laws. By far the larger part of the German administrative bureaucracy is at the state level. So, too, are a number of important sources of tax revenue. Finally, the *Länder* have very extensive and diverse means of influencing legislation at the federal level, powers which they use with skill and effectiveness, especially in parliament.

The Federal Parliament

Like so much else in the Federal Republic, present-day parliamentary institutions have been influenced by a rather extraordinary diversity of historical experience. In part they derive from the national legislatures of prior regimes. The parliamentary provisions of the Basic Law (Articles 38–53) also draw heavily on the experiences of other democracies, especially those of the occupying powers. The resulting amalgam is a unique mixture of indigenous and foreign factors, and it includes several novel arrangements.

Certainly the strongest historical influence on these provisions of the Basic Law was the apparent failure of the parliamentary institutions of the Weimar Republic. As has been seen, the Weimar institutions were both too strong and too weak. The potency of the Reichstag in the fourteen years of the first Republic was best exemplified by its negative powers. It could, and often did, undermine a government even without formally unseating it. The Reichstag was able to prevent the emergence of a strong Chancellor and cabinet who could induce, if not compel, parliamentary support for a legislative program. At the same time parliament remained weak within the overall political system. In the presence of a stalemate, or in the absence of a clear and stable legislative majority, the President was able to assume virtually dictatorial emergency powers. Even in its best years, the Weimar Republic had been characterized by a kind of dualism between government and parliament, and at its worst, it was susceptible to arbitrary rule by the decrees of one man alone.

The Parliamentary Council sought to remedy the major faults of this system. While it strengthened the role of parliament, it also firmed the position of the Chancellor in relation to the legislature. In this it struck a much healthier balance, and on the whole its purposes have been realized. Parliament has emerged as a more reliable and effective institution than its predecessor under the Weimar constitution, but at the same time it has become more subordinate and responsive to the Chancellor and the government bureaucracy.

In part this is the result of the parliamentary provisions codified in the Basic Law, and as such it reflects the intent of those who drafted them. But the stability and compliance of parliament is also the result of several other factors. To a large degree it is made possible by changes in the party system and electoral law, which have proved far more conducive to stable politics than before. Also, the fourteen-year incumbency of Konrad Adenauer as Chancellor helped to shape an orderly and very workable pattern of relationships between the cabinet and the legislature. Especially in view of the force, skill, and prestige of Adenauer, the Chancellor's office grew substantially in power. This pattern was reinforced by the increasing complexity of many of the issues that had to be resolved and on which parliament was far less well equipped to act than the executive agencies of the government. Indeed, the decline of parliamentary prerogatives, which can be seen in most advanced political systems, has had a marked impact on the Federal Republic. However, here it has been seen as less of a problem, for two reasons. First, the interlude of sixteen years without free elections and a parliamentary system meant that the decline was less obvious and measurable. Second, the fact that the accretion of executive powers in Germany was identified with political stability and economic prosperity was sufficient to satisfy the majority of the electorate, which could still recall the chaos associated with parliamentary politics under the Weimar regime. Only more recently, as the memory of past failures receded and new problems of leadership developed, has concern begun to grow over the substantial imperfections of the current parliamentary arrangements in the Federal Republic.

The Bundesrat

The Bundesrat, or Federal Council, is the upper chamber of parliament. In its structure and role it very much resembles German institutions of the past. Since unification, the German parliament has always had a strong federal component. This was particularly the case in the Bismarckian system, in which the Bundesrat played a very vital role. The prerogatives of the second chamber, renamed the Reichsrat, were substantially reduced in 1919 in an effort to firm the hand of the national government. As a result, the upper house remained a rather ineffective institution, although the power of the larger *Land* governments, especially those of Prussia and Bavaria, was not effectively curbed.

The framers of the Basic Law sought quite deliberately to strengthen the role of the second chamber for several reasons. First, the *Länder* predated the establishment of federal institutions, and, therefore, the Parliamentary Council, which was entirely composed of *Land* representatives, had an interest in providing the state governments with a strong voice at the federal level. However, the danger that the larger *Länder* would regain predominant influence in parliament was diminished by the elimination of Prussia from Germany and by certain provisions that gave the smaller *Länder* a larger voice in the Bundesrat.

This development was encouraged by the Allied Occupation authorities, who were reluctant to cede too much power to national institutions and who, in any case, sought to counterbalance the accretion of power at the center by a strong involvement of *Länder* representatives in the decision-making process at the federal level. For this purpose the Bundesrat has served very well. It has injected a strong state voice into the federal parliament as well as increasing parliament's expertise on complex issues of legislation.

The four articles of the Basic Law dealing with the Bundesrat are brief and explicit. They provide that each of the *Länder,* now eleven in number, shall be represented by three to five members. Each *Land* is entitled to at least three delegates. Those with a population of more than 2 million have four, while the states with populations above 6 million are entitled to five representatives. This arrangement clearly favors the smaller states. Thus, for example, the three smallest *Länder,* the Saarland, Bremen, and Hamburg, have nine representatives for a combined population of 3.7 million, or one member for every 410,000 inhabitants; whereas the four largest *Länder* have only twenty representatives for a population of 44 million, or one for every 2.2 million people. By contrast, the Reichsrat in the Weimar Republic allocated seats in direct proportion to population, with one seat for every 700,000 citizens, which provided Prussia and Bavaria with great influence.

This overrepresentation of the smaller *Länder* is reinforced by the fact that each *Land* is entitled to membership on each of the committees of the Bundesrat. Therefore, since most of the legislative activity is concentrated in the committees, Bremen has as strong a voice as North Rhine-Westphalia. This originally served the purposes of the S.P.D., which was assured a majority in the three smaller *Länder* of Hamburg, Bremen, and Berlin, and thus modified its initial opposition to an arrangement that ceded such important powers to the *Länder* at the federal level.

Article 51 provides that the Bundesrat will consist of members of the *Länder* governments that appoint and recall them. Members may be alternated from session to session: but what is important is that they are usually also members of their state executive governments and often bring substantial executive expertise to the consideration of federal legislation, which the elected members of the lower house generally do not. Furthermore, the Basic Law provides that each *Land* delegation must cast its vote in the Bundesrat plenary sessions as a bloc, which means that even where a state government is a coalition of two or more parties, such partisan division is not reflected in the votes of the Bundesrat. This provision has served to cast the Bundesrat member much more into the role of a representative of his state's interests, substantially cutting across party lines.

This arrangement has given the state governments a major voice in federal legislation. It has also facilitated the shifting of senior political figures between federal and *Land* politics. For example, both Willy Brandt and Kurt Georg Kiesinger became the Chancellor candidates of their parties while heading *Land* governments and both had the opportunity to gain greater national prestige through positions taken in the Bundesrat, in which Brandt served a one-year term as President. Although this post is largely ceremonial, it does provide for substantial national exposure. But more than that, the Bundesrat, through its composition, requires the *Länder* governments to take a stand on a great variety of national issues and thus reduces the provincialism that would otherwise characterize

Land politics. It has also made it even more attractive for national political leaders to move to state office without relinquishing a voice in national legislation.

One difficulty with this arrangement is that the composition of the upper house
is very much affected by the outcome of the *Land* elections, which occur periodically during the usual four-year term of office of the lower house. Indeed, the
majority in the upper house may shift several times within this period, which can
pose some problems for a Chancellor and his cabinet. The impact of state elections
at the federal level has meant that the state campaigns are waged much more on
national issues and that the election results are seen as a kind of approval or
rejection of the national government. Such a continuous process of elections can
prove somewhat destabilizing for the political system in the long run and has been
the subject of substantial critical debate in the Federal Republic.

It is really more the frequent referenda implied by this procedure than the
possible loss of a supporting majority in the upper house that is most complicating
for the national government. The loss of a majority in the Bundesrat need not be
crippling. The upper house has a limited mandate on legislation. Its approval is
required only on those issues on which the states possess the concurrent right of
legislation. Here its veto can be absolute. But on all other issues the Bundesrat
stands possessed of only a suspensive veto. This means that its negative vote can
be overridden by the lower house. If the Bundesrat rejects legislation by a majority,
a simple majority of the lower chamber can override. If the rejection is by two-
thirds—which would be a very rare instance—a two-thirds vote in favor is required
in the Bundestag. In fact, the Brandt government that came into office in 1969 had
to contend with a one-vote minority in the Bundesrat for an extended period
without risking the defeat of important legislation in the upper house. This is
because most points of conflict between the two chambers of parliament are
resolved in a standing committee of conciliation comprising eleven members from
each house.

The great asset of the Bundesrat is the expertise that it brings to bear on legislation. Most of its members are senior civil servants from the *Länder* and, as such,
they are well equipped to scrutinize legislation introduced by the federal bureaucracy. Other persons commissioned by the *Länder* may also participate in the
committee sessions of the Bundesrat, which have the power to secure the participation of members of the federal government. It is here that legislation is usually
first considered and it is in the committees of the Bundesrat that the government
bureaucracy often encounters its most substantial examination and challenge,
especially where planned legislation affects the interests of the states.

The expertise of its members compensates for the lack of prestige that attaches
to service in the Bundesrat. There is no German equivalent to an English lord or
an American, or even a French, senator. The sole exception is the office of President of the chamber, to which candidates are elected for a one-year term from
among the Minister-Presidents of the eleven *Länder*. The mayor of West Berlin is
eligible for this post, even though the Bundesrat delegation from that city has a
limited mandate without the right to vote on certain issues in plenary session.

The Bundesrat rarely introduces legislation itself, but it usually considers federal drafts before they are passed on to the lower house. This occurs during a three-week period in which the Bundesrat members consult their *Land* governments before deliberating in committee on the legislation. Their views, especially on matters of important state interest, tend to have great influence on the lower house, where the real political power lies. Armed with the substantial expertise of its members and its equal representation in the standing conciliation committee, the Bundesrat can exercise a very weighty voice on federal legislation. In most instances in which the federal government might contemplate the suspension of constitutional rights and the declaration of a state of national emergency, it could only do so with the approval of the Bundesrat, that is to say, with the agreement of a majority of the *Land* governments. Federalism in Germany thus plays a very substantial role in the parliamentary system, primarily, but not exclusively, through the upper house.

The Bundestag

It was in the drafting of the provisions pertaining to the lower house, renamed the Bundestag, that the framers of the Basic Law gave particular attention to the experience of the Weimar Republic. The negative powers of the Reichstag had been altogether too great and far too often had succeeded in nullifying the program of Weimar Chancellors and their cabinets. Although the Reichstag could prevent action, its position in the political system was not strong because under Article 48 recourse could so easily be had to extraparliamentary rule by decree reinforced by national plebiscites.

The Parliamentary Council sought to remedy these defects. First of all, it sought to increase the constructive powers of the lower house. This was done in a number of ways. The responsibility of the chamber in electing the Chancellor was substantially augmented, and the powers of the federal President in proposing candidates very much circumscribed. While the President still retains the authority to propose an initial nominee to the house, if such a candidate fails to receive a majority the Bundestag can, under the terms of Article 63, elect a Chancellor of its own choosing within fourteen days of the first ballot. If the candidate receiving the largest number of votes does not obtain a majority, the President has the option of either appointing him Chancellor or dissolving the chamber.

These provisions very much reduce the role and influence of the President in the appointment of the Chancellor. In fact, the President is not likely to propose to the Bundestag a candidate who cannot secure a majority if there is another figure who will clearly obtain more than half of the votes in the chamber. The power to select a Chancellor really rests with the Bundestag. But it has been substantially circumscribed by the party and election system. Actually, since 1949 it has been the parties that nominate their candidates and the voters who determine the outcome of the election, although there is some scope for subsequent negotiation among the various party leaders in those situations where federal elections fail to provide any one party with a majority of the seats in the Bundestag. In these instances the President has never played a critical role. When in 1961 President Lübke sought to intervene on behalf of a grand coalition, his efforts were seen as obstructive and proved rather counterproductive.

The Chancellor need not be a member of the Bundestag. Indeed, Kurt Georg Kiesinger was not a member of the house at the time of his election. This was often the case in the Weimar Republic as well. However, since 1949 a much larger percentage of the cabinet has been composed of members of the lower house, which reflects the strength of the Bundestag in the system. The negotiations for selecting the cabinet often take many weeks and can prove quite complicated. Only once, in 1957, did one party command a majority in the chamber, which means that coalition government has been an almost constant feature of the Federal Republic. There have been a few cabinet members from outside parliament, such as Gustav Heinemann, Kai Uwe von Hassel, Horst Ehmke and Hans Leussink, but this has been the case much less frequently than in the Weimar Republic. The cabinet must maintain close rapport with its parliamentary majority, and this can most effectively be achieved by rewarding parliamentary leaders with ministerial posts.

It is difficult to dissolve the Bundestag. As mentioned, one instance would be if the Bundestag failed to provide a majority for the election of a Chancellor, but this is a fairly unlikely contingency. Article 68 provides that if a motion of the Chancellor for a vote of confidence is not assented to by a majority of the Bundestag, the President can, upon the proposal of the Chancellor, dissolve the chamber within twenty-one days. However, the right to dissolve lapses as soon as the Bundestag elects another Chancellor by a majority vote; therefore, this is not a very reliable weapon for the Chancellor except with the prior agreement of the opposition, since he may find himself displaced rather than able to compel a dissolution and new elections.

These provisions have all served to enhance the role of the Bundestag and to create greater stability for government in the Federal Republic. There is no escape to presidential emergency government. Although the Chancellor can wield extraordinary powers in a state of emergency, there are legal safeguards that make it unlikely that such a state would be declared if normal parliamentary procedure produced a stalemate—as so often happened under Weimar. While all of this has served to stabilize the role of parliament, a number of measures were drafted by the Parliamentary Council to firm the position of the Chancellor as against that of the Bundestag.

By far the most important of these is provided by Article 67, which states that the Bundestag can declare its lack of confidence in the Chancellor only by electing a successor by a majority and then requesting the President to dismiss the incumbent. Under these circumstances the President must comply with this request. In the Weimar Republic it was always a great deal easier to establish a negative majority than a constructive one. But in the Federal Republic, given the strength of the parliamentary parties, it does not seem plausible that this procedure would be invoked to remove a Chancellor. In any case, if it were, there would be no crippling interregnum, but rather a new candidate ready to replace the incumbent. Such a situation would be likely to develop only in the face of a substantial defection of members from one party or a realignment of coalitions within parliament.

There are a number of additional factors that have served to limit the powers of the Bundestag vis-à-vis the Chancellor and his cabinet. First, the parliamentary parties represented in the government have little incentive to cause difficulties for their own cabinet. Party voting in the Bundestag has been highly disciplined. Even the Brandt government, with a bare majority of six, did not sustain one defeat in the Bundestag during its first two years, and this was achieved without recourse to a single vote of confidence and in the face of several defeats in state elections during that period.

Second, the increasing complexity of the issues on which votes are taken has served to limit the powers of the Bundestag. Most of its members are no match for the bureaucracy, which can deliver expert advice to its parliamentary parties. This places the opposition at a substantial disadvantage, especially as most members of the Bundestag have very limited staffs. This has also meant that a great deal of the real work of the Bundestag occurs in committees, where legislation can be amended in time if it appears to be encountering substantial resistance.

Indeed, the average member of the Bundestag is not a very powerful figure. He is poorly compensated, which reflects a German tradition opposing paid professionalism in parliament. Staff assistance is not adequate for the legislative responsibilities that confront members of parliament. This has meant that most members pursue a second career, often merely to secure a sufficient income. It has also made service in parliament attractive for civil servants. Although civil servants must take leave from their bureaucratic posts to enter parliament, they receive the equivalent of their pensions as a súpplementary salary while they serve, which eases the economic strain. Another solution is to take a second salary for working for an interest group: a union, business, or trade association. This has enabled German interest groups to play a very direct role in influencing legislation.

These factors have contributed to making the position of backbencher in the Bundestag less than attractive. They have led to a high level of absenteeism and have created a two-tiered system in the Bundestag. In the outer circle are the many relatively uninfluential, often poorly informed, and frequently absent members, whose primary involvement tends to be on a few select issues of direct concern to some professional or interest group. Real power is deferred by this group to an inner circle constituting the party parliamentary leadership, which wields a great deal of power. Together with the officers of the Bundestag and its Council of Elders, the latter group constitutes a highly effective elite that runs the Bundestag and largely determines the outcome of legislation.

The party professionals at the helm are clearly favored in this system, and they have little interest in its reform. It is they who control committee appointments, determine the agenda of the house, and decide on who within the party delegation may speak in plenary debates. In the case of the party or parties supporting the government, its parliamentary leaders play an important role in shaping the legislation that the cabinet presents to parliament.

The parliamentary front benches include most of the opposition leaders who would constitute a cabinet should their party come into office. However, unlike the British system, here there is no shadow cabinet among the opposition ranks, although in 1972 the C.D.U. did attempt to name one. While there are often specific spokesmen on certain issues, the allocation of prospective cabinet posts cannot be made before an election, since it may depend on negotiations with a coalition party that can be conducted only once the election results are known. It would also be difficult to name a shadow cabinet composed only of Bundestag members, since the recruitment of a cabinet may include party figures from outside parliament. In the case of the S.P.D., its national leader in opposition for many years, Willy Brandt, was not a member of the Bundestag. Given the federal structure of government, a party may wish to reach out to one or several of the *Länder* regimes in allocating cabinet posts.

It has proven difficult under these circumstances for an outsider or a young recruit to rise rapidly in parliament. There have been some exceptions, such as Heinrich Köppler, Gerhard Jahn, and Katharine Focke, who moved swiftly through the Bundestag to important government positions. But on the whole, the parliamentary party leadership has not been easy to penetrate.

This is often seen as a defect of the Bundestag. It appears private and unspontaneous in its deliberations, very much in the grip of a small, self-recruiting hierarchy of party leaders. In the absence of direct primaries, the party parliamentary leadership cannot easily be challenged from outside, except by the interest groups, whose power within this system, and especially within the parties, is considerable. Indeed, the Bundestag often behaves in a manner that suggests that it sees these groups as its chief clients and constituents, especially in the rather hidden committee deliberations in which the content of most legislation is determined. Throughout, "the sense of public participation in politics through parliament is not well developed."[5]

Indeed, a kind of public apathy has characterized popular attitudes toward politics and, in particular, toward parliament, in the Federal Republic. There has been poor communication between parliament and the people. In part this is a consequence of the decline of plenary debates and an increase in the technical complexity of most legislation. The Bundestag has never achieved the kind of educative function of the British House of Commons or the U.S. Senate.

But this is also caused by the reluctance of the German public to become involved in politics, which is partially explained by the historical experience of the years before 1945. Several studies have shown that the willingness to become active in community affairs is much lower in the Federal Republic than in either

---

[5]Gerhard Loewenberg, *Parliament in the German Political System* (Ithaca, 1966), p. 434.

Britain or the United States. In Germany, the public has repeatedly expressed much more confidence in administrators than in legislators. German political culture has cast the parliamentarian into the role of a *Staatsdiener,* or "servant of the state." There is an inherent mistrust of opposition where it might threaten to destabilize politics or undermine a regime. Orderly procedure is greatly preferred in this system to ideological controversy.

All this has served to diminish the role of opposition and to foster a seeming consensus and identity of interest among the several competing parliamentary parties. It helps to explain the absence of extremist or ideological parties in parliament, and recently it has given rise to a marginal movement to create a voice of opposition altogether outside of parliament, the so-called Ausser-parlamentarische Opposition (A.P.O.). But within the Bundestag the consequence has been a kind of bureaucratization. Those who know how to operate through the system have succeeded, whereas those who have sought to challenge it have tended to find themselves thwarted. The expert and the party professional have done well, but the orator or critic or member who disregards the established leadership has gotten nowhere. Under these conditions parliament has functioned smoothly but at a substantial cost.

The grip of the party leadership within the Bundestag is reinforced by party control of the electoral process. Only those parties which secure three seats in direct election or 5 percent of the total vote may be represented in the Bundestag. This rule has served to eliminate a great number of the smaller parties that so plagued the Weimar Republic. But it means that an independent candidate not supported by one of the three major parties cannot succeed. Thus, anyone aspiring to a parliamentary career is ineluctably drawn into one of the three parties, and one of these, the F.D.P., is in constant danger of falling below the 5 percent voter-support level.

The pivotal control of the nominating procedure by the central party hierarchy makes penetration from without very difficult indeed. Only one-half of the seats in the Bundestag are contested as single-member constituencies. The other half are allocated on the basis of proportional representation to the parties that secure more than 5 percent of the vote, taking into account any disparities that may occur in the direct-constituency elections. Each voter casts two ballots. He votes once for the candidate of his choice in his constituency (there are 248 contituencies throughout the Federal Republic). He also casts a second ballot for the party of his choice, on the basis of a list ranking the nominees of the parties within his *Land.* The composition of the *Land* list is critical, for high placement on it is the equivalent of assured victory. Yet the sequence of names on the *Land* list is not decided by means of a popular primary but is controlled by the party leadership. This is exactly as in the Weimar Republic, except that at that time there were no direct constituencies at all.

This procedure means that in Germany, in contrast to the situation in Britain, the national party leadership can allocate a safe seat to any candidate of its choosing.

Indeed, the *Land* lists need not be headed by prominent politicians of that particular state, although as a rule they are. For example, in the 1969 Bundestag elections the S.P.D. *Land* list for North Rhine-Westphalia was headed by Willy Brandt, the former mayor of Berlin, and by Karl Schiller of Hamburg, because they were deemed the two best vote-getters in the party and, therefore, particularly valuable at the top of a slate from the most populous of the German *Länder*.

Turnover in the Bundestag has been fairly low and is carefully controlled. Less than one-quarter of its membership is new every four years. But even this figure is somewhat deceptive, for it does not suggest the high continuity of party leadership within the house. Furthermore, most of those who enter for the first time are substantially in debt to the party leaders or to some interest group, although recently there has been more emphasis on ceding to the constituencies a larger voice in the designation of their candidates and on broadening democratic procedures in selecting nominees.

The average age of a Bundestag member is about fifty, roughly the same as that of a member of Congress in the United States but higher than the average in the French and Italian parliaments. There is a relatively high representation of women —who make up 7 percent of the membership—despite a comparatively low level of participation in politics among German women. Most often they enter through the *Land* lists, which also tend to reflect considerations of regional and denominational balance. What is most unusual in the composition of the Bundestag is the substantial representation of civil servants, who constitute about one-tenth of the membership.

The positions of real power within the Bundestag are narrowly held. They include the party caucus leaders; the Präsidium and the Council of Elders of the chamber; and the committee chairmen, some thirty in number. Altogether they comprise a small elite that controls legislation, rules on procedure, and determines advancement within the house. The impression is one of deliberate and careful control. Membership within this elite is usually decided by the party leadership, and once appointed, incumbents tend to remain in their positions for relatively long periods. Eugen Gerstenmaier, for example, served as President of the Bundestag for almost fifteen years. It would be difficult to point to another European parliamentary system with such extended tenures in office.

The Council of Elders (Ältestenrat) serves as a kind of steering committee for the house. It determines the agenda for each week and distributes the committee assignments, but with the prior agreement of the party leaders. Committee assignment is a crucial power because of the vital role exercised by the committees. Indeed, the committee system has often been cited as one of the most successful features of the German parliamentary tradition. It even functioned quite well during the Weimar Republic, when everything else in parliament seemed to be faltering.

A peculiar feature of the present system is that committee chairmanships are assigned on the basis of party representation in the Bundestag as a whole. This means that even minority opposition parties, provided they have no less than fifteen members, are eligible to head one or several of these committees. Even during the period of an absolute majority of the C.D.U./C.S.U., in the legislative period between 1957 and 1961, the opposition S.P.D. controlled nine committee chairmanships.

Because the committees are among the few areas of the Bundestag where staffing is adequate, this control of committee chairmanships is especially crucial. For the opposition lacks access to the ample expertise possessed by the government bureaucracy and available to its parties. Another source of expert information in the committees are the interest-group representatives. This representation is particularly high on the committees that specialize in areas of interest to particular groups. Thus, while only 10 percent of the membership of the Bundestag elected in 1957 represented farming, more than three-fifths of the members of the agriculture committee had farm backgrounds.

Committee sessions can be open or secret. Usually, members of the government bureaucracy participate in them. From time to time a committee will choose to hold open hearings on pending legislation, but these are not frequent in Germany. Committees of investigation, which are provided for in the Basic Law, are also relatively rare. Indeed, the entire control function of parliament, best evidenced by the formal interpellations of cabinet ministers during plenary sessions, has not posed a serious challenge to the government's prerogatives.

In fact, the involvement of the executive in parliament is very extensive. Usually assured of majority support, capitalizing on its superior command of information and expertise, and having free access to the committees and the Council of Elders, the government is in a far stronger position to exert its will than is the opposition. Most legislation is introduced by the government, not by members of parliament. A great deal of it is enacted into law. Since 1949, almost 90 percent of all the legislation introduced by the government has been passed by parliament, whereas less than one-third of those bills proposed by members have made their way into law.

Usually, legislation is first presented to the Bundesrat, after which it is considered in either two or three readings, with intermediate deliberation in committee by the lower house. The most frequent parliamentary intervention is in the area of finance. The German parliament has considerably greater control over spending and the budget than do the British or the French legislatures, though less than does the United States Congress.

On the whole, there are few surprises and rarely any reverses for a government in parliament. In the absence of free votes on important legislation and given the grip of the party leadership, the outcome of most votes can be safely forecast. Indeed, during its first two years, the S.P.D./F.D.P. coalition established in 1969, with a majority that shrank to only six, did not lose a single major vote. This is strong evidence of the power of the government vis-à-vis parliament in the German system. It is a situation in which legislative opposition has consistently become weaker and less effective. Given a strong and stable party system, the Chancellor and his cabinet have been the main beneficiaries of this development. It is really more the contending pressures within their own party or coalition than the formal opposition in parliament that poses constraints that may force the hand of a Chancellor or his cabinet colleagues. The success or failure of a government depends to a great degree on the capacity of its leaders to prevail within their own camp. It was primarily in instances where the leaders failed to do so that a government was enfeebled and began to falter. Thus in the German system it is not so much parliamentary as intraparty dissidence that will most often set the real limits on legislation and policy. Keeping a cabinet or a coalition satisfied may prove much more difficult than securing a Bundestag mandate for government legislation.

The Chancellor and the Cabinet

Without question the chancellorship has emerged as a very powerful position in the Federal Republic. This is largely a realization of the intent of the Parliamentary Council. The Basic Law is relatively brief in the eight articles (62 through 69) that deal with this office, but they confer great powers upon the Chancellor. Once a Chancellor is elected by the Bundestag, it is exceedingly difficult for that body to remove him. According to the Basic Law the Chancellor's removal by the lower house can occur in only one of two ways. First, there is the possibility of a so-called constructive vote of nonconfidence, as provided by Article 67. This stipulates that the Bundestag must first elect an alternative candidate by a majority vote before it can displace an incumbent Chancellor.

This provision was designed to preclude the kind of negative majorities that were so common in the Weimar Reichstag. It would serve as an important safeguard if there were many small parties and few large ones in the Bundestag, because it would force the parties to agree on a new candidate prior to casting their negative vote. In the Federal Republic, given the consolidation of the party system, this provision is likely to be invoked only if there is a realignment within a governing coalition or substantial defections from the party or parties supporting a government in the Bundestag. It has never been used at the federal level, although it was applied twice in North Rhine-Westphalia, whose constitution contains a similar article.

The other provision for the removal of a Chancellor, which is included in Article 68, applies only after the Chancellor has called for and lost a vote of confidence. Should the Bundestag then elect a new candidate by a majority vote, the Chancellor is replaced. However, if the Bundestag cannot do this—and, again, the party system makes it unlikely—the Chancellor may ask the President to dissolve the chamber and call for new elections. This article is a very balanced instrument because it places certain constraints on both the Chancellor and the Bundestag.

While these provisions insulate the Chancellor from an easy erosion of his parliamentary majority, the strength of his position depends to a large degree on his control and influence within his own party or coalition. In each of the two cases when a Chancellor resigned while in office, it was due to internal party pressures.

Konrad Adenauer made way for Ludwig Erhard in 1963 largely at the behest of his own party, which, for various reasons, was eager to induce the retirement of a figure who had stood at the helm for fourteen years. When Erhard then faltered three years later, it was the defection of the Free Democrats from the governing coalition and the substantial criticism from within the ranks of his own C.D.U. that left the Chancellor little choice but to resign.

Both of these examples show how much it is party control and personal qualifications of leadership that determine the strength and effectiveness of a Chancellor. Where an incumbent has a firm grip on his party, a strong working agreement with its coalition partners, and the capacity for effective leadership, the Chancellor's office provides wide-ranging powers and prerogatives. These have grown very considerably over time for a number of reasons.

First, there is the fact that the first Chancellor of the Federal Republic, Konrad Adenauer, was a particularly forceful figure who remained in office for fourteen years, during which time his party, the C.D.U./C.S.U., won four successive elections. Second, Adenauer knew well how to use foreign policy to strengthen his position, and he successfully wrested important concessions from the Allies, which lent greater prestige and popularity to his position. In a country whose sovereignty was once so restricted, that remains divided, and that stands as a point of confrontation between East and West in Europe, it is not surprising that issues of foreign and national policy play an important role in shaping public support for a Chancellor.

Third, the power of the Chancellor within the cabinet is strongly defined in Germany. Federal ministers are appointed and dismissed by the President at the request of the Chancellor, and Article 65 states that the Chancellor determines, and assumes responsibility for, general policy. While individual cabinet ministers can exert powerful influence on policy, it is the Chancellor who retains ultimate control, provided his position within his party and his popularity among the electorate remains strong. The position of Vice-Chancellor, often allocated to the leader of the smaller party joining a coalition, carries some prestige but relatively little formal power. Certain of the traditional ministries, especially those dealing with foreign affairs, defense, the interior, economics, and finance, carry special weight. Overall, the German cabinet system is less collegial than Britain's, although again much depends on the respective power of the Chancellor and his ministers within their parties. The Federal Republic has had the greatest continuity and stability of cabinet membership of any European parliamentary system. Since 1949 there have only been eighty-two figures who have served in the cabinet, and in some cases members have remained in one office for more than a decade.

Within the cabinet the role of the Chancellor has grown measurably. It very much suited Adenauer's personality and style to retain as much power for his own office within the cabinet as possible. The key chancellery position of state secretary is one of the most powerful in Germany. Under Chancellor Brandt the post was upgraded to ministerial rank, and Horst Ehmke, a leading political figure within the S.P.D. who had been a member of the previous cabinet, was placed in this post. Under his direction, the Bundeskanzleramt has made a more systematic effort to plan policy and coordinate efforts among the ministries, a task which seems more urgent in view of the growing complexity of government today.

A second innovation, introduced in the late sixties and adapted in part from British practice, has been the appointment of parliamentary state secretaries, who play the role of junior ministers and maintain close liaison with the Bundestag. But the pivotal position within the ministries often is still that of the state secretaries, who stand at the head of the federal bureaucracy. It is they who, to a large degree, command the fundamental loyalty and respect of the vast ministerial bureaucracy. Often they, too, are members of the major political parties, although it is generally assumed, though not always the case, that the civil service will act in a nonpartisan manner. But the distinction between the senior political and purely administrative bureaucracy is somewhat blurred in Germany, certainly more so than in Britain.

This has posed some serious problems for the S.P.D., which first entered a cabinet in 1966 and did not head one until three years later. It found that twenty years of C.D.U. domination of government had affected the political outlook and party preferences of some of the senior administrative personnel. This was particularly important because the German minister is more closely surrounded by bureaucrats than are ministers in Britain or France. Often, the prestige of a senior civil servant may exceed that of his minister. Furthermore, there is a general reverence for administration and mistrust of partisan criteria for selecting or promoting administrative personnel. Thus, the S.P.D. was hard put to remove or reassign many civil servants. The decision of the new F.D.P. foreign minister Walter Scheel to retire twenty-six senior diplomats was attacked as unwarranted political patronage by the C.D.U. opposition. The removal of twelve of the state secretaries who had served C.D.U. ministers raised a shrill political outcry. Yet it would seem that these moves were unavoidable if the new cabinet was to have fundamental confidence in its bureaucratic and diplomatic personnel.

The power of the German civil service is often criticized as a weakness of the government system. Its prestige derives from a period that predates the unification of Germany. In many respects it has more continuity with the past than any other institution in the land. Although its administrative competence is high, it has remained somewhat castelike, with access to its higher echelons very restricted. Recruitment for the top ranks has been closely geared to the educational system, which itself has retained certain class features. The higher service has a vast preponderance of law graduates, and entry is dependent on passing examinations that generally require substantial legal expertise.

Administrative service in the Federal Republic still offers considerable status and security. The official has assured tenure until he reaches retirement age and very generous pension rights. The bureaucracy itself remains subdivided into several tiers, and membership in its highest rank brings special prerogatives and exclusive access to the key positions in government. All this has provided the senior bureaucrat with a special sense of esprit de corps, of membership in a privileged group. It has provided the government with a powerful and effective administrative machine, but one whose ingrained preference is to keep things as they are and that often remains resistant to extensive change, especially of the sort that seems to derive from a partisan motivation.

This can, of course, pose problems for a Chancellor and his government. It set a particular challenge for the new regime, an S.P.D./F.D.P. coalition, that came into office in 1969. For the first time in forty years, a Social Democrat, Willy Brandt, assumed the chancellorship. His government had to contend with some popular mistrust of its programmatic intentions and with some administrative resistance. Yet its capacity to govern was facilitated by several factors. First, it had already shared in the cabinet under Chancellor Kiesinger. It was also able to draw upon some administrative personnel from those *Länder* regimes that had been under its control. This aspect of the federal system proved a real asset for the opposition when it came into power. The Chancellor himself had gained substantial government experience from his many years as mayor of West Berlin.

The key factor in government remains the Chancellor himself. Increasingly, distinctions among the parties have become muted. As ideology has faded and as telecommunications have improved, the image projected by the contender for the chancellorship has become a powerful factor. For a popular Chancellor, the frequency of state elections may be a useful means of demonstrating his strength to party and cabinet colleagues. It is not unusual for a Chancellor to have much wider support than his party has. This is a kind of personalization of politics, which is matched by an overall decline in party identification. It is also a manifestation of a historical pattern in German politics. Not only has there been a "cult of the strong man" in politics, but those periods which are generally regarded by the electorate as having been most successful are linked with the rule of a forceful leader. The nadir always seemed to be associated with weak leadership. This propensity of the German electorate has created greater opportunities for an assertive and vigorous Chancellor. In the cases of Adenauer and Brandt, it was a major asset. For Ludwig Erhard, who was unable to personify strength while Chancellor, it posed a fatal handicap.

Is this proclivity toward strong, one-man rule a healthy phenomenon? Given the dangerous excesses of the past, might it again prove corrosive of democratic politics? Here the institutional safeguards designed for the Federal Republic should be sufficient to contain the problem. To be sure, under Adenauer's tutelage, the powers of the Chancellor created some imbalance in the system. But this was checked by other forces that set limits on the extent of one-man rule. The federal system, the provision for judicial review, the capacity of the opposition to exercise some control in parliament, the power of interest groups identified with each of the two major parties, and the frequency of elections all pose substantial curbs on government prerogatives. It is not so much the potential abuse of power by the

Chancellor as the incapacity of the system to operate well without a strong leader that remains a source of concern. The demise of Erhard in 1966 led directly to the establishment of a grand coalition of the two major parties, leaving the opposition inadequately represented by the Free Democrats, who represented less than 10 percent of the Bundestag.

More than the rise of the strong man, it is the decline of the opposition that is a serious problem in Germany today. This is not just a matter of the growing similarity of the major parties and the receding role of parliament. A far deeper cause is the decrease of viable alternatives as industrial societies grow more complex. The dissatisfaction of the voter with government has not diminished, but his capacity to discern meaningful alternate courses has decreased. Affluence, stability, and the growing complexity of controlling the conditions of modern life have reduced the options for consensus-seeking mass parties. Under these circumstances, opposition has lost much of its ideological sting. While controversy has not been muted, the personification of politics remains one of the few methods available for generating broad-based support in the political arena. In Germany this has worked for the government, not only because of the great visibility of the Chancellor, but also because of the preference for order and respect for office that remain an important heritage of the past. All this has served to create a system that is perhaps best described as a "Chancellor democracy."

The President

The President's office has been very much reduced in power since the Weimar Republic. The Parliamentary Council felt that presidential politics under Weimar had served to weaken the Chancellor and had led to an easy abuse of the parliamentary system through recourse to emergency rule under Article 48 of the Weimar constitution. The drafters of the Basic Law also sought to place the symbol of the state above partisan politics, which meant removing the presidency from any important involvement in the poltical process.

As a result, the President has emerged as a relatively weak and rather symbolic figurehead, but as such, he has served well in the Federal Republic. While he is the head of state, his responsibilities are largely ceremonial, which relieves the Chancellor of a number of time-consuming formalities. The President has extensive powers to appoint and dismiss officials, including the Chancellor, but, in fact, these are dependent on decisions taken elsewhere. While he designates ambassadors, some federal judges, and senior civil servants, he does so at the behest of the Chancellor and the cabinet. Occasionally, he may forestall an appointment or promote his own candidate, but such instances are relatively rare. His cooperation, however, would be important if a Chancellor sought a dissolution of the Bundestag under Article 68.

The President is elected for a five-year term by a special federal convention composed of the members of the Bundestag and an equal number of delegates from the various *Land* parliaments. He may serve for only two successive terms and must be elected by a secret vote requiring a majority on the first two ballots and a plurality thereafter. Any German citizen over the age of forty who is entitled to vote in the Bundestag elections is eligible to stand as a candidate for the presidency, but the choice of nominees is predetermined by the parties represented in the federal convention.

The President can serve as a symbolic moral force in the German political system if his qualifications lend themselves to such a role. Certainly in the case of the first incumbent, the distinguished academician and statesman Theodor Heuss, the President served an important educative function. But one of the problems of the position has been the difficulty of recruiting prestigious candidates in view of the weakness of the President's prerogatives.

While the President formally designates the Chancellor, the Bundestag can override his choice. Thus invariably his proposal reflects the preference of the lower house, and his power is, therefore, very restricted. When in 1961 President Lübke sought to convey his preference for a grand coalition to the party leaders before the election, he was chided for intruding in the political process. Indeed, his contact with the Chancellor and cabinet, which was dominated by his own party, remained formal and distant. When in 1969 the election of the new President threatened to coincide with the Bundestag elections, Lübke was willing to resign before the end of his term so that the election of a successor could be kept out of the oncoming Bundestag election campaign.

This led to the election as President of a Social Democrat and former member of the C.D.U., Gustav Heinemann, by a narrow majority of four votes. Heinemann was supported by the F.D.P., which thereby signaled its preference for joining with the Social Democrats to form a government should the two together secure sufficient votes in the forthcoming Bundestag election. F.D.P. backing of the Social Democratic candidate was a substantially political act that foreclosed some of the freedom of action of the F.D.P. in the electoral campaign.

The weakness of the presidency is very much influenced by history. It is an important factor in explaining the strength of the Chancellor and has contributed to the smooth functioning of the political system. The memory of the interference by Kaiser Wilhelm and President Hindenburg was too vivid to permit the ceding of any substantial powers to this post. Yet institutionally it remains useful to differentiate the head of state from the head of government. And while the division of functions strongly favors the latter, the distinction between the two positions has served a constructive purpose in the Federal Republic.

Indeed, it may be said that the political institutions designed for the new state in 1949 were well conceived. For the first time Germany stood possessed of a constitution that preserved individual rights, secured democratic processes, and provided for effective governance. In a country that gives such weight to the written law and attaches such importance to order, the success of the institutional

provisions laid down in 1949 and amended since then has been of critical importance. While these institutions have revealed defects and substantial new problems
have developed, the formal pattern of government has proved very workable and
reasonably balanced. Yet this explains only one part of politics in the Federal
Republic. To a large degree the real determinants of the political system rest with
the parties and the informal pattern of interests that really control the institutions
of government.

Five

The Party System

To gain an adequate understanding of the political system of the Federal Republic, it is essential to give close attention to important changes that have occurred since 1945 in the pattern of interests. It is always difficult when judging a parliamentary democracy, especially one as recent in origin as the Federal Republic, to know how much weight to assign to its political institutions and how much to the underlying social and economic forces. In a way the explanation always tends to be somewhat circular and interdependent. While well-designed institutions can set the framework for the effective articulation and integration of political demands, these demands remain very much the expression of basic social and economic factors. Between these two strata, the institutional framework and the socioeconomic base, rest the political parties and groups, which in a parliamentary democracy largely determine whether the government can function effectively.

Changes in these parties and groups are particularly important in explaining the apparent success of the Federal Republic as a political system. Here the heritage from the past was especially inauspicious. The party system before World War I was relatively weak. During the war it was largely ineffective, and then, during the Weimar Republic, it proved badly flawed and was an important contributing factor in the chronic instability of its regimes. As we have seen, the Weimar parties were ideological, divisive, and rent with factionalism. The Catholics, the industrialists, and the Bavarians sought to organize their own interest groups. The Left was torn by dissidence, the Right infused with animosity toward the parliamentary republic.

These features were reinforced by an electoral system that gave no incentive to consensus politics or to the emergence of strong individual leaders within the parties. Instead, it firmed the grip of the central party bureaucrats and reduced that of the parliamentary leadership. Narrow interests, reflecting a variety of rending social cleavages, prevailed, and it became increasingly difficult to integrate or harmonize such interests on a basis broad enough to command majority support. Thus the power represented by the parties could not be converted into a viable coalition government. The resulting pattern of instability, dissension, and turmoil undermined confidence in the party system, which seemed ever more impotent and nihilistic. *Parteipolitik* soon became a disreputable but ingrained feature of what was widely seen as a defective political system.

This helped create the conditions for an even more pernicious party system, the National Socialistic dictatorship. Twelve years of Nazi rule eradicated the roots of the old parties and replaced them with a single, totalitarian monolith, which was in turn destroyed through military defeat and occupation. By 1945 there was little in the German past on which to build a healthy and dynamic party system. Here, more than anywhere, a new beginning seemed essential. Remarkably, it was achieved.

The Reemergence of Political Parties

The reestablishment of political parties in occupied Germany came quickly. During the summer of 1945 a number were licensed by the Allied authorities. The first to organize was the Social Democratic party, which had been founded in 1863 and banned by the Nazis seventy years later. Some of its members returned from exile, while others emerged from the underground or from Nazi incarceration. In many respects it was much the same party as before, with a mass membership, a tight hierarchical structure, a working-class base, and a concentration of membership in the now war-ravaged cities. Its leader, Kurt Schumacher, had been one of the most courageous younger members of its Reichstag delegation who had spoken out vehemently against the Nazis in the early thirties. But he was also, in the tradition of his party, very wary of Communist intentions and control.

Germany in the immediate postwar period seemed fertile terrain for the reestablished Social Democrats. The enormity of the task of reconstruction made planning seem indispensable. The complicity of the industrialists in Hitler's rise to power and the sweeping reach of state control of the economy under Nazi rule made socialization of industrial assets a plausible undertaking. Shortages of food and displacement of much of the rural population suggested the timeliness of land reform. All these objectives were proclaimed by the S.P.D. in its first postwar party program, in May 1946.

What is more, capitalism and the bourgeois parties seemed to be in disrepute because of the manner in which they had faltered in the last years of the Weimar Republic. The S.P.D. virtually alone among the democratic parties had voted against the legislation that had enabled Hitler to suspend parliamentary rights in 1933. The Social Democratic record seemed clean, and its leaders had little to fear from the denazification proceedings that the Allies had begun to impose.

But circumstances swiftly shifted in a direction that limited the opportunities available for the S.P.D. Most significant was the effort made by the Soviet authorities to force through a merger of the Social Democrats with the newly reestablished Communist party (K.P.D.). Schumacher immediately realized that this would mean Communist domination. He prevented an amalgamation of the two parties in the western zones, a move that reflected the overwhelming preference of his party cohorts. But this meant that the S.P.D. would be deprived of its eastern wing, for the Soviets compelled the merger of the two parties in their zone of occupation. Through this action the Social Democratic party lost many of its former strongholds in Prussia and Saxony. The division of Germany meant that the S.P.D. as it emerged after the war would at least initially remain a minority party in the western zones, despite the fortuitous circumstances that suggested that its program might find very broad acceptance.

A striking new development in 1945 was the establishment of the Christian Democratic Union (C.D.U.). This party was rather loosely structured at the federal level with strong local units, as in Bavaria, where the affiliated party was launched as the Christian Social Union (C.S.U.), a distinction that has remained to date. The early programmatic impetus within the C.D.U. was not dissimilar to the ethos of the postwar S.P.D. Especially under the influence of its Berlin wing, led by Jakob Kaiser and Ernst Lemmer, the C.D.U. at first adopted several Socialist objectives. It, too, was critical of capitalism and advocated limited state control of the giant firms that had dominated German industry. The C.D.U. favored codetermination, which offered to extend to organized labor an important voice in the control of the larger factories, and it sought support among the working class. This approach also characterized much of the western C.D.U., especially in the industrial Ruhr, where Karl Arnold became leader of the party. Arnold, like Kaiser, had been active before 1933 in the Catholic trade-union movement.

Indeed, the C.D.U. represented a rather variegated amalgam of political components. As such, it was a new phenomenon in German politics. It was the first successful effort to broaden a Christian party beyond the ranks of Catholicism; it derived as much from Protestant political forces as from Catholic. This was not just a postwar recrudescence of the old Center party, which, in fact, sought also to revive itself. Christian Democracy from the beginning attempted to reach out to a broader constituency. In this it paralleled developments in France and Italy. But it also remained emphatically conscious of a lesson from the German past, namely, that the divisiveness among the non-Socialist forces in the Weimar Republic had vitiated their efforts and had created insurmountable obstacles to stable government. This time these forces would have to coalesce.

As a mass movement Christian Democracy would emerge as a rather heterodox, loose-knit, and decentralized party. In attempting to integrate forces that had so long been divided, it had to make substantial concessions to each. The common denominator that remained was not clearly defined. Party organization initially was not tight or well formed. Instead, the C.D.U. remained a rather collegial federation that sought to embrace divergent elements, including the conservative Protestants of north Germany, the old liberals of southwest Germany, and the traditional Catholic forces from Bavaria and the Rhineland.

What gave the party form and definition and an opportunity for real success was the division of Germany. First, this removed a great Protestant bastion, leaving the Catholics, who comprised the more dynamic core of the C.D.U., almost a majority in the three western zones. Second, Soviet actions and the division provided the party with an effective, albeit negative, integrating ideology, that of anticommunism. Third, the division and the aggressiveness of Soviet policy gave credence to those forces within the C.D.U. which sought a pro-Western policy. This served to hasten the rise of Konrad Adenauer and to consolidate his position as leader of the new party. His foremost competitor was not, as many had expected, former Center Chancellor Heinrich Brüning, who had now returned to Germany; rather, it was Jakob Kaiser, the Catholic trade unionist in Berlin, who called for a neutral policy for Germany between East and West. But Soviet harassment of the C.D.U. in its zone and the expulsion of Kaiser undermined Kaiser's policy and destroyed his base, leaving Adenauer, the spokesman of a more conservative, free-enterprise–oriented, and emphatically pro-Western outlook, as the uncontested leader of the Christian Democrats.

By 1947 Adenauer had made his breakthrough, and two years later he was the first Chancellor of the Federal Republic. This success was critical for his party. Loosely federated and largely heterogeneous as it was, the C.D.U. was greatly assisted by the common purpose of constituting a government and by the prestige of office. These provided the cement to hold together what was originally a decentralized and unassimilated coalition of contending forces. Indeed, it was not until 1950, after the first C.D.U.-dominated government had been established, that the party was able to hold its first national convention. Even so, its Bavarian wing, the Christian Social Union, remained an independent affiliate.

The opportunities of office and the effectiveness of its leaders gave the C.D.U. a common incentive to cohere rather than splinter. This was the most significant factor in the postwar reconstruction of the German party system. By 1953 one party was able to command a majority of the seats in the Bundestag. Four years later it would receive an absolute majority of the votes cast in the Bundestag elections. Never before in German history had this occurred. It was a singular achievement, but one that would not have been possible without the division of Germany and the opportunities created by Soviet hostility.

Indeed, foreign policy was critical for the formation of the Federal Republic and for the success of its party system. While it created sudden opportunities for the Christian Democrats, the division of Germany effectively removed the extreme Left as a factor in West German politics and thereby freed the S.P.D. from one of its most onerous problems, a constant internecine battle with a formidable left-wing antagonist. As part of a divided country with limited sovereignty, West Germany was greatly influenced by foreign policy. Throughout the 1950s it tended to consolidate the position of the Christian Democrats. The Berlin blockade, the rising in

East Berlin in 1953, and the brutal Soviet repression of the Hungarian revolution all closely preceded Bundestag elections that produced increasing C.D.U. victories. It was not until the mid-1960s, when the opportunities of détente and of rapprochement with the East became viable alternatives, that foreign policy began to favor the Social Democrats, who sought a more flexible and less antagonistic approach to the Soviet Union, Eastern Europe, and East Germany.

By that time the trend toward a two-party system was firmly developed, and the S.P.D. for the first time could seriously contemplate winning a plurality of the Bundestag votes and perhaps constituting a government. This was due to several substantial changes that had occurred within the major parties, especially within the S.P.D. It was also a consequence of the changing social and economic complexion of the Federal Republic by the mid-sixties. But above all, the emergence of large, unified parties and the stability of the political process were the result of changes in the electoral system.

The Electoral System

The electoral system has been a crucial factor in determining the pattern and success of party politics in the Federal Republic. The present system has evolved with a continuing awareness of the defects of the election law as defined in the past. From 1871 to 1918, members of the Reichstag were elected by majority vote, if necessary through a runoff second ballot, in single-member constituencies. During the Weimar Republic a strict proportional system of party lists was instituted, with one seat allocated for every 60,000 votes won.

The Parliamentary Council was divided on the electoral issue. The Christian Democrats preferred the British system of relative majorities in single-member constituencies. The Social Democrats, on the other hand, demanded proportional representation. As a result of this division, the Parliamentary Council contented itself with drafting the law for the first Bundestag election only, leaving to that chamber the task of further legislation. Therefore, the Basic Law says little about the electoral system, stipulating only in Article 38 that elections to the Bundestag shall be universal, direct, free, equal, and secret; that any person having reached the age of twenty-one be entitled to vote, and that those over the age of twenty-five may stand for election; and that all further details were to be determined by subsequent federal law.

Since 1949 there has been a substantial body of legislation dealing with the electoral process. Basically it has been guided by three aims. First, there has been an effort to correct the depersonalized pattern of the Weimar Republic by allocating to local constituencies one-half of the seats in the Bundestag. Second, the other half of the seats (originally only 40 percent) are filled from the party lists in such a way that each party receives a number of seats in proportion to the total number of votes cast for it. Third, only parties that either receive 5 percent of the list vote or win three constituencies outright are represented in the Bundestag. Votes for the parties that do not surmount this hurdle are reallocated to the parties that do, so that in the Bundestag each party is always represented by a slightly larger percentage of the seats than it has gained in the election.

Each of the two major parties contests all 248 election districts. Through 1965 the C.D.U. (with its Bavarian affiliate) always outpolled the Social Democrats in these direct constituency elections. However, in 1969 this pattern was reversed for the first time, with the S.P.D. winning 127, or slightly over half, of the 248 seats. In addition it has won most of the 22 seats indirectly elected by the Berlin Assembly, but these delegates have only limited voting rights.

The nomination of the candidates in the districts is left to the local constituency selection conference. In the larger cities several districts will combine to form one conference. But the size of these conferences has remained small, ranging from 25 to 360 party members. There are no primaries. This means that less than 3 percent of the 1.2 million members of the two larger parties actually participate in the selection of candidates.

There has been a real effort in constituency nominations to develop a strong link between the candidate and his locality. In 1969, of the 496 candidates nominated by the two major parties in constituencies, only 22 percent did not live in their districts, and of these over half maintained a nearby residence. The remaining candidates tended to be prominent national figures within their parties or experts whom the national party was eager to have elected to the Bundestag.

The compliance of the local selection conferences in this process is important because constituency nomination has become a more frequent prerequisite for safe placement on the party lists, which determine how the other 248 seats are allocated. This is particularly true for the S.P.D. It is less the case for the Christian Democrats, who elected forty-two members in 1969 on the basis of a list candidacy alone. This is explained by the greater influence within the C.D.U. of a diverse range of interest groups, whose support of the party may depend on receiving a safe seat, and thus on strong placement on the *Land* list. Generally, nomination in the S.P.D. depends more on a candidate's relations within the party, whereas in the C.D.U. a candidate's relations outside the party carry considerable weight. But overall the importance of a strong local party base is growing. Of the 156 new candidates elected to the sixth Bundestag in 1969, 60 percent held important party posts. Fifty-five percent of the Bundestag members elected since 1949 have entered politics at the local or community level, whereas in the Weimar Republic only 40 percent did so. This is an indicator of the decreased importance of the central party bureaucracy as compared to that of the local party organization, which is a natural concomitant of a direct constituency system.

The composition of the lists is quite complex. Here a variety of factors and calculations must be considered. First is the party's prospect for victory in the constituency elections. In those *Länder* where one of the two major parties tends to win more direct districts than its share of the total vote, placement on the list is meaningless for its candidates. Thus in Bremen, for example, the Social Democrats have won only through the constituencies, whereas in Bavaria or Baden-

Württemberg they have little hope of winning any districts outside the larger cities and must depend on the lists. Other considerations involve the popularity of those heading a *Land* list; the allocation of safe seats to certain groups, especially to women; and the reinsurance of those candidates whom the party is particularly eager to place in the Bundestag and who are contesting difficult or hopeless constituencies. Thus Fritz Erler, for years the major foreign policy spokesman and deputy leader of the S.P.D. in the Bundestag, always failed to win in his district, but gained reelection through safe placement high on the list.

This system of dual election has worked reasonably well. No distinction has developed between those members directly elected and those who gain entry to the Bundestag through the lists, as was originally feared. The method of constituency candidate selection, which is the key process, has worked on a more democratic basis than in many other parliamentary systems. The lists also serve as a party reservoir in the case of death, removal, or resignation of a member of the Bundestag, thereby obviating by-elections.

The two hurdles, 5 percent of the votes or three constituencies won, have been particularly important features of this system. Except in the case of regionally concentrated parties they have meant that the smaller parties can only win through the lists and, therefore, tend not to contest many constituencies. Since 1961 the process has eliminated all but one of the smaller parties from the Bundestag. Today only the Free Democrats (F.D.P.) (who won some 5.8 percent of the vote and thirty seats in 1969) are represented in the lower house, but without them the S.P.D. would probably not be able to constitute a government in which it retained the chancellorship, so that the survival of the F.D.P. has become an important issue for the Social Democrats. This has induced the party to try to win votes for its weaker coalition partner, especially in the frequent *Landtag* elections. Curiously, had the fourth party, the right-wing National Democrats (N.P.D.), secured but 226,000 more votes in 1969, the coalition between the Social Democrats and the F.D.P. would not have been possible since it was only through the reallocation of the 4.8 percent vote of the N.P.D. that these two parties obtained a narrow majority in the Bundestag. Finally, it should be said that these hurdles can be manipulated. If, for example, one of the two major parties sees an electoral advantage in assuring Bundestag representation for a smaller party, there is no restriction preventing it from *not* running a candidate in three districts in which it has a strong majority and in which it could urge its voters to cast their ballots for the smaller party.

Perhaps a more serious problem is a predilection to keep changing the electoral law. The entry requirements for the Bundestag have been successively tightened over the years. A recent constitutional amendment has extended the vote to all those between the ages of eighteen and twenty-one. State financing of parties has been redefined several times. More serious has been the attempt under the grand coalition of the C.D.U. and S.P.D. that came into office in 1966 to raise the issue of fundamental and radical reform of the electoral system, replacing the lists entirely with single member constituencies. There are many experts and forces in the Federal Republic that have been advocating this reform for many years. However, in 1966 when the grand coalition came into office, it had strongly partisan reasons for considering such a change: It would have permanently eliminated the two smaller parties, the F.D.P., which had demonstrated itself to be an illoyal coalition partner, and the N.D.P., which suggested too strong a revival of right-wing nationalism for inclusion in any government. As elsewhere, the foremost problem of a multiparty system in Germany has been that of assuming stable coalition government.

But even without electoral reform, it seems likely that a two-party system will emerge in the framework of the present system. The two major parties have consistently enlarged their joint share of the seats in the Bundestag, rising from 60 percent in 1949 to 94 percent twenty years later. With almost seven-eighths of the electorate voting in the 1969 Bundestag election (an indication of the high turnout typical of German elections), the C.D.U. and the S.P.D. together gained some 29.2 million votes of the total 33 million that were cast. This is a striking feat in view of Germany's record in the past, and it is very largely the consequence of an electoral system designed to maximize the coalescing of votes (and interests) and the consolidation of the larger parties.

The Parties and the State

In the Federal Republic state institutions and the government play a considerable role in determining important features of the party system. First of all, the Basic Law provides for their existence. Article 21 states explicitly that "the parties participate in the forming of the political will of the people. They can be freely formed. Their internal organization must conform to democratic principles. They must publicly account for the sources of their funds. Parties which, according to their aims and the conduct of their members, seek to impair or abolish the libertarian democratic basic order or to jeopardize the existence of the Federal Republic of Germany are unconstitutional."

It is the Federal Constitutional Court that holds the power to rule on the constitutionality of party practices. Its rulings have been very significant. During the 1950s, two parties, the extreme right-wing Socialist Reich party (S.R.P.) and the Communists (K.P.D.), were decreed in violation of Article 21 and banned as unconstitutional. In the case of the former it was the fear of a renascent Nazi movement that motivated its prohibition. The case of the K.P.D. was more complex and controversial. It was explained in part by the desire of the court and the government to appear evenhanded in banning extremist parties on both Right and Left. However, the political efficacy of this action was widely challenged, because the Communists seemed such a negligible political force in the Federal Republic. By declaring their party illegal, the court actually helped to camouflage the electoral weakness of the K.P.D. This is the reason why several prominent politicians welcomed the reestablishment of a new Communist party (now labeled the D.K.P.) in 1967, hoping that it would secure scant support while removing a propaganda weapon of the East Germans.

The Federal Constitutional Court has also ruled frequently on matters of party finance. Here the relationship between the government and the parties has been a particularly close and somewhat unique one in the Federal Republic. The first decision of the court in 1958 merely declared that contributions to political parties were not to be considered tax exempt, which had been the practice up to that date. This judgment worsened the financial condition of the parties, though least of all the S.P.D., which derives the larger part of its income from the dues paid by its members. However, the two coalition parties, the C.D.U. and the F.D.P., were especially threatened and, therefore, pressed for new state subsidies to the parties for the "political education" work that they sponsored.

Beginning in 1959 and lasting for the next six years, the parties received a total of 131 million marks from the government, ostensibly for this purpose. Then, in July 1966, the court ruled again, forbidding this form of support. It did, however, sanction payments by the government to the parties to defray the costs of election campaigns. This has become a major source of party income. Each party is entitled to two-and-a-half marks for each vote won in a federal election for the Bundestag (and one-and-a-half marks per vote cast in elections for the *Land* parliaments). Only parties that receive half of 1 percent of the vote or more are eligible for such government subsidy. As there are now some 40 million enfranchised voters in Germany, the total amount available for the parties over a four year period is about 100 million marks, and, indeed, nearly this amount was paid out during the 1969 election. A further 60 million is available for the state elections held every four years. In the event of an interim election caused by the dissolution of parliament, this amount would increase.

This practice is very important for party development in the Federal Republic. It has greatly eased the burden of financing the costly election campaigns and reduced the dependency of the parties on those interest groups and wealthy individuals who were, heretofore, an important source of monetary support. It has been estimated that total party spending at the federal level in 1968 was about 150 million marks. But the contributions reported by the three major parties for that year, in which no federal election was fought, only came to 11 million marks, or about 8 percent of the total. Even assuming substantial underreporting, it is clear that private contributions are a very secondary source of income for the parties —which is a healthy development. Dues tend to be more important. The S.P.D. reports that almost 40 percent of its income derives from this source, but for the other parties the figure is closer to 12 percent.

It has been argued that this arrangement has substantial faults. First, it may create a greater susceptibility toward a state orientation within the parties. Conceivably it also discriminates against new parties, which would find it difficult to amass one-half of 1 percent of the vote, the minimum requirement for a subsidy. It is not this hurdle, however, but the 5 percent-vote clause for entry into the Bundestag, that is the major obstacle for any new political grouping.

In fact, state support actually is of greater advantage to the opposition. The provision of funds is more important for it in any election because the government parties have certain cost-free advantages available to them through the regular government public relations machinery. It is always more costly to popularize an opposition leader and usually more difficult to obtain contributions for an opposition party. Thus, state support serves as a kind of equalizer. But it can, occasionally, cause difficulties, as in 1969 when the Free Democrats polled less votes than they had expected and, as a result, found that they had substantially overspent in the campaign, having overcalculated the amount that would be available from government coffers.

Party Organization

The two major parties are organized along rather similar lines, although the S.P.D. has a more cohesive and integrated structure. The composition of each reflects its historical evolution, regional strength, and social bases. Initially, the C.D.U. was organized as a rather loose coalition, held together by the prerogatives, prestige, and patronage of the government that it had headed for twenty years. It yielded substantial influence to its various components, and especially to its Bavarian affiliate, the C.S.U., with which it caucuses in the Bundestag in order to retain the privileges of the largest parliamentary party. In many ways the C.S.U. is really an autonomous component of the C.D.U., but it has utilized its independent position to maximum effect and, occasionally, has threatened to pursue its own course.

In other ways as well the C.D.U. structure has remained somewhat bizarre. For example, in North Rhine-Westphalia, Lower Saxony, and Baden-Württemberg, it has no statewide organizations, but rather operates through party units that do not encompass the entire state. Thus, in the largest *Land* there are separate organizations for Rhineland and for Westphalia, which adds to the problems of an overall coordination of policy. Furthermore, since the C.S.U. is organized more effectively than any other state unit, its leverage is all the greater on issues that concern the party nationally.

The C.D.U. also yields important powers to various groups that are represented within the party. The influence of the Protestant working group and of the social committee that derives from the Christian trade-union movement and from the socialism of the early postwar years has remained considerable. Likewise, in view of the importance of business and agrarian constituents within the party, the C.D.U. tends to incorporate their wishes in its programs and to allocate positions of influence to their delegates within party councils.

The greater homogeneity of the S.P.D., while limiting its electoral base, has eased its organizational problems. Its state organizations, which exist in each *Land* except Hesse, tend to have less autonomous power within the party. It is only where there is a significant difference of outlook between a local unit and the national leadership that regional tensions tend to emerge. Controversies within the S.P.D. have dealt more with policy than with structure. Its greatest organizational problems have been in contending with its own left-wing dissidents, who, since the early 1960s, have become more outspoken in their criticism of party policy.

The S.P.D. has a substantially larger membership than the C.D.U., with some 780,000 to the latter's 420,000. Its paid professional staff is also more elaborate. For both parties, the party congress, which is usually convened once or twice in every electoral period, is the highest organ, but for the Social Democrats the congress has greater significance in view of its role in debating programmatic issues. Actually the key governing body of each party is its executive committee. That of the C.D.U. contains some thirty-one members, half of whom also comprise the leadership of the party in the Bundestag. Thus federal and state politicians are fairly evenly matched in numbers, although the former are more heavily represented on the smaller presidium, which is the inner core of the party leadership. Roughly the same pertains for the S.P.D. Nineteen of the thirty-six members of its executive committee are members of the Bundestag. As in the C.D.U., the executive committee has shown a high continuity in membership and relatively little mobility. It is rare and difficult for anyone under forty to penetrate these inner ranks of party leadership, which has been a source of complaint among many younger members of the parties.

Each party has a relatively large youth organization. The Junge Union, affiliated with the C.D.U., has some 120,000 members, whereas the Jung Sozialisten of the S.P.D. is half again as large. The median age for members in these organizations is over twenty-five, with an age limit of forty, and the tendency here, too, has been toward an older leadership. For the Social Democrats its youth organization has been a source of growing radical criticism. The Jusos, as they are popularly known, have challenged the party leadership on a broad range of issues, finding support in more radical party organizations, such as the ones in South Hesse and Schleswig-Holstein. To some degree this represents a replay of the party's experience with its student affiliate in the 1950s, the S.D.S., whose party connection was eventually severed when its criticism became too strident.

This reflects the continuing decline of ideological issues in the party programs and policies. Catchy slogans and a pragmatic posture have replaced ideological premises and programmatic commitment in German political parties. For the S.P.D., which traces its origins and heritage to the last century, this transformation has been much more painful than for the others. Its Marxist *Weltanschauung* was a central feature of party ideology for almost a century. But a great deal changed during this period, and eventually it, too, found the lure of the electorate greater than the conceptions of its party theoreticians. By the 1960s, the Social Democrats had adapted their program primarily to the purposes of achieving maximum electoral advantage.

The Composition of the Electorate

In changing its course, the S.P.D. has had to take into account shifts in the German electorate, some of which have posed special problems for the party. Because of the decimation of the male population in the two world wars, women comprise fifty-five percent of the electorate in postwar Germany. They have tended to be more conservative, less class-conscious, more concerned with inflation than with social reform, and, generally, more religious than the male voter. This last factor is important, since several surveys have revealed that it is the intensity of the religious tie that is most relevant in determining voter preference. About two-thirds of those Catholics who attend church regularly vote C.D.U., while one-half of those who attend rarely opt for the S.P.D.

If the female voter has been an important asset to the C.D.U., so have the growing number of employees and government officials who tend to prefer this party. With development and affluence, the percentage of the population that regards itself as working class has decreased, and with higher incomes and relatively full employment, the attitudes of the workers themselves have changed. This shift has been reflected in the changing composition of the S.P.D. In 1961 55 percent of its membership was working class. By the end of the sixties, this group represented less than 45 percent of the party membership. In the same period the party substantially increased its membership among the sectors of the population that were growing most rapidly in terms of employment and social position. Today, white-collar employees and government officials comprise almost one-third of its membership.

In terms of income, the S.P.D. membership today conforms more closely to that of the Federal Republic as a whole. In 1970, 31 percent of its members had monthly incomes below 800 marks, and only 17 percent were above 1,400 marks. The national composite figures were 36 and 12 percent respectively, whereas those for the C.D.U. membership were considerably weighted in favor of the more affluent. Only 15 percent of its members received less than 800 marks a month, and over one-third earned more than 1,400.

These figures suggest that economic factors can be critical for the success of the Social Democrats. Any substantial downturn in the economy that threatened the large lower-income groups would broaden the appeal of the S.P.D. if it were in opposition. This was the cause for its major electoral victory in North Rhine-Westphalia in June 1966, in which it won almost 50 percent of the vote, a development which paved the way for the party's inclusion in the grand coalition that was established in Bonn five months later.

Other sociological and demographic factors seem to be favoring the S.P.D. The imbalance between male and female voters will in time correct itself. The new youth vote of those between eighteen and twenty-one may align itself more easily with a party advocating social reform, as the S.P.D. tends to do, especially when it is in the opposition. But this would also require a process of rejuvenation within the party, only 18 percent of whose members are today under the age of thirty-four. In fact, one of the great inner problems of the S.P.D. has been the preponderance of the old *Parteigenossen* ("party comrades"). Over half of its membership is over fifty years of age, whereas in the C.D.U. this age group comprises only 40 percent of its smaller membership. However, the Social Democrats are trying to meet this problem in their recruiting of new members. Of the new members who have joined the party since 1967, four out of ten are under thirty, which represents a 30 percent increase in this category over a ten-year period.

The S.P.D. should also benefit from the increasing urbanization of Germany. The demise of the farmer and of the rural sectors will deplete an important reservoir of C.D.U. strength and will probably serve to weaken the religious factor in determining party preference. In fact, as the S.P.D. moves away from its working-class base, the C.D.U. will have to readdress itself to the problems of a more modern, industrialized, and urban society, which will probably give greater weight to those groups within it that played such an important part in its establishment and that have always sought to emphasize social reform as a central credo of the party.

What seems clear is that these two parties have become more similar to each other over time. They have successfully reached out to broaden their constituency and to appeal to the uncommitted voters, who today represent between 15 and 20 percent of the electorate. In this process, both parties tend to appeal to an identical audience. Such is often the fate of two-party systems, and it can produce problems of disaffection, splintering, and antisystem politics if the range of choice between the major contending parties appears too narrow to a significant portion of the electorate. In the Federal Republic this problem has not yet become severe. The more extreme manifestations of political disaffection, such as the N.P.D. on the Right or the A.P.O. on the Left, have been epiphenomenal, brief, and highly overrated. Indeed, it has been the success of the two major parties in integrating diverse political forces that has helped shape a stable pattern of politics, which is increasingly developing into a two-party system.

Toward a Two-Party System

The process of consolidation of the two major parties has been very consistent. During the 1950s it was the C.D.U. that steadily expanded its base, capitalizing on the popularity of its leader, the domestic appeal of its foreign policy, and the success of its economic efforts. The S.P.D., by contrast, was poorly led from 1952, after the death of Schumacher, until the selection of Willy Brandt as its Chancellor candidate and chairman of the party in the sixties. The key reversal for the party was its Godesberg program, adopted amid a great deal of shrill controversy, in 1959. Basically, the party congress meeting at Bad Godesberg jettisoned its Marxist program in favor of a program seeking a modern, mixed economy that combined free enterprise with state planning.

This shift in policy enabled the party to make a substantial breakthrough in its voter support, which rose from a low point of 23 percent in 1957 to almost 43 percent of the votes cast twelve years later. It also meant that from the early sixties onward the possibility of a grand coalition spanning the C.D.U. and the S.P.D. was a reasonable possibility.

This option became important because of three factors: the leadership crisis within the C.D.U., the uncertainty of a continued coalition with the F.D.P., and the brief but sudden rise of the National Democrats. Basically, the C.D.U. found it very difficult to hasten the retirement of Chancellor Adenauer, which seemed desirable in view of his long tenure in office, advanced age, and poor showing in the 1961 Bundestag elections. After Adenauer's retirement in 1963, Ludwig Erhard, long identified with the brilliant economic recovery of Germany, became Chancellor. He faltered badly in 1966, which led important factions within his own party to favor a coalition with the S.P.D. in order to effect his removal.

For this purpose a renewed coalition of the Christian Democrats with the F.D.P., which had been a junior partner in all the cabinets since 1949, did not seem feasible. After seventeen years of partnership, relations between the two parties had eroded badly. This was reflected in the complex negotiations to establish a C.D.U./F.D.P. coalition in both 1961 and 1965, which had taken an average of seven weeks of intensive interparty negotiation. Furthermore, the Free Democrats sustained substantial defeats in the Hessian and Bavarian *Landtag* elections that were held in November 1966, just at the time when the Erhard coalition had broken down. Under these circumstances the C.D.U. turned to the S.P.D. to establish a grand coalition under Chancellor Kurt Georg Kiesinger.

The rise of the right-wing N.P.D. was an important factor in the establishment of this coalition. Capitalizing on the economic recession of 1966, the National Democrats scored some impressive electoral gains, receiving more than 7 percent of the vote in both the Hessian and Bavarian *Landtag* elections. This prompted a sense of alarm about a further downturn in the economy. Many leaders spoke of the impending economic crisis. A grand coalition was deemed the only way to deal effectively with the situation.

As a transitory phenomenon the grand coalition was a success. It restored vitality to the economy and began a readjustment of foreign policy that seemed long overdue. Perhaps more importantly, it demonstrated that the S.P.D. was also highly competent to govern. Long castigated by the C.D.U. for its purportedly radical ideology, the S.P.D. seized the opportunity of partnership in government to shed this distorted image and present itself as a more skillful and expert, but not very different party from the C.D.U.

The weakness of the grand coalition was the enormous reduction in the size of the parliamentary opposition. Forty-nine Free Democrats, less than 10 percent of the Bundestag, became the minute voice of parliamentary opposition. This was not a healthy situation. Yet it was one that was forced upon the system by the increasing weakness of the third party, the F.D.P. The role of this small party with a membership of only 80,000 is important disproportionately to its size. It can, barring a clear majority vote for one of the two giant parties, determine the composition of a coalition, as it did in 1969, when it refused to consider a renewed alliance with the C.D.U. Thus the power of the party was enormous, even though it had lost 38 percent of its voters over the previous four years. Rarely has a defeated party played so critical a role in the formation of a government. However, had the party done slightly worse, or the N.P.D. slightly better, the coalition that was constituted in the fall of 1969 between the S.P.D. and the F.D.P. would not have been possible. Indeed, the 5 percent hurdle for entry into the Bundestag remains a very significant factor in the political process.

It is really the demise of the small parties, which was not foreseen in 1949, which has made this so. Originally, in the early fifties, when Allied licensing of political parties had ceased, there were over thirty parties competing for electoral support. Eleven were represented in the first Bundestag. By 1953 only five survived, and by 1957, when the C.D.U. won an absolute majority, only four parties remained in the Bundestag. After the 1961 elections, the number dropped to three.

Most of the vote of these small, special-interest parties was absorbed during the fifties by the C.D.U. If the F.D.P. were to disappear, it is likely that a part of its constituency would also flow to the Christian Democrats, therefore raising the prospects of their regaining an absolute majority in the Bundestag. But the S.P.D. has been surprisingly successful in the sixties in winning voters away from the C.D.U., which means that in a two-party system with a growing urban concentration and a larger ratio of independent voters, each of the major parties could reasonably vie for more than 50 percent of the vote. This development, remarkable in the context of Germany's past, is partially the result of well-designed institutions and the capacity of the parties to develop as consensus-building, multi-interest mass movements. But it is also due to the decline of conflict-producing cleavages in German society. The homogeneity of the German electorate has made possible the hegemony of two parties alone.

Six

Economic and Social Forces

The absence of meaningful social cleavages in the Federal Republic is due to a number of factors. Foremost among these has been its striking economic recovery and transformation during the two-and-a-half decades since the war. No other country in Europe has experienced a comparable postwar economic resurgence. It is not surprising, therefore, that the West German achievement is often described as "miraculous." After the enormous destruction wrought by the war, the dislocations brought by division, the proscriptions enforced by the occupying authorities, and the massive influx of displaced refugees from the East, the prognosis for the German economy in the early 1950s was far from sanguine. Yet remarkably, the West German economy was able to grow at an average annual rate of more than 10 percent under conditions of controlled price inflation; succeeded in absorbing more than 11 million refugees in the fifteen postwar years and still achieved full employment by 1957; and was able to gain levels of affluence and an overall standard of living higher than that of either Britain or France by the end of the 1960s.

The Economic Miracle

How was all this achieved? What explains the German economic "miracle"? A number of factors must be cited to comprehend a process that has been fundamental to the social stability and political harmony that have characterized the first two decades of the Federal Republic and that have produced a seemingly durable equilibrium unknown in Germany's recent past.

First, it is important to note that the wartime destruction, while very extensive, seemed greater than it really was. Sixty-one percent of all industrial assets in prewar Germany were located in what was to become the Federal Republic. Many of these had been rationalized and modernized under National Socialism. While factories and mines were ravaged by the bombings, production in the later years of the war was actually greater than before. According to the economist Karl Roskamp, "West German industry actually had, in 1946, a greater industrial capacity than in 1936."[1] And what had been destroyed could be replaced in the postwar years by more modern and productive equipment. The rebuilding of German industry, which was concentrated during the first decade after the war, permitted widespread introduction of the most modern techniques and machinery, many imported, together with massive economic assistance, from the United States.

American financial aid was of vital significance. In the first seven years after the termination of hostilities, Germany received more than 3.5 billion dollars from the United States, of which about one-third came in the form of Marshall Plan loans. Furthermore, in striking contrast to, but largely because of, the grim experience after World War I, reparations payments were initially deferred. It was not until after 1952, when the German economy had begun to recover, that reparations began to be made on a substantial basis. The dismantling of industry and the forced payment of goods and services, which was extracted on a vast level by the Soviet Occupation government in its zone, had quickly been brought to an end in the western zones.

The Federal Republic had certain special advantages when compared with its former occupying powers. It had no costly overseas or colonial commitments. Initially, there was no defense budget at all, only the payments for the costs of the Occupation, a substantial portion of which fed back into the German economy. Even after rearmament was begun in the mid-fifties, the cost of the German defense effort remained less than that of Britain or France. In 1958, for example, less than 3 percent of the German gross national product was allocated for military purposes, while the comparable figure for Britain was close to 7 percent. Ten years later the gap had narrowed, although, in the absence of a nuclear program and foreign commitments, the German defense budget still remained smaller in proportion to gross national product than the defense budgets of most of its major N.A.T.O. allies.

A second asset of even greater importance was the availability of a skilled labor reservoir throughout the 1950s. Some economists, such as Charles Kindleberger, have seen this as the key factor in accounting for German growth since the war. During the sixteen years between the end of the war and the construction of the Berlin wall, some 12 million German expellees and refugees moved westward from

---

[1] Karl W. Roskamp, *Capital Formation in West Germany* (Detroit, 1965), p. 36.

Eastern Europe and East Germany to the Federal Republic. Of this number, 7 million eventually entered the work force. Initially, the refugees were seen as a potential burden upon the German economy. Destitute and often homeless, they had to be provided with basic social services: food, which was sometimes scarce; and housing. Many of them chose to settle in the poorer, rural areas of West Germany, in Bavaria, Lower Saxony, and Schlewsig-Holstein, creating additional pressures on the limited resources of these *Länder*.

But, in fact, the refugees proved to be a uniquely valuable resource. Speaking the same language and having sought refuge from oppressive conditions elsewhere, they were relatively easy to assimilate and to satisfy. What is more, they were usually willing to relocate and often had special skills. The latter was particularly the case among the 3 million refugees who fled from the German Democratic Republic before departure was barred in 1961.

The availability of a large reservoir of labor was doubtless a factor of vital importance for German economic recovery. Not only did it allow for a rapid increase in production; this pool of unemployed also contributed to the tempering of labor demands for wage increases and to the prevailing disinclination to strike. Indeed, the conditions under which postwar recovery began had a great impact on the labor movement, accounting for the docility and the common enterprise of the working force. The vivid memories of vast unemployment and uncontrolled inflation coupled with the experience of enormous postwar deprivation created conditions congenial to an unprecedented labor harmony, which in turn contributed significantly to the marked increase in productivity. It was not so much the purported German ethos, or national character, that accounted for the consistent record of hard work and increasing output. Rather, it was the absence of workdays lost through strikes. Here, the postwar German record was unmatched by any other industrial nation.

The low incidence of strikes can be attributed to a number of factors, several of which have already been enumerated. An important additional explanation can be found in the attitude of the trade unions. When the union movement was reorganized after the proscriptions of the Third Reich, it had special reasons to avoid strikes. First, the position of the Federation of German Trade Unions (*Deutscher Gewerkschafts Bund*, or D.G.B) was unchallenged, and, therefore, its leadership did not have to resort to strikes to assert its position against potential competitors. This was, to some degree, a change from the situation that prevailed before 1933. Second, union coffers were largely empty, so that the damage to the union membership of a prolonged strike would have been particularly severe. More importantly, the unions on the whole tended to seek objectives other than mere wage increases or social benefits. Much of their energy was directed toward achieving labor representation in the management of companies and other quasi-political goals.

The moderation of labor demands in terms of compensation was also the result of the widespread fear of inflation. In Germany alone of all the industrial nations of Europe, this prevalent attitude toward inflation, which was conditioned by the experiences of 1923 and 1947, greatly facilitated the task of the government in

pursuing a growth-oriented policy while avoiding inordinate cost-and-price inflation. Monetary stability in Germany carried a very special value of its own, and
compliance with antiinflationary actions could be assumed there, when it could not
be elsewhere in Europe. Thus, while the German economy has grown faster than
those of France and Britain, the rate of inflation in consumer goods, for which
demand was even higher in Germany, has been less than half that of its Western
neighbors.

This has been a great asset, especially in the period of increasing labor scarcity
after 1957. It was critical for the success of the German drive for a major export
market, which, in turn, was a key factor in stimulating growth. Export prices
remained strongly competitive, while the domestic market was less attractive to
foreign producers because of price restraints. This balance was achieved with a
minimum of government-imposed controls. In short, the same factors that permitted accelerated growth with minimal inflation provided Germany with the opportunity to concentrate on policies conducive to continued expansion without fearing
their consequences.

One of the ironies of German postwar experience was that consumer demand,
which had been intensified by the privations of war and the Occupation, could be
deferred in favor of a policy that emphasized investment in capital goods. In part
this was the result of a determined government policy of providing a substantial
amount of basic and urgently required social services and products, such as housing. This, in turn, was made possible by a stringent tax system. Since the war
Germany has had the highest tax rate of any West European country. According
to Andrew Shonfield, taxes in 1960 represented no less than 34 percent of the
gross national product.[2] Public awareness of the need for state action in bringing
about the economic recovery of Germany made such levies seem acceptable and
rendered to the state a substantial role in the economy.

This public awareness was reflected in the widespread compliance with government efforts to encourage savings. By the late fifties, German public saving totaled
about 8 percent of G.N.P., a figure roughly twice the level in France and Italy and
about four times that in Britain. This made additional funds available for investment
and helped further to reduce inflation.

Once the system began to work, it seemed to provide its own rewards. Well-
placed investment in new machinery and capital goods made possible consistent
increases in labor productivity. At an annual rate of increase of almost 6 percent
throughout the 1950s, the productivity of labor grew far more rapidly in Germany
than anywhere else in Europe. This, in turn, permitted wages to rise without
creating inflationary pressures. Between 1950 and 1966 real wages rose by some
140 percent, while the work week was reduced by 10 percent. This was a sufficient
reward for most of the labor force, sufficient at least to deter it from pursuing costly
strikes.

---

[2]Andrew Shonfield, *Modern Capitalism* (London, 1965), p. 265.

German economic growth was indeed prodigious. For the first fifteen years after the establishment of the Federal Republic, annual growth averaged 7.5 percent. This compared to a rate of 4 percent in France and less than 3 percent in Britain, and it was exceeded only by the rate of recovery of the Japanese economy. This remarkable achievement took place in the context of an economic policy that rejected overall planning. Elsewhere in Europe governments adopted elaborate machinery to plan economic growth, but the German government, under a Christian Democratic–dominated coalition, adhered to an economic outlook of neoliberalism that strongly emphasized free enterprise. To be sure, capitalism was tempered with social-purpose policies, but planning and even national forecasting were mostly rejected. Instead, the policies long identified with Ludwig Erhard, who served as Minister of Economics for fourteen consecutive years, affirmed the virtues of competition and the free market mechanism and advocated the removal of government restraints and controls. It was a policy that worked extremely well for a decade and a half, taking Germany from the debacle of defeat to a position of economic leadership in Europe. When it finally began to fail, in the mid-sixties, it had run a uniquely successful course. This was a distinctive policy, an amalgam of various theories and impulses, and its aim came to be known as *Sozialmarktwirtschaft,* or "social-market economy."

The Social Market Economy

Erhard's liberal economic doctrine sought to create conditions of maximum freedom in the economy while simultaneously promoting certain limited social goals. A small dosage of social welfare was blended into an overall program designed to foster the resurgence of free enterprise. The fundamental premises of this program reflected a great faith in the virtues of competition and private ownership and in the incentives of an economic system geared to the maximization of profit. The policies that were pursued sought an overall reduction in the role of the state in direct management of the economy and the systematic removal of government controls on production, prices, and profits.

Although initially this course was vigorously opposed by the Social Democrats, it had special appeal in postwar Germany. In view of the experience of twelve years of stringent Nazi controls and planning and the subsequent restrictions placed on economic activity by the Allies, there was a strong sentiment against what was seen as excessive government intrusion into the economic sphere. This was reinforced by the growing antipathy in western Germany toward the state-imposed economic policies that the Soviet occupying authorities rigorously applied in their zone.

It was further strengthened by the perception in important quarters that the Americans very much favored a free enterprise system for Germany. As anticommunism became the ideological ethos of the Federal Republic, an economic doctrine that seemed to emphasize freedom and liberty seemed both congenial and efficacious. If the German business community—which was an important constituency of the C.D.U. and the F.D.P., the twin pillars of the ruling coalitions for the first seventeen years of the Federal Republic—was to expedite the process by which it regained control over the German economy, it made sense to reject extensive planning, which was largely antithetical to American thinking at the time. Thus the neoliberal approach of Erhard and his cohorts, with its apparent affirmation of laissez faire, seemed particularly attractive.

What is more, the policy soon proved itself remarkably successful in promoting growth and development. It therefore became increasingly difficult for the opposition to attack and reject it. Throughout the 1950s all the economic indicators suggested that Erhard had found the magic formula for a government economic policy. Removing controls, promoting capital formation, and encouraging investment, but otherwise restraining government intervention in the economy, seemed to fit the needs of the time. Even the S.P.D. began to acknowledge the effectiveness of this policy. At the Berlin party congress in 1954, Karl Schiller, a prominent economic theoretician of the party, proclaimed that Germany required a policy that sought "as much competition as possible, and only as much planning as was necessary."[3] Five years later at Bad Godesberg his party jettisoned its residual and waning commitment to a Marxist program. The astounding success of the *Sozialmarktwirtschaft* had overwhelmed the appeals of a Socialist program.

But while the government disclaimed any interest in planning and desisted from adopting an incomes policy (which was actually unnecessary in view of the temperance of labor's demands), its intervention in the economy was, in fact, rather substantial. First of all, there was extensive planning in various sectors. The government adopted "green plans" for agriculture, pursued medium-term planning in its railway and road-building programs, and set fixed targets in the ambitious provision of state-subsidized public housing. Extensive plans were developed for Berlin, the Saar, and lagging regional areas and territories bordering on the German Democratic Republic. Various kinds of subsidies were provided by the federal and *Länder* budgets, sometimes to reward important political constituencies but more often to achieve economic and social goals, such as effective integration of the continuing flood of refugees.

Monetary and fiscal policy was also carefully calibrated to curb the extreme gyrations of an uncontrolled business cycle. Usually in close collusion with the powerful central bank, established as an independent authority in 1957, interest rates were constantly readjusted either to spur or restrain the level of economic activity. Indeed, it is fair to summarize the policy of the fifties and early sixties as one of "positive, coordinated state intervention carefully moulded to achieve specific and limited objectives."[4]

---

[3]Leo Brawand, "Gespräch mit Karl Schiller," in Leo Brawand, *Wohin steuert die deutsche Wirtschaft?* (Munich, 1971), p. 26.

[4]Malcolm MacLennan, Murray Forsyth, and Geoffrey Denton, *Economic Planning and Policies in Britain, France, and Germany* (New York, 1968), p. 77.

This policy was designed not only to maximize stable growth but also to achieve certain other aims. A very conscious effort was made to encourage the development of a prosperous middle class. The government sought deliberately to support medium and small producers in trade, business, and agriculture. Public contracts often were placed with small or medium-sized firms. Several state-owned assets were distributed to small owners. The partial denationalization of giant government companies such as Volkswagen, Pressag, Veba, and Lufthansa were part of this effort, which came to be known as *Mittelstandspolitik*. An anticartel law was passed, establishing a federal cartel office (Bundeskartellamt) in Berlin, although its effectiveness was substantially reduced by the successful efforts of business interests lobbying against it in Bonn.

A deliberate effort was made to support lagging sectors as well. Agriculture in particular was heavily subsidized, partially to ease the plight of the small farmers, but also because of the political influence of their well-organized pressure group, the Bauernverband, which regularly delivered substantial pluralities for C.D.U. candidates in rural districts. Nonetheless, the subsidies for agriculture, which rose to more than 5 billion marks in 1968, could not curb the exodus from the countryside nor improve the economic condition of the small farmer. More than one-third of the 1.5 million farms of less than ten hectares ceased to operate during the first two decades of the Federal Republic, while the farming population declined from almost 5 to less than 3 million.

Subsidies were also lavished on other depressed areas of the economy. The coal industry, threatened by American exports and cheaper fuel oil, was largely sustained by payments from Bonn. So were some other inefficient producers. With large tax revenues to distribute, the federal government displayed a predilection to use public finance to subsidize industry and trade, but without a coherent plan. By 1965 this pattern had begun to become enormously costly and highly political. Andrew Schonfeld has estimated that by that year no less than one-fourth of the federal budget was being used to support agriculture, industry, and commerce through subsidies, cheap loans, discriminating tax allowances, and other procedures. This was a form of massive state intervention through ad hoc concessions, without any developed blueprint for structural reforms or purposeful reorientation of the lagging sectors.

The state has also intervened in the economy in other ways. Despite its emphatic preference for free enterprise, the C.D.U.-dominated governments of the fifties and early sixties did not dismantle the bulk of state-owned enterprise. Instead, the federal government has continued to own and operate about 50 billion marks worth of assets, with occasional efforts to denationalize some of these. About one out of ten workers is employed by a state enterprise, if the railroad and postal systems are included. One-fourth of coal producing, almost half of all iron-ore mining, 77 percent of all aluminum mining, and one-third of all shipbuilding is done by government-owned firms. In addition the *Länder* and local communities control substantial assets of their own. Their role in controlling local savings and loan associations and institutions is particularly marked. Finally, the government, even under the more conservative Christian Democrats, exercises a major role in the provision of social services. Here the Federal Republic has followed upon a strongly developed German tradition that began more than a century ago. Indeed, Article 20 of the Basic Law refers to the Federal Republic as "a social federal state." This document is, in fact, rather specific, by comparison with other constitutions, in stipulating the social rights to which German citizens are entitled.

With a budget approaching 100 billion marks today (which represents a seven-fold increase over twenty years), about one-third of all federal spending is presently allocated for social services. In part this is a consequence of the war. Beginning in 1952, a program to equalize burdens was introduced in the Federal Republic. By 1971, somewhat over 6 billion marks was provided annually for indemnification and support of war victims, who today still number some two and a half million. Large payments have also been made to the refugees who emigrated to West Germany in such large numbers after the war. A peculiar innovation has also sought to redress imbalances among the *Länder*. Here the redistribution of certain revenues has benefitted the more indigent states. The *Länder* with relatively high per capita incomes, such as North Rhine-Westphalia, Baden-Württemberg, Hesse, and Hamburg, have provided assistance for those which are poorer. Under this arrangement, Lower Saxony received, for example, more than 500 million marks in 1965, or roughly 70 marks per inhabitant, many of whom were former refugees.

In 1952 state child support was also introduced. While this assistance is less generous than that provided in France, the federal budget in 1971 allocated almost 3 billion marks for family allowances. This is in keeping with Article 6 of the Basic Law, which states that "marriage and family are under the special protection of the state" and that "every mother has a claim to the protection and assistance of the community."

By comparison with France work accident insurance is lower in the Federal Republic, while unemployment compensation is more comprehensive (but, since 1957, rarely required because there has been so little unemployment). On the whole, the Federal Republic today spends slightly more of its national income on social welfare than does France and far outdistances the United States and Britain in such expenditures. Indeed, the amount allocated for old age, sickness, and disability alone is close to 8 percent of national income in Germany, while less than 4 percent in the other three countries. And the percentage has been increasing. In 1950, despite the depressed condition of the economy and the enormity of the postwar burden, the Federal Republic spent 11.6 percent of its gross national product on social welfare. By 1970 this figure was close to 16 percent, and this of a G.N.P. that had swelled enormously.

A comparable increase has been registered in the provision of pensions. Here payments have increased by more than 350 percent since 1950, totaling almost 40 billion marks in 1971. A progressive system, linking the rate of pension payment to the rise in the cost of living, accounts for a substantial portion of this increase; but it is also the consequence of a conscious state policy that seeks to avert the pauperization of the retired working class, which took such a grievous toll and proved so destabilizing during the Weimar Republic.

In housing policy, too, the government has been particularly enterprising. Some 10 million dwellings were constructed during the first two decades of the Federal Republic, and of these about 35 percent were erected with state support. Here intervention has been wide ranging but carefully measured. As a recent study concluded, "the restoration of market forces has been deliberately and systematically encouraged, though controls were maintained as long as the market was structurally out of balance; and social intervention has been such as to prevent those with low incomes from suffering, but carefully adapted so as to distort the market as little as possible."[5]

All these factors suggest that the neoliberal Erhard model of the German economy has ineluctably moved toward a social-welfare state. To be sure, the ethos of the system emphasizes free enterprise, the profit motive, and competition. But to a substantial degree, it has failed to realize these goals, for economic concentration, the reemergence of cartels, and the grip of oligopolistic firms have become characteristic of the system. Nonetheless, from the outset the outspoken capitalism of the Erhard years was tempered by a broadly developed social policy. The social-market economy has evolved as a mixed system. As Alfred Grosser has argued, "the German 'welfare state' is more reminiscent of the British Socialist model than of traditional liberalism."[6] Yet, curiously, this is a welfare state in which the Social Democrats, at least until 1966, played a relatively minor role. And when finally they entered the government, their prescriptions and policies were directed more toward refining and reforming the system that had been established, rather than seeking its replacement with a radically different program.

But while German economic policy over the past two decades has made enormous strides and gained unanticipated achievements, it has not been free of problems. Some of these have been the consequence of rapid growth. Others are the result of the kinds of policy that were pursued, of the compromises that were struck and of the accommodations that were made. For the future the resolution of these problems will be of critical significance.

Economic and Social Dilemmas

One of the more serious problems of the German economy is the restricted capacity of the government to control the private sector. This is largely the result of the continuous pattern of amalgamation and concentration, which has rendered vast power to a relatively small number of giant firms. The initial postwar efforts of the Allies to break up the monolithic companies, especially in the steel, coal,

---

[5] *Ibid.,* p. 58.

[6] Alfred Grosser, *Germany in Our Time* (New York, 1971), p. 193.

and chemical industries, had no lasting effect. Many of the Allied edicts made little sense and were quickly set aside as Germany regained sovereign control over its own industry. The requirements of maximizing growth in the wake of the Cold War provided an acceptable rationale for suspending limitations on the size of firms. A trend toward concentration soon took hold. By 1960 four chemical companies (including the three firms into which the I.G. Farben trust had been divided) controlled 40 percent of all chemical production. Within the next decade their share of this sector had grown to 70 percent.

Similar figures reveal the pattern of concentration in iron and steel production. Originally, the Allies had subdivided the twelve giant heavy industrial firms concentrated in the Ruhr into twenty-eight companies. But within a decade of the establishment of the Federal Republic many of these had merged again. By 1960 the four largest steel companies controlled more than half of all German production. Today they produce 90 percent of all German steel. Four companies control 50 percent of the output of the electrical industry. Concentration in the automotive industry is even greater. And even in retailing the pattern of amalgamation is marked. Here fifteen giant chains control one-third of all retail sales.

In part the pattern of amalgamation may be attributed to the German aspiration to gain and preserve a strong, favorable balance of trade. The desire to remain competitive abroad and to protect domestic producers against foreign goods within Germany and the Common Market has reinforced the trend in favor of large firms. Here government preferences combined with those of industry. Today the 100 largest companies produce about 50 percent of all German exports, a fact which helps to explain the benevolent attitude of the government toward amalgamation. It is an attitude reminiscent of the past, for German governments have always sought to support industry in its efforts to protect its markets and to seek new ones. As tariffs tumbled, rationalization through concentration seemed a necessary measure to secure the competitive position of German industry.

Antitrust legislation has remained weak and ineffective. Since 1958 all companies seeking to merge must request permission from the Berlin Kartellamt if together they employ more than 10,000 workers, control 20 percent of the market, or have sales exceeding .5 billion marks annually. But because of the way in which the relevant legislation was drafted, it is difficult for the Kartellamt to withhold its permission. So the pattern toward concentration has continued and, in fact, recently has substantially accelerated. In the two-year period beginning in 1970, some 168 mergers were registered in Germany, representing a three-fold increase from the level of two years before. All together more than 100,000 firms have been liquidated since 1949. This suggests that the ostensible commitment of the C.D.U. and the F.D.P. to maximum free competition may have been more theoretical than real.

Similarly, the reestablishment of cartels in the postwar period has been relatively unhindered. To date more than 230 cartels have been registered. Less than 10 percent of those that were proposed to the Kartellamt have been rejected by it. In part this has been the result of pressure from those business groups which sought cartel arrangements in restraint of trade. It seems apparent that where the government was confronted by a choice between assuring competition within Germany and strengthening German producers vis-à-vis foreign firms, it strongly favored the latter.

Most significant is the concentrated power within the banking system. Here the three giant banks, the Deutsche Bank, the Dresdner, and the Commerzbank, not only dominate the provision of credit but also exert an enormous influence on business activity in Germany. In part this is made possible by the voting of custodial shares held for customers by these banks. An exhaustive inquiry conducted in 1964 indicated that German banks held 70 percent of the voting power of the 425 quoted joint-stock companies. But 87 percent of the shares controlled by the banks were not actually owned by them but held in custody. For 58 firms, the banks actually held a majority of the voting shares. For 138 others, they retained more than a quarter interest, which is sufficient to exercise a veto power over decisions.

This pattern renders great power to the banks. For example, among the nineteen companies in which the Deutsche Bank alone holds more than one-quarter of the shares are such giants as Daimler-Benz, Hapag-Lloyd, Karstadt, and the Bavarian Electrical Works, each of which is dominant in its own sector. The Dresdner and the Commerzbank are in equivalent positions. Furthermore, the trend toward concentration among the banks is continuing. Some 150 private banks have been absorbed since 1949.

Concentration of this sort within the private sector can and does set limits on the freedom of action and the capacity to plan of the federal government. There are additional economic constraints as well. First among these is the entrenched fiscal powers of the states. Article 109 cedes substantial taxing authority to the *Länder.* This accords with the postwar Allied preference to strengthen centrifugal and local forces in the Federal Republic, but it can impair the effectiveness of central government policy. Originally, personal income and corporate taxes, property taxes, and some additional revenues were assigned to the *Länder,* although Article 106 allowed the federal government to claim a certain portion of these receipts. This arrangement has had two adverse consequences. First, it has led to continuous disputes between Bonn and the *Länder.* Second, it has left the federal government with insufficient revenue and has conferred substantial fiscal power on the *Länder* in a way that may impede overall coordination, especially when opposition parties at the federal level constitute the government in several states. This can be critical in those instances when fiscal policy is pursued to achieve an anticyclical effect. The relatively small size of the central government sectors as compared to other sectors is "by itself an obstacle to demand management by means of the budget."[7] The imbalance is becoming more pronounced. Whereas the role of the federation in total state expenditure was 48 percent in 1955, it stood at less than 42 percent ten years later.

This is in part because of the heavy social-service burden carried by the *Länder.*

---

[7]Bent Hansen, *Fiscal Policy in Seven Countries 1955–65* (Paris, 1969), p. 210.

But it is also a reflection of the inadequate sources of revenue for the federal budget. As tariffs have declined, the federal government has become more dependent on the added-value and excise taxes and on obtaining a larger portion of the income taxes collected by the *Länder*. Its share has increased steadily from one-third to some 43 percent of income tax receipts.

Even so, federal revenues have been insufficient. This is particularly critical because the Basic Law does not permit budgetary deficits. Article 110 stipulates that "revenue and expenditure must be balanced." This is a strange proviso in a constitution and may be explained by the abiding fear of the kind of deficit spending that characterized German government policy at the beginning and the end of the Weimar Republic. Nonetheless, since 1963 government expenditure has been rising more rapidly than income. This has created particular problems for the government in periods of economic slowdown, such as occurred in 1966 and 1971. At such times it is especially difficult to reduce spending without further adverse effects on the level of economic activity, yet a substantial decline in the economy will, of course, reduce available government revenues.

This dilemma has led the federal government in recent years to move further in the direction of middle-range planning and to give greater attention to accurate forecasting. The government was substantially assisted by the establishment of the central bank (the Bundesbank), which replaced the more decentralized Bank deutscher Länder in 1957. While the Bundesbank has retained great independence of action, it has sought on the whole to develop precise forecasts regarding the direction of the economy and has been amenable to close cooperation with the federal government.

A five-member Council of Economic Advisors (Wirtschaftsrat) was established in 1964 to render advice to the central government. But the most significant development was the adoption by the grand coalition three years later of a program of middle-range financial planning, which requires projections of budgetary planning over a five-year period. This has made possible the anticipation of future deficits several years before they arise. Indeed, it was an awareness of the enormity of the deficit projected for 1975 that caused the federal Finance Minister, Alex Möller, to resign his post in May 1971, when the federal cabinet refused to invoke the reduction in expenditure that he had urged. This resulted in the hasty consolidation of the Ministries of Finance and Economics, which had traditionally remained separate in the German cabinet system. The resulting "superministry" under Karl Schiller and then Helmut Schmidt has been regarded as a somewhat unwieldy instrument, which, its critics argue, possesses too much power within the cabinet as a whole.

Nevertheless, these institutional innovations and programs have moved Germany far in the direction of a planned economy. Andrew Shonfield has argued that in Germany "the basic bits of apparatus which are required for systematic economic planning are more readily available than in many other countries."[8] In his

---

[8]Shonfield, *op. cit.*, p. 296.

view, the German system lends itself better than the British to collective economic planning because of the size and concentration of firms; the pattern of collaboration within the private sector; the powerful role of the banks; and the high priority of, and past experience with, rationalization within the economy to make it more efficient. Thus there is a kind of tension between the doctrinal predilection in favor of free enterprise and the gradual movement toward planning. If the recent decline of the rate of growth of the economy persists, it is likely that, despite all the stated inhibitions, German economic policy will continue to move further in the direction of central planning, although it remains unclear whether the federal government is in fact equipped with the powers necessary to effect its will and its plans in the present system.

Labor and the Unions

The labor movement has been another critically important component in the remarkable postwar recovery of the German economy. The trade unions were quickly reorganized after the war. Although the Basic Law does not specifically refer to the unions, Article 9 provides that "the right to form associations to safeguard and improve working and economic conditions is guaranteed to everyone." By 1949 a single, mammoth labor federation, the Deutsche Gewerkschaftsbund, had been established under the able leadership of Hans Böckler. The D.G.B. was actually an amalgamation of sixteen existing unions, which continued to retain their autonomy as unions do in the American system. As a result the D.G.B. has had much less direct control over its member unions.

This is necessary in part because of the great discrepancies in power and size among the member unions. Total D.G.B. membership numbers close to 7 million, and the membership of its largest component, the giant I.G. Metall, comprises almost one-third of this figure. Indeed, the metalworkers union—with 2 million members, many of them foreign "guest" workers—is the largest labor union in Europe. Without doubt, its leader, Otto Brenner, was the most powerful figure within German labor, much more so than Ludwig Rosenberg, who headed the D.G.B.

German unions today possess substantial wealth. Each member contributes the equivalent of one hour's wages per week as dues. The low past incidence of strikes has enabled the unions to amass fortunes, which have been invested with impressive ingenuity. For example, the union-owned Bank für Gemeinwirtschaft, organized in 1958, is the fourth largest private bank in Germany. The D.G.B. owns a quarter-million housing units, a substantial shipping fleet, and more than 6,000 cooperative stores. Union leaders sit on the boards of some of the large German enterprises. Otto Brenner, for example, was a member of the board of both Krupp and Volkswagen.

German unions have fought vigorously for the right of codetermination, or *Mitbestimmung,* in the management of German industry. The notion of a shared responsibility for directing major industry derives from the early part of the century. The experiments of the Weimar Republic, both the *Zentralarbeitsgemeinschaft* and the formation of the shop councils *(Betriebsräte)* proved sadly abortive. However, after World War II labor was determined to wrest for itself the right to participate in the management of private industry. *Mitbestimmung* was one of the four central planks of the original D.G.B. platform drafted in 1949.

Initially, union efforts met with some success. In May 1951, under the threat of a massive strike, the Bundestag passed legislation with the acquiescence of the C.D.U., which provided that both the employees and the shareholders would be equally represented on the supervisory board (Aufsichtsrat) of the major companies in the mining, iron, and steel industries. This was hailed as a great victory by the unions. It was also seen as a novel innovation in the German system. However, the union members of the supervisory boards rarely intervene in the ordinary conduct of business. Instead, they concentrate on issues that affect employment and the conditions of work. Thus *Mitbestimmung* has served as a useful way to associate labor with management decisions at a relatively early stage in the decision-making process, which has contributed to labor harmony. Seen another way, "codetermination basically resulted in a sort of cartel of all those involved in the production process directed against the consumers."[9] In any case, *Mitbestimmung* remained limited to heavy industry. The unions' efforts to establish the practice in other industrial sectors has not succeeded. While codetermination has been a modest success where it was attempted, its impact on the German economy as a whole has been relatively marginal.

Limited codetermination was achieved in 1951, but the unions fared rather less well on other political fronts. Originally, the D.G.B. had called for the nationalization of major industry, especially in the mining, metal, and energy fields. This endeavor proved unsuccessful. Indeed, the government has systematically sought to sell off certain assets in the form of *Volksaktien,* or small-holding "people's shares," thereby to further the spread of capitalism. The unions also failed in their efforts in the early fifties to combat the C.D.U. on such issues as rearmament and German entry into N.A.T.O.

The failure of such political action had several causes and consequences. In part, the inability of the unions to succeed with a political program derived from the substantial political apathy characteristic of the German public after years of totalitarian rule, war, and occupation. But also, union acquiescence was secured in place of political confrontation by the economic success that began to take hold in the mid-fifties. Wages grew rapidly, even at a time when there was still considerable unemployment. Real wages by 1970 were at a level almost twice that of two decades before. Meanwhile, the number of those gainfully employed had increased from 14 to 22 million. Such growth offered sufficient incentives to labor

---

[9]Gustav Stolper, Karl Häuser, and Knut Borchardt, *The German Economy: 1870 to the Present* (New York, 1967), p. 293.

to satisfy important economic demands, even in the absence of major political concessions.

This led to a situation in which the D.G.B. began to temper its more radical political prescriptions. A policy of political activism was toned down in favor of "compliance with the political realities of the Federal Republic with a residue of radical rhetoric."[10] In this course, the unions followed the lead of the S.P.D. At its 1963 congress in Düsseldorf, the D.G.B. basically adopted the non-Marxist Godesberg program of political conciliation that the Social Democrats had accepted four years before.

This reflected the close symbiosis between the unions and the S.P.D. Yet it is a relationship that is far less intimate or uniform than in Britain, where the trade unions are such a critical force within the formal Labor party structure. In Germany the unions, while leaning very much toward the S.P.D., are also represented in the other parliamentary parties. Indeed, the labor wing of the C.D.U., led today by Hans Katzer and in the past by such imposing figures as Karl Arnold and Jakob Kaiser, remains a force of considerable influence within the party. This has meant that a separate Catholic union movement has not developed as a strong, independent force in the Federal Republic. The one effort to organize a Christian union movement, in the form of the Christliche Gewerkschaftsbewegung, or C.G.D., in 1955 has been of little real effect. Its membership has not exceeded some 200,000.

This has posed no serious threat to the D.G.B., with its membership totaling almost 7 million. Neither have the separate union organizations for employees (Deutsche Angestelltengewerkschaft, or D.A.G.) and for civil servants (Deutsche Beamtenbund), which together contain somewhat over a million members. Twelve percent of the D.G.B. membership today consists of employees and some 8 percent of civil servants. However, women are poorly represented, constituting less than one-sixth of the D.G.B. membership, which is considerably less than their share of the working force as a whole.

The unions have not been particularly successful in recruiting an enlarged membership to keep pace with the increasing numbers of the working force. In part this is a consequence of the full employment and high wages that have characterized German growth in the fifties and early sixties, which created less need for union action. It is also a consequence of the growth of employment in service industries, where the unions have never been as well represented. More recently, new difficulties have emerged. Since 1965, the German economy has experienced two recessions. Second, price inflation has begun to manifest itself as a serious problem since the late sixties. These problems, taken together, have posed new dilemmas for the management of the economy and for the policy pursued by the unions. By 1971, union demands for wage increases began to exceed growth in the G.N.P. by a considerable amount. During 1970 Lufthansa employees received a wage

[10]Theo Pirker, *Die SPD nach Hitler* (Munich, 1965), p. 197.

increase of almost 16 percent upon threat of strike. In that year the printers' union demanded a 23 percent increase. By 1971, when growth in the economy had slowed considerably, the metalworkers, armed with a strike chest of almost 500 million marks, closed down the automotive industry in Baden-Württemberg with a demand for an 11 percent rise in wages—a figure that had been achieved before, but only in years of substantial boom.

The observation that the Federal Republic is blessed with a strike-free labor posture may no longer be valid. In the absence of continued prodigious strides in economic growth and with the waning of effective centralized control within the unions, a pattern of wildcat strikes and local restiveness has developed in certain sectors.

A more serious problem may be posed by the presence in Germany of a massive number of foreign workers. This is not, in fact, a totally new phenomenon. Even before World War I, almost 1 million non-Germans found employment in the Reich. Today there are more than twice that number working in Germany. Of these, the largest nationality groups are Turks, Yugoslavs, Italians, and Greeks. Their numbers have increased steadily from some 70,000 in 1954 to more than 2.2 million, one-fourth of whom are women. These "guest" workers, as they are known, are highly concentrated at the lower end of the labor scale. They tend to be manual workers, street cleaners, waiters, and maintenance men, and they are particularly heavily represented in the metal, construction, and textile industries.

The foreign workers, an indispensable source of labor supply in the period after the waning of the refugee influx, now pose very special problems. They are more difficult to assimilate, rarely speak German well, and tend to live under more deprived conditions. While they annually send some 5 billion marks of their earnings to their home countries, many have chosen to remain in Germany for years on end, and often they develop skills for which there is no market in their native lands. Increasingly, they have joined German unions, for which they present a particular problem because of their vulnerability to unemployment in periods of recession. In the years that lie ahead the mitigation of serious ethnic strife between German-born and foreign workers will pose a challenge for the unions and the government, a challenge which both must recognize if a potential source of political unrest is to be kept quiescent.

Social Patterns and Problems

The Federal Republic has emerged as a remarkably homogeneous society in view of the deep cleavages and bitter strife of the past. In part this is the result of the social leveling that occurred during the Third Reich. Furthermore, defeat and postwar impoverishment created a brief period in which a kind of social and economic equalization was imposed upon the entire population. The uprooting and transferring of population that followed, and especially the vast influx of refugees from the east, further eradicated historic factors of social differentiation.

Many members of the old, landowning aristocracy from the lands east of the Elbe suddenly found themselves not only geographically, but also socially, dispossessed.

It was to a very large degree Germany's remarkable economic recovery that created the means and conditions for effective integration of the many potentially discordant and socially diverse forces. The primacy of economic recovery as an overall objective, the increasing opportunity of securing material gains, and the political weariness and apathy that characterized public opinion, all eased the process of social integration. So did the prevailing sense of animosity toward communism and Soviet policy in the 1950s. The resulting pattern suggests that Germany, at least in that portion which remains in the Federal Republic, has come a long way in developing a reasonably harmonious domestic social setting.

Still, it would be wrong to overlook important structural problems that remain. First, there is the issue of the lagging sectors. Agriculture has been in steady decline. By 1970, the agricultural sector was producing less than 4 percent of the gross national product, yet it was still employing about one out of every ten members of the working force. Meanwhile, as has been seen, subventions from Bonn have risen to more than 5 billion marks annually. This pattern is an unhealthy one and seriously in need of basic reform.

There are other sectors confronted with chronic problems of overproduction. Coal and shipbuilding, both important components of German economic recovery, have been in serious crisis. Both have been heavily subsidized by government, a method that cannot alone resolve the basic problems of these industries in the absence of more comprehensive planning. Planning will also be required to assure the development of the low-income regional areas scattered throughout the Federal Republic. If social integration is to continue, economic progress must be increased in rural Germany. Social programs will have to be expanded and plans developed to meet the growing demands of the 2 million foreign workers. And the swelling ranks of the aged and the retired will pose increasing problems in a period of greater affluence and mounting inflation.

Success on these fronts is of particular significance in Germany if political stability is to be assured. The manifestations of right-wing radicalism in 1966 with the sudden, though short-lived, rise of the N.P.D. suggest how easily social frustration and economic fears can be triggered into antisystem and antidemocratic politics. Indeed, the recession of 1966 was very mild by comparison with the experience of other countries. Yet it produced a shrill political reaction.

But if recession is to be particularly feared in the Federal Republic, so is inflation. The memory of the 1920s and of the immediate postwar crisis remains vivid, so that a government must be particularly vigorous in combatting price increases if it is to survive. In the Federal Republic the stability and success of economic policy is of greater significance than elsewhere in Europe, for historical reasons. It remains to be seen whether the economic priorities of German governments can be harmonized with those of its European partners in a period of increasing supranational integration.

While the trend toward social homogeneity has increased in the Federal Republic, important factors of differentiation remain. It has been said by the German sociologist Helmut Schelsky and others that an important attribute of modern German society has been the "leveling" of its middle class. With the decline of the self-employed craftsman, shopkeeper, or farmer has come the rise of the affluent worker. However, if overall similarities have increased, fundamental inequalities persist. The pattern of income distribution has remained uneven. While overall taxes are high, ceilings are not. The maximum income tax of 53 percent, is well below the comparable level in Britain. Similarly, there has been an almost total neglect of inheritance taxation. Indeed, it may be argued that virtually from the outset, the very wealthy have been favored. The currency reform of 1948 greatly increased the value of real assets, while reducing that of savings. The subsequent effort to encourage capital reinvestment created unusual opportunities for the amassing of wealth by private industry. Today, some 16,000 industrialists, businessmen, bankers, and landowners have annual incomes in excess of 1 million marks.

Inequities also persist in the distribution of jobs. Educational opportunity has served as a critical filter. For example, only 8 percent of the sons of workers and farmers attend university. Yet higher education is a prerequisite for advancement at the higher echelons of business and government. A sample of only those who hold law degrees indicates how narrow the recruitment process tends to be. Twenty-two percent of all members of the Bundestag hold law degrees, and the same figure pertains for managers in industry. The percentage of law graduates within the federal cabinet is twice as high. And no less than 85 percent of the higher civil service, which controls the administration of government, is trained in law. Self-recruitment is also high. For example, 24 percent of all cabinet members, 30 percent of all managers, and 43 percent of all professors are the sons of higher civil servants. By contrast, the lower classes, Catholics, and women are substantially underrepresented in this elite work force.

Yet membership in the German upper class does not imply a combination of power, wealth, and respect. It is not a homogeneous group like the British and French upper classes; it is not an establishment. For the Federal Republic lacks the elite schools, the great cosmopolitan capital, and the historical tradition of closely shared values and habits that are features of the British and French social systems. Class rule in Germany has always left competing groups at the helm. Today, it is a more open society, but clearly more open for some than for others.

Seven

Modernity Facing the Future

During the past century, the German people have lived under an extraordinary diversity of regimes. The Kaiserreich was succeeded briefly by the military dictatorship of General Ludendorff. This was followed in turn by the abortive revolution of 1918 and the establishment of the Weimar Republic. Fifteen years of chaotic republicanism brought on twelve of totalitarian frenzy. Then came the four-year hiatus of Allied Occupation with its several zones of administration. Even after 1949, Germany remained divided into two states, shorn of much of its former territory and with a separate and special status for its traditional capitol, Berlin. No other European people has experienced so much impermanence of boundaries or such frequent and extensive transfigurations of its political way of life.

For Germany it has been a century of prodigious growth and vast destruction. No other country grew as fast during the period of industrialization, nor was any other as completely militarized during World War I. No other suffered as bitter a disappointment in its first experiment with democratic institutions nor experienced as deep an economic dislocation in the wake of the Depression. Certainly nowhere else has totalitarianism produced so monolithic a system in so short a period of time, nor one that was based to such a degree on war, genocide, terror, and destructive megalomania. No other European nation was left as dismembered by World War II, nor did any other confront as massive a postwar forced transfer of population. Yet since the war, no European country has had an economic recovery comparable to that achieved by the Federal Republic.

A pattern of recurrent instability and of constant change has characterized German experience in the hundred years since unification. It was as though the forces unleashed by nationhood had created pressures so powerful that they could not be effectively controlled or contained. And yet while Germany appeared to be in motion all the time, its population seemed to yearn for nothing so much as order and stability. In a way, that which was most ardently sought was least available. A manifestly traditional society could not easily cope with such frequent and often radical change.

Virtually from the outset Germany as a unified nation was confronted by a dual dilemma. Internally, it had somehow to modernize its institutions and political system if it was successfully to integrate the forces of change. Externally, the German nation had to make certain that its quest for unity did not unsettle and threaten the rest of Europe. However, it failed from the start in achieving either of these tasks.

The intense scope and speed of industrialization had rapidly transformed the structure of German society. It suddenly produced a host of new claimants for participation in the political process. This further reinforced the need for overdue political reforms. Yet the capacity of the German system to modernize did not extend to the political realm. Deep social cleavages, entrenched special interests, an inept monarchy, and the grip of authoritarian habits stood in the way of an evolutionary transformation of the political way of life.

Unable and unwilling to effect reform from within, Germany's leaders sought gains abroad that might quell internal dissension and deflect pressure for political change at home. Nation, state, and *Volk* were held above the pursuit of pluralistic rights and liberal values. The cult of the military, the quest for economic expansion, and the fostering of a shrill, romantic nationalism were the components of an ideology that was meant to unify a restive and divided nation. This seemed to require tension abroad, so gradually, an aggressive foreign policy became a pillar of the domestic peace. But this produced a dangerous and highly unstable situation that could not long endure. In 1914 it led to a war from which Germany was never fully to recover.

When Germany took the path of reform during the Weimar Republic, conditions were extremely inauspicious. It was a noble experiment, but one that faltered very early. By 1920, with the abortive Kapp Putsch, the forces of the Right were able to mount the first onslaught of their counterrevolution. But it was less the conspiracies of the Right than the failings of the system that signaled the demise of this venture in democracy. Long before Hitler seized power, the Weimar Republic had ceased to function as a democratic, parliamentary system. This is not to say that Nazism was inevitable or somehow immanent in the German soul or system. Rather, events had created a situation in which the most pathological and authoritarian factors and forces became predominant.

Twelve years of macabre Nazi rule served as a kind of catharsis for Germany. Its vicious fanaticism and destructive mania removed a great deal of that which had been traditional in the German system. It not only consumed the forces of constructive change, but also obliterated the fundamental elements of the old order.

Thus, when the regime was itself eradicated through the total defeat of 1945, the opportunity for a new beginning was at hand.

This brief review suggests how critical foreign policy has been in shaping the course of German history since the separate German states were first unified. To a large degree it was the international situation prevailing in the years just after World War II that led to the establishment of the Federal Republic and that created important opportunities for its regaining of sovereign powers. For Konrad Adenauer and Willy Brandt, the two most effective leaders among the four postwar German Chancellors, foreign policy played a central role in the consolidation of their domestic political positions. But in stark contrast to the past, this course did not prove unsettling and destablizing to Germany's neighbors. For in the postwar epoch Germany was no longer in a position to dominate others in Europe. The changed nature of the international system precluded an independent, aggressive policy pursued by any one European state. And in the case of Germany, its own division, becoming increasingly permanent over time, and its limited sovereignty greatly reduced the power available for the pursuit of an autonomous foreign policy.

This was a very significant change. For the first time in almost a century Germany was no longer a predominant military power. Although some irredentist claims and aspirations were kept alive, the Federal Republic did not pose an actual threat to any of its neighbors. Foreign policy still remained an important domestic factor, but no longer in the virulent and pernicious sense of the past. Indeed, despite its longtime official pretensions and pronouncements in favor of reunification, the Federal Republic has hardly, at least until recently, played a major political role in international affairs.

Ironically, this may have been a factor greatly to its advantage. While Britain and France had to cope with costly and cumbersome problems of decolonization and dwindling empires, the Federal Republic could concentrate on the tasks of domestic reconstruction. Having foresworn nuclear weapons and the maintenance of an independent military force outside the N.A.T.O. Alliance, it has been able to economize substantially on defense costs. In a period in which the pursuit of sovereign foreign-policy aims brought few gains and ample frustrations to other European nations, the Federal Republic seemed blessed by the postwar restrictions placed on its own freedom to maneuver.

Instead of pursuing purely national aims abroad, the Federal Republic has sought to mute its regained sovereign powers within the context of a larger European entity. The movement toward European integration created an entirely new framework for German aspirations. The Federal Republic alone among the six signatories of the Treaty of Rome regarded itself at the time as a somewhat provisional state. It was difficult to engender a real sense of permanent West German separateness. In part this was because the German nation remained divided into two states. But it was also the consequence of the fact that at the time of its entry into the Common Market, the Federal Republic was still not a fully sovereign state. Thus, it surrendered less and stood to gain more from the process of western integration.

To the degree that the Common Market has been a success, the Federal Republic has been able to derive a real sense of achievement from its foreign policy. Its efforts in the East have been less successful. Not until the late 1960s did the Federal Republic embark on a policy of détente toward the Soviet Union and Eastern Europe. This was accelerated under the government of Chancellor Brandt, whose efforts on behalf of *Ostpolitik* rendered to the Federal Republic a new sense of initiative in the realm of foreign policy. Suddenly, what had seemed to be a restrictive burden upon the Bonn government—namely its relations with the East—was transformed into a sense of special opportunity. But even so, German *Ostpolitik* has remained clearly subordinate to the primary purposes of achieving futher integration in the West and of maintaining the close alliance with the United States.

In the postwar epoch, foreign policy has served to reinforce the pattern of stable and liberal democratic politics within the Federal Republic. Whereas in the past external tensions were utilized to justify the thwarting of domestic reform, the Federal Republic has pursued policies of accommodation and cooperation. This has removed the traditional isolation of Germany from its Western neighbors. Instead, a powerful sense of transnational identification and symbiosis emerged, which has helped to consolidate the liberal, democratic parliamentary system in the Federal Republic. Today, despite the division of Germany, the special status of Berlin, and the continuing limited Allied rights with reference to issues of German reunification, the problems of the Federal Republic have come more and more to resemble those of other countries in Europe. There is no longer the acute sense of an ominous and intractable "German problem" that prevailed throughout the first half of this century. To be sure, there are issues still to be resolved, especially with regard to the relationship between the two German states and the matters of access to, and the status of, West Berlin. But German attitudes toward these issues are far more temperate than would have been conceivable several decades ago. The belligerent nationalism that sought the regaining of the Polish corridor or Alsace-Lorraine in the years following World War I does not exist today. It may be unpalatable for West Germans to recognize the Oder-Neisse frontier separating the German Democratic Republic from Poland. But there are no responsible leaders or groups who would advocate the use of force to regain the lost territories of the East, which are far greater in size than those lost after 1918. And for the first time in a century, relations with France have become amicable. This is indeed a profound and salutary development.

In many other ways the Federal Republic has proven a rather remarkable success. Its political system, despite the parliamentary crisis of 1972, has emerged as relatively stable. The tenure in office of Chancellors and cabinets has been relatively long. Not once has a government resorted to emergency measures, despite the frequent stress produced by Soviet machinations in the past. Parliament has never (before 1972) been dissolved by the government, nor to date removed a Chancellor through a constructive vote of no confidence. Indeed, until the spring of 1972, no motion of constructive nonconfidence had ever been introduced in the Bundestag. Federalism seems to have worked well, allowing a useful inter-

change between state and national governments. The party system, too, has functioned relatively well. Coalitions have been unusually stable, and if the pattern of
consolidation continues, it is likely that only the two major parties will soon remain,
precluding the necessity, in most cases, of coalition government at all.

In terms of economic development and social transformation, the Federal
Republic has also come a long way. Its growth rate is unmatched in Europe and
has rendered to West Germany a position of leadership in trade and a high standard
of living. The process of social integration has been highly successful. As Juan Linz
has shown, in the 1950s "the cross-cutting of group affiliations and the absence
of overly organized and closed subcultures" already characterized the political
system of the Federal Republic.[1] This was a striking departure from the patterns
of the past. It was the more surprising insofar as a number of groups—including
labor, industry, the farmers, and the refugees—were extremely well organized in
this period. However, each had a sufficient capacity to identify with the common
purposes and aims of the system as a whole to accept compromise and to acquiesce in favor of national priorities and prescriptions. Ironically, the Federal
Republic, with a very weak symbolic manifestation of the national interest, was
able to secure much greater compliance from a diversity of groups than its more
outspokenly nationalistic predecessors.

In large part this was because material reconstruction was broadly accepted as
the primary task of the Federal Republic. It proved easier to integrate diverse social
forces in pursuit of economic growth than on behalf of a highly articulated definition of German nationalism. But this was only possible because economic growth
was so successfully achieved. The sheer quantity of material betterment was sufficiently great to provide concrete rewards even for those most opposed to acceptance of the political status quo. This was a great asset in the quest for political
stability in the Federal Republic.

Will this success endure? To be sure, important problems remain. They are not
so much those of the division of Germany, but rather uncertainties about the
quality of change that has occurred within the Federal Republic. Ralf Dahrendorf
has expressed his concern that "German society has not yet accepted the reality
of conflict and the necessity of its rational regulation. Many of the most striking
changes in the structure of the economy and society in the Federal Republic are,
therefore, most liable to be undone again."[2] This is entirely possible. The great
emphasis on material values poses dangers. First, it may falsely accustom the
population to a continuous improvement in the standard of living, which can lead
to abrupt and exaggerated disappointment such as occurred during the brief recession of 1966. Second, material satisfaction in itself should not be mistaken for a
fundamental reorientation of political values.

---

[1]Juan J. Linz, "Cleavage and Consensus in West German Politics: The Early Fifties," in
Seymour M. Lipset and Stein Rokkan, *Party Systems and Voter Alignments* (New York,
1967), p. 316.

[2]Dahrendorf, *Society and Democracy in Germany* (London, 1967), pp. 446–447.

In a sense public values seem to be largely missing, or at least poorly articulated, in the Federal Republic. There is a marked absence of any ideological commitment or vision. A kind of prosaic political culture has resulted. Even the scope of the nation is not clearly resolved. And, as Sidney Verba has observed, "the politics of Germany reflects a pragmatism and passivity to governmental authority."[3] Thus, a great deal depends on how that authority is used.

So far, it has been used with constructive effect. But the past record has been one of uninterrupted economic growth and a firm Western presence and pattern of continued integration. If one or the other were to be seriously thwarted, substantial instability might reemerge in German politics. Even with continued economic prosperity and success in foreign policy, it is not certain that the past pattern of stability will endure.

The prospect of political polarization is a serious one. This could manifest itself in a splintering of the two major parties or in a significant decline in party loyalty and an increase in extra-party activity. The vociferous challenge of the S.P.D. leadership by new, militant forces within the party, and especially among its younger members, has posed grave problems for the Social Democratic leaders. While the decade following the adoption of the Godesberg Program in 1959 was one of consensus-building movement toward the political center for the party, it seems that in the years ahead the S.P.D. will be confronted with a vigorous internal challenge by those seeking a more radical and ideological definition of the party program. How this movement of radical dissent will be absorbed or resisted by the party will be of critical importance for the development and success of the S.P.D. in the decade ahead.

Similarly, the C.D.U./C.S.U. must contend with increasingly vocal forces on the Right. The success of the German political system in containing the appeals of the N.P.D. and other right-wing parties in the past has, in part, been due to the capacity of the C.D.U./C.S.U. to absorb the reservoir of right-wing voters. But here, too, further polarization would pose serious dilemmas. The potential force of a right-wing reaction against some of the manifestations of modern, industrial life may grow among those social groups which are threatened or which still yearn for a more traditional social order and cannot accept the demise of effective national symbols in present-day Germany. And here the extremism of the Left, fostered by a small minority and manifested in a series of violent acts, can contribute to a dangerous overreaction on the Right.

It is also possible that a diminution in the effectiveness of the present political institutions may occur. The recent crisis, beginning in the spring of 1972, demonstrated that some of the institutional provisions of the Basic Law may not continue to function as well in the future as they seemed to in the past. For the first time, in April 1972, a motion of constructive nonconfidence was placed by the opposi-

---

[3]Sidney Verba, "Germany: the Remaking of Political Culture," in Lucien W. Pye and Sidney Verba, *Political Culture and Development* (Princeton, 1969), p. 153.

tion. In the secret vote on this motion, the opposition came within two votes of the absolute majority of the Bundestag membership required for the election of a new Chancellor. Yet the results of this vote demonstrated that the government also no longer possessed a majority in the lower house. Thus, in a sense, three wavering members who cast ballots of abstention largely determined who would govern the Federal Republic in the absence of new elections.

Yet the crisis demonstrated how difficult it is for a Chancellor to secure new elections without the cooperation of the opposition. Should he move for and lose a vote of confidence and request a dissolution, the opposition could again, under the terms of Article 68, attempt to elect a new Chancellor before the President could dissolve the house. And under these circumstances, it is not unlikely that several Bundestag members, fearing the loss of their seats or their parliamentary pensions, would defect from the government ranks in the secret vote in order to avert new elections. A new Chancellor elected under such conditions would stand no stronger in Parliament than his predecessor. This situation was evidently not foreseen by those who drafted the Basic Law. Articles 67 and 68 were designed with a multiparty Parliament in mind.

In the absence of a constitutional change, the crisis of 1972 suggests that a stalemate can develop in Parliament, in which a Chancellor, lacking a clear majority cannot easily achieve new elections. Instead, he may be compelled to continue to govern with the occasional support or acquiescence of a basically hostile parliamentary opposition that has sufficient power to block his legislation while lacking the necessary votes to displace him. A paralyzed parliamentary situation of this sort, which resulted in 1972 from the gradual defection over a two-year period of six members from the S.P.D./F.D.P coalition, could further reduce confidence in the parliamentary system as a whole. This factor, combined with the general trend toward a decline in the role of Parliament and the concomitant increase in the overall bureaucratization of politics, could have seriously destabilizing consequences in Germany.

The catalogue of potential social problems is large as well. Rancor against the foreigners working in ever greater numbers within the Federal Republic, the prospect of further rural stagnation, the radicalization of the universities, the persistence of educational imbalances, and the growth of crime are new problems that may well continue to afflict the Federal Republic in the years ahead. But they are in no sense unique to Germany. Rather, they are to a substantial degree the products of a highly advanced industrial society. Germany today is certainly not problem-free. But its foremost problems are also common to other countries. There is still a great deal that is peculiar to the German system, but its predominant concerns are not so much of German origin as they are the result of processes of modernization. The Federal Republic today is in this sense a more "normal" society than any of its predecessors have been. To be afflicted by common ailments is, in the German case, symptomatic of a state of comparative good health—given the diseased record of the past.

Select Bibliography

The Period before 1945

Bracher, Karl Dietrich. *The German Dictatorship*. New York: Praeger, 1970.

Bullock, Allan. *Hitler—A Study in Tyranny*. New York: Harper & Row, 1964.

Eyck, Erich. *A History of the Weimar Republic*. 2 vols. Cambridge, Mass.: Harvard University Press, 1962.

Feldman, Gerald D. *Army, Industry and Labor in Germany 1914–1918*. Princeton, N. J.: Princeton University Press, 1966.

Fischer, Fritz. *Germany's Aims in the First World War*. New York: W. W. Norton, 1967.

Gay, Peter. *Weimar Culture*. New York: Harper & Row, 1968.

Gerschenkron, Alexander. *Bread and Democracy in Germany*. New York: Howard Fertig, 1966.

Heberle, Rudolf. *From Democracy to Nazism*. New York: Howard Fertig, 1967.

Krieger, Leonard. *The German Idea of Freedom*. Boston: Beacon Press, 1957.

Mann, Golo. *The History of Germany Since 1789*. New York: Praeger, 1968.

Moore, Barrington, Jr. *Social Origins of Dictatorship and Democracy*. Boston: Beacon Press, 1967.

Neumann, Franz. *Behemoth*. New York: Harper & Row, 1966.

Peterson, Edward N. *The Limits of Hitler's Power*. Princeton, N. J.: Princeton University Press, 1969.

Rosenberg, Arthur. *Imperial Germany: The Birth of the German Republic 1871–1918*. Boston: Beacon Press, 1964.

Rosenberg, Hans. *Bureaucracy, Aristocracy and Autocracy: The Prussian Experience 1660–1815*. Cambridge, Mass.: Harvard University Press, 1958.

Ryder, A. J. *The German Revolution of 1918*. Cambridge, England: Cambridge University Press, 1967.

Schoenbaum, David. *Hitler's Social Revolution*. New York: Doubleday, 1966.

Schorske, Carl. *German Social Democracy 1905–1917*. Cambridge, Mass.: Harvard University Press, 1955.

Stern, Fritz. *The Politics of Cultural Despair.* Garden City, N. Y.: Anchor Books, 1965.

Taylor, A. J. P. *The Course of German History.* New York: Capricorn Books, 1962.

Turner, Henry Ashby, Jr. *Stresemann and the Politics of the Weimar Republic.* Princeton, N. J.: Princeton University Press, 1963.

The Period from 1945 to 1949

Conze, Werner. *Jakob Kaiser: Politiker zwischen Ost und West 1945–1949.* Stuttgart: W. Kohlhammer Verlag, 1969.

Gimbel, John. *A German Community Under American Occupation.* Stanford, Calif.: Stanford University Press, 1961.

_____. *The American Occupation of Germany: Politics and the Military 1945–1949.* Stanford, Calif.: Stanford University Press, 1968.

Golay, John Ford. *The Founding of the Federal Republic of Germany.* Chicago: University of Chicago Press, 1958.

Merkl, Peter H. *The Origin of the West German Republic.* New York: Oxford University Press, 1963.

Schwarz, Hans-Peter. *Vom Reich zur Bundesrepublik.* Neuwied, West Germany: Luchterhand Verlag, 1967.

Willis, F. Roy. *The French in Germany 1945–1949.* Stanford, Calif.: Stanford University Press, 1962.

Government and Political Institutions

Ellwein, Thomas. *Das Regierungssystem der Bundesrepublik Deutschland.* Cologne: Westdeutscher Verlag, 1965.

Fromme, Friedrich Karl. *Von der Weimarer Verfassung zum Bonner Grundgesetz.* Tübingen, West Germany: J. C. B. Mohr (Paul Siebeck) Verlag, 1960.

Grosser, Alfred. *Die Bonner Demokratie.* Düsseldorf: Karl Rauch Verlag, 1960.

_____. *Germany in Our Time.* New York: Praeger, 1971.

Heidenheimer, Arnold J. *The Governments of Germany.* New York: Thomas Y. Crowell, 1961.

Holborn, L., G. Caster and J. Herz. *German Constitutional Documents Since 1871.* New York: Praeger, 1970.

Loewenberg, Gerhard. *Parliament in the German Political System.* Ithaca, N. Y.: Cornell University Press, 1966.

Political Parties

Chalmers, Douglas A. *The Social Democratic Party of Germany.* New Haven, Conn.: Yale University Press, 1964.

Edinger, Lewis J. *Kurt Schumacher: A Study in Personality and Political Behavior.* Stanford, Calif.: Stanford University Press, 1965.

Heidenheimer, Arnold J. *Adenauer and the C.D.U.* The Hague: Martinus Nijhoff, 1960.

Kaack, Heino. *Geschichte und Struktur des deutschen Parteiensystems.* Cologne: Westdeutscher Verlag, 1971.

Schellenger, Harold Kent. *The S.P.D. in the Bonn Republic: A Socialist Party Modernizes.* The Hague: Martinus Nijhoff, 1968.

Social and Economic Forces

Arndt, Hans-Joachim. *West Germany: Politics of Non-Planning.* Syracuse, N. Y.: Syracuse University Press, 1966.

Beyme, Klaus von. *Die Politische Elite in der Bundesrepublik Deutschland.* Munich: R. Piper Verlag, 1971.

Boarman, Patrick. *Germany's Economic Dilemma: Inflation and the Balance of Payments.* New Haven, Conn.: Yale University Press, 1964.

Dahrendorf, Ralf. *Society and Democracy in Germany.* New York: Doubleday, 1967.

Edinger, Lewis J. *Politics in Germany: Attitudes and Processes.* Boston: Little, Brown, 1968.

MacLennan, Malcolm, Murray Forsyth, and Geoffrey Denton. *Economic Planning and Policies in Britain, France and Germany.* New York: Praeger, 1968.

Roskamp, Karl W. *Capital Formation in West Germany.* Detroit: Wayne State University Press, 1965.

Stolper, Gustav, Karl Häuser, and Knut Borchardt. *The German Economy: 1870 to the Present.* New York: Harcourt, Brace & World, 1967.

Wallich, Henry C. *Mainsprings of the German Revival.* New Haven, Conn.: Yale University Press, 1955.

Zapf, Wolfgang. *Wandlungen der deutschen Elite 1919–1961.* Munich: R. Piper Verlag, 1965.

Foreign Policy

Baring, Arnulf. *Aussenpolitik in Adenauers Kanzlerdemokratie.* Munich: R. Oldenbourg Verlag, 1969.

Besson, Waldemar. *Die Aussenpolitik der Bundesrepublik.* Munich: R. Piper Verlag, 1970.

Deutsch, Karl W., Lewis J. Edinger, Roy C. Macridis, and Richard L. Merritt. *France, Germany and the Western Alliance.* New York: Charles Scribner's Sons, 1967.

Hanrieder, Wolfram. *German Foreign Policy 1949–1963.* Stanford, Calif.: Stanford University Press, 1967.

_____. *The Stable Crisis: Two Decades of German Foreign Policy.* New York: Harper & Row, 1970.

Kaiser, Karl. *German Foreign Policy in Transition.* New York: Oxford University Press, 1968.

Richardson, James. *Germany and the Atlantic Alliance.* Cambridge, Mass.: Harvard University Press, 1966.

Willis, F. Roy. *France, Germany and the New Europe.* Stanford, Calif.: Stanford University Press, 1964.

Windsor, Philip. *Germany and the Management of Detente.* New York: Praeger, 1971.

5

The Russian
Political System

Adam B. Ulam

Accounting and control—that is the *main* thing required for the "setting up" and correct functioning of the *first phase* of Communist society. *All* citizens are transformed into the salaried employees of the state, which consists of the armed workers. *All* citizens become employees and workers of a *single* national state "syndicate." All that is required is that they should work equally—do their proper share of work—and get paid equally. . . . The whole of society will have become a single office and a single factory, with equality of labour and equality of pay.—V.I. Lenin, *The State and Revolution, August 1917*

In every branch of industry, in every factory, in every department of a factory, there is a leading group of more or less skilled workers who must be first and foremost attached to production if we want to make sure of having a permanent staff of workers. . . . And how can we manage to attach them to the factory? It can be done by advancing them, by raising their wages, by introducing such a system of payment as will give the skilled worker his due. . . . *And so our task is to put an end to the instability of labour power, to abolish equalitarianism, to organize wages properly, and to improve the living conditions of the work-ers.*—J. V. Stalin, Speech Delivered in June 1931

One

Tradition and Modernity in Soviet Political Culture

When we speak of Soviet Russia (for it takes too long to say or write The Union of Soviet Socialist Republics), we underline the twofold character of the history and government of the communist state. There is Russia the builder and dominant part of the empire: "An unbreakable union of free republics was forged forever by the great Rus," proclaimed the first words of the Soviet national anthem adopted during World War II.[1] The earlier ideological scruples were then fully displaced by proud glorification of Russia's past, and the *Internationale* was no longer deemed suitable for the national anthem. And there is "Soviet," the term that brings to mind the complex of ideas and institutions having to do with Marx, Engels, and Lenin, with the Revolution of 1917, and with a movement that claims to be universal and supranational and has an ideology that claims to present a picture of the future of all mankind.

Thus the political culture of the U.S.S.R. contains elements of the history of the state and nation that trace their beginnings to the tenth century; yet, at the same time, it has the imprint of an ideology that has developed within the last century. The two major foundations of the Soviet political system lie in the history of the Russian people and of Marxism-Leninism.

How to assess their relative importance has been the major point of dispute among the commentators on Russian affairs and Russian historians themselves. Is

---

[1]The word *Rus* has been used traditionally to describe the medieval Russian state in contrast to its modern form, *Rossiya*.

Marxism merely a thin veneer for the latest manifestation of forces apparent throughout the course of Russian history, or is the Communist regime a definite break with the historical tradition of Russia? The proponents of the first view have stressed the parallel between Soviet totalitarianism epitomized in Stalin and the high points of despotism and reform in Russian history found under Ivan the Terrible (1533–1584) and Peter the Great (1682–1725). Even such characteristic institutions of Soviet Russia as the *kolkhoz* (the collective farm) are for them but a continuation of the old system of peasant tenancy—the *mir* of old Russia. The proponents of basic continuity of Russian history have not infrequently characterized the dictatorship of the Communist party as the up-to-date expression of the traditional organization of Russian society, where the sense of community and social union, often with religious undertones, has assertedly been prized above the "Western" values of personal freedom and individualism.

It has been pointed out with equal force that there is but a faint resemblance between modern totalitarianism and old despotism; that the kolkhoz, which is an attempt to apply the factory system to agriculture, has nothing to do with the *mir;* and that it is a gross oversimplification to take the relative absence of liberal and representative institutions in Russian history as an indication of something inherently undemocratic or collectivistic in the Russian national character. And indeed, though no revolution can destroy the accumulated weight of ten centuries of history, both Marxism and totalitarianism are modern phenomena. Russian history explains why they came to Russia and the modifications they have undergone there. But neither Marxism nor totalitarianism are "typically" Russian. To understand them we must look at the social and economic forces that gave birth to the doctrine and have guided its growth and that of the most influential socialist movement.

Marxism

There has always been a feeling in some circles, both Marxist and non-Marxist, that the victory of a Marxist party in Russia was something of a historical "mistake." Marxism was born in the West. It was the product of political and economic conditions of Western society in the nineteenth century. By its own premises the doctrine of Karl Marx (1818–1883) and Friedrich Engels (1820–1895) was supposed to triumph in a fully industrialized society. How can one explain, then, the popularity of Marxism in pre-1917 Russia and, finally, the victory of a Marxist party in a largely peasant economy undergoing only the intermediate stages of industrialization? Does it make any sense to talk about historical forces and the role of ideologies? Or should we consider the prevalence of Marxism in pre-1917 Russia an intellectual fad and the victory of the Bolsheviks in 1917 a historical accident?

What characterized Marxism in its beginning, both as a theory and a political movement, were three main elements: (1) an economic theory, (2) a philosophy of history, and (3) a philosophy of revolution.

The economic doctrine is based on the famous labor theory of value. Capitalism, resting as it does upon private ownership of the means of production, is not only, or mainly, unjust, but primarily self-destructive. The capitalist's profit is considered an unjust extortion from the worker, who has the right to the total product, since labor is the only source of value. But far more important than the ethical aspect of the problem are its economic consequences: The inevitable exploitation of capitalism creates periodic and successively more severe crises of overproduction. Mature capitalism cannot but lead to increasing unemployment and increasing poverty of the masses, since in order to retain their profits the capitalists must keep depressing the level of wages. At the other end of the social scale this leads to increasing monopoly and concentration of the means of production in fewer and fewer hands. It was the economic aspect of their doctrine that led Marx and Engels to differentiate sharply between their own and other brands of socialism. The others, they held, pleaded for socialism on ethical or political grounds, while only Marxism saw that, quite apart from moral postulates and political conditions, socialism—the ownership of the means of production by the community—is the *inevitable* sequel of fully developed capitalism.

Marx and Engels produced their work at a period when it was widely believed, and not only among socialists, that the social sciences could have the validity and predictability of the natural sciences and that the laws governing the development of society could be laid down with the rigor of physical laws. That conviction was likewise the basis of their philosophy of history and politics. "Scientific socialism" was built on the broad framework of economic determinism, which provided the main clue to the workings of history. Material factors, specifically, the character and ownership of the principal means of production, constitute for the Marxist the master key of the social development of mankind. Hegelian dialectic and nine-teenth-century materialism are joined in Marxism to provide the gigantic frame-work of history, where, as their economic underpinnings change, civilizations develop, mature, and then collapse. The economic forces determining the content of history are, then, themselves triggered off by changes in science and technology. The industrial use of steam spells the final end of feudal society, in which land is the principal means of production. Further inventions and the adoption of industrial techniques bring about the triumph of a new civilization and economic organiza-tion—capitalism. Yet *when fully developed,* capitalism is doomed by the same technological and economic forces that had predestined its success, and it must yield to a new way of life—socialism. Whatever its philosophical and political postulates, Marxism is unusually sensitive to and conscious of the development of science and technology. Its frame of mind is both historical and scientific.

The forces of history find their tangible embodiment in the social classes. Hence "the history of all hitherto existing society is the history of class struggles;"[2] for the dominant class does not capitulate once its economic basis becomes less important

---

[2] *The Communist Manifesto.*

and its political role obsolete. In Marx's lifetime the middle class in Western Europe, especially in England and France, was winning political concessions from the landowning aristocracy and became the dominant political class in the state. The struggles for parliamentary and social reforms, for the ending of aristocratic privileges, and for civil rights were viewed by Marxism as mere reflections of the basic and immemorial class struggle—itself echoing the evolution of the forces of production. To Marx the triumph of the middle class (which he witnessed and in a way applauded as rendered inevitable by the forces of history) was but a prelude to the ultimate class struggle between the bourgeoisie and the new class produced by the Industrial Revolution: the working proletariat.

The intricate combination of philosophical, historical, and economic arguments culminated in Marxism in a plea for political action. Even before its theoretical structure was fully complete, Marxism appeared in the *Communist Manifesto* (1848) as a philosophy of revolution. Though Marx considered as inevitable the eventual destruction of the capitalist system by the forces of history, he worked for and at times expected the imminent overthrow of capitalism by the workers. The language of the economist and philosopher is often subdued by the language of the politician and revolutionary who wants to give history a push. If the theoretical part of Marx's writings is flavored by one word, *inevitability*—the inevitability of the Marxian scheme of history, of forces dwarfing human efforts and making the downfall of capitalism certain—the political side of his argument is colored by the word *exploitation:* The capitalists and industrialists are not mere agents of historical forces but are also malevolent oppressors and exploiters of the workers. The workers, once they gain the consciousness of their real situation, will smash decaying capitalism and its props, the state and organized religion.

Throughout his life the need for a revolution in which the working classes would seize the reins of the state remained for Marx an article of faith. As to the character and methods of this revolution, he did not remain of one mind. When the revolutionary excitement in Western Europe began to subside after the 1840s and 1850s, Marx's revolutionary optimism subsided with it. At one point he was ready to grant that in some highly industrialized countries with parliamentary institutions revolution might come through nonviolent and parliamentary means; that is, by the working classes' securing a majority in the parliaments of their countries. After his death his "alter ego," Engels, was to go even further in the expectation of a peaceful transition to socialism. But the most persistent elements in original Marxism are its appeal for revolution and its distrust of the institutions of the modern state, whether parliamentary or judicial, as being based not on impartiality, but on the vested interests of the economically dominant class. Only when the workers capture the state will democracy and equality become a reality. Until then they are for Marx merely hypocritical phrases used by the bourgeoisie to strengthen its political and economic oppression.

Any large-scale social doctrine is open to many interpretations. Translated into political action, it becomes of necessity detached from the mere opinions of its author and his immediate disciples. Marxist parties, not only in Russia, have justified actions most inconsistent with one another in the name of the same theory and the same body of writings. Already in Marx's life economic and political facts were impinging upon some of his principal theories and prophecies. It was a cardinal point of Marx's theory that the growth of capitalism brings with it the inevitable lowering of the standard of living and increasing unemployment for the workers. Yet the second half of the nineteenth century, which saw the flourishing of capitalism and industrialism in Western Europe, witnessed also an undeniable increase in the material well-being of the masses. Along with it came the widening of the parliamentary franchise, rudimentary measures of social security, and the legalization of labor unions—measures that Marx had held unlikely to be allowed by the bourgeois state. Socialist parties, even when they adopted the "orthodox" Marxist program (as in Germany) and refused to dilute it with liberalism, tacitly discarded Marx's more revolutionary and undemocratic prescriptions. Marxism in Western Europe appeared toward the end of the nineteenth century as merely a radical expression of the cosmopolitan, democratic, and egalitarian tendencies of the era, capable of being absorbed into the mechanics of a constitutional state. It was as such, clothed in democratic and constitutional phraseology, that it traveled into the economically and politically backward regions of Eastern Europe.

Even a summary account of Marxism provides some clues as to what made it so important to Russia, then a predominantly agrarian country, and what caused Marxism *as a political movement* to be born in the context, not of a fully industrialized society with democratic institutions, but in a society in the initial stages of industrialization and with semi-feudal political institutions. Its revolutionary appeal echoed the discontent of the former peasant or artisan whom mysterious economic forces had deprived of his previous livelihood and had compelled to seek employment in industry. Here he found himself, even if better paid, without the security of his previous occupation, usually unprotected against sickness and accident, unprovided for in old age, and prohibited by the state and his employer from joining a labor union. Politically, the industrial worker was then without the right to vote, and it is logical that parliamentary institutions must have appeared to him merely as an arena of struggle between the middle and the upper classes. By the end of the nineteenth century the status and material conditions of the working class *in the West* presented a considerably different picture and precluded a ready response to the revolutionary appeal of Marxism. But the Russia of 1900 was similar in some respects to the West of the 1840s and 1850s, so that Marxism in its original revolutionary and conspiratorial form could well take root in Russian soil.

A critical analysis of Marxism and of the validity of its postulates is not needed to perceive its twofold significance as a political movement. In a society undergoing the transition from the agricultural to the industrial order, Marxism offers the lower classes an effective and appealing exposition of their grievances and frustrations. It shares this characteristic with many other socialist and anarchist movements. But unlike the latter, Marxism does not urge blind opposition to the necessary phenomena of modern life—the state and industry. On the contrary, while it advocates the destruction of capitalism and the bourgeoisie by revolution, it also speaks of the inevitability and benevolent effects of both industrialism and the state after capitalism has been destroyed.[3] Marx's qualifications about the withering away of the state and about complete economic equality, both of them inconsistent with modern industrial society, were to provide a useful rationalization for Stalin when he was building his totalitarian state and grossly inegalitarian society. But without burdening Marxism with the full responsibility for totalitarianism, it is clear that Marxism has considerable tactical advantages over other forms of socialism and radicalism. In a society where the mass of inhabitants are denied the right of participation in politics, and where the birth pangs of industrialism are in evidence, Marxism appeals both to the past, in denouncing the evils of factory discipline and the wage system, and to the future, in promising that in a socialist society industrialism will bring with it democracy and abundance.

Russian Traditions

That Russian history is in some sense "different," that it does not fit into the categories employed for other countries, has been the assumption of many writers, Russian and non-Russian, conservative and socialist. To the nineteenth-century historian with a liberal bias, history meant steady progress from despotism and superstition to democracy and enlightenment. Since Russia did not appear to conform to the pattern, Russian history had to be qualitatively different from that of the West. Today we no longer share the optimism that made such overgeneralizations possible. Nor do we believe in the notion that every country has its own "genius" and historical mission imprinted in the unique character of its political institutions. Russian history *is* different from that of the West, but not because of the "Russian soul" or the presence of factors absent elsewhere. It is different because the same social and economic forces found in the West appeared in Russia at different times and with different intensity.

We should not minimize the importance of the most obvious differences: a religion accepted from Constantinople rather than Rome and a Church and society that had undergone neither the Renaissance nor the Reformation; a social system in which the mass of the peasants was not emancipated from serfdom until 1861, long after those of Western Europe; and the relative absence or fragility of repre-

---

[3]Though Marx believes, as do the anarchists, that the state should wither away, the practical consequences of this notion are nullified by his admission that victorious socialism will need the state for a while, and a powerful centralized state at that—owner of all the means of production. A similar admission takes most of the strength out of Marxism's message of egalitarianism: Complete equality cannot be achieved immediately after the victory of socialism and destruction of capitalism. Only communism, the final stage of socialism—the time schedule is again not specified—will realize the slogan "from each according to his ability, to each according to his needs."

sentative institutions and of an independent judiciary. But we need not resort to mysticism or the exaggerated theory of the uniqueness of the Russian national character to explain the heritage of Russian history that the Soviets took over in 1917. The analytical apparatus of the social sciences is quite adequate for that purpose.

The most striking characteristics of Russian society on the eve of the revolutions of the twentieth century were centralization and the autocratic character of political authority; a social structure in which the mass of the freshly emancipated peasantry was still under severe economic and political restrictions and the middle class far weaker than, and different in character from, its Western European counterpart; and the rudimentary character of institutions of political and economic representation. The sources of these "peculiarities" that leave an undeniable imprint on today's Soviet institutions can be found in Russian history. Let us therefore spotlight some problems in the development of Russia and examine how the social and political forces that agitated the rest of Europe made their appearance in Russia.

Centralization of Political Authority and the Autocratic Tradition

In the West the principal beginnings of the modern state date from the Renaissance. Every student of history knows how the Tudor monarchy in England and figures such as Louis XI and Richelieu in France strove to overcome the heritage of feudalism and dispersion. The necessary elements of a modern state—a sense of national unity and centralization of political authority with the attendant institutions of the bureaucracy and the standing army—began to emerge only slowly and painfully toward the end of the Middle Ages. Roughly at the same time the task of state and nation building also confronted Russia but under vastly different conditions.

Ever since its recorded beginnings in the tenth century, the Russian state struggled for survival and expansion against its neighboring Finnish- and Turkish-speaking tribes and states. After the Mongol invasions the most notable setback in this struggle resulted in the subjugation of most of the country to the Tartars. For two centuries (from the middle of the thirteenth to the middle of the fifteenth century) most of Russia was isolated from the rest of Europe. Her previous and quite extensive commericial and cultural intercourse was almost entirely interrupted, and her princes were reduced to Tartar vassals and tribute collectors. Only in the fifteenth and sixteenth centuries did modern Russia begin to take shape, around the nucleus of the Grand Duchy of Moscow. This building of a state took place under conditions that, much more than in the West, facilitated, if not demanded, the erection of a strong and despotic monarchical authority. There was continuous warfare with the Tartars and sporadic war with Russia's northern and western neighbors, Sweden, and the kingdom of Poland-Lithuania, which contained extensive Russian-speaking lands. It is no wonder that even in sixteenth-century Europe, where absolute monarchy was the rule, the government of the Russian tsars, epitomized in the reign of Ivan the Terrible, became the byword for despotism.

In the West the Middle Ages had bequeathed to the Renaissance states social and political institutions that, centuries later, became the bases on which constitutionalism and representative institutions could, and did, grow. Such institutions were not unknown in medieval Russia. The monarchy was counterpoised by the Church, with the Metropolitan of Moscow, later on the Patriarch, as its head. The estates and diets of the rest of Europe were paralleled by the Russian Assembly of the Land and the Council of the Magnates. Even the rising middle class, in Western Europe the fermenting element of the social and political change, found its counterpart in the merchant republics of Novgorod and Pskov, which acknowledged only nominal sovereignty of the prince. But in Russia these institutions were considerably weaker and lacked a wide enough social basis. They were either eliminated (as in the loss of autonomy by Novgorod and Pskov) or subjugated through terror and economic sanctions by Ivan III (1462–1505) and Ivan the Terrible (1533–1584). The latter's reign is not atypical of certain other great periods of Russian history: Though he was a great social and political reformer and the military leader who finally destroyed the Tartar power, his reign abounds in instances of violent and systematic terror. It is a pattern to be found again in Peter the Great and Stalin and one that is not entirely absent from the reigns of the great state builders in the West, Louis XI in France and Henry VIII in England.

Ivan's reign with its centralization and despotism was followed, again not atypically, by a period of reassertion by the nobles, internal anarchy, and foreign invasions. Early in the seventeenth century it appeared as if Russia was to be joined to her western neighbor, the Polish-Lithuanian state. At that point something approaching modern nationalism was born in Russia. A wave of popular feeling, largely religious in its foundations, since the rival Polish monarchy was Catholic, established the Romanov dynasty in Russia and preserved the independence of the country. The inheritance of a prolonged national or religious struggle is likely to be an exaggerated and parochial sense of nationalism. The struggle against the Poles erected the autocracy and Orthodoxy into national symbols and strengthened the isolation from the political and cultural currents from the West.

It fell to Peter the Great (1682–1725) to modernize the Russian monarchy, but also to clamp tighter the shackles of absolutism. One aspect of his reforms was the imposition of the externals of Western civilization upon his subjects. An example was the enforced shaving of beards by the nobility. Modern industry and technology were imported into Russia, not through the action of private citizens, but by the state. In one reign Russia, a backward and ignored country, became a major power and a member of the European community of states—a historical development unparalleled until the rise of Japan in the late nineteenth century. Peter's reforms, however, also resulted in the destruction of the still existing social and political particularisms and, consequently, in the strengthening of the principle of autocracy. The Church was deprived of the patriarch and subjected to a lay official appointed by the emperor. Noblemen's privileges were made dependent on their direct service to the state, and the nobility, as a class, was amalgamated with a bureaucratic caste. Violent repression followed the slightest sign of semi-feudal or religious (one is tempted to say "counterrevolutionary") reaction against the reforms. Serfdom remained the chief prop of the economy, and the gap between the upper classes, forcibly westernized and educated, and the mass of the people became wider.

In a sense the pattern established under Peter has characterized Russian history during the past two centuries, and its traces are evident under the Soviet regime: The state became the main planner and executor of social and economic policy. In the West a similar situation prevailed during the heyday of mercantilism in the seventeenth and eighteenth centuries, but it was drastically changed in the nineteenth century when the social classes developed stronger viewpoints and pressures of their own. As compared with Western European countries, a sharp contrast marks Russia's development down to our own times. Russia was now in the forefront of the European community of nations; from Peter's time onward her upper classes participated in the most advanced European intellectual and political currents. Yet the mass of the people were left far behind. Revolutionary outbreaks, in which seventeenth- and eighteenth-century Russia abounded were like medieval risings and jacqueries—sporadic outbreaks of disgruntled nobles or oppressed peasants or Cossacks, rather than modern revolutionary movements with their specific political and economic postulates.

The principle of autocracy, now embellished with the latest bureaucratic techniques, remained unimpaired throughout the reign of Catherine the Great (1762–1796). Contacts with Europe increased, and indeed the partitions of Poland brought Russia much farther west. But if Catherine and her advisers thought of modernizing the state, they thought so in terms of the enlightened absolutism of the century, which sought to increase education and efficiency but neither decentralization nor the subjects' rights. The French-speaking and Westernized nobility was tied more firmly to the throne by economic and social concessions, but any half-hearted attempts at basic social reforms were defeated by the fears arising from the outbreak of the French Revolution.

Only at the beginning of the nineteenth century was the possibility of modern representative assemblies first discussed by the Russian government. This brief era of liberalism under Alexander I and his Minister, Mikhail Speransky, was succeeded by a period of reaction, and the fundamental parts of the latter's constitutional proposals were shelved. At the end of the Napoleonic wars the empire was increased by the addition of Finland and a part of Poland. In these areas the tsar was a constitutional monarch, and representative institutions functioned while he remained the autocrat of a Russia that did not possess anything remotely resembling a parliament!

The reign of Nicholas I (1825–1855) began with the first modern revolutionary attempt. The Decembrists of 1825, who failed in an armed *putsch,* were composed mostly of young aristocrats and army officers. They had some constitutional and reformist notions gathered from the West, and they stand at the beginning of the great Russian revolutionary tradition. Their abortive attempt provided the justification for a new technique and routine of repression. The Russia of Nicholas

I became an autocracy in which the passivity of the citizen was no longer taken for granted. The police state, with its administrative judgments, its secret police, and its all-embracing censorship, became the means through which the tsarist bureaucracy strove to preserve the status quo and to repress the social and intellectual ferment. The tsarist state under Nicholas considered itself (and was so considered by Europe) the bulwark of absolutism. The Polish uprising of 1830–1831 was put down by arms and Poland's constitutional privileges were abrogated. A Russian army helped the Austrian emperor to put down the Hungarian rebellion of 1848–1849. In contrast to a Europe bustling with democratic movements and liberal reforms, Russia stood as the fortress of militarism and national and social oppression, a seeming exception to all the rules of historical development as propounded by liberalism.

A cursory look at Russian history reinforces one's first impression of the passivity of the population and the consequent ability of the government to exercise absolute and at times tyrannical power. The revolutionary movement of the second half of the nineteenth century, though now almost continuous and punctuated by violent incidents, such as the assassination of Alexander II in 1881, was the work of small groups drawn for the most part from the thin layer of the educated and upper classes. At the end of the nineteenth century, just as at its beginning, Russia was an autocracy. The reforms of Alexander II supplied the rudiments of local government and judicial independence, but they did not affect the reality of the police state and the absence of civil rights. Into this society, politically static but in economic and social revolution, came Marxism.

The Social Structure and Representative Institutions

Russia's political development becomes intelligible only in terms of her social history, the main characteristics of which are familiar in the history of the West—though the parallel development stops at a certain point. Social classes and their status became frozen in Russia, and it was only the coming of the Industrial Revolution in the second half of the nineteenth century that propelled society forward at a feverish speed, ultimately creating a political crisis. An oversimplified explanation, not without elements of truth, would run in a circle: Society was weak in Russia because the government was strong, and the government could be so strong and oppressive because society was so weak. The actual story is more complicated.

Economic conditions peculiar to Eastern Europe made Russia lag in her commercial and industrial development. By the same token, the structure of Russian agrarian society relied on serfdom. A great majority of the cultivators of the soil —hence a majority of the population—were unfree: They belonged to the state or the landlords. These serfs, besides working their own land, had to work for their masters. The latter had a variety of powers over their peasants amounting almost to that of life and death. In direct opposition to what happened in the West, the legal status of the Russian peasant had deteriorated since the Middle Ages. The building of modern Russia that took place in the eighteenth century did not lead, as one might have expected, to the destruction or alleviation of serfdom. On the contrary, the submission of the nobility to the new autocratic system was won not only through force but also through concessions, at the expense of the peasants. The alliance of the government and the nobility made serfdom far more rigid and the powers of the landlords more extensive. A Russian landowner of the eighteenth century, indeed until 1861, could whip his serfs and could send them into the army (where until 1874 the term of service was twenty-five years) or, in extreme cases, into exile to Siberia. He was not allowed, at least in theory, to ruin them economically or to evict them from their land, as could be done to the tenant farmers in England or Ireland. In short, the lack of rights was mitigated by an extremely low but still real form of economic security, a situation that was to recur in Russian history.

Serfdom and its consequences were the central facts of tsarist Russia's politics and economics, just as the collectivized agriculture of the U.S.S.R. constitutes the main dilemma of the Communist regime. Largely because of serfdom, the nobility remained an obedient tool of the government and could not assume an independent posture toward the throne. It made social mobility almost impossible and hampered commercial and industrial progress. Last but not least, in an age of nationalism as well as liberalism, serfdom was felt to be, and was, a derogation of human dignity, an institution that set a majority of Russians apart from the national community. Yet the government could not bring itself to abolish the institution on which the whole social order was grounded and the destruction of which might threaten the survival of autocracy.

It was as much the pressure of economic forces as a deliberate decision of the government that led to the Emancipation Edict of 1861. The action of the government of Alexander II was greeted at first with enthusiasm and was considered, even by some of the political exiles, as a rebirth of Russia. Yet the manner of emancipation was to have grave results for Russian society.

Economically, the result of emancipation was far from satisfactory to the peasant. The government took all too great care to protect the landlords. The peasants were given land, but in many places not even all the land that they had held as serfs. The government paid off the landlords, while the peasants were to be weighed down for years with redemption dues to the state. But the main point of grievance was to remain the scarcity of land and the peasants' feeling that somehow they had been cheated because so much land remained in the hands of the landlords. The impact of the industrial age was already felt in Russia through a prodigious growth in population. Even with the growth of industry and mass migrations to the new areas in Asiatic Russia, the need and hunger for land was deeply felt among the peasant masses.

Politically and socially, the Act of 1861 preserved some of the features of the old village system, a decision endowed with far-reaching consequences. We may be justified in using a twentieth-century term and speaking of "nationalization" of the peasants, rather than of "emancipation"; for the reform in 1861 did not give them full civic and social rights but made them more directly wards of the government. Equally important, the old form of village organization, the *mir*, was preserved and even strengthened. The *mir* was a form of communal self-government that exercised a variety of economic as well as judicial decisions, although in tsarist Russia its more important decisions were naturally guided, first by the landlord and then by the government agent. The *mir* collected taxes, sent recruits to the army, judged minor disputes, and so on. In addition it periodically redistributed the land of the peasants, decided on the character and methods of cultivation, and, in general, acted as the joint possessor of both the land and labor of its members. To a conservative the *mir* appeared as the bulwark of old Russia, which preserved the peasant in his "native" customs and allegiances and saved him from the contamination of modern ideas. But even some of the revolutionaries thought of the institution as a Russian form of socialism and democracy that should be preserved. Karl Marx said in a weak moment that the *mir* could enable Russia to pass into socialism without undergoing the full rigors of capitalism.

The truth is that the *mir* had nothing to do with democracy or socialism—particularly Marxian socialism—as the terms are properly understood. It was an institution at once egalitarian and conservative, but in both senses running against the tendencies of modern times. It was certainly different from the kolkhoz, the collective farm, imposed by Stalin and based on the application of industrial factory methods to agriculture. The *mir* prevented the application of better agricultural methods and inhibited the development of enterprise among its members. It hampered social mobility and the growth of an enlightened farmer class. It was, in brief, a powerful anti-industrial influence and, hence, not only anitcapitalist but also antisocialist in spirit. Its preservation in 1861 for reasons of expediency and conservative ideology did not help the regime but was bound to prevent the rise of a strong middle class, which both enlightened conservatism and liberalism require. It was only a few years before World War I that the tsarist regime made a resolute attempt to remedy the mistakes of 1861. On the initiative of Peter Stolypin, the ablest social statesman of prewar Russia, the peasants were enabled and encouraged to break up the *mir* and to become individual farmers. But the war interrupted what would have been the building of a peasant middle class.

The imperfect emancipation of 1861 was only one of the measures by which the government belatedly recognized that an economic and social revolution was going on in Europe and that Russia could not escape its effects. The lament of a provincial governor is characteristic: The building of railways was a threat to established institutions, because railways enable people to travel and travel in turn exposes them to subversive ideas. Railways, however, had to be built, and with them came manufacturing and banking and other disturbing paraphernalia of progress. The growth of the middle class never caught up with the advances in industry and commerce. Russia entered the Industrial Revolution during its more advanced stage. The average size of a manufacturing or commercial unit was much greater than the average size of such a unit during a corresponding period in the industrial development of the West. There were few who could be compared to the self-made small and medium-sized manufacturers of France and England. Rather, the Russian middle class of the late nineteenth century had an educational and intellectual status and was composed mainly of members of the liberal professions and of the middle and lower bureaucracy. The intelligentsia was unusually susceptible to the intellectual currents and political ideas of the West. Their frustrated thirst for political activity often found its expression in literature and journalism, which flourished both at home and in exile.

To its educated classes with their growing social aspirations the tsarist government, even in the reforming period of Alexander II, offered but half measures of reform. The jury system and a very limited scheme of local self-government, in the country (councils called *zemstvos*) and cities, heavily weighted in favor of the propertied classes, were substantial advances over the past; but they were insignificant even when compared with recent reforms in the former fellow autocracies of Austria-Hungary and Prussia. Instead of becoming a safety valve, Alexander's reforms stimulated the pressure for more basic reforms. The latter half of his reign (from the late sixties to 1881) was full of revolutionary activity and violent repression. The revolutionary movement was as yet the work of small groups, but it reflected the discontent of several sections of society. Western anarchist and socialist ideas, which in the West had become tamed or insignificant, were being adopted in Russia in their original revolutionary and violent character. When Alexander II fell to the last of several attempts on his life by the revolutionary group called the People's Will, his assassins included a man of peasant antecedents, the daughter of a high tsarist official, a scientist, a Pole, and a Jew. The composition of the group symbolized the diversity of revolutionary premises within the Russian Empire.

It is useful to insert a note of caution: Because the Revolution came in 1917, we tend to think of many preceding years as years solely of oppression on one side and of revolutionary strivings on the other. A more balanced view would take into account the strength of the nationalist and conservative tradition in nineteenth-century Russia and popular attachment to the tsar and the Orthodox church as the symbols of Russian nationhood. The century was also the period of the great flowering of Russian culture, which in literature, music, and even the sciences made imperishable contributions to European civilization.

Once Russia entered the industrial race, the growth of her economy was rapid indeed. The *rate of growth* of Russia's industry between 1890 and 1914 does not compare unfavorably with that of the United States for the same period. Perhaps the total picture points up one of the "contradictions" of which the Marxists love to speak—a vigorous and growing society and economy shackled by obsolete political forms. But even in politics the picture is not of one color. After 1905 Russia had a degree of constitutionalism. Her parliament (Duma) was neither democratically elected nor very effective, but it provided the promise of political progress. Censorship was relaxed. The lot of political prisoners, while still grim, was considerably better after 1905 than it was to be in Stalin's Russia. In the Constitutional Democrats (*Kadets*) liberalism was the most potent influence among Russia's educated classes.

In brief, the coming and popularity of Marxism in Russia are explicable in terms of historical and social forces, but the Revolution of 1917 and the triumph of the Bolsheviks are as much, if not more, the result of a fortuitous arrangement of events and personalities.

Two

The Origins of Soviet Political Structure

The history of the Soviet state begins, paradoxically, nineteen years before the Revolution. It was in 1898 at a meeting in Minsk that a handful of delegates organized the Russian Social-Democratic party, out of which grew the Bolsheviks —the Communist party of our day. The years of clandestine activity, of conspiracy against tsarism, and of internal strife that characterized the growth of Bolshevism left their indelible mark on the state the Party created. Hence the "prenatal" period of the U.S.S.R. and the habits of thought and action the Bolsheviks acquired before coming to power are of much more than academic interest. The Marxism that has stamped its imprint upon the minds of millions of Soviet citizens is not that of Marx. Much as Soviet ideology today owes to Marx, it owes perhaps even more to the powerful genius of Lenin, who boldly interpreted, altered, and distorted the original doctrine. In so doing, he not only dictated the tactics of the revolutionary move-ment in Russia, but also formulated the political values and beliefs upon which the Soviet dictatorship was founded and in large measure still rests. To follow the fortunes of the tiny handful of conspirators that he led is to witness the emergence in embryo of most of the essential ideals, structures, and practices of the massive Soviet state of today.

Marxism in Russia

The genealogy of Russian Marxism runs back at least to the small groups of revolutionaries who fought and conspired against tsarism during the last decade of

Alexander II's reign. In 1879 the most notable of these groups, the People's Will, split into two factions. One of them conducted a campaign of terror that culminated in the assassination of the tsar in 1881. The other, the so-called Black Partition, under the leadership of George Plekhanov, abandoned terrorism and became the nucleus of the Marxist movement in Russia. The original People's Will, like its predecessor the Land and Freedom group, had a vague populistic ideology that did not go much beyond a plea to summon a constitutional assembly for Russia. Though socialistic in character, the ideology of the group centered upon the peasant and paid scant attention to the rising industrial proletariat. The People's Will perished in the wave of repression that followed the assassination of the tsar, though some of its ideas and terrorist tendencies were reborn shortly after the turn of the century in the Social Revolutionary party. Black Partition, on the other hand, became the progenitor of Liberation of Labor, the first Russian Marxist group, formed in 1883 by Plekhanov, Paul Axelrod, and Leo Deutsch. Plekhanov, in a series of books, laid the foundations of theoretical Marxism in Russia.

Thus from the beginning the attitude of the Russian Marxists toward populism, indeed toward the peasant, was an ambivalent one. Having sprung from a *narodnik* (populist) movement Marxism in Russia inherited some of the latter's conspiratorial flavor as well as a preoccupation with the peasant. On the other hand, the separation from Black Partition meant that Plekhanov and some others felt that conspiring was not enough and that the vague, partly sentimental and partly utopian, philosophy of populism had to be replaced with the systematic philosophy of history and economics of Marxism. While recognizing the revolutionary potentialities of the peasant problem, the Marxists came to feel that the *active element* in a revolution would be provided by the rising working class, and not by the discontented but dispersed and basically conservative peasantry. As we have seen, Russia in the eighties and nineties of the last century was a rapidly industrializing country. Since Russia had entered the industrial race late, her industry was of the new large-unit type, which created large conglomerations of workers in the main cities of the empire. Thus Moscow, St. Petersburg (today's Leningrad), Warsaw, Lodz in Russian Poland, Baku in the Caucasus, and others became highly industrialized; and these large concentrations of workers of many nationalities provided fruitful ground for revolutionary propaganda.

Little circles of mostly young intellectuals, some of them university and high-school students, were the first to absorb and then spread Marxian propaganda. The oppressive intellectual atmosphere of Russia in the nineties, with its censorship and suppression of all political activity on the part of students, merely increased resentment among young people and led them to search for a revolutionary solution. Marx's doctrine, with its intellectual intricacies, its comprehensive scope and theological flavor, was the very thing to appeal to young intellectuals living in revolt against their society. They in turn carried a simplified version of Marxism to the workers, who, scantily protected by the state and forbidden to form unions, were equally responsive to the revolutionary call. In contrast to populism, Russian Marxism did not rely on terrorism, nor did it expect a sudden and dramatic reversal in the government and society. Its propaganda was of a long-range nature. It worked through discussion and persuasion, stressed the need for organization, and taught that the struggle, though it would be long and arduous, was bound to end in victory because the forces of history were on its side. Economic distress and political persecution combined to create a wave of strikes in 1895–1898, and they in turn increased the influence of the socialists among the workers.

The foundation of the Social-Democratic party in 1898 was an attempt to unite the different strains of Marxism within the Russian Empire. The new party was to house not only the various shades of socialism but the Marxist groups based on nationality associations, such as the Jewish Bund and various socialist groups in Russian Poland, the Caucasus, and so forth. The very diversity of the elements the Party was attempting to hold together augured from the outset that its internal life was to be one of ideological and tactical quarrels, of schisms, divisions, and expulsions. There arose a situation quite paradoxical at first glance and yet common among ideological and revolutionary parties: A group of conspirators pitted against a powerful state was so rent by discords and quarrels that at times the various factions tended to make their struggle against the autocracy secondary to their internecine quarrels. What became known as Bolshevism emerged from two such struggles within the Party: one over the issue of the meaning of Marxism in Russian society, the other over the character and organization of the Marxist party.

Orthodox Marxist doctrine held that as capitalism progresses, the working class will organize itself *spontaneously,* and the workers will acquire the class viewpoint —that is, they will realize the necessity and inevitability of putting an end to capitalism. Drawing upon this interpretation of Marxism, a group of Russian socialists, who were to become known as "Economists," held that the primary task of the Socialist party in Russia should be to operate not on the political but on the economic plane. Trade unions, not conspiracies, should be the weapons with which to fight for the immediate *material* interests of the workers—better pay, shorter working hours, the legal right to organize, and social security. Inherent in the position of the Economists were two assumptions. First, Russia was as yet unprepared for socialism, because she was just entering the capitalist stage of development. They interpreted Marxism as meaning that a fairly long capitalist development, with the state dominated by the middle class and parliamentarianism, must precede any successful attempt to set up socialism.

The second assumption of the Economists was equally repugnant to revolutionary socialists. In line with the ideas then prevailing among Western socialists,[1] they appeared to hold that the very logic of economic and social development would bring about democracy and then socialism and that revolutionary activity was consequently unnecessary, if not harmful. Industrialization and social pressures

---

[1] Best illustrated in the writings of the Fabians, in England, and of Eduard Bernstein and other Revisionists in Germany.

would first temper and ultimately abolish the barbarities of Russian tsarism. The road to socialism lay through peaceful organization and education, not through coups d'état.

Had the ideas of the Economists prevailed and become basic to Russian socialism, it would have followed the democratic and evolutionary path of many socialist parties in Western Europe and elsewhere. But as a matter of fact, the Economists, though influential among the intelligentsia, were soon to find themselves outside the pale of the Social-Democratic party, and their subsequent story belongs to the history of Russian liberalism rather than to that of socialism. The reasons for their defeat were fairly obvious. In the first place Russian autocracy was not willing, at least not until after the Revolution of 1905, to allow any political activity even of the most moderate kind. The tsarist bureaucracy was also blind enough to prohibit independent labor unions and to procrastinate before extending the most rudimentary type of protection to the worker. The soil of parliamentarianism, social legislation, and progress in which democratic socialism could grow simply did not exist in Russia at the time; even after 1905 there was little opportunity for free political and professional life.

The answer of the revolutionary wing of the Party to the Economists was uncompromisingly hostile. The great authority of the founder of Russian Marxism, Plekhanov, was thrown against them. The future Bolsheviks and Mensheviks combined in denouncing the Economists as traitors to Marxism. It was in this polemic that Vladimir Ilich Lenin laid the theoretical foundations of the Soviet version of Marxism.

In 1902 Lenin was only thirty-two and already a veteran revolutionary. His membership in the socialist circles dated from the early 1890s, and his career included a period of exile in Siberia. Since he came from an intellectual middle-class family one of whose members (his elder brother) was executed for participation in a plot against Tsar Alexander III, his choice of the life of a revolutionary was neither atypical nor difficult to understand. Reading Plekhanov had drawn him toward Marxism. He had already established himself as a theoretician, and in 1900, with Plekhanov and others, he began in exile to edit the Social-Democratic paper *Iskra* (Spark). In 1902 Lenin came out with *What Is To Be Done?*, probably his most important work, fundamental to the understanding of the history of the Bolshevik party and the Communist state.

What Is To Be Done? was a book addressed to the current problems of the Social-Democratic party, which at that time, we must repeat, was a small group of revolutionaries, partly in Russia, partly in exile. Neither their most pessimistic enemies nor they themselves would have dreamed that in the course of one generation this group would grow into a party of millions and into the absolute master of a vast state. Yet the argument and the flavor of *What Is To Be Done?* have remained imbedded in the values and beliefs of the Soviet system. They are as evident in the pronouncements of Khrushchev as they were in those of Stalin and Lenin.

First, the flavor and tone of the book: We are struck by its *dogmatism*. The theory of Marxism is not to be trifled with. The use of Marx's writings as if they were infallible scriptures, the heavy pedantic tone, and the vituperation of those who would dilute or modify Marx (i.e., those who disagreed with Lenin's interpretation of the master) are already in evidence. We can already see in the book the *undemocratic* temperament that Lenin was to implant in the movement. When he wrote it, Lenin was officially and by conviction a Social-Democrat: His socialism was coupled with the belief in and postulates of democratic institutions. But temperamentally he was opposed to the premises of democracy, in particular its rationalism, which teaches that the mass of people are capable of seeing and resolving the main issues of politics, and its humanitarianism, which holds that human values and feelings should not be sacrificed too readily, even at the altar of social and economic progress.

The argument of the book revolves about the concept and role of the Party. In a remarkable passage in which he attacks the main theses of the Economists, Lenin lays the foundations of Bolshevism. The masses, if left to themselves, he argues, cannot acquire the proper class consciousness or work out a revolution. They must be led by a body of professional revolutionaries. In fact, Lenin is quite ready to reinterpret Marx, while claiming that he is merely following the letter of the doctrine. Marx had assumed that class consciousness comes to the workers in the course of their economic struggle with the capitalists. But, says Lenin, *spontaneously* the workers will develop only *trade union consciousness,* that is, the desire to improve their economic conditions, to legalize their organizations, and to secure other material and status concessions. To rely on the spontaneous growth of class feeling among workers, as the Economists would have done, is to abandon the hope for revolution, the hope for socialism, and to resign oneself—though Lenin does not say it in so many words—to a slow *evolutionary* development toward something which, though an improvement on autocracy, will be neither socialism nor Marxism. The first task of revolutionary socialism, therefore, must be the creation of a disciplined party of professional revolutionaries who will instill revolutionary consciousness into the masses. This party cannot be a debating society or a party on the Western model, but must possess a conspiratorial as well as legal organization. Lenin's concept of the Party—that of a quasi-religious order of conspirators devoted to revolution—harks back to the traditions of revolutionary groups of Russian populists. Thus the tradition of a conspiratorial group ready to undertake a coup d'état was linked with the doctrine of Marx—the mixture that constitutes Bolshevism.

What Lenin had to say about the composition of his ideal revolutionary party has likewise been imprinted on the history of the Communist movement, not only in Russia but elsewhere. The workers constitute the best material for membership, not only because of the reasons Marxism traditionally gives, but also because their very mode of life—the routine of the factory—accustoms them to discipline and organization. Thus they make good soldiers of revolution. Yet the class origin, Lenin implies, is of secondary importance as a qualification for the revolutionary. A socialist party devoted to the cause of revolution must send its detachments into every segment and class of society. Intellectuals as a rule may be too individualistic and opportunistic to submerge themselves in a group, but, by the same token, they have the necessary intellectual tools for conducting revolutionary propaganda. In a sense, a revolutionary party must disregard the class origin of its members and must look to the qualities of mind and will and the capacity for obedience.

In short, the recipe is for a centralized hierarchical and conspiratorial organization whose highest organs will lay down not only organizational directives but the doctrine as well. To repeat: This is not a political party in the Western sense of the word, not even in the sense in which the contemporary German and French Socialists were parties, but a quasi-religious, almost military, order of revolutionaries. The notion of *elitism,* of subordination of the mass of members to a small directorate, is clearly present. Marxism, born in the era of rationalism, receives in Lenin's hands a definitely irrationalist twist. If the majority of the people cannot see clearly their real interest—that is, the necessity of revolution—but have to be propagandized and shown the path, does it not follow that the mass of mankind will always have to listen to the dictates of a few? Such a conclusion is not spelled out by Lenin, but it is inherent in the argument of *What Is To Be Done?*

In its totalitarian intolerance of differences of opinion, in its antidemocratic contempt for the capacities of the masses and its stress on disciplined obedience to an elite, Lenin's pamphlet formulated the conception of authority that was to triumph in the Soviet dictatorship. This conception defined the role of the Communist party in relation to the rest of society, endowing it with the unquestioned right to govern. At the same time, it also set the movement on its way to a centralization of authority in the top leadership of the Party itself, unchecked by any effective participation from below. This is not to say that Lenin had already conceived the dictatorship of Stalin. There were still traces of democracy and freedom within the Party, if not in the Party's relation to the masses. In time these remnants of liberalism were eliminated from the structure of Soviet absolutism. Still, for the house that Stalin built, Lenin laid the foundation well.

The Bolsheviks Before November

The Second Congress of the Russian Social-Democratic party, which met in 1903 in Brussels and then in London (after the Belgian police drove the delegates out), was the decisive turning point in the history of Russian Marxism. The Economists had for the most part been defeated or had left the Party. The splits that appeared at the Brussels Congress were thus between various branches of *revolutionary socialists.* The most notable among them was the controversy and the division between the Mensheviks and the Bolsheviks. These names, meaning, respectively, "Minoritarians" and "Majoritarians," do not convey accurately what happened at the Congress; for on some issues the Bolsheviks, led by Lenin, were in a minority. So, for example, the definition of a Party member followed the Menshevik draft rather than that of the Bolsheviks. Lenin wanted the Party membership restricted to those who were *actively* participating in the political and conspiratorial work. His Menshevik opponent, Julius Martov, sponsored a slightly different phrase that would have allowed sympathizers as well as activists to enroll in the organization, and he carried the day. On some other issues, notably on the personnel of the Central Committee and the Party organ *(Iskra),* the Bolsheviks, supported by Plekhanov, prevailed, but only after some of their opponents had walked out and refused to participate in the balloting.

It should be kept in mind that in view of conditions then prevalent in Russia, it had not been possible for the delegates to the Party Congress to be elected in any regular and orderly fashion. The Congress that produced the Party program and crystallized the two main tendencies of Russian Marxism was composed of the revolutionaries who happened to be abroad at the time or who had been able to smuggle themselves out of the country. The basic split in the Party between the Bolsheviks and the Mensheviks was to persist until 1912, when the former declared themselves a separate Party.[2] It is difficult to give a simple reason for the split: The causes are not exhausted either by the ideological differences or by the personalities involved. Thus it would be erroneous to assume that the Mensheviks were, as a body and on every issue, less radical than the Bolsheviks or less prone to revolutionary action. It is by and large correct to say that the Bolshevik faction was Lenin's group and that he dominated it to an extent not even approximated by any single leader within the Menshevik group. Thus Lenin's dictatorial ways led to an early split with Plekhanov, who soon joined the Mensheviks, thereby isolating Lenin on the editorial board of the *Iskra*. Many other prominent socialists, some of whom were to rejoin the Bolsheviks in 1917, became estranged from them in the pre-Revolution days simply because they felt that the Party was unduly dominated by one man.[3] In fact, it was said among the European socialists that Lenin was ruining the cause of Russian Marxism and that his personal ambition and vindictiveness would destroy Social Democracy in the empire. Yet it should be kept in mind that *prior* to the victory of Bolshevism in November 1917 Lenin did not have at his disposal any instruments of coercive power, and if a sizable body of Marxists followed him both inside Russia and in exile, it must have been because his arguments appealed to them. It would not be far wrong to discern two opposing temperaments in the camp of pre-Revolution Russian Marxism: The Bolsheviks, on the one hand, were more akin to the old populist groups in their revolutionary impatience; they were less democratically minded and more prone to divest Marxism of its elements of humanism and rationalism. On the other hand, the Mensheviks were closer in spirit to their Western colleagues—revolution in their minds did not take an absolute priority over democracy.

But we have to keep in mind that such judgments are based on hindsight. It was

---

[2]On many issues, though, especially within Russia, the two factions continued to collaborate until the Revolution.

[3]The outstanding example is Leon Trotsky.

not until 1917 and afterward that the full extent of antidemocratic tendencies lurking in Bolshevism was exposed. Prior to the Revolution neither of the two Marxist groups appeared as dangerous and radical, either to the government or to the upper classes, as did the Social Revolutionary party, the inheritor of the populist tradition. One branch of the Social Revolutionary party conducted a systematic terroristic campaign against the government, and several high officials fell prey to assassination.[4] Though led by intellectuals, the Social Revolutionaries were mainly a peasant-oriented party, and their influence on the peasants, still a decided majority of the population, was a matter of profound concern to both Marxist groups.

The revolution of 1905 was a sign that revolutionary feeling was endemic in Russian society. That revolution was a preview of the conditions that were to destroy tsarism in 1917. First there was a wave of peasant unrest, reaching its crest in lootings, land seizures, and so forth. As usual, the peasant rising was uncoordinated, elemental, and ineffective in its character. Nationalist stirrings of revolutionary character came into the open in Russian Poland. Other non-Russian parts of the empire also experienced trouble. The defeat of Russia in the war with Japan became the catalyst of tension. Peasant unrest proved to be merely the broader canvas against which the decisive revolutionary action took place in the cities, especially in the two capitals, St. Petersburg and Moscow. It was among the workers that the revolutionary movement that had permeated all classes of society took the most drastic expression. The striking workers of St. Petersburg formed a *soviet*. The word is merely Russian for *council*, but its more specific meaning, illustrated in 1905 and 1917, could be loosely translated as "a workers' council of action"—a revolutionary body elected ad hoc in a time of crisis from among the delegates of factory workers.[5] The soviet in a revolutionary situation was elected with little attention to democratic safeguards. It tended to be a fluid group in its composition, likely to be dominated by a party that possessed the advantages of strict discipline and superior techniques of agitation. The latter characteristics were to be fully evident only in 1917. In 1905 the almost spontaneous growth of soviets astonished the Russian Marxists and especially the Bolsheviks. The latter could not be expected to be too friendly to the new phenomenon. Didn't Lenin distrust "spontaneity"? Yet they joined in the movement. In the St. Petersburg soviet the leadership was assumed by the Mensheviks, but soon a brilliant newcomer, Leon Trotsky, then only twenty-six and temporarily estranged from both

---

[4] The attitude of the Bolsheviks toward terror was not without ambiguities. Thus in some areas —e.g., in the Caucasus—Lenin evidently countenanced terroristic activity designed to secure funds for the Party. Yet sporadic acts of terror against government officials were held by Lenin, along with other Marxists, to be harmful to the revolutionary cause. Even before the Revolution some of the Bolsheviks indicated that they were not opposed to *preventive terror*, i.e., the use of extralegal and drastic punishments against political opponents once the socialists were in power.

[5] In 1917 delegates of soldiers were to join the workers in the soviets.

factions, became its moving spirit. For a time St. Petersburg was ruled by the soviet, the authorities being fearful of moving against it. The general strike, followed by an insurrection, broke out in Moscow.

The revolution failed for several reasons. First, the government disarmed the more moderate of its opponents by promising constitutional concessions. Second, the armed forces had not been demoralized, as they were to be in 1917 by three years of a sanguinary war, and remained, with a few notable exceptions, disciplined and obedient to the government.[6] Third, the process of social dissolution had not reached the level of 1917. With its opponents divided, the government proceeded to arrest the soviet of St. Petersburg and to suppress in blood the Moscow uprising. The revolution of 1905 proved to be a great rehearsal.

Viewed as such, it is difficult to overestimate its influence on the Bolsheviks. For Lenin and his followers it was an eye-opening revelation that in a revolutionary situation one has to transcend Marxist formulas and employ flexible and daring tactics. One must swim with the revolutionary current and seize its direction. The discontent of the peasant masses (and the majority of soldiers were peasants) can not be channeled into Marxist slogans. Hence, when an opportunity arises the Bolsheviks must forget Marx for a while and appeal to the peasant with a slogan that will assure them of, at least, his benevolent neutrality. The middle classes showed themselves ready to abandon the revolution when promised parliamentarianism. But bourgeois parliamentarianism is less suitable as an arena for revolutionary action than the flexible and volatile system of representation embodied in the soviets. The idea of an alliance with the progressive part of the middle class became for the Bolsheviks entirely secondary to the need of winning the support of *workers and poorer peasants.* Unlike the Mensheviks, they decided that liberalism was *not* a natural ally of socialism.

The period of 1906 to 1917 was the only period in the history of modern Russia when something resembling constitutionalism and free political life was in existence. The tsarist government did not have the slightest intention of introducing democracy, nor even a constitutional and parliamentary system in our own sense of the word. The *Duma,* or Parliament, convoked in 1906 had very limited powers. Since there was no ministerial responsibility, executive powers continued to reside in the tsar and his advisers. Even in legislative and budgetary fields, the government could still by-pass the Parliament. Most important of all, the complicated electoral law was rigged in favor of the more conservative classes, and when the first two Parliaments proved unduly radical and obstreperous, the law was still further changed so that the Third and Fourth Dumas were dominated by moderate conservatives. But if Russia in the period immediately preceding the War and Revolution did not become a democracy or shed the vestiges of despotism, it must be kept in mind that for the first and only time in the twentieth century

---

[6] That revolutionary stirrings were particularly potent in the Russian navy was already demonstrated in 1905. There was a mutiny in the naval fortress of Kronstadt, and the famous revolt of the battleship *Potemkin* took place.

(excluding the short period between March and November 1917), political parties could operate in the open and literature critical of the government could be distributed legally. In the Duma there was at least the germ of genuine national representation and a platform for voicing social and political demands. Those who hold that the Bolshevik regime, while repressive, freed Russia from unrestrained monarchical absolutism forget that between 1906 and 1917 the civic freedoms, while not sufficient or considerable, were infinitely more extensive than they were ever to become in the Soviet period.

The fortunes of the Bolsheviks during the period illustrate the axiom that the party was already so constructed both ideologically and organizationally that it was bound to prosper in periods of acute revolutionary excitement and to decline in periods of political and economic progress. Like the Mensheviks and the Social Revolutionaries, the Bolsheviks finally agreed to participate in the work of the Duma, though, with their radical colleagues, they considered the emasculated Parliament a platform for propaganda rather than a genuine parliamentary forum. It is significant—bearing in mind that the franchise was far from democratic and the elections could not accurately portray the division of political sentiment in the country—that in the elections to the Second Duma the Bolsheviks obtained half as many deputies as the Mensheviks and that in the subsequent elections they never topped the number of deputies elected by their socialist rivals. Both Marxist parties were outdistanced by the Social Revolutionaries and their allies, who had what amounted to a monopoly of political influence among the radically minded peasants. The middle class followed the Kadets (the Constitutional Democrats), the leading party in the first two Dumas, who professed liberal ideas and would have been content to transform Russia into a constitutional monarchy on the English pattern. Even in the freest and most democratic elections, the Bolsheviks would never have received more than a small minority of votes, and they and their sympathizers were a minority even among those who saw a drastic revolutionary change as the only solution.

This fact in itself never bothered the Bolsheviks, who considered the parliamentary struggle as entirely secondary to clandestine revolutionary activity. Lenin reproved some Bolsheviks who would have boycotted the Duma elections, but he was much more severe with those who would have liquidated illegal activities and concentrated on open political life. What was profoundly more disturbing to the Bolsheviks than their numerical weakness or the government's tampering with the electoral law was the possibility that revolutionary feeling would abate and that reform, whether put into effect by the government or forced by the moderates, would relegate them to a small, uninfluential group.

Such prospects were quite real in Russia in 1906–1917. For once, the tsarist government adopted the policy of intelligent reform in addition to repression to deal with the revolutionary situation. The new premier, Peter Stolypin (in office from 1906 to 1911), while a man of the most conservative and reactionary ideas, saw clearly that the police, the Cossacks, and the *agents provocateurs* would not by themselves preserve the monarchy and the social order. He realized that the source, if not the active carrier, of the lingering revolutionary feeling was the peasant imprisoned in the *mir,* denied more land, and kept under all sorts of social and political disqualifications. The solution was to free the more enterprising peasants from the *mir,* to give them some semblance of civic rights, and, most important of all, to transform them into farmers with land of their own and opportunities of acquiring more. The peasant would then have a stake in the political and social order, and Russia would have a rural middle class antagonistic to revolutionary changes. A series of laws enabled and encouraged the peasants to break up the *mirs* and to set themselves up as individual proprietors. The peasants' remaining financial obligations to the state (dating from the time of the emancipation) were canceled, and the government now extended credit facilities to the peasants so that they could buy up the nobles' lands. The peasants' land hunger was being at least partly satisfied, and a new peasant class, more conservative in its outlook, was rising in the villages.

Had Stolypin's social engineering been accompanied by a willingness on the part of the regime to introduce genuine constitutionalism and to invite the moderates into the government, there is little doubt that Russia would have been launched on a period of peaceful liberal reform. There was an undoubted decline of revolutionary feeling beginning in 1907. Membership in the revolutionary organizations, especially among the Bolsheviks, declined. Some Party leaders turned to other pursuits. Even though there was a renewal of radical feeling in 1912 and Lenin reorganized his faction into a separate party in the same year, it appeared as if no major chance, on the order of 1905, for a dramatic overthrow of the regime would ever recur. Lenin himself, while not abandoning Bolshevism, more than once indicated that he did not expect an overthrow of tsarism in his lifetime.

All such calculations were completely upset by the outbreak of the war in 1914. The war brought for Bolshevism the sense of final and complete separation from the main current of Western socialism. It had been fondly imagined prior to the summer of 1914 that the working masses in every country would make a world war impossible, that under the leadership of the socialists, they would refuse to fight in the quarrels of their capitalist masters. The war demonstrated, on the contrary, that the Marxist notion of the workers' solidarity transcending national boundaries was largely a dream and that the appeal of nationalism was infinitely greater than that of any other social or political idea. The majority of socialists in France, England, and Germany followed their country's policy, some of them entering the war governments. Especially painful and disillusioning to Lenin was the "defection" of the German Social Democracy, until 1917 the leading Marxist party in Europe, whose spokesmen now vied with the bourgeois and conservative parties in the intensity of their chauvinism. Nor was Russian socialism free of the same influence: Many radicals, including Plekhanov, urged that the political struggles be postponed until the war was brought to a victorious conclusion.

To Lenin and his followers the war marked the end of a stage in the development of socialism. Marxian socialism had to be reborn in a more radical and revolutionary form. The body uniting all the socialist parties, the Second International, had to be replaced by a new international, uniting the "true Marxists." In neutral Switzerland, where he spent the first three years of the war, Lenin held conferences with other socialists who opposed the war. His position, a radical one even within the context of a radical assembly, was that pacifism and prevention of war was not enough and that the world war should be utilized for the purposes of a socialist revolution. More and more he considered the world-wide struggle as the final and suicidal convulsion of world capitalism—an opportunity for revolution and socialism.[7] During the early stages of the war there was little to justify his hopes. It was socialism and not the old order that seemed to be disintegrating. But the collapse of tsarism in Russia provided a new and unexpected opportunity for Bolshevism and, as it seemed then, for a world-wide socialist revolution.

The Revolution

The first Russian revolution of March 1917 was in no sense the work of the Bolsheviks nor of any organized political movement. Exhausted by its military defeats and its corruption and inefficiency, the tsarist regime simply collapsed in the face of some riots and strikes in Petrograd that at another time could have been easily suppressed. The blood baths of the war, in which after initial successes Russian armies were being continuously beaten, had deprived the regime of the army's support. The soldier's disgust with his leaders and the scandalously inefficient and corrupt system communicated itself to the villages. Moderates and even conservatives now saw tsarism as an obstacle to a military victory and a barrier to reform that would save them from a revolution. Hence it fell easily after a slight push.

What was to take its place? The Duma formed a Provisional Government composed of liberals (the Kadets) and moderate conservatives. The war, it was thought, would continue, and in due time Russia would have a constitution and a democratic state. Yet revolutionary pressures soon gave the lie to such hopes and pushed toward a more radical solution. A war period is not the time for successful constitutional experimentation. The Provisional Government was from the beginning only a shadow authority, political power having become fragmented and distributed among the soviets, which sprang up all over the country. This time the soviets extended to the army, where they were called the Soviets of the Workers' and

---

[7]During the war years Lenin wrote his *Imperialism*. The main thesis of the book—that imperial expansion and hence wars are a direct result of the search for investment markets and sources of raw materials by the capitalists of advanced industrial countries—was taken verbatim from the book of the same title by an English radical, J. A. Hobson (with Lenin barely acknowledging his debt). But in Lenin's formulation, Hobson's argument was to serve the Marxist cause: Imperialism is the last critical stage of capitalism—the quarrels and wars of rival imperialist powers present a wonderful opportunity for revolutionary socialism, which in backward colonial territories should exploit local nationalism and anticolonialism.

Soldiers' Delegates, and even into the front lines. In the villages the *mirs* received a new lease on life, the peasants who under the Stolypin reforms had become "separators" being in many cases forced by their less progressive and less prosperous brethren to come back to the traditional organization. In retrospect it is easy to see that Russia between March and November of 1917 was in a state of anarchy and that only a very determined action on the part of the democratically minded politicians could have prevented a dictatorship of the Right or the Left. Yet the democratically minded politicians both in the Provisional Government and in the Soviets were of divided counsel and separated by ideological differences. Popular sentiment was in favor of an end to the war, but the liberals and some socialists felt that they were bound to their allies and were now fighting for the cause of liberalism against Germany. The peasants as usual wanted land, but the Provisional Government was unwilling to carry out an agricultural reform during the war. The leading person of the "Government" was a moderate Social Revolutionary, Alexander Kerensky, who in July became Prime Minister and who secured for a while the collaboration of the leading Mensheviks and Social Revolutionaries. But the temper of the times was revolutionary, and the most extreme suggestions were likely to become most popular. The Bolshevik party, which in the beginning of the Revolution was a tiny element in the political picture, was to become within a few months, through revolutionary audacity and unabated demagoguery, the state.

Before March the Bolsheviks' numbers are estimated to have been between 20,000 and 25,000. Its leaders were in exile (like Lenin and Zinoviev), in Siberia (like Kamenev and Stalin), or in jail. In the first elections to the Soviets they ran a rather poor third behind the Mensheviks and the Social Revolutionaries. In the villages the latter still overwhelmed both the Marxist groups. Until Lenin's arrival in April, the Bolsheviks were in a quandary as to what their policy should be. According to the Marxist scheme, here was the bourgeois-democratic revolution. Presumably the socialist revolution was to come, but not in the immediate future. Should not the Bolsheviks in the meantime collaborate with the Mensheviks and other radical groups? The first Bolshevik leaders to reach the capital were Kamenev and Stalin, who as members of the Central Committee assumed temporary command and pursued a rather hesitant and ambiguous policy both on the issue of collaboration and on the continuance of the war.[8]

In the middle of April Lenin arrived in Petrograd, formerly St. Petersburg. His very first words at the railway station indicated the new tactics: No compromise

---

[8]Joseph Vissarionovich Stalin was at the time neither an obscure Party hack, as he has been pictured by some, nor the leading collaborator of Lenin, as he has been presented in servile official biographies. Since 1912 he had been a member of the Bolshevik Central Committee and one of the leading Bolsheviks. In the overall hierarchy of Bolshevik leaders he occupied an intermediate position. Certainly people like Kamenev, Zinoviev, and Trotsky were much more prominent during and immediately after the Revolution, and the first two had been much closer to Lenin.

with the Provisional Government, "all power to the Soviets"; immediate peace, confiscation of privately owned land, and abolition of the coercive organs of the state. It was clear that to Lenin the Bolsheviks, Marx or no Marx, should try to seize power at the first propitious moment and for that purpose should not hesitate to outbid everybody else with the most demagogic and anarchist slogans. Lenin's postulates were at first greeted with amusement by his enemies and with incomprehension and protests by the Bolsheviks. The "old man" seemed to have lost touch with reality, and once again his fanaticism was going to doom Russian Marxism. By the force of his personality Lenin gained the majority among the Bolsheviks, though tactical and ideological scruples lingered on among his closest associates until, and after, November.

The ridiculous dream of a fanatic who thought that he and his small group could conquer and rule Russia soon became a real threat. The Provisional Government was losing what little power and prestige it had; the armed forces, demoralized by the bloodletting of an unsuccessful offensive and undermined by the revolutionary agitators, were in a mutinous mood. The Bolsheviks' peace agitation was especially effective in gaining converts among the garrison of Petrograd and among the sailors. The moderate leaders of the Social Revolutionaries who had joined the Provisional Government in May were being undermined in their own party because of their failure to carry out a land reform. The Bolsheviks in the summer of 1917 received an accession of strength from a group of socialists who had previously oscillated between the Bolsheviks and the Mensheviks and who now brought into their ranks a group of brilliant leaders. Outstanding among these was Trotsky, who, along with Lenin, was to be the moving spirit of the Bolshevik Revolution and of the first few years of the new regime. The Bolsheviks gained vastly in membership. On the eve of the second revolution they were still a decided minority in the country. But they were now a sizable and strategically located minority that enjoyed the advantages of almost military discipline, while their enemies were divided and confused.

The Government, composed of people with democratic doubts and hesitations, was not only unable but also unwilling to proceed resolutely against the Bolsheviks, who made no secret of their intentions. Only in July, after an unsuccessful Bolshevik rising, were some Bolsheviks imprisoned and was Lenin forced to go into hiding. The structure of the Party was left undamaged. An attempted rightist rising by General Kornilov in September forced Kerensky to relax his half-hearted attempts against the Bolsheviks. The unsuccessful insurrection showed the weakness of the army as a political instrument, but also the hopeless position of Kerensky's Provisional Government and the moderates. Russia was in the throes of anarchy. By late September the Bolsheviks obtained the majority in the Petrograd and Moscow Soviets. On October 23, 1917, the Bolshevik Central Committee decided upon an uprising. The plans for the uprising became a public secret, since they were revealed by Zinoviev and Kamenev, who had opposed them within the Central Committee. Still, the Government was powerless to prevent it. On November 7,

1917, the "Government," which by this time meant the city of Petrograd and the control of some arsenals and offices, fell to the Bolsheviks, who had presumed to act in the name of the Petrograd Soviet. The struggle was brief and almost bloodless. Kerensky's Government fled the city, and the Bolsheviks could appear before the All-Russian Congress of Soviets as victors. The Congress, in which the Bolsheviks and their temporary allies, the left wing of the Social Revolutionaries, had a majority, proclaimed the transfer of power to soviets throughout Russia, in fact to the Bolsheviks.

The new Government, the Council of Commissars, was purely Bolshevik in its composition, with Lenin as chairman. The opposition—the Mensheviks, the moderate Social Revolutionaries—left the Congress. The Bolsheviks had "power." At the end of 1917 power meant a strategic position in the civil war that was to engulf Russia for the next three years and that began while the German armies were advancing deeper into Russian territory. The new regime had no army to speak of and no administrative machinery. In the country as a whole the Bolsheviks, at the end of 1917, when they were more popular than ever before or after, were still a decided minority. The proof came in the elections to the Constituent Assembly held before the Bolsheviks established their monopoly of power. The elections produced a majority for the Social Revolutionaries, with about 25 percent of the vote going to the Bolsheviks. Thus the only free and democratic election held in the twentieth century in Russia produced a decided anti-Bolshevik majority. In January 1918 the Assembly met for its only session and was promptly dissolved and driven out by the Bolshevik Government. January 1918 marks the demise of the last lingering democratic impulses in Bolshevism. No more *free* and *multiparty* elections were to be allowed, and the Party self-professedly assumed an absolute dictatorship.

The rise of the Bolsheviks to power and the final stage of victory offer certain lessons important to an understanding of the Soviet Union and the Communist movement of today. Lenin had succeeded in creating a party that, unlike so many socialist and radical parties, managed to preserve discipline and to follow its leaders in all their tactical and ideological shifts and maneuvers. The price paid for the achievement was to give up what was left of the democratic element in Marxism. But the Party *itself,* though run dictatorially, had not as yet achieved the totalitarian spirit characteristic of the Stalin period. Zinoviev and Kamenev, although they had disagreed with Lenin on the eve of the revolution, were immediately after the November coup again his closest collaborators. A few weeks after the November Revolution some Bolshevik leaders still felt that the Government should include representatives of the other socialist parties, and they felt so strongly about it that they resigned temporarily from the Council of Commissars. It would take several more years before the Party, now the instrument of dictatorship, would in itself become so monolithically totalitarian that honest disagreement with the dictator would be branded as treason. But the foundations of totalitarianism were already there.

Another point to be stressed is that the Party did not win power and relative popularity under the banner of Marxism but with anarchist slogans that appealed to the war-weary and demoralized nation. Lenin had preached defeatism and desertion, the taking over of the land and factories by the peasants and the workers, abolition of the bureaucracy and the standing army, and complete economic egalitarianism. Once in power the stark realities confronted the Bolsheviks. Like any government, they had to defend the country against the enemy, keep the national economy going, and reconstruct the machinery of the state—all tasks that would have been made impossible by literal fulfillment of their own slogans. Powerful brakes had to be applied, and the manner of their application is the history of the decades that followed the November coup. From the most thorough-going, most anarchical of all revolutions was born the most dominating and exacting state of modern times.

Three

The Development of Policy

The Struggle with the Peasant

The Bolsheviks seized power in November 1917 with the idea of instituting a new type of society in Russia and eventually in the world. The basis of that society was to be Marxian socialism, and the society's eventual aim, communism. We have already seen[1] why Marxian socialism should have won in a society that Marx and Engels thought unlikely to be among the first seized by socialism. But whatever doubts, conflicting schemes, and theories the Bolsheviks might have had before November 1917—as to whether Russia was ripe for a socialist revolution, whether the bourgeois revolution should be prolonged, whether they should share power with liberal and other socialist parties, whether the Russian Revolution could survive in the absence of a world-wide revolution, and so forth—they were faced in November with the fact of having power and of being called on to build a socialist society from the ruins of what they regarded as having been, not a fully developed capitalist society, but a mixture of feudal and capitalist elements.

Now there was precious little in their own ideology to facilitate the task or to guide them through the first step. Marx and Engels had been socialists, but they had written mostly about capitalism. There is very little in Marx to indicate *con-*

---

[1] In Chapter 1.

crete steps that a socialist party should undertake upon seizing power in a predominantly agricultural country. There is no discussion in the scriptures of Marxism as to how a *socialist country* should *industrialize,* how the mass of small peasant holdings can be brought into large-scale units run by the state, or what kind of price system a socialist administration would evolve. And beyond the vague and contradictory hints in those same scriptures, there is little to indicate, economics aside, what kind of society the dictatorship of the proletariat would bring about. What about the family under socialism? What kind of arts and amusements would the new society have? Of bourgeois ideas and institutions under those headings Marx had written voluminously and scathingly. But he offered no blueprints for the future except to assert that socialism would free man from all his bonds and release his highest creative powers.

All this, understandably, did not help the Communists, who had inherited a government and society in complete ruin and had civil and foreign wars on their hands, with industry and agriculture producing at a fraction of their pre–World War I level. As to all revolutionary leaders, it fell to Lenin and his colleagues to restrain the revolutionary impatience of their followers and to point out that first things come first, that reconstruction and victory in the war must precede social experimentation and the building of a new life. Yet, at first, the broad sweep of the Revolution poured past all the cautions and restraints. The peasants seized the landlords' lands and in effect reinstituted the communal organization of the villages. The workers drove out their employers and directors and attempted to run factories on an ideological rather than technical *expertise.* The more militant among the Communists pushed the official policy of repression of the church to the point of severe persecution of religious cults and their faithful. Wars, famines, and the collapse of established social values led to the decline of the family and to drastic experimentation in the arts, education, and so forth.

In the midst of all the troubles and changes the most stringent measures had to be resorted to, and sometimes this gave the impression that the regime, prompted by the crisis as well as by its ideological scruples, was drawn despite its better judgment to install socialism and communism right away, skipping several historical periods. Thus in agriculture all land was legally nationalized, and the heavy grain requisitions imposed upon the peasant gave the impression that he was to be communized by compulsion. Agricultural communes with land, implements, and dwellings held in common were encouraged. In industry a high degree of egalitarianism was in fashion, with any disparity in pay or difference in status, even if justified by function, considered unproletarian, if not outright counterrevolutionary. This was the period (1917–1921) of "War Communism," when the inexperience of the new rulers, their ideological premises, and most of all the social and economic chaos gave rise to the impression that the Communists were impractical fanatics determined to establish the final stage of communism without having industrialized their country, without having gone through the stage of socialism.

A halt was called in 1921 with the institution of the New Economic Policy, the period of 1921–1928 taking consequently the name of the *Nep.* Aside from the need for an economic reconstruction, Lenin and his associates were motivated in establishing the Nep by the anarchistic tendencies they saw in the Party (the Workers' Opposition) and the Kronstadt Revolt. Hence their decision to eschew the most radical policies for the moment. The peasants were to be appeased by being required to pay to the state only a specified portion of their crops, rather than having to meet an arbitrary quota regardless of the size of their crop. Trade and even small-scale industry run by private operators were legalized. In brief, the state reserved banking, transportation, and heavy industry for its ownership and allowed free enterprise elsewhere. The march toward socialism was not given up but merely suspended until the country could catch its breath and fully recover from the ravages of the preceding years.

The Nep represented a strategic retreat, during which the forces of socialism in Russia would retrench, recuperate, and then resume their march. Yet both within Russia and abroad the adoption of moderate economic policies was often condemned or praised as indicating that the Bolsheviks had realized the "impracticability" of socialism and were content to establish a mixed economy or state capitalism. Such judgments were based on a gross misunderstanding of the basic ideological premises of the Soviet leaders or—in the case of those who argued the point in Russia—on purely political motivations. Being Marxists by temperament as well as by conviction, the Soviet leaders, whether led by Stalin, Trotsky, or Zinoviev, were bound in the long run to insist on full-scale industrialization and socialization of the country. The reasons for their determination were found not only in their ideology and their economic views but also in their most deeply held *social* and *political* opinions. It is almost axiomatic for a Marxist to hold that socialism can come only in an *industrialized* country. It was equally axiomatic for Russian Marxists to have held that the power of any socialist party must be based on a mass of industrial proletarians and that in a country where the mass of the population was composed of petty landholders—no matter how strong the dictatorship of the Party, no matter how exclusive its monopoly of political power— the forces of history would act against socialism and would eventually bring about the downfall of the Soviet regime. This obsession of the Communists regarding the individual peasant holder had the tenacity of a religious dogma, the strength of which no one who does not share it can fully appreciate. The Communists of all factions held this belief: In the long run Russia must be industrialized and private ownership in agriculture must be abolished. If not, Soviet power would collapse, either before an external enemy, for a nonindustrialized state is weak, or before an internal enemy, for peasants, no matter how poor, if they have land, are against socialism and have all the instincts and aspirations of the petty bourgeois.

Thus the Nep, for its short duration, 1921–1928, was obviously an expedient. Yet even as such it was bitterly assailed by various factions of the Communist party, especially when to ideological scruples was joined the resentment of the ruling clique. First Trotsky and then Kamenev and Zinoviev attacked the ruling group and its policy as favoring the peasant, and especially the rich peasant, the *kulak,* while neglecting the industrial worker. Stalin and his then ally, Nikolai Bukharin, were accused in 1924–1925 of encouraging the growth of rich peasants by their policy, which legalized the leasing of land and the hiring of help by peasants who could afford it. This was decried as the legalization of exploitation of man by man, a fine state of affairs for the first socialist country in the world!

The reasons that brought the Nep to an end and determined the regime to proceed full speed with collectivization and industrialization are manifold and complex. The ensuing period, 1928–1933, has been called with a great deal of justice the "Third Russian Revolution" (the first one having been in March, the second in November, 1917). In the space of five years individual ownership of land was practically eliminated, collective farms and state farms taking its place, and Russia was launched on a gigantic industrialization drive that was to make her over from a mainly agricultural country into one of the two leading industrial countries of the world. The scope of this program and the speed with which it was to be accomplished involved tremendous dangers. The regime declared an open war on the majority of the population—the peasants. Industrialization was financed by lowering the standard of living of the masses and thus imperiling the Soviet regime. Why should a power-conscious regime embark on such a perilous course? And having done so, why the feverish and reckless pace?

There are three *groups* of reasons behind the decisions reached in 1927 and 1928. *Economically,* by 1927 Russia had recovered from the ravages of war, and her production, both agricultural and industrial, had reached the prewar level. Further advance could, the Soviet government became convinced, proceed only on the basis of thorough industrialization. Furthermore the type of economy that became stabilized during the Nep did not allow the Soviet government that *full control over the economic life of the country that every Communist government craves.* The tempo of economic development was dependent not only on the government but on the peasant. If the peasant felt that he was getting enough money for his crops and if he could purchase some goods with that money, he would sell his grain. If not, he could consume it on the farm or feed it to his animals rather than sell it at the government-fixed price. In 1927 and 1928 on the basis of such reasons the peasants were reluctant to sell. The socialist government in bondage to the peasant! The Communists forced to appease the peasant economically! And if he is appeased economically, won't he tomorrow demand political concessions as the price for his grain? It is no wonder that Stalin's regime fell upon the peasant with the same fury that it displayed in fighting its opponents within the Party.

Politically, then, the decision to industrialize and *collectivize* was based on the natural aversion of Communism to any independent source of economic or political power in the state. Instead of millions of individual farmers with all their anitsocialist instincts there would be fewer but more efficient collective and state farms. Labor would be released to industry; the government would, so it was hoped, be able to contol the production and distribution of food; and, most important of all, the Soviet regime would not be dependent upon the good will of millions of peasants.

General power and international considerations were also not lacking behind the resolution. Stalin's dictatorship was firmly established. But it was a dictatorship over a relatively weak and backward country. Until Russia was industrialized, until she had reached the industrial level of the West, she would be, so ran the thinking of the Communists, at the mercy of the capitalist world. Hence Stalin's slogan that the U.S.S.R. had "to catch up and to leave behind" the leading capitalist countries in the industrial race. Hence his appeal to national pride in evoking the memory of Russia's past defeats because of her weakness and making the pledge that a powerful industrialized and socialized U.S.S.R. would never have to endure a similar fate.

Thus economic, military, and politico-social reasons, as well as the natural impulse of a totalitarian system to grow stronger and vaster, all played their parts. In view of the weak position of agriculture and the lack of capital, the decision to industrialize rapidly and to telescope into ten years what in the West took generations undoubtedly represented a vast gamble. But the gamble was undertaken by a regime confident of its ideological premises and conscious of its great resources, among which not the least important was coercive power. This power was almost, but not quite, unlimited, as the resistance of the peasants was to show.

The decision to industrialize a country involves a choice not unlike that facing an individual who decides to buy a house or a car. He will finance it out of a loan, his savings if he has any, or simply by curtailing his expenditures by reducing his standard of living. To the Soviet government beginning its industrialization in 1928, the last choice was the only feasible one. The sinews of industrialization—mainly heavy industry—had to be developed from the internal resources of U.S.S.R., a country that in 1928 already enjoyed, if that is the phrase, one of the lowest standards of living in Europe. From then on the Soviet workers had to work harder and longer. For a time, and it turned out to be quite a long time, fewer among them would be producing commodities to feed, clothe, and shelter people; and more of them would be producing heavy machinery and the commodities that could be sold abroad, for which the Soviets would acquire foreign machines and foreign experts. To repeat, none but a totalitarian system enjoying vast powers of compulsion would have attempted to squeeze the wherewithal of industrialization out of the already pitiful standard of living of its people.

The First Five Year Plan was authorized by the Fifteenth Party Congress in 1927 and was to cover the years 1928–1933. Many of the delegates to the Congress believed that they were sanctioning a cautious progress toward collectivization and industrialization. The mechanics of planning were theoretically to be worked out by the planning organs, especially the Gosplan, or the State Planning Commission. This was an organ staffed mainly by economists, cautious and aware of resources, rates of growth, and other economic realities. But the actual planning and supervision of the plan was soon snatched out of the economists' hands. Decisions about the goals of economic planning, the pace of industrialization and collectivization, and the means to be employed came to be arrived at—and still are—in the Politburo of the Communist party, with the planning experts just filling in the details.

Thus sometime in 1929 the dictator and his entourage reached the conclusion that the original pace of collectivization prescribed in the First Five Year Plan was too slow. It was decided to accomplish the major part of collectivization before 1933. The ostensible slogan was to exterminate the kulaks as a class. But the fury of the Party and the state fell not only upon the rich (by Russian standards) peasant, but also upon the broad masses of peasantry. In his incredible tenacity for his land, the peasant refused to be propagandized or "educated" into the collective, where his land and his livestock would be pooled. The government increased its compulsion, and the peasant resisted by the only means he knew: by refusing his grain to the state, by slaughtering his animals. In 1929 and 1930 the conflict became violent. Wholesale deportations transferred to Siberia and elsewhere hundreds of thousands, if not millions, of kulaks, now a catchall term for any peasants who resisted collectivization. Famine gripped the Ukraine. The losses of livestock endured during those terrible years have not, in some categories, been made up even today.

The war against the peasant was not merely an incident in Russia's industrialization, and the problem requires a few words. Deeply ingrained in the Marxists has been the habit of thought that socialism cannot be achieved, nor can the power of the Communist party be secure, if there is in society a considerable element that owns one of the means of production. Thus the millions of peasant households, each tilling its small plot, were not only a bar to rapid industrialization but the breeder of antisocialist attitudes. The collective farms, on the contrary, communism believes, are not only more efficient, as they can produce more with less labor and can be profitably worked with mechanical appliances because of their larger size, but they give the peasant the psychology of the worker rather than that of the small property owner—deadly enemy of socialism. But complete elimination of the private element from agriculture proved beyond the means of even the Soviet regime. True, by 1936 more than 90 percent of the land in Russia was in the collective and state farms, and as of today there are, practically speaking, no individual farmers in the U.S.S.R. But the government and the Party had to make two important concessions to the peasant.

In the first place, the bulk of arable land is in collective farms rather than state farms. The Communists believed early in the First Five Year Plan that the latter would play a more important role than they have actually assumed. A state farm, where the peasants are just hired hands, is the closest thing in agriculture to an industrial factory, hence preferable to the Marxist and disliked by the peasant. The dominant role of the collectives over the state farms, or *sovkhozes,* is thus a concession.

In the second place, the structure of the collective farm has been modified so as somewhat to appease the peasant. True, the collective farm is not a cooperative farm in our sense of the word. Though theoretically it is run by an assembly of its members, it is subject to the most centralized direction. Its manager in many cases comes from outside the kolkhoz. Insofar as the nature of its crop, the norm of work, and its organization are concerned, the kolkhoz is most stringently subject to regulations that emanate, in the last instance, from Moscow. As the medieval baron's castle stood overawing his serfs in the vicinity, so in the pre-1958 period did the local Machine Tractor Station stand guard over several kolkhozes.[2] The M.T.S. not only provided machinery for the kolkhoz but supervised its plans and performance. Attached to it were special Party workers who carried on propaganda and ideological indoctrination among the villagers. "Collectivization," then, is a euphemism for land nationalization and direction from above. But in the collective the devil—to the Communists the element of private ownership—has not been entirely chased away. In the prevailing type of kolkhoz, the so-called *artel*, though most of the land is pooled, the peasants still retain their dwellings and little garden plots. They grow fruit and vegetables, which they can sell in the open market; and—faced with the implacable resistance of that powerful personage, the peasant woman—even Stalin had to yield and grant that peasant households might own fowl and a cow. Yet in the main, the kolkhoz, in its structure and principle, reminds one of the factory. Peasants work in teams and brigades according to an assignment by the chairman. Their remuneration is adjusted according to the type of job and their individual performance. The net income of the kolkhoz is divided among the members both in cash and in kind. Special bonuses are allotted to the workers and teams that surpass their output quota, and corresponding deductions penalize those who fail to meet the plan. A job that requires some technical skill, for example that of the tractor driver, may have a base pay several times that of an unskilled laborer. In brief, insofar as his collective work is concerned, the peasant is simply in the position of a hired hand rather than a member of a cooperative.

Ridiculous as it may seem to us, the peasant's garden plot and the few pitiful remaining elements of private property in agriculture have been a source of major worry to the Soviet leaders and a matter of major concern to the Soviet economy. For one thing, peasants have spent disproportionately large amounts of time in working their own plots as against working on communal land. For another, the remaining plot, smaller than one acre, and its few appurtenances, stand as a link with the past and with the peasant's nostalgia for individual ownership. Soviet agriculture has not shared in the prodigious growth of the rest of Soviet economy. While Russian industry (especially heavy industry) has increased its production manyfold over its pre-1928 level, many sectors of agriculture have not advanced substantially beyond that year. Collectivization has centralized Soviet agriculture at the disposal of the Government; it has released labor for industry. But it has not solved the problem of agricultural production in a country with a growing population, and it has not eradicated the peasant's longing for his own land.

Confronted with this problem, the Soviet regime has pursued the familiar zigzag course between compulsion and concession to the popular feeling. Thus at times the government would limit more sharply the size of the garden plot, tax its

---

[2]In 1958 the M.T.S.s were abolished and their machinery sold to the individual collective farms.

produce more heavily, and tighten the discipline of the collective farm. At other times the peasants would be granted tax benefits and encouraged to grow more on their plots. A major debate on the future of Soviet agriculture must have divided the inner circle in 1949–1950. One Soviet leader, Andrey Andreyev, came out publicly for a loosening of the kolkhoz structure in a direction that might transform it into a genuine cooperative farm rather than a government grain factory. But Andreyev was publicly denounced, and the opposite tendency prevailed for a time. A great movement to merge collective farms into larger units combining perhaps several villages was initiated and carried through. The main objective was clear: In a gigantic kolkhoz the peasants working in brigades some miles away from their homestead would find it impossible to devote much time to their individual plots. Nikita Khrushchev in 1950 formulated an even more drastic remedy. He advocated *agrogorods,* or agro-cities, in which the collectives would be combined into still larger units, peasants would live in apartment houses and be taken out to cultivate the outlying fields. The garden plot and its appurtenances would now completely disappear, and the Communists' dream would be realized: The peasant would be assimilated in his habits, way of living, and psychology to the city dweller. But Khrushchev's plan was in turn repudiated.

The post-Stalin era inherited the dilemma of agriculture. Again a variety of remedies has been tried: tax concessions, promises of more consumer goods under Malenkov's primacy, reduced requisitions from the kolkhozes to the government so that the rest of their produce could be sold in the open market, and so forth. To increase total agricultural yield, the regime, especially Khrushchev, who identified himself with the project, has sponsored the settlement and cultivation of "virgin land"—lands in Kazakhstan and elsewhere that were previously thought unsuitable for agricultural production because of their climate and soil.

In a country where the ordinary political processes are denied or are meaningless, people will often express their satisfaction or dissatisfaction with the regime by their economic performance. In that sense the Soviet peasant has up to now "voted" against the government. It remains to be seen whether any structural changes in Soviet agriculture, or a greater flow of consumer goods, or a greater liberality of the regime would change their vote. In Russian history until now the peasant has been the central, though passive, figure. Most of the social and political problems, though often fought out by others, had their source in the status and feelings of the preponderant majority of the nation who dwelt in the villages. Today, with industrialization, the peasants no longer constitute that majority. Yet with their status not entirely satisfactory to the regime and unsatisfactory to them, they constitute a vast social segment that has not quite fitted into socialism and hence a question mark in the uncertain future of the Soviet regime.

How were the Soviet leaders able to win their long and bitter struggle with the vast majority of the population? What was the source of their power? Their principal instrument was the Communist party, whose weapons and techniques of control we shall examine in detail in Chapter 5. But how did the leadership hold together this huge organization and win from it the emotional commitment and the disciplined devotion necessary to carry out their grandiose plans? We can understand this only if we look at the drive for industrialization, which under Stalin became for millions in and outside the Party a compelling national purpose, inspiring fanatic loyalty and legitimizing privation, terror, and rigid conformism.

Industrialization

The appeal of Soviet communism to people in other countries has often reflected not so much the attraction of the ideas of communism, but the admiration for a country that in the space of one generation has raised itself from a backward agricultural community to a great industrial power. Though the achievement of the Soviets has undoubtedly been great, it should be kept in mind that it was not created from nothing. Pre-Revolutionary Russia, backward as she was in *absolute* terms by comparison with the West, was in *relative* terms a rapidly growing industrial country. Entering the industrial race late in the nineteenth century, Russia progressed very fast; her industrial production in some years prior to World War I grew at a faster pace than that of the most advanced Western countries, including the United States. It is reasonable to assume that with some industrial base and with her scientific talent, post–World War I Russia under any social and economic system would have become a major industrial power. Still the achievement of the Bolsheviks in absolute terms, and in view of the two devastating wars that have intervened, is very great—as great as their ability to squeeze the sinews of industrialization out of the already pitiful standard of living of the Russian masses. The price in human terms has been enormous, but in one respect the fondest expectations of the authors of the November Revolution have been fulfilled: Russia is an industrial power, one of the two greatest in the world.

The original impulse to industrialize was for the Bolsheviks grounded in their Marxist ideology but also in something else. By and large the Communist leaders hated—and their hatred was shared by many non-Communist intellectuals—pre-Revolutionary Russia with its backwardness, its social torpor, and the majority of its population sunk in passivity and superstition. Those exotic social traits that charm many a Western reader of nineteenth-century Russian novels were exactly the ones that the Bolsheviks detested. From the intelligentsia, who, as the saying went, "knew about everything, but could do nothing," to the peasant masses clinging to their immemorial habits, the Russian Marxists saw nothing but backwardness and apathy. Their view, as we have seen, may have been exaggerated, but they were impatient to "give history a push," to establish a modern scientifically organized society. Though they detested the capitalist West, they looked with admiration upon its industry and its scientific spirit. Years after the Revolution, when the pendulum had swung back and when Russian history was again being glorified, Stalin could still speak with approval of the American spirit of enterprise and wish for its presence in the Russians—together, to be sure, with socialist consciousness.

It is no wonder then that the first years of rapid industrialization after 1928, the years of great suffering, of the persecution of the peasantry, were also years of great ideological fervor and élan, especially among the Communist young. If it had not aroused strong enthusiasm among at least part of its supporters, the regime, cruel and in many ways inefficient, would undoubtedly have collapsed. But the Communists, for all their transgressions and inefficiencies, managed at the time to convey the impression that they were doing something—lifting Russia by its bootstraps. And from the despot himself came the slogans that underlined the grandiose task: "To catch up and to overcome" the West, the U.S.S.R. must within a decade perform the work of industrialization that elsewhere took generations. And since every struggle needs a visible, tangible enemy to justify the privations and sacrifices, Stalin proclaimed the thesis that as socialism progresses, the class struggle becomes sharper and the "enemy" becomes more desperate and unscrupulous— the "enemy" being whomever it was convenient to brand as such at the moment: the rich peasant in Russia, the capitalist powers, and so forth. Hence the great question was, in Stalin's words: "Who will get whom?" Shall "we," the Communists, succeed in building a modern industrial state? Or shall "they" defeat our attempts to collectivize, to industrialize, and to destroy the hostile classes and forces? "They" were then not only the kulak or a foreign-paid saboteur, but those Communists of little faith who pitied the peasant, who felt that industrialization was proceeding too fast or too inhumanly. "They" were all the traditional forces of apathy and backwardness in Russian society.

The drive toward industrialization proceeded then at a high pitch and, initially, with a kind of religious fervor. But beyond the initial fervor the campaign to industrialize rapidly and at a high cost in human freedom and comfort obviously requires other things. If you want a whole nation to strain everything to produce more and more, to measure success in life and national well-being by production figures, then you must adjust the whole mentality of the nation to the task. Thus industrialization cannot be performed rapidly in a society that is permeated by ascetic values. Nor can it come easily where people believe that equality is the highest social good, that it is ignoble for a man to strive to have more in goods and services than his neighbor, and that comfort and leisure are more important than production. The Soviet leaders accordingly set about creating a system of sanctions and incentives that had as its main objective the maximization of production. At the altar of industrialization there had to be sacrificed those parts of the Marxist dogma that proclaimed equality and the protection of the worker against the employer. For industrialization demands incentives based on performance, and very rapid industrialization demands at times the sacrifice of the worker's health and comfort to the demands of production.

The first to go overboard was the remaining autonomy of the trade unions vis-à-vis the state. In 1930 the Stalinists acquired complete control of the Soviet trade unions. From then on they became but an auxiliary branch of the government, with their main function not the protection of the worker against the employer, that is, the state, but the maximization of production and the indoctrination of the workers in attitudes appropriate to rapid industrialization. The right to strike, though legally not abolished, in fact disappeared, and we hear of no strikes until the post-Stalin era. In 1931 Stalin spelled out a few more of the consequences of the drive for industrialization: Workers must be subject to some discipline; they cannot be allowed to flounder from one job to another, and their pay must correspond to their performance at work. Thus arose the institution of labor passports, which limit the worker's freedom of choice of work, and the institution of work norms, which the worker has to meet to earn his full pay, and the excess over which is rewarded by a bonus. Both these devices have always been resisted by the trade unions in every country on the ground that, unless in a real emergency such as wartime, they make the worker into a beast of burden and are likely to limit his freedom and injure his health. But in the socialist state they became the basis of labor relations, and evolution away from them did not begin until two years after Stalin's death. Indeed, they were soon supplemented by a rigorous labor code that subjected the worker to fines for absenteeism or lateness to work and, for repetition of these offenses, to imprisonment. It goes without saying that the length of the working day was extended. Since the thirties filled the Soviet forced-labor camps with a mass of inmates, the government could utilize millions of slave laborers for particularly hazardous tasks such as mining and construction in unfavorable climatic conditions and could rely upon prison labor for a large part of its scheduled production.[3]

In 1934 Stalin summarized the whole trend in theoretical terms. Marxism, he proclaimed at the Seventeenth Party Congress, has nothing to do with egalitarianism in wages. This is a petty-bourgeois prejudice. Nor had Marxism anything to do, according to the same authority, with the workers' interfering with management. There had already been proclaimed the dissolution of the "trio" (troika) that used to run the factory: the manager, trade union secretary, and the local Party secretary. The manager assumed full authority, with the latter two becoming his helpers in the task of expanding production. The Soviets have used extensively that bane of the working class in the West—the speed-up system. The middle thirties were full of well-publicized workers who would suddenly break the working norm. The heroes would be properly rewarded, and the *average norm would then be raised* for all the workers in the given occupation. The shock workers became known after one of the first as the Stakhanovites—and they became the aristocracy of Soviet labor, rewarded by higher pay, bonuses, orders, and so forth. "Socialist competition," whereby factories and industrial regions as well as individuals

---

[3]The number of people in forced labor camps has always been a matter of dispute among foreign experts. Some have given fantastic estimates like 20 million, but the most modest guesses for any year between 1932 and 1941 have never gone below 3 million. Authentic Soviet documents, like the secret economic plan for 1941, which was captured by the Germans and then found its way to the West, authorize the assumption that the inmates of the forced labor camps constitute a sizable proportion of the Soviet labor force. Partial dissolution of the camps began with the amnesties following Stalin's death.

"spontaneously" challenged each other to a race in production, became a regular feature of the Soviet labor scene, both in industry and in agriculture. Thus those two proverbial methods of driving the labor force in a capitalist state, the carrot and the stick, found their fullest application in the socialist state. Gone in the process was even the pretense of building a classless society in the real sense of the word. For now a huge difference in the economic status and in the opportunity to obtain the amenities of life separated the common worker from a Stakhanovite, not to mention an industrial director, a successful engineer, or a popular author. The disparities in income grew, and they were fully authorized by the changes in the Soviet tax structure. The change was symbolized by the quiet disregard of the old principle, operative until the late twenties, that a Party member should not be paid more than the equivalent of the wages of an *average industrial worker.* The visible symptoms included the restoration of ranks, orders, and more colorful uniforms in the army and navy; and soon, during World War II, certain branches of the civil service were put in uniform.

In 1936 Stalin proclaimed that socialism had been achieved in the U.S.S.R. and that now, instead of the exploiters and the exploited, there were left only two friendly classes, working peasants and workers, and the Soviet intelligentsia, not a class, but sprung from the other two. The statement was true insofar as it referred to the abolition of private ownership of the means of production. But it was untrue insofar as it implied that the Soviet Union had achieved a society in which the difference in income and status had narrowed or even that it was moving in that direction. It was true that hereditary distinctions had been largely obliterated and that careers were now open to talent on a scale unimaginable in pre-Revolutionary Russia. But it was and is emphatically untrue that the exploitation of man by man —and its source, the exploitation of man by the state—has been abolished in the U.S.S.R.

Sociologists have noticed that often a given stage in the economic development of society is accompanied by specific social customs. Marx and Engels in writing of their contemporary bourgeois societies decried the "philistinism" of their social and moral values. The emphasis on the family tie and on religion, the horror of illicit love and unconventional behavior, even the optimistic and moralistic tone of the literature of Victorian England—all appeared to the makers of Marxism as hypocritical devices through which the exploiting classes kept the workers content with their miserable lot. Yet all those symptoms appeared, and with official encouragement, during the period of socialist industrialization in the thirties. There was one exception: A Marxist regime could never encourage religion. Yet even so the struggle against the Orthodox church was relaxed, and militant propagation of atheism was discouraged.

Prior to the thirties divorce was extremely easy to obtain, and abortion was legal. No sanctions were invoked against unconventional sexual relations. Again the change is drastic in the decade of great industrialization. Divorce was still legal, but the courts discouraged it and it became expensive. Abortion for reasons other than health was declared illegal. Heavy penalties were prescribed for homosexual acts. The sanctity of the family tie was invoked both in official pronouncements and in Soviet literature. It would be too simple to assume that at a certain point the regime had suddenly decided that the grandiose task at hand required social stability and moral orthodoxy. But certainly in comparison with the immediate post-Revolutionary era, the "line" officially sponsored in the thirties and up to now has been extremely conventional and moralistic. It is as if the individual were told that this is no time to indulge personal whim and life: The state and society expect everyone to have a stable and decorous life and to devote his energies to the important social tasks.

The early Bolsheviks included among themselves, or attracted, experimenters in art, literature, and the theater. Every social revolution breeds and brings the desire for the new in the arts. But as in the case of morals, the arts and literature and even science became increasingly subject to the authority of the Party. And in the thirties and forties the official line turned heavily toward traditionalism and conventionality. Soviet writers were told, then ordered, to depict the problems and successes of socialist construction. The depiction of the unusual or the morbid, stress on individual problems unconnected with the building of socialism or the defense of the socialist fatherland became in effect prohibited. The arts and literature became subjugated to the Party, to the extent that distinguished authors were forced to rewrite their works if these did not meet with the Party's approval. The prevailing line became *socialist realism.* Its principal motif in contemporary novels and even poetry was the striving by the new Soviet man toward—and eventually his attainment of—collectivization and industrialization and the subordination of individual life to society. In Plato's *Republic* the author anticipates totalitarianism by prescribing what music a well-ordered state should allow. The rulers of Russia followed by prescribing or banning various styles of musical composition and by requiring the artists to celebrate patriotic or social motifs in their music, for example, Dimitri Shostakovich's composition celebrating Stalin's afforestation plan. The Party's control over the artistic and scientific life of the country duplicated its control over every other aspect of life of the population. Scientific and artistic disputes would be settled not by the judgment of the public but by the dictum of a Party authority, with the dictator himself making pronouncements on the most unexpected subjects.[4]

The main import of the change during the thirties, quite apart from the strictness of totalitarian controls, was the emphasis on stability, conventionality, and optimism in the arts and literature. The question must be posed whether this tendency can be ascribed solely to the dictates of the Party or whether the artistic fashions of the period—which has not yet ended in the U.S.S.R.—are not also due to the

---

[4]Thus in 1950 Stalin all of a sudden delivered himself of a judgment condemning the then leading linguistic theory in the U.S.S.R. and coming out for another one. The baffled sycophants, not quite knowing why, what, and to whom Stalin was addressing his pronouncement, declared his commonplace views to be one of the most important philosophical and scientific documents of the era!

natural reactions of a society undergoing industrialization and acquiring thereby (for all the Marxian phraseology) middle-class values reminiscent of Victorian England. The paradox is hard to stomach if we look at Russia as a socialist state and a totalitarian society. And yet the effect of the great changes that were imposed upon Soviet society beginning with the First Five Year Plan was to inculcate in a considerable part of the society the good bourgeois values of the nineteenth-century West: the importance of hard work; of saving; of measuring one's station in life, among other things, by one's income and the quantity of one's material goods; and so forth. True, all these things have been drilled into the Soviet people in the name of socialism, and, true, no one in the Soviet Union may own a bank or a factory. But otherwise the logic of modernization and industrialization has played a strange joke on Marxism: Decades of socialism and of the "dictatorship of the proletariat" have instilled the attitudes and aspirations of a middle-class society. "Become prosperous," said Stalin to the peasants in 1934. Soviet literature and newspapers are full of moralistic stories—really the Soviet version of the Horatio Alger stories—of poor working or peasant boys who, through hard work and study, advance in life, becoming engineers, doctors, or "shock workers," that is, reaching the status where they have a car of their own and a television set and enjoy, as the phrase goes, "all the amenities of a rich and cultural life." Such is the ideal set before the youth of Russia by the Communist party of the U.S.S.R.!

The return to the traditional values[5] has been accompanied by a *qualified* rehabilitation of Russian history. Soviet historians in the immediate post-Revolutionary era and up to the middle thirties depicted pre-November Russia as a barbarous country, sunk in despotism, poverty, and obscurantism. Except for the revolutionary tradition reaching to the beginning of the nineteenth century, nothing was presented in a positive light. Tsarist Russia was an oppressor of nations; her population groaned under poverty and superstition; whatever was good and progressive, whether in ideas or technology, came from the West. In this respect a fundamental change was ordered in the mid-thirties. The history of the Russian people was to be extolled. Even some of the imperial rulers were classified as having been "progressive" for their period. Thus Peter the Great, for all his despotism, was now a man who reformed Russia and made her a world power (and a Soviet reader could not be unmindful of a contemporary parallel). Even Ivan the Terrible, it was discovered, was terrible and terroristic always toward the nobles, but solicitous of Russia and her people. The dangerous international situation and the imminence of war was the major but not the only reason for this rewriting of the past. In a period of great reconstruction and of great purges, the regime was also instinctively reaching for all the elements of stability it could find, and one of the most important ones was Russian patriotism. It seemed to be saying to the dominant nation of the Soviet Union: "The regime may be tyrannical, and it may

---

[5]Or rather to the traditional values of the West, since, as we have seen, these values were not shared very widely in pre-Revolutionary and preindustrial Russia.

be subjecting you to all kinds of sufferings and privations, but it is your government, and it is doing it for the greatness of your country."

This note was of course sounded even more loudly during the war. During its first, and for the Russians most catastrophic, phase, all the invocations and appeals to stand against the invader were made in the name of *Russian* patriotism, rather than socialism, Marxism, or even the more inclusive *Soviet* patriotism. And at the end, at a victory banquet at the Kremlin, Stalin pronounced a famous eulogy of the *Russian* people, again assigning them major credit for the victory and acknowledging their tolerance toward their government, which, the despot stated—an unusual modesty in Stalin—had made mistakes. Russian patriotism was then rediscovered by the Soviet regime to be its major asset, and the natural instinct of the people to fight for their government, no matter how oppressive, against a foreign foe, to be a surer basis of its power than even Marxism-Leninism.

Following the war the Russian nationalist motif was not muted but intensified. The damages of the war had to be made good in a feverish haste. Instead of easier living and greater liberties, the Soviet people were subjected after 1945 to continuing deprivations, and the continuation of the totalitarian rigor was no longer masked or rationalized by the war effort. As if to offset and justify the disappointed illusions and continued hardships, a violent propaganda of Russian nationalism was launched. The non-Russian nationalities of the Bolshevik empire were reminded that the Russian nation even in tsarist times not only did not oppress them, as the earlier Communist "line" had proclaimed, but even then had brought them civilization and progress. Some of their national heroes previously extolled by the Communists as "progressive" fighters against Russian and tsarist oppression now were declared to have been reactionaries and traitors. The past traditions of the Russian people in the arts, science, literature—in a word, in everything but pre-Revolutionary politics—were extolled and declared to have been in advance of those of other nations. A violent campaign was conducted against "cosmopolitanism," by which for a time was meant any feeling that there was anything in the outside world worthy of admiration or emulation. And an anti-Semitic note, an invariable element of extreme chauvinism and xenophobia in any society, crept into even official pronouncements. It is clear from the admissions made by Soviet officials since the Twentieth Party Congress that discrimination was practiced against people of Jewish origin.

The tightening of totalitarian curbs and the officially sponsored chauvinism appear in retrospect to have been prompted by two major reasons. The first one was the recollection of the war, in which Russian nationalism proved to be intense, even on behalf of a tyrannical regime, while in the non-Russian areas of the U.S.S.R., especially the Ukraine during the first stage of the war, capitulation and even collaboration with the invader occurred on a fairly large scale.[6] But above

---

[6] Though German brutality and exactions soon dissuaded the Ukrainians from the notion that the Nazis were a lesser evil.

and beyond the experience of the war, its end signified the end of the hopes for more liberal policies and for a more abundant life. Barely pausing for a period of reconstruction, the march toward more complete industrialization was resumed, and with it the continuation of a low living standard for the masses. The victory of the state—which made it one of the two superpowers in the world, expanded its territory, gave it satellites in Eastern Europe, and won a Communist ally and protégé in Asia—brought no benefits to the people, save freedom from the invader. It is not inconceivable that to allay and redirect the popular grievances, the Communist authorities sponsored the nationalist campaign with its distinctly anti-Semitic undertones.[7] The movement that has always boasted of its international orientation and that had vowed unyielding struggle against all national and social prejudices thus lent itself to a campaign of chauvinism.

The story of Soviet society between 1945 and 1953 is that of a society that had largely matured economically and socially, leaving behind the backwardness of old Russia and showing both in its resistance to the invader and in its economic recovery and progress its great adaptability and strength. But against this social and economic picture the political system still remained geared to the task of running a primitive society that needed the whiplash of totalitarianism to make it into a modern industrial state. Totalitarianism, fastened on Russian society in the name of social and economic reconstruction, has remained and has intensified, even though the major task of reconstruction has been accomplished.[8]

Policy Trends Since Stalin's Death

The more than seventeen years that have passed since Stalin's death have of course witnessed many changes in Soviet Russia. Is it possible to say that Soviet society and the Soviet governmental system have basically changed? Has Russia become markedly different following the disappearance of the man who had exercised absolute power and control in a manner unparalleled in modern history and unmatched even in other totalitarian systems?

We might anticipate our discussion by the general observation that Soviet society has changed a great deal but that the governmental system remains in its essence

---

[7] Another reason is found in the fact that the propaganda authorities had to overcome the effects of their own *wartime* efforts, when of course friendliness toward and appreciation of the U.S.S.R.'s Western allies was the officially sponsored line.

[8] The other and the major justification for the stringency of police controls and the continued sacrifices in the standard of living, as given by the regime, has always been the alleged "capitalist encirclement" and the hostility of the outside world to the U.S.S.R. That argument has lost much of its propaganda value since World War II and especially since the Russians' acquisition of nuclear and hydrogen weapons in 1949 and 1953 and the subsequent realization that a *major* war would involve universal and unprecedented destruction.

that elaborated and bequeathed to his successors by Stalin. To be sure, the structure is no longer topped by an all-powerful dictator. Even at his most powerful Khrushchev did not possess Stalin's powers, certainly not vis-à-vis his colleagues on the Presidium-Politburo. And Khrushchev's successors constitute even more emphatically what the Soviets call collective leadership, a euphemism for dictatorship by a committee. The fear of repression is also less than it ever was under Stalin, even apart from periods of intense terror such as that of the Great Purge, 1934–1939. But Russia is still very much a police state.

It is well to recognize, though, that there have been considerable shifts in official policy. First there was a determined change, practically from the moment of Stalin's death. The so-called liberalization of 1953–1957 rested upon two closely interwoven facts. One was a recognition, probably unanimous in the highest Party circles, that terror and suppression in the Stalinist manner were no longer necessary and were in fact interfering with the objectives of totalitarianism itself. The other was the struggle for succession, in which each of the contenders for supreme power was anxious to appear as a proponent of liberalization and to ascribe the odium of the defense of the most oppressive features of Stalinism to his opponents or rivals. As a result, the extremes of terror and control over the citizens' lives ended abruptly. Successive amnesties largely emptied the forced labor camps. The well-advertised stress on *socialist legality* has narrowed the range of cases in which penalties are dispensed administratively without juridical procedure (though these have not been entirely abolished, for in a totalitarian state terror can never be completely abolished). The special panels of the secret police that dealt out summary justice were officially abolished, and the powers and role of the secret police curtailed. Greater latitude of views and fashions was allowed in the arts, science, and literature. In brief, the regime, while still totalitarian in its controls and attitudes, sought to impose a sane pattern of totalitarianism, in contrast with the extreme of Stalin's despotism, which undoubtedly imparted something of the psychopathic to the whole society. In other words, the regime probed how far the controls could be relaxed and terror minimized without damaging the essentials of totalitarian power.

After 1957, and coinciding with Khrushchev's undoubted assumption of primacy, the pace of liberalization slackened. Foreign developments such as the troubles in the satellites culminating in the Hungarian revolt of the fall of 1956 had their reverberations within the U.S.S.R. The campaign against Stalinism was soft-pedaled, and it was made abundantly clear that there was no intention to challenge the monopoly of power by the Communist party or its supervision of every aspect of political and social life.

Beginning in 1961 with the Twenty-second Party Congress, Khrushchev resumed attacks on his late boss and his closest collaborators. It was only after Khrushchev's dismissal in 1964 that Western observers came to realize that those attacks by Khrushchev were part of his continuing campaign to strengthen his position within the Party, which was in no way as strong as it was then believed abroad. Khrushchev sought to overcome the opposition within the highest body, but once again appealing for wider support in the Central Committee and, beyond it, with the mass of the lower Party functionaries. As part of his campaign he used a rather ingenious device: meetings of the higher Party organs, eventually of the Presidium itself, were held often, not behind closed doors but in the presence of a *large* number of outsiders, sometimes running into hundreds, supposedly experts and "activists" on the questions the Party organ was at the time discussing. In such a setting it was of course virtually impossible for the First Secretary's opponents to speak their minds freely and to oppose his policies. There must be a strong presumption that Khrushchev's flirting with this peculiar form of participatory democracy served to increase his colleagues' apprehension and their determination to get rid of him.

This was done in a virtual coup by the Politburo in October 1964, while the Chairman and First Secretary was vacationing in the Crimea. But this time, unlike in 1957, the anti-Khrushchev move was approved by the Central Committee.

The Brezhnev-Kosygin team moved to restore the absolute authority of the Central Party organs. Their meetings, for the most part, have, since 1964, been held without outsiders present; and in contrast with previous practice, detailed minutes of the Central Committee meetings have seldom been made public. Since 1966 and the Twenty-third Party Congress, the new leadership has soft-pedaled criticism of Stalin. In fact what might be called a moderate rehabilitation of Stalin has taken place. Names and titles associated with Stalin's era have in some cases been restored: The Presidium has returned to its old name, Politburo; and the highest Party official is once more the General Secretary of the Central Committee.

A similar mixture of causes—a common-sense response to a changed situation, political maneuverings in the struggle for succession, and the conviction that no measures or concessions must injure the framework of totalitarianism—characterized the regime's policy toward the economic aspirations of its citizens. Under Georgi Malenkov (roughly from Stalin's death to the end of 1954) the government promised and in some ways began to furnish more in the way of consumer goods. The fantastically grandiose plans of capital construction initiated or planned under Stalin, uneconomically expensive in manpower and capital, were largely modified or abandoned. The plenum of the Central Committee held in September 1953 ended the merciless exploitation of the peasantry and instituted added material incentives to restore faltering Soviet agriculture. Malenkov's demotion in 1955 was accompanied by admonitions that heavy industry still had priority over the consumer's needs. Yet in the long run the demand for a rise in the standard of living could not be ignored as insistently as it was under Stalin; and barring war, this demand had to be appeased by the Communist party, for such is the logic of the social and economic situation of the U.S.S.R.[9] In 1957 Khrushchev threw in the slogan of surpassing the United States within a few years in the production of meat,

---

[9] This problem is elaborated in Chapter 5.

butter, and milk. The stress on catching up with and overcoming America was now extended to the field of consumer goods as well as heavy industry, and it was linked with the promise of the realization of communism as the final stage of socialist society. Stalin's successors hastened to reduce working time in industry and to increase the wages of the lowest paid workers. There was, in brief, a new sensitivity to the needs of the Soviet consumer and an acknowledgment that the general standard of living must be raised. This reflected a change in attitude from the period before March 1953, when a low priority was assigned to such goals.

The key and troublesome problem in this new campaign remained Soviet agriculture. In December 1958 at a Central Committee meeting Khrushchev revealed, or rather confirmed, what had been suspected for a long time: The statistics for grain production in Stalin's time were regularly falsified. The favorite method of falsification was the identification of the biological yield, that is, grain and produce still in the field, with production for consumption.

Khrushchev tackled the problem of agriculture through several measures. First there were added material incentives for the collective peasant. Then in 1957–1958 it was announced that the Machine Tractor Stations would be sold to the kolkhozes, a measure designed to give the collective farmers a greater feeling of freedom in planning and executing their work.

But apart from such administrative improvisations the first phase of Khrushchev's attack on the problem consisted of two major lines of approach. First, he vigorously sponsored the growing of special crops, some of them not very popular with the Russian peasant and not particularly suited to the soil conditions in large parts of Russia. Thus his enthusiastic sponsorship of corn, which earned him the humorous sobriquet of Nikita the Corn Grower. Then he waged an extensive campaign to bring under cultivation new territories (mostly in Kazakhstan in southeast Russia), a project that involved vast effort and expense.

This "virgin territories" plan from the start attracted criticisms that it was uneconomic, that in the long run many of the areas would turn into dust bowls, and so forth. And to be sure, while in the beginning the virgin territories plan seemed a success and helped the First Secretary to defeat the "anti-Party" group of Vyacheslav Molotov, Georgi Malenkov, and Lazar Kaganovich, who allegedly opposed it, difficulties developed by the late fifties. In 1959 there was a bad crop in Kazakhstan; and by the mid-sixties the whole scheme was recognized as a failure and largely abandoned.

In fact the whole effort to increase agricultural productivity substantially and to increase the well-being of the collective farmer suffered setbacks by 1960. There followed a new series of administrative improvisations. In 1961 the Ministry of Agriculture was reorganized and stripped of most of its administrative functions. Direct supervision of agricultural matters was then shifted to the Party. In 1962 Party organs and officials up to, but not including, the Union Republic level were split into two sectors, one of which was to deal mainly with industrial affairs and the other with agricultural matters. This laid the ground for considerable confusion and duplication of functions: At the regional and lower level of the Party hierarchy

there were now two coequal first secretaries and two parallel sets of Party hierarchy. It was one of the reforms that was most bitterly resented by Party officials
and most speedily repealed after Khrushchev's fall; his successors evidently felt
that this was a classical example of what they labeled Khrushchev's "harebrained
schemes."

The new regime has tackled the problem of agriculture in a less feverish and
more systematic way. Thus it was decreed and, since 1966, gradually instituted in
most collective farms that their members, like the state-farm workers and industrial
workers, should have a guaranteed minimum monthly wage. Previously, most of
the payment was in kind; now increasingly payment is in cash. Also, since 1965
old-age pensions have been extended to the kolkhoz workers.

Apart from providing material incentives, the new regime has attempted to boost
the morale of the collective peasant. To emphasize the importance of collective
farm economy, Brezhnev in 1966 called for a congress of representatives of
collective farms throughout the U.S.S.R. This action evidently encountered opposition. Some bureaucrats may have felt that it was unwise to create in agriculture a
parallel structure to trade unions, thus giving the peasants a *potential* vehicle for
pressing their interests. Anyway, the congress was not held until November 1969,
and its decisions were hardly sensational. It emphasized that the collective farm
would remain the basic unit of Soviet agriculture. The collective peasant's right to
a private plot, something the regime has never been happy about and occasionally
has tried to curtail or abolish, was reaffirmed. The establishment of regional kolkhoz councils topped by an All-Union Council of Collective Farms was proposed.

Such has been, very briefly, the story of Soviet agriculture after Stalin. For all the
increased payments to the peasants and for all the new efforts to help production
through increased investment and increased use of artificial fertilizer, the problem
is far from solved. A bad harvest still means serious food shortages; occasionally
Russia, one of the main grain exporters before the Revolution, is forced to import
food. The principle of the collective farm still, it is fair to say, has not been fully
accepted by the peasant, just as his tiny private plot, the vestige of private property,
is still a source of unhappiness to the regime. Policies in this field best employ the
interplay of motivations of the Soviet regime: Its ideology and the drive toward total
control make the regime begrudge the peasant his own plot and make it still prefer
a "grain factory," that is, the state farm, to the kolkhoz. On the other hand, a
realistic appreciation of the need for material and other incentives to increase
production at times forces the government to conciliate the peasant and to relax
its control over him.

The overall character of the new policies reminds one of the deep-rooted continuity of Soviet totalitarianism. After all, in his social and economic policy Stalin also
moved in a zigzag course: Once the limit of compulsion was reached, a relaxation
was ordered for a time. Thus compulsory and brutal collectivization was arrested
in 1930 to be resumed after a breathing spell, and the Second Five Year Plan was
kinder to the consumer than the First. We have traced similar zigzags in the
post-Stalin era in agriculture, and similar phenomena could be observed in other

fields. Though the main characteristic of the Stalin era was the reliance on compulsion and terror with an occasional recourse to incentives and more "liberal" policies, the post-Stalin regimes have reversed this priority: They rely on the general persuasiveness and concrete appeal of their internal policies, but they do not shy away from compulsion. It is unlikely that the combination of personality and circumstances that created Stalinism could be reproduced in today's U.S.S.R.

One is reminded of the fable of the sorcerer and his apprentice. The sorcerer could evoke a giant of enormous strength but could also render him harmless at will. Lenin and the Bolsheviks activated the masses of the Russian people and carried through a revolution. The task accomplished, they fastened the people to a bureaucratic and oligarchic regime. Stalin poured the enthusiasm and energies of the Communist party into the task of industrializing and collectivizing the countryside. After the foundations of a new industrial society were laid, he decimated the Party. The sorcerer's assistant, it will be remembered, could evoke the monster but forgot how to control him, and the giant threatened his maker with destruction. The fable should not be taken too literally, but it suggests the difficulty of reimposing the full weight of past despotism upon a society that has changed so much in the past generation.

The above suggests the limits of even the most totalitarian regime's power to control and suppress its people. Yet at the same time we must bear in mind that following Khrushchev's fall, his successors continuously and gradually, but firmly, have clamped down on the modest liberalization that had taken place between 1953 and 1964. Stalinism has not returned, but the old despot has been partially rehabilitated. Mass terror has not been reintroduced, but individual dissenters, especially those among the artists, writers, and scientists, have been severely repressed. Many of them have been sentenced to prison terms, deported, or, when not actually deprived of liberty, silenced. Among those persecuted has been the greatest Soviet writer of the present generation, Alexander Solzhenitsyn, whose two latest novels, shattering in their depiction of the realities of life under Stalin, have been banned inside the U.S.S.R. Whatever might be considered dissent is quickly and ruthlessly suppressed. Nothing suggests that barring a cataclysmic occurrence, the internal system of the Soviet Union can evolve internally into something resembling a democracy; certainly this could not happen in the foreseeable future.

In some Communist countries considerable evolution has taken place. Yugoslavia, first to emancipate herself from the U.S.S.R. in 1948, has not turned into a democracy but has a much freer society than the Soviet model. In Hungary in 1956 and in Czechoslovakia in 1968 attempts at far-reaching internal reforms, in the latter case within the framework of the Communist system, were repressed by Soviet troops. But in these cases Communism was rather recent, for the most part imported from the outside, and local nationalism was on the side of reforms.

In the U.S.S.R. Communism has been the way of life for more than fifty years, and *Russian* nationalism is an ally of the Soviet regime. The average Soviet citizen could hardly have a clear-cut idea of an alternative political and social system. But society, even a regimented one, never stands still. Social and cultural pressures can be seen building up and beginning to impinge on the totalitarian regime. In a longer run something like semiautonomous status might be won by institutions like the *state* bureaucracy, the trade unions, and the armed forces. Certainly in the economic sphere, even after Khrushchev's fall, the regime continued to be much more responsive to the people's needs and aspirations than had been the case under Stalin. Still, it is appropriate to conclude this chapter with the conclusion from this book's 1958 edition: There is no prospect in the foreseeable future of the U.S.S.R.'s evolving into a democracy or achieving the rule of law rather than that of men and a doctrine.

Four

The Formal Structure: Soviet Constitutionalism

Soviet Constitutionalism

The constitutional structure of the Soviet Union has always been an elaborate façade behind which one-party rule and totalitarianism have occupied the policial scene. No meeting of the Supreme Soviet has ever even faintly approached in importance a Party congress. Neither the Council of Commissars nor the Council of Ministers has ever rivaled the role of the Central Committee or the Presidium-Politburo of the Party as the supreme maker of policies. It is almost superfluous to add that Stalin, during much of the period of his dictatorial power (1925–1941), never held a high state position. Lenin's function as the leader of the Soviet state was predicated on his personal and Party stature rather than only on the fact that he was Chairman of the Council of People's Commissars. Malenkov's brief primacy after Stalin's death was again based on a number of factors, only one of which was that he headed the government as the Chairman of the Council of Ministers. If the formal aspect of Soviet politics is to be studied, the Statute of the Communist party is a more important document than the Constitution of the U.S.S.R. From the top to the bottom of the Soviet structure the Party has played a more important role than the corresponding state organs.

The question that occurs right away is: Why have an elaborate constitutional structure in a totalitarian regime? Is the Soviet constitution, the whole apparatus of elections, representative bodies, and so forth, merely "propaganda" of no significance whatsoever in the total picture of Soviet politics? And if so, why study the Soviet constitution and its appurtenances?

There can be no simple answer. The evolution of Soviet constitutional institutions has reflected an important evolution in the thinking of the Bolsheviks about the state and its organization. Although in practical terms the state institutions have usually been subordinate to those of the Party and the representative bodies have usually had functions of a declamatory rather than political or deliberative character, the overall significance of the representative institutions has transcended the "propaganda" aspect that is usually stressed by the outside commentators on the Soviet system. Soviet representative institutions as well as Soviet constitutionalism as a whole have several aspects of usefulness for the Communist regime and by the same token, several points of interest for those who want to understand the spirit and mechanics of Russian totalitarianism.

Constitutionalism and the Soviet Philosophy of the State

The Soviet regime has inherited the ambivalent attitude of Marxism toward the state and bourgeois constitutionalism. As for some Christian philosophers the state was a necessary evil and a consequence of our sins, so for Marx and Engels nineteenth-century Western constitutionalism, if not the state itself, was the product of the specific conditions of the class struggle. Economic exploitation by the possessing classes was protected by the state, while constitutionalism with its fictions of civic equality and legality was designed to appease the non-propertied masses. Yet Marxism, unlike anarchism, never maintained that victorious socialism would be able to dispense with the machinery of the bourgeois state right away. Presumably, constitutions, elections, and the administrative machinery of the state would continue until socialism turned into communism, that is, until production, liberated from the fetters of capitalism, became able to provide abundance for everybody and thus dissolve classes and make the state, even the democratic state, superfluous. The presumably long transition from socialism to communism would be characterized by real—as opposed to bourgeois-fake—democracy; in contrast to the situation under bourgeois democracy, elections, civil liberties, and so forth, would flower under the conditions of "proletarian dictatorship," which Marx somewhat paradoxically specifies as the dictatorship of a vast majority of the people.

Marxism, then, offered very little by way of concrete prescription for constitutional experimenting under the conditions of Russia of 1918 or, for that matter, of 1971. It did offer paradoxes: the distrust of Western parliamentarianism, and yet the conviction that under socialism "real" parliamentary institutions and "real" democracy would flourish; the final aim of the withering away of the state, and yet the transitional period during which the socialist state would be extremely powerful, since it would run the economy of the country as well as exercise the usual functions of the state. Within the thinking of Bolshevik leaders, these paradoxes were reflected both before and after the Revolution in a variety of ideas

Figure 4.1 The Formal Structure of the Soviet Government

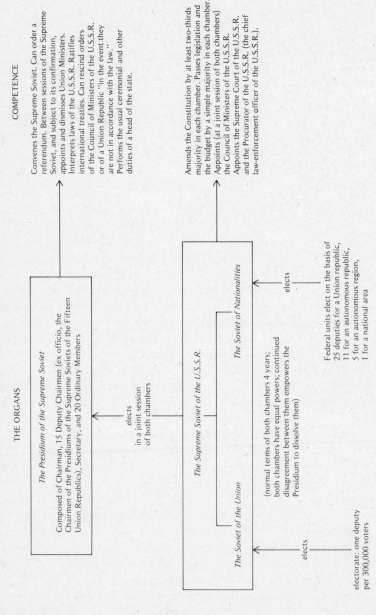

THE ORGANS

COMPETENCE

The Presidium of the Supreme Soviet

Composed of Chairman, 15 Deputy Chairmen (ex officio, the Chairmen of the Presidiums of the Supreme Soviets of the Fifteen Union Republics), Secretary, and 20 Ordinary Members

Convenes the Supreme Soviet. Can order a referendum. Between sessions of the Supreme Soviet, and subject to its confirmation, appoints and dismisses Union Ministers. Interprets laws of the U.S.S.R. Ratifies international treaties. Can rescind orders of the Council of Ministers of the U.S.S.R. or of a Union Republic "in the event they are not in accordance with the law." Performs the usual ceremonial and other duties of a head of the state.

elects
in a joint session
of both chambers

The Supreme Soviet of the U.S.S.R.

The Soviet of Nationalities

The Soviet of the Union

(normal terms of both chambers 4 years; both chambers have equal powers; continued disagreement between them empowers the Presidium to dissolve them)

Amends the Constitution by at least two-thirds majority in each chamber. Passes legislation and the budget by a simple majority in each chamber. Appoints (at a joint session of both chambers) the Council of Ministers of the U.S.S.R. Appoints the Supreme Court of the U.S.S.R. and the Procurator of the U.S.S.R. (the chief law-enforcement officer of the U.S.S.R.).

elects

Federal units elect on the basis of 25 deputies for a Union republic, 11 for an autonomous republic, 5 for an autonomous region, 1 for a national area

elects

electorate: one deputy per 300,000 voters

running the whole gamut from the "abolition" of the state to the most centralized and authoritarian structure. Some problems resolved themselves. Like most secular religions, Bolshevism was for freedom but the "right" kind of freedom, for democratic elections but elections that would end in victory for the "right" side's (i.e., their own). Thus one-party rule became both the reality and the theory of the Bolshevik government a few months after the November Revolution, though at first a few Bolsheviks grumbled and objected that other bona fide revolutionary parties should be allowed to share in the government. The issue was determined when the Bolsheviks drove out the Constituent Assembly in January 1918. Within a few months the temporary alliance of the Bolsheviks and the Left Social Revolutionaries was ended. Up to about 1920 there were still a few stray Mensheviks and Social Revolutionaries in the representative organs (soviets). In effect, however, the two years after the Revolution witnessed the repression and liquidation of *all* other parties, including even those elements in the Social Revolutionary and Menshevik parties that offered qualified submission to Soviet power.

While building the one-party state, Lenin and his associates, even in the midst of a civil war, still considered it supremely important to settle the constitutional framework. No idea of a revolutionary directorate or complete absence of constitutional forms entered their minds. They set about devising a structure of government in which the Party dictatorship would operate within the context of democratic institutions. Their own form of democracy, it was felt, should represent something new and different from Western parliamentary institutions. Yet for all the nomenclature and all the pyramidal arrangement involved, the network of representative institutions evolved in the Constitutions of 1918 and 1924 bore more than a superficial resemblance to the Western pattern. Though the electoral appurtenances favored the workers over the peasants and though members of the former possessing classes and clergy were banned from voting, the base for elections was the mass of people. The Bolshevik leaders thus felt themselves heirs of the Western republican tradition. They early rejected the notion that professional representative institutions, that is, trade-union councils, should replace wider popular assemblies. The new nomenclature, "soviets" for representative institutions and "commissars" for ministers, had a revolutionary flavor, but the structure of assemblies, provisions for amending the constitution, and parliamentary practices indicated the link that, on paper and in theory, existed with the main current of Western constitutionalism.

The first two Soviet constitutions, prepared in the early days of the regime and considered as transitional documents until the final triumph of communism in Russia, illustrate, then, one of the uses of studying the formal side of the government of the U.S.S.R.: Soviet constitutions reflect the basic philosophy of the state of the actual rulers of the Soviet Union—the leaders of the Party and the state—and their estimate of the people's aspirations. Soviet politics is like a vast painted canvas: Action and movement take place on the first plane, but they are balanced by a serene background. Thus the actuality of Party politics, of the real pattern of power, is balanced by the background of constitutionalism.

The trend toward "normalcy" in constitutional institutions was emphasized even more in the Soviet Constitution of 1936. The Stalin Constitution, as it was then called, abandoned the unwieldy network of elections of its predecessors. Instead of retaining a huge Congress of Soviets that seldom met, its also overlarge Executive Committee of two chambers, and the Presidium—the only steadily functioning representative organ—the new Constitution returned to the bourgeois simplicity of two normal-sized parliamentary chambers: the Council (Soviet) of the Union and the Council of Nationalities, which designate the Presidium, the collective president of the U.S.S.R. Under this Constitution suffrage is direct and equal, and the former disqualification from voting of certain classes is abandoned. The Constitution of 1936, adopted incidentally in the period of Popular Front, and the drawing together of the Western democracies and the U.S.S.R. in the face of the threat from the Axis reflected the conviction of the regime that the Soviet Union should receive a "normal" constitution with the echoes of the early revolutionary struggles and revolutionary romanticism muted. As Stalin proclaimed, socialism had been achieved in Russia. There were no longer any exploiting but only two friendly classes—workers and peasants. Hence there was no longer any need to discriminate against the former landowners, the clergy, and so on, nor to give the worker's vote more weight than that of the peasant. The Constitution, which acknowledged the leading role of the Communist party, proclaimed an impressive list of civil rights guaranteed to the citizens; the "bourgeois" freedoms of press, speech, and inviolability of the person were joined by the socialist rights, the state guaranteeing every citizen the right to work and leisure. Again, the value of the Constitution as a beautiful background to the stark political reality is enhanced if we keep in mind that the Stalin Constitution came into effect during the most intense period of terror in the history of the U.S.S.R., when the holocaust, not only within the Party and the state apparatus but also among the population at large, made a mockery of the civil rights and liberties so emphatically guaranteed in the Constitution.

The background is not without its uses. The regime, unlike the Fascist and Nazi philosophies, does not in theory repudiate the democratic and humanitarian tradition of European political thought. It does not explicitly base its claims on an irrationalist philosophy or on elitism. The regime claims that political democracy *does* exist in the U.S.S.R. When it becomes necessary or convenient to repudiate a particularly sordid period of Soviet history, it can put the blame on wanton behavior of individuals and their lack of respect for Soviet legality and constitutionalism. None other than the head of the police forces, and presumably one of the main supervisors of terror, Lavrenti Beria, blossomed out after Stalin's death (though not for long) as the advocate of legality. In the campaign against the cult of personality and in the general repudiation of the excesses of the Stalinist era, the Soviet leaders led by Khrushchev again based their emphasis on the illegality and unconstitutionality of Stalin's actions and the system of terror from 1934 on. Thus the Constitution and the legal underpinnings of the system enable the regime to have its cake and eat it too and to present all the hard political facts that are, in reality, of the essence of the Soviet political system as temporary and transient aberrations arising out of the willful and illegal acts of individuals, rather than as being imposed by the logic of totalitarianism.

With Khrushchev's departure in 1964 the liberalizing (*not* the liberal) period in Soviet political life was definitely if not, one hopes, permanently ended. His successors slowly and cautiously but with determination, moved toward a restoration of full Party authority and totalitarian controls, both of which they believed had been undermined by what they characterized as Khrushchev's "harebrained schemes." Part of the new campaign was the restoration of Stalin's image, not indeed to its pre-1953 status, but to the position Khrushchev adopted in 1956 (but went beyond in subsequent years by denouncing Stalin's career as a whole); Stalin was a great leader who unfortunately made mistakes and in the *latter* part of his activity gave rein to unfounded suspicions.

A more tangible sign of the resurrection of a stricter totalitarian model has been the application of more severe controls over the arts and intellectuals in general. Several writers and intellectuals who either wrote novels and stories depicting Soviet past and present in an unfavorable light (which, of course, were circulated or sent abroad clandestinely) or signed petitions demanding an enlargement of the area of freedom for the artist and writer were tracked down, brought before court, and almost invariably sentenced to prison or detention in labor camps. (The most notorious trial was that of Andrey Sinyavsky, whose stories under the nom de plume A. Tertz won a wide audience in the West as well as clandestinely in Russia, and his fellow writer and critic Yuri Daniel.) Nor had this "dissent" been limited to intellectuals. A retired general, a collective farm chairman, and some ordinary citizens have been among the open dissenters, and most of them also suffered imprisonment for merely expressing their views or protesting trials like those of Sinyavksy's and Daniel's. The protests, and this has been a rather new development in the U.S.S.R., have often been based on invoking the Constitution of the U.S.S.R. and the guarantees it contains of the freedom of speech and other freedoms. It is almost superfluous to add that the regime has indignantly denied the accusation that it is acting against the Constitution or persecuting people for their political views or protests. In each and every such case the dissenters are being punished, it is rebutted, for criminal and not for political transgressions.

The regime's need to countenance and to try to rebut such charges points out the fact that the Soviet Constitution is far from an unimportant document. There is, to be sure, a vast gap between Soviet political reality and the paper guarantees of civil and democratic freedoms contained in the 1936 document. At one time Soviet representative institutions and constitutionalism could have been considered a tribute that totalitarianism paid to universal human aspirations for freedom and democratic institutions. Now they must be considered more than that, for it is in their name that political protest, as yet feeble and quickly suppressed, is being made. Thus Soviet constitutional institutions already possess symbolic importance, and before too long they may become a factor of political importance as well.

Soviet Constitutionalism as a Unifying and Educational Factor

In their origins Western representative and constitutional institutions had little to do with abstract theories of democracy or with the practical necessities of giving the people an opportunity for expressing their preferences as to the system of government. They existed to provide a framework of national or state unity. The monarchs of the Middle Ages summoned parliaments in order to consult their subjects on the most expeditious ways of obtaining money and to give a select body of their subjects an opportunity to acquaint themselves with the complexity of the problems facing the state. This rudimentary function of constitutional institutions is of great importance in assessing the working of the constitutional framework of the U.S.S.R. In the Supreme Soviet of the U.S.S.R. the delegates from Uzbekistan and the Soviet Far East sit alongside Russians and Ukrainians; factory workers and collective-farm peasants who have distinguished themselves in their work are fellow delegates with the highest Party leaders, marshals of the Soviet Union, and academicians. Thus unity and cohesiveness of the Soviet state finds its tangible expression in the constitution and its organs.

The Supreme Soviet serves as a platform for the announcement and demonstration of national policies. Once a motif is thrown out by a leader, the other delegates, in a fashion common to all totalitarian parliaments, join in a chorus expounding and intensifying the official pronouncement, be it a warning to the "warmongers of the West" or, contrariwise, a profession of Soviet friendship and wish for collaboration with the United States; the need for further development of the Soviet consumer industries; or the reassertion of the superior needs and requirements of heavy industry. In an "activist" totalitarian regime, in which the citizen is expected to be not merely a passive subject and observer but a convinced and enthusiastic participant in the official policies and sentiments, the tribune of the national legislature is one more instrument for enmeshing the common man with the machine of the state, of expounding and amplifying the policies that come from above. The same holds for the Soviet courtroom: The dictator, whether an individual or a group, reserves for himself alone the right to proceed extralegally, while the mass of the citizens in their dealings with one another are bound by general rules and regulations. Thus in a highly developed totalitarian regime constitutionalism and legality become themselves handmaidens of the dictatorship.

In the same vein, in a country of the vastness of Russia, of the complexity and ubiquity of the Soviet state machinery, the network of representative and legal institutions serves as one of the most useful devices through which the rulers check on both the behavior of their subordinates and the sentiments of their subjects. A deputy from Odessa will not criticize Stalin or, at different times, Khrushchev or Brezhnev or any of the main figures of the regime. He will not be restrained, but, on the contrary, encouraged to speak of the administrative deficiencies or shortcomings in his city or the failure of some ministry to provide an adequate volume or quality of goods. Legal remedies will not avail against officially sponsored terror, but a worker persecuted by his manager or trade-union secretary will have his day in court. Beyond the rigid frame of the dictatorship itself and beyond the wide scope of official policies, the grievances and aspirations of the people can be aired and redress can be sought.

Soviet Constitutionalism as a Political Factor

We come to the third major consideration of Soviet constitutionalism: its use as a *major* political factor. Admittedly, as implied throughout, *in a stable totalitarian situation* the legal and constitutional framework is secondary to the real complex of political, police, and social forces upon which the regime rests. Yet examples are not lacking in which in a situation of crisis an institution that has existed on paper without interfering with the essence of political power has suddenly become endowed with importance. Throughout many years of the Fascist regime in Italy, it would have been inconceivable for the Grand Fascist Council to have repudiated Mussolini or for the figurehead king to have dismissed the dictator. Yet following Italy's defeats in Sicily in 1943 the constitutional and legal fictions became endowed with temporary reality, and the Fascist regime crumbled at the bidding of those institutions it had so long and so readily commanded.

It is rather far-fetched to draw any possible parallels with the Soviet Union. Throughout the long years of the consolidated Bolshevik reign the representative institutions have never registered any but a unanimous vote, and the courts have never rendered a political verdict except in accordance with the desires of those in power. When the great struggle for power rocked the Communist party and the country in the middle twenties, no reflection of it penetrated the All-Union Congress of Soviets or its Executive Committee, so unimportant were they in the overall political picture. Legal institutions were used during the purges of the thirties as convenient places to publicize and denounce the alleged crimes of the former and potential opponents to Stalin. Nor has the use of such extralegal devices died with Stalin. Beria and his henchmen were tried and sent to death without observing any of the constitutional provisions about guarantees against arbitrary arrest and trial in open court. It is not too much to assume that many a humbler citizen has met with an arbitrary arrest since March 1953, though the frequency of such incidents must have diminished considerably since Stalin's death.

Yet when all is said, the importance of Soviet constitutional devices has increased since the despot died. Essentially, the dictatorship has been in transition, and constitutional offices are endowed with *potential* political significance. On the morrow of Stalin's death a group of senior Communist party officials, after (it is reasonable to assume) some bargaining, rearranged the highest offices in the Party and the state. The new arrangements were in obvious violation of both the Party statute and the Soviet Constitution, though ex post facto they were ratified by the competent body. One office that changed hands was that of the chairman of the Presidium of the Supreme Soviet, that is, the titular head of the Soviet state. That post was never of any political significance, having been held during Stalin's last years by a faithful but indistinguished Stalinist, Nicolai Shvernik. It is significant that with the opening of a new era it was thought important by the highest Party leaders to change the incumbent and to entrust the presidency to the senior member of the Party Presidium—a man who, it was assumed (and, as the events of 1957 were to show, not quite correctly), because of his age and past role would not be directly involved in the coming struggle for power—Marshal of the Soviet Union Kliment Voroshilov. In an unstable situation the post of the titular head of the state became of consequence.

Totalitarian systems are unable to endow their constitutional systems with vitality, not only because of the unwillingness of the rulers, but also because of their real inability to conceive how free representative and legal institutions can operate. Political struggle thus *has* to assume the aspect of intrigue, of matching physical and organizational forces at the disposal of the factions, rather than of a free interplay of ideas and a test of strength within the constitutional framework. It is not too much to say of the rulers of the Soviet Union that they do not wish to grant the real prerequisites of democracy to their people; that they could not afford to grant them if they wished; and, most important of all, that they would not know how to go about instituting *real* constitutionalism and a *really* independent judiciary even if they could afford to. By the same token, the habits of mind and action and the social and political setting that enable constitutional and democratic institutions to operate have at present no root among the peoples of the U.S.S.R., having been extirpated by four decades of dictatorship and having had but a rudimentary development before. Yet history teaches that as the most intensive form of absolutism recedes, social and economic aspirations become translated into political demands. Representative institutions, one of their most famous theorists has asserted, are a tender growth, and it may take a very complicated pattern of events and conditions to bring them to maturity. But the seeds of democratic ideas and institutions possess a vitality that makes them begin their growth even within the freshly opened cracks of totalitarianism.

Federalism

The Constitution of 1936 guarantees each of the fifteen[1] Union republics that constitute the Soviet state the right "freely to secede from the U.S.S.R." More realistic on the subject is the Soviet national anthem when it speaks of "an *unbreakable* union of free republics." The most poignant illustration of both the freedom and the right to secession is seen in the fact that no more serious charge could be preferred against a real or alleged enemy of the regime, whether under Stalin or after him, than that of plotting to separate one of the national republics from the U.S.S.R. As for tsarist Russia, so for the U.S.S.R., the problem of the

---

[1]The number was reduced in 1956 to fifteen through the absorption of the Karelo-Finnish S.S.R. in the Russian S.S.R.

non-Russian nationalities remains a master factor of its politics. The mosaic of nationalities is reflected by the gradations of legal status from the Union Republic, to the Autonomous Republic, to the Autonomous Region and the National District. The intricacies of formal federalism are counterbalanced by the political centralization that is assured by the totalitarian system. As is the case with other political institutions the nationality problem is an example of the peculiar dialectic of Soviet politics: The theory, grounded in the democratic side of Marxism and embodied in the Constitution, confronts the antithesis of totalitarian reality. The interplay of the two will provide one of the keys to the future of the Union of Soviet Socialist Republics.

This dialectic confronted the Bolsheviks at the time of the Revolution, when the Russian empire was in a state of dissolution and when the Soviet leaders by their own declaration had been committed to the principle of self-determination. Though the discussion of nationality problems had in the past divided the Russian Social-Democratic party, Lenin and his partisans had firmly embraced the principle of a free option for each nation to remain within a multinational state or to separate from it. Definitely repudiated was the view of Rosa Luxemburg that national independence is a problem of secondary importance to the working class, and that the triumph of socialism will render the national question superfluous. The official view, enunciated under Lenin's supervision by young Joseph Stalin, had clung to the territorial principle and independence of nations. Yet power brought with it the immediate posing of concrete questions: Should the Bolsheviks sit idly by and see large parts of the Russian empire slip from their grasp? Should self-determination extend to cases in which "reactionary" (i.e., non-Bolshevik) elements would form states out of the former territories of the Russian empire? At first, in view of its weakness, the Bolshevik regime could not but find it good politics to adhere to its announced principles and to agree to the independence of various nationalities of the old empire. The defeat of Germany freed the Soviets from the oppressive conditions of the Treaty of Brest-Litovsk, which, among other things, would have detached the Ukraine and made her in effect a German satellite. Soviet successes in the Civil War infused the regime with more self-confidence and made it solicitous of restoring to the government most of the old empire's territory. There were still in 1919–1920 expectations of a Europe-wide revolution, and hence the independence of Poland, of Finland, and of other Baltic states would presumably be but an interlude to their reintegration as Soviet republics. The 1920–1921 period saw the end of such hopes. The task was now to reconstruct the Soviet state on a new federal basis and to implement in practice the Soviet nationality principle.

This principle was to be enunciated later on by Stalin, the first Commissar of Nationalities and one of the architects of Soviet federalism, as requiring a state "proletarian in content and national in form." The expression "proletarian in content" signified in effect that the various "union" and "autonomous" republics could not expect bona fide political self-determination once they found themselves within the spectrum of Soviet power. The Ukrainians, Georgians, Armenians, the Turkic nations of Central Asia, and so on, would no longer—this is speaking from the perspective of the early twenties—be submitted to forcible russification and denial of cultural rights, but they would be subject, together with the Great Russians, to the political and economic monolith of the Soviet system.

In the early days of the regime, when the foundations of Soviet federalism and their theoretical underpinnings were being laid, ideological considerations still possessed a vitality that only much later gave way to power considerations. Lenin, the supreme revolutionary pragmatist, was anxious that the practical task of consolidation of the Soviet state and its centralistic organization should not be combined with an underestimation of the potent force of nationalism. Before, as a leader of a handful of revolutionaries, he had adhered to a nationality policy that would avoid a disintegration of the revolutionary movement into its national segments while at the same time it endorsed the spirit of nationalism. Now, as the leader of a multinational state, he sanctioned forcible incorporation of the Ukraine and Georgia by the Bolsheviks, while at the same time warning against the excesses of Great-Russian chauvinism. At the Eighth Party Congress in 1919, angered by the arguments of Bukharin and Pyatakov who disparaged self-determination as being strictly secondary to the dictatorship of the proletariat, he exclaimed: "Scratch some Communists and you will find Great-Russian chauvinists." Practically on his deathbed, in 1923, Lenin denounced Stalin's and Dzherzinski's repressive policies in Georgia with the observation that people of non-Russian ethnic origin sometimes became the most intense Russian chauvinists, a particularly suitable remark in view of Stalin's subsequent career.

The theoretical disagreement thus paralleled the differences among personalities of Soviet leaders. Dzherzinski, the Pole, and Stalin, the Georgian, could be the warmest advocates of political centralization and, in effect, of Russian predominance in the Soviet Union. Others, like the veteran Ukrainian Communist Skrypnik and the Georgian Budu Mdivani, professed their native nationalism no less intensely than their Communism. Out of the ideological crosscurrents, out of the specifically Russian conditions following the end of World War I and the Civil War, was born both the theory and the practice of Soviet federalism.

The theory was militantly nationalistic insofar as the cultural rights of each, even the tiniest, nationality were concerned. Not only were the great and ancient non-Russian nations to be given the fullest autonomy in the use of their language, free development of their culture, and so on, but similar rights were to be extended to the Chuvash and the Ostyaks, primitive Asian tribes. Siberian tribes barely emerged from the Stone Age were to be encouraged to have their own written language and literature and to have some form of national organization. The early, most ideologically tinged days of the Soviet state were the days of enthusiastic nation building, when federalism was to join in a harmonious union nationalities at most disparate stages of development and to guide them in a joint socialist experiment. The Bolsheviks went out of their way to provoke and establish the feeling of national separateness, even in such cases as that of the Byelorussians, where this feeling was not very strongly developed. If socialism was eventually (and "eventually" in the early twenties was thought to mean rather soon) to unite all nations of the world in one great union, why be afraid of Ukrainian, Armenian, or Kazakh nationalism? Remove economic exploitation, proclaimed Marxism, and the state becomes an instrument of social justice and of progress—progress that will gradually make the state itself superfluous. By the same token, remove national oppression, which is but one form of economic exploitation, and various nationalities will abide peacefully together and, through their free development, will hasten the day when the triumph of socialism will secure one supranational socialist culture and language. Russia, the jailer of nations under the tsarist regime, would become a Soviet federation, a prototype of the future universal union of socialist states.[2]

The practice of Soviet federalism saw at the end of the Civil War several state units nominally independent of each other, but in fact already united, or about to be united through the agency of the Communist party and the Red Army. By the end of 1922 the process of consolidation, either peaceful or forceful, by the Bolsheviks transformed their empire into four units. The giant among them was the Russian Socialist Federated Soviet Republic, which received its constitution in July 1918. The R.S.F.S.R. contained several autonomous republics and districts, many of them created out of the Turkic-inhabited territories of Central Asia. United in fact, but nominally entirely independent, were the Ukrainian, the Byelorussian, and the Transcaucasian Soviet Socialist Republics. The last was composed of three previously separate and really independent states, which the Bolsheviks conquered once the Civil and Polish wars were over. The edifice was crowned by a formal union, and as of January 31, 1924, the Soviet state became the Union of Soviet Socialist Republics.

The formal pattern of Soviet federalism has changed but little between 1924 and 1972. The number of Union republics has grown from four to eleven on the eve of World War II, and is now fifteen. The sources of accession have been: "promotion" of autonomous republics to the status of Union republics, as in the case of the Central Asiatic republics; subdivision of existing republics, as in the case of the Transcaucasian republic, resolved into its historic components Azerbaijan, Georgia, and Armenia; and conquest, as in the case of the Moldavian republic (part of which had been in the Ukrainian S.S.R. before 1939) and the three Baltic states annexed to the U.S.S.R. in 1940. Some changes of status have taken place among the lesser gradations within the federal structure. The most noteworthy has been the dissolution during and after the war of some autonomous republics and national

---

[2]It is a highly academic question, but one that has occasioned some debate, whether Marxism postulates that the final stage of socialism-communism will see the withering away not only of the state but also of national differences. Certainly Stalin in one of his speeches once forecast the development of a universal language superseding the national one. Late in life, as in his famous article on linguistics, he repudiated the view that the progress of socialism would erase cultural separateness of nations or construct one nation. Like all the more extreme and utopian prognoses of Marxism, the notion of the withering away of the state and of national differences has been allowed in the Soviet Union to fall into desuetude.

regions, whose inhabitants allegedly collaborated with the Germans. This fate befell, among others, the Volga German and the Crimean Tatar autonomous republics and was accompanied by a wholesale deportation and dispersal of the surviving population throughout Russia.

Within the framework of the Constitution the federal principle is represented in the Council (Soviet) of Nationalities, one of the two representative chambers. Within this Council each of the Union republics is represented by twenty-five members, autonomous republics by eleven members, autonomous regions by five, and each national district by one member. The 1936 Constitution thus enthrones the federal principle in a more clearcut form than its predecessor of 1923–1924, in which the Council of Nationalities was one of the two branches of the Executive Committee of the unwieldy Congress of Soviets. The council of Nationalities has coequal powers with the Council of the Union, which is elected on the basis of population. The attractiveness of Soviet federalism was enhanced during the discussion of the 1936 Constitution by Stalin's pointed references to the right of secession of the Union republics and the need, therefore, of their being fairly large and homogeneous units.

The division of competence between the All-Union and the republic authorities was sketched again in an atmosphere of unreality that has pervaded the whole history of Soviet constitution making. The administrative organs are divided into three large classes: the All-Union ministries (e.g., heavy industry)[3] reserved to the competence of the central organs; the Union-republic ministries (e.g., agriculture), in which the administrative organs in the republics report to the corresponding ministries in Moscow; and finally republican ministries (e.g., education), where authority, theoretically, is vested exclusively in the hands of the republics. The Union-republic governments parallel the central organs with their single-chamber Supreme Council and the Council of Ministers. More or less the same arrangement prevails in the case of the autonomous republics.

Political literature has been rich in discussion occasioned by problems of federalism. Thus the American, Swiss, Canadian, and German systems have since their beginnings been characterized by conflicts and debate as to the extent of federal versus state or provincial powers. Within the Soviet Union the secondary character of the constitutional arrangements has prevented any possibility of such conflicts and has rendered almost superfluous a serious discussion of the division of authority between the center and the Union republics. It is nevertheless appropriate to make some remarks concerning the problem. Even within the letter of the Constitution, the autonomy of the constituent units appears shaky. The Union republics have the right to secede from the Union (Article 17), but the Presidium of the Supreme Soviet of the U.S.S.R. has the power to rescind decisions of the Councils of Ministers of the Union Republics (Article 49–e), and similar powers belong to

---

[3]Some heavy-industry ministries have recently become Union-republic ones, others from Union-republic have become republican, and thus the trend toward greater decentralization of economic organization still continues in the U.S.S.R.

the Council of Ministers of the U.S.S.R. (Article 69). The Procurator of the U.S.S.R., the chief law-enforcing official of the state, *appoints* the procurators of the Union and autonomous republics (Article 115). The amount of centralization envisaged in the Constitution is so considerable that an argument could be advanced that, even if one takes into account the strict letter of law and disregards everything else, the Soviet Union is more of a unitary than a bona fide federal state.

The federal aspect of the Constitution is largely a backdrop against which is played the real and vital problem of nationalities. Whenever foreign or domestic exigencies require it, Soviet federalism is dramatically exhibited to the world as proof that the nationality problem has been solved in the Soviet Union. It is difficult to interpret otherwise the amendment of the Constitution in 1944 whereby the Union republics were granted the right to conduct foreign relations and to possess military forces and the ministries of defense and foreign affairs were transformed into Union-republic agencies. No federation in the world grants its federal units the right to conduct independent foreign and defense policies. Behind the amendment were obvious political reasons: Soviet Russia was soon to claim seats in the United Nations for each of her sixteen constituent republics and was actually to obtain two additional seats, one for the Ukraine and one for Byelorussia.[4] Stalin's ingenious reasoning at the Yalta conference, that he might have political trouble in the Ukraine if that war-devastated republic did not become one of the charter members of the world organization, illustrates one of the uses to which the regime has put its federal pretensions. No one in his right mind, either in the U.S.S.R. or abroad, is today willing to believe that Kiev or Minsk have policies, or even agencies capable of conducting policies, independent of Moscow.

Even more mysterious has been the fate of the Union-republic defense ministries. The inextricable combination of fiction, propaganda, and potential importance that is Russian federalism was given yet another illustration in 1954. On that date, in celebration of the three-hundredth anniversary of the first union of the Ukraine and Muscovy, the Crimea, which is geographically part of the Ukraine but which until then had been a district of the Russian Socialist Federated Soviet Republic, was ceremoniously transferred to the Ukrainian S.S.R. The practical political consequence was somewhat parallel to the gesture of a man transferring some change from one pocket to another, but it served as a reminder that the nationality-federal problem remains of great significance for the Soviet state.

The problem of non-Russian nationalities has three main focuses in the Soviet Union. The most important non-Russian ethnic group is the Ukrainian. Numbering more than 40 million and closely related to the Russians in speech and culture, the Ukrainians are still a separate nationality with national consciousness and national aspirations that originated at least a century ago.

---

[4] The U.S.S.R. is thus represented in the United Nations by three member states: the federation and the two republics. The paradox, which escaped comment at the time, is that the largest federal unit, the R.S.F.S.R., was not pushed for admission, while two smaller ones were.

The two main nations of Transcaucasia, the Armenians and the Georgians, though much less numerous, have memories of a national existence and culture dating back to the first centuries of the Christian era. And both in the Caucasus and in Central Asia there are several Turkic-speaking nationalities: the Uzbeks, Azerbaijanis, Kazakhs, Turkmen, and others, all closely related and with a common background of Moslem culture.

In all three cases local nationalisms have been watched eagerly by the Soviet regime to detect and inhibit any signs of a desire for separate statehood or even a real, as distinguished from a paper, autonomy. This supervision has reached deeply even into the cultural life of the non-Russian nationalities, with anything suggesting past as well as present incompatibility of interests between the given nation and the Russians being declared treason. The process of russification of national cultures and indoctrination of the youth in the primacy of, and the indissoluble union with, the Russian nation has been especially pronounced since World War II. Yet while these means can be effective in the case of small, until recently primitive tribes, or smaller nations, like the three small Baltic countries annexed during the war, they cannot be entirely efficacious when dealing with national groups, like the Ukrainians and the Turkic peoples, that have populations in the millions.

In some cases the Soviet regime has resorted to or allowed demographic changes to strengthen the preponderance of the Russian element. Thus in the enormous Kazakh republic, the Texas of the U.S.S.R., the Kazakhs are now in a minority, with more than half of the population being relatively recent settlers from the Ukraine and Russia. And this process is likely to go on, with the progress of industrialization and the settlement of the "virgin lands." The Russian element seems to predominate also in the larger industrial cities of the Ukraine. Yet in the age of nationalism even the most powerful totalitarian regime cannot resettle, extirpate, or completely eradicate the national feelings of a group of 20 million or 40 million people.

Here it is necessary to pause once again to observe the use of Soviet "constitutional formalism." The letter of the law stands in stark contrast to the reality of politics. Whether in Uzbekistan, the Ukraine, or Georgia, political authority proceeds from Moscow. But at times the grant, on paper, of national sovereignty has served to relieve the fissiparous tendencies of non-Russian nationalisms and even to gain enthusiastic adherents for Communism from among the more backward nationality groups, for whom even a paper sovereignty represents an advance and promise over their pre-Revolution status. By the same token, the institutions and liberties that exist on paper sometimes have the knack of becoming transformed into live and menacing demands. No other aspect of the Soviet system is a likelier candidate for this role of Frankenstein monster than its national and federal problem.

Administration

The Soviet state has been, because of the size and complexity of its administrative structure, *the* administrative state of recent times. Modern technology and the consequently enormously involved economic and political systems under which we live have everywhere increased the importance of administration: the art and procedures of doing things political and economic. Some have argued that the very focus of politics has shifted from the public forums and halls of legislatures, where politicians discuss principles and enact laws, to the offices and institutions, where administrators devise the ways and means of keeping the complex economic and political machinery of the modern state going. This development in the pattern of policy has been noticeable even in the democracies. It has reached its highest point in the Soviet Union. The totalitarian state is also the administrative state: a hierarchy of administrators—whether Party bureaucrats, officials charged with the planning and development of the economy, army and police officers, or whatever—rules Russia. They are accountable, in the last resort, to the highest group of administrators. In the Presidium of the Communist party the old revolutionary leaders (who themselves had served as Stalin's deputies over a large administrative domain) now play a secondary role to the new generation, whose whole career had been within the administrative apparatus of the state and the Party until their ability or the whim of the dictator, or both, endowed them with a political significance as well.

It was not as a charismatic leader or a victorious general that Stalin ascended the pinnacle of power. Though most accounts of his rise neglect his considerable political ability, it is generally true that his main avenue was his skill as an *"apparatchik,"* a man of the "apparatus" (of the Party) who through his ability at running the routine business of the Party gained an upper hand over his competitors, who shone more brilliantly as theoreticians or orators. Several years of anonymous work in Stalin's secretariat preceded Malenkov's emergence as a major Party figure. Khrushchev had been an obscure Party worker before he was selected by the dictator, at the height of the purges in the thirties, to be the head of the Ukrainian party organization. Bulganin's career prior to his disgrace in 1958 may serve as a prototype of the curriculum vitae of a successful politician in the Soviet Union: a stint with the Secret Service, work at the managerial level, director of the State Bank, chairman of the Moscow City Soviet, and finally national prominence as a political general and minister of war, accompanied of course by membership in the highest Party councils. The new generation of the highest Soviet leaders, the Kosygins and Suslovs—and one of the Shelepins and the Mazurovs today—are for the most part people who have arrived at prominence through long years of administrative work and whose political prominence was a prize for their technical (in the broad sense of the word) usefulness. To be sure, the ability to advance or even to survive within the Soviet administrative system cannot have been unconnected, especially during the period of the Great Purge of the thirties, with political ability, at least in the sense of choosing the right protectors, special usefulness and docility to the dictator, and so on. But the fact remains that the ascent to high posts has been apolitical in the Western sense of the word "political": no struggle for votes, no interplay of political ideas has enabled a man in the Soviet Union to achieve prominence during the last generation. Politics in our sense of the word atrophied during the Stalin era. Administration has become preeminent.

That this should be is one of the poignant ironies of the history of the Soviet state. For along with the conviction that under socialism the repressive and military tasks of government should wither away, the early Bolsheviks have inherited the notion that there is nothing specialized or special in the task of governing. Lenin's dictum that a kitchen servant can easily be transformed into a political expert is well known. That amateurs could perform the most involved functions of government was clearly expressed in Lenin's *State and Revolution.* Administration would wither away before the state. Popularly elected councils would run the whole complex of governmental functions, executive and legislative, and even judges would be elected. Thus members of the local city soviet (i.e., city councilmen) would give part of their time freely to the task of administering various branches of the city administration. The principle of separation of powers, *at any level,* was felt by the Bolshevik to be obsolete and smacking of fraudulent, bougeois parliamentarianism. The highest administrative organ could not be dispensed with, even in the early beginnings—but no bourgeois-sounding title of "minister" for the land of the soviets. The official appellation was at first the "Provisional Workers' and Peasants' Government." Branches of the central government were called Commissariats, presided over by the People's Commissars, each assisted by a council-collegium. The Soviet of People's Commissars soon became in effect a council of ministers, and the fact was officially recognized in March 1946, when the name itself was changed to conform to the accepted world-wide usage. About the same time uniforms were introduced for members of various branches of administration including those the most "bourgeois" countries are content to leave ununiformed. The symbolism of titles and uniforms has reflected the great change both in actuality and in official thinking on the subject of administrations.[5]

Russia is, then, a much-administered country. We will examine here the structure of state administration, leaving the structure of the Party for the next chapter. The interrelationship of the Party and state machinery is one of those topics in politics that cannot be described by laying down a set of rules. The Party leads and controls the government. All the state officials, even of the middling rank, are its members. The highest officers of the state are important Party officials (though the converse is not always so). Yet the exact way in which the two machines intermesh and react upon each other varies with each important change in the political atmosphere, the personality of the incumbents of the given positions, and so on. A few examples will illustrate the problem.

---

[5] That the first generation of Bolsheviks should have believed the problems of governing to be relatively simple at the same time that they espoused the notion of a *professional* and *centralized* revolutionary party, is one of those paradoxes that illuminate the twofold character of their Marxist heritage.

The Chairman of the Council of Commissars—that is, the prime minister—following Lenin's death was Alexei Rykov. As early as 1928 Rykov disagreed with Stalin (then already in complete ascendance) over questions of agricultural policy and fell into disgrace. Yet Rykov retained his chairmanship until December 1930. The head of the executive branch of the government was powerless when confronted with the hostility of the Secretary-General of the Party. While still in office, Rykov had no alternative but to carry out policies and instructions of which he disapproved. He was succeeded by Molotov, a faithful pupil and follower of Stalin. It was not until May 1941 that the dictator himself assumed the chairmanship. It is possible that the general European situation—Russia was to be plunged into war within a few weeks—may have persuaded Stalin that he should assume immediate and overt leadership of the government. But in terms of real power, the chairmanship was in fact insignificant. No one would argue that Stalin was more powerful on May 6, 1941, when he assumed the office, than he had been on May 5.

In February 1950 an article in *Pravda* attacked A. A. Andreyev for his views on the organization of the collective farms. Andreyev was then a member of the Politburo but, what is more important from our point of view, he was also Chairman of the Council on Kolkhoz Affairs, then the highest governmental organ dealing with collectivized agriculture. A simple notice in the Party organ was a sufficient indication that Andreyev's views no longer had the support of the very highest Party circles. Andreyev promptly recanted his views and was replaced as the chief spokesman for the regime on agricultural affairs by N. S. Khrushchev. The latter in turn was criticized within a year by a Party official much inferior to him in status, but who was obviously acting on instructions from higher quarters. The incident illuminates not only Soviet politics in the last years of the Stalin era, but also the atmosphere in which policies are formulated and executed under the Soviet system. The Ministry of Agriculture is not an independent policy-formulating organization. It goes along formulating and supervising policies until at a crucial point the highest Party organ, or the dictator himself, steps in. Here a matter of great economic and, incidentally, ideological, importance is settled by a decision of one, or at most a few, persons. The Party then lays down the policies and provides the "tone" in which they are administered. What is true at the top is also true at lower levels. The secretary of a local Party committee is likely to be a more important person than the chairman of the given city's council. The former attends not only to Party matters in the strict sense of the word, but economic, educational, and other problems of the city or district are also within his responsibilities.

The enormous growth of administration in the Soviet Union is a logical consequence of the concept of the state, which controls and administers every aspect of the national economy. If the state strives at the same time to direct all forms of its citizens' activities from their beliefs to chess playing, it cannot dispense with a vast army of officials. The logic of totalitarianism as well as that of socialism makes the U.S.S.R. a bureaucratic state.

The administrative history of the Soviet state has exhibited one of those "inherent contradictions" of which Marxists love to talk when they discuss nonsocialist countries. In the Soviet concept socialism means "doing things": increasing production, expanding the industrial plant, training scientists, athletes, soldiers. Action rather than deliberation, construction rather than the reconciliation of conflicting interests, has been the desired characteristic of the Soviet administrator. The emphasis on quantitative achievement has characterized not only economic administration. It would be comical if it did not involve so huge a number of human tragedies to relate how at the height of the Great Purge (1936–1938), Party and security officials set themselves regular quotas of "enemies of the people" and "wreckers" they "had" to discover and liquidate to gain the approval of their superiors. The emphasis on production, in the widest sense of the word, that has characterized Soviet society in the last generation has necessitated the institution of one-man direction in most administrative institutions and the discarding of many devices designed to prevent administrative abuse of powers and corruption. Gone or diminished in importance are the collegial arrangements in ministries whereby the minister was merely a chairman of a collegium of senior officials. The same has happened to the famous *troika,* the arrangement under which major industrial enterprises were run by a committee composed of the director, the secretary of the Party cell, and the trade-union representative. One-man management was prescribed in a famous speech of Stalin's in 1931 as an imperative in the struggle for rapid industrialization, and it has been a rule ever since.

But vesting in one man complete authority for a certain area of administration is an excellent incentive for efficiency *only up to a certain point.* After that point has been reached the lack of institutionalized restraints is liable to breed complacency, corruption, and, a cardinal sin in a totalitarian regime, a feeling of independence vis-à-vis the central organs. The story of Soviet official utterances on public administration and administrators has consisted in the interplay of two ostensibly contrasting *motifs.* One has been the harping on the need of one-man management and the inadmissibility of diluting authority, whether in a ministry or in a plant. The other insistent note has been the complaint of officials' "losing touch with the masses," of nepotism and high living among Party and state officials, of their arbitrary behavior, contempt for the rank and file of their subordinates, and so forth. In place of normal administrative restraints, a system of controls peculiar to a totalitarian state had to be constructed. Officially, the task of control lies in an institution, like the Ministry of State Control, which checks administrative performances of various agencies and has the right to audit their books, and the Procuracy of the U.S.S.R., which checks on the legality of administrative actions and ordinances. But in fact the most, if not the only, effective way of controlling high officials has been the fear of political disgrace and liquidation that could befall them upon discovery of an administrative failure. Failure, under Soviet totalitarianism, has often been equated with political heresy and treason. A high official—say a Party Secretary of a sizable region or a minister controlling an important segment of the economy—was, especially in Stalin's era, like the proverbial Oriental vizier. While in favor he enjoyed unlimited power over his subordinates and, if he so desired, the appurtenances of luxurious living. An incautious utterance, an administrative mistake, or bad luck that could be seized upon by the envious or by his rivals could bring his instant downfall, followed by imprisonment or worse.

The system under Stalin, as his successors who had sweated it out were perceptive enough to realize, did not really *control* the administrators, it *terrorized* them. It was not the control agencies and regulations that exercised restraints over the body of bureaucrats but the secret police and the fear of denunciation. Thus in the last resort the system often defeated itself. For an administrator endowed with the power to make a prompt decision in an economic or other matter would yet be so terrified of making a miscalculation, which might cost him not only his job but also his head, that he would refer the matter to his superior, he to his, until relatively trivial decisions would have to be decided by the Politburo or the dictator himself. The secret police spread its network of informers over all administrative institutions. From a less dramatic viewpoint the obsession with fulfilling and overfulfilling production quotas—the main avenue of success for an ambitious manager and director—often resulted in falsifying statistics, shoddy quality of the product, and corrupt practices in the struggle to obtain scarce raw materials. Soviet administration worked in an atmosphere of nervous tension, conducive to success over shorter periods and emergencies like the War, but insufferable and self-defeating as a long-run practice.

It is this fact, among others, that persuaded Stalin's successors to carry out their campaign against the "cult of personality," that is, to spell out and to publicize the crimes and abuses of their great predecessor. Their objective has *not* been to change the totalitarian character of the regime, but to reintroduce a degree of "normalcy" and legality into the Soviet system. Some German political theorists of many years ago formulated the concept of *Rechtsstaat,* of a state, that, while not democratic in character, would be ruled by laws and whose bureaucracy would have its powers and competence strictly defined. The objective of the new masters of the Soviet Union has been to have a form of Communist *Rechtsstaat.* The campaign against Stalin's ghost had the concrete result of exposing thousands of little Stalins who in their spheres acted arbitrarily and corruptly. The relaxation of terror and the imposition of stricter controls on the power of the organs of state security has served to relieve the tension and to assure the rank and file of Soviet administrators that they could now work with at least a modicum of physical security. The new regime has grasped the dangers and inefficiencies of overcentralization. While not for a moment relaxing the totality of political centralization, the bosses of the country—members of the Politburo of the Communist party of the U.S.S.R.—have allowed and encouraged a degree of economic and administrative decentralization. More emphasis on the quality of work and production and the restoration of the morale of the administration—these have been the aims of the new leaders, and, as we shall see, behind the new policy there has been not only the desire for administrative efficiency but political considerations as well.

In brief, the objective of the rulers has been what might be called sane Stalinism: policies oriented to preserve the totalitarian character of the state and to assure its economic growth but stripped of the aberrations and excesses that emanated from the despot's personality. It is legitimate to pose the question, is it in the nature of things political to have a halfway house between unbridled totalitarianism and a government of laws? and a related question: What effect have the new policies had up to now? No simple answer will suffice. It is reasonable to assume that in the administrative sphere as elsewhere, Soviet totalitarianism is in a fluid condition and capable of retrogressing into some of the excesses of the Stalin era as well as progressing to a pattern more closely approximating bureaucracies of the West. The lessened fear of the secret police, greater freedom of criticism, and the encouragement of more initiative and decision making at the lower and local levels of administration: All these reforms cannot but improve the morale and efficiency of Soviet administration. But the Khrushchev era also saw a rapid turnover of high Party and administrative officials, some of them within the highest circle of power. The bad harvest in 1959 in Kazakhstan was blamed directly on the First Party Secretary of the Republic. A member of the Presidium, Nikolai Belyayev, was subsequently dismissed from his high post. The year 1960 witnessed the disgrace and demotion of a yet higher official: A. Kirichenko, Secretary of the Central Committee, member of the Presidium, and a long time associate of Khrushchev, was, for reasons not fully divulged, removed to a post of lesser importance and dismissed from the Presidium. In the wake of unsatisfactory agricultural performance and of the revelations of a widespread falsification of statistics, a wholesale removal of local Party officials took place in the spring of 1961. The most drastic illustration is provided by the case of the Party boss of Tadjikistan, Uldzhabayev. Accused of systematic falsification of the figures relating to the harvesting and production of cotton, Uldzhabayev and some of his subordinates were stripped of their Party and government posts and faced with criminal prosecution.

The Soviet official, especially in a crucial economic sphere, is still expected to perform at a feverish pace. The analogy of an Oriental potentate may no longer be suitable, but insofar as his security and peace of mind are concerned, he may not unfairly be compared to an American baseball manager or football coach. Failure to produce may not always be excused by references to the poor material available or to the hard schedule. He may find himself accused of an improper attitude or the inability to work with people, and no civil service regulations will protect him from a curt dismissal. And the element of terror has not of course been entirely eliminated. The main subordinates of Beria were hunted down and eliminated with the same thoroughness that in Stalin's times characterized the persecution of real and alleged Trotskyites and Bukharinites. Malenkov's replacement as top man of the regime by Khrushchev was followed by a shake-up in several important Party and state positions. The fall of Khrushchev in October 1964 was of a somewhat different type. What evidently led to his fall was the fairly unanimous conviction of other members of the Presidium that their leader was, through his constant administrative reorganizations and other reforms and designs (more on some of them below), undermining the power of the Party as a whole and threatening their own position. Hence with the exception of a few officials of secondary rank (one of them Khrushchev's son-in-law), the hierarchy was not purged following the dismissal of the man who dominated Soviet politics for more than a decade. This was, then, yet another variant in the incessant struggle for power that never really ceases at the top of the Soviet pyramid. It was not a case of Stalin's crushing any *potential* opposition and rivals, nor of the outmaneuvering of Beria and then Malenkov in the struggle for *the* top spot. It was a case where oligarchy acted fairly unanimously to get rid of an increasingly unstable boss before he could start purging them. Unlike under Stalin but somewhat similar to the pattern of dismissal of Malenkov in 1955, the 1964 coup had a *thin* veneer of legality, though the official version that Khrushchev himself requested to retire on account of his age and ill health could not be long maintained, even by the Soviets. (Malenkov had been prevailed upon or compelled to request *publicly* his release as Prime Minister and was retained for two years in high Party and government posts. Khrushchev evidently could not be prevailed upon to make a similar gesture of acquiescence and was dismissed from all his positions immediately and simultaneously.) Insofar as the vast mass of Soviet citizens was concerned, the man who had been their highest political leader and guide one day disappeared the next, without bidding his farewell, presenting his side of the case, or indeed without being alluded to by name in the press after his dismissal.

Ministers and Ministries

The structure of the Soviet administration bears witness to the complexity of functions assumed by the state and to the undercurrents of totalitarian politics. Since the state controls *directly all* the spheres of economic life, the Soviet administrative apparatus includes all the agencies of production and consumption. Every store and every factory in the U.S.S.R. is owned and administered by the state. Every acre of land is under control of the state, while most cultivated soil and forest is owned and run either by state agencies or by collective enterprises like the collective farms, which for all purposes are units in the state economic administration.

To supervise this vast network of enterprises, the Soviets until recently resorted to centralized economic administration as well as planning. The number of ministries both of the U.S.S.R. and the Union republics was consequently large. They included in addition to departments common to all states, such as finance, war, interior, and commerce, ministries covering every region of economic activity, such as ministries of chemical and heavy industry, the automobile industry, and so forth. The total roster of central ministries (i.e., both All-Union and Union-Republic) has oscillated between twenty-five and fifty, and the number would be considerably larger if we included a number of special commissions and committees whose heads have ministerial status (e.g., the Gosplan—the Committee to Plan National Economy—and the Committee for State Security). Some of the ministries used to be, and a few still are, not administrative agencies in the Western sense of the word but headquarters of gigantic economic enterprises that cover all of the

Soviet Union.[6] Others are great preserves of political power, and their heads, by virtue of their position, are among the leading men of the regime. Thus at the height of his power in the late forties and again for a few months after Stalin's death, Lavrenti Beria was clearly more than just a Deputy Prime Minister and minister in charge of security matters. He was a man who controlled a vital segment of power in a totalitarian state. The police and the special armed forces of his ministry were at his disposal. Some of his closest subordinates were his personal protégés and friends. It was only gradually and cautiously that Stalin himself moved to diminish the enormous concentration of power in Beria's hands, and the security chief's ultimate downfall evidently required a concerted action of all other major leaders of the regime. In a somewhat similar sense the Ministry of Defense, for so long jealously preserved by Stalin against any potential Bonaparte, enjoys, under currently fluid conditions of Soviet totalitarianism, a special status. Its head had been for a long time Stalin's crony Klimenti Voroshilov, followed by ministers who were either technicians or political generals. That the ministry of armed forces has now become a preserve of political power and its incumbent a figure of great influence has been demonstrated in both the political rise and downfall of Georgi Zhukov. Elected an alternate member of the Presidium at the Twentieth Congress, he was promoted to a full member in the July 1957 crisis and removed as well as dismissed as Minister a few months later. While the reasons for his dismissal are not clear, the Party bosses obviously did not enjoy the presence in the highest organ of a man who was primarily a general and only secondarily a Party man and who, worst of all, enjoyed a wide popularity in the country.

The problem of coordination and of relative competence of various ministries is posed in sharper focus in a totalitarian society than it is in the framework of democratic administration. In England a war minister who feels that he is being imposed upon by the Treasury will carry his case to the Prime Minister and the Cabinet, or as a last resort, he can resign and explain his case to Parliament. In the U.S.S.R. the major decisions are reached outside the context of the ministerial council, and the given ministers participate in them only insofar as they are important members of the Presidium of the Communist party. Thus in the middle thirties when Russian transportation was in a deplorable state and was proving to be a major obstacle in rapid industrialization of the country, Lazar Kaganovich was appointed Commissar of Transportation. Kaganovich had the reputation of a capable administrator, but what is more important, he was then a person of enormous political importance: a member of the Politburo and right hand of Stalin in economic affairs. Thus he had the ability to make decisions and commandeer resources far beyond the reach of an "ordinary" minister of transport.

The Council of Ministers even from a mechanical point of view is not the proper body to debate and determine policies. Even in the post-Stalin days it remains a

---

[6]Something like the Atomic Energy Commission in the United States, which is charged with the production of atomic products as well as the extraction of fission-producing materials, comes close to the *type* of economic agency in the U.S.S.R.

large body to perform the functions, say, of the British Cabinet, which, though only between one-third and one-half of its size, has been accused of being too large for efficient policy formulation. It may be assumed that insofar as *administrative* policies are concerned they are determined by a smaller group, composed of the Chairman, first deputy chairmen, and deputy chairmen.[7] This group in October 1956 totaled fourteen, seven of whom were, until June 1957, members of the Presidium of the Communist party and all of whom were members of the Party Central Committee. The Chairman of the Council is traditionally, though as we have seen not always, one of the highest men in the regime. Bulganin, the Premier until March 1958, was for the most part of his tenure considered second man in the Soviet hierarchy. Khrushchev's assumption of the office was significant, not for its own sake but simply because it showed a considerable deviation from the current theory of collective leadership, insofar as the highest positions both in the Party and in the administration were for the moment combined as they were during the latter part of the Stalin era.[8]

The administrative reforms and the party crisis of 1957 have affected the structure of the Council of Ministers. Most of the deputy chairmen happened to be in a group opposed to Khrushchev and lost their ministerial positions as well as their party posts. Thus the two senior first deputy chairmen, Molotov and Kaganovich, were dismissed, as well as deputy chairmen Malenkov, Saburov, and Pervukhin. Previous reforms had added to the All-Union Council of Ministers (not inconceivably to increase Khrushchev's influence) chairmen of Councils of Ministers of the Union Republics. Again, the years from 1957 have demonstrated the constriction-expansion pattern of Soviet administration. The number of deputy chairmen at first dropped to four and the title "first deputy chairman" disappeared. The overall number of ministers has been raised again by bringing into the Council of Ministers the chairmen of various state councils and commissions and subdivisions of the Gosplan. The current setup is not likely to remain fixed. For one thing, if the Council of Ministers meets frequently, it is difficult to see how the chairmen of the Council of Ministers of the Union Republics can be in regular attendance. Also, in view of the vastness of the Soviet administrative machinery, it is quite likely that the number of deputy chairmen of the All-Union Council of Ministers will be expanded still further. Each of the deputies is likely to wear several hats: Some are still heads of ministries or committees; all of them are high Party officials. Multiplication of

---

[7] The Chairman and first deputy chairmen constitute the Presidium of the Council.

[8] The relative ranking of the Soviet oligarchs was for a long time easy to assess by simply following the official order of names at a function as given in the Soviet press. Thus in the thirties the names of Molotov, Voroshilov, and L. Kaganovich invariably followed that of the dictator. Stalin's death brought about the ranking (1) Malenkov, (2) Beria, (3) Molotov. Sometime after Beria's imprisonment in the summer of 1953, the pattern was set whereby members of the Presidium of the Party are listed first and alphabetically, then members of the Party Secretariat, then deputy chairmen of the Council of Ministers who are not members of the preceding bodies, etc. Official etiquette thus conforms to "collective leadership."

offices in one person is not as pronounced as in Stalin's time. Jealous though he was of his subordinates' becoming too prominent, the dictator, himself a man of enormous energy and industry, required his lieutenants to imitate his working habits. L. Kaganovich, for instance, was at one time in the thirties Secretary of the Moscow Party organization and member of the Central Party Secretariat, in addition to being in overall supervision of heavy industry. But Soviet administrators are still, as a rule, overworked.

There have been but a few glimpses of the decision-forming process at the highest levels of Soviet administration. We know, for instance, that important decisions used to be reached under Stalin (and there is no reason to believe that the procedure is now greatly different) at a meeting of either the plenum or a committee of the Politburo. The specialists, the ministers in charge, would report or recommend, and the Politburo would decide. In his "secret" speech denigrating Stalin at the Twentieth Congress, Khrushchev criticized his erstwhile boss for, among other things, his completely chaotic way of assigning responsibility for various matters or of simply by-passing even the Politburo and settling vital decisions on his own. Yet there is little to indicate that administratively things have changed very much. There is no more Stalin to act completely arbitrarily, but there has not been and there cannot be in a totalitarian system a nice division of functions between the government and the Party. Khrushchev did not find it inconsistent to address himself to matters of administration as well as policy. Thus he spelled out the way in which new areas were to be brought under cultivation and prescribed the main crops for them. He upbraided the Soviet construction industry for not using enough structural steel and cement. And so it will be as long as the Soviet system continues; the Party will not leave any branch of administration to its own devices, whether its head is Khrushchev, Brezhnev, or anyone else.

The same confused line of authority runs through the ministries and through the councils of ministers of Union and autonomous republics. One might imagine that the improvement of dairy cultivation in the Ukraine is the primary responsibility of the Minister of Agriculture of the Ukrainian S.S.R. But it is the First Secretary of the Ukrainian Party who makes the authoritative statement on the subject. Somewhat in the manner of a dog chasing its tail, the regime is forever trying to establish clearer lines of authority and to free its administrative machinery from the insufferable amount of red tape the system entails. Ministries are merged into larger units to assure greater flexibility and more scope of action; then it is found that the unit is too large and unwieldy or that, for political reasons, it is unwise to concentrate so much authority under one minister. It is useless to recount how many times light industry has been split and then reunited into one ministry or how, for different reasons, the Ministry of the Interior has fissioned into Internal Affairs and State Security, only to regroup again.[9] In 1957 *administrative* decentralization again

---

[9]The Ministry of Internal Affairs was re-created on the morrow of Stalin's death out of the ministries of Internal Affairs (N.K.V.D.) and of State Security (M.G.B.). The former had specialized in the more routine functions of the Ministry of the Interior; the latter's functions

became the order of the day in the U.S.S.R. The ground had been prepared previously by the transformation of several Union-Republic ministries into republican ones by putting them within the full administrative competence of the Union republics. The decisive step prescribed in the spring of 1957 abolished most of the central economic ministries, such as those of the chemical industry, food products, and textile industry. Most of the functions of the former industrial and economic ministries were split up among a number of economic councils corresponding to the major industrial and production regions of the country—the sovnarkhozes. Each territorial council administers multiple economic enterprises within the region. The original plan envisaged in 1957 was ninety-two sovnarkhozes, sixty-eight within the Russian S.S.R., eleven within the Ukrainian S.S.R., and one for each of the remaining federal republics. By the spring of 1961 the number had grown to 104. Thus huge industrial complexes like Moscow or Leningrad as well as some of the smaller Union republics like Estonia or Moldavia constituted an economic unit within the new structure.

The reform was prompted by several factors. Economically it was felt desirable to bring administration closer to the units of production. Under it a chemical plant, say in Minsk, no longer is directly administered by a ministry in Moscow but is run by a department of the Byelorussian Economic Council with its seat right in Minsk. Savings in personnel, the avoidance of wasteful duplication of production facilities, and greater powers of initiative for the people on the spot are among the gains of the new system. Like everything about Soviet administration, the decision to decentralize was also motivated by political reasons. When it was formulated in 1957, it meant a weakening of the central administrative apparatus, then not firmly in Khrushchev's control. It was also an appeal for political support among the local interests, especially among the local Party secretaries, whose help during the June 1957 crisis did in fact enable Khrushchev to swing the majority of the Central Committee against the Malenkov-Molotov group.[10] Economic reasons combined with administrative and political ones to make the reform desirable.

---

were devoted to the more political tasks: the tracking down of espionage and subversion, the supervision of the forced-labor camps, and so on. Their reunification in the hands of Beria indicated his reassertion of power, just as their previous separation reflected the realization that complete and immediate control over *all* the security apparatus made its incumbent dangerously powerful. Following Beria's downfall the political importance of the security apparatus was decisively reduced and the still important segment of police and security powers again split up. Thus there was the Ministry of Internal Affairs, with its usual tasks and supervision of ordinary police, and the Committee of State Security (K.G.B.), which has inherited the function of the old M.G.B. More recently the functions of the Ministry of Internal Affairs were brought within the competence of the Union republics and the Ministry dissolved.

[10]Disgraced or demoted were not only the old Party leaders like Malenkov, Molotov, and Kaganovich, but also the principal administrative leaders, Mikhail Pervukhin, until June in overall control of economic administration, Saburov, and finally Bulganin himself. The latter three, it was announced in December 1958, had supported the Molotov-Malenkov group during the crisis.

The 1957 reform, however, not only failed to overcome what Alec Nove, a British expert on the Soviet economy, has called the "original weaknesses deriving from the inner logic of a command economy and its centralizing trend," but also created additional problems and shortcomings. In particular, there was now a tendency for the various economic regions to put local interests ahead of those of the U.S.S.R. as a whole. Khrushchev's response to this situation basically took the form of tinkering and experimenting with economic (and political) administration during the remaining years of his reign. To a large extent this involved a drive toward recentralization. Along the way, republican sovkhozes were created in the Ukraine, the R.S.F.S.R., and Kazakhstan (1960); the National Economic Council was set up to supervise the fulfillment of the annual plan (1962); the number of sovnarkhozes was reduced to approximately forty and a Central Asian sovkhoz was set up (1962); and a Supreme Economic Council was established as the highest state organ for the management of industry and construction (1963). Rather than solving the regime's economic (and in some instances, political) problems, Khrushchev's attempts at administrative reform resulted in the creation of further administrative confusion and chaos—and indeed would prove to be one of the major factors leading to his downfall in October 1964.

In the wake of Khrushchev's ouster, there occurred a full-fledged attack on his administrative policy. What took place in September 1965 essentially involved a reversion to the pre-1957 administrative system. With the exception of the retention of regional supply depots, the entire sovnarkhozy system was abolished, and instead control over the industrial sphere was vested in ministries. In all, seventeen All-Union and twelve Union-Republic ministries were created in the industrial realm, compared with sixteen All-Union and eleven Union-Republic ministries in 1957. These measures together with the economic reforms discussed in Chapter 3 must be viewed as an attempt on the part of the post-Khrushchev collective leadership to improve the country's economic position through the introduction of a greater degree of rationality and stability both in the administrative sphere and in the operation of the Soviet economic plan.

In the last few years of the Khrushchev era another, more basic, approach to problems of economic efficiency was proposed by a number of Soviet economists. Quite apart from the distribution of authority as between Moscow and regional economic organizations and councils, the crux of the difficulty lay, the economists argued, in the insufficient authority granted to the individual enterprise, that is, to its manager, whose hands on all vital elements of production, pricing, and so forth, were tied by plans and directives from above. In this context it was unimportant whether the plan originated wholly in Moscow or only partly. These economists, among whom the most prominent was Evey Liberman, argued in favor of freeing the director's hands in several managerial respects and thus allowing more scope for local initiative and a greater incentive for skillful and efficient management. Between 1962 and 1964 the Liberman plan, as it became known, was tried in a few enterprises. Following Khrushchev's ouster the new leaders decided to try the plan on a wholesale basis and eventually to introduce it to all industrial enterprises.

The reforms still, from our point of view, left a huge area of economic decision making in the hands of the central authorities. They, rather than the given industrial enterprise, still plan and set figures for the volume of prospective roles, output, the total wage fund, the rate of profit, and so forth. But the director of the individual enterprise could now regulate on his own the size of his working force and exercise some other functions that in noncommunist countries are assumed to be within the prerogative of management. The special incentive built into the plan was that the profits of the given enterprise, rather than its record of fulfillment of the production plan, would be the basis for awarding bonuses to the managers and workers, who would thus have a very real stake not only in meeting and surpassing production goals, but also in having their product be of attractive quality and in economizing on their costs.

This policy of decentralization (again if we use the term with proper qualifications) was to be extended by 1970 to the whole Soviet industrial and public sector (with the exception of agriculture). Yet it is evident that this schedule was not met. Even a, by our standards, modest measure of decentralization runs under the Soviet conditions into some basic obstacles that are noted in the political features of the system, its inherent tendency toward centralization and the real indecision of the Soviet leaders as to how far the objective of economic efficiency should be pursued at the expense of their complete control.

Behind the problem of Soviet administration stands the larger issue of the Soviet administrator. In the early days of the regime the administrator was of two varieties —the specialist taken over from the tsarist or pre-November days, indispensable because of his technical qualifications but watched and suspected by the regime; or a professional revolutionary, well-versed in Marx and Plekhanov but not necessarily competent to run a ministry or factory. Both types have become extinct, either through natural attrition or through the Great Purge of the thirties. In their place has arisen the new Soviet bureaucrat, a product of the Stalin era. He is a man almost equally distant from pre-Revolutionary society and from the struggles and ideological excitement of the Revolution and the first years after it. His training, often even in the noneconomic and nontechnical branches of the administration, is likely to have been scientific or in the social sciences. Questions of ideology, the great doctrinal disputes of the past, are for him matters of, at most, historical interest. He is, in brief, not greatly dissimilar to a bureaucrat, business executive, or army officer in the West *insofar as his training* and his *objectives* in life are concerned. If he belongs to the Party, it is more often than not a consequence of his job and the desire to advance, rather than of a deeply thought-out ideological preference. Communism in Russia has managed to produce in its officialdom a new middle class not startlingly different in its aspirations and viewpoint from the middle classes elsewhere, though it is superficial to speak of a managerial revolution and unwise to consider this new class as a monolithic whole in its attitudes and interests.

Soviet administration is thus an important factor in the changing social scene of the U.S.S.R. Here, as in other aspects of the Soviet political scene, the relentless terror of the Stalin era has obscured but has not stopped the growth of new social forces and aspirations. Russia's industrialization and growth as a great world power would have been inconceivable without the creation of the enormous and intricate administrative machinery. For all its shortcomings, for all the tenseness and insecurity in which the Soviet administrator has worked, this machinery has performed the day-to-day tasks of administration and planning. It has served the state well, and the Soviet administrator may soon feel and demand that his rewards should go beyond the enhanced social status and relative physical security accorded to him by the post-Stalin regime. His technical ability and his vital function in the system give him a base of power from which to press such a demand.

Five

The Informal Structure: The Communist Party

The Character and Function of the Party

In the years that have passed since Lenin wrote his *What Is To Be Done?* the Bolsheviks have grown from a handful of conspirators, partly in exile abroad and partly in the underground in Russia, into a huge party of several million members. No longer fugitives and in the background, the Communists rule Russia and control or guide other Communist parties that have sprung up in all countries of the world, some of which have since World War II achieved power in their own countries. It is certainly no longer the party of the hunted, of the Marxian intellectual and the revolutionary worker. Its resources are in effect the resources of the largest country of the world, and for its funds it no longer has to beg from rich sympathizers or stage "expropriation" raids on banks, like the ones in which young Dzugashvili-Stalin first achieved revolutionary renown. Over the years the Party has grown and changed until it is today the party of business managers, ministers, generals; of the elite of skilled workers and collective farm officials; of professors and engineers. Membership in the Party has become almost synonymous with achieving success and status in Soviet society. The symbolism that the Party retains of being the representative of the oppressed, of the "prisoners of starvation"— as the *Internationale,* the Party hymn, still proclaims—is clearly obsolete and paradoxical.[1]

---

[1] The evolution of the name of the Party is an interesting story. Until 1918 the Bolsheviks

And yet if the Party's composition and function have changed, the spirit of its organization and its professed aims still remain based on the principles postulated by Lenin in 1902, fought for and evolved by him in 1903 and the succeeding years. Democratic centralism—that is, strict discipline and unquestioned and absolute authority of the central organs of the Party—remains the official dogma of the 6 to 7 million Party members, just as it was for a few thousand before the Revolution. The Party is still officially the vanguard of the working class, and as such it cannot be content just to express and execute what the masses want: Its official aim is to propel them to what they "really" want (i.e., what they ought to want), and as such it is the teacher and censor of the people. Officially, again, socialism in Russia has been achieved, but the final goal of the Party remains as it was in 1903—further expansion and strengthening of socialism and, eventually, its transformation into communism, when "from each according to his ability, to each according to his needs" will become the basis of social relations. Thus the split personality of the Communist party—the party of conspiracy—in power. The champion of the oppressed is now an organization thoroughly bureaucratized, its high officials enjoying the privileges and perquisites of good living; the party aiming to bring about the most absolute and perfect democracy is still organized with the strictest discipline and a lack of inner democracy surpassing that of the most rigorous military organizations and religious orders.

The Communist party of the U.S.S.R. is, then, many things. It is certainly not a political party in the American, English, or French sense of the word. It does not seek and solicit members the way a democratic party does. To gain membership in the Party is an achievement and privilege. There is a period of probation, and any member who fails to live up to the standard of behavior set for the Party member, whether in his public or private life, faces expulsion. In theory, even the rank-and-file member is an "activist"—a man who takes a leading part in public activities of his city, town, or village; who on any job is an example to his fellow workers in industry and diligence; who has at least a rudimentary knowledge of Marxism-Leninism and hence is capable of explaining political situations in his country and the world at large. The Bolshevik is, then, expected to be a *superior citizen,* if not a superior type of human being. There are many descriptions of this idealized version of a Party member in Soviet literature. In Mikhail Sholokhov's

---

remained the "Social-Democratic Workers Party–Bolshevik faction." To demonstrate the Bolsheviks' drastic break with the "reformist" Socialists of the West as well as with the Mensheviks, Lenin prevailed at the Seventh Party Congress (not without protests from some Bolsheviks) in having the name changed to the "Communist party (of Bolsheviks)." The change was designed to emphasize that while the Bolsheviks remained Socialists and Marxists, they repudiated the name allegedly stolen by "opportunistic" and non-Marxist socialist parties and by their new name emphasized *revolutionary* and nonreformist Marxism and socialism. At the Nineteenth Party Congress the parenthesis "(of Bolsheviks)," so full of history, disappeared from the Party's name, which is now officially the "Communist party of the U.S.S.R."

Upturned Virgin Soil[2] the author describes the struggle for collectivization in a small Cossack village. The period is that of the great collectivization drive of the late twenties and early thirties. The Party representatives encounter all sorts of opposition in their attempt to persuade the peasants to join in a collective: sabotage by the rich peasants, "wrecking" activities of the emissaries of counterrevolution, and simply ignorance and attachment to their own land on the part of the mass of peasants. One *non*-Party man stands out in helping the Party officials to overcome these obstacles and to make the peasants see the justice and wisdom of pooling their land and cattle in a communal organization. At the end of the book this patriotic Soviet citizen is invited, as a reward, to join the Party. He begs off for the moment, saying that he is still not worthy of membership in the Party of Lenin and Stalin, because whenever he sees his cow, now a part of the communal herd, he still has a twinge of regret that his property has been "communalized." The old Adam of bourgeois mentality is not entirely dead, and until he is laid to rest, the new Communist man cannot take his place!

The process of indoctrination begins not too long after the cradle with the organization of the Little Octobrists, following which, Soviet children may at age nine join the Young Pioneers. But the burden of indoctrination of the young falls upon the *Komsomol,* the League of Communist Youth, its members ranging in age from fourteen to twenty-six. An organization patterned in its structure upon the Party itself and strictly controlled by it, the Komsomol is even larger, having over 15 million members. The organization has its congresses and central committee. Though as the relative size of the two groups indicates, by no means all of the Komsomol graduates join the Party, the former is the main recruiting ground for the ruling group.

Totalitarianism is especially watchful in indoctrinating the young. And the young are perhaps less convinced by paper theories than by the romanticism of action, of working and playing together. Hence to the Komsomol have been addressed the special calls for action, as during the First Five Year Plan, during the War, when the membership in it grew by leaps and bounds in the Armed Forces, and most recently when the call went out to settle and cultivate "virgin land" in Kazakhstan and elsewhere. Physical culture and paramilitary training emphasize the "activist" character of the Komsomol. It is definitely *not* merely a discussion group or an assembly of political sympathizers of a "grown-up" party, like the Young Conservatives or the Young Republicans.

In brief, the mystique of communism is propagated from the earliest days. It is a mystique of an active and devoted life—devoted to the service of the Party and the Soviet Fatherland. The young Komsomol member is supposed to be a junior replica of the image of the Communist: enthusiastic, eternally watchful (against the enemies of the Party and the state), and joyfully creative and enterprising at whatever post he finds himself in.

---

[2]Published in the United States under the title *Seeds of Tomorrow.*

This mystique of communism, strange in an ideology claiming its descent from the most rationalistic and materialistic creed of the nineteenth century, is very deeply ingrained in the official myth. The Communists, as the popular saying had it about the Seabees in this country, are supposed to be able to do the impossible in only a little more time than it takes them to do the difficult! The Communist is a dedicated builder of a new society and a new life. He is a man whose mind is free of superstitions about private property and religion, a perfect repository of the scientific truths inherent in Marxism-Leninism. So much for the official picture, the picture the Party presents especially to its ancillary youth organizations, the Pioneers and the Komsomol, which are designed to train young devotees for its membership. The actual picture is more complicated.

The concept of the Communist party emphasizes that it is the party of workers. In the early days before the Revolution, while most of the leaders came from the intelligentsia, the bulk of membership was in fact found among the factory workers. After the Revolution, when the Party was in power, it still put a premium upon recruitment among workers. The Party was now governing a predominantly rural country, yet it shrank from admitting too many peasants into its ranks. They were a "hostile class element." The Bolsheviks in order to govern had to employ tens of thousands of former tsarist officials, engineers, and officers, who as a group were also debarred from membership. In the rules about admission to Party membership, until the mid-thirties one finds inherent the theory of what might be called hereditary and occupational taint: Except in unusual circumstances, no one who had been born into a middle-class environment or who had at one time possessed real property, even if only a few acres, could be expected to become as trustworthy a Communist as a *real worker*—the son of a worker or of a landless peasant.[3] The more the prospective candidate was removed from the worker, the more difficult were the conditions for admission and the longer was the probationary period before full membership. Already in the early days there were voices on both sides of the question: The Workers' Opposition cried as early as 1921 and 1922 that the Party and the country were run not by workers but by bureaucrats. Zinoviev and Kamenev in 1924 and 1925 exclaimed that the rich peasants were penetrating the Party. On the other side Leonid Krassin, an early Commissar of Trade, an old Bolshevik but an engineer by profession, protested that a country like Russia could not be run without the help of a technical intelligentsia and that the Party should not scorn the administrators, industrialists, and engineers. Yet the Party's attitude on qualifications for membership continued substantially unchanged into the thirties. The beginning of the great drive for industrialization and collectivization and the First Five Year Plan were bound to have an effect on the problem. In 1936 Stalin

---

[3]The injunction did not apply of course to the old Bolsheviks themselves, among whom could be found Lenin, sprung from a family of tsarist bureaucrats; Trotsky, son of a kulak, i.e., a prosperous farmer; Leonid Krassin, who had before World War I been an engineer and industrial manager; and even somebody like V. V. Ossinsky, whose real name was Obolensky, and who came from the famous princely family.

proclaimed that exploitation of man by man was extinguished in Russia. Socialism had been achieved, and instead of *antagonistic* classes, two friendly classes now existed—the peasants and workers; and the intelligentsia was not like the old intelligentsia, the product of a class society, but came out of the working classes and hence was entirely trustworthy. The change in the attitude of diffidence toward the nonworker was coming about slowly, even amid the tremendous revolution that was transforming Soviet society and the vast purge that was decimating the old revolutionaries among the Bolsheviks.[4] The watershed was represented by the Eighteenth Party Congress, held in 1939. The discriminatory regulations about accepting new Party members from among the nonworkers were abolished, and the attitude of distrust toward the intellectuals, engineers, and so forth, was proclaimed to be non-Soviet.

The Party has thus both in practice and in theory abandoned social discrimination when it comes to accepting new members. With industrial growth and the passage of years, the Communists no longer feel, as they most certainly did in the 1920s, that they are a garrison in a country peopled either by the class enemy or the ignorant and that, consequently, it is courting disaster to let the enemy or wavering elements into the ruling group.

What does remain is the conviction that the broad basis of the Party must still remain the worker. Even amid the most total terror and most absolute one-man dictatorship, the Bolsheviks paid more than lip service to this principle. Stalin expressed it when in a speech he compared the Communists to Antaeus of Greek mythology: Antaeus was invincible when he was in contact with Mother Earth; only by lifting him up and depriving him of this strength-giving connection could Hercules defeat him. And so this thoroughly totalitarian and oligarchically run organization is forever seeking to have its contacts with the masses of the population. Clearly an elite body, it still considers it supremely important to have workers and collective farmers as the bulk of its membership. In his report to the Twentieth Party Congress, Khrushchev again pointed out that unless the Party penetrates every sphere of national life and unless it has members everywhere, both Soviet power and Russia's economic progress will be endangered. The standard complaint reappears in Khrushchev's remarks: The Party is becoming too bureaucratized, too distant from the common worker: "It is an abnormal state of affairs that in a number of branches of national economy a considerable number of Commu-

---

[4]The late twenties and the early thirties thus witnessed quite a series of trials of engineers accused of "wrecking" the growing industry of the Soviet Union. Quite apart from the substance of the accusations, the trials represented a propaganda effort to picture the failures and privations of the First Five Year Plan as being largely caused by the "class enemy" rather than by its inherent defects. In the purges of the thirties, including the trials of the old Bolsheviks, a subsidiary charge leveled against the accused was the concealment of their class origin upon joining the Party. X joined the Party pretending to be the son of a poor peasant while in reality his father was an exploiting kulak. Not surprisingly, X, several years later while a high official, turned out to be a "wrecker" bent upon sabotaging the Soviet people's victorious march toward socialism!

684   The Russian Political System

nists working in these branches are doing work which is not directly connected with the decisive sectors of production. For instance, at coal industry enterprises there are nearly 90,000 Communists, but *only* 38,000 are employed underground. Over 3 million Party members and candidate members live in rural areas, *but less than half of them are working directly on collective farms, M.T.S.* [Machine Tractor Stations], *and state farms.'*[5] And in an attempt to revivify the Party that still recalls the terrible sufferings and oppression of the Stalin era, the Party boss once again emphasized the cardinal point of the Communist creed: Nothing can go well in Russia unless the Party is directly connected with it and unless every Party member has a sense of mission and responsibility: "The C.P.S.U. is a governing party, and what is done in our Soviet land is of vital interest for the Party as a whole and for every Communist. *A Communist has no right to be an onlooker.'*[6] The attempt to spread its membership widely in the occupational sense is emphasized in the renewed attempt to strengthen the Party organization in the villages. Traditionally, and still distrustful of the peasant and peasant mentality, the Party believes that the performance of the agricultural sector of Russian economy, which still lags behind the industrial, would improve if there were more Communists and more Party activity in the countryside. The beginning of the great collectivization drive of 1928–1929 was signalized by the sending of thousands of Party activists and agitators from the cities to the villages to explain to, to cajole, and, as it turned out in most cases, to coerce the peasants into pooling their land and cattle in collective farms.

The injection of the Party into the most crucial sectors of the nation's economy has been paralleled by saturation with Party members of the most important segments of the power structure. It goes without saying that a vast majority of high-ranking officers in the Army are now card-carrying Communists. The situation is thus drastically different from the days of the Civil War and the twenties, when a majority of officers were still outside the Party circle, many of them still veterans of the tsarist army, and when the institution of the political commissar was created largely to watch over the apolitical officer. The security organs have always been the part of the state apparatus most heavily saturated with Party members, and in the early days of the regime they were, at the higher level, a special preserve for the old Bolsheviks.

The story of the changing national composition of the Bolsheviks is another interesting sidelight of the changing function of the Communist party. Along with other revolutionary movements in pre–World War I Russia, the Bolsheviks drew heavily, especially within their leading circles, on the national minorities within the tsarist empire. It is not surprising that disproportionate numbers of Jews, Poles, Letts, Georgians, and Armenians flowed into the ranks of the revolutionary movement.[7] The national character of the Party immediately after the Revolution and

---

[5]Italics added.

[6]Italics added.

[7]If any generalization is possible, it could be stated that the Bolsheviks were more "Russian"

throughout the twenties continued to reflect the numerically disproportionate contribution that the erstwhile persecuted minorities and nations had brought into the Bolshevik party. The trend began to be reversed with the growing ascendance of Stalin. A Georgian by birth who to his death spoke Russian with an accent, Stalin became in effect an exponent of Great-Russian chauvinism within the Party. In the struggle for leadership, first against Trotsky and then against the so-called Left Opposition, the Stalinist faction was not above using anti-Semitic arguments, capitalizing on the fact that the "left" leaders, Trotsky, Kamenev, Zinoviev, and many of their supporters were Jews. The purges of the thirties fell with particular vehemence upon non-Russian Communists. The Party had now clearly embraced Great-Russian nationalism, and what was implicit in Communism before now became explicit: the continuation and intensification of Russian imperialism both internally and externally.

In the early days of Soviet power a fugitive Hungarian or Polish Communist would be welcomed in the Soviet Union and quite often pass into a high Party or even state position. In the mid and late thirties the majority of these honored guests were liquidated, often after an absurd charge that they were spies for the very governments from which they had fled. While the purge hit the Party hard as a whole, it was particularly ferocious in the Ukraine and the Central Asian republics. By the end of the thirties the Party was overwhelmingly and disproportionately Great-Russian in its composition. One expert concludes that numerically the Party was especially strong in Russia proper and in Transcaucasia, weaker in the Ukraine and, especially, in Byelorussia and in the Central Asian republics; and presumably even in these last Great Russians accounted for a considerable proportion of its membership.[8] The trend continued unabated until Stalin's death. While victory over the Germans was officially the triumph of all nationalities of the Soviet Union, it was to the Russian nation in particular that Stalin raised his toast at the famous victory celebration at the Kremlin in 1945. The last years of the tyrant's life witnessed a renewed campaign against the alleged nationalist aberrations among the non-Russian nationalities and a clearly officially sponsored anti-Semitic campaign.

A fuller story of these events belongs to a discussion of social changes in Russia. What should be stressed is that the Communist party has become predominantly Russian. It is an ironic fact that the Party that claims to represent the proletariat of the whole world, and in its ideology the humanistic tradition of all mankind, conducted in the late 1940s a deliberate campaign against cosmopolitanism and for, in effect, Russian chauvinism. The years that have passed since Stalin's death have brought some changes in the nationality policy of the Party. Russian chauvin-

---

in their leadership and composition than their rivals the Mensheviks and, insofar as the leadership was concerned, than the Social Revolutionaries, the representatives *par excellence* of the peasants.

[8] Merle Fainsod, *How Russia Is Ruled,* Cambridge, 1953, p. 229.

ism has become muted. In the local Party organizations, especially in the Ukraine, more prominence is given to the natives. It is impossible to say how far this policy has been reflected in the national distribution of Party members. It is clear, however, that the Russian predominance within the Communist party as a whole is here to stay. One factor that worked against Beria in his struggle for Party leadership was undoubtedly his non-Russian origin. And Russian nationalism, as well as its broader version, Soviet patriotism, remains one of the leitmotifs of the Party.

The evolution of the character of the Communist party and the distribution of its membership among various social and national groups already throw a considerable light on the role of the Party in Soviet society. But in what sense are its some 14 million members the "governing party," as phrased by Khrushchev? To be sure, *all* officeholders in Russia in every branch at every level of government are either Party members or in fact nominees of the Party. To be sure, *all* political and economic decisions in Russia are made either by the Party directly, or indirectly through the state organs staffed and led by Party members. But, as distinguished from the small group at the top, be it the Politburo, the Presidium, or the Central Committee, how do the millions of individual members "govern"? And what is the basis of their power as a party?

We have seen the idealized concept of the Party member, and we shall see in the next section how an individual Party member fits into the machine of Party organization. Here we want to define the personality and the role of the Party member in Soviet society. For all the machinery of terror and police, for all the armed might of the state, political power rests in Russia, in some sense, upon these some 14 million members. If their sense of identification with the Party weakens or disappears, if the Party member who is a trade unionist thinks of himself mostly as a unionist, the one who is an officer mostly as an army man, and so on, then the structure of monolithic totalitarianism will be weakened beyond recovery. History is full of examples of revolutionary parties that carried through victorious revolutions and ruled for a while until their revolutionary élan weakened or degenerated, and they themselves atrophied, eventually yielding to new social or political forces. The regime has always boasted and boasts today, more than fifty years after the November coup d'état, that in the Communist party there is still enshrined the *Revolution;* that the revolutionary regime has not given way to a military dictatorship or a bureaucratic clique, that the Communist party—the spirit of Revolution—not only reigns but rules.[9] An impartial observer will not accept the

---

[9]It is interesting to note how the Communists have clung to the democratic and progressivist symbolism. Their periodical organs have traditionally borne names like *Forward, Truth,* and *Worker's Cause.* Their propaganda, even at times of the greatest terror in the Soviet Union, has always been couched in terms of democratic and humanitarian trends bringing to mind the dynamic, forward-moving character of the movement. And those who are, or who are alleged to be, opposed to the Soviet regime are branded not as revolutionaries but as *counterrevolutionaries,* implying that they are not only traitors but people who stupidly and vainly oppose the inevitable march of history.

regime's self-estimation. He will point out that Russia is in fact ruled by a clique or, today, by several cliques of Party bureaucrats and that the high idealism of the Revolution has often given way to disenchantment, cynicism, and, in the high places, cynical enjoyment of the fruits of victory and power. But he will also be forced to admit that there has been some truth in the regime's boast: The Party's composition has changed, its rule has become vested in dictators and oligarchies, but the Communist party, even during the worst periods of oppression and terror, has remained the catalyst of the vital forces in Russian society. It has led the Soviet Union through enormous economic growth and to the position of a great world power. The Party has often succumbed to corruption and terror, but never to lassitude. And if the Party is to continue to be the vital force in Russia, the rank-and-file members must continue to see in their Party card something meaningful beyond an acknowledgment of status and an open door to personal success.

"A Communist has no right to be an onlooker." The individual member must have a sense of mission. Is this as true today as it was in the days of the Revolution and in the days following it? The average member of the Party throughout the twenties was still very much of a revolutionary. Any party in power will attract careerists, and even pure opportunists, but in its general tone the Communist party of the earlier years was still very much like a religious order with a special mission. An average member, even if a laborer with no formal education, was still assumed to be something of an intellectual, with a knowledge of the principles of Marxism and an acquaintance with the politics and economy not only of Russia but of the capitalist world as well. In theory no Communist, no matter what his official position or formal salary, was supposed to live on a scale surpassing the income of the average skilled worker. Marxism in its most theoretical aspect was still very much a live force in Party life. The great struggle for power that took place following Lenin's death was accompanied by the protagonists' tossing citations from Marx, Engels, and Lenin at each other. Not only Party congresses but small Communist cells debated the theoretical as well as practical aspects of such problems as whether socialism could be fully realized in Russia before a proletarian revolution took place in the West; whether a social revolution could succeed a national one in China and what the role of the Communists should be in it, and so forth. Of freedom of discussion, in the wide sense of the word, there was always very little in the Communist party, but there was certainly a lot of *ideological* excitement, which must have seeped down to the humblest member. The Party, then, in the earliest days of the regime was bound by the cohesive force of ideology and the sense of mission both in Russia and in the world at large. This embryonic political culture enabled the Communists, while still weak numerically, to preserve their power, first against their Civil War foes and then in a country beginning to recover from the ravages of the wars, weak and rather primitive in its economy.

The ascendancy of Stalin, which must be marked as definitive from the Fourteenth Party Congress in 1925 and as absolute from the Sixteenth Congress in 1930, brought a different emphasis. The age of discussion, of ideological fervor, was over. What replaced it was the fascination of concrete tasks, the gigantic enterprise of collectivizing Russian agriculture and industrializing Russia. The average Party member in 1930 already felt the tightening of Party discipline and the beginning of relentless terror, which was directed against anybody who opposed the dictator. In the country at large terroristic measures were in full swing against the recalcitrant peasants. But for all the sufferings and famines and privations the Party had a new and concrete task to uphold its élan: the vision of a Russia full of factories, of manufactured goods, with all the major means of production really socialized—a gigantic step in the realization of socialism. It is doubtful that any society in modern times has undergone such a shock of privation, of a lowered standard of living, and of oppression as did Russia during the years 1928 to 1933 without overthrowing the regime that was causing the sufferings. The tightness of police controls does not provide the entire explanation. Part of it must be found in the fact that throughout the terrible years the ruling order—the Communist party—could still operate with zeal and cohesion inspired by the awesome task.

The ability of Stalin to push the country and the Party close to the brink of disaster and yet avoid a catastrophe was vividly demonstrated again in the midthirties and late thirties when, while the economic situation was considerably improved (over the conditions of the early thirties) and industrialization was gathering momentum, terror of unprecedented proportions gripped the Party and society.[10] But aside from terror, the Communist party was kept as a functioning organism by the magnitude of the task still at hand and by the knowledge that to slacken in the effort toward economic power would be to risk defeat in a war that was clearly approaching. To the incentive of socialist construction the regime added the note of Soviet—and even plain Russian—patriotism. Russia's past was rehabilitated. No longer was Russia's history to be presented, as it had been in the twenties by official Marxist historians, as a story of backwardness and oppression. The Bolsheviks were now cast in the role of perpetuators of the great figures of Russia's past, like Peter the Great. The Russian nation was allowed to have had a great history, with some of the most tyrannical tsars being presented as having played a "progressive" role for their time. In other words, through the most trying times the Communist party could still play a leading role and through its existence assure the regime and the state of a degree of cohesion. World War II and its immediate aftermath recharged the Party with patriotic élan. The struggle against the invader and then the reconstruction of the ravaged country were again the kind

---

[10]Incidents illustrating the extent of terror were given by Stalin's right-hand man, Andrei Zhdanov, at the Eighteenth Party Congress in 1939, when the most acute phase of terror had been concluded, and the regime had piously denounced its excesses. In some Party organizations regular quotas were set for the percentage of "wreckers" and "spies" that had to be discovered in the Party membership. In one district hysterical Communists would provide themselves with medical certificates testifying that Comrade X, because of the poor state of his physical and mental health, could not conceivably become a tool of the class enemy! Stalin himself acknowledged that some errors had been made.

of aims to spur the Communists, to give them some feeling that they were still a "governing party" and not onlookers.

In some sense the Communist party through its long years in power has been like an athletic team that preserves its morale throughout all the privation of training, despite all the bullying by the coach or manager, as long as the aim is concrete and visible and the performance of the team satisfactory. But if there is no game in sight or the discipline and privations are obviously excessive for the desired purpose, the spirit of rebellion or sullen apathy replaces that of purpose. This in some way was the story of the Communist party in the last years of Stalin's rule. The Party had long before ceased to be a revolutionary corps, a handpicked elite of activists. It was, and it is now, composed mostly of people who have grown up under the Soviet regime and for whom the old ideological struggles and issues have no meaning. The asceticism of old days and the feeling of a special mission are also gone. Russia has been modernized and industrialized, and an average Russian does not have to be a fervent Communist or a reader of Marx to feel that it is a good thing for his country to produce more steel or to have more institutions of higher learning. During the last generation Russia has leaped into the front rank of modern industrial states. But this success of communism has by the same token created its greatest problem: What is the rationale for the iron discipline within the Party or for privations in terms of the standard of living, if the main struggle has been won?

The fondest dream of the Communist leaders of a generation ago was to create an administrative and technical elite that should not yield anything in terms of competence and skill to its Western counterpart. That elite has now been created, and its members comprise a large part of the Communist party membership. But by the same token, why should an engineer or an administrator or a factory manager who is also a Communist have aspirations different from those of his Western confrere? In what sense is he different *because he is a Communist?* To be sure, though socialism has been realized in Russia, the officially proclaimed goal—communism—still remains ahead. But how realistic or how desirable is it to an average member of the Party to conceive a society where the state will "wither away" and where "from each according to his ability, to each according to his needs" will be the fundamental law? What does communism have to offer now to justify further privations, the continuance of the police state, and the stringent duties inherent in being a member of the Party? The desirable achievements of communism from the point of view of a convinced Communist—public ownership of the means of production, the widespread system of social security, modernization and industrialization of Russia—do not have to be fought for anymore. They exist, and they will go on of their own momentum even if the Communist party disappears tomorrow.

The problem that faces the Communist party is, then, the problem of preserving cohesion and the sense of purpose without which the Party, though it would continue to exist, would degenerate in importance and would ultimately yield as the ruling organ to some other force—the bureaucracy, the army, or something else—with incalculable consequences for the whole Soviet system. The problem is not new. What marked its existence in Stalin's last years was the reign of terror exerted by the dictator. By the same token the degree of suppression exerted by the despot, while it masked the crisis, deepened its nature, and it was inevitable that with Stalin gone and a more fluid situation confronting the leadership in the country and in the Communist party, the crisis would appear with full force.

How the late dictator appraised the nature of the crisis in the Party and the means that he proposed to undertake in order to deal with it are described in some detail later on. To his successors it appeared imperative, as the first step, to lift the excessive amount of terror exerted within and without the Party by Stalin and to demonstrate to the rank and file of the members that while the Party would continue to be run according to "democratic centralism," that is, from the top, a certain degree of latitude and freedom would be allowed in intra-Party relationships. When the Presidium of the Party took their seats on the opening day of the Twentieth Party Congress in February 1956, they were greeted as during the Stalin days by the servile applause of the delegates; but Nikita Khrushchev admonished the members to act with more dignity and restraint, since they were masters and not servants of the Presidium! Nothing could be more symbolic of the changed times. Under Stalin frenetic applause for the leader was the prescribed form at a Party Congress, and his closest subordinates would receive ovations, the intensity of which was proportionate to the official's closeness to the dictator.[11] Apart from the official etiquette, the charted course of the new leaders of the Party became obvious from two speeches by Khrushchev, first his official report as the First Secretary of the Party and then his speech to the closed session of the Congress in which he berated the late Joseph Stalin and attacked the "cult of personality," a euphemism for the craven worship of the despot in which Khrushchev along with all other Communists had to engage for more than a generation. The same leitmotif appeared in other speeches at the Congress.

By hacking at the Stalin legend, the leaders were in effect undermining their own position. For had they not been the most servile helpers of the despot, and did they not reveal the abject terror in which the Party, along with the whole society, had lived for more than twenty years? Why? Part of the reason must be sought in the developments in the Party leadership just before and after Stalin's death. But beyond those reasons it is clear that the partial denigration of Stalin had a wider and more profound reason. Because of the developments we shall discuss later, it is no longer possible to exert, either in Russia or among the foreign Communists, the degree of terror with which the late dictator had ruled. If the Communist party, the Soviet state, indeed the whole Communist world, is to be held together, a new spirit, a new sense of mission, a new conception of purpose has to be poured into

---

[11]Thus at the Sixteenth Party Congress in 1930 Stalin was greeted according to the official transcript by "loud, long-lasting applause turning into a long ovation; shouts 'Hurrah'; the whole Congress greeting him standing up." Molotov and Kaganovich and a few others received "long applause," while a mere member of the Central Committee in good standing (with Stalin) had to be content with "applause." In the subsequent congresses the art and nuances of "spontaneous ovations" became considerably more developed.

the Communists. What Khrushchev and other leaders attempted to say could be translated as follows: "Look, Communism is not terror, forced-labor camps, and the whole nation prostrate before one man. Those things were just an accident traceable to the personality of one man. Communism is a live, creative doctrine; it requires discipline and privations to be sure, but not servility and complete negation of legal and rational processes. We as Communists still have great tasks to perform, and we can perform them best if we return to the Leninist purity of our Party and its doctrine." In other words, in place of terror, though its *moderate* use can never be abandoned by a totalitarian regime, the Soviet leaders are trying to revive ideological fervor and a sense of mission. Khrushchev quoted approvingly the criticism of Party officials by the great Soviet poet, Vladimir Mayakovsky. Though written many years ago, it has become particularly applicable to the Stalin and post-Stalin era: "They have rooted themselves in their own spot and see nothing beyond their own nose. Having passed his exams on Communism according to the book, having learned 'the isms' by heart, he has finished forever with thoughts about Communism. What is the use of looking further? Sit and wait for the circular. You and I do not have to think if the leaders think." It might be added that under Stalin it was not always safe "to look further." The current line is to encourage initiative of Party members and to appeal especially to the youth. Great tasks like the settlement and agricultural development of new virgin lands are designed, quite apart from their economic desirability, to rekindle the sense of mission among young Communists.

It might be objected that the post-Stalin leaders want to have their cake and eat it too. They do not dream of abandoning the substance of the police state or of replacing oligarchic rule with real Party democracy. At the same time they want all the advantages that in a democratic system accrue from free discussion and individual initiative. In a sense this has been a perennial dilemma of the Soviet system, hence the alternate periods, even under Stalin, of relative liberalization and of extreme terror. What makes the present system different is that there have been economic and social changes in Russia that impinge upon the Party and that make a return to full-fledged Stalinism impractical.

The role of the Party as the guiding force of the Soviet state and society is, then, in a state of flux. There is in the foreseeable future no alternative to the rule of the Communist party. But to repeat: If the Party does not recover its vitality and *esprit de corps,* it will lose ground to other social forces and other institutions, like the army; and eventually the point will be reached when it will be "a governing party" only in name, and its members will feel a prior loyalty to other social and political groups with which they are associated. It is often said that the monopoly of education and propaganda enjoyed by the regime can ward off such dangers and can continue to bring up generations of Communist fanatics. But the most powerful and penetrating propaganda machinery in the world will still be ineffective if social and economic conditions make its postulates unrealistic and distant from the circumstances of life of the persons being propagandized. The regime is quite explicit in its concept of the Communist party. It wants an active and ideologically motivated elite, or, as Mikhail Suslov, member of the Presidium, stated at the Twentieth Party Congress: "The Party does not admit all who declare their wish to join its ranks. It selects for itself the most advanced and active people; it regulates admission in conformity with the tasks facing it at one or another stage of its work. During the industrialization and collectivization of agriculture, the Party admitted mainly workers and peasants; during the years of war preferential admittance to the Party was given to those who were at the front line. It is hardly necessary to prove that at present, when the problem of a steep improvement of material benefits is being solved, it is wise to lay stress primarily on the admittance of the direct producers of these benefits—workers and peasants." But will the new members, under changed social and economic conditions, respond as readily as of old to indoctrination and the old appeals of communism? Suslov himself—and it is well worth noting that for many years he had been in charge of propaganda and agitation for the Party—gives examples of how boring the old stock in trade of Communist propaganda is to the average member. Thus he quotes approvingly the criticism of a rank-and-file member: "I am now in my thirteenth year of study of the history of the Party, and for the thirteenth time propagandists are talking about the Bund. Have we no more important problems than the criticism of the Bund? We are interested in the problems of our M.T.S., *rayon,* and *oblast. We want to live in the present and future.* Yet our propagandists are so stuck in the bog of the affairs of the Narodniki and Bund that they cannot get out of it."[12] But if Party members are bored by the stories of what was after all the heroic period of the Party, are they likely to be more interested in the intricate theories of Marx and Engels? If they begrudge the time spent at countless educational and propaganda meetings, are they likely to remain attached to the Party that forces them to go through what are now largely meaningless motions? They want to live in the present and the future as engineers, students, workers, men with concrete needs and aspirations, and they will remain attached to the Party only if the Party shows that it responds to those needs and aspirations.

The future of the Communist party is thus bound up with the changes the whole Soviet society is undergoing. And in turn this future is bound up with the wider question of whether Communism has still something to offer to Soviet society or whether it, instead of the state, will "wither away." By relaxing one of the traditional levers of power in a totalitarian society, terror, the regime hopes to use more effectively the supplementary mechanism of propaganda and indoctrination. It explains to the millions of Party members that Communism is not blind obedience or bureaucratic self-satisfaction or learning by rote, but healthy self-criticism and accomplishment of great tasks of socialist construction. The success or failure of the new campaign will go a long way in determining the future of politics in the U.S.S.R.

---

[12]Italics added.

The Power Structure

In its structure and the spirit of its organization the Communist party bears an indelible stamp of having been born as the party of conspiracy, pitted against the resources of a powerful state, and forced to operate in secrecy and illegality. Today it is the ruling party, a body of several million members that monopolizes all political power in the Soviet Union, and yet its organization preserves the tone inherited from the years of illegality, of the struggle against overwhelming odds, of the years when the Party, in power but still a small group, was transforming the social and economic character of the vast country. The character of the struggle many years ago imposed upon the Party the need of deliberating in secret. Today, though the Party is no longer a group of hunted conspirators but the ruler, still, insofar as the deliberations of its highest bodies are concerned, the Politburo or the Central Committee, it reaches its decisions in secret, the mass of the membership and the world outside learning only the final conclusions—and not always even that. The conditions of the revolutionary struggle were presented by Lenin in 1902 and 1903 as necessitating iron discipline and firm control of the central organs. But the victory of the Bolsheviks and then, by their own account, of socialism in Russia has not weakened the discipline nor relaxed, up to now, the iron grip of the central organs over the whole organization. The early Bolsheviks could not have bothered, even if they had wanted to, about the niceties of the democratic process. Terror, though not considered by them as a major means of reaching their objectives, was still held to be legitimate and useful under certain circumstances. And terror both within and without the Party was never used as extensively as during the period when the Communist rule was unchallenged in the 1930s, and, though relaxed, it was not abandoned either in theory or in practice by Stalin's successors.[13]

---

[13]In his speech to the Twentieth Congress denouncing Stalin, Khrushchev contrasted the circumstances justifying terror as practiced by Lenin with Stalin's illegitimate use of the technique: ". . . Lenin without hesitation used the most extreme methods against the enemies. Lenin used such methods, however, only against actual class enemies and not against those who blunder, who err, and whom it was possible to lead through ideological influences and even retain in the leadership. Lenin used severe methods only in the most necessary cases, when the exploiting classes were still in existence and were vigorously opposing the Revolution, when the struggle for survival was decidedly assuming the sharpest forms, even including a civil war. Stalin, on the other hand, used extreme methods and mass repressions at a time when the Revolution was already victorious, when the Soviet state was strengthened, when the exploiting classes were already liquidated and socialist relations were rooted solidly in all phases of national economy, when our party was ideologically consolidated and had strengthened itself both numerically and ideologically. It is clear that here Stalin showed in a whole series of cases his intolerance, his brutality, and his abuse of power." Yet the speaker himself and his colleagues, despite the fact that "the Revolution was already victorious" applied methods not much different from Stalin's against Lavrenti Beria and his associates. Beria and his real or alleged associates were denounced as guilty the day after their arrest, tried in secret, and executed.

Thus the early pattern has perpetuated itself, and though in recent years it has begun to give way under the pressure of new social forces being generated in Russia, the "ruling party" is still the party of conspiracy.

The statements above cover the general behavior of the Communist party in the almost fifty-five years that it has been in power. Yet within the general pattern there have been considerable variations in detail: periods when there was savage struggle for power within the ruling oligarchy, times when the hand of one man lay heavily upon the whole organization, times when there was at least a semblance of inner-Party democracy, other times when terror and intimidation restrained a member of the Politburo as well as a rank-and-file worker.

Like the Soviet state institutions, the Party institutions and laws exhibit a twofold character. The language of the statute, the concept of organization, is, more often than not, democratic. The reality behind very often limits or negates the democratic phraseology. Thus the cardinal organizational principle of the Party is "democratic centralism." As defined in the Party statutes its meaning is: "(a) Election of all Party governing bodies from bottom to top. (b) Periodic accountability of Party bodies to their Party organizations. (c) Strict Party discipline and subordination of the minority to the majority. (d) The decisions of higher bodies are unconditionally binding upon lower ones."[14] There is nothing in the bald statement of the principle with which a democratically minded person would quarrel. But the crucial word is "election." Here our usage of the term and its meaning within the Communist party differ sharply. Just as in the election to the Supreme Soviet, or for that matter to any legislative body in the Soviet Union, there is only one list; thus the pattern of election to any Party office is monotonously simple: one candidate, or one list, and a unanimous election. It is likely that a small Party cell of a few members would be free to elect any one of them to be the secretary of the cell, but—and in this "but" there is the whole story of the Party structure—his election would not be binding until and unless it received the sanction of a higher Party organ. When we reach the upper levels of the Party organization, the picture becomes even clearer. Nobody in the Soviet Union, at least for a generation, could have imagined the election of a secretary of a sizable Party unit, be it territorial or a great factory, as the result of a free play of sentiments and interests of the members of the given organization. The secretary of the Party, say in the city of Krasnodar, will be selected by a higher Party organization, most likely by the central secretariat of the Communist party of the U.S.S.R. At the time of his selection he will not necessarily be a resident of the area. Quite likely he will be doing Party work thousands of miles away from Krasnodar, which he may never have visited. An emissary of the central organs will appear before the Party committee of Krasnodar with the "suggestion" that Comrade X be elected, and elected he will be—unanimously. The same procedure applies with variations in the bureaus, committees, and other organs of the Party at the local and national levels. To be pedantic, those officials are

---

[14]Quoted in *Current Soviet Policies,* ed. Leo Gruliow, New York, 1953, p. 29.

elected by members of the given organization but *selected* by somebody else, the somebody else being in the last resort the dictator or the ruling oligarchy.

If the word "election" is a euphemism for something else, the next principle of democratic centralism, "periodic accountability of Party bodies to their Party organizations," also requires an appraisal. Again, there is no doubt that members of a small Party cell would ordinarily feel no compunction about criticizing or removing their secretary or their bureau (i.e., the executive committee) for inefficiency or corruption. When, however, it comes to a "higher up"—an official who is a considerable Party functionary—criticism or removal will have to come from above. An institution of which the Soviets are very proud and which they cite very often as a proof of their superiority over the Western forms of democracy throws a glaring light on democratic centralism. This is the famous *samokritika,* or self-criticism. As applied to Party organization, a typical example would be a letter by a worker to a local or national newspaper pointing out that the Party secretary in the factory is falling down on his job, or is a person of low moral standards, and inquiring why *the regional or central Party committee does not undertake a corrective action.* The letter will be published or spoken criticism allowed, but not before the responsible Party officials determine that there is enough substance in the accusation. What is most characteristic is the fact that the call is always for *superior* Party organization to take action. Our worker will seldom, if ever, start agitating against the official within the Party organization and call for a free vote of members to remove or chastise the culprit. Again, it is an emissary of the higher Party organs who is to investigate and chastise. It hardly needs to be added that this form of self-criticism is not infrequently a put-up job to remove for political reasons somebody who has become suspect or inconvenient to the higher-ups. And if the person concerned is really in the upper levels of the Party hierarchy, say a regional or republic secretary, the chances are overwhelming that his liquidation through self-criticism is at the order of the ruling hierarchy.

Democratic centralism has thus meant, in practice, centralism and domination of the Party by a small group at the top, which, *as long as it is united,* can and has been able to exercise an absolute sway over the whole vast body of the membership and hence over the U.S.S.R. The qualification is important, for as we shall see, the pattern might be altered only during periods when a serious breach occurred within the very top group—this group usually being smaller than the membership of the Central Committee and usually identical with the Politburo (renamed "Presidium" at the Nineteenth Congress in 1952 and subsequently renamed Politburo in 1966). Then politics, or rather politicking, could take place within the Party. Various factions reflecting the views of the leaders would try to gain adherents at the Central Committee and local levels, offering in effect competing ideological and political platforms, with the consequence that, as in earlier times, heated debates and conferences would take place at the Party conferences and congresses. Some writers when referring to such periods, especially the years following the November Revolution and up to the beginning of Stalin's dictatorship (usually dated from the Fourteenth Party Congress in 1925), have seen in them an intra-Party democracy, which was then restrained and finally destroyed only by the iron hand of the dictator. Yet it is stretching the term a great deal to see in disagreements and struggles within a narrow elite an essential part of the democratic process. It is true that under Lenin Party members who disagreed with the leader and the majority group in the Central Committee were not physically liquidated, instantly imprisoned, or forced to degrade themselves by humiliating recantations. Yet in most cases they were demoted from their Party posts and sent to diplomatic posts abroad or assigned Party work in remote parts of the U.S.S.R. What Stalin often accomplished through terror and arrest, his great predecessor often did through lesser chicanery and through persuasion. The return to Lenin's ways as advertised by Stalin's successors is a return to more humane, more rational ways of ruling the Party, but still ruling it undemocratically.

The problem of power in the structure of the Communist party is then a subject of considerable fascination. How was it that a group of revolutionaries—people who, we are always told by social psychologists, are unstable, liable to be quarrelsome, and, as history always has shown, liable to fall out among themselves once the victory is secure—managed to preserve an organizational unity over so vast a country? To pose the question thus is partly to answer it, for the magnitude of the task as well as the danger held the Bolsheviks together. And before the instruments of terror and bureaucratic controls could be perfected by his successor, the Party had been held together by the extraordinary personality of Lenin. He had held his flock together not only during the wanderings in the wilderness of exile, the Revolution, and the Civil War, but also, what was even more difficult, during the first years in the promised land of absolute power and during the beginnings of the recasting of Russia's economy and society. By his very success in being a moderate dictator, he laid the foundations for a thorough despotism.

The development of the power structure in the Party and the shifting role of the Party organs can best be studied in the light of the major crises that have shaken the Communist party ever since its victory. The latest of these, a crisis of ideology as well as a struggle for power, is still continuing as this is being written.

The first crisis, for all its undramatic resolution and in spite of the fact that among the Bolsheviks it claimed no human sacrifices, was in a sense the most important one in the forty years that the Communist party has been in power. For in breaking, though through fairly humane methods, the various factions and opposition groups in the Party, and in reaffirming the organizational principles postulated in 1902 and 1903, Lenin cut off all possibility that a different, democratic spirit might begin to grow in the Party. The methods employed had none of the perfidy that Stalin exhibited in outmaneuvering the "Left Opposition" in 1924–1925 and the Right Opposition in the late twenties. Certainly they had none of the bloodthirstiness and sadism of Stalin when he sent the old Bolsheviks, then already discredited and impotent, to their death by the thousands during the Great Purge. Yet the latter phenomenon would not have been possible except for the developments in 1920–1922, which determined that there could be no "loyal opposition" within the Communist party, that any disagreement on political or ideological grounds would be branded by the prevailing group in the leadership as heresy and then treason, and that the defeated faction would be forced to recant or face expulsion or worse. The crisis had as a far-reaching side effect Lenin's sanctioning the erection of an elaborate apparatus of Party bureaucracy that would help prevent the recurrence of dissidence and of his entrusting the leadership of it to Joseph Stalin, who in 1922 became the Secretary-General of the Communist party.

There were two arenas of struggle: the Party Congress and the Central Committee. The Party Congress was then, as it is now officially, the sovereign organ of the Communist party. During the first post-Revolutionary era the Congress was no longer the motley assembly it had been before, of a few exiles and revolutionaries who managed to get out of Russia to hold a conclave on foreign soil, nor was it yet the assembly of delegates summoned to worship and applaud the great man and his lieutenants that it was to become under Stalin. It was still a live and reasonably democratically elected body. Under Lenin it met every year, and for all the dissonance and bitterness of debate, the magic personality and enormous prestige of Lenin were still sufficient to secure a majority for the leader's postulates and policies. But increasingly the focus of power was shifting to a much smaller group, the Central Committee elected by the Congress but liable to be more subservient to Lenin than the parent body. Those organs of the Party that were to be manipulated so skillfully by Stalin to secure his predominance—the Secretariat, the Organizational Bureau, and the Party Control Commission—were during the period 1919–1923 thought to be mainly of administrative importance, inferior to the Central Committee in fact as well as in theory. The Congress as the sovereign policy-determining body and the Central Committee as the executive and policy-formulating organ enjoyed real importance during Lenin's postwar leadership. Beginning with Lenin's incapacitating illness in 1922, their real political importance declined, until they eventually were to serve as additional tools of personal dictatorship for Stalin and the oligarchy that succeeded him.

The issue of the struggle was nothing other than the character of the Soviet state being born and consequently of the Communist party that was guiding it. The Communist party, as we observed before, inherited from Marxism its twofold character. It was the party of revolution, of opposition to the state, the party that embraced the anarchistic slogans of complete equality, abolition of all social distinction and rank, and abolition of the standing army. At the same time, paradoxically, it was the party that believed in the creation of a modern industrialized state as a prerequisite to socialism. Such a state, especially under the conditions of Russia of 1920, required many things directly opposed to the anarchistic side of the postulates of Bolshevism, the postulates under which it won the Revolution and the Civil War. Instead of weakening the state and hence the central organs of the Party, the vision of an industrialized and socialist Russia required a strong state, hence the unchallengeable authority of the central Party organs. Instead of economic equality and socialism right away, it required economic stability and reconstruction and incentives for hard work. Instead of the dissolution of bureaucracy and the standing army, it required the erection of an administrative and planning machinery. Lenin very early perceived the necessity of abandoning the "campaign oratory" in which the Bolsheviks had indulged during the Revolution and of facing the facts. When the Kronstadt sailors, who in the crucial days of the fall of 1917 had been the staunchest supporters of the Bolsheviks, revolted in 1921 and tossed in the face of the Bolsheviks the very same anarchistic slogans they themselves had employed, their uprising was mercilessly suppressed. In 1921 Lenin had sanctioned the New Economic Policy, which was premised on the belief that before Russia could advance toward socialism her economy must be reconstructed, and hence private trade and private ownership in agriculture must be tolerated for an indefinite period of time. The same line of reasoning persuaded Lenin and, especially, Trotsky that the Red Army could not become a revolutionary mob but had to have officers and discipline and that the factories had to have skilled workers and engineers, who had to have salaries above the wages of a common laborer.

These common-sense conclusions were opposed by a number of Bolshevik leaders, not only because of the persistence in the Bolshevik ranks of anarchistic and egalitarian sentiments, but also because of their more reasonable belief that the ruling group among the Communists was already settling down to the enjoyment of power and its appurtenances and was inclined to defer the realization of socialism to an indefinite future. As in all dissensions within the Communist party, we find in those early struggles an inextricable mixture of the power drive and ideological and temperamental dissonances. It would take too long to give a reasonably full story of the early Party schisms. The most characteristic and important were those of the Workers' Opposition, which provides the best opportunity for study of the early structure of the Party and the ways then employed in managing it.

At the Eighth and Ninth Party Congresses in 1919 and 1920 there were already voices decrying bureaucratization of the Party, admission of former tsarist officers into the Red Army, and so on. With the end of the Civil War the discontent within the Party found expression in a new movement sponsored by some Party leaders. The two most prominent names were those of Alexandra Kollontai, an upper-class intellectual who had joined the Bolsheviks,[15] and Alexander Shlyapnikov, a true proletarian in origin and a member of the Central Committee. The Workers' Opposition had as its first and most important postulate the plea that the trade unions should be fairly independent of the state and the Party, that they should run the economy of the country. As secondary postulates they advocated scaling down the wage differential[16] and democratization of the Party. Repeated in the propaganda of the Worker's Opposition was the charge that the Party was run by an oligarchy

---

[15]Mme. Kollontai gained notoriety also by her strenuous advocacy of free love and her literary efforts dedicated to that theme.

[16]Though from our point of view, or from that of the U.S.S.R. since the thirties, Russia in the period under discussion was economically as egalitarian a society as one could find.

and that the country freshly freed from the rule of landlords and tsarist officials was in the process of getting a new official caste of Communist functionaries.

Their position was condemned by Lenin, not unjustifiably, as anarchist-syndicalist rather than Marxian. At the Tenth Party Congress, which met in 1921 in the shadow of the Kronstadt revolt, Lenin's position that the trade unions should be autonomous but not independent of the Party received overwhelming approval. Lenin's motion prevailed not only against the Workers' Opposition but also against the views of Trotsky. Trotsky would have made explicit what was implicit in Lenin's motion and what became an accepted maxim in Stalin's period, namely, that the trade unions are strictly subordinate to the Party and are to help carry out the government's economic policies, rather than to have any policies of their own. Sentiments akin to those reflected by the Opposition were strong among the rank and file of the Party. Yet characteristically the Workers' Opposition could muster only a handful of votes at the Congress when the great prestige of Lenin was thrown against them, and they had almost no support within the Central Committee. The Tenth Congress condemned the Workers' Opposition as a "syndicalist and anarchist" deviation and forbade further propaganda of their ideas.

The dispute had its most concrete application in the adoption by the Congress of a provision still in the Party statute in a revised form, stating that a joint plenum of the Central Committee of the Party and its Control Commission could by a majority of two-thirds expel a member of the Central Committee from his post or even from the Party. Thus was formalized a provision that enabled the Party oligarchy, without recourse to the Congress, to deal summarily even with Party notables should they set themselves in opposition to the dominant fashion. This weapon was to be used frequently by Stalin. The Tenth and Eleventh Congresses sanctioned an extended purge of the Party and of its "anarchist and syndicalist" deviationists. Thus, what began as a common-sense position of Lenin's against extreme radicalism ended as the negation of any democratic opportunities in the Party, the consolidation of the position of the Central Committee, and the forging of the weapon of the Party purge, by which the leaders could always rid the Party of elements they did not desire. It is not accidental that, at the same time, Lenin entrusted the direction of the Party apparatus to a man he did not particularly like, but who among the top Party leaders showed the least propensity for ideological quarrels and the most for quiet organizational work. In 1922 Joseph Stalin, already a member of the Political and Organizational Bureaus, became the Secretary-General. The expectation was that he would bring order out of the chaos into which routine administrative affairs of the Party had fallen, and also that he would help curtail the factional strife the Tenth and Eleventh Congresses had demonstrated.

Stalin's emergence as the top administrator of the Party was the culmination of an organizational career. Before 1922 he already belonged to the Party's Organization Bureau and had held various important political posts, chief among them the

Commissariats of Nationalities and of the Workers' and Peasants' Inspection, the latter devised as a control organ to check the performance of Soviet administration. His rise to power coincided with and was partly based on the growing importance of the administrative and control organs within the Party and the state. An indefatigable worker, master of detail and routine, Stalin struck a vivid contrast with the rest of the first-rank Communist leaders, who were much more impressive as speakers or writers but lacked the patience or temperament to attend to dull administrative work. Within a short time the Secretariat of the Communist party ceased to be a simple organization where a few people received provincial delegations and attended to the grievances and problems of various local Party organizations. It became the veritable nerve center of the Party. The Secretariat assumed the responsibility for instructional and propaganda work; it sent out emissaries to check on the performance of Party organizations. The Secretary-General was in a position to determine who was to head Party work in various organizations (except during the first few years for the capitals of Moscow and Leningrad), and his work gave him an enhanced opportunity to make wide contacts and recruit partisans among the important Communist activists. If to Stalin's supremacy in the Secretariat and the Organizational Bureau is added his considerable influence in the Party Control Commission, the body charged with standing watch over the activities and performance of the Party members, it becomes understandable how an ambitious and able man was capable of building a tremendous power base and the foundations for an absolute dictatorship.

But the explanation cannot be given entirely in terms of Stalin's mastery of the apparatus. At any time between 1922 and 1925 the Central Committee or the Party Congress could have dismissed Stalin from his powerful position as Secretary-General. None of those bodies was dominated as yet by Stalin. Shortly before his death, Lenin, irked by Stalin's rudeness to his wife, Nadezhda Krupskaya, and alarmed by the reports that Stalin was building a personal machine, did in fact propose the replacement of the Secretary-General in a letter that was certainly known to the Central Committee.[17] But none of the aspirants for Lenin's mantle could be enticed to take on the strenuous job of day-to-day administration of the Party. Among the Party leaders of secondary importance Stalin did at the time enjoy a certain popularity. In the light of what was to happen later this reputation of Stalin in the years 1922–1925 may appear incredible. But his views and activities were, as a matter of fact, of the kind to appeal to a Communist administrator. He appeared then as a man of moderate views, desirous of rebuilding the Russian economy before taking drastic steps, such as the expropriation of the peasants. In brief he was the advocate of moderate social policies. While the others were planning grandiose foreign revolutions, Stalin, though all for the support of foreign Communists, directed attention primarily to the tasks of socialist construction in

[17]The new generation of Communists heard of it for the first time in Khrushchev's indictment of Stalin at the Twentieth Party Congress.

Russia.[18] In terms of personality, Stalin, for all his scheming propensities, had, so it seemed at the time, none of Trotsky's intellectual arrogance, or Zinoviev's and Kamenev's vacillation. He stood—and it is not surprising that so many Communists were taken in—as an advocate of Communist "normalcy," of moderate policies, neither too much to the Left nor too much to the Right; in brief, he stood for the continuation of Lenin's policies and tactics. It is no accident that after Lenin's death it was mainly Stalin who inaugurated a veritable cult of the dead leader, who, for all his faults, had detested sycophancy and religious veneration of personalities.

Despite its democratic phraseology, the Communist party was then, as it is now, an organization calling for a united leadership. Stalin's management of the problem of succession combined all the elements necessary to the guidance of a totalitarian movement: the seizure of the administrative structure, a degree of acceptance and popularity among the Party activists, and the erection of a quasi-religious cult of the departed leader that would facilitate the acceptance of a new one. Within the highest circles of the Party he skillfully exploited the distrust of the majority of the top Communist leaders toward Leon Trotsky. The latter, the leader of the Red Army and Lenin's right hand during the Revolution and the Civil War, aroused the admiration of certain circles of the Red Army, the Soviet youth, and foreign Communists. A brilliant and many-sided man, Trotsky proved to be poorly equipped for the kind of infighting into which Communist party politics resolves itself at times of transition. To the Party hierarchy he appeared as a potential Bonaparte of the Russian Revolution, a man who was not "really" a Bolshevik, as he had rejoined Lenin only on the eve of the Revolution, and all his enormous services to the cause did not diminish their envy and fear of his brilliant abilities. In contrast to Trotsky, Stalin stood out as a solid but rather drab personality, capable through hard work and attention to administrative detail of warding off the brilliant rhetoric and charismatic personality of the Commissar of War. It was thus that the two senior Communist leaders Kamenev (a brother-in-law of Trotsky) and Zinoviev joined with Stalin to provide the collective leadership of the Party during Lenin's incapacity and after his death. The triumvirate (in Russian *troika*) was the product of the fear of Trotsky and of the assumption that through a division of leadership personal dictatorship could be avoided.

The story has often been told how Stalin maneuvered his allies into committing themselves too far against Trotsky, how he disposed of them in turn with the help

---

[18]Stalin's position on this issue, his famous "socialism in one country" plea, is almost invariably misrepresented. It is made to appear as if Stalin in the period under discussion was for the abandoning of the revolutionary work abroad, while his antagonist, Trotsky, believed that a socialist reconstruction of Russia must be postponed until after a world revolution. The position of neither man was that categorical and one-sided, and, as a matter of fact, there was but little difference between their real views on the subject. Once in opposition Trotsky was maneuvered into arguing that Stalin was betraying the revolution, an argument that further weakened Trotsky's position, for it gave Stalin an opportunity to present Trotsky's followers as adventurists who, instead of attending to concrete tasks at home, wanted to engage in dangerous adventures abroad.

of the right wing of the Party, and how then, in sole possession of power, he crushed his erstwhile right-wing allies in 1929–1930.[19] But personalities and personal struggles provide only part of the story. What is necessary for an understanding of the mechanics of Party politics is the realization that personal factors, ideological issues, and administrative controls all play their part, and it is impossible neatly to separate one factor from the others. Stalin's ambition and diabolical cunning are usually isolated as the key factor in his rise to power. Stalin's defeated enemies have traced his perfidy and deception throughout his whole career. Charges have been made, some absurd and others unverifiable, about Stalin's early career, such as the stories of his poisoning Lenin or having been a tsarist police agent. But at the crucial point—to repeat—Stalin stood as morally no better and no worse than the other would-be successors of Lenin. Far from the future author of purges that decimated the Old Bolsheviks, it was Stalin who restrained his allies, Zinoviev and Kamenev, from taking too drastic steps against Trotsky, whom they wanted to expel from the Party. When in 1925 Zinoviev and Kamenev turned against Stalin and his new allies, the future Right opposition, Stalin the moderate again presented his erstwhile allies as extremists. In a dramatic moment at the Fourteenth Congress he exclaimed that Zinoviev and Kamenev wanted the "blood of Bukharin," his then ally on the Politburo, and having aroused the horror of the Congress at the idea of a revered Bolshevik leader's being assailed as if he were a counterrevolutionary, he announced that "we will not give you the blood of Bukharin."[20]

But Stalin's personal skill and the equally sordid but less skillful intrigues of his opponents provide just one part of the picture. In 1923–1925 the policies embraced by Stalin, his political "platform," were of the kind to appeal to the great mass of Communists: cautious progress toward socialism, but certainly no drastic break with the New Economic Policy designed to set Russia on her feet before a wholesale socialist transformation. When Zinoviev and the Left finally turned on

---

[19]The discussion of Communist leaders and policies in terms of right and left wings and deviations is likely to appear puzzling. Thus Nikolai Bukharin, when he opposed Lenin on the signing of the Treaty of Brest-Litovsk in 1918, was described as the leader of the Left Communists. In 1929 and 1930 we find Bukharin denounced by Stalin's faction as a "Right opportunist" for his opposition to rapid collectivization. In line with the usual semantic jugglery at which the Communists are so adept, the Party's course, i.e., the course of the prevailing faction of the Party, is *always* correct and *always* in the middle. Those Communists who are fearful that the policies are too drastic or rapid are denounced as the "Right opportunists"; those who at other times believe them to be too cautious are branded as "left-wing adventurers." Most of the proposals advanced by Trotsky, Kamenev, and Zinoviev in 1924–1925 and decried by Stalin as senselessly "left" were put into effect by Stalin in *much more drastic form* in 1929–1930, but as emanating from himself alone. These policies were no longer either "left" or "right"—they were "correct," and any criticism of them (often in the very words of the Stalin of 1925) was piously described as "right-wing" opportunism.

[20]In 1938 Bukharin and a whole group of Old Bolshevik leaders were tried and shot, thus following the fate of Zinoviev and Kamenev.

the Secretary-General, they pictured the country as reverting to a capitalist economy, with rich peasants becoming stronger and stronger and dictating the pace of Russia's economy. Stalin imperturbably met the charge by justifying his policies, as he justified everything he did, in the name of Leninism. Thus in 1925 private property in agriculture and the allowing of richer peasants to hire help and lease more land (strange doings under a socialist regime) was Leninism, just as in 1929–1930 it was Leninism to expropriate the peasants and to force them into collectives. On the previous occasion Stalin informed the assembled Communists that Zinoviev and Kamenev obviously intended to force and rob the peasant, to attempt to coerce him into socialism instead of educating him through example and persuasion as Vladimir Ilich Lenin had taught should be done. And in the spirit of revolutionary pragmatism, answering the opposition's charge that Marx and Engels, were they alive, would be alarmed at what was happening in Russia under an allegedly socialist regime, Stalin maintained that Marx and Engels would say: "May the devil take the old formulas; long live victorious socialism in the U.S.S.R." Quite apart from the administrative and personal intrigues of the Stalinists, the program thus presented and thus stated would always gain some popularity, especially in a country still recovering from the ravages of war and still mainly peasant in its population.

The struggle for succession reached its peak at the Fourteenth Party Congress, held in December 1925. It repays the effort to examine the proceedings of the Congress, for it was the culminating point in Stalin's rise to power, the most opportune moment when his rise could have been checked by a determined, skillful, and united opposition to him within the Party. For the first, and up to the present day the last, time the division within the Communist ranks spilled out from the Central Committee into the larger body. To an extent not approximated in the days of the Workers' Opposition nor in the feeble last movements of opposition of the next few years, this division threatened to split the victorious Communist party. The Fourteenth Congress was the last one about which there was still some of the air of a gathering of revolutionaries. Debates were heated, and yet there was some remnant of the free and comradely spirit of the underground and the Revolution. Future Congresses were to prostrate themselves before the dictator, and, like gatherings of Oriental satraps, respond to his slightest whim.

The Communist party and the world Communist movement were treated to the spectacle of the Central Committee split into two factions. Thus in place of a single report of the Central Committee, traditionally the token of united leadership of the movement delivered by its leading figure, two reports were presented: the majority's by Stalin, and the minority's by Zinoviev. All the negotiations in advance had not been able to prevent the split's becoming public and violent. Zinoviev and Kamenev felt that it was now or never: Organizationally and politically they were being surrounded. Their frantic attempts to garner and convert delegates before and during the Congress were not successful. Stalin's machine now assured him of a strong majority. It was only in Leningrad, where Zinoviev had been the Party boss, that the Opposition, through methods similar to those used by Stalin in the Party at large, had secured very strong support—hence its name, the "Leningrad Opposition." Moscow, the other capital, where Kamenev's influence had been strong in the Party organization, at first gravitated somewhat to the Opposition, but just before the Congress the Stalinists obtained the adherence of the Moscow Party boss, Nikolai Uglanov, and with him went the majority of his delegation. It was thus a struggle of Party bosses, of Party "machines," in which what had once been the Social-Democratic party of Russia finally surrendered the last vestige of its democracy.

The substance of the debate has already been presented. Ranged with Stalin against the Left, or Leningrad Opposition, were the Party leaders whom in a few years he would denounce as "right-wing opportunists"—Chairman of the Council of Commissars, Alexei Rykov; leader of the trade unions, Mikhail Tomsky; and an outstanding Communist writer and theoretician, Bukharin. They joined Stalin, seeing in him the advocate of moderate policy and a believer in collective leadership. Silent throughout the Congress remained Leon Trotsky, still a man of influence in the Party, who refused to join Kamenev and Zinoviev, his persecutors of only a few months before. The Opposition's fire at first was directed mainly at Bukharin, in whom they saw the author of the lenient policy toward the peasant. It was only toward the end that an open attack was made upon the already fearsome figure of the Secretary-General. It was related how the Party's control organs abused their powers in persecuting and ejecting partisans of the Opposition. And the essence of the struggle was revealed when Kamenev proclaimed that the Secretariat of the Party had become *a political organ,* and its head had raised himself to a position unheard of in a free revolutionary movement, that of a totalitarian leader. We believe, stated Kamenev, that the party should be run by its senior officials (i.e., the Politburo), and we are against the theory of a leader. An oligarchy rather than a personal dictatorship was the best that the Opposition could prescribe for the Party, and it was brought out by the Stalinists, not without justification, that Kamenev and Zinoviev were piqued at having had their personal ambitions thwarted and that Stalin's ascendancy in the Party's councils was largely the product of their own organizational ineptitude and indolence. Stalin himself modestly denied any intention or possibility of dictatorship within the Party.

Five years later, at the Sixteenth Party Congress, the effect of the Fourteenth was fully demonstrated. The old Left Opposition had been fully shattered, its leaders had been stripped of their posts and many of its followers imprisoned. Trotsky was in exile. Russia was in the midst of forced collectivization, which was to lead to a famine in the Ukraine and the deportation of hundreds of thousands, if not millions, of peasant families. No longer the genial compromiser, the middle-of-the-road man who eschewed all extremism, Stalin now appeared as a resolute dictator, a man who would brook no opposition. Throughout his speech lashing out at his recent allies, Rykov, Tomsky, Bukharin and Uglanov, he kept repeating with terrible intensity the phrase: "If you don't press those people, you don't get anywhere." The obedient delegates responded with jeers and abuse directed at the culprits, all of them at one time trusted lieutenants of Lenin and men of great popularity and influence within the Party.

It is instructive to compare Stalin's destruction of the Left Opposition with another great crisis in the Party, the crisis that occurred before and after Stalin's death and that as this is being written, is still unresolved. The details of the latest crisis are largely a matter of conjecture. We do not possess, as we do for the period of the twenties, Party Congress speeches and minutes of the Central Committee and even of the Politburo, with the position of contestants for power and their political moves clearly delineated. The struggle of the late forties and the fifties has been taking place in secrecy, illuminated only occasionally by a public announcement of the removal and execution of a high official. Yet it is possible to reconstruct the general outlines of the struggle for power within the Communist party during the last years of Stalin and the current period of collective leadership. Like the preceding crisis, the current one has had the ingredients of personal rivalry, political and administrative maneuvering, and an ideological debate.

In the background of the crisis lay the absolute dictatorship of Stalin, which, since 1934, had liquidated physically not only all the members of opposing factions but many of Stalin's closest collaborators, who, for one reason or another, incurred the dictator's distrust or displeasure. To be specific and to list only those leaders who at one time or another had occupied the highest positions in the Party: to their deaths, after trials in which they had to confess to the most improbable crimes, went Zinoviev and Kamenev, as well as Rykov and Bukharin. Liquidated without a trial and in secrecy were Stalin's erstwhile closest collaborators and members of the Politburo: S. V. Kossior, Yan Rudzutak, and Vlas Chubar. If we add to the list Valentin Kuibyshev and Gregory Ordzhonikidze, who assertedly died of natural causes but actually under suspicious circumstances, we get an impressive picture of the decimation of Lenin's and the post-Lenin Politburo.[21] It would be superfluous to list all the other high officials of the army, Party, and government who were purged, or to elaborate on what has now been admitted by the Soviets themselves, that the purge not only attacked the big people, but spread to all layers of Soviet society. Terror, as a regular philosophy of government, and the secret police and an elaborate system of spying and denunciation, as the means of controlling the Party and the state, became the routine features of Soviet society. Even after the massive purge that ended in 1939, the dictator continued these practices on a more moderate scale, and indeed they are the essential ingredients of Soviet totalitarianism.

But apart from terror and concentration camps and the frightening reality of the power structure, Soviet society underwent profound changes during the Stalin era. Social changes continued to exert a mounting pressure on the Communist party of the U.S.S.R. To use a favorite Marxist term, an "inherent contradiction" devel-

---

[21]Leon Trotsky died in exile, murdered by a hired assassin; Sergei Kirov, whom Stalin had delegated to clean up the Leningrad organization after Zinoviev's deposal, was assassinated allegedly by an anti-Stalinist in 1934.

oped between Russian society and the system of government. As society was modernized and industrialized, a new pattern of interests emerged. The Russian people, including the mass of members of the Communist party, obviously longed to enjoy the fruits of progress: to acquire a higher standard of living, to achieve a modicum at least of personal security, of "normalcy," and a release from the continuous dread of terror. Yet this social pressure—which is merely another name for the needs and aspirations of Soviet citizens of all walks of life—was simply unavailing against what appeared then as a cast-iron system of dictatorship, buttressed by the secret police and fortified by the people's fear and downright inability to conceive of an alternative to Stalin's personal rule. In the eyes of the dictator and the ruling hierarchy, the situation, though secure, had two grave contradictions in it. There was, first of all and quite understandably, a decline of the esprit de corps of the Communist party, a loss of vitality in the organization almost synonymous with Soviet power. And how could it be otherwise? The Party was terrorized. Its leading organs almost stopped functioning. In defiance of the Party statute no Party congress took place between 1939 and 1952. If the Central Committee met between the end of the War and Stalin's death, we have no record of it. Even the Politburo functioned irregularly, with some members sometimes forbidden to attend because of the dictator's whim. The most crucial decisions were often taken by Stalin himself with whoever at the moment was closest to him. The day-to-day task of running the country was evidently in the hands of the secret police. The two ministries comprising it, the M.V.D. (the Ministry of Internal Affairs) and the M.G.B. (the Ministry of State Security), were rapidly becoming a state within a state. If the situation bothered Stalin and some of his lieutenants, it was not because of democratic scruples. It was because of the simple realization that the economic growth of the country and the development of stability of Soviet society could not be assured by bayonets, prisons, and concentration camps and that somehow the role of the Communist party would have to be revived.

Closely connected with the preceding problem was that of leadership of the Party and succession to the despot. At the close of World War II Stalin was sixty-six. Whatever his health, his age would no longer allow him to exercise a continuous and detailed supervision of the many departments of the Party and the state. Authority had to be delegated, and at the same time Stalin, with a true dictator's instinct, lived in constant apprehension of a subordinate's becoming too powerful. His technique had always been to liquidate or demote those closest to him as soon as they became too influential. Thus the period immediately after the Great Purge, 1939–1941, saw reduction in status of those who in the thirties had been closest to him—Kaganovich, Molotov, and Voroshilov—and the emergence of new men in the leading positions: Zhdanov, Malenkov, Beria, and Khrushchev. At the same time the logic of the situation and the tyrant's advanced age tended necessarily to enable his lieutenants to build strong personal followings. In the immediate postwar years Lavrenti Beria obtained a powerful hold on the vast machinery of the security forces, as well as on the Party organizations in Transcaucasia, while the Party apparatus was the scene of an undercover struggle between Zhdanov and Malenkov. The competing factions vied for strategic positions as well as for the despot's favor. The latter was always distributed with the object of keeping any one of the powerful aides from becoming too powerful. Thus after Zhdanov's death in 1948 (under circumstances that have not been fully clarified), Malenkov appeared for a while in sole control of the Party apparatus. But not for long, for he was soon joined in the Party Secretariat by Nikita Khrushchev. Beginning in 1949–1950, if not before, steps were taken to weaken Lavrenti Beria's hold on the security apparatus, and purges were carried out in his special preserve, the Georgian Communist party.

The picture of the Party situation in conjunction with social and economic developments in the country at large may have inclined Stalin and the people who had his ear at the time to give yet another drastic turn to the development of the Communist regime. The reform was to conform to the usual recipes of Stalin's reforms, in part terror, in part an ideological offensive. In 1950–1951 there was the reopening of the discussion of the future of Soviet agriculture. Amalgamation of the collective farms was designed to weaken elements of private property that still lingered in agriculture.[22]

At the same time, the leadership of the Party was to be changed and a new wave of terror perhaps on the scale of the Great Purge was to shake the Party. There are several solid pieces of evidence that this was what Stalin had in mind. The Nineteenth Party Congress, convened in the fall of 1952, doubled the size of the top organ, the Politburo, now renamed Presidium of the Central Committee. The old leaders were still there, but they were swamped by "new men," mostly younger bureaucrats and regional Party secretaries; the latter were obviously to be given on-the-job training and were then to replace the old guard, whose scheming and intrigues may have wearied Stalin.[23] But the purge was not only to be political. In January 1953 a group of leading Soviet medical specialists was "unmasked" and promptly confessed to some successful and some planned assassinations of various leading figures in the Party, army, and so forth. Judged by the sad precedent of the thirties, the investigation would undoubtedly link the "criminal doctors" to some other currently leading figures. On the eve of Stalin's death in March 1953 a new

---

[22]The rulers were casting about for a solution to a most pressing problem of the Soviet economy *and at the same time were seeking something that would restore the sense of ideological mission and purpose to the Party.* Stalin's *Economic Problems of Socialism in the U.S.S.R.,* a pamphlet written in 1952, was designed to inspire new ideological fervor into the rank and file of the Party.

[23]From Khrushchev's indictment of Stalin at the Twentieth Congress: "Stalin evidently had plans to finish off the old members of the Political Bureau. He often stated that Political Bureau members should be replaced by new ones. His proposal, after the Nineteenth Congress, concerning the election of twenty-five persons to the Central Committee Presidium, was aimed at the removal of the old Political Bureau members and the bringing in of less experienced persons so that these would extol him in all sorts of ways."

purge was in the offing, and it was to be accompanied by a redirection of the Party's efforts and leadership.

Stalin's death cut short both processes at one blow. Its immediate consequence was a veritable coup d'état, in which the old leaders, some of them probably intended victims of the purge, proceeded to rearrange the highest state and Party positions. The Presidium was cut down to its old size, most of the newcomers from the Nineteenth Congress being ejected. From the bargaining that must have followed, Malenkov emerged as the head of the government but had to relinquish his seat on the Party Secretariat. Beria once again assumed what appeared to be full control of the security forces; even the position of the titular head of the state, unimportant in a stable totalitarian system but potentially important in an unstable situation, changed hands and was entrusted to the senior member of the Presidium, Voroshilov. It was clear on the morrow of Stalin's death that none of his successors inherited all or even most of the tyrant's powers. None of them was in a position, as Stalin had been, to consign the majority of his colleagues to political obscurity or liquidation. None of them could, alone and at will, chart the future of the Communist party and Soviet society. It was obvious that in public the leaders would strive to preserve the appearance of solidarity and unanimity, but at the same time sparring for position and political maneuvering would go on.

It is sometimes assumed in the West that political power in the Soviet Union is like a concrete object locked in the offices of the Presidium of the Communist party of the U.S.S.R. and that anybody who seizes it becomes the absolute dictator. But the first effect of Stalin's death was that the arena of political maneuvering in Russia was considerably enlarged. Previously the struggle for influence had gone on in the closest entourage of the dictator. It was relatively unimportant what a Party secretary in Odessa may have felt about the relative virtues of policies advocated by Khrushchev and Malenkov. For one thing, any public disagreement among the Bolshevik leaders on policies reflected only a temporary hesitation on the given issue by the dictator. His closest collaborators had no indentifiable ideological personalities. After his death the picture became different. With the situation fluid at the top it *does* become important to the aspirants for power not only to have their men in the strategic positions in the Party and state apparatus but also to woo the whole mass of officialdom by appealing to their interests and convictions.

The classical case of a "political campaign" in a totalitarian system is the career of Beria between March and the summer of 1953. Like any politician in any country, the Minister of the Interior knew the requirement for success was twofold: strengthen your organization and have an attractive political platform. The widespread agencies of the Ministry of the Interior and the security forces were cleansed (though, as it turned out later, not completely) of the anti-Beria or neutral elements. But, in addition, Beria became both in his public pronouncements and official acts an advocate of "socialist legality" and national equality. He appeared desirous of taking for himself most of the credit for the curbing of the worst abuses of official terrorism—as shown by his repudiation of the doctors' case—and for the greater opportunities offered to non-Russian officials in the state and Party. It is not far-fetched to suggest that he realized the political appeal of measures that held out to the middle ranks of the Soviet hierarchy the promise of a modicum of security for their lives and their positions. And against the background of frantic Russian chauvinism of Stalin's last years, Beria's policies must likewise have suggested greater opportunities for advancement and more freedom from Great-Russian supervision for the non-Russian elements of the officialdom. The dramatic fall of Beria and his associates in June 1953 indicates, paradoxically, the success of those policies. Rehabilitation of the victims of Stalinist terror and greater latitude on the nationality issue have continued under the "collective leadership." It is unnecessary to postulate an attempted coup by Beria as an explanation for his liquidation. He was becoming too well entrenched in his administrative machinery and was courting popularity too strenuously not to arouse the deepest apprehension of his colleagues. It does not matter that the propaganda machine has managed to picture him as an exponent of terror and author of the plan to dismember the Soviet Union. The measures he had advocated have proved appealing and have been endorsed as their own by the rest of the leadership.

The elimination of Beria did not bring harmony to the ruling elite. The vacuum created by Stalin's death continues down to our own day, and the impression of harmony that the ruling hierarchy attempts to convey conceals considerable strains.[24] Beria's personal empire was dismantled and his partisans throughout Russia purged.[25] The realization that the leadership of the vast security apparatus conferred enormous power upon an individual and that the secret police were abhorred by the population and—what in the context of Russia's politics is much more important—by influential Party and army leaders has led the regime to weaken the principal arm of terror, to disband some of its armed forces, and to make sure that no single person or organization should have exclusive control over the security apparatus.

If terror is weakened as the principal lever of totalitarian power, other instrumentalities must take its place. The leaders must have realized that a mixed policy of concessions to the population and the strengthening of the Communist party was

---

[24]It is interesting to list several instances of both the confusion produced by the lack of a single absolute leader and of the oligarchy's frantic attempts to conceal discords. On the morrow of Stalin's death the official communiqué spoke of the changes in Party and government leadership as having been executed to insure prevention of "disorder and panic." In the funeral orations over Stalin's bier delivered by the triumvirs Malenkov, Beria, and Molotov, it was Beria who made warm personal remarks about Malenkov, and it was on Beria's motions in the Supreme Soviet that Malenkov was confirmed as Chairman of the Council of Ministers. One is reminded of Stalin's warm eulogies of Bukharin in the twenties.

[25]The extent to which the secret police had penetrated all aspects of the governmental machinery is best indicated by the fact that among those tried and executed with Beria as his principal aides was one Dekanozov, Beria's personal appointee as Minister of the Interior in Georgia. Dekanozov's previous posts had included that of Ambassador to Germany and Deputy Commissar of Foreign Affairs. He had been, it is not too much to surmise, delegated to operate within the diplomatic corps.

the most fruitful approach. Concessions included a modest attempt to raise the standard of living, the attempt with which Malenkov especially identified himself, and the general relaxation of the most obnoxious features of the police state, including abolition of special police courts that meted out penalties in secret, reduction of the drastic labor discipline, and partial disbanding of forced-labor camps. We cannot tell how far these decisions were the result of a united decision of the Politburo-Presidium and how far they reflected maneuvering among the rulers and pressure of outside elements, such as the army. It is characteristic that Malenkov's degradation in February 1955—when he stepped down as chairman of the Council of Ministers though remaining in the government and the Presidium —was justified on the grounds of his alleged preference for the development of consumer goods over heavy industries. As Stalin's favorite during his last years, and conceivably as the only member of the late dictator's entourage not slated for the purge he had been preparing, Malenkov must have been eyed suspiciously by his colleagues in the "collective leadership." Perhaps in his identification with the masses' desire for greater amenities of life his colleagues saw again a political campaign designed to secure absolute power, very much in the style of Stalin's moderation and middle-of-the-road position of the early 1920s. The mildness of his "punishment" indicates that perhaps, unlike Beria, Malenkov did not attempt to fight back. A wave of changes in Party posts followed the change at the top. In their peregrinations throughout the Soviet Union, it was not unusual for Khrushchev and Bulganin to meet with the Party Committee of a republic or region, the result being very often a new First Secretary of the given organization.

But the main effort of the new leadership, divided and fluctuating as it is, has obviously been to infuse new spirit into the Party. The Twentieth Congress, which met in February 1956, was to chart the new course. For a long time prior to the Congress there had been a silent de-emphasis of Stalin. During the dictator's absolute rule no public speech, no book on any subject, no leading article failed to refer to Comrade Stalin. Not long after his death the references became scarcer and scarcer, and even implied criticism of the late dictator was allowed. The Twentieth Congress was to mark a definite break with this cautious de-emphasis and criticism by implication. For reasons known only to themselves, the leaders decided to attack Stalin's memory openly. Thus in the public speeches at the Congress Khrushchev and Mikoyan referred scathingly to the personality cult and the atrophy of Party organs that prevailed during the last twenty years of Stalin's reign. Mikoyan assailed Stalin's version of the Party's history, *History of the Communist Party, A Short Course,* published under his name and filled with adulatory references to himself. Stalin's *Economic Problems of Socialism in the U.S.S.R.,* hailed in 1952 by the same speakers as a work of genius, was now described as containing serious theoretical errors.

These speeches were only a prelude to a special address by Khrushchev about Stalin. Though delivered before a closed session of the Congress, it was circulated to all the Party organizations in the U.S.S.R. and thus became a public secret.[26] Khrushchev's speech was not an unqualified condemnation of Stalin. The great dictator was pictured as a man who, for all his faults, until 1934 performed great services for socialism in the U.S.S.R. But beginning with 1934 and the opening of the Great Purge, Stalin is presented as a tyrant and sadist, dispatching people to death out of whim and increasingly thirsty for adulation. In his last years the picture is that of a psychologically sick man contemplating on the eve of his death a wholesale liquidation of his associates.

Khrushchev's account cannot be entirely trusted. It should be borne in mind that those who now denounced Stalin were coauthors, and at times probably instigators, of his purges. Nikita Khrushchev had himself been Stalin's chosen instrument of purge in the Ukraine; Georgi Malenkov, for many years an official of his personal secretariat. Many of the liquidations and executions of the period can be traced not only to Stalin's undoubted sadism, but also to the intense rivalry of those closest to him. Yet some of the facts cited by Khrushchev are supported by other evidence. Thus of the Central Committee elected in 1934 at the Seventeenth Party Congress, 70 percent of the membership was arrested or liquidated within the next five years. The same fate befell 1,108 delegates out of 1,966 who attended the same Congress. We have a confirmation of the fact that the Central Committee and even the Politburo practically ceased to function during Stalin's last years and that the despot transacted the most important business by himself, or with whoever enjoyed his confidence at the moment. Thus in 1949 Nicolai Voznesensky, the head of Russia's economic planning and a member of the Politburo, was liquidated along with a number of other high officials at a period when, Khrushchev asserts, "Stalin became even more capricious, irritable and brutal; in particular his suspicion grew," and "everything was decided by him alone without any consideration for anyone or anything."[27] In short, out of the mouth of the highest Party functionary, Soviet and foreign Communists heard the confirmation of the worst attacks of their enemies and an avowal that for a long time the U.S.S.R. and world communism had been ruled by a bloodthirsty tyrant who had thought nothing of ordering tortures for veteran Bolsheviks.

Some other details of Khrushchev's speech may or may not be confirmed by a future historian. There are two questions pertinent to the study of the Soviet government. First, though we cannot know the exact reasons for the revelations, what lines of reasoning could have persuaded the leaders to admit so much and thus, as they must have realized, to threaten their own positions as formerly the closest servants of Joseph Vissarionovich Stalin—not to mention shocking millions of Party activists by telling them authoritatively that all they had been taught about

---

[26]All the quotations from the speech are from the version published by the *New Leader* under the title *The Crimes of the Stalin Era,* edited by Boris I. Nicolayevski.

[27]The reason why Stalin's "suspicion grew" may have been a fairly rational feeling on his part that as he grew older his closest collaborators were maneuvering for power positions in the eventuality of his death.

the Party's history during the preceding twenty years was a big lie? As suggested before, the only reasonable explanation is twofold: (1) In condemning the cult of the individual, the collective leadership may have thought that it was acquiring a collective insurance against any one of its member's trying to emulate the late dictator and ascend the summit of power in Stalin's fashion. (2) The revival of the Party's spirit under conditions that would not allow one absolute dictator would have indicated the necessity for a dramatic break with the past, a surgical operation on the Party's history, painful and dangerous no doubt, but in the long run, it was hoped, to prove salutary.

The other question turns on the hypothetical reasons and how far they have been and are likely to be justified by the events. There is no doubt that the regime gained in popularity through its new policies. The attempt to ascribe most of the repressive and unpleasant things of the preceding twenty years to Stalin's personal foibles has also been a qualified success. The deliberative organs of the Communist party have been revived. We hear of meetings of the Central Committee; there is more of the air of real discussion of issues in the Party press and less of the craven sycophancy that characterized Party speeches and writings in Stalin's time. These developments have undoubtedly increased the administrative efficiency of the Party machinery and encouraged the development of more initiative and spirit at the lower levels. As a whole the Party is now a healthier organism. The average member is driven less by mere compulsion than he was prior to 1953.

At the same time the fundamental problem has not been solved. Much has been said and written about a return to the Leninist principles and spirit. But the circumstances of today's Russia make the condition of the Party as it was in Lenin's time simply inapplicable and irrelevant to today's problems. By publicly confirming the terrible excesses of the past, the Party has not only shattered the incredible if not feigned innocence of many foreign Communists, but must have injured itself in the eyes of the younger and more credulous of Soviet Communists. Human gratitude for the removal of the worst type of repression is notoriously short-lived and succeeded by demands for more substantial freedoms.

The slogan "back to Lenin," that is, back to the Leninist principles and spirit, which underlay Khrushchev's revelations and projected reforms could not, however, prove of much practical help in the more than fifteen years that separate us from the Twentieth Party Congress. The period has witnessed new struggles for power, Khrushchev's triumph and then his very far-reaching designs for even more basic reforms of the Party, his fall in 1964, and the much more conservative "don't rock the boat" attitude of his successors. The circumstances of today's Russia and the character of the Communist party now are so vastly different from what they were in Lenin's time that there is little from Lenin's era that can help or illuminate the problems of today.

Not long after the Twentieth Party Congress, a new crisis shook the very top leadership in the summer of 1957. The story (and it was not to emerge in full until 1961) concerned an attempt by a *majority* of the Presidium members, led by Molotov, Malenkov, and Kaganovich, to oust Khrushchev. The vote in the

Presidium was seven to four in favor of the ouster. But the surprised First Secretary fought back and succeeded in convening the full Central Committee, which over-ruled the Presidium—something that had not happened for a long time—and sent, instead of Khrushchev, his opponents into political wilderness. Among them were not only the three veterans of Stalin's highest councils (mentioned above) but Prime Minister Bulganin, whose "treacherous" role was not fully revealed until 1959, and Voroshilov, the titular head of state, whose very active part in those proceedings was to be described by Khrushchev only in 1961 when the old man (then eighty) was publicly humiliated. The "Anti-Party group," as it was officially dubbed, contained also some younger oligarchs, some of them until then assumed by everybody, including Khrushchev, to have been the First Secretary's protégés.

It is unlikely that the plotters (who of course were given no opportunity to tell publicly their side of the story) were united by any ideological pro-Stalin platform as the official version of the crisis claimed. It was largely a power struggle in which Khrushchev's opponents were probably united by their conviction that the First Secretary's course was too erratic and dangerous, his de-Stalinization tactics un-desirable insofar as they undermined the prestige of the Party as a whole. The events of the previous fall in Poland and Hungary led them to believe that Khrushchev acted incautiously in talking so much about the excesses of Stalinism instead of liquidating them quietly and without much fuss. His plans to decentralize economic administra-tion threatened the economic power base of Presidium members Maxim Saburov and Mikhail Pervukhin, who joined in the plot. All in all the scenario of the intrigue, its colorful course in which evidently Khrushchev won largely because he obtained the Army's assistance in rounding up and bringing to Moscow "his" Central Com-mittee members, was more reminiscent of a gangland coup—even though the plotters paid only with their high positions and not their lives—than a political dispute surrounding supreme power in one of the world's greatest states.

For the next five years Khrushchev, now Prime Minister as well as the Party boss, enjoyed undisputed supremacy. At the Twenty-second Congress in 1961 he went even more deeply into the story of Stalin's crimes, now associating with them his deposed opponents of 1957. Stalin's body was removed from its place of honor next to Lenin's in the mausoleum. Members of the Anti-Party group of 1957, mainly Malenkov, Molotov, and Kaganovich, were now identified as having participated in Stalin's crimes. Indeed for a time there was every appearance that there would be a series of political trials in which those old Stalinists would be called to account.

In 1962 Khrushchev's position, still in the West considered unassailable, became more precarious. The conflict with China now became public knowledge; and indirectly Soviet inability to resolve it, to bring the Chinese back at least to formal and verbal agreement within the Communist bloc, reflected on the top Soviet official, who was soon to become an object of personal attacks by the Chinese.

But the most fundamental blow to Khrushchev's position was probably rendered by Soviet retreat in the Cuban missile crisis in the fall of 1962. We can only conjecture that the idea of placing nuclear missiles in Castro's Cuba was largely Khrushchev's own and that it was connected with a very ambitious foreign policy design of his. In any case the U.S.S.R. suffered the humiliation of a retreat. Chinese attacks now became virulent; and after the Test Ban Agreement with the United States and Great Britain in 1963, relations between the two Communist superpowers became openly hostile and Chinese references to Khrushchev surpassed in vilification what they had to say about Western statesmen.

Foreign failures were accompanied by domestic ones. During the early sixties the Soviet economic growth slowed down. Always an innovator and improviser, Khrushchev plunged into new moves in both policy and administration to improve the picture. With the now obvious failure of the virgin territories to solve the basic dilemma of Soviet agriculture, he sought to stress greater investments in the chemical industry so as to increase greatly the production of artificial fertilizer. A self-proclaimed expert on agronomy, Khrushchev's great enthusiasm for corn subsided, and he called for and enforced cultivation of other fodder foods.

In administration one reform adopted in 1962, and the one most speedily undone after Khrushchev's fall, was the division of the party hierarchical organization up to the Union-Republic level into two parallel structures, one to deal mainly with agriculture, the other with industrial as well as other matters. Thus at the Soviet region and county level there were now two coequal First Party secretaries and so two parallel Party committees. This destruction of unity of leadership at lower levels of the Party organization was a prime example of what were subsequently characterized as the First Secretary's "harebrained schemes." It evidently increased rather than diminished confusion and did not have any effect in improving the picture of Soviet agronomic production.

But perhaps the main direct cause of Khrushchev's precipitous fall is to be sought in another technique that he spawned in the last years of his rule, and which must have been seen by the Party hierarchs as a direct threat to their power and indeed their jobs. This consisted in giving increasingly public character to the Central Committee meetings. No longer were many of them held in secret, attendance limited strictly to their full and alternate members. Now many nonmembers, sometimes running into hundreds, would be invited to attend and on some questions even to vote on resolutions. The outsiders were allegedly specialists and other people whose interest lay in the subject under discussion, but the practice, whatever its rationale, ran counter to the hierarchical tradition and penchant for secrecy in matters of high policy that are so characteristic of the Soviet system. It is clear that Khrushchev, probably increasingly challenged by the inner-Party council, wanted to eschew meetings behind closed doors. In the presence of outsiders for whom he was of course the undisputed leader, the oligarchs were loath to venture their disagreements or to challenge their leader. Shortly before his fall, Khrushchev extended this version of participatory democracy to the meetings of the Presidium and the Council of Ministers. That must have been the last straw. The malcontents must have realized that Khrushchev now aspired to rule as the popular leader, to cow them into absolute submission or perhaps to deal with them the way he had with Molotov, Malenkov, and Kaganovich in 1957. In October 1964 during Khrushchev's absence on vacation, the other members of the Presidium struck. The duped leader was brought to the meeting of the Central Committee only after it had begun and after his fate had been reached, and this time he was incapable of turning the tide. The man who shook the country and the whole world with his policies and improvisations for more than ten years became overnight an obscure emeritus.

Khrushchev's successors moved quickly to undo many of his "harebrained" reforms. It was decided again to keep the two top positions in the Party and government separate. Succeeding as First Secretary was Leonid Brezhnev, a veteran Party official, at one time the titular head of the Soviet state and then a member of the Secretariat of the Central Committee. Another who first reached the high councils of Soviet power under Stalin, Alexei Kosygin, became chairman of the Council of Ministers. Both men, then in their fifties, were somewhat colorless in comparison with their buoyant predecessor. The two were undoubtedly elected by their fellow oligarchs as safe men unlikely to rock the boat in the Khrushchev manner. They seem as of now to have justified those expectations.

The first of Khrushchev's reforms to go was the bifurcation of the Party apparatus on the lower levels; it was abolished in 1964. The single secretaryship and single Party bureau were restored from the regional level on. Meetings of the central Party bodies would no longer be held in the presence of hundreds of outsiders, but in decorous privacy. The Central Committee debates were no longer published *in extenso*. In 1966 took place the first post-Khrushchev Party Congress, the Twenty-third. Some changes were symbolic insofar as they reintroduced nomenclature familiar from the Stalin era. The First Secretary became once more Secretary-General; the Presidium was again called the Politburo. Another feature from the old times, the Party Conference, was reintroduced, though it has not been used in the last five years.

This reintroduction of terms familiar from the old era was symbolic of the new leaders' determination to rehabilitate Stalin partially and to cut short any lengthy discussion and reminiscing about the "bad old times." There has been no idea of letting a single man achieve the position held by Stalin, or even by Khrushchev from 1957 to 1962. In fact one of the main accusations against Khrushchev has been that the former leader often treated Party bigwigs with scant respect. The idea of collegial dictatorship, rather than dictatorship by a single person, is the one currently in favor, though the General Secretary is very much the number-one man in the regime.

Since 1964 the regime and top leadership has, then, been conservative as the term is used in the Soviet context, eschewing violent changes and reemphasizing the role of the Party, its omniscience, its controlling voice in all aspects of Soviet life. It has been wary of younger people; newcomers into the charmed circle of the Politburo have been people of mature years and long service in the officialdom. Typical is a person co-opted in 1966, A. J. Pelshe, a man in his mid sixties and a veteran Bolshevik, with a background of service in the Secret Police and as regional Party official. Younger members of the Politburo such as Alexander Shelepin—once seemingly a rising star and hardly a youth, now in his fifties—have been confined to administrative responsibilities not of the highest political importance, in his case leadership of the Soviet Trade Unions. In brief this is the regime of Party secretaries, people of mature years who came into prominence for the most part under Stalin and who therefore have no reason to look at his era with just revulsion. They feel that anyway terror and all those other unpleasant things happened a long time ago and that people now concentrate on positive things about communism, rather than stirring up old ghosts.

At one time it was possible to think of other Soviet institutions as at least challenging the undisputed role of the Party. In the brief interlude after Stalin's death the secret police under Beria evidently wielded considerable political influence; but with his liquidation its political influence at the highest level was curtailed. The KGB, as it is generally known (from the initials of the Russian name for the Office of the Committee on State Security), though all pervasive in Soviet life, is strictly controlled by the highest Party officials.

The Army has always played a curious role in the Soviet political context. At times it appeared close to wielding political power, only to be reduced again to an obedient servant of the Party. Along with other agencies in the U.S.S.R., Stalin purged it mercilessly. In 1937–1938 three out of five marshals of the Soviet Union were liquidated. The whole officer corps was purged thoroughly in the 1930s. Even after World War II some of the most prestigious commanders were shunted off into obscurity and some arrested, though nothing on the order of the Great Purge of 1934–1939 took place. In the post-Stalin period of confusion and uncertainty the Party leaders felt that they needed the prestige of such war heroes as Marshal Zhukov, brought from the obscurity of a provincial command to be First Deputy and then Minister of Armed Forces. In 1957 he played a crucial role in helping Khrushchev defeat his opponents and as a reward was made a full member of the Party Presidium. In that position he evidently claimed more autonomy from political controls over his domains. Anyway, within a few months he was dismissed in his turn, stripped of his state and Party offices, and accused of having had "Bonapartist" ambitions. Here again the Party was quick to reassert its full authority and to cast back into shadows a man who conceivably might have aspired to combine his national prestige and his power base into a bid for the top spot.

It is perhaps not accidental that the top military positions are still occupied by people who were important commanders in World War II, people often beyond the mandatory retirement age for military personnel in the United States. Napoleons are not made from people in their sixties. The armed forces are honeycombed with political officers. It would, however, be incorrect to assert that the army—that is, its top commanders—plays no political role or does not exercise a certain influence, say, when it comes to the formulation of foreign policy. And should another crisis on the order of 1953 or 1957 shake the Party, who knows whether the Soviet generals might not try their hand at resolving it. Soviet political history since Stalin's death is a vivid proof of how within the outwardly placid and seemingly monolithic picture at the top of the Soviet pyramid are concealed conflicts and tensions that may erupt at any time, bringing about a sudden change in the top leadership and perhaps even someday a more fundamental transformation of the political picture.

The Formal Organization

Congresses and Conferences

Nothing would be more deceptive than to judge the importance and actual role of various organs of the Communist party on the basis of their competence as laid

Figure 5.1 Formal Organization of the Communist Party at the Time of the Twenty-fourth Congress—March 1971

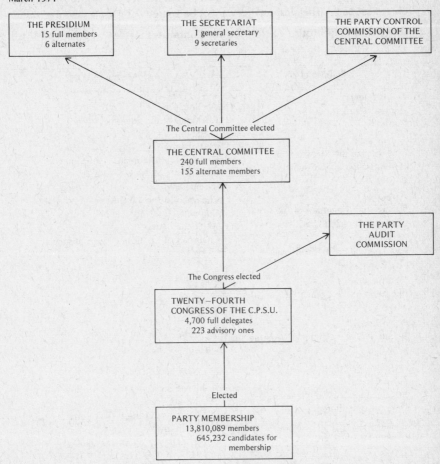

down in the Party statute. It would be almost as misleading to ignore the flux of Soviet politics, which makes the role of, say, the Central Committee of the Party —though its official competence has changed but little throughout the years—quite different today from what it was in Lenin's time, or, we may add, from what it is likely to be in a year or two. A student of British government may write about the role in British politics of the Cabinet, the House of Lords, or the National Executive of the Labour party, confident that their importance, barring a cataclysmic development, will change but little, and in a quite foreseeable fashion, within the immediate future. Students of totalitarian systems would be wise to avoid such confidence. It falls to them to sketch the general *trend of the development* of the political institutions of a totalitarian state, taking into account both the formal and the informal (that is, not expressed in formal statutes or constitutions) aspects of politics. As with the institutions of the Soviet state, so with the *institutions of the Communist party:* Their importance cannot be entirely assessed either in terms of

Table 5.1 The Politburo of the Central Committee After the Twenty-Fourth Party Congress

Full Members	Full Members, cont.
L. I. Brezhnev General Secretary of the Central Committee	N. V. Podgorny Chairman of the Supreme Soviet Presidium
G. I. Voronov Chairman of the Russian Soviet Federated Republic Council of Ministers	D. S. Polyanski First Deputy Chairman of the Council of Ministers of the U.S.S.R.
K. T. Mazurov First Deputy Chairman of the Council of Ministers of the U.S.S.R.	A. N. Shelepin Chairman of the All-Union Central Committee of Trade Unions
V. V. Grishin First Secretary of the Moscow City Committee	V. V. Shcherbitzky Chairman of the Council of Ministers of the Ukraine
A. N. Kosygin Chairman of the Council of Ministers of the U.S.S.R.	**Alternate Members**
A. P. Kirilenko Secretary of the Central Committee	A. A. Andropov Chairman of the K.G.B.
F. D. Kulakov Secretary of the Central Committee	P. N. Demichev Secretary of the Central Committee of the C.P.S.U.
P. Y. Shelest First Secretary of the Ukrainian Central Committee	Sh. R. Rashidov First Secretary of the Uzbek Party
M. K. Suslov Secretary of the Central Committee	P. M. Masherov First Secretary of the Byelorussian Party
A. J. Pelshe Chairman of the Commission of Party Control	V. P. Mzhavanadze First Secretary of the Georgian Party
D. A. Kunaev First Secretary of the Kazakh Central Committee	D. F. Ustinov Secretary of the Central Committee of the C.P.S.U.

the statute and constitutional phraseology or in terms of the role they have actually played in the power struggle of the totalitarian system. As we have seen, the organs that at one point constituted the battle scene of Soviet politics have in many cases become tame and ornamental adjuncts of the dictatorship. On the other hand, the paper realities of today may become vital and important factors of Soviet politics tomorrow. Therefore an appraisal of the most important Party institutions both in terms of the Party statute and in terms of their past and present evolution presents a perspective for the future.

The Party Congress, as noted before, is in theory, as it has been from the very beginning, the sovereign organ of the Party. Delegates to the Congress are elected in a specified ratio per number of Party members. Party rules used to specify that the Congress should meet at least once every three years. As amended in the statutes of 1952 they provide that ordinary congresses are to be convoked every four years. So much for the constitutional provisions. A student of Soviet politics will draw conclusions from the fact that following the Revolution, Party congresses met every year until 1925. Following the Fourteenth Congress, which marks a watershed in the real importance of congresses, there was a two-year hiatus before the Fifteenth in 1927; then a three-year hiatus until 1930. In defiance of the Party statute no congress met for four years between the Sixteenth and the Seventeenth, which met in 1934. Then came a five-year period coinciding with the Great Purge, until the Eighteenth in 1939, and after that a thirteen-year hiatus until Stalin's last Congress in 1952.

The lengthening and unstatutory interval has an eloquence of its own. For the congresses until 1925 still were fairly genuine representative assemblies. They had a life of their own, often a lively discussion, and at times a clash of points of view: as between Lenin and the Workers' Opposition at the Ninth and Tenth Congresses (1920 and 1921) and between Trotsky's partisans and those of the ruling *troika* in 1923 and 1924; and as in the decisive clash between Stalin and the Leningrad Opposition led by Zinoviev and Kamenev in 1925. Beginning with the Sixteenth Congress in 1927, the picture changes. Congresses are triumphant reviews by the Stalinist rulers of their subordinates. There is no discussion in the sense of a controversy, but only obedient reports and unanimity on the theses presented by the leader. Former opponents of Stalin as long as they are alive are given the opportunity to recant and to crawl in the dirt to the revilings and amusement of those assembled. At the Eighteenth Congress, held on the morrow of the blood bath, no opposition voices are heard. Veteran Communist leaders, as if incredulous that they are still alive, recite little poems in praise of Stalin, and a delegation of schoolchildren intones: "Thank you Comrade Stalin for our happy childhood!"

The mechanics of the Congress stay the same. The Presidium and the Secretariat (the former including the most prominent leaders) having been elected, the central point of the proceedings is the report of the Central Committee delivered by the acknowledged leader of the Party. Thus it was Lenin who reported, until his fatal illness; then in 1923 Zinoviev, followed in succeeding congresses by Stalin. At the Nineteenth Congress the report was presented by Malenkov, Stalin contenting himself with a brief speech at the end. Reasons for this may not be difficult to find. The report requires a not inconsiderable physical effort, which in 1952 might have been beyond the powers of the seventy-three-year-old despot. For example, Khrushchev's report at the Twentieth Congress covers 116 pages in English translation. The delivery usually occupies two separate sessions, and the speaker reviews both the world situation and domestic politics as well as the state of the Party, usually in some detail and with elaborate statistical data. Following the report a lengthy debate takes place, with scores of delegates participating. Since 1925 the debate increasingly consisted in the speakers' agreeing with the report, praising Stalin, and actually giving reports of their own on conditions in their particular organization and part of the country. Another major speech might be delivered by a Party leader on, say, the directives for a new economic plan, and that in turn would be discussed, that is, agreed to by numerous speakers. It used to be said of members of Hitler's Reichstag that they were the best paid male chorus in the world, for they met infrequently, heard the Fuehrer speak, sang the national anthem, and went home. The same claim cannot be made for members of the Party Congress, for when one reads the minutes of Stalin's congresses and even of the post-Stalin Twenty-fourth Congress, one is struck by the massive monotony and tedium of the proceedings, which must have constituted hard work for the participants.

The mechanics of the Congress include minor routine things such as the report of the Audit and Mandate Commissions, greetings from foreign Communist parties, factories, army units, and so forth. In the earlier and spontaneous days these indeed helped give an air of holiday and comradely meeting to the Congress; in Stalin's days they became a travesty. And at the end comes the concluding word of the leader or leaders, followed by a unanimous agreement on the reports and unanimous election of the Central Committee and other organs of the Party. The Twentieth Congress, held in 1956, did not change the pattern. Here again was unanimity, which included a unanimous condemnation of the "cult of personality" and thus of Stalin. Even though the speeches differed somewhat from the old monotonous pattern, it was still a propaganda show arranged and directed down to the smallest detail by the (this time collective) dictator, and not a Congress, not a deliberation, in the proper sense of the word. At the Twenty-second Congress, held in 1961, there was a case of publicly voiced disagreement, but it came from a foreign guest, the Chinese Prime Minister, Chou En-lai. He criticized Khrushchev's utterances on foreign policy and especially his attack on the Albanian-Communist party, with which the Soviets broke relations in 1960 because of its pro-Chinese stand. And later Chou ostentatiously left Moscow with the rest of the Chinese Communist delegation while the Congress was still in session. At the Twenty-third Party Congress, in 1966, the Chinese simplified the situation by refusing to attend, instead publicly denouncing Khrushchev's successors as revisionists as bad as the man they had ousted. The Congress then passed in the traditional fashion, that is, with everybody agreeing with the general line of the Party, though in some of the foreign Communists' speeches there were undertones of criticism of Soviet foreign policy. But on the domestic front good old unanimity prevailed; and it was certainly an achievement of some sort that Khrushchev, though amply and often criticized in a roundabout way, was not mentioned by name even once.

Aside from the Party Congress, an assembly that has played an important role in Bolshevik history has been the *Party Conference*. The Conference is a less formal and smaller version of the Party Congress. Instead of being elected by the body of the membership of the Party, it is a conclave of the Party hierarchy; its membership includes representatives of the Party's central organs and delegates from the committees and bureaus of regional and territorial organizations. In the twenties, the days of the struggle for power, the Conference was a more pliable and convenient assembly for the Party apparatus to manipulate than the Congress. The latter, as we have seen, still had some vestigial remnants of a democratic gathering, some delegates still could be swung by oratory, while the Party Conference, because of its character, could be relied upon to be more responsive and submissive to the *apparatus* headed by Stalin. That is how it worked at the Fifteenth Party Conference in 1926, when Zinoviev and Kamenev, previously crushed at the Fourteenth Congress, made one last effort at defiance of Stalin. They were joined this time by Trotsky. But this combination, which two or three years before could have swung any congress or conference of the Party, was in 1926 impotent to break the hold that the Stalinist machine had on the majority of Party officials.

The Conference became something of a fifth wheel. It was abolished in 1934, restored by the Party Congress in 1939, again abolished in 1952, and restored in 1966. As the 1962 edition of this book suggested, a Party Conference is a useful device that could bridge the gap between the Congress and the Central Committee. (It is *not* suggested that its restoration in 1966 is due to this book.) But though restored on paper in 1966, no conference has been held since then. The last one on record, the Eighteenth Conference, was way back in February 1941.

The Central Committee

To the Central Committee belongs a more essential and continuous part in the history of the Party. Just as the constitutional fiction of the Party statutes proclaims that the Congress is the supreme body, so in theory the Central Committee is the executive arm of the Party; but in this case the theory has a more substantial link with reality. The Secretariat, the Politburo, or the Presidium are thus in theory only organs and servants of the Central Committee. When Stalin between 1934 and 1939 imprisoned, dismissed, or sent to death two-thirds of the committee elected by the Party in 1934, he was in the eyes of the law merely a Secretary of the Central Committee, "removable" by a simple majority of its members.

Again, the genealogy of the institution is an impressive reminder of change in history. The Central Committee of pre–World War I days was a handful of revolutionaries holding its meetings in a shabby room in London or somewhere else outside Russia. Today it is an assembly of potentates, of ministers, marshals, and men who direct vast domains of power in the U.S.S.R. But the growth in splendor and numbers, has not always coincided with the growth in real power. The few men who met in a shabby room abroad did really direct the activities of the Party, though their adherents may have been just a few thousand clandestine revolutionaries. The assemblage of Party bigwigs, marshals, and directors of enterprises often surpassing (in size) the General Motors Corporation has been, at least for a generation, the servant of one man or a handful of men, officially just their colleagues and their executive officers, but in truth their masters. That it should have become so will not surprise a student of government who remembers that the British Cabinet, officially the servant and executive committee of Parliament, is in fact the master of the House of Commons. But it is the extent and the character of subjugation of the Central Committee that require some comment.

As organized originally the Committee was a relatively small group that met very frequently. After the Seventh Congress, in 1918, it consisted of twenty-three people, fifteen full members and eight alternates. The earlier Party statutes required it to meet at first twice a month, then once every two months, and so forth. In fact in those early days it met usually more often than statutorily required. If, even in those early days, it was a bit too large to decide and execute really important decisions with speed and secrecy, it was still small enough to decide on most executive matters, and of an ideal size to debate and decide policy issues within the scope defined by the Congress. The Central Committee was then an active, powerful body. Elected by the Congress, it contained partisans of various viewpoints in the Party, though Lenin's views had almost always enjoyed a majority. Another factor of vital importance in the years immediately after the Revolution was that the personnel of the Central Committee was in its vast majority composed of persons domiciled in the capitals of Moscow and Leningrad. Many of its members, certainly more than after 1927, were people with no day-to-day administrative work.

The Stalinist period profoundly altered the nature of the Central Committee and it work. It is best to look at the end result—the Central Committee of today—though there has been an evolution from the most extreme Stalinist pattern. For an executive body the Central Committee is enormous and unwieldy. Already in 1927 it was decreed that it should have seventy-one members and sixty-eight alternates. Since the Twenty-fourth Congress it has had 245 full members and 155 alternates. The rules adopted at the same time specify that it should meet ordinarily once every six months. But even this decrease over the earlier required frequency of meetings gives no idea of the decline of the Central Committee's meetings during the later Stalin era. As a matter of fact for several years before 1952 there is no authenticated report of the Committee's meetings. It is not too much to say that from the end of World War II to 1952 it existed largely on paper and that various acts announced as having been done by the Committee were simply decrees issued by the dictator and his associates. Stalin's death brought new life to the Central Committee. It now undoubtedly exists and meets fairly frequently, and in the era of post-Khrushevian *collective leadership* its importance is undoubtedly enhanced, though still not what it was in Lenin's time.

This point is underlined if we look at the list of members at the time of Stalin's last Congress in 1952 or at the latest one in 1971. They are almost without exception people who have at least one other full-time job, often at a great distance from Moscow. Once Stalin's rule was firmly planted, membership became a reward for faithful service, whether in the state, the Party, or the armed forces. It was a recognition—though often a fleeting one, for the despot was whimsical and sadistic —that the man "had arrived." Thus a Party secretary 6,000 miles away from Moscow, an ambassador to London, and an admiral of the Black Sea Fleet might sit on the Committee, though it is difficult to see how they could have performed their functions if the Committee had been a regularly meeting and active body.

Stalin's death has not changed the occupational pattern of the Committee. There are now perhaps more military and naval personnel among its *full* members.[28] Secret-service bureaucrats now appear in much smaller numbers than before. But the character of the bulk of membership is still very much the same: bureaucrats from the central state and Party organs and most of the important local Party functionaries. While the will and choice of one man is no longer the key to all posts and honors, it is not too much to surmise that most of those on the Committee are there as protégés of one or another of the ruling group.

The Central Committee has undoubtedly gained in importance since Stalin's death. To repeat, as long as the ruling group in the Politburo is united or dominated by one man, the Central Committee acts as a ratifying body and a sounding board of Soviet notables. Whenever there is factional strife in the Politburo, the Central Committee may be called upon to decide the dispute. Thus, it is highly probable that the downfall of Beria and the demotion of Malenkov were preceded by discussion in the Committee. The crisis of 1957 was decided in and by the Central Committee. Finding himself outvoted in the Presidium by a vote of seven to four, Khrushchev managed to convoke a special session of the Central Committee, which reversed the Presidium's decision and ejected, instead, his main enemies. Khrushchev successfully imitated Stalin's tactics of the early and mid-twenties when, surrounded by rivals in the Politburo, he played against it the larger body, where the majority of the Party bureaucrats were his partisans.

While the June crisis was followed by the official admonition that the Central Committee is the parent body of and superior to the Presidium, it still remains true that the former is too large and too dispersed to function *continually* as the highest policy organ in the intricate Soviet structure. At each occasion when there is factional strife within the ruling hierarchy, the Central Committee may be called upon to decide and may thus become a decisive factor in a crisis of the Soviet system. And as we have seen, in October 1964 the Central Committee served this

---

[28]In Stalin's days an admiral or marshal of the Soviet Union, unless a special pet of the dictator, had to be content with the status of an alternate member.

time to ratify the verdict of the Presidium ousting Khrushchev. The Central Committee elected at the Twenty-third Congress consisted of 195 full and 165 alternate members. More than 50 percent of them were over fifty years old, and only two full members were born after 1932. It might be interesting to add a few more statistics. Sixty-five percent of the full members were of Russian nationality. (The percentage of Russians compared to the total population of the U.S.S.R. is now just under 50 percent.) High Party and government functionaries constituted a great majority of the full members: There were eighty-one and seventy-five, respectively, some of course being listed under both categories. Fourteen full members could be classified as primarily military by profession. Only three full and eleven alternate members were workers and peasants in their current employment.

The Politburo-Presidium-Politburo

In justifying his decision in 1916 to run the British war effort with a war cabinet of five to seven members instead of the usual fifteen- to twenty-member Cabinet, Prime Minister Lloyd George stated that you cannot run a war "with a Sanhedrin." This assertion about the relations of arithmetic to the mechanics of a war is equally true of the mechanics of a totalitarian society. The latter, in a sense, lives in a continuous state of emergency. It cannot be "run" by a parliament or by a many-member committee. It requires a unified direction by one person or, at most, by a handful of people. Hence it is not surprising that it has been assumed that of all the organs of the Soviet government and the Communist party of the U.S.S.R., it is in the Politburo-Presidium-Politburo that the ultimate decision-making power has resided. This small group of people, usually of about ten full members, has been assumed to be the repository of all power, the kingpin of the political structure of the U.S.S.R. Like all generalizations, this one requires some elaboration and correction, though in the main it is true.

The original Politburo, or, to give it its full name, the Political Bureau of the Central Committee, was set up for a specific purpose. On the eve of the November uprising in 1917 a special committee of seven members was set up by the Central Committee to provide guidance to the insurrection. The Eighth Party Congress in 1919 sanctioned a permanent Politburo, as a subcommittee of the Central Committee, to which it would regularly report and of which it would remain a subordinate organ. But the list of members already indicated then that the new organization could not be thought of as "subordinate" to any other. Elected as full members were Lenin, Kamenev, Trotsky, Stalin, and Krestinsky; as alternates Zinoviev, Bukharin, and Kalinin. All of them were persons of the highest importance, though Nikolai Krestinsky, then the Party's Secretary, not long afterward dropped from the most important political plane, and Mikhail Kalinin, long the figurehead president of the Soviet Union, remained content to play a passive role and received his reward by being the only member of the original group—in addition to Lenin and (probably) Stalin—to die a natural death in his old age.

The personnel of the organization assured it from the beginning of a decisive role in the structure of the Party and government organization. Once united, the Polit-buro could settle everything, since other members of the Central Committee were for the most part either secondary figures or protégés and friends of the Politburo members. But by the same token, the Politburo could not initially assume absolute power over the Party, since most of its initial members were, except for Lenin, personal rivals and unlikely to agree on the most fundamental questions. The main arenas of struggle were the Party congresses and the Central Committee meetings. In the struggle for succession after Lenin's stroke, Stalin could not use the Politburo as his instrument of rise, for every other member was his competitor! Hence his policy of working for power through the Secretariat and control organs of the Party. The Party leaders in the Politburo were increasingly "surrounded" as more and more of Stalin's partisans were put in the Central Committee. At the same time it was decreed that on certain important questions the Presidium of the Central Control Commission (then already filled with Stalin's partisans) would sit with the Politburo. At the Fourteenth Congress Kamenev in his attack upon Stalin demanded a "collective leadership" of the Party by the Politburo. Stalin piously denounced the proposal as smacking of oligarchical rule and not consonant with inner-Party democracy. The Politburo was the last of the power positions in the Party con-quered by Stalin. It was only in 1925 and 1926, with the ejection from it of Zinoviev, Kamenev, and Trotsky and the addition of Molotov, Voroshilov, Kalinin, and Rudzutak, that he gained a majority on the Politburo; and it was not until 1930, when Bukharin, Rykov, and Tomsky were dismissed, that the Politburo, like every-thing else in the Party, became solidly Stalinist.

It was natural then that the Politburo would become the focus of all govern-mental action, arrogating to itself most of the functions belonging to other Party organs such as the Central Committee and the Council of Commissars. The Polit-buro came to be composed of the leader and his principal lieutenants. We have very little to go on to illustrate the manner of its operation during Stalin's ascend-ancy. We know, however, that in the previous era, in the twenties, the Politburo already functioned as the supreme political and economic organ. It was the su-preme decision-making body in political and economic matters; it required reports from the governmental and Party organs; and it supervised as a body or through subcommittees the most important spheres of action. It is natural to surmise that with the dictatorship firmly established after 1930 and with just one faction estab-lished in the Politburo, the supreme functions of that body were still further aggran-dized. Even the most absolute despot needs advice and help in directing his government, and a small group of intimates, people who had been Stalin's main help in his rise to power, were the best instrument of despotic government. Mem-bership in the Politburo became the most exalted and powerful position in the Soviet hierarchy, and those who achieved it became beings apart from the other, even the highest, Party and state officials. One thing even the highest office in a despotic system cannot bestow is physical security and safety from the tyrant's whim or wrath. And thus among the officials destroyed in the Great Purge of the thirties were Stalin's colleagues on the Politburo—people who had gotten there because they had been his most faithful and useful servants and creatures. Liqui-dated in secrecy were Stanislav V. Kossior, Vlas I. Chubar, and Ian E. Rudzutak among the full members. Two other full members, Valerian V. Kuibyshev and Georgi "Sergo" Ordzhonikidze, died in good graces but under suspicious circum-stances. Among the alternate members of the Politburo who met their end sud-denly, their name one day dropping out of the news and the well-informed simply forgetting that they ever existed, was the main instrument of terror and Commissar of the Interior, the unspeakable Nicolai Yezhov.

From Khrushchev's secret speech we get some occasional, though unverifiable, accounts of the functioning of the highest Party organ under Stalin. Thus, says Khrushchev, Stalin was in 1936 vacationing in the Caucasus with Andrei Zhdanov, then Stalin's favorite, head of the Leningrad Party organization and alternate mem-ber of the Politburo. From there they sent a telegram to the Politburo demanding the immediate dismissal of the then Commissar of the Interior, Henryk Yagoda, and his replacement by Yezhov. The Politburo complied, and terror was intensified under Yezhov until he, like his predecessor, was sent to his reward. Whether the other members of his Politburo were ever able to restrain or temper Stalin remains unclear, though there are unverified reports that the slackening of the terror in late 1938 and the liquidation of Yezhov were due to the intervention of Molotov and Kaganovich. But the incident, if true, illustrates what was undoubtedly the case most of the time: Stalin could dominate and overrule even the Politburo, and at times his closest advisers could be chosen from among others than full members of the Politburo. Thus in 1936 Zhdanov was only an alternate.

During the war the supreme function of the Politburo was largely superseded by the State Committee of Defense. As originally composed in June 1941, it comprised Stalin, Molotov, Voroshilov, Beria, and Malenkov, the last two at the time alternate members of the Politburo. With victory the Committee was dissolved and the prewar structure of authority evidently restored. Of the postwar Politburo we know only scraps of information given by Khrushchev. Thus he informs us that the arrest and liquidation of Nikolai Voznesensky was not even brought before his colleagues on the supreme body but was a decision of the dictator himself. Khrushchev also confirms what could be suspected from other sources: A man nominally a member of the Politburo might still be forbidden by Stalin to attend its sessions, or he might simply be ejected from it without any public notice. The latter was the fate of Andreyev in 1950. The former was the fate of Kliment Voroshilov, toward whom the dictator took a dislike just before his death.[29]

---

[29]The career of A. A. Andreyev is one of the proverbial exceptions to the rule. An Old Bolshevik, involved in opposition activities in the early twenties, criticized for administrative incompetence in the thirties, Andreyev not only survived but continued in very important Party positions. Until 1950 he was in the Politburo and head of the Party Control Commis-sion. He incurred disgrace in that year, allegedly for his views on agriculture (he was also the head of the Commission on the Kolkhoz Economy), yet he was merely demoted, and survived.

The Nineteenth Party Congress took measures that, had they survived Stalin's death, would have drastically changed the nature of the Politburo. Renamed the Presidium, it was now composed of twenty-five full members and eleven alternates. Co-opted into the supreme body were some veteran Communist party functionaries but also a number of the younger and rising Party and state bureaucrats. As stated above and confirmed by Khrushchev, the warning must have been plain: The dictator contemplated a change of the guard, and most of the surviving members of the pre–1952 Politburo were going to be pushed out. In the enlarged Presidium there was evidently a smaller directing body—the bureau of the Presidium. Who its members were we do not know. Before the new pattern could jell, Stalin died, and on the morrow of his death the veteran members threw out most of the newcomers added at the Nineteenth Congress. The Presidium was restored to more or less its previous size; ten full members and four alternates.

The Presidium after the Twentieth Congress remained of mixed character. Of the Old Bolsheviks who helped Stalin in his rise to power, four remained: Vyacheslav Molotov, erstwhile Premier and Foreign Minister; Lazar Kaganovich, long the chief economic planner and previously Stalin's chief helper in Party affairs; Marshal Kliment Voroshilov, formal head of the Soviet state; and Anastas Mikoyan, expert on trade. In the second group were those who rose to prominence when Stalin's dictatorship was already firmly established during the purges of the thirties: Georgi Malenkov, who had worked long in Stalin's personal secretariat and was probably his intended successor; Nikolai Bulganin, Premier until March 1958; and the head of the Party, Nikita Khrushchev. In the third group were pure products of the Stalin era who climbed the rungs of the Party and state hierarchy to merge into prominence after the war: M. G. Pervukhin and Maxim Saburov, both of whom have been connected with industrial affairs; and Party bureaucrats Mikhail Suslov and Alexei Kirichenko.

This crisis of June 1957 changed the composition of the Presidium. The alleged leaders of the anti-Khrushchev faction, Molotov and Kaganovich, each of whom had served on the powerful council for over a generation, were ejected, as was Georgi Malenkov. Dropped, though without any charges, was Maxim Saburov. Mikhail Pervukhin was demoted to alternate member. Pervukhin and Dimitri Shepilov, who was dismissed as an alternate member, were presumably potential candidates for Khrushchev's job.

The post–June 1957 Presidium was not, from the point of view of personnel, very stable. Some of "Khrushchev's men" elected in 1957–1958 had already managed to incur disgrace prior to the Twenty-second Party Congress and were dismissed. The most prominent of them was A. I. Kirichenko, a long-time associate of the dictator in the Ukraine and one of the minority of the Presidium who supported the dictator in the June 1957 crisis. Kirichenko's dismissal in 1960 and demotion to a lower-Party position was possibly an outcome of a struggle for the role of the heir apparent to Khrushchev in which Kirichenko might have lost to Kozlov. Marshal Zhukov, raised to full membership in June, was dismissed in October 1957 for his alleged "Bonapartism" and his intention to turn the army into his political preserve. Whatever the truth of the charges, it is not likely that Khrushchev would have tolerated in the highest council of communism a man whom many Russians regarded as a national hero and who could have become a focus of opposition to the dictator.

Some of the demotions from the Presidium must be ascribed to reasons of efficiency rather than politics. Thus dismissed in 1960 was N. I. Belyayev, who was blamed for the disastrous harvest of 1959 in Kazakhstan where he had been First Secretary. Others like Madame Y. A. Furtseva, Minister of Culture, and A. B. Aristov were dropped at the Twenty-second Congress, not in disgrace, but simply because they evidently had not measured up to the stature expected of a member of the highest Party organ. In the wake of Khrushchev's ouster as First Secretary and Prime Minister in October 1964, he was, of course, immediately dropped from the Presidium. From then until now (March 1971) the body has been rather stable. Death has claimed F. R. Kozlov, once considered a likely successor to Khrushchev, and the Presidium's senior member from the point of view of age is O. Y. Kuusinen. After the Twenty-third Congress two other senior members, Mikoyan and N. M. Shvernik, retired because of their age, both being well into their seventies. Promotions to the body have been routine. Thus in 1966 we find a former alternate member, Mazurov, elevated to full membership. At the Congress itself the former head of the Latvian Communist party, A. Pelshe, a man in his sixties, joined the top body. Though the Politburo (as it became known again after the Twenty-third Congress) has a clear Russian majority, some consideration is given to the geographic and national principles. A. J. Pelshe, a Lett, N. V. Podgorny, a Ukrainian, and Mazurov, a Byelorussian, are full members; among the alternate members are heads of the Party organization of Georgia, Byelorussia, and Uzbekistan. The Twenty-fourth Congress continued the pattern and elevated to full membership two previous alternates, Dinmukhamed Kunoyev and V. V. Shcherbitzky, and a Secretary of the Central Committee, F. D. Kulakov.

The relative stability of the Politburo in the last six to seven years has reflected a certain degree of consensus or, at least, an agreement as to the limits of (secret) disagreement at the top of the Party hierarchy. Yet it would be hazardous to venture a guess that this condition will continue and that we will not sometime witness a more fluid condition, like that of the fifties or even, if the element of physical terror is abstracted from the picture, on the order of the purges of the thirties.

The Party Control Organs

The Party Control Committee is a continuation in its ostensible function of the Central Control Commission, which existed until 1934. Insofar as its political powers and significance are concerned, it is but a feeble imitation of its predecessor, which in the twenties enjoyed a status almost equal to that of the Central Committee and members of whose Presidium were summoned to the sessions of the Politburo.

It would take too long to recite the full history of both Party and state control organs. But the moral of their evolution is very clear: No machinery of control, however elaborate, can substitute for the element of control that is provided by the multi-party system and by the give-and-take of democratic politics. The Party control organs were evolved originally to "guard the guardians," to save the Party from the evils of bureaucratism, corruption, and abuse of power. Yet operating within a totalitarian society, the control organs did not prevent, but hastened, the shackling of the Party and the rise of absolute personal dictatorship.

The Central Control Commission was organized in 1920. It stood at the top of a control organization that paralleled the territorial organization of other Party organs. The personnel and the functions of the Commission soon expanded. It was given the additional duties of ferreting out anti-Party activities—in effect, of probing into the lives of Party functionaries and even rank-and-file members in order to see if their behavior, as well as their politics, was of a kind expected of a Bolshevik. The Commission was to be independent of other Party institutions. Thus a member of it could not simultaneously be a member of the Central Committee. The apparatus and the size of the Commission grew prodigiously. At the Sixteenth Party Congress in 1930 it reached the size of 187 members, some of them attached to the central organ, others delegated to tasks of local supervision. In its original concept as envisaged by Lenin, the control organs were to function so as to curtail and point out various abuses, to act as a check on the very considerable power of the "political" organs like the Central Committee. The Central Control Commission was to function as a restraint on political power, performing some of the role that an independent judiciary performs in democratic states. Lenin's last moments were occupied in thinking about the ways and means of controlling the inner-Party strife and of erecting a bar both against fatal dissensions that would split the Party wide open and against the seizure of power by one man.

Yet in a totalitarian system nothing can be apolitical. From its inception the Central Control Commission interpreted its task as that of enforcing the Party "line," that is, rooting out various oppositionists, beginning with Lenin's opponents in the very early twenties and ending with Stalin's. From a censor of Communist morals and guardian of revolutionary morality, the control organs became almost from the beginning an instrument of political purges.

The Central Control Commission very early came to be dominated by Stalin's faction. It would be too simple to attribute this only to Stalin's personal machinations. In the control organs just as in the other branches of the Party's administration the dominant type very soon became the *apparatchik,* "man of the machine," with a bureaucratic mentality, seeing politics in terms of practical administrative problems and distrustful of intellectuals in the Party (and Trotsky, Zinoviev, and Kamenev were *par excellence* revolutionary intellectuals). It was natural for such men to feel an affinity with Stalin and to see in him a man of practicality and moderation. In the struggle for power in the twenties the control organs regularly supported Stalin, chastised or expelled from the Party his opponents, and overlooked the transgressions of the Secretary-General's partisans. Quite apart from the "control" functions the Commission had an important political role. Certain important political decisions such as demotion of a Central Committee member could be transacted only at a joint meeting of the Central Committee and the Commission. Three members of the Presidium of the Commission had the right to sit in with the Politburo. Thus the relative strength of Stalin's opponents in the Central Committee and the Politburo was effectively neutralized or overcome by his domination of the Control Commission.

With the end of all open opposition to dictatorship, the political function of the control organs became superfluous. The control organs could return to their administrative duties, without, however, abandoning the task of rooting out disloyal and would-be disloyal Party members. In connection with the latter, the personnel of the Central Control Commission was increasingly penetrated by high officials of the N.K.V.D. (the Commissariat of the Interior—the security forces). By 1934 the Commission was renamed the Committee of Party Control. The fiction of its independent status was abandoned, and though still elected by the Party Congress, it was now officially inferior to the Central Committee and charged with implementing its directives. The statutes of 1952 made the Party Control Committee fully a creature of the Central Committee. Unlike the Central Auditing Commission, a body of minor importance, the Party Control Committee is no longer elected by the Congress, but organized by the Central Committee of the Communist party. In the structure of Soviet power the Control Committee no longer has any independent political role. It confines itself to its stated duties, that is, the preservation of Party discipline and ethics,[30] supervises the fulfillment of the decrees of the central organs, and so forth. It is not impossible, however, that any deep split within the present leadership and factional strife could again awaken the political role of the control organs, and that the dossiers and files of the Party Control Committee could again become the instrument of factional strife.

Between November 1962 and the Twenty-third Party Congress in 1966 another control body, the Forty-State Control Committee, was in existence. It was under the leadership of Alexander Shelepin, who *then* seemed a rising star on the Soviet political firmament. In 1966 this body was abolished, and the Party Control Committee reverted to its role as the central control organ but still subordinate to the Central Committee.

The Secretariat

The nerve center of the Communist party has been since the beginning of the twenties the Secretariat of the Central Committee. Prior to the Nineteenth Congress of 1952 there existed in addition to the Secretariat the Organizational Bureau (Orgburo) of the Central Committee. But the latter body, extremely important during the post-Revolutionary period and again one of the avenues through which

---

[30]A violation of Party ethics is defined as "dishonesty and insincerity in relation to the Party, slander, bureaucracy, moral turpitude, etc."

Stalin rose to power, was later increasingly superseded in its functions by both the Secretariat and the Politburo, and at the time of its abolition was actually a fifth wheel.

The Secretariat, on the other hand, has preserved its crucial importance. The First Secretary of the Communist party in the U.S.S.R. is the leading man in the country, whether he holds another office or not. The same pattern prevails in almost all Communist-ruled countries (except occasionally, as in China, where there is the office of Chairman of the Party). The word "secretary" evokes in our mind a rather clerical person occupied with shuffling papers. Actually the General or First Secretary of the Communist party is not only the chief administrative officer, but also the man with the dominant voice in formulating the policies of his Party and, if the Party is in power, of the country.

The pattern was set in 1922 when Joseph Stalin became the General Secretary of the Central Committee of the Russian Communist party. The Party, which had inherited so much of the anarchistic contempt for problems of political organization, had given but little thought to its own administration prior to the Revolution. Following November 1917 the functions of the chief administrative officer of the Party were discharged by Jacob Sverdlov, a close collaborator of Lenin. His death in 1919 left the Party without a first-rate figure charged with administration. Lenin had all the cares of the state and policies to be busy with. Trotsky was running the Red Army, and other leading figures of the regime were much more at home making speeches, writing pamphlets, and preparing revolutions abroad than in attending to day-to-day administrative routine. Yet the Party was not longer a small conspiratorial organization that could be run informally. One of the central problems was that of liaison between the center and the local organizations. Another was the problem of admission of new members; of ideological education of Party members, their apportionment to the government apparatus, and so forth. To deal with the broader organizational problems, the Eighth Congress created the Orgburo, one of whose original members was Stalin. To deal with immediate administrative problems, a Secretariat of the Central Committee was set up.

Under its first leaders the Secretariat remained very much what it had been intended to be: an administrative and liaison organ. The change came in 1921, when three secretaries were appointed (one of whom was Molotov) who were closely linked to Stalin. In 1922 Stalin himself became Secretary-General, and the office underwent a transition.

The Secretariat rapidly arrogated to itself the function not only of administrative but also of general guidance of the Party. The tasks of agitation, propaganda, and ideological education were taken over by the rapidly expanding institution. From a modest office where unassuming secretaries sat ready to counsel and comfort visiting Party officials from the provinces, the Secretariat became a veritable command post, which transferred Party leaders from the Caucasus to the Ukraine, changed ideological instructors, and even disciplined and dismissed Party functionaries. A list of departments of the Secretariat between 1924 and 1930 gives a fair idea of this Frankenstein-like growth of an administrative department that came to engulf the whole Party. The departments included: organization—assignment one —village affairs, statistical, general administration, agitation and propaganda, and information.[31] From the writing of newspaper articles to the appointment of a Party secretary in a small town, all these affairs—the very lifeblood of a political organism —were regulated by the Secretariat. Complaints of the opposition, cries that the Secretariat should return to a purely administrative role and leave politics to political organs, went unheeded. The Secretariat more and more absorbed the real task of governing Russia as well as the Party.

With the effective elimination of opposition in the Party, the remnants of which task could now be handed over to the secret police, the Secretariat was adjusted largely to propelling the country toward industrialization. Thus the reorganization of 1930 split the organization-instruction section into two, one of which, the assignment department, had several subdepartments dealing with the assignment of Party workers to several major areas of the Russian economy, for example, heavy industry, light industry, and agriculture, and subdepartments as well as sections devoted to Soviet administration, foreign Communist activities, and so forth.[32] Soviet government was thus reduced to the typical bureaucratic model. The main function of the Party organization became the selection of personnel, and this in turn would be decided in the offices of the Secretariat, which was now running not only the Party, but also almost directly the whole country's administration and economy. Even a more direct functional principle was introduced in 1934, when this time special departments rather than subdepartments were created in the Secretariat paralleling large areas of the Soviet economy, that is, agriculture, transport, industry, and finance and trade. The Secretariat thus became not merely the power behind the throne, but a body *directly* supervising and staffing all branches of the Soviet government, expanding directly into industry, agriculture, and so on. The resulting confusion of authority led to the scheme's being temporarily abandoned in 1939, and most of the departments again corresponded to purely Party affairs. But in 1948 the functional setup was restored, and among the departments there now appeared a special one devoted to political administration of the armed forces.[33]

The whole development since 1930 again demonstrates the dilemma of a totalitarian regime, even at an administrative level. The regime feels the need of checking and double-checking every sphere of activity. Everything is controlled by the government apparatus, which in turn is supervised by the Party apparatus— and then there is the secret police. It is likely that during Stalin's last years there was a special personal secretariat surrounding the leader and independent of the Party apparatus. The result, however, when you come to concrete tasks of administration and economy, is often inefficiency and confusion. So periodically the cry

---

[31]Fainsod, *op. cit.,* p. 167.

[32]*Ibid.,* p. 168.

[33]*Ibid.,* pp. 173 and 195.

is raised that the Party should not stick its fingers into the details of running the economic machinery, and just as periodically it is exclaimed that things are not going well because the Party does not evidence enough care for economic problems. But the administrative history of the Secretariat shows how a modest administrative office, in a system where there are no effective checks on power, may grow into the kingpin of the whole political and economic system of a vast country.

The actual work of the Secretariat at the highest level has been shrouded in something of a mystery. Since the office has been the locus of political power in the Soviet Union for at least thirty years, its innermost operations have been secret, and the only conjectures we can form are on the basis of changes in its personnel. Stalin's ascendancy in the Secretariat was immediate and unqualified. As Secretary-General in 1922 he was assisted by two secretaries, Molotov and V. V. Kuibyshev, both of them members of his faction. From then on the pattern of Secretary-General and two, three, or four "plain" secretaries of the Central Committee persisted. The latter were invariably the closest associates of the dictator, though for reasons that are obvious none of them was allowed to warm up his seat in the Secretariat for more than a few years before being transferred to other work. In the regional and republic party organizations there has often been the pattern of designating a hierarchy of secretaries, one of them being designated as first secretary, another as second, and sometimes there even being an official third secretary. In the central secretariat, except for Stalin, other secretaries were not differentiated in status. Yet with the dictatorship in full swing and Stalin occupied with other vast responsibilities, it becomes possible to identify his chief deputy for organizational matters in the Party. In the early thirties that function was performed by Lazar M. Kaganovich. It was Kaganovich who first selected for higher Party posts many of the subsequent leaders like Khrushchev and Malenkov. In the later thirties Andrei Zhdanov succeeded to the post of Stalin's main Party lieutenant. A Party secretary, since 1934 head of the Leningrad organization, he played a large but still unexplained role during the Great Purge of 1936–1938 and in the immediate postwar era. During the latter period he was in open (insofar as anything in the Soviet system can be open) rivalry with Georgi Malenkov, Party secretary since 1939, but temporarily dropped from the Secretariat in 1946. Zhdanov died, assertedly of a heart attack, in the summer of 1948, and Malenkov, until Stalin's death, enjoyed the position of the main Party administrator and presumably Stalin's intended successor. He was soon, however, joined on the Secretariat by another Party figure of importance, Nikita Khrushchev.

The story of the top personnel of the Secretariat preceding and immediately following Stalin's death has a little of the air of a mystery story. At the Nineteenth Congress the number of secretaries was raised to ten, all of them members of the Presidium. On the morrow of Stalin's death the communiqué about the changes in other branches of the government and the Party was quite explicit, but on the reconstruction of the Secretariat its language was unclear and confused. Some secretaries were dropped, some were added, but it was impossible to tell whether anyone would occupy the chief position in the Secretariat and whether Malenkov, just made Prime Minister, was retained on this body or not. The leaders, who evidently agreed after Stalin's death and for the moment on the redistribution of other government and Party positions, were evidently unable to come to a full agreement on the redistribution of power in the most important office of all. Only one week later, on March 14, 1953, it was announced that Comrade Malenkov requested and was granted permission to resign from the Secretariat. One of the secretaries freshly appointed in March, S. D. Ignatiev, was dismissed on April 7.[34]

The office of the General Secretary was not then restored. As a matter of fact, for reasons that are difficult to divine, that title was not used by Stalin in the postwar era; he was referred to in his Party capacity as *a* secretary of the Central Committee. Among the secretaries appointed or confirmed after his death none was designated as the chief one. It was only after Beria's liquidation in the summer of 1953, and possibly as a part of another political bargain between the leaders, that Nikita Khrushchev was appointed as First Secretary; and in 1966 the title General Secretary was reintroduced. The personnel of the Secretariat following the Twentieth Congress confirms the impression that the other secretaries are mostly, but not entirely, Khrushchev's creatures and that the same situation prevails in the regional and local Communist organizations. It is equally clear that the days of the greatest power of the Secretariat are over and that lacking a Stalin it cannot enjoy the absolute supremacy it had in the thirties and forties vis-à-vis the Central Committee and the Politburo.

With Khrushchev's removal, Leonid Brezhnev became the First Secretary. And in 1966 there was an obvious effort to return to some of the nomenclature of Stalin's time and thus to signify that *intense* de-Stalinization was definitely over and that Stalin, though discreetly, was rehabilitated. The highest official of the Communist party became again General Secretary. To be sure no one could mistake Brezhnev for a real or even potential Stalin. In fact during the past seven years his stature, despite some occasional efforts at a modest personality cult of his own, could not approach even that of Khrushchev at the height of his power, from 1957 to 1962. Brezhnev, a much less flamboyant man, has been content or constrained to play the first among equals of the leading group of the Politburo. The group, in addition to Brezhnev, consists of Prime Minister Kosygin; M. K. Suslov, the next senior Party secretary and a veteran of the Secretariat since Stalin's time; and N. V. Podgorny, the official head of state.

This sketch of the main organs of the Communist party leads to certain conclusions. History has witnessed an atrophy of the deliberative organs of the Party almost to the same degree as of those of the state. The Party Congress, a lively and

---

[34]S. D. Ignatiev was Minister of State Security at the time of the "Doctors' Plot" and was made a member of the Presidium at the Nineteenth Congress. Chastised for political blindness on account of his role in the preparation of a new purge before Stalin's death, he made a modest comeback after Beria's downfall. At the time of the Twentieth Congress he was head of the Party organization in Bashkiria.

often turbulent body under Lenin, became, insofar as it was summoned at all, a rubber stamp under Stalin. After Stalin the Party Congress gained in interest, but not really in importance insofar as making political decisions has been concerned. The Central Committee has certainly recovered some of its importance since 1953; on one occasion in 1957 the debate in the Central Committee did indeed prove decisive. But since 1964 it again declined in real significance vis-à-vis the Politburo, which unlike the other two bodies has again become very important and is not just an appendage of the dictator, as it was between about 1930 and 1953. The control organs instead of being checks on despotism, whether of one person or an oligarchy, became tools of despotism. Power became withdrawn into a tight administrative clique, and Khrushchev's attempt to break through this ring of the Politburo's rule and, to a lesser extent, the rule of the regional parties' secretaries led to his downfall. Though uniquely efficient as an instrument of power, this pyramid of the Party officialdom has obviously serious deficiencies.

Much of the enthusiasm and the feeling of mission that was so evident in the Communist party during the *earlier* part of Lenin's leadership (say until 1921) later became diluted and then suppressed by the Party bureaucracy. Then came Stalin's rule of terror, which turned the Party into an obedient tool of the dictator. Following his death there has been more flexibility and certainly some gain in the morale of the rank-and-file members. But the general spirit remains heavily bureaucratic; the main threads of power, while no longer in the hands of one man, remain in the hands of a few.

It would be a bold person who would try to predict the Party's future course and whether and for how long it can remain the absolute master of the state and society. Events in other Communist countries, not excluding China, have demonstrated in the last few years that the structure, while it looks monolithic and unshakeable from the outside, need not be so in fact. But to be sure, the rule of the Soviet Communist party is of much longer standing, its controls much firmer than those in Poland, Czechoslovakia, or even China.

Six

The Challenge to the Soviet System

In theory, at least, the Soviet Union is ruled not only by the Communist party, by a specific set of men, or according to certain procedures. Its development is assumed to reflect the stages of development as laid down by Marxism-Leninism. The doctrine, both in itself and as interpreted by the rulers, has not always been consistent in describing what stages of development the U.S.S.R. has undergone. The November 1917 Revolution did not introduce socialism because, according to Marxist canons, the country was obviously not ripe for it economically and hence socially and politically. In such terms what Russia was between 1917 and 1921 is rather difficult to describe, and her rulers were not clear about it themselves. There was some attempt at what the Chinese were to call many years later a "Great Leap Forward," an effort to skip a historical phase, from capitalism to socialism, through various economic measures described collectively as "war communism." But it was probably intended primarily as an expedient during the Civil War and anyway was shelved in 1921 with the institution of the NEP, the New Economic Policy. Here some Marxian clarity returns to what the regime thinks is the given stage of the country's development. From 1921 until 1928 there was what Marxism describes as state capitalism; that is, most of the economic functions exercised elsewhere by private enterprise (banking, heavy industry, etc.) are in the hands of the state, but large areas of economic activity (agriculture, most small-scale commerce, and even some industry) are in private hands. During 1928–1929, with the plan for intensive industrialization and collectivization of agriculture, began the socialist phase that was supposedly "completed" in 1936. When most private ownership of the means of production and distribution were put under state control, the Soviet Union officially entered the era of socialism. Exploitation, according to the then ideological exegesis, had been ended and the exploiting classes abolished. From 1936 on, runs the official view, there were basically two friendly classes in Russia, workers and peasants. The administrators and intellectuals, according to the official terminology, were not a class in the Marxist sense of the word.

The next stop on the Marxist scheme of stages of development should be the period of communism—the era when there should be progressive equalization of the economic status of all citizens culminating in "from everybody according to his ability, to everybody according to his need," and when various coercive and regulatory functions of the state would drop off, so to speak, with the final goal "the withering away of the state." The latter would be unnecessary at the stage of human development where the achievement of abundance through technology, on the one hand, and of the social and cultural improvement of mankind, on the other, would make force and regulation of human affairs superfluous.

In 1961 the Twenty-second Party Congress unveiled a new program of the Communist party. It was the third in the series, the first having been voted at the Second Party Congress in 1903, when the Russian Marxists were not as yet split and when they were, of course, out of power. The second program was adopted in 1919, following the Bolsheviks' victory. Such a program had traditionally been a statement of the goals of the Party and a prophecy of the future problems and achievements of Soviet society. The third program was thus not only an ideological self-appraisal by the regime but also a propaganda document. It postulated that the U.S.S.R. would find itself in an advanced phase of communism—not, to be sure, in the final phase.

The program recognized realistically that the state, not to mention the Party, would not have withered away by 1980. But it talked enticingly about the development of cooperation, of spontaneous social forms, and bodies taking over one after another of the state's functions. When it came to specifics, it could promise only several economic boons by 1980, such as free education, free health services, free transportation, and free utilities. As to the actual disappearance of agencies of the state, the program specified that the state committee on sports would be replaced by an independent agency!

The program's boasts and promises soon became of academic importance. The document was associated with Khrushchev's flamboyant style of leadership. After his removal in 1964 nothing further was heard about the Soviet Union's entering an advanced phase of communism by 1980.

But the problem of projection to the future remains, both for the Soviet leaders and for those abroad who try to analyze Soviet developments. Though the two aspects of the problem cannot be neatly separated and though they also depend on things that will happen in the world at large, it is useful to consider perspectives for the future of Soviet politics first from the domestic, then from the foreign policy–world communism points of view.

Today Russia is ruled by an oligarchy, but this rule of about twenty men (i.e.,

Politburo members and secretaries of the Central Committees) rests on a broader base of a strong Party and state bureaucracy. The thousands of people occupying ministerial and near ministerial positions at the center and in the various subdivisions of the U.S.S.R., the personnel of the Central Committee, and Party secretaries down to the town and county level have a strong vested interest in the perpetuation of the main features of the Soviet regime as it is. This is not to say that there are no serious divisions of opinion on the most crucial policy matters, both at the top and throughout the pyramid. But a *drastic* alternative to the system, say, a two-party system or such concessions as complete abolition of internal censorship, is simply inconceivable to anybody within this group.

The issues that divide the ruling group can be identified to some extent by observing the zigzag policies of the regime and the differing emphasis in some of the leaders' pronouncements and tactics. There is, first of all, a division between what might be called the "hard" and "soft" schools on domestic policies, between those who in informal parlance are called "conservatives" and "liberals." They are divided, for example, on the limits of what constitutes tolerable dissent within the Soviet Union. No one in either group would argue that a basically anticommunist ideology or expression of opinion should be allowed. But should writers be allowed to dwell at length on the inhumanities of the Stalin period, on the primitiveness and deficiencies of life in rural Russia? Should artists follow the prescriptions of socialist realism in the arts? Or should nonobjective painting and more modern trends be occasionally allowed? Is considerable intellectual intercourse with the West desirable? Or does it threaten especially the younger generation with ideological pollution?

To us these are hardly world-shaking questions. Yet in the context of Soviet politics and life they are vitally important. The more liberal faction in the Soviet officialdom, and one which has been in retreat ever since 1964, has held that rigid controls over artistic and intellectual matters are no longer necessary and are in fact counterproductive. The Soviet state is no longer a backward and isolated country, but one of the two greatest military and industrial powers. The regime would not collapse if an occasional novel critical of the Soviet past or present were published, if an atonal music poem were performed, or if a nonobjective painting were exhibited. Those, they hold, would not only be cultural policies befitting Russia's new status and strength but prudent measures bridging the gap between the regime and the intelligentsia, judicious letting off of steam, a convincing proof to the young that they live in a modern society, not in one that stamps out the slightest nonconformity.

The prevailing view in the oligarchy, however, has held such liberalism in cultural matters not only unwise but endowed with grave political dangers. "If one yields a little bit today, what concessions will one be called upon to make tomorrow?" may summarize the argument of the conservative faction of the Soviet Establishment. Quite apart from supporting the need for ideological vigilance, the conservatives feel that the recent cultural trends in the West bespeak decadence and are demoralizing to the young. Soviet society, one which by definition does not admit of alienation or generational conflicts, cannot afford the infusion of such bourgeois poison, which breeds pessimism and defeatism about life and about the desirability of a positive, optimistic outlook on society and man—the socialist man.

The last few years have seen quite a sprouting of intellectual dissent in the Soviet Union. It has taken two main forms, one of which might by analogy be called "legal" dissent. This dissent has consisted in the continuance in certain literary and artistic circles of the tradition of moderate critique of the Soviet past and present that had occasionally been encouraged by Khrushchev. The main focus of this critique within the system has been the Soviet literary magazine *Novyi Mir (The New World)*. For long edited by Alexander Tvardovsky, a talented poet, it printed short stories, novels, and travel literature that fairly often came close to the limits of allowable criticism and in some cases went beyond it. Tvardovsky and his closest collaborators were people of unimpeachable Communist loyalty (he himself served for a while on the Central Committee). By encouraging a critique, not of the Soviet system or ideology but of what they believed had been Stalinist and bureaucratic excrescences upon it, they sought a reform from within, a return to Lenin's original ideas of Communist society. What might be called the Neo-Leninist idea led to the publication in *Novyi Mir* of stories dealing with suppression under Stalin, as well as of critiques of contemporary life in Soviet villages, describing the abuses in collectivization.

The most notable example of this legal criticism was Alexander Solzhenitsyn's famous novel *One Day in the Life of Ivan Denisovich,* a startling account of life in a forced-labor camp. The great Soviet author had himself suffered such imprisonment because, in a *private* letter, he made one incautious remark about Stalin. The decision to print the story was authorized by Khrushchev. Solzhenitsyn's two subsequent novels, *The Cancer Ward* and *The First Circle,* going even beyond *One Day* in their depiction of the horrors of the Stalinist past, failed, however, to receive an official imprimatur. In 1969 Tvardovsky was removed as editor of the journal, and in 1970 Solzhenitsyn, recognized not only in the U.S.S.R. but universally as one of the greatest living authors, was ejected from the Union of Soviet Writers. And on being awarded the Nobel Prize in literature, the writer was not able to travel to Stockholm to receive it for fear that he would be barred from returning to his native land and thus forced to become a political exile—a role he has resolutely eschewed.

The story epitomizes the evolution of Soviet society and the predicament of the regime as well as of those who, though they feel they remain loyal to the ideas of communism, refuse to ignore or acquiesce in its abuses. Such a story could not have taken place under Stalin, for then the slightest criticism of the regime would have led to the imprisonment or execution of the hero. Even a parallel case in the fifties, that of Boris Pasternak, shows how the situation has changed since then. The great poet's *Dr. Zhivago,* a much less direct criticism of the Soviet past than *One Day,* was never published in the U.S.S.R., and Pasternak, upon receiving the Nobel Prize, was forced to decline it. Solzhenitsyn's defiance testifies to how cultural dissent has advanced and how the regime has become hesitant to use *pure* terror measures in suppressing it. Yet the sequel to the publication of *One Day* illustrates, likewise, how the post-Khrushchev regime has held previous gestures of liberalism to have been a mistake and how, unable or unwilling to apply outright police measures to eminent figures, it seeks to perpetuate and even strengthen intellectual repression.

The story of moral pressures applied to Solzhenitsyn in recent years has an eloquence of its own. Publicly in the press he has been called a renegade. At meetings of Soviet writers, conformists among them called upon him to remove the objectionable parts of his novels. He has been accused of being a leader of an antiregime opposition and provocatively assailed for not denouncing those in the West who have praised him for showing the dark side of Soviet life. All such imputations and pleas have been indignantly rejected by the writer, who eloquently reasserted his patriotism and his right and duty to write about the travails and sorrows of his people.

Literature provides us with some insight into the nature of dissent in the Soviet Union. It has to be repeated that Solzhenitsyn, even in his last books, which have not been cleared for publication, writes from the point of view of a critic rather than an enemy of the system. He is protesting both the distortion of Lenin's heritage by Stalin and the current leadership's attempt to impose silence about abuses and crimes of the past.

But there have been some protests of an out-and-out political nature. Some clandestine pamphlets have been circulated, criticizing the Soviet system in principle, and not just on account of abuses and alleged departures from the Leninist norms. A handful of courageous or reckless (depending on how one looks at their actions) dissenters have even staged political demonstrations. One such demonstration, which was followed by prison and exile for its participants, took place in protest against the Soviet military occupation of Czechoslovakia in 1968.

Quantitatively this form of political dissent is far from imposing. Even such an extreme opponent of the regime as Andrei Amalrik—the author of *Will the Soviet Union Survive until 1984?* which gained some celebrity in the West—estimates the number of political opponents of the regime at a few dozen active participants and a few hundred sympathizers. This open defiance is important, not in itself, but as a symptom of a much deeper malaise and of the readiness of at least a few individuals to take on the all-powerful state.

The Jewish problem in the U.S.S.R. provides us with another demonstration of tensions and dissent that, though they have existed for a long time, have become visible to the outside world only fairly recently. Insofar as the official viewpoint is concerned, there is and there can be no such thing as a Jewish problem in the U.S.S.R. That some Soviet Jews have become attracted to the idea of Zionism and that in recent years some of them have become emboldened to profess their allegiance openly, to request permission to emigrate to Israel, and to suffer the consequences of their boldness is at once a demonstration of the government's no longer inspiring the same fear as in Stalin's time and a demonstration of how unfree Soviet society still remains. The government, while licensing in some cases, and even on a fairly sizable scale, the migration of individuals to Israel, in principle cannot admit the right of any Soviet citizen to foreswear his allegiance to the state, which, according to the official ideology, guarantees and secures full equality and free cultural development to every national group.

What can be said as a whole about those various manifestations of political dissent and opposition in Russia and of their relation to any possible change within the political system? In the first place, we must note that all the activities mentioned above have been the work of isolated individuals or of rather small groups of people. The very nature of the Soviet system now and in the foreseeable future excludes the possibility of *organized* political opposition, of more than a handful of people getting together even to address a petition to the Supreme Soviet or the Central Committee of the Communist party on a subject or in a tone that clashes with the official Party line. We must thus discount the possibility of political protest that challenges the basic premises of the Soviet system and that would be aimed at directly effecting a change in the political reality. It is instructive to recall that Khrushchev for much of the period of his primacy was associated with the liberalizing (not liberal!) tendency. Yet his removal, effected in the style of a palace coup d'état, aroused not a whisper of popular opposition, nor indeed any reaction on the part of the population. It is dangerous in our fast-changing era to project this passivity of the Soviet people into the future. But it is at least as imprudent to assume that because a number of prominent intellectuals, writers, and so forth, have expressed their unhappiness with things as they are, the system must change or is in imminent danger.

The mechanics of political change have traditionally come from within the hierarchy itself. In the struggle for political supremacy a group or an individual might make liberalization the basis of appeal, as Khrushchev did between 1953 and 1956, or, contrariwise, might try to exploit fears that such liberalization had gone too far, as Khrushchev's successors successfully claimed in 1964. But the audience to which they all addressed themselves was not the people or a legislature, but the top of the bureaucracy, as represented by the Central Committee and, especially, its dominant segment of Party officials. The arguments would hinge not only on personalities or ideological preferences but also on the record of performance by those at the top.

Such then are the prospects for change or reform within the Soviet system that can be projected on the basis of past experience and an estimate of the forces currently at work in Soviet politics.

But we must bear in mind that quite apart from any domestic causes that may precipitate an internal shakeup, the impetus for a drastic change or reform may come from developments in the international situation, and specifically, within international communism. The Russian Revolution in the form it took would have been inconceivable without World War I. The Bolsheviks' seizure of power and successful defense of that power were in turn made possible by the circumstances, first of wartime and then of civil war, which continued until 1921. Stalinism, in turn, if not caused was certainly shaped to a large extent by Soviet Russia's isolation in post–World War I Europe and by the feeling, which Stalin successfully exploited, that the country was a besieged fortress and that hence any privations and drastic reforms were justified to defend and strengthen the world's only socialist state. Today the official rationale of the Soviet state, the basis of the claim to legitimacy of its rulers, remains officially, as it did on the first days after the November Revolution, the unique role of the Soviet Union as the center and the leader of a world-wide movement. Successes and failures of this movement, its ability to preserve unity or, contrariwise, its splitting into rival or even warring sects and states, are thus factors of vast importance for the preservation or alteration of the Soviet system of government and Soviet society as we currently know them. If international communism prospers and gains ground on a world-wide scale, if it maintains or, rather, speaking from today's perspective, regains its unity under Soviet leadership, then the average citizen of the U.S.S.R. might well feel that whatever his privations or dissatisfactions, he would in opposing his government oppose history itself. If, on the contrary, communism proves less dynamic than competing systems and ideologies, if, most important of all, its present splits and internal rivalries, of which the Sino-Soviet conflict is but the most important, become perpetuated or intensified, the reverberations of this situation are bound to affect internal politics. Internal pressures for liberalization and for more consumer goods and disillusionment with the official rationale for the authoritarian regime will grow, and eventually these sentiments might undermine both the ideological and the organizational foundations of the regime.

The Soviet Union emerged from World War II no longer an isolated Communist state, but a leader of a bloc of states, where within a few years after the war's end the domination of the Soviet leaders became as absolute as within their own state. And in 1949 another huge country, China, was conquered by communism. But it soon became obvious that while the U.S.S.R. easily dominated the international movement when she was the *only* Communist state in the world, the problem of controlling Communist parties that became bosses in their own countries would be infinitely more intricate and difficult. As long as Stalin was at the helm, the pattern of Soviet domination of Eastern European satellites was one simply of repression and exploitation. But even so, Soviet exactions brought one of them, Yugoslavia, to break away from the bloc in 1948, and neither Soviet threats nor attempts at internal subversion were successful in overthrowing Marshal Tito's regime. With the emergence of Communist China, it became obvious that even Stalin's Russia could not make this huge, if still backward and improverished, country behave like a simple dependency of the Kremlin.

There arose a phenomenon that foreign observers called, with a bit of oversimplification, national communism. Foreign Communist leaders who while out of power had been the most faithful followers of Moscow's dictates and the most slavish adulators of Stalin, now as bosses in their own countries developed their own points of view and interests. As long as Stalin lived, Yugoslavia may have appeared as an isolated case, and even Sino-Soviet disagreements, though already present and serious, remained veiled to the outside world while both sides continued to emphasize the unbreakable unity of the Communist world and Soviet leadership of the "camp of socialism." But with the old despot gone, his successors were both unwilling and unable to preserve the pattern of absolute control and repression. Khrushchev attempted to develop a new pattern of relationships within the Communist camp. Instead of dominating both internal and external policies of other Communist states, the U.S.S.R. now sought to have its primacy acknowledged mainly in the fields of foreign policy and defense. Internally the local Communist regimes would be left a wide degree of autonomy. The old practice of brutal economic exploitation through unequal terms of trade and through joint economic companies, whereby the Russians at a very small cost to themselves were able to exploit the natural resources of their satellites, now gave way to a more equitable system of economic partnership. The Soviets abandoned their effort to subvert the Yugoslav regime and counted on Tito—correctly, as it turned out—to restore friendly and intimate relations between the U.S.S.R. and the Balkan federation. But this time the relationship was based on equality. Other Communist states were no longer required to imitate the Soviet example in every detail of their social and economic policies. Khrushchev proclaimed the permissibility of "separate ways to socialism." Underlying the new policy was the fond expectation that the new pattern of relations would preserve the essence of Soviet domination, but instead of terrorized satellites requiring constant Soviet vigilance and policing, the U.S.S.R. would be surrounded by grateful and satisfied junior partners. The case of China was recognized as a special one. The Soviets finally abandoned the bases and special privileges on Chinese soil that they had secured by a treaty with Chiang Kai-shek's regime in 1945; though the Soviets had promised to give up the bases as part of their treaty with the Chinese *Communist* regime in 1950, they were still being held when Stalin died in 1953. The U.S.S.R. now also extended massive economic and technological help to Peking.

In brief, Soviet intra-Communist bloc policies after 1953 aimed at the substitution of an ideological link for sheer terror as the main element of cohesion within the bloc. Yet as almost twenty years of experience have shown, this link has not proved strong enough to secure even a very loose, compared with the pre-1953 situation, unity and cohesion of the Communist world. As terror abated, the people's raised expectation of a freer life and strivings for national independence could not be contained within the new formula. In 1956 Soviet troops had to intervene to put down a national revolution in Hungary that, having started as a movement to reform the Communist regime there, threatened to overthrow it, something the Kremlin was not ready or able to tolerate. And a decade later the Soviets were confronted with a similar problem in Czechoslovakia. They had to decide whether to let an internal evolution within a Communist country carry the country to the threshold of democracy or whether to use force, and the latter was the choice. Soviet intervention in Czechoslovakia in 1968 was based on a very realistic—from Moscow's point of view—assumption that if the Dubcek regime were allowed to "get away" with such concessions as abolishing censorship, granting freedom of the press and of speech, and, as it appeared to be on the verge of doing, licensing genuine opposition parties, pressures for similar concessions would become irresistible throughout the rest of the bloc. And eventually the ideas of "humanistic communism" might prove contagious even within the U.S.S.R. Following the invasion of Czechoslovakia by the Warsaw Pact forces and the abrogation of the Dubcek reforms, the Soviet leaders reiterated the right and duty of the Soviet Union to intervene militarily whenever in the Soviets' opinion Communist rule in any of the bloc countries became endangered. This so-called Brezhnev doctrine makes it clear, first, that the ultimate guarantor of Communist regimes in Eastern Europe remains the armed might of the U.S.S.R. and, second, that there are definite limits even on domestic reforms that the local Communist parties may undertake if they do not want to risk a repetition of the Budapest events of 1956 or the Prague ones of 1968.

But even the vast predominance of Soviet strength vis-à-vis its East European allies (if "allies" is the proper word) has not enabled the U.S.S.R. to preserve the Communist bloc in the form in which it was hoped it could be kept after Stalin's demise. The smallest of Communist states, Albania, slipped out of Soviet control in 1960–1961; and due in equal measure to her lack of a common frontier with Russia and to Chinese support, she has been able to retain her independent and defiant stance vis-à-vis the Communist Goliath. Even in those Communist countries that have continued to acknowledge Soviet leadership, there has been an occasional defiance of Moscow's wishes. It is again against the background of the Sino-Soviet dispute that Rumania has managed to assert a considerable degree of independence of Moscow, though retaining her membership in the Warsaw Pact organization and the COMECON (the organization for economic collaboration uniting the European Soviet bloc countries). Rumania has defiantly refused to follow the Soviet example in breaking diplomatic relations with China and friendly ones with the United States, and she was the only one of the Warsaw bloc countries to refuse to furnish a military contingent for the subduing of Czechoslovakia in 1968.

Under Stalin, and perhaps until 1956, it could be claimed that the Communist countries of Eastern Europe were the source of added prestige and certainly of profit to the U.S.S.R. But today they are becoming increasingly a source of worry, vexation, and, occasionally, expense. The old pattern of straightforward exploitation has gone, and at times the Soviet Union has had to pour in economic aid to salvage the ailing economy of a given country and to avoid the danger of destitution and despair, which could give birth to an outright rebellion. This happened following the Czechoslovak invasion in 1968 and, more recently, following the change of leadership in Poland in December 1970—which was brought about by what amounted to popular revolt in several cities against the economic hardships. And there is always the danger that the opposition to Soviet domination may not remain isolated, resistance to armed intrusion passive, as in Czechoslovakia in 1968, but that the flame of armed rebellion may spread from the Baltic to the Black Sea. Communism has not proved stronger than nationalism; the ideological link has proved ineffective as a substitute for force to ensure cohesion of the socialist camp.

The implications of this fact strike at the very foundation of the ideology itself and hence at the rationale of the Soviet system.

This problem is put in the most vivid relief in connection with the Sino-Soviet conflict, which has been one of the main facts of international politics within the last decade. We cannot give here even a very general outline of the momentous crisis. Suffice it to say that Communist China began by challenging Soviet supremacy within the world Communist movement, but then put in its own bid for its leadership. Mao Tse-tung has purged his party of those leaders who were allegedly pro-Russian and has proclaimed unequivocally that the brand of communism practiced in the Soviet Union since the death of Stalin has been "revisionist," hence false to the foundations of Marxism-Leninism. The Soviets, on their part, proclaimed Peking's theory and practice of ideology as "dogmatist" and "sectarian." But behind the abstruse terminology there is the basic fact of a sharp conflict of national interests between the two giant countries: China asserting at least in theory her claims to vast areas of Asiatic U.S.S.R. that were wrested in the past from the Manchu Empire; Russia, quite apart from indignant denials of those claims, plainly apprehensive of the technological and military growth of her giant neighbor. And ironically, as many a Soviet citizen must ruefully realize, the Chinese threat is largely enhanced by the fact that the world's most populous country is Communist. Without communism imparting its ruthless cohesion and drive to society, pushing it, no matter what the sacrifices, toward rapid industrialization and advanced nuclear and other military technology, there would be little reason for the U.S.S.R. to be more apprehensive of China than she is, say, of India. The greatest triumph of communism since the 1917 Revolution thus must be seen by many Russians as the source of the greatest threat to the security of their country. Publicly, both countries, that is, the leaders of both countries, profess to see their conflict as temporary and due to the ideological aberration of the opposite ruling group; once Mao and his group are gone, say the Soviets, healthy elements within the Chinese Communist party are bound to bring it back to the correct path and reestablish fraternal relations with the U.S.S.R. Once the present Kremlin crew is replaced, retort the Chinese, the Soviets will realize the correctness of Peking's position and act accordingly. But despite such professions and despite occasional rapprochements, it is difficult to see how the movement which, because of its strongly ideological complexion, needs a single authoritative source of doctrinal authority, if not indeed also of decision making, can ever recoup its unity if it is to contain two such huge powers. Whatever the future of Sino-Soviet relations, and the possibilities range all the way from a strained accommodation to a cataclysmic conflict, it is safe to say that world communism will never recoup the unity of authority and direction that it *seemed* to preserve until about 1960, but which it in fact lost irretrievably when the Chinese Communists completed their conquests of the mainland in 1949.

In our day foreign and domestic affairs have become more intermixed than ever before. We have seen in the case of the United States how the political system and American society have been powerfully affected by events taking place thousands of miles away from home. In the case of the Soviet Union this relationship has been even more pronounced. The Soviet system, when it began, was proclaimed as only the nucleus, the first installment, of what was to be a world-wide system of socialist states that would banish forever not only exploitation and poverty, but also war and national conflicts. For a long time the Soviet leaders could enjoy the enviable position of having at their disposal not only the resources of their vast country, but also the allegiance of a world-wide movement. Imperfections and sufferings of their own society could always be rationalized as inevitable sacrifices on the road toward the achievement of this great historical goal. Even the dreadful holocausts of the Stalin era could be partly rationalized as a necessary price for the ultimate goal of a Communist-dominated world, which, whatever its imperfections or lack of freedom, would banish mankind's greatest scourge—war. Now the international side of the ideology can no longer offer much hope or consolation.

The erosion of the international side of Marxism-Leninism poses, then, a challenge to the very ideological foundations of the Soviet system. Marxism has traditionally dwelt on the inherent contradictions of the capitalist economy: its inability to accommodate the growing productive power of modern industry within the relationship of private property and the struggle for markets between capitalist states, which brings about worse and worse conflicts and wars. Whatever the truth of this analysis, we are now entitled to talk about the inherent contradictions of communism, both internally and on a world scale. The growing productivity of the Soviet economy brings with it not only demands for a more equitable share for the consumer, but also for the freedoms that have traditionally accompanied a higher standard of living. And the spread of communism has sharpened rather than attenuated national conflicts between the states that profess it as their ruling ideology. It is these contradictions which form the background against which the Soviet system will have to evolve and which pose problems that the regime will eventually have to try to resolve.

Select Bibliography

The most essential materials toward the study of Soviet government are in Russian. Among them may be mentioned *Sbornik Zakonov S.S.S.R., I Ukazov Prezidiuma Verkhovnogo Soveta S.S.S.R. (Collection of the Laws of the U.S.S.R. and Decrees of the Supreme Soviet of the U.S.S.R.),* Moscow: Soviet Government Printing Office, 1945; *Vsesoyuznaya Kommunisticheskaya Partiya V Rezolutsiyakh I Resheniyakh S' ezdov, Konferentsii, I Plenumov Tsk 1898–1939 (All-Union Communist Party (B) in Resolutions and Decrees of Congresses, Conferences, and Plenums of the Central Committee 1898–1939),* Moscow: Soviet Government Printing Office, 1941. Stenographic reports of congresses and conferences of the Communist party of the U.S.S.R. are available in Russian, and they provide the most illuminating guide to the Soviet system.

Among the many studies in English *How Russia Is Ruled* by Merle Fainsod and *Soviet Politics—the Dilemma of Power* by Barrington Moore, Jr., are the most perceptive and comprehensive treatments of the Soviet government. The already existing volumes of E. H. Carr's *A History of Soviet Russia* provide the most detailed account of the development of Soviet power, though some of Carr's interpretations, especially in the first volume, are questioned by other authorities. Bertram Wolfe's *Three Who Made a Revolution* is an excellent treatment of the origins of Bolshevism. My own work *The Bolsheviks* bears on the same problem and carries the story to 1924. A valuable tool for the student who does not have a command of Russian is the *Current Digest of the Soviet Press,* which translates the most important articles appearing in the Soviet press. Bibliographic material available in English is indicated in the list below.

Abramov, F. *The New Life—A Day on a Collective Farm.* New York: Praeger, 1963.

Armstrong, John A. *The Politics of Totalitarianism.* New York: Random House, 1962.

Barghoorn, Frederick C. *The Soviet Image of the United States.* New York: Harcourt, Brace & World, 1950.

————. *Politics in the U.S.S.R.* Boston: Little, Brown, 1966.

Bauer, Raymond A., Alex Inkeles, and Clyde Kluckholhn. *How the Soviet System Works.* Cambridge, Mass.: Harvard University Press, 1956.

Berliner, Joseph. *Factory and Manager in the U.S.S.R.* Cambridge, Mass.: Harvard University Press, 1957.

Berman, Harold J. *Justice in Russia.* Cambridge, Mass.: Harvard University Press, 1950.

Bienstock, Gregory, Solomon M. Schwarz, and Aaron Yugow. *Management in Russian Industry and Agriculture.* London and New York: Oxford University Press, 1944.

Burns, Emile. *A Handbook of Marxism.* New York: International Publishers, 1935.

Carr, E. H. *A History of Soviet Russia: The Bolshevik Revolution.* Vols. I–III. New York: Macmillan, 1951–1953.

————. *A History of Soviet Russia: The Interregnum 1923–24.* New York: Macmillan, 1955.

————. *Socialism in One Country.* Vols. I–III. New York: Macmillan, 1958–1964.

Chamberlin, W. H. *The Russian Revolution, 1917–1921.* 2 vols. New York: Macmillan, 1935.

Conquest, Robert. *Power and Policy in the U.S.S.R.* New York: St. Martin's Press, 1961.

————. *The Great Terror.* New York: Macmillan, 1968.

Current Soviet Policies: The Documentary Record of the XIXth Communist Party Congress and the Reorganization After Stalin's Death. New York: Praeger, 1953.

Curtiss, J. W. *Church and State in Russia, 1900–1917.* New York: Columbia University Press, 1940.

Dallin, David, and Boris I. Nicolaevsky. *Forced Labor in Soviet Russia.* New Haven, Conn.: Yale University Press, 1947.

Daniels, Robert. *Conscience of the Revolution.* Cambridge, Mass.: Harvard University Press, 1960.

————. *Red October: The Bolshevik Revolution of 1917.* New York: Scribner, 1967.

Deutscher, Issac. *Soviet Trade Unions.* London and New York: Royal Institute of International Affairs, 1950.

————. *Stalin: A Political Biography.* New York: Oxford University Press, 1949.

Erickson, John. *The Soviet High Command.* New York: St. Martin's Press, 1962.

Fainsod, Merle. *How Russia Is Ruled.* Cambridge, Mass.: Harvard University Press, 1953. Rev. ed., 1964.

————. *Smolensk Under Soviet Rule.* Cambridge, Mass.: Harvard University Press, 1958.

Fischer, Ruth. *Stalin and German Communism.* Cambridge, Mass.: Harvard University Press, 1948.

Florinsky, Michael T. *The End of the Russian Empire.* New Haven, Conn.: Yale University Press, 1931.

Friedrich, Carl J., and Zbigniew K. Brzezinski. *Totalitarian Dictatorship and Autocracy.* Cambridge, Mass.: Harvard University Press, 1956.

History of the Communist Party of the Soviet Union (Bolsheviks); Short Course. New York: International Publishers, 1939.

Holzman, Franklyn D. *Soviet Taxation.* Cambridge, Mass.: Harvard University Press, 1955.

Hunt, R. N. Carew. *The Theory and Practice of Communism.* New York: Macmillan, 1951.

Inkeles, Alex. *Public Opinion in Soviet Russia.* Cambridge, Mass.: Harvard University Press, 1950.

Kennan, George. *Russia and the West*. Boston: Little, Brown, 1960.

Kolars, Walter. *Russia and Her Colonies*. New York: Praeger, 1952.

Laird, Roy D., ed. *Soviet Agricultural and Peasant Affairs*. Lawrence, Kansas: University of Kansas Press, 1963.

Lane, D. *Politics and Society in the U.S.S.R.* New York: Random House, 1971.

Lenin, V. I. *State and Revolution*. New York: International Publishers, 1935.

Linden, Karl. *Khrushchev and the Soviet Leadership*. Baltimore: Johns Hopkins Press, 1966.

Lowenthal, Richard. *World Communism*. New York: Oxford University Press, 1964.

Lyashchenko, P. I. *History of the National Economy of Russia to the 1917 Revolution*. New York: Macmillan, 1949.

Marx, Karl. *Capital*. 3 vols. Chicago: C. H. Ken & Co., 1908–1909.

_____. *The Civil War in France*. London: International Publishers, 1941.

_____. *Critique of the Gotha Programme*. London: International Publishers, 1943.

Masaryk, Thomas G. *The Spirit of Russia*. 2 vols. London: G. Allen & Unwin, 1919.

Mavor, James. *An Economic History of Russia*. 2 vols. London and Toronto: Dutton, 1914.

Meyer, Alfred. *The Soviet Political System*. New York: Random House, 1965.

Moore, Barrington, Jr. *Soviet Politics—The Dilemma of Power*. Cambridge, Mass.: Harvard University Press, 1950.

_____. *Terror and Progress: the U.S.S.R.* Cambridge, Mass.: Harvard University Press, 1955.

Plamenatz, John. *German Marxism and Russian Communism*. London: Longmans, 1954.

Report of Court Proceedings in the Case of the Anti-Soviet "Bloc of Rights and Trotskyites." Moscow, 1938.

Report of Court Proceedings, the Case of the Trotskyite—Zinovievite Terrorist Centre, Heard before the Military Collegium of the Supreme Court of the USSR, August 19–24, 1936. Moscow, 1936.

Robinson, Geroid T. *Rural Russia under the Old Régime*. New York: Longmans, 1932.

Russian Institute. *The Anti-Stalin Campaign and International Communism*. New York: Columbia University Press, 1956.

Schapiro, Leonard. *The Communist Party of the Soviet Union*. New York: Random House, 1959.

Schumpeter, Joseph. *Capitalism, Socialism, and Democracy*, 3rd ed. New York: Harper & Row, 1950.

Seton-Watson, Hugh. *From Lenin to Malenkov*. New York: Praeger, 1953.

Solzhenitsyn, A. *One Day in the Life of Ivan Denisovich*. New York: Praeger, 1963.

Souvarine, Boris. *Staline: Aperçu historique du bolchévisme*. Paris: Plon, 1935.

Stalin, Joseph. *Foundations of Leninism*. New York: International Publishers, 1932.

_____. *Problems of Leninism*. New York: International Publishers, 1934.

Swearer, Howard R. *The Politics of Succession in the USSR*. Boston: Little, Brown, 1964.

Towster, Julian. *Political Power in the USSR*. New York: Oxford University Press, 1948.

Treadgold, Donald W. *Lenin and His Rivals*. New York: Praeger, 1955.

Trotsky, Leon. *The History of the Russian Revolution*. 3 vols. New York: Simon and Schuster, 1936.

Tucker, Robert. *The Soviet Political Mind*. New York: Praeger, 1963.

Ulam, Adam. *The Unfinished Revolution*. New York: Random House, 1960.

_____. *The Bolsheviks*. New York: Macmillan, 1965.

_____. *Expansion and Coexistence, a History of Soviet Foreign Policy*. New York: Praeger, 1968.

Vernadsky, George. *A History of Russia*, rev. ed. New Haven, Conn.: Yale University Press, 1961.

Werth, A. *Russia at War*. New York: Dutton, 1964.

White, D. Fedotoff. *The Growth of the Red Army*. Princeton, N. J.: Princeton University Press, 1944.

Wolfe, Bertram D. *Three Who Made a Revolution*. New York: Dial Press, 1948.

Wollenberg, Erich. *The Red Army*. London: Seeker & Warburg, 1938.

Yevtushenko, Ye. *A Precocious Autobiography*. New York: Dutton, 1963.

Zagoria, Donald. *The Sino-Soviet Conflict, 1956–1961*. Princeton, N. J.: Princeton University Press, 1962.

Statistical
Appendixes

Appendix A A Comparison of the United States, the United Kingdom, France, Germany, and the Soviet Union

	Year	United States	United Kingdom	France	Germany	Soviet Union
I. Population						
(in Thousands)	1970	203,184	55,534	50,320	58,707	241,748
Population Growth (Average Annual Percent)	1963–1969	1.2	0.6	0.9	0.9	1.1
II. Area (in Thousands of Square Miles)		3,675	94	210	96	8,599
Population Density (Inhabitants Per Square Mile)	1970	57	593	239	602	29
III. Urbanization[1]						
Population in Metropolitan Areas Over 100,000 (in Percent)	1969	55.5	53.3	31.4	32.8	25.2
IV. Industrialization						
Civilian Labor Force by Main Sectors of Economic Activity (in Percent)	1969					
Agriculture		4.5	2.9	14.7	9.5	11.9
Industry		32.6	45.9	39.9	48.8	42.5
Services		59.4	49.1	44.0	41.1	45.6
V. National Accounts						
Gross National Product (in Billions of U.S. Dollars)	1969	947.8	109.8	140.0	152.9	358.0[2]
G.N.P. Per Capita (in U.S. Dollars)	1969	4,664	1,976	2,783	2,512	1,520[2]
Breakdown of G.N.P.	1969					
Private and Government Consumption (in Percent)		82	81	74	71	72
Capital Formation (in Percent)		18	18	26	26	27
Public Services (as Percent of G.N.P.)						
General Government	1968	32.0	39.0	38.9	37.5	—
National Defense	1969	8.6	5.1	4.4	3.5	8.5
Social Security Expenditure	1966	7.2	12.6	15.5	15.5	11.1
Education	1969	5.8	5.8	4.4	3.6	7.3

	Year					
VI. Economic Growth						
Average Annual Rates of Growth in G.N.P., Market Prices						
1950–1960		2.9	2.7	4.4	7.7	10.4
1960–1968		5.1	3.0	5.6	4.5	7.1
Average Annual Rates of Growth in G.N.P., Constant Prices						
1959–1969		4.3	3.0	5.9	5.1	—
Per Capita		2.9	2.3	4.8	4.0	5.8
VII. Education						
Numbers Attending School and University Full-time (in Thousands)	1967	55,070	10,098	11,205	10,506	61,344
Total Population (in Percent)		28.4	18.2	19.6	14.4	26.1
Numbers in Higher Education (in Thousands)	1967	6,085	267	509	219	4,123
VIII. Health						
Population Per Hospital Bed	1968	120	100	150	80	107
Population Per Physician	1968	650	860	770	620	433
IX. Material Indexes (U.S. = 100)						
Energy Consumption	1968	100	50	38	44	—
Steel Production	1968	100	62	53	86	63
Motor Vehicles	1968	100	49	54	51	1.4
Newspapers	1968	100	160	80	108	105

[1] Based on national calculations furnished by the United Nations. German and Soviet data include only cities, not their metropolitan areas.

[2] 1967 Estimate; Institute of Strategic Studies.

[3] Based on estimates; actual union membership statistics are unreliable.

[4] No data reported for 1968.

DATA SOURCES: United Nations, *Statistical Yearbook, 1970*; United Nations, *Yearbook of National Accounts Statistics, 1970*; United Nations, *Compendium of Social Statistics, 1968*; International Labour Office, *Yearbook of Labour Statistics, 1970*; Statistical Office of the European Communities, *Basic Statistics of the Community, 1970*; United States, Department of Commerce, *Statistical Abstract of the United States, 1971*; United Kingdom, Central Statistical Office, *Annual Abstract of Statistics, 1970*; France, *Annuaire Statistique de la France, 1969*; Germany, *Statistisches Jahrbuch für die Bundesrepublik Deutschland, 1970*; Institute of Strategic Studies, *The Strategic Balance, 1969–1970*.

The Statistical Appendixes were prepared especially for this book by Glenn A. Robinson.

Appendix A (*continued*)

	Year	United States	United Kingdom	France	Germany	Soviet Union
Televisions	1968	100	71	50	66	32
X. Labor Statistics						
Working Population (in Thousands)	1969	69,877	25,825	20,439	26,342	99,130
Salaried Employees (as Percent of Working Population)	1969	82.8	89.4	74.4	81.0	66.4
Self-Employed (as Percent of Working Population)	1969	11.3	6.8	17.0	11.2	2.7
Unemployment, Average Rate	1961–1969	4.7	1.8	1.4	1.0	—
Trade Union Membership (in Thousands)	1967	19,181	9,970	3,880[3]	6,482	80,000
Industrial Disputes: Average Working Days Lost Annually Per 1,000 Workers in Mining, Manufacturing, Construction, Transport	1960–1969	1010	272	262[4]	22	—
Hourly Wage, Average in Nonagricultural Sectors (in U.S. Dollars)	1970	3.21	1.29	.84	1.66	—
Labor Productivity, Growth (1960 = 100)	1969	130	111	159	152	—
XI. Breakdown of Government Expenditures and Revenues (All Levels of Government) Expenditures (in Percent)	1969					
National Defense		24.1	11.7	11.8	9.5	12.4
External Relations		1.1	1.5	1.0	0.3	
Highways, Transport, Commerce		7.6	7.3	4.2	7.2	
Industry and Trade		1.3	9.4	7.4	6.9	43.0
Agriculture, Natural Resources		2.7	2.7	4.0	4.5	
Housing		0.6	5.7	2.7	4.2	
Education		20.6	11.8	11.9	7.6	16.9
Social Welfare		26.2	19.7	24.9	34.0	14.6
Health		6.2	11.6	12.8	15.7	6.4
Debt Interest		6.8	10.2	5.6	6.8	—
Other		2.8	8.4	13.7	3.3	6.7
		100.0	100.0	100.0	100.0	100.0

	Year					
Revenues (in Percent)						
Direct Taxes on Households		36.2	28.5	12.5	22.3	8.8
Social Security Contributions		17.8	13.5	38.4	28.4	—
Direct Taxes on Corporations		15.6	6.6	4.9	6.1	—
Indirect Taxes		30.2	43.5	42.0	36.8	32.2
Income from Public Enterprise		—	7.5	1.6	5.1	34.8
Other		0.2	0.4	0.6	1.3	24.2
		100.0	100.0	100.0	100.0	100.0
XII. Public Expenditure						
Total Public Expenditure						
(Billions of U.S. Dollars)	1969	334.8	—	40.9	64.3	—
(as Percent of G.N.P.)		35.3	43.2	40.3	42.1	—
Defense Expenditure per Capita (in U.S. Dollars)	1969	393	100	123	116	164
Social Security Benefits Per Capita (in U.S. Dollars)	1966	260	228	321	334	238
XIII. Degree of Centralization						
Central Government Expenditures, Current Account (as Percent of Government Expenditures)	1969	54.0	73.0	55.1	35.8	—
Employees at Different Levels of Government (in Percent)	1967					
National		24.2	42.3	59.3	9.4	—
State		21.8	—	—	54.4	—
Local		54.0	57.7	40.7	36.2	—
XIV. Government Employees (as Percent of Working Population)	1967	17.7	5.8	7.2	11.1	18.3
XV. Annual Rates of Growth in Government Expenditures, Market Prices						
1950–1960		3.2	0.7	2.5	4.9	—
1960–1968		5.7	2.6	3.3	4.4	—

[1] Based on national calculations furnished by the United Nations. German and Soviet data include only cities, not their metropolitan areas.

[2] 1967 Estimate; Institute of Strategic Studies.

[3] Based on estimates; actual union membership statistics are unreliable.

[4] No data reported for 1968.

Appendix B British General Election Results
(Selected Elections 1832–1895; All Elections 1900–1970)

Year	Percent Share of Party Vote						M.P.s Elected						
	Conservative	Liberal Unionist	Liberal	Irish Nationalist	Labour	Other	Conservative	Liberal Unionist	Liberal	Irish Nationalist	Labour	Other	Unopposed Seats
1832	32.1		67.9				172		473				200
1841	51.0		48.8			0.2	360		295				325
1852	57.4		42.5			0.1	346		286				243
1868	40.8		59.2				286		365				199
1874	45.6		49.3	3.5		1.6	345		242	48		4	181
1880	43.8		53.2	2.4		0.6	248		325	56		4	107
1886	37.5	14.0	44.9	3.6			316	79	190	85			223
1895	49.2		45.4	3.9	1.1	0.4	341	70	177	82			185
1900	51.1		45.9	2.5	0.5		334	68	184	82	2		243
1906	43.7		49.0	0.6	5.9	0.8	134	24	399	83	30		114
1910	46.9		43.1	1.9	8.0	0.1	242	31	275	82	40		55
1910	46.4		43.8	2.5	7.1	0.2	240	34	270	84	42		163
1918	38.7		25.6	6.7	23.7	5.3	383		161	80	73	10	107
1922	38.2		29.1		29.5	3.2	345		116		142	12	57
1923	38.1		29.6		30.5	1.8	258		159		191	7	50
1924	48.3		17.6		33.0	1.1	419		40		151	5	32
1929	38.2		23.4		37.1	1.3	260		59		288	8	7
1931	55.2		10.7		32.2	1.7	473		72		64	5	67
1935	53.8		6.4		38.6	1.3	432		21		158	5	40
1945	39.8		9.0		47.8	2.8	213		12		393	22	3
1950	43.5		9.1		46.1	1.3	298		9		315	3	2
1951	48.0		2.5		48.8	0.7	321		6		295	3	4
1955	49.7		2.7		46.4	1.2	344		6		277	3	0

1959	49.4	5.9	43.8	0.9	365	6	258	1	0
1964	43.4	11.2	44.1	0.3	304	9	317		0
1966	41.9	8.5	47.9	1.7	253	12	363	2	0
1970	46.4	7.5	43.1	3.0	330	6	287	6	0

NOTE: Data for the eight elections of the nineteenth century reported in this table were compiled from constituency results published in McCalmont's *Parliamentary Poll Book* for the 1832–1874 elections and Dod's *Parliamentary Companion* for the 1880–1895 elections. Party affiliations were based on the respective author's determinations. Appropriate adjustments were made for multiple-member constituencies. Comparisons with other election data indicate a margin of error of about 5 percent.

These statistics should be interpreted as indicative rather than definitive. Historians have cautioned that the absence of formal political organizations, changes in the mode of election, and local constituency practices preclude the use of election data as a substantive measure of political opinion. The data do offer, however, a useful perspective of party development over a 150-year period.

DATA SOURCES: Frederick H. McCalmont, *The Parliamentary Poll Book of All Elections 1832–1895* (London: 1895); Dod's *Parliamentary Companion 1843, 1852, 1874, 1880, 1886, 1895; David Butler and Jennie Freeman, *British Political Facts, 1900–1968* (London: 1969).

Appendix C French Legislative Election Results, 1893–1968
Percent Share of Party Vote

Year	Communists	Extreme Left	Socialists		Socialist Radicals	Radicals	Center (Moderate Republicans)	Ralliés	Conservatives Nationalists	Conservatives Extreme Right	Other
1893			8.5		2.4	20.5	45.3	6.5		16.8	
1898			11.3		9.6	17.9	41.5	6.9		12.8	
1902		4.1	6.3		10.1	16.8	29.7	4.6	14.2	14.1	
1906			10.0	2.3[1]	28.5	7.9	22.0[2]			29.2	0.1
1910			13.3	4.1[1]	20.1	18.4	22.5[3]			20.9	0.6
1914			16.9	3.9[4]	17.9	16.8	28.5[3]			15.6	0.4
1919	9.8		22.7		11.0	—[5]	6.0		33.4[5]	26.9	
1924	11.4				38.1		11.5		39.5		1.0
1928	8.4	0.9	18.2	4.4[4]	17.7		22.9		23.1		1.4
1932		0.9	20.7	5.3[4]	19.2		23.4		22.1		
1936	15.4		19.9	7.5[4]	14.6			42.6[6]			0.2

Year	Communists		Socialists S.F.I.O.	Radicals	Christian Democrats (M.R.P.)	Gaullists	Moderates (Right Independents)	Extreme Right	Other
1945	26.2		23.4	10.5	23.9		15.6		0.1
1946[14]	25.9		21.1	11.6	28.2		12.8		0.1
1946[15]	28.2		17.8	11.1	25.9	3.0	12.9		0.8
1951	26.9		14.6	10.0	12.6	21.7	14.1		
1956	25.9	1.7	15.2	13.5	11.1		14.6	13.9[7]	4.3[8]
1958	19.2	1.2	15.7	7.3	11.1	20.4	22.1	2.6	
1962	21.7	2.4	12.6	7.5	8.9	36.3[9]	9.5	0.9	

1967	22.4	2.2[10]	18.7[11]		13.4[12]	38.1	3.9	0.8	0.5
1968	20.0	4.0[10]	16.5[11]	0.6	10.3[13]	43.7	4.1	0.1	0.5

[1]Independent Socialists.
[2]Left and Moderate Republicans.
[3]Moderate Right and the Republican Federation.
[4]Socialist Republicans.
[5]Bloc National (combined Radical and Right lists).
[6]National Front.
[7]Includes the Poujadists (11.6%).
[8]Includes Social Republicans.
[9]Includes Republican Independents (Gaullists).
[10]Parti socialiste unifié.
[11]Fédération de la gauche démocrate et socialiste (F.G.D.S.).
[12]Centre démocrate.
[13]Centre progrès et démocratie moderne.
[14]June 1946.
[15]November 1946.

DATA SOURCES: Peter Campbell, *French Electoral Systems and Elections Since 1789* (Hamden: 1958); François Goguel and Alfred Grosser, *La Politique en France* (Paris: 1964); L'*Année Politique*; Georges LaChapelle, *Les Élections Législatives: Resultats Officiels*. (Paris: 1914, 1919, 1928, 1932, 1936); *Annuaire statistique de la France, 1969*.

Appendix D German Parliamentary Election Results
(Selected Elections 1871–1912; All Elections 1919–1969)
Percent Share of Party Vote

Year	Social Democratic Party	Regional Parties	Center Party (Catholic)	German People's Party	Progressives (Liberal Parties)	National Liberal Party	Conservative Parties	Other Parties
1871	3.2	6.6	18.6	0.5	7.2	30.0	23.0	2.0
1881	6.1	8.8	23.2	2.0	21.1	14.6	23.7	0.5
1890	19.7	6.6	18.6	2.0	16.0	16.3	19.8	1.0
1903	31.7	6.0	19.7	1.0	8.3	13.9	16.1	3.5
1912	34.8	5.7	16.4	12.3		13.7	12.6	4.5

Year	Communist Party (K.P.D.)	Social Democratic Party	Bavarian People's Party	Center Party	German People's Party	German State Democratic Party	Special Interest Parties	National People's Party	National Socialists	Other Parties
1919		45.5		19.7	4.4	18.6	1.1	10.3		0.4
1920	2.1	39.5	4.4	13.6	13.9	8.3	1.7	14.9		1.6
1924[1]	12.6	20.5	3.2	13.4	9.2	5.7	5.3	19.5	6.5	4.0
1924[2]	9.0	26.0	3.7	13.6	10.1	6.3	5.7	20.5	3.0	2.0
1928	10.6	29.8	3.0	12.1	8.7	4.9	8.9	14.2	2.6	4.8
1930	13.1	24.5	3.0	11.8	4.5	3.8	11.3	7.0	18.3	3.1
1932[3]	14.6	21.6	3.2	12.5	1.2	1.0	2.3	5.9	37.4	0.9
1932[4]	16.9	20.4	3.1	11.9	1.9	1.0	2.5	8.8	33.1	2.2
1933[5]	12.3	18.3	2.7	11.7	1.1	0.8	1.6	8.0	43.9	0.3
1933[6]									92.2	

	Communist Party	Social Democratic Party	Christian Democratic Union/Christian Social Union	German Party	Free Democratic Party	Extreme Right Parties	Other Parties
1949	5.7	29.2	31.0	4.0	11.9	1.1	17.1
1953	2.2	28.8	45.2	3.2	9.5		11.1
1957		31.8	50.2	3.4	7.7		6.9
1961		36.2	45.3	12.8	12.8		2.9
1965		39.3	47.6		9.5	2.0	1.6
1969		42.7	46.1		5.8	4.3	1.2

[1] May 1924
[2] December 1924
[3] July 1932
[4] November 1932
[5] March 1933
[6] November 1933

DATA SOURCES: Walter Tormin, *Geschichte der deutschen Parteien seit 1848* (Stuttgart: 1964); *Statistisches Jahrbuch fur das deutsche Reich, 1933; Statistisches Jahrbuch fur die Bundesrepublik Deutschland, 1970.*

Appendix E Growth of the Electorates: Great Britain, France, and Germany, 1870–1970

Great Britain

Year	Registered Electorate (in Thousands)	% of Population in Electorate	% Voting in Election
1832	813	3.3	
1868	2,298	7.5	
1874	2,810	8.6	
1880	3,032	8.8	
1886	5,734	15.8	
1895	6,412	16.4	74.6
1900	6,731	16.4	82.6
1906	7,264	16.8	
1910	7,694	17.0	86.6
1918	21,392	45.6	58.9
1924	21,731	48.5	76.3
1929	28,850	62.4	76.1
1931	29,960	65.0	76.7
1935	31,379	67.8	71.2
1945	33,240	67.8	72.7
1950	33,269	66.7	84.0
1955	34,858	68.5	76.7
1959	35,397	68.1	78.8
1964	35,892	66.4	77.1
1966	35,965	65.6	75.8
1970	39,384	70.9	72.0

France

Year	Registered Electorate (in Thousands)	% of Population in Electorate	% Voting in Election
1877	9,948	25.6	80.8
1881	10,124	27.2	68.5
1886	10,181	26.2	77.5
1893	10,443	27.2	71.5
1902	10,863	27.9	77.6
1910	11,327	28.8	77.3
1919	11,436	29.2	71.3
1924	11,070	27.7	83.0
1928	11,396	28.0	83.8
1932	11,741	28.2	83.5
1936	11,768	28.1	84.2
1945	24,623	61.4	79.1
1951	24,531	58.1	80.2
1956	26,775	61.2	82.8
1958	27,736	62.1	77.1
1962	27,535	59.5	68.7
1967	28,291	57.5	80.9
1968	28,171	56.7	80.1

Germany

Year	Registered Electorate (in Thousands)	% of Population in Electorate	% Voting in Election
1871	7,975	19.5	50.7
1881	9,090	20.0	56.1
1890	10,146	20.6	71.2
1903	12,531	21.4	75.8
1912	14,441	21.8	84.5
1919	36,766	59.4	82.6
1924	38,987	61.5	76.3
1928	41,224	63.4	74.6
1932	44,227	67.8	83.4
1949	31,207	63.5	78.5
1953	33,121	64.8	86.0
1957	35,401	66.0	87.8
1961	37,441	66.8	87.7
1965	38,510	65.0	86.8
1969	38,677	63.8	86.7

DATA SOURCES: See data sources for Appendixes B, C, and D.

Index

Adenauer, Konrad: early role in Federal Republic, 515, 533; prestige of, 544; mentioned, 512, 514, 546, 563, 585

Aereopagitica (John Milton), 250, 264

Alexander I, Tsar, 606

Alexander II, Tsar, 607, 608, 610

Alexander III, Tsar, 615

Alford, Robert R., 308

Algeria, and French political conflict, 335–336, 367, 378, 379

Allen, Kevin, 345

Allied Control Commission, 508, 510

Almond, Gabriel, 25n

Amalrik, Andrei, 740

Amery, L. S.: on Conservative party policy, 277–278; mentioned, 139, 140

An Inquiry into the Nature and the Causes of the Wealth of Nations, 63

Andreyev, Andrey, 635, 667, 726

Aragon, Louis, 395

Arendt, Hannah, 245

Aristocracy, as stage in political development, 91–92

Aristov, A. B., 728

Armstrong, Sir William, 194n

Arnold, Karl, 511, 552, 579

Aron, Raymond, 479

Attlee, Clement: Attlee government and rebellious Labourites, 228–229; legislative program, 276; and foreign policy, 301; mentioned, 147, 166, 196, 207, 247, 252, 280, 293, 300, 301

Austria: idea of sovereignty in, 78; mentioned, 474, 475, 482

Authoritarianism, in Soviet Russia, 107–110

Authority: conceptions of, 39, 261–262, in Russia, 107–110, in France, changed by Revolution, 350, expressed in constitutional models, 356; and law, 59; problems of in

Authority (*continued*)
modernity, 110–115; bipolar in Great Britain, 139–141, 143; of Whigs and Tories, 265–266, 278; and functional representation, 274–275. *See also* Legitimacy

Axelrod, Paul, 613

Bagehot, Walter, 24, 41, 56, 206

Baldwin, Stanley, 140–141

Balfour, Arthur, 202, 296

Barber, Anthony, 238

Beattie, Alan, 196n

Bebel, August, 486

Beeching Report, 318

Behavioralism, in political science, 24

Belief systems: defined, 26–28; distinguished from value systems, 29

Belyayev, Nikolai, 670, 728

Benn, Anthony Wedgewood, 321n

Bentham, Jeremy, hypothesis of modernity: 126, 137, applied to welfare state, 132–133, as inspiration for reform, 258

Bentley, Arthur F., 24n

Beria, Lavrenti: elimination of, 708–709, 734; mentioned, 654, 657, 671, 675n, 693n, 706, 707, 710, 716, 723, 726

Berlin: status in Federal Republic, 526–528; Kartellamt, 574; mentioned, 478, 508

Bernard, André, 408n

Bernstein, Eduard, 486, 614n

Berrington, Hugh, 271

Bevan, Aneurin; leadership of Labour rebels, 229; mentioned, 36, 149–150, 201

Bevin, Ernest: advocate of N.A.T.O., 279–280; mentioned, 147, 233, 272

Bias, ideological, sources of, 30–31

Bismarck, Otto von: and tradition of strong man, 480–481; mentioned, 108, 476

Black, Cyril E., 58n

About the Authors

Samuel H. Beer, general editor of *Patterns of Government* and author of Part 1, "Modern Political Development," and Part 2, "The British Political System," is Eaton Professor of the Science of Government at Harvard University. He studied at the University of Michigan and Oxford University and won his Ph.D. at Harvard. Chairman of the Department of Government at Harvard from 1954 to 1958, he is the author of *The City of Reason, Treasury Control,* and *British Politics in the Collectivist Age,* which was given the Woodrow Wilson Award as the "best book on politics, government or international affairs published in the United States in 1965." He served as Vice-President of the American Political Science Association in 1964–1965, has held Fulbright and Guggenheim Fellowships, and was Messenger Lecturer at Cornell University in 1969. His principal fields of interest are comparative politics and American federalism, and he has published articles on political parties, economic planning, the British Parliament, the methodology of social science, state government, and American political thought. He has been active in Democratic party politics and recently served as a member of the McGovern-Fraser Commission on Delegate Selection and Party Structure.

Suzanne Berger, author of Part 3, "The French Political System," received a B.A. from the University of Chicago and an M.A. and Ph.D. from Harvard University. She began teaching at Harvard University and is now Associate Professor in the Department of Political Science at the Massachusetts Institute of Technology. She is a member of the Center for International Studies at the Massachusetts Institute of Technology and a Research Associate of the West European Studies Center, Harvard University. She is the author of *Peasants Against Politics: Rural Organization in Brittany, 1911–1967* and of various articles on French politics.

Guido Goldman, author of Part 4, "The German Political System," was granted his B.A., M.A., and Ph.D. by Harvard University. In addition, he has studied at the University of Munich. He is a Lecturer in the Government Department, Executive Director of West European Studies, and Advisor to the German Kennedy Memorial Fellows, all at Harvard University. During 1972–1973 he will be on leave from the University in order to serve as the Acting President of the new German Marshall Fund of the United States, which Chancellor Willy Brandt announced at Harvard on June 5, 1972, the twenty-fifth anniversary of the Marshall Plan. Dr. Goldman played a central role in negotiating and planning the establishment of the new Fund.

Adam B. Ulam, co-editor of *Patterns of Government* and author of Part 5, "The Russian Political System," received his B.A. from Brown University and his Ph.D. from Harvard University. He began teaching at the University of Wisconsin and since 1947 has been on the faculty of Harvard University. In 1948 he joined the Russian Research Center at Harvard as a Research Associate, and in 1953–1955 he was a Research Associate for the Center for International Studies at the Massachusetts Institute of Technology. He received the Rockefeller Fellowship in Political Theory for 1956–1957 and was granted a Guggenheim Fellowship in 1956–1957. Among his books are *The New Face of Soviet Totalitarianism, The Bolsheviks, Expansion and Coexistence,* and *The Rivals.* He has contributed to *Continuity and Change in Russian and Soviet Thought* (Ernest J. Simmons, ed.) and to *Constitutions and Constitutional Trends since World War II* (Arnold J. Zurcher, ed.). In addition, he has published many articles in professional journals.